CURRENT LAW STATUTES ANNOTATED
1986

VOLUME THREE

AUSTRALIA AND NEW ZEALAND
The Law Book Company Ltd.
Sydney : Melbourne : Perth

CANADA AND U.S.A.
The Carswell Company Ltd.
Agincourt, Ontario

INDIA
N. M. Tripathi Private Ltd.
Bombay
and
Eastern Law House Private Ltd.
Calcutta and Delhi

M.P.P. House
Bangalore

ISRAEL
Steimatzky's Agency Ltd.
Jerusalem : Tel Aviv : Haifa

MALAYSIA : SINGAPORE : BRUNEI
Malayan Law Journal (Pte.) Ltd.
Singapore

PAKISTAN
Pakistan Law House
Karachi

CURRENT LAW
STATUTES
ANNOTATED
1986

VOLUME THREE

EDITOR IN CHIEF
PETER ALLSOP, C.B.E., M.A.
Barrister

GENERAL EDITOR
KEVAN NORRIS, LL.B.
Solicitor

ASSISTANT GENERAL EDITOR
JULIE HARRIS, LL.B.

ADMINISTRATION
GILLIAN BRONZE, LL.B.

LONDON

SWEET & MAXWELL   STEVENS & SONS

EDINBURGH
W. GREEN & SON

1987

Published by
SWEET & MAXWELL LIMITED
and STEVENS & SONS LIMITED
of 11 New Fetter Lane, London,
and W. GREEN & SON LIMITED
of St. Giles Street, Edinburgh,
and Printed in Great Britain
by The Eastern Press Ltd.,
London and Reading

ISBN This Volume only : 0 421 38040 3
As a set : 0 421 38060 8

©
Sweet & Maxwell Limited
1987

CONTENTS

CHRONOLOGICAL TABLE

VOLUME THREE

STATUTES

INDEX OF SHORT TITLES

VOLUME THREE

References are to chapter numbers of 1986

COMPANY DIRECTORS DISQUALIFICATION ACT 1986*

(1986 c. 46)

---

* Annotations by Christopher Ryan, LL.M., Barrister and Solicitor (N.Z.), University of Liverpool.

An Act to consolidate certain enactments relating to the disqualification of persons from being directors of companies, and from being otherwise concerned with a company's affairs.   [25th July 1986]

PARLIAMENTARY DEBATES

Hansard: H.L. Vol. 474, col. 1038; H.L. Vol. 475, col. 714; H.L. Vol. 477, col. 1036; H.C. Vol. 102, col. 153.

INTRODUCTION AND GENERAL NOTE

The year 1985 was a noteworthy and difficult one for anyone involved in the promotion and management of companies and in particular for those advising them because almost simultaneously the Government consolidated the law relating to companies and the law relating to insolvency. The latter was the first full-scale statutory enactment in which the two branches of insolvency law—individual and corporate—were deliberately gathered together. This meant combining what had previously been in the Bankruptcy Act 1914 (for individuals) with those provisions in the Companies Act (dealing with corporate insolvency). Despite the fact that the Insolvency Act effected major amendments to, and repeals of, many of the provisions in the Companies Act relating to corporate insolvency, the opportunity was missed at that time to place into a single statute all the statutory provisions governing insolvency, even though that had been advocated in the final Report of the Review Committee on Insolvency Law and Practice, published in 1982, Cmnd. 8558 ("the Cork Report") which proposed that the law and practice relating to individual and corporate debtors alike should be harmonised wherever possible. The new Insolvency Act 1986 together with the Company Directors Disqualification Act 1986 amend substantially the contents of what was the Insolvency Act 1985 (now repealed) and parts of the Companies Act 1985 which together with the Business Names Act 1985, and the Company Securities (Insider Dealing) Act 1985 were the product of the project begun in 1981 to consolidate company law. Both the Companies Act 1985 and the Company Securities (Insider Dealing) Act 1985 will be further amended by the Financial Services Bill currently before Parliament and likely to become law in November 1986.

The Company Directors Disqualification Act 1986 brings together and consolidates the provisions formerly found in the Companies Act 1985 and the Insolvency Act 1985 relating to the disqualification of persons from being company directors or from otherwise being concerned with a company's affairs.

Preliminary

Disqualification orders: general

1.—(1) In the circumstances specified below in this Act a court may, and under section 6 shall, make against a person a disqualification order, that is to say an order that he shall not, without leave of the court—

(*a*) be a director of a company, or

(*b*) be a liquidator or administrator of a company, or

(*c*) be a receiver or manager of a company's property, or

(*d*) in any way, whether directly or indirectly, be concerned or take part in the promotion, formation or management of a company,

for a specified period beginning with the date of the order.

(2) In each section of this Act which gives to a court power or, as the case may be, imposes on it the duty to make a disqualification order there is specified the maximum (and, in section 6, the minimum) period of disqualification which may or (as the case may be) must be imposed by means of the order.

(3) Where a disqualification order is made against a person who is already subject to such an order, the periods specified in those orders shall run concurrently.

(4) A disqualification order may be made on grounds which are or include matters other than criminal convictions, notwithstanding that the person in respect of whom it is to be made may be criminally liable in respect of those matters.

DEFINITIONS
   "company": s.22(2).
   "Director": s.22(4) and (5).

GENERAL NOTE
   This section re-enacts subss. (1), (2) and (4) of s.295 of the Companies Act 1985. In that Act ss.295–302 dealt with disqualification. Their original blueprint was s.188 of the 1948 Act as altered by s.93 of the 1981 Act into a series of shorter sections. This current section like ss.295–302 of the 1985 Act follows the 1981 Act's extension of disqualification to preclude unsatisfactory persons acting as liquidators, receivers, and the managers of property of a company as well as preventing them (without the court's permission) from acting as directors.
   As to who may apply to the court to have a disqualification order made against a person to prevent that person from holding office or acting as a director, liquidator, receiver or manager, see s.16 and the note to that section. In certain instances the right to apply to the court is very limited, see ss.6–8.

DERIVATIONS
   Companies Act 1985, s.295(1), (2) and (4).

Disqualification for general misconduct in connection with companies

Disqualification on conviction of indictable offence

   2.—(1) The court may make a disqualification order against a person where he is convicted of an indictable offence (whether on indictment or summarily) in connection with the promotion, formation, management or liquidation of a company, or with the receivership or management of a company's property.
   (2) "The court" for this purpose means—
     (a) any court having jurisdiction to wind up the company in relation to which the offence was committed, or
     (b) the court by or before which the person is convicted of the offence, or
     (c) in the case of a summary conviction in England and Wales, any other magistrates' court acting for the same petty sessions area;
and for the purposes of this section the definition of "indictable offence" in Schedule 1 to the Interpretation Act 1978 applies for Scotland as it does for England and Wales.
   (3) The maximum period of disqualification under this section is—
     (a) where the disqualification order is made by a court of summary jurisdiction, 5 years, and
     (b) in any other case, 15 years.

DEFINITIONS
   "company": s.22(2).
   "court": s.2(2).
   "Indictable offence": Interpretation Act 1978, Sched. 1.

GENERAL NOTE
   See note to s.1. Some indictable offences are triable either way, *i.e.* they can be tried in either the Crown Court before a judge and jury or summarily by a stipendiary or a group of lay magistrates in the magistrates court. Wherever the trial takes place, conviction for an indictable offence committed while promoting, forming, managing or liquidating a company or while acting as receiver or manager of a company's property may result in the court making an order disqualifying the convicted person from acting as a director or in any of the other capacities itemised in s.1.
   See also *R.* v. *Austen* (1985) 1 B.C.C. 99, 528 where the argument against disqualification under the forerunner to s.2 by a man convicted of dishonesty was to the effect that the wording of the section refers to a conviction in "connection with the . . . management . . . of a company . . ." This must mean some fraud or irregularity in the internal management

of one or more of his companies' affairs and did not include his convictions for offences arising out of the fraudulent raising of finance in connection with the management of his various companies. The court rejected this proposition on the basis that such activities were caught by the words "in connection with the management of a company". These words in the view of Mann J. meant the management of the whole of the companies' affairs without differentiating between internal and external affairs. In other words the fraud or other irregular activity did not have to be committed on or against any of his companies; it is sufficient if it is done in connection with the management of any of their affairs. Therefore the appeal against the 10 year disqualification order was dismissed.

This section does not apply for any crime committed as liquidators, receivers or managers before June 15, 1982, under para. 1 of Sched. 2. It will apply however, where a person is convicted on indictment of an offence which he committed before June 15, 1982 but in such cases any disqualification order made under this section shall not exceed five years maximum (see para. 2(*a*) of Sched. 2) and this section has no application at all to similar situations where a person is convicted summarily for an offence comitted before that date (see para. 2(*b*) of Sched. 2.)

DERIVATIONS
Companies Act 1985, s.296(1), (2) and s.295(2).
See also paras. 9 and 10 of Sched. 12 of that Act.

Disqualification for persistent breaches of companies legislation

3.—(1) The court may make a disqualification order against a person where it appears to it that he has been persistently in default in relation to provisions of the companies legislation requiring any return, account or other document to be filed with, delivered or sent, or notice of any matter to be given, to the registrar of companies.

(2) On an application to the court for an order to be made under this section, the fact that a person has been persistently in default in relation to such provisions as are mentioned above may (without prejudice to its proof in any other manner) be conclusively proved by showing that in the 5 years ending with the date of the application he has been adjudged guilty (whether or not on the same occasion) of three or more defaults in relation to those provisions.

(3) A person is to be treated under subsection (2) as being adjudged guilty of a default in relation to any provision of that legislation if—

   (*a*) he is convicted (whether on indictment or summarily) of an offence consisting in a contravention of or failure to comply with that provision (whether on his own part or on the part of any company), or

   (*b*) a default order is made against him, that is to say an order under any of the following provisions—

      (i) section 244 of the Companies Act (order requiring delivery of company accounts),

      (ii) section 713 of that Act (enforcement of company's duty to make returns),

      (iii) section 41 of the Insolvency Act (enforcement of receiver's or manager's duty to make returns), or

      (iv) section 170 of that Act (corresponding provision for liquidator in winding up),

   in respect of any such contravention of or failure to comply with that provision (whether on his own part or on the part of any company).

(4) In this section "the court" means any court having jurisdiction to wind up any of the companies in relation to which the offence or other default has been or is alleged to have been committed.

(5) The maximum period of disqualification under this section is 5 years.

DEFINITIONS
"company": s.22(2).
"court": s.3(4).
"default": s.3(3).
"persistently": s.3(2).

GENERAL NOTE
See note to s.1. "Default" is defined in subs. (3). "Persistent default" is defined in subs. (2) as three or more defaults during the five years prior to the application to the Court. See also *Re Arctic Engineering* (1985) 1 B.C.C. 99, 563; [1986] 1 W.L.R. 686, in which the issue before the Chancery Division was the meaning of the words "persistently in default" in what was the forerunner to s.3. There the Secretary of State had applied for a disqualification order to prevent a named person acting as a liquidator, receiver or manager of a company's property for five years. (Although the facts concern a liquidator the provision applies equally to persons acting as, or wanting to act as, directors.) The person in question was an accountant specialising in liquidation work who had failed to file or send 35 returns as required by the Companies Act to the Registrar of companies in the five years prior to application for disqualification. No enforcement order however, had ever been made against him and he had never been convicted of default. The Secretary of State relied only on that person's neglect. The judge (Hoffmann J.) said that such conduct did amount to a culpable disregard for the requirements of the Act but that was not an essential ingredient of persistent default. A finding of the latter entitled the court to disqualify at its discretion, therefore culpability was relevant as to whether to disqualify and if so, for how long. "Persistently" in his view connoted some degree of continuance or repetition which might involve the same default or a series of defaults. The section suggested the kind of conduct the legislature had in mind as amounting to persistent default. The omission to prosecute default (as in this case) could not affect the question of persistence (see *Re Grantham (Wholesale)* [1972] 1 W.L.R. 559). Despite the defaults Hoffmann J. felt that the consequences of disqualification were so serious that in this case an order would not be made but this decision was made subject to the general caveat that a disqualification order may be made on similar facts in the future. Under para. 5 of Sched. 2 no account is taken of any offence committed, or any default order made, before June 1, 1977. Note that according to para. 6 of Sched. 2 an order made under s.28 of the Companies Act 1976 has the effect as if made under this section and an application made for such an order before June 15, 1982, now is to be treated as an application for an order under this section.

DERIVATION
Companies Act 1985, s.297.

Disqualification for fraud, etc., in winding up

4.—(1) The court may make a disqualification order against a person if, in the course of the winding up of a company, it appears that he—

    (*a*) has been guilty of an offence for which he is liable (whether he has been convicted or not) under section 458 of the Companies Act (fraudulent trading), or

    (*b*) has otherwise been guilty, while an officer or liquidator of the company or receiver or manager of its property, of any fraud in relation to the company or of any breach of his duty as such officer, liquidator, receiver or manager.

(2) In this section "the court" means any court having jurisdiction to wind up any of the companies in relation to which the offence or other default has been or is alleged to have been committed; and "officer" includes a shadow director.

(3) The maximum period of disqualification under this section is 15 years.

DEFINITIONS
"company": s.22(2).
"court": s.4(2).
"fraudulent trading": s.458, Companies Act 1985.
"officer": s.22(6) and s.744, Companies Act 1985.
"shadow director": s.22(5).

GENERAL NOTE
See note to s.1. By virtue of para. 1 of Sched. 2, s.4(1)(*b*) does not apply to acts done as liquidator, receiver or manager before June 15, 1982, and under para. 3 of Sched. 2. The maximum period of disqualification for an offence committed before June 15, 1982, is five years.

DERIVATIONS
Companies Act 1985, s.298 and ss.297(4) and 295(2).

Disqualification on summary conviction

5.—(1) An offence counting for the purposes of this section is one of which a person is convicted (either on indictment or summarily) in consequence of a contravention of, or failure to comply with, any provision of the companies legislation requiring a return, account or other document to be filed with, delivered or sent, or notice of any matter to be given, to the registrar of companies (whether the contravention or failure is on the person's own part or on the part of any company).

(2) Where a person is convicted of a summary offence counting for those purposes, the court by which he is convicted (or, in England and Wales, any other magistrates' court acting for the same petty sessions area) may make a disqualification order against him if the circumstances specified in the next subsection are present.

(3) Those circumstances are that, during the 5 years ending with the date of the conviction, the person has had made against him, or has been convicted of, in total not less than 3 default orders and offences counting for the purposes of this section; and those offences may include that of which he is convicted as mentioned in subsection (2) and any other offence of which he is convicted on the same occasion.

(4) For the purposes of this section—

   (*a*) the definition of "summary offence" in Schedule 1 to the Interpretation Act 1978 applies for Scotland as for England and Wales, and

   (*b*) "default order" means the same as in section 3(3)(*b*).

(5) The maximum period of disqualification under this section is 5 years.

DEFINITIONS
"company": s.22(2).
"companies legislation": s.22(6).
"default order": s.5(4)(*b*) and s.3(3)(*b*).
"summary offence": s.5(4)(*a*) and Interpretation Act 1978, Sched. 1.

GENERAL NOTE
If, in the five years prior to a person's conviction for a summary offence he has been previously convicted or received default orders totalling three or more, then the court may disqualify him.

See note to s.1. Under para. 4 of Sched. 2, the powers under this section are not exercisable where a person is convicted of an offence committed before June 15, 1982; in any event, under para. 5 of that Schedule, no account is taken of an offence committed or default order made before June 1, 1977.

DERIVATIONS
Companies Act 1985, s.299 and s.295(2).

Disqualification for unfitness

Duty of court to disqualify unfit directors of insolvent companies

6.—(1) The court shall make a disqualification order against a person in any case where, on an application under this section, it is satisfied—

(*a*) that he is or has been a director of a company which has at any time become insolvent (whether while he was a director or subsequently), and

(*b*) that his conduct as a director of that company (either taken alone or taken together with his conduct as a director of any other company or companies) makes him unfit to be concerned in the management of a company.

(2) For the purposes of this section and the next, a company becomes insolvent if—

(*a*) the company goes into liquidation at a time when its assets are insufficient for the payment of its debts and other liabilities and the expenses of the winding up,

(*b*) an administration order is made in relation to the company, or

(*c*) an administrative receiver of the company is appointed;

and references to a person's conduct as a director of any company or companies include, where that company or any of those companies has become insolvent, that person's conduct in relation to any matter connected with or arising out of the insolvency of that company.

(3) In this section and the next "the court" means—

(*a*) in the case of a person who is or has been a director of a company which is being wound up by the court, the court by which the company is being wound up,

(*b*) in the case of a person who is or has been a director of a company which is being wound up voluntarily, any court having jurisdiction to wind up the company,

(*c*) in the case of a person who is or has been a director of a company in relation to which an administration order is in force, the court by which that order was made, and

(*d*) in any other case, the High Court or, in Scotland, the Court of Session;

and in both sections "director" includes a shadow director.

(4) Under this section the minimum period of disqualification is 2 years, and the maximum period is 15 years.

DEFINITIONS

"administration order: Pt. II, ss.8–12, Insolvency Act 1986.
"company": s.22(2).
"court": s.6(3).
"director": s.22(4).
"insolvent": s.6(2).
"shadow director": s.22(5).

GENERAL NOTE

This provision marks an important stage in the evolution of the law concerning directors' answerability for the manner in which a company's affairs are conducted. It enables the court to make an order disqualifying a person from direct or indirect involvement in company promotion, formation or management for a period of up to 15 years. The procedure established by this section is a controlled one, however: see the note to s.7.

The original clause from which this section evolved was the most controversial provision in the Insolvency Bill, and underwent considerable alteration throughout all Parliamentary stages. In chap. 45 of this Cork Report it was recommended that delinquent directors should be punished by disqualification from company management for up to 15 years. The Report also recommended that in certain serious cases of misconduct disqualification should be mandatory, while in others it would be a matter for the court's discretion. In their White Paper (paras. 12–14 and 46–51) the Government adopted a more draconian and mechanical approach whereby all directors of companies undergoing compulsory liquidation would suffer automatic disqualification unless they could exculpate themselves before a court. Clause 7 of the Insolvency Bill 1985 as first published duly embodied this principle. However, a concerted opposition in Parliament led to a radical recasting of the clause through progressive stages in which the Government, having first been defeated on a division

(*Hansard*, H.L. Vol. 459, col. 628), withdrew its original clause (*Hansard*, H.L. Vol. 461, cols. 711–719) and subsequently procured the enactment of s.12 of that Act which was the parent of what are now ss.6–7, providing a restrictively controlled procedure for the disqualification of directors of insolvent companies. The concept of insolvency used here is a broad one, embracing both compulsory and voluntary liquidation and any situation where the company becomes the subject of an administration order, or where an administrative receiver is appointed (subs. (2)). Among the reasons stated by the Government for restricting the right to seek a disqualification order so that applications can only be made by or on the directions of the Secretary of State was the concern that other interested parties—especially creditors—might use it as a means of putting pressure upon the directors of a failing company, or of conducting a form of personal vendetta against any of them.

The provisions of s.15 are also of relevance in that if any person acts in contravention of a disqualification order he becomes personally liable for all the relevant debts of the company in relation to which he so acts.

Subs. (1)
He is or has been a director
It may be observed that para. (*a*) is so drafted as to render it possible for a person to incur disqualification regardless of whether he retains any ties or association with the company at the time when it becomes insolvent within the meaning of this section (see subs. 1(*a*)).

His conduct as a director
Although the duty of the court to make a disqualification order is expressed as a mandatory one, this is dependent upon the court first forming the judgment that the conduct of the person in question makes him unfit to be concerned in the management of a company. It is therefore left to the courts in the final analysis to determine the standards of proper conduct which directors (and also those in the position of shadow directors) must attain in order to escape the penalty of disqualification if the company with which they are associated should at any time become insolvent. The matters listed in Sched. 1 to which the court is required to have particular regard in the course of forming its judgment, include many matters identified during the course of protracted Parliamentary debates regarding the characteristic hallmarks of incompetent or delinquent company management. A further, important, provision is that contained in subs. (2), whereby it is made clear that the notion of a person's "conduct as a director" extends to that person's conduct in relation to any matter connected with or arising out of the insolvency of any company with which he is associated.

The terms of para. (6) authorise the court to undertake the widest possible review of the overall behavioural record in business of the person whose case is under examination. Thus, if his conduct in relation to any other company is suggestive of his overall unfitness, this may be taken into account notwithstanding that the other company may not in fact have become insolvent. Present or past involvement with several companies, only one of which becomes insolvent within the meaning of this section, may thus serve to place a person's entire business history under scrutiny, and if a composite picture of unfitness emerges a disqualification order must follow.

Subs. (3)
Court having jurisdiction to wind up company
The applicable provisions to determine jurisdiction in company winding up are ss. 512 (for England and Wales) and 515 (for Scotland) of the Companies Act 1985, together with the County Courts (Bankruptcy and Companies Winding Up Jurisdiction) Order 1971 (S.I. 1971 No. 656) as amended and currently in force (see S.I. 1971 No. 1983; S.I. 1976 No. 852; S.I. 1977 No. 151; S.I. 1977 No. 350; S.I. 1981 No. 1624; S.I. 1983 No. 713). These provisions therefore indicate which court or courts would have constituted the venue for a compulsory winding up of the company which, in the event under contemplation, is being wound up voluntarily. The court or courts so indicated represent the proper forum for making an application for a disqualification order.

Subs. (3) concludes with the words that the term "director" includes a shadow director.

Shadow director
The definition given in s.22(5) coincides with that contained in s.741(2) of the Companies Act 1985. See s.19(*c*) and Sched. 2 which preclude any applications for disqualification orders under this section and s.8 where the relevant company went into liquidation before April 28, 1986.

DERIVATIONS
Insolvency Act 1985, s.12(1), (2), (7)–(9), 108(2) and Companies Act 1985, s.295(2).

Applications to court under s.6; reporting provisions

7.—(1) If it appears to the Secretary of State that it is expedient in the public interest that a disqualification order under section 6 should be made against any person, an application for the making of such an order against that person may be made—

(*a*) by the Secretary of State, or

(*b*) if the Secretary of State so directs in the case of a person who is or has been a director of a company which is being wound up by the court in England and Wales, by the official receiver.

(2) Except with the leave of the court, an application for the making under that section of a disqualification order against any person shall not be made after the end of the period of 2 years beginning with the day on which the company of which that person is or has been a director became insolvent.

(3) If it appears to the office-holder responsible under this section, that is to say—

(*a*) in the case of a company which is being wound up by the court in England and Wales, the official receiver,

(*b*) in the case of a company which is being wound up otherwise, the liquidator,

(*c*) in the case of a company in relation to which an administration order is in force, the administrator, or

(*d*) in the case of a company of which there is an administrative receiver, that receiver,

that the conditions mentioned in section 6(1) are satisfied as respects a person who is or has been a director of that company, the office-holder shall forthwith report the matter to the Secretary of State.

(4) The Secretary of State or the official receiver may require the liquidator, administrator or administrative receiver of a company, or the former liquidator, administrator or administrative receiver of a company—

(*a*) to furnish him with such information with respect to any person's conduct as a director of the company, and

(*b*) to produce and permit inspection of such books, papers and other records relevant to that person's conduct as such a director.

as the Secretary of State or the official receiver may reasonably require for the purpose of determining whether to exercise, or of exercising, any function of his under this section.

DEFINITIONS
"administrative receiver": s.251, Insolvency Act 1986.
"becomes insolvent": s.6(2).
"court": s.6(3).
"director": s.22(4).

GENERAL NOTE
This section limits the capacity to invoke s.6 by confining the exercise of the power to apply to the court for a disqualification order to the Secretary of State, or, in defined circumstances, the Official Receiver acting under authority delegated by the Secretary of State. It should be noted however that s.6 indirectly extends the scope for initiating proceedings from which a disqualification order may ensue since the court may make such an order of its own motion following the making of a declaration that a person is liable to contribute to the company's assets. Compare this with the right to make application for such a declaration under ss.213–214 of the Insolvency Act 1986 which is enjoyed by a wider range of interested parties, and is not confined to the Secretary of State alone.

In order to ensure that the requisite information is supplied to the Secretary of State so as to enable him to determine whether it is expedient in the public interest that a disqualification order should be made against any person, a duty is imposed upon all office holders who have charge of company insolvency proceedings—the Official Receiver, the liquidator, the administrator, or the administrative receiver, as the case may be—to report to the Secretary of State if they discover that any present or past director or shadow director of the company has engaged in conduct which makes him unfit to be concerned in the management of companies. The function of deciding whether a person's conduct satisfies this statutory formula is vested in the court to which the application is made in accordance with the terms of ss.6(1) and 7(1). In performing this task the court is required by s.9 to have regard to the matters mentioned in Sched. 1 to the Act. If on this basis the court is satisfied that the conduct of the person concerned matches the statutory formula embodied in s.6(1)(*b*), the combined effect of s.6(1) and (2) is to render obligatory the making of a disqualification order for a minimum of two years, albeit according to s.6(4) the court may exercise a discretion as to the duration of the disqualification between the statutory minimum of two years and the maximum of 15 years.

Subs. (1)
If it appears to the Secretary of State

This provision is designed to ensure that a centralised control is maintained over the making of all applications for a disqualification order under this section. This is achieved by confining the power to initiate such applications to the Secretary of State alone. It is true that para. (*b*), which will in practice be the basis for the majority of applications made to the court, authorises the making of the application by the Official Receiver in the case where a compulsory winding up is taking place, but the provision is so worded that the Official Receiver can only act at the direction of the Secretary of State. It should be noted therefore that, although s.7(3)(*a*) imposes upon the Official Receiver in a compulsory winding up a duty to report to the Secretary of State if it appears to him that any present or past director is guilty of conduct making him or her unfit to be concerned in company management, the actual decision whether to make an application for a disqualification order has to be taken by the Secretary of State albeit the latter may thereupon direct the Official Receiver who has had charge of the winding up to undertake the conduct of the application to the court for a disqualification order to be made.

Subs. (3)

The purpose of this provision is to ensure that there is a proper flow of information to the Secretary of State so that decisions can be taken regarding the making of applications for disqualification orders. A duty is then imposed upon the office holder in each respective type of insolvency proceeding (the Official Receiver, liquidator, administrator, or administrative receiver, as the case may be) to report to the Secretary of State if he discovers evidence of misconduct on the part of any present or past director (or shadow director) of the company. It may be observed that, while provision has been made to render it a duty to report for those who are generally best positioned to uncover relevant evidence and information concerning the conduct of a company's affairs, no restriction has been imposed on the right of other persons who may have knowledge or suspicions about misconduct to make independent submissions to the Secretary of State. It is likely, however, that in most cases such submissions will be channelled via the office holder, who should be informed of all matters relevant to his investigation of the company and its affairs. If the office holder declines to take appropriate action on the basis of reasonably sound evidence submitted to him, the person by whom he has been vainly urged to fulfil his obligations under this subsection could legitimately proceed to make a direct approach to the Secretary of State, coupling this with a formal complaint against the office holder himself (*cf.* H.C. Standing Committee E, cols. 151–152, May 23, 1985).

Subs. (4)
The Secretary of State or official receiver may require . . .

This provision operates as a counterpart to that contained in subs. (3), whereby an office holder in insolvency proceedings is subject to a duty to report certain matters to the Secretary of State. The present subsection enables the Secretary of State or the Official Receiver to take the initiative in seeking to elicit information about any person's conduct as a director of the company. The office holder is subject to the further duty of responding to all such specific requests for information and documents, subject only to the qualification that the request must not transcend the limits of reasonableness, in the context in which it is issued.

DERIVATIONS
Insolvency Act 1985, s.12(3)–(6).

Disqualification after investigation of company

8.—(1) If it appears to the Secretary of State from a report made by inspectors under section 437 of the Companies Act, or from information or documents obtained under section 447 or 448 of that Act, that it is expedient in the public interest that a disqualification order should be made against any person who is or has been a director or shadow director of any company, he may apply to the court for such an order to be made against that person.

(2) The court may make a disqualification order against a person where, on an application under this section, it is satisfied that his conduct in relation to the company makes him unfit to be concerned in the management of a company.

(3) In this section "the court" means the High Court or, in Scotland, the Court of Session.

(4) The maximum period of disqualification under this section is 15 years.

DEFINITIONS
"company": s.22(2).
"court": s.8(3).
"director": s.22(4).
"shadow director": s.22(5).
"unfit": s.9, s.6(2), Pts. I and II of Sched. 1.

GENERAL NOTE
See note to ss.6 and 7. Under Pt. XIV of the Companies Act 1985 provision is made for the investigation of companies and their affairs and powers given to question persons and to requisition and seize company documents. It provides several methods in ss.431–432 by which a company may come under the scrutiny of inspectors appointed by the Secretary of State and ss.433–441 specify the wide powers of such inspectors and the consequences that may follow an investigation. One consequence is that under s.437 the inspectors may, and if directed by the Secretary of State, must make an interim report and it is mandatory on the conclusion of their investigation for them to make a written report to the Secretary of State. It is on the basis of such reports or material requisitioned or seized under ss.447–448 that the Secretary of State may apply to the court for a disqualification order to be made against any person who is or has been a director.

Note, the Financial Services Bill which should become law in October 1986 will amend s.8. It will add several more methods to those contained in the Companies Act 1985 by which the Secretary of State may appoint inspectors to report or seek information. Based on either he may apply to the court for a disqualification order to be made against persons who either engaged in insider dealing or found wanting in their managerial or supervisory functions relating to a collective investment business. Such an order will prevent them acting as company directors.

Matters to be considered for determining unfitness of directors are set out in Pt. I and II of Sched. 1 to this Act.

Note, however, s.19(*c*) and Sched. 2 which preclude any application for disqualification under this section or s.6, where the relevant company went into liquidation before April 28, 1986.

DERIVATIONS
Insolvency Act 1985, ss.12(9), 13, 108(2) and Companies Act 1958, s.295(2).

Matters for determining unfitness of directors

9.—(1) Where it falls to a court to determine whether a person's conduct as a director or shadow director of any particular company or companies makes him unfit to be concerned in the management of a company, the court shall, as respects his conduct as a director of that company or, as the case may be, each of those companies, have regard in particular—

    (*a*) to the matters mentioned in Part I of Schedule 1 to this Act, and

    (*b*) where the company has become insolvent, to the matters mentioned in Part II of that Schedule;

and references in that Schedule to the director and the company are to be read accordingly.

(2) Section 6(2) applies for the purposes of this section and Schedule 1 as it applies for the purposes of sections 6 and 7.

(3) Subject to the next subsection, any reference in Schedule 1 to an enactment contained in the Companies Act or the Insolvency Act includes, in relation to any time before the coming into force of that enactment, the corresponding enactment in force at that time.

(4) The Secretary of State may by order modify any of the provisions of Schedule 1; and such an order may contain such transitional provisions as may appear to the Secretary of State necessary or expedient.

(5) The power to make orders under this section is exercisable by statutory instrument subject to annulment in pursuance of a resolution of either House of Parliament.

DEFINITIONS

    "company": s.22(2).
    "conduct": s.6(2).
    "director": s.22(4).
    "insolvent": s.6(2), Pt. II, Sched. 1.

GENERAL NOTE

    This section imposes upon the court which is deciding an application for a disqualification order a mandatory requirement to have regard to the relevant provisions of Sched. 1 for the purpose of determining whether a person's conduct as a director makes him unfit to be concerned in the management of a company. The transitional provision in subs. (3) allows for the fact that courts will frequently have to take into account conduct which took place before the present Act, the Companies Act 1985 and the Insolvency Act 1986, came into effect, and it is accordingly provided that all past conduct is to be judged in relation to the law then in force. Power to modify, and to make further transitional provisions to, the section and its accompanying Schedule is delegated to the Secretary of State by subss. (4) and (5).

Subs. (1)
Conduct as a director

    By virtue of subs. (2) the extended notion of "conduct" embodied in s.6(2) is incorporated into this section and into Sched. 1. Therefore where any of the companies concerned has become insolvent any references in the relevant statutory provisions to a person's "conduct as a director" include references to his conduct in relation to any matter connected with or arising out of the insolvency of that company.

Where the company has become insolvent

    By virtue of subs. (2) the special definition of "becomes insolvent" which is contained in s.6(2) is made applicable also to this section and to Sched. 1.

DERIVATIONS

    Insolvency Act 1985, s.14 and s.12(9).

Other cases of disqualification

Participation in wrongful trading

    10.—(1) Where the court makes a declaration under section 213 or 214 of the Insolvency Act that a person is liable to make a contribution to a company's assets, then, whether or not an application for such an order is made by any person, the court may, if it thinks fit, also make a disqualification order against the person to whom the declaration relates.

(2) The maximum period of disqualification under this section is 15 years.

DEFINITION
   "disqualification order: s.1.

GENERAL NOTE
   The effect of this section is to empower the court to make a disqualification order of its own motion in any case in which it has made a declaration against a person under s.214 (for wrongful trading) or under s.213 (for fraudulent trading) of the Insolvency Act 1986. Since the right to make applications for such a declaration is enjoyed by the liquidator he may become indirectly responsible for the court utilising its power under this section to make a disqualification order against the director in question. This is of interest because, as we have seen, the right to make a direct application for a disqualification order under ss.6 or 8 of the Act is effectively confined to the Secretary of State. The provisions of s.15 also apply to a disqualification order made under this section with the consequence that any person who contravenes the order becomes personally liable for all the relevant debts of the company.

If it thinks fit
   Although there is no specific reference to s.10 in the provisions of s.9, it is surely desirable in the interests of ensuring consistency that in exercising the discretion it enjoys under this section the court should have regard to the criteria for determining unfitness of directors, which are set out in Sched. 1 to the Act for use in relation to the tasks which the court is called upon to perform under ss.6 and 8. It must be admitted however that the way in which the Act is actually drafted appears to give the court a wider discretion when acting under this section than when acting under s.6 or s.8.

DERIVATIONS
   Insolvency Act 1985, s.16 and s.108(2) and Companies Act 1985, s.295(2).

Undischarged bankrupts

   11.—(1) It is an offence for a person who is an undischarged bankrupt to act as director of, or directly or indirectly to take part in or be concerned in the promotion, formation or management of, a company, except with the leave of the court.
   (2) "The court" for this purpose is the court by which the person was adjudged bankrupt or, in Scotland, sequestration of his estates was awarded.
   (3) In England and Wales, the leave of the court shall not be given unless notice of intention to apply for it has been served on the official receiver; and it is the latter's duty, if he is of opinion that it is contrary to the public interest that the application should be granted, to attend on the hearing of the application and oppose it.

DEFINITIONS
   "company": s.22(2).
   "court": s.11(2).
   "director": s.22(4).
   "official receiver": s.21 and ss.399–401, Insolvency Act 1986.
   "undischarged bankrupt": ss.278–281, Insolvency Act 1986.

GENERAL NOTE
   This section aims to stop undischarged bankrupts from acting as company directors or in any way being involved in the setting-up of a company. In order to be so involved the permission of the court must be first obtained but by subs. (3) the official receiver is given an opportunity to oppose such an application.
   This was s.302 of the Companies Act 1985 which in turn derived from the 1948 Act, s.187, the 1981 Act, Sched. 3, para. 9; and the Companies Acts (Pre-Consolidation Amendments) (No. 2) Order 1984 (S.I. 1984 No. 1169). The latter amendment had enabled the fine to be made additional to imprisonment in Scotland, as well as an alternative.

DERIVATION
Companies Act 1985, s.302.

Failure to pay under county court administration order

12.—(1) The following has effect where a court under section 429 of the Insolvency Act revokes an administration order under Part VI of the County Courts Act 1984.

(2) A person to whom that section applies by virtue of the order under section 429(2)(*b*) shall not, except with the leave of the court which made the order, act as director or liquidator of, or directly or indirectly take part or be concerned in the promotion, formation or management of, a company.

DEFINITIONS
"administration order": Pt. II, ss.8–12, Insolvency Act 1986.
"director": s.22(4).

GENERAL NOTE
S. 429 of the Insolvency Act 1986 provides that where a person fails to make any payment which he is required to make under an administrative order made against him under Pt. VI of the County Courts Act 1984 then the court administering his estate may revoke the administration order and substitute an alternative. The alternative is a dual order under s.429(2)(*b*) which provides for an order under s.12 of the Company Directors Disqualification Act 1986 for a specified period up to two years together with an order under s.429(3) directing that the person so disqualified shall not either alone or jointly obtain credit above the amount prescribed in s.360(1)(*a*) or enter any transaction in connection with any business without disclosing to the other party the fact that this disability has been imposed on him by s.429. While the former order precludes such a person participating in the formation or management of a company, the latter disability, while not preventing him from participating in some other form of business organisation, makes it incumbent on him to disclose that money has not been paid by him under an administrative order.

DERIVATION
Insolvency Act 1985, s.221(2).

Consequences of contravention

Criminal penalties

13.—(1) If a person acts in contravention of a disqualification order or of section 12(2), or is guilty of an offence under section 11, he is liable—

(*a*) on conviction on indictment, to imprisonment for not more than 2 years or a fine, or both; and

(*b*) on summary conviction, to imprisonment for not more than 6 months or a fine not exceeding the statutory maximum, or both.

GENERAL NOTE
See note to s.12 for a guide as to what constitutes acting in contravention of s.12(2). This section prescribes the maximum penalties imposable on indictment or summarily on those who act in contravention of a disqualification order made under this Act or arising from a failure to pay under an administrative order under the Insolvency Act 1986 or for the offence of acting as a director while still an undischarged bankrupt.

DERIVATIONS
Companies Act 1985, ss.295(7) and 302(1) and Sched. 24 to that Act.

Offences by body corporate

14.—(1) Where a body corporate is guilty of an offence of acting in contravention of a disqualification order, and it is proved that the offence occurred with the consent or connivance of, or was attributable to any neglect on the part of any director, manager, secretary or other similar officer of the body corporate, or any person who was purporting to act in any such capacity he, as well as the body corporate, is guilty of the offence and liable to be proceeded against and punished accordingly.

(2) Where the affairs of a body corporate are managed by its members, subsection (1) applies in relation to the acts and defaults of a member in connection with his functions of management as if he were a director of the body corporate.

DEFINITIONS
  "body corporate": s.22(6) and Companies Act 1985, s.740.
  "disqualification order": s.1.
  "officer": s.22(6) and Companies Act 1985, s.744.

GENERAL NOTE
  This section previously was s.733(1)–(3) of the 1985 Companies Act which had re-enacted s.81 of the 1981 Companies Act. It provides not only for corporate liability but also for the lifting of the veil of incorporation to allow for the prosecution of the individuals who are responsible for the company's failure to comply with a disqualification order imposed upon it. Those individuals who run the affairs of the company, and who should have ensured that the obligation was met, will be liable together with the company itself, this includes any director, manager, secretary, officer or member (in the case of a company managed by members) responsible by his act, omission or negligence.

DERIVATIONS
  Companies Act 1985, s.733(1)–(3).

Personal liability for company's debts where person acts while disqualified

15.—(1) A person is personally responsible for all the relevant debts of a company if at any time—
  (*a*) in contravention of a disqualification order or of section 11 of this Act he is involved in the management of the company, or
  (*b*) as a person who is involved in the management of the company, he acts or is willing to act on instructions given without the leave of the court by a person whom he knows at that time to be the subject of a disqualification order or to be an undischarged bankrupt.

(2) Where a person is personally responsible under this section for the relevant debts of a company, he is jointly and severally liable in respect of those debts with the company and any other person who, whether under this section or otherwise, is so liable.

(3) For the purposes of this section the relevant debts of a company are—
  (*a*) in relation to a person who is personally responsible under paragraph (*a*) of subsection (1), such debts and other liabilities of the company as are incurred at a time when that person was involved in the management of the company, and
  (*b*) in relation to a person who is personally responsible under paragraph (*b*) of that subsection, such debts and other liabilities of the company as are incurred at a time when that person was acting or was willing to act on instructions given as mentioned in that paragraph.

(4) For the purposes of this section, a person is involved in the management of a company if he is a director of the company or if he is concerned, whether directly or indirectly, or takes part, in the management of the company.

(5) For the purposes of this section a person who, as a person involved in the management of a company, has at any time acted on instructions given without the leave of the court by a person whom he knew at that

time to be the subject of a disqualification order or to be an undischarged bankrupt is presumed, unless the contrary is shown, to have been willing at any time thereafter to act on any instructions given by that person.

DEFINITIONS
"company": s.22(2).
"disqualification order": s.1.
"involved in the management of a company": s.15(4).
"the relevant debts": s.15(3).

GENERAL NOTE
This section creates a potent sanction against various kinds of misconduct by persons in relation to company management. It does so by providing that certain individuals shall be denied the privileges normally associated with limited liability, and shall be personally liable for the relevant debts of any company in relation to which they act in a prohibited manner. The prohibited manner of acting is cast in two modes. The first mode (expressed in subs. (1)(*a*)) consists of being personally involved in the management of a company in contravention of a disqualification order, or in contravention of s.11 whereby an undischarged bankrupt is forbidden to act as a director of, or to be in any way concerned in the promotion, formation or management of a company without the leave of the court. The second mode (expressed in subs. (1)(*b*)) consists of knowingly acting or being willing to act on the instructions given without leave of the court by a person on whom any of the foregoing disqualifications or prohibitions are in force, thereby becoming the medium through which that person is able to assert an influence on the affairs of the company. Thus personal liability will be incurred not only by any person who, while subject to disqualification or prohibition, acts as a director or as a shadow director within the meaning of s.22(4) and (5), but also by any person who, though not personally the subject of any such legal disability, consciously lends himself to the arrangement whereby the disqualified party contrives to circumvent the law's intentions.

Subs. (2)
Shall be jointly and severally liable
This provision ensures that whenever two or more persons incur personal responsibility for the same debts of a company by virtue of this section, liability shall be shared on an equal basis as between those persons themselves. But by providing that their liability shall be several as well as joint, the process of recovery is greatly facilitated since proceedings can be directed against any one of them who is both traceable and solvent. The full amount of the sum which constitutes the "relevant debts" of a company (as defined in subs. (3)) may be recovered from any such person, leaving him in his turn to seek contribution from any other persons who may have incurred joint liability with him.

Subs. (5)
This subsection establishes a significant presumption with regard to the concept of a person's willingness to act on the instructions of another for the purposes of this section (see subss. (1)(*b*) and 3(*b*)). Effectively, once it is established that a person involved in the management of a company has at any time acted on such instructions in a manner which contravenes subs. (1)(*b*), he is presumed to have been willing to act on any instructions of a similar character given by that other person at any time thereafter. Thus, having once comprised himself, anyone to whom this subsection applies will continue to incur personal liability for the company's debts unless he can prove to the court that his subsequent actions in relation to the company were not accompanied by a willingness on his part to act on the instructions given by the person who was barred from involvement in company management for the time being.

DERIVATION
Insolvency Act 1985, s.18(1) (part), (2)–(5).

Supplementary provisions

Application for disqualification order

16.—(1) A person intending to apply for the making of a disqualification order by the court having jurisdiction to wind up a company shall give not less than 10 days' notice of his intention to the person against whom the order is sought; and on the hearing of the application the last-mentioned person may appear and himself give evidence or call witnesses.

(2) An application to a court with jurisdiction to wind up companies for the making against any person of a disqualification order under any of sections 2 to 5 may be made by the Secretary of State or the official receiver, or by the liquidator or any past or present member or creditor of any company in relation to which that person has committed or is alleged to have committed an offence or other default.

(3) On the hearing of any application under this Act made by the Secretary of State or the official receiver or the liquidator, the applicant shall appear and call the attention of the court to any matters which seem to him to be relevant, and may himself give evidence or call witnesses.

DEFINITIONS
    "default": s.3(3).
    "disqualification order": s.1.
    "liquidator": ss.100 and 165, Insolvency Act 1986.
    "official receiver": s.21 and ss.399–401, Insolvency Act 1986.

GENERAL NOTE
    This section prescribes the persons who may apply to the court to have a disqualification order made against another person on the grounds set out in ss.2–5, namely, for being convicted of an indictable offence; for persistent breaches of companies legislation, for fraud in a winding up and for summary conviction.
    Note that this section is a natural justice type provision in that subs. (1) specifies the number of days notice that an applicant seeking a disqualification order must give the person against whom the order is sought and it further specifies that the latter is entitled, if he chooses, to appear, give evidence and call witnesses.
    Subs. (3) states that in relation to certain applications (*e.g.* under s.8), the Secretary of State, Official Receiver or liquidator must appear at the hearing of the application and must provide the court with relevant information but they may also give evidence and call witnesses.

DERIVATIONS
    Companies Act 1985, s.295(6) (part), Sched. 12, para. 1–3; Insolvency Act 1985, s.108(2), Sched. 6, para. 1(4).

Application for leave under an order

17.—(1) As regards the court to which application must be made for leave under a disqualification order, the following applies:—
    (*a*) where the application is for leave to promote or form a company, it is any court with jurisdiction to wind up companies, and
    (*b*) where the application is for leave to be a liquidator, administrator or director of, or otherwise to take part in the management of a company, or to be a receiver or manager of a company's property, it is any court having jurisdiction to wind up that company.

(2) On the hearing of an application for leave made by a person against whom a disqualification order has been made on the application of the Secretary of State, the official receiver or the liquidator, the Secretary of State, official receiver or liquidator shall appear and call the attention of the court to any matters which seem to him to be relevant, and may himself give evidence or call witnesses.

DEFINITIONS
    "company": s.22(2).
    "disqualification order": s.1.
    "liquidator": ss.100 and 165, Insolvency Act 1986.
    "official receiver": s.21 and ss.399–401, Insolvency Act 1986.

GENERAL NOTE
This section provides for a procedure whereby a disqualified person may seek the permission of the court to set up a company or to act as a liquidator, administrator or director, or participate in the management of a company or in the other prescribed activities. In the situation outlined in subs. (2) the Secretary of State, official receiver or liquidator must attend the court hearing.

DERIVATIONS
Companies Act 1985, s.295(6) (part), Sched. 12, paras. 4, 5; Insolvency Act 1985, s.108(2), Sched. 6, paras. 1(4) and 14.

Register of disqualification orders

18.—(1) The Secretary of State may make regulations requiring officers of courts to furnish him with such particulars as the regulations may specify of cases in which—

(*a*) a disqualification order is made, or

(*b*) any action is taken by a court in consequence of which such an order is varied or ceases to be in force, or

(*c*) leave is granted by a court for a person subject to such an order to do any thing which otherwise the order prohibits him from doing;

and the regulations may specify the time within which, and the form and manner in which, such particulars are to be furnished.

(2) The Secretary of State shall, from the particulars so furnished, continue to maintain the register of orders, and of cases in which leave has been granted as mentioned in subsection (1)(*c*), which was set up by him under section 29 of the Companies Act 1976 and continued under section 301 of the Companies Act 1985.

(3) When an order of which entry is made in the register ceases to be in force, the Secretary of State shall delete the entry from the register and all particulars relating to it which have been furnished to him under this section or any previous corresponding provision.

(4) The register shall be open to inspection on payment of such fee as may be specified by the Secretary of State in regulations.

(5) Regulations under this section shall be made by statutory instrument subject to annulment in pursuance of a resolution of either House of Parliament.

GENERAL NOTE
This section requires the Secretary of State to keep a public register of disqualification orders, empowers him to require relevant information from court officers and requires him to delete entries and related particulars once they are no longer in force.

DERIVATIONS
Companies Act 1985, s.301; 1976 Act, s.29; 1981 Act, Sched. 3, para. 36; Companies Act 1984 (Pre-consolidation amendments) Order (S.I. 1984 No. 134) which substituted for the text of s.29 of the 1976 Act the text which has been incorporated into the present provision (subject to consequential modifications).

Special savings from repealed enactments

19. Schedule 2 to this Act has effect—

(*a*) in connection with certain transitional cases arising under sections 93 and 94 of the Companies Act 1981, so as to limit the power to make a disqualification order, or to restrict the duration of an order, by reference to events occurring or things done before those sections came into force,

(*b*) to preserve orders made under section 28 of the Companies Act 1976 (repealed by the Act of 1981), and

(*c*) to preclude any applications for a disqualification order under section 6 or 8, where the relevant company went into liquidation before 28th April 1986.

DERIVATION
Companies Act 1985, s.295(6); and see Sched. 2.

Miscellaneous and general

Admissibility in evidence of statements

20. In any proceedings (whether or not under this Act), any statement made in pursuance of a requirement imposed by or under sections 6 to 10, 15 or 19(*c*) of, or Schedule 1 to, this Act, or by or under rules made for the purposes of this Act under the Insolvency Act, may be used in evidence against any person making or concurring in making the statement.

GENERAL NOTE
   This section provides for the admissibility in evidence of statements made pursuant to the specified provisions of this Act or under a requirement imposed by any subsidiary rules. This section largely re-enacts s.231 of the Insolvency Act 1985 which in turn had largely re-enacted the provisions of s.663(3) of the Companies Act 1985 (repealed) and of the decision in *R.* v. *Pike* [1902] 1 K.B. 552, decided under the Bankruptcy Act 1914.

DERIVATION
Insolvency Act 1985, s.231 (part).

Interaction with Insolvency Act

21.—(1) References in this Act to the official receiver, in relation to the winding up of a company or the bankruptcy of an individual, are to any person who, by virtue of section 399 of the Insolvency Act, is authorised to act as the official receiver in relation to that winding up or bankruptcy; and, in accordance with section 401(2) of that Act, references in this Act to an official receiver includes a person appointed as his deputy.

(2) Sections 6 to 10, 15, 19(*c*) and 20 of, and Schedule 1 to, this Act are deemed included in Parts I to VII of the Insolvency Act for the purposes of the following sections of that Act—

section 411 (power to make insolvency rules);
section 414 (fees orders);
section 420 (orders extending provisions about insolvent companies to insolvent partnerships);
section 422 (modification of such provisions in their application to recognised banks); and
section 431 (summary proceedings).

(3) Section 434 of that Act (Crown application) applies to sections 6 to 10, 15, 19(*c*) and 20 of, and Schedule 1 to, this Act as it does to the provisions of that Act which are there mentioned.

GENERAL NOTE
   Subs. (1) defines "official receiver" and together with subs. (2) they chart the inter-relationship between this Act and the Insolvency Act 1986.
   Subs. (3) contains the customary declaration, for the avoidance of doubt, that certain provisions of the Act bind the Crown.

DERIVATION
Insolvency Act 1985, ss.106, 107, 108(1), (2), 221(1), 224(2), 227, 229, 234.

Interpretation

22.—(1) This section has effect with respect to the meaning of expressions used in this Act, and applies unless the context otherwise requires.

(2) The expression "company"—
  (*a*) in section 11, includes an unregistered company and a company incorporated outside Great Britain which has an established place of business in Great Britain, and
  (*b*) elsewhere, includes any company which may be wound up under Part V of the Insolvency Act.

(3) Section 247 in Part VII of the Insolvency Act (interpretation for the first Group of Parts of that Act) applies as regards references to a company's insolvency and to its going into liquidation; and "administrative receiver" has the meaning given by section 251 of that Act.

(4) "Director" includes any person occupying the position of director, by whatever name called, and in sections 6 to 9 includes a shadow director.

(5) "Shadow director", in relation to a company, means a person in accordance with whose directions or instructions the directors of the company are accustomed to act (but so that a person is not deemed a shadow director by reason only that the directors act on advice given by him in a professional capacity).

(6) Section 740 of the Companies Act applies as regards the meaning of "body corporate"; and "officer" has the meaning given by section 744 of that Act.

(7) In references to legislation other than this Act—
  "the Companies Act" means the Companies Act 1985;
  "the Companies Acts" has the meaning given by section 744 of that Act; and
  "the Insolvency Act" means the Insolvency Act 1986;
and in sections 3(1) and 5(1) of this Act "the companies legislation" means the Companies Acts (except the Insider Dealing Act), Parts I to VII of the Insolvency Act and, in Part XV of that Act, sections 411, 413, 414, 416 and 417.

(8) Any reference to provisions, or a particular provision, of the Companies Acts or the Insolvency Act includes the corresponding provisions or provision of the former Companies Acts (as defined by section 735(1)(*c*) of the Companies Act, but including also that Act itself) or, as the case may be, the Insolvency Act 1985.

(9) Any expression for whose interpretation provision is made by Part XXVI of the Companies Act (and not by subsections (3) to (8) above) is to be construed in accordance with that provision.

GENERAL NOTE
  This is the definition section with respect to the entire Act, and supplies the statutory meaning of terms and expressions which are used in a consistent sense throughout the Act and also those terms which are consistent and compatible with the Companies Act 1985 and the Insolvency Act 1986.

DERIVATION
  Insolvency Act 1985, s.108(1)–(4).

Transitional provisions, savings, repeals

23.—(1) The transitional provisions and savings in Schedule 3 to this Act have effect, and are without prejudice to anything in the Interpretation Act 1978 with regard to the effect of repeals.

(2) The enactments specified in the second column of Schedule 4 to this Act are repealed to the extent specified in the third column of that Schedule.

24.—(1) This Act extends to England and Wales and to Scotland.
(2) Nothing in this Act extends to Northern Ireland.

General Note
This Act does apply to Scotland but not to Northern Ireland.

Derivation
Insolvency Act 1985, s.236(4)(*a*).

Commencement

25. This Act comes into force simultaneously with the Insolvency Act 1986.

Citation

26. This Act may be cited as the Company Directors Disqualification Act 1986.

SCHEDULES

Section 9   SCHEDULE 1

MATTERS FOR DETERMINING UNFITNESS OF DIRECTORS

PART I

MATTERS APPLICABLE IN ALL CASES

1. Any misfeasance or breach of any fiduciary or other duty by the director in relation to the company.
2. Any misapplication or retention by the director of, or any conduct by the director giving rise to an obligation to account for, any money or other property of the company.
3. The extent of the director's responsibility for the company entering into any transaction liable to be set aside under Part XVI of the Insolvency Act (provisions against debt avoidance).
4. The extent of the director's responsibility for any failure by the company to comply with any of the following provisions of the Companies Act, namely—
   (*a*) section 221 (companies to keep accounting records);
   (*b*) section 222 (where and for how long records to be kept);
   (*c*) section 288 (register of directors and secretaries);
   (*d*) section 352 (obligation to keep and enter up register of members);
   (*e*) section 353 (location of register of members);
   (*f*) sections 363 and 364 (company's duty to make annual return);
   (*g*) section 365 (time for completion of annual return); and
   (*h*) sections 399 and 415 (company's duty to register charges it creates).
5. The extent of the director's responsibility for any failure by the directors of the company to comply with section 227 (directors' duty to prepare annual accounts) or section 238 (signing of balance sheet and documents to be annexed) of the Companies Act.

PART II

MATTERS APPLICABLE WHERE COMPANY HAS BECOME INSOLVENT

6. The extent of the director's responsibility for the causes of the company becoming insolvent.
7. The extent of the director's responsibility for any failure by the company to supply any goods or services which have been paid for (in whole or in part).
8. The extent of the director's responsibility for the company entering into any transaction or giving any preference, being a transaction or preference—
   (*a*) liable to be set aside under section 127 or sections 238 to 240 of the Insolvency Act, or
   (*b*) challengeable under section 242 or 243 of that Act or under any rule of law in Scotland.
9. The extent of the director's responsibility for any failure by the directors of the company to comply with section 98 of the Insolvency Act (duty to call creditors' meeting in creditors' voluntary winding up).
10. Any failure by the director to comply with any obligation imposed on him by or under any of the following provisions of the Insolvency Act—

(*a*) section 22 (company's statement of affairs in administration);
(*a*) section 47 (statement of affairs to administrative receiver);
(*c*) section 66 (statement of affairs in Scottish receivership);
(*d*) section 99 (directors' duty to attend meeting; statement of affairs in creditors' voluntary winding up);
(*e*) section 131 (statement of affairs in winding up by the court);
(*f*) section 234 (duty of any one with company property to deliver it up);
(*g*) section 235 (duty to co-operate with liquidator, etc.).

GENERAL NOTE
This Schedule provides detailed formulations of the matters which are to be taken into account by the court when determining whether a person's conduct as a director of any particular company or companies makes him unfit to be concerned in the management of a company. The consequence of such a finding would be the making of a disqualification order under s.6 and the direction to the court to have regard to the provisions of this Schedule is contained in s.9(1). The Schedule is divided into two parts, Pt. I of which contains matters which are applicable in all cases, while Pt. II lists matters which are applicable only where the company has become insolvent. Although s.6 applies only in the case where a person is or has been a director of a company which has at any time become insolvent, the provisions of s.8 do not operate so restrictively, and are capable of giving rise to an application for a disqualification order even where the company which has undergone investigation did not in fact become insolvent. In such cases, the provisions of Pt. I only will be applicable, and the matters mentioned in Pt. II should not, strictly speaking, be taken into account even where, as in the case of para. 7 they may seem capable of application to cases where insolvency has not occurred.

DERIVATION
Insolvency Act 1985, Sched. 2.

Section 19   SCHEDULE 2

SAVINGS FROM COMPANIES ACT 1981, SS.93, 94, AND INSOLVENCY ACT 1985, SCHEDULE 9

1. Sections 2 and 4(1)(*b*) do not apply in relation to anything done before 15th June 1982 by a person in his capacity as liquidator of a company or as receiver or manager of a company's property.
2. Subject to paragraph 1—
  (*a*) section 2 applies in a case where a person is convicted on indictment of an offence which he committed (and, in the case of a continuing offence, has ceased to commit) before 15th June 1982; but in such a case a disqualification order under that section shall not be made for a period in excess of 5 years;
  (*b*) that section does not apply in a case where a person is convicted summarily—
      (i) in England and Wales, if he had consented so to be tried before that date, or
      (ii) in Scotland, if the summary proceedings commenced before that date.
3. Subject to paragraph 1, section 4 applies in relation to an offence committed or other thing done before 15th June 1982; but a disqualification order made on the grounds of such an offence or other thing done shall not be made for a period in excess of 5 years.
4. The powers of a court under section 5 are not exercisable in a case where a person is convicted of an offence which he committed (and, in the case of a continuing offence, had ceased to commit) before 15th June 1982.
5. For purposes of section 3(1) and section 5, no account is to be taken of any offence which was committed, or any default order which was made, before 1st June 1977.
6. An order made under section 28 of the Companies Act 1976 has effect as if made under section 3 of this Act; and an application made before 15th June 1982 for such an order is to be treated as an application for an order under the section last mentioned.
7. Where—
  (*a*) an application is made for a disqualification order under section 6 of this Act by virtue of paragraph (*a*) of subsection (2) of that section, and
  (*b*) the company in question went into liquidation before 28th April 1986 (the coming into force of the provision replaced by section 6),

the court shall not make an order under that section unless it could have made a disqualification order under section 300 of the Companies Act as it had effect immediately before the date specified in sub-paragraph (*b*) above.

8. An application shall not be made under section 8 of this Act in relation to a report made or information or documents obtained before 28th April 1986.

GENERAL NOTE

This Schedule is concerned with certain transitional provisions. It is important to read it in conjunction with ss.2, 3, 4, 5, 6 and 8 of this Act because this Schedule specifies certain cut off dates which affect the applicability of those provisions.

DERIVATIONS

Companies Act 1985, Sched. 12, Pt. III and Insolvency Act 1985, Sched. 9, paras. 2 and 3.

Section 23(1) SCHEDULE 3

TRANSITIONAL PROVISIONS AND SAVINGS

1. In this Schedule, "the former enactments" means so much of the Companies Act, and so much of the Insolvency Act, as is repealed and replaced by this Act; and "the appointed day" means the day on which this Act comes into force.

2. So far as anything done or treated as done under or for the purposes of any provision of the former enactments could have been done under or for the purposes of the corresponding provision of this Act, it is not invalidated by the repeal of that provision but has effect as if done under or for the purposes of the corresponding provision; and any order, regulation, rule or other instrument made or having effect under any provision of the former enactments shall, insofar as its effect is preserved by this paragraph, be treated for all purposes as made and having effect under the corresponding provision.

3. Where any period of time specified in a provision of the former enactments is current immediately before the appointed day, this Act has effect as if the corresponding provision had been in force when the period began to run; and (without prejudice to the foregoing) any period of time so specified and current is deemed for the purposes of this Act—

(*a*) to run from the date or event from which it was running immediately before the appointed day, and

(*b*) to expire (subject to any provision of this Act for its extension) whenever it would have expired if this Act had not been passed;

and any rights, priorities, liabilities, reliefs, obligations, requirements, powers, duties or exemptions dependent on the beginning, duration or end of such a period as above mentioned shall be under this Act as they were or would have been under the former enactments.

4. Where in any provision of this Act there is a reference to another such provision, and the first-mentioned provision operates, or is capable of operating, in relation to things done or omitted, or events occurring or not occurring, in the past (including in particular past acts of compliance with any enactment, failures of compliance, contraventions, offences and convictions of offences) the reference to the other provision is to be read as including a reference to the corresponding provision of the former enactments.

5. Offences committed before the appointed day under any provision of the former enactments may, notwithstanding any repeal by this Act, be prosecuted and punished after that day as if this Act had not passed.

6. A reference in any enactment, instrument or document (whether express or implied, and in whatever phraseology) to a provision of the former enactments (including the corresponding provision of any yet earlier enactment) is to be read, where necessary to retain for the enactment, instrument or document the same force and effect as it would have had but for the passing of this Act, as, or as including, a reference to the corresponding provision by which it is replaced in this Act.

          SCHEDULE 4

Repeals

Chapter	Short title	Extent of repeal
1985 c.6	The Companies Act 1985.	Sections 295 to 299. Section 301. Section 302. Schedule 12. In Schedule 24, the entries relating to sections 295(7) and 302(1).
1985 c.65.	The Insolvency Act 1985.	Sections 12 to 14. Section 16. Section 18. Section 108(2). Schedule 2. In Schedule 6, paragraphs 1, 2, 7 and 14. In Schedule 9, paragraphs 2 and 3.

TABLE OF DERIVATIONS

Note: The following abbreviations are used in this Table:—
"CA" — The Companies Act 1985 (c.6).
"IA" — The Insolvency Act 1985 (c.65).

Provision	Derivation
1	CA s.295(1), (2), (4); IA Sch. 6 para.1(1)–(3).
2	CA ss.295(2), 296.
3	CA ss.295(2), 297.
4	CA ss.295(2), 298.
5	CA ss.295(2), 299.
6	CA s.295(2); IA ss.12(1), (2), (7)–(9), 108(2).
7	IA s.12(3)–(6).
8	CA s.295(2); IA ss.12(9), 13, 108(2).
9	IA ss.12(9), 14.
10	CA s.295(2); IA ss.16, 108(2).
11	CA s.302.
12	IA s.221(2).
13	CA ss.295(7), 302(1), Sch. 24.
14	CA s.733(1)–(3); IA Sch. 6 para. 7.
15	IA s.18(1) (part), (2)–(6).
16	CA s.295(6) (part), Sch. 12 paras. 1–3; IA s.108(2), Sch. 6 para. 1(4).
17	CA s.295(6) (part), Sch. 12 paras. 4, 5; IA s.108(2), Sch. 6 paras. 1(4), 14.
18	CA s.301; IA s.108(2), Sch. 6 para. 2.
19	CA s.295(6); and see Sch. 2.
20	IA s.231 (part).
21	IA ss.106, 107, 108(1), (2), 222(1), 224(2), 227, 229, 234.
22	IA 108(1)–(4).
23	—
24	IA s.236(4)(*a*).
25	—
26	—
Sch. 1	IA Sch. 2.
Sch. 2	CA Sch. 12 Pt. III; IA Sch. 9 paras. 2, 3.
Sch. 3	—
Sch. 4	—

TABLE OF DESTINATIONS

1986 references are to the Company Directors Disqualification Act 1986.

COMPANIES ACT 1985 (c.6)

1985	1986	1985	1986	1985	1986
s.295(1)	s.1	297	ss.2, 3	Sch. 2	19
(2)	ss.1, 2, 3, 4, 5, 6, 8, 10	298	s.4	Sch. 12	
(4)	s.1	299	5	paras. 1–3	16
(6)	19	301	18	paras. 4, 5	17
(6) (part)	ss.16, 17	302	11	Pt.III	Sch. 2
(7)	s.13	(1)	13	Sch. 24	s.13
		733(1)–(3)	14		

INSOLVENCY ACT 1985 (c.65)

1985	1986	1985	1986	1985	1986
s.12(1)	s.6	106	21	234	21
(2)	6	107	21	236(4)(a)	24
(3)	7	108(1)	ss.21, 22	Sch. 2	Sch. 1
(4)	7	(2)	6, 8, 10, 16, 17, 18, 21, 22	Sch. 6,	
(5)	7	(3)	s.22	para. 1(1)–	
(6)	7	(4)	22	(3)	s.1
(7)	6	222(1)	21	(4)	ss.16, 17
(8)	6	(2)	12	para. 2	s.18
(9)	ss.6, 8, 9	224(2)	21	para. 7	14
13	s.8	227	21	para. 14	17
14	9	229	21	Sch. 9,	
16	10	231 (part)	20	paras. 2, 3	Sch. 2
18(1) (part)	15				
(2)–(6)	15				

LEGAL AID (SCOTLAND) ACT 1986*

(1986 c. 47)

ARRANGEMENT OF SECTIONS

PART I

SCOTTISH LEGAL AID BOARD

The Board

PART II

ADVICE AND ASSISTANCE

PART III

CIVIL LEGAL AID

PART IV

CRIMINAL LEGAL AID

PART V

EMPLOYMENT OF SOLICITORS BY THE BOARD

---

* Annotations by Alistair R. Brownlie, S.S.C., Edinburgh.

An Act to establish the Scottish Legal Aid Board and the Scottish Legal Aid Fund; to make new provision in connection with the availability of criminal legal aid in Scotland; to repeal and re-enact with modifications certain enactments relating to legal aid and to advice and assistance in Scotland; and for connected purposes.   [25th July 1986]

INTRODUCTION AND GENERAL NOTE

The Legal Aid (Scotland) Act 1986 received the Royal Assent on July 25, 1986 after a speedy Parliamentary passage of about eight months. It gives effect to most of the proposals outlined in a consultation paper "Legal Aid in Scotland" issued by the Scottish Home & Health Department in March 1985. It transfers responsibility for the provision of legal aid in Scotland from the Law Society of Scotland in whose hands it has rested since 1949 (the Law Society having been called into existence partly to shoulder that responsibility) to the newly created Scottish Legal Aid Board to be set up exclusively for that purpose. In general, the legislation re-enacts the framework of the former statutory code which is entirely repealed with only a few major and some minor modifications. It also improves the logical scheme of the legislation and to a minor extent simplifies the statement of the law. The Act, however, is a general framework into which the fine details of the practical arrangements for considering and granting legal aid are to be fitted on the basis of some 23 regulations to be provided by the Secretary of State for Scotland. To such an extent is this the case that during its Parliamentary passage there were frequent criticisms that the whole scheme of legal aid in Scotland is to be at the whim of the Secretary of State. The Government's reply to this criticism was that such was the case under the previous statutory code.

Pt. I of the Act deals with the creation of the Scottish Legal Aid Board and of the Fund.

Pt. II of the Act provides for a form of advice and assistance which is treated as ancillary to but distinct from legal aid.

Pt. III of the Act covers legal aid in connection with civil proceedings in Court, now known as Civil Legal Aid and the financial conditions and provisions in relation to expenses and conditions necessary to fit in with existing court procedures.

Pt. IV of the Act describes the form of criminal legal aid now to be available not from the courts themselves but from the Scottish Legal Aid Board both at first instance and in appeals.

Pt. V of the Act reproduces the provisions which have existed from the beginning but have not yet been used to enable solicitors to be employed to provide services in relation to legal aid.

Pt. VI is a miscellaneous section dealing with legal aid for children, contempt of court, the arrangements for solicitors and counsel who wish to participate in providing legal aid, information received in the course of providing legal aid and offences in relation to it, power to the Secretary of State to promulgate the numerous regulations needed to provide flesh on the bare bones of the Act, and Parliamentary scrutiny of these, and to the courts to make the necessary rules of court to facilitate the working of legal aid; and miscellaneous matters such as rights of indemnity, finance and so forth.

Sched. 1 provides the constitution, status and make up of the new Scottish Legal Aid Board, its membership, remuneration and staff.

Sched. 2 specifies the courts in which legal aid is to be available and the proceedings for which legal aid is not to be available.

Sched. 3 deals with minor and consequential amendments.

Sched. 4 deals with transitional provisions and savings.

Sched. 5 sets out the repeals including the whole of the previous statutory apparatus of legal aid.

PARLIAMENTARY DEBATES

Hansard: H.L. Vol. 470, col. 1138; H.L. Vol. 471, col. 756; H.L. Vol. 472, cols. 308, 336, 1205; H.L. Vol. 473, cols. 451, 492, 1106; H.L. Vol. 479, col. 186; H.C. Vol. 98, col. 365; H.C. Vol. 101, col. 773.

The Bill was considered by the first Scottish Standing Committee between June 10, 1986 and July 1, 1986.

PART I

SCOTTISH LEGAL AID BOARD

The Board

The Scottish Legal Aid Board

1.—(1) There shall be established a body to be known as the Scottish Legal Aid Board (in this Act referred to as "the Board").

(2) The Board shall have the general functions—

    (*a*) of securing that legal aid and advice and assistance are available in accordance with this Act; and

    (*b*) of administering the Fund.

(3) The Board shall consist of not less than 11 and not more than 15 members appointed by the Secretary of State; and the Secretary of State shall appoint one of the members to be chairman.

(4) The Secretary of State shall appoint to membership of the Board—

    (*a*) at least two members of the Faculty of Advocates;

(*b*) at least two members of the Law Society; and

(*c*) at least one other person having experience of the procedure and practice of the courts.

(5) Before appointing persons to be members of the Board in pursuance of either paragraph (*a*) or paragraph (*b*) of subsection (4) above, the Secretary of State shall consult with the professional body mentioned in that paragraph.

(6) Schedule 1 to this Act shall have effect with respect to the Board.

DEFINITION

"Scottish Legal Aid Board": Sched. 1.

GENERAL NOTE

From its inception in 1949 until the present time the Law Society of Scotland has had the responsibility of supervising the provision of legal aid in Scotland in accordance with a scheme prepared by them and for establishing a statutory Central Committee to administer their scheme. The Central Committee consisted of not more than 16 persons of whom two were laymen and the remainder were solicitors and advocates, the former being in the majority. The functions of the Law Society of Scotland and of the Central Committee are now to be taken over by a newly created Scottish Legal Aid Board of not more than 15 persons appointed by the Secretary of State after consultation with professional bodies. The stated purpose of the Government in so arranging was that the Scottish Legal Aid Board should be independent. The inference from this that the Law Society of Scotland had not acted independently and in the public interest was somewhat resented since no substantial criticism had been voiced over the years of the Law Society's conduct. Much time was spent in Parliament debating whether such a change was necessary or desirable. In introducing the Bill in the House of Lords the Lord Advocate specified the aims of the measure to be to achieve consistency in award of legal aid, to increase efficiency effectiveness and economy, and to eliminate abuse. The Report of the Royal Commission on Legal Services in Scotland (May 1980), had supported the view that it was wrong in principle for the Law Society as the governing body of the legal profession to be responsible for payment of public funds to its own members, a view which gives little credit to the ability of the professional legal man to act in a fiduciary capacity. The contrary view strongly advanced that a Board hand-picked and with a chairman appointed by the Secretary of State to operate the framework of an Act whose details are to be provided by 23 sets of regulations framed by the Secretary of State could scarcely be regarded as a more independent creature. However, that may be, the Solicitor General in the Scottish Standing Committee insisted that legal aid should not be the preserve of lawyers alone. The Law Society of Scotland, recognising the Government's resolve, has undertaken to support the new Board.

One of the concerns about having a Board composed mainly of laymen arises from the experience of the Central Committee that a substantial proportion of their time both in committee and in plenary session was occupied in considering or reviewing problems arising from particular or general difficulties of law thrown up from the throughput of applications, and in interpretation of the law affecting such points. With fewer lawyers on the Board much more outside help may be required.

The major functions of the Board are to ensure that legal aid and advice and assistance are available to the public, and to administer the Fund. These are broadly similar to the functions previously laid upon the Law Society as administrators of legal aid, but in their case provision was made for the establishing of local committees. No such provision appears in regard to the Scottish Legal Aid Board and it is not known how the Board will organise its workload. The Government are apparently taking the advice of management consultants before revealing their plans in detail.

Powers of the Board

2.—(1) Subject to the provisions of this Act, the Board may do anything—

(*a*) which it considers necessary or expedient for securing the provision of legal aid and of advice and assistance in accordance with this Act; or

(*b*) which is calculated to facilitate or is incidental to or conducive to the discharge of its functions.

(2) Without prejudice to the generality of subsection (1) above, the Board shall have power—

(*a*) to enter into any contract or agreement, including, subject to subsection (3) below, any contract or agreement to acquire or dispose of land;

(*b*) to invest money;

(*c*) to promote or assist in the promotion of publicity relating to the functions of the Board;

(*d*) to undertake any inquiry or investigation which the Board considers necessary or expedient in relation to the discharge of its functions; and

(*e*) to give to the Secretary of State such advice as it may consider appropriate in relation to the provision of legal aid and advice and assistance in accordance with this Act.

(3) The power under subsection (2)(*a*) above to enter into any contract or agreement to acquire or dispose of land shall not be exercised without the approval in writing of the Secretary of State.

DEFINITION
"the Board": Sched. 1.

GENERAL NOTE
The powers of the Board are enumerated more specifically than were the powers of the Law Society. They are suitably extensive. It is curious that power is given to publicise the Board's functions rather than the benefits which legal aid may bring to the public. By a provision added by the Government in the House of Lords the Board may, if it identifies areas where changes should be made, so advise the Secretary of State. This goes a small way to meet the criticism made of the Law Society that they were concerned only with running the legal aid scheme and not at all with planning how it might be improved. To be fair, no such function was accorded to them.

The power to invest money relates to the depositing of principal sums received until such time as they can be paid out from the Fund.

Duties of the Board

3.—(1) The Board shall, from time to time, publish information as to the discharge of its functions in relation to legal aid and advice and assistance including the forms and procedures and other matters connected therewith.

(2) The Board shall, from time to time, furnish to the Secretary of State such information as he may require relating to its property and to the discharge and proposed discharge of its functions.

(3) It shall be the duty of the Board to provide to the Secretary of State, as soon as possible after 31st March in each year, a report on the exercise of its functions during the preceding 12 months.

(4) The Board shall have regard, in the exercise of its functions, to such guidance as may from time to time be given by the Secretary of State.

(5) Guidance under subsection (4) above shall not relate to the consideration or disposal (whether in general or in respect of individual applications) of—

(*a*) applications for legal aid or advice and assistance;

(*b*) supplementary or incidental applications or requests to the Board in connection with any case where legal aid or advice and assistance has been made available.

(6) For the purposes of subsection (2) above, without prejudice to the requirements of section 5 of this Act, the Board shall permit any person authorised in that behalf by the Secretary of State to inspect and make copies of any accounts or documents of the Board and shall furnish such explanation of them as that person or the Secretary of State may require.

DEFINITIONS

"advice and assistance": s.6(1).
"legal aid": s.41.
"the Board": Sched. 1.

GENERAL NOTE

This section lays upon the Board the duty of reporting publicly upon various aspects of its work as well as on its domestic arrangements. The provision that the Board shall have regard to such guidance as may from time to time be given by the Secretary of State was debated at length in both Houses of Parliament. The provision was seen as objectionable if it meant that the Board must follow guidance and unnecessary if it meant that the Board may follow such guidance. Subs. (5) makes clear that guidance cannot be used to influence disposal of particular applications.

The Fund

Scottish Legal Aid Fund

4.—(1) The Board shall establish and maintain a fund to be known as the Scottish Legal Aid Fund (in this Act referred to as "the Fund").

(2) There shall be paid out of the Fund—

(*a*) such sums as are, by virtue of this Act or any regulations made thereunder, due to any solicitor or counsel in respect of fees and outlays properly incurred by him, in connection with the provision, in accordance with this Act, of legal aid or advice and assistance;

(*b*) expenses awarded to any person under section 19 of this Act; and

(*c*) such other payments for the purposes of this Act as the Secretary of State may, with the concurrence of the Treasury, determine.

(3) There shall be paid into the Fund—

(*a*) any contribution payable to the Fund by any person in pursuance of section 17 of this Act;

(*b*) any sum recovered under an award of a court or an agreement as to expenses in any proceedings in favour of any party who is in receipt of civil legal aid;

(*c*) any sum which is to be paid in accordance with section 17 of this Act out of property recovered or preserved for any party to any proceedings who is in receipt of civil legal aid;

(*d*) the sums to be paid by the Secretary of State in pursuance of section 40(1)(*a*) of this Act; and

(*e*) such other receipts of the Board as the Secretary of State may, with the concurrence of the Treasury, determine.

DEFINITIONS

"advice and assistance": s.6(1).
"civil legal aid": s.13(2).
"legal aid": s.41.
"the Board": Sched. 1.

GENERAL NOTE

This description of the Scottish Legal Aid Fund (which will take the place of the previous Legal Aid (Scotland) Fund) is much clearer and more straightforward than the description set out in ss.9 and 10 of the 1967 Act. The important provision of subs. (3)(*d*) means that the Government undertake to supply the Fund with such moneys as are needed to pay for legal aid and advice and assistance, *i.e.* these services are not cash limited.

Accounts and audit

5.—(1) The Board shall keep separate accounts with respect to—

(*a*) the Fund; and

(*b*) the receipts and expenditure of the Board which do not relate to the Fund, and shall prepare in respect of each financial year a statement of accounts.

(2) The accounts shall be kept and the statement of accounts shall be prepared in such form as the Secretary of State may, with the approval of the Treasury, direct.

(3) The accounts shall be audited by persons to be appointed in respect of each financial year by the Secretary of State in accordance with a scheme of audit approved by him, and the auditors shall be furnished by the Board with copies of the statement and shall prepare a report to the Secretary of State on the accounts and the statement.

(4) No person shall be qualified to be appointed auditor under subsection (3) above unless he is a member of one of the following bodies—

(a) the Institute of Chartered Accountants of Scotland;
(b) the Institute of Chartered Accountants in England and Wales;
(c) the Chartered Association of Certified Accountants;
(d) the Institute of Chartered Accountants in Ireland.

(5) Upon completion of the audit of the accounts, the auditors shall send to the Secretary of State a copy of the statement of accounts and of their report, and the Secretary of State shall send a copy of the statement and of the report to the Comptroller and Auditor General.

(6) The Secretary of State and the Comptroller and Auditor General may inspect the accounts and any records relating thereto.

(7) The Secretary of State shall lay before each House of Parliament a copy of every—

(a) annual report of the Board under section 3(3) of this Act;
(b) statement of accounts under subsection (1) above; and
(c) report of the auditors under subsection (3) above.

(8) In this section "financial year" means the period beginning with the commencement of this section and ending with 31st March next following and each subsequent period of 12 months ending with 31st March in each year.

DEFINITIONS
  "the Board": Sched. 1.
  "the fund": s.4.

GENERAL NOTE
  These provisions virtually repeat the corresponding provisions of the 1967 Act. The Secretary of State's report to Parliament each year shall include the Board's report and the audited accounts. These details will thus be made public.

PART II

ADVICE AND ASSISTANCE

Definitions

6.—(1) In this Act—
  "advice and assistance" means any of the following—
    (a) oral or written advice provided to a person by a solicitor (or, if and so far as may be necessary, by counsel)—
      (i) on the application of Scots law to any particular circumstances which have arisen in relation to the person seeking the advice;
      (ii) as to any steps which that person might appropriately take (whether by way of settling any claim, instituting, conducting or defending proceedings, making an agreement or other transaction, making a will or other instrument, obtaining further legal or other advice and assistance, or otherwise) having regard to the application of Scots law to those circumstances;

(*b*) assistance provided to a person by a solicitor (or, if and so far as may be necessary, by counsel) in taking any steps mentioned in paragraph (*a*)(ii) above, by taking such steps on his behalf or by assisting him in so taking them; and

"assistance by way of representation" means advice and assistance provided to a person by taking on his behalf any step in instituting, conducting or defending any proceedings—
  (*a*) before a court or tribunal; or
  (*b*) in connection with a statutory inquiry, whether by representing him in those proceedings or by otherwise taking any step on his behalf (as distinct from assisting him in taking such a step on his own behalf).

(2) In this Part of this Act—

"client" means a person who seeks or receives advice and assistance in accordance with this Part of this Act;

"statutory inquiry" has the meaning assigned to it by section 19(1) of the Tribunals and Inquiries Act 1971;

"the solicitor" means the solicitor by whom any advice and assistance is provided or, where it is provided by counsel, the solicitor on whose instruction counsel provides it;

"tribunal" includes an arbiter or oversman, however appointed.

GENERAL NOTE

This part of the Act for the first time brings legal advice and assistance into the main statutory framework. It re-enacts in almost identical language the definition of advice and assistance used in the 1972 Act and adds the concept of ABWOR (Advice and assistance by way of representation), which was a new import from England in 1979 mid way between advice and assistance and civil legal aid, designed to give limited representation in certain court or tribunal matters but on the basis of the straightforward means forms used in connection with advice and assistance rather than the more complicated assessments required for issue of a full legal aid certificate. ABWOR has not hitherto been brought into operation in Scotland.

Advice and assistance on the application of Scots law to a client's problems was first introduced by the 1972 Act. It excludes actual representation at court or before a tribunal but is available for almost all kinds of legal work including general advice, correspondence, preparation of wills and other documents and even certain limited items of conveyancing. It is of particular value in that it is granted by the solicitor (not by the committee) on a simplified assessment form. The control of expenditure is achieved by requiring prior authority to exceed £50. This valuable form of help is to be continued under the Scottish Legal Aid Board. For financial control see s.10. In 1984–85 the cost of such assistance was £3·2m., the average account being only £45.

Application of Part II

7.—(1) Subject to subsections (2) to (4) below, and to any exceptions and conditions prescribed by regulations made under this section or under section 9 of this Act, this Part of this Act applies to any advice and assistance.

(2) This Part of this Act does not apply to advice and assistance provided to a person in connection with proceedings before a court or tribunal at a time when he is receiving legal aid in connection with those proceedings.

(3) Subject to subsection (4) below and to section 9 of this Act, this Part of this Act does not apply to assistance by way of representation.

(4) Except where subsection (2) above applies, this Part of this Act does apply, in the case of civil proceedings before a court or tribunal, to any step which consists only of negotiating on behalf of a person with a view to the settlement of a claim to which the proceedings relate.

DEFINITIONS
"advice and assistance": s.6(1).
"legal aid": s.41.

GENERAL NOTE
   This difficult section prevents a party having a civil legal aid certificate as well as receiving advice and assistance in the same matter.
   Subs. (4) advice and assistance, however, is available to negotiate settlement of a claim in court. This proceeds on the view that assistance ought always to be available to settle or compromise proceedings where it may save much expense.

Availability of advice & assistance

8. Subject to section 11(2) of this Act, advice and assistance to which this Part applies shall be available in Scotland for any client if—
   (*a*) his disposable income does not exceed £114 a week; or
   (*b*) he is (directly or indirectly) in receipt of supplementary benefit under the Supplementary Benefits Act 1976 or of family income supplement under the Family Income Supplements Act 1970.
and his disposable capital does not exceed £800.

DEFINITIONS
   "advice and assistance": s.6(1).
   "disposable capital": s.41(1).
   "disposable income": s.41(1).

GENERAL NOTE
   The financial parameters for the grant of advice and assistance are here set out. These limits will of course be amended from time to time. It has been a recurring criticism that these financial limits are fairly low.
   Once advice and assistance is given it continues irrespective of financial changes in the client's affairs until the work for which it is given is done or the authorised expenditure is exhausted.

Regulations may apply Part II to representation

9.—(1) Regulations made under this section may provide for this Part of this Act to apply to assistance by way of representation; and regulations so made may make different provision for different cases or classes of case.
   (2) Such regulations may—
   (*a*) describe the proceedings (or stages of proceedings) in relation to which this Part of this Act shall so apply by reference to the court, tribunal or statutory inquiry, to the issues involved, to the capacity in which the person requiring the assistance is concerned, or in any other way;
   (*b*) specify, in relation to any proceedings so described, the assistance by way of representation which may be provided;
   (*c*) prescribe the criteria to be applied in determining whether assistance by way of representation should be provided;
   (*d*) require that the approval of the Board or of such other appropriate authority as may be prescribed shall be obtained, in certain classes of case, as a pre-condition of the provision of assistance by way of representation; and
   (*e*) modify the financial limits under sections 8 and 10(2) of this Act in their application to assistance by way of representation by substituting for the sums specified therein such other sums as may be prescribed, and such modification of the financial limit under the said section 10(2) may substitute different sums in relation to different proceedings or stages of proceedings.
   (3) Such regulations may also make provision, for the purposes of paragraph (*d*) of subsection (2) above, as to—
   (*a*) the procedure to be followed in applying for approval and the criteria for determining whether approval should be given;

(*b*) the conditions which should or may be imposed; and

(*c*) the circumstances in which approval may be withdrawn and the effect of its withdrawal.

DEFINITIONS

"assistance by way of representation": s.6(1).

"the Board": Sched. 1.

GENERAL NOTE

Special regulations may be made in terms of this section to define the terms on which ABWOR may be provided. These may differ from the terms of the regulations for advice and assistance itself.

Financial limit

10.—(1) Where at any time (whether before or after advice and assistance has begun to be provided to a client) it appears to the solicitor that the cost of giving it is likely to exceed the limit applicable under this section—

(*a*) the solicitor shall determine to what extent that advice and assistance can be provided without exceeding that limit; and

(*b*) shall not give it (or, as the case may be, not instruct counsel to provide it) so as to exceed that limit except with the approval of the Board.

(2) The limit applicable under this section is £50.

(3) For the purposes of this section, the cost of providing advice and assistance shall be taken to consist of such of the following as are applicable in the circumstances—

(*a*) any outlays (including the fees and outlays of counsel) which may be incurred by the solicitor or his firm or incorporated practice in, or in connection with, the providing of the advice and assistance;

(*b*) any fees (not being charges for outlays) which, apart from section 11 of this Act, would be properly chargeable by the solicitor or his firm or incorporated practice in respect of the advice and assistance; and

(*c*) in the case of advice and assistance given by a solicitor employed by the Board, any fees (not being charges for outlays) which, if the solicitor had been employed by a firm of solicitors or by an incorporated practice, would, apart from section 11 of this Act, have been properly chargeable by that firm or practice in respect of the advice and assistance.

DEFINITIONS

"advice and assistance": s.6(1).

"the Board": Sched. 1.

GENERAL NOTE

This section re-enacts the control of advice and assistance by requiring prior consent of the Board before £50 is exceeded.

Clients' contributions

11.—(1) A client shall not be required to pay any fees or outlays in respect of advice and assistance received by him in pursuance of this Part of this Act except in accordance with subsection (2) below.

(2) Where—

(*a*) a client's disposable income exceeds £54 a week; and

(*b*) he is not (directly or indirectly) in receipt of supplementary benefit under the Supplementary Benefits Act 1976 or of family income supplement under the Family Income Supplements Act 1970, he shall be liable to pay, in respect of the advice and assistance, fees or outlays up to, but not in aggregate exceeding, such amount as may be prescribed by regulations made under this section, and such regulations may prescribe different maximum payments for different amounts of disposable income and for different cases or classes of case.

DEFINITIONS
"advice and assistance": s.6(1).
"disposable income": s.42(1).

GENERAL NOTE
If a client's disposable income (calculated in accordance with regulations made under s.42) does not exceed £54 per week or he is in receipt of supplementary benefit he pays nothing for advice and assistance however much is authorised. If it does exceed that figure and he does not receive supplementary benefit the client pays a contribution calculated in accordance with a prescribed table.

Payment of fees or outlays otherwise than through clients' contributions

12.—(1) In this section, in relation to advice and assistance provided by a solicitor employed by—
  (*a*) a firm of solicitors;
  (*b*) an incorporated practice; or
  (*c*) the Board,
in the course of that employment (or by counsel on instructions given to him by such a solicitor), "the solicitor" includes the firm, incorporated practice or the Board, as the case may be.

(2) This section applies to any fees or outlays properly chargeable (in accordance with section 33 of this Act), in respect of advice and assistance given to a client in pursuance of this Part of this Act.

(3) Except in so far as regulations made under this section otherwise provide, fees or outlays to which this section applies shall be paid to the solicitor as follows—
  (*a*) *first*, out of any contribution payable by the client in accordance with section 11(2) of this Act;
  (*b*) *secondly*, in priority to all other debts, out of any expenses which (by virtue of a judgment or order of a court or an agreement or otherwise) are payable to the client by any other person in respect of the matter in connection with which the advice and assistance is provided;
  (*c*) *thirdly*, in priority to all other debts, out of any property (of whatever nature and wherever situated) which is recovered or preserved for the client in connection with that matter, including his rights under any settlement arrived at in connection with that matter in order to avoid or bring to an end any proceedings;
  (*d*) *fourthly*, by the Board out of the Fund, following receipt by it of a claim submitted by the solicitor.

DEFINITIONS
"advice and assistance": s.6(1).
"the Board": Sched. 1.
"the Fund": s.4.

GENERAL NOTE
As in earlier legislation the solicitors' account for advice and assistance is to be paid (1) from any contribution; (2) from any winnings; (3) from any property recovered for the client, and only as regards what the 1972 Act called "the deficiency", from the Fund. With advice and assistance (unlike civil legal aid) recoveries are not paid to the fund.
This follows the former pattern.

PART III

CIVIL LEGAL AID

Meaning of "civil legal aid"

13.—(1) This Part of this Act applies to civil legal aid.

(2) In this Act, "civil legal aid" means representation by a solicitor and (so far as is necessary) by counsel in any proceedings mentioned in Part I of Schedule 2 to this Act, on the terms provided for in this Act, and includes all such assistance as is usually given by solicitor or counsel in the steps preliminary to or incidental to proceedings, or in arriving at or giving effect to a settlement to prevent them or bring them to an end.

(3) Subject to sections 14 and 15 of this Act and to regulations made under this section, civil legal aid shall be available in connection with any proceedings mentioned in subsection (2) above, except insofar as Part II of Schedule 2 to this Act otherwise provides.

(4) Schedule 2 to this Act may be varied by regulations made under this section, so as to extend or restrict the categories of proceedings in which civil legal aid is available, by reference to the court or tribunal, to the issues involved, to the capacity in which the person seeking civil legal aid is concerned, or otherwise.

(5) Regulations under subsection (4) above may not have the effect of adding any reference to proceedings in any court or tribunal before which persons have no right to be and are not normally represented by counsel or a solicitor.

GENERAL NOTE

The first form of legal aid to be provided in 1949 was civil legal aid. This part of the Act re-enacts the outlines of the arrangements for this basic form of legal aid in slightly simpler form than the earlier legislation. In 1984–85 over 16,000 people received legal aid of this kind, about two-thirds of these being matrimonial cases. The initial cost was over £11,000,000.

Availability of civil legal aid

14.—(1) Subject to section 15 of this Act and to subsection (2) below, civil legal aid shall be available to a person if, on an application made to the Board—

(*a*) the Board is satisfied that he has a *probabilis causa litigandi*; and

(*b*) it appears to the Board that it is reasonable in the particular circumstances of the case that he should receive legal aid.

(2) The Board may require a person receiving civil legal aid to comply with such conditions as it considers expedient to enable it to satisfy itself from time to time that it is reasonable for him to continue to receive civil legal aid.

(3) The Board shall establish a procedure under which any person whose application for legal aid under this section has been refused may apply to the Board for a review of his application.

DEFINITIONS

"civil legal aid": s.13(2).
"the Board": Sched. 1.

GENERAL NOTE

The traditional criteria for granting civil legal aid are reproduced here *viz. probabilis causa litigandi* and reasonableness. There is provision for possible review of the client's financial position to make sure that it continues to be reasonable that he should go on receiving legal aid.

One of the major criticisms of this Part of the Bill in Parliament was the absence of a procedure to review the refusal of legal aid by the Board. This was eventually conceded by

Government. The Legal Aid Central Committee operated an appeal system under subordinate legislation but it is an advance to have a specific right of review enacted. A corresponding right of review is provided where criminal legal aid is refused: see s.24(5).

Financial conditions

15.—(1) A person shall be eligible for civil legal aid if his disposable income does not exceed £5,415 a year.

(2) A person may be refused civil legal aid if—

(*a*) his disposable capital exceeds £4,710; and

(*b*) it appears to the Board that he can afford to proceed without legal aid.

(3) For the purposes of this section, a person's disposable income and disposable capital shall be determined by the Board.

DEFINITIONS
"a person": s.41.
"civil legal aid": s.13(1).
"disposable capital": s.42(1).
"disposable income": s.42(1).
"the Board": Sched. 1.

GENERAL NOTE

The financial parameters for the grant of civil legal aid are here set out. These limits will of course be amended from time to time. The Board have here assumed the functions of determining the assessment of an applicant's financial situation previously undertaken by the Department of Health and Social Security.

"A person" is defined to make it clear that legal aid is available only to individuals and not to bodies, corporate or unincorporate, except where these are acting in a representative, fiduciary or official capacity.

Expenses

Expenses in favour of certain assisted persons

16.—(1) Any sums recovered under an award of a court or an agreement as to expenses in favour of a legally assisted person in receipt of civil legal aid shall be paid to the Fund.

(2) In this section and in sections 17 to 20 of this Act—

"court" includes tribunal;

"legally assisted person" means a person in receipt of civil legal aid in the proceedings in question or a person in receipt of assistance by way of representation in any proceedings to which this Part applies.

DEFINITIONS
"assistance by way of representation": s.6(1).
"civil legal aid": s.13(2).
"the Fund": s.4.

GENERAL NOTE

Sums payable to a legally assisted person under a decree for expenses or an agreement relating to expenses are to be paid in to the Fund. It may be that the definition covers a person who at any time was in receipt of civil legal aid or ABWOR. A person receiving advice and assistance is not for the purposes of this, and the following four sections, to be regarded as a legally assisted person.

Contributions and payments out of property recovered

17.—(1) Legally assisted persons may be required by the Board to contribute to the Fund in accordance with this section in respect of any proceedings in connection with which they are granted civil legal aid.

(2) A legally assisted person's contribution under this section shall be determined by the Board, and may include—

    (*a*) if his disposable income exceeds £2,255 a year, a contribution in respect of income which shall not be more than one-quarter of the excess (or such other proportion of the excess, or such amount, as may be prescribed by regulations made under this section); and

    (*b*) if his disposable capital exceeds £3,000, a contribution in respect of capital which shall not be more than the excess (or such proportion of the excess or such lesser amount as may be prescribed by regulations made under this section).

(3) A legally assisted person may be required to make his contribution to the Fund in one sum or by instalments.

(4) If the total contribution to the Fund made by a person in respect of any proceedings exceeds the net liability of the Fund on his account, the excess shall be repaid to him.

(5) Except insofar as regulations made under this section otherwise provide—

    (*a*) any sums remaining unpaid in respect of a person's contribution to the Fund in respect of any proceedings; and

    (*b*) any deficiency by reason of his total contribution being less than the net liability of the Fund on his account,

shall be paid, in priority to any other debts, out of any property (wherever situate) which is recovered or preserved for him—

    (i) in the proceedings; or

    (ii) under any settlement to avoid them or bring them to an end.

(6) Nothing in subsection (5) above shall prejudice the power of the court to allow any damages or expenses to be set off.

(7) In this section references to the net liability of the Fund on a legally assisted person's account are references to the aggregate amount of—

    (*a*) the sums paid or payable to a solicitor or counsel out of the Fund on his account, in respect of the proceedings in question; and

    (*b*) any sums so paid or payable, for advice and assistance in connection with the proceedings in question or any matter to which those proceedings relate,

being sums not recouped by the Fund out of expenses in respect of those proceedings, or as a result of any right which he may have to be indemnified against such expenses.

(8) Where the solicitor acting for a legally assisted person is employed by the Board for the purposes of Part V of this Act, references in subsection (7) above to sums payable out of the Fund include references to sums which would have been so payable had he not been so employed.

DEFINITIONS

  "advice and assistance": s.6(1).

  "civil legal aid": s.13(2).

  "disposable capital": s.42(1).

  "disposable income": s.42(1).

  "legally assisted person": s.16(2).

  "the Board": Sched. 1.

  "the Fund": s.4.

GENERAL NOTE

  A person's contributions for civil legal aid are to be paid into the Fund and these, together with any recoveries, are to be used to meet the cost of giving that person legal aid and also any sums paid or payable for giving him advice and assistance on or related to the matter in issue; but the court's power to allow set off of one award against another is preserved.

Expenses of unassisted party

18.—(1) This section and section 19 of this Act apply to proceedings to which a legally assisted person is party and which are finally decided in favour of an unassisted person.

(2) The liability of a legally assisted person under an award of expenses in proceedings to which this section applies shall not exceed the amount (if any) which in the opinion of the court or tribunal making the award is a reasonable one for him to pay, having regard to all the circumstances including the means of all the parties and their conduct in connection with the dispute.

(3) None of the following, namely a legally assisted person's house, wearing apparel, household furniture and the tools and implements of his trade or profession shall—

(a) be taken into account in assessing his means for the purposes of subsection (2) above; or

(b) be subject to diligence or any corresponding process in any part of the United Kingdom in connection with any award of expenses in proceedings to which this section applies,

except insofar as regulations made under this section may prescribe.

DEFINITION
"legally assisted person": s.16(2).

GENERAL NOTE
In a question with an unassisted person, a legally assisted person's liability for an award of expenses may be modified to such sums as the court thinks it reasonable for him to pay having regard to circumstances and conduct. This is the secondary benefit of legal aid to an assisted person. This section seems to restrict that benefit slightly as compared with s.2(6)(e) of the 1967 Act which did not have the restriction set out in subs. (1) above.

Expenses out of the Fund

19.—(1) In any proceedings to which this section applies, subject to subsections (2) and (3) below, the court may make an award out of the Fund to an unassisted party of the whole or any part of any expenses incurred by him (so far as attributable to any part of the proceedings in connection with which another party was a legally assisted person).

(2) Before making an order under this section, the court shall consider making an award of expenses against the legally assisted person.

(3) An order under this section may be made only if—

(a) an order for expenses might be made in the proceedings, apart from this Act; and

(b) in the case of expenses of proceedings in a court of first instance, those proceedings were instituted by the legally assisted person, and the court is satisfied that the unassisted party will suffer severe financial hardship unless the order is made; and

(c) in any case, the court is satisfied that it is just and equitable in all the circumstances that the award should be paid out of public funds.

(4) The provisions of subsection (3)(b) above regarding financial hardship may be modified, in their application to persons who are concerned in proceedings only in a fiduciary, representative or official capacity, by regulations made under this section.

(5) No appeal may be made against an order made under this section, or against a refusal to make such an order, except on a point of law.

(6) In this section, "expenses" means expenses as between party and party, and includes the expenses of applying for an order under this section.

DEFINITIONS
"legally assisted person": s.16(2).
"the Fund": s.4(1).

GENERAL NOTE
This section re-enacts, in a simpler form, the provision first introduced in 1964 to allow a payment from the fund to rectify the injustice that an assisted person might involve an unassisted person in legal proceedings which failed and then have his liability to pay expenses modified, so that the unassisted litigant was left without redress. There are stringent conditions to be met, principally in proceedings on appeal that it is just and equitable that such a payment should be made, and in proceedings at first instance that it is just and equitable, and also that severe financial hardship would follow if no payment were allowed. The conditions of s.20 must also be satisfied.
Special provision may now be made for persons acting in a trust capacity.

Provisions supplementary to sections 18 and 19

20.—(1) For the purposes of sections 18 and 19 of this Act, civil proceedings are finally decided in favour of an unassisted party—

(*a*) if no appeal may be made against the decision in his favour;

(*b*) if an appeal may be made against the decision with leave, and the time limit for applications for leave expires and either no application has been made, or leave has been refused;

(*c*) if leave to appeal against the decision is granted or is not required and no appeal is made within the time limit for appeals; or

(*d*) if an appeal is made but is abandoned before it is determined.

(2) Where an appeal is allowed to be made late, the court by which the appeal (or any further appeal in those proceedings) is determined may make an order for the repayment by the unassisted party to the Fund of the whole or any part of any sum previously paid to him under section 19 of this Act in respect of those proceedings.

(3) Where a court decides any proceedings in favour of the unassisted party and an appeal may be made (with or without leave) against that decision, the court may, if it thinks fit, make or refuse to make an order under section 19 of this Act, but any order so made shall not take effect unless—

(*a*) where leave to appeal is required, the time limit for applications for leave to appeal expires and no application has been made or leave is refused;

(*b*) where leave to appeal is granted or is not required, the time limit for appeals expires without an appeal being made; or

(*c*) an appeal is made but is abandoned before it is determined.

(4) It shall be competent, at any time within such period after the making of an award of expenses to which section 18(2) of this Act applies as may be prescribed by regulations made under this section, for any party concerned with the award to apply to the court or tribunal which made the award for re-assessment of its amount, on the ground that since the award was made there has been a relevant change of circumstances, and on such application the court or tribunal may make such re-assessment of the amount of the award as seems to them proper.

DEFINITION
"the Fund": s.4(1).

GENERAL NOTE
This section expresses the other conditions which must be satisfied before an order for payment from the fund under s.19 can be made. The provisions of subs. (4) for re-assessment are new.

PART IV

CRIMINAL LEGAL AID

Scope and nature of criminal legal aid

21.—(1) This Part of this Act applies to legal aid in connection with—
(*a*) criminal proceedings before any of the following—
    (i) the High Court of Justiciary;
    (ii) the sheriff;
    (iii) the district court; and
(*b*) any reference in connection with such proceedings under Article 177 of the EEC Treaty,
and such legal aid is referred to in this Act as "criminal legal aid".

(2) The Secretary of State may, by regulations made under this section, prescribe by reference to such considerations as appear to him to be appropriate any class or stage of proceedings in connection with which criminal legal aid shall or, as the case may be, shall not be available.

(3) Subject to regulations made under this section, and to sections 22 and 23 of this Act, criminal legal aid shall not be available in connection with summary criminal proceedings until the conclusion of the first diet at which the accused has tendered a plea of not guilty.

(4) Criminal legal aid shall consist of representation, on terms provided for by this Act—
(*a*) by a solicitor and (so far as necessary) by counsel;
(*b*) by a solicitor at any identification parade held, by or on behalf of the prosecutor (within the meaning of section 462 of the Criminal Procedure (Scotland) Act 1975), in connection with or in contemplation of criminal proceedings against the person so represented,
and shall include all such assistance as is usually given by a solicitor or counsel in the steps preliminary to or incidental to criminal proceedings.

GENERAL NOTE

This part of the Act re-enacts the earlier provisions regarding criminal legal aid with the important variation that in summary proceedings criminal legal aid is no longer to be granted as formerly by the court at first instance and by the Law Society of Scotland in appeals. These functions are now assumed by the Scottish Legal Aid Board. In solemn proceedings criminal legal aid may be available from the court in accordance with the following sections.

The sweeping powers in subs. (2) which allow the Secretary of State to regulate (or abolish) criminal legal aid came in for much criticism in Parliament. These powers are however, almost exactly what were contained in earlier legislation. They will be used *inter alia* to make regulations to prescribe exactly how ABWOR may be allowed for certain circumstances rather than criminal legal aid. To avoid duplication they will remove the possibility of receiving criminal legal aid in these circumstances.

Under existing regulations criminal legal aid in summary or solemn proceedings could be granted through a solicitor of the accused's choice from the earliest point in a case to its conclusion, if the court were minded to grant it. One of the changes wrought by this section is that in summary cases there can be no criminal legal aid for an accused pleading not guilty before the conclusion of the first diet, except through the duty solicitor should the accused be in custody.

As previously, criminal legal aid is to consist of representation by solicitor and so far as necessary by counsel and to cover all steps necessary to carry out the duties which fall upon solicitor and counsel in relation to their client. The latter reassurance does not rule out the necessity of obtaining sanction as at present for certain steps or facilities and it is expected that regulations will prescribe how sanctions for counsel, expert witnesses and the like are to be procured from the Board.

In 1984–85 over 71,000 people received legal aid of this kind at a cost of over £19,600,000.

Automatic availability of criminal legal aid

22.—(1) Subject to regulations made under section 21(2) of this Act, criminal legal aid shall be available to every accused person—

(a) where he is given representation as mentioned in paragraph (b) of section 21(4) of this Act;
(b) where his case is being prosecuted under solemn procedure until either—
    (i) an application for legal aid under section 23(1)(a) of this Act has been determined; or
    (ii) he is admitted to bail or he is committed until liberated in due course of law,
whichever first occurs;
(c) where he is being prosecuted under summary procedure, and either is in custody or has been liberated under section 295(1)(a) of the Criminal Procedure (Scotland) Act 1975 (liberation by police on undertaking to appear)—
    (i) until the conclusion of the first diet at which he tenders a plea of guilty or not guilty; or
    (ii) where he has tendered a plea of guilty at that diet, until his case is finally disposed of;
(d) where he is in custody and he is being prosecuted under summary procedure and he has—
    (i) tendered a plea of not guilty; and
    (ii) made an application to the Board for legal aid in connection with the proceedings,
until his application has been determined by the Board; and
(e) where he is being prosecuted under section 255 or 452B of the Criminal Procedure (Scotland) Act 1975 (new prosecution for same or similar offence), until his case is finally disposed of.

(2) Criminal legal aid made available in the circumstances referred to in paragraph (c)(i) of subsection (1) above shall also be available in connection with any steps taken in the making of and representation in connection with any application for liberation following upon the diet referred to in that paragraph.

DEFINITION
"criminal legal aid": s.21(1).

GENERAL NOTE
This section prescribes the circumstances in which accused persons will receive what the rubric describes as "automatic availability" of criminal legal aid. This is the work previously covered by the duty solicitor, namely attendance at a Crown identification parade, in solemn procedure and until full committal unless criminal legal aid has been sooner granted or refused by the court. In summary procedure automatic legal aid will cover the accused who is in custody or liberated on his undertaking to appear until conclusion of the first diet if he pleads not guilty (including an application for liberation) or if he has applied to the Board until his application is determined by the Board. Also in the very special case where following an appeal against conviction the court authorises a new prosecution for the same or similar offence.

Power of the court to grant legal aid

23.—(1) Criminal legal aid shall be available on an application made to the court—
(a) where a person is being prosecuted under solemn procedure; or
(b) where a person who has not previously been sentenced to imprisonment or detention has been convicted in summary proceedings, and the court is considering a sentence of imprisonment or detention or the imposition of imprisonment under section 396(2) of the Criminal Procedure (Scotland) Act 1975 (failure to pay a fine when no time for payment is allowed),

if the court is satisfied after consideration of the person's financial circumstances that the expenses of the case cannot be met without undue hardship to him or his dependants.

(2) In subsection (1) above, "the court" means—

(*a*) in relation to solemn proceedings—

(i) the sheriff before whom the person is brought for examination; or

(ii) where criminal legal aid has not been made available at any earlier stage of the proceedings in a case before it, the High Court of Justiciary;

(*b*) in relation to summary proceedings, the court before which the proceedings are being taken,

and references in that subsection to detention shall be construed in accordance with section 41(2)(*b*) of the Criminal Justice (Scotland) Act 1980.

DEFINITION
"criminal legal aid": s.21(1).

GENERAL NOTE
This section defines the remaining circumstances in which the courts will still be able to grant criminal legal aid. These are in solemn procedure cases or in circumstances in which the court, following conviction, is considering a first sentence of imprisonment. In either case the court will have to be satisfied that the accused cannot pay his own expenses without undue hardship.

Except in the case of contempt procedings (see s.30), there is no provision to allow the court to award criminal legal aid in the form of a "dock brief" in exceptional circumstances, and such situations would have to be met by allowing an adjournment to allow the accused to approach the Board: see s.24(6).

Legal aid in summary proceedings

24.—(1) Subject to regulations made under section 21(2) of this Act, to section 21(3) of this Act and to subsection (3) below, criminal legal aid shall be available to an accused person in summary proceedings on an application made to the Board if the Board is satisfied—

(*a*) after consideration of the financial circumstances of the accused person, that the expenses of the case cannot be met without undue hardship to him or his dependants; and

(*b*) that in all the circumstances of the case it is in the interests of justice that legal aid should be made available to him.

(2) The Board may require a person receiving criminal legal aid under this section to comply with such conditions as it considers expedient to enable it to satisfy itself from time to time that it is in the interests of justice for him to continue to receive criminal legal aid.

(3) The factors to be taken into account by the Board in determining whether it is in the interests of justice that criminal legal aid be made available in any case shall include—

(*a*) the offence is such that if proved it is likely that the court would impose a sentence which would deprive the accused of his liberty or lead to loss of his livelihood;

(*b*) the determination of the case may involve consideration of a substantial question of law, or of evidence of a complex or difficult nature;

(*c*) the accused may be unable to understand the proceedings or to state his own case because of his age, inadequate knowledge of English, mental illness, other mental or physical disability or otherwise;

(*d*) it is in the interests of someone other than the accused that the accused be legally represented;

(*e*) the defence to be advanced by the accused does not appear to be frivolous;

(*f*) the accused has been remanded in custody pending trial.

(4) The Secretary of State may, by regulations made under this section, vary the factors listed in subsection (3) above by amending factors in the list or by adding new factors to the list.

(5) The Board shall establish a procedure under which any person whose application for criminal legal aid in summary proceedings has been refused may apply to the Board for a review of his application.

(6) Where a person who is being prosecuted under summary procedure is not represented by a solicitor or counsel and has either—

(*a*) not applied for criminal legal aid in connection with proceedings; or

(*b*) applied for criminal legal aid but been refused it on the grounds that it is not in the interests of justice,

the court at the trial diet may, if it considers that owing to the exceptional circumstances of the case it would be inequitable to proceed with the trial without such representation and without legal aid being made available to him, adjourn the diet to enable an application for legal aid to be made to the Board, which shall consider the application expeditiously.

(7) Where the trial of an accused person is adjourned as is mentioned in subsection (6) above, and he has made an application to the Board, criminal legal aid shall be available to him until his application is determined by the Board.

(8) Where any person to whom criminal legal aid has been made available in pursuance of subsection (7) above has his application for criminal legal aid under subsection (6) above refused by the Board on the ground that it is satisfied that subsection (1)(*a*) above does not apply in his case, the Board may require him to pay to the Fund the whole or part of the amount of any sums paid out of the Fund under section 4(2)(*a*) of this Act in respect of the criminal legal aid so made available.

DEFINITIONS
    "criminal legal aid": s.21(1).
    "the Board": Sched. 1.

GENERAL NOTE
    In summary proceedings this section allows application for criminal legal aid to be made to the Board who may grant subject to being satisfied on the undue hardship financial test, *and* that it is in the interests of justice to allow the application. The latter of these tests under previous legislation gave rise to much difficulty and inconsistency amongst judges. The elements of that test are now spelled out for the benefit of the Board and may be varied by the Secretary of State. Conditions may be attached to the grant of legal aid to ensure that it continues to be in the interests of justice that it should subsist.

    The Board are to establish a procedure to review refusals of criminal legal aid in summary proceedings. If this is not to hold up court procedures it will have to operate at fairly short notice.

    Following considerable Parliamentary debate, subs. (6) allows an unrepresented accused at his trial, in exceptional circumstances where it would be equitable to do so, to have the diet adjourned to allow an application to the Board. In these circumstances, where an application has been made to the Board, criminal legal aid should be available to the accused until his application is determined. Should it be refused, the Board can recover the cost of such temporary cover from him. Following this procedure thus adds another element of chance to the hazards inherent in all court proceedings.

Legal aid in appeals

25.—(1) This section shall apply to criminal legal aid in connection with an appeal against conviction, sentence or acquittal in criminal proceedings.

(2) Subject to regulations made under section 21(2) of this Act criminal legal aid to which this section applies shall be available on an application made to the Board if the Board is satisfied—

(a) subject to subsection (4) below, after consideration of the financial circumstances of the applicant, that the expenses of the appeal cannot be met without undue hardship to the applicant or his dependants; and

(b) where the applicant is the appellant, that he has substantial grounds for making the appeal and that it is reasonable, in the particular circumstances of the case, that legal aid should be made available to him.

(3) The Board may require a person receiving criminal legal aid under this section to comply with such conditions as it considers expedient to enable it to satisfy itself from time to time that it is reasonable for him to continue to receive criminal legal aid.

(4) Subsection (2)(a) above does not apply where criminal legal aid was made available under section 23 or 24 of this Act in connection with the proceedings in respect of which the appeal is being made.

(5) Subsections (2) to (4) above shall apply in relation to an application for criminal legal aid in connection with—

(a) a petition to the *nobile officium* of the High Court of Justiciary (whether arising in the course of any proceedings or otherwise); or

(b) a reference by the Secretary of State under section 263 of the Criminal Procedure (Scotland) Act 1975,

as they apply for the purposes of subsection (1) above.

DEFINITIONS
"criminal legal aid": s.21(1).
"the Board": Sched. 1.

GENERAL NOTE
In criminal appeals against conviction, sentence or acquittal, applications for criminal legal aid are to be made to the Board who will apply the undue hardship financial test and will also have to be satisfied that there are substantial grounds for appeal and that it is reasonable to grant such legal aid. Conditions may be attached to the grant of legal aid to ensure that it continues to be in the interests of justice that it should subsist. The undue hardship test is not applied where the accused had criminal legal aid at first instance.

Similar arrangements cover petitions to the *nobile officium* and references by the Secretary of State to the High Court of Justiciary.

PART V

EMPLOYMENT OF SOLICITORS BY THE BOARD

Employment to which Part V applies

26.—(1) This Part of this Act applies to the employment of solicitors by the Board for any of the following purposes—

(a) giving advice and assistance to which Part II of this Act applies;

(b) acting for persons receiving legal aid, either generally or in cases of any such description as may be prescribed by regulations made under this section;

(c) providing any such services as are mentioned in subsection (2) below.

(2) The services referred to in subsection (1)(c) above are services provided by a solicitor for or in connection with any local organisation and consisting of—

(*a*) assisting the organisation in its function of giving advice and guidance to applicants;

(*b*) promoting contacts between the organisation and solicitors practising in the locality for which the organisation is established, with a view to enabling applicants to obtain the professional services of those solicitors in cases where those services are required;

(*c*) giving oral advice to applicants, instead of referring them to other solicitors, in cases which can be readily disposed of by such advice.

(3) In subsection (2) above—

(*a*) "local organisation" means an organisation concerned in the giving of advice or guidance (whether generally or with respect to any particular classes of matters) to persons residing in the locality for which the organisation is established; and

(*b*) "applicants", in relation to such an organisation, means persons who apply to the organisation for advice or guidance or are referred to it with a view to their receiving advice or guidance from it.

(4) In this section "organisation" includes a branch or section of an organisation; and, in relation to such a branch or section, any reference to the locality for which the organisation is established shall be construed as a reference to the locality for which the branch or section is established.

DEFINITIONS
"advice and assistance": s.6(1).
"the Board": Sched. 1.

GENERAL NOTE
This and the two following sections set out the arrangements under which the Board could employ solicitors to provide advice and assistance or legal aid or to act generally for individuals or local organisations. Somewhat similar provisions have existed in the previous legislation but have never been operated. There is no present likelihood of such employment.

Arrangements for employment to which Part V applies

27.—(1) The Secretary of State may, by regulations made under this section, make provision as to the employment of solicitors under this Part of this Act and as to the circumstances in which solicitors may be so employed.

(2) Section 32(*a*) of this Act shall not apply to the remuneration of a solicitor by the Board in respect of any employment to which this Part of this Act applies.

(3) Notwithstanding section 33(1) of this Act, a solicitor who, in the course of employment to which this Part of this Act applies, acts for a person in receipt of legal aid or advice and assistance shall not be paid out of the Fund for so acting.

DEFINITIONS
"advice and assistance": s.6(1).
"legal aid": s.41.
"the Board": Sched. 1.

General provisions relating to employment to which Part V applies

28.—(1) In relation to any solicitor who is employed by the Board in employment to which this Part of this Act applies, and in relation to any work performed, or other thing done or omitted to be done, by any such solicitor in the course of that employment—

(*a*) the enactments relating to solicitors, and

(*b*) any rule of law which relates to solicitors, or is applicable to things done, or omitted to be done, by solicitors in their capacity as solicitors, shall have effect as if the Board were a firm of solicitors.

(2) Nothing in subsection (1) above shall prohibit 2 or more solicitors employed by the Board in employment to which this Part of this Act applies from acting (including acting in any proceedings) for different parties having opposing or otherwise different interests in relation to the same matter.

DEFINITION
"the Board": Sched. 1.

GENERAL NOTE
Solicitors employed by the Board may separately act for persons having conflicting interests.

PART VI

MISCELLANEOUS

Proceedings in relation to children

Legal aid in certain proceedings relating to children

29.—(1) This section applies to legal aid in connection with—

   (*a*) proceedings before the sheriff in respect of any matter arising under Part III of the Social Work (Scotland) Act 1968 (in this section referred to as "the 1968 Act"); and

   (*b*) any appeal to the Court of Session in connection with such proceedings.

(2) Subject to subsections (3) to (5) below, legal aid to which this section applies shall be available to a child or his parent—

   (*a*) in connection with an appeal to the sheriff under Part III of the 1968 Act—

   (i) against a decision of a children's hearing to grant a warrant for the detention of the child; or

   (ii) against any other decision of a children's hearing;

   (*b*) in connection with an application to the sheriff under section 42 of the 1968 Act for a finding as to whether the grounds for a referral (or any of them) are established; and

   (*c*) in connection with an appeal to the Court of Session against a decision of the sheriff under Part III of the 1968 Act.

(3) Legal aid shall be available under subsection (2)(*a*)(i) above on an application made to the sheriff without inquiry into the resources of the child or his parent.

(4) Legal aid shall be available under subsection (2)(*a*)(ii) or (*b*) above on an application made to the sheriff if the sheriff is satisfied—

   (*a*) that it is in the interests of the child that legal aid be made available; and

   (*b*) after consideration of the financial circumstances of the child and his parent that the expenses of the case cannot be met without undue hardship to the child or his parent or the dependants of either.

(5) Legal aid shall be available under subsection (2)(*c*) above on an application made to the Board if it is satisfied—

   (*a*) after consideration of the financial circumstances of the child and his parent that the expenses of the appeal cannot be met without undue hardship to the child or his parent or the dependants of either; and

   (*b*) that the child or, as the case may be, his parent has substantial grounds for making or responding to the appeal and that it is reasonable, in the particular circumstances of the case, that legal aid should be made available to him.

(6) The Board may require a person receiving legal aid under subsection (2)(*c*) above to comply with such conditions as it considers expedient to enable it to satisfy itself from time to time that it is reasonable for him to continue to receive such legal aid.

(7) Where, in connection with any proceedings, the sheriff or the Board has been satisfied as is mentioned in subsection (4)(*b*) above or, as the case may be, subsection (5)(*a*) above and has made legal aid available to a child or his parent, it shall not be necessary for the Board or, as the case may be, the sheriff to be so satisfied in respect of an application for legal aid by the child or his parent in connection with any subsequent proceedings arising from such proceedings.

(8) Legal aid to which this section applies shall consist of representation by a solicitor and (so far as is necessary) by counsel in any proceedings (including any appeal) mentioned in subsection (1) above and shall include all such assistance as is usually given by solicitor or counsel in the steps preliminary to or incidental to proceedings.

(9) In this section "child" and "parent" shall be construed in accordance with section 30 of the 1968 Act.

DEFINITIONS
"legal aid": s.41.
"the Board": Sched. 1.

GENERAL NOTE
This section sets out the circumstances in which legal aid is available to a child or a child's parents in respect of the various procedures arising under the Social Work (Scotland) Act 1968 or in appeals from these procedures. Where warrant for detention is involved no financial enquiry is necessary. In proceedings other than appeal, the sheriff is to grant legal aid if satisfied that it is in the child's interests and on an undue hardship test. In appeals to the Court of Session the Board will grant legal aid if satisfied on the undue hardship test and that there are substantial grounds for appeal. As with other kinds of legal aid, conditions may be attached to the grant of legal aid to ensure that it continues to be in the interest of justice that it should subsist.

Where legal aid was granted at first instance the hardship test will not be applied in subsequent proceedings arising from these at first instance.

Although the provision of legal aid for children is of great importance to the children concerned, the cost in 1984–85 of £245,000 can be regarded as modest.

Contempt of court

Legal aid in contempt proceedings

30.—(1) Where a person is liable to be dealt with for contempt of court during the course of or in connection with any proceedings, legal aid shall be available to him on an application being made to the court if it is satisfied—

    (*a*) after consideration of the person's financial circumstances that the expenses of the proceedings for contempt of court cannot be met without undue hardship to him or his dependants; and

    (*b*) that in all the circumstances of the case it is in the interests of justice that legal aid should be made available to him.

(2) In making legal aid available under subsection (1) above, the court may order in any case that the legal aid shall consist of representation by counsel only or, in a court where solicitors have a right of audience, by a solicitor only; and, notwithstanding section 31 of this Act, the court may assign for the purpose any counsel or solicitor who is within the precincts of the court at the time when the order is made.

(3) Section 25 of this Act shall apply in relation to legal aid in connection with an appeal against a decision of a court in proceedings for contempt of court as it applies in relation to legal aid in connection with an appeal against conviction, sentence or acquittal in criminal proceedings, and in such application—

(a) for the reference in subsection (4) of that section to criminal legal aid having been made available under section 23 or 24 of this Act there shall be substituted a reference to legal aid having been made available under subsection (1) above; and

(b) in subsection (5) of that section the reference to the *nobile officium* of the High Court of Justiciary shall include a reference to the *nobile officium* of the Court of Session.

(4) Subject to subsection (2) above legal aid made available under this section shall consist of representation by a solicitor and (so far as necessary) by counsel and shall include all such assistance as is usually given by a solicitor or counsel in the steps preliminary to or incidental to proceedings for contempt of court or, in the case of legal aid made available under subsection (3) above, any appeal in connection with such proceedings.

DEFINITIONS
 "interests of justice": s.24(3).
 "legal aid": s.41.

GENERAL NOTE
 In recognition of the fact that contempt proceedings are serious and often lead to imprisonment, this section allows the court to grant legal aid on the undue hardship financial test and where it is in the interests of justice to do so. The court may restrict the legal aid to counsel only or solicitor only and may assign counsel or solicitor who may be present in the precincts of the court to deal at once with the matter. Arrangements are also made to cover appeals from contempt proceedings and petitions to the *nobile officium*.

Solicitors and counsel

Solicitors and counsel

31.—(1) Subject to section 30(2) of this Act and to regulations made under subsection (9) below, a person to whom legal aid or advice and assistance is made available may select—

(a) the solicitor to advise or act for him; and

(b) if the case requires counsel, his counsel,

and he shall be entitled to make the selection himself.

(2) Nothing in subsection (1) above shall prejudice any right of a solicitor or advocate to refuse or give up a case or to entrust it to another solicitor or advocate.

(3) The relevant body may decide to exclude any advocate or solicitor either from being selected under subsection (1) above, or from giving advice and assistance to or from acting for a person to whom legal aid is made available on the ground that there is good reason for excluding him arising out of—

(a) his conduct when acting or selected to act for persons to whom legal aid or advice and assistance is made available;

(b) his professional conduct generally;

(c) in the case of a member of a firm of solicitors or a director of an incorporated practice, such conduct on the part of any person who is for the time being a member of the firm or a director of the practice.

(4) The relevant body may decide to exclude a solicitor or advocate under subsection (3) above in respect of any specified period or without limit of time.

(5) A solicitor or advocate who is aggrieved by a decision of the relevant body under subsection (3) above may appeal against his exclusion or the period of such exclusion to the Court of Session; and the court in determining such an appeal may make such order as it thinks fit.

(6) Where the relevant body decides or the Court of Session, on an appeal against such a decision, orders that an advocate or solicitor be excluded under subsection (3) above, the relevant body shall inform the Board of the decision or order.

(7) Except in so far as expressly provided under this Act, the fact that the services of counsel or a solicitor are given by way of legal aid or advice and assistance shall not affect the relationship between or the respective rights in that connection of counsel, solicitor and client.

(8) The Board may arrange that, in such circumstances as it may specify, a solicitor shall be available for the purposes of providing legal aid or advice and assistance.

(9) Where a solicitor is available as is mentioned in subsection (8) above, the Secretary of State may, by regulations made under this section, provide that—

    (*a*) subsection (1) above shall not apply; and

    (*b*) legal aid or, as the case may be, advice and assistance shall be provided only by the solicitor so made available.

(10) In this section, "the relevant body" means—

    (*a*) in relation to an advocate, the Faculty of Advocates;

    (*b*) in relation to a solicitor, the Law Society or the Scottish Solicitors' Discipline Tribunal,

and in considering whether to exclude a solicitor under subsection (3) above, section 52 of and Part II of Schedule 4 to the Solicitors (Scotland) Act 1980 shall apply in relation to the procedure of that Tribunal as they apply in relation to its procedure in respect of a complaint under section 51(1) of that Act.

DEFINITIONS
    "advice and assistance": s.6(1).
    "legal aid": s.41.
    "the Board": Sched. 1.

GENERAL NOTE
    Solicitors and counsel who act in giving advice and assistance and legal aid need not register with the Board and may be selected by the client, although they have the right to refuse to act or to give up acting or to entrust the case to another solicitor or advocate. This important right for the client to exercise *delectus personae* in all but the situations of the duty solicitor or the dock brief in contempt cases is rightly preserved. It seems that the system of complaints about solicitors and counsel has been scrapped and discipline will be dealt with by the Law Society of Scotland or the Faculty of Advocates according to their customary procedures. They can exclude a member from being selected either for a limited period or without limitation of time subject to a right of appeal to the Court of Session.

    Subs. (7) preserves the relationship between counsel, solicitor and client where legal aid or advice and assistance are given except so far as disturbed by the Act.

    Subs. (8) allows the Board to arrange for what used to be called the duty solicitor.

Restriction on payment and employment of solicitor or counsel

32. Where legal aid is available to a person in connection with any proceedings (whether legal aid is available in connection with all or only part of the proceedings)—

    (*a*) the solicitor or counsel providing legal aid shall not take any payment in respect of any advice given or anything done in connection with such proceedings during any period when legal aid was so available except for such payment as may be made, in accordance with this Act, out of the Fund; and

(b) except as is mentioned in section 31(2) of this Act, no solicitor or counsel other than the solicitor or counsel referred to in paragraph (a) above shall advise or act for him in connection with the proceedings.

DEFINITIONS
  "legal aid": s.41.
  "the Fund": s.4(1).

GENERAL NOTE
  This section re-establishes the rule which used to prevail which was that a client either has legal aid or he does not. If he accepts legal aid he accepts it as it stands and he cannot supplement it by privately funded extras. A client may of course have legal aid for only part of a case and may fund an earlier part of the case prior to legal aid himself.

Fees and outlays of solicitors and counsel

33.—(1) Any solicitor or counsel who acts for any person by providing legal aid or advice and assistance under this Act shall be paid out of the Fund in accordance with section 4(2)(a) of this Act in respect of any fees or outlays properly incurred by him in so acting.

(2) The Secretary of State may, by regulations made under this section, make such provision as seems to him appropriate in respect of the fees and outlays of solicitors and counsel—

(a) acting in any proceedings for a person to whom legal aid has been made available; or

(b) providing advice and assistance in accordance with Part II of this Act.

(3) Without prejudice to the generality of subsection (2) above, regulations made under this section may—

(a) prescribe the work in respect of which fees may be charged;

(b) prescribe rates or scales of payment of fees and outlays allowable and the conditions under which such fees and outlays may be allowed;

(c) provide for the assessment and taxation of fees and outlays, and for the review of any such assessment or taxation, either by the Secretary of State or by any other person;

(d) prescribe general principles to be applied in connection with any such assessment, taxation or review;

(e) prescribe forms to be used for the purposes of any regulations made under this section; and

(f) make different provision for different cases.

(4) In subsection (1) above the reference to acting for a person includes, in relation to a solicitor, a reference to acting for such a person on the instructions of another solicitor.

(5) Where a person is in receipt of legal aid in connection with any proceedings, any expenses incurred in connection with the proceedings which would, if he were not in receipt of legal aid, be paid, in the first instance, by or on behalf of the solicitor acting for him, shall be so paid.

DEFINITIONS
  "advice and assistance": s.6(1).
  "legal aid": s.41.
  "the Fund": s.4(1).

GENERAL NOTE
  This section lays down the entitlement to remuneration of the solicitors and counsel who render legal aid and advice and assistance. The Secretary of State is empowered to regulate the remuneration, to set the table of fees and to provide for assessment and taxation thereof.

Discussions are now proceeding between the legal profession and the Scottish Home and Health Department regarding the proper basis of such remuneration.

Information

Confidentiality of information

34.—(1) Subject to subsection (2) below, no information furnished for the purposes of this Act to the Board or to any person acting on its behalf shall be disclosed—

(a) in the case of such information furnished by, or by any person acting for, a person seeking or receiving legal aid or advice and assistance, without the consent of the person seeking or receiving legal aid or advice and assistance; or

(b) in the case of such information furnished otherwise than as mentioned in paragraph (a) above, without the consent of the person who furnished it,

and any person who, in contravention of this subsection, discloses any information obtained by him when employed by, or acting on behalf of, the Board shall be guilty of an offence and liable, on summary conviction, to a fine not exceeding level 4 on the standard scale.

(2) Subsection (1) above shall not apply to the disclosure of information—

(a) for the purpose of the proper performance or facilitating the proper performance by the Secretary of State, the Board, any court or tribunal or by any other person or body of duties or functions under this Act;

(b) for the purpose of investigating, prosecuting or determining any complaint of professional misconduct—

(i) against a solicitor, by the Law Society or the Scottish Solicitors' Discipline Tribunal;

(ii) against an advocate, by the Faculty of Advocates;

(c) for the purpose of investigating or prosecuting any offence or for the report of any proceedings in relation to such an offence.

(3) For the purposes of this section, information furnished to any person in his capacity as counsel or a solicitor by or on behalf of a person seeking or receiving legal aid or advice and assistance is not information furnished to the Board or to a person acting on its behalf.

DEFINITIONS
"advice and assistance": s.6(1).
"legal aid": s.41.
"the Board": Sched. 1.

GENERAL NOTE
Information supplied to the Board in connection with legal aid or advice and assistance is to remain confidential. This section creates an offence should an employee of the Board improperly disclose information received for the purpose of legal aid. Complaints may be taken to the professional bodies.

False information etc.

35.—(1) If any person seeking or receiving legal aid or advice and assistance—

(a) wilfully fails to comply with any regulations as to the information to be furnished by him; or

(b) for the purpose of obtaining legal aid or advice and assistance knowingly makes any false statement or false representation, he shall be guilty of an offence and liable, on summary conviction, to a fine not exceeding level 4 on the standard scale or to imprisonment for a term not exceeding 60 days or to both.

(2) Notwithstanding section 331 of the Criminal Procedure (Scotland) Act 1975, proceedings for an offence under subsection (1) above may be commenced at any time within 2 years from the date of the commission of the offence or within 6 months from the date when evidence sufficient in the opinion of the Lord Advocate to justify proceedings comes to his knowledge, whichever period is the shorter; and for the purposes of this subsection a certificate by the Lord Advocate as to the date on which such evidence came to his knowledge shall be conclusive evidence of that fact.

DEFINITIONS
    "advice and assistance": s.6(1).
    "legal aid": s.41.

GENERAL NOTE
    This section creates an offence of wilful failure to comply with any regulations and in seeking legal aid knowingly making any false statement or representation and specifies the limitation period to apply to such offences.

Regulations and rules of court

Regulations

36.—(1) The Secretary of State may make such regulations under this section as appear to him necessary or desirable for giving effect to, or for preventing abuses of, this Act; and regulations made under this section may make different provision—
    (*a*) in relation to legal aid and to advice and assistance respectively; and
    (*b*) for different cases or classes of case.

(2) Without prejudice to subsection (1) above or to any other provision of this Act authorising the making of regulations, regulations made under this section may—
    (*a*) make provision as to the exercise by the Board of its functions under this Act;
    (*b*) substitute different amounts for any of the amounts specified in section 8, 10(2), 11(2), 15 and 17(2) of this Act;
    (*c*) make provision as to the proceedings which are or are not to be treated as distinct proceedings for the purposes of legal aid, and as to the matters which are or are not to be treated as distinct matters for the purposes of advice and assistance;
    (*d*) make provision as to the manner of making applications for legal aid or advice and assistance under this Act and the time when such applications may be made and disposed of;
    (*e*) make provision as to the information to be furnished by a person seeking or receiving legal aid or advice and assistance;
    (*f*) make provision as to the cases in which a person may be refused legal aid or advice and assistance by reason of his conduct when seeking or receiving legal aid or advice and assistance (whether in the same or in a different matter or proceedings);
    (*g*) make provision in connection with the recovery of sums due to the Fund and making effective the priorities conferred by this Act on the payment of such sums out of awards of expenses or property recovered or preserved for a person receiving legal aid, including—

    (i) provision in connection with the enforcement (by whatever means) for the benefit of the Fund of any award of expenses or any agreement as to expenses in favour of a person who has received legal aid; and

    (ii) provision making a solicitor's right to payment out of the Fund dependent, in whole or in part, on his performing any duties imposed on him by regulations made for the purposes of this paragraph;

(*h*) modify any provision of this Act so far as appears to the Secretary of State necessary to meet any of the special circumstances mentioned in subsection (3) below.

(3) The special circumstances referred to in subsection (2)(*h*) above are where a person seeking or receiving legal aid or advice and assistance—

(*a*) is not resident in Scotland;

(*b*) is concerned in a representative, fiduciary or official capacity;

(*c*) is concerned jointly with or has the same interest as other persons, whether receiving legal aid or advice and assistance or not;

(*d*) has available to him rights and facilities making it unnecessary for him to take advantage of the provisions of this Act, or has a reasonable expectation of receiving financial or other help from a body of which he is a member;

(*e*) seeks legal aid or advice and assistance in a matter of special urgency;

(*f*) begins to receive legal aid or advice and assistance after having consulted a solicitor in the ordinary way with respect to the same proceedings, or ceases to receive legal aid or advice and assistance before the proceedings in question are finally settled;

(*g*) has, while receiving legal aid or advice and assistance, any change of circumstances such that, had the changed circumstances subsisted at the time the application for legal aid or advice and assistance was made, the original disposal of the application would have been likely to have been affected.

(4) Regulations made under this section may also modify this Act or any instrument having effect under this Act (including so much of any of those provisions as specifies a sum of money) for the purposes of its application—

(*a*) in cases where such modification appears to the Secretary of State necessary for the purpose of fulfilling any obligation imposed on the United Kingdom or Her Majesty's government therein by any international agreement; or

(*b*) in relation to proceedings for securing the recognition or enforcement in Scotland of judgments given outside the United Kingdom for whose recognition or enforcement in the United Kingdom provision is made by any international agreement.

DEFINITIONS
    "advice and assistance": s.6(1).
    "legal aid": s.41.
    "the Board": Sched. 1.
    "the Fund": s.41(1).

GENERAL NOTE
    This section enables the Secretary of State for Scotland to make regulations to give effect to (or even to alter) the Act. These regulations will put flesh on much of the skeleton of the Act which is presently not filled out. The Secretary of State is not obliged to consult the Law Society of Scotland or the Faculty of Advocates but is known to be doing so.

Parliamentary procedure

37.—(1) Regulations under this Act shall be made by the Secretary of State by statutory instrument and, except as provided in subsection (2) below, shall be subject to annulment in pursuance of a resolution of either House of Parliament.

(2) No regulation shall be made under section 7, 9, 11(2), 13(4), 17(2), 21(2), 24(4) or 36(2)(*b*) of this Act unless a draft of it has been laid before, and approved by a resolution of, each House of Parliament.

(3) Regulations made under section 42 of this Act shall be made with the concurrence of the Treasury.

GENERAL NOTE

This section prescribes the method by which the draft regulations will be submitted to Parliamentary scrutiny.

Rules of court

38.—(1) The court may by act of adjournal or, as the case may be, by act of sederunt—

(*a*) regulate the procedure of any court or tribunal in relation to legal aid, and in particular may make provision as to the cases in which and the extent to which a person receiving legal aid may be required to find caution, and the manner in which caution in such cases may be found;

(*b*) make provision as to the cases in which a person may be treated as having disentitled himself to a continuance of legal aid by his conduct in connection with his receipt of legal aid;

(*c*) make provision as to the apportionment of sums recovered or recoverable by virtue of any award of expenses made generally with respect to proceedings or matters which are to be treated as distinct by virtue of regulations made under section 36(2)(*c*) of this Act;

(*d*) make provision as to the proceedings which are or are not to be treated as having been instituted by the legally assisted person for the purposes of section 19(3)(*b*) of this Act;

(*e*) regulate the procedure to be followed in connection with an order under section 19 of this Act, in particular to enable the Board to be heard in connection with such an order.

(2) The court may by act of adjournal or, as the case may be, by act of sederunt restrict the fees to be paid to auditors of court, messengers-at-arms, sheriff officers and shorthand writers in any case where such fees are payable in the first instance by or on behalf of a person receiving legal aid to such proportion thereof as may be provided for the time being.

(3) Before making rules of court regulating the procedure of any court or tribunal, the court shall, so far as practicable, consult any rules council or similar body by whom or on whose advice rules of procedure for the court or tribunal may, apart from this Act, be made or whose consent or concurrence is required to any such rules so made.

(4) In this section "the court" means in relation to criminal proceedings, the High Court of Justiciary, and in relation to civil proceedings, the Court of Session.

DEFINITIONS

"legal aid": s.41.
"the Board": Sched. 1.

GENERAL NOTE

This section empowers the court to make orders regulating procedure in respect of legal aid including the extent to which a person receiving legal aid may have to find caution and other matters. Before making such orders there must be consultation.

47–31

Such orders for caution have been extremely rare, but see *Stevenson* v. *Midlothian District Council,* 1983 S.L.T. 433.

Rights of indemnity

Adaptation of rights to indemnity

39.—(1) This section shall have effect in relation to any right (however and whenever created or arising) which a person may have to be indemnified against expenses incurred by him in connection with any proceedings.

(2) In determining in respect of any such right the reasonableness of any expenses, the possibility of avoiding them or part of them by taking advantage of the provisions of this Act shall be disregarded.

(3) Where a person, having any such right to be indemnified against expenses, receives legal aid in connection with the proceedings, then the right shall enure also for the benefit of the Fund as if the expenses incurred by the Fund on his behalf in connection with the proceedings had been incurred by him.

(4) Where—

(*a*) such a right to be indemnified against expenses arises by virtue of an agreement and is subject to any express provision conferring on those liable under the agreement any right with respect to the bringing or conduct of the proceedings; and

(*b*) those liable have been given a reasonable opportunity of exercising the right so conferred and have not availed themselves of that opportunity,

the right to be indemnified shall be treated, for the purposes of subsection (3) above, as not being subject to that provision.

DEFINITIONS
  "legal aid": s.41.
  "the Fund": s.4(1).

GENERAL NOTE
A person who receives legal aid and has a right to indemnity against expenses must allow that right to enure for the benefit of the Fund.

General

Finance

40.—(1) The Secretary of State shall pay to the Board out of moneys provided by Parliament—

(*a*) such sums as are required (after allowing for payments into the Fund under paragraphs (*a*) to (*c*) and (*e*) of section 4(3) of this Act) to meet payments out of the Fund under this Act; and

(*b*) such sums as he may, with the approval of the Treasury, determine are required for the other expenditure of the Board.

(2) The Secretary of State may, with the approval of the Treasury—

(*a*) determine the manner in which and times at which the sums referred to in subsection (1)(*a*) above shall be paid to the Board; and

(*b*) impose conditions on the payment of the sums referred to in subsection (1)(*b*) above.

(3) The Secretary of State shall pay to the Law Society in accordance with paragraph 1(2)(*b*) of Schedule 4 to this Act out of moneys provided by Parliament the amount required to make up any deficit in the Legal Aid (Scotland) Fund.

(4) Any payments received by the Secretary of State from the Law Society in accordance with paragraph 1(2)(*a*) of Schedule 4 to this Act shall be paid by him into the Consolidated Fund.

DEFINITIONS
"the Board": Sched. 1.
"the Fund": s.41(1).

GENERAL NOTE
This section authorises the Secretary of State to pay to the Board from moneys provided by Parliament the sums required to fund the operations of the Board. The distinction between funds for legal aid and for administration is maintained.

Interpretation

41. In this Act, unless the context otherwise requires—
"advice and assistance" has the meaning given to it in section 6(1) of this Act;
"assistance by way of representation" has the meaning given to it in section 6(1) of this Act;
"the Board" has the meaning given to it in section 1(1) of this Act;
"civil legal aid" has the meaning given to it in section 13(2) of this Act;
"criminal legal aid" has the meaning given to it in section 21(1) of this Act;
"the Fund" has the meaning given to it in section 4(1) of this Act;
"incorporated practice" has the same meaning as in the Solicitors' (Scotland) Act 1980;
"the Law Society" means the Law Society of Scotland;
"legal aid" means civil legal aid, criminal legal aid, or legal aid given in connection with proceedings for contempt of court or proceedings under Part III of the Social Work (Scotland) Act 1968;
"person" does not include a body corporate or unincorporate, except where such body is acting in a representative, fiduciary or official capacity, so as to authorise legal aid or advice and assistance to be provided to such a body.

Disposable income and capital

42.—(1) In this Act "disposable income" or "disposable capital" in relation to any person means his income or, as the case may be, the amount of his capital, after making such deductions and allowances as regulations made under this section may prescribe—
  (*a*) in respect of maintenance of dependants, interest on loans, income tax, rates, rent and other matters for which that person must or reasonably may provide;
  (*b*) to take account of the nature of his resources,
and does not include the subject matter of the dispute.

(2) Regulations made under this section may make provision as to the determination of a person's income and the amount of his capital and in particular for determining whether any resources are to be treated as income or capital and for taking into account fluctuations of income, and different provision may be made for legal aid and for advice and assistance.

(3) Except in so far as regulations made under this section otherwise provide, the resources of a person's spouse shall be treated for the purposes of this section as that person's own resources, and such regulations may also make provision, in relation to minors and pupils and other special cases, for taking into account the resources of other persons.

Act not to affect certain taxations etc.

43. Nothing in this Act shall affect the sum recoverable by virtue of—
(*a*) an award of expenses in favour of a person to whom legal aid has been made available; or
(*b*) an agreement as to expenses in favour of such a person which provides for taxation,
and for the purpose of any such award or agreement, the solicitor who acted for the person in whose favour it is made shall be treated as having paid any counsel's fees.

Crown application

44. This Act shall bind the Crown.

Amendments, transitional provisions, savings and repeals

45.—(1) The enactments mentioned in Schedule 3 to this Act shall have effect subject to the amendments there specified (being minor amendments and amendments consequential on this Act).

(2) Without prejudice to sections 16 and 17 of the Interpretation Act 1978 (effect of repeals) and section 46(3) of this Act, the transitional provisions and savings contained in Schedule 4 to this Act shall have effect.

(3) The enactments set out in columns 1 and 2 of Schedule 5 to this Act are repealed to the extent specified in the third column of that Schedule.

Short title, commencement and extent

46.—(1) This Act may be cited as the Legal Aid (Scotland) Act 1986.

(2) This Act, apart from this section, shall come into force on such day as the Secretary of State may, by order made by statutory instrument, appoint; and different days may be so appointed for different purposes and for different provisions.

(3) An order under subsection (2) above may contain such transitional provisions and savings as appear to the Secretary of State necessary or expedient.

(4) This Act, except section 18(3), extends only to Scotland.

SCHEDULES

Section 1   SCHEDULE 1

THE SCOTTISH LEGAL AID BOARD

Incorporation and Status

1. The Board shall be a body corporate with a common seal.
2.—(1) The Board is not an emanation of the Crown and shall not act or be treated as the servant or agent of the Crown.
(2) Accordingly—
(*a*) neither the Board, nor any of its members, nor any member of its staff as such is entitled to any status, immunity, privilege or exemption enjoyed by the Crown;
(*b*) the members of the Board and the members of its staff are not, in such capacity, Crown servants; and
(*c*) the Board's property is not the property of or held on behalf of the Crown.
(3) Subject to sub-paragraph (4) below, the Board shall not be exempt from any tax, duty, rate, levy or other charge whatever (whether general or local).

(4) Notwithstanding sub-paragraph (2)(*c*) above, all lands and heritages occupied by the Board shall, for the purposes of the Lands Valuation (Scotland) Act 1854, the Acts amending that Act and any other enactment relating to valuation of lands and heritages, be treated as if they were occupied by or on behalf of the Crown for the purposes of the Crown.

Tenure of Members

3. Subject to paragraphs 4 and 5 below any member of the Board shall hold and vacate office in accordance with the terms of his appointment, but a person shall not be appointed a member of the Board for a period of more than 5 years.

4.—(1) The chairman or a member may resign office by giving notice in writing to the Secretary of State, and if the chairman ceases to be a member he shall cease to be the chairman.

(2) A person who ceases to be the chairman or a member shall be eligible for reappointment.

5. The Secretary of State may terminate the appointment of a member of the Board if satisfied that—

(*a*) he has had his estate sequestrated, or has been adjudged bankrupt or has granted a trust deed for or entered into an arrangement with his creditors;

(*b*) he is unable to carry out his duties as a Board member by reason of physical or mental illness;

(*c*) he has been absent from meetings of the Board for a period longer than six consecutive months without the permission of the Board; or

(*d*) he is otherwise unable or unfit to discharge the functions of a member of the Board, or is unsuitable to continue as a member.

Remuneration of members

6.—(1) The Board may—

(*a*) pay to its members such remuneration; and

(*b*) make provision for the payment of such pensions, allowances or gratuities to or in respect of its members,

as the Secretary of State may, with the approval of the Treasury, determine.

(2) Where a person ceases to be a member of the Board otherwise than on the expiry of his term of office, and it appears to the Secretary of State that there are special circumstances which make it right for that person to receive compensation, the Secretary of State may, with the consent of the Treasury, direct the Board to make that person a payment of such amount as the Secretary of State may, with the consent of the Treasury, determine.

Staff

7.—(1) The Board shall, after consultation with, and subject to the approval of, the Secretary of State, appoint on such terms and conditions as it may determine a person to be the principal officer of the Board.

(2) The principal officer shall be responsible to the Board for the exercise of its functions.

8.—(1) Subject to paragraph 9 below, the Board may appoint, on such terms and conditions as it may determine, such other employees as it thinks fit.

(2) A determination as to terms and conditions under paragraph 7(1) or sub-paragraph (1) above shall be subject to the approval of the Secretary of State given with the consent of the Treasury.

(3) The Board shall, in respect of such of its employees as it may determine, with the approval of the Secretary of State and the consent of the Treasury make such arrangements for providing pensions, allowances or gratuities as it may determine; and such arrangements may include the establishment and administration, by the Board or otherwise, of one or more pension schemes.

(4) The reference in sub-paragraph (3) above to pensions, allowances or gratuities in respect of employees of the Board includes a reference to pensions, allowances or gratuities by way of compensation to or in respect of any such employee who suffers loss of office or employment.

(5) If any employee of the Board becomes a member of the Board and was by reference to his employment by the Board a participant in a pension scheme established and administered by it for the benefit of its employees—

(*a*) the Board may determine that his service as a member shall be treated for the purposes of the scheme as service as an employee of the Board whether or not any benefits are to be payable to or in respect of him by virtue of paragraph 6 above; but

(*b*) if the Board determines as aforesaid, any discretion as to the benefits payable to or in respect of him which the scheme confers on the Board shall be exercised only with the consent of the Secretary of State given with the approval of the Treasury.

9.—(1) The Board shall, not later than such date as the Secretary of State may determine, make an offer of employment by the Board to each person employed immediately before that date—

    (*a*) by the Law Society for the purpose of their functions under the Legal Aid (Scotland) Act 1967; and

    (*b*) in the civil service of the State wholly or mainly in connection with the assessment of a person's means under section 4 of that Act.

(2) The terms of the offer shall be such that they are, taken as a whole, not less favourable to the person to whom the offer is made than the terms on which he is employed on the date on which the offer is made.

(3) For the purposes of sub-paragraph (2) above no account shall be taken of the fact that employment with the Board is not employment in the service of the Crown.

(4) An offer made in pursuance of this paragraph shall not be revocable during the period of 3 months commencing with the date on which it is made.

10.—(1) Where a person becomes an employee of the Board on acceptance of an offer made under paragraph 9 above, then, for the purposes of the Employment Protection (Consolidation) Act 1978, his period of employment with the Law Society or, as the case may be, in the civil service of the State, shall count as a period of employment by the Board, and the change of employment shall not break the continuity of the period of employment.

(2) Where an offer is made in pursuance of paragraph 9(1) above to any person employed as is mentioned in that paragraph, none of the agreed redundancy procedures applicable to such a person shall apply to him and—

    (*a*) where a person employed as is mentioned in sub-paragraph (*a*) of that paragraph ceases to be so employed—

        (i) on becoming a member of the staff of the Board in consequence of that paragraph; or

        (ii) having unreasonably refused the offer,

    Part VI of the Employment Protection (Consolidation) Act 1978 shall not apply to him and he shall not be treated for the purposes of any scheme under section 12 of the Legal Aid (Scotland) Act 1967 as having been retired on redundancy;

    (*b*) where a person employed as is mentioned in sub-paragraph (*b*) of that paragraph ceases to be so employed on becoming a member of the staff of the Board in consequence of that paragraph, he shall not be treated for the purposes of any scheme under section 1 of the Superannuation Act 1972 as having been retired on redundancy.

(3) Without prejudice to sub-paragraph (2) above, where a person has unreasonably refused an offer made to him in pursuance of paragraph 9 above, the Law Society or, as the case may be, the Secretary of State shall not terminate that person's employment unless it or, as the case may be, he has first had regard to the feasibility of employing him in a suitable alternative position with the Law Society or, as the case may be, in the civil service of the State.

(4) Where a person continues in employment in the Law Society or, as the case may be, the civil service of the State either—

    (*a*) not having unreasonably refused an offer made to him in pursuance of this paragraph, or

    (*b*) having been placed in a suitable alternative position as mentioned in sub-paragraph (3) above,

he shall be treated for all purposes as if the offer mentioned in paragraph 9(1) above had not been made.

11.—(1) Any dispute as to whether an offer under sub-paragraph (1) of paragraph 9 above complies with sub-paragraph (2) of that paragraph shall be referred to and be determined by an industrial tribunal.

(2) An industrial tribunal shall not consider a complaint referred to it under sub-paragraph (1) above unless the complaint is presented to the tribunal before the end of the period of 3 months beginning with the date of the offer of employment or within such further period as the tribunal considers reasonable in a case where it is satisfied that it was not reasonably practicable for the complaint to be presented before the end of the period of 3 months.

(3) Subject to sub-paragraph (4) below there shall be no appeal from the decision of an industrial tribunal under this paragraph.

(4) An appeal to the Employment Appeal Tribunal may be made only on a question of law arising from the decision of, or in proceedings before, an industrial tribunal under this paragraph.

Proceedings

12.—(1) Subject to anything in regulations made by the Secretary of State under this Act, the Board may regulate its own proceedings.

(2) The Board may make such arrangements as it considers appropriate for the discharge of its functions, including the delegation of specified functions.

(3) Committees may be appointed and may be dissolved by the Board, and may include, or consist entirely of, persons who are not members of the Board.

(4) A committee shall act in accordance with such directions as the Board may from time to time give, and the Board may provide for anything done by a committee to have effect as if it had been done by the Board.

(5) The validity of any proceedings of the Board or of any committee appointed by the Board shall not be affected by any vacancy among its members or by any defect in the appointment of any member.

Allowances

13. The Board may pay to each of its members and the members of any committee such reasonable allowances in respect of expenses or loss of remuneration as the Secretary of State may, with the approval of the Treasury, determine.

Instruments

14.—(1) The fixing of the seal of the Board shall be authenticated by the Chairman or another member of the Board and by some other person authorised either generally or specially by the Board to act for that purpose.

(2) A document purporting to be duly executed under the seal of the Board, or to be signed on the Board's behalf, shall be received in evidence and, unless the contrary is proved, be deemed to be so executed or signed.

Board not dominus litis

15. Nothing done by the Board for the purpose of securing that legal aid or advice and assistance is available to any person in connection with any proceedings shall render it liable to be held to be *dominus litis* in relation to the proceedings.

Section 13   SCHEDULE 2

Part I

Courts in which Civil Legal Aid is Available

1. Civil legal aid shall be available in relation to civil proceedings in—
    the House of Lords, in appeals from the Court of Session;
    the Court of Session;
    the Lands Valuation Appeal Court;
    the Scottish Land Court;
    the sheriff court,
and in relation to proceedings—
    before any person to whom a case is referred in whole or in part by a court mentioned above;
    in the Restrictive Practices Court under Part III of the Fair Trading Act 1973 (including any proceedings in that court in consequence of an offer made or undertaking given to the court under that Part of that Act);
    in the Lands Tribunal for Scotland;
    in the Employment Appeal Tribunal.

2. For the purposes of section 13 of this Act, proceedings in the European Court of Justice on a reference, under Article 177 of the EEC Treaty, made by a court mentioned in paragraph 1 above are part of the proceedings in the court making the reference.

Part II

Excepted Proceedings

1. Subject to paragraph 2 below, civil legal aid shall not be available in proceedings which are wholly or partly concerned with defamation or verbal injury.

2. The making of a counterclaim for defamation or verbal injury in any proceedings shall not of itself affect the availability of legal aid to the other party, and legal aid may be granted for the purposes of defending such a counterclaim.

3. Civil legal aid shall not be available in relation to—
    election petitions under the Representation of the People Act 1983;
    simplified divorce applications under the rules of procedure of the Court of Session or the sheriff court.

Section 45   SCHEDULE 3

MINOR AND CONSEQUENTIAL AMENDMENTS

The Maintenance Orders (Reciprocal Enforcement) Act 1972 (c.18)

1.—(1) In section 31(1) of the Maintenance Orders (Reciprocal Enforcement) Act 1972 for the words from "secretary" where it first occurs to "taking" there shall be substituted the words:—
    "Secretary of the Law Society of Scotland who shall send the application and any accompanying documents to a solicitor practising in the sheriff court within the jurisdiction of which that other person resides or to such other solicitor practising in Scotland as appears to the Secretary to be appropriate, for the purposes of enabling the solicitor to take".

(2) In section 32 of that Act—

(*a*) after subsection (7) there shall be inserted the following subsections—
    "(7A) The Secretary of State on receiving notice under subsection (6) above shall send a copy of the registered order and of the related documents to the Secretary of the Law Society of Scotland who shall send the copy of the order and of the related documents to a solicitor practising in the registering court or to such other solicitor practising in Scotland as appears to the Secretary to be appropriate for the purpose of enabling the solicitor to take, on behalf of the person entitled to the payments for which the order provides, such steps as appear to the solicitor appropriate to enforce the order.

    (7B) Where an order is registered in the sheriff court by virtue of subsection (3) above, any provision of the order by virtue of which the payments for which the order provides are required to be made through or to any officer or person on behalf of the person entitled thereto shall be of no effect so long as the order is so registered.";

(*b*) subsection (9)(*e*) of that section shall be omitted.

(3) In section 34(5) of that Act, for paragraph (*b*) there shall be substituted the following paragraph—
    "(*b*) for subsection (3) there shall be substituted the following subsection—
        '(3) Where the Secretary of State receives from the appropriate authority in a convention country an application by a person in that country for the variation of a registered order, he shall, if the registering court is a sheriff court, send the application, together with any documents accompanying it, to the Secretary of the Law Society of Scotland who shall send the application and any accompanying documents to a solicitor practising in the registering court or to such other solicitor practising in Scotland as appears to the Secretary to be appropriate, for the purpose of enabling the solicitor to take on behalf of the applicant such steps as appear to the solicitor appropriate in respect of the application.'.".

2.—(1) Section 43A of that Act shall be amended as follows.

(2) In subsection (1) for the words "section 2(1) and (6)(*c*), 3 and 4 of the Legal Aid (Scotland) Act 1967" there shall be substituted the words "section 15 and 17 of the Legal Aid (Scotland) Act 1986".

(3) In subsection (2) for the words "section 2(1) and (6)(*c*), 3 and 4 of the said Act of 1967", there shall be substituted the words "section 15 and 17 of the said Act of 1986".

(4) In subsection (3) for the words from "legal advice" to "said Act of 1972)", where they second occur, there shall be substituted the words "advice and assistance under the said Act of 1986, shall, notwithstanding any financial conditions or requirements to make contributions imposed by sections 8 and 11 of that Act,".

The House of Commons Disqualification Act 1975 (c.24)

3. In Part III of Schedule 1 to the House of Commons Disqualification Act 1975 (other disqualifying offices) there shall be inserted (at the appropriate place in alphabetical order) the following entry—
    "Chairman of the Scottish Legal Aid Board".

The Northern Ireland Assembly Disqualification Act 1975 (c.25)

4. In Part III of Schedule 1 to the Northern Ireland Assembly Disqualification Act 1975 (other disqualifying offices) there shall be inserted (at the appropriate place in alphabetical order) the following entry—
    "Chairman of the Scottish Legal Aid Board".

The Sex Discrimination Act 1975 (c.65)

5. In section 75(4) of the Sex Discrimination Act 1975 for the words "the Legal Aid and Advice (Scotland) Acts 1967 and 1972" there shall be substituted the words "the Legal Aid (Scotland) Act 1986".

The Race Relations Act 1976 (c.74)

6. In section 66(6) of the Race Relations Act 1976 for the words "the Legal Aid and Advice (Scotland) Acts 1967 and 1972" there shall be substituted the words "the Legal Aid (Scotland) Act 1986".

The Solicitors (Scotland) Act 1980 (c.46)

7. In section 35(4) of the Solicitors (Scotland) Act 1980 for paragraph (*b*) there shall be substituted—
    "(*b*) who is in employment to which Part V of the Legal Aid (Scotland) Act 1986 applies;".

8.—(1) Section 51 of that Act shall be amended as follows.

(2) In subsection (2) after the word "client" there shall be inserted the words "or against the Scottish Legal Aid Fund".

(3) In subsection (3) after paragraph (*d*) there shall be inserted the following paragraph—
    "(*e*) the Scottish Legal Aid Board.".

The Tenants' Rights, Etc. (Scotland) Act 1980 (c.52)

9. In section 9B(4) of the Tenants' Rights, Etc. (Scotland) Act 1980 for the words "Legal Aid and Advice (Scotland) Acts 1967 and 1972 and to any provision of those Acts for payment of any sum into the legal aid fund" there shall be substituted the words "Legal Aid (Scotland) Act 1986 and to any provision of that Act for payment of any sum into the Scottish Legal Aid Fund".

Section 45   SCHEDULE 4

TRANSITIONAL PROVISIONS AND SAVINGS

The Legal Aid (Scotland) Fund

1.—(1) On the appointed day the Legal Aid (Scotland) Fund ("the Old Fund") established under section 9 of the Legal Aid (Scotland) Act 1967 ("the 1967 Act") shall be wound up.

(2) If, as at the appointed day, after taking account of all receipts and expenses of the Law Society attributable to the 1967 Act or to their functions under the Legal Advice and Assistance Act 1972 ("the 1972 Act"), there is in relation to the Old Fund any surplus or deficit—
    (*a*) such surplus shall be paid by the Law Society to the Secretary of State; and
    (*b*) such deficit shall be made up by payment to the Law Society by the Secretary of State of the amount of the deficit.

(3) Notwithstanding their repeal by this Act—
    (*a*) section 8(10) and (11) and 11 of the 1967 Act shall continue to have effect for the purposes of requiring the Law Society to account for the Old Fund and to report on its discharge of its functions under that Act up to the appointed day; and

(*b*) section 9(5) of that Act shall continue to have effect for the purposes of any
    determination as to the expenses or receipts of the Law Society,
and, if the appointed day falls on a day which is not the last day of the financial year (for the
purposes of the said section 11), references in those sections to the financial year shall be
construed as references to the period commencing on the day immediately following the end
of the last complete financial year and ending with the appointed day.

Rights, obligations and property

2. Subject to paragraph 1 above, on the appointed day all rights, obligations and property
of the Law Society which are referable to its functions under the 1967 Act or under the 1972
Act shall become rights, obligations and property of the Board.

Legal aid and advice and assistance

3.—(1) Nothing in this Act shall affect any legal aid under the 1967 Act or advice and
assistance under the 1972 Act in respect of which an application has been determined before
the appointed day; and, notwithstanding the repeal by this Act of these Acts, they and any
schemes, regulations, orders or rules of court made under them shall continue to have effect
for the purposes of such legal aid or advice and assistance.

(2) For the purposes of sub-paragraph (1) above, where the 1967 Act or the 1972 Act or
any such scheme, regulation, order or rule of court—

(*a*) requires or enables anything to be done by the Law Society or any of its committees
    or by any person on its behalf; or

(*b*) requires or enables the person in receipt of such legal aid or advice and assistance to
    do anything in relation to the Law Society,

that thing shall, on and after the appointed day, be required or, as the case may be, enabled
to be done by or in relation to the Board.

(3) Any payments which are required to be made into or out of the Old Fund in
connection with such legal aid or advice and assistance shall, on and after the appointed
day, be made into or out of the Fund; and for the purposes of this sub-paragraph, any
reference in the 1967 Act or the 1972 Act to the Old Fund shall be construed as a reference
to the Fund.

4.—(1) Any application for legal aid duly made under the 1967 Act or for advice and
assistance duly made under the 1972 Act which has been made, but not determined, before
the appointed day shall be treated as an application duly made under this Act.

(2) For the purposes of this paragraph and paragraph 3 above an application for legal aid
is determined—

(*a*) in the case of legal aid in connection with—
        (i) civil proceedings (including an appeal in such proceedings);
        (ii) an appeal in criminal proceedings; or
        (iii) an appeal against the decision of the sheriff under Part III of the Social
        Work (Scotland) Act 1968,
    when a legal aid certificate is issued or refused;

(*b*) in the case of legal aid in connection with—
        (i) criminal proceedings; or
        (ii) proceedings before the sheriff under Part III of the Social Work (Scotland)
        Act 1968,
    when the court grants or refuses legal aid.

(3) For the purposes of this paragraph and paragraph 3 above an application for advice
and assistance is determined when the solicitor to whom the application is made agrees or,
as the case may be, refuses to accept the application and to provided advice and assistance.

Pensions

5. Any arrangements made by the Law Society under section 12 of the 1967 Act in respect
of any person shall be treated on and after the appointed day (so far as may be necessary
to preserve their effect) as having been made under paragraph 8 (3) of Schedule 1 to this
Act, and any pension scheme administered by the Law Society immediately before the
appointed day shall be deemed to be a pension scheme established and administered by the
Board under that paragraph and shall continue to be administered accordingly.

General

6.—(1) In this Schedule "the appointed day" means the day appointed by the Secretary
of State under section 46(2) of this Act for the coming into force of section 4 thereof.

(2) Subject to sub-paragraph (1) above, expressions used in this Schedule and in the 1967 Act or, as the case may be, in the 1972 Act shall have the same meaning in this Schedule as they do in that Act.

Section 45   SCHEDULE 5

REPEALS

Chapter	Short title	Extent of repeal
1967 c.43.	The Legal Aid (Scotland) Act 1967.	The whole Act.
1968 c.49.	The Social Work (Scotland) Act 1968.	Section 53. Schedule 4.
1972 c.11.	The Superannuation Act 1972.	Section 18(2).
1972 c.18.	The Maintenance Orders (Reciprocal Enforcement) Act 1972.	Section 32(9)(*e*).
1972 c.50.	The Legal Advice and Assistance Act 1972.	The whole Act.
1973 c.41.	The Fair Trading Act 1973.	In section 43(1), paragraph (*b*). Section 43(2).
1975 c.20.	The District Courts (Scotland) Act 1975.	Section 21.
1977 c.38.	The Administration of Justice Act 1977.	Section 1(2). In Schedule 1, Part II.
1979 c.26.	The Legal Aid Act 1979.	Part II. Section 12(2). In section 14(2), the words "and may be cited together with the Act of 1967 and the Act of 1972 as the Legal Aid and Advice (Scotland) Acts 1967 to 1979.". Section 14(3)(*b*). In section 14(4), the words ", or as the case may be the Secretary of State". Section 14(5)(*b*). In Schedule 1, paragraphs 1 to 8.
1980 c.30.	The Social Security Act 1980.	In Schedule 4, paragraph 4.
1980 c.55.	The Law Reform (Miscellaneous Provisions) (Scotland) Act 1980.	Section 26.
1980 c.62.	The Criminal Justice (Scotland) Act 1980.	Section 10(4).
1981 c.49.	The Contempt of Court Act 1981.	Section 13(4). In Schedule 2, Part II.
1982 c.27.	The Civil Jurisdiction and Judgments Act 1982.	Section 40(2).
1983 c.12.	The Divorce Jurisdiction, Court Fees and Legal Aid (Scotland) Act 1983.	Section 3. In the Schedule, paragraph 11 and paragraphs 14 to 17.

WAGES ACT 1986*

(1986 c. 48)

ARRANGEMENT OF SECTIONS

Part I

PROTECTION OF WORKERS IN RELATION TO THE PAYMENT OF WAGES

PART II

WAGES COUNCILS

Scope of operation of wages councils

Wages orders

Enforcement

Miscellaneous and supplemental

PART III

REDUNDANCY REBATES, ETC.

PART IV

GENERAL

* Annotations provided by Sandra Fredman, B.A. (Rand), M.A.; B.C.L. (Oxon), Lecturer in Law, King's College, University of London.

SCHEDULES:
Schedule 1—Enactments repealed by section 11.
Schedule 2—Constitution etc. of wages councils.
Schedule 3—Wages orders: supplementary provisions.
Schedule 4—Minor and consequential amendments.
Schedule 5—Repeals.
Schedule 6—Transitional provisions and savings.

An Act to make fresh provision with respect to the protection of workers in relation to the payment of wages; to make further provision with respect to wages councils; to restrict redundancy rebates to employers with less than ten employees and to abolish certain similar payments; and for connected purposes. [25th July 1986]

INTRODUCTION AND GENERAL NOTE
The Wages Act is in four parts. Part I repeals the Truck Acts 1831 to 1940 and other enactments imposing restrictions connected with the payment of wages, replacing them with a new regulatory system, based primarily on the contract of employment. Part II substantially narrows the jurisdiction of wages councils, removing their power to determine wages or other conditions of work of workers under 21, and restricting their powers in respect of adult workers to the determination of a single minimum basic rate and a single minimum overtime rate. Part III limits the payment of statutory redundancy rebates by the Secretary of State to employers with fewer than ten employees. Part IV contains general and supplementary provisions.
There are six Schedules. Sched. 1 lists the enactments repealed by s.11; Sched. 2 sets out the constitution of wages councils; Sched. 3 contains supplementary provisions concerning wages orders. Sched. 4 contains minor and consequential provisions; Sched. 5 lists the enactments repealed by s.32(2); and Sched. 6 contains transitional provisions and savings.

ABBREVIATIONS
Employment Protection (Consolidation) Act 1978 (c.44): EPCA
Standing Committee A: SC
Trade Union and Labour Relations Act 1974 (c.52): TULRA 1974
Wages Councils Act 1979 (c.12): WCA 1979.

PARLIAMENTARY DEBATES
Hansard: H.C. Vol. 90, col. 1114; H.C. Vol. 91, col. 798; H.C. Vol. 97, cols. 731, 877; H.C. Vol. 102, col. 470; H.L. Vol. 474, col. 1438; H.L. Vol. 475, col. 1203; H.L. Vol. 477, cols. 158, 423; H.L. Vol. 478, col. 180; H.L. Vol. 479, col. 123.
The Bill was considered by Standing Committee K between February 18, 1986, and April 29, 1986.

PART I

GENERAL NOTE
Part I regulates deductions from pay and receipts by employers of payments from workers, replacing the Truck Acts 1831 to 1940, and the assortment of other legislation covering remuneration of specific workers. (Merchant seamen remain separately regulated by the Merchant Shipping Act 1970 (ss.7–18)—see s.30(3) below). Section 1 authorises deductions from wages provided they are required or authorised by virtue of a statutory provision or a provision in the worker's contract, or the worker has previously given written consent to the making of it. Similar provisions apply to the receipt by employers of payments from their workers (s.1(2)). In the case of retail workers, deductions or payments in respect of stock deficiencies or cash shortages are limited to ten per cent. of wages payable on any pay day (ss.2, 3), although deductions may be made by instalments, and no limit is placed on the amount deductible from the final pay packet on termination of employment (s.4).
The major feature distinguishing the new framework from that provided by the Truck Act 1896 is the assertion by the present Act of the "central nature of contract." (SC45) Under the 1896 Act, it was not sufficient for deductions to be authorised by contract. In addition, they had to relate to the employer's loss and be "fair and reasonable." In the case of fines, the Act required the contract to specify the acts or omissions in respect of which the fine might be imposed, and the amount of the fine or the particulars from which that amount

might be ascertained. Moreover, the Act was policed by an inspectorate, and breach was a criminal offence. The present Act removes the "fair and reasonable" criterion and the other constraints on the contract as well as the criminal sanctions. Redress is to an industrial tribunal, which can award only what has been unlawfully deducted, with no punitive or compensatory elements.

The Act eliminates the distinction found in the Truck Acts between manual and non-manual workers, and between fines and deductions for negligent work, categories which had spawned numerous technical distinctions. A broad definition of "worker" is adopted (s.8). However, the Act adopts a new potentially difficult distinction, between retail and non-retail workers.

Note the exclusions in s.30.

COMMENCEMENT
To be appointed (see s.33(5)).

PROTECTION OF WORKERS IN RELATION TO THE PAYMENT OF WAGES

General restrictions on deductions made, or payments received, by employers

1.—(1) An employer shall not make any deduction from any wages of any worker employed by him unless the deduction satisfies one of the following conditions, namely—

(*a*) it is required or authorised to be made by virtue of any statutory provision or any relevant provision of the worker's contract; or

(*b*) the worker has previously signified in writing his agreement or consent to the making of it.

(2) An employer shall not receive any payment from any worker employed by him unless the payment satisfies one of the conditions set out in paragraphs (*a*) and (*b*) of subsection (1).

(3) In this section "relevant provision", in relation to a worker's contract, means any provision of the contract comprised—

(*a*) in one or more written terms of the contract of which the employer has given the worker a copy on any occasion prior to the employer making the deduction in question, or (where subsection (1)(*a*) applies for the purposes of subsection (2)) prior to his receiving the payment in question, or

(*b*) in one or more terms of the contract (whether express or implied and, if express, whether oral or in writing) whose existence and effect, or (as the case may be) combined effect, in relation to the worker the employer has notified to the worker in writing on any such occasion.

(4) For the purposes of this section—

(*a*) any relevant provision of a worker's contract having effect by virtue of any variation of the contract, or

(*b*) any agreement or consent signified by a worker as mentioned in subsection (1)(*b*),

shall not operate to authorise the making of any deduction, or the receipt of any payment, on account of any conduct of the worker, or any other event occurring, before the variation took effect or (as the case may be) the agreement or consent was signified.

(5) Nothing in this section applies—

(*a*) to any deduction from a worker's wages made by his employer, or any payment received from a worker by his employer, where the purpose of the deduction or payment is the reimbursement of the employer in respect of—

(i) any overpayment of wages, or

(ii) any overpayment in respect of expenses incurred by the worker in carrying out his employment,

made (for any reason) by the employer to the worker;

(*b*) to any deduction from a worker's wages made by his employer, or any payment received from a worker by his employer, in consequence of any disciplinary proceedings if those proceedings were held by virtue of any statutory provision;

(*c*) to any deduction from a worker's wages made by his employer in pursuance of any requirement imposed on the employer by any statutory provision to deduct and pay over to a public authority amounts determined by that authority as being due to it from the worker, if the deduction is made in accordance with the relevant determination of that authority;

(*d*) to any deduction from a worker's wages made by his employer in pursuance of any arrangements which have been established—

    (i) in accordance with any relevant provision of his contract to whose inclusion in the contract the worker has signified his agreement or consent in writing, or

    (ii) otherwise with the prior agreement or consent of the worker signified in writing,

and under which the employer is to deduct and pay over to a third person amounts notified to the employer by that person as being due to him from the worker, if the deduction is made in accordance with the relevant notification by that person;

(*e*) to any deduction from a worker's wages made by his employer, or any payment received from a worker by his employer, where the worker has taken part in a strike or other industrial action and the deduction is made, or the payment has been required, by the employer on account of the worker's having taken part in that strike or other action; or

(*f*) to any deduction from a worker's wages made by his employer with his prior agreement or consent signified in writing, or any payment received from a worker by his employer, where the purpose of the deduction or payment is the satisfaction (whether wholly or in part) of an order of a court or tribunal requiring the payment of any amount by the worker to the employer.

(6) This section is without prejudice to any other statutory provision by virtue of which any sum payable to a worker by his employer but not falling within the definition of "wages" in section 7 is not to be subject to any deduction at the instance of the employer.

DEFINITIONS
"deduction": s.8(3) and (4).
"employed": s.8(1).
"employer": s.8(1).
"relevant provision": s.1(3).
"statutory provision": s.8(1).
"wages": s.7.
"worker", "worker's contract": s.8(1) and (2).

GENERAL NOTE
See General Note to Part I above.

Subs. (1).
"required or authorised to be made by virtue of . . . any relevant provision in the worker's contract": Provided it is authorised by the contract, the Act does not require the deduction to be fair or reasonable, as required by the Truck Act 1896, nor, if misconduct is alleged, that it be proved. Similarly, where a deduction is on account of a cash shortage or stock deficiency, there is no requirement that the deduction reflect the exact amount of the deficiency, nor that the worker be informed of the way in which the deduction is calculated.

(Contrast *Sealand Petroleum Co.* v. *Barratt* [1986] 2 All E.R. 360) (*Hansard,* H.L., Vol. 477, No. 115, col. 215; Vol. 478, No. 125, col. 195).

Some constraints, however, are placed on the substance of the contract by the common law restrictions on "penalty clauses" (See Hepple and O'Higgins, *Employment Law* (1981) para. 483). This doctrine applies to clauses in a contract which stipulate that a sum of money be paid to the injured party by the party in breach of contract. Such clauses are "subject to the rule of public policy that the court will not enforce it . . . if it is satisfied that the stipulated sum was not a genuine estimate of the loss likely to be sustained by the party not in breach, but was a sum in excess of such anticipated loss and thus, if exacted would be in the nature of a penalty or punishment imposed upon the contract breaker." (*Robophone Facilities Ltd.* v. *Blank* [1966] 1 W.L.R. 1428, *per* Diplock L.J.). In any case, the amount of the penalty must be specified in the contract or readily ascertainable in accordance with its terms. It is submitted that a penalty clause which is unenforceable at common law cannot be said to be "authorised" by the contract for the purposes of s.1(1)(*a*). However, the principle requires that the penalty be payable on breach of contract (*Bridge* v. *Campbell Discount Company Ltd.* [1962] A.C. 600). Where the deduction is part of the contractual consideration, not dependent on breach of contract, the common law restrictions do not operate. (See for example, *Sagar* v. *Ridehalgh* [1931] 1 Ch. 310).

A further constraint is potentially found in s.3 of the Unfair Contract Terms Act 1977, which applies to contracts between a party in business and a person who deals as a consumer or on the other party's standard terms and conditions. S.3(2) UCTA refers to a term of a contract which seeks to allow one party to render no performance at all, or a performance substantially different from that which was reasonably expected. Such a term is unenforceable unless it satisfies the reasonableness requirement in s.11 UCTA. It is arguable that a worker is a consumer for the purposes of s.12 of this Act. (*Chitty on Contract,* vol. II, p.669 at note 54.) Alternatively, the worker may deal on the employer's written standard terms of business, if he or she signs a standard application form or if the relevant term is in the company handbook. In such a case, a clause which falls within s.3(2) would have to be reasonable. (See Tamara Goriely "Deductions from Pay and Repeal of the Truck Acts" [1983] *Industrial Law Journal* 236 at 241).

"*statutory provision*": Note the exception in subs. (5)(*c*) for deductions in pursuance of a statutory provision requiring the employer to pay over the amount deducted to a public authority. The effect of these two subsections is that a worker who contests whether a deduction is authorised by statute may only appeal to an industrial tribunal if the statute does not require the employer to pay over the amount deducted to a public authority. In other cases, the appeals procedure of the relevant public body (such as the Inland Revenue or Department of Health and Social Security) is applicable. (See also note to subs. (5) (*c*)).

"*previously signified*": By subs. (4), consent must be given prior to the conduct in respect of which the deduction is made (Contrast subs. (3)).

"*agreement or consent to the making of it*": If the consent amounted to a variation of the contract of employment, it would fall into subs. (1)(*a*). (See also the distinction drawn in subs. (4) between a variation of contract and agreement or consent under subs. (1)(*b*)). This provision therefore captures non-contractual documents or collateral contracts. (*Hansard,* H.L. Vol. 477, No. 115, col. 185) For example, if a non-contractual bonus is payable to a worker for good work, such a bonus cannot be withdrawn unless the worker has signified consent in writing. (See notes to ss.2(4), 2(5) and 7(3)). In the appropriate case, such documents may be governed by the Unfair Contract Terms Act 1977. See note to "required or authorised" above. (*Hansard,* H.L. Vol. 478, No. 125, col. 218). One difficulty concerns cases in which a worker is covered by a wages council order (s.14 *post*), and the employer has paid the worker less than the statutory minimum. Such an underpayment is a "deduction" for the purposes of Part I (s.8(3)), and cannot be authorised by statute or contract for the purposes of s.1(1). (See s.16(1)). However, it may be possible to argue that consent signified in a non-contractual document may make the deduction lawful by virtue of s.1(1)(*b*). It is submitted that s.6(3) precludes this argument (see note to s.6(3)).

Subs. (2)
As in the Truck Act 1896, these provisions apply equally to situations in which an employer requires the worker to pay back money instead of deducting it at source.

Subs. (3)
The relevant contractual provision may be oral or written, and express or implied. Where the relevant provision is contained in a written term of the contract, the employer is required

to give the worker a copy on an occasion prior to making the deduction or receiving the payment (subs. (3)(*a*)). In the case of oral terms, whether express or implied, the employer is required to notify the worker in writing of their existence as well as their effect. There is no further provision in this statute requiring the employer to notify the worker of the details of each particular deduction or why it was made. (Contrast Truck Act 1896, s.1(1)(*b*), which required the contract to specify the acts or omissions in respect of which the fine might be imposed and the amount of the fine or the particulars from which that amount might be ascertained. For retail workers, see s.3.) This is covered to some extent by EPCA 1978, ss.8 and 9, which give employees the right to an itemised pay statement in writing at or before any payment of wages or salary is made. This statement should specify any variable or fixed deductions and the purposes for which they are made. Alternatively, the employer may give a standing statement of fixed deductions, in which case, the itemised statement need only specify an aggregate deduction (EPCA 1978, s.9). However, this section does not apply to the extended definition of "worker" in the present Act, but only to "employees" (employed under a contract of service) who fulfil the eligibility requirements of EPCA. (See, *e.g.* s.146).

"*prior to making the deduction*": It appears that, unlike subs. (4) below, the notification may be after the conduct in respect of which the deduction occurs, provided it is prior to the deduction itself. No time-scale is specified; but it must be a separate "occasion."

"*implied*": A deduction may be made even in respect of an implied contractual term, for example, a term implied from custom and practice (*Sagar* v. *Ridehalgh* [1931] 1 Ch. 310), or from a relevant collective agreement or from the employer's rules, provided the worker has been notified in writing of its existence and effect. This may involve the tribunal in applying the complex principles relating to implied terms.

Subs. (4)

This subsection provides that where a contract has been varied to require or authorise a deduction or payment, that variation cannot operate retrospectively to authorise deductions in respect of events occurring before the variation (subs. (4)(*a*)). Similarly, any agreement or consent of the worker under subs. (1)(*b*) can only authorise deductions or payments in respect of events occurring thereafter. However, the subsection is limited to variation of contract. Where a contract is terminated and a new contract entered into between the same parties, this provision does not apply. (For example, a worker may be employed under a series of short contracts.) (*Hansard,* H.L. Vol. 477, No. 116, col. 200).

Subs. (5)

This subsection lists the exceptions to s.1. Its main aim is to delineate the respective jurisdictions of industrial tribunals, the civil courts and other bodies such as the Inland Revenue or Department of Health and Social Security Appeals Tribunals.

Para. (*a*): The example given in the House of Commons was of the practice of some firms, for reasons of administrative convenience, to make small overpayments of wages that are later recovered. For example, where information on bonus or overtime payment is not available until after payday, a standard sum is paid, with a small adjustment, up or down, the following week. The exception applies equally to overpayments of expenses incurred by the worker in the course of employment. The effect of this subsection is to remove the worker's right to complain to an industrial tribunal on the grounds that s.1 has not been complied with (*e.g.* the notification provisions have not been complied with) (*Hansard,* H.C. Vol. 97, No. 113, col. 789). However, the common law right to complain to the ordinary courts that there has been a breach of contract, is unaffected. Moreover, where the worker asserts that the employer has deducted more than what was overpaid, he or she retains the right to complain to an industrial tribunal under s.1 (*Hansard,* H.L. Vol. 478, No. 125, col. 192). This may lead to complex jurisdictional disputes, in cases where the distinction between reimbursements of overpayments and deductions is unclear.

Para. (*b*): Thus workers covered by statutory disciplinary procedures, such as the police or fire service, have no right to complain to an industrial tribunal.

Para. (*c*): Examples would include deductions in respect of social security contributions, pay-as-you-earn tax, and attachment of earnings orders made by a court to enforce maintenance orders and other judgments. Disputes in respect of such payments are dealt with by the Inland Revenue, the Department of Health and Social Security or the relevant court rather than industrial tribunals. (See also Note to subs. (1)(*a*)).

Para. (*d*): Although this provision constitutes an exception to s.1, it substitutes requirements which are in one sense stricter in that the worker's written consent is required to any arrangement, whether contractual or non-contractual. The chief example of this subsection is the "check-off," where the employer deducts union dues on behalf of the worker and pays them over to the union. This section therefore follows the existing law, the Truck Acts having been interpreted by the courts to permit union subscriptions to be deducted at the worker's request (*Williams* v. *Butlers Ltd.* [1975] I.C.R. 308). It is not, however, limited to the check-off. Indeed, there is no requirement that the recipient be independent of the employer. The safeguards against abuse of this power is the need for written consent from the worker which may be withdrawn if desired. (*Hansard,* H.L. Vol. 477, No. 115, col. 203).

Para. (e): The justification for this exclusion was that "it is not right, fair or proper for an industrial tribunal to deal with an industrial dispute . . . where tempers flair; it is better for a court of law to do so" (SC 129). Thus if the worker disputes any deduction made on account of having taken part in a strike or other industrial action, the remedy is a claim for breach of contract in an ordinary court of law and the extra safeguards contained in s.1 do not apply. The section is modelled on s.62 EPCA 1978, which states that an industrial tribunal shall not have jurisdiction over a dismissal which has taken place while an employee is "taking part in a strike or other industrial action." However, s.62 only applies if the employer treats all workers alike, thus preventing victimisation. By contrast, this section contains no similar protection against discriminatory deductions (*Hansard,* H.L. Vol. 477, No. 115, col. 204). A complex caselaw exists as to the meaning of "has taken part in a strike or other industrial action". (*e.g. Power Packing Casemakers Ltd.* v. *Faust* [1983] 2 All E.R. 166; *Midland Plastics* v. *Till* [1983] I.C.R. 188).

Para. (f): This exception allows an employer who has obtained an order of court or tribunal against a worker to deduct the relevant sums or require them to be repaid, provided the prior written agreement of the worker has been given. (*Hansard,* H.C. Vol. 97, No. 113, col. 790).

Deductions from wages of workers in retail employment on account of cash shortages etc.

2.—(1) Where (in accordance with section 1(1)) the employer of a worker in retail employment makes, on account of one or more cash shortages or stock deficiencies, any deduction or deductions from any wages payable to the worker on a pay day, the amount or aggregate amount of the deduction or deductions shall not exceed one-tenth of the gross amount of the wages payable to the worker on that day.

(2) In this Part—

"cash shortage" means a deficit arising in relation to amounts received in connection with retail transactions;

"pay day", in relation to a worker, means a day on which wages are payable to the worker;

"retail employment", in relation to a worker, means employment involving (whether on a regular basis or not)—

(*a*) the carrying out by the worker of retail transactions directly with members of the public or with fellow workers or other individuals in their personal capacities, or

(*b*) the collection by the worker of amounts payable in connection with retail transactions carried out by other persons directly with members of the public or with fellow workers or other individuals in their personal capacities;

"retail transaction" means the sale or supply of goods, or the supply of services (including financial services); and

"stock deficiency" means a stock deficiency arising in the course of retail transactions.

(3) Where the employer of a worker in retail employment makes a deduction from the worker's wages on account of a cash shortage or stock deficiency, the employer shall not be treated as making the deduction in accordance with section 1(1) unless (in addition to the requirements of that provision being satisfied with respect to the deduction)—

(*a*) the deduction is made, or

(*b*) in the case of a deduction which is one of a series of deductions relating to the shortage or deficiency, the first deduction in the series was made,

not later than the end of the period of 12 months beginning with the date when the employer established the existence of the shortage or deficiency or (if earlier) the date when he ought reasonably to have done so.

(4) This subsection applies where—

(*a*) by virtue of any agreement between a worker in retail employment and his employer, the amount of the worker's wages or any part of them is or may be determined by reference to the incidence of cash shortages or stock deficiencies, and

(*b*) the gross amount of the wages payable to the worker on any pay day is, on account of any such shortages or deficiencies, less than the gross amount of the wages that would have been payable to him on that day if there had been no such shortages or deficiencies.

(5) In a case where subsection (4) applies—

(*a*) the amount representing the difference between the two amounts referred to in paragraph (*b*) of that subsection ("the relevant amount") shall be treated for the purposes of this Part as a deduction from the wages payable to the worker on that day made by the employer on account of the cash shortages or stock deficiencies in question, and

(*b*) the second of the amounts so referred to shall be treated for the purposes of this Part (except subsection (4)) as the gross amount of the wages payable to him on that day;

and section 1(1) and (if the requirements of that provision and subsection (3) above are satisfied) subsection (1) above shall have effect in relation to the relevant amount accordingly.

DEFINITIONS
"cash shortage": s.2(2).
"deduction": See ss.4(6), 8(3).
"employer": s.8(1)
"gross amount": s.8(1).
"pay day": s.2(2).
"retail employment": s.2(2).
"retail transaction": s.2(2).
"stock deficiency": s.2(2).
"wages": s.7.
"worker": s.8(1) and (2).

GENERAL NOTE
This section provides that, in the case of retail workers, deductions made on account of cash shortages or stock deficiencies should not exceed 10 per cent. of the gross amount of wages payable on a pay day (subs. (1)). Deductions may, however, be made by instalments, and, by s.5, any outstanding amount may be recouped on the final pay packet if the employment is terminated. A deduction may not be made more than 12 months after a shortage or deficiency has been discovered, or, if earlier, should reasonably have been discovered (subs. (3)). The protection is limited to deductions on account of cash shortages or stock deficiencies, Deductions for any other purposes, such as absenteeism or bad workmanship, may be deducted from the pay of retail workers without limit; and non-retail workers may be subject to unlimited deductions for any reason including suspected dishonesty. (In all these cases, it is necessary to comply with s.1.)

Subs. (1)
"On account of one or more cash shortages or stock deficiencies": This is relatively widely drawn, broadening the range of situations in which the 10 per cent. limit applies in addition to the constraints in section 1. (See s.4(6) and note thereto).

"Gross amount of the wages payable": By s.8(1), "gross amount" means the total amount before any deductions of whatever nature. Since tax and national insurance payments are

calculated on the gross amount before any deductions, a worker is in effect required to pay tax on the deductions. Depending on the individual circumstances, the Inland Revenue may consider such deductions to be expenses and therefore tax deductible. (SC 237) "Wages" as defined in s.7 excludes certain sums (s.7(2)); such sums would therefore not be part of the gross amount.

"one tenth": This figure appears to reflect the wishes of the majority of employers who made representations, although some employers, such as the Motor Agents Association, would have preferred a limit of 20 per cent. (SC 204).

Subs. 2
"pay day": The relevant day is that in which wages are payable, not the day on which they are paid. Thus where payment is by direct debit, it is not necessary to determine which day payment was authorised or received. (*Hansard*, H.C. Vol. 97, No. 113, col. 791).

"retail employment":
"fellow workers or individuals in their personal capacities": This includes workers in factory or hospital canteens who sell or supply goods or services to fellow workers rather than direct to the public.
"whether on a regular basis or not": For example, a worker who covers for a colleague during a lunch break (*Hansard,* H.L. Vol. 477, No. 115, col. 218).
"involving the carrying out of ... retail transactions": Hence a worker is fully protected in respect of all sales even if some sales are to individuals and some are to companies.
"the collection by the worker of amounts payable in connection with retail transactions carried out by other persons": Thus cashiers are covered even if they do not themselves supply goods or services.
There are likely to be some fine distinctions between retail and non-retail workers. Shop assistants are clearly covered, but warehouse staff or clerks involved in backup services in retail establishments are, depending on the circumstances, likely to be excluded (*Hansard,* H.L. Vol. 477, No. 115, col. 219.) Similarly, if there is an office or factory canteen, the workers supplying the food and taking the money in the canteen are retail workers, but those who merely use the canteen are not. (H.L. Vol. 479, No. 135, col. 124).

"retail transaction": The definition is not limited to sales, but includes the supply of goods or services.

Subs. (3)
The time period of 12 months was imposed in order to "prevent employers . . . who decide to victimise a worker, dredging up old events and eventually starting to make deductions in the distant future . . In addition, the provision will help to prevent disputes over events that happened so far back in the past that memories have become blurred." (SC 781). At the same time, the Government was anxious to preserve the employer's right to make deductions for cash shortages or stock deficiencies which are only ascertained on an annual stock-taking. (This may be contrasted with the three months allowed to workers to complain to an industrial tribunal (s.5(2))).

Subs. (4) and (5)
These two subsections prevent the circumvention of the 10 per cent. limit in cases in which pay is calculated after taking account of any cash shortages or stock deficiencies. (For example, a basic wage might be payable which reflects the incidence of shortages, and an extra bonus may be available if there are no shortages.) In such cases, the "gross wage" payable is deemed to be the wage which would be payable if there were no cash shortages or stock deficiencies. (In the above example, "gross wages" would include any bonus payable in the absence of shortages.) The difference between the deemed gross wage and the pay actually received is then treated as a deduction and should comply with s.1. In addition, the deduction, as here defined, together with any other deductions, must be no more than 10 per cent. of the deemed gross wage. (SC 149) (For example, if the bonus is not paid, this counts as a deduction and should not exceed 10 per cent. of the basic pay plus the bonus.)

"is or may be": These subsections apply even if the bonus is discretionary or conditional on a number of different factors, one of which is the absence of cash shortages or stock deficiencies. (*Hansard,* H.C. Vol. 102, No. 57, col. 475).

Payments by workers in retail employment on account of cash shortages etc.

3.—(1) Where the employer of a worker in retail employment receives from the worker any payment on account of a cash shortage or stock deficiency the employer shall not be treated as receiving the payment in accordance with section 1(2) unless (in addition to the requirements of that provision being satisfied with respect to the payment) he has previously—

    (*a*) notified the worker in writing of the worker's total liability to him in respect of that shortage or deficiency; and

    (*b*) required the worker to make the payment by means of a demand for payment made in accordance with this section.

(2) Any demand for payment made by the employer of a worker in retail employment in respect of a cash shortage or stock deficiency—

    (*a*) shall be made in writing, and

    (*b*) shall be made on one of the worker's pay days.

(3) A demand for payment in respect of a particular cash shortage or stock deficiency, or (in the case of a series of such demands) the first such demand, shall not be made—

    (*a*) earlier than the first pay day of the worker following the date when he is notified of his total liability in respect of the shortage or deficiency in pursuance of subsection (1)(*a*) or, where he is so notified on a pay day, earlier than that day, or

    (*b*) later than the end of the period of 12 months beginning with the date when the employer established the existence of the shortage or deficiency or (if earlier) the date when he ought reasonably to have done so.

(4) Where the employer of a worker in retail employment makes on any pay day one or more demands for payment in accordance with this section, the amount or aggregate amount required to be paid by the worker in pursuance of the demand or demands shall not exceed—

    (*a*) one-tenth of the gross amount of the wages payable to the worker on that day, or

    (*b*) where one or more deductions falling within section 2(1) are made by the employer from those wages, such amount as represents the balance of that one-tenth after subtracting the amount or aggregate amount of the deduction or deductions.

(5) Once any amount has been required to be paid by means of a demand for payment made in accordance with this section on any pay day, that amount shall not be taken into account under subsection (4) as it applies to any subsequent pay day, notwithstanding that the employer is obliged to make further requests for it to be paid.

(6) For the purposes of this Part a demand for payment shall be treated as made by the employer on one of the worker's pay days if it is given to the worker, or posted to, or left at, his last known address—

    (*a*) on that pay day, or

    (*b*) in the case of a pay day which is not a working day of the employer's business, on the first such working day following that pay day.

DEFINITIONS
    "cash shortage": s.2(2).
    "deduction": See s.4(6), s.8(3).
    "employer": s.8(1).
    "gross amount": s.8(1).
    "pay day": s.2(2).
    "retail employment": s.2(2).
    "retail transaction": s.2(2).

"stock deficiency": s.2(2).
"wages": s.7.
"worker": s.8(1) and (2).

GENERAL NOTE

This section contains protections for retail workers in situations in which an employer demands payment for cash shortages or stock deficiencies, instead of deducting at source. An employer is required, in addition to the provisions of s.1(2), to notify the worker in writing of the total liability in respect of the cash shortage or stock deficiency for which payment is demanded (subs. (1)(*a*)), and to make a written demand for payment (subs. (1)(*b*) and (2)(*a*)). The demand should be made on a pay day no earlier than the date of the written notification (subs. (3)(*a*)).

There is no provision for advance warning of a demand; the employer may pursue the demand immediately. (For the definition of the date on which a demand is made, see subs. (6)). This may be compared with the provisions in respect of deductions in s.8 EPCA, which, however, applies only to a limited class of "employees." (See note to s.1(3)). It is noteworthy that no similar requirement applies to payments demanded of non-retail workers.

As in the case of deductions, the demand for payment must be made not later than 12 months after the cash shortage or stock deficiency has been established or ought to have been established (subs. (3)(*b*), see also s.4(4)). Furthermore, the total amount of any payment should not exceed 10 per cent. of the gross amount of wages payable. (subs. (4)). Where a deduction on account of a cash shortage or stock deficiency is made at the same time as a demand for payment, the total of payments and deductions should not exceed 10 per cent. (subs.(4)(*b*)). By subs. (5), a demand for payment which has not been met is not counted into the 10 per cent. limit for the next pay day, even if the employer is obliged to make further requests for payment.

Provisions supplementary to ss.2 and 3

4.—(1) In this section "final instalment of wages", in relation to a worker, means—

 (*a*) the amount of wages payable to the worker which consists of or includes an amount payable by way of contractual remuneration in respect of the last of the periods for which he is employed under his contract prior to its termination for any reason (but excluding any wages referable to any earlier such period), or

 (*b*) where an amount in lieu of notice is paid to the worker later than the amount referred to in paragraph (*a*) the amount so paid,

in each case whether the amount in question is paid before or after the termination of the worker's contract.

(2) Section 2(1) shall not operate to restrict the amount of any deductions that may (in accordance with section 1(1)) be made by the employer of a worker in retail employment from the worker's final instalment of wages.

(3) Nothing in section 3 shall apply to any payment falling within subsection (1) of that section that is made on or after the day on which any such worker's final instalment of wages is paid, but (notwithstanding that the requirements of section 1(2) would otherwise be satisfied with respect to it) his employer shall not be treated as receiving any such payment in accordance with section 1(2) if the payment was first required to be made after the end of the period referred to in section 3(3)(*b*).

(4) Legal proceedings by the employer of a worker in retail employment for the recovery from the worker of any amount in respect of a cash shortage or stock deficiency shall not be instituted by the employer after the end of the period referred to in section 3(3)(*b*) unless the employer has within that period made a demand for payment in respect of that amount in accordance with section 3.

(5) Where in any legal proceedings the court finds that the employer of a worker in retail employment is (in accordance with section 1(2), as it applies apart from section 3(1)) entitled to recover an amount from the worker in respect of a cash shortage or stock deficiency, the court shall,

in ordering the payment by the worker to the employer of that amount, make such provision as appears to the court to be necessary to ensure that it is paid by the worker at a rate not exceeding that at which it could be recovered from him by the employer in accordance with section 3.

This subsection does not apply to any amount which is to be paid by a worker on or after the day on which his final instalment of wages is paid.

(6) References in this Part to a deduction made from any wages of a worker in retail employment, or to a payment received from such a worker by his employer, on account of a cash shortage or stock deficiency include references to a deduction or payment so made or received on account of—

(a) any dishonesty or other conduct on the part of the worker which resulted in any such shortage or deficiency, or

(b) any other event in respect of which he (whether together with any other workers or not) has any contractual liability and which so resulted,

in each case whether the amount of the deduction or payment is designed to reflect the exact amount of the shortage or deficiency or not; and references in this Part to the recovery from a worker of an amount in respect of a cash shortage or stock deficiency accordingly include references to the recovery from him of an amount in respect of any such conduct or event as is mentioned in paragraph (a) or (b).

DEFINITIONS
"cash shortage": s.2(2).
"deduction": See s.4(6), s.8(3).
"demand for payment": s.3.
"employer": s.8(1).
"final instalment": s.4(1).
"gross amount": s.8(1).
"retail employment": s.2(2).
"retail transaction": s.2(2).
"stock deficiency": s.2(2).
"wages": s.7.
"worker": s.8(1) and (2).

GENERAL NOTE
Subsections (1) to (3) of this section provide that the 10 per cent. limit in ss.2 and 3 above is not applicable to the final instalment of wages on termination of employment, although the more limited protections in s.1 continue to apply. The section applies regardless of the reason for termination, leaving it open to the employer to terminate the contract in order to recover the full amount from the final instalment or to demand payment of the full amount after the payment of the final instalment. In such circumstances, a worker may claim to have been unfairly dismissed under EPCA 1978, s.54 but only if he or she is eligible (EPCA, ss.64–65, 141–149). The dismissal is not automatically fair but it is submitted that a tribunal is likely to find that such a dismissal is unreasonable (EPCA s.57).

Subs. (1)
"consists of or includes an amount payable by way of contractual remuneration": By s.7, wages include non-contractual payments.

"termination for any reason": This applies even if an employer has not been given lawful notice. Where a contract has been unlawfully terminated without notice, the worker has a separate claim for breach of contract to the ordinary courts, or to an industrial tribunal under the statutory notice provisions in EPCA 1978, s.49. In neither case, however, would a worker be able to recover the deductions, provided they are authorised by the contract. It is arguable that "for any reason" excludes "for no reason". Thus some reason is required, even if it is not a reason which would entitle the employer to terminate the contract without notice at common law.

Subs. (2)
The requirements of s.1 must be complied with, but the 10 per cent. limit need not be. Note that s.2(3) continues to apply; so that an employer may not deduct from the final instalment in respect of a cash shortage or stock deficiency which was discovered or ought to have been discovered more than 12 months before the final instalment is paid.

Subs. (3)
In the case of payments made by the worker to the employer on or after the final instalment of wages is paid, the employer is not required to notify the worker, nor make a demand for payment as required by s.3(1), (2) or (3). Similarly, the 10 per cent. limit in s.3(4) is inapplicable. However, the employer cannot require the payment to be made outside of the 12 month time limit in s.3(3)(*b*). This corresponds to the case of deductions in subs (2) above. (Note that s.1(2) continues to apply.)

Subs. (4)
The limitation period for ordinary contractual claims is six years from the date of breach. This is qualified in this case by the requirement that an employer either institute proceedings or make a demand for payment within the period of 12 months referred to in s.3(3)(*b*).

"in respect of a cash shortage or stock deficiency": This is defined in subs. (6).

Subs. (5)
This subsection applies to cases in which a court finds that an employer is entitled to recover sums of money from a worker in respect of a cash shortage or stock deficiency. In such cases, the court should ensure that the payment does not exceed the 10 per cent. limit on any pay day. This does not apply to the final instalment, as defined in subs. (1) above.

"in respect of a cash shortage or stock deficiency": See subs. (6)

Subs. (6)
The definition of deductions or payments on account of a cash shortage or stock deficiency is drawn relatively widely, with the result that the 10 per cent. limit applies in all such cases. Where the deduction or payment does not fall within this definition, it is not subject to the 10 per cent. limit. It will, however, be subject to the provisions of s.1.

"include": The definition is not comprehensive.

"any dishonesty or other conduct": Whenever a deduction is made for a shortage or deficiency which resulted from dishonesty or other conduct, the 10 per cent. limit applies even if the deduction is not contractual. By s.1, however, such deductions would require statutory authority or written consent from the worker.

"whether the amount of the deduction or payment is designed to reflect the exact amount of the shortage or deficiency or not": The employer cannot sidestep the 10 per cent. limit by making a deduction which does not reflect the exact amount of the cash shortage or stock deficiency. (For example, a standard sum may be deducted.)

"an amount in respect of a cash shortage or stock deficiency": The definition is parallel to the definition of an amount "on account" of a cash shortage or stock deficiency. See subs. (4) and (5).

Complaints to industrial tribunals in respect of unauthorised deductions etc.

5.—(1) A worker may present a complaint to an industrial tribunal—
    (*a*) that his employer has made a deduction from his wages in contravention of section 1(1) (including a deduction made in contravention of that provision as it applies by virtue of section 2(3)), or
    (*b*) that his employer has received from him a payment in contravention of section 1(2) (including a payment received in contra-

vention of that provision as it applies by virtue of section 3(1)), or

(c) that his employer has recovered from his wages by means of one or more deductions falling within section 2(1) an amount or aggregate amount exceeding the limit applying to the deduction or deductions under that provision, or

(d) that his employer has received from him in pursuance of one or more demands for payment made (in accordance with section 3) on a particular pay day, a payment or payments of an amount or aggregate amount exceeding the limit applying to the demand or demands under section 3(4).

(2) An industrial tribunal shall not entertain a complaint under this section unless it is presented within the period of three months beginning with—

(a) in the case of a complaint relating to a deduction by the employer, the date of payment of the wages from which the deduction was made, or

(b) in the case of a complaint relating to a payment received by the employer, the date when the payment was received,

or within such further period as the tribunal considers reasonable in a case where it is satisfied that it was not reasonably practicable for the complaint to be presented within the relevant period of three months.

(3) Where a complaint is brought in respect of—

(a) a series of deductions or payments, or

(b) a number of payments falling within subsection (1)(d) and made in pursuance of demands for payment subject to the same limit under section 3(4) but received by the employer on different dates,

subsection (2) shall be read as referring to the last deduction or payment in the series or to the last of the payments so received (as the case may require).

(4) Where a tribunal finds that a complaint under this section is well-founded, it shall make a declaration to that effect; and (subject to subsections (5) and (6))—

(a) in the case of a complaint under subsection (1)(a) or (b), the tribunal shall order the employer to pay to the worker the amount of any deduction, or to repay to him the amount of any payment, made or received in contravention of section 1; and

(b) in the case of a complaint under subsection (1)(c) or (d), the tribunal shall order the employer to pay or (as the case may be) repay to the worker any amount recovered or received from him in excess of any such limit as is mentioned in that provision.

(5) Where, in the case of any complaint under subsection (1)(a) or (b), a tribunal finds that, although neither of the conditions set out in section 1(1)(a) and (b) was satisfied with respect to the whole amount of a deduction or payment, one of those conditions was satisfied with respect to any lesser amount, the amount of the deduction or payment shall for the purposes of subsection (4)(a) be treated as reduced by the amount with respect to which that condition was satisfied.

(6) An employer shall not under subsection (4)(a) or (b) be ordered by a tribunal to pay or repay to a worker any amount in respect of a deduction or payment, or (as the case may be) in respect of any combination of deductions or payments, in so far as it appears to the tribunal that he has already paid or repaid any such amount to the worker.

(7) Where a tribunal has under subsection (4)(a) or (b) ordered an employer to pay or repay to a worker any amount in respect of a particular deduction or payment falling within subsection (1)(a) to (d) ("the relevant amount") the amount which the employer shall be entitled to recover (by

whatever means) in respect of the matter in respect of which the deduction or payment was originally made or received shall be treated as reduced by the relevant amount.

(8) Where a tribunal has under subsection (4)(*b*) ordered an employer to pay or repay to a worker any amount in respect of any combination of deductions or payments falling within subsection (1)(*c*) or (*d*) ("the relevant amount") the aggregate amount which the employer shall be entitled to recover (by whatever means) in respect of the cash shortages or stock deficiencies in respect of which the deductions or payments were originally made or required to be made shall be treated as reduced by the relevant amount.

DEFINITIONS
"cash shortage": s.2(2).
"deduction": See ss.4(6), 8(3).
"employer": s.8(1).
"gross amount": s.8(1).
"stock deficiency": s.2(2).
"wages": s.7.
"worker": s.8(1) and (2).

GENERAL NOTE
This section sets out the remedies available for breach of ss.1–4. Note that in addition to the major provisions in ss.1 and 2, a worker may bring a complaint in respect of deductions or payments which contravene the 12 month limit in s.2(3) and the provisions for demands for payment under s.3(1). Unlike the Truck Acts, there is no inspectorate nor any criminal remedy (Truck Act 1896, ss.6–10), nor is the term of the contract avoided. Instead, the worker may complain to an industrial tribunal. Tribunals were regarded as preferable because of their cheapness and accessibility. The drawback is that there is no legal aid and no costs may be awarded, even if the worker is successful.

Where a complaint is well-founded, the tribunal should order the employer to pay back any unlawful deductions or payments received (subs. (4)–(6)). However, there is no provision for compensation for consequential loss, as is the case for unfair dismissal (EPCA 1978, s.74) nor any element of deterrent in the awards, comparable to the high levels of compensation in cases of dismissal for belonging to or refusing to belong to a trade union (EPCA 1978, s.58A). (If a worker is dismissed for protesting against a deduction, he or she may have a remedy under EPCA s.54 (unfair dismissal), if the eligibility criteria for that section are fulfilled.)

Note that an underpayment of a worker whose remuneration is governed by a wages council order (Part II, below) amounts to a "deduction" by virtue of s.8(3). This means that such a worker may complain to an industrial tribunal under this section as well as to the wages inspectorate. (see note to s.8(3)). This dual jurisdiction was initially unintended and leads to some difficulties. First, a tribunal is required to adjudicate on a matter which is also a criminal offence. Secondly, it involves the tribunal in applying the highly complex provisions of Part II, particularly s.17. Thirdly, if the worker complains to a tribunal under this section, the Advisory, Conciliation and Arbitration (ACAS) is automatically involved. If the worker has also complained to the Wages Inspectorate, the two organisations will have to co-ordinate their efforts. On the other hand, the industrial tribunal remedy opens up a welcome new avenue for redress for workers, decreasing the extent to which they will have to rely on a diminishing number of wages inspectors.

There are three points to be noted in respect of the dual jurisdiction. First, a complaint to the wages inspectorate remains confidential, whereas a worker who complains to an industrial tribunal is vulnerable to victimisation by the employer. Secondly, the costs of an application to a tribunal are borne by the worker. Thirdly, the worker has only three months to claim under this section, although where there is a series of underpayments, time only runs from the last of these.

Subs. (1)
"received from him a payment": In the case of payments in subs. (1)(*b*), the remedy hinges on a wrongful receipt by an employer, rather than a wrongful demand. A difficulty arises if a worker refuses to make a payment in pursuance of a demand which breaches s.3, but which is nevertheless authorised by the contract. In such a case, the employer may in theory

pursue a claim in the ordinary courts for breach of contract. If an order of court is made requiring the payment, the provisions of s.1 no longer apply. (s.1(5)(*f*)). It is submitted that a court would be unlikely to order the worker to make a payment in such circumstances.

Para. (d): "in accordance with section 3": Where s.3(1) has not been complied with, the complaint is under subs. (1)(*b*). The Minister assured the House of Lords that a complaint could be made under this subsection even if payment was made in pursuance of a demand which did not satisfy s.3. (*Hansard* H.L. Vol. 477, No. 116, col. 250).

Subs. (2)
The three month limit is the same as that in EPCA 1978, s.67 (unfair dismissal). This limit may be contrasted with the 12 months during which the employer is permitted to make a deduction or demand for payment (ss.2 and 3 above) and the six years limitation period (subject to s.4(4)) for a claim in contract.

Subs. (3)
"*a series of deductions*": It is submitted that where a wages council order applies, and the worker has been underpaid over a period of time, this amounts to a "series of deductions" for the purposes of this section. The three months runs from the last of these deductions. (See General Note above, and note to s.8(3) below.)

"*Not reasonably practicable*": These words are identical to those in EPCA 1978, s.67(2) and have been interpreted strictly in that context.

Subs. (4)
The compensation is the exact amount lost. Consequential loss to the worker as a result of having been wrongfully kept out of possession of his or her money is not recoverable. (See General Note to s.5 above).

"*any deduction*": It is submitted that where there has been a series of deductions, the tribunal may award all of these, provided the time limit in subs. (3) is complied with. Thus where a wages council order applies, and the worker has been underpaid over a period of time, it is submitted that all such underpayments may be recovered. (see note to sub. (3) and s.8(3)). (This may be contrasted with s.16(3), which gives the wages inspector the power to claim two years arrears on behalf of the worker.)

Subs. (7)
This subsection envisages a case in which the employer sues the worker for a payment which is authorised by the contract, but which does not comply with ss.1, 2 or 3 of the present Act. Such a term is not avoided by the Act, but any amount which the employer is entitled to recover is reduced by the amount awarded by the tribunal. This prevents an employer from using the civil courts to recover money which has been repaid to a worker pursuant to a tribunal finding. The problem here is that this only occurs when a tribunal has actually made such an order; not merely when the employer has contravened the statute. This leaves out of account the fact that by subs. (1) of this section, a worker can only put in a claim to a tribunal if an employer has wrongfully received a payment, not if a wrongful demand has been made. If a worker has refused to pay in response to a demand which breaches s.3, an employer may in theory be able to claim the full amount in a claim in contract. Similarly, a worker may have failed to apply to an industrial tribunal at all. However, it is submitted that a court would not allow an employer to succeed in a claim which would subvert the present Statute. (See note to subs. (1).)

Subs. (8)
See note to subs. (7) above. It is arguable, moreover, that a term which purports to entitle an employer to recover an amount which does not comply with the Act is void under s.6(3) as purporting to limit the operations of this Part.

Supplementary provisions relating to complaints

6.—(1) The remedy of a worker in respect of any contravention of section 1(1) or (2) of section 2(1) or 3(4) shall be by way of a complaint under section 5 and not otherwise.

(2) Section 5 shall not affect the jurisdiction of an industrial tribunal to entertain a reference under section 11 of the 1978 Act in relation to any deduction from the wages of a worker, but the aggregate of any amounts ordered by an industrial tribunal to be paid under section 11(8)(b) of that Act and under subsection (4) of section 5 of this Act (whether on the same or different occasions) in respect of a particular deduction shall not exceed the amount of the deduction.

(3) Any provision in an agreement shall be void in so far as it purports to exclude or limit the operation of any provision of this Part, or to preclude any person from presenting a complaint under section 5; but this subsection shall not apply to an agreement to refrain from presenting or continuing with a complaint where a conciliation officer has taken action in accordance with section 133(2) or (3) of the 1978 Act.

DEFINITIONS
   "deduction": See s.4(6).
   "wages": s.7.
   "worker": s.8(1) and (2).

Subs. (1)
   The remedy for contravention of provisions of this Part is confined to a complaint under s.5. However, it is submitted that an ordinary claim for breach of contract is unaffected. Thus a worker who claims that a deduction is not authorised by the contract may complain to an ordinary court within the six years limitation period; but a worker who claims contravention of, for example, the notification provisions or the 10 per cent. limit, may only complain to an industrial tribunal. This is particularly relevant to wages council workers, whose contractual remedy in the civil courts is unaffected.

Subs. (2)
   Section 11(8)(b) of the EPCA provides that where a tribunal finds that an employer has made deductions from an employee's pay which have not been specified in a pay statement or standing statement of deductions, the tribunal may order the employer to repay the deductions made during the 13 preceeding weeks. This subsection prevents double recovery.

Subs. (3)
   This follows the usual form in employment protection statutes (*e.g.* EPCA 1978 s.140). It is submitted that a contractual term which purports to permit the employer to recover more than permitted by this Part is void under this section.

Meaning of "wages"

7.—(1) In this Part "wages", in relation to a worker, means any sums payable to the worker by his employer in connection with his employment, including—

(a) any fee, bonus, commission, holiday pay or other emolument referable to his employment, whether payable under his contract or otherwise;

(b) any sum payable in pursuance of an order for reinstatement or re-engagement under section 69 of the 1978 Act;

(c) any sum payable by way of pay in pursuance of an order under section 77 of that Act for the continuation of a contract of employment;

(d) any of the payments referred to in paragraphs (a) to (d) of section 122(4) of that Act (guarantee payments and other statutory payments in lieu of wages);

(e) statutory sick pay under Part I of the Social Security and Housing Benefits Act 1982; and

(f) in the case of a female worker, maternity pay under Part III of the 1978 Act,

but excluding any payments falling within subsection (2).

(2) Those payments are—
- (*a*) any payment by way of an advance under an agreement for a loan or by way of an advance of wages (but without prejudice to the application of section 1(1) to any deduction made from the worker's wages in respect of any such advance);
- (*b*) any payment in respect of expenses incurred by the worker in carrying out his employment;
- (*c*) any payment by way of a pension, allowance or gratuity in connection with the worker's retirement or as compensation for loss of office;
- (*d*) any payment referable to the worker's redundancy;
- (*e*) any payment to the worker otherwise than in his capacity as a worker.

(3) Where any payment in the nature of a non-contractual bonus is (for any reason) made to a worker by his employer, then, for the purposes of this Part, the amount of the payment shall—
- (*a*) be treated as wages of the worker, and
- (*b*) be treated as payable to him as such on the day on which the payment is made.

(4) For the purposes of this Part any monetary value attaching to any payment or benefit in kind furnished to a worker by his employer shall not be treated as wages of the worker except in the case of any voucher, stamp or similar document which is—
- (*a*) of a fixed value expressed in monetary terms, and
- (*b*) capable of being exchanged (whether on its own or together with other vouchers, stamps or documents, and whether immediately or only after a time) for money, goods or services (or for any combination of two or more of those things).

DEFINITION
"worker": s.8(1) and (2).

GENERAL NOTE
The definition of wages is significant in several respects. First, deductions or payments are only permissible in accordance with s.1 and, where relevant, s.2. Deductions or payments from any sums which fall outside the definition may be made without complying with those sections (although a worker may have a civil claim if a deduction is made in breach of contract). Secondly, the 10 per cent. limit in s.2 operates as a percentage of gross wages as here defined. The inclusion of fees, bonuses, commissions, holiday pay, maternity pay, etc., (subs. (1)) means that a higher proportion may be deducted than would have been the case if the definition only included basic and overtime pay. At the same time, deductions made from payments which are not "wages" as here defined, may exceed the 10 per cent. limit.

Subs. (1)
"*including*": Thus any sums payable in connection with employment fall within the definition unless excluded by subs. (2).

"*whether payable under his contract or otherwise*": Note that non-contractual sums are only lawful under s.1 if they are authorised by statute or the worker has previously signified consent. By subs. (3) below, pay day will be the day on which payment is made.

Subs. (2)
The payments listed in this section are not subject to the controls in this Act. Thus deductions may be made from such sums without the restrictions imposed by this Act, but subject to contractual constraints. Similarly, these sums are not counted as "gross wages" when calculating the 10 per cent. limit of s.2. (See General Note above).

Para. (a): "any payment by way of an advance . . . but without prejudice to the application of s.1(1) . . ." Thus if an employer makes a loan or advance of wages to a worker, this does not count as wages; so that deductions may be made regardless of ss.1 and 2, and the loan is not part of "gross wages" for s.2. However, s.1(1) continues to apply to any deductions made from the worker's wages in order to repay the principal or interest on the loan or advance.

Para. (c): "Pensions" "We do not want to ask industrial tribunals, for example, to decide whether an obligation to pay a pension has been properly discharged." (*Hansard,* H.L. Vol. 477, No. 116, col. 248).

"Gratuity" The relationship between subs. (2) and (3) is not made clear. Subs. (3) includes in the definition of "wages" any non-contractual bonus (for any reason), whereas subs. (2) includes non-contractual payments, such as gratuities in connection with retirement or loss of office and payments referable to redundancy, which may be a non-contractual bonus (subs. (2)(*d*)). It is submitted that a non-contractual bonus which is specifically referred to in subs. (2) is excluded from the definition, notwithstanding subs. (3).

Subs. (3)
On the relationship with subs. (2) see note to subs. (2) above. This subsection prevents evasion from the Act in cases in which for example, a non-contractual bonus is payable for good work instead of making a deduction for bad work. In such cases, if all or part of the bonus is not paid, it counts as a deduction and must comply with the provisions of the statute. (See note to ss.2(4) and (5).) The date of payment for the purposes of ss.1 and 2 is the date on which the payment is made.

General interpretation of Part I

8.—(1) In this Part—
"the 1978 Act" means the Employment Protection (Consolidation) Act 1978;
"cash shortage" has the meaning given by section 2(2);
"employer", in relation to a worker, means the person by whom the worker is (or, where the employment has ceased, was) employed;
"employment", in relation to a worker, means employment under his contract and "employed", in relation to a worker, accordingly means employed under his contract;
"gross amount", in relation to any wages payable to a worker, means the total amount of those wages before deductions of whatever nature;
"pay day", "retail employment" and "retail transaction" have the meaning given by section 2(2);
"statutory provision" means a provision contained in or having effect under any enactment;
"stock deficiency" has the meaning given by section 2(2);
"wages" shall be construed in accordance with section 7;
"worker" means an individual who has entered into or works under (or, where the employment has ceased, worked under) one of the contracts referred to in subsection (2), and any reference to a worker's contract shall be construed accordingly.
(2) Those contracts are—
(*a*) a contract of service;
(*b*) a contract of apprenticeship; and
(*c*) any other contract whereby the individual undertakes to do or perform personally any work or services for another party to the contract whose status is not by virtue of the contract that a client or customer of any profession or business undertaking carried on by the individual,
in each case whether such a contract is express or implied and, if express, whether it is oral or in writing.

(3) Where the total amount of any wages that are paid on any occasion by an employer to any worker employed by him is less than the total amount of the wages that are properly payable by him to the worker on that occasion (after deductions) then, except in so far as the deficiency is attributable to an error of computation, the amount of the deficiency shall be treated for the purposes of this Part as a deduction made by the employer from the worker's wages on that occasion.

(4) In subsection (3) the reference to an error of computation is a reference to an error of any description on the part of the employer affecting the computation by him of the gross amount of the wages that are properly payable by him to the worker on that occasion.

(5) Any reference in this Part to an employer receiving a payment from a worker employed by him is a reference to his receiving such a payment in his capacity as the worker's employer.

GENERAL NOTE
Subs. (1)
"Gross amount": Thus in effect, the worker pays tax on the deductions made. In individual cases, the Inland Revenue may consider treating such deductions as expenses for tax purposes.

Subs. (2)
The inclusion of subs. (2)(c) makes the definition of "worker" in this Statute broader than that in EPCA 1978, s.153(1), being closer to the definitions in SDA 1975 (s.82(1)), RRA 1976 (s.78(1)) and TULRA 1974 (s.30).

"do or perform personally any work or services": In the context of SDA 1975 and RRA 1976, this phrase has been interrupted to exclude cases in which a worker may under the contract delegate the work to another, whether or not he or she in fact does so. *(Tanna* v. *Post Office* [1981] I.C.R. 374).

"whose status is not by virtue of the contract that of a client or customer of any profession or business undertaking carried on by the individual": This differs from other similar formulations, which do not include the references to "customer" or "business undertaking." The aim is to exclude those who are "genuinely operating a business or offering a professional service on their own account."(*Hansard* H.L. Vol. 477, No. 116, col. 263) However, the status of some workers is left in doubt. For example, homeworkers would have to show that they were not in business on their own account. (Contrast the specific inclusion of "homeworkers" for the purposes of Part II (s.26).

Subs. (3)
The aim of this section is to distinguish between deliberate deductions on the one hand, and genuine errors of computation on the other. The former are covered by this Act, whereas the latter are considered to be contractual disputes to be resolved in the High Court. (See *Hansard* H.L. Vol. 477, No. 116, col. 265). The worker is thus required to make a difficult choice of jurisdiction on the basis of available evidence as to the reason for the shortfall. Since the time limit for claims under this Act is only three months, as against six years for contractual claims, it is advisable in doubtful cases to make a claim under this Act.

One important effect of this submission is that it enables a worker whose minimum remuneration is determined by a wages council to complain to an industrial tribunal if he or she has been paid less than the statutory minimum. This is because the difference between the amount actually paid and the amount "properly payable" by virtue of the relevant wages order is a "deduction" as defined in this subsection. Such a deduction will not be lawful under s.1(1), since it is not authorised by contract or statute (see s.16)1)). (*Hansard* H.C. Vol. 97, No. 113, col. 788.) It is arguable that if a worker signifies consent in writing in a non-contractual document, the deduction is lawful under s.1(1)(b). However, it is submitted that such a document should be construed as an agreement to preclude the presentation of a complaint under s.5 and therefore void under s.6(3). (The use of "agreement" rather than "contract" in s.6(3) indicates that the technical requirements of contract need not be present.) Thus a worker who is underpaid has three possible remedies, namely, a complaint to an industrial tribunal, a claim in contract to the county court and a complaint to the wages inspectorate. (See further note to s.5) (SC 787).

"properly payable": It is arguable that this provision may be sidestepped where the contract provides that the amount of wages payable depends on how well finished a piece of work is. In such a case, a lower wage for a badly finished piece is "properly payable" for the purposes of this provision and any shortfall is outside of this section. (See, *e.g. Sagar* v. *Ridehalgh* [1931] 1 Ch. 310.) (In the case of retail workers, s.2(4) and (5) prevent a similar result. See note to s.2(4)). It may be possible to argue in some circumstances that a differential paid according to how well or badly a piece has been finished is a "non-contractual bonus" for s.7(3) and therefore counts as "wages".

Crown employment

9.—(1) Subject to subsection (4), this Part shall apply to Crown employment.

(2) In this section "Crown employment" means employment under or for the purposes of a government department or any officer or body exercising on behalf of the Crown functions conferred by any statutory provision.

(3) Without prejudice to the generality of subsection (2), "Crown employment" includes employment by any of the bodies specified in Schedule 5 to the 1978 Act (National Health Service employers).

(4) This Part does not apply to service as a member of the naval, military or air forces of the Crown, but does apply to employment by any association established for the purposes of Part VI of the Reserve Forces Act 1980.

(5) For the purposes of the application of this Part to Crown employment in accordance with subsection (1)—

(*a*) any reference to a worker shall be construed as a reference to a person in Crown employment;

(*b*) any reference to a worker's contract shall be construed as a reference to the terms of employment of a person in Crown employment;

(*c*) any reference to the termination of a worker's contract shall be construed as a reference to the termination of his Crown employment; and

(*d*) any reference to redundancy shall be construed as a reference to the existence of such circumstances as, in accordance with any arrangements for the time being in force as mentioned in section 111(3) of the 1978 Act (payments equivalent to redundancy payments in respect of civil servants etc.), are treated as equivalent to redundancy in relation to Crown employment.

GENERAL NOTE

The Statute applies to Crown employment as provided for in this section. It is broadly similar to other equivalent provisions (*e.g.* EPCA 1978 s.121), with the additional specific reference to National Health Service employees.

Power to extend provisions to employment outside United Kingdom

10.—(1) Section 137 of the 1978 Act (power to extend employment legislation to employment for purposes of activities in territorial waters etc.) shall apply in relation to this Part as it applies in relation to the enactments referred to in subsection (1) of that section, but as if—

(*a*) any reference to employment were a reference to employment within the meaning of this Part; and

(*b*) subsection (3)(*g*) of that section were omitted.

(2) Any Order in Council made by virtue of subsection (1) above may modify or exclude the operation of any provision of section 30 of this Act

(as it applies to this Part) in relation to persons to whom the Order applies.

Repeal of Truck Acts 1831 to 1940 etc.

11. The enactments listed in Schedule 1 to this Act (which impose restrictions in relation to the payment of wages to manual and other workers and make other provision in connection with the payment of wages to such persons) shall cease to have effect.

GENERAL NOTE
The most important effect of the repeal of the Truck Acts, apart from the provisions concerning deductions, relates to cashless pay. The Truck Act 1831 required manual workers to be paid in the "coin of the realm", the aim being to prevent workers being paid in "truck", *i.e.* in goods or tokens only valid in the company shop. The Payment of Wages Act 1960, however, permitted payment by cheque or into an account or by other methods if requested by the worker. The present Act repeals these provisions. The method of pay is therefore governed by the contract. It should be noted that where a worker is currently paid in cash, the method of payment may only be changed if the worker agrees to a variation of contract.

PART II

WAGES COUNCILS

GENERAL NOTE
This Part repeals the Wages Councils Act 1979 and narrowly circumscribes the powers and scope of operation of wages councils, while stopping short of outright abolition. No new wages councils may be established, and those which do exist will henceforth apply only to workers who have reached the age of 21 (s.12). Existing wages councils are limited to setting a single minimum basic rate and a single overtime rate for all the workers within their sphere of operation, as well as a limit to the amount which may be charged for accommodation (s.14). The power to create statutory joint industrial councils is also removed, but there are in any case no such councils. (W.C.A. 1979, ss.10–13). (The operation of Agricultural Wages Boards, which have similar powers to wages councils under the Agricultural Wages Act 1948 and the Agricultural Wages (Scotland) Act 1949 are unaffected by this Act.)
In 1985, there were 26 wages councils in Great Britain, covering about 2.75m workers, primarily in retailing, catering and hairdressing. About two-thirds of wages council workers were part-time, and 80 per cent. were women. Wages Councils rates tend to be low: in March 1985, most minimum full time rates for adults ranged from £63 to £72 per week. No figures are given in Government Consultative papers as to the number of workers under 21 who will be affected; however, in 1986 about five per cent. of the wages council workforce were full time employees under 18, representing about 20 per cent. of all young people in employment. (Government Consultative paper on Wages Councils, 1985, paras. 4 and 5).
Withdrawal of minimum wage protection, from workers under 21 in particular, sets Britain apart from many other countries. (Contrast France, Luxembourg and Spain, where adult minimum pay rates apply from aged 18, with a fixed percentage (ranging from 30–90 per cent.) for workers under 18; and the Netherlands and Portugal, where similar fixed percentage rates apply for "young" workers (under 23 in the Netherlands and 20 in Portugal). (European Industrial Relations Review 145, February 1986, pp.21–24)). Indeed, in order to pave the way for this legislation, the government was obliged to deratify International Labour Organisation (ILO) Convention No. 26, which required the creation or maintenance of minimum wage fixing machinery. Notice of deratification was given in June 1985 and took effect in June 1986.
Similarly, the Act removes all statutory holiday entitlement, in contrast with many European countries where workers have the right to minimum holiday periods (*e.g.* France, Denmark, Sweden, Luxembourg, Spain, Greece, Norway, West Germany, Netherlands, Portugal and Italy; SC 657).
Note the exclusions in s.30.

COMMENCEMENT:
Apart from ss.24 and 25(1) to (3), at the end of two months beginning with July 25, 1986
(see s.33(4)). Sections 24 and 25(1) to (3), on July 25, 1986.

Scope of operation of wages councils

Continued existence of wages councils after repeal of Wages Councils Act 1979

12.—(1) The Wages Councils Act 1979 shall cease to have effect, but, subject to the following provisions of this Part—

(*a*) any council in existence immediately before the commencement of this section by virtue of an order made or having effect as if made under section 1 of that Act (establishment of wages councils) shall continue in existence; and

(*b*) any order made or having effect as if made under that section or under section 4 of that Act (variation of field of operation of wages councils) and then in force in relation to that council shall continue in force;

and in this Part (except where the context requires otherwise) "wages council" means such a council as is mentioned in paragraph (*a*).

(2) Subject to the following provisions of this Part, there shall be exercisable by such a council, in relation to the workers and employers within its scope of operation by virtue of subsection (1), the functions conferred on wages council by this Part.

(3) A wages council shall not, however, exercise any functions under this Part in relation to workers under the age of 21.

(4) Schedule 2 shall have effect with respect to the constitution, proceedings and officers of a wages council.

DEFINITIONS
"employer": s.26(1).
"organisation": s.26(1).
"wages council": s.12(1)(*a*).
"worker": s.26(1).

GENERAL NOTE
Subs. (1) and (2)
These subsections repeal the Wages Councils Act 1979, but retain existing wages councils (subs. (1)), with the more limited powers applying under this Act (subs. (2)).

Subs. (3)
Workers under the age of 21 are excluded from the sphere of operation of wages councils, the rationale being that minimum wages tend to price young workers out of jobs. The evidence concerning the employment effect of excluding young workers from wages councils is, however, unclear and conflicting. (*e.g.* SC 494, 550, 567, *Hansard,* H.L. Vol. 477, No. 117, col. 445; H.L. Vol. 478, No. 125, cols. 236–237). This subsection comes into effect immediately on the coming into force of the Act (s.24(5), s.33).

Subs. (4)
The constitution and procedure, set out in Sched. 2, are substantially similar to the provisions under the 1979 Act. There are three notable changes. First, para. 2(2) states that unless inappropriate, the employers' association nominated to appoint the employers' representatives on a wages council should be representative of small businesses within the scope of operation of the wages council. Secondly, members of wages councils may only hold office for a maximum of three years instead of five as previously provided (para. 8(1)), and thirdly there is to be a maximum of five independent members rather than three (para. 1(*b*); *Hansard* H.L. Vol. 477, No. 117, col. 451).

Abolition, or variation of scope of operation, of wages councils

13.—(1) The Secretary of State may at any time by order abolish, or vary the scope of operation of, any wages council.

(2) Before making an order under this section the Secretary of State shall have regard to—

(*a*) the current levels of remuneration among any workers in relation to whom the wages council concerned would cease to operate, or (as the case may be) begin to operate, as a result of the order, and

(*b*) such other matters as appear to him to be appropriate,

and shall consult such persons or organisations as appear to him to be appropriate.

(3) An order under this section may vary the scope of operation of a wages council by reference to any matters or circumstances whatever, and in particular may do so by excluding from its scope of operation employers who are either—

(*a*) specified in the order, or

(*b*) members of an organisation so specified, or

(*c*) represented on an organisation so specified.

(4) Where an order of the Secretary of State under this section abolishes, or varies the scope of operation of, one wages council and directs that any workers previously within the scope of operation of that council shall be brought within the scope of operation of another, the order may—

(*a*) provide that anything done by, or to give effect to proposals made by, the first of those councils shall have effect in relation to those workers as if it had been done by, or to give effect to proposals made by, the second of those councils; and

(*b*) make such further provisions as appear to the Secretary of State to be expedient in connection with the order, including provision for renaming any council to which the order relates.

(5) Where an order of the Secretary of State under this section abolishes a wages council or directs that a wages council shall cease to operate in relation to any workers, then, except as is otherwise provided by the order, anything done by, or to give effect to proposals made by, that wages council shall cease to have effect or (as the case may be) cease to have effect in relation to the workers in relation to whom the council ceases to operate.

(6) Nothing in subsection (5) shall be construed as affecting any rights or liabilities which have accrued to any person in consequence of anything done or omitted to be done before the coming into operation of the order.

DEFINITIONS
"employer": s.26(1).
"organisation": s.26(1).
"wages council": s.12(1)(*a*).
"worker": s.26(1).

GENERAL NOTE
This section gives the Secretary of State the power to abolish or vary the scope of operation of any wages council. Subss. (4)–(6) make provision in respect of workers transferred from one wages council to another. Any order made under this power is exercisable by statutory instrument and is subject to annulment by either House (s.25(2) and (3). In addition, where the Secretary of State proposes to abolish a wages council, without directing that all or any of the workers within its scope of operation are brought under the aegis of another wages council, a draft order must first be laid before and approved by both Houses (s.25(4)–(6)).

Subs. (1)
The Secretary of State no longer has the power to establish new wages councils. This makes it impossible to establish wages councils in low paid areas not presently covered or to break up large wages councils, such as the Retail Food and Allied Trade Wages Council, which covered 519,300 workers in 1982, and establish new wages councils covering more easily manageable areas (*Hansard* H.L. Vol. 477, No. 117, col. 449). The Secretary of State

does, however, have power to vary the scope of operation of existing wages councils to include workers not previously covered.

Subs. (2)

The Secretary of State is given a wide discretion in the exercise of the power to abolish or vary the scope of operation of wages councils. There is no requirement to consult either the Advisory, Conciliation and Arbitration Service (ACAS) or representatives of workers or employers involved; instead, there is an open-ended discretion to consult as he or she considers apppropriate. By subs. (2)(*a*) current levels of remuneration must be considered; but there is no requirement that the standards of remuneration be reasonable (compare WCA 1979 s.5(2)) nor that collective bargaining machinery be adequate.

"begin to operate"; The Secretary of State has power to include workers not previously included, or to transfer workers from another wages council.

Subs. (3)

This section differs from WCA 1979 in that under that Act the power to exclude employers from the scope of wages councils depended on their being members of an employers' association which was a party to a collective agreement regulating remuneration or the terms or conditions of employment of their employees (WCA 1979, s.4(3)). The Secretary of State may now exclude employers "by reference to any matters or circumstances whatever."

Subs. (4)

This subsection is substantially similar to WCA 1979 s.4(6), with the extra power to change the name of a wages council.

Subs. (5)

This subsection is identical to WCA 1979 s.4(7).

Subs. (6)

Orders under this section do not retrospectively affect rights or liabilities accrued before the coming into operation of the order.

Wages orders

Wages orders

14.—(1) A wages council may make an order—
    (*a*) fixing a single minimum hourly rate of remuneration in respect of all the time worked by a worker in any week;
    (*b*) fixing—
        (i) a single minimum hourly rate of remuneration in respect of time worked by a worker in any week up to a total amount not exceeding such number of hours as may be fixed by the order ("the basic hours"), and
        (ii) a single minimum hourly overtime rate of remuneration in respect of time worked by a worker in any week in excess of the basic hours;
    (*c*) fixing, for the purposes of section 17(2)(*b*) and (3)(*b*), a limit applying to amounts which are deducted from a worker's remuneration by his employer, or paid by a worker to his employer, in respect of the provision of living accommodation for him by his employer, being a limit framed by reference to the amount recovered by the employer by means of any such deductions or payments in respect of any period of 24 hours for the whole or part of which any such accommodation is so provided.
(2) Any such order may—
    (*a*) make different provision under subsection (1) in relation to periods of time beginning with different dates;
    (*b*) provide for any matter fixed by the order in pursuance of that

subsection to have effect only as from a date later than that on which the order comes into force;

but no such order shall provide for a limit fixed in pursuance of paragraph (*c*) of that subsection to have effect at a time when no rate or rates fixed in pursuance of paragraph (*a*) or (*b*) of that subsection will have effect under the order.

(3) Any order made by a wages council under this section shall apply—

(*a*) to all time workers in relation to whom the council operates, and

(*b*) in accordance with the provisions of this Part relating to the remuneration of piece workers, to all piece workers in relation to whom the council operates;

and shall so apply whether any such workers work on a full-time or part-time basis.

(4) References in this Part to the statutory minimum remuneration provided for a worker by an order under this section shall, in the case of a time worker to whom such an order applies, be construed as references to the remuneration due under the order in respect of any time worked by him in a week, as determined by the application, in relation to any time so worked—

(*a*) of the rate for the time being fixed by the order in pursuance of subsection (1)(*a*) or (*b*)(i); or

(*b*) where a rate is so fixed in pursuance of subsection (1)(*b*)(i) and the time so worked exceeds the basic hours, of a combination of that rate (as respects the basic hours) and the rate for the time being fixed by the order in pursuance of subsection (1)(*b*)(ii) (as respects any time worked in excess of those hours).

(5) In this Part any reference, in relation to a time worker, to time worked by that worker shall be construed as including a reference to time during which he is required (whether in accordance with his contract or otherwise) to be available for work and is so available at his place of work.

(6) Before making an order under this section fixing any such rate as is mentioned in paragraph (*a*) or (*b*)(i) or (ii) of subsection (1) a wages council shall have regard to—

(*a*) the effect that that rate will have on the level of employment among the workers to whom it will apply, and in particular in those areas where the remuneration received by such workers is generally less than the national average for such workers; and

(*b*) such other matters as appear to it to be appropriate.

(7) An order under this section may amend or revoke a previous order under this section, and any such order may, in particular, amend any rate or limit fixed in pursuance of subsection (1)(*b*)(ii) or (*c*) without also amending the rate for the time being fixed in pursuance of subsection (1)(*a*) or (*b*)(i), as the case may be.

(8) An order under this section shall not prejudice any rights conferred on any worker by or under any other enactment.

(9) Schedule 3 (supplementary provisions relating to wages orders) shall have effect.

DEFINITIONS
  "employer": s.26(1).
  "organisation": s.26(1).
  "piece-worker": s.26(1).
  "statutory minimum remuneration": 26(4).
  "time worker": s.26(1).
  "wages council": s.12(1)(*a*).
  "week": s.26(1).
  "worker": s.26(1).

GENERAL NOTE

This section confines the powers of wages councils to the setting of either a single minimum rate (subs. (1)(*a*)) or a single minimum basic rate of remuneration and a single minimum overtime rate (subs. (1)(*b*)) for all workers within their sphere of operation, as well as a limit to the amount which may be demanded for accommodation (subs. (1)(*c*)). By contrast, under the 1979 Act, wages councils had power to fix remuneration, holidays and any other terms and conditions of employment for all or any of the workers within their scope. (WCA 1979, s.14(1)). The effect of this section is that wages councils no longer have the power to fix mimimum holiday entitlement, nor to set separate rates for different occupations (such as those presently set by some wages councils, such as the Retail Food and Allied Trades Wages Council and the Boot and Shoe Repairing Wages Council). (*Hansard* H.L. Vol. 477, No. 117, col. 456). Similarly, wages councils may no longer set premium rates for anti-social working time (such as Sundays or public holidays) or difficult shift work.

For computation of remuneration, see s.17.

Existing wages councils orders remain in effect as provided for by s.24(2), although workers under 21 are excluded with immediate effect (s.24(5)). For commencement, see s.33. For provisions in respect of accrued rights see Sched. 6, paras. 5 and 6.

Subs. (1)

Para. (c): Where accommodation is provided, the employer is entitled to deduct only the amount specified in the wages council order. The minimum rate fixed by virtue of subs. (1)(*a*) and (*b*) may be reduced by this amount. The statute is, however, infringed if more than this is deducted, and as a result the worker's pay falls below the minimum rate. (See s.17(2)(*b*) and (3)(*b*)).

Subs. (2)

This subsection allows wages councils to stagger their awards, with different provisions coming into effect at different dates.

Subs. (3)

Wages council orders cover both workers who are paid by time and those who are paid on a piecework basis, whether full-time or part-time (for definition see s.26). By s.26(1), this includes homeworkers. (Note the qualification in s.26(3).)

Subs. (4)

The "statutory mimimum remuneration" is calculated, for time workers, on a weekly basis, by multiplying the number of basic hours worked by the basic hourly rate, plus, where appropriate, the number of overtime hours worked multiplied by the overtime rate. To determine whether the worker has in fact been paid the statutory minimum, see s.17.

Subs. (5)

Time worked by a worker includes not only time during which work was actually done, but also time during which a worker is required to be available for work at the place of work.

Subs. (6)

This section introduces guidelines for wages councils in making their decisions. The Government was particularly concerned throughout this Act with the ostensible negative effects of minimum wages on employment levels; hence the wages council is required to have regard to the effect on the level of employment. Particular regard must be had to the effect on the level of employment in areas where workers are generally paid less than the national average for such workers. The statute does not, however, specify how much weight should be attached to these factors, nor whether they should point to an increase or decrease in the rate set. In any case, under subs. (6)(*b*), wages councils may have regard to any other appropriate matters too.

Subs. (9)

Sched. 3 follows along similar lines to the procedure under the WCA 1979 (see, *e.g.* WCA 1979, s.14(4) and (5)), but modifies it in some respects, particularly in connection with the extent of consultation with interested parties.

Application of wages orders to piece workers

15.—(1) Subject to subsection (4), references in this Part to the statutory minimum remuneration provided for a worker by an order under section 14 shall, in the case of a piece worker to whom such an order applies, be construed as references to remuneration, in respect of work executed by him, at such one or more piece rates as are appropriate to secure the result mentioned in subsection (2).

(2) That result is that an ordinary worker executing the work in question would be able to earn, in any given time worked by him in any week, not less than the amount of remuneration due under the order in respect of the time so worked, as determined by the application, in relation to that time, of any such rate or combination of rates as is mentioned in section 14(4)(*a*) or (*b*).

(3) In subsection (2) the reference to an ordinary worker in relation to any work is a reference to a worker of ordinary competence to execute the work who has no disability affecting the speed at which he is able to execute it.

(4) In relation to any time during which—

> (*a*) a piece worker (other than a homeworker) is required, whether in accordance with his contract or otherwise, to be available for work and is so available at his place of work, but
>
> (*b*) no work is available to be executed by the worker,

references in this Part to the statutory minimum remuneration provided for him by an order under section 14 shall be construed as references to remuneration in respect of any such time at the rate for the time being fixed by the order in pursuance of section 14(1)(*a*) or (*b*)(i).

(5) In the application of subsection (4) to a piece worker whose remuneration is calculated by reference to items of work executed by a number of workers of whom he is one ("the group"), the reference to the worker in paragraph (*b*) shall be construed as a reference to the group.

DEFINITIONS
"homeworker": s.26(1).
"piece rate": s.26(1).
"piece worker": s.26(1).
"statutory minimum remuneration": s.26(4).
"time worker": s.26(1).
"wages council": s.12(1)(*a*).
"week": s.26(1).
"worker": s.26(1) and (2).

GENERAL NOTE
This section adapts the formula for statutory minimum remuneration to cases in which a worker is not paid according to hours worked, but solely by reference to the number of items produced ("piecework"). (Note that the definition of "piece rate" in s.26(1) includes cases in which pay is calculated by reference to work done by a group.) The rate per piece must be fixed at a level so that for a given number of hours worked in a week, an ordinary worker would earn the same as a time worker working the same number of hours. The ordinary worker, according to subs. (3), is a worker of ordinary competence who has no disability affecting the speed of work. The use of the concept of an "ordinary worker" means that slow or less competent workers may earn less than the statutory minimum. Subs. (4) deals with remuneration for the time during which a worker is required to be available at the place of work, but no work is available. In such a case, the worker should be paid by the hour according to the basic time rate set by the wages council. No parallel protections exist for workers who hold themselves available at home for work which in the event is not forthcoming. Subs. (5) adapts subs. (4) to cases in which remuneration is calculated by reference to items of work executed by a group.

The Act only deals with time working and piece work. Other more complex payment systems are taken into account to some extent in s.17.

Effect and enforcement of wages orders

16.—(1) If, in the case of any worker to whom an order under section 14 applies, the amount of remuneration paid to the worker by his employer in respect of any week is less than the statutory minimum remuneration provided for him by the order in respect of that week, the worker shall be taken to be entitled under his contract to be paid the difference between those two amounts as additional remuneration in respect of that week.

(2) Any employer who, in respect of any week, fails to pay any worker to whom an order under section 14 applies an amount of remuneration equal to, or exceeding, the statutory minimum remuneration provided for him by the order shall be guilty of an offence and liable on summary conviction to a fine not exceeding the third level on the standard scale.

(3) Where proceedings are brought in respect of any offence under subsection (2) and the employer, or any other person charged as a person to whose act or default the offence was due, is found guilty of the offence, the court may (subject to subsection (5)) order the employer to pay to the worker the appropriate sum in respect of the week in relation to which the offence was committed, and (subject to subsections (5) and (6))—

(a) evidence may be given of any other failure on the part of the employer such as is mentioned in subsection (3) which occurred, in relation to any week falling within the period of two years ending with the date of the offence, in the case of the worker in relation to whom the offence was committed or in the case of any other worker employed by the employer; and

(b) on proof of any such failure the court may order the employer to pay to the worker or (as the case may be) to each of the workers in question the appropriate sum in respect of the week in relation to which the failure occurred.

(4) In subsection (3) "the appropriate sum", in relation to any worker, means such sum as is found by the court to represent the difference between the following amounts, namely—

(a) the statutory minimum remuneration provided for the worker in respect of the week in question by the relevant order under section 14; and

(b) the amount of remuneration paid to the worker in respect of that week.

(5) A court shall not make an order in the case of any time worker under subsection (3) in respect of any such offence or failure as is mentioned in that subsection if—

(a) the offence was committed or the failure occurred in relation to a week forming part of a cycle of weeks (not exceeding four) during which the time worked by that worker in a week was different in different weeks; and

(b) the total remuneration paid to that worker in respect of the total time worked by him during the cycle was not less than the aggregate of the statutory minimum remuneration provided for him by the relevant order under section 14 in respect of the time worked in the constituent weeks of the cycle.

(6) Evidence of any such failure as is mentioned in subsection (3) may be given under that subsection only if notice of intention to adduce such evidence has been served with the summons or warrant.

(7) The powers given by this section for the recovery of sums due from an employer to a worker shall not be in derogation of any right to recover such sums by civil proceedings.

(8) Any reference in this section, in relation to a worker, to remuneration or statutory minimum remuneration in respect of a week shall be

construed as a reference to remuneration or statutory minimum remuneration in respect of the following, namely—
  (a) in the case of a time worker, time worked by the worker in that week; and
  (b) in the case of a piece worker—
      (i) work executed by the worker in that week, and
      (ii) any such time as is mentioned in section 15(4) occurring during that week.
(9) In the application of this section to Scotland—
  (a) in subsection (3), the words ", or any other person charged as a person to whose act or default the offence was due," shall be omitted; and
  (b) in subsection (6), for "summons or warrant" there shall be substituted "complaint".

DEFINITIONS
  "employer": s.26(1).
  "piece rate": s.26(1).
  "piece worker": s.26(1).
  "statutory minimum remuneration": s.26(4).
  "time worker": s.26(1).
  "week": s.26(1).
  "worker": s.26(1) and (2).

GENERAL NOTE
There are three methods of enforcing wages council orders, namely, by criminal proceedings (subs. (2) and (3)), by civil proceedings for breach of contract (subs. (1)), and by a claim to an industrial tribunal by virtue of ss.5 and 8(3) above. The right to complain to an industrial tribunal, which was an unintended consequence of the definition of "deduction" in s.8(3) (see note to s.8(3)), did not exist under WCA 1979. (Compare WCA 1979, s.15.) (For the advantages and disadvantages of the different claims, see note to s.5.)

Subs. (1)
Wages councils orders operate on the worker's contract of employment. Where the employer pays less than the statutory minimum under the relevant wages council order, the worker is taken to be contractually entitled to the shortfall as additional remuneration. The worker may thus enforce the contract at civil law (*cf.* WCA 1979, s.15(1)).
See subs. (8) for the meaning of remuneration in respect of a week.
"the amount of remuneration paid to the worker by his employer": For computation, see s.17 below.

Subs. (2)
The employer who pays less than the minimum commits an offence and is liable on summary conviction to a fine (*c.f.* WCA 1979, s.15(3)). In fact, the policy of the inspectorate is to avoid prosecutions if possible. Thus only two prosecutions reached the courts in 1984, leading to average fines of £107. In the same year, however, of almost 417,000 workers whose wages were checked, over 18,000 (4·3 per cent.) were underpaid. A total of £1·87m in arrears were paid.
It is noteworthy that the Act does not protect a worker who is victimised or dismissed for informing the inspectorate of alleged underpayment. Such a worker may be able to claim compensation for unfair dismissal, under EPCA, s.54, but only if he or she fulfils the eligibility requirements in respect of that section (EPCA, ss.64–65, 141–147).

Subs. (3)
Where the employer is found guilty under subs. (3), and proof is adduced of underpayments in the preceding two years, the court has power to award the worker arrears of pay in respect of any week during which the worker has been underpaid (*cf.* WCA 1979, s.15(4)). (Compare awards under s.5.) Note that by subs. (6), notice of intention to adduce such evidence must be served with the summons or warrant.

Computation of remuneration

17.—(1) For the purpose of determining, for the purposes of this Part, the amount of remuneration paid to a time worker by his employer in respect of time worked by the worker in any week there shall be added together—

(a) the total amount of any money payments made by the employer to the worker, on or before the relevant pay day, by way of remuneration in respect of time worked by him in that week, and

(b) the total amount of any deductions made by the employer (whether in accordance with Part I or not) when making the payment of wages which consisted of or included those money payments, apart from deductions falling to be left out of account under this paragraph by virtue of subsection (2),

and then, from the aggregate of those amounts, there shall be subtracted the aggregate of—

(i) the worker's necessary expenditure in connection with his employment to the extent that such expenditure consists of payments to persons other than the employer, is attributable to that week and is not met, or designed to be met, by an allowance paid to him by the employer, and

(ii) the total amount of any payments received from the worker by the employer (whether in accordance with Part I or not) and falling to be taken into account under this paragraph by virtue of subsection (3).

(2) The following deductions shall be left out of account under subsection (1)(b), namely—

(a) any deduction in respect of the worker's necessary expenditure in connection with his employment to the extent that the deduction is attributable to the week in question;

(b) any deduction in respect of the provision of living accommodation for the worker by the employer to the extent that the deduction exceeds any limit for the time being in force in relation to the worker by virtue of section 14(1)(c), and

(c) subject to subsection (4), any other deduction made by the employer for his own use and benefit (and accordingly not attributable to any amount paid or payable by him to any other person, or to any authority, on behalf of the worker).

(3) The following payments by the worker shall be taken into account under subsection (1)(ii), namely—

(a) any payment in respect of the worker's necessary expenditure in connection with his employment to the extent that the payment is attributable to the week in question;

(b) any payment due from the worker in that week in respect of the provision of living accommodation for him by the employer to the extent that the payment exceeds any limit for the time being in force in relation to the worker by virtue of section 14(1)(c), and

(c) subject to subsection (4), any other payment due from the worker in that week and retained by the employer for his own use and benefit (and accordingly not attributable to any amount paid or payable by him to any other person, or to any authority, on behalf of the worker).

(4) Subsections (2)(c) and (3)(c) do not apply—

(a) to deductions made or payments received by the employer on account of any of the following matters, namely—

(i) any conduct of the worker or any other event in respect of which he (whether together with any other workers or not) has any contractual liability,

(ii) any advance under an agreement for a loan or any advance of wages, or

(iii) the purchase by the worker of any shares or other securities or of any share in a partnership; or

(b) to deductions made or payments received by the employer on account of any goods or services supplied by the employer with the worker's prior agreement or consent to the extent that any such deductions or payments do not result in the employer recovering from the worker an amount exceeding the cost to the employer of supplying the goods or services in question;

and accordingly any such deductions shall not be left out of account under subsection (1)(b) and any such payments shall not be taken into account under subsection (1)(ii).

(5) For the purposes of subsection (4)(b) the cost to an employer of supplying any goods or services shall—

(a) where he supplies goods or services of the kind in question in the course of his business, be taken to be the amount which he would have obtained for the goods or services if they had been supplied in the course of that business; and

(b) in any other case, be taken to be the amount of expenditure incurred by the employer in connection with the supply by him of the goods or services.

(6) The preceding provisions of this section shall apply to a piece worker as they apply to a time worker but as if, in subsection (1), any reference to remuneration in respect of time worked by the worker in any week were a reference to remuneration in respect of—

(a) work executed by him in any week, and

(b) any such time as is mentioned in section 15(4) that occurs during the week.

(7) In this section—

"deduction" does not include any such deficiency in the payment of wages as is mentioned in section 8(3);

"money payment" means—

(a) a payment in cash,

(b) a payment by cheque or by a money or postal order issued by the Post Office, or

(c) a payment (however effected) into any account kept with a bank or other institution;

"relevant pay day", in relation to any week of a worker's employment, means the day on which his remuneration in respect of that week is payable;

"wages", has the same meaning as in Part I.

DEFINITIONS

"deduction": s.17(7).
"employer": s.26(1).
"money payment": s.17(7).
"piece rate": s.26(1).
"piece worker": s.26(1).
"relevant pay day": s.17(7).
"statutory minimum remuneration": s.26(4).
"time worker": s.26(1).
"wages": s.17(7).
"wages council": s.12(1)(a).
"week": s.26(1).
"worker": s.26(1) and (2).

GENERAL NOTE

The purpose of this section is to set out a formula to determine whether a worker has been paid the statutory minimum remuneration. This complex computation is best understood by considering two categories: those sums of money which may be taken into account for the purposes of determining whether a worker has been paid the statutory minimum, and those sums which may not be taken into account. The starting point is the amount actually received by the worker (the "take-home pay"). The next step is to consider deductions made at source. If sums deducted are to be taken into account, they are added on to take-home pay, thus increasing the available total. For example, any sums deducted for tax and national insurance are added on to the take-home pay. If sums deducted are not to be taken into account, they are ignored, and the take-home pay must be correspondingly higher to reach the minimum. The converse is true for payments made by the worker out of take-home pay. Where a worker makes a payment which is taken into account, it is ignored. For example, if a worker pays the employer rent for accommodation which is within the limit prescribed in the order, the statutory minimum is calculated before the payment is made. On the other hand, if a payment is not taken into account, it is deducted from take-home pay, and the latter must be correspondingly higher to reach the minimum. For example, any sums paid by the worker for accommodation in excess of the prescribed minimum are deducted from take-home pay. (The formula is adapted for pieceworkers in subs. (6).) (Compare WCA 1979, s.17.)

I. The following sums are not taken into account for the purposes of determining whether a worker has been paid the statutory minimum:

(1) The worker's necessary expenditure in connection with his or her employment as far as it is attributable to the week in question. Subs. (1)(i) refers to such expenditure paid to persons other than the employer, to the extent that this is not met or designed to be met by an allowance paid by the employer; subs. (3)(*a*) concerns such expenditure paid to the employer. In both these cases, the sums expended are subtracted from take-home pay. Subs. (2)(*a*) referes to deductions made in respect of necessary expenditure; such sums are ignored.

(2) Sums demanded for accommodation in excess of the limit set by the wages council. Where this takes the form of a deduction, the excess amount is ignored (subs. (2)(*b*)); where the worker is required to pay the employer from take-home pay, the excess is subtracted from that pay (subs. (3)(*b*) and subs. (1)(ii)).

(3) Sums demanded by the employer for the latter's own use or benefit, except those listed in II (numbers (3) to (6)) below. Again, if this takes the form of a deduction, it is ignored (subs. (2)(*c*)), and if it is a payment, it is subtracted from take-home pay (subs. (3)(*c*) and (1)(ii)).

(4) Any difference between payment actually made and payment properly payable is ignored unless it is due to an error of computation (subs. (7) and s.8(3)). (See note to subs. (7) below.)

II. The following sums may be accounted for in determining the remuneration received by the worker:

(1) The total amount of money payments actually made by the employer to the worker on or before the relevant pay day in respect of time worked in that week (subs. (1)(*a*)).

(2) All deductions made at source, whether lawful under Part I or not, except those specified in Group I above. For example, sums deducted for tax and national insurance are added back to take-home pay in order to decide if the total has reached the minimum (subs. (1)(*b*)).

(3) Deductions made or payments received on account of any conduct of the worker or any other event in respect of which he or she has any contractual liability (subs. (4)(*a*)(i)).

(4) Deductions made or payments received on account of a loan or advance on wages made by the employer to the worker. (subs. (4)(*a*)(ii)).

(5) Deductions made or payments received on account of the purchase of shares, etc., (subs. (4)(*a*)(iii)).

(6) Deductions made or payments received on account of goods or services supplied to the worker by the employer with the worker's prior agreement or consent, provided they do not exceed the cost to the employer as defined in subs. (5). (subs. (4)(*b*)) (See note to subs. (4)(*b*)).

Note: The sums mentioned in Group II nos. (3) to (6) above are accounted for despite the fact that they may be for the employer's own use or benefits; thus they override the sums in Group I no. (3).

Subs. (1)(a)
"in any week": The calculation relates specifically to the amount paid for time worked in any week (or for a piece worker, for work done in a week), and to deductions or payments

which are attributable to or have been made in the same week. (*Hansard* H.C. Vol. 102, No. 157, col. 498).

"Whether in accordance with Part I or not": All deductions not specifically excluded are added back on to take-home pay even if they fail to comply with Part I. The aim is to ensure that the remedy for an unlawful deduction is solely by way of a complaint to an industrial tribunal. The worker cannot rely on the wages inspectorate or the criminal courts to recover wrongful deductions. Subs. (7) (definition of "deduction") does, however, provide a necessary exception to this. Where the employer has deliberately paid the worker less than the statutory minimum, the shortfall is not a "deduction" for the purposes of this section (despite being so for s.8(3)), and the lawfulness is clearly an issue for the wages inspectorate.

Subs. (4)(a)
"contractual liability": Note that it is not necessary for such deductions to fulfil the provisions of Part I (See note to subs. (1) above).

Subs. (4)(c)
"any goods or services supplied by the employer with the worker's prior agreement or consent": The aim of this requirement is to prevent the employer from sidestepping the minimum pay limit by supplying goods or services in lieu of pay against the worker's will. Note that if the employer recovers from the worker more than the "cost" to the employer of supplying such goods or service, the excess is not taken into account (subs. (4)(*b*)). For the formula for calculating the cost to the employer, see subs. (5).

Subs. (7)
"deduction": By s.8(3), a deliberate underpayment is included in the definition of "deduction" for the purposes of Part I. This allows a worker to make a claim to an industrial tribunal under Part I where a deliberate underpayment has been made. However, the object of s.17 is to prevent deliberate underpayments. Hence, notwithstanding subs. (1)(*b*), such sums are not taken into account in determining whether a worker has been paid the statutory minimum, and a deliberate underpayment will contravene this Part.

"wages": For the definition of wages in Part I, see s.7. Note that the present section generally refers to "remuneration," "money payments" and "payments" rather than "wages."

Apportionment of remuneration

18.—(1) This section applies where—
    (*a*) in respect of part of the time worked by a time worker in any week ("the relevant period") the worker is entitled to the statutory minimum remuneration provided for him by an order under section 14, and
    (*b*) in respect of the remainder of the time worked by him in the week ("the remaining period") the worker is not entitled to any such remuneration or is entitled to any such remuneration by virtue of another such order;
and in this section any reference to the worker's computed remuneration is a reference to the amount of the remuneration paid to the worker in respect of the time worked by him in the week in question as determined in accordance with section 17.

(2) Subject to subsections (3) to (5), the amount of the worker's computed remuneration that is to be attributed to either the relevant period or the remaining period for the purposes of this Part shall, if not apparent from the terms of the worker's contract, be the amount which bears to the total amount of the worker's computed remuneration the same proportion as the relevant period, or (as the case may be) the remaining period, bears to the total time worked by the worker in the week in question.

(3) Where any particular amount falling to be added or subtracted under section 17(1), as it applies to any week, is exclusively referable to the relevant period, the amount of the worker's computed remuneration

to be attributed to that period for the purposes of this Part shall be determined by either—

(a) adding the unattributed balance of that particular amount to the amount to be attributed to that period in accordance with subsection (2) above, or

(b) subtracting the unattributed balance of that particular amount from the amount to be attributed to that period in accordance with that subsection,

according to whether that particular amount falls to be added or subtracted under section 17(1); and a corresponding adjustment shall be made in the amount of the worker's computed remuneration to be attributed for the purposes of this Part to the remaining period.

(4) In subsection (3) "the unattributed balance", in relation to the particular amount in question, means so much of that amount as is not taken into account for the purpose of determining the amount to be attributed to the relevant period in accordance with subsection (2).

(5) Where any particular amount falling to be added or subtracted under section 17(1), as it applies to any week, is exclusively referable to the remaining period, subsections (3) and (4) shall apply to any such particular amount as if—

(a) any reference to the relevant period were a reference to the remaining period; and

(b) the reference in subsection (3) to the remaining period were a reference to the relevant period.

(6) The preceding provisions of this section shall apply to a piece worker as they apply to a time worker but as if—

(a) any reference to time worked by the worker in any week were a reference to work executed by him in any week; and

(b) the word "work" were substituted for the word "period" wherever occurring;

and for the purposes of those provisions as they apply to a piece worker in accordance with this subsection the worker shall be treated as executing work during any such time as is mentioned in section 15(4).

DEFINITIONS
"piece rate": s.26(1).
"piece worker": s.26(1).
"statutory minimum remuneration": s.26(4).
"time worker": s.26(1).
"wages council": s.12(1)(a).
"week": s.26(1).
"worker": s.26(1) and (2).

GENERAL NOTE
Despite rationalisation of wages councils in recent years, the boundaries of existing wages councils remain complex and at times arbitrary. As a result, it is quite possible for a worker to spend part of his or her time in a job which is covered by a wages council and the remainder in a job which is not. For example, a worker may work for an employer who runs a retail food shop and a florist next door. Only the former is covered by a wages council. (*Hansard* H.L. Vol. 478, No. 125, col. 261). Similarly, a worker may be employed in work which lies within the scope of more than one wages council. This section sets out the formula for apportioning remuneration between time spent on a wages council job (the "relevant period") and the rest of the time ("the remaining period"). The basic formula is that, unless the contract states otherwise, remuneration (as calculated by s.17 above) should be apportioned in the same ratio as the time spent in each type of work (subs. (2)). The complexity arises in respect of deductions or payments which are relevant to the statutory minimum (by s.17 above) but are attributable exclusively to one or other part of the work. The aim of subs. (3)–(5) is to ensure that the whole amount of such a deduction or payment is attributable to the period to which it refers, rather than apportioned according to the ratio of time spent in either. This is achieved by first apportioning the whole amount, and then

transferring the fraction which has been wrongly attributed ("the unattributed balance") to the correct period. Subs. (6) adapts the formula for piece-workers. (Compare WCA 1979, s.18).

Enforcement

Obligation to keep records etc.

19.—(1) The employer of any workers to whom an order under section 14 applies shall keep such records as are necessary to show—

(*a*) whether or not the provisions of this Part are being complied with in relation to the payment of remuneration to those workers, and

(*b*) the amount of any deductions or payments made in the case of those workers in respect of the provision of living accommodation by the employer;

and the records shall be retained by the employer for a period of 3 years beginning with the date of the payments or deductions in question.

(2) The employer of any such workers shall post in the prescribed manner such notices as may be prescribed for the purpose of informing the workers—

(*a*) of any order under section 14, or proposal under paragraph 1 of Schedule 3, that affects them; or

(*b*) of such other matters (if any) as may be prescribed.

(3) Where any such workers are homeworkers, the employer shall notify them in the prescribed manner of the matters mentioned in subsection (2).

(4) An employer who fails to comply with any of the requirements of this section shall be guilty of an offence and liable on summary conviction to a fine not exceeding the third level on the standard scale.

DEFINITIONS
"employer": s.26(1).
"homeworker": s.26(1).
"worker": s.26(1) and (2).

GENERAL NOTE
This section is similar to provisions under WCA 1979, s.20. As in that Act, employers are only required to keep records for three years, a period which may, it is submitted, frequently be inadequate. The duty to inform homeworkers is a welcome new addition (subs. (3)). Prosecutions under this section are rare.

Officers

20.—(1) The Secretary of State, with the approval of the Treasury as to numbers and salaries, may appoint officers to act for the purposes of this Part, and may, instead of or in addition to appointing any officers under this section, arrange with any government department that officers of that department shall act for those purposes.

(2) When acting for the purposes of this Part any such officer shall, if so required, produce some duly authenticated document showing his authority so to act; and if it appears to any such officer that any person with whom he is dealing while so acting does not know that he is an officer acting for the purposes of this Part he shall identify himself as such to that person.

(3) An officer acting for the purposes of this Part shall have power for the performance of his duties—

(*a*) to require the production of—

(i) wages sheets or other records of remuneration kept by an employer, or

(ii) records of payments made to homeworkers by persons giving out work, or

(iii) any other records such as are required by this Part to be kept by employers,

and to inspect and examine those sheets or records and to copy any material part of them;

(*b*) to require any person giving out work and any homeworker to give any information which it is in his power to give with respect to the names and addresses of the persons to whom the work is given out or (as the case may be) of the persons from whom work is received by the homeworker, and with respect to the payments made or to be made for the work;

(*c*) where the officer has reasonable cause to believe that an order under section 14 applies to any employer, at all reasonable times to enter any premises at which that employer carries on his business (including any place used, in connection with that business, for giving out work to homeworkers, and any premises which the officer has reasonable cause to believe to be used by, or by arrangement with, the employer to provide living accommodation for workers);

(*d*) to inspect and copy any material part of any list of homeworkers kept by an employer or person giving out work to homeworkers;

(*e*) to examine (either alone or in the presence of any other person, as he thinks fit) with respect to any matters under this Part any person whom he has reasonable cause to believe to be or to have been—

(i) a worker to whom an order under section 14 applies or applied, or

(ii) the employer of any such person, or

(iii) a servant or agent of any such employer employed in the employer's business,

and to require every such person to be so examined, and to sign a declaration of the truth of the matters in respect of which he is so examined;

but no person shall be required under paragraph (*e*) to give any information tending to incriminate that person or, if married, that person's spouse.

(4) Where an officer acting for the purposes of this Part has reasonable cause to believe that an order under section 14 applies to an employer, he may, for the purpose of, or in connection with, the enforcement of that order, by notice in writing require the employer to furnish him with such information as may be specified or described in the notice; and any such notice—

(*a*) may specify the way in which, and the time within which, it is to be complied with; and

(*b*) may be varied or revoked by a subsequent notice under this subsection.

(5) In England or Wales, an officer acting for the purposes of this Part may institute proceedings for any offence under this Part and may, although not a barrister or solicitor, conduct any such proceedings.

(6) An officer acting for the purposes of this Part and being authorised in that behalf by general or special directions of the Secretary of State may, if it appears to him that a sum is due from an employer to a worker on acccount of the payment to the worker of an amount of remuneration less than the statutory minimum remuneration provided for him by an order under section 14, institute on behalf of and in the name of the worker civil proceedings for the recovery of that sum; and in any such proceedings the court may make an order for costs (or, in Scotland, expenses) to be paid by the officer as if he were a party to the proceedings.

(7) The power conferred by subsection (6) for the recovery of sums due from an employer to a worker shall not be in derogation of any right of the worker to recover such sums by civil proceedings.

DEFINITIONS
"employer": s.26(1).
"homeworker": s.26(1).
"statutory minimum remuneration": s.26(4).
"wages council": s12(1)(*a*).
"worker": s.26(1) and (2).

GENERAL NOTE
The appointment and powers of officers are substantially similar to those under WCA 1979, s.22. Subs. (4), which was introduced in 1979, gives the inspectorate the power to conduct investigations by postal questionnaire, a power which has become the central means of checking wages.

The number of wage inspectors in post fell from 158 in 1979 to 120 in 1985 (figures supplied by Department of Employment) as a result of severe cuts in available resources. As a result, only 10·8 per cent. of the register was checked in 1984, with about 150,000 workers checked by visit and a further 270,000 checked in other ways (*e.g.* by questionnaire). Nevertheless, Lord Young, the Secretary of State for Employment, announced in the House of Lords that the number of inspectors is to be reduced from 120 to 71, and the number of indoor support staff from 104 to 68. The emphasis is to be on inspections by telephone and questionnaire, rather than by visit. (*Hansard* H.L. Vol. 478, No. 136, cols. 249–250).

Offences in connection with enforcement of Part II

21.—(1) Any person who—
  (*a*) makes, or knowingly either causes or allows to be made, in a record required by this Part to be kept by employers any entry which he knows to be false in a material particular, or
  (*b*) for purposes connected with the preceding provisions of this Part produces or furnishes, or knowingly either causes or allows to be produced or furnished, any wages sheet, record, list or information which he knows to be false in a material particular.
shall be guilty of an offence and liable on summary conviction to a fine not exceeding the fifth level on the standard scale.

(2) Any person who—
  (*a*) intentionally obstructs an officer acting for the purposes of this Part of this Act in the exercise of any power conferred by section 20, or
  (*b*) fails to comply with any requirement of such an officer made in the exercise of any such power,
shall be guilty of an offence and liable on summary conviction to a fine not exceeding the third level on the standard scale; but it shall be a defence for a person charged under this subsection with failing to comply with a requirement to prove that it was not reasonably practicable to do so.

(3) Any person who, in purported compliance with a requirement of a notice under section 20(4), knowingly or recklessly makes any statement which is false in a material particular shall be guilty of an offence and liable on summary conviction to a fine not exceeding the fifth level on the standard scale.

DEFINITION
"employer": 26(1).

GENERAL NOTE
This section follows the WCA 1979 (ss.23, 22(6), 24(3) and (4)). Again, prosecutions are rare.

Miscellaneous and supplemental

Application of Part II to superior employers: liability of employers and others in respect of offences

22.—(1) Where—
    (*a*) the immediate employer of a worker is himself in the employment of some other person; and
    (*b*) the worker is employed on the premises of that other person,
that other person shall be deemed for the purposes of this Part to be the employer of the worker jointly with the immediate employer.

(2) Where the commission by any person of an offence under section 16(2) or 19(4) is due to the act or default of some other person, that other person shall be guilty of the offence; and a person may be charged with and convicted of the offence by virtue of this subsection whether or not proceedings are taken against the first-mentioned person.

(3) In any proceedings for an offence under section 16(2) or 19(4) it shall be a defence for the person charged to prove that he exercised all due diligence and took all reasonable precautions to secure that the provisions of this Part, and of any relevant regulations or order made under it, were complied with by himself and by any person under his control.

DEFINITION
    "employer": s.26(1).
    "worker": s.26.(1).

GENERAL NOTE
    This section re-enacts the relevant sections of the 1979 Act (*e.g.* ss.21(1), (4), (5)).

Offences by bodies corporate

23.—(1) Where an offence under this Part which has been committed by a body corporate is proved to have been committed with the consent or connivance of, or to be attributable to any neglect on the part of, any director, manager, secretary or other similar officer of the body corporate, or any person purporting to act in any such capacity, he as well as the body corporate shall be guilty of the offence and shall be liable to be proceeded against and punished accordingly.

(2) Where the affairs of the body corporate are managed by its members, subsection (1) shall apply in relation to the acts and defaults of a member in connection with his functions or management as if he were a director of the body corporate.

GENERAL NOTE
    This section re-enacts the relevant sections of the 1979 Act (s.24(6) and (7)).

Transitory provisions relating to existing wages councils and wages orders

24.—(1) As from the date of the passing of this Act—
    (*a*) a wages council within the meaning of the Wages Councils Act 1979 shall not exercise any functions under that Act; and
    (*b*) the following provisions of this section shall apply to any wages order in force on that date under section 14 of that Act ("an existing order").

(2) An existing order shall, subject to the following provisions of this section, continue in force until whichever is the later of the following times, namely—
    (*a*) the end of the period of six months beginning with the date of the passing of this Act, and

(*b*) the end of the period of twelve months beginning with the date of the coming into force of the order,

and shall so continue in force notwithstanding the repeal of that Act by section 12 of this Act.

(3) If, before the later of those times, there comes into force an order made under section 14 of this Act by the wages council that made the existing order, the existing order shall cease to have effect at that time.

(4) The Secretary of State may by order—

> (*a*) provide for all or any of the provisions of any existing order to cease to have effect;
>
> (*b*) restrict the operation of all or any of the provisions of any such order by reference to any matters or circumstances whatever.

(5) As from the date of the passing of this Act nothing in any existing order shall apply to workers under the age of 21.

DEFINITION
"wages council": s.26(1).

GENERAL NOTE
This section provides for the continuation of existing orders under WCA 1979 for six months from the passing of this Act, or 12 months from the commencement of the order, whichever is sooner. The Secretary of State, however, is given power to terminate or restrict existing orders sooner than this "by reference to any matters whatsoever". In addition, any new order by the relevant wages council which comes into force before the existing order has passed supercedes the existing order. Workers under 21 are excluded with immediate effect. (For the effect on accrued rights, see paras. 5 and 6 of Sched. 6.)

Subs. (4)
"By order": By statutory instrument (s.25(2)).

Regulations and orders made by Secretary of State under Part II

25.—(1) The Secretary of State may make regulations for prescribing anything which by this Part is authorised or required to be prescribed.

(2) Any power to make an order or regulations conferred on the Secretary of State by this Part shall be exercisable by statutory instrument.

(3) A statutory instrument containing—

> (*a*) an order made by the Secretary of State under section 13 (other than an order to which subsection (4) below applies) or under section 24(4), or
>
> (*b*) any regulations made by him under this Part,

shall be subject to annulment in pursuance of a resolution of either House of Parliament.

(4) No order to which this subsection applies shall be made by the Secretary of State unless a draft of the order has been laid before and approved by a resolution of each House of Parliament.

(5) Subsection (4) applies to an order under section 13 which—

> (*a*) abolishes a wages council, and
>
> (*b*) does not direct that all or any of the workers previously within the scope of operation of that wages council shall be brought within the scope of operation of another wages council.

(6) A draft of such an order which would, apart from the provisions of this subsection, be treated for the purposes of the Standing Orders of either House of Parliament as a hybrid instrument shall proceed in that House as if it were not such an instrument.

(7) Any power conferred by this Part to prescribe the manner in which anything is to be published shall include power to prescribe the date which is to be taken for the purposes of this Part as the date of publication.

Interpretation of Part II

26.—(1) In this Part—
  "employer", in relation to a worker, means the person by whom the worker is (or, where the employment has ceased, was) employed;
  "employers' association" means any organisation representing employers and any association of such organisations or of employers and such organisations;
  "employment", in relation to a worker, means employment under his contract and "employed", in relation to a worker, accordingly means employed under his contract;
  "homeworker" means an individual who—
      (*a*) contracts with a person, for the purposes of that person's business, for the execution of work to be done in a place not under the control or management of the person with whom he contracts, and
      (*b*) does not normally make use of the services of more than two individuals in the carrying out of contracts for the execution of work in relation to which statutory minimum remuneration is provided by any order under section 14;
  "organisation", in relation to workers, means a trade union and, in relation to employers, means an employers' association;
  "piece rate", means a rate where the amount of a worker's remuneration is to be calculated by reference to the number of items of work executed either by him alone or by a number of workers of whom he is one, and "piece worker" means a worker whose contract provides for the remuneration payable to him in respect of work executed by him to be calculated only by reference to one or more such rates;
  "prescribed" means prescribed by regulations made by the Secretary of State;
  "time worker" means a worker other than a piece worker (whether the worker's remuneration is determined by reference to the actual number of hours worked by him or not);
  "wages council" (except where the context requires otherwise) means such a wages council as is mentioned in section 12(1)(*a*);
  "week" means—
      (*a*) in relation to a worker whose remuneration is calculated weekly by a week ending with a day other than Saturday, a week ending with that other day; and
      (*b*) in relation to any other worker, a week ending with Saturday;
  "worker" means (subject to subsection (2)) an individual who—
      (*a*) has entered into or works under (or, where the employment has ceased, worked under) one of the contracts referred to in section 8(2), or
      (*b*) whether or not he falls within paragraph (*a*) above, is a homeworker,
and any reference to a worker's contract shall be construed as a reference to any such contract as is referred to in paragraph (*a*) above or, in the case of a homeworker, to the contract by virtue of which he is a homeworker.

(2) In this Part "worker" does not include an individual who is wholly employed otherwise than for the purposes of the business of the person employing him.

(3) Notwithstanding section 14(3)—

 (*a*) where a worker is employed partly for the purposes of his employer's business and partly not, nothing in any order under section 14 shall apply to the worker in his employment otherwise than for the purposes of that business, and

 (*b*) where a worker is employed for the purposes of his employer's business both in an employment to which an order under section 14 applies and in one to which that order does not apply, nothing in that order shall apply to the worker in the second of these employments.

(4) References in this Part to the statutory minimum remuneration provided for a worker by an order under section 14 shall—

 (*a*) in relation to a time worker, be construed in accordance with subsection (4) of that section, and

 (*b*) in relation to a piece worker, be construed in accordance with section 15.

DEFINITION

"employer", "employment": These definitions are the same as those in s.8(3).

GENERAL NOTE

"homeworker": This definition retains the definition used in WCA 1979. Note that, although called "homeworkers", the definition does not require the worker to work at home, merely that the work be done in a place not under the control or management of the employer. This would include outworkers and freelance workers, *e.g.* drivers and delivery workers, sales representatives, taxicab drivers and market research workers. The outworker is excluded if he or she normally makes use of the service of more than two others in the execution of the work. Note also that the definition of "worker" includes homeworkers even if they do not work under the contracts described in s.8(2) above. This avoids some of the problems in recent case-law as to the nature of the homeworker's contract (*e.g. Nethermere St. Neots Ltd.* v. *Gardiner* [1984] I.C.R. 365).

"Piece-rate", "timeworker": Given the wide variety of payment systems, there may be some difficulty with the simple distinction between pieceworkers and others. Piecework does include payments in respect of the number of items produced by a group of workers, but pay by commission or profit sharing schemes do not fit easily in either category.

"worker": See note to s.8(2) and to homeworker above. Note the exclusion in subs. (2).

PART III

REDUNDANCY REBATES, ETC.

Restriction of redundancy rebates to employers with less than ten employees

27.—(1) For section 104(1) of the Employment Protection (Consolidation) Act 1978 (duty of Secretary of State to pay redundancy rebates) there shall be substituted—

 "(1) Where an employer—

 (*a*) is liable under the foregoing provisions of this Part to pay, and has paid, a redundancy payment to an employee, or

 (*b*) under an agreement in respect of which an order is in force under section 96, is liable to make, and has made, a payment to an employee on the termination of his contract of employment, and that payment is a qualifying payment within the meaning of section 104A, then, subject to the provisions of this section, the Secretary of State shall make a payment out of the fund to the employer (in this Part referred to as a "redundancy rebate")."

(2) In section 104(3) of that Act (discretion of Secretary of State to pay redundancy rebates in certain cases), for the words from "satisfied that" onwards there shall be substituted "satisfied—

(*a*) that, had the payment been a payment falling within subsection (1)(*a*), it would have been a qualifying payment within the meaning of section 104A, and

(*b*) that it would be just and equitable to pay a redundancy rebate in respect of the payment having regard to all the relevant circumstances."

(3) After section 104 there shall be inserted—

"Qualifying payments for purposes of redundancy rebates

104A.—(1) A payment made by an employer to an employee and falling within subsection (1)(*a*) or (*b*) of section 104 shall be treated as a qualifying payment if at no time on the appropriate date did the number of employees employed by the employer, added to the number employed by any associated employer, exceed nine.

(2) In subsection (1) "the appropriate date"—

(*a*) in the case of a payment falling within section 104(1)(*a*), means the date which is the relevant date in relation to that payment by virtue of section 90(1) or (2); and

(*b*) in the case of a payment falling within section 104(1)(*b*), means the date on which the termination of the employee's contract of employment is treated as having taken effect for the purposes of the agreement referred to in that provision.

(3) In determining for the purposes of subsection (1) the number of employees employed by any individual on any date an employee who is employed by that individual for the purposes of his own household shall be disregarded if—

(*a*) the employee's contract of employment normally involves employment for less than eight hours weekly, and

(*b*) not more than one other employee is so employed for the purposes of that household (whatever the number of hours of employment which any such other employee's contract of employment normally involves in a week)."

(4) In section 117 of that Act (employees paid by person other than employer), after subsection (2) there shall be inserted—

"(2A) Section 104A shall have effect in relation to a payment falling within section 104(1)(*a*) or (*b*) and made to an employee to whom this section applies as if, in subsection (1)—

(*a*) any reference to the employer were a reference to the person responsible for paying the remuneration, and

(*b*) the reference to employees employed by the employer were a reference to employees who are employed by that person or whose remuneration is payable by him as mentioned in subsection (1) above.

(2B) In the application of section 104A(1) in relation to a payment falling within section 104(1)(*a*) or (*b*) and made by an employer to an employee, the reference to employees employed by the employer shall be construed as including a reference to employees whose remuneration is payable by the employer as mentioned in subsection (1) above."

DEFINITIONS

"associated employer": s.153(4) EPCA 1978.
"contract of employment": s.153(1) EPCA 1978.
"employee": s.153(1) EPCA 1978.
"employer": s.153(1) EPCA 1978.
"redundancy fund": s.103 EPCA 1978.
"redundancy payment": s.81(1) EPCA 1978.

GENERAL NOTE

The section amends EPCA 1978, s.104(1), which provided for rebates to be payable from the Redundancy Fund to employers who had made statutory redundancy payments. The amendment provides that only employers with fewer than 10 employees will be entitled to the rebate in respect of redundancies occurring after the commencement. The Fund will, however, continue to make payments in respect of insoivencies (EPCA 1978, s.106).

Employees' rights to statutory redundancy payments are unaffected by this provision. With the increase in redundancies since 1980, the Fund has been in financial difficulties. It was originally financed by contributions from employers, but in order to increase the available funds, employee contributions were instituted in April 1982, at the rate of 0·35 per cent. of earnings (Social Security (Contributions) Act 1982). Since then, employee contributions have exceeded those of employers, as a percentage both of earnings and of the Fund. In addition, the amount of the rebate has progressively declined, to its current value of 35 per cent. in respect of redundancies occurring on or after April 1985 (Paul Lewis, "Twenty Years of Statutory Redundancy Payments in Great Britain," Universities of Leeds and Nottingham 1985, pp.19–21.)

The Secretary of State for Employment, Lord Young, stated in the House of Lords that an estimated £200m a year would be saved as a result of the amendment and about £10m a year would continue to be payable in rebates under the new arrangement (*Hansard* H.L. Vol. 478, No. 126, col. 267). The choice of ten as a cut-off point reflects the particular concern of the present Government that redundancy payments represent an unduly large burden on small employers, although Lord Young acknowledged that some very small companies, such as computer firms, may not be among the poorest of companies. It is estimated that about 1.8m employees are employed in firms of this size (1981 Labour Force Survey.)

COMMENCEMENT

August 1, 1986 (see s.33(3)).

Subs. (1)

Apart from the proviso added by subs. (3) (new s.104A), this section is substantially similar to the unamended s.104.

Subs. (3)

"*the number of employees employed by the employer*": The definition of "employees" in EPCA, s.153 is limited to those employed under a contract of service. Thus all other workers are disregarded in determining whether the employer qualified for the rebate. However, employees who do not fulfil the other eligibility requirements for redundancy payments, such as length of service, are not disregarded. Note that by s.104A(3), employees employed for the purposes of the employer's own household must be added into the total unless only one person is so employed, and his or her contract normally involves employment for fewer than eight hours a week. See also not to subs. (4) below.

"*associated employer*": This is defined in EPCA 1978, s.153(4).

"*the appropriate date*": This is defined by reference to EPCA, s.90 which sets out criteria for determining the date of dismissal of a redundant employee.

"*at no time on the appropriate date*": Thus the redundant employee is to be included in the total of those employed, since his or her termination takes place at some point on the relevant date.

Subs. (4)

Section 117 applies to employees whose remuneration is, by virtue of a statutory provision, payable by a person other than the employer. Then the reference to "employer" in this section is read as if it referred to that person.

Abolition of payments equivalent to redundancy rebates

28. No payment shall be made by the Secretary of State under—

(*a*) section 111(2) of the Employment Protection (Consolidation) Act 1978 (payments equivalent to redundancy rebates in respect of civil servants, etc.), or

(*b*) section 113(1) of that Act (similar payments in respect of employees of foreign governments),

in respect of any termination of employment occurring after the commencement of this section.

GENERAL NOTE

Sections 111(2) and 113(1) continue in force, but not in respect of termination of employment occurrring after the commencement of this section (namely August 1 1986: see s.33(3)).

Power to make corresponding provision for Northern Ireland

29. An Order in Council under paragraph 1(1)(*b*) of Schedule 1 to the Northern Ireland Act 1974 (legislation for Northern Ireland in the interim period) which states that it is made only for purposes corresponding to those of sections 27 and 28 of this Act—

(*a*) shall not be subject to paragraph 1(4) and (5) of that Schedule (affirmative resolution of both Houses of Parliament); but

(*b*) shall be subject to annulment in pursuance of a resolution of either House.

Part IV

General

Excluded employments

30.—(1) Parts I and II do not apply to employment where under his contract the person employed ordinarily works outside Great Britain.

(2) For the purposes of subsection (1) a person employed to work on board a ship registered in the United Kingdom (not being a ship registered at a port outside Great Britain) shall, unless—

(*a*) the employment is wholly outside Great Britain, or

(*b*) he is not ordinarily resident in Great Britain,

be regarded as a person who under his contract ordinarily works in Great Britain.

(3) Parts I and II do not, however, apply to a person employed under a crew agreement within the meaning of the Merchant Shipping Act 1970.

GENERAL NOTE
Subs. (1)
Compare EPCA 1978, s.141(2).

Subs. (2)
Compare EPCA 1978, s.141(5).

Financial provisions

31. There shall be paid out of money provided by Parliament—

(*a*) any expenses incurred by the Secretary of State in consequence of Part II;

(*b*) any expenses incurred by wages councils (within the meaning of Part II) in accordance with the terms of any authorisation given by the Secretary of State with the consent of the Treasury; and

(*c*) any increase attributable to this Act in the sums payable out of money so provided under any other Act.

Amendments, repeals, transitional provisions and savings

32.—(1) The enactments mentioned in Schedule 4 shall have effect subject to the minor and consequential amendments there specified.

(2) The enactments mentioned in Schedule 5 are hereby repealed to the extent specified in the third column of that Schedule.

(3) The transitional provisions and savings contained in Schedule 6 shall have effect; but nothing in that Schedule shall be taken as prejudicing the operation of sections 16 and 17 of the Interpretation Act 1978 (which relate to repeals).

Short title, commencement and extent

33.—(1) This Act may be cited as the Wages Act 1986.

(2) The following provisions of this Act shall come into force on the day on which this Act is passed—

section 24;

section 25(1) to (3);

section 29;

section 31;

section 32(3) and Schedule 6;

this section.

(3) The following provisions of this Act, namely—

sections 27 and 28

paragraphs 8 and 11 of Schedule 4 and section 32(1) so far as relating thereto, and

Part I of Schedule 5 and section 32(2) so far as relating thereto,

shall come into force on the day on which this Act is passed or on 1st August 1986, whichever is the later.

(4) The following provisions of this Act shall come into force at the end of the period of two months beginning with the day on which this Act is passed—

Part II (excluding sections 24 and 25(1) to (3) but including Schedules 2 and 3);

section 30 so far as relating to Part II;

paragraphs 4 to 7 of Schedule 4 and section 32(1) so far as relating thereto;

Part II of Schedule 5 and section 32(2) so far as relating thereto.

(5) The following provisions of this Act shall come into force on such a day as the Secretary of State may appoint by order made by statutory instrument, namely—

Part I (including Schedule 1);

section 30 so far as relating to Part I;

paragraphs 1 to 3, 9 and 10 of Schedule 4 and section 32(1) so far as relating thereto;

Part III of Schedule 5 and section 32(2) so far as relating thereto.

(6) An order under subsection (5) may—

(*a*) appoint different days for different provisions or for different purposes;

(b) contain such transitional and supplementary provisions as appear to the Secretary of State to be necessary or expedient.

(7) With the exception of—

section 29 (which extends only to Northern Ireland),

paragraphs 5 and 6 of Schedule 4 and section 32(1) so far as relating thereto,

section 32(2) and Part II of Schedule 5 so far as they repeal any provision of the Wages Councils Act 1979 extending to Northern Ireland, and

this section,

this Act does not extend to Northern Ireland.

SCHEDULES

Section 11

SCHEDULE 1

ENACTMENTS REPEALED BY SECTION 11

The Truck Act 1831 (c.37).
The Hosiery Manufacture (Wages) Act 1874 (c.48).
The Payment of Wages in Public-houses Prohibition Act 1883 (c.31).
Sections 12 and 13 of the Stannaries Act 1887 (c.43).
The Truck Amendment Act 1887 (c.46).
Sections 12 to 14 of the Coal Mines Regulation Act 1887 (c.58).
The Coal Mines (Check Weigher) Act 1984 (c.52).
The Truck Act 1896 (c.44).
The Shop Clubs Act 1902 (c.21).
The Coal Mines (Weighing of Minerals) Act 1905 (c.9).
The Checkweighing in Various Industries Act 1919 (c.51).
The Truck Act 1940 (c.38).
Section 51(2) of the Mines and Quarries Act 1954 (c.70).
The Payment of Wages Act 1960 (c.37).
Sections 135 and 135A or the Factories Act 1961 (c.34).

Section 12(4)

SCHEDULE 2

CONSTITUTION ETC. OF WAGES COUNCILS

1. A wages council shall consist of—
   (a) such numbers of persons appointed to represent employers and workers respectively as may be specified in relation to the council by the Secretary of State; and
   (b) not more than 5 persons appointed by the Secretary of State as being independent persons.

2.—(1) Subject to sub-paragraph (4), the persons appointed under paragraph 1(a) shall be appointed as follows, namely—
   (a) those appointed to represent employers shall be appointed by one or more employers' associations for the time being nominated for the purposes of this paragraph by the Secretary of State; and
   (b) those appointed to represent workers shall be appointed by one or more trade unions (within the meaning of the Trade Union and Labour Relations Act 1974) for the time being so nominated;
and in this Schedule references to the nominated body or bodies in relation to any appointment in pursuance of paragraph (a) or (b) above are references to the body or bodies falling within that paragraph.

(2) Unless it appears to the Secretary of State to be inappropriate in all the circumstances for this sub-paragraph to apply to the wages council—
   (a) the employers' association nominated by him for the purposes of sub-paragraph (1)(a), or
   (b) where two or more employers' associations are so nominated, at least one of those associations,

shall be an employers' association appearing to him to be representative of small businesses within the scope of operation of the wages council.

(3) On making an appointment in pursuance of sub-paragraph (1)(*a*) or (*b*) the nominated body or bodies shall inform the secretary of the wages council in writing of that appointment.

(4) If for any reason there is a deficiency in the number of persons appointed to a wages council in pursuance of sub-paragraph (1)(*a*) or (*b*), the Secretary of State shall, after consulting such persons or organisations as he thinks fit, appoint on behalf of the nominated body or bodies such number of persons to represent employers or (as the case may be) workers as will remedy that deficiency.

3. Of the independent persons appointed under paragraph 1(*b*) one shall be appointed by the Secretary of State to act as chairman, and another may be appointed by the Secretary of State to act as chairman in the absence of the chairman.

4. The Secretary of State may appoint a secretary for a wages council and such other officers as he thinks fit.

5. The proceedings of a wages council shall not be invalidated by any vacancy among the members or by any defect in the appointment of a member.

6.—(1) A wages council may delegate any of its functions, other than the power to make orders under section 14, to a committee or sub-committee consisting of such number of members of the council as the council thinks fit.

(2) On any such committee or sub-committee there shall be an equal number of members representing employers and workers respectively.

7. The Secretary of State may make regulations as to the meetings and procedure of a wages council and of any committee or sub-committee of such a council, including regulations as to the quorum and the method of voting; but, subject to the provisions of this Part of this Act and to any regulations under this paragraph, a wages council and any committee or sub-committee of such a council may regulate its procedure in such manner as it thinks fit.

8.—(1) A member of a wages council shall hold and vacate office in accordance with the terms of his appointment, but a member shall not be appointed to hold office for more than three years at a time.

(2) Where the term of office of any members of a wages council comes to an end before their successors are appointed, then, unless—

(*a*) in the case of members appointed in pursuance of paragraph 2(1)(*a*) or (*b*), the nominated body or bodies directs or direct otherwise, or

(*b*) in the case of members appointed by the Secretary of State, the Secretary of State directs otherwise,

those members shall continue in office until the new appointments take effect.

9. The Secretary of State may pay—

(*a*) to the members of a wages council appointed by him under paragraph 1(*b*) such remuneration, and

(*b*) to any member of a wages council such travelling and other allowances,

as the Secretary of State may determine with the consent of the Treasury.

Section 14(9)   SCHEDULE 3

WAGES ORDERS: SUPPLEMENTARY PROVISIONS

Preliminary inquiries and notices

1.—(1) Before making an order under section 14 a wages council shall make such inquiries as it thinks fit and shall—

(*a*) publish in the prescribed manner notice of any rate or limit which the council proposes to fix under subsection (1) of that section (whether for the first time or in substitution for any existing rate or limit); and

(*b*) give the prescribed notice for the purpose of informing, so far as practicable, all persons affected by the council's proposals, stating the place where copies of the proposals may be obtained and the period within which written representations with respect to the proposals may be sent to the council, being a period of not less than 28 days beginning with the date of publication of the notice.

(2) Once the council has considered any written representations made with respect to the proposals within the period referred to in sub-paragraph (1)(*b*) and made any further

inquiries which the council considers necessary, or once that period has ended without any such representations being so made, the council may—

(*a*) make an order under section 14 giving effect to the proposals; or

(*b*) make such an order giving effect to the proposals with such modifications as the council thinks fit having regard to any such representations.

(3) Sub-paragraph (2)(*b*) is without prejudice to section 14(6).

Publication of notice of making of order

2. As soon as a wages council has made an order under section 14 it shall publish in the prescribed manner notice of the making and contents of the order and shall then and subsequently so publish notice of such other matters affecting the operation of the order as may be prescribed.

Coming into operation of orders

3.—(1) Subject to sub-paragraph (2), any such order shall come into force on such date as may be specified in the order, being a date falling not less than 28 days after the date when it is made.

(2) Where—

(*a*) any such order applies to any worker whose remuneration is paid at intervals not exceeding seven days, and

(*b*) the date specified by virtue of sub-paragraph (1) does not correspond with the beginning of any period for which his remuneration is so paid,

the order shall have effect in relation to that worker as from the beginning of the next such period following the date so specified.

Proof of orders

4. A document purporting to be a copy of an order made by a council under section 14 and to be signed by the secretary of the council shall be taken to be a true copy of the order unless the contrary is proved.

Section 32(1)   SCHEDULE 4

Minor and Consequential Amendments

Coal Mines Regulation Act 1908 (c.57)

1. In section 2 (register of times of descent and ascent), subsection (2) shall be omitted.

2. In section 8 (application of Act etc.), for subsection (1) substitute—

"(1) The mines to which the Act applies are mines of coal, mines of stratified ironstone, mines of shale and mines of fire-clay."

Mines and Quarries Act 1954 (c.70)

3. In section 187(2) (application of Part XIV of that Act to certain enactments), for "the said Acts" substitute "the Coal Mines Regulation Act 1908".

Attachment of Earnings Act 1971 (c.32.)

4. In Part I of Schedule 3 (scheme of deductions), for paragraph 3(*c*) substitute—

"(*c*) amounts deductible under any enactment, or in pursuance of a request in writing by the debtor, for the purposes of a superannuation scheme, namely any enactment, rules, deed or other instrument providing for the payment of annuities or lump sums—

(i) to the persons with respect to whom the instrument has effect on their retirement at a specified age or on becoming incapacitated at some earlier age, or

(ii) to the personal representatives or the widows, relatives or dependants of such persons on their death or otherwise,

whether with or without any further or other benefits."

HOUSE OF COMMONS DISQUALIFICATION ACT 1975 (c.24)

5. In Part III of Schedule 1 (other disqualifying offices), for the first entry beginning "Member of a Wages Council" substitute—
    "Member of a Wages Council appointed under paragraph 1(*b*) of Schedule 2 to the Wages Act 1986."

NORTHERN IRELAND ASSEMBLY DISQUALIFICATION ACT 1975 (c.25)

6. In Part III of Schedule 1 (other disqualifying offices), for the first entry beginning "Member of a Wages Council" substitute—
    "Member of a Wages Council appointed under paragraph 1(*b*) of Schedule 2 to the Wages Act 1986."

EMPLOYMENT PROTECTION (CONSOLIDATION) ACT 1978 (c.44)

7. In section 18(2) (exemption orders), for paragraph (*a*) substitute—
    "(*a*) section 14 of the Wages Act 1986;".
8. In section 108(1)(*a*) (references etc. to tribunal relating to payments out of Redundancy Fund), after "payment" insert "and the payment is a qualifying payment within the meaning of section 104A".
9. In section 133(1) (general provisions as to conciliation officers), after paragraph (*d*) insert "; or
    (*e*) arising out of a contravention, or alleged contravention, of section 1(1) or (2) or section 2(1) or 3(4) of the Wages Act 1986.".
10. In section 136(1) (appeals to Employment Appeal Tribunal), after paragraph (*e*) insert—
    "(*f*) the Wages Act 1986.".
11. In section 153(1) (interpretation), in the definition of "employer's payment", for "(*a*), (*b*) or (*c*)" substitute "(*a*) or (*b*)".

Section 32(2)   SCHEDULE 5

PART I

REPEALS COMING INTO FORCE IN ACCORDANCE WITH S.33(3)

Chapter	Short title	Extent of repeal
1975 c.71.	Employment Protection Act 1975.	Section 104. Section 105(4) and (5).
1978 c.44.	Employment Protection (Consolidation) Act 1978.	In section 104(2) the words "or paragraph (*c*)". In section 106(2)(*c*), the words "or paragraph (*c*)". Section 113. In Schedule 6, in paragraph 6, the words "or paragraph (*c*)", and in paragraph 7(*a*) the words from "or (as" to "that subsection". In Schedule 16, paragraph 23(5).
1982 c.2.	Social Security (Contributions) Act 1982.	In Schedule 1, paragraph 2(2).

PART II

REPEALS COMING INTO FORCE TWO MONTHS AFTER ROYAL ASSENT

Chapter	Short title	Extent of repeal
1970 c.41.	Equal Pay Act 1970.	Section 4.
1975 c.71.	Employment Protection Act 1975.	In Part IV of Schedule 16, in paragraph 13(2) and (3) the figure "4", and paragraph 13(6) to (11).
1979 c.12.	Wages Councils Act 1979.	The whole Act.
1982 c.23.	Oil and Gas (Enterprise) Act 1982.	In Schedule 3, paragraph 41.

PART III

REPEALS COMING INTO FORCE ON A DAY APPOINTED UNDER S.33(5)

Chapter	Short title	Extent of repeal
1831 c.37.	Truck Act 1831.	The whole Act.
1874 c.48.	Hosiery Manufacture (Wages) Act 1874.	The whole Act.
1883 c. 31.	Payment of Wages in Public-houses Prohibition Act 1883.	The whole Act.
1887 c.43.	Stannaries Act 1887.	Sections 12 and 13.
1887 c.46.	Truck Amendment Act 1887.	The whole Act.
1887 c.58.	Coal Mines Regulation Act 1887.	The whole Act.
1894 c.52.	Coal Mines (Check Weigher) Act 1894.	The whole Act.
1896 c.44.	Truck Act 1896.	The whole Act.
1902 c.21.	Shop Clubs Act 1902.	The whole Act.
1905 c.9.	Coal Mines (Weighing of Minerals) Act 1905.	The whole Act.
1908 c.57.	Coal Mines Regulation Act 1908.	Section 2(2).
1919 c.51.	Checkweighing in Various Industries Act 1919.	The whole Act.
1940 c.38.	Truck Act 1940.	The whole Act.
1951 c.39.	Common Informers Act 1951.	In the Schedule, the entry relating to the Hosiery Manufacture (Wages) Act 1874.
1954 c.70.	Mines and Quarries Act 1954.	Section 51(2). Section 185. In section 187(1), the words from "the Coal Mines Regulation" to ", and of ".
1960 c.37.	Payment of Wages Act 1960.	The whole Act.
1961 c.34.	Factories Act 1961.	Sections 135 and 135A.
1969 c.48.	Post Office Act 1969.	In Schedule 4, paragraph 67.
1973 c.38.	Social Security Act 1973.	Section 70.
1975 c.20.	District Courts (Scotland) Act 1975.	In Schedule 1, paragraph 6.
1975 c.21.	Criminal Procedure (Scotland) Act 1975.	In Schedule 7A, paragraph 2.
1977 c.45.	Criminal Law Act 1977.	In Schedule 1, paragraph 2.
1980 c.43.	Magistrates' Courts Act 1980.	In Schedule 1, paragraph 17.
1982 c.24.	Social Security and Housing Benefits Act 1982.	Section 23A(2).

Section 32(3)   SCHEDULE 6

TRANSITIONAL PROVISIONS AND SAVINGS

Members and officers of wages councils

1. Any appointment of a member or officer of a wages council made under any provision of Schedule 2 to the Wages Councils Act 1979 (referred to in this Schedule as "the 1979 Act") and in force immediately before the commencement of Part II of this Act shall continue in force as if made under the corresponding provision of Schedule 2 to this Act.

Enforcement officers appointed by Secretary of State

2. Any appointment of an officer made under section 22 of the 1979 Act and in force immediately before the commencement of Part II of this Act shall continue in force as if made under section 20 of this Act.

Anticipatory exercise of powers relating to making of orders

3. Without prejudice to section 13 of the Interpretation Act 1978 (anticipatory exercise of powers), any of the steps required by paragraph 1 of Schedule 3 to this Act to be taken before the making of an order under section 14 of this Act may be taken by a wages council (within the meaning of the 1979 Act) at any time before the commencement of Part II of this Act, as if Part II were then in force in relation to that council.

Failure to pay minimum remuneration occurring before commencement of Part II

4.—(1) Where at any time during the period of two years ending with the date of an offence under section 16(2) of this Act an order under section 14 of the 1979 Act applied to the worker in relation to whom the offence was committed, or to any other worker employed by that worker's employer, section 16 of this Act shall have effect in relation to any such time as if—

    (*a*) in subsections (3) and (6), any reference to any other failure on the part of the employer to pay an amount of remuneration equal to, or exceeding, the statutory minimum remuneration provided for a worker by an order under section 14 of this Act were a reference to any failure on the part of the employer to pay an amount of remuneration equal to, or exceeding, the remuneration for the time being fixed in relation to a worker by an order under section 14 of the 1979 Act or by a permit under section 16(1) of that Act;

    (*b*) in subsection (4), the reference to the statutory minimum remuneration so provided were a reference to the remuneration so fixed; and

    (*c*) subsection (5) were omitted.

(2) For the purposes of subsections (3) and (4) of section 16 of this Act, as they have effect in accordance with sub-paragraph (1), the following matters, namely—

    (*a*) the question whether an employer has failed to pay an amount of remuneration equal to, or exceeding, that fixed by any such order or permit under the 1979 Act as is mentioned in that sub-paragraph, and

    (*b*) the amount referred to in subsection (4)(*b*).

shall be determined in accordance with sections 17 and 18 of the 1979 Act, and not in accordance with sections 17 and 18 of this Act.

General saving for accrued rights and related provisions of 1979 Act

5.—(1) The repeal of the 1979 Act by this Act shall not affect—

    (*a*) any right of a worker arising out of the payment to him of an amount of remuneration less than that fixed by any such order or permit under the 1979 Act as is mentioned in paragraph 4(1) and accruing before the commencement of Part II of this Act, or

    (*b*) any liability of an employer or other person in respect of any offence under that Act committed before that commencement,

and, subject to sub-paragraph (3), the provisions of that Act relating to the enforcement of any such right or to any such offence shall continue to have effect as if this Act had not been passed.

(2) Where at any time after that commencement any order made under section 14 of the 1979 Act continues in force by virtue of section 24(2) of this Act, then, notwithstanding the repeal of that Act by this Act—

    (*a*) that Act, and

(*b*) anything having effect under that Act in relation to the order,
shall (subject to sub-paragraph (3)) continue to have effect in relation to the order, as for the time being in force in accordance with section 24(4) and (5), as if that repeal had not come into force.

(3) Where the 1979 Act continues to have effect in accordance with sub-paragraph (1) or (2) it shall, in relation to any time after the commencement of Part II of this Act, have effect as if references to an officer acting for the purposes of Parts III and IV of that Act were references to an officer acting for the purposes of Part II of this Act.

4. Nothing in section 24(5) of this Act, or in any order made under section 24(4), shall affect—

(*a*) any such right of a worker as is mentioned in sub-paragraph (1), or

(*b*) any right of a worker to any annual holidays or to any holiday remuneration in respect of those holidays,

which accrued before the commencement of section 24(5) or (as the case may be) before the commencement of any such order.

Power to preserve accrued rights under wages orders

6.—(1) In the case of any provision contained in an order under section 14 of the 1979 Act and ceasing to have effect (whether wholly or in part) at any time in accordance with section 24 of this Act, the Secretary of State may by order provide, for the purpose of, or in connection with, preserving the effect of rights accruing under that provision before that time, for that provision to continue in force as from that time subject to such modifications and transitional provisions as may be specified in the order.

(2) Without prejudice to the generality of sub-paragraph (1), an order under this paragraph may make provision in connection with preserving the effect of rights to which paragraph 5(4)(*b*) above applies.

(3) A provision contained in an order under this paragraph may be made with retrospective effect as from the date on which this Act is passed or any later date.

(4) Any order under this paragraph shall be made by statutory instrument which shall be subject to annulment in pursuance of a resolution of either House of Parliament.

Exemption orders

7. Paragraph 7 of Schedule 4 shall not affect the operation of section 18 of the Employment Protection (Consolidation) Act 1978 in relation to any such order as is referred to in paragraph 5(2) above.

References to trade boards

8. Any reference to a trade board in any enactment or document made before 28th March 1945 (the date of the passing of the Wages Councils Act 1945), other than an enactment repealed by that Act, shall be construed as including a reference to a wages council within the meaning of Part II of this Act.

Redundancy rebates

9.—(1) In subsection (1) of section 104 of the Employment Protection (Consolidaton) Act 1978, as substituted by section 27 of this Act, the requirement that a payment falling within paragraph (*a*) or (*b*) of that subsection should be a qualifying payment within the meaning of section 104A of that Act shall not apply to—

(*a*) any payment falling within either of those paragraphs in respect of which a claim for a redundancy rebate has been made in accordance with regulations under section 104(5) before the commencement of section 27 of this Act, or

(*b*) any other payment so falling in relation to which the relevant date (as defined in sub-paragraph (2)) falls before that commencement.

(2) In sub-paragraph (1)(*b*) "the relevant date"—

(*a*) in the case of a payment falling within subsection (1)(*a*) of section 104, means the date which for the purposes of section 81(4) of that Act is the relevant date in relation to that payment by virtue of any provision of section 90 of that Act, and

(*b*) in the case of a payment falling within subsection (1)(*b*) of section 104, means the date on which the termination of the employee's contract of employment is treated as having taken effect for the purposes of the agreement referred to in that provision.

Payments equivalent to redundancy rebates

10.—(1) Section 28 of this Act shall not affect the operation of provisions of section 111 of the Employment Protection (Consolidation) Act 1978 for purposes other than those of the making by the Secretary of State of payments under section 111(2).

(2) The repeals made by this Act shall not affect the operation of section 113 of that Act in relation to any termination of employment occurring before the commencement of section 28 of this Act.

AGRICULTURE ACT 1986

(1986 c. 49)

ARRANGEMENT OF SECTIONS

An Act to make further provision relating to agriculture and agricultural and other food products, horticulture and the countryside; and for connected matters.   [25th July 1986]

PARLIAMENTARY DEBATES
Hansard: H.C. Vol. 86, col. 118; H.C. Vol. 87, col. 614; H.C. Vol. 95, col. 1036; H.C. Vol. 102, col. 509; H.L. Vol. 473, col. 948; H.L. Vol. 474, col. 620; H.L. Vol. 476, cols. 392, 592, 1047; H.L. Vol. 477, col. 893; H.L. Vol. 479, col. 167.
The Bill was considered by Standing Committee B between December 10, 1985 and January 30, 1986.

Provision of agricultural services and goods

Provision of services and goods connected with agriculture and countryside

1.—(1) The Minister may make provision for the supply to any person of any services or goods relating to—

(a) the production and marketing of agricultural produce and other food;

(b) the conservation and enhancement of the natural beauty and amenity of the countryside; or

(c) any other agricultural activity or other enterprise of benefit to the rural economy.

(2) The provision which may be made under this section includes, in particular, provision for—

(a) the giving of information, advice, instruction and training;

(b) the undertaking of research and development;

(c) the examination or testing of any substance;

(d) the supply of veterinary services and of goods required for veterinary purposes;

(e) the performance of any service required in connection with the drainage of agricultural land.

(3) The provision which may be made under this section includes provision for the supply of such services and goods as are mentioned in subsection (1) above through any organisation; and the Minister shall establish an organisation through which such a supply may be made.

(4) Any services or goods provided by virtue of this section may be provided free of charge or for such reasonable charge as the Ministers may determine.

(5) For the purposes of this section the conservation of the natural beauty of the countryside includes the conservation of flora and fauna and geological and physiographical features.

(6) In this section—

"agriculture" has the same meaning as in the Agriculture Act 1947;

"food" has the same meaning as in the Food Act 1984; and

"the Minister" means—

(a) in relation to services or goods provided in England, the Minister of Agriculture, Fisheries and Food; and

(b) in relation to services or goods provided in Wales, the Secretary of State,

and "the Ministers" means those Ministers acting jointly.

Fees and charges to meet costs of statutory functions connected with agriculture

Fees under seeds regulations

2. In section 16 of the Plant Varieties and Seeds Act 1964 (seeds regulations) after subsection (5) there shall be inserted—

"(5A) In determining any fees to be charged under seeds regulations the Minister may have regard to the costs incurred by him in connection with the enforcement of the regulations.".

Fees and charges under Plant Health Act 1967

3. After section 4 of the Plant Health Act 1967 there shall be inserted the following section—

> **"Charges in connection with import and export licences and certificates**
>
> 4A. Without prejudice to section 4(1) above, an order under this Act may impose such reasonable fees or other charges as the competent authority may, with the consent of the Treasury, prescribe—
>
> (a) in connection with applications for and the issue of any licence or certificate which may be issued in pursuance of such an order in connection with the import or export of any article; and
>
> (b) in respect of the performance by the authority of any service without the performance of which any requirement for the issue of such a licence or certificate would not be met.".

Agricultural marketing

Constitution and functions of Home-Grown Cereals Authority

4.—(1) The Cereals Marketing Act 1965 shall have effect subject to the following amendments (which relate to the constitution and functions of the Home-Grown Cereals Authority).

(2) In subsection (1) of section 1 of that Act (establishment of the Authority for the purpose of improving the marketing of home-grown cereals) for the word "marketing" there shall be substituted the words "production and marketing".

(3) For subsections (2) to (4) of that section (membership of the Authority) there shall be substituted—

> "(2) The Authority shall consist of not less than twelve and not more than twenty-one members appointed by the Ministers.
>
> (3) Of those members—
>
> (a) not less than two and not more than three shall be appointed as being independent; and
>
> (b) an equal number (being not less than five and not more than nine) shall be appointed as being respectively—
>
> > (i) persons capable of representing the interests of growers of home-grown cereals, and
> >
> > (ii) persons capable of representing the interests of persons who are either dealers in or processors of home-grown cereals.
>
> (4) Of the members appointed under paragraph (b) of subsection (3) of this section as being persons capable of representing the interests of growers of home-grown cereals—
>
> (a) such number as appears to the Ministers to be adequate shall be appointed as being also capable of representing the interests of farmers who use home-grown cereals for feeding livestock kept by them; and
>
> (b) at least one shall be appointed as being capable of representing, in particular, the interests of growers of home-grown cereals in Scotland, one the interests of such growers in Wales and one the interests of such growers in Northern Ireland.
>
> (4A) The Ministers shall appoint one of the members appointed under paragraph (a) of subsection (3) of this section to be chairman and another to be deputy chairman of the Authority.".

(4) Sections 2 to 5 (bonus payments in respect of forward contracts and deliveries of cereals) and Part II (trading functions of Home-Grown Cereals Authority) of that Act shall cease to have effect.

(5) In section 6 of that Act (non-trading functions of Home-Grown Cereals Authority) in subsection (5)—

> (*a*) after the words "work in" there shall be inserted the words "connection with any matter relating to—
> > (*aa*) the breeding and cultivation of cereals,";
> (*b*) for the words "the marketing of cereals" there shall be substituted the words "the production or marketing of cereals"; and
> (*c*) for paragraph (*b*) there shall be substituted—
> > "(*b*) the invention of new uses of, or processes which might be applied to, home-grown cereals or straw or the development or assessment of such uses or processes or existing uses or processes,".

(6) In paragraph 10 of Schedule 1 to that Act (appointment by the Home-Grown Cereals Authority of advisory committees)—

> (*a*) at the beginning of sub-paragraph (1) there shall be inserted the words "Subject to sub-paragraph (1A) below,"; and
> (*b*) after that sub-paragraph there shall be inserted—
> > "(1A) The Authority shall appoint a committee to determine programmes for and report on research and development in connection with home-grown cereals and shall, if the Ministers so direct, appoint a committee to determine programmes for and report on the encouragement of the marketing of such cereals.
> > (1B) Different committees may be appointed under this paragraph in respect of different kinds of cereals.".

Levies under Cereals Marketing Act 1965

5.—(1) Section 14 (alternative methods of raising levy) and section 15 (levy recovered wholly or mainly by deduction) of the Cereals Marketing Act 1965 shall cease to have effect.

(2) For subsection (1) of section 16 of that Act (preparation and submission of schemes for imposing levies) there shall be substituted—

> "(1) The Authority may at any time prepare and submit to the Ministers a scheme for imposing a levy on persons specified in the scheme who are growers or processors of, or dealers in, home-grown cereals of a kind so specified or who in the course of their business act as intermediaries in the selling and buying of such cereals.
> (1A) Before submitting a scheme under subsection (1) above, the Authority shall in such manner as they consider appropriate consult such persons or organisations as appear to them to represent the interests concerned.".

(3) In subsection (2) of that section (by virtue of which such schemes may provide for the registration of such growers, dealers and processors and require them to furnish information and keep records) for the words "any persons who are growers of, or dealers in, home-grown cereals or who process home-grown cereals" there shall be substituted the words "any such persons as are mentioned in subsection (1) above".

(4) After that subsection there shall be inserted—

> "(2A) A scheme under this section—
> > (*a*) may authorise such of the persons on whom the levy is imposed as may be specified in the scheme to recover all or part of the levy payable by them from such other persons (being persons mentioned in subsection (1) above) as may be so specified and may provide for direct collection from those other persons; and

(b) may authorise the deduction from the levy payable by persons with such a right of recovery, or the repayment to them, of—
    (i) such amounts as may be determined in accordance with the scheme in respect of expenses incurred by them in exercising that right, and
    (ii) any sums which are in accordance with the scheme to be treated as irrecoverable.".

(5) For section 20(2) of that Act (disclosure of information to Home-Grown Cereals Authority) there shall be substituted—

"(2) Any information obtained by the Intervention Board for Agricultural Produce may be disclosed to the Authority for the purpose of assisting them in collecting any levy imposed under this Act; and any such disclosure shall not be treated as a breach of contract, trust or confidence.".

(6) In section 24 of that Act (interpretation)—
  (a) in subsection (4)(a) (under which orders under section 13 may include provision as to the circumstances in which cereals shall be treated as delivered) after the words "specified in" there shall be inserted the words "the order";
  (b) in subsection (5) (which defines a dealer in home-grown cereals as a person trading as a wholesale buyer and seller of such cereals and a processor of home-grown cereals as a person who applies an industrial process to such cereals with a view to selling the processed cereals in the course of his business) for the words "wholesale buyer and seller" there shall be substituted the words "wholesale buyer or seller" and the words "with a view to selling the processed cereals" shall be omitted.

(7) In Schedule 3 to that Act (supplementary provisions concerning levies), for paragraphs 4 to 6 there shall be substituted—

"4. For the purposes of sections 13 to 17 of this Act and of this Schedule a crop which consists of two or more kinds of home-grown cereals shall be treated as if it were a separate kind of home-grown cereals.".

Extension of Cereals Marketing Act 1965 to new cereals and other crops

6.—(1) The Ministers may, if they think fit, by order provide that the provisions of the Cereals Marketing Act 1965 shall apply in relation to any such crop falling within subsection (2) below as may be specified in the order as if it were a kind of cereals and, in the case of a crop grown in the United Kingdom, a kind of home-grown cereals within the meaning of that Act.

(2) The crops referred to in subsection (1) above are—
  (a) herbage seed, flax and any seed grown with a view to the production of oil from it;
  (b) peas and beans grown for harvesting in a dried state;
  (c) any crop (except grass) normally grown only for use in feeding livestock;
  (d) any other arable crop (except sugar, hops, potatoes or any horticultural produce within the meaning of section 8(1) of the Horticulture Act 1960).

(3) Before making an order under this section in respect of any crop the Ministers shall consult the Home-Grown Cereals Authority and such persons or organisations as appear to them to represent the interests concerned.

(4) An order under this section may make such modifications of the Cereals Marketing Act 1965 as the Ministers consider necessary or expedient in consequence of the provisions of the order.

(5) The power to make an order under this section shall be exercisable by statutory instrument and no such order shall be made unless a draft of it has been laid before and approved by a resolution of each House of Parliament.

(6) In this section "the Ministers" has the same meaning as in that Act.

(7) In section 24 of that Act (interpretation)—

    (*a*) in subsection (2)—

        (i) in the definition of "home-grown cereals" for the words "or rye" there shall be substituted the words "rye, maize or triticale", and

        (ii) after the definition of "related product" there shall be inserted—

        " 'wheat' includes durum wheat"; and

    (*b*) in subsection (3) for the words "and rye" there shall be substituted the words "rye, maize and triticale".

Constitution and levy schemes of Meat and Livestock Commission

7.—(1) In section 1(3) of the Agriculture Act 1967 (maximum number of members of the Meat and Livestock Commission) for the word "ten" there shall be substituted the word "fifteen".

(2) In section 13 of that Act (levy to meet the Commission's expenses)—

    (*a*) at the end of subsection (1) there shall be inserted the words "; and a levy scheme may make different provision in relation to charges to be imposed to meet expenses incurred by the Commission for different purposes";

    (*b*) after that subsection there shall be inserted—

        (1A) Before submitting a levy scheme under subsection (1) above the Commission may in such manner as they consider appropriate consult such persons as appear to them to represent the interests concerned";

    (*c*) in subsection (4) (maximum charges)—

        (i) the word "and" at the end of paragraph (*a*) shall be omitted, and

        (ii) at the end of paragraph (*b*) there shall be inserted the words "and

        (*c*) may differ between the different classes or descriptions of persons chargeable";

    (*d*) in subsection (6) (provision in levy schemes for persons on whom levy imposed to recover all or a specified part of sums paid by them from others) the words "all or a specified part of" shall be omitted; and

    (*e*) after that subsection there shall be inserted—

        "(6A) Where a levy scheme makes such provision as is mentioned in subsection (6) above it shall—

        (*a*) authorise the Commission from time to time to determine the proportion of the sums paid under the levy scheme which shall be recoverable;

        (*b*) specify whether the Commission may determine that the whole of those sums shall be recoverable and, if not, the maximum proportion of them which they may determine shall be recoverable; and

        (*c*) specify whether the Commission may determine that none of those sums shall be recoverable and, if not, the minimum proportion of them which they may determine shall be recoverable.".

Constitution and funding of Food from Britain

8.—(1) The Agricultural Marketing Act 1983 shall have effect subject to the following amendments (being amendments relating to the constitution and funding of Food from Britain).

(2) In section 1(2) (Food from Britain to consist of no fewer than thirteen and no more than fifteen members) for the word "fifteen" there shall be substituted the words "twenty-one".

(3) In section 7 (grants etc. by Ministers)—

  (a) at the end of subsection (1) there shall be inserted the words "and such grants may be made subject to such conditions as the Ministers may with the approval of the Treasury impose"; and

  (b) at the end of subsection (2) there shall be inserted the words "and any such sums may be lent subject to such conditions as the Ministers may with the approval of the Treasury impose".

(4) For paragraph 5 of Schedule 1 (payment by Ministers of remuneration etc. to members of Food from Britain) there shall be substituted—

  "5. Food from Britain may—

  (a) pay to its members such remuneration (whether by way of salary or fees) and such travelling or other allowances as it may determine;

  (b) pay such pension, or make such payments towards the provision of a pension, to or in respect of any of its members as it may determine; and

  (c) if it appears to it that there are special circumstances which make it right that a person should receive compensation on ceasing to be a member, pay him such amount by way of compensation as it may determine.".

(5) In paragraph 6 of that Schedule (amount of remuneration etc. of members of committees of Food from Britain to be determined by Food from Britain with the approval of the Ministers and the Treasury) the words "with the approval of the Ministers and the Treasury" shall be omitted.

(6) In paragraph 11(2) of that Schedule (amount of remuneration etc. of officers and servants of Food from Britain to be determined by Food from Britain with the approval of the Ministers and the Treasury) the words "with the approval of the Ministers and the consent of the Treasury", in each place where they occur, and the words "with such approval" shall be omitted.

Abolition of Eggs Authority

9.—(1) On the appointed date the property, rights and liabilities of the Eggs Authority shall vest in the Ministers.

(2) The accounting period of the Authority in which the day preceeding the appointed date falls shall end with that day (if it would not otherwise have done so) and as soon as the Ministers are satisfied that the requirements of section 20 of the Agriculture Act 1970 (reports and accounts) have been complied with in respect of that and previous accounting periods, they shall by order abolish the Authority; and any liabilities incurred by the Authority after the appointed date in complying with that section or otherwise shall become liabilities of the Ministers.

(3) Until an order is made under subsection (2) above abolishing the Authority they shall exercise their functions solely in accordance with directions given to them by the Ministers with a view to bringing the activities of the Authority to an end.

(4) If after the abolition of the Authority it appears to the Ministers that any property vested in them by virtue of this section is not required

for the purpose of satisfying the liabilities vested in them by virtue of this section, the Ministers may dispose of that property for the benefit of persons engaged by way of business in the production, marketing or processing of eggs in such manner as the Ministers think appropriate.

(5) In this section "appointed date" means such date as the Ministers may by order specify for the purposes of subsection (1) above and any expressions used in this section which are defined in section 1 of the Agriculture Act 1970 shall be construed in accordance with that section.

(6) The power to make an order under this section shall be exercisable by statutory instrument.

Repeal of certain ministerial powers concerning eggs

10. Section 25 (power to regulate retail sales of eggs) and section 26 (assistance for certain transport of eggs by sea) of the Agriculture Act 1970 shall cease to have effect.

Consolidation of agricultural marketing scheme

11. After paragraph 5 of Schedule 1 to the Agricultural Marketing Act 1958 (amendment and revocation of agricultural marketing schemes) there shall be inserted—

"5A.—(1) Where the Minister considers it appropriate to do so he may—

(*a*) prepare a consolidation of any scheme as it has effect with amendments ("the amended scheme"); and

(*b*) by order revoke the amended scheme and approve the consolidated scheme.

(2) An order made by virtue of this paragraph—

(*a*) shall state that it is made only for the purposes of consolidation; and

(*b*) may contain such transitional and consequential provision as the Minister considers necessary or expedient.".

Validation of Apple and Pear Development Council orders

12. The Apple and Pear Development Council Order 1980 and the Apple and Pear Development Council (Amendment) Order 1980 shall be deemed to have been validly made notwithstanding that they were made by the Minister of Agriculture, Fisheries and Food acting alone rather than by that Minister and the Secretary of State acting jointly.

Compensation to tenants for milk quotas

Compensation to outgoing tenants for milk quota

13. Schedule 1 to this Act shall have effect in connection with the payment to certain agricultural tenants on the termination of their tenancies of compensation in respect of milk quota (within the meaning of that Schedule).

Compensation to outgoing tenants for milk quota: Scotland

14. Schedule 2 to this Act shall have effect in connection with the payment to outgoing tenants who are—

(*a*) tenants of agricultural holdings within the meaning of the Agricultural Holdings (Scotland) Act 1949;

(*b*) landholders within the meaning of section 2 of the Small Landholders (Scotland) Act 1911;

(*c*) statutory small tenants within the meaning of section 32(1) of that Act;

(*d*) crofters within the meaning of section 3(2) of the Crofters (Scotland) Act 1955,
of compensation in respect of milk quotas.

Rent arbitrations: milk quotas

15.—(1) Where there is a reference under section 12 of the Agricultural Holdings Act 1986 (arbitration of rent) in respect of land which comprises or is part of a holding in relation to which quota is registered under the Dairy Produce Quotas Regulations 1986 which was transferred to the tenant by virtue of a transaction the cost of which was borne wholly or partly by him, the arbitrator shall (subject to any agreement between the landlord and tenant to the contrary) disregard—

(*a*) in a case where the land comprises the holding, any increase in the rental value of the land which is due to that quota (or, as the case may be, the corresponding part of that quota); or

(*b*) in a case where the land is part of the holding, any increase in that value which is due to so much of that quota (or part) as would fall to be apportioned to the land under those Regulations on a change of occupation of the land.

(2) In determining for the purposes of this section whether quota was transferred to a tenant by virtue of a transaction the cost of which was borne wholly or partly by him—

(*a*) any payment made by the tenant in consideration for the grant or assignment to him of the tenancy or any previous tenancy of any land comprised in the holding, shall be disregarded;

(*b*) any person who would be treated under paragraph 2, 3 or 4 of Schedule 1 to this Act as having had quota transferred to him or having paid the whole or part of the cost of any transaction for the purposes of a claim under that Schedule shall be so treated for the purposes of this section; and

(*c*) any person who would be so treated under paragraph 4 of that Schedule if a sub-tenancy to which his tenancy is subject had terminated, shall be so treated for the purposes of this section.

(3) In this section—
   "quota" and "holding" have the same meanings as in the Dairy Produce Quotas Regulations 1986;
   "tenant" and "tenancy" have the same meanings as in the Agricultural Holdings Act 1986.

(4) Section 95 of that Act (Crown land) applies to this section as it applies to the provisions of that Act.

Rent arbitrations: milk quotas, Scotland

16.—(1) Paragraph 1 and the other provisions of Schedule 2 to this Act referred to therein shall have effect for the interpretation of this section, as they do in relation to that Schedule.

(2) This section applies where an arbiter or the Scottish Land Court is dealing with a reference under—

(*a*) section 6 of the 1886 Act;
(*b*) section 32(7) of the 1911 Act;
(*c*) section 7 of the 1949 Act; or
(*d*) section 5(3) of the 1955 Act,

(determination of rent) and the tenant has milk quota, including transferred quota by virtue of a transaction the cost of which was borne wholly or partly by him, registered as his in relation to a holding consisting of or including the tenancy.

(3) Where this section applies, the arbiter or, as the case may be, the Land Court shall disregard any increase in the rental value of the tenancy which is due to—

(*a*) where the tenancy comprises the holding, the proportion of the transferred quota which reflects the proportion of the cost of the transaction borne by the tenant;

(*b*) where such transferred quota affects part only of the tenancy, that proportion of so much of the transferred quota as would fall to be apportioned to the tenancy under the 1986 Regulations on a change of occupation of the tenancy.

(4) For the purposes of determining whether transferred quota has been acquired by virtue of a transaction the cost of which was borne wholly or partly by the tenant any payment by a tenant when he was granted a lease, or when a lease was assigned to him, shall be disregarded.

(5) Paragraph 3 of Schedule 2 to this Act (in so far as it relates to transferred quota) shall apply in relation to the operation of this section as it applies in relation to the operation of that Schedule.

(6) This section shall apply where paragraph 4 of Schedule 2 to this Act applies, and in any question between the original landlord and the head tenant, this section shall apply as if any transferred quota acquired by the sub-tenant by virtue of any transaction during the subsistence of the sub-lease had been acquired by the head tenant by virtue of that transaction.

(7) Section 86 of the 1949 Act (Crown land) shall have effect in relation to this section as it does in relation to that Act.

Conservation

Duty to balance interests in exercise of agricultural functions

17.—(1) In discharging any functions connected with agriculture in relation to any land the Minister shall, so far as is consistent with the proper and efficient discharge of those functions, have regard to and endeavour to achieve a reasonable balance between the following considerations—

(*a*) the promotion and maintenance of a stable and efficient agricultural industry;

(*b*) the economic and social interests of rural areas;

(*c*) the conservation and enhancement of the natural beauty and amenity of the countryside (including its flora and fauna and geological and physiographical features) and of any features of archaeological interest there; and

(*d*) the promotion of the enjoyment of the countryside by the public.

(2) In this section—

"agriculture" has the same meaning as in the Agriculture Act 1947 or, in Scotland, the Agriculture (Scotland) Act 1948; and

"the Minister" means—

(*a*) in relation to land in England, the Minister of Agriculture, Fisheries and Food; and

(*b*) in relation to land in Wales or Scotland, the Secretary of State.

Designation and management of environmentally sensitive areas

18.—(1) If it appears to the Minister that it is particularly desirable—

(*a*) to conserve and enhance the natural beauty of an area;

(*b*) to conserve the flora or fauna or geological or physiographical features of an area; or

(*c*) to protect buildings or other objects of archaeological, architectural or historic interest in an area, and that the maintenance or adoption of particular agricultural methods is likely to facilitate such conservation, enhancement or protection, he may, with the consent of the Treasury and after consulting the persons mentioned in subsection (2) below as to the inclusion of the area in the order and the features for which conservation, enhancement or protection is desirable, by order designate that area as an environmentally sensitive area.

(2) The persons referred to in subsection (1) above are—

    (a) in the case of an area in England, the Secretary of State, the Countryside Commission and the Nature Conservancy Council;

    (b) in the case of an area in Wales, the Countryside Commission and the Nature Conservancy Council; and

    (c) in the case of an area in Scotland, the Countryside Commission for Scotland and the Nature Conservancy Council.

(3) If the Minister considers that any of the purposes mentioned in paragraphs (a) to (c) of subsection (1) above is likely to be facilitated in a designated area by doing so, he may make an agreement with any person having an interest in agricultural land in, or partly in, the area by which that person agrees in consideration of payments to be made by the Minister to manage the land in accordance with the agreement.

(4) An order under this section designating an area may specify—

    (a) the requirements as to agricultural practices, methods and operations and the installation or use of equipment which must be included in agreements under subsection (3) above as respects land in the area;

    (b) the period or minimum period for which such agreements must impose such requirements;

    (c) the provisions which must be included in such agreements concerning the breach of such requirements; and

    (d) the rates or maximum rates at which payments may be made by the Minister under such agreements and the matters in respect of which such payments may be made.

(5) Subject to the foregoing provisions of this section, an agreement under subsection (3) above may contain such provisions as the Minister thinks fit and, in particular, such provisions as he considers are likely to facilitate such conservation, enhancement or protection as is mentioned in subsection (1) above.

(6) The Minister shall not make an agreement with any person under subsection (3) above in respect of any land unless that person has certified to the Minister—

    (a) that no person other than he is the owner of the land; or

    (b) that he has notified any other person who is an owner of the land of his intention to make an agreement under subsection (3) above in respect of the land;

and in this subsection references to the owner of the land are to the estate owner in respect of the fee simple in the land or, in Scotland, the absolute owner of the land within the meaning of section 93 of the Agricultural Holdings (Scotland) Act 1949.

(7) The provisions of an agreement under subsection (3) above with any person interested in any land in England or Wales shall, unless the agreement otherwise provides, be binding on persons deriving title under or from that person and be enforceable by the Minister against those persons accordingly.

(8) Where agreements have been made under subsection (3) above with persons having an interest in land in a designated area the Minister shall arrange for the effect on the area as a whole of the performance of the agreements to be kept under review and shall from time to time publish such information as he considers appropriate about those effects.

(9) Schedule 2 to the Forestry Act 1967 (power for tenant for life and others to enter into forestry dedication covenants, or, in Scotland, forestry dedication agreements) shall apply to agreements under subsection (3) above as it applies to forestry dedication covenants or, as the case may be, forestry dedication agreements.

(10) This section applies to land an interest in which belongs to Her Majesty in right of the Crown or to the Duchy of Lancaster, the Duchy of Cornwall or a Government department or which is held in trust for Her Majesty for the purposes of a Government department, but no agreement under subsection (3) above shall be made as respects land to which this subsection applies without the consent of the appropriate authority.

(11) In this section—

"agricultural" has the same meaning as in the Agriculture Act 1947 or, in Scotland, the Agriculture (Scotland) Act 1948;

"the appropriate authority" has the same meaning as in section 101(11) of the National Parks and Access to the Countryside Act 1949;

"the Minister" means—

(a) in relation to an area in England, the Minister of Agriculture, Fisheries and Food; and

(b) in relation to an area in Wales or Scotland, the Secretary of State.

(12) The power to make an order under this section shall be exercisable by statutory instrument and any statutory instrument containing such an order shall be subject to annulment in pursuance of a resolution of either House of Parliament.

(13) An Order in Council under paragraph 1(1)(b) of Schedule 1 to the Northern Ireland Act 1974 (legislation for Northern Ireland in the interim period) which states that it is made only for purposes corresponding to those of this section—

(a) shall not be subject to paragraph 1(4) and (5) of that Schedule (affirmative resolution of both Houses of Parliament); but

(b) shall be subject to annulment in pursuance of a resolution of either House.

Supplementary provisions regarding agreements under s.18(3) in Scotland

19.—(1) Where a person having an interest of a kind described in section 18(3) above in land in Scotland, being an interest which enables him to bind the land, enters into an agreement under that subsection—

(a) where the land is registered in the Land Register of Scotland, the agreement may be registered in that Register;

(b) in any other case the agreement may be recorded in the appropriate Division of the General Register of Sasines.

(2) An agreement registered or recorded under subsection (1) above shall be enforceable at the instance of the Secretary of State against persons deriving title to the land (including any person acquiring right to a tenancy by assignation or succession) from the person who entered into the agreement; provided that such an agreement shall not be enforceable against a third party who shall have in good faith and for value acquired right (whether completed by infeftment or not) to the land prior to the agreement being registered or recorded as aforesaid, or against any person deriving title from such third party.

(3) Notwithstanding the terms of any agreement registered or recorded under subsection (1) above, the parties to the agreement or any persons deriving title from them may at any time agree to terminate it; and such

an agreement to terminate it shall be registered or recorded in the same manner as was the original agreement.

(4) A grazings committee appointed under section 24 of the Crofters (Scotland) Act 1955 may, with the consent of a majority of the crofters ordinarily resident in the township, enter into an agreement under section 18(3) above in relation to any part of the common grazings and may agree to the revocation or variation of any such agreement, and such agreement, revocation or variation shall be binding upon all their successors.

(5) In the case of an agreement of a kind referred to in subsection (4) above, the payments by the Secretary of State shall be made to the grazings committee and shall be applied by them either—

(*a*) by division among the crofters who share in the common grazings in proportion to their respective rights therein; or

(*b*) subject to subsection (6) below, in carrying out works for the improvement of the common grazings or the fixed equipment required in connection therewith.

(6) A grazings committee to whom such a payment as is referred to in subsection (5) above has been made and who are proposing to apply the payment in carrying out works in accordance with paragraph (*b*) of that subsection shall give notice in writing to each crofter sharing in the common grazings of their proposals: and any such crofter may within one month of the date of such notice make representations in respect of the proposals to the Crofters Commission who may approve them with or without modifications or reject them.

(7) "Crofter" and other expressions used in any of subsections (4) to (6) above and in section 3 of the Crofters (Scotland) Act 1955 have the same meaning in this section as they have in that section as read with section 15(6) of the Crofters (Scotland) Act 1961.

EEC farm grants relating to areas of special scientific interest or National Parks etc.

20.—(1) The provisions of this section shall have effect for the purpose of amending certain provisions of the Wildlife and Countryside Act 1981 which apply to grants under schemes made under section 29 of the Agriculture Act 1970 so as to apply them to certain agricultural grants under regulations made under section 2(2) of the European Communities Act 1972.

(2) In subsection (1) of section 32 of the said Act of 1981 (duties of agriculture Ministers to exercise functions so as to further conservation where applications are made to them for grants under such schemes with respect to areas of special scientific interest)—

(*a*) for the words "a grant under a scheme made under section 29 of the Agriculture Act 1970 (farm capital grants)" there shall be substituted the words "a farm captal grant"; and

(*b*) in paragraph (*a*) for the words "the scheme and section 29 of the said Act of 1970" there shall be substituted the words "the grant provisions".

(3) For subsection (3) of that section (definition of "the appropriate Minister") there shall be substituted—

"(3) In this section—

'the appropriate Minister' means the Minister responsible for determining the application;

'farm capital grant' means—

(*a*) a grant under a scheme made under section 29 of the Agriculture Act 1970; or

(*b*) a grant under regulations made under section 2(2) of the European Communities Act 1972 to a person carrying on an agricultural business within the meaning of those regulations in respect of expenditure incurred or to be incurred for the purposes of or in connection with that business, being expenditure of a capital nature or incurred in connection with expenditure of a capital nature;

'grant provisions' means—

(i) in the case of such a grant as is mentioned in paragraph (*a*) above, the scheme under which the grant is made and section 29 of the Agriculture Act 1970; and

(ii) in the case of such a grant as is mentioned in paragraph (*b*) above, the regulations under which the grant is made and the Community instrument in pursuance of which the regulations were made.".

(4) In subsection (3) of section 41 of the said Act of 1981 (which makes similar provision in relation to land which is in a National Park or an area specified for the purposes of that subsection)—

(*a*) for the words "a grant under a scheme made under section 29 of the Agriculture Act 1970 (farm capital grants)" there shall be substituted the words "a farm capital grant";

(*b*) in paragraph (*a*) for the words "the scheme and the said section 29" there shall be substituted the words "the grant provisions".

(5) In subsection (5) of the said section 41 (definitions) for the definitions of "agricultural business" and "the appropriate Minister" there shall be substituted—

" 'agricultural business' has the same meaning as in section 29 of the Agriculture Act 1970;

'the appropriate Minister', 'farm capital grant' and 'grant provisions' have the same meanings as in section 32;".

(6) For the definition of "farm capital grant" in subsection (4) of section 50 of that Act (payments under certain agreements offered by authorities where applications for grants under section 29 of the said Act of 1970 are refused) there shall be substituted—

" 'farm capital grant' has the same meaning as in section 32;".

Amendment of s.135 of Highways Act 1980

21. In subsection (1) of section 135 of the Highways Act 1980 (temporary diversion of path or way ploughed up under section 134) for the words "3 weeks", in each place where they appear, there shall be substituted the words "2 weeks".

Farm grants

Farm capital grants: ancillary businesses etc.

22.—(1) In section 28 of the Agriculture Act 1970 (interpretation of provisions relating to capital and other grants) at the end of the definition of "agricultural business" there shall be inserted the words "and includes any other business, of a kind for the time being specified by an order made by the appropriate authority, which is carried on by a person also carrying on a business consisting in or partly in the pursuit of agriculture and is carried on on the same or adjacent land".

(2) The existing provisions of that section shall become subsection (1) of that section and after that subsection there shall be inserted—

"(2) An order under subsection (1) above shall be made by statutory instrument and any statutory instrument containing such an order shall be subject to annulment in pursuance of a resolution of either House of Parliament.".

Supplemental

Financial provisions

23.—(1) There shall be paid out of money provided by Parliament—
(*a*) any expenses incurred by a Minister by virtue of this Act; and
(*b*) any increase attributable to this Act in the sums payable out of money so provided under any other Act.

(2) Any sums received by a Minister under this Act shall be paid into the Consolidated Fund.

Short title, commencement, consequential amendments, repeals and extent

24.—(1) This Act may be cited as the Agriculture Act 1986.

(2) Sections 8, 10, 13 to 16 above and the repeals consequential on sections 8 to 10 above shall come into force on such date as the Ministers acting jointly may by order made by statutory instrument appoint and the remaining provisions of this Act (except for sections 12 and 18(13)) shall come into force at the end of the period of two months beginning with the day on which it is passed; and in this subsection "the Ministers" means the Ministers responsible for agriculture in the parts of the United Kingdom to which the provision in question extends.

(3) An order under subsection (2) above may appoint different dates for the coming into force of different provisions.

(4) The provisions mentioned in Schedule 3 to this Act shall have effect subject to the amendments there specified (being amendments consequential on the provisions of this Act).

(5) The enactments mentioned in Schedule 4 to this Act (which include some spent provisions) are hereby repealed to the extent specified in the third column of that Schedule.

(6) Sections 1, 13, 15, 18(7) and 21 above and Schedule 1 to this Act do not extend to Scotland.

(7) The provisions of this Act do not extend to Northern Ireland except for sections 4 to 6, 8, 9, 11, 18(13) and 22, this section and the provisions of Schedules 3 and 4 which affect enactments extending there.

SCHEDULES

Section 13   SCHEDULE 1

TENANTS' COMPENSATION FOR MILK QUOTA

PART I

RIGHT TO COMPENSATION

Tenants' rights to compensation

1.—(1) Subject to the following provisions of this Schedule, where on the termination of the tenancy of any land the tenant has milk quota registered as his in relation to a holding consisting of or including the land, the tenant shall be entitled, on quitting the land, to obtain from his landlord a payment—
   (*a*) if the tenant had milk quota allocated to him in relation to land comprised in the holding ("allocated quota"), in respect of so much of the relevant quota as consists of allocated quota; and
   (*b*) if the tenant had milk quota allocated to him as aforesaid or was in occupation of the land as a tenant on 2nd April 1984 (whether or not under the tenancy which is terminating), in respect of so much of the relevant quota as consists of transferred quota transferred to him by virtue of a transaction the cost of which was borne wholly or partly by him.

(2) In sub-paragraph (1) above—

"the relevant quota" means—
> (*a*) in a case where the holding mentioned in sub-paragraph (1) above consists only of the land subject to the tenancy, the milk quota registered in relation to the holding; and
> (*b*) otherwise, such part of that milk quota falls to be apportioned to that land on the termination of the tenancy;

"transferred quota" means milk quota transferred to the tenant by virtue of the transfer to him of the whole or part of a holding.

(3) A tenant shall not be entitled to more than one payment under this paragraph in respect of the same land.

Succession on death or retirement of tenant

2.—(1) This paragraph applies where on the termination of the tenancy of any land after 2nd April 1984 a new tenancy of the land or part of the land has been granted to a different tenant ("the new tenant") and that tenancy—

(*a*) was obtained by virtue of a direction under section 39 or 53 of the Agricultural Holdings Act 1986 (direction for grant of tenancy to successor on death or retirement of previous tenant);

(*b*) was granted (following a direction under section 39 of that Act) in circumstances within section 45(6) of that Act (new tenancy granted by agreement to persons entitled to tenancy under direction); or

(*c*) is such a tenancy as is mentioned in section 37(1)(*b*) or (2) of that Act (tenancy granted by agreement to close relative).

(2) Where this paragraph applies—

(*a*) any milk quota allocated or transferred to the former tenant (or treated as having been allocated or transferred to him) in respect of the land which is subject to the new tenancy shall be treated as if it had instead been allocated or transferred to the new tenant; and

(*b*) in a case where milk quota is treated under paragraph (*a*) above as having been transferred to the new tenant, he shall be treated for the purposes of any claim in respect of that quota—

> (i) as if he had paid so much of the cost of the transaction by virtue of which the milk quota was transferred as the former tenant bore (or is treated as having borne); and

> (ii) in a case where the former tenant was in occupation of the land on 2nd April 1984 (or is treated as having been in occupation of the land on that date), as if he had been in occupation of it on that date.

(3) Sub-paragraph (1) above applies in relation to the grant of a new tenancy before the date on which the Agricultural Holdings Act 1986 comes into force as if the references in that sub-paragraph to sections 39, 53 and 45(6) of that Act were references to section 20 of the Agriculture (Miscellaneous Provisions) Act 1976, paragraph 5 of Schedule 2 to the Agricultural Holdings Act 1984 and section 23(6) of the said Act of 1976 respectively.

Assignments

3. Where the tenancy of any land has been assigned after 2nd April 1984 (whether by deed or by operation of law)—

(*a*) any milk quota allocated or transferred to the assignor (or treated as having been allocated or transferred to him) in respect of the land shall be treated as if it had instead been allocated or transferred to the assignee; and

(*b*) in a case where milk quota is treated under paragraph (*a*) above as having been transferred to the assignee, he shall be treated for the purposes of any claim in respect of that quota—

> (i) as if he had paid so much of the cost of the transaction by virtue of which the milk quota was transferred as the assignor bore (or is treated as having borne); and

> (ii) in a case where the assignor was in occupation of the land on 2nd April 1984 (or is treated as having been in occupation of the land on that date), as if he had been in occupation of it on that date;

and accordingly the assignor shall not be entitled to a payment under paragraph 1 above in respect of that land.

Sub-tenancies

4. Where the sub-tenancy of any land terminates after 2nd April 1984 then, for the purposes of determining the sub-landlord's entitlement under paragraph 1 above—

(*a*) any milk quota allocated or transferred to the sub-tenant (or treated as having been allocated or transferred to him) in respect of the land shall be treated as if it had instead been allocated or transferred to the sub-landlord;

(*b*) in the case where milk quota is treated under paragraph (*a*) above as having been transferred to the sub-landlord, he shall be treated for the purposes of any claim in respect of that quota—

(i) as if he had paid so much of the cost of the transaction by virtue of which the milk quota was transferred as the sub-tenant bore (or is treated as having borne); and

(ii) in a case where the sub-tenant was in occupation of the land on 2nd April 1984 (or is treated as having been in occupation of the land on that date), as if he had been in occupation of it on that date;

(*c*) if the sub-landlord does not occupy the land after the sub-tenancy has ended and the sub-tenant has quitted the land, the sub-landlord shall be taken to have quitted the land when the sub-tenant quitted it.

Part II

Amount of Compensation Payable

Calculation of payment

5.—(1) The amount of the payment to which the tenant of any land is entitled under paragraph 1 above on the termination of his tenancy shall be determined in accordance with the following provisions of this paragraph.

(2) The amount of the payment to which the tenant is entitled under paragraph 1 above in respect of allocated quota shall be an amount equal—

(*a*) in a case where the allocated quota exceeds the standard quota for the land, to the value of the sum of—

(i) the tenant's fraction of the standard quota, and

(ii) the amount of the excess;

(*b*) in a case where the allocated quota is equal to the standard quota, to the value of the tenant's fraction of the allocated quota; and

(*c*) in a case where the allocated quota is less than the standard quota, to the value of such proportion of the tenant's fraction of the allocated quota as the allocated quota bears to the standard quota.

(3) The amount of the payment the tenant is entitled to under paragraph 1 above in respect of transferred quota shall be an amount equal—

(*a*) in a case where the tenant bore the whole of the cost of the transaction by virtue of which the transferred quota was transferred to him, to the value of the transferred quota; and

(*b*) in a case where the tenant bore only part of that cost, to the value of the corresponding part of the transferred quota.

"Standard quota"

6.—(1) Subject to the following provisions of this paragraph the standard quota for any land for the purposes of this Schedule shall be calculated by multiplying the relevant number of hectares by the prescribed quota per hectare; and for the purposes of this paragraph—

(*a*) "the relevant number of hectares" means the average number of hectares of the land in question used during the relevant period for the feeding of dairy cows kept on the land or, if different, the average number of hectares of the land which could reasonably be expected to have been so used (having regard to the number of grazing animals other than dairy cows kept on the land during that period); and

(*b*) "the prescribed quota per hectare" means such number of litres as the Minister may from time to time by order prescribe for the purposes of this sub-paragraph.

(2) Where by virtue of the quality of the land in question or climatic conditions in the area the amount of milk which could reasonably be expected to have been produced from one hectare of the land during the relevant period ("the reasonable amount") is greater or less than the prescribed average yield per hectare, then sub-paragraph (1) above shall not apply and the standard quota shall be calculated by multiplying the relevant number of hectares

by such proportion of the prescribed quota per hectare as the reasonable amount bears to the prescribed average yield per hectare; and the Minister shall by order prescribe the amount of milk to be taken as the average yield per hectare for the purposes of this sub-paragraph.

(3) Where the relevant quota of the land includes milk quota allocated in pursuance of an award of quota made by the Dairy Produce Quota Tribunal for England and Wales which has not been allocated in full, the standard quota for the land shall be reduced by the amount by which the milk quota allocated in pursuance of the award falls short of the amount awarded (or, in a case where only part of the milk quota allocated in pursuance of the award is included in the relevant quota, by the corresponding proportion of that shortfall).

(4) In sub-paragraph (3) above the references to milk quota allocated in pursuance of an award of quota include references to quota allocated by virtue of the amount awarded not originally having been allocated in full.

(5) In this paragraph—

(a) references to land used for the feeding of dairy cows kept on the land do not include land used for growing cereal crops for feeding to dairy cows in the form of loose grain; and

(b) references to dairy cows are to cows kept for milk production (other than uncalved heifers).

(6) An order under this paragraph may make different provision for different cases.

(7) The power to make an order under this paragraph shall be exercisable by statutory instrument and any instrument containing such an order shall be subject to annulment in pursuance of a resolution of either House of Parliament.

"Tenant's fraction"

7.—(1) For the purposes of this Schedule "the tenant's fraction" means the fraction of which—

(a) the numerator is the annual rental value at the end of the relevant period of the tenant's dairy improvements and fixed equipment; and

(b) the denominator is the sum of that value and such part of the rent payable by the tenant in respect of the relevant period as is attributable to the land used in that period for the feeding, accommodation or milking of dairy cows kept on the land.

(2) For the purposes of sub-paragraph (1)(a) above the rental value of the tenant's dairy improvements and fixed equipment shall be taken to be the amount which would fall to be disregarded under paragraph 2(1) of Schedule 2 to the Agricultural Holdings Act 1986 on a reference made in respect of the land in question under section 12 of that Act (arbitration of rent), so far as that amount is attributable to tenant's improvements to, or tenant's fixed equipment on, land used for the feeding, accommodation or milking of dairy cows kept on the land in question.

(3) Where—

(a) the relevant period is less than or greater than 12 months; or

(b) rent was only payable by the tenant in respect of part of the relevant period,

the average rent payable in respect of one month in the relevant period or, as the case may be, in that part shall be determined and the rent referred to in sub-paragraph (1)(b) above shall be taken to be the corresponding annual amount.

(4) For the purposes of sub-paragraph (2) above "tenant's improvements" and "tenant's fixed equipment" have the same meanings as in paragraph 2 of Schedule 2 to the 1986 Act, except that—

(a) any allowance made or benefit given by the landlord after the end of the relevant period in consideration of the execution of improvements wholly or partly at the expense of the tenant shall be disregarded for the purposes of sub-paragraph 2(a) of that paragraph;

(b) any compensation received by the tenant after the end of the relevant period, in respect of any improvement or fixed equipment shall be disregarded for the purposes of sub-paragraph (3) of that paragraph; and

(c) where paragraph 2 above applies in respect of any land, improvements or equipment which would be regarded as tenant's improvements or equipment on the termination of the former tenant's tenancy (if he were entitled to a payment under this Schedule in respect of that land) shall be regarded as the new tenant's improvements or equipment.

"Relevant period"

8. In this Schedule "the relevant period" means—
   (a) the period in relation to which the allocated quota was determined; or
   (b) where it was determined in relation to more than one period, the period in relation to which the majority was determined of, if equal amounts were determind in relation to different periods, the later of those periods.

Valuation of milk quota

9. The value of milk quota to be taken into account for the purposes of paragraph 5 above is the value of the milk quota at the time of the termination of the tenancy in question and in determining that value at that time there shall be taken into account such evidence as is available, including evidence as to the sums being paid for interests in land—
   (a) in cases where milk quota is registered in relation to the land; and
   (b) in cases where no milk quota is so registered.

Part III

Supplemental Provisions

Determination of standard quota and tenant's fraction before end of tenancy

10.—(1) Where, on the termination of a tenancy of any land, the tenant may be entitled to a payment under paragraph 1 above, the landlord or tenant may at any time before the termination of the tenancy by notice in writing served on the other demand that the determination of the standard quota for the land or the tenant's fraction shall be referred to arbitration.

(2) On a reference under this paragraph the arbitrator shall determine the standard quota for the land or, as the case may be, the tenant's fraction (so far as determinable at the date of the reference).

(3) Section 84 of the Agricultural Holdings Act 1986 (arbitrations) shall apply as if the matters mentioned in this paragraph were required by that Act to be determined by arbitration under that Act.

Settlement of tenant's claim on termination of tenancy

11.—(1) Subject to the provisions of this paragraph, any claim arising under paragraph 1 above shall be determined by arbitration under the Agricultural Holdings Act 1986 and no such claim shall be enforceable unless before the expiry of the period of two months from the termination of the tenancy the tenant serves notice in writing on his landlord of his intention to make the claim.

(2) The landlord and tenant may within the period of eight months from the termination of the tenancy by agreement in writing settle the claim but where the claim has not been settled during that period it shall be determined by arbitration under the Agricultural Holdings Act 1986.

(3) In any case where on the termination of the tenancy in question a new tenancy of the land or part of the land may be granted to a different tenant by virtue of a direction under section 39 of the Agricultural Holdings Act 1986 then, as respects any claim in respect of that land or part, references in sub-paragraphs (1) and (2) above to the termination of the tenancy shall be construed as references to the following time, namely—
   (a) in a case where no application is made under that section within the period within which such an application may be made, the expiry of that period;
   (b) in a case where every such application made within that period is withdrawn, the expiry of that period or the time when the last outstanding application is withdrawn (whichever is the later);
   (c) in a case where the Agricultural Land Tribunal refuse every such application for a direction under that section, the time when the last outstanding application is refused; and
   (d) in a case where the Tribunal give such a direction, the relevant time for the purposes of section 46 of that Act;
and no notice may be served under sub-paragraph (1) above before that time.

(4) Where a tenant lawfully remains in occupation of part of the land subject to the tenancy after the termination of the tenancy or, in a case where sub-paragraph (3) above applies, after the time substituted for the termination of the tenancy by virtue of that sub-paragraph, the references in sub-paragraphs (1) and (2) above to the termination of the tenancy shall be construed as references to the termination of the occupation.

(5) Section 84 of the Agricultural Holdings Act 1986 (arbitrations) shall apply as if the requirements of this paragraph were requirements of that Act, but paragraph 18 of Schedule 11 to that Act (arbitration award to fix day for payment not later than one month after award) shall have effect for the purposes of this paragraph as if for the words "one month" there were substituted the words "three months".

(6) Where—
    (*a*) before the termination of the tenancy of any land the landlord and tenant have agreed in writing the amount of the standard quota for the land or the tenant's fraction or the value of milk quota which is to be used for the purpose of calculating the payment to which the tenant will be entitled under this Schedule on the termination of the tenancy; or
    (*b*) the standard quota or the tenant's fraction has been determined by arbitration in pursuance of paragraph 10 above,
the arbitrator determining the claim under this paragraph shall, subject to sub-paragraph (7) below, award payment in accordance with that agreement or determination.

(7) Where it appears to the arbitrator that any circumstances relevant to the agreement or determination mentioned in sub-paragraph (6) above were materially different at the time of the termination of the tenancy from those at the time the agreement or determination was made, he shall disregard so much of the agreement or determination as appears to him to be affected by the change in circumstances.

Enforcement

12. Section 85 of the Agricultural Holdings Act 1986 (enforcement) and section 86(1), (3) and (4) of that Act (power of landlord to obtain charge on holding) shall apply to any sum which becomes due to a tenant by virtue of this Schedule as they apply to the sums mentioned in those sections.

Termination of tenancy of part of tenanted land

13. References in this Schedule to the termination of a tenancy of land include references to the resumption of possession of part of the land subject to the tenancy—
    (*a*) by the landlord by virtue of section 31 or 43(2) of the Agricultural Holdings Act 1986 (notice to quit part);
    (*b*) by the landlord in pursuance of a provision in the contract of tenancy; or
    (*c*) by a person entitled to a severed part of the reversionary estate in the land by virtue of a notice to quit that part given to the tenant by virtue of section 140 of the Law of Property Act 1925;
and in the case mentioned in paragraph (*c*) above this Schedule shall apply as if the person resuming possession were the landlord of the land of which he resumes possession.

Severing of reversionary estate

14.—(1) Where the reversionary estate in the land is for the time being vested in more than one person in several parts, the tenant shall be entitled, on quitting all the land, to require that any amount payable to him under this Schedule shall be determined as if the reversionary estate were not so severed.

(2) Where sub-paragraph (1) above applies, the arbitrator shall, where necessary, apportion the amount awarded between the persons who for the purposes of this Schedule together constitute the landlord of the land, and any additional costs of the award caused by the apportionment shall be paid by those persons in such proportions as the arbitrator may determine.

Powers of limited owners

15. Notwithstanding that a landlord of any land is not the owner in fee simple of the land or, in a case where his interest is an interest in a leasehold, that he is not absolutely entitled

to the leasehold, he may for the purposes of this Schedule do anything which he might do if he were such an owner or, as the case may be, were so entitled.

Notices

16.—(1) Any notice under this Schedule shall be duly served on the person on whom it is to be served if it is delivered to him, or left at his proper address, or sent to him by post in a registered letter or by the recorded delivery service.

(2) Any such notice shall be duly served on an incorporated company or body if it is served on the secretary or clerk of the company or body.

(3) Any such notice to be served on a landlord or tenant of any land shall, where an agent or servant is responsible for the control of the management or farming, as the case may be, of the land, be duly served if served on that agent or servant.

(4) For the purposes of this paragraph and of section 7 of the Interpretation Act 1978 (service by post), the proper address of any person on whom any such notice is to be served shall, in the case of the secretary or clerk of an incorporated company or body, be that of the registered or principal office of the company or body, and in any other case be the last known address of the person in question.

(5) Unless or until the tenant of any land has received—
  (a) notice that the person who before that time was entitled to receive the rents and profits of the land ("the original landlord") has ceased to be so entitled; and
  (b) notice of the name and address of the person who has become entitled to receive the rents and profits.
any notice served on the original landlord by the tenant shall be deemed for the purposes of this Schedule to have been served on the landlord of the land.

Crown land

17.—(1) The provisions of this Schedule shall apply to land which belongs to Her Majesty in right of the Crown or to the Duchy of Lancaster, the Duchy of Cornwall or a Government department or which is held in trust for Her Majesty for the purposes of a Government department, subject in each case to such modifications as the Minister may by regulations prescribe.

(2) For the purposes of this Schedule—
  (a) as respects land belonging to Her Majesty in right of the Crown, the Crown Estate Commissioners or the proper officer or body having charge of the land for the time being, or if there is no such officer or body, such person as Her Majesty may appoint in writing under the Royal Sign Manual, shall represent Her Majesty and shall be deemed to be the landlord,
  (b) as respects land belonging to Her Majesty in right of the Duchy of Lancaster, the Chancellor of the Duchy shall represent Her Majesty and shall be deemed to be the landlord;
  (c) as respects land belonging to the Duchy of Cornwall, such person as the Duke of Cornwall or the possessor for the time being of the Duchy of Cornwall appoints shall represent the Duchy and shall be deemed to be the landlord and may do any act or thing which a landlord is authorised or required to do under this Act.

(3) Any sum payable under this Schedule by the Duke of Cornwall (or any other possessor for the time being of the Duchy of Cornwall) may be raised and paid as if it were an expense incurred in permanently improving the possessions of the Duchy as mentioned in section 8 of the Duchy of Cornwall Management Act 1863.

(4) Any sum payable under this Schedule by the Chancellor of the Duchy of Lancaster may—
  (a) be raised and paid as if it were an expense incurred in the improvement of land belonging to Her Majesty in right of the Duchy within section 25 of the Duchy of Lancaster Act 1817; or
  (b) be paid out of the annual revenues of the Duchy.

(5) The power to make regulations under this paragraph shall be exercisable by statutory instrument and any statutory instrument containing such regulations shall be subject to annulment in pursuance of a resolution of either House of Parliament.

Interpretation

18.—(1) In this Schedule—
  "allocated quota" has the meaning given in paragraph 1(1) above;

"holding" has the same meaning as in the 1986 Regulations;

"landlord" means any person for the time being entitled to receive the rents and profits of any land and "sub-landlord" shall be construed accordingly;

"milk quota" means—

    (*a*) in the case of a tenant registered in the direct sales register maintained under the 1986 Regulations, a direct sales quota (within the meaning of the 1986 Regulations); and

    (*b*) in the case of a tenant registered in the wholesale register maintained under those Regulations, a wholesale quota (within the meaning of those Regulations);

"the Minister" means—

    (*a*) in the case of land in England, the Minister of Agriculture, Fisheries and Food; and

    (*b*) in the case of land in Wales, the Secretary of State;

"registered", in relation to milk quota, means—

    (*a*) in the case of direct sales quota (within the meaning of the 1986 Regulations) registered in the direct sales register maintained under those Regulations; and

    (*b*) in the case of a wholesale quota (within the meaning of those Regulations) registered in a wholesale register maintained under those Regulations;

"relevant quota" has the meaning given in paragraph 1(2) above;

"standard quota" has the meaning given in paragraph 6 above;

"the 1986 Regulations" means the Dairy Produce Quotas Regulations 1986;

"tenancy" means a tenancy from year to year (including any arrangement which would have effect as if it were such a tenancy by virtue of section 2 of the Agricultural Holdings Act 1986 if it had not been approved by the Minister) or a tenancy to which section 3 of that Act applies (or would apply apart from section 5 of that Act); and "tenant" and "sub-tenant" shall be construed accordingly;

"tenant's fraction" has the meaning given in paragraph 7 above;

"termination", in relation to a tenancy, means the cesser of the letting of the land in question or the agreement for letting the land, by reason of effluxion of time or from any other cause;

"transferred quota" has the meaning given in paragraph 1(2) above.

(2) In this Schedule references to land used for the feeding of dairy cows kept on the land and to dairy cows have the same meaning as in paragraph 6 above.

(3) The designations of landlord and tenant shall continue to apply to the parties until the conclusion of any proceedings taken under or in pursuance of this Schedule.

Section 14   SCHEDULE 2

TENANTS' COMPENSATION FOR MILK QUOTA: SCOTLAND

Interpretation

1.—(1) In this Schedule, except where the context otherwise requires or provision is made to the contrary—

"allocated quota" has the meaning given in paragraph 2(1) below;

"holding" has the same meaning as in the 1986 Regulations;

"landlord" means—

    (*a*) in the case of an agricultural holding to which the 1949 Act applies, the landlord within the meaning of section 93(1) of that Act;

    (*b*) in the case of a croft within the meaning of the 1955 Act, the landlord within the meaning of section 37(1) of that Act;

    (*c*) in the case of a holding within the meaning of the 1911 Act to which the 1949 Act does not apply, the same as it means in the 1911 Act;

"milk quota" means—

    (*a*) in the case of a tenant registered in the direct sales register maintained under the 1986 Regulations, a direct sales quota within the meaning of those Regulations; and

    (*b*) in the case of a tenant registered in the wholesale register maintained

under those Regulations, a wholesale quota within the meaning of those
   Regulations;
"registered", in relation to milk quota, means—
      (*a*) in the case of direct sales quota within the meaning of the 1986
      Regulations, registered in the direct sales register maintained under those
      Regulations; and
      (*b*) in the case of a wholesale quota within the meaning of those Regulations,
      registered in a wholesale register maintained under those Regulations;
"relevant quota" has the meaning given in paragraph 2(2) below;
"standard quota" means standard quota as calculated under paragraph 6 below;
"tenancy" means, as the case may be—
      (*a*) the agricultural holding, within the meaning of section 1 of the 1949
   Act;
      (*b*) the croft within the meaning of section 3(1) of the 1955 Act;
      (*c*) the holding within the meaning of section 2 of the 1911 Act;
      (*d*) the holding of a statutory small tenant under section 32 of the 1911 Act;
      (*e*) any part of a tenancy which is treated as a separate entity for purposes
   of succession, assignation or sub-letting;
"tenant" means—
      (*a*) in the case of an agricultural holding to which the 1949 Act applies, the
      tenant within the meaning of section 93(1) of that Act;
      (*b*) in the case of a croft within the meaning of the 1955 Act, the crofter
      within the meaning of section 3(2) of that Act;
      (*c*) in the case of a holding within the meaning of the 1911 Act to which the
      1949 Act does not apply, the landholder within the meaning of section 2(2) of
      the 1911 Act;
"tenant's fraction" has the meaning given in paragraph 7 below;
"termination" means the resumption of possession of the whole or part of the tenancy
      by the landlord by virtue of any enactment, rule of law or term of the lease
      which makes provision for removal of or renunciation by a tenant, or
      resumption of possession by a landlord, and in particular includes resumption
      of possession following—
      (*a*) vacancy arising under section 11(5) of the 1955 Act;
      (*b*) termination of a lease in pursuance of section 16(3) of the Succession
      (Scotland) Act 1964;
"transferred quota" has the meaning given in paragraph 2(2) below;
"the 1886 Act" means the Crofters Holdings (Scotland) Act 1886;
"the 1911 Act" means the small Landholders (Scotland) Act 1911;
"the 1949 Act" means the Agricultural Holdings (Scotland) Act 1949;
"the 1955 Act" means the Crofters (Scotland) Act 1955;
"the 1986 Regulations" means the Dairy Produce Quotas Regulations 1986.
   (2) For the purposes of this Schedule, the designations of landlord and tenant shall
continue to apply to the parties to any proceedings taken under or in pursuance of it until
the conclusion of those proceedings.

Tenant's right to compensation

   2.—(1) Subject to this Schedule, where, on the termination of the lease, the tenant has
milk quota registered as his in relation to a holding consisting of or including the tenancy,
he shall be entitled, on quitting the tenancy, to obtain from his landlord a payment—
   (*a*) if the tenant had milk quota allocated to him in relation to a holding consisting of or
   including the tenancy ("allocated quota"), in respect of so much of the relevant quota
   as consists of allocated quota; and
   (*b*) if the tenant had quota allocated to him as aforesaid or was in occupation of the
   tenancy as a tenant on 2nd April 1984 (whether or not under the lease which is
   terminating), in respect of so much of the relevant quota as consists of transferred
   quota by virtue of a transaction the cost of which was borne wholly or partly by him.
   (2) In sub-paragraph (1) above—
   "the relevant quota" means—
      (*a*) where the holding consists only of the tenancy, the milk quota registered
      in relation to the holding; and
      (*b*) otherwise, such part of that milk quota as falls to be apportioned to the
      tenancy on the termination of the lease;

"transferred quota" means milk quota transferred to the tenant by virtue of the transfer to him of the whole or part of a holding.

(3) A tenant shall not be entitled to more than one payment under this paragraph in respect of the same tenancy.

(4) Nothing in this paragraph shall prejudice the right of a tenant to claim any compensation to which he may be entitled under an agreement in writing, in lieu of any payment provided by this paragraph.

Succession to lease of tenancy

3.—(1) This paragraph applies where a person (the successor) has acquired right to the lease of the tenancy after 2nd April 1984—
   (a) under section 16 of the Succession (Scotland) Act 1964;
   (b) as a legatee, under section 20 of the 1949 Act or under section 16 of the 1886 Act;
   (c) under a bequest of a croft under section 10 of the 1955 Act, or following nomination under section 11 of that Act;
   (d) under a lawful assignation of the lease,
and the person whom he succeeded or, as the case may be, who assigned the lease to him is described in this paragraph as his "predecessor".

(2) Where this paragraph applies—
   (a) any milk quota allocated or transferred to the predecessor (or treated as having been allocated or transferred to him) in respect of the tenancy shall be treated as if it had been allocated or transferred to his successor;
   (b) where, under (a) above, milk quota is treated as having been transferred to the successor, he shall be treated as if he had paid so much of the cost of the transaction by virtue of which the milk quota was transferred as his predecessor bore (or is treated as having borne).

Sub-tenants

4. In the case of a tenancy which is sub-let, if the sub-tenant quits the tenancy—
   (a) paragraph 2 above shall apply so as to entitle the sub-tenant to obtain payment from the head tenant, and for that purpose, references to the landlord and the tenant in this Schedule shall be respectively construed as references to the head tenant and the sub-tenant; and
   (b) for the purposes of the application of paragraph 2 above as between the original landlord and the head tenant—
      (i) the head tenant shall be deemed to have had the relevant quota allocated to him, and to have been in occupation of the tenancy as a tenant on 2nd April 1984; and
      (ii) if the head tenant does not take up occupation of the tenancy when the sub-tenant quits, the head tenant shall be treated as if he had quitted the tenancy when the sub-tenant quitted it.

Calculation of payment

5.—(1) The amount of the payment to which a tenant is entitled under paragraph 2 above on the termination of the lease shall be determined in accordance with this paragraph.

(2) The amount of the payment in respect of allocated quota shall be equal to the value of—
   (a) where the allocated quota exceeds the standard quota for the tenancy—
      (i) the tenant's fraction of so much of the allocated quota as does not exceed the standard quota; together with
      (ii) the amount of the excess;
   (b) where the allocated quota is equal to the standard quota, the tenant's fraction of the allocated quota;
   (c) where the allocated quota is less than the standard quota, such proportion of the tenant's fraction of the allocated quota as the allocated quota bears to the standard quota.

(3) The amount of the payment in respect of transferred quota shall be equal to the value of—
   (a) where the tenant bore the whole of the cost of the transaction by virtue of which the transferred quota was transferred to him, the transferred quota; and

(*b*) where the tenant bore only part of that cost, the corresponding part of the transferred quota.

Standard quota

6.—(1) Subject to this paragraph, the "standard quota" for any tenancy for the purposes of this Schedule shall be calculated by multiplying the relevant number of hectares by the standard yield per hectare.

(2) Where by virtue of the quality of the land in question or of climatic conditions in the area the amount of milk which could reasonably be expected to have been produced from one hectare of the tenancy during the relevant period ("the reasonable amount") is greater or less than the average yield per hectare then sub-paragraph (1) above shall not apply and the standard quota shall be calculated by multiplying the relevant number of hectares by such proportion of the standard yield per hectare as the reasonable amount bears to the average yield per hectare; and the Secretary of State shall by order prescribe the amount of milk to be taken as the average yield per hectare for the purposes of this sub-paragraph.

(3) Where the relevant quota includes milk quota allocated in pursuance of an award of quota made by the Dairy Produce Quota Tribunal for Scotland which has not been allocated in full, the standard quota shall be reduced by the amount by which the milk quota allocated in pursuance of the award falls short of the amount awarded (or, in the case where only part of the milk quota allocated in pursuance of the award is included in the relevant quota, by the corresponding proportion of that shortfall).

(4) In sub-paragraph (3) above the references to milk quota allocated in pursuance of an award of quota include references to quota allocated by virtue of the amount awarded not originally having been allocated in full.

(5) For the purposes of this paragraph—

(*a*) "the relevant number of hectares" means the average number of hectares of the tenancy used during the relevant period for the feeding of dairy cows kept on the tenancy or, if different, the average number of hectares of the tenancy which could reasonably be expected to have been so used (having regard to the number of grazing animals other than dairy cows kept on the tenancy during that period); and

(*b*) "the standard yield per hectare" means such number of litres as the Secretary of State may from time to time by order prescribe for the purposes of this sub-paragraph.

(6) In this and in paragraph 7 below—

(*a*) references to the area of a tenancy used for the feeding of dairy cows kept on the tenancy do not include references to land used for growing cereal crops for feeding to dairy cows in the form of loose grain; and

(*b*) "dairy cows" means milking cows and calved heifers.

(7) An order under this paragraph may make different provision for different cases.

(8) The powers to make an order under this paragraph shall be exercisable by statutory instrument and any statutory instrument containing such an order shall be subject to annulment in pursuance of a resolution of either House of Parliament.

Tenant's fraction

7.—(1) For the purposes of this Schedule "the tenant's fraction" means the fraction of which—

(*a*) the numerator is the annual rental value at the end of the relevant period of the tenant's dairy improvements and fixed equipment; and

(*b*) the denominator is the sum of that value and such part of the rent payable by the tenant in respect of the relevant period as is attributable to the land used in that period for the feeding, accommodation or milking of dairy cows kept on the tenancy.

(2) For the purposes of sub-paragraph (1)(*a*) above, in the case of an agricultural holding within the meaning of the 1949 Act, the annual rental value of the tenant's dairy improvements and fixed equipment shall be taken to be the amount which would be disregarded, on a reference to arbitration made in respect of the tenancy under section 7 of the 1949 Act (variation of rent), as being—

(*a*) an increase in annual rental value due to dairy improvements at the tenant's expense (in terms of subsection (2)(*a*) of that section); or

(*b*) the value of tenant's fixed equipment and therefore not relevant to the fixing of rent under that section, so far as that amount is attributable to tenant's dairy improvements and fixed equipment which are relevant to the feeding, accommodation or milking of dairy cows kept on the tenancy.

(3) Where—

    (*a*) the relevant period is less than or greater than 12 months; or

    (*b*) rent was payable by the tenant in respect of only part of the relevant period,

the average rent payable in respect of one month in the relevant period or, as the case may be, in that part shall be determined and the rent referred to in sub-paragraph (1)(*b*) above shall be taken to be the corresponding annual amount.

(4) For the purposes of this paragraph—

    (*a*) "dairy improvement"—

        (i) in the case of an agricultural holding or a statutory small tenancy, means a "new improvement" or an "old improvement" within the meaning of section 93 of the 1949 Act;

        (ii) in the case of a croft, means a "permanent improvement" within the meaning of section 37 of the 1955 Act;

        (iii) in the case of a holding under the 1911 Act to which the 1949 Act does not apply, means a "permanent improvement" within the meaning of section 34 of the 1886 Act,

    so far as relevant to the feeding, accommodation or milking of dairy cows kept on the tenancy;

    (*b*) "fixed equipment" means fixed equipment, within the meaning of section 93 of the 1949 Act, so far as relevant to the feeding, accommodation or milking of dairy cows kept on the tenancy;

    (*c*) all dairy improvements and fixed equipment provided by the tenant shall be taken into account for the purposes of sub-paragraph (1)(*a*) above, except for such improvements and fixed equipment in respect of which he has, before the end of the relevant period, received full compensation directly related to their value.

(5) For the purposes of this paragraph—

    (*a*) any allowance made or benefit given by the landlord after the end of the relevant period in consideration of the execution of dairy improvements or fixed equipment wholly or partly at the expense of the tenant shall be disregarded;

    (*b*) any compensation received by the tenant after the end of the relevant period in respect of any dairy improvement or fixed equipment shall be disregarded; and

    (*c*) where paragraph 3 above applies, dairy improvements or fixed equipment which would be regarded as tenant's dairy improvements or fixed equipment on the termination of a former tenant's lease (if he were entitled to a payment under this Schedule in respect of the land) shall be regarded as the new tenant's dairy improvements or fixed equipment.

Relevant period

8. In this Schedule "the relevant period" means—

    (*a*) the period in relation to which the allocated quota was determined; or

    (*b*) where it was determined in relation to more than one period, the period in relation to which the majority was determined or, if equal amounts were determined in relation to different periods, the later of those periods.

Valuation of milk quota

9. The value of milk quota to be taken into account for the purposes of paragraph 5 above is the value of the milk quota at the time of the termination of the lease and in determining that value there shall be taken into account such evidence as is available, including evidence as to the sums being paid for interests in land—

    (*a*) in cases where milk quota is registered in relation to land; and

    (*b*) in cases where no milk quota is so registered.

Determination of standard quota and tenant's fraction before end of lease

10.—(1) Where it appears that on the termination of a lease, the tenant may be entitled to a payment under paragraph 2 above, the landlord or tenant may at any time before the termination of the lease by notice in writing served on the other demand that the determination of the standard quota for the land or the tenant's fraction shall be referred—

(*a*) in the case of an agricultural holding within the meaning of the 1949 Act to arbitration under that Act or, under section 78 of that Act to the Scottish Land Court;

(*b*) in any other case, to the Scottish Land Court, for determination by that court,

and where (*a*) above applies, section 75 (or, where the circumstances require, sections 77 and 87) of the 1949 Act shall apply, as if the matters mentioned in sub-paragraph (1) above were required by that Act to be determined by arbitration.

(2) On a reference under this paragraph the arbiter or, as the case may be, the Scottish Land Court shall determine the standard quota for the land or, as the case may be, the tenant's fraction (as nearly as is practicable at the end of the relevant period).

Settlement of tenant's claim on termination of lease

11.—(1) Subject to this paragraph, any claim arising under paragraph 2 above shall be determined—

(*a*) in the case of an agricultural holding within the meaning of the 1949 Act by arbitration under that Act or, under section 78 of that Act, by the Scottish Land Court;

(*b*) in any other case, by the Scottish Land Court,

and no such claim shall be enforceable unless before the expiry of the period of 2 months from the termination of the lease the tenant has served notice in writing on the landlord of his intention to make the claim specifying the nature of the claim.

(2) The landlord and tenant may within the period of 8 months from the termination of the lease by agreement in writing settle the claim but where the claim has not been settled during that period it shall be determined as provided in sub-paragraph (1) above.

(3) Where a tenant lawfully remains in occupation of part of the tenancy after the termination of the lease, the references in sub-paragraphs (1) and (2) above to the termination of the lease shall be construed as references to the termination of the occupation.

(4) In the case of an arbitration under this paragraph, section 75 (or, where the circumstances require, sections 77 and 87) of the 1949 Act (arbitrations) shall apply as if the requirements of this paragraph were requirements of that Act, but paragraph 13 of the Sixth Schedule to that Act (arbitration awards to fix day for payment not later than one month after award) shall have effect for the purposes of this paragraph with the substitution for the words "one month" of the words "three months".

(5) In the case of an arbitration under this paragraph, section 61 of the 1949 Act (determination of claims for compensation where landlord's interest is divided) shall apply, where the circumstances require, as if compensation payable under paragraph 2 above were compensation payable under that Act.

(6) Where—

(*a*) before the termination of the lease of any land the landlord and tenant have agreed in writing the amount of the standard quota for the land or the tenant's fraction or the value of milk quota which is to be used for the purpose of calculating the payment to which the tenant will be entitled under this Schedule on the termination of the lease; or

(*b*) the standard quota or the tenant's fraction has been determined by arbitration in pursuance of paragraph 10 above,

the arbiter or, as the case may be, the Scottish Land Court in determining the claim under this paragraph shall, subject to sub-paragraph (7) below, award payment in accordance with that agreement or determination.

(7) Where it appears to the arbiter or, as the case may be, the Scottish Land Court that any circumstances relevant to the agreement or determination mentioned in sub-paragraph (6) above were materially different at the time of the termination of the lease from those at the time the agreement or determination was made, he shall disregard so much of the agreement or determination as appears to him to be affected by the change in circumstances.

Enforcement

12. Section 69 of the 1949 Act (enforcement) and section 70 of that Act (power of tenant to obtain charge on holding) shall apply to any sum which becomes due to a tenant by virtue of this Schedule as they apply to the sums mentioned in those sections.

Powers of limited owners

13. Whatever his interest in the tenancy, the landlord may, for the purposes of this Schedule, do or have done to him anything which might be so done if he were absolute owner of the tenancy.

Notices

14.—(1) Any notice or other document required or authorised by this Schedule to be served on any person shall be duly served if it is delivered to him, or left at his proper address, or sent to him by post in a recorded delivery letter or a registered letter.

(2) In the case of an incorporated company or body, any such document shall be duly served if served on the secretary or clerk or the company or body.

(3) Any such document to be served by or on a landlord or tenant shall be duly served if served by or on any agent of the landlord or tenant.

(4) For the purposes of this paragraph and of section 7 of the Interpretation Act 1978, the proper address of a person is—

(*a*) in the case of a secretary or clerk to a company or body, that of the registered or principal office of the company or body;

(*b*) in any other case, the person's last known address.

(5) Unless and until the tenant receives notice of a change of landlord, any document served by him on the person previously known to him as landlord shall be deemed to be duly served on the landlord under the tenancy.

Crown land

15.—(1) This Schedule shall apply to land belonging to Her Majesty in right of the Crown, subject to such modifications as may be prescribed; and for the purposes of this Schedule the Crown Estates Commissioners or other proper officer or body having charge of the land for the time being or, if there is no such officer or body, such person as Her Majesty may appoint in writing under the Royal Sign Manual, shall represent Her Majesty and shall be deemed to be the landlord.

(2) Without prejudice to sub-paragraph (1) above, subject to such modifications as may be prescribed, section 14 of this Act and this Schedule shall apply to land where the interest of the landlord or of the tenant belongs to a government department or is held on behalf of Her Majesty for the purposes of a government department.

Section 24(4)   SCHEDULE 3

CONSEQUENTIAL AMENDMENTS

1. In section 2(15) of the Agricultural Marketing Act 1958 for the words "or revoked" there shall be substitued the words "revoked or consolidated".

(2) In the Cereals Marketing Act 1965—

(*a*) in section 1(5) for the words "paragraphs (*b*) and (*c*) of subsection (2)" there shall be substituted the words "paragraph (*b*) of subsection (3)";

(*b*) in section 7(5) for the words "sections 2 to 6" there shall be substituted the words "section 6";

(*c*) in section 16(6) for the words from the beginning to "under this section" there shall be substituted the words "Where for any year the Ministers have made an order under section 13 of this Act specifying a rate of levy for that year in respect of any kind of home-grown cereals";

(*d*) in Schedule 1, in paragraph 5(3) for the words "and the chairman or deputy chairman" there shall be substitiuted the words "and in a case where there is another person eligible to be appointed as chairman, the chairman, and the deputy chairman";

(*e*) in Schedule 3, in paragraph 3 for the words "sections 15 and 16" there shall be substituted the words "section 16."

3. In subsection (3) of section 43 of the Land Drainage Act 1976 for the words "by a scheme under section 103 of the Agriculture Act 1947" there shall be substituted the words "under section 1 of the Agriculture Act 1986".

4. In subsection (2) of section 41 of the Wildlife and Countryside Act 1981 for the words from "such advice" onwards there shall be substituted the words—

"(a) advice to persons carrying on agricultural businesses on the conservation and enhancement of the natural beauty and amenity of the countryside;

(b) advice to such persons on diversification into other enterprises of benefit to the rural economy; and

(c) advice to government departments and other bodies exercising statutory functions on the promotion and furtherance of such diversification as is mentioned in paragraph (b).".

Section 24(5)   SCHEDULE 4

REPEALS

Chapter	Short title	Extent of repeal
7 & 8 Geo. 6. c.28.	The Agriculture (Miscellaneous Provisions) Act 1944.	Section 1. Schedule 1.
10 & 11 Geo. 6. c.48.	The Agriculture Act 1947.	Section 103.
5 & 6 Eliz. 2. c.57.	The Agriculture Act 1957.	In Part II of Schedule 1, the words "Eggs (Hen and Duck in Shell)".
1965 c.14.	The Cereals Marketing Act 1965.	Sections 2 to 5. Sections 8 to 11. In section 12(1) the words from "except" onwards. In section 13, in subsection (1) the word "either" and the words from "or" onwards, in subsection (3)(a) the words from "and (where applicable)" to "Act", in subsection (3)(b) the words from "(or" to "amounts)" and in subsection (3)(c) the words from "(or" to "amount)". Sections 14 and 15. In section 18(1), the words from "and may" onwards. Section 19(2), (3) and (4). In section 23(4), the words "section 8" and "or section 19". In section 24(2) the definitions of "cereals (guarantee payments) order", "deficiency payment", "forward contract" and "registered grower". In section 24(4), in paragraph (a) the words from "any scheme" to "Act, and", the words "scheme or" and the words "the scheme" in the second place where they occur, paragraph (b) and the word "and" immediately preceding it. In section 24(5) the words "with a view to selling the processed cereals". Schedule 2. In Schedule 3, in paragraphs 1 and 2 the words "or, as the case may be, Part II".
1967 c.22.	The Agriculture Act 1967.	In section 13, in subsection (4), the word "and" at the end of paragraph (a) and in subsection (6) the words "all or a specified part of".

Chapter	Short title	Extent of repeal
1970 c.40.	The Agriculture Act 1970.	Sections 1 to 27. Section 103. Section 107. Schedule 1.
1972 c.62.	The Agriculture (Miscellaneous Provisions) Act 1972.	In section 16, in subsection (1) the words "subsection (1) of", the words from "(which" to "accordingly" and the words "of that section".
1973 c.65.	The Local Government (Scotland) Act 1973.	In Schedule 27, paragraph 197.
1975 c.24.	The House of Commons Disqualification Act 1975.	In Part II of Schedule 1, the words "The Eggs Authority".
1975 c.25.	The Northern Ireland Assembly Disqualification Act 1975.	In Part II of Schedule 1, the words "The Eggs Authority".
1976 c.34.	The Restrictive Trade Practices Act 1976.	In Schedule 5, the entries relating to the Agriculture Act 1970.
1981 c.69.	The Wildlife and Countryside Act 1981.	In section 41, subsection (1) and in subsection (6) the words from the beginning to "Wales and".
1983 c.3.	The Agricultural Marketing Act 1983.	In section 7(3), the words from "or" onwards. In Schedule 1, in paragraph 6 the words "with the approval of the Ministers and the Treasury" and in paragraph 11(2) the words "with the approval of the Ministers and the consent of the Treasury" in each place where they occur and the words "with such approval".

SOCIAL SECURITY ACT 1986*

(c. 50)

ARRANGEMENT OF SECTIONS

PART I

PENSIONS

Personal pension schemes

---

* Annotations by Keith Ewing, LL.B., Ph.D. and Douglas Brodie, LL.B.

Housing benefit

PART III

THE SOCIAL FUND

PART IV

BENEFITS UNDER SOCIAL SECURITY ACT 1975

PART V

MATERNITY PAY ETC.

PART VI

COMMON PROVISIONS

Administration

Subordinate legislation

General provisions as to operation of social security

PART VII

MISCELLANEOUS, GENERAL AND SUPPLEMENTARY

Miscellaneous

General

Northern Ireland

Supplementary

Part IV—Statutory maternity pay, statutory sick pay etc.
Part V—Common provisions.
Part VI—Miscellaneous.
Schedule 11—Repeals.

An Act to make provision in relation to personal pension schemes, to
amend the law relating to social security, occupational pension schemes
and the provision of refreshments for school pupils, to abolish maternity
pay under the Employment Protection (Consolidation) Act 1978 and
provide for the winding-up of the Maternity Pay Fund, to empower the
Secretary of State to pay the travelling expenses of certain persons,
and for connected purposes.

[25th July 1986]

PARLIAMENTARY DEBATES
  Hansard, H.C. Vol. 89, col. 1347; H.C. Vol. 90, col. 819; H.C. Vol. 95, col. 746; H.C.
Vol. 96, col. 137; H.C. Vol. 98, cols. 29, 123, 206; H.C. Vol. 102, col. 383; H.L. Vol. 475,
cols. 533, 594, 647; H.L. Vol. 476, col. 731; H.L. Vol. 477, cols. 12, 589; H.L. Vol. 478,
cols. 679, 797; H.L. Vol. 479, cols. 9, 384.
  The Bill was considered in Committee by the House of Commons in Standing Committee
B between February 4, 1986 and May 1, 1986.

GENERAL NOTE
  The Act follows the government White Paper "Reform of Social Security" (Cmnd. 9691).
Part One of the Act makes significant changes to the law on pensions. The government sees
the aims of these reforms as being " . . . a reduction in the emerging cost of the state
earnings-related scheme; a significant increase in the number of people with an occupational
or personal pension; and more flexibility and choice generally in pension provision for
employers and employees" (White Paper, para. 2.7). Various modifications are made to
SERPS and, in particular, the state additional pensions will be based on lifetime average
earnings, rather than the best 20 years of earnings. In future, personal pension schemes will
be allowed to contract-out in the same way as occupational pension schemes. The Act also
enables occupational schemes which provide money purchase benefits to contract-out.
  Part Two of the Act deals with three income-related benefits: housing benefit, income
support and family credit. The latter two will replace supplementary benefit and family
income supplement. The Act is content to set out the general framework, leaving the details
to be provided by regulations. Income support will provide fixed payments, with no
discretion in the scheme to meet any special or emergency needs. Part III of the Act
provides for the social fund which will cater for such needs. Payments from the social fund
will, effectively, replace single payments under the supplementary benefit scheme. Contro-
versially, claimants to the social fund will have no right of appeal to social security appeal
tribunals. The government has stated that " . . . a formal system on the lines of the
adjudication system for other social security decisions is not appropriate for reviewing the
exercise of judgment by social fund officers." (White Paper, para. 4.50).
  Part Four of the Act makes changes to various benefits under the Social Security Act
1975. Part Five provides for statutory maternity pay which will replace maternity allowance
and maternity pay. In the eyes of the government this " . . . is a logical and sensible
extension of the statutory sick pay arrangements which have worked well." (White Paper,
para. 5.20). Part Six sets out common provisions for the administration of social security
benefits. Part Seven contains miscellaneous provisions and includes the controversial
alterations to the provision of school meals.

COMMENCEMENT
  Most of the Act's provisions will come into force on a day to be appointed. The provisions
listed in s.88(5) come into force with the passing of the Act.

PART I

PENSIONS

Personal pension schemes

Minimum contributions to personal pension schemes

1.—(1) Subject to the following provisions of this Part of this Act, the Secretary of State shall pay, except in such circumstances as may be prescribed, minimum contributions in respect of an employed earner for any period during which the earner—

(a) is over the age of 16 but has not attained pensionable age;

(b) is not a married woman or widow who has made an election which is still operative that her liability in respect of primary Class 1 contributions shall be a liability to contribute at a reduced rate; and

(c) is a member of an appropriate personal pension scheme which is for the time being the earner's chosen scheme.

(2) Regulations may make provision as to the manner in which, and time at which or period within which, minimum contributions are to be paid.

(3) Subject to subsection (4) below, the Secretary of State shall pay minimum contributions in respect of an earner to the trustees or managers of the earner's chosen scheme.

(4) In such circumstances as may be prescribed the Secretary of State shall pay minimum contributions to a prescribed person.

(5) Where any of the conditions mentioned in subsections above ceases to be satisfied in the case of an earner in respect of whom the Secretary of State is required to pay minimum contributions, the duty of the Secretary of State to pay them shall cease as from a date determined in accordance with regulations.

(6) If the Secretary of State pays an amount by way of minimum contributions which he is not required to pay, he may recover it from the person to whom he paid it or from any person in respect of whom he paid it.

(7) If he pays in respect of an earner an amount by way of minimum contributions which he is required to pay, but does not pay it to the trustees or managers of the earner's chosen scheme, he may recover it from the person to whom he paid it or from the earner.

(8) A personal pension scheme is an appropriate scheme if there is in force a certificate (in this Act referred to as an "appropriate scheme certificate") issued by the Occupational Pensions Board in accordance with section 2 below that it is such a scheme.

(9) Where an earner and the trustees or managers of an appropriate personal pension scheme have jointly given notice to the Secretary of State, in such manner and form and with such supporting evidence as may be prescribed—

(a) that the earner is, or intends to become, a member of the scheme and wishes minimum contributions in respect of him to be paid to the scheme;

(b) that the trustees or managers have agreed to accept him as a member of the scheme and to receive minimum contributions in respect of him,

that scheme is the earner's chosen scheme as from a date determined in accordance with regulations and specified in the notice, unless at that date some other appropriate scheme is the earner's chosen scheme.

(10) Either an earner or the trustees or managers of a scheme may cancel a notice under subsection (9) above by giving notice to that effect to the Secretary of State at such time and in such manner and form as may be prescribed.

(11) Where a notice under subsection (10) above is given, the scheme ceases to be the earner's chosen scheme as from a date determined in accordance with regulations and specified in the notice.

DEFINITIONS

"employed earner": s.84(1).
"minimum contributions": s.84(1).
"personal pension scheme": s.84(1).
"prescribed": s.84(1).
"primary Class 1 contributions": s.84(1).
"regulations": s.84(1).

GENERAL NOTE

The section deals with personal pension schemes and provides for the Secretary of State to pay minimum contributions where an employed earner is a member of an "appropriate" scheme. Women paying national insurance contributions at the reduced rate are excluded. An employer will pay the full rate of national insurance just as if the employee with a personal pension were fully in SERPS. The D.H.S.S. will then pay the amount of the contracted-out rebate to the personal pension scheme.

Some concern has been expressed that employees under the age of 18 may have difficulty in making a sound assessment of the options. Concern has also been expressed that a spouse's position may be unfairly prejudiced by an election for a personal pension. The opposition, unsuccessfully, sought to amend the Bill by providing that the employee's intention to contribute to a personal pension scheme would have to be confirmed first by the employee's spouse. A "cooling-off period", whereby the employee could retract his agreement to the contract, was also sought and this is to be provided in the Financial Services legislation.

Finally, one may note that some fear that if large numbers of young employees opt for personal pension schemes, this could have a serious impact on existing occupational pension schemes.

Appropriate schemes

2.—(1) Regulations shall provide—
(a) for the issue of appropriate scheme certificates by the Occupational Pensions Board;
(b) for the cancellation, variation or surrender of any such certificate, or the issue of an amended certificate, on any relevant change of circumstances; and
(c) that any question whether a personal pension scheme is or at any time was an appropriate scheme shall be determined by the Board.

(2) A scheme can be an appropriate scheme only if the requirements imposed by or by virtue of Schedule 1 to this Act are satisfied in its case.

(3) An appropriate scheme certificate may be withheld or cancelled by the Board if they consider that there are circumstances which make it inexpedient that it should be or continue to be an appropriate scheme, notwithstanding that they would otherwise issue such a certificate or not cancel such a certificate.

(4) Where by or by virtue of any provision of Schedule 1 to this Act a scheme's being an appropriate scheme depends on the satisfaction of a particular condition, the scheme's continuing to be an appropriate scheme shall be dependent on continued satisfaction of the condition; and if the condition ceases to be satisfied that shall be a ground (without prejudice to any other) for the cancellation or variation of an appropriate scheme certificate.

(5) Except in prescribed circumstances, no appropriate scheme certificate and no cancellation, variation or surrender of such a certificate shall

have effect from a date earlier than that on which the certificate is issued or the cancellation, variation or surrender is made.

(6) An appropriate scheme certificate for the time being in force in relation to a scheme shall be conclusive that the scheme is an appropriate scheme.

(7) Every assignment of or charge on and every agreement to assign or charge protected rights or payments giving effect to protected rights shall be void.

(8) On the bankruptcy of a person who is entitled to protected rights or a payment giving effect to protected rights, any protected rights or payment the assignment of which is or would be made void by subsection (7) above shall not pass to any trustee or person acting on behalf of his creditors.

(9) In the application of this section to Scotland—
 (a) references to assignment shall be construed as references to assignation and "assign" shall be construed accordingly; and
 (b) the reference to a person's bankruptcy shall be construed as a reference to the sequestration of his estate or the appointment on his estate of a judicial factor under section 41 of the Solicitors (Scotland) Act 1980.

DEFINITIONS
 "personal pension scheme": s.84(1).
 "prescribed": s.84(1).
 "protected rights": s.84(1).
 "regulations": s.84(1).

GENERAL NOTE
 S.1(8) provides that a personal pension scheme is an appropriate scheme if there is in force an appropriate scheme certificate issued by the Occupational Pensions Board. S.2, with Sched. 1, deals with the issue, variation, surrender, etc., of such certificates. The Occupational Pensions Board must determine whether any scheme is appropriate. Regulations are to impose requirements concerning the investments, administrative costs, etc., of such schemes.
 It was argued that personal pension schemes should be required to provide guaranteed minimum pensions for the member and his widow or widower in the same way as contracted out salary related occupational schemes. This was rejected by the government and a government spokesman stated that " . . . I do not believe that it is possible to reconcile money purchase pensions with any sort of guaranteed return of that sort." He continued ". . . money purchase pensions inevitably carry risks although they can also bring substantial rewards." (Standing Committee B, February 11, 1986, col. 102).

Amount of minimum contributions

3.—(1) Subject to subsection (2) below, in relation to any tax week falling within a period for which the Secretary of State is required to pay minimum contributions in respect of an earner, the amount of those contributions shall be the aggregate of—
 (a) the rebate percentage of so much of any earnings paid to or for the benefit of the earner with respect to any employment which is not contracted-out employment in relation to him as exceeds the lower earnings limit but does not exceed the upper earnings limit; and
 (b) where the tax week ends before 6th April 1993, 2 per cent. of any such earnings or, if 2 per cent. of any such earnings is less than £1·00 and the prescribed person applies within such time, in such form and manner and with such supporting evidence as may be prescribed, £1·00.

(2) In relation to earnings paid with respect to any such employment as may be prescribed, subsection (1) above shall have effect as if the words "the aggregate of" and paragraph (b) and the word "and" immediately preceding it were omitted.

(3) In subsection (1) above—
"employment" means employed earner's employment; and
"rebate percentage" means the percentage arrived at by adding—
    (*a*) the percentage by which for the time being under section 27(2) of the Social Security Pensions Act 1975 the contracted-out percentage of primary Class 1 contributions is less than the normal percentage; and
    (*b*) the percentage by which for the time being under that subsection the contracted-out percentage of secondary Class 1 contributions is less than the normal percentage.

(4) The references to the upper and lower earnings limits in subsection (1)(*a*) above are references, in the case of an earner who is paid otherwise than weekly, to their prescribed equivalents under section 4(2) and (6) of the Social Security Act 1975.

(5) Regulations may provide—

  (*a*) that earnings shall be calculated or estimated in such manner and on such basis as may be prescribed for the purpose of determining whether any, and if so what, minimum contributions are payable in respect of them;

  (*b*) for the adjustment of the amount which would otherwise be payable by way of minimum contributions so as to avoid the payment of trivial or fractional amounts;

  (*c*) for the intervals at which, for the purposes of minimum contributions, payments of earnings are to be treated as made;

  (*d*) for this section to have effect, in prescribed cases, as if for any reference to a tax week there were substituted a reference to a prescribed period and as if in any case so prescribed for the references to £1·00 in subsection (1)(*b*) above there were substituted references to such other sum as may be prescribed.

DEFINITIONS
"employed earner": s.84(1).
"minimum contributions": s.84(1).
"prescribed": s.84(1).
"primary Class 1 contributions": s.84(1).
"regulations": s.84(1).
"secondary Class 1 contributions": s.84(1).

GENERAL NOTE
This section deals with the amount of minimum contributions paid by the Secretary of State to a personal pensions scheme and provides that the amount is to be the same as the contracted out rebate. That is calculated by applying the rebate percentage to any earnings between the lower and upper earnings limits in non-contracted-out employment. The rebate percentage is the difference between the normal and contracted-out percentage rates of Class 1 contributions under s.27(2) of the Social Security Pensions Act 1975. In addition, up to April 5, 1993 the Secretary of State will also pay two per cent. of any such earnings or £1 (whichever is the higher amount).

The two per cent. addition has been strongly criticised but the government believed it to be necessary " . . . to provide encouragement to launch the new arrangement and to overcome the inertia which faces a major reform that offers new choices to individuals, employers and financial institutions" (Mr. Fowler, Secretary of State for Social Services, Standing Committee B, February 18, 1986, col. 202). Mr. Archy Kirkwood, on the other hand, expressed the view that if personal pension schemes are " . . . meritorious, they should stand or fall in their own right." (Standing Committee B, February 18, 1986, col. 203).

It should be noted that the two per cent. incentive will not be available for someone who has been in a contracted-out scheme for a reasonable period and who is still eligible for membership of that scheme after leaving it. S.3(2) stipulates that regulations will prescribe when the incentive is to be withheld.

Effect of payment of minimum contributions on rate of certain benefits

4.—(1) Where for any period minimum contributions have been paid in respect of an earner, sections 16(2B), 28(7A) and 59(1A) of the Social Security Act 1975 and section 29 of the Social Security Pensions Act 1975 shall have effect—

(a) in relation to him, as from the date on which he reaches pensionable age, as if he were entitled to a guaranteed minimum pension at a prescribed weekly rate arising from that period;

(b) in prescribed circumstances, in relation to any widow or widower of the earner—

(i) if the earner died after reaching pensionable age, as if the widow or widower were entitled to a guaranteed minimum pension at a rate equal to one-half of the rate prescribed under paragraph (a) above; and

(ii) if the earner died before reaching pensionable age, as if the widow or widower were entitled to a guaranteed minimum pension at a prescribed weekly rate arising from that period.

(2) The power to prescribe a rate conferred by subsection (1)(a) above includes power to prescribe a nil rate.

DEFINITIONS
 "minimum contributions": s.84(1).
 "prescribed": s.84(1).

GENERAL NOTE
 The purpose of the section is to provide for a reduction in the personal pension holder's additional pension under the SERPS scheme to take account of the minimum contributions paid. This is to be done by deeming the personal pension holder (or the widow or widower) to be in receipt of a guaranteed minimum pension, which will then be deducted from the additional pension under SERPS. The reduction will be by a notional amount, even though the real amount may be larger or smaller. The opposition sought to limit the reduction to the amount actually received.

Personal pension protected rights premium

5.—(1) In the case of a personal pension scheme which is or has been an appropriate scheme the Occupational Pensions Board may, for the event of, or in connection with, its ceasing to be an appropriate scheme, approve any arrangements made or to be made in relation to the scheme, or for its purposes, for the preservation or transfer of protected rights under the scheme.

(2) If the scheme ceases to be an appropriate scheme (whether by being wound up or otherwise) and the Board either—

(a) have withdrawn their approval of previously approved arrangements relating to it; or

(b) have declined to approve arrangements relating to it,
the Board may issue a certificate to that effect.

(3) A certificate issued under subsection (2)(a) or (b) above shall be cancelled by the Board if they subsequently approve the arrangements.

(4) If the scheme ceases to be an appropriate scheme (whether by being wound up or otherwise), a state scheme premium shall be payable, except in prescribed circumstances—

(a) in respect of each earner whose protected rights under the scheme are not subject to approved arrangements; and

(b) in respect of each person who has become entitled to receive a pension under the scheme giving effect to protected rights which are not subject to approved arrangements.

(5) A premium under subsection (4) above may be referred to as a "personal pension protected rights premium".

(6) If at any time regulations are in force by virtue of which section 52C of or paragraph 16 of Schedule 1A to the Social Security Pensions Act 1975 has effect in relation to personal pension schemes, subsection (4)(*a*) above shall have effect as if after the word "arrangements" there were inserted the words "and have not been disposed of so as to discharge the trustees or managers of the scheme under section 52C of or paragraph 16 of Schedule 1A to the Social Security Pensions Act 1975".

(7) A personal pension protected rights premium shall be paid by the prescribed person, within the prescribed period, to the Secretary of State.

(8) The amount of a personal pension protected rights premium payable in respect of any person shall be the cash equivalent of the protected rights in question, calculated and verified in the prescribed manner.

(9) Where a personal pension protected rights premium is paid in respect of a person—

(*a*) the rights whose cash equivalent is included in the premium shall be extinguished; and

(*b*) section 4 above and section 29(2) and (2A) of the Social Security Pensions Act 1975 shall have effect in relation to that person and a widow or widower of that person as if any guaranteed minimum pension to which that person or any such widow or widower is treated as entitled under those provisions and which derives from the minimum contributions, minimum payments (within the meaning of the Social Security Pensions Act 1975) or transfer payment or payments from which those rights derive were reduced by the appropriate percentage.

(10) In subsection (9) above "the appropriate percentage" means, subject to the following provisions of this section,

$$\frac{X}{Y} \times 100, \text{ where—}$$

(*a*) X = the amount of the premium together with, if the person in respect of whom it falls to be paid gives notice to the prescribed person within the prescribed period—

(i) the cash equivalent, calculated and verified in the prescribed manner and paid to the Secretary of State within the prescribed period, of any other rights which he has under the scheme and specifies in the notice; and

(ii) the amount of any voluntary contribution paid to the Secretary of State within the prescribed period by, or in respect of, the person concerned; and

(*b*) Y = the cost of providing any guaranteed minimum pension such as is mentioned in subsection (9) above.

(11) If the appropriate percentage, as calculated under subsection (10) above, would fall between two whole numbers, it is to be taken to be the lower number.

(12) If it would be over 100, it is to be taken to be 100.

(13) The remainder after the reduction for which subsection (9) above provides—

(*a*) if it would contain a fraction of 1p, is to be treated as the nearest lower whole number of pence; and

(*b*) if it would be less than a prescribed amount, is to be treated as nil.

(14) The power to make regulations conferred by subsections (8) and (10) above includes power to provide that cash equivalents are to be calculated and verified in such manner as may be approved in particular cases—

(*a*) by prescribed persons;

(b) by persons with prescribed professional qualifications or experience; or

(c) by persons approved by the Secretary of State,

and power to provide that they shall be calculated and verified in accordance with guidance prepared by a prescribed body.

(15) The cost of providing the appropriate percentage of the guaranteed minimum pension shall be certified by the Secretary of State, and in calculating and certifying it the Secretary of State—

(a) shall apply whichever of the prescribed actuarial tables (as in force at the time when the scheme ceases to be appropriate) is applicable in accordance with the regulations prescribing the tables; and

(b) may make such adjustments as he thinks necessary for avoiding fractional amounts.

DEFINITIONS
"personal pension scheme": s.84(1).
"prescribed": s.84(1).
"protected rights": s.84(1).
"regulations": s.84(1).

GENERAL NOTE
Where a personal pension scheme ceases to be an appropriate scheme the Occupational Pensions Board has power to approve any arrangements made for the preservation or transfer of protected rights under the scheme. Where no arrangements are approved a state scheme premium, which will be referred to as a personal pension protected rights premium, shall be payable. The amount of the premium payable shall be the cash equivalent of the protected rights. The government have explained that because " . . . these are money-purchase rights, they may in practice . . . be worth either less or more than the GMP which is deducted from the person's SERPS pension". (Standing Committee B, February 18, 1986, col. 252). Depending on its amount, the premium will reduce or extinguish the deduction that would otherwise be made from a person's SERPS pension.

Occupational pension schemes

Money purchase contracted-out schemes

6. Schedule 2 to this Act has effect to make amendments of the Social Security Pensions Act 1975 in relation to the contracting-out of schemes which provide money purchase benefits.

DEFINITION
"money purchase benefits": s.84(1).

GENERAL NOTE
This section allows occupational pension schemes which provide money purchase benefits to contract-out of SERPS. To contract-out a scheme will have to comply with the conditions set out in Sched. 1 as modified by Sched. 2. Opposition attempts to impose a requirement that such schemes provide a guaranteed minimum pension were unsuccessful. The opposition were again unsuccessful in trying to amend the legislation so that the managers and trustees of a contracted-out salary related scheme would have to obtain the consent of a majority of scheme members, before changing the scheme to enable it to contract-out on a money-purchase basis.

Schemes becoming contracted-out between 1986 and 1993

7.—(1) Subject to subsection (3) below and except in such cases as may be prescribed, where an occupational pension scheme becomes a contracted-out scheme under Part III of the Social Security Pensions Act 1975 during the period beginning on 1st January 1986 and ending on 5th April 1993, having not previously been contracted-out during any part of that period, the Secretary of State shall make in relation to any tax week falling within the period beginning on 6th April 1988 and ending on 5th

April 1993 a payment under this section in respect of each earner who is in employment which—

(a) is contracted-out by reference to the scheme during that tax week; and

(b) has not previously been contracted-out employment by reference to any other scheme during any part of the period beginning on 1st January 1986 and ending on 5th April 1993.

(2) The Secretary of State shall make a payment under this section to the trustees or managers of the scheme except that in such circumstances as may be prescribed he shall make such a payment to a prescribed person.

(3) A payment under this section shall not be made unless the prescribed person makes a claim for it in such manner and form, and at such time or within such period, as may be prescribed.

(4) The amount of a payment under this section in respect of a tax week is—

(a) 2 per cent. of so much of any earnings paid to or for the benefit of the earner in respect of the employment which is contracted-out by reference to the scheme in the tax week as exceeds the lower earnings limit for that week but does not exceed the upper earnings limit for it; or

(b) if 2 per cent. of any such earnings is less than £1·00, £1·00.

(5) The references to the upper and lower earnings limits in subsection (4) above are references, in the case of an earner who is paid otherwise than weekly, to their prescribed equivalents under section 4(2) and (6) of the Social Security Act 1975.

(6) Regulations may make provision—

(a) for earnings to be calculated or estimated in such manner and on such basis as may be prescribed for the purpose of determining whether any, and if so what, payments under this section are to be made in respect of them;

(b) for the adjustment of amounts which would otherwise be the amounts of payments under this section so as to avoid the payment of fractional amounts;

(c) for the intervals at which, for the purposes of payments under this section, payments of earnings are to be treated as made;

(d) for this section to have effect, in prescribed cases, as if for any reference to a tax week there were substituted a reference to a prescribed period and as if in any case so prescribed for the references to £1·00 in subsection (4)(b) above there were substituted references to such other sum as may be prescribed; and

(e) as to the manner in which, and time at which or period within which, payments under this section are to be made.

(7) Where in the case of a scheme a payment has been made under this section in relation to an earner—

(a) if a premium is paid under section 42 of the Social Security Pensions Act 1975 in relation to him, the amount of the premium shall be increased by the amount of the payment; and

(b) if a premium is paid under section 44 or 44A of that Act in relation to him, the amount of the premium shall be increased by the amount of the payment and by a further amount representing interest on the payment and calculated in accordance with regulations.

(8) If the Secretary of State makes a payment under this section which he is not required to make, he may recover the amount of the payment from the person to whom he paid it, or from any person in respect of whom he paid it.

(9) If he makes in respect of an earner a payment under this section which he is required to make, but does not make it to the trustees or managers to whom he is required to make it, he may recover the amount of the payment from the person to whom he paid it or from the earner.

DEFINITIONS
"occupational pension scheme": s.84(1).
"prescribed": s.84(1).
"regulations": s.84(1).

GENERAL NOTE
The section provides that from April 6, 1988 until April 5, 1993, where an occupational pension scheme had become a contracted-out scheme between January 1, 1986 and April 5, 1993, the Secretary of State shall pay an "incentive" payment. The payment is to be made in respect of each employee who has not previously been in contracted-out employment in the relevant period. The amount of payment is to be two per cent. of the earnings between the lower and upper earnings limit or £1·00 (whichever is the higher). The section provides the same incentive to occupational pension schemes contracting-out as is provided for personal pension schemes.

Abolition of requirement relating to requisite benefits

8. The requirement of the Social Security Pensions Act 1975 that for an occupational pension scheme to be contracted-out in relation to an earner's employment it must provide requisite benefits shall cease except so far as it relates to guaranteed minimum pensions and except to that extent shall be treated for the purposes of section 50 of that Act (requirement of consent of Occupational Pensions Board to alterations of rules of schemes) as if it had never existed.

DEFINITION
"occupational pension scheme": s.84(1).

GENERAL NOTE
As a result of this section, it will no longer be a condition of contracting-out that requisite benefits must be provided. Occupational pension schemes providing salary related benefits need only provide a guaranteed minimum pension. A government spokesman commented that in general terms, the requisite benefit test under the Social Security Pensions Act 1975 required " . . . final salary schemes, as well as providing GMPs, to provide pensions worth one-eightieth of final pensionable salary for each year of service—up to a maximum of 40 years". (Standing Committee B, February 20, 1986, col. 305). This was viewed as being unduly complicated. For the opposition, Mr. Michael Meacher expressed the view that the true aim of the section was " . . . to encourage higher contracting-out by occupational schemes and further to weaken adherence to the state scheme." (Standing Committee B, February 20, 1986, col. 307).

Guaranteed minimum pensions

9.—(1) The following subsection shall be substituted for subsection (3) of section 35 of the Social Security Pensions Act 1975 (earner's guaranteed minimum)—
    "(3) In subsection (2) above—
    "the appropriate percentage" means—
      (*a*) in respect of the earner's earnings factors for any tax year not later than the tax year 1987–88—
        (i) if the earner was not more than 20 years under pensionable age on 6th April 1978, $1\frac{1}{4}$ per cent.;
        (ii) in any other case $\frac{25}{N}$ per cent.;

      (*b*) in respect of the earner's earnings factors for the tax year 1988–89 and for subsequent tax years—

(i) if the earner was not more than 20 years under pensionable age on 6th April 1978, 1 per cent.;

(ii) in any other case $\frac{25}{N}$ per cent.;

where N is the number of years in the earner's working life (assuming he will attain pensionable age) which fall after 5th April 1978; and—

"derived" means derived in accordance with the rules to be embodied in regulations.".

(2) The following subsections shall be inserted after subsection (6) of that section—

"(6A) Where an earner's guaranteed minimum pension is increased under subsection (6) above, the increase of that part of it which is attributable to earnings factors for the tax year 1987–88 and earlier tax years shall be calculated separately from the increase of the rest.

(6B) Where one or more orders have come into force under section 37A below during the period for which the commencement of a guaranteed minimum pension is postponed, the amount of the pension for any week in that period shall be determined as if the order or orders had come into force before the beginning of the period.".

(3) In section 36 of that Act (widows)—

    (*a*) the following subsections shall be substituted for subsection (1)—

"(1) Subject to the provisions of this Part of this Act, for an occupational pension scheme to be contracted-out in relation to an earner's employment it must provide, in the event of the earner dying (whether before or after attaining pensionable age) and leaving a widow or widower, for the widow or widower to be entitled to a guaranteed minimum pension under the scheme.

(1A) A scheme need not provide for widowers of earners who die before 6th April 1989 to be entitled to guaranteed minimum pensions.";

    (*b*) the following subsection shall be substituted for subsection (3)—

"(3) To comply with this section the scheme must also contain a rule to the effect that—

    (*a*) if the earner is a man who had a guaranteed minimum under section 35 above, the weekly rate of the widow's pension will be not less than her guaranteed minimum, which shall be half that of the earner;

    (*b*) if the earner is a woman who had such a guaranteed minimum, the weekly rate of the widower's pension will be not less than his guaranteed minimum, which shall be one-half of that part of the earner's guaranteed minimum which is attributable to earnings factors for the tax year 1988–89 and subsequent tax years."; and

    (*c*) the following subsections shall be inserted after subsection (7)—

"(7A) The scheme must provide for the widower's pension to be payable in prescribed circumstances and for the prescribed period.

(7B) The trustees or managers of the scheme shall supply to the Secretary of State any such information as he may require relating to the payment of pensions under the scheme to widowers.".

(4) The following provisions of that Act shall be construed as if the references to "widow" included references to "widower"—
- (*a*) section 26(2);
- (*b*) section 32(2)(*a*);
- (*c*) section 36(8);
- (*d*) section 38(3);
- (*e*) section 39(4)(*b*);
- (*f*) section 41B(1)(*c*), (2)(*a*) and (*b*) and (3);
- (*g*) section 44(9);
- (*h*) section 52D,

and with consequential modifications.

(5) The reference in section 29(1) of that Act to a person entitled to a guaranteed minimum pension shall be construed as including a reference to a person so entitled by virtue of being the widower of an earner in any case where he is entitled to a widower's invalidity pension, but that reference shall be so construed where he is entitled to any other benefit only if—
- (*a*) at the time of the earner's death she and her husband had both attained pensionable age; or
- (*b*) he is also entitled to a Category A retirement pension by virtue of section 16(5) of that Act.

(6) The following provisions of that Act shall be construed as if the references to a person entitled to receive a guaranteed minimum pension included references to a person so entitled by virtue of being the widower of an earner only in such cases as may be prescribed—
- (*a*) section 44(1)(*b*) and (2)(*b*); and
- (*b*) section 49(1); and
- (*c*) section 50(3);

and the references to "widow" in section 44(5) of that Act shall be construed as including references to "widower", and the reference in section 49(6) of that Act to guaranteed minimum pensions as including a reference to the guaranteed minimum pension of such a person, only in those cases.

(7) The following section shall be inserted after section 37 of that Act—

"Annual increases of guaranteed minimum pensions

37A.—(1) The Secretary of State shall in the tax year 1989–90 review the general level of prices obtaining in Great Britain for a period of twelve months commencing in the previous tax year.

(2) The Secretary of State shall in each subsequent tax year review the general level of prices obtaining in Great Britain for the period of twelve months commencing at the end of the period last reviewed under this section.

(3) Where it appears to the Secretary of State that the general level of prices is greater at the end of the period under review than it was at the beginning of that period, he shall lay before Parliament the draft of an order specifying a percentage by which there is to be an increase of the rate of that part of guaranteed minimum pensions which is attributable to earnings factors for the tax year 1988–89 and subsequent tax years for—
- (*a*) earners who have attained pensionable age; and
- (*b*) widows and widowers.

(4) The percentage shall be—
- (*a*) the percentage by which the general level of prices is greater at the end of the period under review than it was at the beginning of that period; or
- (*b*) 3 per cent.,

whichever is less.

(5) If a draft order laid before Parliament in pursuance of this section is approved by a resolution of each House, the Secretary of State shall make the order in the form of the draft.

(6) An order under this section shall be so framed as to bring the alterations to which it relates into force on the first day of the tax year next following the making of the order.

(7) Where the benefits mentioned in sections 16(2B), 28(7A) and 59(1A) of the Social Security Act 1975 and section 29(1) above are not increased on the day on which an order under this section takes effect, the order shall be treated for the purposes of those subsections as not taking effect until the day on which the benefits mentioned in them are next increased.

(8) Except as permitted by subsection (13), (14) or (15) below, the trustees or managers of a scheme may not make an increase in a person's pension which is required by virtue of this section out of money which would otherwise fall to be used for the payment of benefits under the scheme to or in respect of that person unless—

    (a) the payment is to an earner in respect of the tax year in which he attains pensionable age and the increase is the one required to be made in the following year; or

    (b) the payment is to a person as the widow or widower of an earner who died before attaining pensionable age in respect of the tax year in which the person became a widow or widower and the increase is the one required to be made in the next following tax year.

(9) Subsection (8) above overrides any provision of a scheme to the extent that it conflicts with it.

(10) The Occupational Pensions Board may at any time, and shall if requested by the trustees and managers of a scheme, advise on any question whether or not subsection (8) above overrides any provision of the scheme.

(11) On an application made to them in respect of a scheme (other than a public service pension scheme) by persons competent to make such an application in respect of it, the Board shall issue a determination on any such question as is mentioned in subsection (10) above.

(12) The persons competent to make an application under subsection (11) above in respect of a scheme are—

    (a) the trustees or managers of the scheme;

    (b) any person other than the trustees or managers who has power to alter any of the rules of the scheme;

    (c) any person who was an employer of persons in service in an employment to which the scheme applies;

    (d) any member or prospective member of the scheme; and

    (e) such other persons as may be prescribed, in relation to any category of schemes into which the scheme falls, as being proper persons to make an application for the purposes of this section in respect of a scheme of that category.

(13) Where in the tax year 1989–90 the trustees or managers of an occupational pension scheme make an increase in the rate of pensions currently payable to the members of the scheme who have attained pensionable age or to the widows or widowers of members, they may deduct the amount of the increase from any increase which, but for this subsection, they would be required to make under this section in the tax year 1990–91.

(14) Where the trustees or managers of such a scheme make an increase otherwise than in pursuance of this section in a tax year

subsequent to 1989–90, they may deduct the amount of the increase from any increase which, but for this subsection, they would be required to make under this section in the next following tax year.

(15) Where in any tax year subsequent to 1989–90 the trustees or managers of a scheme make an increase which is partly made otherwise than in pursuance of this section, they may deduct the part of the increase made otherwise than in pursuance of this section from any increase which, but for this subsection, they would be required to make under this section in the next following year.

(16) Where by virtue of subsection (13), (14) or (15) above guaranteed minimum pensions are not required to be increased in pursuance of this section, their amount shall be calculated for any purpose as if they had been so increased.

(17) Where by virtue of any of those subsections guaranteed minimum pensions are required to be increased in pursuance of this section by an amount less than they otherwise would be, their amount shall be calculated for any purpose as if they had been increased by that full amount.".

(8) In section 59 of that Act (increase of official pensions) the following subsection shall be inserted after subsection (5)—

"(5A) Nothing in section 37A(13), (14) or (15) above authorises any deduction from an increase in the rate of an official pension under this section.".

(9) In section 59A of that Act (modification of effect of section 59(5)) the following subsection shall be inserted after subsection (2)—

"(2A) Where in any tax year—

(*a*) an increase is calculated in accordance with a direction under this section; and

(*b*) the amount by reference to which the increase is calculated, or any part of it, is increased in that tax year under section 37A above,

the increase calculated in accordance with the direction shall be reduced by the amount of the increase under section 37A above.".

DEFINITIONS
"employer": s.84(1).
"occupational pension scheme": s.84(1).
"prescribed": s.84(1).
"regulations": s.84(1).
"tax year": s.84(1).

GENERAL NOTE
The government have explained that the purpose of this section is to make changes to GMPs under contracted-out occupational schemes which correspond to the changes to SERPS.

The section provides for a reduction in the accrual rate of guaranteed minimum pensions to be provided by contracted-out occupational schemes for the tax years from 1988–89. It also provides for contracted-out occupational schemes to provide widowers' benefits on the same basis as widows' benefits, but not if the wife dies before April 6, 1989.

Short-service benefit: qualifying service

10. In paragraphs 6(1)(*b*) and 7 of Schedule 16 to the Social Security Act 1973 (preservation of benefits under occupational pension scheme) for "5" wherever occurring there shall be substituted "2".

DEFINITION
"occupational pension scheme": s.84(1).

This section amends the Social Security Act 1973 to require occupational pension schemes to preserve the pension rights, rather than to refund the contributions, of everybody who has been a member of the scheme for two years or more.

Auditors

11. The following shall be inserted after section 56N of the Social Security Pensions Act 1975—

"Auditors

Regulations as to auditors

56P. The Secretary of State may by regulations make provision as to—

(*a*) the appointment, resignation and removal of auditors of occupational pension schemes;

(*b*) the duty of employers and auditors of employers to disclose information to the trustees or managers of occupational pension schemes and the auditors of such schemes;

(*c*) the duty of trustees or managers of an occupational pension scheme to disclose information and to make available documents to the auditors of the scheme.".

This section enables the Secretary of State to make regulations which will ensure that auditors have access to the information necessary to enable them to carry out an audit of an occupational pensions scheme. The regulations will also prescribe the conditions for the appointment and termination of auditors of such schemes.

Provisions applying to personal and occupational pension schemes

Voluntary contributions

12.—(1) Except in such cases as may be prescribed, and except so far as is necessary to ensure that a personal or occupational pension scheme has, or may be expected to qualify for, tax-exemption or tax-approval, the rules of the scheme—

(*a*) must not prohibit, or allow any person to prohibit, the payment by a member of voluntary contributions;

(*b*) must not impose, or allow any person to impose, any upper or lower limit on the payment by a member of voluntary contributions;

(*c*) must secure that any voluntary contributions paid by a member are to be used by the trustees or managers of the scheme to provide additional benefits for or in respect of him; and

(*d*) must secure that the value of the additional benefits is reasonable, having regard—

(i) to the amount of the voluntary contributions; and

(ii) to the value of the other benefits under the scheme;

and the requirements specified in this subsection may be referred to as "the voluntary contributions requirements".

(2) Where the rules of a personal or occupational pension scheme do not comply with the voluntary contributions requirements it shall be the responsibility of—

(*a*) the trustees and managers of the scheme; or

(*b*) in the case of a public service pension scheme, the Minister, government department or other person or body concerned with its administration,

to take such steps as are open to them for bringing the rules of the scheme into conformity with those requirements.

(3) The Occupational Pensions Board may at any time, and shall if requested by any such persons as are mentioned in subsection (2) above, advise whether the rules of a scheme do or do not in the Board's opinion conform with the voluntary contributions requirements and, where the Board advise that the rules do not conform, they shall indicate what steps they consider should be taken with a view to securing conformity.

(4) On application made to them in respect of a personal or occupational pension scheme (other than a public service pension scheme) by persons competent to make such an application in respect of it, the Occupational Pensions Board shall issue a determination as to whether or not the rules of the scheme conform with the voluntary contributions requirements.

(5) The persons competent to make an application under this section in respect of a scheme are—

(*a*) the trustees or managers of the scheme;

(*b*) any person other than the trustees or managers who has power to alter any of the rules of the scheme;

(*c*) in the case of an occupational pension scheme, any person who is an employer of persons in service in an employment to which the scheme applies;

(*d*) any member or prospective member of the scheme;

(*e*) such other persons as may be prescribed, in relation to any category of schemes into which the scheme falls, as being proper persons to make an application for the purposes of this section in respect of a scheme of that category.

(6) The Board may at any time of their own motion issue in respect of a scheme which has come to their notice any determination which they could issue in the case of that scheme on an application made to them under subsection (4) above.

(7) If the Occupational Pensions Board determine under subsection (4) or (6) above that the rules of a scheme do not conform with the voluntary contributions requirements they shall, either at the time of issuing their determination or as soon thereafter as they think expedient—

(*a*) by order direct the trustees or managers of the scheme, or any such persons as are referred to in subsection (5)(*b*) above, to exercise such powers as they possess for modifying the scheme with a view to bringing it into conformity with those requirements (for which purpose the Board shall include in their order such directions as they think appropriate to indicate the modification appearing to them to be called for); or

(*b*) if there is no person with power to modify the scheme as required by the Board, by order authorise the trustees or managers, or other persons named in the order (who in relation to an occupational pension scheme may in particular include such an employer as is specified in subsection (5)(*c*) above), to make that modification; or

(*c*) themselves by order modify the scheme with a view to achieving the purpose above-mentioned.

(8) The Board may exercise their powers under subsection (7) above from time to time in relation to any scheme in respect of which they have issued a determination under subsection (4) or (6) above, and may exercise the powers together or separately.

(9) Any modification of a scheme made in pursuance of an order of the Board under subsection (7)(*b*) or (*c*) above shall be as effective in law as if it had been made under powers conferred by or under the scheme; and such an order may be made and complied with in relation to a scheme—

(*a*) notwithstanding any enactment or rule of law, or any rule of the scheme, which would otherwise operate to prevent the modification being made;

(*b*) without regard to any such enactment, rule of law or rule of the scheme as would otherwise require, or might otherwise be taken to require, the implementation of any procedure, or of the obtaining of any consent, with a view to the making of the modification.

(10) An order of the Board under subsection (7)(*a*) above may require persons to exercise a power retrospectively (whether or not the power could otherwise be so exercised), and an order under subsection (7)(*b*) or (*c*) above may operate retrospectively; and in this subsection "retrospectively" means with effect from the date before that on which the power is exercised or, as the case may be, the order is made, not being in either case a date earlier than the coming into operation of this section.

(11) In section 64(3) of the Social Security Act 1973 (modification and winding up by order of Occupational Pensions Board) the following paragraph shall be inserted after paragraph (*f*)—

"(*g*) to comply with the voluntary contributions requirements specified in subsection (1) of section 12 of the Social Security Act 1986, but without prejudice to anything in subsections (2) to (10) of that section,".

DEFINITIONS
"employer": s.84(1).
"modifications": s.84(1).
"occupational pension scheme": s.84(1).
"personal pension scheme": s.84(1).
"prescribed": s.84(1).
"tax approval": s.84(1).
"tax exemption": s.84(1).

GENERAL NOTE
This section provides that personal or occupational pension schemes must not prohibit the payment by members of voluntary contributions. In addition, there must not be any upper or lower limit on the payment of such contributions. Exceptions to these rules may be made in cases prescribed by regulations. It has been explained that this power will be used to exclude public service schemes on the grounds that separate arrangements will be made to allow additional voluntary contributions up to the normal revenue limits since those schemes do not have to obtain tax approval.

Regulations as to form and content of advertisements

13. Regulations may be made relating to the form and content of advertisements and such other material as may be prescribed issued by or on behalf of the trustees or managers of a personal or occupational pension scheme for the purposes of the scheme.

DEFINITIONS
"occupational pension scheme": s.84(1).
"personal pension scheme": s.84(1).
"prescribed": s.84(1).
"regulations": s.84(1).

GENERAL NOTE
This section enables regulations to be made controlling the form and content of advertisements concerning personal and occupational pension schemes.

Information

14. Regulations may require the furnishing by prescribed persons to the Secretary of State or the Occupational Pensions Board of such information as he or they require for the purposes of the preceding provisions of this Part of this Act.

DEFINITIONS
    "prescribed": s.84(1).
    "regulations": s.84(1).

GENERAL NOTE
    This section enables regulations to be prescribed requiring the provision of information to the Secretary of State or Occupational Pensions Board where it is required for the purposes of ss.1–13 of the Act.

Terms of contracts of service or schemes restricting choice to be void

15.—(1) Subject to such exceptions as may be prescribed—
  (a) any term of a contract of a service (whenever made) or any rule of a personal or occupational pension scheme to the effect that an employed earner must be a member of a personal or occupational pension scheme, of a particular personal or occupational pension scheme or of one or other of a number of particular personal or occupational pension schemes shall be void; and
  (b) any such term or rule to the effect that contributions shall be paid by or in respect of an employed earner to a particular personal or occupational pension scheme of which the earner is not a member, or to one or other of a number of personal or occupational pension schemes of none of which he is a member, shall be unenforceable for so long as he is not a member of the scheme or any of the schemes.
  (2) Subsection (1) above shall not be construed so as to have the effect that an employer is required, when he would not otherwise be—
  (a) to make contributions to a personal or occupational pension scheme; or
  (b) to increase an employed earner's pay in lieu of making contributions to a personal or occupational pension scheme.

DEFINITIONS
    "contract of service": s.84(1).
    "employed earner": s.84(1).
    "employer": s.84(1).
    "occupational pension scheme": s.84(1).
    "personal pension scheme": s.84(1).
    "prescribed": s.84(1).

GENERAL NOTE
    This section prohibits any term of an employment contract or any rule of a personal or occupational pension scheme from compelling an employee to be a member of, or to contribute to, a particular personal or occupational pension scheme. The government have explained that the intention is to give every employee the right to take a personal pension if he wishes.
    Exceptions may be prescribed by regulations and the government have stated that there are circumstances where " . . . the freedom to opt out of an employer's scheme may not be justified" (Standing Committee B, February 25, 1986, col. 372). The example given was that of a compulsory scheme which provided only lump sum benefits.

Actuarial tables

16.—(1) Regulations prescribing actuarial tables for the purposes of any of the provisions to which this section applies—
  (a) shall be made only after consultation with the Government Actuary; and
  (b) shall not be made unless a draft of them has been laid before Parliament and approved by a resolution of each House.
  (2) This section applies—

    (*a*) to sections 44, 44ZA, 44A and 45 of the Social Security Pensions Act 1975; and

    (*b*) to section 5 above.

(3) The tables—

    (*a*) shall embody whatever appears to the Secretary of State to be the best practical estimate of the average cost, expressed in actuarial terms and relative to a given period, of making such provision as is mentioned in section 44(5)(*a*) or (*b*), 44ZA(9)(*b*), 44A(3) or 45(2) of the Social Security Pensions Act 1975 or in section 5(10)(*b*) above, as the case may be; and

    (*b*) shall assume for any period an average yield on investments which is not less than the average increase during that period in the general level of earnings obtaining in Great Britain,

but the regulations may provide for them to be adjusted according to whatever is from time to time the actual yield on prescribed investments or the average yield, as shown in prescribed published indices, on prescribed classes of investments.

(4) The Secretary of State may from time to time, and shall when required by subsection (6) below, lay before each House of Parliament—

    (*a*) a report by the Government Actuary on any changes in the factors affecting any of the actuarial tables prescribed for the purposes of any of the provisions to which this section applies (including changes affecting adjustments under the regulations); and

    (*b*) a report by the Secretary of State stating whether he considers that the regulations ought to be altered in view of the Government Actuary's report and, if so, what alterations he proposes.

(5) The changes referred to in subsection (4)(*a*) above are, in the case of the first report under that paragraph, changes since the last report under section 46(3)(*a*) of the Social Security Pensions Act 1975 and, in the case of a subsequent report under this section, changes since the preparation of the last such report.

(6) The Secretary of State shall lay the first report under this section not later than 6th April 1987 and subsequent reports at intervals of not more than five years.

(7) If in a report under this section the Secretary of State proposes alterations in the regulations, he shall prepare and lay before each House of Parliament with the report draft regulations giving effect to the regulations and to be in force—

    (*a*) from the beginning of such tax year as may be specified in the regulations not earlier than the second tax year after that in which the regulations are made; or

    (*b*) where it appears to him to be expedient for reasons of urgency, an earlier date not earlier than the date on which the regulations are made.

(8) If the draft regulations are approved by resolution of each House, the Secretary of State shall make the regulations in the form of the draft.

DEFINITIONS

  "prescribed": s.84(1).

  "regulations": s.84(1).

  "tax year": s.84(1).

GENERAL NOTE

  This section modifies and replaces s.46 of the Social Security Pensions Act 1975. It enables regulations to be prescribed containing actuarial tables concerning the calculation of state scheme premiums. The tables are to show the cost of providing guaranteed minimum pensions.

General power to modify statutory provisions

17.—(1) Regulations may provide that any provision which is contained in the Social Security Act 1973 or the Social Security Acts 1975 to 1986, other than a provision contained in this Part of this Act, and which relates to occupational pension schemes—

(a) shall have effect in relation to personal pension schemes subject to prescribed modifications;

(b) shall have effect subject to such other modifications as the Secretary of State may consider necessary or expedient in consequence of this Part of this Act.

(2) Regulations may provide that any provision contained in an Act to which this subsection applies shall have effect subject to such modifications as the Secretary of State may consider necessary or expedient in consequence of this Part of this Act or in consequence of any corresponding enactment extending to Northern Ireland.

(3) The Acts to which subsection (2) above applies are—

(a) the Fire Services Act 1947;

(b) the Sheriffs' Pensions (Scotland) Act 1961;

(c) the Superannuation Act 1972;

(d) the Parliamentary and other Pensions Act 1972;

(e) the Police Pensions Act 1976;

(f) the Parliamentary Pensions Act 1978;

(g) the Judicial Pensions Act 1981.

DEFINITIONS
"modifications": s.84(1).
"occupational pension scheme": s.84(1).
"personal pension scheme": s.84(1).
"regulations": s.84(1).

GENERAL NOTE
This section enables regulations to be prescribed amending existing legislation concerning occupational pension schemes. The regulation making power of s.17(2) will be used where necessary to ensure that the public service schemes, listed in s.17(3), offer the range of pension options which must now be offered in the private sector. The government have stated that "it may be necessary to amend the Acts to ensure that membership is not compulsory, that members are able to pay additional voluntary contributions up to revenue limits and to ensure that widowers' benefits are provided". (Standing Committee B, February 25, 1986, col.384.)

State earnings-related pension scheme

Additional pensions

18.—(1) In any enactment or instrument made under an enactment—

(a) a reference to a basic pension shall be substituted for any reference to the basic component of a long-term benefit; and

(b) a reference to an additional pension shall be substituted for any reference to an additional component of such a benefit.

(2) In subsection (2) of section 6 of the Social Security Pensions Act 1975 (rate of Category A retirement pension) the words "for a pensioner who attained pensionable age in a tax year before 6th April 1999" shall be inserted before the word "shall".

(3) The following subsections shall be inserted after that subsection—

"(2A) The additional pension for a pensioner who attained pensionable age in a tax year after 5th April 1999 shall be—

(a) in relation to any surpluses in the pensioner's earnings factors for the tax years in the period beginning with the tax year

1978–79 and ending with the tax year 1987–88, the weekly equivalent of $\dfrac{25}{N}$ per cent. of the amount of those surpluses; and

(b) in relation to any surpluses in the pensioner's earnings factors in a tax year after the tax year 1987–88, the weekly equivalent of the relevant percentage of the amount of those surpluses; and in this paragraph "relevant percentage" means—

(i) where the pensioner attained pensionable age in the tax year 2009–10 or any subsequent year, $\dfrac{20}{N}$;

(ii) where the pensioner attained pensionable age in a tax year falling within the period commencing with the tax year 1999–2000 and ending with the tax year 2008–2009, $\dfrac{20 + X}{N}$.

(2B) In this section—

$X = 0{\cdot}5$ for each tax year by which the tax year in which the pensioner attained pensionable age precedes the tax year 2009–10; and

$N = $ the number of tax years in the pensioner's working life which fall after 5th April 1978;

and regulations may direct that in prescribed cases or classes of cases any tax year shall be disregarded for the purpose of calculating N, if it is a tax year after 5th April 1978 in which the pensioner—

(a) was credited with contributions or earnings under the principal Act by virtue of regulations under section 13(4) of that Act (credits to enable a person to satisfy contribution conditions); or

(b) was precluded from regular employment by responsibilities at home; or

(c) in prescribed circumstances, would have been treated as falling within paragraph (a) or (b) above,

but not so as to reduce the number of years below 20.".

(4) In subsection (3) of that section, after "(2)" there shall be inserted "or (2A)".

(5) For the purpose of determining the additional pension falling to be calculated under section 6 of the Social Security Pensions Act 1975 by virtue of section 7, 13 or 16(4) of that Act in a case where the deceased spouse died under pensionable age, the following definition shall be substituted for the definition of

"N" in section 6(2B)—

"N = the number of tax years which begin after 5th April 1978 and end before the date when entitlement to the additional pension commences, except that where—

(a) in a case in which the deceased spouse was a man, that number would be greater than 49; or

(b) in a case in which the deceased spouse was a woman, that number would be greater than 44,

N = 49 or 44, as the case may be;".

(6) For the purpose of determining the additional pension falling to be calculated under section 6 of that Act by virtue of section 14 of that Act (invalidity pension for persons under pensionable age), the following definition shall be substituted for the definition of "N" in section 6(2B)—

"N = the number of tax years which begin after 5th April 1978 and
end before the first day of entitlement to the additional
pension in the period of interruption of employment in which
that day falls, except that where—

(*a*) in a case in which the person entitled to the pension
is a man, that number would be greater than 49; or

(*b*) in a case in which the person so entitled is a woman,
that number would be greater than 44,

N = 49 or 44, as the case may be;".

DEFINITIONS
"prescribed": s.84(1).
"regulations": s.84(1).
"tax year": s.84(1).

GENERAL NOTE
This section, together with s.19, sets out the modifications to SERPS. It is said that the
cost of SERPS will be reduced by about half, reducing it from an estimated £25·5 billion in
year 2033 to around £15 billion. This is to be done by calculating the earnings related
pension by averaging out earnings for all years worked rather than the best 20 years and by
altering the accrual rate. S.18 amends existing legislation for people who attain pensionable
age on or after April 6, 1999 so that the additional pension of Category A retirement pension
for the tax years 1978–79 to 1987–88 shall be the weekly equivalent of 25 per cent. of the
amount of any surpluses in the pensioner's earnings factors for those years, divided by the
number of tax years in the pensioner's working life after April 5, 1978. For the tax year
1988–89 and subsequent tax years it shall be the weekly equivalent of 20 per cent. of any
surpluses in the pensioner's earnings factor, for those years divided by the number of tax
years in the pensioner's working life after April 5, 1978. However, for those reaching
pensionable age between April 6, 1999 and April 5, 2009 the percentage shall be 20, plus 0·5
for each complete tax year by which the tax year in which he attains pensionable age
precedes the tax year 2009–10.

Regulations may prescribe that any tax year shall be disregarded if it is a tax year where
the pensioner was credited with contributions or where he was precluded from regular
employment by responsibilities at home.

Additional pensions supplementary

19.—(1) The additional pension falling to be calculated under section
6 of the Social Security Pensions Act 1975 by virtue of any of the following
provisions—

(*a*) section 7 (rate of widow's Category B retirement pension);
(*b*) section 8 (Category B retirement pension for widower);
(*c*) section 13 (rate of widowed mother's allowance and widow's
pension); and
(*d*) section 16(4) (invalidity pension for widowers),

shall be one-half of the amount so calculated if the deceased spouse died
after 5th April 2000.

(2) In paragraph 4 of Schedule 1 to that Act—

(*a*) the words "Subject to sub-paragraph (2A) below, where" shall
be substituted for the word "Where", in sub-paragraphs (1)
and (2); and

(*b*) the following sub-paragraph shall be inserted after sub-paragraph (2)—

"(2A) If a married person dies after 5th April 2000, the
rate of the retirement pension for that persons's widow or
widower shall be increased by an amount equivalent to the
sum of—

(*a*) the increase in the basic pension to which the
deceased spouse was entitled; and

(*b*) one-half of the increase in the additional
pension.".

(3) In sub-paragraph (1) of paragraph 4A of that Schedule after the word "increased" there shall be inserted the words ", subject to sub-paragraph (1A) below,".

(4) The following sub-paragraph shall be inserted after that sub-paragraph—

"(1A) Where the husband dies after 5th April 2000, sub-paragraph (1) above shall have effect in relation to his widow as if for the words from "the following amounts" onwards there were substituted the words "the following amounts—

(i) one-half of the appropriate amount after it has been reduced by the amount of any increases under section 37A of this Act; and

(ii) one-half of any increase to which he had been entitled under this paragraph.".

(5) In sub-paragraph (2), after the word "increased" there shall be inserted the words ", subject to sub-paragraph (2A) below,".

(6) The following sub-paragraph shall be inserted after that sub-paragraph—

"(2A) Where the wife dies after 5th April 1989, sub-paragraph (2) above shall have effect as if for the words from "an amount", in the first place where those words occur, to the end there were substituted—

(*a*) if she dies before 6th April 2000, the words "an amount equal to the sum of—

(i) that increase, so far as attributable to employment before 6th April 1988;

(ii) one-half of that increase, so far as attributable to employment after 5th April 1988;

(iii) the appropriate amount reduced by the amount of any increases under section 37A of this Act; and

(iv) any increase to which she had been entitled under this paragraph."; and

(*b*) if she dies after 5th April 2000, the words "an amount equal to the sum of—

(i) one-half of that increase so far as attributable to employment before 6th April 1988;

(ii) one-half of the appropriate amount after it has been reduced by the amount of any increases under section 37A of this Act; and

(iii) one-half of any increase to which she had been entitled under this paragraph.".".

GENERAL NOTE

This section amends existing legislation so that for a person who dies after April 5, 2000 the additional pension of a widow's or widower's category B retirement pension, a widowed mother's allowance, a widow's pension or a widower's invalidity pension shall be one-half of the amount that would have been payable if the spouse had died before April 6, 2000.

PART II

INCOME-RELATED BENEFITS

General

Income-related benefits

20.—(1) Prescribed schemes shall provide for the following benefits (in this Act referred to as "income-related benefits")—

(a) income support;
(b) family credit; and
(c) housing benefit.

(2) The Secretary of State shall make copies of schemes prescribed under subsection (1)(a) or (b) above available for public inspection at local offices of the Department of Health and Social Security at all reasonable hours without payment.

(3) A person in Great Britain is entitled to income support if—
   (a) he is of or over the age of 16;
   (b) he has no income or his income does not exceed the applicable amount;
   (c) he is not engaged in remunerative work and, if he is a member of a married or unmarried couple, the other member is not so engaged; and
   (d) except in such circumstances as may be prescribed—
      (i) he is available for employment;
      (ii) he is not receiving relevant education.

(4) Circumstances may be prescribed in which a person must not only satisfy the condition specified in subsection (3)(d)(i) above but also be registered in the prescribed manner for employment.

(5) Subject to regulations under section 51(1)(a) below, a person in Great Britain is entitled to family credit if, when the claim for it is made or is treated as made—
   (a) his income—
      (i) does not exceed the applicable amount; or
      (ii) exceeds it, but only by such an amount that there is an amount remaining if the deduction for which section 21(3) below provides is made;
   (b) he or, if he is a member of a married or unmarried couple, he or the other member of the couple, is engaged and normally engaged in remunerative work; and
   (c) he or, if he is a member of a married or unmarried couple, he or the other member, is responsible for a member of the same household who is a child or a person of a prescribed description.

(6) Family credit shall be payable for a period of 26 weeks or such other period as may be prescribed, beginning with the week in which a claim for it is made or is treated as made and, subject to regulations, an award of family credit and the rate at which it is payable shall not be affected by any change of circumstances during that period.

(7) A person is entitled to housing benefit if—
   (a) he is liable to make payments in respect of a dwelling in Great Britain which he occupies as his home;
   (b) there is an appropriate maximum housing benefit in his case; and
   (c) either—
      (i) he has no income or his income does not exceed the applicable amount; or
      (ii) his income exceeds that amount, but only by so much that there is an amount remaining if the deduction for which section 21(5) below provides is made.

(8) In subsection (7) above "payments in respect of a dwelling" means such payments as may be prescribed, but the power to prescribe payments does not include power to prescribe mortgage payments or, in relation to Scotland, payments under heritable securities.

(9) Except in prescribed circumstances the entitlement of one member of a family to any one income-related benefit excludes entitlement to that benefit for any other member for the same period.

(10) Regulations may provide that an award of family credit shall terminate—

(*a*) if a person who was a member of the family at the date of the claim becomes a member of another family and some member of that family is entitled to family credit; or

(*b*) if income support becomes payable in respect of a person who was a member of the family at the date of the claim for family credit.

(11) In this Part of this Act—

"child" means a person under the age of 16;

"family" means—

    (*a*) a married or unmarried couple;

    (*b*) a married or unmarried couple and a member of the same household for whom one of them is or both are responsible and who is a child or a person of a prescribed description;

    (*c*) except in prescribed circumstances, a person who is not a member of a married or unmarried couple and a member of the same household for whom that person is responsible and who is a child or a person of a prescribed description;

"married couple" means a man and a woman who are married to each other and are members of the same household;

"unmarried couple" means a man and a woman who are not married to each other but are living together as husband and wife otherwise than in prescribed circumstances.

(12) Regulations may make provision for the purposes of this Part of this Act—

(*a*) as to circumstances in which a person is to be treated as being or not being in Great Britain;

(*b*) continuing a person's entitlement to benefit during periods of temporary absence from Great Britain;

(*c*) as to what is or is not to be treated as remunerative work or as employment;

(*d*) as to circumstances in which a person is or is not to be treated as engaged or normally engaged in remunerative work or available for employment;

(*e*) as to what is or is not to be treated as relevant education;

(*f*) as to circumstances in which a person is or is not to be treated as receiving relevant education;

(*g*) as to circumstances in which a person is or is not to be treated as occupying a dwelling as his home;

(*h*) for treating any person who is liable to make payments in respect of a dwelling as if he were not so liable;

(*i*) for treating any person who is not liable to make payments in respect of a dwelling as if he were so liable;

(*j*) for treating as included in a dwelling any land used for the purposes of the dwelling;

(*k*) as to circumstances in which persons are to be treated as being or not being members of the same household;

(*l*) as to circumstances in which one person is to be treated as responsible or not responsible for another.

DEFINITIONS

"applicable amount": s.84(1).

"dwelling": s.84(1).

"income-related benefit": s.84(1).

"prescribed": s.84(1).

"regulations": s.84(1).

GENERAL NOTE

S.20 introduces three income—related benefits: income support, family credit, and housing benefit. The first two will replace supplementary benefit and family income supplement. Income support is to be made available to people over the age of 16. To be entitled to support the applicant's income must not exceed "the applicable amount"; he must not be engaged in remunerative work; and must be available for employment (but not receiving "relevant education"). Family credit may be paid to those engaged in full-time work, provided that their income does not exceed the applicable amount and provided also that there is a child of the household of which the claimant is a member. Family credit is payable for 26 weeks. So far as housing benefit is concerned, entitlement arises where the claimant is liable to make payments in respect of a house which he or she occupies as home. The payments which are to qualify for this purpose are to be prescribed by regulations, but it is expressly provided that they are not to include mortgage payments, and it is not clear whether this includes mortgage interest payments. Again the payment may be made if the claimant has no income or if the income does not exceed the prescribed amount.

The section in fact does very little but set out the general framework, the details of which are to be filled out by regulations. It is intended by the government that the present provisions will significantly simplify the law—making it easier to understand for both officers and claimants alike. But this may be achieved at not inconsiderable cost to both. The effect of the Act may be to reduce staff, and also benefit. Mr Fowler has claimed that "Income support will be based on standard rates rather than the array of weekly additions and the addition of single payments". (*Hansard,* H.C. Vol. 90, col. 826. (January 1986). In the House of Lords, Baroness Trumpington has indicated that "income support will take the form of a basic allowance supplemented by *standard* additions according to the particular group to which people belong. There will be, for example, a family premium, a lone parent's premium and additions as well for each dependent child. It is why there will be a pensioner's premium with a higher premium for pensioner's over 80. It is why there will be a premium for disabled people and an extra family premium for every disabled child in a family". (*Hansard,* H.L. Vol. 475, col. 598. (June 2, 1986). (Emphasis added). In other words, there are to be fixed payments, with no discretion in the scheme to meet any special or emergency needs. This is a task to be fulfilled by the social fund, on which see Part III.

Amount etc.

21.—(1) Where a person is entitled to income support—

  (*a*) if he has no income, the amount shall be the applicable amount; and

  (*b*) if he has income, the amount shall be the difference between his income and the applicable amount.

(2) Where a person is entitled to family credit by virtue of section 20(5)(*a*)(i) above, the amount shall be the amount which is the appropriate maximum family credit in his case.

(3) Where a person is entitled to family credit by virtue of section 20(5)(*a*)(ii) above, the amount shall be what remains after the deduction from the appropriate maximum family credit of a prescribed percentage of the excess of his income over the applicable amount.

(4) Where a person is entitled to housing benefit by virtue of section 20(7)(*c*)(i) above, the amount shall be the amount which is the appropriate maximum housing benefit in his case.

(5) Where a person is entitled to housing benefit by virtue of section 20(7)(*c*)(ii) above, the amount shall be what remains after the deduction from the appropriate maximum housing benefit of prescribed percentages of the excess of his income over the applicable amount.

(6) Regulations shall prescribe the manner in which—

  (*a*) the appropriate maximum family credit;

  (*b*) the appropriate maximum housing benefit,
are to be determined in any case.

(7) Where the amount of any income-related benefit would be less than a prescribed amount, it shall not be payable except in prescribed circumstances.

DEFINITIONS
"applicable amount": s.84(1).
"income-related benefit": s.84(1).
"prescribed": s.84(1).
"regulations": s.84(1).

GENERAL NOTE
S.21 deals with the amount of entitlement to income related benefits. So far as income support is concerned, the amount shall be the applicable amount (as defined by s.22) or the applicable amount less any income. The amount of family credit will depend upon whether the claimant income exceeds the applicable amount. If it does not, the amount shall be the appropriate maximum family credit in his case, the details of which are yet to be prescribed, but which presumably will involve raising the claimant to a departmental plimsoll line. If the claimant's income does exceed the applicable amount (by virtue of s.20(5)(*a*)(ii), family credit shall be what remains after deducting from the appropriate maximum family credit a percentage of the excess of the claimant's income over the applicable amount. Similar arrangements to these for family credit apply to housing benefit (subss. (4) and (5)). S.21 also provides (subs. (7)) that where any income related benefit would be less than a prescribed amount, it shall not be payable except in prescribed circumstances.

Calculation

22.—(1) The applicable amount shall be such amount or the aggregate of such amounts as may be prescribed.

(2) The power to prescribe applicable amounts conferred by subsection (1) above includes power to prescribe nil as an applicable amount.

(3) In relation to income support and housing benefit the applicable amount for a severely disabled person shall include an amount in respect of his being a severely disabled person.

(4) Regulations may specify circumstances in which persons are to be treated as being or as not being severely disabled.

(5) Where a person claiming an income-related benefit is a member of a family, the income and capital of any member of that family shall, except in prescribed circumstances, be treated as the income and capital of that person.

(6) No person shall be entitled to an income-related benefit if his capital or a prescribed part of it exceeds the prescribed amount.

(7) Regulations may provide that capital not exceeding the amount prescribed under subsection (6) above but exceeding a prescribed lower amount shall be treated, to a prescribed extent, as if it were income of a prescribed amount.

(8) Income and capital shall be calculated or estimated in such manner as may be prescribed.

(9) Circumstances may be prescribed in which—
   (*a*) a person is treated as possessing capital or income which he does not possess;
   (*b*) capital or income which a person does possess is to be disregarded;
   (*c*) income is to be treated as capital;
   (*d*) capital is to be treated as income.

DEFINITIONS
"applicable amount": s.84(1).
"income-related benefit": s.84(1).
"prescribed": s.84(1).
"regulations": s.84(1).

GENERAL NOTE
This provides that the applicable amount of any income-related benefit is such an amount as is to be prescribed. The section confers a very wide discretion on the Minister, a discretion

which is simply extended by the substantive provisions of subsections (2) to (9). Particularly important are:
  (i)   subs. (5) which provides that the income and capital of any member of the claimant's family may be treated as if it were the claimant's;
  (ii) subs. (6) which excludes from income-related benefit those whose capital exceeds a prescribed amount;
  (iii) subs. (9) which provides that capital may be treated as income for the purpose of a claim.

Income support

Trade disputes

23.—(1) This section applies to a person, other than a child or a person of a prescribed description—
  (*a*) who is disqualified under section 19 of the Social Security Act 1975 for receiving unemployment benefit; or
  (*b*) who would be so disqualified if otherwise entitled to that benefit,
except during any period shown by the person to be a period of incapacity for work by reason of disease or bodily or mental disablement or to be within the maternity period.
  (2) In subsection (1) above "the maternity period" means the period commencing at the beginning of the sixth week before the expected week of confinement and ending at the end of the seventh week after the week in which confinement takes place.
  (3) For the purpose of calculating income support—
  (*a*) so long as this section applies to a person who is not a member of a family, the applicable amount shall be disregarded;
  (*b*) so long as it applies to a person who is a member of a family but is not a member of a married or unmarried couple, the portion of the applicable amount which is included in respect of him shall be disregarded;
  (*c*) so long as it applies to one of the members of a married or unmarried couple—
            (i) if the applicable amount consists only of an amount in respect of them, it shall be reduced to one-half; and
            (ii) if it includes other amounts, the portion of it which is included in respect of them shall be reduced to one-half and any further portion of it which is included in respect of the member of the couple to whom this section applies shall be disregarded;
  (*d*) so long as it applies to both the members of a married or unmarried couple—
            (i) if neither of them is responsible for a child or person of a prescribed description who is a member of the same household, the applicable amount shall be disregarded; and
            (ii) in any other case, the portion of the applicable amount which is included in respect of them and any further portion of it which is included in respect of either of them shall be disregarded.
  (4) Where a reduction under subsection (3)(*c*) above would not produce a sum which is a multiple of 5p, the reduction shall be to the nearest lower sum which is such a multiple.
  (5) Where this section applies to a person for any period, then, except so far as regulations provide otherwise—
  (*a*) in calculating the entitlement to income support of that person or a member of his family the following shall be treated as his income and shall not be disregarded—

(i) any payment which he or a member of his family receives or is entitled to obtain by reason of the person to whom this section applies being without employment for that period; and

(ii) without prejudice to the generality of paragraph (i) above, any amount which becomes or would on an application duly made become available to him in that period by way of repayment of income tax deducted from his emoluments in pursuance of section 204 of the Income and Corporation Taxes Act 1970; and

(*b*) any payment by way of income support for that period or any part of it which apart from this paragraph would be made to him, or to a person whose applicable amount is aggregated with his—

(i) shall not be made if the weekly rate of payment is equal to or less than the relevant sum; or

(ii) if it is more than the relevant sum, shall be at a weekly rate equal to the difference.

(6) In subsection (5) above "the relevant sum" means the amount which immediately before this section comes into force is specified in section 6(1)(*b*) of the Social Security (No. 2) Act 1980 increased by the percentage by which any order under section 63 below which brings alterations in the rates of benefits into force on the day on which this section comes into force increases the sums specified in subsection (3) of that section.

(7) If an order under section 63 below has the effect of increasing payments of income support, from the time when the order comes into force there shall be substituted, in subsection (5)(*b*) above, for the references to the sum for the time being mentioned in it references to a sum arrived at by—

(*a*) increasing that sum by the percentage by which applicable amounts have been increased by the order; and

(*b*) if the sum as so increased is not a multiple of 50 pence, disregarding the remainder if it is 25 pence and, if it is not, rounding it up or down to the nearest 50 pence,

and the order shall state the substituted sum.

(8) If a person returns to work with the same employer after a period during which this section applies to him, then, until the end of the period of 15 days beginning with the day on which he returns to work with that employer, section 20(3) above shall have effect in relation to him as if the following paragraph were substituted for paragraph (*c*)—

"(*c*) he is a member of a married or unmarried couple and the other member is not engaged in remunerative work; and"

but any sum paid by way of income support for that period shall be recoverable in the prescribed manner from him or from any prescribed person.

DEFINITIONS
"applicable amount": s.84(1).
"prescribed": s.84(1).
"regulations": s.84(1).

GENERAL NOTE
S.23 is based on the supplementary benefit rules. Where a person is engaged in a trade dispute his applicable amount will be disregarded. If only one of a married couple is engaged in a trade dispute the amount to be disregarded is half the requirements of the couple, together with the personal premiums of the striker. In calculating entitlement to income support, any payment received by that striker (or his partner), or to which he is entitled because of the dispute, must be taken into account. This will include any income tax repayments. In addition, the weekly rate is to be reduced by the continuation of the provisions first introduced in the Social Security (No. 2) Act 1980, s.6(1)(*b*). Thus £17 will be deducted from the support payable, on the assumption that this will be paid by the union in a strike. This sum of £17 (originally £6) may be uprated annually. One final point here is

that the disqualifications in s.23 will not apply during any period of incapacity for work by reason of disease or bodily or mental disablement. Nor shall they apply during the maternity period.

Recovery of expenditure on benefit from person liable for maintenance

24.—(1) Subject to the following provisions of this section, if income support is claimed by or in respect of a person whom another person is liable to maintain or paid to or in respect of such a person, the Secretary of State may make a complaint against the liable person to a magistrates' court for an order under this section.

(2) Except in a case falling within subsection (3) below, this section does not apply where the person who is liable to be maintained is an illegitimate child of the liable person.

(3) A case falls within this subsection if—

(*a*) the liable person is someone other than the child's father; or

(*b*) the liable person is liable because he is a person such as is mentioned in section 26(3)(*c*) below.

(4) On the hearing of a complaint under this section the court shall have regard to all the circumstances and, in particular, to the income of the liable person, and may order him to pay such sum, weekly or otherwise, as it may consider appropriate, except that in a case falling within section 26(3)(*c*) below that sum shall not include any amount which is not attributable to income support (whether paid before or after the making of the order).

(5) In determining whether to order any payments to be made in respect of income support for any period before the complaint was made, or the amount of any such payments, the court shall disregard any amount by which the liable person's income exceeds the income which was his during that period.

(6) Any payments ordered to be made under this section shall be made—

(*a*) to the Secretary of State in so far as they are attributable to any income support (whether paid before or after the making of the order);

(*b*) to the person claiming income support or (if different) the dependant; or

(*c*) to such other person as appears to the court expedient in the interests of the dependant.

(7) An order under this section shall be enforceable as an affiliation order.

(8) In the application of this section to Scotland, subsections (2), (3) and (7) shall be omitted and for the references to a complaint and to a magistrates' court there shall be substituted respectively references to an application and to the sheriff.

(9) On an application under subsection (1) above a court in Scotland may make a finding as to the parentage of a child for the purpose of establishing whether a person is, for the purposes of this section and section 26 below, liable to maintain him.

GENERAL NOTE

This repeats the provisions of the Supplementary Benefits Act 1976, s.18. If income support is paid to one person when another is liable to maintain, the Department may proceed against the liable person in a magistrates' court or a sheriff's court for an order. The order will require the liable person to make a payment of an amount representing some or all of the income support. The order may require the payment to be made to the Secretary of State, the person claiming support, or such other person as appears to the court to be expedient. On the operation of s.18 of the 1976 Act, see Mesher, *CPAG's Supplementary Benefit and Family Income Supplement: The Legislation* (3rd ed., 1985).

Affiliation orders

25.—(1) If—
  (*a*) income support is claimed by or in respect of an illegitimate child or paid in respect of such a child; and
  (*b*) no affiliation order is in force; and
  (*c*) the case does not fall within section 24(3) above,
the Secretary of State may, within three years from the time of the claim or payment, make application to a justice of the peace appointed for the commission area (within the meaning of the Justices of the Peace Act 1979) in which the mother of the child resides for a summons to be served under section 1 of the Affiliation Proceedings Act 1957.

(2) In any proceedings on an application under subsection (1) above the court shall hear such evidence as the Secretary of State may produce, and shall in all respects, subject to the provisions of subsection (3) below, proceed as on an application made by the mother under section 1 of the Affiliation Proceedings Act 1957.

(3) An affiliation order—
  (*a*) made on an application by the Secretary of State under subsection (1) above; or
  (*b*) made on an application made by the Secretary of State in proceedings brought by the mother of the child under section 1 of the Affiliation Proceedings Act 1957,
may be made so as to provide that the payments or a part of the payments to be made under the order shall, instead of being made to a person entitled under section 5 of that Act, be made to the Secretary of State or to such other person as the court may direct.

(4) Any affiliation order, whether made before or after the commencement of this section, may, on the application of the Secretary of State, be varied so as to provide for the making of payments, or part of them, as mentioned in subsection (3) above; and an application by the Secretary of State under this subsection may be made—
  (*a*) notwithstanding that the mother has died and no person has been appointed to have the custody of the child; and
  (*b*) where the child is not in the care of the mother and she is not contributing to his maintenance, without making her a party to the proceedings.

(5) An affiliation order which provides for the making of payments, or part of them, as mentioned in subsection (3) above, may, on the application of the mother of the child, be varied so as to provide that the payments shall be made to a person entitled under section 5 of the Affiliation Proceedings Act 1957.

GENERAL NOTE
  This section repeats the provisions of Supplementary Benefits Act 1976, s.19, on which, see Mesher, *op. cit.*, pp. 22–24.

Failure to maintain—general

26.—(1) If—
  (*a*) any person persistently refuses or neglects to maintain himself or any person whom he is liable to maintain; and
  (*b*) in consequence of his refusal or neglect income support is paid to or in respect of him or such a person,
he shall be guilty of an offence and liable on summary conviction to imprisonment for a term not exceeding three months or to a fine of an amount not exceeding level 4 on the standard scale or to both.

(2) For the purposes of subsection (1) above a person shall not be taken to refuse or neglect to maintain himself or any other person by reason only of anything done or omitted in furtherance of a trade dispute.

(3) For the purposes of this section and sections 24 and 25 above—

(*a*) a man shall be liable to maintain his wife and his children;

(*b*) a woman shall be liable to maintain her husband and her children; and

(*c*) a person shall be liable to maintain another person throughout any period in respect of which the first-mentioned person has, on or after 23rd May 1980 (the date of the passing of the Social Security Act 1980) and either alone or jointly with a further person, given an undertaking in writing in pursuance of immigration rules within the meaning of the Immigration Act 1971 to be responsible for the maintenance and accommodation of the other person.

(4) In subsection (3) above—

(*a*) the reference to a man's children includes a reference to children of whom he has been adjudged to be the father; and

(*b*) the reference to a woman's children includes a reference to her illegitimate children.

(5) Subsection (4) above does not apply to Scotland, and in the application of subsection (3) above to Scotland any reference to children shall be construed as a reference to children whether or not their parents have ever been married to one another.

(6) A document bearing a certificate which—

(*a*) is signed by a person authorised in that behalf by the Secretary of State; and

(*b*) states that the document apart from the certificate is, or is a copy of, such an undertaking as is mentioned in subsection (3)(*c*) above,

shall be conclusive of the undertaking in question for the purpose of this section and section 24 above; and a certificate purporting to be so signed shall be deemed to be so signed until the contrary is proved.

GENERAL NOTE

This section repeats the provisions of Supplementary Benefit Act 1976, ss.17(1) and 25, on which see Mesher, *op. cit.,* pp. 19–20, and 29–30.

Prevention of duplication of payments

27.—(1) Where—

(*a*) a payment by way of prescribed income is made after the date which is the prescribed date in relation to the payment; and

(*b*) it is determined that an amount which has been paid by way of income support would not have been paid if the payment had been made on the prescribed date,

the Secretary of State shall be entitled to recover that amount from the person to whom it was paid.

(2) Where—

(*a*) a prescribed payment which apar' from this subsection falls to be made from public funds in the United Kingdom or under the law of any other member State is not made on or before the date which is the prescribed date in relation to the payment; and

(*b*) it is determined that an amount ("the relevant amount") has been paid by way of income support that would not have been paid if the payment mentioned in paragraph (*a*) above had been made on the prescribed date,

then—

(i) in the case of a payment from public funds in the United Kingdom, the authority responsible for making it may abate it by the relevant amount; and

> (ii) in the case of any other payment, the Secretary of State shall be entitled to receive the relevant amount out of the payment.

(3) Where—

> (a) a person (in this subsection referred to as A) is entitled to any prescribed benefit for any period in respect of another person (in this subsection referred to as B); and
>
> (b) either—
>
> > (i) B has received income support for that period; or
> >
> > (ii) B was, during that period, a member of the same family as some person other than A who received income support for that period; and
>
> (c) the amount of the income support has been determined on the basis that A has not made payments for the maintenance of B at a rate equal to or exceeding the amount of the prescribed benefit,

the amount of the prescribed benefit may, at the discretion of the authority administering it, be abated by the amount by which the amounts paid by way of income support exceed what it is determined that they would have been had A, at the time the amount of the income support was determined, been making payments for the maintenance of B at a rate equal to the amount of the prescribed benefit.

(4) Where an amount could have been recovered by abatement by virtue of subsection (2) or (3) above but has not been so recovered, the Secretary of State may recover it otherwise than by way of abatement—

> (a) in the case of an amount which could have been recovered by virtue of subsection (2) above, from the person to whom it was paid; and
>
> (b) in the case of an amount which could have been recovered by virtue of subsection (3) above, from the person to whom the prescribed benefit in question was paid.

(5) Where a payment is made in a currency other than sterling, its value in sterling shall be determined for the purposes of this section in accordance with regulations.

DEFINITIONS
"prescribed": s.84(1).
"regulations": s.84(1).

GENERAL NOTE
This is similar to the Supplementary Benefits Act 1976, s.12 and provides for the recovery of income support which was paid because some prescribed income has not been received by the claimant in circumstances where the income support would not have been paid had the prescribed income been received earlier.

Housing benefit

Arrangements for housing benefit

28.—(1) Housing benefit provided by virtue of a scheme under section 20(1) above (in this Act referred to as "the housing benefit scheme")—

> (a) is to be in the form of a rate rebate funded and administered by the appropriate rating authority, if it is in respect of payments by way of rates;
>
> (b) is to be in the form of a rent rebate funded and administered by the appropriate housing authority, if it is in respect of payments, other than payments by way of rates, to be made to a housing authority; and
>
> (c) is in any other case to be in the form of a rent allowance funded and administered by the appropriate local authority.

(2) Regulations may provide that in prescribed cases a payment made by a person entitled to a rent allowance shall be treated for the purposes of subsection (1)(*a*) above as being, to such extent as may be prescribed, a payment by way of rates.

(3) For the purposes of this section in its application to any dwelling—

(*a*) the appropriate rating authority is the rating authority for the area in which it is situated;

(*b*) the appropriate housing authority is the housing authority to whom the occupier of the dwelling is liable to make payments; and

(*c*) the appropriate local authority is the local authority for the area in which the dwelling is situated.

(4) Authorities may agree that one shall carry out responsibilities relating to housing benefit on another's behalf.

(5) Circumstances may be prescribed in which a rate rebate may be treated as if it fell to be paid as a rent allowance.

(6) An authority may modify any part of the housing benefit scheme administered by the authority—

(*a*) so as to provide for disregarding, in determining a person's income (whether he is the occupier of a dwelling or any other person whose income falls to be aggregated with that of the occupier of a dwelling), the whole or part of any war disablement pension or war widow's pension payable to that person;

(*b*) to such extent in other respects as may be prescribed,

and any such modifications may be adopted by resolution of an authority.

(7) Modifications other than such modifications as are mentioned in subsection (6)(*a*) above shall be so framed as to secure that, in the estimate of the authority adopting them, the total of the rebates or allowances which will be granted by the authority in any year will not exceed the permitted total of rebates or allowances for that year.

(8) An authority who have adopted modifications may by resolution revoke or vary them.

(9) If the housing benefit scheme includes power for an authority to exercise a discretion in awarding housing benefit, the authority shall not exercise that discretion so that the total of the rebates or allowances granted by them in any year exceeds the permitted total of rebates or allowances for that year.

(10) In relation to any authority the permitted total of rebates or allowances for any year shall be calculated, in the manner specified by an order made by the Secretary of State, by reference to the total housing benefit granted by that authority during the year, less such deductions as are specified in the order.

DEFINITIONS

"dwelling": s.84(1).
"housing authority": s.84(1).
"housing benefit scheme": s.84(1).
"local authority": s.84(1).
"modifications":s.84(1).
"prescribed": s.84(1).
"rate rebate": s.84(1).
"rates": s. 84(1).
"rating authority": s.84(1).
"rent allowance": s.84(1).
"rent rebate": s.84(1).
"regulations": s.84(1).
"war disablement pension": s.84(1).
"war widow's pension": s.84(1).

GENERAL NOTE

This section provides for the housing benefit scheme to be in the form of rent and rate rebates funded and administered by housing and rating authorities, and rent allowances funded and administered by local authorities.

The section ends the general power of local authorities to run local housing benefit schemes funded by their own resources. Special provision is made for war pensioners.

Adjudication and over-payments

29.—(1) Regulations shall require authorities to notify a person who has claimed housing benefit of their determination of that claim.

(2) Any such notification shall be given in such form as may be prescribed.

(3) Regulations shall make provision for reviews of determinations relating to housing benefit.

(4) Except where regulations otherwise provide, any amount of housing benefit paid in excess of entitlement may be recovered in such manner as may be prescribed either by the Secretary of State or by the authority which paid the benefit.

(5) Regulations may require such an authority to recover such an amount in such circumstances as may be prescribed.

(6) An amount recoverable under this section is in all cases recoverable from the person to whom it was paid; but, in such circumstances as may be prescribed, it may also be recovered from such other person as may be prescribed.

(7) Any amount recoverable under this section may, without prejudice to any other method of recovery, be recovered by deduction from prescribed benefits.

DEFINITIONS

"prescribed": s.84(1).
"regulations": s.84(1).

GENERAL NOTE

This section enables regulations to be made concerning notification of the determination of housing benefit claims, the review of claims and the recovery of excess payments.

Housing benefit finance

30.—(1) For each year the Secretary of State shall pay—
   (a) a subsidy to be known as "rate rebate subsidy" to each rating authority;
   (b) a subsidy to be known as "rent rebate subsidy" to each housing authority; and
   (c) a subsidy to be known as "rent allowance subsidy" to each local authority.

(2) The subsidy under subsection (1) above which is to be paid to an authority—
   (a) shall be calculated, in the manner specified by an order made by the Secretary of State, by reference to the total housing benefit granted by that authority during the year with any additions specified in the order but subject to any deductions so specified; and
   (b) shall be subject to deduction of any amount which the Secretary of State considers it unreasonable to meet out of money provided by way of subsidy under subsection (1) above.

(3) For each year the Secretary of State may pay to an authority as part of the subsidy under subsection (1) above an additional sum calculated, in the manner specified by an order made by the Secretary of State, in respect of the costs of administering housing benefit.

(4) The Secretary of State may pay to an authority, for the financial year 1987–88, a subsidy, calculated in the manner specified by an order made by the Secretary of State, in connection with the costs incurred by the authority in implementing the housing benefit scheme.

(5) Rent rebate subsidy shall be payable—

    (a) in the case of a local authority in England and Wales—

        (i) for the credit of their Housing Revenue Account to the extent that it is calculated by reference to Housing Revenue Account rebates and any costs of administering such rebates; and

        (ii) for the credit of their general rate fund to the extent that it is not so calculated;

    (b) in the case of a local authority in Scotland, for the credit of their rent rebate account;

    (c) in the case of a new town corporation in England and Wales or the Development Board for Rural Wales, for the credit of their housing account; and

    (d) in the case of a new town corporation in Scotland or the Scottish Special Housing Association, for the credit of the account to which rent rebates granted by them are debited.

(6) Every local authority shall make for each year a rate fund contribution to their Housing Revenue Account of an amount equal to the difference between—

    (a) so much of their rent rebate subsidy for the year as is credited to that Account; and

    (b) the total of—

        (i) the Housing Revenue Account rebates granted by them during the year; and

        (ii) the cost of administering such rebates.

(7) Rent allowance subsidy shall be payable—

    (a) in the case of a local authority in England and Wales, for the credit of their general rate fund; and

    (b) in the case of a local authority in Scotland, for the credit of their rent allowance account.

(8) Subsidy under this section shall be payable by the Secretary of State at such time and in such manner as the Treasury may direct, but subject—

    (a) to the making of a claim for it in such form and containing such particulars as the Secretary of State may from time to time determine; and

    (b) to such conditions as to records, certificates, audit or otherwise as the Secretary of State may, with the approval of the Treasury, impose.

(9) The amount of any subsidy payable to an authority shall be calculated to the nearest pound, by disregarding an odd amount of 50 pence or less and by treating an odd amount exceeding 50 pence as a whole pound.

(10) If an order made by the Secretary of State so provides—

    (a) the rate fund contribution under subsection (6) above made by a local authority for any year; and

    (b) the rent allowances granted by a local authority during any year,

or such proportion of them as may be calculated in the manner specified by the order, shall not count as relevant expenditure for the purposes of section 54 of the Local Government, Planning and Land Act 1980 (rate support grant).

"housing authority": s.84(1).
"housing benefit scheme": s.84(1).
'Housing Revenue Account rebate": s.84(1).
"local authority": s.84(1).
"new town corporation": s.84(1).
"rating authority": s.84(1).
"rent allowance": s.84(1).
"rent rebate": s.84(1).

GENERAL NOTE
This section makes important changes to the arrangements for meeting local authorities' costs. The government believe change is necessary to give greater incentives to monitor and control the costs of housing benefit. (White Paper, para. 3.60) The section enables the Secretary of State to determine the level of direct benefit subsidy in an annual order.

Information

31.—(1) The Secretary of State may supply to authorities such information of a prescribed description obtained by reason of the exercise of any of his functions under the benefit Acts as they may require in connection with any of their functions relating to housing benefit.

(2) Authorities shall supply to the Secretary of State such information of a prescribed description obtained by reason of the exercise of their functions relating to housing benefit as he may require in connection with any of his functions under the benefit Acts.

(3) It shall also be the duty of an authority to supply the Secretary of State, in the prescribed manner and within the prescribed time—

(a) with such information as he may require concerning their performance of any of their functions relating to housing benefit; and

(b) with such information as he may require to enable him—

(i) to prepare estimates of likely future amounts of housing benefit expenditure; and

(ii) to decide questions relating to the development of housing benefit policy.

(4) Every authority granting housing benefit—

(a) shall take such steps as appear to them appropriate for the purpose of securing that persons who may be entitled to housing benefit from the authority become aware that they may be entitled to it; and

(b) shall make copies of the housing benefit scheme, with any modifications adopted by them under section 28 above, available for public inspection at their principal office at all reasonable hours without payment.

(5) In order to assist authorities to give effect to the housing benefit scheme, where a rent is registered under Part IV of the Rent Act 1977, there shall be noted on the register the amount (if any) of the registered rent which, in the opinion of the rent officer or rent assessment committee, is fairly attributable to the provision of services, except any amount which is negligible in the opinion of the officer or, as the case may be, the committee.

DEFINITIONS
"the benefit Acts": s.84(1).
"housing benefit scheme": s.84(1).
"modifications": s.84(1).
"prescribed": s.84(1).

GENERAL NOTE
The section deals with the provision of information to the Secretary of State by the authorities and vice versa. It also imposes a duty on the authorities to publicise housing benefit.

PART III

THE SOCIAL FUND

The social fund and social fund officers

32.—(1) There shall be established a fund, to be known as the social fund.

(2) Payments may be made out of that fund, in accordance with this Part of this Act—

(a) to meet, in prescribed circumstances, maternity expenses and funeral expenses; and

(b) to meet other needs in accordance with directions given or guidance issued by the Secretary of State.

(3) Payments under this section shall be known as "social fund payments".

(4) Social fund payments to meet funeral expenses may in all cases be recovered, as if they were funeral expenses, out of the estate of the deceased, and (subject to section 53 below) by no other means.

(5) The social fund shall be maintained under the control and management of the Secretary of State and payments out of it shall be made by him.

(6) The Secretary of State shall make payments into the social fund of such amounts, at such times and in such manner as he may with the approval of the Treasury determine.

(7) Accounts of the social fund shall be prepared in such form, and in such manner and at such times, as the Treasury may direct, and the Comptroller and Auditor General shall examine and certify every such account and shall lay copies of it, together with his report, before Parliament.

(8) The Secretary of State shall appoint officers, to be known as "social fund officers", for the purpose of performing functions in relation to social fund payments such as are mentioned in subsection (2)(b) above; and the Secretary of State may allocate an amount, or allocate different amounts for different purposes, for such payments by a particular social fund officer or group of officers in a financial year.

(9) A social fund officer may be appointed to perform all the functions of social fund officers or such functions of such officers as may be specified in his instrument of appointment.

DEFINITIONS
"prescribed": s.84(1).
"social fund payment": s.84(1).

GENERAL NOTE
This section represents the government's answer to social security claims which cannot be met by other benefits. In the White Paper the government recognised that "however effective the main structure of income support, there will always be some people who run into particular difficulties or who have special needs which cannot sensibly be met by normal weekly payments". (para. 4.6). Payment from the social fund will effectively replace the single payment under the supplementary benefit scheme, of which the government has been strongly critical. The aim is to raise the level of benefit so that there will be no need to rely on single payment, expenditure on which has doubled at a time when the claimant population has increased by no more than one-tenth (White Paper, para. 4.7). It remains to be seen whether any increase in benefit rates will be sustained, or indeed whether the level of benefit will in fact eliminate the need for single payments.

Subs. (2) provides that regulations may be made authorising social fund payment to be made to meet maternity expenses, funeral expenses, and other needs. According to the White Paper the social fund will make grants of around £75 to families on low incomes towards the expenses of having a baby. Payments will be made automatically to those on income support or family credit. Full help will be given if savings do not exceed £500, but savings above this amount will be taken into account. Payment will be made 11 weeks before the birth of the baby and a payment may be made to adoptive parents, provided the child is under one year of age. The arrangement will replace the state maternity grant, though it will do so only partially.

So far as funeral expenses are concerned, social fund payments will take the place of the death grant which is to be abolished (see s.41). According to the White Paper, it is proposed that anyone in receipt of any of the income-related benefits will qualify for help. There will, however, be some account taken of the applicant's own savings, and in this respect the same rule will apply as applies to a person's maternity needs. The amount payable will be decided locally, though some "guidance on what costs should be covered will be provided to local offices and made available to funeral directors." (White Paper, para. 4.23). An important feature of the proposals is that although payments will not be recovered from the personal resources of the person seeking help, they may be recovered from the estate of the deceased.

So far as "other needs" are concerned, two situations appear to be anticipated. The first relates to community care, the details being fully discussed in the Green Paper (vol. 2, para. 2.98). The second situation relates to financial crisis, with help to be made available in circumstances covered by urgent needs payments (Green Paper, vol. 2, para. 2.106). According to the White Paper, help will be provided where money is lost or stolen; where there is a need for funds after a fire or flood; or where someone is stranded away from home without any funds. Payment will not be restricted to people receiving income support, but will be made "only to people who have no resources to draw on and they will be recovered when circumstances allow" (White Paper, para. 4.35). Authority for the recovery of payment is provided by s.33(5) below.

Awards by social fund officers

33.—(1) A social fund payment such as is mentioned in section 32(2)(*b*) above may be awarded to a person only if an application for such a payment has been made by him or on his behalf.

(2) The questions whether such a payment is to be awarded and how much it is to be shall be determined by a social fund officer.

(3) A social fund officer may determine that an award shall be payable in specified instalments at specified times.

(4) A social fund officer may determine that an award is to be repayable.

(5) An award which is repayable shall be recoverable by the Secretary of State.

(6) Without prejudice to any other method of recovery, the Secretary of State may recover an award by deduction from prescribed benefits.

(7) The Secretary of State may recover an award—

    (*a*) from the person to or for the benefit of whom it was made;

    (*b*) where that person is a member of a married or unmarried couple, from the other member of the couple;

    (*c*) from a person who is liable to maintain the person by or on behalf of whom the application for the award was made or any person in relation to those needs the award was made.

(8) Subsections (3) to (6) of section 26 above have effect for the purposes of subsection (7)(*c*) above as they have effect for the purposes of sections 24 to 26 above.

(9) In determining whether to make an award to the applicant or the amount or value to be awarded an officer shall have regard, subject to subsection (10) below, to all the circumstances of the case and, in particular—

    (*a*) the nature, extent and urgency of the need;

    (*b*) the existence of resources from which the need may be met;

    (*c*) the possibility that some other person or body may wholly or partly meet it;

    (*d*) where the payment is repayable, the likelihood of repayment and the time within which repayment is likely;

    (*e*) any relevant allocation under section 32(8) above.

(10) An officer shall determine any question under this section in accordance with any general directions issued by the Secretary of State and in determining any such question shall take account of any general guidance issued by him.

(11) Payment of an award shall be made to the applicant unless the social fund officer determines otherwise.

(12) In this section "married couple" and "unmarried couple" are to be construed in accordance with Part II of this Act and regulations made under it.

DEFINITIONS
"prescribed": s.84(1).
"regulations": s.84(1).
"social fund payment": s.84(1).

GENERAL NOTE
This section deals with the procedure for making social fund payments. The question of whether a payment is to be made, and how much, is to be determined by a social fund officer, who will be specially trained departmental officers. The officer has a wide discretion. He or she may decide, for example, that a payment is to be made by instalments, and in some cases that it is to be repayable (see above). Where an award is repayable, subs. (7) deals with the persons from whom the payment may be recovered. These are respectively the person to or for the benefit of whom the payment was made; the other member of a married or unmarried couple of which the person is a member; a person who is liable to maintain the claimant.

Subs. (9) requires the social benefit officer to take into consideration five relevant factors in determining whether to make an award. Subs. (10) then provides that officers are to determine questions in accordance with regulations made by the Secretary of State, and must also take into account any general guidance issued by the Secretary of State. According to the White Paper "Guidance will be prepared on the administration of the fund. The guidance will be published and will be in two parts. Specific directions on certain points will be issued to provide a clear basis for officers' decisions. This will be particularly relevant in areas such as maternity and funeral payments. But for more complex issues the guidance will set out the purposes for which the fund is intended and the factors to be taken into account. Unlike the current arrangements, the guidance will not attempt to cover every conceivable situation. It will recognise that there will be cases where the social fund officer has to exercise judgment. In these cases, it will set the broad approach to be followed, leaving the decision to the officer on the spot in the light of the circumstances of each case and the spirit of the guidance." (White Paper, para. 4.42).

Reviews

34.—(1) A social fund officer—

    (*a*) shall review a determination made under this Part of this Act by himself or some other social fund officer, if an application for a review is made to him within such time and in such form and manner as may be prescribed by or on behalf of the person who applied for the social fund payment to which the determination relates; and

    (*b*) may review such a determination in such other circumstances as he thinks fit;

and may exercise on a review any power exercisable by an officer under section 33 above.

(2) The power to review a determination conferred on a social fund officer by subsection (1) above includes power to review a determination made by a social fund officer on a previous review.

(3) On an application made by or on behalf of the person to whom a determination relates within such time and in such form and manner as may be prescribed a determination of a social fund officer which has been reviewed shall be further reviewed by a social fund inspector appointed by the social fund Commissioner under section 35 below.

(4) On a review a social fund inspector shall have the following powers—

(*a*) power to confirm the determination made by the social fund officer;

(*b*) power to make any determination which a social fund officer could have made;

(*c*) power to refer the matter to a social fund officer for determination.

(5) A social fund inspector may review a determination under subsection (3) above made by himself or some other social fund inspector.

(6) In determining a question on a review a social fund officer or social fund inspector shall have regard, subject to subsection (7) below, to all the circumstances of the case and, in particular, to the matters specified in section 33(9)(*a*) to (*e*) above.

(7) An officer or inspector shall determine any question on a review in accordance with any general directions issued by the Secretary of State under section 33(10) above and any general directions issued by him with regard to reviews and in determining any such question shall take account of any general guidance issued by him under that subsection or with regard to reviews.

(8) Directions under this section may specify—

(*a*) the circumstances in which a determination is to be reviewed; and

(*b*) the manner in which a review is to be conducted.

DEFINITIONS

"prescribed": s.84(1).

"social fund payment": s.84(1).

GENERAL NOTE

The view was expressed in the White Paper " . . . that a formal system on the lines of the adjudication system for other social security decisions is not appropriate for reviewing the exercise of judgment by social fund officers". (Para. 4.50). S.34 provides, however, for the right of review of a determination under the social fund. Reviews will be undertaken by a social fund officer. Claimants who remain dissatisfied have the right to a further review by a social fund inspector appointed by the social fund commissioner under s.35.

The social fund Commissioner

35.—(1) There shall be an officer known as the social fund Commissioner (in this section referred to as "the Commissioner").

(2) The Commissioner shall be appointed by the Secretary of State.

(3) The Commissioner—

(*a*) shall appoint such social fund inspectors;

(*b*) may appoint such officers and staff for himself and for social fund inspectors, as he thinks fit, but with the consent of the Secretary of State and the Treasury as to numbers.

(4) Appointments under subsection (3) above shall be made from persons made available to the Commissioner by the Secretary of State.

(5) It shall be the duty of the Commissioner—

(*a*) to monitor the quality of decisions of social fund inspectors and give them such advice and assistance as he thinks fit to improve the standard of their decisions;

(*b*) to arrange such training of social fund inspectors as he considers appropriate; and

(*c*) to carry out such other functions in connection with the work of social fund inspectors as the Secretary of State may direct.

(6) The Commissioner shall report annually in writing to the Secretary of State on the standards of reviews by social fund inspectors and the Secretary of State shall publish his report.

This section provides for the creation of the office of social fund Commissioner. The Commissioner is given the duty to appoint social fund inspectors, to ensure that they are given appropriate training and to monitor the quality of their decisions. The government has indicated that the social fund inspectors will operate " . . . not only outside the local D.H.S.S. office, but outside and independent from the normal D.H.S.S. local office network and management". (*Hansard,* H.C. Vol. 102, col. 428.)

No provision has been made for a right of appeal to the social security appeal tribunals.

PART IV

BENEFITS UNDER SOCIAL SECURITY ACT 1975

Widowhood

36.—(1) The following section shall be substituted for section 24 of the Social Security Act 1975—

"Widow's payment
24.—(1) Subject to subsection (2) below, a woman who has been widowed shall be entitled to a widow's payment of the amount specified in relation thereto in Schedule 4, Part IA, if—
  (*a*) she was under pensionable age at the time when her late husband died, or he was then not entitled to a Category A retirement pension (section 28); and
  (*b*) her late husband satisfied the contribution condition for a widow's payment specified in Schedule 3, Part I, paragraph 4.

(2) The payment shall not be payable to a widow if she and a man to whom she is not married are living together as husband and wife at the time of her husband's death.".

(2) The following shall be inserted after Part I of Schedule 4 to that Act—

"PART IA

WIDOW'S PAYMENT

Widow's payment (section 24). | £1,000·00.".

(3) In section 26—
  (*a*) in subsection (1), for "40", where occurring in paragraphs (*a*) and (*b*), there shall be substituted "45"; and
  (*b*) in subsection (2), for "50", in both places where it occurs, there shall be substituted "55".

This section abolishes the widow's allowance (on which see Ogus and Barendt, p. 230) and replaces it with a tax-free lump sum widow's payment of £1,000. The payment will be made only if the widow's late husband satisfied the contribution conditions for the payment.

By virtue of subs. (2) a widow may be disqualified from payment if she is living with another man as husband and wife at the time of her husband's death.

Invalid care allowance for women

37.—(1) Section 37(3) of the Social Security Act 1975 shall have effect, and shall be treated as having had effect from 22nd December 1984, as if the words from "and a woman" to the end were omitted.

(2) The Social Security Benefit (Dependency) Regulations 1977 shall have effect, and shall be treated as having had effect from 22nd December

1984, as if the following sub-paragraphs were substituted for sub-paragraphs (*a*) and (*b*) of paragraph 7 of Schedule 2 (increases of invalid care allowance)—

"(*a*) a spouse who is not engaged in any one or more employments from which the spouse's weekly earnings exceed that amount; or

(*b*) some person (not being a child) who—

(i) has the care of a child or children in respect of whom the beneficiary is entitled to child benefit, being a child or children in respect of whom the beneficiary is entitled to an increase of an invalid care allowance or would be so entitled but for the provisions of any regulations for the time being in force under the Act relating to overlapping benefits;

(ii) is not undergoing imprisonment or detention in legal custody;

(iii) is not engaged in any one or more employments (other than employment by the beneficiary in caring for a child or children in respect of whom the beneficiary is entitled to child benefit) from which the person's weekly earnings exceed that amount;

(iv) is not absent from Great Britain, except for any period during which the person is residing with the beneficiary outside Great Britain and for which the beneficiary is entitled to an invalid care allowance.".

DEFINITION
"regulations": s.84(1).

GENERAL NOTE
This section was introduced at the Report stage in the House of Lords, implementing a commitment which had been given by the government on June 23. The commitment was in turn made in anticipation of the decision of the European Court of Justice in the *Drake* case.

Under s.37 of the 1975 Act, invalid care allowance is payable to a person who is engaged in caring for a severely disabled person provided that the carer is not in gainful employment. The statute is, however, sexist in the sense that by s.37(3) a woman was not entitled if for example, she was married and living with her husband. The effect of s.37 is to extend invalid care allowance to married women, and those living with a man as his wife, on equal terms with men and single women.

An important feature of the amendment is that it is back-dated to December 22, 1984. According to the Minister "any married woman whose claim is received by the 31st December 1986 will be able to have arrears back to 22nd December 1984, if she satisfied all the conditions at that date" (*Hansard* H.L., vol. 478, col. 853 (July 15, 1986)). Married women who satisfied the conditions for invalid care allowance on December 22, 1984 but who ceased to be carers in the meantime, will be able to claim for any period during which they satisfied the conditions (*ibid.*, col. 856). The Minister also said that the government would be "writing individually to as many attendance allowance beneficiaries as we can to bring this to the attention of their carers" (*ibid.*, col. 853).

Abolition of maternity grant

38.—(1) The provisions to which this subsection applies shall cease to have effect.

(2) The provisions to which subsection (1) above applies are—

(*a*) in the Social Security Act 1975—

(i) section 21; and

(ii) Schedule 4, Part II, paragraph 1; and

(*b*) section 5 of the Social Security Act 1980.

(3) If a woman is confined after the commencement of subsection (1) above, she shall nevertheless be entitled to maternity grant if—

(*a*) her expected date of confinement was before the commencement of that subsection; and

(b) she has claimed the grant before the date of her confinement.

(4) No regulations made under section 21(5) of the Social Security Act 1975 shall apply to a woman whose expected date of confinement is after the commencement of subsection (1) above.

DEFINITION
"regulations": s.84(1).

GENERAL NOTE
This section abolishes the state maternity grant. Subs. (3) makes transitional arrangements whereby the grant may continue to be paid after the commencement of the section. Entitlement will survive if the expected date of confinement was before the commencement of the section *and* the woman has claimed the grant before the date of her confinement. Presumably the second condition may be satisfied if the claim is made *after* the commencement date, but *before* the confinement. Those in receipt of income support or family credit will qualify for the £75 payment from the Social fund. See s.32 above.

Industrial injuries and diseases

39. Schedule 3 to this Act shall have effect in relation to Chapters IV and V of Part II of the Social Security Act 1975 and associated enactments.

GENERAL NOTE
Together with Sched. 3 this section makes a number of important amendments to the industrial injuries scheme. The first area of amendment relates to disablement benefit, now the main industrial injuries benefit. Para. 3 of the Schedule provides that disablement benefit will no longer be payable for disablement below 14 per cent. Two other points are worth noting about para. 3. Those suffering from disablement of between 14 per cent. and 19 per cent. will benefit from being paid at the 20 per cent. rate. In addition, the effect of successive accidents will be aggregated so that benefit could be paid where the overall industrial disablement equalled or exceeded 14 per cent.

The second area of amendment relates to unemployability supplement. This is to be abolished except for beneficiaries (presently about 100) at the time the measure comes into force. The reasoning behind this is that s.50A of the 1975 Act has given the industrially disabled automatic entitlement to national insurance benefits for any incapacity resulting from injury at work. As a result "payment of invalidity benefit is now the norm in cases of long-term incapacity." (Official Reports Standing Committee B, April 29, 1986, col. 1807).

The third area of amendment relates to special hardship allowance, which is to be renamed "reduced earnings allowance". It will continue to be payable at all levels of disablement.

The fourth area of amendment relates to constant attendance allowance. Para. 6 gives power to alter by regulations the provision for paying constant attendance allowance.

Fifthly, para. 7 abolishes hospital treatment allowance.

The final area of amendment is the abolition of industrial death benefit. Existing industrial widows are transferred to the National Insurance Scheme and special provision is made for new industrial widows.

Abolition of child's special allowance except for existing beneficiaries

40. A child's special allowance under section 31 of the Social Security Act 1975 shall not be payable for any period after this section comes into force except to a beneficiary who—

(a) immediately before the date on which this section comes into force satisfied the conditions for entitlement set out in paragraphs (a) to (c) of that section and was not barred from payment of the allowance by the proviso to it; and

(b) has so continued since that date.

GENERAL NOTE
Child special allowance was introduced in 1957. It was designed for women with dependent children where the women was divorced and where the former husband had died. The women in question would receive provision for the children from their former partners, but this would cease on death of the husband. Such women would not, however, qualify for widows benefit on the ground that they were not widows. S.40 abolishes the allowance, in

line with proposals made in both the Green Paper and the White Paper. According to the government the proposal "did not arouse comment or opposition" (Official Report, Standing Committee B, April 17, 1986, col. 1462). The abolition was, however, criticised in Standing Committee, though, for its part, the government pointed out that "Abolition will not affect families which receive supplementary benefit, which constitute a large portion of recipients, nor will it affect recipients of invalidity benefit—severe disablement allowance or invalid care allowance—because increases to those beneficiaries' children are paid instead at the same rate as child special allowance. Mothers in full-time work will be able to claim FIS or family credit" (Official Report, Standing Committee B, April 17, 1986, col. 1462).

Abolition of death grant

41. Death grant shall not be payable in respect of a death which occurs after the commencement of this section.

GENERAL NOTE
The death grant attracted a lot of criticism and concern, due mainly to the low rate at which it was paid. In 1986 this stood at £30. Rather than increase the benefit, the government has responded to this criticism by abolishing the benefit altogether. According to the government "It is not sensible to maintain a miniscule universal help for hundreds of thousands of people for whom it manifestly makes little difference, while giving too little help to significant numbers of people who need more help" (Official Report, Standing Committee B, April 17, 1986, cols. 1468–1469). Low income families must now rely on the social fund for payments.

Abolition of reduced rate of short-term benefits

42. Paragraphs (*a*) to (*c*) of section 33(1) of the Social Security Act 1975 (reduced rate of short-term benefits payable on partial satisfaction of contribution conditions) shall cease to have effect.

GENERAL NOTE
This section abolishes the right to a reduced rate of certain benefit (unemployment benefit, sickness benefit and maternity allowance) for people who had paid reduced contributions during the qualifying period. Part of the reason for the introduction of this measure "was the disproportionate administrative cost of paying contributory benefit in quite modest sums" to the people involved (Official Report, Standing Committee B, April 17, 1986, col. 1498). It was pointed out, however, that "Many of those affected will gain in supplementary benefit what they lose in contributory benefit" (*ibid.*) There are, however, "2,000 people, most of whom will be married women, [who] will receive less. But some will be men—or single women—excluded from supplementary benefit because of their capital, or their wives' earnings." (Official Report, Standing Committee B, April 17, 1986, col. 1499).

Unemployment benefit—disqualification

43.—(1) The following subsection shall be substituted for section 18(4) of the Social Security Act 1975—

"(4) Regulations may provide for a person who would be entitled to unemployment benefit but for the operation of any provision of this Act or of regulations disentitling him to it or disqualifying him for it to be treated as if entitled to it for the purposes of this section.".

(2) "13" shall be substituted for "6"—
  (*a*) in section 20(1) of that Act; and
  (*b*) in regulation 8(4)(*b*) of the Supplementary Benefit (Requirements) Regulations 1983.

(3) In the Social Security Act 1975—
  (*a*) the following subsection shall be inserted after section 20(1)—

"(1A) The Secretary of State may by order substitute a longer or shorter period for the period for the time being mentioned in subsection (1) above."; and (*b*) in section 167(1)(*b*) (affirmative procedure for certain orders) the words "section 20(1A)" shall be inserted before the word "or", in the second place where it occurs.

GENERAL NOTE
This section was introduced in Committee in the House of Commons. It was strongly condemned by the Opposition as being harsh and nasty. (Official Report, Standing Committee B, April 30, 1986, cols. 1835–1836). What it does is to extend the period of disqualification of the so-called voluntary unemployed from the present maximum of six weeks (which has existed since the scheme was introduced in 1911) to 13 weeks. It will also increase from six to 13 weeks the period for which voluntary employment deductions may be applied.

Two other points are to be noted about s.43. First, subs. (1) deals with the situation where disqualification may lead to a postponement of benefit. In Committee the Minister explained that if a person is disqualified, he or she may receive a year's benefit delayed by the period of disqualification and so never lose benefit at all. In the government's view this is "anomalous", and subs. (1) provides the authority to deal with the "anomaly". It is not proposed to use the power immediately, though the government does wish to make use of it as soon as is practicable. (Official Report, Standing Committee B, April 30, 1986, cols. 1833–1835). The other point of note in s.43 is subs. (3) which authorises the Minister to make regulations to extend, up or down, the 13-week disqualification period.

Unemployment benefit—trade disputes

44.—(1) The following subsections shall be substituted for subsection (1) of section 19 of the Social Security Act 1975 (disqualification for unemployment benefit)—

"(1) Subject to the following provisions of this section—
>   (*a*) an employed earner who has lost employment as an employed earner by reason of a stoppage of work due to a trade dispute at his place of employment is disqualified for receiving unemployment benefit for any day during the stoppage unless he proves that he is not directly interested in the dispute; and
>   (*b*) an employed earner who has withdrawn his labour in furtherance of a trade dispute but does not fall within paragraph (*a*) above is disqualified for receiving unemployment benefit for any day on which his labour remains withdrawn.

(1A) A person disqualified under subsection (1)(*a*) above for receiving unemployment benefit shall cease to be so disqualified if he proves that during the stoppage—
>   (*a*) he has become bona fide employed elsewhere; or
>   (*b*) his employment has been terminated by reason of redundancy within the meaning of section 81(2) of the Employment Protection (Consolidation) Act 1978; or
>   (*c*) he has bona fide resumed employment with his employer but has subsequently left for a reason other than the trade dispute.".

(2) The following shall be inserted after section 49 of that Act—

"Trade disputes

Effect of trade disputes on entitlement to increases

49A. A beneficiary shall not be entitled—
>   (*a*) to an increase in any benefit under sections 44 to 48 above; or
>   (*b*) to an increase in benefit for an adult dependant by virtue of regulations under section 49 above,

if the person in respect of whom he would be entitled to the increase—

    (i) is disqualified under section 19 above for receiving unemployment benefit; or

    (ii) would be so disqualified if he were otherwise entitled to that benefit.".

GENERAL NOTE

This section makes the first substantial change to the trade dispute disqualification from unemployment benefit since 1975. The new drafting is designed to cover a loophole whereby "a person participates in a dispute by withdrawing his labour although there is no stoppage of work. That sometimes happens when some people go on strike while others keep working." (Official Report, Standing Committee B, April 17, 1986, col. 1505). Essentially, however, the disqualification remains the same, claimants will be disqualified if there is a stoppage due to a trade dispute in which they are directly interested, or if they are participating in industrial action. It is interesting to note that in this redrafting of the disqualification, the government has not seen fit to narrow the definition of a trade dispute (and so the range of disqualification) along the lines of the amended definition in the Trade Union and Labour Relations Act 1974, s.29. The other interesting feature of the amendment is that it relaxes the disqualification in one important respect. Thus, a person disqualified by reason of direct interest shall cease to be disqualified if the employment is terminated by reason of redundancy within the meaning of s.81(2) of the Employment Protection (Consolidation) Act 1978. This effectively reverses the decision of the Court of Appeal in *Cartlidge* v. *Chief Adjudication Officer* [1986] 2 All E.R. 1.

Guardian's allowance—adoption

45. In section 38 of the Social Security Act 1975 (guardian's allowance)—

    (*a*) in subsection (6), for the word "No" there shall be substituted the words "Subject to subsection (7) below, no"; and

    (*b*) the following subsection shall be inserted after subsection (6)—

        "(7) Where a person—

            (*a*) has adopted a child; and

            (*b*) was entitled to guardian's allowance in respect of the child immediately before the adoption,

    subsection (6) above shall not terminate his entitlement".

GENERAL NOTE

In the words of the Minister, this measure "gives legal sanctification to a current provision which we thought was legal, but over which some doubt was cast." (Official Report, Standing Committee B, April 17, 1986, col. 1512). It has been the practice for a person who adopts a child not to lose entitlement to the allowance in respect of that child. In the words of the Minister "A guardian should not suffer financially if he adopts his ward because that could be a significant disincentive to adoption especially for less well-off people" (*ibid.*) S. 45 is designed to remove doubts about the validity of this practice, doubts fuelled by s.38(6) of the 1975 Act. About 90 families are known to have adopted children for whom guardian's allowance is in payment (*ibid.*)

PART V

MATERNITY PAY ETC.

Statutory maternity pay—entitlement and liability to pay

46.—(1) Subject to the following provisions of this Act, where a woman who is or has been an employee satisfies the conditions set out in this section, she shall be entitled to payments to be known as "statutory maternity pay".

    (2) The conditions mentioned in subsection (1) above are—

    (*a*) that she has been in employed earner's employment with an employer for a cc·'tinuous period of at least 26 weeks ending with the week immediately preceding the 14th week before the expected week of confinement but has ceased to work for him, wholly or partly because of pregnancy or confinement;

(b) that her normal weekly earnings for the period of 8 weeks ending with the week immediately preceding the 14th week before the expected week of confinement are not less than the lower earnings limit in force under section 4(1)(a) of the Social Security Act 1975 immediately before the commencement of the 14th week before the expected week of confinement; and

(c) that she has become pregnant and has reached, or been confined before reaching, the commencement of the 11th week before the expected week of confinement.

(3) The liability to make payments of statutory maternity pay to a woman is a liability of any person of whom she has been an employee as mentioned in subsection (2)(a) above.

(4) Except in such cases as may be prescribed, a woman shall be entitled to payments of statutory maternity pay only if—

(a) she gives the person who will be liable to pay it notice that she is going to be absent from work with him, wholly or partly because of pregnancy or confinement; and

(b) the notice is given at least 21 days before her absence from work is due to begin or, if that is not reasonably practicable, as soon as is reasonably practicable.

(5) The notice shall be in writing if the person who is liable to pay the woman statutory maternity pay so requests.

(6) Any agreement shall be void to the extent that it purports—

(a) to exclude, limit or otherwise modify any provision of this Part of this Act; or

(b) to require an employee or former employee to contribute (whether directly or indirectly) towards any costs incurred by her employer or former employer under this Part of this Act;

but section 23A of the Social Security and Housing Benefits Act 1982 shall have effect in relation to paragraph (a) above as it has effect in relation to section 1(2)(a) of that Act but as if the reference to statutory sick pay were a reference to statutory maternity pay.

(7) Regulations shall make provision as to a former employer's liability to pay statutory maternity pay to a woman in any case where the former employer's contract of service with her has been brought to an end by the former employer solely, or mainly, for the purpose of avoiding liability for statutory maternity pay.

(8) The Secretary of State may by regulations—

(a) specify circumstances in which, notwithstanding the foregoing provisions of this section, there is to be no liability to pay statutory maternity pay in respect of a week;

(b) specify circumstances in which, notwithstanding the foregoing provisions of this section, the liability to make payments of statutory maternity pay is to be a liability of his;

(c) specify in what circumstances employment is to be treated as continuous for the purposes of this Part of this Act;

(d) provide that a woman is to be treated as being employed for a continuous period of at least 26 weeks where—

(i) she has been employed by the same employer for at least 26 weeks under 2 or more separate contracts of service; and

(ii) those contracts were not continuous;

(e) provide that subsection (2)(a) or (b) above or both shall have effect subject to prescribed modifications—

(i) where a woman has been dismissed from her employment;

(ii) where a woman is confined before the beginning of the 14th week before the expected week of confinement; and

(iii) in such other cases as may be prescribed;

(*f*) provide for amounts earned by a woman under separate contracts of service with the same employer to be aggregated for the purposes of this Part of this Act; and

(*g*) provide that the amount of a woman's earnings for any period, or the amount of her earnings to be treated as comprised in any payment made to her or for her benefit, shall be calculated or estimated in such manner and on such basis as may be prescribed and that for that purpose payments of a particular class or description made or falling to be made to or by a woman shall, to such extent as may be prescribed, be disregarded or, as the case may be, be deducted from the amount of her earnings.

DEFINITIONS

"confinement: s.50(1).
"contract of service": s.84(1).
"dismissed": s.50(1).
"employed earner": s.84(1).
"employee": s.50(1).
"employer": s.50(1).
"modifications": s.84(1).
"prescribed": s.84(1).
"regulations": s.84(1).
"week": s.50(1).

GENERAL NOTE

Section 46 introduces statutory maternity pay. This will replace the maternity allowance (Social Security Act 1975, s.22) and maternity pay under the Employment Protection (Consolidation) Act 1978, ss.34–44. Mr. Tony Newton, for the government, explained that one of the reasons for this change was that the maternity allowance was unsatisfactory and was becoming "increasingly poorly targeted." (H.C. Official Report, Standing Committee B, April 29, 1986, col. 1756). Thus, the "advent of earnings-related contributions and the use of more distant tax years for the satisfaction of the contribution test means that many women who gave up work well before becoming pregnant can still receive the allowance, and that a number of women who worked continuously over the 12 months prior to the birth of the baby fail to qualify for maternity allowance." (*ibid.*) Responsibility for the payment of statutory maternity pay will be on employers, and the measure is seen by the government as "a logical extension of the arrangements for statutory sick pay".

Section 46(1) provides that a woman will be entitled to statutory maternity pay if she satisfies the three conditions laid down in subs. (2). The first is that she must have been employed by the same employer for a continuous period of at least 26 weeks ending with the week before the fourteenth week before the expected week of confinement. Although the service qualification is less than the threshhold required for maternity pay (under EPCA 1978), it is not something which was required under the 1975 Act. The government argued that the threshhold was necessary in the interest of fairness and to prevent abuse. The employer may however recover any statutory maternity pay from the State by reduced national insurance contributions, following the precedent set by statutory sick pay.

The second condition is that in the eight weeks immediately preceding the fourteenth week before the expected week of confinement, the normal weekly earnings of the employee must be not less than the lower earnings limit. At the time of writing, this stands at £38 per week. The government pointed out that "there is no requirement for a woman to have paid full rate contributions during those eight weeks. That means that married women who opted out of full national insurance contributions and thus are presently excluded from state maternity allowance will qualify for statutory maternity pay as they do for SSP." (*ibid.*, col. 1758). On the other hand, it is to be noted that the scheme under the 1978 Act did not have an earnings threshhold, though it did apply only to those who worked 16 hours (in some cases eight hours) per week. The third condition is that the employee is pregnant and that the pregnancy has advanced to the eleventh week before the baby is due.

S.46(3) provides that the employer will be liable to pay statutory maternity pay as is the case with statutory sick pay, though as is also the case with statutory sick pay, provision is made for the reimbursement of the employer (see Sched. 4). S.46(4) and (5) require the employee to give notice that she will be absent from work and require the notice to be given at least 21 days before the absence is due to begin, or as soon as reasonably practicable. S.46(6) also deals with the employer's liability and seeks to prevent agreements which aim to exclude or modify the provision of statutory maternity pay or which aim to require the employee to make a contribution towards the costs of the employer. S.46(7) deals with the possible abuse where the employer ends the contract of employment in order to avoid paying statutory maternity pay. Regulations may be made requiring statutory maternity pay to be paid in such circumstances. Finally, s.46(8) empowers the Secretary of State to make regulations dealing with a range of issues. These include the power to specify in what circumstances employment is to be treated as continuous.

The maternity pay period

47.—(1) Subject to the provisions of this Part of this Act, statutory maternity pay shall be payable in respect of each week during a prescribed period ("the maternity pay period") of a duration not exceeding 18 weeks.

(2) Subject to subsections (3) and (7) below, the first week of the maternity pay period shall be the 11th week before the expected week of confinement.

(3) Cases may be prescribed in which the first week of the period is to be a prescribed week later than the 11th week before the expected week of confinement, but not later than the 6th week before the expected week of confinement.

(4) Statutory maternity pay shall not be payable to a woman by a person in respect of any week during any part of which she works under a contract of service with him.

(5) It is immaterial for the purposes of subsection (4) above whether the work referred to in that paragraph is work under a contract of service which existed immediately before the maternity pay period or a contract of service which did not so exist.

(6) Except in such cases as may be prescribed, statutory maternity pay shall not be payable to a woman in respect of any week after she has been confined and during any part of which she works for any employer who is not liable to pay her statutory maternity pay.

(7) Regulations may provide that this section shall have effect subject to prescribed modifications in relation—

(a) to cases in which a woman has been confined before the 11th week before the expected week of confinement; and

(b) to cases in which—

(i) a woman is confined between the 11th and 6th weeks before the expected week of confinement; and

(ii) the maternity pay period has not then commenced for her.

DEFINITIONS
  "confinement": s.50(1).
  "contract of service": s.84(1).
  "employer": s.50(1).
  "maternity pay period": s.50(1).
  "modifications": s.84(1).
  "prescribed": s.84(1).
  "regulations": s.84(1).
  "week": s.50(1).

GENERAL NOTE
  This section deals with the period during which statutory maternity pay is payable, and is to be read with s.48 which deals with the rate of payment, which is set at two different levels. Statutory maternity pay is payable for a maximum of 18 weeks, the general rule being that the first week of the maternity pay period shall be the eleventh week before the expected week of confinement. The other major feature of s.47 is that it contains a number of disqualifications from statutory maternity pay (subss. (4)–(6)).
  These provide first that it is not payable by an employer if during the week in question the woman has done any work under a contract of employment for him or her. So if a woman

works on one day a week, she loses payment for the whole week. It may have been more appropriate to disqualify only for the day during which the woman is employed. The second disqualification is that a payment shall not be made to a woman who takes up work after confinement with any other employer who is not liable to pay her statutory maternity pay.

Rates of payment

48.—(1) There shall be two rates of statutory maternity pay, in this Act referred to as "the higher rate" and "the lower rate".

(2) The higher rate is a weekly rate equivalent to nine-tenths of a woman's normal weekly earnings for the period of 8 weeks immediately preceding the 14th week before the expected week of confinement.

(3) The lower rate is such weekly rate as may be prescribed.

(4) Subject to the following provisions of this section, statutory maternity pay shall be payable at the higher rate to a woman who for a continuous period of at least 2 years ending with the week immediately preceding the 14th week before the expected week of confinement has been an employee in employed earner's employment of any person liable to pay it to her, and shall be so paid by any such person in respect of the first 6 weeks in respect of which it is payable.

(5) Statutory maternity pay shall not be payable at the higher rate to a woman whose relations with the person liable to pay it are or were governed by a contract of service which normally involves or involved employment for less than 16 hours weekly unless during a continuous period of at least 5 years ending with the week immediately preceding the 14th week before the expected week of confinement her contract of service normally involved employment for 8 hours or more weekly.

(6) The Secretary of State may by regulations make provision as to when a contract of service is to be treated for the purposes of subsection (5) above as normally involving or having involved employment—

(*a*) for less than 16 hours weekly; or

(*b*) for 8 hours or more weekly,

or as not normally involving or having involved such employment.

(7) Statutory maternity pay shall be payable to a woman at the lower rate if she is entitled to statutory maternity pay but is not entitled to payment at the higher rate.

(8) If a woman is entitled to statutory maternity pay at the higher rate, she shall be entitled to it at the lower rate in respect of the portion of the maternity pay period after the end of the 6 week period mentioned in subsection (4) above.

DEFINITIONS
    "confinement": s.50(1).
    "contract of service": s.84(1).
    "employed earner": s.84(1).
    "employee": s.50(1).
    "prescribed": s.84(1).
    "regulations": s.84(1).
    "week": s.50(1).

GENERAL NOTE
    This section deals with the rate of payment of statutory maternity pay. In so doing the section integrates the arrangement existing under the old schemes, with the result that the position is relatively complex. The higher rate is equivalent to nine-tenths of the woman's normal weekly earnings, with the lower rate yet to be prescribed.

    (*a*) The higher rate is to be paid (for a maximum of six weeks) to
        (i) women who have been continuously employed by the employer in question for a period of at least two years ending with the week immediately before the fourteenth week before the expected week of confinement; provided that
        (ii) the woman in question is employed under a contract of employment which

normally provides for 16 or more hours per week. If the woman has worked for five years or more, the normal contractual hours must be eight or more.
(*b*) The lower rate is to be paid:
  (i) for the entire period if the woman does not qualify for the higher rate;
  (ii) for 12 weeks in the case of women entitled to the higher rate for the first six weeks of the maternity pay period.

Further provisions relating to statutory maternity pay etc.

49.—(1) Part I of Schedule 4 to this Act shall have effect for supplementing this Part of this Act.

(2) The Social Security Act 1975 shall have effect subject to the amendments set out in Part II of that Schedule.

(3) Part III of that Schedule shall have effect in relation to maternity pay under the Employment Protection (Consolidation) Act 1978 and to the Maternity Pay Fund.

GENERAL NOTE

The section together with Part I of Sched. 4 enables regulations to be made entitling employers to offset their expenditure on statutory maternity pay against their national insurance contributions, or for payments to be made to reimburse employers.

The schedule also lays down rules dealing with the interchange of information between employees and employers and with the D.H.S.S. It may be noted that any day which falls within the maternity pay period shall not be treated as a day of unemployment or of incapacity for work for the purpose of determining whether it forms part of a period of interruption of employment.

Part II of the schedule sets out the provisions for payment of state maternity allowance to those women who do not qualify for statutory maternity pay. The qualifying conditions are set out in paras. 13 and 14 of the schedule. First, the woman must have worked as an employed or self-employed earner for at least 26 of the 52 weeks immediately preceding the fourteenth week before the expected week of confinement. Secondly, she must have paid full rate contributions at the class 1 or 2 rate in at least 26 weeks in the 52 week period immediately preceding the fourteenth week before the expected week of confinement. Finally, she must not be entitled to statutory maternity pay.

Part III of the schedule deals with the abolition of maternity pay and the winding up of the maternity pay fund.

Interpretation of Part V

50.—(1) In this Part of this Act (including Schedule 4 to this Act)—
  "confinement" means labour resulting in the issue of a living child, or labour after 28 weeks of pregnancy resulting in the issue of a child whether alive or dead, and "confined" shall be construed accordingly; and where a woman's labour begun on one day results in the issue of a child on another day she shall be taken to be confined on the day of the issue of the child or, if labour results in the issue of twins or a greater number of children, she shall be taken to be confined on the day of the issue of the last of them;
  "dismissed" is to be construed in accordance with section 55(2) to
    (7) of the Employment Protection (Consolidation) Act 1978;
  "employee" means a woman who is—
    (*a*) gainfully employed in Great Britain either under a contract of service or in an office (including elective office) with emoluments chargeable to income tax under Schedule E; and
    (*b*) over the age of 16;
  but subject to regulations which may provide for cases where any such woman is not to be treated as an employee for the purposes of this Part of this Act and for cases where a woman who would not otherwise be an employee for those purposes is to be treated as an employee for those purposes;

"employer", in relation to a woman who is an employee and a contract of service of hers, means a person who under section 4 of the Social Security Act 1975 is, or but for subsection (2)(*b*) of that section would be, liable to pay secondary Class 1 contributions in relation to any of her earnings (within the meaning of that Act) under the contract;

"maternity pay period" has the meaning assigned to it by section 47(1) above;

"week" means a period of 7 days beginning with midnight between Saturday and Sunday or such other period as may be prescribed in relation to any particular case or class of cases.

(2) Without prejudice to any other power to make regulations under this Part of this Act, regulations may specify cases in which, for the purposes of this Part of this Act or of such provisions of this Part of this Act as may be prescribed—

(*a*) two or more employers are to be treated as one;

(*b*) two or more contracts of service in respect of which the same woman is an employee are to be treated as one.

(3) For the purposes of this Part of this Act a woman's normal weekly earnings shall, subject to subsection (5) below, be taken to be the average weekly earnings which in the relevant period have been paid to her or paid for her benefit under the contract of service with the employer in question.

(4) For the purposes of subsection (3) above "earnings" and "relevant period" shall have the meanings given to them by regulations.

(5) In such cases as may be prescribed a woman's normal weekly earnings shall be calculated in accordance with regulations.

GENERAL NOTE

This section provides definitions of some of the terms used in Part V of the Act.

PART VI

COMMON PROVISIONS

Administration

Regulations about claims for and payments of benefit

51.—(1) Regulations may provide—

(*a*) for requiring a claim for a benefit to which this section applies to be made by such person, in such manner and within such time as may be prescribed;

(*b*) for treating such a claim made in such circumstances as may be prescribed as having been made at such date earlier or later than that at which it is made as may be prescribed;

(*c*) for permitting such a claim to be made, or treated as if made, for a period wholly or partly after the date on which it is made;

(*d*) for permitting an award on such a claim to be made for such a period subject to the condition that the claimant satisfies the requirements for entitlement when benefit becomes payable under the award;

(*e*) for a review of any such award if those requirements are found not to have been satisfied;

(*f*) for the disallowance on any ground of a person's claim for a benefit to which this section applies to be treated as a disallowance of any further claim by that person for that benefit until the grounds of the original disallowance have ceased to exist;

(*g*) for enabling one person to act for another in relation to a claim for a benefit to which this section applies and for enabling such a claim to be made and proceeded with in the name of a person who has died;

(*h*) for requiring any information or evidence needed for the determination of such a claim or of any question arising in connection with such a claim to be furnished by such person as may be prescribed in accordance with the regulations;

(*j*) for a claim for any one benefit to which this section applies to be treated, either in the alternative or in addition, as a claim for any other such benefit that may be prescribed;

(*k*) for the person to whom, time when and manner in which a benefit to which this section applies is to be paid and for the information and evidence to be furnished in connection with the payment of such a benefit;

(*l*) for notice to be given of any change of circumstances affecting the continuance of entitlement to such a benefit or payment of such a benefit;

(*m*) for the day on which entitlement to such a benefit is to begin or end;

(*n*) for calculating the amounts of such a benefit according to a prescribed scale or otherwise adjusting them so as to avoid fractional amounts or facilitate computation;

(*o*) for extinguishing the right to payment of such a benefit if payment is not obtained within such period, not being less than 12 months, as may be prescribed from the date on which the right is treated under the regulations as having arisen;

(*p*) for suspending payment, in whole or in part, where it appears to the Secretary of State that a question arises whether—
(i) the conditions for entitlement are or were fulfilled;
(ii) an award ought to be revised;
(iii) an appeal ought to be brought against an award;

(*q*) for withholding payments of a benefit to which this section applies in prescribed circumstances and for subsequently making withheld payments in prescribed circumstances;

(*r*) for the circumstances and manner in which payments of such a benefit may be made to another person on behalf of the beneficiary for any purpose, which may be to discharge, in whole or in part, an obligation of the beneficiary or any other person;

(*s*) for the payment or distribution of such a benefit to or among persons claiming to be entitled on the death of any person and for dispensing with strict proof of their title;

(*t*) for the making of a payment on account of such a benefit—
(i) where no claim has been made and it is impracticable for one to be made immediately;
(ii) where a claim has been made and it is impracticable for the claim or an appeal, reference, review or application relating to it to be immediately determined;
(iii) where an award has been made but it is impracticable to pay the whole immediately;

(*u*) for treating any payment on account made by virtue of para-graph (*t*) above as made on account of any benefit to which this section applies that is subsequently awarded or paid.

(2) This section applies to the following benefits—
(*a*) benefits under the Social Security Act 1975;

  (*b*) child benefit;
  (*c*) income support;
  (*d*) family credit;
  (*e*) housing benefit;
  (*f*) a payment under paragraph 2 of Schedule 6 to this Act
       (Christmas bonus);
and any social fund payments such as are mentioned in section 32(2)(*a*)
above.

  (3) Subsection (1)(*p*) above shall have effect in relation to housing
benefit as if the reference to the Secretary of State were a reference to the
authority paying the benefit.

  (4) Subsection (1)(*g*), (*k*), (*n*), (*r*) and (*s*) above shall have effect as if
statutory sick pay and statutory maternity pay were benefits to which this
section applies.

DEFINITIONS
  "prescribed": s.84(1).
  "regulations": s.84(1).
  "social fund payment": s.84(1).

GENERAL NOTE
  This section provides for regulations to be made for claiming and paying social security
benefits. It applies to benefit under the 1975 Act, child benefit, income support, family
credit, housing benefit and the pensioners' Christmas bonus. In the White Paper the
government stated that an important element in its plans "is a further move towards
simplification by applying common rules to all benefits. These include matters like the time
for claiming and paying benefits . . . " (para. 6–7).

Adjudication

  52.—(1) Part I of Schedule 5 to this Act (which makes amendments of
enactments relating to social security adjudications) shall have effect.

  (2) The questions to which section 93(1) of the Social Security Act 1975
(questions for determination by the Secretary of State) applies shall
include any question specified in Part II of that Schedule.

  (3) Subject to subsections (7) and (8) below, the following provisions of
the Social Security Act 1975 shall have effect for the purposes of the
benefits to which this subsection applies as they have effect for the
purposes of benefit under that Act—
  (*a*) sections 97 to 104 and 116 (adjudication officers, tribunals and
       Commissioners);
  (*b*) section 114 (regulations as to determination of questions);
  (*c*) section 115(1) and (2) and (4) to (7) and Schedule 13 (procedure);
  (*d*) section 117(1) and (2) (finality of decision);
  (*e*) section 119 (regulations in connection with adjudications); and
  (*f*) section 160 (age, marriage and death).

  (4) Procedure regulations made under section 115 of the Social Security
Act 1975 by virtue of subsection (3) above may make different provision
in relation to each of the benefits to which subsection (3) above applies.

  (5) Section 148(1) of the Social Security Act 1975 (determinations of
Secretary of State to be final) shall have effect in relation to offences
under Part I of the Social Security and Housing Benefits Act 1982 and
offences under this Act as it has effect in relation to offences under the
Social Security Act 1975.

  (6) Subsection (3) above applies to the following benefits—
  (*a*) child benefit;
  (*b*) statutory sick pay;
  (*c*) statutory maternity pay;
  (*d*) income support;
  (*e*) family credit;

and any social fund payments such as are mentioned in section 32(2)(*a*) above.

(7) In their application to statutory sick pay and statutory maternity pay the provisions of the Social Security Act 1975 mentioned in subsection (3) above shall have effect as if—

(*a*) the following subsection were substituted for section 98(1)—

"(1) Any question as to, or in connection with, entitlement to statutory sick pay or statutory maternity pay may be submitted to an adjudication officer—

(*a*) by the Secretary of State; or

(*b*) subject to and in accordance with regulations, by the employee concerned,

for determination in accordance with sections 99 to 194 below.";

(*b*) in section 99(3), for the words, "notice in writing of the reference shall be given to the claimant" there were substituted the words "the employee and employer concerned shall each be given notice in writing of the reference.";

(*c*) in section 100—

(i) in subsection (1), for the words "claimant may" there were substituted the words "employee and employer concerned shall each have a right to";

(ii) in subsection (2), for the words "claimant shall" there were substituted the words "employee and employer concerned shall each"; and

(iii) subsection (7) were omitted; and

(*d*) the following subsection were substituted for section 101(2) to (4)—

"(2) The persons at whose instance an appeal lies under this section are—

(*a*) an adjudication officer;

(*b*) the employee concerned;

(*c*) the employer concerned;

(*d*) a trade union, or any other association which exists to promote the interests and welfare of its members, where—

(i) the employee is a member at the time of the appeal and was so immediately before the question at issue arose; or

(ii) the question at issue is a question as to or in connection with entitlement of a deceased person who was at death a member;

(*e*) an association of employers of which the employer is a member at the time of the appeal and was so immediately before the question at issue arose.".

(8) In its application to family credit section 104(1)(*b*) of the Social Security Act 1975 shall have effect subject to section 20(6) above.

DEFINITIONS
"regulations": s.84(1).
"social fund payment": s.84(1).

GENERAL NOTE
This section, together with Sched. 5, deals with the adjudication and appeal system. In the first place, it extends the list of questions for determination by the Secretary of State (see 1975 Act, s.93(1)). The questions concerned are various matters arising under Part I of this Act (see Sched. 5, Part II(a)); and matters arising under Part V (dealing with statutory maternity pay). The statutory maternity pay provisions are modelled on the statutory sick

pay arrangements, initially contained in Social Security and Housing Benefits Act 1982, s.11, but not reproduced in Sched. 5, Part II(b) of the 1986 Act.

Secondly, the section harmonises the existing law on the adjudication of claims. Under the existing law for some purposes (contributory benefits, child benefit and statutory sick pay) an appeal lies on a question of fact and law, whereas for other purposes (supplementary benefit and family income supplement) an appeal lies only on a point of law. The government sought to rationalise this anomaly with the justification that this is the most "substantial improvement in the tribunal mechanism in recent years" and the fact that most "areas of civil adjudication that operate a tribunal system allow appeals from a tribunal to a higher authority only on matters of law." (Official Report, Standing Committee B, 22 April, 1986, col. 1343). Leave to appeal will be required in all cases.

Over-payments

53.—(1) Where it is determined that, whether fraudulently or otherwise, any person has misrepresented, or failed to disclose, any material fact and in consequence of the misrepresentation or failure—

(*a*) a payment has been made in respect of a benefit to which this section applies; or

(*b*) any sum recoverable by or on behalf of the Secretary of State in connection with any such payment has not been recovered,

the Secretary of State shall be entitled to recover the amount of any payment which he would not have made or any sum which he would have received but for the misrepresentation or failure to disclose.

(2) An amount recoverable under subsection (1) above is in all cases recoverable from the person who misrepresented the fact or failed to disclose it.

(3) In relation to cases where payments of a benefit to which this section applies have been credited to a bank account or other account under arrangements made with the agreement of the beneficiary or a person acting for him, circumstances may be prescribed in which the Secretary of State is to be entitled to recover any amount paid in excess of entitlement; but any such regulations shall not apply in relation to any payment unless before he agreed to the arrangements such notice of the effect of the regulations as may be prescribed was given in such manner as may be prescribed to the beneficiary or to a person acting for him.

(4) Except where regulations otherwise provide, an amount shall not be recoverable under subsection (1) above or regulations under subsection (3) above unless the determination in pursuance of which it was paid has been reversed or varied on an appeal or revised on a review.

(5) Regulations may provide—

(*a*) that amounts recoverable under subsection (1) above or regulations under subsection (3) above shall be calculated or estimated in such manner and on such basis as may be prescribed;

(*b*) for treating any amount paid to any person under an award which it is subsequently determined was not payable—

(i) as properly paid: or

(ii) as paid on account of a payment which it is determined should be or should have been made,

and for reducing or withholding any arrears payable by virtue of the subsequent determination;

(*c*) for treating any amount paid to one person in respect of another as properly paid for any period for which it is not payable in cases where in consequence of a subsequent determination—

(i) the other person is himself entitled to a payment for that period; or

(ii) a third person is entitled in priority to the payee to a payment for that period in respect of the other person, and for reducing or withholding any arrears payable for that period by virtue of the subsequent determination.

(6) Circumstances may be prescribed in which a payment on account made by virtue of section 51(1)(*t*) above may be recovered to the extent that it exceeds entitlement.

(7) Where any amount paid is recoverable under—

(*a*) section 27 above;

(*b*) subsection (1) above; or

(*c*) regulations under subsection (3) or (6) above,

it may, without prejudice to any other method of recovery, be recovered by deduction from prescribed benefits.

(8) Where any amount paid in respect of a married or unmarried couple is recoverable as mentioned in subsection (7) above, it may, without prejudice to any other method of recovery, be recovered, in such circumstances as may be prescribed, by deduction from prescribed benefits payable to either of them.

(9) Any amount recoverable under the provisions mentioned in subsection (7) above—

(*a*) if the person from whom it is recoverable resides in England and Wales and the county court so orders, shall be recoverable by execution issued from the county court or otherwise as if it were payable under an order of that court; and

(*b*) if he resides in Scotland, shall be enforced in like manner as an extract registered decree arbitral bearing a warrant for execution issued by the sheriff court of any sheriffdom in Scotland.

(10) This section applies to the following benefits—

(*a*) benefits under the Social Security Act 1975;

(*b*) child benefit;

(*c*) income support;

(*d*) family credit;

and any social fund payments such as are mentioned in section 32(2)(*a*) above.

(11) A scheme under section 2 or section 5 of the Industrial Injuries and Diseases (Old Cases) Act 1975 may make provision in relation to allowances under that Act corresponding to the provision made by this section in relation to the benefits to which it applies.

DEFINITIONS

"prescribed": s.84(1).

"regulations": s.84(1).

"social fund payment": s.84(1).

GENERAL NOTE

This section harmonises existing legislation governing the recovery of overpaid benefit and establishes misrepresentation or failure to disclose a material fact as a general test for recovering overpayments. This formulation is the same as that found in s.20(1) of the Supplementary Benefit Act 1976. The Minister for Social Security (Mr. Tony Newton) has stated that " . . . the misrepresentation or failure to disclose test as distinct from a subjective test, is easier for everyone to understand and to operate because it is clearer and effectively more factual. . . . It is more rigorous at the margin but that is not unreasonable" (Official Report, Standing Committee B, April 22, 1986, col. 1363).

Breach of regulations

54.—(1) Regulations under any of the benefit Acts may provide for contravention of, or failure to comply with, any provision contained in regulations under that Act to be an offence under that Act and for the recovery, on summary conviction of any such offence, of penalties not exceeding—

(*a*) for any one offence, level 3 on the standard scale; or (*b*) for an offence of continuing any such contravention or failure after conviction, £40 for each day on which it is so continued.

(2) Subsection (1) above shall have effect in relation to the Industrial Injuries and Diseases (Old Cases) Act 1975 as if the references in that subsection to regulations were to schemes.

DEFINITIONS
"the benefit Acts": s.84(1).
"regulations": s.84(1).

GENERAL NOTE
This section allows regulations made under this Act and also under earlier Social Security Acts to provide for an offence of contravening or failing to comply with the provisions in the regulations. The section provides for the summary conviction of such an offence, and fixes a maximum penalty.

False representations for obtaining benefit etc.

55.—(1) If a person for the purpose of obtaining any benefit or other payment under any of the benefit Acts, whether for himself or some other person, or for any other purpose connected with any of those Acts—
  (*a*) makes a statement or representation which he knows to be false; or
  (*b*) produces or furnishes, or knowingly causes or knowingly allows to be produced or furnished, any document or information which he knows to be false in a material particular,
he shall be guilty of an offence.

(2) A person guilty of an offence under subsection (1) above shall be liable on summary conviction to a fine not exceeding level 5 on the standard scale, or to imprisonment for a term not exceeding three months, or to both.

DEFINITION
"the benefit Acts": s.84(1).

GENERAL NOTE
S.55 creates an offence of knowingly making a false statement or producing false information for the purpose of obtaining benefit. The section provides for summary conviction of such an offence, and fixes a maximum penalty. It is to be noted that as originally drafted the clause was much wider, and would have applied to reckless behaviour. The government resisted an attempt to strike this out in Committee in the Commons (Official Report, Standing Committee B, April 22, 1986, cols. 1592–1593), but not in the Lords. (*Hansard* H.L., vol. 478, col. 880).

Legal proceedings

56.—(1) Any person authorised by the Secretary of State in that behalf may conduct any proceedings under the benefit Acts before a magistrates' court although not a barrister or solicitor.

(2) Notwithstanding anything in any Act—
  (*a*) proceedings for an offence under the benefit Acts other than an offence relating to housing benefit may be begun at any time within the period of three months from the date on which evidence, sufficient in the opinion of the Secretary of State to justify a prosecution for the offence, comes to his knowledge or within a period of twelve months from the commission of the offence, whichever period last expires; and
  (*b*) proceedings for an offence under the benefit Acts relating to housing benefit may be begun at any time within the period of three months from the date on which evidence, sufficient in the opinion of the appropriate authority to justify a prosecution

for the offence, comes to the authority's knowledge or within a period of twelve months from the commission of the offence, whichever period last expires.

(3) For the purposes of subsection (2) above—

(*a*) a certificate purporting to be signed by or on behalf of the Secretary of State as to the date on which such evidence as is mentioned in paragraph (*a*) of that subsection came to his knowledge shall be conclusive evidence of that date; and

(*b*) a certificate of the appropriate authority as to the date on which such evidence as is mentioned in paragraph (*b*) of that subsection came to the authority's knowledge shall be conclusive evidence of that date.

(4) In subsections (2) and (3) above "the appropriate authority" means, in relation to an offence concerning any dwelling—

(*a*) if the offence relates to rate rebate, the authority who are the appropriate rating authority by virtue of section 28(3) above;

(*b*) if it relates to a rent rebate, the authority who are the appropriate housing authority by virtue of that subsection; and

(*c*) if it relates to rent allowance, the authority who are the appropriate local authority by virtue of that subsection.

(5) In the application of this section to Scotland, the following provisions shall have effect in substitution for subsections (1) to (4) above—

(*a*) proceedings for an offence under the benefit Acts may, notwithstanding anything in section 331 of the Criminal Procedure (Scotland) Act 1975, be commenced at any time within the period of three months from the date on which evidence sufficient in the opinion of the Lord Advocate to justify proceedings comes to his knowledge, or within the period of twelve months from the commission of the offence, whichever period last expires;

(*b*) for the purposes of this subsection—

(i) a certificate purporting to be signed by or on behalf of the Lord Advocate as to the date on which such evidence as is mentioned above came to his knowledge shall be conclusive evidence thereof;

(ii) subsection (3) of section 331 of the said Act of 1975 (date of commencement of proceedings) shall have effect as it has effect for the purposes of that section.

DEFINITIONS
"the benefit Acts": s.84(1).
"dwelling": s.84(1).
"housing authority": s.84(1).
"local authority": s.84(1).
"rate rebate": s.84(1).
"rating authority": s.84(1).
"rent allowance": s.84(1).
"rent rebate": s.84(1).

GENERAL NOTE
S.56 makes arrangements for the prosecution of social security offences. It provides that the Secretary of State may authorise someone other than a barrister or solicitor to conduct his case, and it lays down a time limit within which prosecution must be brought.

Offences by bodies corporate

57.—(1) Where an offence under any of the benefit Acts which has been committed by a body corporate is proved to have been committed with the consent or connivance of, or to be attributable to any neglect on the part of, a director, manager, secretary or other similar officer of the body corporate, or any person who was purporting to act in any such capacity, he, as well as the body corporate, shall be guilty of that offence and be liable to be proceeded against accordingly.

(2) Where the affairs of a body corporate are managed by its members, subsection (1) above applies in relation to the acts and defaults of a member in connection with his functions of management as if he were a director of the body corporate.

DEFINITION
"the benefit Acts": s.84(1).

GENERAL NOTE
This section deals with the liability of the officers of a company where an offence has been committed by a corporate body.

Inspection

58.—(1) For the purposes of the benefit Acts, the Secretary of State may appoint such inspectors, and pay to them such salaries or remuneration, as he may determine with the consent of the Treasury.

(2) An inspector appointed under this section shall, for the purposes of the execution of the benefit Acts, have the following powers—
  (*a*) to enter at all reasonable times any premises liable to inspection under this section;
  (*b*) to make such examination and enquiry as may be necessary—
      (i) for ascertaining whether the provisions of any of those Acts are being, or have been, complied with in any such premises; or
      (ii) for investigating the circumstances in which any injury or disease which has given or may give rise to a claim for industrial injuries benefit was or may have been received or contracted;
  (*c*) to examine, either alone or in the presence of any other person, as he thinks fit, in relation to any matters under any of those Acts on which he may reasonably require information, every person whom he finds in any such premises or whom he has reasonable cause to believe to be or to have been a person liable to pay—
      (i) contributions under the Social Security Act 1975;
      (ii) a state scheme premium,
    and to require every such person to be so examined;
  (*d*) to exercise such other powers as may be necessary for carrying any of the benefit Acts into effect.

(3) The premises liable to inspection under this section are any where an inspector has reasonable grounds for supposing that—
  (*a*) any persons are employed;
  (*b*) there is being carried on any agency or other business for the introduction or supply to persons requiring them of persons available to do work or to perform services; or
  (*c*) a personal or occupational pension scheme is being administered,
but do not include any private dwelling-house not used by, or by permission of, the occupier for the purposes of a trade or business.

(4) Every inspector shall be furnished with a certificate of his appointment, and on applying for admission to any premises for the purpose of any of the benefit Acts shall, if so required, produce the certificate.

(5) Where any premises are liable to be inspected by an inspector or officer appointed or employed by, or are under the control of, some other government department, the Secretary of State may make arrangements with that department for any of the powers or duties of inspectors to be carried out by an inspector or officer employed by that department.

(6) In accordance with this section, persons shall furnish to an inspector all such information, and produce for his inspection all such documents, as he may reasonably require for the purpose of ascertaining—

(a) whether—
    (i) any contribution under the Social Security Act 1975;
    (ii) any state scheme premium,
is or has been payable, or has been duly paid, by or in respect of any person; or

(b) whether benefit under any of the benefit Acts is or was payable to or in respect of any person.

(7) The following persons are under the duty imposed by subsection (6) above—

(a) the occupier of any premises liable to inspection under this section;

(b) any person who is or has been an employer or an employee within the meaning of any of the benefit Acts;

(c) any person carrying on an agency or other business for the introduction or supply to persons requiring them of persons available to do work or perform services;

(d) any person who is or has at any time been a trustee or manager of a personal or occupational pension scheme;

(e) any person who is or has been liable to pay such contributions or premiums;

(f) the servants or agents of any such person as is specified in any of the preceding paragraphs;

but no-one shall be required under this section to answer any questions or to give any evidence tending to incriminate himself, or, in a case of a person who is married, his or her spouse.

(8) If a person—

(a) wilfully delays or obstructs an inspector in the exercise of any power under this Act; or

(b) refuses or neglects to answer any question or to furnish any information or to produce any document when required to do so under this Act,

he shall be guilty of an offence and liable on summary conviction to a fine not exceeding level 3 on the standard scale.

(9) Where a person is convicted of an offence under subsection (8)(b) above and the refusal or neglect is continued by him after his conviction, he shall be guilty of a further offence and liable on summary conviction to a fine not exceeding £40 for each day on which it is so continued.

DEFINITIONS
"the benefit Acts": s.84(1).
"dwelling": s.84(1).
"employee": s.84(1).
"employer": s.84(1).
"occupational pension scheme": s.84(1).
"personal pension scheme": s.84(1).

GENERAL NOTE
This section is based on the 1975 Act, ss.144 and 145, and on the 1982 Act, s.19. It enables the Secretary of State to appoint inspectors with power to enter at all reasonable times premises of employers, employment agencies, businesses and pension administrators to ascertain that the provisions of this Act and earlier Social Security legislation are being complied with. They are also empowered to investigate the circumstances surrounding any industrial injury or disease. It is an offence to wilfully delay an inspector or obstruct him in his duty.

Disclosure of information

59.—(1) No obligation as to secrecy imposed by statute or otherwise on a person employed in relation to the Inland Revenue shall prevent information obtained in connection with the assessment or collection of income tax from being disclosed to the Secretary of State, or the

Department of Health and Social Services for Northern Ireland, or to an officer of either of them authorised to receive such information in connection with the operation of any of the benefit Acts or of any corresponding enactment of Northern Ireland legislation.

(2) In relation to persons who are carrying on or have carried on a trade, profession or vocation income from which is chargeable to tax under Case I or II of Schedule D, disclosure under subsection (1) above relating to that trade, profession or vocation shall be limited to information about the commencement or cessation of the trade, profession or vocation, but sufficient information may also be given to identify the persons concerned.

(3) Subsection (1) above extends only to disclosure by or under the authority of the Commissioners of Inland Revenue; and information which is the subject of disclosure to any person by virtue of that subsection shall not be further disclosed to any other person, except where the further disclosure is made—

(*a*) to a person to whom disclosure could by virtue of this section have been made by or under the authority of the Commissioners of Inland Revenue;

(*b*) for the purposes of any proceedings (civil or criminal) in connection with the operation of any of the benefit Acts or of any corresponding Northern Ireland legislation; or

(*c*) for any purposes of Part III of the Social Security Act 1975 including that Part as extended by section 52(3) above, and any corresponding provisions of Northern Ireland legislation.

DEFINITION
"the benefit Acts": s.84(1).

GENERAL NOTE
This section broadly re-enacts old provisions in allowing information to be passed from the Inland Revenue to the DHSS. But as was pointed out in Standing Committee, however, the new power is wider than that previously contained in the earlier legislation. See Official Report, Standing Committee B, April 22, 1986, col. 1599.

Regulations as to notification of deaths

60.—(1) Regulations may provide that it shall be the duty of any of the following persons—

(*a*) the Registrar General for England and Wales;
(*b*) the Registrar General of Births, Deaths and Marriages for Scotland;
(*c*) each registrar of births and deaths,

to furnish the Secretary of State, for the purpose of his functions under the benefit Acts and the functions of the Department of Health and Social Services in Northern Ireland under any corresponding Northern Ireland legislation, with the prescribed particulars of such deaths as may be prescribed.

(2) The regulations may make provision as to the manner in which and times at which the particulars are to be furnished.

DEFINITIONS
"the benefit Acts": s.84(1).
"prescribed": s.84(1).
"regulations": s.84(1).

GENERAL NOTE
This section is consequential upon the abolition of the death grant. See s.41 above. The section provides that deaths are to be notified to the DHSS by individual registrars or by the Registrars-General.

Consultations on subordinate legislation

61.—(1) Nothing in any enactment shall require any proposals in respect of regulations to be referred to the Committee, the Council or the Board if—

(*a*) it appears to the Secretary of State that by reason of the urgency of the matter it is inexpedient so to refer them; or

(*b*) the relevant advisory body have agreed that they shall not be referred.

(2) Where by virtue only of subsection (1)(*a*) above the Secretary of State makes regulations without proposals in respect of them having been referred, then, unless the relevant advisory body agree that this subsection shall not apply, he shall refer the regulations to that body as soon as practicable after making them.

(3) Where the Secretary of State—

(*a*) has referred proposals to the Committee or the Board, he may make the proposed regulations before the Committee or Board have made their report;

(*b*) has referred proposals to the Council, he may make the proposed regulations before the Council have given their advice,

only if after the reference it appears to him that by reason of the urgency of the matter it is expedient to do so.

(4) Where by virtue of this section regulations are made before a report of the Committee or Board has been made, the Committee or Board shall consider them and make a report to the Secretary of State containing such recommendations with regard to the regulations as the Committee or Board think appropriate; and a copy of any report made to the Secretary of State on the regulations shall be laid by him before each House of Parliament together, if the report contains recommendations, with a statement of the extent (if any) to which the Secretary of State proposes to give effect to the recommendations and, in so far as he does not propose to give effect to them, his reasons why not.

(5) Nothing in any enactment shall require the reference to the Committee, the Council or the Board of regulations made by virtue of an enactment contained in this Act or in an Act passed before this Act, if they are—

(*a*) contained in a statutory instrument made before the end of a period of 12 months from the commencement of the enactment under which it is made; or

(*b*) contained in a statutory instrument which—

(i) states that it contains only provisions consequential on a specified enactment or such provisions and regulations made under that enactment; and

(ii) is made before the end of a period of 12 months from the commencement of that enactment.

(6) Nothing in any enactment shall require the reference to the Committee, the Council or the Board of regulations made by virtue of an enactment contained in an Act passed after this Act, if they are—

(*a*) contained in a statutory instrument made before the end of the period of 6 months from the commencement of the enactment under which it is made; or

(*b*) contained in a statutory instrument which—

(i) states that it contains only provisions consequential on a specified enactment or such provisions and regulations made under that enactment; and

(ii) is made before the end of the period of 6 months from the commencement of that enactment,
unless the Act containing the enactment by virtue of which the regulations are made excludes this subsection in respect of the regulations.

(7) Subject to subsection (8) below, before making—

    (*a*) regulations relating to housing benefit (other than regulations of which the effect is to increase any amount specified in regulations previously made);

    (*b*) an order under section 28(10) or 30 above,

the Secretary of State shall consult with organisations appearing to him to be representative of the authorities concerned.

(8) Nothing in subsection (7) above shall require the Secretary of State to undertake consultations if—

    (*a*) it appears to him that by reason of the urgency of the matter it is inexpedient to do so; or

    (*b*) the organisations have agreed that consultations should not be undertaken.

(9) Where the Secretary of State has undertaken such consultations, he may make any regulations or order to which the consultations relate without completing the consultations if it appears to him that by reason of the urgency of the matter it is expedient to do so.

(10) In this section—

    "the Board" means the Occupational Pensions Board;

    "the Committee" means the Social Security Advisory Committee;

    "the Council" means the Industrial Injuries Advisory Council.

DEFINITION
"regulations": s.84(1).

GENERAL NOTE
S.61 provides that regulations may be made before they have been referred to or before a response has been received from the Social Security Advisory Committee, the Industrial Injuries Advisory Council or the Occupational Pensions Board if the Secretary of State considers that by reason of urgency it is expedient to do so. Any report on the regulations that is made to the Secretary of State is to be laid before each House of Parliament together with a statement on the effect to be given to any recommendations. Regulations made within 12 months of the coming into force of the enactment under which they are made need not be referred to any advisory body. There will be an obligation before making regulations on housing benefit to consult with organisations representative of authorities unless because of the urgency of the matter the Secretary of State considers it inexpedient to do so.

In Standing Committee an attempt was made to limit the power of the Secretary of State to the extent that regulations might be made before being referred only if both the Minister and the relevant advisory committee consider that it is not expedient on grounds of urgency to make the reference.

Subordinate legislation—miscellaneous

62.—(1) The following subsection shall be inserted after subsection (3) of section 166 of the Social Security Act 1975 (general provisions about orders and regulations)—

    "(3A) Without prejudice to any specific provisions in this Act, a power conferred by this Act to make an Order in Council, regulations or an order includes power to provide for a person to exercise a discretion in dealing with any matter.".

(2) The following subsection shall be inserted after subsection (7) of section 22 of the Child Benefit Act 1975 (regulations and orders)—

    "(7A) Without prejudice to any specific provisions in this Act, a power conferred by this Act to make an Order in Council or regulations includes a power to provide for a person to exercise a discretion in dealing with any matter.".

(3) In subsection (1) of section 167 of the Social Security Act 1975 (Parliamentary control of orders and regulations)—

(a) for the words from the beginning to "namely" there shall be substituted the words "Subject to the provisions of this section, a statutory instrument containing (whether alone or with other provisions)—

    (a) regulations made by virtue of";

(b) in paragraph (b), for the words "no order shall be made wholly or partly by virtue of" there shall be substituted the words "an order under";

(c) in paragraph (c), for the words "no order shall be made" there shall be substituted the words "an order"; and

(d) for the words "unless a draft of the regulations or order" there shall be substituted the words "shall not be made unless a draft of the instrument".

GENERAL NOTE

This section authorises regulations to confer discretionary powers on the executive. This applies to regulations made under the Social Security Act 1975 and the Child Benefit Act 1975.

General provisions as to operation of social security

Annual up-rating of benefits

63.—(1) The Secretary of State shall in each tax year review the sums—

(a) specified—

    (i) in Schedule 4 to the Social Security Act 1975;

    (ii) in section 30(1) of that Act;

    (iii) in sections 2(6)(c) and 7(2)(b) of the Industrial Injuries and Diseases (Old Cases) Act 1975;

    (iv) in section 6(1)(a) of the Social Security Pensions Act 1975;

(b) which are the additional pensions in long-term benefits;

(c) which are the increases in the rates of retirement pensions under Schedule 1 to the Social Security Pensions Act 1975;

(d) which are—

    (i) payable by virtue of section 35(6) of that Act to a person who is also entitled to a Category A or Category B retirement pension (including sums payable by virtue of section 36(3)); or

    (ii) payable to such a person as part of his Category A or Category B retirement pension by virtue of an order made under this section by virtue of this paragraph or made under section 126A of the Social Security Act 1975;

(e) specified in section 41(2B) of the Social Security Act 1975;

(f) specified by virtue of section 5(1) of the Child Benefit Act 1975;

(g) specified in section 7(1) of the Social Security and Housing Benefits Act 1982;

(h) specified in regulations under section 48(3) above;

(i) prescribed for the purposes of section 21(6)(a) above or specified in regulations under section 22(1) above,

in order to determine whether they have retained their value in relation to the general level of prices obtaining in Great Britain estimated in such manner as the Secretary of State thinks fit.

(2) Where it appears to the Secretary of State that the general level of prices is greater at the end of the period under review than it was at the beginning of that period, he shall lay before Parliament the draft of an up-rating order—

(a) which increases each of the sums to which subsection (3) below

applies by a percentage not less than the percentage by which the
general level of prices is greater at the end of the period than it
was at the beginning; and

(b) if he considers it appropriate, having regard to the national economic situation and any other matters which he considers relevant,
which also increases by such percentage or percentages as he thinks
fit any of the sums mentioned in subsection (1) above but to which
subsection (3) below does not apply; and

(c) stating the amount of any sums which are mentioned in subsection
(1) above but which the order does not increase.

(3) This subsection applies to sums—

(a) specified in Part I, paragraph 1, 2, 3, 4 or 5 of Part III, Part IV
or Part V of Schedule 4 to the Social Security Act 1975;

(b) mentioned in subsection (1)(a)(iii) or (iv), (b), (c) or (d) above.

(4) Subsection (2) above shall not require the Secretary of State to
provide for an increase in any case in which it appears to him that the
amount of the increase would be inconsiderable.

(5) The Secretary of State may, in providing for an increase in pursuance
of subsection (2) above, adjust the amount of the increase so as to round
any sum up or down to such extent as he thinks appropriate.

(6) Where subsection (2) above requires the Secretary of State to lay
before Parliament the draft of an order increasing any sum that could be
reduced under section 17(1) of the Child Benefit Act 1975, the order may
make such alteration to that sum as reflects the combined effect of that
increase and of any reduction that could be made under that subsection.

(7) An increase in a sum such as is specified in subsection (1)(d)(ii)
above shall form part of the Category A or Category B retirement pension
of the person to whom it is paid and an increase in a sum specified such
as is specified in subsection (1)(d)(i) above shall be added to and form
part of that pension but shall not form part of the sum increased.

(8) Where any increment under section 35(6) of the Social Security
Pensions Act 1975—

(a) is increased in any tax year by an order under section 37A of that
Act; and

(b) in that tax year also falls to be increased by an order under this
section,

the increase under this section shall be the amount that would have been
specified in the order, but for this subsection, less the amount of the
increase under section 37A.

(9) Where sums are payable to a person by virtue of section 35(6) of
the Social Security Pensions Act 1975 (including such sums payable by
virtue of section 36(3) of that Act) during a period ending with the date
on which he became entitled to a Category A or Category B retirement
pension, then, for the purpose of determining the amount of his Category
A or Category B retirement pension, orders made under this section
during that period shall be deemed to have come into force (consecutively
in the order in which they were made) on the date on which he became
entitled to that pension.

(10) If the Secretary of State considers it appropriate to do so, he may
include in the draft of an up-rating order, in addition to any other
provisions, provisions increasing any of the sums for the time being
specified in regulations under Part II of this Act.

(11) The Secretary of State shall lay with any draft order under this
section a copy of a report by the Government Actuary giving the latter's
opinion on the likely effect on the National Insurance Fund of such parts
of the order as relate to sums payable out of that Fund.

(12) If a draft order laid before Parliament in pursuance of this section is approved by a resolution of each House, the Secretary of State shall make the order in the form of the draft.

(13) An order under this section—

    (*a*) shall be framed so as to bring the alterations to which it relates into force—

        (i) in the week beginning with the first Monday in the tax year; or

        (ii) on such earlier date in April as may be specified in the order;

    (*b*) shall make such transitional provision as the Secretary of State considers expedient in respect of periods of entitlement—

        (i) to statutory sick pay;

        (ii) to family credit,

running at the date when the alterations come into force.

DEFINITIONS

"prescribed": s.84(1).
"regulations": s.84(1).
"tax year": s.84(1).

GENERAL NOTE

This section provides for the annual review of benefits in order to determine whether they have retained their value in relation to the general level of prices. In the case of some benefits the Secretary of State is required to up-rate the benefits, and in the case of others he has a discretion to do so if he thinks it appropriate, having regard to the considerations referred to in subs. (2)(*b*) and (*c*).

Effect of alteration of rates of benefit

64.—(1) This section applies where the rate of any relevant benefit is altered—

    (*a*) by an Act subsequent to this Act;

    (*b*) by an order under section 63 above; or

    (*c*) in consequence of any such Act or order altering any maximum rate of benefit;

and in this section "the commencing date" means the date fixed for payment of benefit at an altered rate to commence.

(2) Subject to such exceptions or conditions as may be prescribed where—

    (*a*) the weekly rate of a relevant benefit is altered to a fixed amount higher or lower than the previous amount; and

    (*b*) before the commencing date an award of that benefit has been made (whether before or after the passing of the relevant Act or the making of the relevant order),

except as respects any period falling before the commencing date, the benefit shall become payable at the altered rate without any claim being made for it in the case of an increase in the rate of benefit or any review of the award in the case of a decrease, and the award shall have effect accordingly.

(3) Where—

    (*a*) the weekly rate of a relevant benefit is altered; and

    (*b*) before the commencing date (but after that date is fixed) an award is made of the benefit,

the award either may provide for the benefit to be paid as from the commencing date at the altered rate or may be expressed in terms of the rate appropriate at the date of the award.

(4) Where in consequence of the passing of an Act, or the making of an order, altering the rate of disablement pension under section 57 of the

Social Security Act 1975, regulations are made varying the scale of disablement gratuities under subsection (5) of that section, the regulations may provide that the scale as varied shall apply only in cases where the period taken into account by the assessment of the extent of the disablement in respect of which the gratuity is awarded begins or began after such day as may be prescribed.

(5) Subject to such exceptions or conditions as may be prescribed, where—

(*a*) for any purpose of any Act or regulations the weekly rate at which a person contributes to the cost of providing for a child, or to the maintenance of an adult dependant, is to be calculated for a period beginning on or after the commencing date for an increase in the weekly rate of benefit; but

(*b*) account is to be taken of amounts referable to the period before the commencing date,

those amounts shall be treated as increased in proportion to the increase in the weekly rate of benefit.

(6) In this section "relevant benefit" means benefit under the Social Security Act 1975 or the Industrial Injuries and Diseases (Old Cases) Act 1975.

DEFINITIONS
"prescribed": s.84(1).
"regulations": s.84(1).

GENERAL NOTE
This section provides that where the rate of benefit has been altered, it shall become payable at the altered rate without a fresh claim having to be made.

Reciprocal arrangements

65.—(1) At the end of subsection (4)(*b*) of section 142 of the Social Security Act 1975 (co-ordination with Northern Ireland) there shall be added "(but not so as to confer any double benefit) and for determining, in cases where rights accrue both in relation to Great Britain and in relation to Northern Ireland, which of those rights shall be available to the person concerned."

(2) In subsection (1) of section 143 of that Act (reciprocity with other countries)—

(*a*) for the words from "reciprocity" to the end of paragraph (*c*) there shall be substituted the words "reciprocity in matters relating to payments for purposes similar or comparable to the purposes of this Act"; and

(*b*) the words "relating to social security" shall be omitted.

(3) The words "relating to child benefit" shall be omitted from subsection (1) of section 15 of the Child Benefit Act 1975 (reciprocal agreements with countries outside the United Kingdom).

(4) Sections 14 and 15 of the Child Benefit Act 1975 (reciprocal arrangements with Northern Ireland and reciprocal agreements with countries outside the United Kingdom) shall have effect in relation to income support, family credit and housing benefit as they have effect in relation to child benefit, references in them to Part I of that Act being construed as including references to this Act.

GENERAL NOTE
This section amends the Social Security Act 1975, ss.142 and 143 and the Child Benefit Act 1975, ss.14 and 15. In so doing, it makes further arrangements to ensure co-ordination with Northern Ireland and reciprocity with other countries.

PART VII

MISCELLANEOUS, GENERAL AND SUPPLEMENTARY

Miscellaneous

Pensioners' Christmas bonus

66. Schedule 6 to this Act (which makes provision relating to payments for pensioners) shall have effect.

GENERAL NOTE
This section, together with Sched. 6, re-enacts existing legislation making provision for the Christmas bonus.

Rates of payments of statutory sick pay and provisions as to recovery

67.—(1) The following subsections shall be inserted after subsection (1) of section 7 of the Social Security and Housing Benefits Act 1982 (rate of payment of statutory sick pay)—

"(1A) The Secretary of State may by regulations—

(*a*) substitute alternative provisions for subsection (1)(*a*) to (*c*) above; and

(*b*) make such consequential amendments of any provision contained in this Act as appear to him to be required.

(1B) A statutory instrument containing (whether alone or with other provisions) regulations under subsection (1A) above shall not be made unless a draft of the instrument has been laid before Parliament and approved by a resolution of each House.".

(2) The following paragraph shall be substitued for subsection (1A)(*a*) of section 9 of that Act (recovery by employers of amounts paid by way of statutory sick pay)—

"(*a*) giving any employer who has made a payment of statutory sick pay a right, except in prescribed circumstances, to an amount, determined in such manner as may be prescribed—

(i) by reference to secondary Class 1 contributions paid in respect of statutory sick pay; or

(ii) by reference to the aggregate of secondary Class 1 contributions so paid and secondary Class 1 contributions paid in respect of statutory maternity pay;".

GENERAL NOTE
This section amends the Social Security and Housing Benefits Act 1982, ss.7 and 9. So far as s.7 is concerned, the new measure enables the government to substitute by affirmative regulations new provisions for those contained in s.7(1) (which deals with the rate of statutory sick pay). In Standing Committee, it was explained that this will enable the government to alter the present three rates of payment to two or four, should this be necessary. It was also explained, however, that there are no such plans at the present, though "The greater flexibility of the proposed new clause will give us more scope to consider alternatives at future upratings, should that be necessary in the interest of what we believe to be a more coherent structure." (Official Report, Standing Committee B, April 29, 1986, col. 1797.) So far as s.9 of the 1982 Act is concerned, subs. (2) provides for employees to be compensated for the national insurance contributions that they will pay on statutory maternity pay. The precise way in which the compensation will be calculated will not be finally determined without further consultation with employers organisations. (*ibid.*, col. 1796).

Liability of Secretary of State to pay statutory sick pay in prescribed circumstances

68. The following subsections shall be added at the end of section 1 of the Social Security and Housing Benefits Act 1982—

"(5) Circumstances may be prescribed in which, notwithstanding the foregoing provisions of this section, the liability to make payments of statutory sick pay is to be a liability of the Secretary of State.

(6) Any sums paid under regulations made by virtue of subsection (5) above shall be paid out of the National Insurance Fund.".

GENERAL NOTE

In the House of Lords, Baroness Trumpington explained that "where an employer fails to comply with the adjudicating authorities' decision that he is liable to pay SSP, regulations made under this provision will enable the Secretary of State to take over payments." (*Hansard*, H.L. Vol. 478, col. 880). The corresponding provision in relation to statutory maternity pay is s.46(8) of this Act.

Repeal of section 92 of Social Security Act 1975

69. Section 92 of the Social Security Act 1975 (which relates to arrangements to forgo benefit in return for unabated sick pay) shall cease to have effect.

GENERAL NOTE

This section repeals Social Security Act 1975, s.92. The measure was introduced in Committee, with the Parliamentary Under-Secretary of State explaining that the provision " . . . abolishes the arrangements under which civil servants and some other groups, including Members of Parliament and Ministers, undertake not to claim DHSS benefit while receiving full pay during the first months of sickness. Those arrangements are no longer necessary because statutory sick pay has been extended to 28 weeks. They are known as "Estains". I am reliably informed that that is an abbreviation of "establishment and insurance" dating back to 1947." (Official Report, Standing Committee B, April 24, 1986, col. 1649).

Child benefit in respect of children educated otherwise than at educational establishments

70.—(1) In section 2 of the Child Benefit Act 1975 (meaning of "child")—

(*a*) in paragraph (*b*) of subsection (1), for the words "by attendance at a recognised educational establishment" there shall be substituted the words "either by attendance at a recognised educational establishment or, if the education is recognised by the Secretary of State, elsewhere"; and

(*b*) the following subsections shall be inserted after that subsection—

"(1A) The Secretary of State may recognise education provided otherwise than at a recognised educational establishment for a person who, in the opinion of the Secretary of State, could reasonably be expected to attend such an establishment only if the Secretary of State is satisfied that education was being so provided for that person immediately before he attained the age of sixteen.

(1B) Regulations may prescribe the circumstances in which education is or is not to be treated for the purposes of this Act as full-time.".

(2) Regulations purporting to be made under section 24(1) of that Act and made before the passing of this Act shall be treated as validly made.

DEFINITION

"regulations": s.84(1).

GENERAL NOTE

This section amends the definition of "child" in s.2 of the Child Benefit Act 1975. At present a child includes someone who is under 19 and is receiving full-time education at a recognised educational establishment. In addition, it will now also include someone receiving an education elsewhere which is recognised by the Secretary of State.

Entitlement to mobility allowance general

71.—(1) In paragraph (*a*) of section 37A(2) of the Social Security Act 1975 (duration of inability or virtual inability to walk for the purposes of entitlement to mobility allowance) for the words "time when a claim for the allowance is received by the Secretary of State" there shall be substituted the words "relevant date".

(2) The following subsections shall be inserted after that subsection—

"(2A) Subject to subsection (2B) below, in subsection (2)(*a*) above "the relevant date" means the date on which the claimant's inability or virtual inability to walk commenced or the date on which his claim was received or treated as received by the Secretary of State, whichever is the later.

(2B) Where—

(*a*) a claimant is awarded an allowance for a period; and

(*b*) he subsequently claims an allowance for a further period, the relevant date is the first date not earlier than the end of the period for which the allowance was awarded on which the claimant was unable or virtually unable to walk.

(2C) Regulations may make provision—

(*a*) for permitting an award on a claim for a mobility allowance to be made either as from the date on which the claim is received or treated as received by the Secretary of State or for a period beginning after that date subject to the condition that the person in respect of whom the claim is made satisfies the prescribed requirements for entitlement when benefit becomes payable under the award;

(*b*) for the review of any such award if those requirements are found not to have been satisfied.".

(3) Section 37A(7) (under which, except so far as may be provided by regulations, the question of a person's entitlement to a mobility allowance falls to be determined as at the time when a claim for the allowance is received by the Secretary of State) shall cease to have effect.

(4) Where—

(*a*) it has been determined that a person was entitled to mobility allowance; and

(*b*) the claim should have been determined as at the date when it was received by the Secretary of State, but was determined as at a later date,

the fact that the claim was determined as at that date shall not invalidate the determination.

(5) Where the Secretary of State has made a payment to a person who has claimed mobility allowance on the ground that, if the person's claim had been received by the Secretary of State at a date later than that on which it was in fact received, the person would have been entitled to mobility allowance—

(*a*) the payment shall be treated as a payment of mobility allowance; and

(*b*) the person shall be treated as having been entitled to mobility allowance for the period in respect of which the payment was made.

DEFINITION
"regulations": s.84(1).

GENERAL NOTE
This section amends s.37A of the Social Security Act 1975 to enable regulations to make provision for permitting an award on a claim for a mobility allowance to be made either as from the date on which the claim is received or from a later date.

The section reverses a recent Court of Appeal decision which held that entitlement to mobility allowance could be considered only as at the date on which a claim is received. Subs. (4) validates, retrospectively, payment of mobility allowance to claimants who satisfied the condition for entitlement from a date later than the date of their claim.

The government has been making extra-statutory payments to people who would only have qualified on a "later-date" basis, on account of, and at the same amount, as the mobility allowance which would have been paid had the existing law permitted "later-date" awards. Subs. (5) puts these payments on a statutory basis, by treating them as payments of mobility allowance, and treats the recipients of the payments as entitled to the allowance for the period the payments are made.

Entitlement of certain women to mobility allowance

72. In relation to women born after 6th June 1918 but before 21st December 1919 sections 22 and 65(1) of the Society Security Pensions Act 1975, paragraphs 47, 49 and 51 to 53 of Schedule 4 to that Act and section 3(3) of the Social Security Act 1979 shall be deemed to have come into force—

(*a*) for the purposes of the making of claims for, and the determination of claims and questions relating to, mobility allowance, on 29th March 1979; and

(*b*) for all other purposes, on 6th June 1979.

GENERAL NOTE
This section validates retrospectively the payment of mobility allowance to women born after June 6, 1918 and before December 21, 1919.

Application of provisions of Act to supplementary benefit etc.

73. Schedule 7 to this Act shall have effect for the purpose of making provision in relation to the benefits there mentioned.

GENERAL NOTE
Together with Sched. 7 this makes continuing provision for former benefits, including supplementary benefit.

National Insurance contributions

74.—(1) The subsection set out in subsection (2) below shall be inserted in the Social Security Act 1975—

(*a*) in section 4 (Class 1 contributions) after subsection (6H), as subsection (6HH); and

(*b*) in section 123A (further power to alter certain contributions) after subsection (6), as subsection (6A).

(2) The subsection is—

"Where the Secretary of State lays before Parliament a draft of an order under this section he shall lay with it a copy of a report by the Government Actuary on the effect which, in the Actuary's opinion, the making of such an order may be expected to have on the National Insurance Fund.".

(3) In section 134 of that Act (appropriate employment protection allocation) the following subsections shall be inserted after subsection (5)—

"(5A) Without prejudice to section 122(3) and (4) above, the Secretary of State may, with the consent of the Treasury, by order amend this section, in relation to any tax year beginning after the tax year 1986–87—

(*a*) by substituting a different percentage for the percentage for

the time being specified in paragraph (i) or (ii) of subsection (4) above or for each of the percentages specified in those paragraphs;
(*b*) by directing that there shall be no appropriate employment protection allocation; or
(*c*) by directing that there shall be an appropriate employment protection allocation only in the case of primary Class 1 contributions or only in the case of secondary Class 1 contributions.

(5B) At any time when an order under subsection (5A) above containing a direction under paragraph (*b*) of that subsection is in force, the Secretary of State may, with the consent of the Treasury, by order direct that there shall be an appropriate employment protection allocation of such percentage in the case of primary Class 1 contributions or secondary Class 1 contributions, or both, as may be specified in the order.

(5C) At any time when an order under subsection (5A) above containing a direction under paragraph (*c*) of that subsection is in force, the Secretary of State may, with the consent of the Treasury, by order direct that there shall be an appropriate employment protection allocation of such percentage as may be specified in the order in the case of the description of contributions in whose case there is, by virtue of the direction, no such allocation.

(5D) Any percentage specified as an allocation by an order under subsection (5B) or (5C) above shall be deemed to be inserted at the appropriate place in subsection (4) above and an order under subsection (5A)(*a*) above may accordingly be made in respect of it.".

(4) In section 167(1)(*b*) of that Act (orders subject to affirmative procedure) after "134 (4A)" there shall be inserted "(5A), (5B) or (5C)".

(5) The powers to prescribe equivalents of a limit or bracket under section 4 of and paragraph 1(1C) of Schedule 1 to that Act include power to prescribe an amount not more than £1·00 more than the amount which is the arithmetical equivalent of the limit or bracket.

(6) In section 1(2) of the Social Security Pensions Act 1975 (lower earnings limit) for "49p" there shall be substituted "99p".

DEFINITION
"prescribed": s.84(1).

GENERAL NOTE
This section provides for the laying before Parliament of a copy of the report by the Government Actuary on the effect on the National Insurance Fund of an order altering the structure of reduced percentage rates and related earnings introduced from October 1985 and for a new power to alter the employment protection allocation.

Earnings factors

75. The Social Security Acts 1975 and the Social Security (Miscellaneous Provisions) Act 1977 shall be amended in accordance with Schedule 8 to this Act in relation to earnings factors for the tax year in which this section comes into force and subsequent tax years.

DEFINITION
"tax year": s.84(1).

GENERAL NOTE
Together with Sched. 8 this provides for earnings factors to be calculated from the earnings on which Class 1 contributions are payable rather than from the contributions themselves.

Amendments relating to forfeiture of benefits

76.—(1) The Forfeiture Act 1982 shall be amended as follows.

(2) The following subsections shall be inserted after subsection (1) of section 4 (Social Security Commissioner to determine whether forfeiture rule applies to social security benefits)—

"(1A) Where a Commissioner determines that the forfeiture rule has precluded a person (in this section referred to as "the offender") who has unlawfully killed another from receiving the whole or part of any such benefit or advantage, the Commissioner may make a decision under this subsection modifying the effect of that rule and may do so whether the unlawful killing occurred before or after the coming into force of this subsection.

(1B) The Commissioner shall not make a decision under subsection (1A) above modifying the effect of the forfeiture rule in any case unless he is satisfied that, having regard to the conduct of the offender and of the deceased and to such other circumstances as appear to the Commissioner to be material, the justice of the case requires the effect of the rule to be so modified in that case.

(1C) Subject to subsection (1D) below, a decision under subsection (1A) above may modify the effect of the forfeiture rule in either or both of the following ways—

(*a*) so that it applies only in respect of a specified proportion of the benefit or advantage;

(*b*) so that it applies in respect of the benefit or advantage only for a specified period of time.

(1D) Such a decision may not modify the effect of the forfeiture rule so as to allow any person to receive the whole or any part of a benefit or advantage in respect of any period before the commencement of this subsection.

(1E) If the Commissioner thinks it expedient to do so, he may direct that his decision shall apply to any future claim for a benefit or advantage under a relevant enactment, on which a question such as is mentioned in subsection (1) above arises by reason of the same unlawful killing.

(1F) It is immaterial for the purposes of subsection (1E) above whether the claim is in respect of the same or a different benefit or advantage.

(1G) For the purpose of obtaining a decision whether the forfeiture rule should be modified the Secretary of State may refer to a Commissioner for review any determination of a question such as is mentioned in subsection (1) above that was made before the commencement of subsections (1A) to (1F) above (whether by a Commissioner or not) and shall do so if the offender requests him to refer such a determination.

(1H) Subsections (1A) to (1F) above shall have effect on a reference under subsection (1G) above as if in subsection (1A) the words "it has been determined" were substituted for the words "a Commissioner determines".".

(3) In subsection (2) of that section, after the words "that subsection" there shall be inserted the words "or any decision under subsection (1A) above".

(4) In section 5 (exclusion of murderers) after the word "Act", in the second place where it occurs, there shall be inserted the words "or in any decision made under section 4(1A) of this Act".

<small>GENERAL NOTE</small>

In introducing this section Baroness Hooper explained that it " . . . amends the Forfeiture Act 1982 to give the Social Security Commissioners the same powers in relation to granting relief from forfeiture of benefit as the courts already enjoy in relation to property rights. It will enable the commissioners to decide in cases where the rule of public policy applies whether, and if so for how long, an offender should forfeit benefit." (*Hansard* H.L. vol. 477, col.726).

Refreshments for school pupils

77.—(1) The words "and may do so either on the premises or at any place other than the school premises where education is being provided" shall be inserted—

(*a*) after "refreshment" in subsection (1)(*a*) of section 22 of the Education Act 1980; and

(*b*) after "management" in subsection (1)(*a*) of section 53 of the Education (Scotland) Act 1980.

(2) The following subsections shall be substituted for subsections (2) and (3) of each of those sections—

"(2) Subject to subsection (3) below, an authority must charge for anything provided by them under subsection (1)(*a*) above and must charge every pupil the same price for the same quantity of the same item.

(3) In relation to a pupil whose parents are in receipt of income support or who is himself in receipt of it an authority shall so exercise the power conferred by subsection (1)(*a*) above as to ensure that such provision is made for him in the middle of the day as appears to the authority to be requisite and shall make that provision for him free of charge.".

GENERAL NOTE
The section provides an entitlement to free school meals to families on income support and removes the discretionary powers of local education authorities to extend the eligibility to free school meals to families not on income support.

Travelling expenses

78. The Secretary of State may pay such travelling expenses as, with the consent of the Treasury, he may determine—

(*a*) to persons required by him to attend an interview in connection with the operation of any of the benefit Acts;

(*b*) to persons attending local offices in connection with the operation—

(i) of any of those Acts; or

(ii) of any prescribed enactment.

DEFINITIONS
"the benefit Acts": s.84(1).
"prescribed": s.84(1).

GENERAL NOTE
This section enables the Secretary of State to reimburse travelling expenses to persons attending local offices.

General

Crown employment

79.—(1) A person who is employed by or under the Crown shall be treated as an employed earner for the purposes of sections 1 to 17 above.

(2) A person who is serving as a member of Her Majesty's forces shall, while he is so serving, be treated for the purposes of sections 1 to 16 above as an employed earner in respect of his membership of those forces.

(3) The provisions of this Act relating to family credit apply in relation to persons employed by or under the Crown as they apply in relation to persons employed otherwise than by or under the Crown.

(4) Subject to subsection (5) below, the provisions of Part V of this Act apply in relation to persons employed by or under the Crown as they apply in relation to persons employed otherwise than by or under the Crown.

(5) The provisions of that Part of this Act do not apply in relation to persons serving as members of Her Majesty's forces, in their capacity as such.

(6) For the purposes of this section Her Majesty's forces shall be taken to consist of such establishments and organisations as may be prescribed, being establishments and organisations in which persons serve under the control of the Defence Council.

DEFINITIONS
"employed earner": s.84(1).
"prescribed": s.84(1).

Application of Parts I and V to special cases

80.—(1) Regulations may modify Parts I and V of this Act, in such manner as the Secretary of State thinks proper, in their application to any person who is, or has been, or is to be—

(*a*) employed on board any ship, vessel, hovercraft or aircraft;

(*b*) outside Great Britain at any prescribed time or in any prescribed circumstances; or

(*c*) in prescribed employment in connection with continental shelf operations.

(2) Regulations under subsection (1) above may in particular provide—

(*a*) for any provision of either of those Parts of this Act to apply to any such person, notwithstanding that it would not otherwise apply;

(*b*) for any such provision not to apply to any such person, notwithstanding that it would otherwise apply;

(*c*) for excepting any such person from the application of any such provision where he neither is domiciled nor has a place of residence in any part of Great Britain;

(*d*) for the taking of evidence, for the purposes of the determination of any question arising under any such provision, in a country or territory outside Great Britain, by a British consular official or such other person as may be determined.

(3) In this section "continental shelf operations" means any activities which, if paragraphs (*a*) and (*b*) of subsection (6) of section 23 of the Oil and Gas (Enterprise) Act 1982 (application of civil law to certain off-shore activities) were omitted, would nevertheless fall within subsection (2) of that section.

DEFINITIONS
"prescribed" : s.84(1).
"regulations" : s.84(1).

Northern Ireland

Orders in Council making corresponding provision for Northern Ireland

81. An Order in Council under paragraph 1(1)(*b*) of Schedule 1 to the Northern Ireland Act 1974 (legislation for Northern Ireland in the interim period) which states that it is made only for purposes corresponding to those of this Act—

(*a*) shall not be subject to paragraph 1(4) and (5) of that Schedule (affirmative resolution of both Houses of Parliament); but

(*b*) shall be subject to annulment in pursuance of a resolution of either House.

Amendments of enactments relating to social security in Northern Ireland

82. The enactments relating to social security in Northern Ireland specified in Schedule 9 to this Act shall have effect subject to the amendments there specified.

Supplementary

Orders and regulations general provisions

83.—(1) Section 166(1) to (3A) of the Social Security Act 1975 (extent of powers) shall apply to powers conferred by this Act to make regulations or orders as they apply to any power to make regulations or orders conferred by that Act but as if for references to that Act there were substituted references to this Act.

(2) Any power conferred by this Act to make orders or regulations relating to housing benefit shall include power to make different provision for different areas.

(3) A statutory instrument containing (whether alone or with other provisions)—

(*a*) regulations under section 5(15)(*a*) above;

(*b*) regulations under Part II of this Act which are made before the coming into operation of that Part;

(*c*) orders under section 30(2) or (3) above which are made before the coming into operation of those subsections;

(*d*) an order under section 63 above;

(*e*) an order under paragraph 2(3)(*b*) of Schedule 6 to this Act,

shall not be made unless a draft of the instrument has been laid before Parliament and approved by a resolution of each House.

(4) All regulations and orders made under this Act, other than those to which subsection (3) above applies and orders under section 88 below, shall be subject to annulment in pursuance of a resolution of either House of Parliament.

(5) An order under section 30 or 63 above or section 85 below shall not be made without the consent of the Treasury.

(6) A power conferred by this Act to make any regulations or order, where the power is not expressed to be exercisable with the consent of the Treasury, shall if the Treasury so direct be exercisable only in conjunction with them.

DEFINITION
"regulations" : s.84(1).

General interpretation

84.—(1) In this Act, unless the context otherwise requires,—

"applicable amount" shall be construed in accordance with Part II of this Act;

"average salary benefits" means benefits the rate or amount of which is calculated by reference to the average salary of a member of a pension scheme over the period of service on which the benefits are based;

"the benefit Acts" means—

(*a*) the Social Security Act 1973;

(*b*) the Social Security Acts 1975 to 1986;

(*c*) the Industrial Injuries and Diseases (Old Cases) Act 1975;

(*d*) the Child Benefit Act 1975;

"contract of service" has the same meaning as in the Social Security Act 1975;

"dwelling" means any residential accommodation, whether or not consisting of the whole or part of a building and whether or not compromising separate and self-contained premises:

"employed earner" has the same meaning as in the Social Security Act 1975;

"employee" means a person gainfully employed in Great Britain either under a contract of service or in an office (including an elective office) with emoluments chargeable to income tax under Schedule E;

"employer" means—

(*a*) in the case of an employed earner employed under a contract of service, his employer;

(*b*) in the case of an employed earner employed in an office with emoluments—

(i) such person as may be prescribed in relation to that office; or

(ii) if no person is prescribed, the government department, public authority or body of persons responsible for paying the emoluments of the office;

"housing authority" means a local authority, a new town corporation, the Scottish Special Housing Association or the Development Board for Rural Wales;

"housing benefit scheme" shall be construed in accordance with Part II of this Act;

"Housing Revenue Account dwelling", in relation to a local authority, means a dwelling which is within the authority's Housing Revenue Account (within the meaning of Part XIII of the Housing Act 1985) and is not—

(*a*) a dwelling for the time being let on a long tenancy at a low rent within the meaning of the Leasehold Reform Act 1967; or

(*b*) a dwelling no longer owned by the authority;

"Housing Revenue Account rebate", in relation to a local authority in England and Wales, means a rent rebate for a tenant of a Housing Revenue Account dwelling of that authority;

"income-related benefit" shall be construed in accordance with Part II of this Act;

"insurance company" has the meaning assigned to it by section 96(1) of the Insurance Companies Act 1982;

"local authority" means—

(*a*) in relation to England and Wales, the council of a district or London borough, the Common Council of the City of London or the Council of the Isles of Scilly; and

(*b*) in relation to Scotland, an islands or district council;

"long-term benefit" has the meaning assigned to it by Schedule 20 to the Social Security Act 1975;

"minimum contributions" shall be construed in accordance with Part I of this Act;

"modifications" includes additions, omissions and amendments, and related expressions shall be construed accordingly;

"money purchase benefits", in relation to a member of a personal or occupational pension scheme or the widow or widower of a member of such a scheme, means benefits the rate or amount of which is calculated by reference to a payment or payments made by the member or by any other person in respect of the member and which are not average salary benefits;

"new town corporation" means—

(a) in relation to England and Wales, a development corporation established under the New Towns Act 1981 or the Commission for the New Towns; and

(b) in relation to Scotland, a development corporation established under the New Towns (Scotland) Act 1968;

"occupational pension scheme" has the same meaning as in section 66(1) of the Social Security Pensions Act 1975;

"personal pension scheme" means any scheme or arrangement which is comprised in one or more instruments or agreements and which has, or is capable of having, effect so as to provide benefits, in the form of pensions or otherwise, payable on death or retirement to or in respect of employed earners who have made arrangements with the trustees or managers of the scheme for them to become members of the scheme;

"prescribed " means specified in or determined in accordance with regulations;

"primary Class 1 contributions" and "secondary Class 1 contributions" have the same meanings as in the Social Security Act 1975;

"protected rights" shall be construed in accordance with Schedule 1 to this Act;

"qualifying benefit" has the meaning assigned to it by Schedule 6 to this Act;

"rate rebate", "rent rebate" and "rent allowance" shall be construed in accordance with section 28 above;

"rates" and "rating authority"—

(a) in relation to England and Wales, have the same meaning as in the General Rate Act 1967; and

(b) in relation to Scotland, have respectively the same meanings as "rate" has in section 379 of the Local Government (Scotland) Act 1947 and "rating authority" has in section 109 of the Local Government (Scotland) Act 1973;

"regulations" means regulations made by the Secretary of State under this Act;

"social fund payment" means a payment under Part III of this Act;

"tax-exemption" and "tax-approval" mean respectively exemption from tax and approval of the Inland Revenue in either case under any such provision of the Income Tax Acts as may be prescribed;

"tax year" means the 12 months beginning with 6th April in any year;

"trade dispute" has the same meaning as in the Social Security Act 1975;

"war disablement pension" means—

(a) any retired pay, pension or allowance granted in respect of disablement under powers conferred by or under the Air Force (Constitution) Act 1917, the Personal Injuries (Emergency Provisions) Act 1939, the Pensions (Navy, Army, Air Force and Mercantile Marine) Act 1939, the Polish Resettlement Act 1947, or Part VII or section 151 of the Reserve Forces Act 1980;

(b) without prejudice to paragraph (a) of this definition, any retired pay or pension to which subsection (1) of section 365 of the Income and Corporation Taxes Act 1970 applies;

"war widow's pension" means any widow's pension or allowance granted in respect of a death due to service or war injury and payable by virtue of any enactment mentioned in paragraph (*a*) of the preceding definition or a pension or allowance for a widow granted under any scheme mentioned in subsection (2)(*e*) of the said section 365.

(2) Expressions used in Part I of this Act and in the Social Security Pensions Act 1975 have the same meanings in that Part as they have in that Act.

(3) References in this Act to the general rate fund of an authority shall be construed—

    (*a*) in relation to the Council of the Isles of Scilly, as references to their general fund; and

    (*b*) in relation to the Common Council of the City of London, as references to their general rate.

(4) In this Act—

    (*a*) references to the United Kingdom include references to the territorial waters of the United Kingdom; and

    (*b*) references to Great Britain include references to the territorial waters of the United Kingdom adjacent to Great Britain.

Financial provision

85.—(1) There shall be paid out of money provided by Parliament—

    (*a*) any sums payable by way of the following—
        (i) income support;
        (ii) family credit;
        (iii) rate rebate subsidy;
        (iv) rent rebate subsidy;
        (v) rent allowance subsidy;

    (*b*) payments by the Secretary of State into the social fund;

    (*c*) any sum payable to a person under Schedule 6 to this Act if the relevant qualifying benefit to which he is entitled or treated as entitled is a benefit payable out of such money;

    (*d*) any sums falling to be paid by the Secretary of State under or by virtue of this Act by way of travelling expenses;

    (*e*) any other expenses of the Secretary of State attributable to this Act;

    (*f*) any expenses of the Lord Chancellor attributable to this Act; and

    (*g*) any increase attributable to this Act in the sums payable out of money provided by Parliament under any other Act.

(2) Any increase attributable to this Act in the sums to be charged on and paid out of the Consolidated Fund under any other Act shall be charged on and paid out of that Fund.

(3) There shall be paid out of the National Insurance Fund—

    (*a*) minimum contributions paid by the Secretary of State under Part I of this Act;

    (*b*) payments by him under section 7 above;

    (*c*) sums falling to be paid by or on behalf of the Secretary of State under regulations made by virtue of section 46(8)(*b*) above or paragraph 1(*b*) or (*e*) of Schedule 4 to this Act; and

    (*d*) any sums paid to a person under Schedule 6 to this Act if the relevant qualifying benefit to which the person is entitled or treated as entitled is a benefit payable out of that fund.

(4) There shall be paid out of the National Insurance Fund into the Consolidated Fund, at such times and in such manner as the Treasury may direct, such sums as the Secretary of State may estimate (in accordance with any directions given by the Treasury)—

    (*a*) to be the amount of the administrative expenses incurred by the

Secretary of State under Part V of this Act, excluding any category of expenses which the Treasury may direct, or any enactment may require, to be excluded from the Secretary of State's estimate under this subsection; and

(*b*) to be the amount of the administrative expenses incurred by a government department under Schedule 6 to this Act.

(5) Subject to subsections (6) and (7) below, so far as it relates to payments out of money provided by Parliament, any sum recovered by the Secretary of State under or by virtue of this Act shall be paid into the Consolidated Fund.

(6) So far as any such sum relates to a payment out of the National Insurance Fund, it shall be paid into that fund.

(7) So far as any such sum relates to a payment out of the social fund, it shall be paid into that fund.

(8) There shall also be paid into the National Insurance Fund sums recovered under section 1(6) or (7) or 7(8) or (9) above any personal pension protected rights premium and sums recovered by the Secretary of State by virtue of a scheme under section 2 or section 5 of the Industrial Injuries and Diseases (Old Cases) Act 1975 making provision corresponding to that made by or by virtue of this Act.

(9) There shall be made out of the National Insurance Fund into the Consolidated Fund or out of money provided by Parliament into the National Insurance Fund such payments by way of adjustment as the Secretary of State determines (in accordance with any direction of the Treasury) to be appropriate in consequence of the operation of any enactment or regulations relating to family credit, statutory sick pay or statutory maternity pay.

(10) Where such adjustments fall to be made, the amount of the payments to be made shall be taken to be such, in such cases or classes of case as may be specified by the Secretary of State by order, and payments on account thereof shall be made at such times and in such manner, as may be determined by the Secretary of State in accordance with any direction given by the Treasury.

(11) There shall be made—

(*a*) out of the social fund into the Consolidated Fund or the National Insurance Fund;

(*b*) into the social fund out of money provided by Parliament or the National Insurance Fund,

such payments by way of adjustment as the Secretary of State determines (in accordance with any directions of the Treasury) to be appropriate in consequence of any enactment or regulations relating to the repayment or offsetting of a benefit under any of the benefit Acts or other payments under any of those Acts.

(12) Where in any other circumstances payments fall to be made by way of adjustment—

(*a*) out of the social fund into the Consolidated Fund or the National Insurance Fund; or

(*b*) into the social fund out of money provided by Parliament or the National Insurance Fund,

then, in such cases or classes of case as may be specified by the Secretary of State by order, the amount of the payments to be made shall be taken to be such, and payments on account of it shall be made at such times and in such manner, as may be determined by the Secretary of State in accordance with any direction given by the Treasury.

(13) In this section "Act" includes an Act of the Parliament of Northern Ireland.

DEFINITIONS
"the benefit Acts" : s.84(1).
"rate rebate" : s.84(1).
"regulations" : s.84(1).
"rent allowance" : s.84(1).
"rent rebate" : s.84(1).

Minor and consequential amendments and repeals

86.—(1) The enactments mentioned in Schedule 10 to this Act shall have effect with the amendments there specified.

(2) The enactments mentioned in Schedule 11 to this Act (which include enactments already obsolete or unnecessary) are repealed to the extent specified in the third column of that Schedule.

Extent

87.—(1) The following provisions of this Act extend to Northern Ireland—

(a) section 17(2) above, so far as relating to Acts which extend to Northern Ireland;

(b) section 61 above;

(c) section 66 above, so far as relating to paragraph 3(6) of Schedule 6;

(d) section 81 above;

(e) sections 83 to 86 above;

(f) this section;

(g) sections 88 to 90 below.

(2) Section 82 above (with Schedule 9) extends to Northern Ireland only.

(3) Sections 25 and 30(6) and (10) above do not extend to Scotland.

(4) Where any enactment repealed or amended by this Act extends to any part of the United Kingdom, the repeal or amendment extends to that part.

(5) Except as provided by this section, this Act extends to England and Wales and Scotland, but not to Northern Ireland.

Commencement

88.—(1) Subject to the following provisions of this section, the provisions of this Act shall come into force on such day as the Secretary of State may by order made by statutory instrument appoint, and different days may be appointed in pursuance of this section for different provisions or different purposes of the same provision.

(2) In relation to section 52 above (including Schedule 5) and section 82 above (including Schedule 9) for the reference to the Secretary of State in subsection (1) above there shall be substituted a reference to the Lord Chancellor and the Secretary of State, acting jointly.

(3) Without prejudice to the generality of subsection (1) above, different days may be appointed under that subsection for the purposes of Part III of this Act in relation to different descriptions of persons, and those descriptions of persons may be determined by any criteria that appear to the Secretary of State to be appropriate.

(4) If an order under subsection (1) above brings paragraph 8 of Schedule 3 to this Act into force on the same day as section 36 above, the former shall be deemed to have come into force immediately before the latter.

(5) The following provisions of this Act—

section 30(4), (8), (9) and (10);

section 37;

section 38(4);
section 45;
section 61;
sections 63 and 64;
section 70;
section 71(4) and (5);
section 72;
section 74;
section 76;
section 81;
section 83 to 85;
section 86(1) so far as relating to paragraphs 2, 22, 23(3), 26(1) and
    (2), 27, 30(*b*), (*c*) and (*d*)(ii), 82, 86, 94(*a*), 98, 99, 106 and
    107 of Schedule 10;
section 86(2) so far as relating—

> (*a*) to section 37(3) of the Social Security Act 1975 and
> the reference to paragraph (*b*) of that subsection in section
> 22(2) of the Social Security (Miscellaneous Provisions) Act
> 1977;
> (*b*) to section 141(2) of the Social Security Act 1975;
> (*c*) to section 52D(2) and (3) of the Social Security
> Pensions Act 1975 and paragraph 12 of Schedule 1A to that
> Act;
> (*d*) to section 10 of the Social Security Act 1980; and
> (*e*) to section 29 of the Social Security and Housing
> Benefits Act 1982;

section 87;
this section; and
sections 89 and 90;

shall come into force on the day this Act is passed.

Transitional

89.—(1) Regulations may make such transitional and consequential
provision (including provision modifying any enactment contained in this
or any other Act) or saving as the Secretary of State considers necessary
or expedient in preparation for or in connection with the coming into
force of any provision of this Act or the operation of any enactment which
is repealed or amended by a provision of this Act during any period when
the repeal or amendment is not wholly in force.

(2) The reference to regulations in subsection (1) above includes a
reference—

(*a*) to regulations made by the Lord Chancellor; and
(*b*) to regulations made by the Lord Chancellor and the Secretary of
    State, acting jointly.

DEFINITION.
    "regulations": s.84(1).

Citation

90.—(1) This Act may be cited as the Social Security Act 1986.

(2) This Act, except section 77 above, may be cited together with the
Social Security Acts 1975 to 1985 as the Social Security Acts 1975 to 1986.

SCHEDULES

SCHEDULE 1

APPROPRIATE PERSONAL PENSION SCHEMES

Interpretation

1. In this Schedule—
"member" means a member of a scheme;
"rules" means the rules of a scheme; and
"scheme" means a personal pension scheme.

Requirements: general

2. The Secretary of State may prescribe descriptions of persons by whom or bodies by which a scheme may be established and, if he does so, a scheme may only be established by a person or body of a prescribed description.

3. A scheme must comply with such requirements as may be prescribed as regards the investment of its resources and with any direction of the Occupational Pensions Board that—

    (*a*) no part, or no more than a specified proportion, of the scheme's resources shall be invested in investments of a specified class or description;

    (*b*) there shall be realised, before the end of a specified period, the whole or a specified proportion of investments of a specified class or description forming part of the scheme's resources when the direction is given.

4. A scheme must comply with such requirements as may be prescribed as regards the part—

    (*a*) of any payment or payments that are made to the scheme by or on behalf of a member;

    (*b*) of any income or capital gain arising from the investment of payments such as are mentioned in sub-paragraph (*a*) above; or

    (*c*) of the value of rights under the scheme,

that may be used—

      (i) to defray the administrative expenses of the scheme;

      (ii) to pay commission; or

      (iii) in any other way which does not result in the provision of benefits for or in respect of members.

5.—(1) Subject to sub-paragraph (2) below, all minimum contributions which are paid to a scheme in respect of one of its members must be applied so as to provide money purchase benefits for or in respect of that member, except so far as they are used—

    (*a*) to defray the administrative expenses of the scheme; or

    (*b*) to pay commission.

(2) If regulations are made under paragraph 4 above, minimum contributions may be used in any way which the regulations permit, but not in any way not so permitted except to provide money purchase benefits for or in respect of the member.

6. A scheme must satisfy such other requirements as may be prescribed.

Requirements: protected rights

7.—(1) Unless the rules make provision such as is mentioned in sub-paragraph (2) below, the protected rights of a member are his rights to money purchase benefits under the scheme.

(2) Rules may provide that a member's protected rights are his rights under the scheme which derive from any payment of minimum contributions to the scheme, together with any rights of his to money purchase benefits which derive from protected rights under another personal pension scheme or protected rights (within he meaning of the Social Security Pensions Act 1975) under an occupational pension scheme which have been the subject of a transfer payment and such other rights as may be prescribed.

(3) Where rules make such provision as is mentioned in sub-paragraph (2) above, they shall also make provision for the identification of the protected rights.

(4) The value of protected rights such as are mentioned in sub-paragraph (2) above—

    (*a*) shall be calculated in a manner no less favourable than that in which the value of any other rights of the member to money purchase benefits under the scheme are calculated;

    (b) subject to that, shall be calculated and verified in such manner as may be prescribed.

(5) The power to make regulations conferred by sub-paragraph (4) above includes power to provide that protected rights such as are mentioned in sub-paragraph (2) above are to be calculated and verified in such manner as may be approved in particular cases—

    (a) by prescribed persons; or

    (b) by persons with prescribed professional qualifications or experience; or

    (c) by persons approved by the Secretary of State,

and power to provide that they shall be calculated and verified in accordance with guidance prepared by a prescribed body.

8. Rules must provide for effect to be given in a manner permitted by paragraph 9 below to the protected rights of every member and must not provide for any part of any member's protected rights to be discharged in any other way.

9.—(1) Effect may be given to protected rights—

    (a) by the provision by the scheme of a pension which—

        (i) complies with the requirements of sub-paragraph (7) below; and

        (ii) satisfies such conditions as may be prescribed; or

    (b) in such circumstances and subject to such conditions as may be prescribed, by the making of a transfer payment—

        (i) to another personal pension scheme; or

        (ii) to an occupational pension scheme,

where the scheme to which the payment is made satisfies such requirements as may be prescribed.

(2) If—

    (a) the rules of the scheme do not provide for a pension; or

    (b) the member so elects,

effect may be given to protected rights by the purchase by the scheme of an annuity which—

        (i) complies with the requirements of sub-paragraphs (7) and (8) below; and

        (ii) satisfies such conditions as may be prescribed.

(3) Effect may be given to protected rights by the provision of a lump sum if—

    (a) the lump sum is payable on a date which is either the date on which the member attains pensionable age or such later date as has been agreed by him; and

    (b) the annual rate of a pension under sub-paragraph (1) above or an annuity under sub-paragraph (2) above giving effect to the protected rights and commencing on the date on which the lump sum is payable would not exceed the prescribed amount; and

    (c) the circumstances are such as may be prescribed; and

    (d) the amount of the lump sum is calculated in a manner satisfactory to the Occupational Pensions Board by reference to the amount of the pension or annuity.

(4) If the member has died without effect being given to protected rights under sub-paragraph (1), (2) or (3) above, effect may be given to them in such manner as may be prescribed.

(5) No transaction is to be taken to give effect to protected rights unless it falls within this paragraph.

(6) Effect need not be given to protected rights if they have been extinguished by the payment of a personal pension protected rights premium.

(7) A pension or annuity complies with this sub-paragraph if—

    (a) it commences—

        (i) on the date on which the member attains pensionable age; or

        (ii) on such later date as has been agreed by him,

and continues until the date of his death;

    (b) in a case where the member dies while it is payable to him and is survived by a widow or widower—

        (i) it is payable to the widow or widower in prescribed circumstances and for the prescribed period at an annual rate which at any given time is one-half of the rate at which it would have been payable to the member if the member had been living at that time; or

        (ii) where that annual rate would not exceed a prescribed amount and the circumstances are such as may be prescribed, a lump sum calculated in a manner satisfactory to the Occupational Pensions Board is provided in lieu of it.

(8) An annuity complies with the requirements of this sub-paragraph if it is provided by an insurance company which—

(*a*) satisfies prescribed conditions;

(*b*) complies with such conditions as may be prescribed as to the calculation of annuities provided by it and as to the description of persons by or for whom they may be purchased; and

(*c*) subject to sub-paragraph (9) below, has been chosen by the member.

(9) A member is only to be taken to have chosen an insurance company if he gives notice of his choice to the trustees or managers of the scheme within the prescribed period and in such manner and form as may be prescribed, and with any such supporting evidence as may be prescribed; and, if he does not do so, the trustees or managers may themselves choose the insurance company instead.

10. The Occupational Pensions Board must be satisfied that a scheme complies with any such requirements as may be prescribed for meeting the whole or a prescribed part of any liability in respect of protected rights under the scheme which the scheme is unable to meet from its own resources—

(*a*) by reason of the commission by any person of a criminal offence;

(*b*) in such other circumstances as may be prescribed.

11. Rules must not allow, except in such circumstances as may be prescribed, the suspension or forfeiture of a member's protected rights or of payments giving effect to them.

General

12. Nothing in this Schedule shall be taken to prejudice any requirements with which a scheme must comply if it is to qualify for tax-exemption or tax-approval.

Section 6   SCHEDULE 2

MONEY PURCHASE CONTRACTED-OUT SCHEMES

1. The Social Security Pensions Act 1975 shall be amended as follows.

2. In subsection (1) of section 26 (contracting-out of full contributions and benefits) after the word "provides" there shall be inserted the words "or falls to be treated as providing".

3. In section 29 (contracted-out rates of benefit) the following subsections shall be inserted after subsection (2)—

"(2A) Subject to subsection (2B) below, where for any period minimum payments have been made in respect of an earner to an occupational pension scheme which, in relation to the earner's employment, is a money purchase contracted-out scheme, then, for the purposes of this section and sections 16(2B), 28(7A) and 59(1A) of the principal Act—

(*a*) the earner shall be treated, as from the date on which he reaches pensionable age, as if he were entitled to a guaranteed minimum pension at a prescribed weekly rate arising from that period in that employment; and

(*b*) in prescribed circumstances, in relation to any widow or widower of the earner—

(i) if the earner died after reaching pensionable age, any widow or widower of the earner shall be treated as entitled to a guaranteed minimum pension at a rate equal to one-half of the rate prescribed under paragraph (*a*) above; and

(ii) if the earner died before reaching pensionable age, any widow or widower of the earner shall be treated as entitled to a guaranteed minimum pension at a prescribed weekly rate arising from that period.

(2B) Where the earner is a married woman or widow, subsection (2A) above shall not have effect in relation to any period during which an election that her liability in respect of primary Class 1 contributions shall be a liability to contribute at a reduced rate is operative.

(2C) The power to prescribe a rate conferred by subsection (2A)(*a*) above includes power to prescribe a nil rate.".

4. In section 30 (contracted-out employment)—

(*a*) in subsection (1)(*a*), after the word "scheme" there shall be inserted the words "or his employer makes minimum payments in respect of the earner's employment to a money purchase contracted-out scheme";

(*b*) the following subsections shall be inserted after subsection (1)—

"(1A) The minimum payment in respect of an earner for any tax week shall be the rebate percentage of so much of the earnings paid to or for the benefit of the earner as exceeds the lower earnings limit for the tax week but does not exceed the upper earnings limit for it; and in this subsection "rebate percentage" means the percentage arrived at by adding—

(a) the percentage by which for the time being under section 27(2) above the contracted-out percentage of primary Class 1 contributions is less than the normal percentage; and

(b) the percentage by which for the time being under that subsection the contracted-out percentage of secondary Class 1 contributions is less than the normal percentage.

(1B) The references to the upper and lower earnings limits in subsection (1A) above are references, in the case of an earner who is paid otherwise than weekly, to their prescribed equivalents under section 4(2) and (6) of the principal Act.

(1C) Regulations may make provision—

(a) for the manner in which, and time at which or period within which, minimum payments are to be made;

(b) for the recovery by employers of amounts in respect of the whole or part of minimum payments by deduction from earnings;

(c) for calculating the amounts payable according to a scale prepared from time to time by the Secretary of State or otherwise adjusting them so as to avoid fractional amounts or otherwise facilitate computation;

(d) for requiring that the liability in respect of a payment made in a tax week, in so far as the liability depends on any conditions as to a person's age on retirement, shall be determined as at the beginning of the week or as at the end of it;

(e) for securing that liability is not avoided or reduced by a person following in the payment of earnings any practice which is abnormal for the employment in respect of which the earnings are paid;

(f) without prejudice to sub-paragraph (e) above, for enabling the Secretary of State, where he is satisfied as to the existence of any practice in respect of the payment of earnings whereby the incidence of minimum payments is avoided or reduced by means of irregular or unequal payments of earnings, to give directions for securing that minimum payments are payable as if that practice were not followed;

(g) for the intervals at which, for the purposes of minimum payments, payments of earnings are to be treated as made; and

(h) for this section to have effect, in prescribed cases, as if for any reference to a tax week there were substituted a reference to a prescribed period."

5. In section 32 (contracted-out schemes)—

(a) in subsection (2), the words "or it satisfies subsection (2A) below." shall be inserted after paragraph (b) (but not as part of it);

(b) the following subsections shall be inserted after that subsection—

"(2A) An occupational pension scheme satisfies this subsection only if—

(a) the requirements imposed by or by virtue of Schedule 1 to the Social Security Act 1986, modified under subsection (2B) below, are satisfied in its case;

(b) it complies with section 40(1) below; and

(c) the rules of the scheme applying to protected rights are framed so as to comply with the requirements of any regulations prescribing the form and content of rules of contracted-out schemes and with such other requirements as to form and content (not inconsistent with regulations) as may be imposed by the Occupational Pensions Board as a condition of contracting-out, either generally or in relation to a particular scheme.

(2B) The modifications of Schedule 1 are—

(a) that for the references to a personal pension scheme there shall be substituted references to an occupational pension scheme;

(b) that for the references in paragraph 5 to minimum contributions there shall be substituted references to minimum payments and any payments by the Secretary of State under section 7 of the Social Security Act 1986;

(c) that for paragraph 7(2) there shall be substituted—

"(2) The rules of the scheme may provide that a member's protected rights are his rights under the scheme which derive from the payment of minimum payments (within the meaning of the Social Security Pensions Act 1975) together with any payments by the Secretary of State to the scheme under section 7 of this Act in respect of the member and any rights of the member to money purchase benefits which derive from protected rights (within the meaning of the Social Security Pensions Act 1975) under another occupational pension scheme or protected rights under a personal pension scheme which have been the subject of a transfer payment and such other rights as may be prescribed.";

(*d*) that in paragraph 9—

(i) for the reference to an occupational pension scheme there shall be substituted a reference to a personal pension scheme; and

(ii) for the reference to a personal pension protected rights premium there shall be substituted a reference to a contracted-out protected rights premium; and

(*e*) that paragraph 10 shall not apply to public service pension schemes.

(2C) A contracting-out certificate shall state whether the scheme is contracted-out by virtue of subsection (2) or subsection (2A) above; and where a scheme satisfies both of those subsections the employers, in their application for a certificate, shall specify one of the subsections as the subsection by virtue of which they desire the scheme to be contracted-out.

(2D) A scheme which has been contracted-out by virtue of one of those subsections may not become contracted-out by reason of the other, except in prescribed circumstances.".

6.—(1) The words "which is not a money purchase contracted-out scheme" shall be inserted after the words "occupational pension scheme" in—

(*a*) section 33(1);
(*b*) section 36(1);
(*c*) section 40(3) and (4);
(*d*) section 41A(1);
(*e*) section 42(1);
(*f*) section 44(1);
(*g*) section 44A(1);
(*h*) section 45(1);
(*j*) section 51;
(*k*) paragraph 4(1) and (2) of Schedule 2.

(2) If section 9 above comes into force after this paragraph, the amendment to section 36(1) made by sub-paragraph (1) above shall be made in the subsection both as amended by section 9 above and as unamended.

(3) The words "or a money purchase contracted-out scheme" shall be inserted after the words "public service pension scheme" in—

(*a*) section 40(2);
(*b*) section 41(1);
(*c*) section 41E(1).

7. The following section shall be inserted after section 44—

"Money purchase schemes: contracted-out protected rights premium

44ZA.—(1) In the case of a scheme which is or has been a money purchase contracted-out scheme the Occupational Pensions Board may, for the event of, or in connection with, its ceasing to be contracted-out, approve any arrangements made or to be made in relation to the scheme, or for its purposes, for the preservation or transfer of protected rights under the scheme.

(2) If the scheme ceases to be a contracted-out scheme (whether by being wound up or otherwise) and the Occupational Pensions Board either—

(*a*) have withdrawn their approval of previously approved arrangements relating to it; or

(*b*) have declined to approve arrangements relating to it,

the Board may issue a certificate to that effect.

(3) A certificate issued under subsection (2)(*a*) or (*b*) above shall be cancelled by the Board if they subsequently approve the arrangements.

(4) If the scheme ceases to be a contracted-out scheme (whether by being wound up or otherwise), a state scheme premium shall be payable, except in prescribed circumstances,—

(*a*) in respect of each earner whose protected rights under the scheme are not subject to approved arrangements and have not been disposed of so as to discharge the trustees or managers of the scheme under section 52C of or paragraph 16 of Schedule 1A to this Act; and

(*b*) in respect of each person who has become entitled to receive a pension under the scheme giving effect to protected rights which are not subject to approved arrangements.

(5) A premium under subsection (4) above may be referred to as a "contracted-out protected rights premium".

(6) A contracted-out protected rights premium shall be paid by the prescribed person, within the prescribed period, to the Secretary of State.

(7) The amount of a contracted-out protected rights premium payable in respect of any person shall be the cash equivalent of the protected rights in question, calculated and verified in the prescribed manner.

(8) Where a contracted-out protected rights premium is paid in respect of a person—

(*a*) the rights whose cash equivalent is included in the premium shall be extinguished; and

(*b*) section 29(2) and (2A) above and section 4 of the Social Security Act 1986 shall have effect in relation to that person and a widow or widower of that person as if any guaranteed minimum pension to which that person or any such widow or widower is treated as entitled under those provisions and which derives from the minimum payments, minimum contributions (within the meaning of the Social Security Act 1986) or transfer payment or payments from which those rights derive were reduced by the appropriate percentage.

(9) In subsection (8) above "the appropriate percentage" means, subject to the following provisions of this section,

$$\frac{X}{Y} \times 100,$$

where—

(*a*) X = the amount of the premium together with, if the person in respect of whom it falls to be paid gives notice to the prescribed person within the prescribed period—

(i) the cash equivalent, calculated and verified in the prescribed manner, and paid to the Secretary of State within the prescribed period, of any other rights which he has under the scheme and specifies in the notice; and

(ii) the amount of any voluntary contribution paid to the Secretary of State within the prescribed period by, or in respect of, the person concerned; and

(*b*) Y = the cost of providing any guaranteed minimum pension such as is mentioned in subsection (8) above.

(10) If the appropriate percentage, as calculated under subsection (9) above would fall between two whole numbers, it is to be taken to be the lower number.

(11) If it would be over 100, it is to be taken to be 100.

(12) The remainder after the reduction for which subsection (8) above provides—

(*a*) if it would contain a fraction of 1p, is to be treated as the nearest lower whole number of pence; and

(*b*) if it would be less than a prescribed amount, is to be treated as nil.

(13) The power to make regulations conferred by subsections (7) and (9) above includes power to provide that cash equivalents are to be calculated and verified in such manner as may be approved in particular cases—

(*a*) by prescribed persons;

(*b*) by persons with prescribed professional qualifications or experience; or

(*c*) by persons approved by the Secretary of State,

and power to provide that they shall be calculated and verified in accordance with guidance prepared by a prescribed body.

(14) The cost of providing the appropriate percentage of the guaranteed minimum pension shall be certified by the Secretary of State, and in calculating and certifying it the Secretary of State—

(*a*) shall apply whichever of the prescribed actuarial tables (as in force at the time when the scheme ceases to be appropriate) is applicable in accordance with the regulations prescribing the tables; and

(*b*) may make such adjustments as he thinks necessary for avoiding fractional amounts.".

8. In section 48 (guaranteed minimum pensions to be inalienable)—

    (*a*) in subsection (1)—

        (i) after the word "scheme", in the first place where it occurs, there shall be inserted the words "or to payments giving effect to protected rights under such a scheme"; and

       (ii) after the word "pension", where it occurs in paragraphs (*a*) and (*b*), there shall be inserted the words "or those payments"; and

    (*b*) in subsection (3), for the words from "any", in the first place where it occurs, to "not" there shall be substituted the words "nothing whose assignment is or would be made void by that subsection shall"

9. In section 49 (supervision of schemes which have ceased to be contracted-out)—

    (*a*) the following paragraph shall be substituted for subsection(1)(*b*)—

        "(*b*) there has not been a payment—

        (i) of a premium under section 44 above in respect of each person entitled to receive, or having accrued rights to, guaranteed minimum pensions under the scheme; or

       (ii) of a premium under section 44ZA above in respect of each person who has protected rights under it or is entitled to any benefit giving effect to protected rights under it;";

    (*b*) in subsection (2)(*a*), after the word "above" there shall be inserted the words "or, by virtue of subsections (2A) and (2B) of section 32 above, paragraph 10(1) of Schedule 1 to the Social Security Act 1986"; and

    (*c*) in subsection (5), "32" shall be substituted for "33".

10. At the end of subsection (3) of section 50 (alteration of rules of contracted-out schemes) there shall be added the words "or any person has protected rights under it or is entitled to any benefit giving effect to protected rights under it".

11. In section 66(1) (interpretation)—

    (*a*) the following definition shall be inserted before the definition of "guaranteed minimum pension"—

        " "average salary benefits" means benefits the rate or amount of which is calculated by reference to a member's average salary over the period of service on which the benefits are based;";

    (*b*) the following definitions shall be inserted after the definition of "long-term benefit"—

        " "minimum payments" shall be construed in accordance with section 30 above;

        "money purchase benefits" in relation to an occupational pension scheme, means benefits the rate or amount of which is calculated by reference to a payment or payments made by a member of the scheme or by any other person in respect of a member, other than average salary benefits;

        "money purchase contracted-out scheme" means an occupational pension scheme which is contracted-out by virtue of satisfying section 32(2A) above;";

    (*c*) the following definition shall be inserted after the definition of "the principal Act"—

        " "protected rights" has the meaning given by Schedule 1 to the Social Security Act 1986 with the substitution made by section 32(2B) above.".

12. In paragraph 2 of Schedule 3 (priority in bankruptcy etc.).—

    (*a*) the following sub-paragraph shall be inserted after sub-paragraph (1)—

        "(1A) This Schedule applies to any sum owed on account of an employer's minimum payments to a contracted-out scheme falling to be made in the period of twelve months immediately preceding the relevant date."; and

    (*b*) in sub-paragraph (2)—

        (i) the words "or payments" shall be inserted after the word "contributions"; and

       (ii) the words "or (1A)" shall be inserted after the words "sub-paragraph (1)".

Section 39   SCHEDULE 3

INDUSTRIAL INJURIES AND DISEASES

Social Security Act 1975 (c.14)

1. The Social Security Act 1975 shall have effect as provided by this Schedule.

2. The following subsection shall be substituted for section 50(1)—

"(1) Subject to the provisions of this Act, industrial injuries benefit shall be payable where an unemployed earner suffers personal injury caused after 4th July 1948 by accident arising out of and in the course of his employment, being employed earner's employment.".

3.—(1) In subsection (1) of section 57 (disablement benefit) "14 per cent." shall be substituted for "1 per cent.".

(2) The following subsections shall be inserted after that subsection—

"(1A) In the determination of the extent of an unemployed earner's disablement for the purposes of this section there may be added to the percentage of the disablement resulting from the relevant accident the assessed percentage of any present disablement of his resulting from any other accident after 4th July 1948 which arose out of and in the course of his employment, being employed earner's employment, and in respect of which a disablement gratuity was not paid to him under this Act after a final assessment of his disablement.

(1B) Subject to subsection (1C) below, where the assessment of disablement is a percentage between 20 and 100 which is not a multiple of 10, it shall be treated—

(*a*) if it is a multiple of 5, as being the next higher percentage which is a multiple of 10; and

(*b*) if it is not a multiple of 5, as being the nearest percentage which is a multiple of 10,

and where it is a percentage of 14 or more but less than 20 it shall be treated as a percentage of 20.

(1C) Where subsection (1A) above applies, subsection (1B) above shall have effect in relation to the aggregate percentage and not in relation to any percentage forming part of the aggregate.".

(3) Subsection (5) of that section shall cease to have effect except in relation to cases where the claim for benefit was made before this paragraph comes into force.

(4) Subsection (6) shall have effect, except in relation to such cases, as if the words "Where disablement benefit is payable for a period, it shall be paid" were substituted for the words from the beginning to "payable".

4. Sections 58 and 59 and 64 to 66 (unemployability supplement) shall cease to have effect, except in relation to beneficiaries in receipt of unemployability supplement immediately before this paragraph comes into force.

5.—(1) The following section shall be inserted after section 59—

"Reduced earnings allowance

59A.—(1) Subject to the provisions of this Part of this Act, an employed earner shall be entitled to reduced earnings allowance if—

(*a*) he is entitled to a disablement pension or would be so entitled if that pension were payable where disablement is assessed at not less than 1 per cent.;

(*b*) as a result of the relevant loss of faculty, he is either—

(i) incapable, and likely to remain permanently incapable, of following his regular occupation; and

(ii) incapable of following employment of an equivalent standard which is suitable in his case,

or is, and has at all times since the end of the period of 90 days referred to in section 57(4) above been, incapable of following that occupation or any such employment.

(2) The Secretary of State may by regulations provide that in prescribed circumstances employed earner's employment in which a claimant was engaged when the relevant accident took place but which was not his regular occupation is to be treated as if it had been his regular occupation.

(3) In subsection (1) above—

(*a*) references to a person's regular occupation are to be taken as not including any subsidiary occupation, except to the extent that they fall to be treated as including such an occupation by virtue of regulations under subsection (2) above; and

(*b*) employment of an equivalent standard is to be taken as not including employment other than employed earner's employment;

and in assessing the standard of remuneration in any employment, including a person's regular occupation, regard is to be had to his reasonable prospect of advancement.

(4) For the purposes of this section a person's regular occupation is to be treated as extending to and including employment in the capacities to which the persons in

that occupation (or a class or description of them to which he belonged at the time of the relevant accident) are in the normal course advanced, and to which, if he had continued to follow that occupation without having suffered the relevant loss of faculty, he would have had at least the normal prospects of advancement; and so long as he is, as a result of the relevant loss of faculty, deprived in whole or in part of those prospects, he is to be treated as incapable of following that occupation.

(5) Regulations may for the purposes of this section provide that a person is not to be treated as capable of following an occupation or employment merely because of his working thereat during a period of trial or for purposes of rehabilitation or training or in other prescribed circumstances.

(6) Reduced earnings allowance shall be awarded—
   (a) for such period as may be determined at the time of the award; and
   (b) if at the end of that period the beneficiary submits a fresh claim for the allowance, for such further period as may be determined.

(7) The award may not be for a period longer than the period to be taken into account under paragraph 4 or 4A of Schedule 8 to this Act.

(8) Reduced earnings allowance shall be payable at a rate determined by reference to the beneficiary's probable standard of remuneration during the period for which it is granted in any employed earner's employments which are suitable in his case and which he is likely to be capable of following as compared with that in the relevant occupation, but in no case at a rate higher than 40 per cent. of the maximum rate of a disablement pension or at a rate such that the aggregate of disablement pension and reduced earnings allowance awarded to the beneficiary exceeds 140 per cent. of the maximum rate of a disablement pension.

(9) In subsection (8) above "the relevant occupation" means—
   (a) in relation to a person who is entitled to reduced earnings allowance by virtue of regulations under subsection (2) above, the occupation in which he was engaged when the relevant accident took place; and
   (b) in relation to any other person who is entitled to reduced earnings allowance, his regular occupation within the meaning of subsection (1) above.

(10) On any award except the first the probable standard of his remuneration shall be determined in such manner as may be prescribed; and, without prejudice to the generality of this subsection, regulations may provide in prescribed circumstances for the probable standard of remuneration to be determined by reference—
   (a) to the standard determined at the time of the last previous award of reduced earnings allowance; and
   (b) to scales or indices of earnings in a particular industry or description of industries or any other data relating to such earnings.

(11) A person who—
   (a) attains pensionable age after this section comes into force; and
   (b) has retired from regular employment before that day; and
   (c) was entitled to reduced earnings allowance on the day immediately before he retired from regular employment,

shall be treated as entitled as from the day on which he retires from regular employment to reduced earnings allowance at a rate not higher at any time than that at which the allowance was payable to him immediately before he retired from regular employment.".

(2) Section 60 (increase of disablement pension for special hardship) shall cease to have effect.

(3) A person who—
   (a) is over pensionable age on the day on which this paragraph comes into force; and
   (b) has retired from regular employment before that day; and
   (c) was entitled on the day immediately before that day to an increase under section 60,

shall be treated as entitled as from the day on which this paragraph comes into force to reduced earnings allowance at a rate not higher at any time than that at which the increase was payable to him immediately before that day.

(4) Where for any period commencing before 6th April 1987 a person is entitled both to reduced earnings allowance under section 59A and to an additional pension of a long-term benefit or, if the long-term benefit is invalidity pension, to either an invalidity allowance or an additional pension, or both, his reduced earnings allowance shall be reduced in respect of any part of the period falling on or after 6th April 1987 by the amount of any increase in

the additional pension or invalidity allowance as the result of an order under section 63 above taking effect on or after that date.

(5) Where for any period commencing on or after 6th April 1987 a person is entitled as mentioned in sub-paragraph (4) above, his reduced earnings allowance shall be reduced by the amount of any additional pension or invalidity allowance to which he is entitled.

(6) Where a reduction falls to be made under sub-paragraph (4) or (5) above, the person to whom it falls to be made shall be entitled to reduced earnings allowance only if there is a balance after the reduction and, if there is such a balance, of an amount equal to it.

(7) Where the weekly rate of a benefit is reduced under section 29 of the Social Security Pensions Act 1975, there shall be subtracted from the amount which would otherwise fall to be deducted under sub-paragraph (4) or (5) above an amount equal to the reduction under that section.

(8) In the preceding sub-paragraphs references to an additional pension are references to that pension after any increase under section 9(3) of the Social Security Pensions Act 1975 but without any increase under Schedule 1, paragraphs 1 and 2, to that Act.

6. The following subsections shall be inserted after subsection (2) of section 61 (constant attendance allowance)—

"(3) The Secretary of State may by regulations direct that any provision of section 35 above shall have effect, with or without modifications, in relation to increases of pension under this section.

(4) In subsection (3) above "modifications" includes additions and omissions.".

7. Section 62 (increase during hospital treatment) shall cease to have effect, except in relation to a period during which a person is receiving medical treatment as an in-patient in a hospital or similar institution and which—

(a) commenced before the coming into force of this paragraph; or

(b) commenced after it but within a period of 28 days from the end of the period during which he last received an increase of benefit under that section in respect of such treatment for the relevant injury or loss of faculty.

8. The following provisions (which all relate to industrial death benefit)—

(a) sections 67 and 68;

(b) sections 70 to 75; and

(c) Schedule 9,

shall cease to have effect.

9.—(1) This paragraph shall have effect in relation to widows who on the day before paragraph 8 above comes into force are entitled to death benefit under section 67.

(2) A widow who is entitled to a pension at the initial rate specified in Schedule 4, Part V, paragraph 13(a) shall be treated as satisfying the conditions of entitlement to a widow's allowance specified in subsection (1) of section 24 and her entitlement to the allowance under that section shall, subject to the proviso to subsection (2) of that section, continue for so long as she would have been entitled to a pension under section 67 at the initial rate.

(3) A widow who—

(a) is not entitled to a pension at the initial rate but has one or more dependent children; or

(b) is pregnant on the day before paragraph 8 above comes into force,

shall be treated as satisfying the conditions of entitlement to a widowed mother's allowance under section 25 and her entitlement to the allowance shall, subject to the proviso to subsection (3) of that section, continue for so long as she satisfies either of the conditions specified in paragraph (a) or (b) of subsection (1) of that section.

(4) A widow who—

(a) is under 60; and

(b) has no dependent child; and

(c) does not fall to be treated as entitled to a widow's allowance or a widowed mother's allowance,

shall be treated as satisfying the conditions of entitlement to a widow's pension under section 26 and the pension shall be payable for any period during which she satisfies the provisions of subsection (3) of that section.

(5) Subject to sub-paragraph (6) below, the rate of a widow's pension under sub-paragraph (4) above shall be—

(a) in the case of a widow who was entitled to an allowance under section 70 after her husband died, but has ceased to be so entitled, the rate for a widow of the age she was when she so ceased;

(b) in the case of a widow who was not so entitled, the rate for a widow of the age she was when her late husband died, and for the purposes of this subsection a woman who was under the age of 40 at the relevant time shall be treated as having been of the age of 40 at that time.

(6) The rate of pension for a widow who is entitled under section 68(2) to a pension at the higher permanent rate specified in Schedule 4, Part V, paragraph 13(*b*), shall be the rate specified in section 13 of the Social Security Pensions Act 1975 and shall be that rate notwithstanding anything in subsection (3) of that section.

(7) Regulations may provide that a widow who on the day before paragraph 8 above comes into force is entitled to death benefit under section 67 shall be entitled to a prescribed benefit at a prescribed rate.

(8) In this paragraph "dependent child" means a child in respect of whom the widow is entitled to child benefit if one of the conditions specified in section 43(1) is for the time being satisfied with respect to the child and the child is either—

    (*a*) a son or daughter of the widow and her late husband; or

    (*b*) a child in respect of whom her late husband was immediately before his death entitled to child benefit; or

    (*c*) if the widow and her late husband were residing together immediately before his death, a child in respect of whom she was then entitled to child benefit.

10. In any case where—

    (*a*) an employed earner who is married dies as a result—

        (i) of a personal injury of a kind mentioned in section 50(1); or

        (ii) of a disease or injury such as is mentioned in section 76(1);

    (*b*) the contribution conditions are not wholly satisfied in respect of him;

those conditions shall be taken to be satisfied for the purposes of his widow's entitlement to—

    (i) a widow's allowance or widow's payment;

    (ii) a widowed mother's allowance;

    (iii) a widow's pension; or

    (iv) a Category B retirement pension at the same weekly rate as her widow's pension.

11. Section 69 (widower's death benefit) shall cease to have effect, except in relation to widowers in receipt of death benefit immediately before this paragraph comes into force.

12. The Secretary of State may by regulations provide for the payment of prescribed amounts in prescribed circumstances to persons who immediately before the repeal of sections 71 to 73 were entitled to any benefit by virtue of any of those sections, but in determining the amount which is to be payable in any case or class of cases the Secretary of State may take into account—

    (*a*) the extent to which the weekly rate of industrial death benefit has been modified in that case or class of cases by virtue of section 74;

    (*b*) the age of the beneficiary and of any person or persons formerly maintained by the deceased; and

    (*c*) the length of time that entitlement to the benefit would have been likely to continue if those sections had not been repealed.

13. In section 77 (regulations as to industrial diseases) the following subsections shall be inserted after subsection (3)—

    "(4) The regulations may also provide—

        (*a*) that in the determination of the extent of an employed earner's disablement resulting from a prescribed disease or injury there may be added to the percentage of that disablement the assessed percentage of any present disablement of his resulting from—

            (i) any accident after 4th July 1948 arising out of and in the course of his employment, being employed earner's employment;

            (ii) any other prescribed disease or injury due to the nature of that employment and developed after 4th July 1948,

        and in respect of which a disablement gratuity was not paid to him under this Act after a final assessment of his disablement; and

        (*b*) that in the determination of the extent of an employed earner's disablement for the purposes of section 57 above there may be added to the percentage of disablement resulting from the relevant accident the assessed percentage of any present disablement of his resulting from any prescribed disease or injury due to the nature of his employment and developed after 4th July 1948 and in respect of which a disablement gratuity was not paid to him under this Act after a final assessment of his disablement.

    (5) Where the regulations make provision such as is mentioned in subsection (4) above and also make provision corresponding to subsection (1B) of section 57

above, they may also make provision to the effect that the corresponding provisions shall have effect in relation to the aggregate percentage and not in relation to any percentage forming part of the aggregate.".

14. In section 108 (disablement questions)—

(*a*) in subsection (1) the following words shall be added at the end, but not as part of paragraph (*b*)—

"but questions relating to the aggregation of percentages of disablement resulting from different accidents are not disablement questions."; and

(*b*) the following subsection shall be inserted after subsection (4)—

"(4A) In the case of a claimant for disablement benefit the adjudication officer may refer to one or more adjudicating medical practitioners for determination any question as to the extent of any present disablement of his resulting from an accident other than the accident which is the basis of the claim.".

15. In Schedule 8 (assessment of extent of disablement)—

(*a*) paragraph 4 shall be renumbered as sub-paragraph (1) of that paragraph; and

(*b*) the following sub-paragraph shall be inserted after that sub-paragraph—

"(2) Where—

(*a*) the assessed extent of a claimant's disablement amounts to 13 per cent. or less;

(*b*) it seems likely that the assessed extent of a claimant's disablement will be aggregated with the assessed extent of any present disablement of his and the likely aggregate amounts to 13 per cent. or less,

the period to be taken into account by the assessment of the disablement shall not end earlier than any date by which it seems likely that the extent of the disablement or the aggregate will be at least 1 per cent.".

Industrial Injuries and Diseases (Old Cases) Act 1975 (c.16)

16. For the purposes of section 159 and of section 7 of the Industrial Injuries and Diseases (Old Cases) Act 1975 paragraph 4 of this Schedule shall be deemed not to have been enacted.

Pneumoconiosis etc. (Workers' Compensation) Act 1979 (c.41)

17.—(1) Section 2 of the Pneumoconiosis etc. (Workers' Compensation) Act 1979 (conditions of entitlement to lump sum payments) shall be amended as follows.

(2) At the end of subsection (1)(*a*) there shall be added the words "or, subject to subsection (3A) below, would be payable to him in respect of it but for his disablement amounting to less than the appropriate percentage".

(3) At the end of subsection (2)(*b*) there shall be added the words "or, subject to subsection (3A) below, would have been so payable to him—

(i) but for his disablement amounting to less than the appropriate percentage; or

(ii) but for his not having claimed the benefit; or

(iii) but for his having died before he had suffered from the disease for the appropriate period".

(4) In subsection (3) the following definitions shall be inserted before the definition of "death benefit"—

"the appropriate percentage" means, in the case of any disease, the percentage specified in subsection (1) of section 57 of the Social Security Act 1975 or, if regulations have been made under section 77 of that Act specifying a different percentage in relation to that disease, the percentage specified in the regulations;

"the appropriate period" means, in the case of any disease, the period specified in subsection (4) of the said section 57 or, if regulations have been made under the said section 77 specifying a different period in relation to that disease, the period specified in the regulations;".

(5) The following subsection shall be inserted after that subsection—

"(3A) No amount is payable under this Act in respect of disablement amounting to less than 1 per cent.".

         SCHEDULE 4

STATUTORY MATERNITY PAY ETC.

PART I

PROVISIONS SUPPLEMENTARY TO PART V

Recovery of amounts paid by way of statutory maternity pay

1. Regulations shall make provision—
    (a) entitling, except in prescribed circumstances, any person who has made a payment of statutory maternity pay to recover the amount so paid by making one or more deductions from his contributions payments; and
    (b) for the payment, in prescribed circumstances, by the Secretary of State or by the Commissioners of Inland Revenue on behalf of the Secretary of State, of sums to persons who are unable so to recover the whole, or any part, of any payments of statutory maternity pay which they have made;
    (c) giving any person who has made a payment of statutory maternity pay a right, except in prescribed circumstances, to an amount, determined in such manner as may be prescribed—
        (i) by reference to secondary Class 1 contributions paid in respect of statutory maternity pay; or
        (ii) by reference to secondary Class 1 contributions paid in respect of statutory sick pay; or
        (iii) by reference to the aggregate of secondary Class 1 contributions paid in respect of statutory maternity pay and secondary Class 1 contributions paid in respect of statutory sick pay;
    (d) providing for the recovery, in prescribed circumstances, of the whole or any part of any such amount from contributions payments;
    (e) for the payment, in prescribed circumstances, by the Secretary of State or by the Commissioners of Inland Revenue on behalf of the Secretary of State, of the whole or any part of any such amount.

2. Regulations under paragraph 1 above may, in particular provide for any deduction made in accordance with the regulations to be disregarded for prescribed purposes.

3. The power to make regulations conferred by paragraph 5 of Schedule 1 to the Social Security Act 1975 (power to combine collection of contributions with collection of income tax) shall include power to make such provision as the Secretary of State considers expedient in consequence of any provision made by or under this Schedule.

4. Provision made in regulations under paragraph 5 of Schedule 1, by virtue of paragraph 3 above, may in particular require the inclusion—
    (a) in returns, certificates and other documents; or
    (b) in any other form of record;
which the regulations require to be kept or produced or to which those regulations otherwise apply, of such particulars relating to statutory maternity pay or deductions or payments made by virtue of paragraph 1 above as may be prescribed by those regulations.

5. Where, in accordance with any provision of regulations made under this Schedule, an amount has been deducted from an employer's contributions payments, the amount so deducted shall (except in such cases as may be prescribed) be treated for the purposes of any provision made by or under any enactment in relation to primary or secondary Class 1 contributions as having been—
    (a) paid (on such date as may be determined in accordance with the regulations); and
    (b) received by the Secretary of State,
towards discharging the employer's liability in respect of such contributions.

Provision of information by women and their employers and/or former employers

6. A woman shall provide the person who is liable to pay her statutory maternity pay—
    (a) with evidence as to her pregnancy and the expected date of confinement in such form and at such time as may be prescribed; and
    (b) where she commences work after her confinement but within the maternity pay period, with such additional information as may be prescribed.

7. Where a woman asks an employer or former employer of hers to provide her with a written statement, in respect of a period before the request is made, of one or more of the following—

(a) the weeks within that period which he regards as weeks in respect of which he is liable to pay statutory maternity pay to the woman;

(b) the reasons why he does not so regard the other weeks in that period; and

(c) his opinion as to the amount of statutory maternity pay to which the woman is entitled in respect of each of the weeks in respect of which he regards himself as liable to make a payment,

the employer or former employer shall, to the extent to which the request was reasonable, comply with it within a reasonable time.

8. Regulations—

(a) may require employers to maintain such records in connection with statutory maternity pay as may be prescribed;

(b) may provide for—

(i) any woman claiming to be entitled to statutory maternity pay; or

(ii) any other person who is a party to proceedings arising under this Act relating to statutory maternity pay,

to furnish to the Secretary of State, within a prescribed period, any information required for the determination of any question arising in connection therewith; and

(c) may require persons who have made payments of statutory maternity pay to furnish to the Secretary of State such documents and information, at such time, as may be prescribed.

Provision of information by Secretary of State

9. Where the Secretary of State considers that it is reasonable for information held by him to be disclosed to a person liable to make payments of statutory maternity pay for the purpose of enabling that person to determine—

(a) whether a maternity pay period exists in relation to a woman who is or has been an employee of his; and

(b) if it does, the date of its commencement and the weeks in it in respect of which he may be liable to pay statutory maternity pay,

he may disclose the information to that person.

Statutory maternity pay to count as remuneration for purposes of Social Security Act 1975

10. For the purposes of section 3 of the Social Security Act 1975 (meaning of "earnings"), any sums paid to, or for the benefit of, a woman in satisfaction (whether in whole or in part) of any entitlement of hers to statutory maternity pay shall be treated as remuneration derived from employed earner's employment.

Relationship with benefits and other payments etc.

11. Any day which falls within the maternity pay period shall not be treated for the purposes of the Social Security Act 1975 or the Social Security Pensions Act 1975 as a day of unemployment or of incapacity for work for the purpose of determining whether it forms part of a period of interruption of employment.

12.—(1) Subject to sub-paragraphs (2) and (3) below, any entitlement to statutory maternity pay shall not affect any right of a woman in relation to remuneration under any contract of service ("contractual remuneration").

(2) Subject to sub-paragraph (3) below—

(a) any contractual remuneration paid to a woman by an employer of hers in respect of a week in the maternity pay period shall go towards discharging any liability of that employer to pay statutory maternity pay to her in respect of that week; and

(b) any statutory maternity pay paid by an employer to a woman who is an employee of his in respect of a week in the maternity pay period shall go towards discharging any liability of that employer to pay contractual remuneration to her in respect of that week.

(3) Regulations may make provision as to payments which are, and those which are not, to be treated as contractual remuneration for the purposes of sub-paragraphs (1) and (2) above.

PART II

AMENDMENTS OF SOCIAL SECURITY ACT 1975

13. For sections 22 and 23 there shall be substituted—

"State maternity allowance

22.—(1) A woman shall be entitled to a maternity allowance at the weekly rate specified in relation thereto in Schedule 4, Part I, paragraph 4, if—

    (*a*) she satisfies the condition specified in section 46(2)(*c*) of the Social Security Act 1986; and

    (*b*) she has been engaged in employment as an employed or self-employed earner for at least 26 weeks in the 52 weeks immediately preceding the 14th week before the expected week of confinement; and

    (*c*) she satisfies the contribution condition for a maternity allowance specified in Schedule 3, Part I, paragraph 3; and

    (*d*) she is not entitled to statutory maternity pay for the same week in respect of the same pregnancy.

(2) Subject to the following provisions of this section, a maternity allowance shall be payable for the period ("the maternity allowance period") which, if she were entitled to statutory maternity pay, would be the maternity pay period under section 47 of the Social Security Act 1986.

(3) Regulations may provide—

    (*a*) for disqualifying a woman for receiving a maternity allowance if—

        (i) during the maternity allowance period she does any work in employment as an employed or self-employed earner or fails without good cause to observe any prescribed rules of behaviour; or

        (ii) at any time before she is confined she fails without good cause to attend for, or submit herself to, any medical examination required in accordance with the regulations;

    (*b*) that this section and Schedule 3, Part I, paragraph 3 shall have effect subject to prescribed modifications in relation to cases in which a woman has been confined and—

        (i) has not made a claim for a maternity allowance in expectation of that confinement (other than a claim which has been disallowed); or

        (ii) has made a claim for maternity allowance in expectation of that confinement (other than a claim which has been disallowed), but she was confined more than 11 weeks before the expected week of confinement.

(4) Any day which falls within the maternity allowance period shall be treated for the purposes of this Part of this Act as a day of incapacity for work.

(5) Where for any purpose of this Part of this Act or of regulations it is necessary to calculate the daily rate of a maternity allowance—

    (*a*) Sunday or such other day in each week as may be prescribed shall be disregarded; and

    (*b*) the amount payable by way of that allowance for any other day shall be taken as $\frac{1}{6}$th of the weekly rate of the allowance.

(6) In this section "confinement" and "confined" are to be construed in accordance with section 50 of the Social Security Act 1986.

(7) The fact that the mother of a child is being paid maternity allowance shall not be taken into consideration by any court in deciding whether to order payment of expenses incidental to the birth of the child.".

14. The following paragraph shall be substituted for paragraph 3 of Part I of Schedule 3—

    "3. The contribution condition for a maternity allowance is—

    (*a*) that the claimant must in respect of at least 26 weeks in the 52 weeks immediately preceding the 14th week before the expected week of confinement have actually paid contributions of a relevant class; and

    (*b*) in the case of Class 1 contributions, that they were not secondary contributions and were not paid at the reduced rate.".

PART III

ABOLITION OF MATERNITY PAY AND WINDING-UP OF MATERNITY PAY FUND

15. The provisions of Part III of the Employment Protection (Consolidation) Act 1978 shall cease to have effect so far as they relate to maternity pay.

16. A woman who is entitled to maternity pay on the coming into force of paragraph 15 above shall continue to be so entitled notwithstanding that paragraph; but a woman who continues to be entitled to maternity pay by virtue of this paragraph shall not be entitled to statutory maternity pay in respect of any week as respects which she is entitled to maternity pay.

17.—(1) The assets and liabilities of the Maternity Pay Fund (including, in particular, liabilities of the Secretary of State in respect of sums advanced under section 38 of the Employment Protection (Consolidation) Act 1978 or claims under section 39 or 40 of that Act) immediately before the relevant date shall become assets and liabilities of the National Insurance Fund; and on that date the Maternity Pay Fund shall cease to exist.

(2) Not later than such date as the Treasury may direct the Secretary of State shall prepare an account in such form as the Treasury may direct showing the state of the Maternity Pay Fund on the relevant date.

(3) The Secretary of State shall send to the Comptroller and Auditor General a copy of the account prepared under sub-paragraph (2) above; and the Comptroller and Auditor General shall examine, certify and report on the account and lay copies of it and of his report before each House of Parliament.

(4) In this paragraph "the relevant date" means such date in the period of 12 months ending on 5th April 1988 as the Secretary of State may, with the consent of the Treasury, determine.

Section 52   SCHEDULE 5

ADJUDICATION

PART I

AMENDMENT OF ENACTMENTS

Social Security Act 1973 (c.38)

1. In section 67(2) of the Social Security Act 1973 (review of determinations by Occupational Pensions Board) the words "or was erroneous in point of law" shall be inserted at the end of paragraph (*a*).

Social Security Act 1975 (c.14)

2. Section 95 of the Social Security Act 1975 (other questions for Secretary of State) shall cease to have effect.

3. The following subsection shall be substituted for subsection (1) of section 96 of that Act (review of certain decisions of Secretary of State)—

"(1) Subject to subsection (2) below, the Secretary of State may review any decision given by him on any question within section 93(1) above if—
(*a*) new facts have been brought to his notice; or
(*b*) he is satisfied that the decision—
(i) was given in ignorance of some material fact;
(ii) was based on a mistake as to some material fact; or
(iii) was erroneous in point of law.".

4. The following subsections shall be substituted for subsection (2) of section 98 of that Act (claims and questions to be submitted to adjudication officer)—

"(2) Subsection (1) above does not apply to any question which falls to be determined otherwise than by an adjudication officer.
(2A) If—
(*a*) a person submits a question relating to the age, marriage or death of any person; and
(*b*) it appears to the adjudication officer that the question may arise if the person who has submitted it to him submits a claim for benefit,
the adjudication officer may determine the question.".

5. The following subsection shall be substituted for subsection (2) of section 99 of that Act (decision of adjudication officer)—

"(2) Subject to section 103 below (reference of special questions), the adjudication officer may decide a claim or question himself or refer it to a social security appeal tribunal.".

6. In section 100 of that Act (appeal to social security appeal tribunal)—

(a) in subsection (1), the words "adversely to the claimant" shall be omitted;

(b) in subsection (2), for the words from "notified" to the end there shall be substituted the words "given any such notification of a decision and of his right of appeal under this section as may be prescribed.";

(c) for the words from the beginning of subsection (3) to the end of paragraph (b) there shall be substituted the words "Where in connection with the decision of the adjudication officer there has arisen any question which under or by virtue of this Act falls to be determined otherwise than by an adjudication officer";

(d) the following subsection shall be substituted for subsection (4)—

"(4) Regulations may make provision as to the manner in which, and the time within which, appeals are to be brought.";

(e) the following subsection shall be substituted for subsection (7)—

"(7) Where an adjudication officer has determined that any amount is recoverable under or by virtue of section 27 or 53 of the Social Security Act 1986 (over payments) any person from whom he has determined that it is recoverable shall have the same right of appeal to a social security appeal tribunal as a claimant.".

7.—(1) At the end of subsection (1) of section 101 of that Act (appeal from tribunal to Commissioner) there shall be added the words "on the ground that the decision of the tribunal was erroneous in point of law.".

(2) The following paragraph shall be substituted for paragraph (d) of subsection (2) of that section—

"(d) a person from whom it is determined that any amount is recoverable under or by virtue of section 27 or 53 of the Social Security Act 1986.".

(3) The following subsections shall be substituted for subsection (5) of that section—

"(5) Where the Commissioner holds that the decision was erroneous in point of law—

(a) he shall have power—

(i) to give the decision which he considers the tribunal should have given, if he can do so without making fresh or further findings of fact; or

(ii) if he considers it expedient, to make such findings and to give such decision as he considers appropriate in the light of them; and

(b) in any other case he shall refer the case to a tribunal with directions for its determination.

(5A) No appeal lies under this section without the leave—

(a) of the person who was the chairman of the tribunal when the decision was given or, in a case prescribed by regulations, the leave of some other chairman of a social security appeal tribunal; or

(b) subject to and in accordance with regulations, of a Commissioner.

(5B) Regulations may make provision as to the manner in which, and the time within which, appeals are to be brought and applications made for leave to appeal.".

8. The following subsection shall be substituted for subsection (2) of section 102 of that Act (question first arising on appeal)—

"(2) Subsection (1) above does not apply to any question which under or by virtue of this Act falls to be determined otherwise than by an adjudication officer.".

9. The following section shall be substituted for section 103 of that Act—

"Reference of special questions

103.—(1) Subject to subsection (2) below—

(a) if on consideration of any claim or question an adjudication officer is of opinion that there arises any question which under or by virtue of this Act falls to be determined otherwise than by an adjudication officer, he shall refer the question for such determination; and

(b) if on consideration of any claim or question a social security appeal tribunal or a Commissioner is of opinion that any such question arises, the tribunal or Commissioner shall direct it to be referred by an adjudication officer for such determination.

(2) The person or tribunal making the reference shall then deal with any other question as if the referred question had not arisen.

(3) The adjudication officer, tribunal or Commissioner may—

    (*a*) postpone the reference of, or dealing with, any question until other questions have been determined;

    (*b*) in cases where the determination of any question disposes of a claim or any part of it make an award or decide that an award cannot be made, as to the claim or that part of it, without referring or dealing with, or before the determination of, any other question.".

10. In section 104 of that Act (review of decisions of adjudication officers, tribunals or Commissioner)—

(*a*) the following subsection shall be substituted for subsection (1)—

    "(1) Any decision under this Act of an adjudication officer, a social security appeal tribunal or a Commissioner may be reviewed at any time by an adjudication officer, or, on a reference by an adjudication officer, by a social security appeal tribunal, if—

        (*a*) the officer or tribunal is satisfied that the decision was given in ignorance of, or was based on a mistake as to, some material fact; or

        (*b*) there has been any relevant change of circumstances since the decision was given; or

        (*c*) the decision was based on a decision of a question which under or by virtue of this Act falls to be determined otherwise than by an adjudication officer, and the decision of that question is revised,

    but regulations may provide that a decision may not be reviewed on the ground mentioned in paragraph (*a*) above unless the officer or tribunal is satisfied as mentioned in that paragraph by fresh evidence.";

(*b*) in subsection (1A), the words "in prescribed circumstances" shall cease to have effect;

(*c*) the following subsection shall be inserted after subsection (3)—

    "(3A) Regulations may provide for enabling or requiring, in prescribed circumstances, a review under this section notwithstanding that no application under subsection (2) has been made."; and

(*d*) the following subsection shall be added after subsection (4)—

    "(5) Regulations—

        (*a*) may prescribe what are, or are not, relevant changes of circumstances for the purposes of subsection (1)(*b*) above; and

        (*b*) may make provision restricting the payment of any benefit, or any increase of benefit, to which a person would, but for this subsection, be entitled by reason of a review in respect of any period before the review.".

11.—(1) In section 106(1) of that Act (review of decision of Attendance Allowance Board) in paragraph (*b*) before the word "within" there shall be inserted the words "on an application made".

(2) The following paragraph shall be inserted after that paragraph—

    "(*bb*) without an application review such a determination on any ground within the prescribed period;".

12. In section 107(6) of that Act (declaration that accident is an industrial accident)—

    (*a*) the words "or was not" shall be inserted after the words "accident was"; and

    (*b*) the words "by fresh evidence" and paragraph (*b*) shall cease to have effect.

13. In section 109(3) of that Act (medical appeals and references) after the words "by a medical appeal tribunal," there shall be inserted the words "or, if the adjudication officer is of the opinion that any such decision ought to be so considered,".

14. In section 110 of that Act (review of medical decisions)—

    (*a*) in subsection (1), the words "by fresh evidence" shall cease to have effect; and

    (*b*) the following subsections shall be inserted after that subsection—

    "(1A) Any decision under this Part of this Act of an adjudicating medical practitioner may be reviewed at any time by such a practitioner if he is satisfied that the decision was erroneous in point of law.

    (1B) Regulations may provide that a decision may not be reviewed under subsection (1) above unless the adjudicating medical practitioner is satisfied as mentioned in that subsection by fresh evidence.".

15. In section 112 of that Act (appeal etc. on question of law to Commissioner)—

    (*a*) in subsection (1), the following paragraph shall be inserted before paragraph (*a*)—

    "(*za*) an adjudication officer; or"; and

    (*b*) in subsection (3), for the words from "without the leave" to "and regulations" there shall be substituted—

"without the leave—
(*a*) of the person who was the chairman of the medical appeal tribunal when the decision was given or, in a case prescribed by regulations, the leave of some other chairman of a medical appeal tribunal; or
(*b*) subject to and in accordance with regulations, of a Commissioner, and regulations".

16. In section 114 of that Act (regulations as to determination of questions)—
(*a*) the following subsections shall be inserted after subsection (2A)—
"(2B) Regulations under subsection (1) above may provide for the review by the Secretary of State of decisions on questions determined by him.
(2C) The Lord Chancellor may by regulations provide—
(*a*) for officers authorised—
(i) by the Lord Chancellor; or
(ii) in Scotland, by the Secretary of State,
to determine any question which is determinable by a Commissioner and which does not involve the determination of any appeal, application for leave to appeal or reference;
(*b*) for the procedure to be followed by any such officer in determining any such question;
(*c*) for the manner in which determinations of such questions by such officers may be called in question.
(2D) A determination which would have the effect of preventing an appeal, application for leave to appeal or reference being determined by a Commissioner is not a determination of the appeal, application or reference for the purposes of subsection (2C) above."; and
(*b*) subsections (3) and (4) shall cease to have effect.

17. The following subsection shall be inserted after section 166(5) of that Act (regulations)—
"(5A) Where the Lord Chancellor proposes to make regulations under this Act it shall be his duty to consult the Lord Advocate with respect to the proposal.".

18. In paragraph 2(2) of Schedule 12 to that Act (appointment of members of medical appeal tribunals) for the words "Secretary of State" there shall be substituted the word "President".

19. In Schedule 13 to that Act (provision which may be made by procedure regulations)—
(*a*) the following paragraph shall be inserted after paragraph 1—
"1A. Provision as to the striking out of proceedings for want of prosecution.";
(*b*) in paragraph 10, for the words from "the determination" to the end there shall be substituted the words "a determination.".

20. In Schedule 20 to that Act (glossary of expressions), for the definition of "Regulations" there shall be substituted the following definition—

"Regulations"
In relation to regulations with respect to proceedings before the Commissioners (whether for the determination of any matter or for leave to appeal to or from the Commissioners) and to regulations under section 114(2C) above regulations made by the Lord Chancellor under this Act and in relation to other regulations, regulations made by the Secretary of State under this Act.".

PART II

QUESTIONS FOR DETERMINATION BY THE SECRETARY OF STATE

The questions referred to in section 52(2) above are—
(*a*) any question arising in connection with—
(i) minimum contributions;
(ii) any state scheme premium under Part I of this Act; or
(iii) payments under section 7 above,
other than a question which is required under or by virtue of this Act or the Social Security Pensions Act 1975 to be determined by the Occupational Pensions Board;
(*b*) any question arising under any provision of Part I of the Social Security and Housing Benefits Act 1982, or of regulations under that Part of that Act, as to—

(i) whether a person is, or was, an employee or employer of another;

(ii) whether an employer is entitled to make any deduction from his contributions payments in accordance with regulations under section 9 of that Act;

(iii) whether a payment falls to be made to an employer in accordance with the regulations;

(iv) the amount that falls to be so deducted or paid; or

(v) whether two or more employers or two or more contracts of service are, by virtue of regulations made under section 26(5) of that Act, to be treated as one;

(c) any question arising under Part V of this Act (including Schedule 4 to this Act) or regulations under it as to—

(i) whether a person is, or was, an employee or employer of another;

(ii) whether an employer is entitled to make any deduction from his contributions payments in accordance with regulations under Part I of Schedule 4;

(iii) whether a payment falls to be made to an employer in accordance with the regulations;

(iv) the amount that falls to be so deducted or paid;

(v) whether two or more employers or two or more contracts of service are, by virtue of regulations made under section 50(2) above, to be treated as one, and any question arising under regulations made by virtue of paragraph (c), (d) or (f) of section 46(8) above.

Section 66SCHEDULE 6

CHRISTMAS BONUS FOR PENSIONERS

Interpretation

1.—(1) In this Schedule "qualifying benefit" means—

(a) any of the following benefits under the Social Security Act 1975—

(i) a retirement pension;

(ii) an invalidity pension;

(iii) a widowed mother's allowance or widow's pension;

(iv) a severe disablement allowance;

(v) an invalid care allowance;

(vi) an industrial death benefit by way of widow's or widower's pension;

(b) an attendance allowance;

(c) an unemployability supplement or allowance;

(d) a war disablement pension;

(e) a war widow's pension;

(f) income support.

(2) In this Schedule—

"attendance allowance" means—

(a) an attendance allowance under section 35 of the Social Security Act 1975;

(b) an increase of disablement pension under section 61 or 63 of that Act (increases in respect of the need for constant attendance);

(c) a payment under regulations made in exercise of the power in section 159(3)(b) of that Act (constant attendance allowance and an increase for exceptionally severe disablement for certain pre-1948 cases);

(d) an increase of allowance under Article 8 of the Pneumoconiosis, Byssinosis and Miscellaneous Diseases Benefit Scheme 1983 (constant attendance allowance for certain persons to whom that Scheme applies) or under the corresponding provision of any Scheme which may replace that Scheme;

(e) an allowance in respect of constant attendance on account of disablement for which a person is in receipt of war disablement pension, including an allowance in respect of exceptionally severe disablement;

"married couple" and "unmarried couple" are to be construed in accordance with Part II of this Act and any regulations made under it.

"pensionable age" means—

(a) in the case of a man, the age of 65;

(b) in the case of a woman, the age of 60;

"retirement pension" includes graduated retirement benefit, if paid periodically;

"unemployability supplement or allowance" means—
    (*a*) an unemployability supplement payable under section 58 of the Social Security Act 1975 by virtue of paragraph 4 of Schedule 3 to this Act; or
    (*b*) any corresponding allowance payable—
        (i) by virtue of section 7(3)(*a*) of the Industrial Injuries and Diseases (Old Cases) Act 1975;
        (ii) by way of supplement to retired pay or pension exempt from income tax under section 365(1) of the Income and Corporation Taxes Act 1970;
        (iii) under the Personal Injuries (Emergency Provisions) Act 1939; or
        (iv) by way of supplement to retired pay or pension under the Polish Resettlement Act 1947;
and each of the following expressions, namely "attendance allowance", "unemployability supplement or allowance", "war disablement pension" and "war widow's pension", includes any payment which the Secretary of State accepts as being analogous to it.

(3) In this Schedule "the relevant week", in relation to any year, means the week beginning with the first Monday in December or such other week as may be specified in an order made by the Secretary of State.

Entitlement

2.—(1) Any person who in any year—
    (*a*) is present or ordinarily resident in the United Kingdom or any other member state at any time during the relevant week; and
    (*b*) is entitled to a payment of a qualifying benefit in respect of a period which includes a day in that week or is to be treated as entitled to a payment of a qualifying benefit in respect of such a period,
shall, subject to the following provisions of this Schedule, be entitled to payment under this sub-paragraph in respect of that year.

(2) Subject to the following provisions of this Schedule, any person who is a member of a married or unmarried couple and is entitled to a payment under sub-paragraph (1) above in respect of a year shall also be entitled to payment under this sub-paragraph in respect of that year if—
    (*a*) both members of the couple have attained pensionable age not later than the end of the relevant week; and
    (*b*) the other member of the couple satisfies the condition mentioned in sub-paragraph (1)(*a*) above; and
    (*c*) either—
        (i) he is entitled or treated as entitled, in respect of the other member of the couple to an increase in the payment of the qualifying benefit; or
        (ii) the only qualifying benefit to which he is entitled is income support.

(3) A payment under sub-paragraph (1) or (2) above—
    (*a*) is to be made by the Secretary of State; and
    (*b*) is to be of £10 or such larger sum as the Secretary of State may by order specify.

(4) Where the only qualifying benefit to which a person is entitled is income support, he shall not be entitled to a payment under sub-paragraph (1) above unless he has attained pensionable age not later than the end of the relevant week.

(5) Only one sum shall be payable in respect of any person.

3.—(1) For the purposes of paragraph 2 above the Channel Islands, the Isle of Man and Gibraltar shall be treated as though they were part of the United Kingdom.

(2) A person shall be treated for the purposes of paragraph 2(1)(*b*) above as entitled to a payment of a qualifying benefit if he would be so entitled—
    (*a*) in the case of a qualifying benefit other than income support—
        (i) but for the fact that he or, if he is a member of a married or unmarried couple, the other member is entitled to receive some other payment out of public funds;
        (ii) but for the operation of section 30(1) of the Social Security Act 1975;
        (iii) but for the fact that he has not made a claim for the payment;
    (*b*) in the case of income support, but for the fact that his income or, if he is a member of a married or unmarried couple, the income of the other member of the couple was exceptionally of an amount which resulted in his having ceased to be entitled to income support.

(3) A person shall be treated for the purposes of paragraph 2(2)(*c*)(i) above as entitled in respect of the other member of the couple to an increase in a payment of qualifying benefit if he would be so entitled—

(*a*) but for the fact that he or the other member is entitled to receive some other payment out of public funds;

(*b*) but for the operation of any provision of section 30(1), 45(2) or (2A) or 66(4) of the Social Security Act 1975 or any regulations made under section 66(3) of that Act whereby entitlement to benefit is affected by the amount of a person's earnings in a given period; or

(*c*) but for such terms as are mentioned in sub-paragraph (2)(*a*)(iii) above; or

(*d*) but for the fact that he has not made a claim for the increase.

(4) For the purposes of paragraph 2 above a person shall be deemed not to be entitled to a payment of a war disablement pension unless not later than the end of the relevant week—

(*a*) he has attained the age of 70 in the case of a man or 65 in the case of a woman; or

(*b*) he is treated under section 27(3) of the Social Security Act 1975 as having retired from regular employment.

(5) A sum payable under paragraph 2 above shall not be treated as benefit for the purposes of any enactment or instrument under which entitlement to the relevant qualifying benefit arises or is to be treated as arising.

(6) A payment and the right to receive a payment—

(*a*) under paragraph 2 above or any enactment corresponding to it in Northern Ireland; or

(*b*) under regulations relating to widows which are made by the Secretary of State under any enactment relating to police and which contain a statement that the regulations provide for payments corresponding to payments under that paragraph,

shall be disregarded for all purposes of income tax and for the purposes of any enactment or instrument under which regard is had to a person's means.

Administration of payments

4.—(1) A determination by the competent authority that a person is entitled or not entitled to payment of a qualifying benefit in respect of a period which includes a day in the relevant week shall be conclusive for the purposes of paragraph 2 above; and in this sub-paragraph "competent authority" means, in relation to a payment of any description of qualifying benefit, an authority who ordinarily determines whether a person is entitled to such a payment.

(2) Any question arising under this Schedule other than one determined or falling to be determined under sub-paragraph (1) above shall be determined by the Secretary of State whose decision shall except as provided by the following sub-paragraph be final.

(3) The Secretary of State may reverse a decision under sub-paragraph (2) above on new facts being brought to his notice or if he is satisfied that the decision was given in ignorance of, or was based on a mistake as to, some material fact.

Section 73 SCHEDULE 7

SUPPLEMENTARY BENEFIT ETC.

Interpretation

1. In this Schedule—

"the former National Insurance Acts" means the National Insurance Act 1946 and the National Insurance Act 1965; and

"the former Industrial Injuries Acts" means the National Insurance (Industrial Injuries) Act 1946 and the National Insurance (Industrial Injuries) Act 1965.

Prevention of duplication of payments

2. Section 27 above shall have effect in relation to supplementary benefit as it has effect in relation to income support.

Claims and Payments

3.—(1) Section 51 above shall have effect in relation to the benefits specified in sub-paragraph (2) below as it has effect in relation to the benefits to which it applies by virtue of subsection (2).

(2) The benefits mentioned in sub-paragraph (1) above are benefits under—
- (*a*) the former National Insurance Acts;
- (*b*) the former Industrial Injuries Acts;
- (*c*) the National Assistance Act 1948;
- (*d*) the Supplementary Benefit Act 1966;
- (*e*) the Supplementary Benefits Act 1976;
- (*f*) the Family Income Supplements Act 1970.

Adjudication

4.—(1) Section 52(3) above shall have effect for the purposes of the benefits specified in paragraph 3(2) above as it has effect for the purposes of benefit under the Social Security Act 1975.

(2) Procedure regulations made under section 115 of the Social Security Act 1975 by virtue of sub-paragraph (1) above may make different provision in relation to each of the benefits specified in paragraph 3(2) above.

Overpayments

5.—(1) Section 53 above shall have effect in relation to the benefits specified in paragraph 3(2) above as it has effect in relation to the benefits to which it applies by virtue of subsection (10).

(2) The reference to housing benefit in section 29(4) includes a reference to housing benefits under Part II of the Social Security and Housing Benefits Act 1982.

Legal proceedings

6. Section 56 above shall have effect as if the benefit Acts included—
- (*a*) the National Assistance Act 1948;
- (*b*) the Supplementary Benefit Act 1966;
- (*c*) the Supplementary Benefits Act 1976;
- (*d*) the Family Income Supplements Act 1970.

Inspection

7. Section 58 above shall have effect as if the benefit Acts included the Acts mentioned in paragraph 6(*c*) and (*d*) above.

Up-rating

8. Section 63 above shall have effect as if the sums mentioned in subsection (1) included sums payable by way of benefit under—
- (*a*) the Family Income Supplements Act 1970;
- (*b*) the Supplementary Benefits Act 1976; and
- (*c*) Part II of the Social Security and Housing Benefits Act 1982.

Section 75   SCHEDULE 8

EARNINGS FACTORS

Social Security Act 1975 (c.14)

1. The Social Security Act 1975 shall be amended as follows.

2.—(1) In subsection (2) of section 13 (contribution conditions and the earnings factor) for the words from "from" to "above" there shall be substituted the words "in respect of each tax year from those of his earnings upon which primary Class 1 contributions have been paid or treated as paid and from Class 2 and Class 3 contributions".

(2) In subsection (3) of that section, for the words from "primary" to the end there shall be substituted the words "earnings upon which primary Class 1 contributions are paid at the reduced rate".

(3) In subsection (4), for the words "contributions of any class" there shall be substituted the words "earnings or Class 2 or Class 3 contributions".

(4) In subsection (5)—

    (*a*) for the word "contributions", in the first place where it occurs, there shall be substituted the words "earnings or Class 2 or Class 3 contributions";

    (*b*) paragraph (*a*) shall be omitted; and

    (*c*) for the words from "shall be derived" to the end of the subsection there shall be substituted the words "may be derived—

        (i) from earnings upon which primary Class 1 contributions have been paid or treated as paid;

        (ii) from earnings which have been credited;

        (iii) from contributions of different classes paid or credited in the same tax year;

        (iv) by any combination of the methods mentioned in sub-paragraphs (i) to (iii) above.".

(5) The following subsection shall be inserted after subsection (5A)—

    "(5B) Regulations may provide for requiring persons to maintain, in such form and manner as may be prescribed, records of such earnings paid by them as are relevant for the purpose of calculating earnings factors, and to retain such records for so long as may be prescribed.".

(6) In subsection (6)(*c*)—

    (*a*) for the words "person's contribution of any class or classes" there shall be substituted the word "person";

    (*b*) for the words "those contributions" there shall be substituted the words "his earnings upon which primary Class 1 contributions have been paid or treated as paid and from his Class 2 and Class 3 contributions".

3.—(1) The following paragraph shall be substituted for sub-paragraph (2)(*b*) of paragraph 1 (unemployment and sickness benefit) of Schedule 3 (contribution conditions)—

    "(*b*) the earnings factor derived—

        (i) in the case of unemployment benefit, from earnings upon which primary Class 1 contributions have been paid or treated as paid; and

        (ii) in the case of sickness benefit, from such earnings or from Class 2 contributions,

    must be not less than that year's lower earnings limit multiplied by 25.".

(2) In sub-paragraph (3)(*a*) of that paragraph, after the word "class" there shall be inserted the words "or been credited with earnings".

(3) The following paragraph shall be substituted for sub-paragraph (3)(*b*)—

    "(*b*) the earnings factor derived—

        (i) in the case of unemployment benefit, from earnings upon which primary Class 1 contributions have been paid or treated as paid or from earnings credited; and

        (ii) in the case of sickness benefit, from such earnings or from Class 2 contributions,

    must be not less than that year's lower earnings limit multiplied by 50.".

(4) In sub-paragraph (1)(*b*) of paragraph 4 of that Schedule for the words "those contributions" there shall be substituted the words "earnings upon which primary Class 1 contributions have been paid or treated as paid and from Class 2 and Class 3 contributions".

(5) In sub-paragraph (2)(*b*) of paragraph 5 of that Schedule (widowed mother's allowance, widow's pension and retirement pensions) for the words "those contributions" there shall be substituted the words "earnings upon which such of those contributions as are primary Class 1 contributions were paid or treated as paid and any Class 2 or Class 3 contributions".

(6) The following paragraph shall be substituted for sub-paragraph (3)(*b*) of that paragraph—

    "(*b*) in the case of each of those years, the earnings factor derived from—

        (i) any earnings upon which such of those contributions as are primary Class 1 contributions were paid or treated as paid or earnings credited; and

        (ii) any Class 2 or Class 3 contributions for the year,

    must be not less that the qualifying earnings factor for the year.".

(7) In paragraph 8(3) (satisfaction of certain contribution conditions in early years of contribution) for the words "his contributions of a relevant class" there shall be substituted

the words "the aggregate of his earnings upon which primary Class 1 contributions were paid or treated as paid and from Class 2 contributions".

Social Security Pensions Act 1975 (c.60)

4. The Social Security Pensions Act 1975 shall be amended as follows.

5. In subsection (4) of section 3 (married women and widows) for the words from "contributions" to "rate" there shall be substituted the words "earnings upon which primary Class 1 contributions are paid at a reduced rate by virtue of regulations under subsection (2) above or from Class 2 contributions paid at a reduced rate by virtue of such regulations".

6. In subsection (1) of section 5 of that Act (voluntary contributions) after the word "from" there shall be inserted the words "earnings upon which Class 1 contributions have been paid or treated as paid or from Class 2".

7.—(1) In section 6 (rate of Category A retirement pension)—

    (*a*) in subsection (5), for the words "contributions actually paid by him in respect of that year" there shall be substituted the words "earnings upon which primary Class 1 contributions were paid or treated as paid in respect of that year and earnings factors derived from Class 2 and Class 3 contributions actually paid in respect of it"; and

    (*b*) subsection (5A) shall be omitted.

8.—(1) In subsection (2) of section 35 (earner's guaranteed minimum) for the words "contributions paid in respect of such earnings as are mentioned in subsection (1) above" there shall be substituted the words "earnings such as are mentioned in subsection (1) above upon which primary Class 1 contributions have been paid or treated as paid".

9. Section 43(1A) and section 47(2A) shall not apply to any period after the end of the tax year 1986–87.

10. In subsection (3)(*b*) of section 45 (premium where guaranteed minimum pension excluded from full revaluation) for the word "contributions", in the first place where it occurs, there shall be substituted the words "earnings upon which primary Class 1 contributions have been paid or treated as paid".

Social Security (Miscellaneous Provisions) Act 1977 (c.5)

11. In subsection (1)(*b*) of section 21 of the Social Security (Miscellaneous Provisions) Act 1977 (calculation of guaranteed minimum pensions preserved under approved arrangements) after the word "contributions", in the first place where it occurs, there shall be inserted the words "or earnings".

Section 82   SCHEDULE 9

NORTHERN IRELAND

PART I

APPEAL ON QUESTION OF LAW FROM MEDICAL APPEAL TRIBUNAL TO COMMISSIONER

1. After section 112 of the Social Security (Northern Ireland) Act 1975 there shall be inserted the following section—

"**Appeal etc. on question of law to Commissioner**

    112A.—(1) Subject to this section, an appeal lies to a Commissioner from any decision of a medical appeal tribunal on the ground that the decision is erroneous in point of law, at the instance of—

    (*a*) an adjudication officer; or

    (*b*) the claimant; or

    (*c*) a trade union of which the claimant was a member at the time of the relevant accident or, in a case relating to severe disablement allowance, at the prescribed time; or

    (*d*) the Department.

    (2) Subsection (1) above, as it applies to a trade union, applies also to any other association which exists to promote the interests and welfare of its members.

    (3) No appeal lies under subsection (1) above without the leave—

    (*a*) of the person who was the chairman of the medical appeal tribunal when the decision was given or, in a case prescribed by regulations, the leave of some other chairman of a medical appeal tribunal; or

    (*b*) subject to and in accordance with regulations, of a Commissioner, and regulations may make provision as to the manner in which, and the time within which, appeals are to be brought and applications made for leave to appeal.

(4) Where a question of law arises in a case before a medical appeal tribunal, the tribunal may refer that question to a Commissioner for his decision.

(5) On any such appeal or reference, the question of law arising for the decision of the Commissioner and the facts on which it arises shall be submitted for his consideration in the prescribed manner; and the medical appeal tribunal on being informed in the prescribed manner of his decision on the question of law shall give, confirm or revise their decision on the case accordingly.

(6) No appeal lies under subsection (1) from a decision of a medical appeal tribunal given before the date of the coming into operation of Part I of Schedule 9 to the Social Security Act 1986.".

PART II

TRANSFER OF FUNCTIONS RELATING TO COMMISSIONERS

2.—(1) In this Part—
"the Commissioners" means the Chief and other Social Security Commissioners for Northern Ireland;
    "the Department", except in the expression "the Department of Finance and Personnel", means the Department of Health and Social Services for Northern Ireland.

(2) The references in paragraphs 3(1)(*b*) and 4 to service by any person as a Commissioner include references to service treated as service as a Commissioner under paragraph 5(2) of Schedule 10 to the Social Security (Northern Ireland) Act 1975 (service under former enactments).

3.—(1) The following functions of the Department are hereby transferred to the Lord Chancellor—

(*a*) the functions of the Department under paragraphs 4, 6 and 7 of Schedule 10 to the Social Security (Northern Ireland) Act 1975 (payment of remuneration, expenses, and pensions of the Commissioners);

(*b*) the functions of the Department under the provisions of the Judicial Pensions Act (Northern Ireland) 1951 (lump sums and widow's and children's pensions) and paragraph 3 of Schedule 3 to the Administration of Justice Act 1973 (increase of certain widow's and children's pensions) so far as those provisions apply to service by any person as a Commissioner;

(*c*) the administration of the offices of the Commissioners, including the functions of the Department under paragraph 3 of Schedule 10 to the Social Security (Northern Ireland) Act 1975 (payments in connection with work or tribunals etc.) relating to the work of the Commissioners;

(*d*) the making, under or for the purposes of the enactments mentioned in sub-paragraph (2) below, of regulations with respect to proceedings before the Commissioners, whether for the determination of any matter or for leave to appeal to or from the Commissioners.

(2) The enactments referred to in sub-paragraph (1)(*d*) above are—

(*a*) sections 6(1) and 10 of the Family Income Supplements Act (Northern Ireland) 1971;

(*b*) section 5 of the National Insurance Measure (Northern Ireland) 1974;

(*c*) sections 106(2), 112A and 115(1) of the Social Security (Northern Ireland) Act 1975;

(*d*) Articles 9(1) and 24 of the Child Benefit (Northern Ireland) Order 1975;

(*e*) the definition of "regulations" in Article 2(2), and Articles 4(1) and 19(1), of the Supplementary Benefits (Northern Ireland) Order 1977;

(*f*) section 14 of the Social Security Act 1980;

(*g*) Article 11(1) of the Social Security (Northern Ireland) Order 1980;

(*h*) Article 6 of the Forfeiture (Northern Ireland) Order 1982;

(*j*) Articles 17(5) and 36 of the Social Security (Northern Ireland) Order 1982.

4.—(1) The functions of the Department of Finance and Personnel, so far as they relate to the functions transferred by paragraph 3 above, are hereby transferred to the Treasury.

(2) The functions of the Department of Finance and Personnel under the Judicial Pensions Act (Northern Ireland) 1951, so far as it applies to service by any person as a Commissioner, are hereby transferred to the Treasury.

5. The functions of the Secretary of State under paragraph 7(5) of Schedule 10 to the Social Security (Northern Ireland) Act 1975 (power of Secretary of State to require person retired on medical grounds to resume duties of Commissioner) are hereby transferred to the Lord Chancellor.

6.—(1) Subject to any Order made after the passing of this Act by virtue of subsection (1)(*a*) of section 3 of the Northern Ireland Constitution Act 1973, the matters to which this paragraph applies shall not be transferred matters for the purposes of that Act but shall for the purposes of subsection (2) of that section be treated as specified in Schedule 3 to that Act.

(2) This paragraph applies to all matters relating to the Commissioners, including procedure and appeals, other than those specified in paragraph 9 of Schedule 2 to the Northern Ireland Constitution Act 1973.

7. Regulations made by the Lord Chancellor by virtue of this Part of this Schedule shall be subject to annulment in pursuance of a resolution of either House of Parliament in like manner as a statutory instrument and section 5 of the Statutory Instruments Act 1946 shall apply accordingly.

8.—(1) Enactments and instruments passed or made before the coming into operation of this Part of this Schedule shall have effect, so far as may be necessary for the purpose or in consequence of the transfers effected by this Part as if—

(*a*) references to the Department or to the Secretary of State were references to the Lord Chancellor; and

(*b*) references to the Department of Finance and Personnel were references to the Treasury; and

(*c*) references to moneys appropriated by Measure of the Northern Ireland Assembly were references to money provided by Parliament and references to the Consolidated Fund of Northern Ireland were references to the Consolidated Fund of the United Kingdom.

(2) This Part of this Schedule shall not affect the validity of anything done (or having effect as done) by or in relation to the Department, the Department of Finance and Personnel or the Secretary of State before the coming into operation of this Part, and anything which at the time of the coming into operation of this Part is in process of being done by or in relation to either of those Departments or the Secretary of State may, if it relates to a function transferred by this Part, be continued by or in relation to the Lord Chancellor or the Treasury, as the case may require.

(3) Anything done (or having effect as done) by the Department, the Department of Finance and Personnel or the Secretary of State for the purpose of a function transferred by this Part of this Schedule, if in force at the coming into operation of this Part, shall have effect, as far as required for continuing its effect after the coming into operation of this Part, as if done by the Lord Chancellor or by the Treasury, as the case may require.

(4) The amendments specified in Part III of this Schedule are without prejudice to the generality of this paragraph.

PART III

CONSEQUENTIAL AMENDMENTS

Judicial Pensions Act (Northern Ireland) 1951 (c.20)(N.I.)

9. In section 16 of the Judicial Pensions Act (Northern Ireland) 1951 (recommendation required for payments conditional on eligibility for Commissioners' pensions) for the words "Department of Health and Social Services" there shall be substituted the words "Lord Chancellor".

Social Security (Northern Ireland) Act 1975 (c.15)

10.—(1) In paragraphs 4, 6 and 7 of Schedule 10 to the Social Security (Northern Ireland) Act 1975 (payment of remuneration, expenses and pensions of the Commissioners)—

(*a*) for the word "Department" in each place where it occurs (except in the expression "Department of Finance") there shall be substituted the words "Lord Chancellor";

(*b*) for the words "Department of Finance" in each place where they occur there shall be substituted the word "Treasury".

(2) In sub-paragraph (1) of the said paragraph 6 for the words "moneys appropriated by Measure of the Northern Ireland Assembly" there shall be substituted the words "money provided by Parliament".

(3) In sub-paragraph (5) of the said paragraph 7 for the words "Secretary of State" there shall be substituted the words "Lord Chancellor".

Social Security Act 1980 (c.30)

11. In section 14 of the Social Security Act 1980 (appeal from Commissioners etc. on point of law)—
   (*a*) subsection (6) (which provides for modifying the preceding provisions of that section in relation to decisions of medical appeal tribunals appointed under the Social Security (Northern Ireland) Act 1975) shall cease to have effect;
   (*b*) in subsection (7) (which provides for modifying subsections (3) and (5) of that section in relation to decisions of Commissioners on questions of law referred by medical appeal tribunals) after the words "to a Commissioner)" there shall be inserted the words "and in relation to a decision of a Commissioner within the meaning of the Social Security (Northern Ireland) Act 1975 which was given in consequence of a reference under subsection (4) of section 112A of that Act (which makes corresponding provision for Northern Ireland)";
   (*c*) in subsection (8) (which provides for the making of regulations)—
         (i) in paragraph (*b*), for the words from "or a medical appeal tribunal" to "for Northern Ireland" there shall be substituted the words "by the Lord Chancellor";
         (ii) the words from "negative resolution" to the end there shall be substituted the words "annulment in pursuance of a resolution of either House of Parliament in like manner as a statutory instrument and section 5 of the Statutory Instruments Act 1946 shall apply accordingly.".
12. In paragraph 21 of Schedule 3 to that Act (regulations in Northern Ireland corresponding to regulations in Great Britain made by the Secretary of State not requiring prior submission to Social Security Advisory Committee), after the words "Secretary of State" there shall be inserted the words "or the Lord Chancellor".

Forfeiture (Northern Ireland) Order 1982 (S.I. 1982/1082 (N.I. 14))

13. In Article 6(2) of the Forfeiture (Northern Ireland) Order 1982 (regulations for purposes of determinations by Social Security Commissioner), for the words "Department of Health and Social Services" there shall be substituted the words "Lord Chancellor".

Section 86   SCHEDULE 10

                     MINOR AND CONSEQUENTIAL AMENDMENTS

                               PART I

                              PENSIONS

                    Social Security Act 1973 (c.38)

1. The Social Security Act 1973 shall be amended as follows.
2. In section 58(2) (linked qualifying service)—
   (*a*) the following paragraph shall be substituted for paragraph (*a*)—
         "(*a*) under the rules of a scheme applying to him in the earlier period of service—
               (i) there was made a transfer of his accrued rights under that scheme to another scheme applying to him in the later period of service; or
               (ii) those rights were secured by a policy of insurance or an annuity contract and were subsequently transferred to another scheme applying to him in the later period of service;"; and
   (*b*) in paragraph (*b*), for the words "that transfer" there shall be substituted the words "the transfer of his accrued rights to the second scheme.".
3. In section 64 (modification of occupational pension scheme by order of Occupational Pensions Board) the following subsection shall be inserted after subsection (1)—
         "(1A) The Board shall also have power on such an application to make an order—
               (*a*) authorising the modification of the scheme with a view to achieving any one or more of such other purposes as may be prescribed; or

(b) modifying the scheme with a view to achieving any one or more of those purposes.".

4. In section 66—

(a) in subsection (1)(a), for the words "and the Pensions Act" there shall be substituted the words ", the Pensions Act and Part I of the Social Security Act 1986";

(b) in subsection (7)(a), after the words "contracting-out certificates" there shall be inserted the words "and appropriate scheme certificates"; and

(c) the following subsection shall be substituted for subsection (10)—

"(10) References in this section—

(a) to this Part of this Act, the Pensions Act and Part I of the Social Security Act 1986 include references to any provisions in force in Northern Ireland and corresponding to provisions of this Part of this Act, the Pensions Act or Part I of the Social Security Act 1986; and

(b) to contracting-out certificates and appropriate scheme certificates include references to contracting-out certificates and appropriate scheme certificates within the meaning of any such provisions.".

5. In section 67(1)(a) (review of determinations by Board) after the words "contracting-out certificate" there shall be inserted the words "or an appropriate scheme certificate".

6. In section 69 (rule against perpetuities)—

(a) in subsection (1), for the words "an occupational" there shall be substituted the words "a personal or occupational";

(b) in subsection (2), for the words "under this Part of this Act" there shall be substituted the words "or an appropriate scheme under Part I of the Social Security Act 1986"; and

(c) in subsection (5), for the words "which ceases to be contracted-out, or" there shall be substituted the words "which ceases—

(a) if it is an occupational pension scheme, to be contracted-out; or

(b) if it is a personal pension scheme, to be an appropriate scheme,

or".

7. Sections 70 (legal restrictions of doubtful application), 71 (friendly societies) and 72 (fees for official services to schemes) shall have effect in relation to personal pension schemes as they have effect in relation to occupational pension schemes.

8. In section 99(1) the following definitions shall be inserted at the appropriate places—

" "appropriate scheme" shall be construed in accordance with Part I of the Social Security Act 1986;"; and

" "personal pension scheme" has the same meaning as in the Social Security Act 1986;"

9. In paragraph 4 of Schedule 16 (preservation of benefits under occupational pension schemes)—

(a) for the words "requisite benefits" in the first place where they occur in sub-paragraph (2) and in sub-paragraph (3) there shall be substituted the words "a guaranteed minimum pension"; and

(b) for the words "his requisite benefits" in sub-paragraph (2) there shall be substituted the words "the guaranteed minimum pension".

Social Security Act 1975 (c.14)

10. In paragraph 6(1)(h) of Schedule 1 to the Social Security Act 1975 (regulations about return of contributions) after the word "of", in the first place where it occurs, there shall be inserted the words "the whole or any prescribed part of any".

Social Security Pensions Act 1975 (c.60)

11. The Social Security Pensions Act 1975 shall be amended as follows.

12. In section 26 (contracting-out)—

(a) in subsection (1), for the words "the requisite benefits" there shall be substituted the words "a guaranteed minimum pension"; and

(b) in subsection (2), for the words from the beginning to "such pension" there shall be substituted the words " "Guaranteed minimum pension" means any pension which is provided by an occupational pension scheme in accordance with the requirements of sections 33 and 36 below".

13. In section 27(4) (contracted-out rates of Class 1 contributions) for the words from the beginning to "that employment" there shall be substituted the words "Where—

(a) an earner has ceased to be employed in an employment; and

(b) earnings are paid to him or for his benefit within the period of 6 weeks, or such other period as may be prescribed, from the day on which he so ceased, that employment".

14. In section 29 (contracted-out rates of benefit)—

(*a*) in subsection (1)(*a*), for the words "or a widow's pension" there shall be substituted the words ", a widow's pension or a widower's invalidity pension under section 16 above";

(*b*) in subsection (2)—

(i) after the words "this section" there shall be inserted the words "and sections 16(2B), 28(7A) and 59(1A) of the principal Act"; and

(ii) at the end there shall be added the words "or if as a result of a transfer payment or transfer under regulations made by virtue of section 38 below he is no longer entitled to guaranteed minimum pensions under the scheme by which the transfer payment or transfer is made and has not as a result of the transfer payment or transfer become entitled to guaranteed minimum pensions under the scheme to which the transfer payment or transfer is made."

15. In section 30(1)(*a*) (contracted-out employment) for the words "the requisite benefits of" there shall be substituted the words "a guaranteed minimum pension provided by".

16. In section 32 (contracted-out schemes)—

(*a*) in subsection (2)—

(i) for the words "the requisite benefits" in paragraph (*a*); and

(ii) for the words "requisite benefits" in paragraph (*b*), there shall be substituted the words "guaranteed minimum pensions";

(*b*) in subsection (4) the words "relating to the scheme or its management" shall cease to have effect.

17. In section 33 (requirements for contracting-out) the following subsection shall be inserted after subsection (1)—

"(1A) In the case of an earner who is a married woman or widow who is liable to pay primary Class 1 contributions at a reduced rate by virtue of section 3 of this Act, subject to the provisions of this Part of this Act, for a scheme to be contracted-out in relation to her employment it must—

(*a*) provide for her to be entitled to a pension under the scheme if she attains pensionable age; and

(*b*) satisfy such other conditions as may be prescribed.".

18. The following subsection shall be substituted for section 38(1) (transfer of accrued rights)—

"(1) Regulations may prescribe circumstances in which and conditions subject to which—

(*a*) there may be made by one occupational pension scheme to another or by an occupational pension scheme to a personal pension scheme a transfer of or a transfer payment in respect of—

(i) an earner's accrued rights to guaranteed minimum pensions under a contracted-out scheme;

(ii) an earner's accrued rights to pensions under an occupational pension scheme which is not contracted-out, to the extent that those rights derive from his accrued rights to guaranteed minimum pensions under a contracted-out scheme; or

(iii) the liability for the payment of guaranteed minimum pensions to or in respect of any person who has become entitled to them;

(*b*) there may be made to an occupational pension scheme or a personal pension scheme a transfer of or a transfer payment in respect of an earner's accrued rights to guaranteed minimum pensions which are appropriately secured for the purposes of section 52C below.".

19. Sections 41(4) and 49(3) and (7) (powers of Occupational Pensions Board which are no longer required) shall cease to have effect.

20. In section 41A(4) of that Act (protection of earner's pensions) "2" shall be substituted for "5".

21. In section 42(1)(*b*) (premium on termination of contracted-out employment) for the word "five" there shall be substituted the word "two".

22. In section 43(2A) (linked qualifying service)—

(*a*) the following paragraph shall be substituted for paragraph (*a*)—

"(*a*) under the rules of a scheme applying to him in the earlier period of service—

(i) there was made a transfer of his accrued rights under that scheme to another scheme applying to him in the later period of service; or

(ii) those rights were secured by a policy of insurance or an annuity contract

and were subsequently transferred to another scheme applying to him
in the later period of service;"; and

(*b*) in paragraph (*b*), for the words "that transfer" there shall be substituted the words
"transfer of his accrued rights to the second scheme".

23.—(1) In subsection (1) of section 44 (premium on termination of contracted-out
scheme) after the word "is" there shall be inserted the words "or has been" and after the
words "for the event of" there shall be inserted the words ", or in connection with.".

(2) The following subsections shall be inserted after subsection (1B) of the section
(arrangements for scheme's ceasing to be contracted-out)—

"(1C) If the scheme ceases to be a contracted-out scheme (whether by being wound
up or otherwise) and the Occupational Pensions Board either—

(*a*) have withdrawn their approval of previously approved arrangements
relating to it; or

(*b*) have declined to approve arrangements relating to it,

the Board may issue a certificate to that effect.

(1D) A certificate issued under subsection (1C)(*a*) or (*b*) above shall be cancelled
by the Board if they subsequently approve the arrangements.".

(3) In subsection (2)(*a*) of that section, after the word "under", in the second place where
it occurs, there shall be inserted the words "section 52C of or".

(4) In subsection (5) of that section, for the words "The amount" there shall be substituted
the words "Subject to subsection (5A) below, the amount".

(5) The following subsections shall be inserted after that subsection—

"(5A) Where in calculating the costs referred to in subsection (5) above the
Secretary of State cannot readily ascertain the amount of any earnings in a tax week,
he may make the calculation as if the amount of those earnings were equal to the
upper earnings limit for that tax week, and may certify the costs accordingly.

(5B) Where—

(*a*) the Secretary of State subsequently ascertains the amount of those
earnings; and

(*b*) it appears to him that the amount of the premium would have been less
if he had not made the calculation on the basis described in subsection
(5A) above,

he shall refund to the prescribed person the amount by which it would have been
less.".

24. The following subsection shall be inserted after section 49(2) of that Act (duty to
supervise schemes which have ceased to be contracted-out)—

"(2A) Where in the case of any scheme the Board have issued a certificate under
subsection (1C) of section 44 above which has not been cancelled under subsection
(1D) of the section, or a certificate under subsection (2) of section 44ZA above which
has not been cancelled under subsection (3) of that section, the Board shall not be
under the duty which would otherwise be imposed on them by subsection (2) in
relation to that scheme.".

25. In section 50 (alteration of rules of contracted-out schemes)—

(*a*) in subsection (1)—

(i) after the word "Board" there shall be inserted the words "unless it is an
alteration to which the subsection does not apply"; and

(ii) for the words "such alteration" there shall be substituted the words
"alteration to which this subsection applies"; and

(*b*) the following subsection shall be inserted after that subsection—

"(1A) Subsection (1) above does not apply—

(*a*) to an alteration consequential on a provision of the Health and Social
Security Act 1984, the Social Security Act 1985 or the Social Security
Act 1986; or

(*b*) to an alteration of a prescribed description.".

26.—(1) Section 52C (cases where scheme's liability is discharged) shall have effect and
shall be deemed always to have had effect as if the following subsections were substituted
for subsections (1) to (3)—

"(1) A transaction to which this section applies discharges the trustees or managers
of an occupational pension scheme from their liability to provide for or in respect of
any person either the requisite benefits or short service benefit or any alternative to
short service benefit—

(*a*) if it is carried out not earlier than the time when that person's pensionable
service terminates; and

(*b*) if and to the extent that it results in—

      (i) the requisite benefits; or

      (ii) short service benefit, or an alternative to short service benefit, for or in respect of that person being appropriately secured; and

  (c) in a case where the transaction takes place on or after 1st January 1986, if and to the extent that the requirements set out in any one of paragraphs (a), (b) and (c) of subsection (5) below are satisfied.

(2) This section applies to the following transactions—

  (a) the taking out or the transfer of the benefit of a policy of insurance or a number of such policies;

  (b) the entry into or the transfer of the benefit of an annuity contract or a number of such contracts.".

(2) Subsection (5) of that section shall have effect and shall be deemed always to have had effect as if "(1)" were substituted for "(2)(b)".

(3) In relation to transactions which take place after the commencement of section 8 above section 52C(1) of the Social Security Pensions Act 1975 shall have effect with the substitution of the words "guaranteed minimum pensions" for the words "the requisite benefits", in both places where they occur.

27.—(1) Subsection (1) of section 52D (supplementary provisions) shall have effect and shall be deemed always to have had effect—

  (a) as if the following paragraph were substituted for paragraph (b)—

      "(b) either—

        (i) the transaction wholly or partly securing them was carried out before 1st January 1986 and discharged the trustees or managers of the scheme as mentioned in subsection (1) of that section; or

        (ii) it is carried out on or after that date without any of the requirements specified in subsection (5)(a) to (c) of that section being satisfied in relation to it and the scheme has been wound up;"; and

  (b) as if for the words from "entitled" to "which" there were substituted the words "only entitled to such part (if any) of his or her guaranteed minimum pension as".

(2) In that subsection after the words "purposes of" there shall be inserted the words "sections 16(2B), 28(7A) and 59(1A) of the principal Act and".

28. The following definition shall be inserted after the definition of "occupational pension scheme" in section 66(1)—

      ""personal pension scheme" has the meaning assigned to it by section 84(1) of the Social Security Act 1986;";

29. At the end of paragraph 5(1) of Part I of Schedule 1A (revaluation of pensions) there shall be added the words "and which is not an average salary benefit".

30. In Part II of Schedule 1A (transfer values)—

  (a) the following sub-paragraphs shall be inserted after paragraph 12(2)—

      "(2A) Where a member continues in employment to which a scheme applies after his pensionable service in that employment terminates—

      (a) if regulations so provide, he only acquires a right to the cash equivalent of such part of the benefits specified in sub-paragraph (1) above as may be prescribed; and

      (b) if regulations so provide, he acquires no right to a cash equivalent.

      (2B) Regulations may provide for the purposes of sub-paragraph (2A) above that in prescribed circumstances a number of employments (whether or not consecutive) shall be treated as a single employment.";

  (b) paragraph 12(4) and the references to it in paragraph 12(3) shall be omitted and shall be deemed never to have been included;

  (c) in paragraph 13—

      (i) in paragraph (c) of sub-paragraph (2), for the words "such other type or types of pension arrangements as may be prescribed" there shall be substituted the words "other pension arrangements which satisfy prescribed requirements"; and

      (ii) the following sub-paragraph shall be inserted after that sub-paragraph—

        "(2A) Without prejudice to the generality of sub-paragraph (2) above, the powers conferred by that sub-paragraph include power to provide that a scheme, an annuity or pension arrangements must satisfy requirements of the Inland Revenue.";

      (iii) in sub-paragraph (5)(b), for the word "them" there shall be substituted the words "the trustees or managers of the scheme from which he is being transferred"; and

  (d) in paragraph 14—

(i) in sub-paragraph (1), for the words "The cash equivalents mentioned in paragraph 12(1) above" there shall be substituted the words "Cash equivalents";

(ii) at the end of sub-paragraph (2), there shall be added (but not as part of paragraph (*c*)) the words "and power to provide that they shall be calculated and verified in accordance with guidance prepared by a prescribed body,"; and

(iii) the following paragraph shall be substituted for sub-paragraph (3)(*b*)—

"(*b*) that in prescribed circumstances a cash equivalent shall be increased or reduced.".

Employment Protection (Consolidation) Act 1978 (c.44)

31.—(1) In the following provisions of the Employment Protection (Consolidation) Act 1978 (which all relate to payments to pension schemes of contributions which are unpaid on employer's insolvency) the words "or a personal pension scheme" shall be inserted after the words "an occupational pension scheme"—

(*a*) section 123(1) and (3);
(*b*) section 124(2);
(*c*) section 125(3); and
(*d*) section 126(1).

(2) In section 123(2) of that Act for the words "in accordance with an occupational pension scheme" there shall be substituted the words "to an occupational pension scheme or a personal pension scheme".

(3) In section 127(3) of that Act the following definition shall be inserted after the definition of "occupational pension scheme"—

" "personal pension scheme" means any scheme or arrangement which is comprised in one or more instruments or agreements and which has, or is capable of having, effect so as to provide benefits, in the form of pensions or otherwise, payable on death or retirement to or in respect of employees who have made arrangements with the trustees or managers of the scheme for them to become members of the scheme;".

PART II

INCOME-RELATED BENEFITS

National Assistance Act 1948 (c.29)

32.—(1) In subsection (3) of section 22 of the National Assistance Act 1948 (charges to be made for local authority accommodation) for the words "(apart from any supplementation of his resources which he will receive under the Supplementary Benefits Act 1976" there shall be substituted the words "(disregarding income support)".

(2) At the end of subsection (5) of that section there shall be added the words "except that, until the first such regulations come into force, a local authority shall give effect to Part III of Schedule 1 to the Supplementary Benefits Act 1976, as it had effect immediately before the amendments made by Schedule 2 to the Social Security Act 1980.

33. The words ", whether before or after the commencement of the Supplementary Benefits Act 1976," shall be omitted from subsection (6) of section 43 of that Act (recovery of cost of assistance from persons liable for maintenance).

Maintenance Orders Act 1950 (c.37)

34. In subsection (1) of section 3 of the Maintenance Orders Act 1950 (jurisdiction of English courts to make affiliation orders) after "1976" there shall be inserted the words "or section 25 of the Social Security Act 1986".

35. In section 4 of that Act (jurisdiction of English courts to make affiliation orders against persons in Scotland or Northern Ireland)—

(*a*) the following paragraph shall be added at the end of subsection (1)—

"(*d*) for an order under section 24 of the Social Security Act 1986 (which provides for the recovery of expenditure on income support from such persons);" and

(*b*) in subsection (2), after the words "or the said section 18" there shall be inserted the words "or the said section 24".

36. In section 9 of that Act—

(*a*) the following paragraph shall be added at the end of subsection (1)—

"(*d*) for an order under section 24 of the Social Security Act 1986 (which provides for the recovery of expenditure on income support from such persons);" and

(*b*) in subsection (2), after the words "or the said section 18" there shall be inserted the words "or the said section 24".

37. In section 11(1) of that Act (jurisdiction of Northern Ireland courts to make affiliation orders) after "1977" there shall be inserted the words "or any enactment applying in Northern Ireland and corresponding to section 25 of the Social Security Act 1986".

38. In section 12 of that Act (jurisdiction of Northern Ireland courts to make affiliation orders against persons in England or Scotland)—

(*a*) the following paragraph shall be added at the end of subsection (1)—

"(*d*) for an order under any enactment applying in Northern Ireland and corresponding to section 24 of the Social Security Act 1986 (which provides for the recovery of expenditure on income support from such persons);" and

(*b*) the words "or of any order falling within subsection (1)(*d*) of this section" shall be added at the end of subsection (2).

39. In section 16(2) of that Act (enforcement of maintenance orders)—

(*a*) the following sub-paragraph shall be inserted after paragraph (*a*)(vii)—

"(viii) section 24 of the Social Security Act 1986 or section 4 of the Affiliation Proceedings Act 1957 on an application made under section 25(1) of the Act of 1986 ;";

(*b*) the following sub-paragraph shall be inserted after paragraph (*b*)(viii)—

"(ix) an order made on an application under section 24 of the Social Security Act 1986 ;"; and

(*c*) the following sub-paragraph shall be inserted after paragraph (*c*)(vii)—

"(viii) any enactment applying in Northern Ireland and corresponding to section 24 of the Social Security Act 1986 ;".

Ecclesiastical Jurisdiction Measure 1963 (No. 1)

40. In subsection (7) of section 55 of the Ecclesiastical Jurisdiction Measure 1963, as amended by section 1 of the Ecclesiastical Jurisdiction (Amendment) Measure 1974, (deprivation etc. of priests etc. after certain proceedings) in the definition of "affiliation order" the word "or" shall be omitted and at the end there shall be inserted the words "or section 25 of the Social Security Act 1986".

Social Work (Scotland) Act 1986 (c.49)

41.—(1) In section 78(2A) of the Social Work (Scotland) Act 1968 (duty to make contributions in respect of children in care etc.) for words from "of" where second occurring to the end there shall be substituted the words "of income support or family credit.".

(2) In section 87(3) of that Act (charges for service and accommodation)—

(*a*) after the word "by" where first occurring there shall be inserted the words "the Schedule to the Housing (Homeless Persons) Act 1977, paragraph 2(1) of Schedule 4 to the Social Security Act 1980,";

(*b*) after "1983" there shall be inserted "and paragraph 32 of Schedule 10 to the Social Security Act 1986"; and

(*c*) for the words "to 44" there shall be substituted the words "(as amended by paragraph 5 of Schedule 1 to the Law Reform (Parent and Child) (Scotland) Act 1986) and 43".

Administration of Justice Act 1970 (c.31)

42. In Schedule 8 to the Administration of Justice Act 1970 (maintenance orders)—

(*a*) in paragraph 5, the word "or" shall be omitted from both places where it occurs and after "1975" there shall be inserted the words "or section 25 of the Social Security Act 1986"; and

(*b*) in paragraph 6, the word "or", where first occurring, shall be omitted and after "1976" there shall be inserted the words "or section 24 of the Social Security Act 1986".

Attachment of Earnings Act 1971 (c.32)

43. In Schedule 1 to the Attachment of Earnings Act 1971 (maintenance orders)—
    (a) in paragraph 6, the word "or" shall be omitted from both places where it occurs and after "1976" there shall be inserted the words "or section 25 of the Social Security Act 1986"; and
    (b) in paragraph 7, the word "or" where first occurring shall be omitted and after "1976" there shall be inserted the words "or section 24 of the Social Security Act 1986".

Housing (Financial Provisions) (Scotland) Act 1972 (c.46)

44.—(1) In section 24(1)(a) of the Housing (Financial Provisions) (Scotland) Act 1972 (amount to be carried to credit of rent rebate account) for the words "under section 32 of the Social Security and Housing Benefits Act 1982" there shall be substituted the words "under section 30 of the Social Security Act 1986".

(2) In section 25(1)(a) of that Act (amount to be carried to credit of rent allowance account) for the words "under section 32 of the Social Security and Housing Benefits Act 1982" there shall be substituted the words "under section 30 of the Social Security Act 1986".

Employment and Training Act 1973 (c.50)

45. In section 12(2)(b) of the Employment and Training Act 1973 (ancillary and transitional provisions) for the words "supplementary benefit within the meaning of the Supplementary Benefits Act 1976" there shall be substituted the words "income support".

Legal Aid Act 1974 (c.4)

46. In each of the following provisions of the Legal Aid Act 1974, for the words from "supplementary" to "1970" there shall be substituted the words "income support or family credit"—
    (a) section 1(1)(b);
    (b) section 4(2);
    (c) section 11(5).

47. In paragraph 3(c) of Part I of Schedule 1 to that Act for the words "18 of the Supplementary Benefits Act 1976" there shall be substituted the words "24 of the Social Security Act 1986".

Social Security Act 1975 (c.14)

48. The following provisions of the Social Security Act 1975—
    (a) section 87 (benefits to be inalienable); and
    (b) section 165A(1) (necessity of claim for entitlement),
shall have effect in relation to income-related benefits as they have effect in relation to benefits under that Act.

Local Government (Scotland) Act 1975 (c.30)

Rating (Disabled Persons) Act 1978 (c.40)

49. The words "the housing benefit scheme (whether or not modified under section 28 of the Social Security Act 1986)" shall be substituted for the words "a scheme made under section 28(1)(a) of the Social Security and Housing Benefits Act 1982 (whether or not modified under section 30(1)(a) of that Act)"—
    (a) in section 8(4) of the Local Government (Scotland) Act 1975 (payment of rates by instalments);
    (b) in section 1(6) of the Rating (Disabled Persons) Act 1978 (rebates for hereditaments with special facilities for disabled persons); and
    (c) in section 4(9) of that Act (rebates for lands and heritages with special facilities for disabled persons).

Employment Protection (Consolidation) Act 1978 (c.44)

50. In section 132 of the Employment Protection (Consolidation) Act 1978 (recoupment of benefit)—
(*a*) in subsection (2)(*a*) and (*c*), for the words "supplementary benefit" there shall be substituted the words "income support";
(*b*) in subsection (3)—
(i) in paragraphs (*a*) and (*f*), for the words "supplementary benefit" there shall be substituted the words "income support"; and
(ii) in paragraph (*e*), for the words from "who" to the end of the paragraph there shall be substituted the words "a right of appeal to a social security appeal tribunal against any decision of an adjudication officer as to the total or partial recoupment of income support in pursuance of the regulations;"; and
(*c*) in subsection (4), for the words from "supplementary benefit", in the first place where those words occur, to the end there shall be substituted the words "income support, no sum shall be recoverable under the Social Security Act 1986, and no abatement, payment or reduction shall be made by reference to the income support recouped.".

Child Care Act 1980 (c.5)

51. The following subsection shall be substituted for subsection (1A) of section 45 of the Child Care Act 1980 (liability for contributions in respect of children in care)—
"(1A) A person shall not be liable under subsection (1)(i) above to make any contribution during any period when he is in receipt of income support or family credit.".

Local Government, Planning and Land Act 1980 (c.65)

52.—(1) In section 54 of the Local Government, Planning and Land Act 1980 (rate support grant) in subsections (1) and (2) for the words "and subsidies under section 32(1)(*a*) of the Social Security and Housing Benefits Act 1982" there shall be substituted the words "and rate rebate subsidy under the Social Security Act 1986".
(2) The following paragraph shall be substituted for subsection (5)(*d*) of that section—
(*d*) subsection (10) or section 30 of the Social Security Act 1986 (power to exclude rate fund contributions under subsection (6) of that section and certain other items);".
53. In section 154 of that Act (grant of rent rebates by urban developments corporations) for the words "Part II of the Social Security and Housing Benefits Act 1982" there shall be substituted the words "Part II of the Social Security Act 1986".

Magistrates' Courts Act 1980 (c.43)

54. The following paragraph shall be added after subsection 1(*l*) of section 65 of the Magistrates' Courts Act 1980 (domestic proceedings)—
"(*m*) section 24 or 25 of the Social Security Act 1986;".

Civil Jurisdiction and Judgments Act 1982 (c.27)

55. In paragraph 5 of Schedule 5 to the Civil Jurisdiction and Judgments Act 1982 (proceedings excluded from Schedule 4)—
(*a*) in sub-paragraph (*c*), after "1976," there shall be inserted the words "section 24 of the Social Security Act 1986, or any enactment applying in Northern Ireland and corresponding to it,"; and
(*b*) in sub-paragraph (*d*), after "1976," there shall be inserted the words "section 25 of the Social Security Act 1986 or any enactment applying in Northern Ireland and corresponding to it,".

Legal Aid Act 1982 (c.44)

56. In section 7(8) of the Legal Aid Act 1982 (legal aid contribution orders) for the words from "supplementary benefit" to the end there shall be substituted the words "income support or family credit under the Social Security Act 1986.".

57. In section 70(2)(*b*) of the Transport Act 1982 (payments in respect of applicants for exemption from wearing seat belts) for the words from "of" to "and" there shall be substituted the words "of income support or family credit and".

Housing Act 1985 (c.68)

58. In subsection (2)(*b*) of section 425 of the Housing Act 1985 (the local contribution differential) for the words "section 32 of the Social Security and Housing Benefits Act 1982" there shall be substituted the words "section 30 of the Social Security Act 1986".

59. In Item 4 in Part I of Schedule 14 to that Act (items to be credited to the Housing Revenue Account) for the words "Social Security and Housing Benefits Act 1982" there shall be substituted the words "Social Security Act 1986".

60. In paragraph 3 of Part IV of that Schedule (rate fund contributions to the Housing Revenue Account) for the words "section 34(1) of the Social Security and Housing Benefits Act 1982" there shall be substituted the words "section 30(6) of the Social Security Act 1986".

Legal Aid (Scotland) Act 1986 (c.47)

61. In section 8(*b*) (availability of legal advice and assistance) and section 11(2) (clients' contributions) of the Legal Aid (Scotland) Act 1986, for the words from "supplementary" to "1970" there shall be substituted the words "income support or family credit".

PART III

BENEFITS UNDER SOCIAL SECURITY ACT 1975

Social Security Act 1975 (c.14)

62. The Social Security Act 1975 shall have effect subject to the amendments specified in paragraphs 63 to 66 below.

63. In section 12(1) (descriptions of contributory benefits) the following sub-paragraph shall be substituted for sub-paragraph (i) of paragraph (*e*)—
   "(i) widow's payment,".

64. In section 13 (contribution conditions) in subsection (1), in the Table headed "Other benefits" the following entry shall be inserted before the entry relating to widowed mother's allowance—
   "Widow's payment . . . ".

65. The following entry shall be inserted in section 167(1)(*a*) of that Act (regulations subject to affirmative Parliamentary procedure) immediately after the entry relating to section 20(3)—
   "section 61(3) (constant attendance allowance);"

66. In Schedule 3 (contribution conditions)—
   (*a*) in paragraph 4(1) for the words preceding paragraph (*a*) there shall be substituted the words—

"Widow's payment

   4.—(1) The contribution condition for a widow's payment is that—"
   (*b*) "payment" shall be substituted for "allowance"—
       (i) in sub-paragraph (2)(*b*) of paragraph 8; and
       (ii) in the second place where it occurs in sub-paragraph (3) of that paragraph; and
   (*c*) the following paragraph shall be substituted for paragraph 13—
       "13. Where a woman claims a widow's payment, the contributor concerned for the purposes of the claim shall be deemed to satisfy the contribution condition for the payment if on a cl·im made in the past for any short-term benefit he has satisfied the first contribution condition for the benefit, by virtue of paragraph 8 above, with contributions of a class relevant to widow's payment.".

Industrial Injuries and Diseases (Old Cases) Act 1975 (c.16)

67. The words following "pension rate" shall be omitted from sections 2(6)(*b*) and 7(2)(*c*) (weekly rates of benefit) of the Industrial Injuries and Diseases (Old Cases) Act 1975.

68.—(1) In section 4(8)(*a*) of that Act (parliamentary procedure for making of schemes) for the words "an up-rating order under the Social Security Act" there shall be substituted the words "any order or regulations under the Social Security Acts 1975 to 1986".

(2) In section 7 of that Act (amount of benefit)—

(*a*) in subsection (3), the following paragraph shall be substituted for paragraph (*d*)—

"(*d*) where the person is treated under the provisions of the scheme as residing with his or her spouse or contributing at a weekly rate of not less than the relevant amount towards the maintenance of his or her spouse, by the relevant amount (that is to say, an amount equal to any increase which would be payable under section 44 of that Act in respect of the spouse if the person were entitled to sickness benefit)."; and

(*b*) in subsection (4), the following paragraph shall be substituted for the paragraph set out in that subsection—

"(*d*) where the person is treated under the provisions of the scheme as residing with his or her spouse or contributing at a weekly rate of not less than the relevant amount towards the maintenance of his or her spouse, by the relevant amount (that is to say, an amount equal to any increase which would be payable under section 66 of that Act in respect of the spouse if the person were entitled to disablement pension plus unemployability supplement).".

Social Security Pensions Act 1975 (c.60)

69. In section 13(3) of the Social Security Pensions Act 1975 (rate of widowed mother's allowance and widow's pension) for "50" there shall be substituted "55".

70. In section 15 of that Act (invalidity pension for widows)—

(*a*) in subsection (1)—

(i) the following paragraphs shall be substituted for paragraphs (*a*) and (*b*)—

"(*a*) is not entitled to a widowed mother's allowance on her late husband's death or subsequently ceases to be entitled to such an allowance ; and

(*b*) is incapable of work at the time when he died or when she subsequently ceases to be so entitled ;";

(ii) in paragraph (*c*), for "40" there shall be substituted "45";

(*b*) in subsection (2)(*a*), for the words from "she" to the end there shall be substituted the words "her late husband died or she subsequently ceased to be entitled to a widowed mother's allowance ;"; and

(*c*) in subsection (4)(*a*), for "50" there shall be substituted "55".

Part IV

Statutory Maternity Pay, Statutory Sick Pay Etc.

Income and Corporation Taxes Act 1970 (c.10)

71. At the end of section 219A of the Income and Corporation Taxes Act 1970 (which charges certain payments to income tax under Schedule E) there shall be added "and

(*d*) payments of statutory maternity pay under Part V of the Social Security Act 1986 or, in Northern Ireland, any corresponding provision contained in an Order in Council under the Northern Ireland Act 1974.".

Social Security Act 1975 (c.14)

72. The words "(other than maternity allowance)" shall be inserted—

(*a*) after the words "that subsection", in subsection (2) of section 13 of the Social Security Act 1975 ; and

(*b*) after the words "for benefit", in subsection (8) of that section.

73. In section 122(4) of that Act for the words "either or both those Funds" there shall be substituted the words "that Fund".

Social Security (Miscellaneous Provisions) Act 1977 (c.5)

74. In section 18(2)(c) of the Social Security (Miscellaneous Provisions) Act 1977 (certain sums to be earnings for social security purposes) for the words "that Act" there shall be substituted the words "the Employment Protection (Consolidation) Act 1978".

Employment Protection (Consolidation) Act 1978 (c.44)

75. In section 33 of the Employment Protection (Consolidation) Act 1978 (right to return to work) in subsections (3) and (4) for the word "rights" there shall be substituted the word "right" and in subsection (5) for the words "either of the rights" there shall be substituted the words "the right".

76. In subsection (4) of section 123 of that Act (payment of unpaid contributions to pension schemes) for the words "maternity pay" there shall be substituted the words "statutory sick pay, statutory maternity pay under Part V of the Social Security Act 1986, maternity pay under Part III of this Act".

Social Security and Housing Benefits Act 1982 (c.24)

77. The following subsection shall be substituted for section 3(9) of the Social Security and Housing Benefits Act 1982 (definitions relating to period of entitlement to statutory sick pay)—

"(9) In this section—
    "confinement" is to be construed in accordance with section 50 of the Social Security Act 1986 ; and
    "disqualifying period" means—
        (a) in relation to a woman entitled to statutory maternity pay, the maternity pay period ; and
        (b) in relation to a woman entitled to maternity allowance, the maternity allowance period ;
    "maternity allowance period" has the meaning assigned to it by section 22(2) of the principal Act ; and
    "maternity pay period" has the meaning assigned to it by section 47(1) of the Social Security Act 1986.".

78. The following paragraph shall be inserted before paragraph (a) of section 45(2) of that Act (Parliamentary control of subordinate legislation)—
"(za) regulations under section 7 of this Act ;".

Insolvency Act 1985 (c.65)

79. In paragraph 3(2)(d) of Part II of Schedule 4 to the Insolvency Act 1985 (preferential debts) the words from the beginning to "1982" shall cease to have effect.

Bankruptcy (Scotland) Act 1985 (c.66)

80. Paragraph 9(2)(d) of Schedule 3 to the Bankruptcy (Scotland) Act 1985 (preferential debts) shall cease to have effect.

Wages Act 1986 (c.48)

81. In subsection (1)(f) of section 7 of the Wages Act 1986 (meaning of "wages") for the words "maternity pay under Part III of the 1978 Act" there shall be substituted the words "statutory maternity pay under the Social Security Act 1986".

PART V

COMMON PROVISIONS

Social Security Act 1973 (c.38)

82. In section 68(1) of the Social Security Act 1973 (submission to Occupational Pensions Board of proposals to make regulations) for the word "Where" there shall be substituted the words "Subject to section 61 of the Social Security Act 1986, where".

Social Security Act 1975 (c.14)

83. In subsection (6)(*aa*) of section 14 of the Social Security Act 1975 (unemployment benefit and sickness benefit) and in subsection (4)(*aa*) of section 15 of that Act (invalidity pension) for the words "126A of this Act" there shall be substituted the words "63(1)(*d*) of the Social Security Act 1986".

84. In subsection (1) of section 28 of that Act (Category A retirement pension) the words from "(subject" to "rule))" shall be omitted.

85. The following subsection shall be substituted for subsection (3) of section 90 of that Act (obligations of claimant)—

"(3) The regulations relevant under subsection (2) above are—
> (*a*) those made by virtue of the following provisions of this Chapter, namely—
>> (i) section 88(*a*), and
>> (ii) section 89(1) and (2); and
> (*b*) those made by virtue of section 51(1)(*h*), (*k*) and (*l*) of the Social Security Act 1986.".

86. In section 141(2) (reference of proposals to make regulations to Industrial Injuries Advisory Council) for the word "Where" there shall be substituted the words "Subject to section 61 of the Social Security Act 1986, where".

87. The following section shall be substituted for section 165A of that Act—

"General provision as to necessity of claim for entitlement to benefit

165A.—(1) Except in such cases as may be prescribed, no person shall be entitled to any benefit unless, in addition to any other conditions relating to that benefit being satisfied—
> (*a*) he makes a claim for it in the prescribed manner and within the prescribed time; or
> (*b*) by virtue of regulations made under section 51 of the Social Security Act 1986 he is treated as making a claim for it.

(2) Where under subsection (1) above a person is required to make a claim or to be treated as making a claim for a benefit in order to be entitled to it—
> (*a*) if the benefit is a widow's payment, she shall not be entitled to it in respect of a death occurring more than twelve months before the date on which the claim is made or treated as made; and
> (*b*) if the benefit is any other benefit, except disablement benefit or reduced earnings allowance, the person shall not be entitled to it in respect of any period more than twelve months before that date.".

88. The words ", reduced earnings allowance" shall be inserted in section 165A(3)(*c*), as originally enacted, after the words "disablement benefit".

89. In section 167(3) of that Act (parliamentary procedure) for the words ", 123A or 126A or an up–rating order" there shall be substituted the words "or 123A".

90. In paragraph 8 of Schedule 16 (exemption in respect of up–rating regulations from requirements to consult Industrial Injuries Advisory Council) for the words from "one or more" to the end there shall be substituted the words "one or more of the following provisions—
(*a*) section 120 and 122 of this Act; and
(*b*) section 63 of the Social Security Act 1986.".

Social Security Pensions Act 1975 (c.60)

91. In section 23 of the Social Security Pensions Act 1975 (increase of long–term benefits)—
(*a*) in subsections (2) and (3), for the words "the said section 124" there shall be substituted the words "section 63 of the Social Security Act 1986";
(*b*) in subsection (2), for the words "subsection (1)(*b*) above" there shall be substituted the words "section 63(1)(*b*) of that Act"; and
(*c*) in subsection (3), for the words "subsection (1)(*c*) or (*d*) above" there shall be substituted the words "section 63(1)(*c*) or (*d*) of that Act".

92. In section 24(1)(*a*) of that Act (graduated retirement benefit) for the words "124 to 126 of the principal Act" there shall be substituted the words "sections 63 and 64 of the Social Security Act 1986".

93. In subsection (1) of section 59 of that Act (official pension) for the words "that section" there shall be substituted the words "section 63 of the Social Security Act 1986".

94. In section 61(2) of that Act (consultation about regulations)—

    (*a*) for the word "Where" there shall be substituted the words "Subject to section 61 of the Social Security Act 1986, where"; and

    (*b*) after the words "of this Act" there shall be inserted the words "or of Part I of the Social Security Act 1986".

95. In Schedule 1 to that Act (deferred retirement)—

    (*a*) in paragraphs 2(5) and 4(3)(*b*), for the words "124 of the principal Act" there shall be substituted the words "63 of the Social Security Act 1986"; and

    (*b*) in paragraph 4A(3)(*a*), for the words "126A of the principal Act" there shall be substituted the words "63(1)(*d*) of the Social Security Act 1986".

Child Benefit Act 1975 (c.61)

96. At the end of subsection (1) of section 6 of the Child Benefit Act 1975 (child benefit claims and payments) there shall be added the words "and within the prescribed time".

97. In paragraph 1 of Schedule 3 to that Act (increases in rate of benefit), after the word "Act" there shall be inserted the words "or section 63 of the Social Security Act 1986".

Social Security Act 1980 (c.30)

98. In section 10 of the Social Security Act 1980 (consultation with Social Security Advisory Committee on proposals for regulations)—

    (*a*) in subsection (1), after the word "subsection" there shall be inserted the words "and to section 61 of the Social Security Act 1986"; and

    (*b*) in subsection (9), after the word "section" there shall be inserted the words "or section 61 of the Social Security Act 1986".

99. In paragraph 12(2) of Schedule 3 to that Act (regulations not requiring submission to Social Security Advisory Committee) for the words from "sections of" to the end there shall be substituted the words "provisions—

    (*a*) section 120, 122 or 123A of the principal Act;

    (*b*) section 63 of the Social Security Act 1986,

or contained in a statutory rule which states that it contains only provisions in consequence of an order under section 120 of the Social Security (Northern Ireland) Act 1975 or any enactment applying in Northern Ireland and corresponding to section 63 of the Social Security Act 1986.".

Social Security Act 1985 (c.53)

100. In section 9(9) of the Social Security Act 1985 (abatement of invalidity allowance) for the words "sections 124 and 126A of the Social Security Act 1975" there shall be substituted the words "section 63 of the Social Security Act 1986".

PART VI

MISCELLANEOUS

Income and Corporation Taxes Act 1970 (c.10)

101. In section 219 of the Income and Corporation Taxes Act 1970 (taxation of benefits)—

    (*a*) in subsection (1), for the words, "maternity benefit" there shall be substituted the words "maternity allowance, widow's payments"; and

    (*b*) in subsection (2), for the words "in respect of a family income supplement under the Family Income Supplements Act 1970 or the Family Income Supplements Act (Northern Ireland) 1971" there shall be substituted the words "of family credit under the Social Security Act 1986 or any corresponding enactment applying to Northern Ireland,".

Attachment of Earnings Act 1971 (c.32)

102. In section 24(2)(*c*) of the Attachment of Earnings Act 1971 (social security benefits etc. not earnings for purposes of Act) for the words from "of" to the end there shall be substituted "enactment relating to social security;".

National Insurance Act 1974 (c.14)

Social Security Act 1980 (c.30)

Social Security Act 1985 (c.53)

103. The words "the Social Security Acts 1975 to 1986" shall be substituted—
   (*a*) for the words "the Social Security Act 1975" in section 6(1) of the National Insurance Act 1974;
   (*b*) in the Social Security Act 1980—
        (i) in section 9(7), for the words "the Social Security Acts 1975 to 1985" in both places where they occur; and
        (ii) in section 18(1), for the words "the Social Security Acts 1975 to 1982"; and
   (*c*) for the words "the Social Security Acts 1975 to 1985" in section 5 of the Social Security Act 1985.

Social Security Act 1975 (c.14)

104. In section 4(6) of the Social Security Act 1975 (incidence of Class 1 contributions) after the word "under" there shall be inserted the words "subsection (7) below or under".

Supplementary Benefits Act 1976 (c.71)

105. In section 8 of the Supplementary Benefits Act 1976 (persons affected by trade disputes)—
   (*a*) in subsection (1), the following words shall be substituted for the words from the beginning to "period", in the second place where it occurs—
   "So long as this section applies to a person, his requirements"; and
   (*b*) the following subsections shall be substituted for subsection (2)—
        "(2) This section applies to a person—
            (*a*) who is disqualified under section 19 of the Social Security Act 1975 for receiving unemployment benefit; or
            (*b*) who would be so disqualified if otherwise entitled to that benefit,
        except during any period shown by the person to be a period of incapacity for work by reason of disease or bodily or mental disablement or to be within the maternity period.
        (2A) In subsection (2) above "the maternity period" means the period commencing at the beginning of the sixth week before the expected week of confinement and ending at the end of the seventh week after the week in which confinement takes place.".

Social Security Act 1980 (c.30)

106. The following sub-paragraph shall be inserted after paragraph 13(1) of Schedule 3 to the Social Security Act 1980 (regulations not requiring prior submission to Social Security Advisory Committee)—
        "(1A) Regulations under section 3(2)(*a*) of the Pensions Act (which provides for enabling women to continue to make contributions at reduced rate).".
107. The reference to section 9 of the Social Security and Housing Benefits Act 1982 in paragraph 15A of that Schedule shall include a reference to subsection (1A) of that section.

Forfeiture Act 1982 (c.34)

108. In section 4 of the Forfeiture Act 1982—
   (*a*) in subsection (4), for "and (3)" there shall be substituted "to (3A)"; and
   (*b*) in subsection (5), for the words from "the Family Income Supplements Act 1970" to "the Social Security Act 1980" there shall be substituted the words—
   "the Child Benefit Act 1975,
        the Social Security Acts 1975 to 1986,".

50–129

         SCHEDULE 11

REPEALS

REPEALS

Chapter	Short title	Extent of repeal
11 & 12 Geo. 6, c.29.	National Assistance Act 1948.	In section 43(6), the words ", whether before or after the commencement of the Supplementary Benefits Act 1976,". In section 50(4), the words "or subsection (3)" and the words from "less" to the end. Section 53.
1965 c.55.	Statute Law Revision (Consequential Repeals) Act 1965.	The whole Act.
1966 c.20.	Supplementary Benefit Act 1966.	Section 26.
1968 c.49.	Social Work (Scotland) Act 1968.	In section 28(2), the words "and not re-imbursed under section 32 of the Social Security Act 1975".
1970 c.10.	Income and Corporation Taxes Act 1970.	In section 219(1), the words "death grant". In section 219A(1)(*b*), the word "and".
1970 c.55.	Family Income Supplements Act 1970.	The whole Act.
1971 c.32.	Attachment of Earnings Act 1971.	Schedule 4.
1972 c.70.	Local Government Act 1972.	In section 119(2), the words from "having" to the end.
1972 c.75.	Pensioners and Family Income Supplement Payments Act 1972.	The whole Act.
1972 c.80.	Pensioners' Payments and National Insurance Contributions Act 1972.	The whole Act.
1973 c.38.	Social Security Act 1973.	Section 92(3) and (4). In section 99(1), the definition of requisite benefits. Schedule 23.
1973 c.61.	Pensioners' Payments and National Insurance Act 1973.	The whole Act.
1974 c.14.	National Insurance Act 1974.	In section 6(1), the words "the Supplementary Benefits Act 1976, the Family Income Supplements Act 1970," and the words "or the Social Security and Housing Benefits Act 1982".
1974 c.54.	Pensioners' Payments Act 1974.	The whole Act.
1975 c.14.	Social Security Act 1975.	In section 1(1)(*b*), the words "and the Maternity Pay Fund". In section 12, in subsection (1), paragraph (*h*), in subsection (2), the words "and widow's allowance" and subsection (3). In section 13, in subsection (1), the entries relating to widow's allowance and death grant, subsection (5)(*a*) and subsection (5A). Section 21. In section 25(3), the words "and for which she is not entitled to a widow's allowance". In section 26(3), the words "a widow's allowance or".

Chapter	Short title	Extent of repeal
1975 c.14— *cont.*	Social Security Act 1975— *cont.*	In section 28(1), the words from "(subject" to "rule))". Section 32. Section 33(1)(*a*) to (*c*). Section 34(2). In section 37(3), the words from "and a woman" to the end. Section 37A(4) and (7). Section 41(2)(*e*) and (2C). Section 50(2) and (5). Section 57(5). Sections 58 and 59. Section 60. Section 62. Sections 64 to 75. Sections 79 to 81. In section 82, subsections (3) and (4) and subsection (6)(*a*). In section 84, subsection (3) and in subsection (5), the references to sections 65 and 66. Section 86. In section 88(*a*), the words from "or", in the first place where it occurs, to "prescribed", in the third place where it occurs. In section 90, in subsection (2)(*a*), the words from "(including" to the end and in subsection (3), the references to sections 79 and 81. In section 91, subsection (1)(*b*)(i) and in subsection (2), the words "section 58 (unemployability supplement)," and the words from "section 64" to the end. Section 92. Section 95. In section 100 in subsection (1), the words "adversely to the claimant" and subsections (5) and (6). In section 101(3)(*c*), the words "or, in relation to industrial death benefit, the deceased". In section 104(1A), the words "in prescribed circumstances". Section 106(3). In section 107, in subsection (4), the words ", whether or not the claimant is the person at whose instance the declaration was made" and in subsection (6), the words "by fresh evidence" and paragraph (*b*). In section 110(1), the words "by fresh evidence". Section 114(3) and (4). In section 117, subsection (4) and in subsection (5), paragraph (*a*) and the word "and" immediately following it.

Chapter	Short title	Extent of repeal
1975 c.14—*cont.*	Social Security Act 1975—*cont.*	In section 119, subsections (1) to (2A), in subsection (3)(*b*), the words "or out of a requirement to repay any amount by virtue of subsection (2A) above", subsection (4)(*b*) to (*d*) and subsections (5) and (6). In section 122(4), the words "or the Maternity Pay Fund". Sections 124 to 126A. In section 134(5)(*b*), the words from "and the Maternity Pay Fund" to "determine". In section 135, subsections (2)(*g*) and (6). Section 136. In section 141(2), the words from "unless" to the end. In section 143(1), the words "relating to social security". Sections 144 and 145. In section 146, in subsection (1), the words "under Part III of the Pensions Act" and subsections (3)(*c*) and (5). Section 147. In section 151(1), the words "under Part III of the Pensions Act". In section 152(8), the words "of the Pensions Act (including in particular sections 47 and 64(3)" and the words "under that Act". Section 164. In Schedule 3, in Part I, paragraph 7 and, in Part II, in paragraph 8(2), in paragraph (*a*), the words "other than a widow's allowance", in paragraph 8(3), the words "or a maternity allowance," in paragraphs 9 and 10, the words "(other than a widow's allowance)" and paragraph 12. In Schedule 4, in Part I, paragraph 5, Part II, in Part IV, paragraph 4 and in Part V, paragraphs 2, 4 to 6 and 10 to 15. Schedule 5. In Schedule 8, paragraph (*b*) of the proviso to paragraph 5 and the word "and" immediately preceding it. Schedule 9. Schedule 14. In Schedule 16, paragraphs 3 and 4. In Schedule 20, the definitions of "The deceased" and "Industrial death benefit", in the definition of "Relative", the reference to sections 66(8) and 72(6), in the definition of "Short-term benefit" the words "and widow's allowance", the definitions of "Unemployability supplement" and "Up-rating order", and in the definition of "Week", the reference to section 64.
1975 c.16.	Industrial Injuries and Diseases (Old Cases) Act 1975.	In section 4(4), paragraph (*c*)(ii) and the word "or" immediately preceding it. Section 9(3). Section 10.

Chapter	Short title	Extent of repeal
1975 c.18.	Social Security (Consequential Provisions) Act 1975.	In Schedule 2, paragraphs 5, 35, 41 and 44. In Schedule 3, paragraph 18.
1975 c.60.	Social Security Pensions Act 1975.	In section 6, in subsection (2), the words from "or" to the end, in subsection (5), the words "Subject to subsection (5A) below," and subsection (5A). In section 19(2), the words "and (3)(*b*)." Section 22(3) and (5). Section 23(1) and (5). Section 30(2). In section 32(4), the words "relating to the scheme or its management". Section 33(1)(*a*) and (4). Section 34. In section 36, subsections (2), (4) and (5), in subsection (6), in the words "Subject to the following provisions of this section", subsection (7), in subsection (8), the words from "but the scheme" to the end and subsection (9). Section 37. In section 39, subsections (2), (3) and (4)(*a*). Section 41(4). In section 44A(1)(*b*) and (4), the words "to requisite benefits". Section 46. Section 49(3) and (7). Section 52D(2) and (3). Section 56K(4). In section 66(1), the definition of "requisite benefits" and, in the definition of "resources", the words "(whether requisite benefits or other benefits)". In Schedule 1A, in paragraph 12, in sub-paragraph (3), the words "Subject to sub-paragraph (4) below," and sub-paragraph (4). In Schedule 2, paragraph 4. In Schedule 4, paragraphs 14 and 17, in paragraph 31 the definition of "requisite benefits" and paragraphs 32(*a*), 41, 42 and 51.
1975 c.61.	Child Benefit Act 1975.	Section 5(5). Section 6(2), (4) and (5). Sections 7 and 8. Section 9(1). Sections 10 and 11. In section 15(1), the words "relating to child benefit". Section 17(3) to (6). In section 24(1), in the definition of "recognised educational establishment", the words from "and" to the end. In Schedule 4, paragraphs 3 to 6, 11, 27, 29, 31 and 33.

Chapter	Short title	Extent of repeal
1975 c.71.	Employment Protection Act 1975.	In section 40, subsections (2) and (4).
1976 c.36.	Adoption Act 1976.	Section 47(3).
1976 c.71.	Supplementary Benefits Act 1976.	Sections 1 to 21. Sections 24 to 27. Sections 31 to 34. Schedule 1. In Schedule 5, in paragraph 1(2), the words from the beginning to "and" in the first place where it occurs. In Schedule 7, paragraphs 1(*b*) and (*d*), 3(*a*), 5, 19, 21, 23, 24, 31, 33 and 37.
1977 c.5.	Social Security (Miscellaneous Provisions) Act 1977.	Section 9. Section 17(2). In section 18, in subsection (1), in paragraph (*a*) the words "and the Supplementary Benefits Act 1976" and paragraph (*c*) and in subsection (2) paragraphs (*a*) and (*b*). Section 19. In section 22, in subsection (2), the references to sections 24(2) and 37(3)(*b*) of the Social Security Act 1975, and subsection (16).
1977 c.51.	Pensioners' Payments Act 1977.	The whole Act.
1978 c.44.	Employment Protection (Consolidation) Act 1978.	In section 33, subsection (1)(*a*) and the word "and" immediately following it, in subsection (3), paragraph (*c*) and in paragraph (*d*) the words "in the case of the right to return" and in subsection (4), the words "to return". Sections 34 to 44. Section 122(4)(*e*). In section 123(5), the words "occupational pension". In section 127(3), the word "such" in the second place where it occurs. In section 132, in subsection (1)(*b*) ", III" and in subsection (6), the definition of "supplementary benefit". In section 133(1)(*a*), ", 33". In section 138, in subsection (1) the words "(except section 44)", and in subsection (5) the words "(except section 44(3) and (4))". In section 139(1), the words "(except section 44)". In section 153(1) the definitions of "maternity pay", "Maternity Pay Fund" and "maternity pay rebate". In section 155(1), the words "44 to". Section 156(1). Section 157(2)(*a*) and the word "and" immediately following it. In Schedule 14, paragraph 7(1)(*d*). In Schedule 15, paragraph 7 and the heading immediately preceding it.

Chapter	Short title	Extent of repeal
1978 c.58.	Pensioners' Payments Act 1978.	The whole Act.
1979 c.18.	Social Security Act 1979.	Section 3(2). Sections 6 to 8. Sections 12 and 13. In Schedule 3, paragraphs 1, 2, 9, 16 and 24 to 27.
1979 c.41.	Pneumoconiosis etc. (Workers' Compensation) Act 1979.	In section 2(3), the words "industrial death benefit under section 76 of the Social Security Act 1975, or".
1979 c.48.	Pensioners' Payments and Social Security Act 1979.	The whole Act.
1980 c.5.	Child Care Act 1980.	In section 25(2), the words from "less" to the end.
1980 c.30.	Social Security Act 1980.	Section 1. Section 4(4). In section 5, in subsection (1) the words from "and in subsection (2)", in paragraph (i), to the end of the subsection and subsections (2) to (4). Section 7. In section 8, in subsection (1), the words "or 7". In section 9(7), the words "the Family Income Supplements Act 1970" and the words "and the Supplementary Benefits Act 1976". In section 10, in subsection (2) and in subsection (7), in the first place where they occur, the words "the Secretary of State or, as the case may be," and in subsection (7), the words "to the Secretary of State, or as the case may be," and paragraph (*a*). In section 14, subsection (6). Section 15. In section 17(2), the words from "a tribunal" to the end. In section 18, in subsection (1), the words "the Family Income Supplements Act 1970;", the words "the Supplementary Benefits Act 1976" and the word "and" immediately preceding them. Section 20(3). In Schedule 1, in paragraph 9, the words "or section 95(1)(*b*) or (*c*)" and paragraphs 10 and 12. In Schedule 2, paragraphs 1 to 20 and 22 to 30. In Schedule 3, in Part II, paragraphs 11, 15, 15B and 16 to 18.
1980 c.39.	Social Security (No. 2) Act 1980.	Sections 1 and 2. In section 4(2), the words "and no earnings-related addition to a widow's allowance". Section 6.
1981 c.33.	Social Security Act 1981.	Section 1. Section 4. In Schedule 1, paragraphs 1, 2, 3(*b*), 4, 5, 8 and 9.

Chapter	Short title	Extent of repeal
1982 c.24.	Social Security and Housing Benefits Act 1982.	Section 7(3) to (10). Section 8. Section 9(8) to (10). Sections 11 to 16. Sections 19 to 21. Section 25. Part II. Section 38. Section 41. Section 42(1) and (2). Section 44(1)(*a*) and (*f*). In section 45, in subsection (1), the words from "and any power" to the end, in subsection (2), in paragraph (*a*), the words "7 or" and paragraphs (*b*) and (*c*) and subsection (3). In section 47 in the definition of "benefit", the words "Part II and". In Schedule 2, paragraph 6. Schedule 3. In Schedule 4, paragraphs 2, 4, 5, 14, 19, 22 to 28, 35(1) and (2) and 38.
1983 c.36.	Social Security and Housing Benefits Act 1983.	The whole Act.
1983 c.41.	Health and Social Services and Social Security Adjudications Act 1983.	Section 19(2). In Schedule 8, Parts III and IV and paragraphs 18 and 31(3). In Schedule 9, paragraph 20.
1984 c.22.	Public Health (Control of Disease) Act 1984.	In section 46(5), the words from "less" to the end.
1984 c.48.	Health and Social Security Act 1984.	Section 22. In section 27(2), the words "22 and". In Schedule 4, in paragraph 3 the entry relating to section 79 and paragraphs 12 and 14. In Schedule 5, paragraphs 4 to 6.
1985 c.53.	Social Security Act 1985.	Sections 15 to 17. Section 22. Section 27(8)(*e*). In section 32(2), the words "section 15" and the words "section 22(1)(*b*) and (*c*) and (2)". In Schedule 4, paragraph 2. In Schedule 5, paragraphs 6, 7, 10, 16, 19, 28, 37 and 38.
1985 c.65.	Insolvency Act 1985.	In Part II of Schedule 4, the words in paragraphs 3(2)(*d*) from the beginning to "1982".
1985 c.66.	Bankruptcy (Scotland) Act 1985.	In Schedule 3, paragraph 9(2)(*d*).
1986 c.9.	Law Reform (Parent and Child) (Scotland) Act 1986.	In Schedule 1, paragraph 16. In Schedule 2, the entry relating to the Supplementary Benefits Act 1976.

BRITISH COUNCIL AND COMMONWEALTH INSTITUTE SUPERANNUATION ACT 1986

(1986 c. 51)

An Act to enable schemes to be made under section 1 of the Superannuation Act 1972 in respect of persons who are serving or have previously served in employment with the British Council or the Commonwealth Institute. [25th July 1986]

PARLIAMENTARY DEBATES
Hansard: H.C. Vol. 99, col. 1201; H.C. Vol. 101, cols. 419, 1143; H.L. Vol. 478, col. 1076; H.L. Vol. 479, col. 442.

Superannuation of staff of British Council and Commonwealth Institute

1.—(1) The persons to whom section 1 of the Superannuation Act 1972 applies (persons to or in respect of whom benefits may be provided by schemes under that section) shall include persons who at any time after the coming into force of this Act are serving in employment with—

(*a*) the British Council; or

(*b*) the Commonwealth Institute;

and accordingly references to those bodies shall be inserted at the appropriate point in the alphabetical list of "Other Bodies" in Schedule 1 to that Act.

(2) That section shall also apply to persons who at any time before the coming into force of this Act have ceased to serve in employment with either of those bodies.

Financial provisions

2.—(1) There shall be paid out of moneys provided by Parliament any increase attributable to this Act in the sums payable out of such moneys under the said Act of 1972; and the British Council and the Commonwealth Institute shall each pay to the Treasury in respect of that increase, at such times as the Treasury may direct, such sums as the Treasury may determine.

(2) Any sums received by the Treasury by virtue of this Act shall be paid into the Consolidated Fund or used as an appropriation in aid for the purposes of section 1 of the said Act of 1972.

Short title and commencement

3.—(1) This Act may be cited as the British Council and Commonwealth Institute Superannuation Act 1986.

(2) This Act shall come into force on such date as the Secretary of State may by order made by statutory instrument appoint; and different dates may be appointed in relation to the British Council and the Commonwealth Institute respectively.

DOCKYARD SERVICES ACT 1986

(1986 c. 52)

An Act to make provision in connection with any arrangements that may be made by the Secretary of State for or with a view to the provision by contractors of certain dockyard services.   [25th July 1986]

PARLIAMENTARY DEBATES

Hansard: H.C. Vol. 86, col. 463; H.C. Vol. 88, col. 27; H.C. Vol. 95, col. 38; H.C. Vol. 102, col. 547; H.L. Vol. 473, cols. 200, 1384; H.L. Vol. 476, col. 23; H.L. Vol. 477, col. 534; H.L. Vol. 478, col. 521; H.L. Vol. 479, col. 447.

The Bill was considered by Standing Committee D between December 12, 1985 and March 18, 1986.

Transfer of persons engaged in dockyard services

1.—(1) This section applies in relation to such services for or in connection with ships or vessels or related establishments in the service of the Crown, provided at such dockyards, as may, in accordance with subsection (12) below, be designated by the Secretary of State by order; and in this section, in relation to a designated dockyard—

"the dockyard undertaking" means the provision by the Crown of designated dockyard services at the dockyard; and

"the qualified dockyard service employees" means the persons employed in or in connection with the dockyard undertaking in the civil service of the Crown on such day as the Secretary of State appoints by order.

(2) If, as regards a designated dockyard, the Secretary of State makes arrangements—

(*a*) for a company to provide designated dockyard services at the dockyard under contract with him, and

(*b*) for that or another company—

(i) to become the employer of such of the qualified dockyard service employees at the dockyard as are employees to whom the arrangements apply, and

(ii) to acquire from him rights in or over the dockyard or any part of it and any property used for the purposes of the dockyard undertaking,

with a view to their services and that property being made available for the provision of the designated dockyard services at the dockyard,

subsections (4) to (11) below shall have effect in relation to the employees to whom the arrangements apply.

(3) The arrangements made by the Secretary of State as regards a designated dockyard may include the formation of a company with a view to, or for any purpose of, the provision of designated dockyard services at the dockyard.

(4) The Transfer of Undertakings (Protection of Employment) Regulations 1981 shall, subject to subsection (5) below, apply to the transfer of the dockyard undertaking or any part of it whether or not, apart from this provision, the undertaking would be treated as an undertaking in the nature of a commercial venture for the purposes of those Regulations, and, for those purposes, the services of the qualified dockyard service employees together with the rights in or over the dockyard and property used for the purposes of the undertaking shall be treated as a part of that undertaking capable of being transferred as a business whether or not the

company which is to become their employer also provides designated dockyard services.

(5) The Transfer of Undertakings (Protection of Employment) Regulations 1981, in their application to the transfer of the dockyard undertaking or any part of it, shall have effect as if, for regulation 10 (duty to inform and consult trade union representatives), there were substituted the provisions of subsections (6) to (9) below, and (unless the remedy provided by section 2 is invoked) the remedies by way of complaint to an industrial tribunal provided for by, and the other provisions of, regulation 11 shall be available and shall apply in relation to those subsections as they would in relation to regulation 10 or any corresponding provision of it.

(6) Long enough before the transfer to enable consultations to take place between the Secretary of State and the representatives of the independent trade unions recognised by him in respect of the employees, the Secretary of State shall, in accordance with subsection (13) below, inform those representatives of—

(a) the fact that the transfer is to take place, when approximately it is to take place, and the reasons for it;

(b) the legal, economic and social implications of the transfer for the employees;

(c) the measures which he envisages he will, in connection with the transfer, take in relation to those employees or, if he envisages that no measures will be so taken, that fact; and

(d) the measures which the company which is to become their employer envisages that it will, in connection with the transfer, take in relation to those employees or, if the company envisages that no measures will be so taken, that fact.

(7) The company which is to become their employer shall give to the Secretary of State such information at such a time as will enable him to perform the duty imposed on him by virtue of subsection (6)(d) above.

(8) The Secretary of State, where he envisages that he will, in connection with the transfer, be taking measures in relation to employees in respect of whom an independent trade union is recognised by him shall enter into consultations with the representatives of the trade unions and in the course of those consultations shall—

(a) consider any representations made by the trade union representatives, and

(b) reply to those representations, and, if he rejects any of those representations, give his reasons.

(9) If in any case there are special circumstances which render it not reasonably practicable for the Secretary of State to perform a duty imposed on him by subsection (6) or (8) above, he shall take all such steps towards performing that duty as are reasonably practicable in the circumstances.

(10) Where in pursuance of the arrangements referred to in subsection (2)(b) above a company is to become the employer of any person none of the agreed redundancy procedures applicable to persons employed in the civil service of the Crown shall apply to him.

(11) Where in pursuance of the arrangements referred to in subsection (2)(b) above—

(a) a person ceases to be employed in the civil service of the Crown on becoming employed by a company, and

(b) he would not have so ceased if it were not for those arrangements,

he shall not, on so ceasing, be treated for the purposes of any scheme under section 1 of the Superannuation Act 1972 as having retired on redundancy.

(12) The power to make an order under subsection (1) above is exercisable by statutory instrument subject to annulment in pursuance of a resolution of either House of Parliament and the dockyards that may be designated by such an order are those dockyards which are Royal Dockyards when this Act comes into force.

(13) In this Act—

"company" means a company formed under the Companies Acts and "formed", with reference to the purposes of a company, includes the alteration of its objects;

"the Companies Act" means the Companies Act 1985, the Companies Act 1948 or any Act repealed by that Act of 1948;

"designated", with reference to a dockyard or services, means designated under subsection (1) above; and

"dockyard contractor" means a company which for the time being provides services which are designated dockyard services at a designated dockyard under contract with the Secretary of State or, by making the services of employees or property available, enables those services to be provided, whether by a company or by the Secretary of State;

"trade union" and "independent trade union" have the same meaning as in the Trade Union and Labour Relations Act 1974 and "recognised", in relation to an independent trade union, means recognised to any extent for the purpose of collective bargaining (within the meaning of the Employment Protection Act 1975);

and any information which is to be given to the representatives of a trade union shall be delivered to them or sent by post to an address notified by them to the employer, or sent by post to the union at the address of its head or main office.

Failure to inform or consult trade unions: High Court and Court of Session remedies

2.—(1) A trade union as respects which the Secretary of State has a duty under section 1(6) or (8) above to give information or enter into consultations may, where it alleges that the Secretary of State has failed to fulfil that duty, bring an action in the High Court for a declaration as to whether or not he has failed to fulfil that duty, and the Court may make a declaration accordingly.

(2) In Scotland, a trade union as respects which the Secretary of State has a duty under section 1(6) or (8) above to give information or enter into consultations may, where it alleges that the Secretary of State has failed to fulfil that duty, raise an action in the Court of Session for a declarator as to whether or not he has failed to fulfil that duty, and the Court may make a declarator accordingly.

(3) No proceedings may be brought under this section if a complaint to an industrial tribunal has been made under the provisions applied by section 1(5) above.

Provisions as regards premises used for transferred services

3.—(1) All the land in a designated dockyard shall, whatever the respective rights in or over any part of it of the Secretary of State and a dockyard contractor, be treated for the purposes of—

(a) section 3 of the Special Constables Act 1923 (appointment of constables in respect of Her Majesty's dockyards),

(b) Part II of the Military Lands Act 1892 (byelaws for lands under the management of Secretary of State used for service purposes), and

(c) the General Rate Act 1967 or, in Scotland, the Valuation Acts (under which rates are levied except on land occupied by or on behalf of the Crown for public purposes),

as land or, in Scotland, land or heritages under the control or management of the Secretary of State or the Defence Council, or occupied on behalf of the Crown, for naval, military or air force purposes or the purposes of his department or for public purposes, as the case may be, and all instruments, authorities, powers and privileges subsisting under those enactments at the commencement of this Act shall (until revoked) continue in force accordingly.

(2) Part II of the Landlord and Tenant Act 1954 (security of tenure for business tenants) shall not apply to any tenancy granted to a dockyard contractor in respect of any land in a designated dockyard.

Expenses of Secretary of State

4. There shall be paid out of money provided by Parliament any expenses of the Secretary of State—
(a) incurred in connection with the formation of any company formed with a view to, or for any purpose of, the provision of designated dockyard services at a designated dockyard or the operation of any such company wholly owned by the Secretary of State; or
(b) incurred in assuming responsibility for any liabilities of that company or any other company which is or has been a dockyard contractor arising out of the provision of designated dockyard services or to or in respect of persons employed or formerly employed in or in connection with the provision of those services.

Short title and commencement

5.—(1) This Act may be cited as the Dockyard Services Act 1986.

(2) This Act shall come into force at the end of the period of two months beginning with the day on which it is passed.

BUILDING SOCIETIES ACT 1986*

(1986 c. 53)

ARRANGEMENT OF SECTIONS

PART I

THE BUILDING SOCIETIES COMMISSION

PART II

CONSTITUTION OF BUILDING SOCIETIES

Establishment

Raising funds and borrowing

PART III

ADVANCES, LOANS AND OTHER ASSETS

Class 1 advances and class 2 advances secured on land

Other advances secured on land

Other commerical assets

Commerical asset structure requirements

Liquid assets

Liabilities of associated bodies

* Annotations by Elizabeth Ovey, B.A., Barrister and Malcolm Waters, M.A., B.C.L., Barrister.

Part X

Dissolution, Winding Up, Mergers, Transfer of Business

Dissolution and winding up

Mergers

Transfer of business to commercial company

Cancellation of registration

Part XI

Miscellaneous and Supplementary and Conveyancing Services

Miscellaneous and supplementary

Provision of conveyancing services by recognised institutions and practitioners

General

An Act to make fresh provision with respect to building societies and further provision with respect to conveyancing services.

[25th July 1986]

PARLIAMENTARY DEBATES
    Hansard: H.C. Vol. 88, col. 457; H.C. Vol. 89, col. 593; H.C. Vol. 98, cols. 914, 915, 1011; H.L. Vol. 476, cols. 61, 1180; H.L. Vol. 477, col. 1036; H.L. Vol. 478, cols. 457, 1100; H.L. Vol. 479, col. 275.
    The Bill was considered by Standing Committee A between January 21, 1986 and February 25, 1986.

INTRODUCTORY AND GENERAL NOTE
    This Act repeals and replaces the Building Societies Act 1962, which, hitherto, has contained the great bulk of the statutory provisions governing building societies. The 1962 Act, however, was largely a consolidating Act, drawing many of its provisions from nineteenth century legislation: in particular, the Building Societies Act 1874. In substance, the present Act is the first major piece of reforming legislation concerning building societies since the 1874 Act. When that Act was passed, building societies were already well established as mutual institutions offering to small investors a safe home for their investments (as least as a general rule) and to borrowers of modest means their best chance of being able to afford to purchase a house to live in. Building society legislation since 1874 has been concerned primarily to ensure that societies continued to perform those functions and that safeguards were increased.
    It is clear from the reports of the debates which took place during the Bill's passage through Parliament that this Act is not intended to detract from the performance by societies of those functions. But the background against which societies are offering their services has changed out of all recognition since 1874. To produce an exhaustive list of relevant changes would be impossible, but the following recent developments should be noted.
    (1) There has been a considerable increase in recent years in shared ownership schemes, under which one person purchases outright a percentage of the beneficial ownership of a property and acquires rights to purchase the remainder later. Those rights may be of varying kinds. The essential point is that the initial purchase price, and any consequent mortgage commitment, are substantially lower than would be the case if the purchaser acquired the entire property outright.
    (2) The traditional supply of private rented accommodation has almost vanished, leaving a gap in housing provision which is not adequately filled by the alternatives of public sector housing or owner occupation. Persons who come low on local authority waiting lists and who cannot finance the purchase of an ordinary flat or house find it very difficult to obtain accommodation from other sources.
    (3) The financial and commercial world has become very much more sophisticated over the past century. Investors can now select from a much wider range of reasonably secure investments and it is the policy of the present Government to encourage small shareholders.

There is also a much wider range of methods of wholesale borrowing available to large financial institutions for raising funds. Further radical changes are imminent.

(4) There is an increasing demand among building society members for additional services. Many shareholders would like to be offered the same sort of services as banks offer to individuals with a current account. Potential borrowers would be assisted by estate agency and surveying services. In these cases in particular, it is not always obvious to ordinary members why such services are not offered as a matter of course.

(5) The building society movement itself has been so successful that the larger societies today have assets of a value which would probably have been inconceivable to their original members. There has been an increasing tendency in recent years for societies to grow fewer in number and greater in value of assets. The assets of the largest society now exceed £20 billion and the financial power of the movement as a whole is enormous.

The consequence of these and other changes was, in the years immediately preceding this Act, a growing restiveness on the part of building societies, and in particular the larger societies, at the constraints (most recently to be found in the Building Societies Act 1962), within which they were obliged to operate. For example, shared ownership schemes could cause problems as to whether any security taken by a lending society would satisfy the requirements of the 1962 Act; housing schemes were inhibited by the lack of a general power to hold land; certain methods of wholesale borrowing were not permitted to societies; common banking services could not be offered in case the account holder became temporarily overdrawn. Constraints of this nature were found both to limit the competitiveness of building societies and to prevent them from making a fuller contribution to housing provision. A complete re-examination of building society law was therefore appropriate, not only in the interests of building society members, but also in the interests of the public generally.

The ball was officially set rolling on the publication by H.M. Treasury in July 1984 of a Green Paper entitled "Building Societies: A New Framework" (Cmnd. 9316). That Paper made similar points to those mentioned above. It emphasised the importance of ensuring that building societies continued to perform their traditional functions, but threw open for debate all the issues concerning the extension of societies' powers, the supervision of societies, the protection of investors, accountability to members and general management and administration. There followed a long consultation process before the Building Societies Bill was introduced in the House of Commons on December 6, 1985. Comments, recommendations and representations continued to flood in throughout the Bill's Parliamentary progress and the Bill which finally received the Royal Assent (on July 25, 1986) was significantly different in many respects from the Bill as first introduced. The proposals put forward in the Green Paper, however, are still readily to be discerned in the Act, notwithstanding the many changes which followed the consultation process.

It is hoped that the foregoing account of the Act's raison d'être will assist readers in discerning the philosophy underlying the Act. It may be observed as a general point that, while the changes made by the Act are often radical and far-reaching, they have been balanced by provisions which secure, first, that the bulk of a building society's business must still be concentrated in its traditional spheres of operation and, second, that the changes are introduced within an extended and more sophisticated framework of prudential supervision. It should also be noted that the detail of many of the new provisions of the Act has been left to be filled in by statutory instrument: nearly 40 such instruments are intended to be made during the period between August 1986 and late 1987. There now follows a brief account of what is to be found in the Act's various parts. A detailed account of the Act's provisions will be found in the annotations to the individual sections.

Part I: ss.1 to 4. This Part establishes the Building Societies Commission and makes provision for its finance, its accounts and its reports to Parliament. The Building Societies Commission is the new supervisory body for building societies, which are therefore no longer subject to the supervision of the Registry of Friendly Societies, although the central office of the Registry retains many functions in respect of building societies. The Commission's duties are many and varied, and it has extensive powers of control (see in particular Part VI).

Part II: ss.5 to 9. Ss.5 and 6 provide for the establishment, constitution and powers of a society and enable it to hold land for the purposes of its business. S.5 ensures that the purpose or principal purpose of a building society will be the traditional one of enabling members to buy homes; it is to be "that of raising, primarily by the subscriptions of the members, a stock or fund for making to them advances secured on land for their residential use". Ss.7 to 9 govern a society's power to raise funds and borrow money. Again the traditional character of societies is preserved; under s.7, a society's liabilities in respect of its non-retail funds and deposits must not exceed 20 per cent. (subject to variation by statutory instrument) of its total liabilities in respect of shares and deposits, and under s.8 the principal of and interest on deposits must not exceed 50 per cent. of the total of that amount and the principal of and interest on shares.

Part III: ss.10 to 23. These sections contain greatly increased powers for societies to engage in activities which will produce assets (frequently, but not always, in the form of debts owed to societies). Those powers should be distinguished from the powers given by Part V of the Act to provide services; those are dealt with separately, since services may produce income, but they will not produce assets. Under this Part, it is necessary to distinguish fixed assets, commercial assets (which are subdivided into classes 1, 2 and 3) and liquid assets. There is no limit on the fixed assets which a society may hold, provided that they are genuinely held for the purposes of its business. The society's liquid assets, by virtue of s.21, must not exceed one-third of its total assets.

A society's commercial assets are those resulting from the exercise of its powers under ss.10 to 19. Those sections specify the class into which assets resulting from the exercise of each power will fall. Very broadly, class 1 assets are advances to individuals fully secured by a first mortgage of land which is for the residential use of the borrower or a dependant of his: in other words, traditional building society advances. Again very broadly, class 2 assets are advances secured at least in part by a first or second mortgage of land and as to the balance (if any) by some other prescribed security. Those two asset classes are covered by ss.10 to 14. Class 3 assets are those resulting from the exercise of the new powers contained in ss.15 to 18: *i.e.* power to make loans for mobile homes; power to make loans (including unsecured loans) to individuals; power to hold and develop residential land as a commercial asset; and power to invest in subsidiaries and other associated bodies. S.19 enables the Treasury to confer additional powers to hold assets.

The composition of a society's total commercial assets is strictly controlled by s.20. The percentages currently specified in that section are subject to variation by statutory instrument, but as the section now stands at least 90 per cent. of a society's commercial assets must be class 1 assets; thus the traditional character of societies is again preserved. Further, no more than five per cent. of its commercial assets may be class 3 assets (which will usually be of a riskier type).

S.22 in effect obliges any society which has subsidiaries or other bodies associated with it to give a statutory guarantee in respect of the liabilities of those bodies. S.23 empowers societies to make certain contracts in order to reduce the risk of loss arising from changes in interest or currency rates or from other prescribed factors.

Two novel features in respect of powers given in this Part should be noted: (1) many of them must be specifically adopted and (2) some of them are not available to all societies. Members of the public will be able to discover which powers a society has adopted by inspecting the public file maintained pursuant to s.106.

Part IV: ss.24 to 33. This Part contains the provisions for the protection of investors in the event that a building society becomes insolvent. The provisions are very similar to those contained in the Banking Act 1979. There is to be a Building Societies Investor Protection Board (s.24) which will administer the Investor Protection Fund (s.25). Unlike the fund created under the Banking Act, this Fund is not a standing fund but will be brought into existence by the levying of contributions in the case of an insolvency (s.26). The level of investor protection offered is such level as the Board may determine, but is currently subject, in effect, to a maximum of £9,000 per investor (s.27). Societies may continue to maintain voluntary schemes offering additional cover (s.31).

Part V: ss.34 and 35. S.34 empowers societies to provide the range of services specified in Sched. 8, subject to the conditions specified in that Schedule. S.35 prevents societies from "linking" services to class 1 lending, that is to say, making an offer of a class 1 advance on the condition that a service provided by the society or its subsidiary is used by the borrower. S.35 also ensures that potential customers will be informed of the price charged (if any) for each service on offer.

Part VI: ss.36 to 57. These sections contain the Commission's principal powers of control. Ss.36 and 37 concern breaches by a society of the requirements as to the assets, liabilities and principal purpose of a society. The Commission can take steps to compel a society to comply with those requirements or to seek to transfer its business to a commercial company (see s.97). Ss.38 to 40 enable the Commission to determine whether or not a particular activity of a society is within its existing powers and, if it is not, to issue a prohibition order requiring the society not to carry on that activity.

Ss.41 to 45 contain powers in relation to authorisation (*i.e.* authorisation to raise money and accept deposits, which is crucial to a society's normal business). The Commission may require a society to re-apply for authorisation (s.41), may impose conditions on a current authorisation (s.42), may revoke an authorisation (s.43), or may reauthorise a society whose original authorisation has been terminated (s.44). These powers are to be exercised for the purpose of protecting the interests of shareholders and depositors. S.45 introduces the "criteria for prudent management", failure to observe which may put a society's authorisation at risk. Ss.46 to 49 provide an appeals procedure in respect of decisions of the Commission as to authorisation. The appeal is to a specially constituted tribunal in the first instance (s.47), with a right of appeal to the High Court on points of law (s.49).

S.50 gives the Commission power to control advertising by societies and s.51 enables it to direct societies to avoid apparent association with other bodies if the apparent association is misleading. Ss.52 to 54 relate to the obtaining of information by the Commission. Under ss.55 to 57, it can appoint investigators or inspectors or can hold a special meeting of a society to consider its affairs.

Part VII: ss.58 to 70. These sections are similar in many respects to provisions of the Companies Act 1985, as indicated in the annotations. They are also in some measure derived from the Building Societies Act 1962, although they are much more elaborate. Ss.58 to 61 contain provisions as to officers: principally, the election and retirement of directors. Ss.62 to 68 are concerned with dealings between directors and societies. They are designed to ensure that, where permitted, such dealings are fair and are not hidden from the members. S.69 ensures that members will be informed of dealings with related businesses. S.70 is an interpretation provision.

Part VIII: ss.71 to 82. This Part contains the provisions for accounts and audit. Again, the sections are similar in many respects to provisions in the Companies Act 1985 and are in part derived from the Building Societies Act 1962. S.71 deals with accounting records and systems of business control. Ss.72 to 76 deal with the annual accounts. Ss.77 to 79 concern auditors and the audit of the accounts. Finally, ss.80 to 82 cover the procedure on the completion of the accounts.

Part IX: ss.83 to 85. These sections and the accompanying schedules (*i.e.* Scheds. 12 to 14) provide for the investigation of complaints and the settlement of disputes. S.83 introduces "ombudsman" schemes for the investigation of complaints. The ombudsman provisions were brought into the Bill at the Report stage in the House of Commons, after a sustained campaign in Committee. They do not feature in the Green Paper.

Part X: ss.86 to 103. These provisions are a mixture of old and new. They cover dissolution, winding up, mergers and transfers of business. The old provisions relate to dissolution, winding up and mergers; they have been rationalised and, in the case of winding up, have very largely been assimilated with the provisions as to the winding up of companies to be found in the Insolvency Act 1986. The new provisions are those concerning the transfer of a society's business to a commercial company, whether existing or specially formed. The provisions themselves were highly controversial and it is not envisaged that they will be used with any frequency. (A society which reaches the point of making such a transfer will be liable to become an institution of a very different kind from the traditional building society.) The sections dealing with dissolution and winding up are ss.86 to 92; the sections dealing with mergers are ss.93 to 96; and ss.96 to 102 deal with a transfer of business to a commercial company. S.103 provides for the cancellation of a society's registration.

Part XI: ss.104 to 126. The provisions of this Part are very largely miscellaneous and supplementary. There may be noted in passing s.106, which provides for the maintenance of a public file in respect of each society; s.107, which restricts the use of names by bodies or individuals which might misleadingly suggest a connection with a building society; s.108, which empowers the Commission to require a society to change a misleading name; and s.118, which defines the term "qualifying asset holding" (currently £100 million, but subject to variation by statutory instrument). Such a holding is required on the part of a society before it can exercise certain of the powers conferred by Part III and Sched. 8.

The final section to be noted in this outline is s.124, which enables the Lord Chancellor to make rules for the recognition of building societies, other institutions and sole practitioners as suitable to provide conveyancing services. It should be noted that this provision, which has a distinct appearance of being tacked on to the rest of the Act, is *not* limited to building societies. It is included in this Act because of Government undertakings given in late 1983 and early 1984 to widen the field of those entitled to offer conveyancing services and because building societies, together with banks, are the prime example of institutions likely to wish to offer conveyancing services.

Then come the Schedules. Sched. 1 concerns the Building Societies Commission. Sched. 2 deals with establishment of societies, anticipation of powers, members' rights and administrative matters. Scheds. 3 and 4 contain supplementary provisions as to authorisation and advances respectively. Sched. 5 concerns the Building Societies Investor Protection Board. Sched. 6 contains provisions as to insolvency payments in cases of trusts and joint holdings. Sched. 7 concerns the death of members and depositors and receipts from depositors who are under age. Sched. 8 specifies the services which societies can offer, subject as therein provided. Scheds. 9 and 10 specify the particulars required of transactions with directors and of the income of related businesses respectively. Sched. 11 deals with the appointment, tenure and qualifications of auditors. Scheds. 12 and 13 concern ombudsman schemes and Sched. 14 concerns the settlement of disputes. Sched. 15 modifies the company winding up legislation for the purpose of applying it to building societies. Scheds. 16 and 17 contain supplementary provisions relating to mergers and transfers of business respectively. Sched. 18 amends existing legislation and Sched. 19 contains repeals and revocations. Sched. 20 sets out the necessary transitional and saving provisions. Finally, Sched. 21 deals with the provision of conveyancing services by recognised institutions and individuals.

It will be obvious that an Act of this nature could not come fully into force immediately upon receiving the Royal Assent; there must be a transitional period. The notes to individual sections (and in particular to s.126) give such information as to commencement dates as was available by August 8, 1986.

The annotations are prepared primarily with a view to use by persons considering the law in England and Wales and do not deal expressly with the law in Scotland or Northern Ireland.

ABBREVIATIONS

In the annotations, the following abbreviations are used:
"the Green Paper": Cmnd. 9316—Building Societies: A New Framework.
"the 1962 Act": the Building Societies Act 1962.

PART I

THE BUILDING SOCIETIES COMMISSION

The Building Societies Commission

1.—(1) For the purposes of this Act there shall be established a body of Commissioners to be called the Building Societies Commission (in this Act referred to as "the Commission").

(2) The Commission shall consist of not less than four and not more than ten members to be appointed by the Treasury and the Treasury shall appoint one member (to be known as the First Commissioner) to be the chairman, and another member to be the deputy chairman, of the Commission.

(3) Any appointment under subsection (2) above may be on either a full-time or a part-time basis.

(4) The general functions of the Commission shall be—

(*a*) to promote the protection by each building society of the investments of its shareholders and depositors;

(*b*) to promote the financial stability of building societies generally;

(*c*) to secure that the principal purpose of building societies remains that of raising, primarily from their members, funds for making advances to members secured upon land for their residential use;

(*d*) to administer the system of regulation of building societies provided for by or under this Act; and

(*e*) to advise and make recommendations to the Treasury or other government departments on any matter relating to building societies;

and the Commission shall have the other functions conferred on it by or under the subsequent provisions of this Act.

(5) The Commission shall have power to do anything which is calculated to facilitate the discharge of its functions, or is incidental or conducive to their discharge.

(6) The functions of the Commission, and of its officers and employees, shall be performed on behalf of the Crown.

(7) Schedule 1 to this Act has effect with respect to the Commission.

GENERAL NOTE

This section provides for the establishment of a new corporate body, to be known as the Building Societies Commission. The Commission takes over the supervisory and regulatory functions formerly exercised by the Registry of Friendly Societies in respect of building societies. Its area of operation, however, will extend further, and will require greater sophistication, than that of the Registry. The broader range of supervision reflects the fact (i) that this Act confers on building societies powers to carry on a much wider range of activities than they were permitted to undertake by the 1962 Act (ii) that, in consequence, societies will be moving into areas in which they have little or no previous experience and (iii) that, in common with all large-scale financial institutions, societies will be competing for business in financial markets which are undergoing rapid and radical change. In one respect, however, the functions of the Commission are narrower than those formerly carried out by the Registry; the Commission will play no part in determining disputes between a member and his society save in relation to (i) the member's right under Sched. 2, para. 15, to obtain particulars of members from the register and (ii) the right to have circulated a statement in support of a resolution, under Sched. 2, para. 31, or an election address on an election of directors under s.61(7), when circulation is opposed on the ground that it would diminish substantially public confidence in the society. (*C.f.* ss. 93 and 95(1) of the 1962 Act, under which provision was made for the determination of disputes by the Registry, and compare ss.63 and 95(2) of that Act with Sched. 2, para. 15 and Sched. 14, para. 6, of the present Act. Under the 1962 Act, there were no rights comparable to those granted by Sched. 2, para. 31 and s.61(7).)

Subs. (2)

It is anticipated that initially the Commission will comprise seven members of whom four will be part-time. The first Chairman (or "First Commissioner") is to be the present Chief Registrar of Friendly Societies, Mr Michael Bridgeman. The appointment of members to serve on the Commission will no doubt be designed to ensure that the Commission can draw upon a wide range of experience and financial expertise from within its own ranks.

Subs. (4)

Functions of the Commission. The functions of the Commission, as specified in this subsection, are primarily to ensure that a building society remains a safe repository of the money of its shareholders and investors. It will be noted that the functions specified do not include the protection of the interests of building society borrowers. This is intentional. The explanation is that the interests of borrowers are intended to be protected through the operation of market forces. Nor do the functions of the Commission extend to the field of housing policy. It is conceived as an investor-protection body and its functions are specified accordingly.

The principal purpose of building societies. C.f. s.5.

Other functions. See Part VI of the Act (ss.36 to 57) for the powers of control of the Commission. Note also the functions entrusted to the Commission under Part X, and under ss.107 and 108.

Financial provision for Commission

2.—(1) There shall be charged on building societies such a general charge towards the expenses of the Commission and such fees in respect of the exercise of its functions as are authorised under this section.

(2) The Treasury may, by regulations, make provision for—

(*a*) a general charge to be levied, with respect to each accounting year of the Commission, on every authorised building society to be paid at such rate computed by reference to such criteria, at such time and in such manner as may be prescribed; and

(*b*) fees of such amounts as may be prescribed to be paid by building societies in respect of the exercise of the Commission's functions in relation to them.

(3) The provision to be made from time to time under subsection (2) above, by way of the general charge and fees, shall be such as to produce an annual revenue of the Commission sufficient to meet its expenses properly chargeable to revenue account, taking one year with another.

(4) Regulations under subsection (2) above may include—

(*a*) provision for any fees payable by societies to be reduced or for payment of any fees to be waived by the Commission in circumstances determined by or under the regulations; and

(*b*) such incidental, supplementary and transitional provision as appears to the Treasury to be necessary or expedient.

(5) The power to make regulations under subsection (2) above is exercisable by statutory instrument which shall be subject to annulment in pursuance of a resolution of either House of Parliament.

(6) The amounts received by the Commission under this section shall be applied as an appropriation in aid of money provided by Parliament for the expenses of the Commission under this Act, and in so far as not so applied, shall be paid into the Consolidated Fund.

(7) In this section—

"authorised", in relation to an accounting year of the Commission, means authorised at any time during that year; and

"prescribed" means prescribed in regulations under subsection (2) above.

DEFINITIONS

"accounting year": s.3(5).
"authorised building society": ss.9, 41, 44 and 119(1); but *n.b.* subs. (7).
"the Commission": ss.1 and 119(1).

GENERAL NOTE

The purpose of this section is to enable the annual running costs of the Commission to be met by its annual receipts from the building society movement. In other words, the Commission is intended to be self-financing.

The Commission's receipts from building societies will come from two sources.

First, each authorised building society (*i.e.* broadly each building society authorised to take in money from the public) will be liable to pay a general charge towards the expenses of the Commission in accordance with regulations to be made by the Treasury under subs. (2)(*a*). Such regulations may specify the criteria by reference to which the rate of the charge is to be computed: so, for example, the amount of the charge may be linked to the asset size of the societies liable to pay it. Subs. (2)(*a*) contemplates that the regulations will provide for the charge to be levied on every authorised building society "with respect to each accounting year of the Commission"; it seems to follow from the partial definition of "authorised" given in subs. (7), that the regulations may include provision for the charge to be paid by a society which is authorised during part only of an accounting year of the Commission. (Whether subs. (7) is also intended to qualify the meaning of "authorised" in subs. (1), and if so with what effect, is not at all clear.)

Second, building societies will be obliged to pay fees to the Commission in respect of the exercise of the Commission's functions in relation to them. The amount of such fees will be prescribed by Treasury regulations to be made under subs. (2)(*b*). In contrast to the regulations applicable to the general charge, the regulations applicable to fees may provide (i) for fees to be charged on all building societies (*i.e.* not just authorised societies): see subs. (2)(*b*); and (ii) for fees to be waived or reduced: see subs. (4)(*a*).

Subs. (3) is designed to ensure that the annual income of the Commission from the general charge and fees is sufficient to meet its annual revenue expenditure. During the Committee stage of the Bill in the House of Commons, a broad estimate of £1.75 million was given as the annual sum that would need to be raised by the general charge, while the initial fee income of the Commission was estimated at about £60,000 p.a. (see *Official Report*, Standing Committee A, January 23, 1986, col. 55). It will be seen, therefore, that the general charge will be responsible for discharging by far the greater part of the Commission's expenditure. The Commission is not intended to make a profit; but if a surplus is produced in any year, it will be paid into the Consolidated Fund (see subs. (6)).

Accounts of Commission and audit

3.—(1) The Commission shall keep proper accounts and proper accounting records and shall prepare in respect of each accounting year a statement of accounts in such form as the Treasury may direct.

(2) The statement of the accounts required by subsection (1) above may be combined with the statement of the accounts of the Chief Registrar which he is required to prepare as regards his functions.

(3) The Commission shall send to the Treasury and to the Comptroller and Auditor General, before the end of the period of seven months after the end of each accounting year, a copy of the statement of accounts for that year.

(4) The Comptroller and Auditor General shall examine, certify and report on every statement of accounts received by him from the Commission and shall lay ˘ copy of the statement and of his report thereon before each House of Parliament.

(5) In this Part "accounting year", in relation to the Commission, means the period of twelve months ending with 31st March in any year, except that the Commission's first accounting year shall end on 31st March 1987.

DEFINITIONS
"accounting year": subs. (5).
"the Chief Registrar": s.119(1).
"the Commission": ss.1 and 119(1).

GENERAL NOTE
Subs. (1) requires the Commission to keep proper accounts, and proper accounting records. It also requires the Commission to prepare an annual statement of accounts, which (by subs. (3)) must be submitted to the Treasury and to the Comptroller and Auditor General not later than seven months after the end of each accounting year. Subs. (4) requires the C & AG to examine, certify and report on every statement of accounts received from the Commission and to lay a copy of the statement and of his report thereon before Parliament. It follows from the fact that the C & AG is required to examine and certify the statement that he will have the power under s.6(1) of the National Audit Act 1983 to carry out examinations "into the economy, efficiency and effectiveness" with which the Commission has used its resources in discharging its functions: see *ibid.*, s.6(3)(c). So the Commission can be subject to a "value for money" audit, as well as to the annual financial audit of accounts. The intention is to ensure that the Commission is a "lean, taut organisation which is not raising a penny more from the building societies than is absolutely necessary" (Sir George Young, *Official Report,* House of Commons, Standing Committee A, January 23, 1986, col. 60).

The power conferred by subs. (2) to combine the Commission's statement of accounts with that of the Chief Registrar reflects the fact that the Commission and the Registry will (at least in the first instance) form a single department.

Annual and other reports

4.—(1) It shall be the duty of the Commission to lay before the Treasury and before Parliament as soon as possible after the end of each accounting year a report on the discharge of its functions during that year.

(2) The annual report shall include a record of the terms of every determination of the powers of a building society published by the Commission under section 39 during that year.

(3) The Commission may lay before Parliament from time to time such other reports relating to the discharge of its functions, whether in relation to building societies generally or a particular building society, as it thinks fit.

DEFINITIONS
"accounting year": s.3(5).
"the Commission": ss.1 and 119(1).

GENERAL NOTE
Subs. (1)

This subsection may be compared with s.118 of the 1962 Act, under which the Chief Registrar was required to make "an abstract and report of the annual returns of building societies and of the proceedings of the central office", and to lay the same before the Treasury and before Parliament. Subs. (1) imposes a similar requirement on the Commission. However, since the supervisory functions of the Commission extend a good deal further than those formerly exercised by the Registry, it is to be expected that the range of topics covered by the annual report of the Commission will be correspondingly wider. During the Committee stage of the Bill in the House of Commons, the Economic Secretary to the Treasury (Mr. Ian Stewart) said that he would expect the Commission "to discuss any matter relevant to the policy underlying supervision, including the implementation of the Act, and possibly to comment on matters such as where the Commission may feel that it will not be long before regulations need to be made to adjust some of the provisions, as the Bill enables them to do, with Treasury approval." (See *Official Report,* Standing Committee A, January 23, 1986, col. 62.)

Subs. (2)

Published: Since there may be some time-lag between the making of a determination and its publication (see s.39(3) and (4)), a determination will not necessarily be recorded in the annual report for the year in which it was made.

Subs. (3)

This subsection empowers the Commission to lay before Parliament such other reports relating to its function as it thinks fit. This provision would, for example, enable matters too urgent to await publication of the Commission's next annual report to be brought to the attention of Parliament in the form of a special report.

PART II

CONSTITUTION OF BUILDING SOCIETIES

Establishment

Establishment, constitution and powers

5.—(1) A society may be established under this Act if its purpose or principal purpose is that of raising, primarily by the subscriptions of the members, a stock or fund for making to them advances secured on land for their residential use.

(2) A society is established under this Act on compliance by the persons establishing it with the scheduled requirements and is incorporated under this Act as from the date of registration by the central office.

(3) A society incorporated under this Act is referred to in this Act as a "building society".

(4) A society incorporated under the repealed enactments whose principal office, as registered with the central office immediately before the commencement of this section, was in the United Kingdom, shall be deemed to be registered (and accordingly as incorporated) under this Act.

(5) A building society shall have the powers conferred on building societies by or under the subsequent provisions of this Act subject, however, to—

(*a*) any specified restriction assumed by the society;

(*b*) the operation of any provision by virtue of which a power is not available to a building society;

(*c*) compliance with any requirement that, for a power to be exercisable by a building society, it must be adopted by the society; and

(*d*) the exercise by the Commission of any of its functions by virtue of which the society is precluded from exercising or is subject to restrictions on the exercise of any of its powers.

(6) Powers are adopted by a building society for the purposes of this Act by its compliance with the scheduled requirements and, subject to

any provision of this Act to the contrary, may be adopted to any specified extent.

(7) Restrictions on its powers are assumed by a building society for the purposes of this Act by its compliance with the scheduled requirements.

(8) Schedule 2 to this Act has effect as respects the constitution, powers, and regulation of building societies and in that Schedule—

(*a*) Part I makes provision with respect to the constitution, memorandum, rules and certain incidents of membership;

(*b*) Part II makes provision for the purpose of precluding a society from anticipating the adoption of powers; and

(*c*) Part III makes provision with respect to meetings, postal ballots and resolutions;

and in this section "scheduled", with reference to requirements for establishment or for the adoption of powers or the assumption of restrictions on powers, means contained in that Schedule and "specified", with reference to the adoption of powers or the assumption of restrictions on powers, means specified in the memorandum.

(9) Any obligation imposed by this Act or the rules of a building society to give or send notices or other documents to members is subject to paragraph 14 of that Schedule.

(10) In this Act, except sections 10 to 13, "land", in the expression "advance secured on land", means land in the United Kingdom, and, in so far as land in other countries or territories is, under any provision of this Act, land on which advances may be secured, land in that other country or territory.

DEFINITIONS
"adopted": s.119(1) and Sched. 2, para. 1(4).
"advances secured on land": see ss.10(1) and 119(1).
"assumed": Sched. 2, para. 1(4).
"the central office": s.119(1).
"the Commission": ss.1(1) and 119(1).
"land": subs. (10).
"memorandum": s.119(1) and Sched. 2, para. 1(4).
"the repealed enactments": s.119(1).
"residential use": *cf.* s.11(2)(*b*), (3) and s.12(1).
"scheduled": subs. (8).
"specified": subs. (8).

GENERAL NOTE
Subs. (1)
Under the 1962 Act, a building society could be established only for the single purpose stated in s.1(1) of that Act, namely, "raising, by the subscriptions of the members, a stock or fund for making advances to members out of the funds of the society upon security by way of mortgage of freehold or leasehold estate." The position of building societies under the 1962 Act was described thus in Wurtzburg and Mills, *Building Society Law* (14th Ed.), p. 3: "it is necessary to understand . . . that they are special statutory creatures, in a statutory strait-jacket, and that, unlike individuals, partnerships or companies in this respect, they have no choice in the matter of the business which they carry on."

Under the present Act, by contrast, building societies are permitted (though not obliged) to have more than one purpose. For the first time, therefore, they will enjoy some choice in the matter of the business for which they are established. But, although this distinction with the 1962 Act is of paramount importance, it is also important to bear in mind the limitations on the freedom of choice allowed to societies under the new Act. In the first place, the purpose specified in subs. (1) above, if it is not the sole purpose for which a society is established, must still be the "principal" purpose for which it is established. This takes one forward to s.20, which, in effect, requires at least 90 per cent. of any building society's commercial assets to be in the form of "class 1 assets", a class which comprises (broadly speaking) advances to members secured by a first mortgage of land for their residential use (see ss.10(1) and 11(2)). Secondly, any other (subsidiary) purpose for which a building society is established must be drawn from those sanctioned by the Act, many of which require express adoption, and are not open to every building society (see ss.15–19, 23 and 34 below). So there is still a world of difference in this respect between a building society and a commercial company (which may be incorporated for any lawful object stated in its memorandum). The new Act may have loosened the "statutory strait-jacket"; but it has not discarded it. (Note, however, the possible means of escape provided by ss.97–101, Sched. 2, para. 30 and Sched. 17, dealing with the transfer of a building society's business to a commercial company.)

In addition to the crucial distinction discussed above, two further points of difference may be noted between subs. (1) and s.1(1) of the 1962 Act. First, the expression "by the subscriptions of the members" is now qualified by the word "primarily". This, however, appears to be a difference of drafting rather than of substance. The Act does not require a building society to raise the whole of its funds from the subscriptions of its members (though note that s.8, broadly speaking, requires at least 50 per cent. of its funds to be raised in the form of shares). The word "primarily" in subs. (1) no doubt reflects the fact that a society may raise money by taking deposits or loans from persons who are not members (see ss.7–9); but that was equally true under the 1962 Act (see s.39 of that Act). Second, the purpose stated in subs. (1) embodies the requirement that the advances which a society makes to its members should be secured on land "for their residential use". No such requirement was contained in s.1(1) of the 1962 Act. In this respect, therefore, subs. (1) above is framed more narrowly than its predecessor. It seems to follow that a society established *solely* for the purpose specified in subs. (1) (a possibility clearly contemplated by the words "if its purpose or principal purpose") will find itself excluded from lending on the security of land which is not being used for residential purposes by the borrowing member. This is difficult to reconcile with ss.10 and 11, which appear to envisage that all societies will have power, *inter alia*, to make (i) class 1 advances secured on land for the residential use of the borrower's dependants and (ii) class 2 advances secured on land not being used for residential purposes at all.

Note finally that the definition of the expression "advances secured on land" (as to which, see s.10(1)) requires security to be taken by way of a mortgage of a legal estate in land or of an equitable interest of a prescribed description or (in Scotland) by way of a heritable security over land. Again, the new Act may be more narrowly drawn in this respect than the old, since it was at least arguable that the words "by way of mortgage of freehold or leasehold estate" in s.1(1) of the 1962 Act included mortgages of all descriptions of equitable estates: see Wurtzburg and Mills, *supra,* pp. 144–5 and see the notes to s.10.

Subs. (2)
There are two pre-conditions to be satisfied before a building society can be incorporated under the Act. First, the society must be "established". This involves compliance with the requirements set out in Sched. 2, para. 1(1). Second, the society must be registered by the central office of the Registry of Friendly Societies: as to this, see Sched. 2, para. 1(2).

Subs. (4)
A building society incorporated under the Building Societies Acts of 1874 or 1962, or (in Northern Ireland) the Building Societies Act (Northern Ireland) 1967, will, by virtue of this subsection, be deemed to be registered (and hence incorporated) under the new Act. For the transitional provisions applicable to existing building societies, see Sched. 20.

Subs. (5)
any specific restriction assumed by the society. As is apparent from subs. (7), a society assumes restrictions on its powers "by its compliance with the scheduled requirements." The relevant requirements are stated in Sched. 2, paras. 1 and 4. In accordance with those paragraphs, a society may assume restrictions on its powers (whether adoptable or other powers) either (i) by agreement between the persons establishing the society or (ii) by subsequent assumption of restrictions by special resolution. In either case the terms of each restriction must be set out in the society's memorandum. (For the transitional provisions applicable to existing societies, see Sched. 20, paras. 2 and 3.)

the operation of any provision by virtue of which a power is not available to a building society. Certain of the adoptable powers contained in the Act are not capable of being adopted (or of being adopted to their full extent) by societies which do not have a "qualifying asset holding", that is to say total commercial assets of not less than the amount for the time being specified under s.118 (currently £100 million). See ss.15(9), 16(12), 17(9) and (10), 18(10), 23(3) and (4), and 34(1) and Sched. 8, Part III, paras. 4 and 6(2).

compliance with any requirement that, for a power to be exercisable by a building society, it must be adopted by the society. The powers here referred to (described in the Act as "adoptable powers": see Sched. 2, para. 1(4)) are those set out in ss.15–19, 23 and 34. The requirements for their adoption (*viz.* "the scheduled requirements) are stated in Sched. 2, paras. 1 and 4, and are similar to those applicable to the assumption of restrictions on the exercise of powers. See the note above (and see Sched. 20, paras. 2 and 3 for the transitional provisions applicable to existing societies). Again, any adoptable powers for the time being adopted by a society must be specified in its memorandum.

the exercise by the Commission of any of its functions. See for example ss. 9(5) and (6), 41, 42 and 44.

Subs. (10)

The definition of "land" contained in this subsection does not apply to ss.10–13 since those sections are confined to land in the United Kingdom.

Power to hold land etc. for purposes of its business

6.—(1) A building society may acquire and hold premises for the purpose of conducting its business.

(2) A building society may, otherwise than by acquisition, provide itself with premises for the purpose of conducting its business.

(3) A building society which has subsidiaries or other associated bodies, in addition to exercising the powers conferred by subsections (1) and (2) above as regards premises from which the society's business is to be conducted by a subsidiary or associated body, may exercise corresponding powers for the purpose of enabling a subsidiary or other associated body to conduct the business of that body from the premises.

(4) A building society may exercise the powers conferred by subsections (1) and (2) above as regards premises situated outside, as well as premises situated within, the United Kingdom.

(5) If the acquisition or provision of any premises is necessary for the purpose of the conduct of the business of a building society or a subsidiary or other associated body, the society may acquire or otherwise provide itself with and hold the premises under this section notwithstanding that part only of the premises is or will be required for that purpose.

(6) A building society—

(*a*) may dispose of property held under this section; and

(*b*) in the event that no part of the premises comes to be or, as the case may be, is any longer occupied for the conduct of the business of the society or a subsidiary or associated body, shall, subject to subsection (7) below, sell its estate or interest in the premises as soon as it is conveniently practicable to do so without undue loss.

(7) Subsection (6)(*b*) above does not require a building society to sell any property if the society may hold the property under section 17 and elects to do so by a resolution of the board of directors.

DEFINITIONS

"associated body": ss.18(17) and 119(1).

"subsidiary": s.119(1) and Companies Act 1985, s.736(1).

GENERAL NOTE

Subss. (1)–(4)

Subs. (1) clearly empowers a society to acquire premises by outright purchase. It is arguable that it also empowers a society to take premises on lease (*i.e.* to "acquire" premises for a term of years). However, if the power to take premises on lease is not conferred by subs. (1) it must plainly be conferred by subs. (2), whereby a society is empowered to "provide itself" with premises "otherwise than by acquisition." If the power to take premises on lease is conferred by subs. (1), then subs. (2) is presumably intended simply to cover arrangements under which a society is permitted to use premises without acquiring any form of proprietary interest therein. (*C.f.* s.7(2) of the 1962 Act, which empowered societies, *inter alia,* to "hire" buildings for conducting their business.) Note, however, that subs. (6)(*b*) seems to assume that a society will obtain a saleable estate or interest in any premises held by it under this section.

Taken together, the effect of subss. (1)–(3) is that a society may acquire or provide itself with premises for the following purposes:–
  (i) to enable the society to carry on its own business;
  (ii) to enable its subsidiaries or associated bodies to carry on the society's business; and
  (iii) to enable its subsidiaries or associated bodies to carry on their own business.

It seems to be implicit in the wording of subs. (3) that, whereas the acquisition or provision of premises for purpose (ii) will constitute an exercise of the powers conferred by subs. (1) and (2), the acquisition or provision of premises for purpose (iii) will constitute an exercise of the further "corresponding powers" conferred by subs. (3) itself. Since subs. (4) does not empower societies to exercise the powers conferred by subs. (3) (as opposed to those conferred by subs. (1) and (2)) as regards premises situated outside the United Kingdom, it appears to follow that a society has no power under this section to acquire or provide itself with such premises for purpose (iii).

In the usual case, an "associated body" (as defined in s.18(17)) will be either (i) a body in which a society has invested under s.18(1)(*a*); or (ii) a body to which a society is linked by resolution under s.18(9). Curiously, the expression "subsidiary" is not used in s.18; but since a society will have to invest in a body before that body can become its subsidiary, it follows that any subsidiary of a building society must necessarily be an associated body of the society. That is no doubt reflected in the expression "subsidiaries *or other* associated bodies" which appears in subs. (3) of the present section. To avoid repetition, references in the rest of this note to "associated bodies" include references to subsidiaries. (For a fuller discussion of these terms, see the notes to s.18(17).)

Providing an associated body with the use of property is a form of "support" for that body within the meaning of s.18(1)(*b*) (see s.18(1)(*b*)(iv)). It would appear, therefore, that a society will be justified in acquiring or providing premises under the present section for the use of an associated body only in circumstances where the society has power to support that body under s.18 (as to which, see in particular s.18(4)–(8) and (11)).

In the normal case, premises held under this section will be treated as fixed assets (as opposed to commercial assets) of the society, and will not, therefore, be subject to the requirements for the structure of commercial assets imposed by s.20. Note, however, the exception introduced by s.17(6), discussed in the notes to subs. (5) below.

Subs. (5)

Suppose, for example, that premises comprising a ground floor shop with a residential flat above are being offered for sale as a single unit. The society has no need of the flat, but requires the shop for conversion to a branch office for itself or an associated body. This subsection makes clear that in such circumstances the society will have power under the present section to purchase the whole of the premises; and it appears that the whole of the premises (including the flat) will be treated as a fixed rather than a commercial asset of the society. It should be noted, however, that the Commission may (with Treasury consent) make an order under s.17(6) specifying circumstances in which premises held by virtue of the present subsection are to be treated in their entirety (and regardless of their use) as land held under s.17 for the purposes of the requirements for the structure of commercial assets imposed by s.20. Such premises will then be treated for those purposes as a class 3 commercial asset of the society. The power to make such an order has no doubt been conferred to prevent potential abuses of the present subsection, *e.g.* the acquisition of a large office block on the pretext of opening a branch office on the ground floor.

Subss.(6)(b) and (7)

The combined effect of these provisions is that, when a society or an associated body gives up occupation of every part of the premises (or decides not to take up occupation of any part of them), then the premises must be sold, unless the society's board resolves to retain them for use or development for residential purposes under s.17. Note, however, that the power to hold land under s.17 must be adopted before it can be exercised, and is, generally speaking, available only to the larger societies (*i.e.* societies with the qualifying asset holding specified in s.118): see s.17(9) and (11) but *n.b.* s.17(10). It should also be borne in mind that land retained by a society under s.17 will not be treated as a fixed asset of the society, but rather as a class 3 commercial asset: see s.17(5). The words "as soon as it is conveniently practicable to do so without undue loss" in subs. (6)(*b*) show that a society will be allowed a reasonable degree of latitude in effecting a sale under this paragraph: a society will not, therefore, be forced into a precipitate sale in a falling market.

Raising funds and borrowing

Power to raise funds and borrow money and limit on non-retail funds and borrowing

7.—(1) Subject to the provisions of this section and sections 8 and 9, a building society may—

(*a*) raise funds by the issue of shares to members, or

(*b*) borrow money and accordingly receive deposits from any person,

to be applied for the purposes of the society.

(2) The power to raise funds by the issue of shares is a power to issue shares of one or more denominations, either as shares paid up in full or as shares to be paid by periodical or other subscriptions, and with or without accumulating interest; and funds so raised may be repaid when they are no longer required for the purposes of the society.

(3) Subject to subsection (14) below, the liabilities of a building society in respect of its non-retail funds and deposits shall not exceed at any time the prescribed percentage of the society's total liabilities at that time in respect of shares in or money deposited with the society.

(4) For the purposes of subsection (3) above, a building society's liabilities in respect of its non-retail funds and deposits are, subject to subsections (5) and (9) below, its liabilities in respect of the principal of and interest payable on or under—

(*a*) transferable instruments,

(*b*) qualifying time deposits,

(*c*) shares in the society held by, or by a trustee for, and (to the extent the liabilities do not fall within (*a*) or (*b*) above) sums deposited with the society by, or by a trustee for—

(i) any body corporate,

(ii) a friendly society registered under the Friendly Societies Act 1974 or the Friendly Societies Act (Northern Ireland) 1970,

(iii) a trade union (within the meaning of the Trade Union and Labour Relations Act 1974),

(*d*) shares in the society (to the extent the liabilities do not fall within (*c*) above) held by, and (to the extent the liabilities do not fall within (*a*), (*b*) or (*c*) above) sums deposited with the society by—

(i) a body of persons or trust established for charitable purposes only, or

(ii) the administrator of an approved retirement benefits scheme.

(5) If a building society so elects with respect to any financial year its liabilities in respect of shares or deposits falling within paragraphs (*c*) or (*d*) (but no other provision) of subsection (4) above shall, subject to subsections (6) and (7) below, not be counted towards the limit in force under subsection (3) above.

(6) The liabilities of the society to any person shall not, by virtue of an election under subsection (5) above, be disregarded at any time during the financial year to which the election relates if at that time the liabilities to that person exceed the prescribed amount; and in that event all the society's liabilities to that person shall count towards the limit in force under subsection (3) above.

(7) To be effective for the purposes of subsection (5) above, an election must apply to the society's liabilities in respect of all its shareholders and depositors who fall within subsection (4)(*c*) and (*d*) above and notice of it must be given to the Commission before the beginning of the financial year to which it relates.

(8) A copy of the notice shall also be sent to the central office and the central office shall keep the copy in the public file of the society.

(9) The Commission may by order made with the consent of the Treasury amend subsection (4) above by adding to or deleting from it any description of property or right or by varying any description of property or right for the time being specified in it and an order under this subsection may—

(*a*) define property or rights by reference to any criteria including the description of person who holds the property or rights,

(*b*) make any consequential amendment or repeal in that subsection, subsections (5) to (8) above or subsection (19) below, and

(*c*) make such supplementary, transitional and saving provision as appears to the Commission to be necessary or expedient.

(10) In determining for the purposes of subsection (3) above the liabilities of a building society with which another body corporate is associated there shall, subject to subsection (13) below, be attributed to the society, in accordance with aggregation rules made by the Commission with the consent of the Treasury under this subsection, the whole or part of the liabilities of whatever description of the associated body, as provided in the rules and subject to any exceptions provided in the rules.

(11) The power to make aggregation rules under subsection (10) above includes power to make—

(*a*) different rules for different circumstances,

(*b*) provision for liabilities of societies to be disregarded; and

(*c*) such supplementary, transitional and saving provision as appears to the Commission to be necessary or expedient.

(12) The power to make aggregation rules under subsection (10) above is exercisable by statutory instrument which shall be subject to annulment in pursuance of a resolution of either House of Parliament.

(13) The Commission may, on the application of a building society, approve rules to be applied for the purposes of subsection (3) above for the attribution to the society of liabilities of bodies associated with the society; and so long as the rules continue to be approved by the Commission they, and not the aggregation rules in force under subsection (10) above, shall apply for the attribution of liabilities for the purposes of subsection (3) above.

(14) Where money is lent to a building society by another such society in accordance with an authority given by the Commission under section 33 the liabilities in respect of the loan shall be disregarded for the purposes of subsection (3) above.

(15) The prescribed percentage for the purposes of subsection (3) above is 20 per cent. or such other percentage not exceeding 40 per cent. as is for the time being substituted for it by order of the Commission made with the consent of the Treasury.

(16) The prescribed amount for the purposes of subsection (6) above is £50,000 or such other amount as is for the time being substituted for it by order of the Commission made with the consent of the Treasury.

(17) The power to make an order under subsection (9), (15) or (16) above is exercisable by statutory instrument which shall be subject to annulment in pursuance of a resolution of either House of Parliament.

(18) If the liabilities of a building society to which subsection (3) above applies exceed at any time the limit in force under that subsection the powers conferred on the Commission by section 36 shall become exercisable in relation to the society, but exceeding the limit shall not affect the validity of transactions effected in excess of it.

(19) In this section—

"qualifying time deposit" means a deposit in sterling made with the society as to which the following conditions are satisfied, that is to say—

(i) the amount of the deposit is or exceeds £50,000;

(ii) the deposit is repayable at the end of a specified period which expires before the end of the period of 12 months beginning on the date on which the deposit is made; and

(iii) the right to repayment is not assignable;

"retirement benefits scheme" means a retirement benefits scheme within the meaning of Chapter II of Part II of the Finance Act 1970 (occupational pension schemes) and "approved" means approved for the time being by the Commissioners of Inland Revenue for the purposes of that Chapter; and

"transferable instrument" means an instrument which embodies a right, transferable by delivery of the instrument, to receive an amount referable to a deposit with the society.

DEFINITIONS

"approved retirement benefits scheme": subs. (19).
"associated" and "associated body": ss.18(17) and 119(1).
"central office": s.119(1).
"Commission": ss.1 and 119(1).
"deposit": s.119(1).
"financial year": ss.117 and 119(1).
"member": s.119(1).
"non-retail funds and deposits": subs. (4).
"prescribed amount": subs. (16).
"prescribed percentage": subs. (15).
"public file": s.119(1).
"qualifying time deposit": subs. (19).
"share": s.119(1).
"transferable instrument": subs. (19).

GENERAL NOTE

Building societies have traditionally raised their funds both by the issue of shares and by the taking of money on deposit or loan. As is apparent from subs. (1), that will continue to be the position under the new Act. (Note in this connection that the reference to deposits in subs. (1), as throughout the Act, includes a reference to loans: see s.119(1).) Hence, the principal liabilities shown on the balance sheet of a building society will continue to be (i) liabilities in respect of shares and (ii) liabilities in respect of loans and deposits.

In the past, building societies have raised by far the greater part of their funds from individual shareholders and depositors (with shareholders increasingly predominating in more recent years). The present section is intended to preserve the traditional character of building societies as institutions which look to the private savings sector for the bulk of their funds. That objective is achieved by limiting each society's "liabilities in respect of its non-retail funds and deposits" to a fixed percentage (initially 20 per cent.) of its total liabilities in respect of shares and deposits: see subss. (3) and (15). The liabilities which count towards the 20 per cent. limit are set out in subs. (4). That is a relatively complex provision; but in essence, it embraces liabilities for the payment of principal and interest in respect of funds falling within either of the following two categories:

(1) wholesale funds borrowed by means of certain money market instruments and time deposits; and

(2) funds raised otherwise than from individuals, both by the issue of shares and by the receipt of deposits (but excluding deposits which fall within the first category).

It should be noted that the detailed list of items set out in subs. (4) may be amended by order made by the Commission with the consent of the Treasury under subs. (9).

Subs. (2)

This re-states the law as it existed under the 1962 Act: see Wurtzburg & Mills, *Building Society Law* (14th Ed.), p. 41, and s.6 of the 1962 Act.

Subss. (3) and (15)

The broad policy underlying these subsections has already been mentioned. The specific limitation which these provisions impose on wholesale borrowing is new. The 1962 Act imposed a general restriction on the amount of a society's borrowings as a whole (see s.39(2) of that Act and the note to the next section); but it did not seek to limit the proportion of such borrowings which could be raised from wholesale sources. Over the past few years, wholesale funds have been found increasingly attractive by building societies, being both cheaper and more readily available than funds from the private savings sector. Nevertheless, wholesale funds still represent a relatively small proportion of the total funds raised by the building society movement as a whole (some five per cent. to six per cent. at the end of 1985: see *Official Report*, House of Commons, Standing Committee A, January 28, 1986, col.82). The initial 20 per cent. limit imposed by subs. (15) on the liabilities of a building society in respect of wholesale funds ought, therefore, in the case of most societies, to allow considerable scope for expansion in the volume of funds raised from wholesale sources. It should be borne in mind that while wholesale funds may be attractive in current market conditions, they tend to be more volatile than retail funds, and to require more skilful management. In view of the potential risk involved in wholesale borrowing, it appears to be unlikely that the 20 per cent. figure currently prescribed under subs. (15) will be raised in the foreseeable future (see *ibid.*, col. 84).

Subss. (5)–(8) and (16)
    The effect of these provisions is that, if a society so elects, its liabilities to a person in respect of shares and deposits falling within subs. (4) (*c*) and (*d*) will not be counted towards the limit in force under subs. (3), if and so long as its liabilities to that person do not exceed the amount prescribed under subs. (16) (initially £50,000). Such an election may be made in respect of any financial year; but subs. (7) requires notice of the election to be given to the Commission before the beginning of the year. It will be noted that the election must apply to the society's liabilities in respect of *all* its shareholders and depositors who fall within subs. (4)(*c*) and (*d*): so the society cannot pick and choose which of those liabilities are to be caught by the election: subs. (7). It will also be noted that, where an election is made, such liabilities are only disregarded for so long as they do not exceed the prescribed amount: subs. (6). Suppose, for example, that a society's liabilities to a corporate shareholder at the beginning of the year amounted to £49,500, but that interest becoming payable during the year increased those liabilities to a sum in excess of £50,000. If an election had been made for that year under subs. (5), the consequence would be that the society's liabilities to that shareholder would be disregarded for so long as they did not exceed £50,000; but as soon as they exceeded that figure they would count in full towards the limit in force under subs. (3).

Subss. (10)–(13)
    Subss. (10)–(13) empower the Commission, with Treasury consent, to make aggregation rules of general application, whereby some or all of the liabilities of an associated body can be treated, for the purposes of subs. (3), as if they were the liabilities of the society with which that body is associated. Subs. (13) empowers the Commission, on the application of an individual society, to approve special rules applicable to that society and its associated bodies; for so long as such rules continue to be approved, they, and not the general rules in force under subs. (10), will govern the attribution to the society concerned of the liabilities of its associated bodies.

Subs. (18)
    If the limit in force under subs. (3) is exceeded, the Commission may require the society to submit a restructuring plan for the approval of the Commission, or to submit a transfer resolution to its membership: see s.36.

Subs. (19)
    transferable instrument. The definition of this expression appears to be wide enough to include instruments such as negotiable bonds, eurobonds, floating rate notes and certificates of deposits, all of which (together with time deposits) have featured prominently in wholesale borrowing undertaken by societies in recent years.

Proportion of liabilities to be in form of shares

8.—(1) Subject to subsection (2) below, a building society shall secure that the amount of the principal of, and interest payable on, sums deposited with the society does not at any time exceed 50 per cent. of the aggregate of that amount and the principal value of, and interest payable on, shares in the society.

(2) The following liabilities shall be disregarded for the purposes of this section—

  (*a*) deposits of such descriptions as may be prescribed for those purposes by the Commission by order made with the consent of the Treasury,

  (*b*) deferred shares, and

(c) loans made to the society in accordance with an authority given by the Commission under section 33.

(3) In determining for the purposes of subsection (1) above the liabilities in respect of deposits of a building society with which another body corporate is associated there shall, subject to subsection (5) below, be attributed to the society, in accordance with aggregation rules made by the Commission with the consent of the Treasury under this subsection, the whole or part of the liabilities of whatever description of the associated body, as provided in the rules and subject to any exception provided in the rules.

(4) The power to make aggregation rules under subsection (3) above includes power to make—

(a) different rules for different circumstances,

(b) provision for liabilities of societies to be disregarded, and

(c) such supplementary, transitional and saving provision as appears to the Commission to be necessary or expedient.

(5) The Commission may, on the application of a building society, approve rules to be applied for the purposes of subsection (1) above for the attribution to the society of liabilities of bodies associated with the society; and so long as the rules continue to be approved by the Commission they, and not the aggregation rules in force under subsection (3) above, shall apply for the attribution of liabilities for the purposes of subsection (1) above.

(6) If a building society receives deposits in excess of the limit permitted under this section the powers conferred on the Commission by section 36 shall become exercisable in relation to the society, but exceeding the limit shall not affect the validity of transactions effected in excess of it.

(7) The power to make an order under subsection (2)(a) or rules under subsection (3) above is exercisable by statutory instrument which shall be subject to annulment in pursuance of a resolution of either House of Parliament.

DEFINITIONS
"associated body": ss.18(17) and 119(1).
"the Commission": ss.1 and 119(1).
"deferred shares": s.119(1).
"deposits" and "deposited": s.119(1).

GENERAL NOTE
As was explained in the note to the preceding section, the principal liabilities shown on the balance sheet of a building society will be (i) liabilities in respect of shares and (ii) liabilities in respect of loans and deposits. The present section is designed to ensure that, broadly speaking, liabilities falling within the second category should never exceed those falling within the first: see subs. (1) (but note the liabilities that fall to be disregarded under subs. (2)). The purpose of imposing that requirement is to ensure that building societies remain recognisable as mutual institutions, with no less than half their funds being subscribed by their members in the form of shares. That requirement is a new one, although it is thought that the 1962 Act indirectly achieved the same result by the borrowing-to-lending ratio specified in s.39(2) (*viz.* the requirement that the total amount received by a society by way of deposits and loans should not at any time exceed two-thirds of the amount for the time being secured to the society by mortgages from its members): see *Official Report*, House of Commons, Standing Committee A, January 28, 1986, col. 89. Compare also the provisions of para. 2 of the Schedule to the Building Societies (Designation for Trustee Investment) Regulations 1972, whereby 50 per cent. of a society's liabilities had to be in the form of shares before the society could qualify for "trustee status". Since, for the time being, the proportion of a society's funds which can be raised from non-retail sources is limited to 20 per cent. (see s.7(3) and (15) above) it is to be expected that, in practice, societies will continue to raise substantially more than 50 per cent. of their funds by way of shares, with the bulk of those shares being issued to individual savers.

Subs. (2)
   deferred shares. These are to be defined by statutory instrument: see s.119(1). The definition, presumably, will be broadly similar to that embodied in the Building Societies (Authorisation) Regulations 1981, Sched. 1, Part II, para. 2.

Subss. (3)–(5)
   Cf. s.7(10)–(13) and the notes thereto.

Subs. (6)
   Cf. s.7(18) and the notes thereto.

Initial authorisation to raise funds and borrow money

   9.—(1) Except to the extent permitted by subsection (3) below, a building society shall not raise money from members or accept deposits of money unless there is in force an authorisation of the Commission granted under this section or treated as granted under this section by any provisions of this Act.
   (2) Authorisation under this section shall, if granted, be granted unconditionally or subject to conditions as provided by subsection (4) or (5) below.
   (3) Authorisation is not required for—
   (*a*) the acceptance of payments by way of subscription for deferred shares unless the aggregate of the payments exceeds the amount produced by multiplying the prescribed minimum for qualifying capital by the factor of $2\frac{1}{2}$ or such other factor as may be substituted for it by order of the Commission made with the consent of the Treasury;
   (*b*) the acceptance of payments for amounts due in respect of shares which represent interest on, or the repayment of, advances made to the holders of shares;
   (*c*) borrowing from a banking or finance company, or from a director or other officer of the society, if the society has obtained the consent in writing of the Commission; or
   (*d*) borrowing under section 33.
   (4) The Commission, on an application duly made for authorisation under this section, shall grant unconditional authorisation to the building society if it is satisfied that—
   (*a*) the society has qualifying capital of an amount which is not less than the prescribed minimum;
   (*b*) the chairman of the board of directors and any executive directors, the chief executive, the secretary and the managers (if any) are each fit and proper persons to hold their respective offices in the society;
   (*c*) the board of directors, with the chief executive and secretary, have the capacity and intention to direct the affairs of the society in accordance with the criteria of prudent management and, in so far as those criteria fell to be satisfied before the date of the application, have secured that they were satisfied; and
   (*d*) the investments of shareholders and depositors will be adequately protected without the imposition of conditions.
   (5) If the Commission, on an application so made, is not satisfied of the matters specified in subsection (4) above in relation to the society, it shall—
   (*a*) if those matters are or include the matters specified in paragraphs (*a*) and (*b*), refuse to grant authorisation;
   (*b*) in any other case, if it is satisfied that the imposition of conditions would secure the protection of the investments of shareholders and depositors, grant authorisation subject to such conditions to be

complied with by the society as the Commission thinks fit to impose to secure that purpose; or

(c) if not so satisfied, refuse to grant authorisation.

(6) The conditions that may be imposed under subsection (5) above on granting authorisation to a society may—

(a) relate to any activities of the society, whether or not those referred to in subsection (1) above; and

(b) require the society to take certain steps or to refrain from adopting a particular course of action or to restrict the scope of its business in a particular way.

(7) Without prejudice to the generality of subsection (6) above, conditions imposed under subsection (5) above may—

(a) impose limitations on the issue of shares, acceptance of deposits or the making of advances or other loans;

(b) require the society to take steps with regard to the conduct of the business of any subsidiary or associated body; and

(c) require the removal of any director or other officer.

(8) The provisions of Schedule 3 to this Act regulating—

(a) the making and determination of applications for authorisation,

(b) the furnishing of information or additional information in connection with such applications, and

(c) the imposition of conditions of authorisation,

apply in relation to authorisation under this section.

(9) Conditions imposed under subsection (5) above—

(a) may be varied from time to time (and notwithstanding any pending appeal) by agreement between the Commission and the society; and

(b) may be revoked at any time by the Commission if it is satisfied that the investments of shareholders and depositors will be adequately protected without the conditions;

but paragraph (b) above is without prejudice to the power of the Commission, under Part VI, to impose other conditions.

(10) On granting authorisation to a building society under this section the Commission shall inform the central office of the fact and the central office shall record that fact, and the date on which the authorisation was granted, in the public file of the society.

(11) If, in contravention of subsection (1) above, a building society raises money from members or accepts deposits of money, then—

(a) the society shall be liable on conviction on indictment or on summary conviction to a fine not exceeding, on summary conviction, the statutory maximum; and

(b) any officer of the society who is also guilty of the offence shall be liable—

(i) on conviction on indictment, to imprisonment for a term not exceeding two years or to a fine or both, and

(ii) on summary conviction, to a fine not exceeding the statutory maximum;

but such a contravention does not affect any civil liability arising in respect of the acceptance or of the money accepted.

(12) Failure by a society to comply with conditions imposed under this section on granting authorisation to the society shall render it liable, if other conditions are not imposed on it under Part VI, to have its authorisation revoked under that Part.

(13) For the purposes of this section, in relation to a building society—

"business" includes business the society proposes to carry on;

"the prescribed minimum", in relation to qualifying capital, is
£100,000 or such other sum as the Commission may specify by
order made with the consent of the Treasury;
"qualifying capital", in relation to a building society applying for
authorisation, means,

(*a*) the aggregate of the nominal value of the qualifying deferred
shares issued at the date of the application and the amount of the
reserves as shown in the last balance sheet of the society less any
accumulated deficit as so shown; or

(*b*) where there is no balance sheet of the society, the nominal
value of the qualifying deferred shares issued at the date of
application; and
"qualifying deferred shares" means deferred shares other than
deferred shares which, by virtue of regulations under section
45(5), are not included in capital resources aggregated with
reserves for the purposes of the first criterion in subsection (3)
of that section.

(14) Any power of the Commission to make an order under this section
is exercisable by statutory instrument which shall be subject to annulment
in pursuance of a resolution of either House of Parliament.

DEFINITIONS
"associated body": ss.18(17) and 119(1).
"central office": s.119(1).
"Commission": ss.1 and 119(1).
"criteria of prudent management": ss.45(3) and 119(1).
"deferred shares": s.119(1).
"deposits and depositors": s.119(1).
"executive": s.119(1).
"managers": s.119(1).
"members": s.119(1).
"officer": s.119(1).
"prescribed minimum": subs. (13).
"qualifying capital": subs. (13).
"public file": s.119(1).
"qualifying deferred shares": subs. (13).
"shares": s.119(1).
"statutory maximum": Criminal Justice Act 1982, s.74; Magistrates Court Act 1980, s.32.

GENERAL NOTE
In broad terms, the purpose of this section is to ensure that no building society will take
in money from the investing public unless it satisfies a minimum capital requirement, and is
prudently managed by fit and proper persons.
The section, and Parts I–III of Sched. 3, supersede the provisions for the authorisation of
building societies previously embodied in regs. 3, 4, 6, 7 and 13 of the Building Societies
(Authorisation) Regulations 1981 (S.I. 1981, No. 1488). Those Regulations were made to
give effect, for building societies, to the provisions of the EEC First Council Directive of
December 12, 1977, on the co-ordination of laws, regulations and administrative provisons
relating to the taking up and pursuit of the business of credit institutions (77/780/EEC). The
present section continues to give effect to those provisions insofar as they are relevant to the
initial grant of authorisation: the revocation of authorisations is now dealt with separately
in s.43 and Part IV of Sched. 3 (*c.f.* regs. 8 and 9 of the 1981 Regulations). The following
points of difference should be noted between the present section and the corresponding
provisions of the 1981 Regulations:
(i) A minimum capital requirement of £100,000 is now applicable to all societies seeking
authorisation: see subss. (4)(*a*) and (13) (and compare the 1981 Regulations, Sched. 1, Part
I, which, in most cases, specified a minimum of £50,000).
(ii) Reg. 7(*b*) of the 1981 Regulations required merely that the business of the society
should be effectively directed by individuals who were at least two in number and were "of
sufficiently good repute and sufficient experience to perform their duties." The requirements
of subs. (4)(*b*) and (*c*) of the present section are noticeably more stringent. Para. (*b*)
requires, in effect, that the chairman of the board and all persons holding senior management

positions in the society should be "fit and proper persons" to hold their respective offices; para. (*c*) requires that all the society's directors, and its chief executive and secretary should have the capacity and intention to direct the affairs of the society in accordance with the far-reaching criteria of prudent management set out in s.45(3).

(iii) Under the 1981 Regulations, authorisation could either be granted unconditionally or refused altogether. It could not be granted subject to conditions. Subs. (5) of the present section now empowers the Commission, in certain circumstances, to impose conditions on the grant of authorisation. Note, however, that the power to make a conditional grant of authorisation will not be exercisable where the requirements of subs. (4)(*a*) or (*b*) are not satisfied: in such a case, the Commission is required to refuse the grant of authorisation.

Subs. (1)
   treated as granted under this section by any provisions of this Act. Note in particular the provisions of Sched. 20, para. 6(1) whereby a society previously authorised under the 1981 Regulations (or their Northern Ireland equivalent) is to be treated as authorised under the present Act. This applies whether or not the society would satisfy the more stringent requirements of subs. (4) above.

Subss. (3) (4) and (13)
   deferred shares. For the purpose of the Act generally, the expression "deferred shares" is to be defined by statutory instrument: see s.119(1). Note, however, that for the purposes of subs. (4)(*a*), deferred shares will count towards the society's "qualifying capital" only if they are "qualifying deferred shares" within the meaning of subs. (13) : see the definition of "qualifying capital" contained in that subsection.
   Procedure and rights of appeal: As to the procedure to be followed in applications under this section, see Sched. 3, Parts II and III. As to a society's right to appeal against a refusal to grant authorisation, or against the imposition of conditions on a grant of authorisation, see ss.46–49.

PART III

ADVANCES, LOANS AND OTHER ASSETS

Class 1 advances and class 2 advances secured on land

Advances secured on land

   10.—(1) A building society may make advances to members (in this Act referred to as "advances secured on land") secured by—
   (*a*) a mortgage of a legal estate or, as provided under subsection (6) below, an equitable interest in land in England and Wales or Northern Ireland, or
   (*b*) a heritable security over land in Scotland,
and for that purpose may (in England and Wales or Northern Ireland) hold land with the right of foreclosure.
   (2) Advances secured on land may, in accordance with sections 11 and 12—
   (*a*) be fully or partly secured by a mortgage of the legal estate or equitable interest in land in England and Wales or Northern Ireland, or
   (*b*) be fully secured by a heritable security over land in Scotland,
and in this Part "the basic security" means the security constituted by the legal estate in or heritable security over the land or, in a case where an equitable interest in land in England and Wales or Northern Ireland is or is also taken as security by virtue of this section, that constituted by that security or, as the case may be, the combined securities; and a reference to the land which is to secure an advance or on which an advance is secured is a reference to the estate or interest or the heritable security which constitutes or will constitute the basic security.

(3) The power to make an advance secured on land includes power, subject to the restriction imposed by subsection (4) below, to make, as a separate advance, an advance which is to be applied in or towards payment of the deposit for the purchase of the land (in this Part referred to as "an advance for a deposit for the purchase of land.")

(4) The restriction referred to is that an advance for a deposit for the purchase of land must not exceed 10 per cent. of the total amount to be paid for the purchase of the land.

(5) An advance shall be treated for the purposes of this Act as secured by a mortgage of a legal estate in registered land in England and Wales or Northern Ireland notwithstanding that the advance is made before the borrower is registered as proprietor of the estate.

(6) A building society may advance money on the security of an equitable interest in land in England and Wales or Northern Ireland if the equitable interest is an equitable interest in land of a description and is created in circumstances prescribed in an order made by the Commission with the consent of the Treasury under this subsection and any conditions prescribed in the order are complied with.

(7) Any powers conferred on building societies by an order under subsection (6) above may be conferred on building societies of a description specified in the order or all building societies other than those of a description so specified.

(8) The power to make an order under subsection (6) above includes power—

    (*a*) to prescribe the circumstances in which the power conferred by section 17(10) on building societies of the description specified therein is to be available to them; and

    (*b*) to make such incidental, supplementary and transitional provision as the Commission considers necessary or expedient.

(9) An instrument containing an order under subsection (6) above shall be subject to annulment in pursuance of a resolution of either House of Parliament.

(10) The power to make advances secured on land includes power to make them on terms that include provision as respects the capital element in the mortgage debt (with or without similar provision as respects the interest element)—

    (*a*) that the amount due to the society may be adjusted from time to time by reference to such public index of prices other than housing prices as is specified in the mortgage;

    (*b*) that the amount due to the society may be adjusted from time to time by reference to such public index of housing prices as is specified in the mortgage;

    (*c*) that the amount due to the society at any time shall be determined by reference to a share, specified or referred to in the mortgage, in the open market value of the property at that time;

and, in cases where the amount due to the society in respect of capital exceeds the amount advanced, references in this Act to the repayment of an advance include references to payment of the excess.

(11) Advances secured on land shall be classified for the purposes of the requirements of this Part for the structure of commercial assets into—

    (*a*) class 1 advances, and

    (*b*) class 2 advances;

and in this Act "advances fully secured on land" means advances which are class 1 or class 2 advances, and any reference to "fully secured" shall be construed accordingly.

(12) Nothing in this section or section 11 or 12 is to be taken as precluding a society from taking other security for an advance secured on

land than such security as is required for an advance to be a class 1 or a class 2 advance under those sections; but the value of the other security shall be disregarded for the purpose of classifying the advance as a class 1 or a class 2 advance.

DEFINITIONS

"advance for a deposit for the purchase of land": subs. (3).
"advances fully secured on land": subs. (11) and s.119(1).
"advances secured on land": subs. (1) and s.119(1).
"basic security": subs. (2).
"class 1 advances": s.11(2).
"class 2 advances": s.11(4).
"heritable security": s.119(1).
"members": s.119(1).
"mortgage": s.119(1).
"mortgage debt": ss.11(14) and 119(1).

GENERAL NOTE

This section empowers building societies to make advances to their members secured on land situated within the United Kingdom. In any case where the land is for the member's residential use, the making of the advance will fall within the society's primary purpose specified in s.5 Note, however, that the present section covers cases in which the land securing the advance is not for the residential use of the borrowing member: such cases will accordingly fall outside the primary purpose stated in s.5 (*cf.* the notes to that section and s.11 below).

Subs. (11) provides that advances secured on land shall be classified either as class 1 advances or as class 2 advances. These two categories are defined in detail in s.11, and the significance of the distinction is discussed in the notes to that section. Broadly speaking, the policy of the Act is to ensure that first mortgages of residential property (class 1 advances) account for no less than 90 per cent. of a society's total commercial assets (*i.e.* its assets other than fixed and liquid assets).

Subss. (1)–(4)

Advances secured on land. S.1 of the 1962 Act empowered building societies to make advances "upon security by way of mortgage of freehold or leasehold estate." The Act contained no express requirement that those estates should be legal estates, and it was assumed in practice that "equitable estates" were included as well: see Wurtzburg & Mills, *Building Society Law* (14th Ed.), pp.144–5. (It is true that, since the property legislation of 1925, the word "estate" usually connotes a legal estate rather than an equitable interest. Note, however, that s.1(1) of the 1962 Act derives from s.13 of the Building Societies Act 1874. There is no reason why, in 1874, the word "estate" should have been limited to legal estates.) However, to constitute an "advance secured on land" for the purposes of this Act, an advance must generally be secured (though not necessarily fully secured) by a mortgage of a legal estate: see subss. (1) and (2). A mortgage of an equitable interest will qualify only where the interest is of a kind prescribed by order made under subs. (6). The reason for limiting the range of equitable interests that can be taken as security for class 1 and class 2 advances is, it seems, that societies might otherwise have sought to make such advances on the security of interests which are manifestly unsuitable for the purpose of mortgage lending, *e.g.* a right to enforce a restrictive covenant, or a mere option to purchase (see *Official Report*, House of Commons, Standing Committee A, January 28, 1986, cols. 96–8; *sed quaere*). It should be noted, however, that subs. (3) provides that the power to make an advance secured on land includes power to make a separate advance for the payment of the deposit for the purchase of the land. Such an advance will almost invariably be made before the borrower has acquired any legal estate in the land; so, if the advance is to be secured at all, it can be secured only by such equitable interest in the land as the borrower may acquire under his contract of purchase. Although subs. (3) states that the power to make such an advance is included in the power to make advances secured in land, it is in reality a separate power to make an advance which *is to be* secured on land: *cf.* the concluding words of s.11(9).

The 10 per cent. limit imposed by subs. (4) is not, of course, a limit on the size of the deposit that can be paid, but on the size of the advance that can be applied towards its payment.

Subs. (5)

This subsection is designed to deal with a technical problem that could otherwise have arisen in the common case where a building society advance is used to finance the purchase of registered land. In such a case, the mortgage deed will be executed, and the advance made, at the date when the purchase is completed. The purchaser, however, will not have the legal estate vested in him until the date (usually several weeks after completion) when he is registered as proprietor of the land at H.M. Land Registry: see the Land Registration Act 1925, ss.19(1), 22(1) and 69(1). By virtue of the present subsection, the society's advance will nevertheless be treated as if it were secured by a mortgage of a legal estate immediately upon completion of the purchase. It will thus qualify from the outset as an "advance secured on land" within the meaning of subs.(1).

Subss. (6)–(9)

Until an order is made under subs. (6), the transitional provisions embodied in Sched. 20, para. 12 will empower building societies to make advances in connection with certain forms of shared ownership schemes (*e.g.* where the purchaser buys outright a defined beneficial share in the property, but leases the remaining share from the vendor, with the right subsequently to purchase that share from the vendor in specified stages). However, the provisions of para. 12 are limited to schemes where some form of lease is granted to the purchaser and where the advance is secured on an equitable interest in land "in addition to a mortgage of the freehold or leasehold estate." It seems likely that any order made under subs. (6) will extend more widely than this, and will, for example, enable building societies to advance money for worthwhile development projects (such as the construction of sheltered accommodation for the elderly) notwithstanding that the advance is secured solely on an equitable interest arising under a contract for the purchase of the land in question. *Cf. Hansard,* H.L. Vol. 477, cols. 1118–19.

Subs. (10)

Paras. (*a*) and (*b*) make provision for index-linked mortgages. The 1962 Act made no express reference to such mortgages; but there is no objection to them in principle under the general law, and it was held in *Nationwide Building Society* v. *Registry of Friendly Societies* [1983] 1 W.L.R. 1226 that there was nothing in the 1962 Act which prevented building societies from entering into such mortgages, provided that the terms of the mortgage specified that, in the event of a downward movement in the index, the sum repaid by the borrower should be no less than the amount originally advanced. It will be noted that no such requirement is embodied in the present subsection. The reference in para. (*b*) to a "public index of housing prices" presumably excludes an index maintained by one building society for the purposes of its own advances. In a case where it is proposed to link a mortgage to an index of housing prices, both the borrower and the society will need to take care to ensure that the index chosen is appropriate to the type of property to be taken as security: the borrower will be concerned to ensure that, if the mortgaged property is situated in a part of the country where the house market is depressed, the mortgage is not linked to housing prices in an area where the market is buoyant; and the society will be concerned to prevent the converse situation arising. Quite apart from that, the society may not find it easy to raise funds on terms which provide a suitable match with loans linked to housing prices.

Para. (*c*) makes provision for so-called "equity mortgages" (that is, mortgages where the mortgage debt is not quantified in cash terms but is defined by reference to the value of a specified share in the property). It is thought that there is some room for doubt as to the validity of such mortgages under the general law (*cf. Samuel* v. *Jarrah Timber and Wood Paving Corp.* [1904] A.C. 323). However, it is now clear that building societies (if no one else) have power to enter into such mortgages.

Note that advances falling within para. (*a*) may be class 1 advances whereas advances falling within paras. (*b*) and (*c*) can only be class 2 advances: see s.11(2) (closing words).

Subs. (11)

advances fully secured on land. This definition is puzzling since it is perfectly clear that class 2 advances do not have to be fully secured on land: see s.11(4)(*c*) and *cf.* subs. (2)(*a*) above.

Class 1 and class 2 advances

11.—(1) The provisions of this section and section 12 define what is a class 1 advance and what is a class 2 advance for the purpose of the requirements of this Part for the structure of commercial assets and when an advance may, for those purposes, be treated partly as a class 1 advance and partly as a class 2 advance.

(2) Class 1 advances are advances as to which the society when it makes the advance is satisfied that the advance is an advance secured on land and that—

    (*a*) the borrower is an individual;

    (*b*) the land is for the residential use of the borrower or a dependant of his of a prescribed description;

    (*c*) the amount advanced will not exceed the value of the basic security (after deducting from that value any mortgage debt of the borrower to the society outstanding under a mortgage of the land); and

    (*d*) subject to subsection (5) below, no other mortgage of the land which is to secure the advance is outstanding in favour of a person other than the society;

and which are not made on terms as respects the capital element of the mortgage debt authorised by section 10(10)(*b*) or (*c*).

(3) Subject to any order made under section 12(1), the requirement in subsection (2)(*b*) above shall be treated as satisfied if no less than 40 per cent. of the area of the land is used for residential purposes by the borrower or a dependant of his of a prescribed description.

(4) Class 2 advances are advances as to which the society when it makes the advance—

    (*a*) either is not satisfied that the requirements for the time being of subsection (2) above are fulfilled or is satisfied that any of them is not fulfilled, but

    (*b*) is satisfied that the advance is an advance secured on land, and

    (*c*) is satisfied, where the amount advanced will exceed the value of the basic security (after deducting from that value any mortgage debt of the borrower outstanding under a mortgage of the land), that the excess will be secured by the taking of security of a prescribed description in addition to the basic security, and

    (*d*) is satisfied that no, or no more than one, other mortgage of the land which is to secure the advance is outstanding in favour of a person other than the society.

(5) The requirement in subsection (2)(*d*) and (4)(*d*) above shall be treated as satisfied if the advance is made on terms that the other mortgage is redeemed or postponed to the basic security.

(6) An advance for a deposit for the purchase of land is also a class 1 or class 2 advance according as it is made with a view to the making of a class 1 or class 2 advance secured on the land.

(7) Advances which would be class 2, and not class 1, advances by reason only that the extent of the residential use of the land is not such as to satisfy the requirement in subsection (2)(*b*) above shall be treated as class 1 advances if and to the extent prescribed by an order under section 12(5).

(8) For the purposes of the requirements of this Part for the structure of commercial assets—

    (*a*) class 1 advances constitute class 1 assets, and

    (*b*) class 2 advances constitute class 2 assets,

and accordingly the aggregate amount of mortgage debts outstanding in respect of class 2 advances counts in accordance with section 20 towards the limit applicable to class 2 assets under that section.

(9) For the purposes of subsections (2) and (4) above, where a building society makes an advance by instalments, any reference to the time when the society makes the advance is a reference to the time when it pays the first of the instalments, disregarding for this purpose any instalment which is to be applied towards payment of the deposit in respect of the purchase of the land which is to secure the advance.

(10) Subject to subsection (11) below, any land to which a building society becomes absolutely entitled by foreclosure or by release or other extinguishment of a right of redemption—

(a) shall as soon as may be conveniently practicable be sold or converted into money; and

(b) shall, until the sale or conversion, constitute a class 1 asset if the advance secured on the land was a class 1 advance and a class 2 asset if it was a class 2 advance.

(11) Where a building society which has for the time being adopted the powers conferred by section 17 becomes entitled to land as mentioned in subsection (10) above, and the land is land that may be held under that section, then, if the society—

(a) elects to hold the land under that section, or

(b) without such an election, retains the land after the expiry of the period of twelve months immediately following the date on which it so becomes entitled to the land,

the society shall be taken to hold the land under that section.

(12) An election under subsection (11) above shall be made by resolution of the board of directors and shall be irrevocable.

(13) If a building society contravenes subsection (10) above the society shall be liable on summary conviction to a fine not exceeding level 5 on the standard scale and so shall any officer who is also guilty of the offence.

(14) For the purposes of this Act, the mortgage debt at any time, in relation to an advance secured on land, is the total amount outstanding at that time in respect of—

(a) the principal of the advance;

(b) interest on the advance; and

(c) any other sum which the borrower is obliged to pay the society under the terms of the advance.

(15) The reference in subsection (10) above to land to which a building society becomes absolutely entitled by foreclosure includes a reference to land which a building society has acquired by virtue of a decree of foreclosure under section 28 of the Conveyancing and Feudal Reform (Scotland) Act 1970.

DEFINITIONS

"advance for a deposit for the purchase of land": s.10(3).
"advance secured on land": ss.10(1) and 119(1).
"basic security": s.10(2).
"class 1 advance": subs.(2) and s.119(1).
"class 2 advance": subs.(4) and s.119(1).
"land which is to secure the advance": s.10(2).
"mortgage": s.119(1).
"mortgage debt": subs.(14) and s.119(1).
"prescribed" (in subs.(2)(b) and subs.(3)): s.12(1).
"prescribed" (in subs.(4)(c)): s.12(3).
"requirements for the structure of commercial assets": s.20.
"residential use": c.f. subs.(3) and s.12(1).
"standard scale": Criminal Justice Act 1982, s.37.

GENERAL NOTE

As is apparent from s.10(11) above, advances secured on land are to be classified as class 1 advances or class 2 advances. The purpose of the present section is to state how the distinction is to be drawn.

It is perhaps worth mentioning that (subject to the point made in the next paragraph) an advance will not fall within the scope of this section *unless* it is an advance secured on land: see the opening words of subs.(2) and subs.(4)(b). The advance must, therefore, be secured on land in the United Kingdom (see the definition of "advances secured on land" in s.10(1)). It is true that advances made on the security of foreign land may be classified as class 1 or class 2 advances: but, if so classified, they will be classified under the provisions of the relevant enabling order, not under the provisions of this section: see s.14(1)(c).

Class 1 and class 2 advances are defined in subs. (2) and subs. (4) respectively. Both definitions include the requirement that the society making the advance should be "satisfied", *inter alia*, that the advance is an advance secured on land (see the opening words of subs.(2) and subs. (4)(*b*)). The definitions have been framed in that way to cover cases where "a society and a borrower enter into a loan contract in good faith but which later turns out to be invalid because of defective title or otherwise" (see *Official Report*, House of Commons, Standing Committee A, January 30, 1986, col. 123).

As appears from subs. (1), the distinction between class 1 and class 2 advances is primarily relevant to the requirements for the structure of a society's commercial assets (*viz.* its assets other than fixed and liquid assets). For those purposes, a society's commercial assets are categorised as class 1 assets, class 2 assets and class 3 assets. Class 1 advances qualify as class 1 assets and class 2 advances qualify as class 2 assets: see subs. (8). S.20 requires a society's class 2 assets (or, if it has class 3 assets, the aggregate of its class 2 assets and class 3 assets) to be limited to a fixed percentage (initially 10 per cent.) of its total commercial assets. There is, however, no limit on the percentage of a society's total commercial assets which can be in the form of class 1 assets. In fact class 1 and class 2 advances (whether classified under this section or under any order made under s.14) constitute the only significant categories of class 1 and 2 assets. The broad effect, therefore, is that (given the percentages currently specified in s.20) class 1 advances must account for no less than 90 per cent. of a society's total commercial assets whereas class 2 advances and class 3 assets (if any) must account for no more than 10 per cent. of its total commercial assets.

It can be seen, therefore, that class 1 advances will represent the great bulk of a society's lending. With that in mind, the distinction between class 1 and class 2 advances has been drawn with a view to achieving two distinct objectives. The first is to preserve the established character of building societies as lending institutions by ensuring that class 1 advances are typical of the type of mortgage lending traditionally undertaken by the building society movement; the second objective is to ensure that the riskier forms of secured lending are excluded from class 1 and placed in class 2. The first objective is reflected in subs. (2)(*a*) and (*b*), by which class 1 advances are required to be made to borrowers who are individuals (as opposed to corporate bodies) and to be secured on land which is for the residential use of the borrower or a qualifying dependant of his. Both those requirements mirror traditional features of building society lending; indeed, as at July 1984, it appears that over 99 per cent. of building society advances were secured on domestic property, with loans to corporate bodies accounting for a very small proportion of lending (see the Green Paper, para. 3.02). The second objective is reflected by the following:

(1) By subs. (2)(*c*), class 1 advances (including further advances) are required to be fully secured on the mortgaged property. By contrast, subs. (4)(*c*) permits the amount of a class 2 advance (or further advance) to exceed the value of the mortgaged property, provided that the excess is secured by taking additional security of a description prescribed by order made under s.12(3).

(2) Broadly speaking, class 1 advances must be secured by a first mortgage whereas class 2 advances may be secured by a second mortgage. To put the point more exactly, subs. (2)(*d*) provides that a class 1 advance cannot be made at a time when a prior mortgage is outstanding on the land which is to secure the advance, unless either (i) the prior mortgage is redeemed, or else postponed to the society's security (see subs. (5)) or (ii) the prior mortgage is in favour of the society making the advance. (The latter qualification may, incidentally, be compared to the similar one embodied in s.32(1) of the 1962 Act.) By contrast, subs. (4)(*d*) permits a class 2 advance to be made in circumstances where one prior mortgage (other than a mortgage which is in favour of the society, or which is to be redeemed or postponed) is outstanding on the land. (Note that registered local land charges are disregarded when determining for the purposes of subs.(2)(*d*) or (4)(*d*) whether land is subject to a prior mortgage: see s.12(*a*).) It may be added that the power to make advances on the security of a second mortgage is new: under the 1962 Act, such advances (subject to certain limited exceptions) were illegal: see s.32 of that Act.

(3) The effect of the concluding words of subs. (2) is that advances secured by mortgages linked to a public index of housing prices (as to which see s.10(10)(*b*)) and advances made under "equity mortgages" (as to which, see s.10(10)(*c*)) are both relegated to class 2. By contrast, advances secured by mortgages linked to a public index of prices *other* than housing prices (dealt with in s.10(10)(*a*)) are capable of constituting class 1 advances. The reason for the difference in treatment is, no doubt, that the type of mortgage described in s.10(10)(*a*) is more familiar, and may be less risky, than the types of mortgage described in s.10(10)(*b*) and (*c*).

As has been noted above, advances to corporate bodies are excluded from class 1 and are hence capable only of constituting class 2 advances. In this respect, the distinction between class 1 and class 2 advances recalls the provisions of the 1962 Act, under which advances to corporate bodies were classified as "special advances". As such, they were made subject to the percentage restrictions imposed by that Act on special advance lending (see ss.21 and 22–24 of the 1962 Act). In one important respect, however, the present distinction between class 1 and class 2 advances differs markedly from the provisions of the 1962 Act relating to special advances. By s.21(1)(*b*) and (*c*) of that Act, any advance to an individual which took his indebtedness to the society above a specified figure (latterly £60,000) was categorised as a special advance. Under the present section, by contrast, an advance may qualify as a class 1 advance however large the sum lent.

All building societies are empowered to make class 1 and class 2 advances secured on land in the United Kingdom; the power to make class 2 advances on such land is not limited to societies with a qualifying asset holding.

Subs. (3)

This subsection will allow advances to qualify as class 1 even though the borrower (or a dependant of his) is using only 40 per cent. of the property for residential purposes. The choice of the 40 per cent. figure was explained by the Economic Secretary to the Treasury (Mr. Ian Stewart) in the following terms: "if we said 50%, it would be impossible to divide a house exactly in two if there were any common parts of the building, because they would detract from the proportion held by both the families in the same house. Therefore, we chose a figure which meant that, if each had 40%, 20% could be common staircase, kitchens or whatever." (See *Official Report*, House of Commons, Standing Committee A, January 30, 1986, col. 125.) However, the assumption that a borrower does not use a shared kitchen (or indeed a common staircase) "for residential purposes" seems questionable. The potential problems generated by this subsection (*e.g.* whether a garden, or a loft or garage can be said to be used "for residential purposes") may in practice be resolved by order made by the Commission under s.12(1). But establishments such as boarding houses and private hotels would seem unlikely on any footing to meet the 40 per cent. requirement specified in this subsection. (Such cases may, however, be dealt with under subs.(7): see the note on that subsection below.)

Subs. (6)

If the purchase is not completed within six months of the making of an advance for the deposit, the advance will cease to be a class 1 or (as the case may be) a class 2 advance, and will be treated as a loan made under s.16: see s.16(2) and (11). This provision may be troublesome for societies without a qualifying asset holding, who are not empowered to make loans under s.16: see ss.16(12) and 118, and *cf.* the notes to s.16(2) and (9).

Subs. (7)

Subs.(1) contemplates that an advance may be treated partly as a class 1 advance and partly as a class 2 advance. It appears that the only case in which a single advance will be split between the two classes is the case covered by the present subsection, *viz.* where (i) an advance fails to qualify as class 1 solely because the borrower (or a dependant of his) is using less than 40 per cent. of the mortgaged property for residential purposes (see subs.(2)(*b*) and (3)) but (ii) an order made under s.12(5) nevertheless requires part of the advance to be treated as a class 1 advance.

Subs. (9)

Where the advance is payable by instalments, care should be taken to ensure that the mortgage imposes an obligation on the society to pay all the instalments. Otherwise, a risk will arise that later instalments will lose priority to an intervening incumbrance of which the society receives express notice. See the Law of Property Act 1925, s.94 and *c.f.* Wurtzburg and Mills, *Building Society Law* (14th Ed.), p.153. It appears to follow from the present subsection that, even if subsequent instalments do lose priority to an intervening incumbrance, the entire advance will nevertheless still qualify as a class 1 advance.

Subss. (10)–(13)

These subsections make provision for the case in which a society becomes absolutely entitled to the mortgaged property by reason of the borrower losing the right to redeem. The commonest case in which this situation will arise is where the society obtains a foreclosure order absolute; but the right to redeem could also be extinguished by limitation or, of course, by express agreement between the society and the borrower. In any such case, subs.(10) imposes a primary duty (which is backed by the criminal sanction imposed by subs.(13)) to sell the land, or otherwise convert it into money, as soon as conveniently practicable. Pending sale or conversion, the land will fall into the same asset category as the advance which was secured on it: see subs.(10)(*b*). As an alternative to sale or conversion, a society which has adopted the power conferred by s.17 to hold land for residential purposes may elect to retain the land under that section (and in default of an election will be taken to hold the land under that section if it retains the land for more than 12 months after becoming absolutely entitled to it): see subs.(11). The option of holding the land under s.17 will, however, generally be available only to the larger societies, since societies without a qualifying asset holding (*i.e.* societies whose commercial assets are less than £100 million: see s.118) can avail themselves of the powers conferred by s.17 only in the limited circumstances specified in s.17(10). It may be noted that subs.(10) and (13) are based on s.109 of the 1962 Act.

Subs. (11)
Level 5. Currently £2,000.

Subs. (14)
It will be noted that, by virtue of para. (*c*), miscellaneous debits charged to the borrower's account under the terms of the mortgage (*e.g.* insurance premiums, costs etc.) will fall within the definition of the mortgage debt contained in this subsection.

Class 1 and class 2 advances: supplementary provisions

12.—(1) The Commission, by order in a statutory instrument, may as respects class 1 advances—
  (*a*) specify the circumstances in which land is for a person's residential use,
  (*b*) specify who are to be a person's dependants, and
  (*c*) make such other incidental and supplementary and such transitional provision as the Commission considers necessary or expedient,
for the purposes of section 11(2); and in that subsection "prescribed" means prescribed in an order under this subsection.

(2) Without prejudice to the generality of subsection (1)(*c*) above, an order may prescribe evidence on which a building society is to be entitled to be satisfied (in the absence of evidence to the contrary) that the requirements of section 11(2) are fulfilled as respects an advance secured on land.

(3) The Commission, by order in a statutory instrument, may as respects class 2 advances—
  (*a*) specify descriptions of security falling within this subsection which, for the purposes of paragraph (*c*) of section 11(4), may be taken for class 2 advances in addition to the basic security; and
  (*b*) make such other incidental or supplementary and such transitional provision as it considers necessary or expedient for the purposes of paragraph (*c*) or (*d*) of that subsection;
and in that subsection "prescribed" means prescribed in an order under this subsection.

(4) The descriptions of additional security which fall within subsection (3)(*a*) above are guarantees, indemnities or other contractual promises made by virtue of, or by a public body established by or under, any enactment for the time being in force.

(5) The Commission, by order in a statutory instrument, may, as respects advances to be secured on land which is to any extent to be used for the residential use of borrowers or persons who are dependants of theirs for the purposes of section 11(2)—
  (*a*) require so much of the amount to be advanced as is determined by or under the order to be treated as a class 1 advance;
  (*b*) specify the circumstances in which and the conditions subject to which advances are to be so treated; and

(*c*) make such incidental, supplementary and transitional provision as the Commission considers necessary or expedient.

(6) The Commission shall not make an order under this section, except with the consent of the Treasury.

(7) An instrument containing an order under this section shall be subject to annulment in pursuance of a resolution of either House of Parliament.

(8) For the purpose of facilitating the repayment to a building society of a class 1 advance or a class 2 advance, the society may make to the borrower, by way of addition to the advance, a further advance of or towards the cost of a single premium payable in respect of an appropriate policy of life assurance; and a sum added to an advance under this subsection shall be treated as not forming part of the advance for the purpose of determining whether the requirements of section 11(2) or (4) are satisfied with respect to the advance.

(9) Where an advance secured on land in England and Wales or Northern Ireland is made, then, for the purpose of determining whether the land is subject to a prior mortgage for the purposes of section 11(2)(*d*) or (4)(*d*) above, any outstanding charge over the land which is registered—

(*a*) in the case of land in England and Wales, in the appropriate local land charges register, and

(*b*) in the case of land in Northern Ireland, in the statutory charges register under section 87 of, and Schedule 11 to, the Land Registration Act (Northern Ireland) 1970,

shall be disregarded.

(10) If at any time when a class 1 advance or a class 2 advance secured on land is outstanding the building society—

(*a*) is satisfied on a revaluation that the value of the basic security has changed,

(*b*) is satisfied that so much of the mortgage debt as represents the principal of the advance has changed,

(*c*) is satisfied on notice given to it by the borrower that there has been a change in the use of the land, or

(*d*) agrees to a change in the relative priority of the mortgage on which the advance is secured,

and is satisfied that the change is such that, if it were to make an advance equal to the mortgage debt at that time, the advance would instead be a class 2 advance or a class 1 advance, as the case may be, the advance shall be reclassified as from that time.

(11) Nothing in subsection (10) above requires a building society to revalue its securities from time to time.

(12) Every building society shall establish and maintain a system to ensure the safe custody of all documents relating to property mortgaged to the society.

(13) In this section "appropriate policy of life assurance", with reference to an advance, means a policy of insurance which satisfies the following requirements, that is to say—

(*a*) the life assured is that of the person to whom the advance is made or his spouse, his son or his daughter, and

(*b*) it provides, in the event of the death, before the advance has been repaid, of the person on whose life the policy is effected, for payment of a sum not exceeding the amount sufficient to defray the sums which are, at and after the time of the death, payable to the society in respect of the advance and any addition made in respect of the premium.

DEFINITIONS
"advance secured on land": ss.10(1) and 119(1).
"appropriate policy of life assurance": subs.(13).
"basic security": s.10(2).
"class 1 advances": ss.11(2) and 119(1).
"class 2 advances": ss.11(4) and 119(1).
"the Commission": ss.1 and 119(1).
"mortgage": s.119(1).
"mortgage debt": ss.11(14) and 119(1).

GENERAL NOTES
Subs. (1)
See s.11(2)(*b*) and (3).

Subs. (2)
This subsection empowers the Commission to prescribe evidence on which a society is entitled to be satisfied (in the absence of evidence to the contrary) that an advance secured on land meets the requirements for class 1 advances set out in s.11(2). It will be noted that there is no corresponding provision empowering the Commission to specify the circumstances in which a society is entitled to be satisfied that the requirements for class 2 advances set out in s.11(4) are fulfilled.

Subss. (3) and (4)
See s.11(4)(*c*). Subs. (4) would, it seems, cover indemnities given to building societies by local authorities under s.442 of the Housing Act 1985 (or the equivalent Scottish or Northern Irish provisions).

Subs. (5)
See s.11(7).

Subss. (8) and (13)
The effect of these provisions is to enable a society to advance an additional sum to the borrower to meet, or contribute to, the cost of a single premium mortgage protection policy. The additional sum so advanced will not affect the classification of the basic advance as a class 1 or class 2 advance. These provisions may be compared with s.33 of the 1962 Act.

Subs. (9)
Broadly speaking, s.11(2)(*d*) provides that a class 1 advance cannot be made on the security of land which is subject to any prior mortgage, whereas s.11(4)(*d*) provides that a class 2 advance cannot be made on the security of land which is subject to more than one prior mortgage. The present subsection provides that, in determining for the purposes of either subsection whether land is subject to a prior mortgage, local land charges registered in the appropriate register are to be disregarded. Curiously, no provision is made for disregarding unregistered local land charges. (Note in this connection that failure to register a local land charge does not render it unenforceable, so it would seem difficult to disregard such a charge under the general law. See Local Land Charges Act 1975, s.10 and note the provisions for compensation set out in that section. *Cf.* also, *Re Abbots Park Estate* (No. 2) [1972] 1 W.L.R. 1597.)

Subss. (10) and (11)
S.11(2) and (4) make provision for an advance to be classified as a class 1 or class 2 advance at the time when the advance is made. Clearly, however, circumstances may change thereafter, and such changes may have the effect that a class 2 advance comes to satisfy the requirements for a class 1 advance, or conversely that a class 1 advance ceases to satisfy those requirements. Subs. (10) requires building societies in certain cases to reclassify advances to reflect these changes. Paras. (*a*) and (*b*) relate to the requirement (set out in s.11(2)(*c*)) that a class 1 advance must be fully secured. Para. (*a*) makes provision for reclassification in cases where a revaluation of the mortgaged property reveals that an advance has become, or has ceased to be, fully secured; para. (*b*) deals with the case where an advance has become, or has ceased to be, so secured by reason of a reduction or (as the case may be) an increase in the outstanding balance of capital. As subs. (11) makes clear, however, a society is not obliged for these purposes to undertake periodic revaluations of its securities. Para. (*c*) relates to the requirement (set out in s.11(2)(*b*) and (3)) that a class 1 advance must be secured on land which is for the residential use of the borrower or a dependant of his; it makes provision for reclassification in cases where the borrower notifies

the society of a change in the use of the property which has the effect that the residential user requirement has become, or has ceased to be, satisfied. Finally, para. (*d*) relates to the requirement (set out in s.11(2)(*d*)) that a class 1 advance must (broadly speaking) be secured by a first mortgage; it makes provision for reclassification where the society agrees to a change in the priority of the mortgage on which the advance is secured. Curiously, para. (*d*) does not seem apt to cover cases where the society's mortgage is promoted to a first mortgage by the redemption of a prior charge, a process which does not require, and will usually not involve, any agreement on the part of the society.

Subs. (12)
Note that the rules of a society must provide for the custody of the mortgage deeds and other securities belonging to the society: see Sched. 2, para. 3(4). Furthermore, the auditor's report must deal with the system of safe custody of documents maintained under s.12(12): see s.82(2)(*c*).

Security for advances: valuation and supplementary and related provisions

13.—(1) It shall be the duty of every director of a building society to satisfy himself that the arrangements made for assessing the adequacy of the security for any advance to be fully secured on land which is to be made by the society are such as may reasonably be expected to ensure that—

(*a*) an assessment will be made on the occasion of each advance whether or not any previous assessment was made with a view to further advances or re-advances;

(*b*) each assessment will be made by a person holding office in or employed by the society who is competent to make the assessment and is not disqualified under this section from making it;

(*c*) each person making the assessment will have furnished to him a written report on the value of the land and any factors likely materially to affect its value made by a person who is competent to value, and is not disqualified under this section from making a report on, the land in question;

but the arrangements need not require each report to be made with a view to a particular assessment so long as it is adequate for the purpose of making the assessment.

(2) In relation to any land which is to secure an advance, the following persons are disqualified from making a report on its value, that is to say—

(*a*) the directors and any other officer or employee of the society who makes assessments of the adequacy of securities for advances secured on land or who authorises the making of such advances;

(*b*) where the society has made, or undertaken to make, to any person a payment for introducing to it an applicant for the advance, that person;

(*c*) where the advance is to be made following a disposition of the land, any person having a financial interest in the disposition of the land and any director, other officer or employee of his or of an associated employer; and

(*d*) where the advance is to be made following a disposition of the land, any person receiving a commission for introducing the parties to the transaction involving the disposition and any director, other officer or employee of his.

(3) In relation to any land which is to secure an advance where the advance is to be made following a disposition of the land, the following persons are disqualified from making an assessment of the security or authorising the making of the advance, that is to say—

(*a*) any person, other than the building society making the advance, having a financial interest in the disposition of the land and any

director, other officer or employee of his or of an associated employer; and
   (b) any person receiving a commission for introducing the parties to the transaction involving the disposition and any director, other officer or employee of his.
(4) Any person who, being disqualified from doing so—
   (a) makes a report on any land which is to secure an advance,
   (b) makes an assessment of the adequacy of the security for an advance, or
   (c) authorises the making of an advance,
and in the case of a person making a report does so knowing or having reason to believe that the report will be used or is likely to be used for the purposes of the advance, shall be liable on summary conviction to a fine not exceeding level 4 on the standard scale.

(5) For the purposes of this section, any two employers are associated if one is a body corporate of which the other (directly or indirectly) has control or if both are bodies corporate of which a third person directly or indirectly has control; and the expression "associated employer" shall be construed accordingly.

(6) In this section "commission" includes any gift, bonus or benefit and, for its purposes, a person shall be taken to have a financial interest in the disposition of any land if, but only if, he would, on a disposition of that land, be entitled (whether directly or indirectly, and whether in possession or not) to the whole or part of the proceeds of the disposition.

(7) Schedule 4 to this Act, which contains supplementary provisions as to mortgages, shall have effect.

DEFINITIONS
   "advance fully secured on land": ss.10(11) and 119(1).
   "advance secured on land": ss.10(1) and 119(1).
   "associated employer": subs. (5).
   "Commission": subs. (6).
   "financial interest": subs. (6).
   "land which is to secure an advance": s.10(2).
   "officer": s.119(1).
   "standard scale": Criminal Justice Act 1982, s.37.

GENERAL NOTE
   This section is modelled closely on the provisions of s.25 of the 1962 Act. Its purpose is to ensure that proper arrangements are made for assessing the adequacy of the security for any advance which is to be "fully secured" on land. As appears from s.10(11), the words "fully secured" contemplate nothing more than that the advance will qualify as a class 1 or class 2 advance. Confusingly, an advance may qualify as a class 2 advance and thus as a "fully secured" advance even though it is not in fact fully secured on land: as is apparent from s.11(4)(c), an advance which exceeds the value of the land taken as security may still qualify as a class 2 advance where the excess is secured by taking an additional security of a prescribed description (viz. a description prescribed by order made under s.12(3)). Presumably, in such a case the "security" whose adequacy must be assessed under the present section will comprise both the land and the additional security to be taken: but note that the valuation reports mentioned in this section are made only in respect of the land.
   Subs. (1) places every director of a society under a duty to satisfy himself that the arrangements made by the society for assessing the adequacy of its securities meet the requirements set out in paras. (a)–(c) of that subsection. That does not, of course, require the directors of the society to assess personally the adequacy of the society's securities: the duty of the directors is simply to ensure that the "arrangements" for making the necessary assessments comply with the requirements of that subsection. Failure to discharge this duty is not made the subject of any specific penalties (cf. s.25(7) of the 1962 Act). Note, however, that the criteria for prudent management listed in s.45 include the maintenance of the requisite arrangements for assessing the adequacy of securities for advances secured on land. Failure to observe these criteria may lead to the imposition of conditions on a society's authorisation to raise funds and borrow money, or even to revocation of that authorisation: see ss.42 and 43.

As is apparent from subs. (1)(*a*), the society's arrangements should ensure that the adequacy of the security is assessed on the occasion of each advance. In this respect, the present section differs from s.25 of the 1962 Act. S.25(1) required the society's arrangements to ensure merely that an assessment should be made of the adequacy of any security to be taken. It follows that no assessment was required to be made in cases where an advance was made without any further security being taken, *e.g.* where a further advance was made on the security of the original mortgage: see Wurtzburg and Mills, *Building Society Law* (14th Ed.), pp. 153 and 170. Under the new regime, however, an assessment should be made on every occasion when an advance (including a further advance or re-advance) is made, irrespective of whether any further security is taken. As a matter of analysis, advances payable by instalments would seem to involve an original advance followed by a succession of further advances (see *ibid.*, p. 153). In such cases, it appears that the society should arrange for the adequacy of the security to be assessed on the payment of each instalment: s.11(9) cannot be relied upon in this context, since it is concerned solely with the classification of advances payable by instalments either as class 1 or as class 2 advances.

Subs. (1)(*b*) and (*c*) are broadly comparable to s.25(1)(*a*) and (*b*) of the 1962 Act. The following points of difference should, however, be noted:—

(i) Subs. (1)(*b*) now permits the adequacy of the security to be assessed by employees, as well as by officers, of the society.

(ii) For the first time, certain persons are now disqualified from assessing the adequacy of the security. The circumstances in which the disqualification will apply, and the persons subject to it, are set out in subs. (3).

(iii) The range of persons disqualified from preparing the valuation report has been rationalised and slightly modified: compare subs. (1)(*c*) and (2) with s.25(3)–(6) of the 1962 Act.

(iv) While the person who prepares the valuation report is still required by subs. (1)(*c*) to be "competent," he is no longer required to be "prudent" and "experienced" as well.

The concluding words of subs. (1) have the effect that a report may be used for more than one assessment, but only for so long as it remains adequate for the purpose. Hence, where a mortgage applicant withdraws from a planned purchase, a valuation report prepared in connection with that application may (if still adequate for the purpose) be used for assessing the adequacy of the security on a subsequent application. In appropriate cases, it may also be possible for a report prepared in connection with an initial advance to be used on a subsequent assessment of the adequacy of the security for a further advance; this may be particularly useful in the case of an advance by instalments, noted above.

Subs. (3)(a)

other than the building society making the advance. These words have been inserted to cover cases in which a building society wishes to make an advance to a purchaser who is buying property from the society itself. In such a case, the society will plainly have a financial interest in the disposition of the land. The words under discussion, however, make it clear that the society (through its officers and employees) will nonetheless be able to make the necessary assessment of the adequacy of the security, and authorise the making of the advance.

Other advances secured on land

Power to make advances secured on land overseas

14.—(1) The appropriate authority may, with a view to conferring on building societies or building societies of particular descriptions powers to make advances to members secured on land outside the United Kingdom corresponding to the powers to make advances secured on land within the United Kingdom, by order—

(*a*) designate countries or territories outside the United Kingdom as countries or territories as respects which advances under this section may be made secured on the land;

(*b*) specify, or provide for the specification by direction of the Commission under the order of, the forms of security on land which may be taken for advances under this section, in any prescribed circumstances and subject to any prescribed conditions;

(*c*) determine, or provide for the determination under the order of, the classification of the advances (and accordingly of the mortgage debts) as class 1 advances or class 2 advances for the purposes of the requirements of this Part for the structure of commercial assets;

(d) provide for the application of the provisions of this Part applicable to advances secured on land to advances under this section with such modifications as appear to be appropriate;

(e) provide for any other provisions of this Act to have effect in relation to advances under this section with such modifications as appear to be appropriate; and

(f) make such incidental, supplemental or transitional provision as appears to be necessary or expedient.

(2) Any powers conferred on building societies under this section may be conferred on building societies of a specified description or all building societies other than those of a specified description.

(3) Where, by virtue of an order under subsection (1) above, advances are made by a building society on the security of land outside the United Kingdom, the aggregate amount of mortgage debts outstanding in respect of such of those advances as are class 2 advances under the order shall count in accordance with section 20 towards the limit applicable to class 2 assets under that section.

(4) Subsection (3) above is subject to any provision contained in the order.

(5) The "appropriate authority" for making an order under subsection (1) above is—

(a) as regards the relevant British overseas territories, the Commission acting with the consent of the Treasury, and

(b) as regards other countries or territories, the Treasury.

(6) An order under this section made as regards any of the relevant British overseas territories may make all or any of the powers conferred thereby exercisable by building societies without the need for adoption, but, in the absence of such a provision any power conferred under this section must, in order to be exercisable by a building society, be adopted by the society.

(7) The power to make an order under subsection (1) above is exercisable by statutory instrument and, as regards the procedure applicable to such an order,—

(a) if the instrument designates other countries or territories than any of the relevant British overseas territories, the order shall not be made unless a draft of it has been laid before and approved by resolution of each House of Parliament, and

(b) if the instrument designates any relevant British overseas territory and no other country or territory, the instrument shall be subject to annulment in pursuance of a resolution of either House of Parliament.

(8) In this section—

"relevant British overseas territories" means the Channel Islands, the Isle of Man and Gibraltar;

"security of land" includes any right or power in or over land to secure the payment of a debt and "secured on land" has a corresponding meaning;

"specified" means specified in an order under subsection (1) above; and any reference to a provision of this Part is a reference to that provision as applied to advances under this section.

DEFINITIONS
"adopt": s.119(1) and Sched. 2, para. 1(4).
"advance secured on land": ss.10(1) and 119(1).
"appropriate authority": subs. (5).
"class 1 advance": *c.f.* ss.11(2) and 119(1).

"class 2 advance": *c.f.* ss.11(4) and 119(1).
"the Commission": ss.1 and 119(1).
"land": s.5(10).
"member": s.119(1).
"mortgage debt": ss.11(14) and 119(1).
"this Part": subs. (8).
"relevant British overseas territories": subs. (8).
"requirements for the structure of commercial assets": s.20.
"secured on land": subs. (8).
"security on land": subs. (8).
"specified": subs. (8).

GENERAL NOTE

As originally conceived, the Bill contained no provision for societies themselves to make advances on the security of land outside the United Kingdom. It did, however, embody provisions (now contained in s.18(1), (2)(*b*), (6), (7) and (10)) empowering societies to invest in or support bodies formed in EEC countries for the purpose of lending money on the security of foreign land. The thinking behind the Bill in its original form appears to have been that direct participation in foreign lending would cause problems to building societies by bringing foreign currency assets onto their domestic balance sheets. It was thought better, therefore, that societies should participate in foreign lending only through the medium of foreign-based associated bodies, who would be better placed to match their liabilities and assets in a foreign currency (*cf. Official Report,* House of Commons, Standing Committee A, February 4, 1986, col. 171).

The present section originates in an amendment to the Bill introduced at the Report Stage in the House of Commons. The section does not directly authorise building societies to lend on the security of foreign land; but it introduces a measure of flexibility by allowing provision to be made for such lending by statutory instrument. It will be noted that the procedure for making an order relating to "the relevant British overseas territories" (*viz.*, the Channel Islands, the Isle of Man and Gibraltar) differs somewhat from the procedure applicable to orders relating to other foreign countries and territories (see subss. (5) and (7)). Moreover, orders in the former category, unlike those in the latter, may confer powers on building societies which will be exercisable without the need for adoption: see subs. (6).

It may be helpful to note that during Committee Stage of the Bill's passage through the House of Lords, Lord Skelmersdale (speaking for the Government) said that the present intention was to make an early order under this section to allow direct lending in the Channel Islands, the Isle of Man and Gibraltar, but that there was no intention to make an early order in respect of other countries. See *Hansard,* H.L. Vol. 477, col. 1122.

Other commercial assets

Loans for mobile homes

15.—(1) Subject to the provisions of this section, a building society may make mobile home loans to individuals, whether or not they are members of the society.

(2) A mobile home loan is a loan made for the purchase of a mobile home and secured by such security as the Commission may, with the consent of the Treasury, prescribe by order in a statutory instrument.

(3) No such loan shall be made unless the building society, when it makes the loan, is satisfied that—

   (*a*) the borrower or a dependant of his of a prescribed description is or will be entitled under an agreement to which the Mobile Homes Act 1983 applies to station the mobile home on land forming part of a protected site;

   (*b*) the mobile home is for the residential use of the borrower or a dependent of his of a prescribed description;

   (*c*) the amount lent will not exceed the amount likely to be realised on a sale of the mobile home on the open market; and

   (*d*) subject to subsection (4) below, no other security prescribed under subsection (2) above which is to secure the loan is outstanding in favour of a person other than the society.

(4) The requirement in subsection (3)(*d*) above shall be treated as satisfied if the loan is made on terms that the other loan is redeemed or postponed to it.

(5) A building society shall not make a mobile home loan to an individual if the principal exceeds—

    (*a*) the limit for the time being imposed by or under subsection (7) below; or

    (*b*) the balance remaining after deducting from that limit the aggregate of any other sums outstanding in respect of loans made under this section or section 16 by the society to that individual;

and if two or more loans under this section or this section and section 16 are made simultaneously by the society to the same individual they shall be treated for the purposes of this subsection as a single loan of an amount equal to the aggregate of the principal of each of those loans.

(6) Joint borrowers under this section shall be treated, for the purpose of the limit on loans under this section, as a single individual and any sums outstanding in respect of loans made under this section or section 16 by the society to any one of the joint borrowers is to be taken into account in determining the balance available for any further loan to him or to him and any joint borrower with him.

(7) The limit on loans to any one individual under this section is £10,000 or such other sum as the Commission may, with the consent of the Treasury, specify by order in a statutory instrument.

(8) Loans under this section constitute class 3 assets for the purposes of the requirements of this Part for the structure of commercial assets and accordingly the aggregate of the amounts outstanding in respect of—

    (*a*) the principal of loans under this section,

    (*b*) the interest on those loans, and

    (*c*) any other sums which borrowers are obliged to pay the society under the terms of those loans,

counts in accordance with section 20 towards the limits applicable to class 3 assets under that section.

(9) The power conferred by this section is not available to a building society which does not for the time being have a qualifying asset holding, but the cessation of its availability does not require the disposal of any property or rights.

(10) The power conferred by this section on a building society, if available to it, must in order to be exercisable, be adopted by the society.

(11) An instrument containing an order under subsection (2) or (7) above shall be subject to annulment in pursuance of a resolution of either House of Parliament.

(12) In this section—

    "mobile home" has the same meaning as "caravan" in Part I of the Caravan Sites and Control of Development Act 1960;

    "prescribed", in relation to descriptions of dependants of borrowers, means such as are for the time being prescribed in an order under section 12(1) as respects class 1 advances; and

    "protected site" has the same meaning as in the Mobile Homes Act 1983.

DEFINITIONS

    "adopt": s.119(1) and Sched. 2, para. 1(4).

    "the Commission": ss.1 and 119(1).

    "mobile home": subs. (12) and Caravan Sites and Control of Development Act 1960, s.29(1).

    "mobile home loan": subs. (2) and s.119(1).

    "protected site": subs. (12) and Mobile Homes Act 1983, s.5(1).

    "prescribed" (in subs. (3)(*a*) and (*b*)): subs. (12).

    "qualifying asset holding": ss.118 and 119(1).

    "requirements for the structure of commercial assets": s.20.

GENERAL NOTE

This section is new. It confers power on building societies, in certain circumstances, to make home loans to individuals for the purchase of mobile homes. The power is available only to the larger societies (*i.e.* societies with a qualifying asset holding within the meaning of s.118): see subs. (9). Any such society wishing to exercise the power must first adopt it in accordance with Sched. 2, para. 1 or 4, or (in the case of an existing society) Sched. 20, para. 2 or 3: see subs. (10).

Subs. (12) defines the expression "mobile home" by reference to the definition of "caravan" in Part I of the Caravan Sites and Control of Development Act 1960. S.29(1) of that Act provides that a caravan is "any structure designed or adapted for human habitation which is capable of being moved from one place to another (whether by being towed or being transported on a motor vehicle or trailer) and any motor vehicle so designed or adapted, but does not include (*a*) any railway rolling stock which is for the time being on rails forming part of a railway system, or (*b*) any tent."

The conditions for the exercise of the present power include the requirement that the borrower (or a dependant of his of a description prescribed in an order under s.12(1) as respects class 1 advances) is or will be entitled under an agreement to which the Mobile Homes Act 1983 applies to station the mobile home on land forming part of a protected site: see subs. (3)(*a*) and (12). The 1983 Act applies to any agreement under which a person (in the Act called "the occupier") "is entitled (*a*) to station a mobile home on land forming part of a protected site; and (*b*) to occupy the mobile home as his only or main residence": see s.1(1) of the 1983 Act. For the purposes of the 1983 Act (and of the present section: see subs. (12)) a "protected site" means, broadly speaking, a permanent caravan site other than a site made available for gipsies by a local authority: see s.5(1) of the 1983 Act, Caravan Sites Act 1968, s.1(2) and Caravan Sites and Control of Development Act 1960, Part I.

It appears to be implicit in the Mobile Homes Act 1983 that, in the normal case, an occupier to whom the Act applies will be, and remain, the owner of the mobile home which, under his agreement, he is entitled to occupy: see Sched. 1, paras. 8 and 9 of the 1983 Act. The 1983 Act seems to assume, therefore, that the mobile home will not lose its character as a chattel by being stationed on the site in question. However, while the occupier may be the owner of the mobile home itself, he will normally be a mere licensee of the land on which the mobile home is stationed. (It is true that it is possible for a mobile home agreement to involve the grant of a lease, but such cases are rare in practice.) In the usual case, therefore, it will not be possible for an advance by a building society to a mobile home owner to be secured on land, and the advance will hence be incapable of qualifying as a class 1 or class 2 advance: see ss.10(1) and 11(2) and (4).

A loan to a mobile home owner under the present section must, however, be secured in some way (see subs. (2)), and subs. (3)(*c*) appears to contemplate that the security will be, or include, a mortgage of the mobile home itself. At present, the law relating to mortgages of chattels is under review; accordingly, to preserve a measure of flexibility, the precise form of security which will be required for loans under this section has been left to be prescribed by order made under subs. (2): see *Hansard*, H.L. Vol. 478, cols. 1128–9.

Subs. (3)(*b*)–(*d*) and (4) may be compared with the similar provisions applicable to class 1 advances under s.11(2)(*b*)–(*d*) and (5). However, in view of the improbability of a mobile home being divided into separate residential units, the present section does not seek to elaborate the concept of residential use employed in subs. (3)(*b*) (contrast ss.11(3) and 12(1)).

A loan under this section may only be made to an individual (as opposed to a corporate body); but the individual does not need to be a member of the society: subs. (1). Subss. (5) and (7) limit the amount that can be lent under this section to any one individual to £10,000 (or such other sum as may be specified by order under that subsection). The limit is higher than that which applies to loans under s.16 (the limit imposed by that section being, initially, £5,000). The higher limit no doubt reflects the fact that loans under this section must be secured (see above) whereas loans under s.16 need not be. It will be noted that subs. (5)(*b*) had the effect that, where a loan has been made to an individual under this section, *or* under s.16, a fresh loan under this section to the same borrower cannot exceed the sum left after deducting the existing indebtedness from the £10,000 limit (or any substitute limit) imposed by subs. (7). The reason for counting loans under s.16 towards the limit in subs. (7) is presumably to stop societies evading that limit by making an unsecured loan to a mobile home owner under s.16 and then topping up that loan with a further maximum loan under this section. S.16(5) and (6) prevent the converse case of loans under this section being topped up with lending under s.16 to produce an overall indebtedness which exceeds the limit imposed by subs. (7) of this section. Hence, given the limits currently in force, if, say, £4,000 is owing to a building society from a mobile home owner in respect of a loan made under s.16, a further loan to that individual under this section could not exceed £6,000. Conversely, if, say, £8,000 is owing to a society in respect of a loan made under this section, a further loan to the same borrower under this section or under s.16 could not exceed £2,000.

Subs. (8)

Loans under the present section are categorised as class 3 assets of the lending society: subs. (8). Accordingly, sums owing to the society in respect of such loans are counted towards the limit on class 3 assets imposed by s.20(3) (the current limit being that class 3 assets must not exceed five per cent. of a society's total commercial assets).

Power to lend to individuals otherwise than by class 1 or class 2 advances etc.

16.—(1) Subject to the provisions of this section, a building society may, with or without security and whether or not at interest, lend money to individuals, whether or not they are members of the society.

(2) Advances fully secured on land do not constitute loans under this section except that an advance for a deposit for the purchase of land shall, if the purchase is not completed within the period of six months beginning with the date of the advance, be treated after the end of that period as a loan under this section and shall accordingly cease to be a class 1 or class 2 advance.

(3) Mobile home loans do not constitute loans under this section.

(4) The power to lend money under this section includes power, as regards members of and depositors with the society, to lend on overdraft on such terms as the society thinks fit.

(5) Subject to subsection (9) below a building society shall not make a loan to an individual under this section if the principal exceeds—

    (*a*) the limit for the time being imposed by or under subsection (8) below; or

    (*b*) the balance remaining after deducting from that limit the aggregate of any other sums outstanding in respect of loans made under this section by the society to that individual;

and if two or more loans under this section or this section and section 15 are made simultaneously by the society to the same individual they shall be treated for the purposes of this subsection as, in the case of loans under this section, a single loan of an amount equal to the aggregate of the principal of each of those loans and, in the case of loans under this section and section 15, as made on different occasions such that loans under this section precede those made under that section.

(6) Subsection (5) above shall have effect (subject to subsection (9) below) in a case where a building society has made a loan under section 15 as if it precluded a building society from making a loan to an individual under this section if the principal exceeds—

    (*a*) the limit referred to in paragraph (*a*) of it; or

    (*b*) the balance referred to in paragraph (*b*) of it; or

    (*c*) the balance remaining after deducting from the limit imposed by or under subsection (7) of that section the aggregate of any sums outstanding in respect of loans made under that section and under this section by the society to that individual.

(7) Joint borrowers under this section shall be treated, for the purpose of the limit on loans under this section, as a single individual and any sums outstanding in respect of loans made under this section or section 15 by the society to any one of the joint borrowers is to be taken into account in determining the balance available for any further loan to him or to him and any joint borrower with him.

(8) The limit on loans to any one individual under this section is £5,000 or such other sum as the Commission may, with the consent of the Treasury, specify by order in a statutory instrument.

(9) The limit on loans to any one individual under this section does not apply to an advance for a deposit for the purchase of land which has come to be treated as a loan under this section and accordingly no account shall be taken of it for the purposes of subsection (5) above.

(10) An order under subsection (8) above may specify different sums as the limit in relation to individuals in different circumstances.

(11) Loans under this section constitute class 3 assets for the purposes of the requirements of this Part for the structure of commercial assets and accordingly the aggregate of the amounts outstanding in respect of—

(*a*) the principal of loans under this section,

(*b*) the interest on those loans, and

(*c*) any other sums which borrowers are obliged to pay the society under the terms of those loans,

counts in accordance with section 20 towards the limits applicable to class 3 assets under that section

(12) The power conferred by this section is not available to a building society which does not for the time being have a qualifying asset holding, but the cessation of its availability does not require the disposal of any property or rights.

(13) The powers conferred by this section on a building society, if available to it, must, in order to be exercisable, be adopted by the society.

(14) An instrument containing an order under subsection (8) above shall be subject to annulment in pursuance of a resolution of either House of Parliament.

(15) If at any time when a loan under this section which is secured by a mortgage of any land is outstanding, the building society is satisfied—

(*a*) on a revaluation, that the value of the security has changed,

(*b*) on notice given to it by the borrower that there has been a change in the use of the land, or

(*c*) on such notice, that there has been a change in the relative priority of the mortgage,

and that the change is such that, if it were to make a loan equal to the mortgage debt at that time and on that security, the loan would be a class 1 advance, or as the case may be, a class 2 advance, then the outstanding loan shall be reclassified as from that time.

(16) Nothing in subsection (15) above requires a building society to revalue its securities from time to time.

DEFINITIONS

"adopt": s.119(1) and Sched. 2, para. 1(4).

"advance for a deposit for the purchase of land": s.10(3).

"advances fully secured on land": ss.10(11) and 119(1).

"class 1 advance": ss.11(2) and 119(1).

"class 2 advance": ss.11(4) and 119(1).

"the Commission": ss.1 and 119(1).

"depositors": *cf.* s.119(1).

"members": s.119(1).

"mobile home loan": ss.15 and 119(1).

"mortgage": s.119(1).

"qualifying asset holding": ss.18 and 119(1).

"requirements for the structure of commercial assets": s.20.

GENERAL NOTE

This section confers an important new power on building societies, enabling them for the first time to make unsecured loans to their customers. The power is, however, subject to the following limitations:

(i) Loans under this section may be made only to individuals (as opposed to corporate bodies): see subs. (1).

(ii) The power to make such loans is available only to the larger societies (*i.e.* societies with a qualifying asset holding within the meaning of s.118): see subs. (12). Any such society wishing to exercise the power must first adopt it in accordance with Sched. 2, para. 1 or 4, or (in the case of an existing society) Sched. 20, para. 2 or 3: see subs. (13).

(iii) Loans under this section are categorised as class 3 assets of the lending society: subs. (11). Accordingly, sums owing to the society in respect of such loans are counted towards the limit on class 3 assets imposed by s.20(3) (the current limit being that class 3 assets must not exceed five per cent. of the society's commercial assets).

(iv) Loans under this section are subject to a general limit of £5,000 per borrower (or such other sum as may be specified by order): see subss. (5) and (8). It should be noted that where a loan is made to a borrower who already owes money to the society under this section, the new loan must not take the borrower's total indebtedness above the limit for the time being in force under subs. (8): see subs. (5)(*b*). (As to the exemption from the limit which is afforded to advances originally made under s.10(3) and subsequently converted to loans under this section, see the notes to subss. (2) and (9) below. For the application of the limit in cases involving both loans under this section and loans under the preceding section, see subs. (6) and the notes to s.15 above.)

The power to make unsecured loans under this section will enable societies to participate in a wide range of consumer lending (though it should be borne in mind that unsecured loans will be fully subject to the provisions of the Consumer Credit Act 1974: such loans cannot qualify as exempt agreements under s.16 of that Act). The power will also enable societies to provide a more flexible range of banking services than has previously been open to them. It will be noted, however, that while money may generally be lent under this section to individuals having no other connection with the society (see subs. (1)), subs. (4) restricts lending on overdraft to persons who are members of or depositors with the society. It is arguable that the words "members" and "depositors" in this context mean persons who are current members or who currently have money deposited with the society, and do not include persons who ceased to be members or to have any money deposited with the society at the moment when their account became overdrawn. The problem (if it is a problem) could presumably be circumvented by maintaining a separate account with some nominal sum credited to it or by framing a special rule to include "overdrawn members". In considering the power of building societies to provide banking services, reference should also be made to s.34, and Sched. 8, Pt. I, paras. 1 and 3, Pt. III, para. 1 and Pt. IV, paras. 1–3, whereby societies are enabled to adopt the power to provide money transmission services (which includes the power to give guarantees in relation to accounts with the society, and to permit "occasional" overdrawings on such accounts) and to make and receive payments as agents. The combined effect of these provisions is that societies will be able to operate accounts in much the same way as current bank accounts, and will be free to issue their customers with cheque books and cheque guarantee cards. (It has not hitherto been possible for societies to issue such cards, since they require the issuer to meet payments to third parties whether or not sufficient funds are available in the customer's account.)

It is important to remember that, while a loan made under the present section *may* be unsecured, it does not *need* to be unsecured (*cf.* the words "with or without security" in subs. (1) and note the provisions of subs. (15)). The point can perhaps best be illustrated by an example. Suppose that a society makes a straightforward class 1 advance to an individual borrower, secured by a mortgage which is apt to charge the land with payment of all moneys from time to time payable by the borrower to the society. Subsequently, the borrower applies to the society for a modest loan, say £2,000, for the purchase of furniture. If prepared to make the loan, the society will no doubt wish it to be secured by the borrower's existing mortgage, and will accordingly handle the transaction as a further advance made on the original security. The society has, however, a choice between (i) making the further advance as a class 1 or class 2 advance and (ii) making the further advance as a loan under the present section. If the society wishes to adopt the first alternative, it will have to satisfy itself of the matters specified in s.11(2) (for the further advance to rank as a class 1 advance) or in s.11(4) (for the further advance to rank as a class 2 advance); and it will have to undertake a fresh assessment of the adequacy of the security under s.13 (such an assessment being a pre-requisite to the making of any class 1 or class 2 advance). To avoid those complications, the society might well choose to adopt the second alternative and make the further advance under the powers conferred by the present section. The further advance would not then be treated for the purposes of the Act as an "advance secured on land", since that expression includes only class 1 or class 2 advances: see s.10(1) and (11). Nevertheless, the new loan, having been made on the security of the original mortgage, would *in fact* be secured on land (and indeed secured in full if the equity were sufficient).

As to the provision made for re-classifying loans made under this section on the security of a mortgage of land, see subs. (15), and compare s.12(10) and the notes thereto.

Subss. (2) and (9)

By s.10(3) and (4), any society has power to make an advance (not exceeding 10 per cent. of the total purchase price) for the payment of a deposit for the purchase of land. Such an advance is treated as an advance secured on land, and will be classified as a class 1 or class 2 advance depending on whether the advance intended to be made on completion would be class 1 or class 2: see s.11(6). Subs. (2) of the present section, however, provides that, if the purchase has not been completed within six months of the making of the advance for the deposit, then the advance will cease to be a class 1 or class 2 advance and will be treated as a loan under this section. Nevertheless, the loan will not be subject to the limit imposed by subs. (8), and no account of it will be taken for the purposes of subs. (5): see subs. (9). Suppose, therefore, that a society makes an advance of £10,000 to a borrower for the payment of a deposit. If, after six months, the purchase has still not been completed, the advance will come to be treated as a loan under this section. The effect of subs. (9) appears to be that, not only can the society leave the £10,000 loan outstanding, but it can also make a further loan to the borrower under this section up to the maximum permitted under subs. (8). However, as was pointed out in the notes to s.11(6), the provisions of subs. (2) may still prove troublesome to societies who lack the power to make loans of *any* amount under this section (*i.e.* because they are not eligible to adopt, or have not in fact adopted, the power which this section confers). Presumably, any such society which makes an advance for the payment of a deposit will need to call in the loan if the purchase is not completed within the six months period. Even where a society does have power to make loans under this section, the provisions of subs. (2) may cause problems in cases where an advance is made to a corporate body for the payment of a deposit: such an advance will qualify as a class 2 advance during the six month period, but will presumably have to be called in after the expiry of that period since loans under the present section can be made only to individuals and not to corporations.

Subs. (3)

For mobile home loans, see. s.15 and the notes thereto.

Power to hold and develop land as commercial asset

17.—(1) Subject to subsections (2), (9) and (11) below, a building society may acquire, hold and dispose of land in the United Kingdom for purposes other than those for which it may acquire, hold or dispose of land under section 6 or 10.

(2) Land may not be acquired or held or disposed of by way of lease under this section except where the land is or is to be used—

(*a*) primarily for residential purposes, or

(*b*) for purposes incidental to the use of adjoining land held or to be held by the society which is or is to be used primarily for residential purposes.

(3) A building society may develop or participate in developing for use for residential purposes or purposes connected with the residential use of land any land it holds under this section.

(4) If land acquired under this section ceases to be used for the purposes authorised by subsection (2) above the society shall sell its estate or interest in the land as soon as it is conveniently practicable without undue loss to the society.

(5) Land held under this section constitutes a class 3 asset for the purposes of the requirements of this Part for the structure of commercial assets and accordingly the aggregate value of all land so held counts in accordance with section 20 towards the limits applicable to class 3 assets under that section.

(6) Premises held under section 6, by virtue of subsection (5) of that section, shall, in prescribed circumstances, be treated in their entirety (and regardless of their use) as land held under this section for the

purposes of the requirements of this Part for the structure of commercial assets and subsection (5) above applies accordingly.

(7) The Commission, with the consent of the Treasury, may by order made by statutory instrument make such provision for the purposes of subsection (6) above as it thinks fit and in that subsection "prescribed" means prescribed in an order under this subsection.

(8) An instrument containing an order under subsection (7) above shall be subject to annulment in pursuance of a resolution of either House of Parliament.

(9) Except as provided in subsection (10) below, the powers conferred by this section are not available to a building society which does not for the time being have a qualifying asset holding, but the cessation of their availability does not require the disposal of any property or rights.

(10) A building society which does not for the time being have a qualifying asset holding may acquire, hold and dispose of land which is or is to be used for residential purposes if the purpose of the acquisition and holding of the land is to enable the society to make advances on the security of equitable interests in the land in the circumstances authorised by an order under section 10(6).

(11) The powers conferred by this section on a building society, if available to it, must in order to be exercisable, be adopted by the society.

DEFINITIONS

    "adopt": s.119(1) and Sched. 2, para. 1(4).
    "prescribed": subs. (7).
    "qualifying asset holding": ss.118 and 119(1).
    "requirements for the structure of commercial assets": s.20.

GENERAL NOTE

Under the 1962 Act, a building society had power to hold land for the purpose of conducting its business; but it had no general power to acquire and hold land: see s.7 and Wurtzburg and Mills, *Building Society Law* (14th Ed.), p.57. (The origin of that restriction on the powers of building societies under the old legislation is evidently to be found in the crash of the Liberator Building Society in the nineteenth century, following a series of imprudent property deals: see the Green Paper, para. 3.14.) The present section changes the law by introducing an important new power for building societies to hold and develop land for residential purposes.

Before discussing the substance of the power, the following limitations on its availability should be noted:

(i) The power is generally available only to the larger societies (*i.e.* societies with a qualifying asset holding within the meaning of s.118(1)): see subs. (9). An exception to this is provided in subs. (10), by which societies of any size may acquire, hold and dispose of residential land under shared ownership schemes of a type authorised by order under s.10(6). Any society wishing to exercise the powers available to it under this section must first adopt those powers in accordance with Sched. 2, para. 1 or 4, or (in the case of an existing society) Sched. 20, para. 2 or 3: see subs. (11).

(ii) Land held under this section is categorised as a class 3 asset of the society and is hence counted towards the limit on class 3 assets imposed by s.20(3) (the current limit being that class 3 assets must not exceed five per cent. of a society's total commercial assets).

Subs. (1) confers a general power to acquire, hold and dispose of land in the United Kingdom. That power is, however, subject to the provisions of subs. (2), by which land may not be "acquired or held or disposed of by way of lease" except where the land is to be used for the purposes there specified. Although subs. (2) is not perhaps as clear as it might be, it is thought that the words "by way of lease" qualify "disposed of", but do not qualify "acquired" or "held" (the insertion of the word "or" between "acquired" and "held" seems to support this construction). On that footing, the combined effect of subss. (1) and (2) is:

  (i) that a society may acquire land (whether by lease or purchase) only for the purposes specified in subs. (2);
  (ii) that it may hold land so acquired only for those purposes;
  (iii) that it may dispose of land by way of lease only for those purposes, but may dispose of land by outright sale for any purpose whatsoever.

(That construction, incidentally, appears to accord with the view expressed by Lord Brabazon on behalf of the Government during the Report stage of the Bill's progress through the House of Lords: see *Hansard*, H.L. Vol. 478, col. 1129.)

One obvious way in which societies will be able to use the powers conferred by subss. (1) and (2) is by acquiring residential property for letting to individual tenants. The powers will also be important, however, in the operation of shared ownership schemes, since it appears that any society wishing to participate in such a scheme (including the smaller societies: see subs. (10)) will have power under this section: (*a*) to acquire residential property for that purpose (*b*) to vest in the purchaser any share in the property bought by him and (*c*) to grant the necessary lease of any share in the property "rented" by the purchaser. (As to the circumstances in which a society can make advances under s.10 on the security of equitable interests in property subject to shared ownership schemes, see s.10(6) and the notes thereto.)

Subs. (2)(*b*) is presumably intended to empower societies to acquire and hold land to be used for such things as estate roads, parking lots, communal gardens and other common areas serving adjoining residential land. Note, however, that the adjoining residential land must be land which is "held or to be held by the society." A society will not, therefore, be justified in retaining land under subs. (2)(*b*) after it has ceased to hold the adjoining residential land. That limitation may be important in cases where a society exercises the power conferred by subs. (3) to undertake, or participate in, the development of land for residential use. Suppose, for example, that a society were to lay out and develop land as a housing estate, complete with estate roads and common areas. Having regard to the way in which subs. (2)(*b*) is worded, and to the duty imposed by subs. (4), a society would need to ensure that the estate roads and common areas were sold off either before the adjoining residential plots were sold or, failing that, as soon as conveniently practicable thereafter.

For the cases in which land not initially acquired under this section may subsequently come to be held under it, see ss.6(6)(*b*) and (7), and 11(10)–(12).

Subs. (6)
See s.6(5) and the notes thereto.

Power to invest in subsidiaries and other associated bodies

18.—(1) Subject to the following provisions of this section, a building society may—

(*a*) acquire and hold shares or corresponding membership rights in bodies corporate and form or take part in forming bodies corporate, and

(*b*) provide bodies corporate in which it holds shares or such rights or to which it is, for the purpose of any power under this section, linked by resolution with any of the following supporting services—

(i) loans of money, with or without security and whether or not at interest,

(ii) grants of money, whether or not repayable,

(iii) guarantees of the discharge of their liabilities, and

(iv) the use of services or property, whether or not for payment;

and in this section "invest" means the exercise of any of the powers conferred by paragraph (*a*) and "support" means the exercise of any of the powers conferred by paragraph (*b*) above.

(2) A building society may invest in or support the following bodies corporate (referred to as "qualifying bodies") but no others, that is to say—

(*a*) companies or industrial and provident societies;

(*b*) bodies formed in another member State for the purpose of carrying on in another member State businesses which consist wholly or mainly in lending money on the security of land and do not (where that is not the whole business) include lending on land in the United Kingdom (referred to as "corresponding European bodies"), and

(*c*) bodies corporate (whether or not falling within paragraph (*a*) or (*b*) above) designated as suitable for investment and support or for support for the purposes of this section by an order (referred to as "a designation order") made by the Commission with the consent of the Treasury.

(3) A designation order may—

(a) designate a particular body or designate descriptions of bodies corporate,

(b) make different provision for different descriptions of building society,

(c) determine, or provide for the determination under the order of, the extent to which, the purposes for which, and the conditions subject to which, investment or support is permitted, and

(d) make such transitional and consequential provision as the Commission considers necessary or expedient.

(4) Subject to subsection (5) below, a building society shall not invest in or support a qualifying body so as to enable that body on its own account, in the United Kingdom, to—

(a) lend money to members of the public on the security of land by loans corresponding to advances secured on land,

(b) accept deposits of money otherwise than in such circumstances that their acceptance would not constitute its business a deposit-taking business or in the course of or for the purposes of providing a service for the time being specified in Part I of Schedule 8 to this Act;

but, subject to that, it may invest in or support a qualifying body so as to enable that body to carry on any activity which it is within the powers of the society to carry on, but, subject to subsection (5) below, no others.

(5) In the case of a qualifying body designated, or included in a description of bodies designated, by a designation order a building society may also invest in or support it for such purposes as are permitted by or under the designation order.

(6) Subject to subsections (7) and (8) below, a building society shall not invest in or support a qualifying body whose objects enable it—

(a) to carry on activities which are outside the powers of the society,

(b) to invest in other bodies corporate, or

(c) to support other bodies corporate;

but this does not imply that it is unlawful for the society to complete the performance of any contractual obligations lawfully incurred in providing a supporting service.

(7) Subsection (6) above shall not operate so as to restrict a building society's powers under this section in relation to a corresponding European body.

(8) Subsection (6) above shall not prevent a building society from investing in or supporting a qualifying body—

(a) if that body is, in relation to the society, a designated body and the investment or support is made in accordance with the designation order,

(b) if, not being a body whose objects enable it to carry on activities outside the powers of the society, the investment or support is made or given with the consent of the Commission and subject to any conditions specified in the instrument giving the consent, or

(c) for a period of three months, pending the alteration of the objects of that body.

(9) For the purposes of any power conferred by this section a body corporate is "linked by resolution" to a building society if the board of directors of the society has passed a resolution making that power exercisable in relation to that body and the resolution is in force.

(10) No power to invest in or support a corresponding European body is available to a building society which does not for the time being have a qualifying asset holding, but the cessation of its availability by virtue of this subsection does not require the disposal of any property or rights.

(11) The powers conferred by this section on a building society, if available to it, must, in order to be exercisable, be adopted by the society and must be adopted in their entirety without any restriction except a restriction with reference to the description of body corporate in relation to which the powers to invest in or support are to be exercisable.

(12) A building society whose board of directors has passed a resolution in pursuance of subsection (9) above shall send three copies of a record of the resolution signed by the secretary of the society to the central office and paragraph 4(3), (4) and (5) of Schedule 2 to this Act shall apply as it applies to a record of the alteration of a building society's powers.

(13) Where the board of directors of a building society passes a resolution rescinding a resolution passed in pursuance of subsection (9) above the society shall send three copies of a record of the rescinding resolution signed by the secretary of the society to the central office and paragraph 4(3), (4) and (5) of Schedule 2 to this Act shall apply as it applies to a record of the alteration of a building society's powers, but subject to subsection (14) below.

(14) No rescinding resolution shall be registered without the consent of the Commission.

(15) Where, by virtue of this section, property is held by a building society the property shall constitute class 3 assets for the purposes of the requirements of this Part for the structure of commercial assets and accordingly the aggregate value of the property shall count in accordance with section 20 towards the limits applicable to class 3 assets under that section.

(16) The power to make an order under subsection (2)(*c*) above is exercisable by statutory instrument which shall be subject to annulment in pursuance of a resolution of either House of Parliament.

(17) In this section—

"company" means a company within the meaning of the Companies Act 1985 or the Companies (Northern Ireland) Order 1986;

"corresponding membership rights", in relation to a body corporate, means such rights (other than rights arising from the holding of shares) as are attributable to membership of the body;

"deposit" and "deposit-taking business" have the same meaning as in the Banking Act 1979;

"industrial and provident society" means a society registered under the Industrial and Provident Societies Act 1965 or, in Northern Ireland, the Industrial and Provident Societies Act (Northern Ireland) 1969;

"property" includes rights of any description;

and in this Act "associated body", in relation to a building society, means a body as respects which any of the following conditions is satisfied, that is to say—

(i) the body is one in which the society holds shares or corresponding membership rights, or

(ii) the body is one to which the society is linked by resolution, or

(iii) the body is one in which, by virtue of subsection (8)(*b*) above, shares or corresponding membership rights are held by a body which falls within (i) or (ii) above;

and "associated" shall be construed accordingly.

DEFINITIONS
"adopt": s.119(1) and Sched.2, para.1(4).
"advances secured on land": ss.10(1) and 119(1).
"central office": s.119(1).
"the Commission": ss.1 and 119(1).
"company": subs.(17) and Companies Act 1985, s.735(1).
"corresponding European body": subs.(2)(*b*).
"corresponding membership rights": subs.(17).
"deposit" and "deposit-taking business": subs.(17) and Banking Act 1979, s.1
"designation order": subs.(2)(*c*).
"industrial and provident society": subs.(17).
"invest": subs.(1).
"land": s.5(10).
"linked by resolution": subs.(17) and s.119(1).
"member State": European Communities Act 1972, s.1 and Sched.1.
"property": subs.(17).
"qualifying asset holding": ss.118 and 119(1).
"qualifying bodies": subs.(2).
"requirements for the structure of commercial assets": s.20.
"support": subs.(1).

GENERAL NOTE
This section is new and represents another important change in the law made by this Act.
The section confers power on building societies, in certain circumstances, to invest in other
corporate bodies, and to provide financial and other support for such bodies. The power is,
however, hedged about with a number of complex restrictions, and these do little to enhance
the intelligibility of the section as a whole.
For the purposes of the section, a building society *invests* in a body corporate when it
exercises the powers conferred by subs.(1)(*a*), and it *supports* a body corporate when it
exercises the powers conferred by subs.(1)(*b*). These terms are used in the same sense in
this note.
The opening words of subs.(2) have the effect that a building society can invest in or
support only such bodies as are "qualifying bodies" within the meaning of that subsection.
Qualifying bodies fall into three categories, namely:
(*a*) companies or industrial and provident societies;
(*b*) corresponding European bodies (*viz.*, broadly speaking, bodies formed in another
EEC country for the purpose of lending money on the security of foreign land);
(*c*) bodies specially designated by an order made by the Commission with Treasury
consent.
In summary, the combined effect of subss. (1) and (2) is that (subject to the restrictions
discussed below) a building society may:
(i) invest in any qualifying body; and
(ii) support any qualifying body in which it has invested *or* to which it is "linked by
resolution".
The words "linked by resolution" are explained in subs.(9). A corporate body becomes
linked by resolution to a building society when the society's board passes a resolution
making a power conferred by this section exercisable in relation to that body. Subs.(9) does
not in terms require the body corporate to be a qualifying body. However, since the powers
conferred by this section are exercisable only in favour of a qualifying body (see the opening
words of subs.(2)), the net result is that a building society can be linked by resolution only
to a qualifying body. In theory, a board resolution could be passed under subs.(9) for the
purpose of investing in a qualifying body or of supporting a qualifying body in which the
society has already invested. Such a step, however, would be unnecessary, since a building
society is authorised by subs.(1) to exercise these powers without a resolution being passed
under subs.(9). The only case in which such a resolution *needs* to be passed is where the
society wishes to support a qualifying body in which it has *not* previously invested:
subs.(1)(*b*).
The combined effect of subss. (12)–(14) and Sched. 2, para. 4(3)–(5) is that:
(i) Any resolution passed under subs. (9) must specify the date on which the resolution is
intended to take effect ("the specified date").
(ii) Three copies of a record of the resolution, signed by the secretary, must be sent to the
central office for registration.
(iii) If satisfied that the resolution is in conformity with the Act, the central office will
retain and register one of the copies. Another will be returned to the secretary of the society

with a certificate of registration, and a third will be placed (together with a copy of the certificate) in the society's public file.

(iv) The resolution will have effect on the specified date, or (if later) the date of registration.

(v) A similar procedure must be followed in the case of any resolution rescinding a resolution passed under subs. (9). In the case of a rescinding resolution, however, subs. (14) imposes the additional requirement that the consent of the Commission must be obtained before the resolution can be registered.

It is perhaps a little surprising that a society wishing to support a qualifying body can apparently avoid all the foregoing restrictions by the expedient of acquiring a few shares (or "corresponding membership rights") in the body in question: the society will then have invested in that body, and will be free to support it under subs. (1)(*b*) without the need to pass any resolution under subs. (9).

The detailed restrictions imposed on the exercise of the powers conferred by this section can be summarised as follows:

First, while the powers are generally available to all societies, the power to invest in or support a corresponding European body is limited to the larger societies (*i.e.* societies with a qualifying asset holding within the meaning of s.118): subs. (10).

Second, any society wishing to exercise the powers which are available to it under this section must first adopt those powers in accordance with Sched. 2, para. 1 or 4, or (in the case of an existing society) Sched. 20. para. 2 or 3. Moreover, those powers must, generally speaking, be adopted in their entirety or not at all; the only restriction on those powers which a society is allowed to assume is a restriction with reference to the description of body corporate in relation to which the powers are to be exercisable: see subs. (11).

Third, any property held by a society under this section (*e.g.* shares in a qualifying body) is categorised as a class 3 asset of the society, and is accordingly counted towards the limit on class 3 assets imposed by s.20(3) (the current limit being that such assets must not exceed five per cent. of a society's total commercial assets).

Fourth, the opening words of subs. (4) and paras. (*a*) and (*b*) of that subsection impose a general restriction whereby societies are precluded from investing in or supporting a qualifying body so as to enable that body (in effect) to compete with the society's principal business in the United Kingdom. Thus, subs. (4)(*a*) provides that a society may not invest in or support a qualifying body so as to enable that body to make loans in the United Kingdom corresponding to advances secured on land (*i.e.* the advances which societies themselves are empowered to make under ss. 10 and 11). Subs. (4)(*b*) prohibits a society from investing in or supporting a qualifying body so as to enable that body to accept deposits of money in the United Kingdom. The latter prohibition is, however, subject to two exceptions. In the first place, it does not apply where the acceptance of deposits by the qualifying body would not constitute its business a deposit-taking business (*i.e.*, broadly speaking, a business in which money received by way of deposit is lent to others, or in which the money deposited, or the interest on it, is used to any material extent to finance any other activity of the business: see s.1(2) of the Banking Act 1979, but note s.1(3) of that Act, which excludes any business in which, in effect, deposits are accepted only on a "one-off" basis). Secondly, the prohibition does not apply where the qualifying body accepts deposits in the course of or for the purpose of providing a service for the time being specified in Sched. 8, Pt. I. An obvious example of this would be a qualifying body which accepts deposits in the course of an estate agency business (see Sched. 8, Pt. I, para. 13). It should be noted, finally, that the restrictions imposed by subs. (4)(*a*) and (*b*) may be overridden by the terms of any order under subs. (2)(*c*) designating particular bodies as suitable for investment and support: see subs. (5).

Fifth, the concluding words of subs. (4) prohibit a society from investing in or supporting a qualifying body so as to enable it to carry on any activity which is not within the powers of the society. The effect of this prohibition, taken together with the restrictions imposed by the earlier part of subs. (4), is that a society wishing to exercise the powers conferred by this section must tread a rather narrow path, taking care on the one hand to avoid investment or support which enables a qualifying body to carry on activities which fall outside the society's own powers, and on the other hand to avoid investment or support which enables a qualifying body to carry on activities which fall so centrally within the society's own traditional sphere of operation that the restrictions in the earlier part of subs. (4) will be infringed. Once again, it will be noted that the prohibition imposed by the concluding words of subs. (4) may be overridden by the terms of a designation order: see subs. (5).

Sixth, subs. (6)(*a*) prohibits a society from investing in or supporting a qualifying body whose objects enable it to carry on activities which are outside the powers of the society. At first sight, this prohibition seems largely to duplicate that contained in the concluding words of subs. (4). It is, however, somewhat wider in scope since it would prevent a society from investing in or supporting a qualifying body whose objects mean that it *could* carry on activities which are *ultra vires* the society, notwithstanding that the purpose of the investment or support in the particular case is to enable the qualifying body to carry on activities which are in fact *intra vires* the society (so that the provisions of subs. (4) would not be infringed). Note that the prohibition in subs. (6)(*a*) does not apply where the society wishes to invest in or support a corresponding European body: subs. (7). It appears, however, that the less stringent prohibition imposed by the last seven words of subs. (4) *does* apply to investment in or support for a corresponding European body: that prohibition is not affected by subs. (7), and it does not appear to be limited (as the restrictions in the earlier part of subs. (4) are limited) to activities carried on by the qualifying body in the United Kingdom. If this construction is correct, it has the striking consequence that, unless and until a society has been empowered to make advances secured on land in another member State by order made under s.14, it will have no power under this section to invest in or support a corresponding European body to enable that body to make advances secured on land in that member State. Hence, if the corresponding European body's business consisted *wholly* in lending money on the security of land in that member State (a possibility clearly envisaged by subs. (2)(*b*)), the effect would be that the powers conferred by this section could not be exercised at all in respect of that body. It is conceivable that a court pressed with the bizarre consequences of a literal construction of the last seven words of subs. (4) would be prepared to treat the prohibition embodied therein as impliedly limited to activities of the qualifying body within the United Kingdom (*i.e.*, by analogy with the opening words of the subsection); but such a result certainly cannot be guaranteed. Finally, it should be noted that the prohibition in subs. (6) (*a*) may be overridden by the terms of any relevant designation order (see subs. (8)(*a*)), and that the prohibition does not apply where the objects of the qualifying body are to be altered within a period of three months so as to confine that body to activities which are within the powers of the society.

Seventh, subs. (6)(*b*) and (*c*) prevent a society from investing in or supporting qualifying bodies whose objects enable them to invest in or support other corporate bodies. The purpose of these restrictions is to prevent a building society's money from being filtered through a first tier of qualifying bodies into a tangled substructure of subsidiary bodies. There may, however, be circumstances in which there is a legitimate need for a second tier of subsidiaries (*e.g.* in the context of joint development projects), and provision is made in subs. (8)(*b*) for the restrictions imposed by subs. (6)(*b*) and (*c*) to be relaxed in individual cases with the consent of the Commission. For no very obvious reason (since one might have thought that a tangled network of foreign subsidiaries was a more alarming prospect than such a network of domestic ones), the restrictions in subs. (6)(*b*) and (*c*) are wholly inapplicable where a society wishes to invest in or support a corresponding European body: see subs. (7). The restrictions are again made subject to any contrary provision in a designation order, and do not apply where the offending objects of the qualifying body are to be altered within three months: see subs. (8)(*a*) and (*c*) respectively.

Subs. (17)

Associated body. Curiously, this term is not used in any of the substantive provisions of s.18 itself. It features prominently, however, in other provisions of the Act (see, *e.g.* ss.6, 7, 8, 20, 22 and 34 and Part VIII). The expression includes, in effect: (i) any qualifying body in which a society has invested under subs. (1)(*a*); (ii) any qualifying body to which a society is linked by resolution under subs. (9); and (iii) any "second tier" associated body of a society—that is to say, any body in which a qualifying body falling within (i) or (ii) above has invested (note in this connection, that, by virtue of subs. (6)(*b*) and (*c*), the society will need to obtain the consent of the Commission under subs. (8)(*b*) before it can invest in or support the "first tier" qualifying body; the words "by virtue of subs. (8)(*b*)" in para. (iii) of the present subsection evidently refer, though somewhat elliptically, to this requirement).

By the combined effect of s.119(1) and s.736(1) of the Companies Act 1985, a "subsidiary" of a building society is, in effect, either (i) a company of which the society is a member and the composition of whose board is controlled by the society; or (ii) a company in which the society holds more than half in nominal value of the equity share capital. It can be seen, therefore, that, before a company can become a subsidiary of a society, the society must have invested in it (within the meaning of subs. (1) of this section). Hence, any subsidiary of a building society will necessarily be an associated body of that society; however, not all bodies associated with a society will be its subsidiaries.

Power for Treasury to add powers to hold other descriptions of class 3 assets

19.—(1) The Treasury may, with a view to extending or altering, or extending to other descriptions of building societies, the forms of property which are to constitute class 3 assets in the hands of building societies or building societies of particular descriptions, by order—

(*a*) specify forms of property which a building society is to have power to acquire, hold and dispose of as assets of that class, subject to any specified conditions or restrictions;

(*b*) without prejudice to paragraph (*a*) above, specify descriptions of bodies corporate shares or other interests or rights in which a building society is to have power to acquire, hold and dispose of as assets of that class, subject to any specified conditions or restrictions;

(*c*) make any amendments of or repeals in this Act which are consequential on the exercise of its powers under paragraph (*a*) or (*b*) above;

(*d*) make such incidental, supplemental or transitional provision as it considers necessary or expedient.

(2) The powers conferred by subsection (1) above may be exercised so as to apply in relation to property situated or bodies incorporated within the United Kingdom or any other member State or other country or territory and so as to be exercisable for purposes other than the purposes of building societies under the powers conferred on them for the time being by or under this Act.

(3) Any powers conferred on building societies under this section may be conferred on building societies of a specified description or all building societies other than those of a specified description.

(4) Any power conferred on a building society under this section, if available to it, must, in order to be exercisable, be adopted by the society.

(5) Where, by virtue of an order under subsection (1)(*a*) or (*b*) above, property is held by a building society the property shall constitute class 3 assets for the purposes of the requirements of this Part for the structure of commercial assets and accordingly the aggregate value of the property, as determined in accordance with the order, shall count in accordance with section 20 towards the limits applicable to class 3 assets under that section.

(6) Subsection (5) above is subject to any provision contained in the order.

(7) The power to make an order under subsection (1) above is exercisable by statutory instrument but no such order shall be made unless a draft of the order has been laid before and approved by a resolution of each House of Parliament.

(8) In this section—

"property" includes rights of any description; and

"specified" means specified in an order under subsection (1) above.

DEFINITIONS
"adopt": s.119(1) and Sched. 2, para. 1(4).
"member State": European Communities Act 1972, s.1 and Sched. 1.
"property": subs. (8).
"requirements for the structure of commercial assets": s.20.
"specified": subs. (8).

GENERAL NOTE
This section empowers the Treasury by order to extend or alter (i) the forms of property which can be held by building societies (normally as class 3 assets: see subs. (5) and (6)) and (ii) the descriptions of bodies corporate in which building societies may invest. The power

may, it seems, also be used to extend powers which are currently conferred by ss.15–18 above, but are restricted to societies with a qualifying asset holding within the meaning of s.118, to societies (or some societies) which do not have a qualifying asset holding. The purpose of the section is to retain a degree of flexibility in the provisions of the Act to enable account to be taken of legitimate future developments in the building society movement; the section is not intended to be used to permit a reckless diversification of building society activities (see *Official Report*, Standing Committee A, February 4, 1986, col. 180).

Subs. (2)
The concluding words of this section are certainly obscure and quite possibly meaningless.

Subs. (4)
A building society wishing to exercise any power conferred on it under this section must first adopt that power in accordance with Sched. 2, para. 1 or 4, or (if applicable) Sched. 20, para. 2 or 3. It will not, of course, be possible for a society to agree or resolve to adopt "automatically" every future power which becomes available to it by order made under this section. Such powers can be adopted only when their terms become known (and can hence be set out in the society's memorandum) and when a date can be specified for them to become exercisable.

Subs. (6)
It looks as though the purpose of this subsection is to allow property held pursuant to an order made under this section to be classified by the order as a class 1 or class 2 asset of the society. But the matter cannot be regarded as free from doubt in view of the reference to class 3 assets (and only to class 3 assets) in the opening words on subs. (1).

Commercial asset structure requirements

Commercial asset structure requirements for building societies

20.—(1) The requirements for the structure of commercial assets applicable to building societies are the following.

(2) The class 2 assets or, if it has class 3 assets, the aggregate of the class 2 and class 3 assets held by a building society at the end of a financial year shall not exceed whichever is the greater of—

(a) 10 per cent. of the total commercial assets held by the society at that time, or

(b) an amount corresponding to that percentage of the total commercial assets held by the society at the end of the preceding financial year.

(3) The class 3 assets (if any) held by a building society at the end of a financial year shall not exceed whichever is the greater of—

(a) 5 per cent. of the total commercial assets held by the society at that time, or

(b) an amount corresponding to that percentage of the total commercial assets held by the society at the end of the preceding financial year.

(4) The Treasury may by order made by statutory instrument direct that subsection (2) or (3) above shall have effect during the currency of the order as if such percentage as is specified in the order were substituted for the percentage specified in that subsection, not being a percentage greater than 25 per cent. in the case of subsection (2) and 15 per cent. in the case of subsection (3) above.

(5) An order under subsection (4) above may—

(a) divide class 3 assets into sub-classes for the purposes of the order by reference to the provision of or made under this Part from which they arise;

(b) subject to subsection (6) below, prescribe different limits for different sub-classes; and

(c) make such transitional provision as appears to the Treasury to be necessary or expedient;

and any reference in this Act to a limit for a class of commercial assets shall, if a limit is in force under subsection (4) above for any sub-class of class 3 assets, be construed as including a reference to the limit for that sub-class.

(6) No order under subsection (4) above shall prescribe as a limit for a sub-class of class 3 assets a percentage of total commercial assets less than the percentage in force immediately before the making of the order for that sub-class or, if the sub-class is created by the order, for class 3 assets generally.

(7) An order under subsection (4) above shall not be made unless a draft of it has been laid before and approved by a resolution of each House of Parliament.

(8) The amount or value of the assets of any class of a building society for the purposes of this section is the amount or value as shown in the latest balance sheet or such other amount or value as the Commission determines to be the correct or, as the case requires, appropriate amount or value; and where the Commission determines an amount or value under this subsection the appropriate alterations shall be noted against the annual accounts of the society kept in the public file of the society.

(9) In determining for the purposes of this section the asset holding of a building society with which another body corporate is associated there shall, subject to subsection (12) below, be attributed to the society, in accordance with aggregation rules made by the Commission with the consent of the Treasury under this subsection, the whole or part of the assets of whatever description of the associated body, as provided in the rules and subject to any exceptions provided in the rules.

(10) The power to make aggregation rules under subsection (9) above includes power to make—

(a) different rules for different circumstances,

(b) provision for assets of societies to be disregarded,

(c) provision for assets to be attributed to any class of assets of societies, and

(d) such supplementary, transitional and saving provisions as appear to the Commission to be necessary or expedient.

(11) The power to make aggregation rules under subsection (9) above is exercisable by statutory instrument which shall be subject to annulment in pursuance of a resolution of either House of Parliament.

(12) The Commission may, on the application of a building society, approve rules to be applied for the purposes of this section for the attribution to the society of assets of bodies associated with the society; and so long as the rules continue to be approved by the Commission they, and not the aggregation rules in force under subsection (9) above, shall apply for the attribution of assets for the purposes of this section.

(13) If the commercial assets of any class of a building society exceed the limits in force under this section the powers conferred on the Commission by section 36 shall become exercisable in relation to the society, but exceeding the limit shall not affect the validity of transactions effected in excess of it nor require the disposal of any assets.

DEFINITIONS
  "associated" and "associated body": ss.18(17) and 119(1).
  "annual accounts": ss.74(1) and 119(1).
  "the Commission": ss.1 and 119(1).
  "financial year": ss.117 and 119(1).
  "public file": ss.106 and 119(1).
  "total commercial assets": s.119(1).

GENERAL NOTE
  The preceding sections of this Part of the Act classify the commercial assets of a building

society as class 1, class 2 or class 3 assets. The present section, while imposing no limit on a society's holding of class 1 assets, requires its class 2 assets and its class 3 assets (if any) to be limited to specified percentages of its total commercial assets. The expression "total commercial assets" is defined in the Act to include all assets of a society falling within any of the three classes. In effect, the expression covers all assets held by a building society other than its fixed and liquid assets (*cf.* para. 3.01 of the Green Paper).

The limits on class 2 and class 3 assets are imposed by subs.(2) and (3). The percentages specified in those subsections may be increased by order made under subs.(4); but, taking the percentages currently applicable, the effect of the subsections is that, at the end of each financial year of a building society:

(i) the society's class 2 assets or, if it has class 3 assets, the aggregate of its class 2 and class 3 assets, must not exceed the greater of: (*a*) 10 per cent. of the total commercial assets then held by the society or (*b*) an amount equal to 10 per cent. of the total commercial assets which the society held at the end of the preceding financial year (see subs. (2)); and

(ii) the society's class 3 assets (if any) must not exceed the greater of: (*a*) five per cent. of the total commercial assets then held by the society or (*b*) an amount equal to 5 per cent. of the total commercial assets which the society held at the end of the preceding financial year (see subs. (3)).

It will be seen that a society whose holdings of class 2 and class 3 assets at the end of any financial year do not exceed the relevant percentages of its total commercial assets at the end of the *preceding* financial year will satisfy the requirements of this section notwithstanding that its holdings of those assets exceed the relevant percentages of the total commercial assets held by it at the current year end. That may be found a useful safeguard for societies which have experienced a reduction in their total commercial assets during the course of the current year. Quite apart from that, some societies may also find it helpful to be able to use the value of their total commercial assets at the end of the preceding financial year as a bench-mark by which to measure their holdings of class 2 and class 3 assets during the current year (that will be so especially in the case of a society which anticipates that it may have difficulty in making an accurate assessment of its total commercial assets at the current year end: but a society which complies diligently with the requirements of s.71(3) ought not to find itself in that position).

In considering the effect of s.20, it may be helpful to bear in mind the composition of the various asset categories. They comprise the following:

Class 1

Class 1 advances secured on land in the United Kingdom: see s.11(2) and (8)(*a*).

Advances on foreign land classified as class 1 advances by order made under s.14(1)(*c*).

Land held under s.11(10) (foreclosure, etc.) where the original advance was a class 1 advance.

(Possibly) other forms of property permitted to be held as class 1 assets by order made under s.19: see s.19(5) and (6), but note the opening words of s.19(1).

Class 2

Class 2 advances secured on land in the United Kingdom: see s.11(4) and (8)(*b*).

Advances on foreign land classified as class 2 advances by order made under s.14(1)(*c*): see s.14(3).

Land held under s.11(10) where the original advance was a class 2 advance.

(Possibly) other forms of property permitted to be held as class 2 assets by order made under s.19: see again s.19(5) and (6), but note the opening words of s.19(1).

Class 3

Mobile home loans under s.15: see s.15(8).

Secured and unsecured loans to individuals made under s.16: see s.16(11).

Residential land held under s.17: see s.17(5).

Property (*e.g.* shares in a subsidiary) held under s.18: see s.18(15).

Property designated as a class 3 asset by any order made under s.19: see s.19(5).

Bearing in mind the composition of the three classes it can be seen that the percentage limits imposed by this section are designed to achieve two distinct but related objectives. The first is to preserve the established character of building societies as lending institutions by ensuring that traditional mortgage lending continues to account for the great bulk of their business. The second is to limit their exposure to the new, and potentially riskier, types of activity which the Act permits them to carry on.

Subss. (4)–(7)

These subsections make provision for the percentage limits currently specified in subss. (2) and (3) to be increased (though not above 25 per cent. and 15 per cent. respectively) and for sub-classes of class 3 assets to be created in the event of any such increase. In either case, the changes will be effected by order made by the Treasury. There has been pressure from some of the larger societies for a speedy increase in the limits now in force. During the Committee stage of the Bill's passage through the House of Commons, however, Mr. Ian Stewart, speaking on behalf of the Government, said that he doubted whether the five per cent. limit would need to be raised "for a number of years" (*Official Report*, House of Commons, Standing Committee A, February 4, 1986, col. 188).

Subss. (9)–(12)

The purpose of these subsections is to enable provision to be made for the assets of bodies associated with a building society (as to which, see s.18) to be brought on to the society's balance sheet. Similar provision is made with respect to the liabilities of associated bodies by ss.7(9)–(13) and 8(3)–(7).

Subs. (13)

If the limits in force under subss. (2) and (3) are exceeded, the Commission may require the society to submit a restructuring plan for the approval of the Commission, or to submit a transfer resolution to its membership: see s.36.

It should also be noted in this connection that maintenance of a structure of commercial assets which satisfies the requirements of this Part of the Act is one of the criteria of prudent management listed in s.45. Failure to observe these criteria may lead to the imposition of conditions on a society's authorisation to raise funds and borrow money, or even to revocation of that authorisation: see ss.42 and 43.

Liquid assets

Liquid assets

21.—(1) Subject to the following provisions of this section, a building society shall secure that, of its total assets, it keeps such a proportion of them having such a composition as will at all times enable the society to meet its liabilities as they arise.

(2) A building society may keep assets of an authorised character beyond those required for the purpose of complying with subsection (1) above.

(3) Subject to subsections (5) and (6) below, the assets held by a building society under subsection (1) or (2) above—

(a) shall not exceed in the aggregate a proportion of its total assets greater than $33\frac{1}{3}$ per cent., and

(b) shall be composed of assets of an authorised character and no others;

but, subject to that, a building society, in deciding on the composition and proportion appropriate for the purpose of complying with subsection (1) above, shall have regard to the range and scale of its business and the composition and character of its assets and liabilities.

(4) Subsection (3) above, in its application to a building society with which other bodies corporate are associated, is to be read as requiring the society to have regard to the range and scale of the business, and the composition and character of the assets and liabilities, of the society and the associated bodies.

(5) The Commission may, by order made with the consent of the Treasury, direct that this section shall have effect during the currency of the order as if such percentage as is specified in the order were substituted for the percentage specified in subsection (3) above; but any order under this subsection shall expire (unless previously revoked) at the end of the period of twelve months beginning with the day on which the order came into operation.

(6) The Commission may, at any time, by notice to a building society, direct that the limit in force under this section shall not, subject to any conditions specified in the notice, apply to the society during such period as the Commission specifies in the notice.

(7) Regulations to be known as liquid asset regulations shall be made by the Commission, with the consent of the Treasury, for the purposes of this section and such regulations—

(*a*) shall prescribe descriptions of assets as assets of a character which societies may, in any prescribed circumstances and subject to any prescribed conditions, hold under this section for the purpose of meeting their liabilities as they arise,

(*b*) may make different provision for different descriptions of building societies, and

(*c*) may make such supplementary or incidental provision and such transitional provision as appears to the Commission to be necessary or expedient.

(8) The power to make an order or regulations under subsection (5) or (7) above is exercisable by statutory instrument which shall be subject to annulment in pursuance of a resolution of either House of Parliament.

(9) If the assets of a building society which are kept in the form directed by subsection (1) above exceed at any time the percentage in force under this section at that time the powers conferred on the Commission by section 36 shall become exercisable in relation to the society, but exceeding the limit shall not affect the validity of transactions effected in excess of it.

(10) In this section—

"authorised", in relation to the character of assets, means authorised by regulations under subsection (7) above for the purpose specified in paragraph (*a*) of that subsection;

"business" includes business the society proposes to carry on; and

"prescribed" means prescribed in regulations under subsection (7) above.

DEFINITIONS

"authorised": subs.(10).
"associated": ss.18(17) and 119(1).
"business": subs.(10).
"the Commission": ss.1 and 119(1).

GENERAL NOTE

The essence of a building society's business is to borrow short and lend long. The successful accomplishment of that difficult feat requires a society, among other things, to keep sufficient of its assets in liquid form to enable it to meet its liabilities when they arise. The 1962 Act did not impose any express obligation on societies to maintain an adequate margin of liquidity, though certain requirements with respect to liquidity had to be satisfied before a society could qualify for "trustee status", and before a new society could be permitted to advertise (see the Building Societies (Designation for Trustee Investment) Regulations 1972, reg. 2(1)(*a*) and para.3 of the Schedule thereto, and the 1962 Act, s.14 and Sched. 2; note also the provisions contained in ss.58 and 59 of the 1962 Act for the application and investment of a society's "surplus funds").

Subs. (1) of the present section now expressly requires a building society to ensure, in effect, that the proportion of its assets kept in a readily realisable form is sufficient to enable it at all times to meet its liabilities as they arise. In discharging that duty, the society is required by the concluding words of subs. (3) to have regard to the range and scale of its business and the composition and character of its assets and liabilities. Where other bodies are associated with the society, subs. (4) additionally requires the society to have regard to the range and scale of the associated body's business, and the composition and character of that body's assets and liabilities. The latter requirement, no doubt, has been imposed to take account of the possibility that a building society may be called upon under the "statutory guarantee" embodied in s.22 to discharge any of the liabilities of an associated body which that body is unable to discharge itself. (It is perhaps worth noting, however, that, whereas subs. (4) is expressed to extend to all associated bodies, s.22 only covers such of them as are subsidiaries of the society, or are bodies to which the society is linked by resolution: *cf.* s.18(17) and the notes thereto.)

Assets held by a society under subs. (1) must be of a character authorised by regulations to be made under subs. (7): see subss.(3)(*b*) and (10). These regulations, which are to be known as liquid asset regulations, will presumably include the range of assets to which societies have traditionally resorted to maintain their liquidity (*viz.*, cash in hand and at the bank, bills, short dated gilts, etc.). It was, however, indicated during the Committee stage of the Bill's passage through the House of Commons that provision would additionally be made for stock lending (see *Official Report*, Standing Committee A, February 4, 1986, cols. 194–6).

Subs. (2) confers power on societies to maintain holdings of liquid assets beyond those strictly required to enable them to meet their liabilities as they arise. Again, however, a society which holds liquid assets under this subsection must ensure that it does so consistently with the requirements of the liquid asset regulations made under subs. (7): see subss.(3)(*b*) and (10), and note that subs. (2) itself requires that any assets held thereunder must be of an "authorised" character.

Subs. (3)(*a*) imposes an upper limit of 33⅓ per cent. on the proportion of a society's total assets which can be held in liquid form. The purpose of this limitation is apparently to guard against the possibility of societies becoming bloated with cash, and diverting their resources away from their traditional mortgage lending business into speculative money market ventures (*ibid.*, col. 196). It may be worth noting in this connection that the time when the Green Paper was published (July 1984), the liquid assets of building societies were usually in the range of 17–20 per cent. By subs. (5), the Commission may (with Treasury consent) make an order varying the upper limit specified in subs (3)(*a*); the maximum duration of any such order is a period of one year from the date on which the order comes into operation. The purpose of subs. (5) is to enable the Commission to make a temporary change in the 33⅓ per cent. limit, where necessary to take account of abnormal conditions in the financial markets. In addition, the Commission has power under subs. (6) to give notice to a particular society, directing that the limit shall not apply to that society for such period as may be specified in the notice. The purpose of this provision is to allow the Commission to grant a temporary exemption from the 33⅓ per cent. limit to individual societies which, by reason of exceptional circumstances, might otherwise find difficulty in maintaining a margin of liquidity adequate to meet their liabilities.

No specific sanction is provided for breach of the duty imposed by subs. (1). However, the maintenance of adequate assets in liquid form is one of the criteria of prudent management listed in s.45. Failure to observe those criteria may lead to the imposition of conditions on a society's authorisation to raise funds or borrow money, or even to the revocation of that authorisation: see ss.42 and 43.

If a society exceeds the upper limit on liquid assets for the time being in force under this section, it may be required by the Commission to submit a restructuring plan for the approval of the Commission or to submit a transfer resolution to its members: see subs. (9) and s.36.

Liabilities of associated bodies

Obligation to meet liabilities of associated bodies

22.—(1) If a body corporate is linked by resolution with a building society or is a subsidiary of the society, then, subject to subsection (2) below, the building society is under an obligation by virtue of this section to discharge the liabilities of that associated body in so far as that body is unable to discharge them out of its own assets.

(2) The obligation so imposed does not extend to the liabilities of the associated body to its members other than the building society with which it is associated.

(3) Any expression used in this section and section 18 has the same meaning in this section as in that section.

DEFINITIONS

"associated" and "associated body": s.18(17).
"corresponding membership rights": s.18(17).
"subsidiary": s.119(1); Companies Act 1986, s.736.

GENERAL NOTE

This section should be considered together with s.18, which confers power on a building society, subject to the provisions of that section, to invest in, or provide support for, associated bodies (including subsidiaries). In effect, the present section provides a statutory guarantee by a society which has exercised that power of the liabilities of its subsidiaries and associated bodies, to the extent that they are unable to discharge their liabilities from their own assets. Note, however, that the benefit of the section will be enjoyed only by bodies in one of the following categories: (i) associated bodies to which the society is linked by resolution pursuant to s.18(9); (ii) associated bodies which are "subsidiaries" of the society (*i.e.*, usually, bodies in which the society holds more than 50 per cent. of the equity share capital). It should be noted that the statutory guarantee does not extend to the liabilities of a subsidiary or associated body to its members: subs. (2).

Other powers

Power to hedge

23.—(1) Subject to subsections (3) and (4) below, a building society may effect contracts of a prescribed description for the purpose of reducing the risk of loss arising from changes in interest rates, currency rates or other factors of a prescribed description which affect its business.

(2) The Commission, with the consent of the Treasury, may by order—

(*a*) specify as contracts which building societies have power to effect under this section descriptions of contract whose purpose or one of whose purposes is the reduction of the risk to businesses of loss arising from the factors specified in subsection (1) above or other similar factors, and

(*b*) regulate, or provide for the regulation of, the terms on which, the persons or descriptions of persons with whom, and the circumstances in which, contracts of a description specified under paragraph (*a*) above, may be effected by building societies.

(3) Except as provided under subsection (4) below, the powers conferred by this section are not available to a building society which does not for the time being have a qualifying asset holding, but the cessation of their availability does not require the disposal of any property or rights.

(4) The Commission, with the consent of the Treasury, may by order provide that subsection (3) above shall not have effect, as regards prescribed powers, in relation to prescribed descriptions of building societies.

(5) The powers conferred by this section on a building society, if available to it, must, in order to be exercisable, be adopted by the society.

(6) The power to make an order under subsection (2) or (4) above—

(*a*) includes power to make such transitional provision as the Commission considers necessary or expedient, and

(*b*) is exercisable by statutory instrument which shall be subject to annulment in pursuance of a resolution of either House of Parliament.

(7) In this section "prescribed" means prescribed in an order under subsection (2) or (4) above, as the case may be.

DEFINITION

"qualifying asset holding": ss.118 and 119(1).

GENERAL NOTE

The purpose of this section is to enable building societies (though primarily the larger ones: see subss. (3) and (4)) to hedge against the risk of loss arising from interest and exchange rate fluctuations and any other similar factors which may be prescribed by statutory instrument. As the wording of subs.(1) makes clear, the section only gives authority to effect contracts for the purpose of reducing the risk of loss to the society; the section is not a licence to speculate in currency and financial futures markets.

Subs. (2)

An order under this subsection may prescribe not only the types of contract which building societies may effect, but also the terms on which, and the circumstances under which, societies may effect them. It will thus be open to the Commission to impose special restrictions on the freedom of societies to enter into the riskier types of contract.

It was indicated at the Committee stage of the Bill that swap contracts would be included as one of the categories of contract prescribed by order under this subsection. It has since been indicated by the Registry of Friendly Societies that it is proposed to make such an order to cover (with effect from January 1, 1987) interest and currency swaps in cases where the counterparty or guarantor is a recognised bank or licensed deposit taker. Under the 1962 Act, the view taken by the Registry was that building societies had implied power to enter into interest swaps (*e.g.* fixed to floating rate swaps in the eurosterling market), but it was regarded as doubtful whether they had power to enter into currency swaps. Under the new regime, it is to be expected that societies will henceforth be in a position to make more flexible use of the eurobond market as a source of wholesale funds (*e.g.* by borrowing in a foreign currency at a fixed rate of interest and swapping for a sterling obligation at a floating rate).

Subss. (3) and (4)

In its original form, the Bill contained nothing equivalent to the present subs. (4). It was intended that the power conferred by this section should be available only to societies with a qualifying asset holding (*i.e.*, assets exceeding £100 million). The reason for that was that the smaller societies were thought unlikely to be able to attract and employ persons with the skills necessary to operate in the technical and sophisticated markets in which the contracts envisaged by this section will be placed. Subs. (4), however, which was added at the Report stage, introduces a degree of flexibility. It recognises that there may be circumstances in which it will be appropriate to allow the smaller societies to make use (though probably only limited use) of the powers conferred by subs. (1). But it is left to the Commission to make regulations prescribing which of the smaller societies may use these powers and the extent to which they may use them.

The concluding words of subs. (3) make it clear that, if a society makes a contract under this section at a time when it has a qualifying asset holding, the performance of the contract will not be affected by the society's subsequently ceasing to have a qualifying asset holding.

Subs. (5)

See Sched. 2, paras. 1 and 4 and Sched. 20, paras. 2 and 3 for the adoption of powers by a society.

PART IV

PROTECTION OF INVESTORS

Investor Protection Scheme

The Building Societies Investor Protection Board

24.—(1) There shall be a body corporate to be known as the Building Societies Investor Protection Board (in this Part referred to as "the Board") which—

(a) shall hold, manage and apply in accordance with the protective scheme provisions of this Part a fund to be known as the Building Societies Investor Protection Fund (referred to in those provisions as "the Fund"); and

(b) shall, if it so determines under section 26 in relation to a building society which has become insolvent, levy contributions to the Fund from authorised building societies in accordance with that section; and

(c) shall have such other functions as are conferred on the Board by the protective scheme provisions of this Part.

(2) Schedule 5 to this Act shall have effect with respect to the constitution of the Board and the procedural and other matters there mentioned.

(3) In this Act "the protective scheme provisions" means sections 25 to 29.

DEFINITIONS
"authorised": s.119(1).
"the protective scheme provisions": subs. (3).

GENERAL NOTE
This section provides for establishment of a statutory scheme for the protection of building society investors. The scheme will be administered by a new corporate body to be known as the Building Societies Investor Protection Board. The protective scheme provisions in ss.25 to 29 are modelled largely on those of the Banking Act 1979 (ss.21 to 33), but are not identical. In particular, it will be observed that contributions are to be levied at the discretion of the Board after a society has become insolvent; there is no standing fund. This difference apparently derives from the relatively good record of building societies, both as to failure rate and as to voluntary protection for investors, compared with that of banks and deposit-taking institutions generally.

It is unclear what impact the new compulsory scheme will have on the existing voluntary scheme set up in 1982 under the auspices of the Building Societies Association. The voluntary scheme aims at 100 per cent. protection for all building society depositors, 90 per cent. protection for shareholders in participating societies and 75 per cent. protection for shareholders in non-participating societies. (Contrast the protection achieved by the statutory scheme, which is limited to 90 per cent. of an investment not exceeding £10,000: see s.27(2) and (5).) But the weakness of the voluntary scheme has been that not all societies belong to it. See s.31 for the statutory provisions which now apply to voluntary schemes.

The Investor Protection Fund

25.—(1) The Fund shall consist of—
(a) contributions levied from building societies under section 26;
(b) moneys borrowed by the Board under section 26(14);
(c) income credited to the Fund in accordance with subsection (3) below;
(d) payments made to the Board under subsection (6) below; and
(e) money credited to the Fund in accordance with section 29.

(2) The moneys constituting the Fund from time to time shall be placed by the Board in an account with the Bank of England.

(3) So far as possible, the Bank of England shall invest moneys placed with it under subsection (2) above in Treasury bills; and any income from moneys so invested shall be credited to the Fund.

(4) The administrative expenses of the Board shall be defrayed out of the Fund.

(5) There shall be chargeable to the Fund—
(a) payments to meet administrative expenses of the Board in accordance with subsection (4) above;
(b) moneys required for the repayment of the Board's borrowings, and interest thereon, under section 26(14); and
(c) payments to investors under section 27 and any expenses incurred in connection with the making of such payments;
(d) payments to contributory societies under section 29(7);
and, in the protective scheme provisions of this Part—
"the expenses attributable to the insolvency", with reference to a building society insolvency, means all the sums chargeable to the Fund under paragraphs (a) to (d) above in respect of that insolvency except that, in the case of payments to meet administrative expenses of the Board, it means so much only of those expenses as the Board determines shall be attributed to the insolvency; and

"insolvency payments to investors" means the payments under section 27 referred to in paragraph (*c*) above, and "insolvency payment" has a corresponding meaning; and

"recognised bank" and "licensed institution" have the same meaning as in the Banking Act 1979.

(6) The Commission shall, at the request of the Board, make payments to it towards the administrative expenses of the Board.

(7) In so far as the Board authorises any recognised bank, licensed institution or building society to receive on its behalf any contributions levied by the Board and to make on its behalf any of the insolvency payments to investors out of the sums so received, the sums so received need not be paid into the Fund and the payments need not to be made out of the Fund but shall be treated as if they were respectively comprised in and charged on the Fund and shall be accounted for accordingly.

DEFINITIONS

"the Board": s.24(1).
"the Commission": ss.1 and 119(1).
"the Fund": s.24(1).
"insolvency payments to investors": subs. (5).
"licensed institution": subs. (5) and Banking Act 1979, s.50(1).
"protective scheme provisions": s.24(3).
"recognised bank": subs. (5) and Banking Act 1979, s.50(1).

GENERAL NOTE

Subs. (1) sets out the payments that will be made into the Fund, and subs. (5) sets out the payments that will be chargeable to it.

The payments-in comprise:
  (*a*) contributions levied on building societies by the Board under s.26;
  (*b*) moneys borrowed by the Board on a temporary basis under s.26(14);
  (*c*) income arising from the investment of moneys constituting the Fund (see subs. (3));
  (*d*) payments made by the Commission towards the Board's administrative expenses (see subs. (6));
  (*e*) any surplus credited to the Fund under s.29(6) in cases where the sums received by the Board from the liquidator of the insolvent society are more than sufficient to repay the sums paid into the Fund by the contributing societies.

The payments-out comprise:
  (*a*) payments to meet the Board's administrative expenses (see subs. (4));
  (*b*) moneys required to repay the Board's borrowings (see s.26(14));
  (*c*) payments to investors in the insolvent society (see s.27);
  (*d*) payments made to contributing societies in cases where any surplus arising as in (*e*) above falls to be shared out between those societies (see s.29(7)).

The provisions of this section are modelled on s.22 of the Banking Act 1979. Subs. (7) of this section, however, has no counterpart in the 1979 Act; it enables the Board to arrange for the sums raised from contributing societies, and the payments made to investors claiming under the scheme, to "by-pass" the Fund and be handled instead by a recognised bank, licensed institution or building society authorised by the Board for the purpose.

Power to levy contributions and to borrow money in event of insolvency

26.—(1) For the purposes of the protective scheme provisions of this Part a building society becomes insolvent—

(*a*) on the making of a winding-up order against it,

(*b*) on the passing of a resolution for a creditors' voluntary winding up, or

(*c*) on the holding of a creditors' meeting summoned under section 95 of the Insolvency Act 1986 or Article 541 of the Companies (Northern Ireland) Order 1986 (effect of insolvency on members' voluntary winding up);

and the occurrence of any of those events constitutes a "building society insolvency" for the purposes of those provisions.

(2) If a building society becomes insolvent the Board may levy contributions to the Fund for the purposes of making insolvency payments to investors at such level of investor protection as the Board determines under section 27 and meeting the other expenses attributable to the insolvency.

(3) All building societies (other than the insolvent building society) authorised on the date of the insolvency are liable to contribute to the Fund and are in the protective scheme provisions of this Part referred to as "contributory societies".

(4) If, on a building society becoming insolvent, the Board determines to levy contributions under subsection (2) above, then, subject to subsection (10) below, it shall levy a contribution from each of the contributory societies and the amount of the contribution due from a society shall be determined by applying to its share and deposit base a percentage determined by the Board for the purpose of the contributions levied to meet the expenses attributable to the insolvency.

(5) The Board, in determining for the purposes of a building society insolvency—

(*a*) whether or not to levy contributions and, if so,

(*b*) the percentage to be applied under subsection (4) above to the share and deposit bases of the contributory societies, and

(*c*) the level of investor protection to be given by the insolvency payments to investors,

shall have regard to the factors specified in subsection (6) below.

(6) Those factors are—

(*a*) the amount available to meet the expenses attributable to the insolvency from the contributions leviable from contributory societies, and

(*b*) the amount of the expenses attributable to the insolvency at any level of investor protection.

(7) If it appears to the Board, as respects a building society insolvency, that the contributions it has levied will be insufficient to make the insolvency payments to investors at the level of investor protection determined by the Board under section 27, the Board may levy further contributions under subsection (2) above from the contributory societies.

(8) Contributions to the Fund shall be levied on a contributory society by the Board by service on the society of a notice specifying the amount (or further amount) due, which shall be paid by the society not later than twenty-one days after the date on which the notice is served.

(9) In relation to any contribution, the share and deposit base of a contributory society is such amount as represents the aggregate of so much of the society's liabilities as is referable to sums deposited with the society or to shares in the society as shown in the latest balance sheet sent to the Commission in accordance with section 81.

(10) No contributory society shall be required to pay a contribution if, or to the extent that, the amount of that contribution, together with previous contributions levied under this section for the purposes of any building society insolvency, after allowing for any repayments made to it under section 29, amounts to more than 0·3 per cent. of the society's share and deposit base as ascertained for the purposes of the contribution in question.

(11) Nothing in subsection (10) above—

(*a*) shall entitle a society to repayment of any contribution previously made, or

(*b*) shall prevent the Board from proceeding to levy contributions from other contributory societies in whose case the limit in that subsection has not been reached.

(12) The Treasury may, after consultation with the Board, by order made by statutory instrument, amend subsection (10) above so as to substitute for the percentage for the time being specified in that subsection such other percentage as may be specified in the order.

(13) No order shall be made under subsection (12) above unless a draft of it has been laid before and approved by a resolution of each House of Parliament.

(14) If, as respects a building society insolvency, it appears to the Board desirable to do so for the purpose of facilitating the making of insolvency payments to investors, the Board may borrow temporarily for that purpose subject, however, to the limit imposed by subsection (15) below.

(15) The aggregate of the amounts outstanding in respect of the principal of and interest due on sums borrowed under subsection (14) above shall not at any time exceed the aggregate of the sums leviable at that time from contributory societies for the purposes of any insolvency.

(16) Any sums borrowed by the Board under subsection (14) above in respect of a building society insolvency shall be repaid as soon as practicable after the contributions levied in respect of the insolvency have been paid by the contributory societies.

(17) In this section "the level of investor protection", in relation to insolvency payments to investors, means the proportion applicable for the purpose of calculating the amount of those payments under section 27.

DEFINITIONS
"authorised": s.119(1).
"the Board": s.24(1).
"the Commission": ss.1 and 119(1).
"contributory societies": subs.(3).
"deposited": *cf.* s.119(1).
"expenses attributable to the insolvency": s.25(5).
"the Fund": s.24(1).
"insolvency payments to investors": s.25(5).
"insolvent": see subs.(1).
"level of investor protection": subs. (17).
"notice": s.119(1).
"protective scheme provisions": s.24(3).
"share": s.119(1).
"share and deposit base": subs.(9).

GENERAL NOTE
In the event of a building society becoming insolvent, the present section empowers the Board to call up contributions from all authorised building societies (other than the insolvent society itself) to enable payments to be made under s.27 to investors in the insolvent society.

The circumstances in which a building society becomes insolvent for this purpose are set out in subs. (1). For the provisions relating to winding-up, reference should be made to ss.88 and 89 and the notes thereto.

The effect of subs. (2) is that the sums called up from the contributory societies will be determined primarily by reference to the payments which fall to be made to the investors entitled to claim against the Fund under s.27. The expression "the level of investor protection" in subs. (2) is explained in subs. (17): it means, broadly speaking, the percentage of protected investments which claimants will get back from the Fund (see s.27(1), (2), (5) and (8)). The level of investor protection is determined by the Board under s.27(2); however, in making that determination, the Board is required by subs. (5)(*c*) of the present section to have regard to the factors specified in subs. (6). These factors are discussed in the notes to subss. (5) and (6) below.

The amount of the contribution payable by each of the contributory societies is determined in accordance with subs. (4). The amount is computed by applying to each society's "share and deposit base" (*viz.* its total liabilities in respect of shares and deposits as shown in its latest balance sheet: see subs. (9)) a percentage determined by the Board. The effect of subs. (10) is that the amount that can be called up from a contributory society must not exceed 0.3 per cent. of its share and deposit base (and in applying that percentage, account must be taken of sums previously called up, to the extent that they have not already been repaid by the Board under s.29). There is, however, power to substitute a different maximum by order made under subs. (12). It should be noted once again that, in determining the percentage which is to apply in any particular case, the Board must have regard to the factors specified in subs. (6): subs. (5)(*b*) and the following note.

Subss. (5) and (6)

As has already been mentioned, the Board is required by subs. (5)(*b*) and (*c*) to have regard to the factors specified in subs.(6) both in determining what percentage of the share and deposit bases of contributory societies is to be called up in any particular case, and in determining what the level of investor protection is to be. Subs. (5)(*a*) additionally requires the Board to have regard to those factors in determining whether to levy contributions at all. In broad terms, the factors specified in subs. (6) are:

(*a*) the amount that can be raised from contributory societies towards the expenses of a particular insolvency; and

(*b*) the costs that will be incurred by the Fund at any level of investor protection.

It is not entirely clear what impact these factors are intended to have on the Board's decision whether or not to levy contributions in a particular case. There seems, however, to be at least a suggestion that, if the maximum amount that can be raised from the contributory societies is likely only to provide a meagre level of investor protection, then that constitutes a reason for not levying contributions at all (*sed quaere*). It may also be commented that there is a certain element of circularity in taking account of factor (*a*) in the determination referred to in subs. (5)(*b*), just as there is in taking account of factor (*b*) in the determination referred to in subs. (5)(*c*).

Subs. (7)

This subsection empowers the Board to levy further contributions in the event that the contributions previously levied prove insufficient to fund payments to investors at the level of protection determined under s.27(2). However, the aggregate of the further contributions and the previous ones must not exceed the 0.3 per cent. limit (or any substitute limit) in force under subs.(10).

Subss. (14)–(16)

The borrowing powers conferred on the Board by these subsections are strictly limited. The Board is empowered only to borrow "temporarily"; borrowings must be for the sole purpose of making payments under s.27 to investors in the insolvent society; the amounts borrowed (together with interest thereon) must not exceed the contributions for the time being leviable from the contributory societies; and the sums borrowed must be repaid as soon as practicable after those contributions have actually been paid.

Payments to investors

27.—(1) Subject to the provisions of this section, if a building society becomes insolvent and the Board determines under section 26 to levy contributions for the purpose of making payments to investors under this section the Board shall as soon as practicable pay out of the Fund to persons who have at the date of the determination protected investments in the building society amounts equal to the proportion of their protected investments applicable under subsection (2) below for the purpose of calculating the amount of those payments.

(2) The proportion applicable for that purpose is 90 per cent. or such lesser proportion as the Board determines to apply instead of it where it considers it expedient to do so having regard to the factors specified in section 26(6).

(3) A person claiming to be entitled to a payment under this section in respect of his protected investment in an insolvent building society shall make his claim in such form, with such evidence proving it, and within such period, as the Board directs and either to the Board or to such other recognised bank, licensed institution or building society authorised by the Board to make the payments on its behalf, as the Board directs.

(4) The Board may decline to make any payment under subsection (1) above to a person who, in the opinion of the Board, had any responsibility

for, or may have profited directly or indirectly from, the circumstances giving rise to the society's financial difficulties.

(5) For the purposes of this section in its application in relation to a building society which has become insolvent—

(a) a person has at any time a protected investment in the society if he has a deposit with, or a share in, the society; and

(b) his protected investment is the total liability of the society to him, limited to a maximum of £10,000, which is referable to sums deposited with the society or to his shares in the society.

(6) The Treasury, after consultation with the Board, may by order made by statutory instrument—

(a) amend subsection (2) above so as to substitute for the percentage for the time being specified in that subsection such other percentage as may be specified in the order; and

(b) amend subsection (5)(b) above so as to substitute for the sum for the time being specified in that paragraph such other sum as may be specified in the order.

(7) No order shall be made under subsection (6) above unless a draft of it has been laid before, and approved by a resolution of, each House of Parliament.

(8) In determining whether a person has a protected investment in a building society and the amount of it there shall be disregarded—

(a) any shares of his which are deferred shares,

(b) any deposit which, on a winding up, would fall to be repaid only after repayment in full had been made to the holders of shares in the society other than deferred shares; and

(c) any deposit which is evidenced by a certificate of deposit or other negotiable instrument.

(9) In determining what is the protected investment of an investor, no account shall be taken of any liability unless proof of the debt or claim which gives rise to it has been lodged with the liquidator of the society.

(10) Unless the Board otherwise directs in any particular case or class of case, in determining the total liability of an insolvent building society to any person for the purposes of subsection (1) above, there shall be deducted the amount of any liability of that person to the society—

(a) in respect of which a right of set-off existed immediately before the society became insolvent against any such investment of his as is referred to in that subsection, or

(b) in respect of which such a right would then have existed if the investment in question had been repayable on demand and the liability in question had fallen due.

(11) Payments under this section in respect of a protected investment in an insolvent building society may, if the Board thinks fit, be made by such instalments as it determines for the purposes of that insolvency.

(12) Schedule 6 to this Act, which contains provisions about investments held by trustees or jointly or on clients' account, shall have effect.

DEFINITIONS
"the Board": s.24(1)
"contributory societies": s.26(3).
"deferred shares": s.119(1).
"deposit": s.119(1).
"the Fund": s.24(1).
"insolvent": s.26(1).
"licensed institution": s.25(5); Banking Act 1979, s.50(1).
"protected investments": subss. (5) and (8).
"recognised bank": s.25(5); Banking Act 1979, s.50(1).
"share": s.119(1).

GENERAL NOTE

The protection afforded to investors by the statutory scheme is limited in two ways. First, a person is only protected by the scheme if and to the extent that he has a "protected investment" with the insolvent society. A person's protected investment is the total liability of the society to him, limited to a maximum of £10,000, in respect of both shares and deposits (but note (i) that deferred shares, "deferred deposits" and certain wholesale deposits must be disregarded in determining the amount of a person's protected investment and (ii) that allowance must be made for certain rights of set-off available to the society against the investor): see subss. (5), (8) and (10). Second, the proportion of his protected investment which the investor will get back from the Fund cannot be more than 90 per cent., and may be less if the Board thinks it "expedient" to apply a lower percentage having regard to the factors specified in s.26(6). Thus an investor holding £10,000 in shares with an insolvent society will recover a maximum of £9,000 from the Fund; and an investor holding £20,000 in shares with the society will also recover a maximum of £9,000 from the Fund. The £10,000 limit on protected investments is the same as that applicable to protected deposits under the scheme set up by the Banking Act 1979 (see s.29(1) of that Act); under that scheme, however, claimants can only recover 75 per cent. of their protected deposits (see s.28(1) of the 1979 Act, but note that there is no discretion under that Act to reduce the percentage recoverable in particular cases). It may be added that the Bill in its original form would have applied a maximum of 75 per cent. to the level of investor protection available under the present scheme: the figure was increased to 90 per cent. following a vigorous debate during the House of Commons Committee stage (see *Official Report*, Standing Committee A, February 4, 1986, cols. 219–230). It was indicated on behalf of the government, however, that the 90 per cent. figure might need to be reduced in the event of the requirements for the structure of commercial assets imposed by s.20 being relaxed to permit larger holdings of class 2 and class 3 assets than those currently permitted (see *ibid.* cols. 228 and 229). Attempts were made during the Committee stage in both Houses to increase or remove the ceiling of £10,000 imposed on protected investments; these attempts were, however, unsuccessful (see *ibid.*, cols. 230–4 and *Hansard*, H.L. Vol. 477, cols. 1132–1135). It should be noted that the current 90 per cent. limit and the existing £10,000 ceiling may both be changed (in either direction) by statutory instrument made under subs. (6).

Subss. (3) and (9)

It will be noted that, in addition to making a claim against the fund in accordance with subs. (3), the investor must also lodge a proof of his claim with the liquidator of the insolvent society: see subs. (9). If he fails to do the latter, his investment cannot be treated as a protected investment, and he will hence be ineligible to receive any payment under the scheme.

The concluding words of subs. (3) refer back to s.25(7) whereby the Fund may be "by-passed" in the event that the Board authorises a recognised bank, licensed institution or building society to receive contributions from the contributory societies, and to make payments to investors, as agent for the Board.

Subs. (4)

The Board has a wide discretion under this subsection to withhold payment from any investor who, in the Board's opinion, has any responsibility for, or may have derived any profit from, the circumstances giving rise to the financial difficulties of the insolvent society. The provision seems likely to have only limited effect since anyone who has *intentionally* caused, or profited from, the society's financial difficulties will no doubt have had the sense to withdraw his investment well before the crash. A similar provision, however, appears in the scheme set up under the Banking Act 1979: see s.28(2) of that Act.

Subs. (12)

This subsection gives effect to Sched. 6 which makes provision for the purposes of this section for investments held on trust, or held by persons jointly, or held on client account. Note in particular that, by Sched. 6, para. 4, joint investors (not being trustees) are usually treated as if each had a separate investment of an amount determined by dividing the total investment by the number of investors. So if two persons are jointly entitled to an investment of £20,000, each will normally be treated as being entitled to a separate (and fully protected) investment of £10,000.

Liability of insolvent society in respect of payments by Board

28.—(1) This section applies where—

(a) a building society has become insolvent,

(b) the Board has determined under section 26 to levy contributions for the purpose of making insolvency payments to investors in the society, and

(c) the Board, by virtue of the determination, has made, or is under a liability to make, an insolvency payment to an investor in respect of his protected investment.

(2) Where this section applies—

(a) the insolvent society shall become liable to the Board, as in respect of a contractual debt incurred immediately before the society became insolvent, for an amount equal to the amount of the insolvency payment to the investor;

(b) the liability of the society to the investor, whether referable to deposits or referable to shares of his (in this section referred to as "the liability to the investor"), shall be reduced by an amount equal to the insolvency payment made or to be made to him by the Board; and

(c) the respective duties of the liquidator of the insolvent building society—

(i) to make payments to the Board on account of the liability imposed by paragraph (a) above and to the investor on account of the liability to the investor so far as that liability is referable to deposits of his (after taking account of paragraph (b) above), and

(ii) to make payments to the Board on account of the liability imposed by paragraph (a) above and to the investor on account of the liability to the investor so far as that liability is referable to shares of his (after taking account of paragraph (b) above),

shall be varied in accordance with subsection (4) and subsection (5) below;

and in those subsections "the liability to the Board" means the liability imposed by paragraph (a) above on the society.

(3) Where the society's liability to the investor is referable to both shares and deposits, the amount equal to the insolvency payment to him shall, for the purposes of subsection (2)(b) above, be first applied in reduction of the liability referable to his shares then, if that amount exceeds that liability, in reduction of the liability referable to his deposits.

(4) The variation in the liquidator's duty where the liability to the investor is referable to deposits of his is as follows—

(a) in the first instance the liquidator shall pay to the Board instead of to the investor any amounts which, apart from this section, would be payable on account of the liability to the investor referable to deposits of his except in so far as that liability relates to a secured deposit; and

(b) if at any time the total amount paid to the Board by virtue of paragraph (a) above and in respect of the liability to the Board equals the amount of the insolvency payment referable to deposits of the investor, the liquidator shall thereafter pay to the investor instead of to the Board any amount which, apart from this section, would be payable to the Board in respect of the liability to the Board.

(5) The variation in the liquidator's duty where the liability to the investor is referable to shares of his is as follows—

(a) in the first instance the liquidator shall pay to the Board instead of to the investor any amounts which, apart from this section, would be payable on account of the liability to the investor referable to shares of his; and

(b) if at any time the total amount paid to the Board by virtue of paragraph (a) above and in respect of the liability to the Board equals the amount of the insolvency payment referable to shares of the investor, the liquidator shall thereafter pay to the investor instead of to the Board any amount which, apart from this section, would be payable to the Board in respect of the liability to the Board.

(6) In the case of a protected investment which, for the purposes of Schedule 6 to this Act, is held on trust for a person absolutely entitled to it against the trustees or, as the case may be, for two or more persons so entitled jointly, any reference in the preceding provisions of this section to the liability to the investor shall be construed as a reference to the liability of the insolvent society to the trustees.

(7) The Board may by notice served on the liquidator of an insolvent building society require him, at such time or times and at such place as may be specified in the notice,—

(a) to furnish to the Board such information, and

(b) to produce to the Board such books or papers specified in the notice,

as the Board may reasonably require to enable it to carry out its functions under the protective scheme provisions of this Part.

(8) Where, as a result of a building society having become insolvent, any books or papers have come into the possession of—

(a) in England and Wales, the Official Receiver,

(b) in Scotland, the liquidator, or

(c) in Northern Ireland, the Official Assignee for company liquidations,

he shall permit any person duly authorised by the Board to inspect the books or papers for the purpose of establishing—

(i) the identity of those of the society's investors to whom the Board is liable to make an insolvency payment; and

(ii) the amount of the protected investment held by each of those investors.

(9) Rules may be made—

(a) for England and Wales and for Scotland, under section 411 of the Insolvency Act 1986, and

(b) for Northern Ireland, under Article 613 of the Companies (Northern Ireland) Order 1986;

for the purpose of integrating the procedure provided for in this section into the general procedure on winding up.

DEFINITIONS
"the Board": s.24(1).
"deposit": s.119(1).
"insolvency payments to investors": s.25(5).
"insolvent": s.26(1).
"liability to the Board": subs. (2)(c).
"liability to the investor": subs. (2)(b).
"protected investment": cf. s.27(5) and (8).
"protective scheme provisions": s.24(3).
"share": s.119(1).

GENERAL NOTE
This section is modelled on s.31 of the Banking Act 1979. Its operation can perhaps best be illustrated by an example. Suppose that a building society becomes insolvent, and the Board calls up contributions from the contributory societies at the maximum level of investor protection permitted by s.27(2), viz., 90 per cent. An investor with the society who has, say, shares of £15,000 and a deposit account of £5,000 will receive a payment of £9,000 from the

Fund (*i.e.* 90 per cent. of the "protected" £10,000 slice of his total investment of £20,000): see s.27(1), (2) and (5). In those circumstances, the present section produces the following consequences:

(i) The society becomes liable to the Board for an amount equal to the £9,000 paid out of the Fund to the investor; the liability is treated as a contractual debt incurred by the society immediately before the insolvency: see subs. (2)(*a*).

(ii) The liability of the society to the investor is reduced by a corresponding amount; so, instead of owing the investor £20,000, the society will now owe him £11,000: see subs. (2)(*b*). By virtue of subs. (3), the society's liability in respect of the investor's shares will be reduced in priority to its liability in respect of his deposit; so the £11,000 now owed to the investor will be treated as representing a liability of £6,000 due in respect of shares (*i.e.* the original shareholding of £15,000 minus the whole of the insolvency payment of £9,000) and an undiminished liability of £5,000 due in respect of the deposit.

(iii) Since the insolvency payment of £9,000 will have had no effect on the society's liability in respect of the deposit, the liquidator of the society will be under a duty to pay the full amount of the deposit to the investor out of any assets of the society available for the purpose. The duty will not be varied by subs. (4), since that subsection only applies where some or all of the insolvency payment has been applied in reducing the society's liability in respect of the investor's deposits; and that is not the case here because the whole of the payment has been applied in reducing the society's liability in respect of his shares.

(iv) In the case of the shares, however, the position is different, since the insolvency payment has reduced the society's liabilities to the investor from £15,000 to £6,000. In those circumstances, subs. (5) varies the normal duties of the society's liquidator. The effect is that if the liquidator has in his hands assets available for distribution to the society's shareholders, he must first apply what would otherwise be the investor's share of those assets in his capacity as shareholder in reimbursing the Board for the £9,000 insolvency payment made out of the Fund. To that extent, therefore, the Board stands in the investor's shoes in the liquidation. If (but only if) the liquidator's liability to the Board is discharged in full, he may then make payments to the investor in respect of the outstanding £6,000 representing the "unprotected" part of his original shareholding.

Subs. (6)

This provision is rather curious. In a case where a trustee holds an investment on trust for a beneficiary who is absolutely entitled thereto, then, for the purposes of s.27, the beneficiary is treated as being entitled to the investment without the intervention of any trust: see Sched. 6, paras. 2(2) and 3. Accordingly, the beneficiary, and not the trustee, will be entitled to receive any insolvency payment made under s.27. Under the present subsection, however, references to the society's liability to the investor fall to be construed as references to its liability to the trustee. It seems logically to follow that the payment to the investor made under s.27 will have no effect on the society's liability to the trustee since the payment will not have been made "to him" (*i.e.* the trustee) and subs. (2)(*b*) above will hence not apply. It is not clear what effect this would have on the duties of the liquidator of the insolvent society.

Repayments in respect of contributions

29.—(1) Any moneys received by the Board under section 28 in respect of a building society insolvency shall not form part of the Fund but, for the remainder of the financial year of the Board in which they are received, shall be retained for the purposes of this section in its application in relation to that insolvency and, so far as appears to the Board appropriate, shall be invested in Treasury bills; and any income arising from moneys so invested during the remainder of the year shall be credited to the Fund.

(2) The Board shall, in connection with each building society insolvency for the purposes of which it has levied contributions under section 26, prepare a scheme for the making, out of moneys received by the Board under section 28 in respect of that insolvency, of repayments to the contributory societies in proportion to the contributions made by each such society in respect of the insolvency.

(3) As soon as practicable after the end of the financial year of the Board in which any moneys are received by the Board in respect of a building society insolvency, the Board shall, subject to subsection (4) below, make out of those moneys the payments required by the scheme made under subsection (2) above in connection with that insolvency.

(4) Where payments are due under subsection (3) above to building societies from whom contributions are due under section 26 for the purposes of other building society insolvencies, the Board may appropriate out of the moneys retained by it under subsection (1) above amounts not exceeding the contributions due from those societies and apply them as if they had been paid by those societies as contributions for the purposes of the other building society insolvencies.

(5) If the Board makes appropriations under subsection (4) above, then, the amounts so appropriated shall be treated for all purposes as having been paid by the Board to those societies in or towards discharge of its debts to them and paid by the societies to the Board as contributions and corresponding amounts shall be credited to the Fund and debited to the account kept for the purposes of this section.

(6) If in any financial year of the Board the payments made under subsection (3) above (in that and any previous years) in pursuance of a scheme under subsection (2) above are more than sufficient to provide for repayment in full of all the contributions to which the scheme related, the balance remaining of the moneys received and retained by the Board as mentioned in subsection (1) above shall be credited to the Fund.

(7) The Board, having regard to the factors specified in subsection (8) below, shall, as respects sums representing—

    (*a*) any balance credited to the Fund under subsection (6) above and any interest thereon, or

    (*b*) any balance of the contributions received in respect of the insolvency remaining after the making of insolvency payments to investors and the meeting of the other expenses attributable to the insolvency and any interest thereon,

either retain them in the Fund or pay so much of them to the contributory societies in proportion to the contributions made by each such society in respect of the insolvency, as the Board may think fit.

(8) Those factors are—

    (*a*) the likely level of future administrative expenses of the Board, and

    (*b*) the likelihood of other building societies becoming insolvent and, if they did, the amount of the expenses likely to be attributable to those insolvencies and the amounts likely to be available from contributory societies to meet those expenses.

DEFINITIONS

"the Board": s.24(1).
"building society insolvency": s.26(1).
"contributory societies": s.26(3).
"expenses attributable to the insolvency": s.25(5).
"financial year of the Board": *cf.* Sched. 6, para. 6(1).
"the Fund": s.24(1).

GENERAL NOTE

This section is broadly similar in purpose to s.32 of the Banking Act 1979. It is designed to ensure that, where the Board receives payments from the liquidator of an insolvent building society under s.28(2)(*c*), (4) and (5), those payments are applied by the Board primarily in refunding the contributions initially raised from the contributory societies.

As is apparent from subs. (1), moneys received by the Board from the liquidator are not credited to the Fund but are retained by the Board until the end of its current financial year: see subs. (1). (It will be noted, however, that subs. (1) provides for any *income* derived from the investment of the moneys so received during the intervening period to be credited to the Fund.) The Board must then draw up a scheme for making repayments to the contributory societies in proportion to their original contributions (see subs. (2)); and in the normal course the Board must make those repayments as soon as practicable after the end of its current financial year (see subs. (3)).

Subss. (4) and (5) make provision for the exceptional case in which sums are payable to a contributory society under subs. (3) at a time when contributions are also due from that society in respect of another building society insolvency; in such circumstances, subss. (4) and (5) provide, in effect, that the sums payable to the contributory society may be offset against the contributions due from it.

Subs. (6) postulates a case in which the moneys received by the Board from the liquidator of the insolvent society are more than sufficient to repay in full the contributions originally raised from the contributory societies. At first sight, it is difficult to see how such a surplus could arise, given (i) that the liquidator of the insolvent society cannot pay to the Board more than the amount paid to investors out of the Fund (see s.28(4)(b) and (5)(b)) and (ii) that income earned on moneys received by the Board from the liquidator is not retained by the Board for distribution to the contributory societies under subs. (3) but is instead credited straight to the Fund (see subs. (1)). The solution to the problem seems to be that, between the time when contributions are paid into the Fund by the contributory societies and the time when payments are made out of the Fund to investors, income may arise under s.25(2) and (3) on the moneys constituting the Fund. It follows that the payments made to investors may (by virtue of the income earned) exceed the sums raised from the contributory societies; so, if in such a case the liquidator of the insolvent society were to reimburse the Board for the full amount paid out of the Fund to investors, the consequence would be that the payments received from the liquidator would exceed the original contributions of the contributory societies, and the resulting surplus would fall to be credited to the Fund in accordance with subs. (6).

Subss. (7) and (8) make provision for any such surplus either (i) to be repaid to the contributory societies in proportion to their original contributions or (ii) (at the Board's discretion) to be retained in the Fund to meet future administrative expenses of the Board or to cover the possibility of future insolvencies. Similar provision is made with respect to any balance of the contributions raised from the contributory society which remains in the Fund after all the payments chargeable to the Fund have been met (*i.e.* where more money was called up from the contributory societies than was in fact required): see subs. (7)(b).

Tax treatment of contributions and repayments

30. In computing for the purposes of the Tax Acts the profits or gains arising from the trade carried on by a contributory building society—

(a) to the extent that it would not be deductible apart from this paragraph, any sum expended or treated under section 29 as expended by the society in paying a contribution to the Fund may be deducted as an expense; and

(b) any payment which is made or treated as made to the society by the Board under section 29(3) or (7) shall be treated as a trading receipt.

DEFINITIONS

"the Board": s.24(1).
"contributory society": s.26(3).
"the Fund": s.24(1).
"the Tax Acts": Income and Corporation Tax Act 1970, s.526(2).

GENERAL NOTE

Sums expended (or deemed to have been expended by virtue of s.29(5)) in the payment of contributions to the Fund are fully deductible in computing the profits or gains of the contributory society for tax purposes. The corollary is that repayments by the Board are treated as trading receipts. Curiously, para. (b) makes no references to s.29(5), under which repayments may be treated as having been made to a contributory society: s.29(3) and (7) deal only with actual repayments.

The present section is modelled closely on the provisions of s.33 of the Banking Act 1979.

Other provisions

Voluntary schemes

31.—(1) Subject to the provisions of this section, any two or more building societies may enter into arrangements for the purpose of making funds available to meet losses incurred by persons who have deposited money with, or who have shares in, an insolvent building society which is a party to the arrangements (referred to in this section as "voluntary arrangements").

(2) A building society shall have power to make contributions to a fund vested in trustees appointed under voluntary arrangements made in accordance with this section.

(3) Voluntary arrangements shall not come into force, and no contributions shall be made thereunder by a building society, until the arrangements have been approved by the Commission and authorised by a resolution passed at a general meeting of the society as a special resolution.

(4) The maximum payment to any investor that may be provided for by voluntary arrangements is such sum as represents the total liability of the insolvent society to him (of any amount) which is referable to sums deposited with the society or to his shares in the society, after taking into account payments to him under section 27.

(5) No payment under voluntary arrangements shall be made to any person—

    (a) in respect of any investment which would be disregarded for the purposes of section 27(8), or

    (b) where the liability of the insolvent society to him is reduced by any set-off for the purposes of section 27(10); or

    (c) where that person is ineligible for any payment under the protective scheme provisions of this Part by virtue of a decision of the Board under section 27(4).

(6) Voluntary arrangements may include—

    (a) arrangements to constitute, and for contributions to be made to, a fund vested in trustees appointed under the arrangements, being a standing fund or a fund established in the event of an insolvency (or a combination of each);

    (b) arrangements for payments to be made on behalf of the trustees to investors by societies participating in the arrangements;

    (c) arrangements to protect only specified classes of investor or specified classes of investment;

    (d) arrangements providing for a level of protection more limited than the maximum allowed by subsection (4) above;

    (e) arrangements with the Board or any institution making payments to investors on the Board's behalf for the purpose of making payments under the protective scheme provisions of this Part and voluntary arrangements at the same time; or

    (f) arrangements providing, in circumstances specified in them, for payments to be made by the trustees to the societies making contributions.

(7) Any payment by a society participating in arrangements which include arrangements falling within subsection (6)(b) above shall be treated for the purposes of this section as a contribution paid by the society to the trustees and as a payment by the trustees to the investors.

(8) Subject to subsection (9) below, subsections (2) to (6) of sections 28 shall, if the voluntary arrangements so provide, apply to payments to investors made by the trustees as they apply to insolvency payments made by the Board.

(9) In relation to a building society insolvency in respect of which the Board and the trustees have each made payments to investors, the

variation in the liquidator's duty effected by subsections (2)(*c*), (4) and
(5) of section 28 shall be modified as follows, that is to say—

  (*a*) subsection (4) shall have effect as if it required the liquidator,
     before paying the investor and after paying the Board to the extent
     required by that subsection, to pay to the trustees instead of to the
     investor any amount which, apart from this paragraph, would be
     payable to the trustees on account of the liability to the trustees
     referable to deposits of the investor; and

  (*b*) subsection (5) shall have effect with a corresponding modification
     in respect of any such amount referable to shares of the investor,

and, in this subsection, "the liability to the trustees", means the liability
to the trustees which, by virtue of subsection (8) above, corresponds to
the liability to the Board imposed by section 28(2)(*a*).

(10) In this section "insolvent" and "insolvency", in relation to a
building society, have the meanings given by section 26(1); and "the
trustees", in relation to voluntary arrangements, means the trustees
appointed under them.

DEFINITIONS
  "the Commission": ss.1 and 119(1).
  "the Board": s.24(1).
  "deposit": s.119(1).
  "insolvent" and "insolvency": subs. (10) and s.26(1).
  "protective scheme provisions": s.24(3).
  "share": s.119(1).
  "special resolution": s.119(1) and Sched. 2, para. 27.
  "trustees": subs. (10).
  "voluntary arrangements": subs. (1).

GENERAL NOTE
  This section enables any two or more building societies to enter into voluntary arrangements to supplement the protection afforded to their investors by the statutory scheme. The
section has certain affinities with s.43 of the 1962 Act (enabling societies to make arrangements for a guarantee fund), but it allows a greater degree of flexibility to participating
societies than was available under the old legislation (in particular, by removing the
requirement that arrangements be made through insurers). The following points should be
noted when considering the present section:
  (i) the arrangements require the approval of the Commission and must be authorised by
a special resolution of each participating society: see subs. (3).
  (ii) The arrangements must provide for the fund to be vested in trustees; but the fund may
be a standing fund, or a fund to be constituted (like the statutory fund) only in the event of
an insolvency, or it may be a combination of the two: see subss. (2) and (6)(*a*).
  (iii) The protection provided to investors can "top up" the protection available to them
under the statutory scheme; but it cannot duplicate or supplant that protection: see the
concluding words of subs. (4).
  (iv) Payments under a voluntary scheme cannot be made (*a*) in respect of deferred shares
and other forms of investment falling within s.27(8); (*b*) in respect of liabilities of the society
which are cancelled out by a right of set-off against the investor; or (*c*) where the investor
has been disqualified from receiving payments under the statutory scheme by a determination
of the Board under s.27(4): see subs. (5).
  (v) Subject to points (iii) and (iv) above, a voluntary scheme may provide for payments
to be made to an investor of any amount up to (but not exceeding) 100 per cent. of his total
investment in the insolvent society: see subss. (4) and (6)(*d*). Unlike the statutory scheme,
therefore, a voluntary scheme need embody no upper limit on the amount of an investment
for which protection is available, nor on the proportion of his protected investment which
the investor can recover from the fund.
  (vi) Protection may be limited to specified classes of investor, or to specified classes of
investment in the participating societies: see subs. (6)(*c*).
  (vii) The liquidator of the insolvent society must repay to the Board any sum paid to an
investor out of the statutory fund before he can repay to the trustees any sum paid to the
investor out of the voluntary fund. But the liquidator must repay the trustees in full before
paying any money direct to the investor. See subs. (9).

See further the notes to s.24, where reference is made to the existing voluntary scheme set up by the Building Societies Association.

Special provisions as regards investors

32. The provisions of Schedule 7 to this Act relating to shareholders in and depositors with a building society shall have effect.

DEFINITIONS
"depositors": s.119(1).
"shareholders": s.119(1).

GENERAL NOTE
This section gives effect to Sched. 7, which makes provision (i) for small investments to be withdrawn following the death of an investor, without the need to produce any grant of representation to the deceased's estate; and (ii) for the giving of receipts by minors for the withdrawal of sums deposited by them with the society.

Assistance by building societies to other building societies

33. Where it appears to the Commission that a building society is in financial difficulties it may authorise a building society to lend money to that society, and a building society shall have power to do so accordingly.

DEFINITION
"the Commission": see ss.1 and 119(1).

GENERAL NOTE
This section substantially re-enacts s.44 of the 1962 Act, but dispenses with the requirement that the consent of the Treasury be obtained before authorisation can be given for the loan. The section is necessary because a loan to another society in these circumstances will not (or not normally) fall within the scope of the lending society's ordinary powers under the Act to make secured or unsecured loans.

PART V

POWERS TO PROVIDE SERVICES

Powers to provide financial services or services relating to land

34.—(1) A building society may provide services of the descriptions for the time being specified in Part I of Schedule 8 to this Act subject to the restrictions (if any) for the time being specified in Part II or III of that Schedule.

(2) The appropriate authority may by order vary Schedule 8 by adding to or deleting from it any description of service or any provision or by varying any description of service or any provision for the time being specified or contained in it but not so as to confer any power to provide services other than services that appear to the authority making the order to be financial services or services relating to land or to be services similar to any such services.

(3) Any power conferred on building societies under subsection (2) above may be conferred on building societies of a specified description or all building societies other than those of a specified description.

(4) Where a provision of Part III of that Schedule states that a power to provide a specified service is available only to a subsidiary or other associated body of a building society the power to provide that service is to be treated as a power of the society for the purposes of section 18 only.

(5) Any power to provide a specified service, if available to a building society or any subsidiary or other associated body, must, in order to be exercisable, be adopted by the society.

(6) Subject to any specified restriction, any power to provide a specified service shall be exercisable in relation to members of the building society or other persons.

(7) Part IV of Schedule 8 has effect for supplementing Parts I, II and III of that Schedule and the power under subsection (2) above to vary that Schedule includes, without prejudice to the generality of that subsection, power to make such provision as appears to the authority making the order to be appropriate by way of a sanction for contravention of any restriction for the time being contained in Part III.

(8) The "appropriate authority" for the purpose of exercising the powers conferred by this section is the Treasury as regards any variation of Part I of Schedule 8 with or without other provision and the Commission in any other case.

(9) The power to make an order under subsection (2) above is exercisable by statutory instrument and—

(*a*) in the case of an order varying Part I of Schedule 8 with or without other provision no such order shall be made unless a draft of it has been laid before and approved by a resolution of each House of Parliament, and

(*b*) in the case of any other order, the instrument containing it shall be subject to annulment in pursuance of a resolution of either House of Parliament.

(10) An order under subsection (2) above may make such incidental and transitional provision as appears to the authority making the order to be necessary or expedient.

(11) In this section—

"financial services" means any of the following services, that is to say, banking, insurance, investment, trusteeship and executorship;

"services relating to land" means any service relating to the acquisition, management, development or disposal of land; and

"specified" means specified for the time being in Schedule 8 to this Act.

DEFINITIONS

"appropriate authority": subs. (8).
"associated body": ss.18(17) and 119(1).
"the Commission": ss.1 and 119(1).
"financial services": subs. (11).
"member": s.119(1).
"services relating to land": subs. (11).
"specified": subs.(11).
"subsidiary": s.119(1) and Companies Act 1985, s.736(1).

GENERAL NOTE

Under the 1962 Act, a building society had power to provide ancillary services for its customers only in circumstances where such services could be described as necessary or reasonably incidental to the attainment of the society's sole statutory purpose, *viz.*, raising by the subscription of its members "a stock or fund for making advances to members out of the funds of the society upon the security by way of freehold or leasehold estate" (see s.1(1) of the 1962 Act). Moreover, it made no difference whether a society was involved in a particular transaction as principal or as agent, since it had no power to do as agent what it lacked the power to do as principal. Hence, for example, a society could arrange for the insurance of a property mortgaged to it, that being something which (because necessary for the proper protection of its security) could be regarded as reasonably incidental to its basic power to make advances secured on land; nor was there any objection to the society acting also as agent of the borrower for the onward transmission of the premiums to the insurers. But the society lacked any general power to arrange insurances for its customers, or to provide money transmission or other banking services as such: *c.f.* Wurtzburg and Mills, *Building Society Law* (14th Ed.), pp. 3–4.

The present section, in conjunction with Sched. 8, makes an important change in the law by conferring power on building societies to provide a wide range of services which have not hitherto been open to them. These services are set out in fifteen different categories in Part I of Sched. 8, and reference should be made to the notes to that Schedule for a discussion of the individual categories. At this point, however, the following general points may be noted:

(i) Services falling within twelve of the fifteen categories may be provided either directly by building societies or through the medium of their subsidiaries or other associated bodies. The power to provide the services which fall within the remaining three categories (namely, personal equity plan management; unit trust pension scheme management; and estate agency) is, however, available only to subsidiaries of building societies: see Sched. 8, Part III, paras. 6(1), 9 and 11 (and see s.18(17) for the definition of the expression "associated body", and the notes thereto for an explanation of the circumstances in which a body associated with a building society constitutes a "subsidiary" of that society). There is a small technical point which arises in relation to the services falling within these categories. Since building societies themselves lack the power to provide these services, the closing words of s.18(4) and the provisions of s.18(6)(*a*) would, unless modified, have prevented societies from investing in or supporting subsidiaries engaged in the provision of such service. The point is, however, met by subs.(4) of the present section which, for the purposes of s.18 only, deems building societies to have power to provide services which are in fact confined by Part III of Sched. 8 to their subsidiaries.

(ii) Services falling within thirteen of the fifteen categories may be provided by building societies of all sizes. The services which fall within the other two categories (namely, estate management and personal equity plan management) are, however, restricted to the larger societies, *i.e.* societies with a qualifying asset holding within the meaning of s.118: see Sched. 8, Part III, paras. 4 and 6(2).

(iii) Subs. (5) provides that any power to provide a service specified in Sched. 8, "if available to a building society or any subsidiary or other associated body must, in order to be exercisable, be adopted by the society" (*i.e.* adopted in accordance with Sched. 2, para.1 or 4 or Sched. 20, para.2 or 3). It would appear, therefore, that even in the three cases where the power to provide a service is available only to a subsidiary of the society, the power must still be adopted by the society itself. It is a little difficult to see how the society can adopt a power which by definition is not available to it; but presumably the intention is that the society, in these cases, should adopt the power to provide the service through (and only through) the medium of a subsidiary. It may be observed that this approach appears to be consistent with subs. (1), which provides simply that "a building society may provide" the services specified in Sched. 8, Part I, without any attempt being made to discriminate between those services which a building society may provide direct, and those services which can be provided only by a subsidiary. In describing services in the latter class as services which "a building society may provide", subs. (1) can only mean that the society may provide those services through its subsidiaries.

(iv) With one exception (namely the power to provide estate agency services), the power to provide the services specified in Sched. 8, Part I does not include power to maintain a place of business in a country or territory outside the United Kingdom unless the society also conducts "the principal business of a building society" in that country or territory: see Sched. 8, Part II. The words quoted are defined in Sched. 8, Part IV, para.7 to mean: "the business of raising funds (whether by the issue of shares or receiving deposits) for the purposes of the society or of making advances secured on land." It would appear, therefore, that provided a society raises funds for its purposes in a foreign country or territory, it will have power to maintain a place of business there for the provision of services under s.34 and Sched. 8, notwithstanding that the society cannot make advances (or does not in fact make advances) secured on land in the relevant country or territory. (As to the circumstances in which a society may be authorised to make advances secured on foreign land, see s.14 and the notes thereto.) As indicated, the power to provide estate agency services constitutes an exception to the general restriction imposed by Sched. 8, Part II. The exception is, however, more apparent than real, since (*a*) estate agency services can only be provided through a subsidiary (see para. (i) of this note); (*b*) if not formed in the United Kingdom, the subsidiary must be formed in an E.E.C. country or in the Channel Islands, the Isle of Man or Gibraltar (see Sched. 8, Part III, para.12(*a*)); (*c*) if the subsidiary is formed in one of those countries or territories, "the principal business" of the society must, at the time when the society forms or acquires the subsidiary, be conducted in that country or territory (see *ibid.*); and (*d*) at least 40 per cent. of the subsidiary's total income in any financial year must be derived from estate agency work done in countries or territories in which, at any time in that year, the society carries on the business of making advances secured on land (see Sched.

8, Part III, para. 12(*b*)). However, Sched. 8, Part III, para. 12, when read with Sched. 8, Part II, subpara. (2), does appear to admit the possibility of a place of business being maintained in a country or territory in which the society does not conduct any other business, if the subsidiary conducts its estate agency business in that country or territory as well as in the country or territory of its formation. In this limited respect, there is a real difference, as respects the maintenance of foreign places of business, between estate agency services and other services specified in Sched. 8.

(v) In general, the services specified in Sched. 8 may be provided to corporate bodies as well as to individuals. The provision of foreign exchange service is, however, limited to individuals, as is arranging for the provision of investment services (see Sched. 8, Part III, paras. 2 and 5); and the power to arrange for the provision of credit and the power to arrange for the provision of insurance are both limited (save in specified circumstances) to their provision to individuals. While not apparent from the terms of Sched. 8 itself, it may be added that personal equity plans (dealt with in Sched. 8, para. 6) can, in practice, be established and managed only for the benefit of individuals, since investment in such plans is restricted to individuals by the Finance Act 1986, Sched. 8, para. 1.

(vi) As is apparent from subs. (6), any power to provide a service specified in that Schedule may, subject to any restriction specified in Sched. 8, be exercised in relation both to members and non-members of the society. As it now stands, Sched. 8 contains no restriction which would require any of the existing powers to provide services to be exercised only in relation to members. Under subs. (2), however, it would be possible for such a restriction to be imposed at a later date by statutory instrument. It should also be borne in mind that subs. (2) empowers the appropriate authority (in this case, the Treasury: see subs. (8)) to make orders adding new descriptions of services to the list currently set out in Sched. 8, Part I; it is quite possible that such an order would embody a restriction whereby the new service or services could be provided only to members. Note, incidentally, that the power to add new services to the list in Sched. 8, Part I is constrained by the requirement that such services must appear to the Treasury to be "financial services" or "services relating to land" within the meanings given to those expressions by subs. (11).

(vii) It may be noted finally that the provision by a society of the services specified in Sched. 8 will normally have no direct effect on the society's balance sheet. Hence there is no room here for applying the requirements for the structure of commercial assets set out in s.20. However, a society which undertook any of these services without sufficient managerial and professional skills, or which diverted an undue proportion of its management and professional resources away from its primary mortgage lending business into the provision of these services, would find itself in danger of failing to satisfy the criteria of prudent management specified in s.45. So, while the provision of the new services may not be susceptible to control through the society's balance sheet, a society which provides them in a reckless or incompetent fashion will soon find itself attracting the watchful eye of the Commission.

Prohibition on linking services

35.—(1) A building society which, or a subsidiary of which, provides services of any description specified in Part I of Schedule 8 to this Act shall not offer to make a class 1 advance to any person subject to a condition that any services of that description which are or may be required by that person in connection with the making of the advance shall be provided by the society or its subsidiary.

(2) Where, in connection with a class 1 advance by a building society, several services are made available by a building society or by a building society and one or more of its subsidiaries the society shall not, and shall secure that each of its subsidiaries does not, make the services available on terms other than terms which distinguish the consideration payable for each service so made available; nor shall any of its subsidiaries make the services available on terms other than terms which make that distinction.

(3) Nothing in subsection (2) above prevents a service from being provided free of charge or free of charge in particular circumstances.

(4) If a building society contravenes subsection (1) or (2) above the society shall be liable on summary conviction to a fine not exceeding level 4 on the standard scale and so shall any officer who is also guilty of the offence.

(5) If a body corporate which is a subsidiary of a building society contravenes subsection (2) above the body corporate shall be liable on summary conviction to a fine not exceeding level 4 on the standard scale.

DEFINITIONS
"subsidiary": s.119(1) and the Companies Act 1985, s.736.
"class 1 advance": ss.11(2) and 119(1).
"the standard scale": Criminal Justice Act 1982, s.37.
"officer": s.119 (1).

GENERAL NOTE
This section is intended to prevent potential abuses by building societies of the dominant position which they enjoy in the housing finance market.

Subs. (1)
The mischief at which this subsection is aimed is that of "linking" services to advances, *i.e.* offering advances on terms which require the borrower to use services provided by the lender. By this subsection (which is backed by the criminal sanctions provided in subs. (4)) a building society is prohibited from making an offer of a class 1 advance subject to the condition that the applicant uses any service provided by the society or its subsidiaries under s.34. It will be noted that the prohibition on linking applies to offers of class 1 advances (*i.e.* broadly speaking, advances to individuals secured by a first mortgage of residential property); there is nothing to stop a society or its subsidiaries linking the provision of services to offers of class 2 advances or (where applicable) to offers of unsecured loans. It will also be observed that the subsection applies only to services which are provided under s.34, and which are or may be required by the applicant in connection with the advance offered to him. Clearly, therefore, the subsection would not prohibit a society from making an offer of advance conditional on the applicant, say, opening a share account with the society (that not being a service provided under s.34); nor, it seems, would the subsection prohibit a society from imposing a condition that the applicant use a service which *is* provided under s.34 where that service is *not* required by the applicant in connection with the advance offered to him. But market pressures will no doubt guard adequately against the latter possibility.

Subs. (2)
This subsection (which is backed by the criminal sanctions provided in subss. (4) and (5)) is designed to prevent the price charged for individual services being concealed by aggregation with the price charged for other services. The effect of the subsection is that, where a borrower is offered a package deal comprising several services provided by the society or its subsidiaries, the borrower must be told the price charged for each component in the package. Like subs. (1), this subsection only applies where services are offered in connection with a class 1 advance (that being regarded as the sector of the market in which building societies have a dominant influence, and in which an added degree of consumer protection is therefore appropriate). Unlike subs. (1), however, the present subsection applies to all services provided by a building society and its subsidiaries: it is not limited to services provided under s.34.
It will be noted that there is nothing in this subsection which requires the price charged for a service to be related to the cost of providing it (indeed so much is clear from subs. (3), whereby services can be provided free of charge). This subsection will not, therefore, eliminate the cross-subsidisation of services: its objective is the different one of "price transparency", *i.e.* enabling the borrower to compare prices by setting out the price charged for each service.

Subss. (4) and (5)
Level 4: currently £1,000.

Commencement
This section attracted a good deal of criticism from building societies during the course of the Bill's passage through Parliament (such criticism being directed primarily at the fact that no similar restrictions apply to those competing with building societies in the mortgage lending market). In response, no doubt, to the pressure from the movement, the Government has announced that this section will not be brought into force in the event that the Building Societies Association introduces a suitable code of practice by January 1, 1988, and that the code is satisfactorily observed by societies thereafter.

PART VI

POWERS OF CONTROL OF THE COMMISSION

Powers in relation to asset or liability structure requirements

Powers in event of breach of limits on certain assets and liabilities

36.—(1) The provisions of this section have effect where, by reason of—

> (*a*) its liabilities in respect of non-retail funds and deposits being in excess of the limit imposed on them by section 7(3), or
>
> (*b*) its liabilities in respect of sums deposited with the society being in excess of the limit imposed on them by section 8(1), or
>
> (*c*) its commercial assets of any class being in excess of the limits imposed on assets of that class by section 20(2) or (3), or
>
> (*d*) its liquid assets being in excess of the limit imposed on them by section 21,

the powers conferred by this section become exercisable by the Commission in relation to a building society (the limits referred to in paragraphs (*a*), (*b*), (*c*) and (*d*) above being referred to in this section as "the relevant statutory limits").

(2) The Commission may give the society a direction under subsection (3), (5) or (6) below.

(3) A direction by the Commission under this subsection is a direction requiring the society, within a specified period, to submit for its approval a plan (in this section referred to as a "restructuring plan") designed to secure the following purposes, that is to say—

> (*a*) that the assets and liabilities of the society will not, by the end of the period of 12 months beginning with the date of the direction, exceed the relevant statutory limits as applied at the last day of that period, and
>
> (*b*) that they will not thereafter exceed the relevant statutory limits.

(4) For the purpose of applying the relevant statutory limits as directed by subsection (3)(*a*) above—

> (*a*) in the case of a limit which operates by reference to the end of a financial year of a society, the financial year of the society shall be treated as ending on the day as at which the limits are to be applied; and
>
> (*b*) the assets and liabilities of the society shall be determined by reference to a balance sheet prepared by the directors by reference to that day and sent to the Commission within the period of three months beginning with that day;

and section 81(4) shall apply in the event of a default in complying with this provision as it applies in the event of a default in complying with subsection (2) of that section.

(5) A direction by the Commission under this subsection is a direction requiring the society—

> (*a*) within the period of six months beginning with the date of the direction, to submit to its members for their approval at a meeting or by ballot the requisite transfer resolutions for a transfer of the business of the society to a company under section 97; and
>
> (*b*) to notify the Commission of the result of the meeting or ballot.

(6) A direction by the Commission under this subsection is a direction requiring the society, at its option, either—

> (*a*) within a specified period, to submit for approval a restructuring plan, or
>
> (*b*) within the period of six months beginning with the date of the direction, to submit to its members for their approval at a meeting

or by ballot the requisite transfer resolutions for a transfer of the business of the society to a company under section 97;
and, within a specific period, to notify the Commission of the option it has decided to pursue.

(7) Where a restructuring plan is submitted by a society to the Commission under subsection (3) or (6) above then—

(*a*) if it appears to the Commission that the plan is reasonably likely to secure its purposes, the Commission shall approve it and direct the society to carry it out;

(*b*) if it appears to it that the plan is, with modifications, likely to secure its purposes and the Commission and the society agree on appropriate modifications within the period of 21 days from the date on which the Commission notifies the society of the modifications it proposes for the society's agreement, the Commission shall approve the plan as modified and direct the society to carry it out;

but otherwise it shall reject the plan.

(8) Where a meeting or ballot is held, in pursuance of a direction under subsection (5) or (6) above, for the purpose of voting on the requisite transfer resolutions, then—

(*a*) if the resolutions are agreed to and the confirmation of the transfer by the Commission is obtained, the society shall proceed under section 97 to transfer its business to a successor company;

(*b*) if either resolution is disagreed to, the society shall notify the Commission of that fact as soon as it is practicable to do so

(9) In the event of the Commission receiving a notice from a society under subsection (8)(*b*) above, it may, if it thinks fit, serve on the society a direction requiring it, within a specified period, to submit to the Commission for its approval a restructuring plan; and if the Commission does so, subsection (7) above shall apply as if the plan had been submitted under subsection (3) above.

(10) The Commission may, if it thinks fit, extend or further extend, any period during which a building society is to take any steps required of it under any of the foregoing provisions of this section and may do so whether or not application is made to it before the expiry of the period in question.

(11) If a building society fails, within the period allowed to it under the foregoing provisions of this section—

(*a*) where it has been given a direction under subsection (3) above, to submit a restructuring plan,

(*b*) where it has been given a direction under subsection (5) above, to submit to members the requisite transfer resolutions,

(*c*) where it has been given a direction under subsection (6) above, to either submit a restructuring plan or submit to members the requisite transfer resolutions,

(*d*) where it has been directed under subsection (7) above to carry out a restructuring plan, to secure the purpose of it specified in subsection (3)(*a*) above,

(*e*) to agree to the requisite transfer resolutions submitted to the members in pursuance of subsection (5) or (6) above, or

(*f*) where it has agreed to the requisite transfer resolutions, to proceed under section 97 to transfer its business to the successor company,

or if the Commission rejects a restructuring plan under subsection (7) above, the powers conferred on the Commission by section 37 shall become exercisable in relation to the society.

(12) In this section "confirmation", "the requisite transfer resolutions" and "transfer" have the same meaning as in section 97.

DEFINITIONS
"the Commission": ss.1 and 119(1).
"confirmation": subs. (12) and s.97.
"deposits": s.119(1).
"financial year": ss.117 and 119(1).
"members": s.119(1).
"non-retail funds and deposits": s.7(4).
"relevant statutory limits": subs. (1).
"requisite transfer resolutions": subs. (12) and s.97.
"restructuring plan": subs. (3).
"transfer": subs. (12) and s.97.

GENERAL NOTE
This section makes provision for cases in which there is a failure by a building society to comply with the constraints imposed by the Act on the structure of its balance sheet. Those constraints are imposed by the provisions referred to in subs. (1), and they apply to both sides of the balance sheet (ss.7(3) and 8(1) deal with the composition of a society's liabilities, and ss.20(2) and (3) and 21 deal with the composition of its assets). If the limits imposed by those provisions are not complied with, then the powers conferred on the Commission by the present section become exercisable in relation to the defaulting society.

The Commission has a choice of measures open to it under the section: see subs. (2).

Under subs. (3), it can direct the society to submit a "restructuring plan" for the Commission's approval. The objects of such a plan are (*a*) to ensure that the society's non-compliance with the relevant limits ceases within a period of 12 months and (*b*) to ensure that the limits will not thereafter be breached. A small technical point arises in connection with the limits imposed by s.20(2) and (3), since those limits fall to be applied only at the end of a society's financial year (in contrast to the limits imposed by the other provisions referred to in subs. (1) of this section, which apply at any time). For that reason, a direction given under subs. (3) of the present section that a society comply with the limits imposed by s.20 within a period of 12 months from the date of the *direction* could have given rise to difficulty in a case where the direction was not given on the last day of the society's financial year. The difficulty is removed by subs. (4) which provides that, for this purpose, the financial year of the defaulting society will be deemed to end on the day which falls 12 months after the date of the direction. A special balance sheet must be prepared and sent to the Commission in such a case (see subs. (4)(*b*)); failure to do so will expose the society's directors to the criminal sanctions set out in s.81(4) (see the concluding words of subs. (4)).

Under subs. (5), the Commission can take the more drastic course of directing the society to submit to its members a resolution for the transfer of the society's business to a commercial company under s.97. Such a course will presumably be appropriate in cases where a society's activities, as reflected in its balance sheet, have strayed so far beyond the limits imposed by the Act that the society has become, or is in the process of becoming, unrecognisable as a building society. In such a case, the society may no longer be capable of responding to the curative properties of a restructuring plan, with the consequence that the most appropriate course is to give its members the opportunity to complete the society's metamorphosis into a commercial company.

Finally, subs. (6) empowers the Commission to direct the society, at its option, either to submit a restructuring plan for the approval of the Commission or to submit a transfer resolution for the approval of the membership. Such a course will presumably be followed in cases where the society's non-compliance with the relevant limits is serious enough to raise doubts about its continued viability as a building society, but not so serious as to call for an outright direction to submit a transfer resolution to the membership under subs. (5).

Where a restructuring plan is submitted to the Commission (either pursuant to a direction under subs. (3) or pursuant to a direction under subs. (6)), then the Commission may either approve it, approve it with modifications, or reject it (see subs. (7)). If the plan is rejected, then the further powers conferred on the Commission by s.37 will become exercisable (with the consequence that the Commission may present a petition to the court to wind up the society).

Subss. (8)(*b*) and (9) make provision for the case in which a transfer resolution is submitted to the membership (*i.e.*, pursuant to a direction under subss. (5) or (6)), but is rejected by the membership. In those circumstances, the Commission may direct the society to submit a restructuring plan for its approval, and the provisions of subs. (7) will then apply to the plan in the same way as if it had been submitted under subs. (3). Again, therefore, if the plan is rejected, the Commission's further powers under s.37 will become exercisable.

As is apparent from subs. (11)(*a*)–(*f*), the Commission's powers under s.37 will also be activated in the event of society failing to comply with a direction given by the Commission under this section, or failing to agree to, or to implement, a transfer resolution submitted to its members.

Powers in event of breach of limits on assets or liabilities or abuse of purpose of building society

37.—(1) Where—
(*a*) by virtue of section 36(11) the powers conferred by this section become exercisable in relation to a building society, or
(*b*) the Commission has reason to believe that the purpose or principal purpose of a building society has ceased to be that required by section 5(1) for the establishment of a building society under this Act,

the Commission may present a petition to the High Court for the winding up of the society under the applicable winding up legislation or make an application to the High Court for an order giving directions to the society under subsection (2) below; and the power to present a petition or to make an application for such an order is available to the Commission whether or not it has previously made an application for such an order or presented a petition, as the case may be.

(2) An order under this subsection is an order directing the society—
(*a*) in a case where the application is made under subsection (1)(*a*) above, to carry out the restructuring plan as directed in the order, and
(*b*) in a case where the application is made under subsection (1)(*b*) above, to modify its business as directed in the order.

(3) An order under subsection (2)(*b*) above may require the society to take certain steps or to refrain from pursuing a particular course of action or to restrict the scope of its business in a particular way.

(4) Where the High Court makes an order under subsection (2) above, the Commission shall give a copy of it to the central office and the central office shall keep the copy in the public file of the society.

(5) The High Court shall not make an order winding up the society on an application under subsection (1)(*b*) above unless it is satisfied that the purpose or principal purpose of the society has ceased to be that required by section 5(1) for the establishment of a building society under this Act.

(6) In the application of this section to a building society whose principal office is in Scotland, references to the High Court shall be read as references to the Court of Session.

DEFINITIONS
"applicable winding up legislation": ss.90 and 119(1).
"central office": s.119(1).
"the Commission": ss.1 and 119(1).
"public file": ss.106 and 119(1).
"restructuring plan": s.36(3).

GENERAL NOTE
As is apparent from subs. (1), the powers conferred on the Commission by this section will become exercisable in two different types of case.

In the first place, the powers may become exercisable by virtue of s.36(11) (see subs. (1)(*a*) of the present section, and *c.f.* the notes to s.36 above). In such cases, the Commission may either (i) present a petition to the court to wind up the defaulting society under the applicable winding up legislation (as to which, see ss.89 and 90 and the notes thereto); or (ii) apply to the court for an order that the society "carry out the restructuring plan as directed in the order" (see subss. (1)(*a*) and (2)(*a*)). The latter course, however, seems to presuppose the existence of a restructuring plan suitable to be carried out by the society: this course seems likely to be followed, therefore, only in the case specified in s.36(11)(*d*) (failure by a society to carry out a restructuring plan approved by the Commission). In the remaining cases specified in s.36, the position will either be that no restructuring plan has been submitted to the Commission, or that a plan has been submitted but rejected by the Commission. In these cases, therefore, the presentation of a winding up petition seems the only course likely to be followed by the Commission.

Secondly, the powers conferred by the present section may become exercisable where the Commission has reason to believe that the society's purpose or principal purpose has ceased to be that specified in s.5(1) (*viz.*, raising, primarily by the subscriptions of its members, a stock or fund for making to them advances secured on land for their residential use): see subs. (1)(*b*). In such a case, the Commission may either (i) present a winding up petition to the court, as before; or (ii) apply to the court for an order that the society modify its business as directed in the order: see subss. (1)(*b*) and (2)(*b*), and *c.f.* subs. (3). The court cannot make a winding up order in such cases unless it is satisfied that the society's purpose or principal purpose has ceased to be that specified in s.5(1); in other words, the court must be satisfied that the Commission was correct in believing that the society's purposes or principal purpose had deviated from that required by s.5(1): see subs. (5) and *c.f.* subs. (1)(*b*).

The situation envisaged by subs. (1)(*b*) is not, of course, one in which the society's memorandum specifies a purpose or principal purpose which deviates from s.5(1), for, if that were the case, the society (or the memorandum in the case of an existing society) would never be registered. Clearly, what is envisaged is a case in which the society's activities are in fact departing from its purpose or principal purpose as stated in its memorandum.

Note that a copy of any order made under subs. (2) is retained in the public file of the defaulting society: see subs. (4).

Power to determine extent of building society powers

Power to determine building society's powers

38.—(1) The Commission shall have power to determine whether a particular activity of a building society or its subsidiary is or is not within the existing powers of the society and may, if it thinks fit, take such professional advice as it considers it needs to enable it to make the determination.

(2) A determination may be made under this section in relation to an activity which is proposed to be carried on as well as in relation to one which is being carried on.

(3) The powers of the Commission in relation to a building society are exercisable—

(a) on an application made by the society, requesting the Commission to make the determination,

(b) on an application made by the society at the direction of the central office under Part II of Schedule 2 to this Act, or

(c) on the Commission's own motion or on an application made by the society at its direction,

as provided in subsection (4), (5), (6) or (8) below.

(4) A building society may at any time, on complying with the following provisions of this section, make an application to the Commission for a determination under this section whether an activity specified in the application is or is not within its powers if the directors of the society are of the opinion that there is a doubt about the existence or extent of the powers to carry on the activity which requires to be resolved in the interests of the society.

(5) A building society which has been directed by the central office under Part II of Schedule 2 to this Act to make an application to the Commission under this section shall, in accordance with the direction, make an application to the Commission for a determination whether the activity specified in the application is or is not within its powers.

(6) If it appears to the Commission at any time that a building society or its subsidiary is carrying on or is about to carry on an activity which is or may be outside the existing powers of the society, the Commission may, by notice to the society specifying the activity and its opinion, direct

it to make an application for a determination under this section whether the activity is or is not within its powers and it shall be the duty of the society to comply with the direction.

(7) A direction under subsection (6) shall require the application to be made within the period of 21 days beginning with the date on which the notice is given, but the Commission may extend or further extend the period within which the application is to be made.

(8) If a building society fails, within the time allowed by or under subsection (7) above, to make an application as directed under subsection (6) above, the Commission may, of its own motion, proceed to make a determination under this section as if an application had been made by the society.

(9) An application by a building society under subsection (4), (5) or (6) above shall be made in writing, signed by the secretary as such an application, and shall comprise—

(*a*) a statement of the question for determination, specifying the activity and the powers in question, the nature of the doubt and (except in the case of an application under subsection (6)) the arguments for and against the activity being within those powers, as they appear to the society, and

(*b*) such documents or draft documents and such other information as are necessary to enable the determination to be made.

(10) The statement of the question for determination may, with the agreement of the Commission, be amended at any time before the determination is made and in that event further documents and other information may be included in the application.

(11) The Commission may, by notice to the society, require a society making an application under subsection (4), (5) or (6) above to amend the statement of the question for determination or to furnish such further documents or other information or such explanations of the statement, documents or information as appear to it to be necessary to enable the determination of the question to be made; and the Commission may allow or require the explanations to be made orally instead of in writing.

(12) In this section and sections 39 and 40—

"activity" includes the exercise, or purported exercise, of any power under this Act, including the holding of any property or rights;

"existing", with reference to powers, means existing at the relevant date and, in relation to a building society, "existing powers" denotes the powers it has, or has adopted, under this Act, with any restrictions it has assumed, as at that date but disregarding anything done by the Commission and then in force (otherwise than under section 39 or 40) by virtue of which the society is precluded from exercising, or is subject to restrictions on the exercise of, its powers;

"the relevant date", in relation to a building society, means—

(*a*) in a case where the Commission decides to proceed of its own motion, the date when the Commission so decides;

(*b*) in a case where the society makes the application at the direction of the central office, the date specified in the direction; and

(*c*) in any other case, the date on which the society makes the application.

(13) Nothing in this section or section 39 or 40 implies that it is improper for the Commission to give to a building society or building societies generally an indication of the action it might or might not take in relation to any proposed activity of theirs; and if any determination comes to be made in relation to the activity the proceedings shall not be liable to be set aside by reason of the indication having been given.

DEFINITIONS
"the Commission": ss.1 and 119(1).
"central office": s.119(1).
"notice": s.119(1).
"existing"; "activity": subs. (12).
"subsidiary": ss.119(1) and Companies Act 1985, s.736(1).

GENERAL NOTE
This section gives power to the Commission to determine whether an activity, or proposed activity, of a building society or its subsidiary is within the existing powers of the society. Under subs. (3), the Commission's powers to make such a determination may be exercised in the following cases:
(a) Where the society, of its own volition, applies to the Commission under subs. (4). As is apparent from the terms of subs. (4), such an application may be made in cases where the directors think there is a doubt about the society's powers to carry on a particular activity, which requires to be resolved in the interests of the society.
(b) Where the society, pursuant to a direction contained in a notice served by the central office under para. 19(5)(c) of Sched. 2, applies to the Commission under subs. (5). This situation will arise where (i) a society has altered its powers by adopting an adoptable power (as to which, see para. 4 of Sched. 2) and (ii) the Commission believes that the society has exercised the power before the date on which the alteration takes effect. (Note that the same situation may arise under Sched. 20, paras. 2, 3 and 11, although this is not expressly mentioned in s.38.)
(c) Where either (i) the society applies to the Commission pursuant to a direction contained in a notice served by the Commission under subs. (6) or (ii) the Commission proceeds to make the determination of its own motion under subs. (8) following a failure by the society to make an application as directed by the Commission under subs. (6). This situation will arise where the Commission believes that the society or its subsidiary is acting, or is about to act, outside the society's powers.
It will be noted that, where the building society applies to the Commission under subs. (4) or (5) (though not where it applies under subs. (6)), the society's statement of the question for determination must specify the arguments for *and against* the activity being within the powers of the society: see subs. (9)(a).
Note also that, whereas the present section includes provision for a determination to be made whether the activities of a subsidiary are within the powers of its parent society, it makes no provision for such a determination to be made with reference to the activities of an associated body which is not a subsidiary. (As to the respective meanings of the expressions "associated body" and "subsidiary", see the notes to s.18(17).) It may, however, be of some importance to a society to know whether the activities of such an associated body fall within the powers of the society, since, if they do not, the society will generally have no power to invest in or support that body under s.18: see the concluding words of s.18(4).

Subs. (13)
The informal contacts previously maintained between building societies and the Registry were a source of considerable benefit to both; this subsection recognises the desirability of establishing similar contacts between societies and their new supervisory body. First, the subsection makes it clear that there is nothing improper in the Commission giving an informal indication of the attitude which it is likely to adopt towards new activities proposed by a particular society, or by societies generally. Second, the subsection ensures that the Commission can give such guidance without imperilling the validity of any formal determination that it may have to make under this section at a later stage.

The determination: notification, effect, appeal

39.—(1) A determination of the Commission under section 38 shall be in writing and, as soon as practicable after it is made, the Commission shall notify the society of the determination and the reasons for it.

(2) On receiving notice of the determination the society shall, if it is a determination that the activity in question was outside its powers, forthwith send a copy of it to every person who the society has reason to believe will or may be affected by it other than a person whose only interest is as a shareholder in, or depositor with, the society.

(3) Subject to subsection (4) below, the Commission shall, within the period of one month beginning with the date of the notice to the society under subsection (1) above, publish the determination in such manner as it thinks appropriate.

(4) Where the determination is made on an application made by the society under section 38(4), the Commission may, on the application of the society, postpone the publication of the determination for such period as it thinks fit, not exceeding the period of six months beginning with the date of the notice to the society under subsection (1) above, if it appears to the Commission that it is just to do so.

(5) A determination under section 38 shall bind all persons, whether or not (in the case of an application) they were parties to it and, subject to any appeal under subsection (8) below, shall be final and conclusive for all purposes.

(6) Where the activity in question was at the relevant date being carried on by the society and the determination is that the activity is outside the powers of the society the directors of the society shall be personally liable, jointly and severally, for any loss or expense to the society consequent on the activity's being outside its powers (including, if a prohibition order under section 40 is made, any loss or expense consequent on the order).

(7) If it appears to the Commission that proceedings under subsection (6) above have not been, but ought in the interests of the society to be, brought, the Commission may bring such proceedings in the name and on behalf of the society; and if it does so the Commission may indemnify the society against the costs or expenses incurred by the society in, or in connection with, proceedings brought by virtue of this subsection.

(8) Any person affected by a determination under section 38 shall be entitled within the period of six weeks beginning with the date of the notice under subsection (1) above or such further period as the Court may allow, to appeal to the High Court against the determination in accordance with rules of court on the ground that it is erroneous in law and the Commission shall be made respondent on the appeal.

(9) On any appeal to the High Court under subsection (8) above the High Court may confirm, reverse or vary the determination appealed from.

(10) In the application of this section to a building society whose principal office is in Scotland, references to the High Court shall be read as references to the Court of Session.

(11) The Commission may, if it thinks fit, require a building society in whose case it has made a determination under section 38 to pay such fee as the Commission directs.

DEFINITIONS
"the Commission": ss.1 and 119(1).
"depositor": s.119(1).
"relevant date": s.38(12).
"shareholder": s.119(1).

GENERAL NOTE
This section supplements s.38 and should be read with that section.

Subs. (2)
A determination by the Commission that a particular activity is outside the powers of a society may have a material effect on third parties (*e.g.* persons who have entered into a transaction with the society which, because of the determination, the society will be unable to complete). Such persons have a right to appeal against the determination to the court on a point of law (subs. 8); but the time limit for bringing such an appeal (unless extended on application to the court) is only six weeks from the date of the notice of the determination. Accordingly, subs. (2) makes provision for a copy of the notice to be sent by the society

forthwith upon receipt (and hence well in advance of publication of the determination by the Commission under subs. (3) or (4)) to any person which it has reason to believe will or may be affected by the determination, other than a person whose only interest in the determination arises from the fact that he is a shareholder in, or depositor with, the society.

Subs. (4)

This subsection will enable the Commission to provide a degree of protection for a society which has devised a novel scheme (*i.e.*, one not yet known to its competitors) and has obtained a determination from the Commission that the implementation of the scheme will be within its powers. In such a case, the Commission has power to delay publication of the determination for up to six months, thus allowing the society to gain some competitive advantage in the market before the details of the scheme become public knowledge.

Subs. (5)

Final and conclusive for all purposes: for a discussion of the effect of "finality clauses" on the availability of judicial review, see de Smith's *Judicial Review of Administrative Action* (4th Ed.), pp. 364–6 *et seq.*

Subss. (6) and (7)

If the Commission determines that a particular activity was outside the powers of the society, subs. (6) gives the society a right of action against its directors to recover any resultant loss or expense suffered by the society. If the directors liable to be sued are still in office, then, for obvious reasons, they are likely to be reluctant to set the necessary proceedings on foot on behalf of the society. Accordingly, subs. (7) gives power to the Commission to bring the proceedings in the name of and on behalf of the society; in such circumstances, the Commission has power (but no duty) to indemnify the society against any costs incurred by it in connection with the proceedings.

Power to make prohibition orders

40.—(1) On or at any time after making a determination under section 38 that a specified activity is outside the powers of a building society, the Commission shall, if it appears to it—

(*a*) that the activity is being carried on by the society, or

(*b*) that the activity has not been but, unless a prohibition order is made under this section, may be carried on by the society,

serve on the society a notice of the Commission's intention to issue a prohibition order directed to the society.

(2) A prohibition order under this section is an order prohibiting, subject to the saving or transitional provisions of the order, the continuance or, as the case may be, the carrying on of the activity specified in the order, either absolutely or unless conditions specified in the order are complied with, after a date specified in the order and requiring, subject to the saving or transitional provisions of the order, the disposal within a specified period of all assets acquired or otherwise in its possession by virtue of the activity.

(3) A disposal of assets in pursuance of a prohibition order shall vest the assets in the transferee but without prejudice to any claim against the society by a person who had an interest in the assets.

(4) The saving or transitional provisions which may be included in a prohibition order shall be such as appear to the Commission to be just having regard to the interests of shareholders of and depositors with the society and the interests of other persons who will be affected by the order; but the provisions shall not in any respect suspend the operation of the order beyond the period of one year.

(5) A prohibition order may include a direction for treating assets of any description as assets of the class specified in the direction for the purposes of the requirements of Part III for the structure of commercial assets.

(6) A notice under subsection (1) above of the Commission's intention to issue a prohibition order shall—

(*a*) specify the date on which the order is to be issued, being a date not earlier than the end of the period of 21 days beginning with the date of the notice;

(*b*) specify the terms of the order, including any saving or transitional provisions proposed to be included in it;

(*c*) inform the society of its right to make representations to the Commission before the order is issued as to the saving or transitional provisions to be included in the order; and

(*d*) inform the society of its duty under subsection (7) below.

(7) On receiving a notice under subsection (1) above the society shall forthwith send a copy of it to every other person whom it has reason to believe will or may be affected by the determination under section 38 on which the order will be founded.

(8) Any person who may be affected by the determination under section 38 on which the order will be founded may, at any time before the order is made, make representations to the Commission as to the inclusion in it of saving or transitional provisions affecting his interests and they may be made orally or in writing.

(9) After considering any representations made under subsection (8) above the Commission shall make the prohibition order with such saving and transitional provisions (if any) as it thinks just, shall issue the order by causing it to be served on the society and shall direct the central office to keep a copy of it in the public file of the society.

(10) A prohibition order so made and issued shall, subject to subsection (15) below, take effect on the date specified in the order.

(11) A copy of any order issued under subsection (9) above shall also be served on each director and on the chief executive of the society.

(12) The requirement of subsection (11) above, so far as it relates to directors, is satisfied by serving a copy on each director whose appointment has been officially notified and the non-receipt of a copy by a director or the chief executive does not affect the validity of the direction.

(13) Subject to subsection (14) below, a prohibition order shall remain in force until revoked by the Commission.

(14) The Commission may suspend or revoke a prohibition order so far as it relates to an asset the disposal of which appears to it, on the application of the society, to be impracticable.

(15) If, when a prohibition order has been made, an appeal is pending before the High Court under section 39(8) against the determination on which the order is founded the High Court may, on application made to it, order that the operation of the prohibition order be stayed until the determination of the appeal; but it shall not do so unless it is satisfied that it is in the public interest that it be stayed.

(16) If a society contravenes a prohibition order issued against it under this section the Commission may certify the contravention in writing to the High Court; and the Court may thereupon inquire into the case and, after hearing any witnesses who may be produced against or on behalf of the society and after hearing any statement which may be offered in defence, may punish the society in like manner as if it had been guilty of contempt of the court.

(17) In the application of this section to a building society whose principal office is in Scotland, references to the High Court shall be read as references to the Court of Session and references to staying shall be read as references to sisting.

DEFINITIONS
  "central office": s.119(1).
  "chief executive": s.59(1).
  "the Commission": ss.1 and 119(1).

"depositor": s.119(1).
"public file": ss.106 and 119(1).
"requirements for the structure of commercial assets": s.20.
"saving or transitional provisions of the order": subs. (4).
"shareholders": s.119(1).

GENERAL NOTE

This section empowers the Commission to make a "prohibition order" against a society (*viz.*, broadly speaking, an order prohibiting a society from continuing or commencing a particular activity, and requiring it to dispose of any assets which have come into its hands by virtue of the activity: see subs. (2)). Subs. (1) embodies three conditions which must be fulfilled before such an order can be made.

First, the Commission must have made a determination under s.38 that the activity in question is outside the society's powers.

Second, the Commission must be satisfied either that the activity is being carried on by the society, or that it may (*n.b.*, not "will") be carried on by the society if no prohibition order is made: see paras. (*a*) and (*b*).

Third, the Commission must serve notice on the society of its intention to make a prohibition order. The notice may be served on or at any time after the making of the determination under s.38; it will be noted, however, that the subsection appears to place the Commission under a mandatory duty to serve such a notice once it is satisfied of either of the matters specified in paras. (*a*) and (*b*) (note the obligatory words "the Commission shall").

A notice served under subs. (1) must set out the matters specified in subs. (6). These include the date on which the prohibition order is to be issued (which must not be a date earlier than 21 days after the date of the notice), and the terms of the order which is to be made. Forthwith upon receiving the order, the society is required by subs. (7) to send a copy to every person whom it has reason to believe will or may be affected by the determination under s.38 on which the prohibition order will be founded. Two points may be made about the latter requirement. First, the society's task is not to identify the persons who will or may be affected by the prohibition order itself, but rather those persons who will or may be affected by the prior determination under s.38 that the specified activity is outside the society's powers. Second, there is nothing in subs. (7) which exonerates the society from the duty to send a copy of the notice to persons affected by the determination solely by reason of the fact that they are shareholders in, or depositors with, the society. Presumably, it is not intended that such persons should receive a copy of the notice; but it may be difficult to justify that conclusion as a matter of statutory construction given the express exclusion of such persons from the closely analogous provisions of s.39(2).

Both the society and any person to whom a copy of the notice is sent under subs. (7) have the right to make representations to the Commission before the prohibition order is issued (see subss. (6)(*c*) and (8) respectively). However, the representations cannot be directed to the question whether or not the prohibition order should be made, but merely to the question whether the order should contain any and, if so, what transitional and saving provisions (*viz.*, provisions which appear to the Commission to be just having regard to the interests of the society's investors and of any other person affected: see subs. (4), and note the concluding words of that subsection, showing that such provisions may suspend the operation of the order, or at least suspend it in certain respects, for a period of up to a year). Generally speaking, therefore, the issue of a prohibition order will follow inexorably once the notice of the Commission's intention to issue it has been served under subs. (1). Presumably, however, the order cannot be issued (or, if already issued, will be discharged) if the determination on which the order is to be (or has been) founded is overturned on appeal to the court under s.39(8). This seems to be implicit in subs. (15), which empowers the Court to suspend the operation of an order pending the outcome of an appeal under s.39(8): the point of suspending the order pending the appeal must be that the order will go if the appeal succeeds. (Note, incidentally, that a stay may only be ordered under subs. (15) if the Court is satisfied that a stay would be "in the public interest".)

A copy of the prohibition order, once made, will be kept in the society's public file: subs. (9). Copies must also be served on the society's chief executive and each of its directors: subss. (11) and (12). If a society contravenes a prohibition order, the Commission is empowered to certify the contravention to the court; and the court may, after inquiry, punish the society in like manner as if it had been guilty of a contempt of court (see subs. (16)). The effect of the latter provision is, presumably, that the court may deal with the contravention as if it were a breach of a court order (*viz.*, in England, by a fine; or by issue of a writ of sequestration against the property of the society, or against the personal property of the society's officers; or by an order committing the society's officers to prison).

Powers in relation to authorisation

Power to direct application to renew authorisation

41.—(1) If, with respect to a building society for which an authorisation is in force, the Commission has reason to believe that the society's business is or may be being conducted in a way that may not adequately protect the investments of shareholders and depositors then, subject to subsections (2) and (3) below, it may by notice direct the society to make an application under this section to renew its authorisation.

(2) The power conferred on the Commission by this section is not exercisable more than once during any period of five years during the whole of which the society has held a current authorisation except where, during that period, the society has, under section 94, undertaken to fulfil the engagements of another society.

(3) A notice under subsection (1) above shall require the society to make the application for renewal within such period as is specified in the notice, being a period not shorter than three nor longer than six months beginning with the date of the notice, but the Commission may, on representations being made to it, extend or further extend the period within which the application is to be made.

(4) A notice under subsection (1) shall indicate the grounds on which the Commission has decided to give a direction under this section.

(5) Authorisation, if renewed under this section, shall be granted unconditionally or subject to conditions as provided by subsection (6) or (7) below.

(6) Subject to subsection (11) below, the Commission, on an application duly made for renewal of authorisation under this section, shall grant unconditional authorisation to the society if it is satisfied that—

    (*a*) the society has qualifying capital of an amount which is not less than the prescribed minimum;

    (*b*) the society has adequate reserves and other designated capital resources;

    (*c*) the chairman of the board of directors and any executive directors, the chief executive, the secretary and the managers (if any) are each fit and proper persons to hold their respective offices in the society;

    (*d*) the board of directors, with the chief executive and secretary, have the capacity and intention to direct the affairs of the society in accordance with the criteria of prudent management and have secured that those criteria are being satisfied; and

    (*e*) the investments of shareholders and depositors will be adequately protected without the imposition of conditions.

(7) If the Commission, on an application so made, is not satisfied of the matters specified in subsection (6) above in relation to the society, it shall, subject to subsection (10) below—

    (*a*) if it is satisfied that the imposition of conditions would secure the protection of the investments of shareholders and depositors, grant authorisation subject to such conditions to be complied with by the society (whether or not they correspond to any conditions in force as respects the current authorisation) as the Commission thinks fit to impose to secure that purpose; or

    (*b*) if not so satisfied, refuse to grant the authorisation;

and if it refuses to grant authorisation under this section the authorisation current under section 9 shall expire on the date specified by the Commission in the notice of its refusal except where section 46(4) applies.

(8) If the Commission refuses to grant authorisation to a building society under this section it shall inform the central office of the fact and the date on which the current authorisation of the society expires; and the central office shall record that date in the public file of the society.

(9) Subsections (6) and (7) of section 9 apply as respects the imposition of conditions on the renewal of authorisation under this section as they apply as respects the imposition of conditions under that section.

(10) The provisions of Schedule 3 to this Act regulating—

(*a*) the making and determination of applications for authorisation,

(*b*) the furnishing of information or additional information in connection with such applications, and

(*c*) the imposition of conditions of authorisation,

apply in relation to authorisation under this section.

(11) The making of an application under this section at the direction of the Commission shall not preclude the Commission, at any time while the application is pending, from imposing conditions on the society's authorisation under section 42 or revoking the society's authorisation under section 43; but if it revokes the authorisation the proceedings under this section shall abate.

(12) An authorisation granted under this section shall be treated for the purposes of this Act as an authorisation granted under section 9 and in particular subsection (9) of that section shall apply as if any conditions had been imposed under subsection (5) of that section.

(13) Any expression used in this section to which a meaning is given by section 9(13) has that meaning in this section.

(14) This section shall expire at the end of the period of 5 years beginning with the date on which this Act is passed unless continued in force by an order under subsection (15) below.

(15) The Treasury may from time to time by order provide that this section shall continue in force for a period not exceeding 5 years from the coming into operation of the order.

(16) The power to make an order under subsection (15) above is exercisable by statutory instrument but no such order shall be made unless a draft of it has been laid before and approved by a resolution of each House of Parliament.

(17) Section 45 applies for the interpretation of "adequate reserves" and "designated capital resources" in subsection (6) above.

DEFINITIONS

"adequate reserves": subs. (17) and s.45(3) and (10).
"authorisation": ss.9 and 119(1).
"business": subs. (13) and s.9(13).
"central office": s.119(1).
"chief executive": s.59(1).
"the Commission": ss.1 and 119(1).
"criteria of prudent management": ss.45(3) and 119(1).
"depositors": s.119(1).
"designated capital resources": subs. (17) and s.45(3), (5) and (10).
"executive": s.119(1).
"managers": s.119(1).
"prescribed minimum": subs. (13) and s.9(13).
"public file": ss.106 and 119(1).
"qualifying capital": subs. (13) and s.9(13).
"shareholders": s.119(1).

GENERAL NOTE

This section empowers the Commission to direct a society which has been authorised under s.9, or is treated as having been authorised under that section, to make an application for the renewal of its authorisation. It should be noted that the power to make such a direction may be exercised no more than once in any five year period (except where the society, during that period, has accepted a transfer of engagements from another society under s.94): see subs. (2). It will also be noted that the power may not be exercised unless the Commission has reason to believe that the society's business is or may be being conducted in a way that may not adequately protect the investments of its shareholders and depositors (see subs. (1)). In considering the latter requirement, it should be borne in mind that there is nothing in s.45 which entitles the Commission to *assume* for the purposes of the present section that the security of those investments will be prejudiced by a failure on the part of the society or its directors to satisfy the criteria of prudent management set out in s.45(3). (Contrast the position under ss.42(1) and 43(1)(*d*), where the Commission is entitled to make such an assumption by virtue of s.45(1) and (2).) Needless to say, however, a failure by the society or its directors to satisfy one or more of those criteria could well be sufficient to demonstrate that there may *in fact* be a risk to the security of the investments of the shareholders and depositors.

It will be noted that the present section will expire at the end of five years from the date on which the Act was passed (July 25, 1986) unless continued by Treasury order: see subss. (14) and (15). It is thought that this reflects the fact that the section has been conceived primarily as a mechanism to enable the Commission, in appropriate cases, to satisfy itself of the suitability for continued authorisation of societies which qualified automatically for authorisation on the coming into force of the Building Societies (Authorisation) Regulations 1981 (see reg. 5(2) thereof, and *cf.* the notes to s.19 above), and whose authorisation has been continued under the present Act (again automatically) by Sched. 20, para. 6(1). In other words, the object is to enable the Commission to take steps to ensure that the automatic authorisation procedure has not let rotten apples into the barrel (*c.f. Official Report*, House of Commons, Standing Committee A, February 11, 1986, col. 284).

A society which has been directed to apply for the renewal of its authorisation will find itself in a position very similar to that of a new society applying for authorisation under s.9. Thus the conditions for the unconditional renewal of authorisation set out in subs. (6) are comparable to the conditions for the grant of initial authorisation under s.9(4), save that a society applying under this section must satisfy the additional requirement that its reserves and other capital resources (being resources of a description designated by order made under s.45(5)) are adequate having regard to the range and scale of its business: see subss. (9)(*b*) and (17) and s.45(3), (5) and (10). Clearly, that is a sensible prudential requirement to apply to an established society seeking a renewal of authorisation; but it could not, of course, be applied to a new society seeking an initial grant of authorisation (*i.e.* because such a society could not have built up any reserves). If the Commission is not satisfied of the matters specified in subs. (6), but is satisfied that the investment of the shareholders and depositors can be adequately protected by the imposition of conditions, it must grant authorisation subject to those conditions (see subs. (7)(*a*)); otherwise it must refuse to grant the authorisation (see subs. (7)(*b*)). These provisions are comparable to s.9(5)(*b*) and (*c*); curiously, however, the Commission has a discretion to grant conditional authorisation under subs. (7)(*a*) of the present section even if it is not satisfied that the society meets the minimum capital requirements imposed by subs. (6)(*a*) and that its executive directors, etc., are fit and proper persons within the meaning of subs. (6)(*c*). If the comparable conditions imposed by s.9(4)(*a*) and (*b*) are not satisfied by a society applying for an initial grant of authorisation, the Commission has no discretion to grant conditional authorisation but must refuse the application outright: see s.9(5)(*a*). (*C.f.* also s.44(5)(*a*).)

It should be noted that if a society fails to apply for the renewal of its authorisation within the time allowed by a notice given to it under subs. (1), then (by virtue of s.43(3)(*c*)) the Commission must revoke the society's authorisation.

As is apparent from subs. (11), the Commission may impose conditions on a society's authorisation under s.42, or may revoke that authorisation under s.43, notwithstanding that proceedings under the present section are pending at the time. This provision is no doubt intended to preserve the Commission's freedom to take more positive action against a society should the information coming to the Commission's notice in the course of an application under this section indicate that such action is necessary to protect the interests of the society's investors.

As to the procedure to be followed in applications under the present section, see Sched. 3, Parts II and III. As to a society's right to appeal against a refusal to grant authorisation, or against the imposition of conditions on a grant of authorisation, see ss.46–49. It should be noted that, where the Commission refuses to renew a society's authorisation under subs. (7)(*b*) of the present section, the expiry of the society's current authorisation cannot have effect until after the end of the period in which an appeal against the refusal can be brought or (in the event of an appeal in fact being brought) until the appeal has been determined or withdrawn: see the concluding words of subs. (7) and s.46(3) and (4).

Imposition of conditions on current authorisation

42.—(1) If, with respect to a building society for which an authorisation is in force, the Commission considers it expedient to do so in order to protect the investments of shareholders or depositors, it may, subject to subsection (7) below, impose conditions to be complied with by the society.

(2) Section 45 has effect for the purpose of any determination whether or not it is expedient to exercise the powers conferred by this section.

(3) Failure by a society to comply with conditions imposed under this section shall render it liable, if other conditions are not imposed on it under this section, to have its authorisation revoked under section 43(1).

(4) The conditions that may be imposed by the Commission under this section may—

   (*a*) relate to any activities of the society, whether or not those for which authorisation is required; and

   (*b*) require the society to take certain steps or to refrain from adopting or pursuing a particular course of action or to restrict the scope of its business in a particular way.

(5) Without prejudice to the generality of subsection (4) above, conditions imposed under this section may—

   (*a*) impose limitations on the issue of shares, the acceptance of deposits or the making of advances or other loans;

   (*b*) require the society to take steps with regard to the conduct of the business of any subsidiary or other associated body; and

   (*c*) require the removal of any director or other officer.

(6) The Commission may impose conditions under this section where it proceeded under section 41 or where it proceeded under section 43 with a view to revoking the society's authorisation.

(7) The Commission shall not impose conditions under this section except in accordance with the provisions of Part III or, where applicable, Part IV of Schedule 3 to this Act; and the other provisions of that Part shall have effect in relation to the imposition of conditions under this section.

(8) Conditions imposed under this section—

   (*a*) may be varied from time to time (and notwithstanding any pending appeal) by agreement between the Commission and the society; and

   (*b*) may be revoked at any time by the Commission if it is satisfied that the investments of shareholders and depositors will be adequately protected without the conditions.

(9) Any expression used in this section to which a meaning is given by section 9(13) has that meaning in this section.

DEFINITIONS
"associated body": ss.19(17) and 119(1).
"authorisation": ss.9 and 119(1).
"business": subs. (9) and s.9(13).
"the Commission": ss.1 and 119(1).
"deposits" and "depositors": s.119(1).
"officer": s.119(1).
"shares" and "shareholder": s.119(1).
"subsidiary": s.119(1) and Companies Act 1985, s.736(1).

GENERAL NOTE
This section empowers the Commission to impose conditions on the current authorisation of a society. As is apparent from subss. (4) and (5), the Commission has a wide discretion as to the nature of the conditions which it may impose under this section; note, in particular, that the conditions may relate to an activity of the society for which authorisation is not required (*e.g.* the making of advances): see subs. (4)(*a*) and *c.f.* subs. (5)(*a*). Before the

Commission can impose conditions under this section, it must be satisfied that it is expedient to do so to protect the investments of shareholders or depositors: see subs. (1). However, the Commission is entitled to assume for this purpose that, if there has been a failure by the society or its directors to satisfy any one or more of the criteria of prudent management set out in s.45(3), then that failure is such as to prejudice the security of the investments of the shareholders and depositors: see subs. (2) and s.45(1) and (2).

The inclusion of the present section in the Act gives effect to a recommendation in the Green Paper (para. 34 of Appendix 2). It was envisaged that the power to impose conditions would be appropriate in a case where the Commission considered that "the society was a safe home for investments provided that it abided by the conditions, and therefore that it could continue on that basis, so avoiding the ill-effects for existing investors of revocation. This arrangement would have the advantage for the management of the society that it would have the protection of [the Commission] being required to observe the statutory procedures. It would have the advantage for [the Commission] that failure to comply with a condition would be sufficient ground by itself for complete revocation." (As to the latter point, see s.43(1)(c).) The present section contains no provision for recording the existence of conditions imposed on the society in its public file; this gives effect to a further recommendation in the Green Paper that such conditions should not be made a matter of public knowledge.

For the procedure to be followed in cases where the Commission exercises its powers under this section, see Sched. 3, Part III. For the provisions regarding appeals against the imposition of such conditions, see ss.46–49.

Revocation of authorisation

43.—(1) The Commission may, subject to subsection (4) below, revoke a building society's authorisation if—

(a) it appears to the Commission that at no time during a financial year of the society which began and ended during the currency of the authorisation did the society raise funds or accept deposits of money in pursuance of the authorisation;

(b) it appears to the Commission that a period of six months has elapsed since the end of a financial year of the society without the society's having sent to it the annual accounts for that year as required by section 81(2);

(c) the Commission is satisfied that, where the society's authorisation is subject to conditions, a condition has not been complied with by the society; or

(d) the Commission considers it expedient to do so in order to protect the investments of shareholders or depositors.

(2) Section 45 has effect for the purposes of any determination whether or not it is expedient to exercise the power conferred by subsection (1)(d) above.

(3) The Commission shall revoke a building society's authorisation if—

(a) the society has requested it to revoke its authorisation;

(b) the society has requested the central office to cancel its registration;

(c) the society has failed, when directed to do so under section 41, to make an application for the renewal of its authorisation within the period allowed under that section;

(d) the society has, under section 93 or 94 amalgamated with or transferred all its engagements to another building society; or

(e) the requisite initial step has been taken to wind up or dissolve the society.

(4) The Commission shall not revoke a society's authorisation under subsection (1) above except in accordance with the provisions of Part IV of Schedule 3 to this Act; and the other provisions of that Part shall also have effect in relation to revocation under this section or the imposition of conditions under section 42 instead of revocation under this section.

(5) Where a society's authorisation is revoked under subsection (1) or (3) above the provisions of subsections (6), (7) and (8) below shall have effect.

(6) Subject to subsection (7) below, any obligation to make a payment to the society which, by virtue of section 9(1), the society is prohibited from accepting shall be wholly rescinded.

(7) If, when a society's authorisation is revoked, a member is under an obligation to make payments to the society which represent instalments of the amount due by way of subscription for a share in the society and which, by virtue of section 9(1) the society is prohibited from accepting, the obligation shall (subject to anything in the rules of the society or any agreement between the society and the member) be suspended in respect of each instalment for the period during which no authorisation is in force; and accordingly, if reauthorisation is granted, the sum due shall again become payable by instalments.

(8) It shall be the duty of the society to make reasonable arrangements for using the funds of the society to meet applications by depositors with or holders of shares in the society (being applications made in accordance with the rules of the society) for repayment of the money deposited or subscribed by them.

(9) Where a society's authorisation is revoked under this section, the Commission shall inform the central office of the fact and the date on which the revocation takes effect and the central office shall record that date in the public file of the society.

(10) In this section "the requisite initial step", with reference to the winding up or dissolution of a building society, means the following—

(i) in the case of a winding up by the court, the making of the winding-up order;

(ii) in the case of a voluntary winding up, the passing of the resolution for voluntary winding up;

(iii) in the case of dissolution by consent of the members, the execution of the instrument of dissolution.

DEFINITIONS
"annual accounts": ss.72(10) and 119(1).
"authorisation": ss.9 and 119(1).
"central office": s.119(1).
"the Commission": ss.1 and 119(1).
"deposits" and "depositors": s.119(1).
"financial year": ss.117 and 119(1).
"public file": ss.106 and 119(1).
"requisite initial step": subs. (10).
"share": s.119(1).

GENERAL NOTE
This section supersedes the power to revoke the authorisation of a building society formerly contained in reg. 8 of the Building Societies (Authorisation) Regulations 1981. The power of revocation conferred by that regulation substantially duplicated the powers conferred on the Chief Registrar by s.48 of the 1962 Act (suspension of a society's power to accept deposits or subscriptions for shares). Accordingly, the powers conferred by s.48 are not as such continued by the present Act (c.f. the Green Paper, Appendix 2, para. 28; and for a full discussion of the nature and extent of the Chief Registrar's powers under s.48 of the old Act, see R. v. *Chief Registrar of Friendly Societies, ex parte New Cross Building Society* [1984] 2 All E.R. 27).

The power of revocation conferred by the present section is a power of last resort, to be exercised primarily in cases where a society has become moribund, or has ceased to be a safe home for the money of its investors. The effect of an order revoking a society's authorisation is that (save in the exceptional cases specified in s.9(3)) the society will commit a criminal offence if it subsequently takes in money from its members or accepts deposits of money: s.9(1) and (11). Revocation will, therefore, preclude a society from taking in new money from the investing public, and will thus prevent it from carrying on business in the normal way of a building society. (That is not to say, however, that the society will necessarily cease to function altogether, since it will not be obliged to call in its existing mortgages, and may be in a position to make new advances from time to time with moneys becoming available from the redemption of its existing securities at the end of the mortgage term. As to this, however, note (i) the practical constraints arising from the duty imposed by subs. (8) to make reasonable arrangements for using the society's funds to meet withdrawals by investors, and (ii) the possibility of a winding up petition being presented under s.89(1)(*e*) on the ground that the society's authorisation has been revoked.)

Subs. (1) specifies four cases in which a society's authorisation *may* be revoked, and subs. (3) specifies a further five cases in which a society's authorisation *must* be revoked.

So far as subs. (1) is concerned, the following comments may be made:

Para. (*a*): This may be compared with reg. 8(1)(*c*) of the Building Societies (Authorisation) Regulations 1981 (in which, however, the period specified was only six months rather than a complete financial year, as here). The purpose of the provision is to enable the Commission to withdraw authorisation from a society which has become moribund as a fund-raising institution. Note that, in applying this paragraph, the question is whether, during the relevant financial year, the society has raised funds or accepted deposits "in pursuance of the authorisation". Hence funds raised, or deposits accepted, in one of the ways mentioned in s.9(3) (for which no authorisation is required) will be ignored for the purposes of this paragraph.

Para. (*b*): Under s.81(2), the directors must send a copy of the annual accounts for the preceding financial year to the Commission no later than 14 days prior to the annual general meeting for the current year. By Sched. 2, para. 20(1), the annual general meeting must be held in the first four months of each financial year. Those already stringent requirements are further tightened by the present provision, under which failure to send a copy of the annual accounts to the Commission within six months of the end of the financial year to which the accounts relate constitutes a ground on which the Commission may revoke the society's authorisation.

Para. (*c*): Conditions may be imposed on a society's authorisation in the following cases: (i) on the initial grant of the authorisation (see s.9(5)(*b*)); (ii) on a renewal of a current authorisation (see s.41(7)(*a*)); (iii) by order of the Commission under s.42 (see s.42(1) and (3)); (iv) as an alternative to revocation (see Sched. 3, Part IV, paras. 7 and 8); (v) on the reauthorisation of a society whose authorisation has been revoked (see s.44(5)(*b*)); and (vi) pursuant to an order of the appeal tribunal (see s.47(6) and (7)). In any of these cases, a subsequent failure by the society to comply with the conditions of its authorisation will constitute a ground on which the Commission may revoke the authorisation.

Para. (*d*): The Commission is entitled to assume for the purposes of this paragraph that, if there has been a failure by the society or its directors to satisfy any one or more of the criteria of prudent management set out in s.45(3), then that failure is such as to prejudice the security of the investments of the shareholders and depositors: see subs. (2) and s.45(1) and (2).

As to the procedure to be followed in cases where the Commission proposes to revoke a society's authorisation on any of the grounds set out in subs. (1), see Sched. 3, Part IV: see subs. (4). Note that the Commission is empowered to adopt the less draconian course of imposing conditions on a society's authorisation as an alternative to revocation: see the closing words of subs. (4) and Sched. 3, Part IV, paras. 7 and 8.

The mandatory grounds for revocation set out in subs. (3) are largely self-explanatory. As to the ground specified in para. (*e*), note the definition of the expression "the requisite initial step" given in subs. (10). It should also be observed that the procedural provisions of Sched. 3, Part IV do *not* apply where revocation is ordered pursuant to subs. (3).

Subss. (6) *to* (8): These provisions re-enact, with minor variations, s.50(2)–(4) of the 1962 Act (and the corresponding provisions contained in reg. 11(1)–(3) of the 1981 Regulations). It is not clear whether the concluding words of subs. (7) have the effect that, on reauthorisation, the suspended instalments become payable in a lump sum, or continue to be payable periodically.

As to a society's right to appeal against a revocation of its authorisation under subs. (1), see ss.46–49. It should be noted that the revocation of a society's authorisation under subs. (1) cannot have effect until the time for bringing an appeal has expired or (in the event of an appeal being brought) until the appeal has been determined or withdrawn: see s.46(3).

There is no right of appeal against revocation of a society's authorisation on one of the mandatory grounds stated in subs. (3): see s.46(1)(*b*) and the definition of "revoke" in s.46(6).

Reauthorisation

44.—(1) Where the authorisation of a building society has expired under section 41(7) or been revoked under section 43(1), or (3)(c), the Commission may, on an application duly made for the purpose, grant reauthorisation to the society under this section.

(2) Reauthorisation is authorisation to raise funds or accept deposits of money to the extent authorisation to do so is required by section 9(1).

(3) Reauthorisation under this section shall, if granted, be granted unconditionally or subject to conditions as provided by subsection (4) or (5) below.

(4) The Commission shall grant unconditional reauthorisation to the building society if it is satisfied that—

    (a) the society has qualifying capital of an amount which is not less than the prescribed minimum;

    (b) the society has adequate reserves and other designated capital resources;

    (c) the chairman of the board of directors and any executive directors, the chief executive, the secretary and the managers (if any) are each fit and proper persons to hold their respective offices in the society;

    (d) the board of directors, with the chief executive and secretary, have the capacity and intention to direct the affairs of the society in accordance with the criteria of prudent management and, in so far as those criteria fell to be satisfied before the date of the application, have secured that they are being satisfied; and

    (e) the investments of shareholders and depositors will be adequately protected without the imposition of conditions.

(5) If the Commission is not satisfied of the matters specified in subsection (4) above in relation to the society it shall—

    (a) if those matters are or include the matters specified in paragraphs (a) and (c), refuse to grant authorisation;

    (b) in any other case, if it satisfied that the imposition of conditions would secure the protection of the investments of shareholders and depositors, grant reauthorisation subject to such conditions to be complied with by the society as the Commission thinks fit to impose to secure that purpose; or

    (c) if not so satisfied, refuse to grant reauthorisation.

(6) Subsections (6) and (7) of section 9 apply as respects the imposition of conditions on reauthorisation as they apply as respects the imposition of conditions under that section.

(7) The provisions of Schedule 3 to this Act regulating—

    (a) the making and determination of applications for authorisation,

    (b) the furnishing of information or additional information in connection with such applications, and

    (c) the imposition of conditions of authorisation,

apply in relation to reauthorisation under this section.

(8) Reauthorisation granted under this section shall be treated for the purposes of this Act as authorisation granted under section 9 and in particular subsection (9) of that section shall apply as if any conditions had been imposed under subsection (5) of that section.

(9) On granting reauthorisation under this section, the Commission shall inform the central office and the central office shall record that fact, and the date on which the reauthorisation was granted, in the public file of the society.

(10) Section 45 applies for the interpretation of "adequate reserves" and "designated capital resources" in subsection (4) above.

"adequate reserves": subs. (10) and s.45(3) and (10).
"authorisation": ss.9 and 119(1).
"central office": s.119(1).
"chief executive": s.59(1).
"the Commission": ss.1 and 119(1).
"criteria of prudent management": ss.45(3) and 119(1).
"depositors": s.119(1).
"designated capital resources": subs. (10) and s.45(3), (5) and (10).
"executive": s.119(1).
"managers": s.119(1).
"prescribed minimum": *c.f.* s.9(13).
"public file": ss.106 and 119(1).
"qualifying capital": *c.f.* s.9(13).
"shareholders": s.119(1).

GENERAL NOTE
This section makes provision for a society whose authorisation has expired under s.41(7) (*i.e.* following a refusal by the Commission to renew the authorisation on an application for renewal made under that section) or whose authorisation has been revoked under s.43(1) or (3)(*c*), to apply to the Commission for reauthorisation. It will be noted that a society whose authorisation has been revoked on any of the mandatory grounds specified in s.43(3)(*a*), (*b*), (*d*) and (*e*) is not entitled to apply for reauthorisation under this section. The requirements for unconditional reauthorisation are set out in subs. (4). The requirements are the same as those specified for the grant of initial authorisation under s.9(4), except that, for unconditional reauthorisation, the society must satisfy the additional requirement embodied in subs. (4)(*b*). That requirement (which corresponds to the one embodied in s.41(6)(*b*)) is that the society must have reserves and other capital resources (being resources of a description designated by order made under s.45(5)) which are adequate having regard to the range and scale of its business: see subs. (10) and s.45(3), (5) and (10). Provision is made in s.44(5)(*b*) for the grant of conditional reauthorisation. Note that the Commission must refuse any application where it is not satisfied of the matters specified in subs. (4)(*a*) and (*c*): it has no discretion to grant conditional reauthorisation in such a case (see subs. (5)(*a*) and (*b*)). In this respect, the present section corresponds to s.9 (see s.9(5)) but differs from s.41 (see s.41(7)).
In most cases, a society whose authorisation has expired or been revoked will be likely to find it difficult to satisfy the requirements for reauthorisation. Reauthorisation might, however, be appropriate in cases where, for example, there had been a thoroughgoing overhaul of the society's management since the loss of the previous authorisation.
For the procedure to be followed in relation to applications for reauthorisation, see Sched. 3, Parts II and III, as applied by subs. (7). For the provisions regarding appeals against a refusal to grant reauthorisation under this section, or against the imposition of conditions on a grant of reauthorisation, see ss.46–49.

The criteria for prudent management

45.—(1) If it appears to the Commission that there has been or is, on the part of a building society or its directors, a failure to satisfy any one or more of the following criteria of prudent management, it shall be entitled to assume for the purposes of its relevant prudential powers that the failure is such as to prejudice the security of the investments of shareholders or depositors.

(2) The prudential powers relevant for the purposes of this section are its powers—

(*a*) under section 42, to impose conditions on a society's authorisation, and

(*b*) under section 43, to revoke a society's authorisation,

by reference to its expedience for the protection of the investments of shareholders or depositors.

(3) For the purposes of this Act, the criteria of prudent management are—

1. Maintenance of adequate reserves and other designated capital resources.

2. Maintenance of a structure of commercial assets which satisfies the requirements of Part III.

3. Maintenance of adequate assets in liquid form.

4. Maintenance of the requisite arrangements for assessing the adequacy of securities for advances secured on land.

5. Maintenance of the requisite accounting records and systems of control of business and of inspection and report.

6. Direction and management.

> (*a*) by a sufficient number of persons who are fit and proper to be directors or, as the case may be, officers in their respective positions,
>
> (*b*) conducted by them with prudence and integrity.

7. Conduct of the business with adequate professional skills.

(4) Nothing in this section implies that it is improper for a determination for any purpose of the Commission's relevant prudential powers to take account of other factors than the criteria in subsection (3) above.

(5) The Commission, with the consent of the Treasury, may, by order in a statutory instrument, specify descriptions of capital resources of building societies which, for the purpose of the first criterion in subsection (3) above, are to be aggregated with reserves for that purpose, to the extent and subject to any conditions specified in the order.

(6) An instrument containing an order under subsection (5) above shall be subject to annulment in pursuance of a resolution of either House of Parliament.

(7) A failure to satisfy any of the first five criteria in subsection (3) above shall be treated, for the purposes of this section, as a failure on the part of a society's directors prudently to conduct the affairs of the society.

(8) A failure on the part of the society to comply with the conditions to which its authorisation is subject shall be treated, for the purposes of this section, as a failure on the part of the society's directors prudently to conduct the affairs of the society.

(9) Any carrying on by a building society or its subsidiary of an activity which has been determined, whether by the Commission under section 38 or by any court, to have been beyond the powers of the society shall be treated, for the purposes of this section, as a failure on the part of the society's directors prudently to conduct the affairs of the society.

(10) The following provisions apply for the interpretation of the list of criteria in subsection (3) above in their application to a building society, that is to say—

> "adequate", except with reference to liquidity, means adequate having regard to the range and scale of the society's business;
>
> "adequate", with reference to liquidity, means of such proportion and composition as is required by section 21(1) and "liquid form", in relation to assets, means assets which are of an authorised character for the purposes of that subsection;
>
> "business" includes business the society proposes to carry on and references to the business of the society include, where other bodies are associated with it, references to the business of those associated bodies;
>
> "requisite", with reference to the arrangements for assessing the adequacy of securities, means such as are required by section 13;
>
> "requisite", with reference to accounting records and systems of control, means such as are required by section 71;
>
> "sufficient", with reference to the number of directors and officers, means sufficient having regard to the range and scale of the society's business.

DEFINITIONS

"adequate" (in subs. (3), paras. 1, 4 and 7): subs. (10) (first sense).
"adequate" (in subs. (3), para. 3): subs. (10) (second sense).
"advances secured on land": ss.10(1) and 119(1).
"associated bodies": ss.18(17) and 119(1).
"authorisation": ss.9 and 119(1).
"business": subs. (10).
"the Commission": ss.1 and 119(1).
"depositors": s.119(1).
"designated capital resources": subs. (5).
"liquid form": subs. (10).
"officers": s.119(1).
"relevant prudential powers": subs. (1).
"requisite" (in subs. (3), para. 4): subs. (10) (first sense).
"requisite" (in subs. (3), para. 5): subs. (10) (second sense).
"shareholders": s.119(1).
"sufficient": subs. (10).

GENERAL NOTE

The criteria of prudent management set out in subs. (3) lie at the heart of the new system of prudential supervision instituted by the Act. The criteria are relevant in two contexts. First, the Commission can only grant unconditional authorisation to a society if it is satisfied that the society's board of directors, with the chief executive and secretary, have the capacity and intention to direct the affairs of the society in accordance with those criteria, and that they have secured that the criteria (so far as applicable) have been complied with prior to the date of the application for authorisation: see s.9(4)(c) (and note that a similar condition must be satisfied on any application to renew a society's authorisation under s.41, and on any application for reauthorisation under s.44: see ss.41(6)(d) and 44(4) (d)). Secondly, a failure by a society or its directors to satisfy any one or more of the criteria of prudent management will entitle the Commission to assume for the purposes of ss.42(1) and 43(1)(d) that the failure is such as to prejudice the security of the investments of the society's shareholders and depositors. The consequence of the Commission's being entitled to make that assumption is that it will then be able to exercise its power to impose conditions on the society's current authorisation under s.42, or to revoke that authorisation under s.43. (Curiously, however, the Commission is not entitled to make a similar assumption for the purpose of exercising its power under s.41 to direct a society to apply for the renewal of its authorisation: *c.f.* the notes to that section.)

In considering the individual criteria set out in subs. (3), the following points should be borne in mind:

Para. 1: The reference here to "designated capital resources" is a reference to capital resources which fall to be aggregated with a society's reserves in accordance with any order made under subs. (5). The requirement that a society's reserves and other designated capital resources should be "adequate" means that they should be adequate having regard to the range and scale of any business carried on, or proposed to be carried on, by the society and any bodies associated with it: see the first definition of "adequate" given in subs. (10) and the definition of "business" which also appears in that subsection. The need to take account of the business of a society's associated bodies in assessing the adequacy of its reserves no doubt reflects the fact that the society may be called upon to discharge the liabilities of those bodies under the "statutory guarantee" embodied in s.22 (though it will be noted that that section in fact extends only to such associated bodies as are subsidiaries of the society or linked to it by resolution: *cf.* s.18(17) and the notes thereto).

Para. 2: The requirements for the structure of a society's commercial assets will be found in s.20.

Para. 3: The expression "adequate assets in liquid form" is explained in subs. (10) (note that, in this context, it is the second definition of "adequate" which applies). The effect is that a society must keep such proportion of its assets in liquid form (*i.e.* in a form authorised by liquid asset regulations made under s.20(7)) as will at all times enable the society to meet its liabilities as they arise: see s.21(1) (and note the closing words of s.21(3)).

Para. 4: The requisite arrangements for assessing the adequacy of securities are the arrangements required by s.13: see the first definition of "requisite" in subs. (10). The requirement that these arrangements should be "adequate" means that they should be adequate in the sense explained under para. 1 above. In theory, therefore, the arrangements must be adequate having regard not only to the range and scale of the society's business, but also to the range and scale of the business of any bodies associated with the society. It is difficult to see, however, how the business carried on by a society's associated bodies can be relevant to the arrangements made under s.13 for assessing the adequacy of the security for advances made by the society (*c.f.* s.13(1)).

Para. 5: The requisite accounting records and systems of control are those required by s.71: see the second definition of "requisite" in subs. (10). Note that, where a society has subsidiaries or other associated bodies linked to it by resolution, the society must ensure that it can comply with the requirements of s.71 in relation to the business of those bodies as well as in relation to its own business: see.71(10). A failure to maintain the accounting records and systems of control requisite for either purpose will, therefore, involve a failure to satisfy the present criterion of prudent management.

Para. 6: The requirement imposed by the first limb of this paragraph that the direction and management of the society be conducted by a "sufficient" number of fit and proper persons, means that the number of such persons must be sufficient having regard to the range and scale of the society's business: subs. (10). Again, the reference to the society's business includes reference to any business proposed to be carried on by the society, and to the business (actual or proposed) of any body associated with the society: see the definition of "business" in subs. (10). In considering the second limb of this paragraph (which, *inter alia*, requires the direction and management of the society to be conducted with prudence) it should be borne in mind that the directors will automatically be regarded as having failed to conduct the society's affairs with prudence in the event:

(i) that there is a failure to comply with any of the first five criteria of prudent management: see subs. (7);

(ii) that there is a failure by the society to comply with any conditions to which its authorisation is subject: see subs. (8); or

(iii) that the society or any subsidiary has carried on an activity which has been determined (either by the Commission under s.38 or by the court) to have been beyond the society's powers: see subs. (9).

Para. 7: The words "adequate" and "business" in this paragraph again bear the extended meanings given to them by subs. (10); so the professional skills deployed in conducting the business of the society and of any associated body must be adequate having regard to the range and scale of the business (actual or proposed) of the society, or, as the case may be, of the associated body. The present paragraph will cover technical skills not normally deployed in the management structure of a society (and hence not covered by the sixth criterion) but nevertheless necessary for the proper conduct of its business (*e.g.* skills in computing, or in conveyancing and other legal matters).

Appeals

Rights of appeal

46.—(1) A building society which is aggrieved by a decision of the Commission—

(*a*) to refuse to grant authorisation,

(*b*) to revoke authorisation, or

(*c*) to impose conditions or as to the conditions imposed,

may appeal against the decision to a tribunal constituted in accordance with section 47.

(2) Any person in relation to whom the Commission, in deciding to refuse to grant or to revoke authorisation or to impose conditions, makes a determination that a person is not a fit and proper person to hold, or as the case may be, to remain in an office in the society or imposes a requirement that he be removed from an office in the society, may appeal against the decision so far as it relates to that determination or requirement.

(3) The revocation of a society's authorisation shall not have effect until—

(*a*) the end of the period within which an appeal can be brought against the Commission's decision to revoke it; and

(*b*) if such an appeal is brought, until it is determined or withdrawn.

(4) Subsection (3) above applies in relation to the expiry of a society's authorisation on a refusal to grant authorisation under section 41 as it applies to the revocation of a society's authorisation.

(5) Subject to any order of the tribunal made under section 47(5), an appeal under subsection (1)(*c*) or (2) above shall not affect the operation, pending the determination of the appeal, of any condition which is the subject of the appeal; and no determination of an appeal by any person under subsection (2) above shall affect the revocation for the purposes of which the Commission made its determination or requirement in relation to that person.

(6) In this section and section 47—

     "conditions" means conditions to be complied with by a building society and imposed on the grant of authorisation under section 9, on the renewal of authorisation under section 41, on reauthorisation under section 44, or under section 42;

     "grant" includes renew; and

     "revoke" means revoke under section 43(1).

DEFINITIONS

     "authorisation": ss.9, 41, 44 and 119(1).
     "the Commission": ss.1 and 119(1).
     "conditions": subs. (6).
     "grant": subs. (6)
     "office": *cf.* s.119(1).
     "revoke": subs. (6).

GENERAL NOTE

This section gives to a building society (and in some cases to its officers) a right to appeal against certain decisions of the Commission relating to the society's authorisation. The appeal lies to a specially constituted tribunal to be set up under s.47.

Subs. (1)

Reading this subsection together with the definitions given in subs. (6), the effect is that a society has a right of appeal:

(i) where the Commission refuses to grant initial authorisation to the society on an application brought under s.9; or refuses to renew the society's current authorisation on an application brought under s.41; or refuses to reauthorise the society on an application brought under s.44 (note, in applying para. (*a*) of the present section to cases arising under s.44, that "authorisation" is defined by s.119(1) to include "reauthorisation");

(ii) where the Commission revokes the society's authorisation under s.43(1) (but *not* where it revokes that authorisation under s.43(3) since, for the purposes of this section, "revoke" means revoke under s.43(1): see subs. (6));

(iii) where the Commission imposes conditions on the society's current authorisation under s.42, or where it imposes conditions on an authorisation granted pursuant to an application made under any of the sections mentioned in para. (i) above. Note, however, that there appears to be no right of appeal against conditions imposed by the Commission in lieu of revocation under Sched. 3, part IV, para. 7 or 8: the word "conditions" in para. (*c*) of the present subsection only includes conditions imposed under ss. 9, 41, 42 and 44 (see subs. (6) of this section).

Subs. (2)

The Commission must refuse an application for authorisation under s.9, or an application for reauthorisation under s.44, if it is not satisfied that the chairman of the board of directors and any executive directors, the chief executive, the secretary and the managers (if any) are each fit and proper persons to hold their respective positions in the society: see ss.9(4)(*b*) and (5)(*a*), and 44(4)(*c*) and (5)(*a*). The Commission must also refuse to grant the unconditional renewal of a society's authorisation under s.41 if it is not satisfied that the same persons are fit and proper persons to hold their respective offices (though it seems that the Commission does have power in such a case to renew the society's authorisation subject to conditions): see s.41(6)(*c*) and (7) and the notes thereto. Again, the Commission has power to impose conditions on a society's current authorisation under s.42, or to revoke that authorisation under s.43, if satisfied that the society is not being directed and managed by a sufficient number of persons who are fit and proper to be directors or other officers in the society: see ss.45(1)(2) and (3) (criterion 6(*a*)) and 42 and 43. Conditions imposed on a society's authorisation under s.42 may include a condition which requires the removal of any director or other officer (see s.42(5)(*c*)). The effect of the present subsection is that any person who, under any of the foregoing powers, is required to be removed from office or is held to be unfit to hold office, has a right of appeal to the tribunal. It appears, however, from the somewhat obscure concluding words of subs. (5) that, where a society's authorisation is revoked on the basis that a person is not fit to be a director or other officer (*i.e.*, for non-compliance with the sixth criterion of prudent management in s.45(3)), any appeal by that person against the Commission's determination of his unfitness will have no effect on the revocation of the society's authorisation. The point, perhaps, is that if the society wishes to overturn the revocation, it should bring its own appeal under subs. (1), rather than relying on the outcome of any appeal by the officer concerned under subs. (2). It may be noted, however, that the society will be entitled to be heard on the officer's appeal under subs. (2): see s.48(2).

Determination of appeals

47.—(1) Where an appeal is brought under section 46, a tribunal to determine the appeal shall be constituted in accordance with subsection (2) below.

(2) The tribunal shall consist of—

(*a*) a chairman appointed by the Lord Chancellor or the Lord Advocate, and

(*b*) two other members appointed by the Chancellor of the Exchequer.

(3) The chairman shall be a barrister, solicitor or advocate of at least seven years standing; and the other two members shall be persons appearing to the Chancellor of the Exchequer to have respectively experience of accountancy and experience of the business of building societies or of other financial institutions.

(4) On any appeal against any decision of the Commission the question for the determination of the tribunal shall be whether, for the reasons adduced by the appellant, the decision was unlawful or not justified by the evidence on which it was based.

(5) The tribunal may, on the application of the building society concerned, order that the operation of any condition which is the subject of an appeal by the society be suspended pending the determination of the appeal.

(6) The tribunal may confirm or reverse the decision which is the subject of the appeal but shall not have power to vary it except by directing the Commission—

(*a*) in the case of an appeal against a decision to refuse to grant authorisation, to determine the conditions to which the grant of authorisation is to be subject;

(*b*) in the case of an appeal against a decision to revoke authorisation, to determine the conditions or different conditions subject to which the authorisation is to continue in force, as the case may be;

(*c*) in the case of an appeal against the imposition of conditions or as to the conditions imposed by the decision, to determine the conditions or different conditions subject to which the authorisation is to be granted or is to continue, as the case may be.

(7) Where by virtue of subsection (6) above the tribunal directs the Commission to determine conditions or different conditions, the Commission shall by notice to the society concerned impose such conditions to be complied with by the society as it considers expedient in order to protect the investment of shareholders or depositors and—

(*a*) Part III of Schedule 3 to this Act shall apply subject to the modifications made by paragraph 9 of that Schedule; but

(*b*) the society concerned may appeal to the tribunal against any of those conditions;

and on any such appeal the tribunal may confirm or reverse the Commission's decision with respect to the conditions which are the subject of the appeal or may direct the Commission to determine different conditions.

(8) Where by virtue of subsection (7) above the tribunal, on an appeal against any conditions, directs the Commission to determine different conditions, the other provisions of that subsection shall apply as they apply where the tribunal gives such a direction by virtue of subsection (6) above.

(9) Where the tribunal reverses a decision of the Commission to refuse to grant authorisation, it shall direct the Commission to grant it; and where the tribunal reverses a decision of the Commission to make the grant of authorisation subject to conditions, it shall direct the Commission to grant it unconditionally.

(10) Notice of a tribunal's determination, together with a statement of its reasons, shall be given to the appellant and to the Commission; and unless the tribunal has directed the Commission to determine conditions or, in any other case, the tribunal directs otherwise, the determination shall come into operation when the notice is given to the appellant.

(11) The Treasury may out of money provided by Parliament pay to the persons appointed as members of a tribunal under this section such fees and allowances in respect of expenses as the Treasury may determine and any other expenses incurred for the purposes of this section.

DEFINITIONS
"authorisation": ss.9, 41, 44 and 119(1).
"the Commission": ss.1 and 119(1).
"conditions": s.46(6).
"grant": s.46(6).
"revoke": s.46(6).

GENERAL NOTE
Subss. (1) to (3)
These provisions deal with the constitution of the tribunal to hear appeals brought by building societies under s.46(1), and by their officers under s.46(2). The tribunal is a new body which has no counterpart in the 1962 Act. It will be noted that, while its chairman will be a lawyer appointed by the Lord Chancellor or the Lord Advocate, its two other members will be non-lawyers appointed by the Chancellor of the Exchequer. One of the non-lawyers must have experience in accountancy and the other must have experience of the business of building societies or of other financial institutions.

Subs. (4)
On an appeal from the Commission, the tribunal is directed by this subsection to address itself to the question whether the decision of the Commission was "unlawful or not justified by the evidence on which it was based". The precise scope of these words is obscure. Presumably, a decision of the Commission will be "unlawful" for this purpose if it is *ultra vires* (whether on substantive or procedural grounds); and presumably a decision will not be "justified" by the evidence on which it was based if it is one which no reasonable body could have reached on the evidence, or (possibly) if it is one which the Commission could not reasonably have come to on the evidence adduced: *c.f.* de Smith's *Judicial Review of Administrative Action* (4th Ed.), p.137. But the matter is far from clear.

Subs. (5)
This should be read with the first part of s.46(5).

Subss. (6) to (10)
There are three courses open to the tribunal on hearing an appeal by a society against a decision of the Commission. First, the tribunal may confirm the Commission's decision, in which case no further action is required beyond giving notice of the tribunal's determination and a statement of its reasons to the appellant and the Commission under subs. (10). Second, the tribunal may "reverse" the Commission's decision; that is to say, it may decide that authorisation should be granted unconditionally instead of being refused outright, or

that it should be granted unconditionally instead of being granted subject to conditions: see subs. (9). In such a case, the tribunal (in addition to giving the notice and statement required by subs. (10)) must give a direction to the Commission under subs. (9) to grant the authorisation without conditions. Third, the tribunal may vary the Commission's decision; that is to say, it may decide that authorisation be granted conditionally instead of being refused, or that authorisation be continued subject to conditions instead of being revoked, or that authorisation be granted or continued subject to conditions different from those imposed by the Commission. (See the notes to Part V of Sched. 3 for a summary of the circumstances in which these various possibilities may arise.) In such a case, the tribunal (in addition to giving the notice and statement required by subs. (10)) must remit the matter to the Commission with a direction that it determine the requisite conditions to be imposed: (see subs. (6).) The tribunal cannot impose its own conditions: see subs. (7) and Sched. 3, Part V. Note that subs. (7)(*b*) enables the society to bring a second appeal to the tribunal if dissatisfied with any of the conditions imposed by the Commission after the matter has been remitted to it in this way.

Costs, procedure and evidence

48.—(1) A tribunal may give such directions as it thinks fit for the payment of costs or expenses by any party to the appeal.

(2) On an appeal under section 46(2) the building society in relation to which the determination was made, or upon which the requirement was imposed, shall be entitled to be heard.

(3) The Treasury may, after consultation with the Council on Tribunals, make regulations with respect to appeals under section 46; and those regulations may in particular make provision—

(*a*) as to the period within which and the manner in which such appeals are to be brought;

(*b*) as to the manner in which such appeals are to be conducted, including provision for any hearing to be held in private;

(*c*) for requiring any person, on tender of the necessary expenses of his attendance, to attend and give evidence or produce documents in his custody or under his control and for authorising the administration of oaths to witnesses;

(*d*) for granting to any person such discovery or inspection of documents or right to further particulars as might be granted by a county court in England and Wales or Northern Ireland or, in Scotland, for granting to any person such recovery or inspection of documents as might be granted by the sheriff;

(*e*) for enabling an appellant to withdraw an appeal or the Commission to withdraw its opposition to an appeal and for the consequences of any such withdrawal;

(*f*) for taxing or otherwise settling any costs or expenses directed to be paid by the tribunal and for the enforcement of any such direction;

(*g*) for enabling any functions in relation to an appeal to be discharged by the chairman of the tribunal; and

(*h*) as to any other matter connected with such appeals.

(4) A person who, having been required in accordance with regulations under this section to attend and give evidence, fails without reasonable excuse to attend or give evidence shall be liable on summary conviction to a fine not exceeding level 5 on the standard scale.

(5) A person who intentionally alters, suppresses, conceals, destroys or refuses to produce any document which he has been required to produce in accordance with regulations under this section, or which he is liable to be so required to produce, shall be liable—

(*a*) on conviction on indictment, to imprisonment for a term not exceeding two years or to a fine or both;

(*b*) on summary conviction, to a fine not exceeding the statutory maximum.

(6) The power to make regulations under this section is exercisable by statutory instrument which shall be subject to annulment in pursuance of a resolution of either House of Parliament.

DEFINITIONS
  "the Commission": ss.1 and 119(1).
  "the Council on Tribunals": Tribunals and Inquiries Act 1971, s.1.
  "the standard scale": Criminal Justice Act 1982, s.37.
  "statutory maximum": Criminal Justice Act 1982, s.74; Magistrates' Courts Act 1980, s.32.

GENERAL NOTE
  This section supplements ss.46 and 47 and should be read with those sections. It authorises the tribunal to make directions for the payment of the costs of any appeal brought before it under s.46 (see subs. (1)), and confers power on the Treasury (after consultation with the Council on Tribunals) to make provision by statutory instrument for the detailed procedure to be followed in relation to any such appeal (including provision for the discovery of documents and the administration of oaths to witnesses): see subs. (3).

Further appeals on points of law

49.—(1) An appeal shall lie to the High Court at the instance of the building society or other person concerned or of the Commission on any question of law arising from any decision of a tribunal under section 47; and if the court is of the opinion that the decision was erroneous in law, it shall remit the matter to the tribunal for re-hearing and determination by it.

(2) In the application of this section to a building society whose principal office is in Scotland, references to the High Court shall be construed as references to the Court of Session.

(3) No appeal to the Court of Appeal or to the Court of Appeal in Northern Ireland shall be brought from a decision under subsection (1) above except with the leave of that court or of the court or judge from whose decision the appeal is brought.

(4) An appeal shall lie, with the leave of the Court of Session or the House of Lords, from any decision of the Court of Session under this section, and such leave may be given on such terms as to costs, expenses or otherwise as the Court of Session or the House of Lords may determine.

DEFINITION
  "the Commission": ss.1 and 119(1).

GENERAL NOTE
  An appeal lies from the tribunal to the High Court (or the Court of Session in Scotland), but only on a point of law. An appeal lies to the Court of Appeal (or, in Scottish cases, to the House of Lords) with leave only.

Advertising etc.

Powers to control advertising

50.—(1) If, with respect to any building society for which an authorisation is in force, the Commission considers it expedient to do so in the interests of persons who may invest by way of shares in or deposits with the society, the Commission may give the society a direction under this section.

(2) A direction given to a building society under this section may do all or any of the following—

   (a) prohibit the issue by the society of advertisements of all descriptions;
   (b) prohibit the issue by the society of advertisements of any specified description;

(*c*) require the society to modify advertisements of a specified description in a specified manner;

(*d*) prohibit the issue by the society of any advertisements which are, or are substantially, repetitions of a specified advertisement;

(*e*) require the society to take all practicable steps to withdraw any specified advertisement, or any specified description of advertisement, which is on display in any place;

and a direction under this section shall be in writing.

(3) Not less than seven days before giving a direction under this section the Commission shall give the society and, subject to subsection (9) below, every director and the chief executive of the society notice that it proposes to give the direction and stating the grounds for the proposed direction.

(4) In any case where—

(*a*) the Commission has given a society notice under subsection (3) above, and

(*b*) within the period of seven days beginning with the date on which the notice was given, representations (whether made in writing or orally) are made to the Commission by the society,

the Commission shall take those representations into account in deciding whether or not to proceed to give the direction.

(5) On giving a direction under this section the Commission shall give the society and, subject to subsection (9) below, every director and the chief executive of the society, notice of the direction, stating also the grounds for giving it.

(6) The Commission may not give a direction under this section on grounds other than those stated, or grounds included in those stated, in the notice under subsection (3) above.

(7) A direction under this section—

(*a*) may be revoked or varied by a further direction under this section; and

(*b*) shall be revoked by notice to the society.

(8) If a building society fails to comply with a direction under this section, then—

(*a*) the society shall be liable on conviction on indictment or on summary conviction to a fine not exceeding, on summary conviction, the statutory maximum; and

(*b*) any officer of the society who is also guilty of the offence shall be liable—

(i) on conviction on indictment, to imprisonment for a term not exceeding two years or to a fine or both; and

(ii) on summary conviction, to a fine not exceeding the statutory maximum.

(9) Where any provision of this section requires notice of a direction under it to be given to every director of a building society that requirement is satisfied by giving notice to each director whose appointment has been officially notified and the non-receipt of a notice of the direction by a director or the chief executive does not affect the validity of the direction.

(10) In this section—

"advertisement" includes every form of advertisement, whether documentary, by way of sound broadcasting or by television or other pictorial means; and references to the issue of advertisements shall be construed accordingly; and

"specified" means specified in a direction under this section.

DEFINITIONS
    "advertisement": subs. (10).
    "authorisation": ss.9 and 119(1).

"chief executive": s.59(1).
"the Commission": ss.1 and 119(1).
"deposit": s.119(1).
"notice": s.119(1).
"shares": s.119(1).
"specified": subs. (10).
"statutory maximum": Criminal Justice Act 1982, s.74; Magistrates Courts Act 1980, s.32.

GENERAL NOTE

This section confers power on the Commission to control advertising by a society in any case where the Commission considers it expedient to do so in the interests of prospective investors in the society. The section substantially re-enacts ss.51 and 52 of the 1962 Act. The main differences between the present section and its predecessors are (i) that the powers conferred by this section may be exercised without the need to obtain Treasury consent; (ii) that there is a new power (contained in subs. (2)(*c*)) to require a society to modify its advertisements; and (iii) that there is a new definition of "advertisement", which updates the somewhat Dickensian definition given in the 1962 Act (see subs. (10) and *cf.* s.129(1) of the 1962 Act).

The Green Paper envisaged that the power to control advertisements would be appropriate not only to deal with undesirable advertisements relating to specific types of investment in the society, but also to enable the Commission to arrange a general "holding operation" while initiating the full procedures for revocation of a society's authorisation (see Appendix 2, para. 35 of the Green Paper; and *c.f.* s.43 for the power of revocation).

Powers to avoid apparent association with other bodies

51.—(1) If, as regards a building society and another body corporate which is not an associated body by virtue of section 18, it appears to the Commission that persons who might invest in or otherwise deal with that other body may be misled into believing that there is such a business relationship between the society and that body as indicates that the society has assumed an obligation to discharge that body's liabilities in any event, the Commission may give the society a direction under subsection (2) below.

(2) A direction under this subsection is a direction requiring the society—

    (*a*) if they are available to it, to assume and make exercisable, or to make exercisable, as regards a body specified in the direction, the powers conferred by section 18; or

    (*b*) to take such steps as are agreed with the Commission for the purpose of removing the appearance of a business relationship with the specified body which indicates the assumption of an obligation of the description referred to in subsection (1) above;

and, within a specified period, to notify the Commission of the course it has decided to take.

(3) The steps that a building society may be required to take for the purpose of complying with a direction under subsection (2) above may relate to the conduct of its business or to its business relationship (if any) with the other body and, in particular, may require the removal of any person from any office in the society or that body.

(4) A direction under subsection (2) above shall—

    (*a*) specify the matters which appear to the Commission to be capable of giving rise to such a belief as is mentioned in subsection (1) above;

    (*b*) specify the period within which the society must comply with the direction;

    (*c*) require the society, if it decides to comply with the direction by taking steps to secure the purpose mentioned in subsection (2)(*b*) above, to notify the Commission of the steps it proposes to take.

(5) Where a building society, in pursuance of subsection (2)(*b*) above notifies the Commission of steps which it proposes to take to secure the purpose mentioned in that paragraph then—

(*a*) if it appears to the Commission that the steps proposed are reasonably likely to secure that purpose, the Commission shall approve them and direct the society to carry them out;

(*b*) if it appears to the Commission that the steps proposed are, with modifications, likely to secure that purpose and the Commission and the society agree on appropriate modifications within the period of 21 days from the date on which the Commission notifies the society of the modifications it proposes for their agreement, the Commission shall approve the steps as modified and direct the society to carry them out;

but otherwise the Commission shall reject the society's proposals.

(6) If the Commission rejects a society's proposals under subsection (5) above the Commission shall direct the society, within a specified period, to take the steps specified in the direction.

(7) Any direction under subsection (2), (5) or (6) above shall be given by the Commission by notice served on the society.

(8) The Commission may, if it thinks fit, extend, or further extend, any period during which a building society is to take any steps required of it under any of the foregoing provisions of this section and may do so whether or not application is made to it before the expiry of the period in question.

(9) If a building society fails, within the period allowed to it under the foregoing provisions of this section, to comply with a direction under subsection (2) or (6) above, the Commission may serve on the society an aggregation notice to take effect on such date as is specified in the notice.

(10) An aggregation notice under subsection (9) above is a notice directing that, from the date specified in the notice until the notice is withdrawn by the Commission, the assets and liabilities of the body specified in the notice will be aggregated with those of the society for the purposes of the provisions of this Act requiring aggregation of assets or liabilities; and where such a notice is served, and whilst it remains in force, the assets and liabilities of the body specified in the notice shall for the purposes of those provisions be aggregated with those of the society in accordance with the aggregation rules in force under sections 7(10), 8(3) and 20(9).

(11) A copy of any aggregation notice served on a building society under subsection (9) above shall, whilst in force, be kept in the public file of the society.

(12) In this section—

"business relationship" includes the use of business names and the holding by one individual of offices in more than one body;

"specified" means specified in a direction under any provision of this section;

and "the provisions of this Act requiring aggregation of assets or liabilities" are sections 7, 8 and 20.

DEFINITIONS

"aggregation notice": subs. (10).

"associated body": ss.18(17) and 119(1).

"business relationship": subs. (12).

"the Commission": ss.1 and 119(1).

"notice": s.119(1).

"provisions of this Act requiring aggregation of assets or liabilities": subs. (12).

"public file": ss.106 and 119(1).

"specified": subs. (12).

GENERAL NOTE

In broad terms, the object of this section is "to ensure that the public is not misled by an apparent and misleading association between the society and another body—misleading in the sense that it is trying to create the impression that the society stands behind that body when it does not do so" (see *Official Report*, House of Commons, Standing Committee A, February 11, 1986: Mr Ian Stewart, speaking on behalf of the Government). The aim of the present section is to empower the Commission to deal with such cases by directing the society, in effect, either to give substance to the apparent relationship by making the other body an associated body within the meaning of s.18, or else to take steps to remove the appearance of the relationship: see subss. (1) and (2).

It should be noted that the present section does not require the Commission to be satisfied that there is *in fact* a business relationship between the society and the other body, but rather that persons dealing with that body might be misled into *believing* that there is such a relationship: see subs. (1). As against that, however, the mere existence of an apparent business relationship will not suffice to make the Commission's powers exercisable: there has to be the appearance of a relationship which indicates that the society has assumed "an obligation to discharge [the other body's] liabilities in any event" (see *ibid.*). Such an appearance could be created, presumably, by the semblance of a parent-subsidiary relationship between the society and the other body, since, were such a relationship to exist in fact, the society would be obliged by the "statutory guarantee" contained in s.22 to discharge liabilities of the other body which that body could not discharge out of its own assets. The same would be true of a case (difficult to visualise in practice) where the other body appeared to be linked by resolution to the society (see again s.22 and *cf.* s.18(9)). No doubt other cases can be imagined in which the other body gave the appearance of having the benefit of an express guarantee from the society (*i.e.* as opposed to the "statutory guarantee").

The expression "business relationship" is partially defined in subs. (12) to include "the use of business names" and "the holding by one individual of offices in more than one body". There is, however, some difficulty in making a direct substitution of either of these expressions for the words "business relationship" as used in subs. (1) (or indeed in subs. (2)(*b*)). The difficulty stems from the fact that subss.(1) and (2)(*b*) are contemplating the *appearance* of a business relationship which does not in fact exist, whereas subs. (12) seems to be contemplating an *actual* use of business names or holding of dual offices. Presumably, the intention is that the Commission should be able to intervene in cases where the actual use of business names, or the actual holding by one individual of offices in more than one body, creates the appearance of a relationship between the society and the other body in which the former has undertaken to discharge the liabilities of the latter. There is no difficulty where the phrase "business relationship" is used in subs. (3).

Subs. (2)

It will be noted that a direction under this subsection is a direction requiring the society *either* to take the course specified in para. (*a*) *or* to take the course specified in para. (*b*): the choice, therefore, rests with the society and cannot be dictated by the Commission (*c.f.* subs. (4)(*c*) where this point emerges clearly).

It will be noted that the requirement embodied in para. (*a*) of this section is that the society should "assume" (adopt?) and make *exercisable* in relation to the other body the powers conferred by s.18. The paragraph does not require the society actually to *exercise* those powers in relation to the other body. While not entirely clear, it seems that para. (*a*) contemplates that the society's board should pass a resolution under s.18(9) linking the other body to the society—that is to say, a resolution making the powers conferred by s.19 "exercisable in relation to that body" (see the concluding words of s.18(9)). If that is the correct construction of para. (*a*), the effect is that the other body will become a body which enjoys the benefit of the society's "statutory guarantee" under s.22 (since the guarantee covers, *inter alia*, any body linked by resolution to a building society); but the society will not be required to go to the lengths of investing in the other body or providing support for it (either of which would require an actual exercise of the s.18 powers). It is thought that this construction achieves consistency with the policy underlying the section.

If the society adopts the alternative course open to it under para. (*b*) of this subsection, it must take the initiative in formulating steps to remove the appearance of the offending relationship: see subs. (4)(*c*). If the Commission is satisfied with the steps proposed by the society (either initially or after agreeing modifications to them with the society), it must approve them and direct the society to carry them out: see subs. (5)(*a*) and (*b*). If not so satisfied, it must reject the society's proposals and direct the society to carry out such steps as may be specified by the Commission itself: see the concluding words of subs. (5), and subs. (6).

If the society fails to comply with the original direction given to it under subs. (2), or if it fails to comply with a direction subsequently given to it under subs. (6) (*i.e.*, if it fails to carry out the steps specified by the Commission after the Commission has rejected the steps proposed by the society), then the society may be served with an "aggregation notice" under subs. (9). Such a notice will have the effect that, so far as the society's balance sheet is concerned, the other body will be treated in precisely the same way as if it were a body associated with the society: that is to say, the body's liabilities will be brought onto the society's balance sheet to the extent prescribed by aggregation rules in force under ss.7(10) and 8(3), and its assets will be brought onto the society's balance sheet to the extent prescribed by aggregation rules in force under s.20(9). (Note, however, that none of this will actually involve the society undertaking to guarantee the liabilities of the other body.)

It will be noted that subs. (9) refers to a failure by a society to comply with a direction under subs. (2) or (6). It does not refer to a failure by a society to comply with a direction under subs. (5) (*cf*. subs. (7) where separate reference is made to directions under subs. (5)). It may be, therefore, that the section provides no sanction for the case (no doubt unlikely in practice) where the society fails to comply with a direction to carry out steps agreed with the Commission under subs. (5)(*a*) or (*b*). Arguably, however, such a failure could be brought within the scope of subs. (9) by characterising it as a failure to comply with the direction originally given to the society under subs. (2) (*viz.*, the initial direction either to make the s.18 powers exercisable in relation to the other body or "to take such steps as are agreed with the Commission").

This section should be considered in conjunction with s.107 which, subject to the exceptions there stated, makes it a criminal offence for any person to describe himself or hold himself out in such a way as to indicate that he or his business is connected with one or more building societies. That section might well apply to a body which had helped to foster the appearance of a relationship falling within the scope of the present section between itself and a building society.

Information

Powers to obtain information and documents etc.

52.—(1) This section applies to information, documents or other material, or explanations of matters, which relate to the business of a building society or its plans for future development and, in relation to the obtaining under this section of information or explanations or the production under this section of documents or other material to which it applies "the purposes of its supervisory functions" means the purposes of the discharge by the Commission of any of its functions under Part I, section 9, the foregoing sections of this Part, Part X and sections 107 and 108.

(2) Where a building society has subsidiaries or other associated bodies this section also applies to information, documents or other material, or explanations of matters, which relate to, or also relate to, the business, or the plans for future development, of every such subsidiary or associated body.

(3) Where the Commission has grounds under section 51(1) for giving a direction to a building society under subsection (2) of that section in relation to another body corporate this section also applies to information, documents or other material, or explanations of matters, which relate to the business of that other body.

(4) This section does not authorise any requirement in relation to information, documents or other material to be imposed on a subsidiary of or other body associated with a building society unless that body carries on business in the United Kingdom; but a requirement may be imposed under this section on a building society in relation to information, documents or other material in the possession or control of a subsidiary or associated body outside the United Kingdom.

(5) Subject to subsection (4) above, the Commission may by notice to a building society, subsidiary or associated body—

   (*a*) require the body to which it is addressed to furnish to it, within a specified period or at a specified time or times, such specified information as the Commission considers it needs for the purposes of its supervisory functions;

(*b*) require the body to which it is addressed to produce to it, at a specified time and place, such specified documents or other material as the Commission considers it needs for the purposes of its supervisory functions;

(*c*) require the body to which it is addressed to provide to it, within a specified period, such explanations of specified matters as the Commission considers it needs for the purposes of its supervisory functions;

(*d*) require the body to which it is addressed to furnish to it a report by an accountant approved by the Commission on, or on specified aspects of, information or documents or other material furnished or produced to the Commission.

(6) Where, by virtue of subsection (5)(*a*), (*b*) or (*c*) above the Commission has power to require the furnishing of any information, the production of any document or material or the provision of any explanation by a building society or other body, the Commission shall have the like power as regards any person who is or has been an officer or employee or agent of the society or other body, as the case may be, or, in the case of documents or material, appears to the Commission to have the document or material in his possession or under his control.

(7) Where any person from whom production of a document or material is required under subsection (6) above claims a lien on the document or material, the production of it shall be without prejudice to the lien.

(8) Nothing in the foregoing provisions of this section shall compel the production by a barrister, solicitor or advocate of a document or material containing a privileged communication made by him or to him in that capacity or the furnishing of information contained in a privileged communication so made.

(9) Where, by virtue of subsection (5) or (6) above, the Commission requires the production by a building society or other body or any other person of documents or material, the Commission may—

(*a*) if the documents or material are produced, take copies of or extracts from them and require that person or any other person who is a present or past director or officer of, or is or was at any time employed by, the building society or other body to provide an explanation of the documents or material; and

(*b*) if the documents or material are not produced, require the person who was required to produce the documents or material to state, to the best of his knowledge and belief, where the documents or material are.

(10) Any person who, when required to do so under this section, fails without reasonable excuse to furnish any information or accountant's report, to produce any documents or material, or to provide any explanation or make any statement, shall be liable on summary conviction—

(*a*) to a fine not exceeding level 5 on the standard scale; and

(*b*) in the case of a continuing offence, to an additional fine not exceeding £200 for every day during which the offence continues.

(11) Any building society which furnishes any information, provides any explanation or makes any statement which is false or misleading in a material particular shall be liable, on conviction on indictment or on summary conviction, to a fine which, on summary conviction, shall not exceed the statutory maximum.

(12) Any person who knowingly or recklessly furnishes any information, provides any explanation or makes any statement which is false or misleading in a material particular shall be liable—

(a) on conviction on indictment, to imprisonment for a term not exceeding two years or to a fine or both; and

(b) on summary conviction, to a fine not exceeding the statutory maximum.

(13) In this section "specified" means specified in a notice under this section and "agent", in relation to a building society, or any subsidiary or other body associated with it, includes its bankers, its accountants and solicitors and its auditors.

DEFINITIONS
"agent": subs. (13).
"associated body": ss.18(17) and 119(1).
"the Commission": ss.1 and 119(1).
"officer": s.119(1).
"the purposes of its supervisory functions": subs. (1).
"specified": subs. (13).
"subsidiary": s.119(1); Companies Act 1985, s.736(1).
"standard scale": Criminal Justice Act 1982, s.37.
"statutory maximum": Criminal Justice Act 1982, s.74; Magistrates' Courts Act 1980, s.32.

GENERAL NOTE
This section confers extensive powers on the Commission to require building societies and their associated bodies to provide the Commission with:
  (i) information (see subs. (5)(a));
 (ii) documents or other material (see subs. (5)(b)); and
(iii) explanations of matters specified by the Commission (see subs. (5)(c)).
There is, in addition, a supplementary power to require building societies and their associated bodies to furnish the Commission with an accountant's report on any information, documents or other material provided under (i) or (ii) above (see subs. (5)(d)).
The only constraints on these powers are:
(a) that, to fall within the scope of the section, the information, documents, material or explanations in question must relate to the business of a building society or its subsidiaries or other associated bodies, or to their respective plans for future development (see the opening words of subs. (1) and subs. (2));
(b) that the Commission must consider that it needs the information, documents, material or explanations for the purposes of any of its functions under ss.1–4, 9, 36–51, 86–103, 107 and 108 (see subs. (5)(a)—(c) and the closing words of subs. (1));
(c) that the Commission cannot require the provision of information, documents or other material by a subsidiary or other associated body which does not carry on business in the United Kingdom (though a *society* may be required to provide the Commission with information, documents or other material in the possession of its subsidiary or other associated body outside the United Kingdom): see subs. (4);
(d) that the Commission cannot require the production of documents or material protected by legal professional privilege, or the provision of information contained therein: see subs. (8).
It will be noted that the Commission may require information, documents, material and explanations to be provided not only by a building society and its associated bodies, but also by the present and past officers, employees and agents of the society or of any such body: see the first part of subs. (6) (and note the wide definition of "agent" in subs. (13)). Furthermore, in relation to documents and other material, the Commission may require their production by any person) whether or not connected with the society or its associated bodies) who appears to have the document or material in his possession or control: see the latter part of subs. (6). It should also be noted that, in the case of documents and other material, an explanation of their contents may be required not only from the society, associated body or other person directed to produce them, but also from any present or past director, officer or employee of the society or associated body concerned: see subs. (9)(a).
The powers conferred by this section are specially extended by subs. (3) to cover the case where information, documents, material or explanations are required in relation to bodies which are not in fact associated with the society but have an apparent relationship with it of a character which falls within the scope of s.51(1): see subs. (3). In such cases, however, the powers conferred by this section appear to be exercisable only against the society and not directly against the other body (*i.e.* because the other body will not in fact be a subsidiary or associated body of the society and will hence not be caught by the opening words of subs. (5)).

Subs. (10) prescribes criminal penalties for persons who, without reasonable excuse, fail to comply with a requirement of the Commission under this section. Subss. (11) and (12) also prescribe criminal penalties for the provision of false or misleading statements. It appears that a society will commit an offence under subs. (11) whether or not it (through its responsible officers) knew or ought to have known that the information explanation or statement in question was false or misleading (contrast subs. (12) where knowledge or recklessness is required).

Level 5: currently £2,000.

The statutory maximum: currently £2,000.

As to the provisions made for protecting the confidentiality of information obtained by the Commission under this section, see s.53.

Confidentiality of certain information obtained by Commission

53.—(1) Subject to the provisions of this section and section 54, no information obtained by or furnished to the Commission under or for the purposes of this Act and relating to the business of a building society or other body or its or their plans for future development or to any person who is or has been or has been appointed or, in the case of a director, nominated or proposed as, an officer of a building society or other body may be disclosed (otherwise than to an officer or employee of the recipient authority) except—

(*a*) with the consent of the body to which, or person to whom, the information relates and (if different) of the person who furnishes it to the Commission; or

(*b*) to the extent that it is information which is at the time of the disclosure, or has previously been, available to the public from other sources; or

(*c*) in the form of a summary or collection of information so framed as not to enable information relating to any particular body or person to be ascertained from it; or

(*d*) to the extent that it is information which is provided for the purpose, under any provision of this Act, of its being made (in whatever manner) available to the public.

(2) Nothing in subsection (1) above prohibits the disclosure of information—

(*a*) with a view to the institution of, or otherwise for the purposes of, any criminal proceedings, whether under this Act or otherwise;

(*b*) with a view to the institution of, or otherwise for the purposes of, any civil proceedings by or at the relation of or against the Commission or by the Investor Protection Board arising out of the discharge of their respective functions under this Act;

(*c*) in order to enable the Commission to discharge any of its functions under this Act or any Community obligation;

(*d*) in order to enable the central office to discharge any of its functions under this Act;

(*e*) in order to enable any person appointed investigator under section 55 or inspector under section 56 to discharge his duties under that section;

(*f*) in order to enable the auditors of the society to discharge their duties to the Commission;

(*g*) with a view to the institution of, or otherwise for the purposes of, any disciplinary proceedings relating to the exercise by a solicitor, auditor, accountant or valuer of his professional duties.

(3) If, in order to enable the Commission properly to discharge any of its functions under this Act or any such obligation, the Commission considers it necessary to seek advice from any qualified person on any matter of law, accountancy, valuation of property or other matter requiring the exercise of professional skill, nothing in subsection (1) above

prohibits the disclosure to that person of such information as may appear to the Commission to be necessary to ensure that he is properly informed with respect to the matters on which his advice is sought.

(4) Nothing in subsection (1) above prohibits the disclosure of information—

(a) to the Treasury in circumstances where, in the opinion of the Commission, it is desirable or expedient that the information should be disclosed—

(i) in the interests of shareholders or depositors or in the public interest; or

(ii) with a view to the exercise by the Treasury of any of its functions under this Act; or

(b) to the Investor Protection Board in order to enable the Board to discharge any of its functions under the protective scheme provisions of Part IV.

(5) Nothing in subsection (1) above prohibits the disclosure of information to the Bank of England in circumstances where, in the opinion of the Commission, it is desirable or expedient that the information should be disclosed with a view to facilitating the discharge—

(a) by the Commission, of any of its functions under this Act; or

(b) by the Bank, of any of its functions, whether under the Banking Act 1979 or otherwise;

nor does subsection (1) above prohibit further disclosure of the information by the Bank of England with the consent of the Commission and within the limits permitted by section 19 of that Act other than subsection (4)(a) so far as it relates to disclosure in the public interest.

(6) Nothing in subsection (1) above prohibits the disclosure of information, with the consent of the Treasury, to the Secretary of State or the Department of Economic Development in circumstances where, in the opinion of the Commission, it is desirable or expedient that the information should be disclosed in the interests of shareholders or depositors or, in the case of information for the Secretary of State, in the public interest.

(7) Nothing in subsection (1) above prohibits the disclosure of information to the Secretary of State or the Department of Economic Development in circumstances where, in the opinion of the Commission, it is desirable or expedient that the information should be disclosed with a view to facilitating the discharge—

(a) by the Commission, of any of its functions under this Act, or

(b) by the Secretary of State, of any functions of his under—

(i) any provision of the Insurance Companies Act 1982, or

(ii) sections 431, 432(2), 442, 444, 446(1) or 447(2) or (3) of the Companies Act 1985 (appointment of inspectors and requirement to produce documents); or

(c) by the Department, of any of its functions under Articles 424, 425(2), 435, 437, 439(1) or 440(2) or (3) of the Companies (Northern Ireland) Order 1986 (appointment of investigators and requirement to produce documents);

nor does subsection (1) above prohibit further disclosure of the information by the Secretary of State or the Department with the consent of the Commission.

(8) Subject to subsection (9) below, nothing in subsection (1) above prohibits the disclosure of information to a prescribed regulatory authority in circumstances where, in the opinion of the Commission, it is desirable or expedient that the information should be disclosed—

(a) in the public interest, or

(b) in the interests of shareholders or depositors, or

(c) with a view to facilitating the discharge—

(i) by the Commission, of any of its functions under this Act, or

(ii) by the regulatory authority, of any prescribed functions of the authority;

nor does subsection (1) above prohibit further disclosure of the information by a prescribed regulatory authority in prescribed circumstances, subject to prescribed conditions and with the consent of the Commission.

(9) The Commission, with the consent of the Treasury, may, by order designate public and other authorities as prescribed regulatory authorities for the purposes of subsection (8) above and an order under this subsection—

(*a*) shall specify the functions of prescribed regulatory authorities which are prescribed functions for those purposes;

(*b*) may restrict the circumstances in which information may, by virtue of that subsection, be disclosed or further disclosed, whether by excluding any of paragraphs (*a*), (*b*) or (*c*) of that subsection or otherwise; and

(*c*) may impose conditions subject to which the information may be disclosed or further disclosed;

and in that subsection "prescribed" means prescribed by an order under this subsection.

(10) The power to make an order under subsection (9) above is exercisable by statutory instrument which shall be subject to annulment in pursuance of a resolution of either House of Parliament.

(11) Nothing in subsection (1) above prohibits the disclosure to an overseas regulatory authority of information which relates to a building society which, or a building society's subsidiary or associated body which,—

(*a*) carries on or proposes to carry on any business in that country or territory, or

(*b*) has or proposes to acquire an interest in a body corporate which carries on or proposes to carry on in that country or territory any business corresponding to any business of a building society, or

(*c*) appears to the Commission to be associated with a body incorporated under the law of that country or territory or whose principal place of business is, or is proposed to be, in that country or territory,

if it appears to the Commission that the disclosure of the information would assist that authority in the discharge of its functions or would assist the Commission in the discharge of any of its functions under this Act.

(12) Subsection (11) above applies in relation to the disclosure of information which relates to any person who is or has been or has been appointed or, in the case of a director, nominated or proposed as an officer of a building society or other body in the case of which that subsection authorises the disclosure of information which relates to it as it applies to the disclosure of information which relates to the society or other body.

(13) Any person who discloses information in contravention of subsection (1) above shall be liable—

(*a*) on conviction on indictment, to imprisonment for a term not exceeding two years or to a fine or both; and

(*b*) on summary conviction, to a fine not exceeding the statutory maximum.

(14) In this section—

"authority" includes any body (corporate or unincorporate) which is charged with the regulation of the carrying on of any description of financial business or the practice of any profession to which the carrying on of such business is incidental;

"overseas regulatory authority" means any government department
or public or other authority in a country or territory outside
the United Kingdom which is charged under the law of that
country or territory with the regulation of the carrying on there
of any business within the powers conferred on building
societies or their subsidiaries by or under this Act; and
"regulation", in relation to any public or other authority, means
regulation in the public interest or for the protection of private
interests.

DEFINITIONS
"authority": subs. (14).
"central office": s.119(1).
"the Commission": ss.1 and 119(1).
"Community obligation": European Communities Act 1972, s.1 and Sched.1.
"depositors": s.119(1).
"the Investor Protection Board": s.24(1).
"officer": s.119(1).
"overseas regulatory authority": subs. (14).
"prescribed": subs. (9).
"protective scheme provisions": s.24(3).
"regulation": subs. (14).
"shareholders": s.119(1).
"statutory maximum": Criminal Justice Act 1982, s.74; Magistrates' Courts Act 1980,
s.32.

GENERAL NOTE
The broad effect of subs. (1) is to establish the general principle that information of a
confidential nature obtained by the Commission for the purposes of the Act (whether under
s.52 or otherwise) may not be disclosed without the consent of the person to whom it relates
and (if different) of the person who supplied it to the Commission. The general principle is,
however, substantially qualified by the remaining provisions of the section, which authorise
disclosure, *inter alia*, for the purposes of instituting legal proceedings (subs. (2)(*a*) and (*b*));
to enable the auditors of a society to discharge their duties to the Commission (subs. (2)(f));
to enable the Commission to seek professional advice in relation to its functions (subs. (3));
and to enable information to be supplied, in appropriate circumstances, to various other
administrative, supervisory and regulatory authorities (see subss.(4)–(12)).
Disclosure of information in breach of this section is a criminal offence: see subs. (13).
The statutory maximum: currently £2,000.
Note that the operation of the present section is excluded or modified in relation to
information supplied to the Commission by persons and bodies specified in s.54: see s.54(3),
(5) and (6).

Information disclosed to Commission from other sources

54.—(1) If and in so far as it appears to the Secretary of State that the
disclosure of any information will enable the Commission better to
discharge its functions under this Act (but not otherwise),—

(*a*) information obtained by the Secretary of State under section 447
or 448 of the Companies Act 1985 (inspection of companies' books
and papers) may be disclosed to the Commission or further disclosed, notwithstanding the provision as to security of information
contained in section 449 of that Act; and

(*b*) where the information is contained in a report made by inspectors
appointed under section 431, 432, 442 or 446 of the Companies
Act 1985 (investigation of affairs or ownership of companies and
certain other bodies corporate) the Secretary of State may furnish
a copy of the report to the Commission.

(2) If and in so far as it appears to the Department of Economic
Development that the disclosure of any information will enable the
Commission better to discharge its functions under this Act (but not
otherwise),—

    (*a*) information obtained by the Department under Article 440 or 441 of the Companies (Northern Ireland) Order 1986 (inspection of companies' books and papers) may be disclosed or further disclosed to the Commission, notwithstanding the provision as to security of information contained in Article 442 of that Order; and

    (*b*) where the information is contained in a report made by inspectors under Article 424, 425, 435 or 439 of the Companies (Northern Ireland) Order 1986 (investigation of affairs or ownership of companies and certain other bodies corporate) the Department may furnish a copy of the report to the Commission.

  (3) Subsection (1) of section 53 does not apply to information which has been disclosed to the Commission by virtue of subsection (1) or (2) above, but—

    (*a*) except as provided by paragraph (*b*) below, nothing in this Act authorises any further disclosure of that information in contravention of section 449 of the Companies Act 1985 or, as the case may require, Article 442 of the Companies (Northern Ireland) Order 1986; and

    (*b*) with respect to that information the references in subsections (3), (4), (5), (6), (8) and (11) of section 53 to subsection (1) of that section shall be construed as including a reference to the said section 449 or, as the case may require, Article 422, but, in the case of subsections (5), (6) and (8), so far only as they relate to the discharge of the Commission's functions or the interests of shareholders and depositors.

  (4) If and in so far as it appears to the Bank of England that the disclosure of any information will enable the Commission better to discharge its functions under this Act (but not otherwise), information obtained by the Bank under or for the purposes of the Banking Act 1979 may be disclosed to the Commission and, with the Bank's consent, further disclosed by the Commission, notwithstanding the provision as to security of information contained in section 19 of that Act.

  (5) Subsection (1) of section 53 does not apply to information which has been disclosed to the Commission by virtue of subsection (4) above, but—

    (*a*) except as provided in paragraph (*b*) below, nothing in this Act authorises any further disclosure of that information in contravention of section 19 of the Banking Act 1979; and

    (*b*) with respect to that information the references in subsection (3), (4), (6), (7), (8) and (11) of section 53 to subsection (1) of that section shall be construed as including a reference to the said section 19 but, in the case of subsections (6), (7) and (8), so far only as they relate to the discharge of the Commission's functions or the interests of shareholders and depositors.

  (6) If information is disclosed to the Commission by an overseas regulatory authority—

    (*a*) subsection (1) of section 53 applies to that information as it applies to information obtained or furnished under or for the purposes of this Act; but

    (*b*) the references in subsections (4) to (11) of that section to the disclosure of information do not extend to the disclosure of that information.

DEFINITIONS
  "the Commission": ss.1 and 119(1).
  "depositors": ss.1 and 119(1).
  "overseas regulatory authority": *cf.* s.53 (14).
  "shareholders" s.119(1).

This section makes provision for the disclosure to the Commission of information obtained, *inter alia*, by the Secretary of State for Trade and Industry under certain provisions of the Companies Act 1985, and by the Bank of England under the Banking Act 1979: see subss. (1) and (4). Information may only be disclosed to the Commission under this section where the person or body in possession of the information is of the view that its disclosure will enable the Commission better to discharge its functions under the present Act: see subss. (1), (2) and (4).

Inspections, etc

Investigations on behalf of Commission

55.—(1) If it appears to the Commission desirable to do so for the purposes of its supervisory functions in relation to a building society, the Commission may appoint one or more competent persons to investigate and report to it on the state and conduct of the business of the society concerned, or any particular aspect of that business.

(2) If a person appointed under subsection (1) above thinks it necessary for the purposes of his investigation, he may also investigate the business of any body corporate which is or has at any relevant time been—

(*a*) a subsidiary of the building society under investigation or,

(*b*) an associated body (other than a subsidiary) of that society.

(3) It shall be the duty of every officer, employee and agent of a building society or other body which is under investigation—

(*a*) to produce to the persons appointed under subsection (1) above all records, books and papers relating to the body concerned which are in his custody or power; and

(*b*) to attend before those persons when required to do so; and

(*c*) otherwise to give to those persons all assistance in connection with the investigation which he is reasonably able to give.

(4) Any officer, employee or agent of a building society or other body who—

(*a*) without reasonable excuse fails to produce any records, books or papers which it is his duty to produce under subsection (3) above, or

(*b*) without reasonable excuse fails to attend before the person appointed under subsection (1) above when required to do so, or

(*c*) without reasonable excuse fails to answer any question which is put to him by persons so appointed with respect to any building society or other body corporate which is under investigation,

shall be liable on summary conviction to a fine not exceeding level 5 on the standard scale.

(5) Any officer, employee or agent of a building society or other body who knowingly or recklessly furnishes to any person appointed under subsection (1) above any information which is false or misleading in a material particular, shall be liable—

(*a*) on conviction on indictment to imprisonment for a term not exceeding two years or to a fine or both; and

(*b*) on summary conviction to a fine not exceeding the statutory maximum.

(6) In this section—

(*a*) "agent", in relation to a building society or other body whose business is under investigation, includes its bankers, its accountants and solicitors and any persons, where they are not officers of the other body concerned, who are employed as its auditors;

(*b*) "the purposes of its supervisory functions", in relation to the Commission, has the same meaning as in section 52; and

(*c*) any reference to an officer, employee or agent of a building society or other body includes a reference to a person who has been but no longer is an officer, employee or agent of that society or other body.

DEFINITIONS

"agent": subs. (6).
"associated body": ss.18(17) and 119(1).
"Commission": ss.1 and 119(1).
"officer": s.119(1); and see subs. (6).
"the purposes of its supervisory functions": s.52(1).
"the standard scale": Criminal Justice Act 1982, s.37.
"the statutory maximum": Criminal Justice Act 1982, s.74; Magistrates' Courts Act 1980, s.32.
"subsidiary": s.119(1); Companies Act 1985, s.736(1).

GENERAL NOTE

This section empowers the Commission to appoint one or more persons to investigate and report on the state and conduct of the business of a society, or any particular aspect of that business, if it appears to the Commission "desirable to do so for the purposes of its supervisory functions". Compare s.56, empowering the Commission, *inter alia*, to appoint one or more persons to investigate and report on the affairs of a society if so requested by the requisite number of members or if the Commission "is of opinion that an investigation should be held into the affairs of the society". It is not entirely clear how the circumstances in which the powers may be invoked differ. It is suggested, however, that the power under this section arises when the Commission wishes to obtain information about the way in which the society is conducting its business, with a view to the exercise by the Commission of its powers of control; whereas the power under s.56 arises when the Commission suspects some irregularity in the affairs of the society.

Subs. (2)

This subsection enables an investigator also to investigate the business of any body which is or was at any relevant time a subsidiary of or other body associated with the society if he thinks it necessary.

Subs. (3)

This subsection imposes a duty on every officer, employee or agent of the society or other body under investigation to give to the investigators all the assistance he reasonably can (including, in particular, assistance by the production of records, books and papers and by attendance before the investigators). Note the extended meaning of "officer, employee or agent" given by subs. (6).

Subs. (4)

This subsection imposes criminal penalties for the breach of subs. (3).
Level 5: currently £2,000.

Subs. (5)

This subsection imposes criminal penalties for the offence of knowingly or recklessly furnishing to the investigators information which is false or misleading in a material particular.
The statutory maximum: currently £2,000.

Inspections and special meetings: general

56.—(1) In the circumstances mentioned in subsection (2) below, the Commission—
   (*a*) may appoint one or more competent inspectors to investigate and report on the affairs of a building society, or
   (*b*) may call a special meeting of a building society to consider its affairs, or
   (*c*) may (either on the same or on different occasions) both appoint an inspector or inspectors and call a special meeting for those purposes;

and, in the circumstances mentioned in subsection (3) below, the investigation or consideration may extend to the affairs of any body corporate which is or at any relevant time has been a subsidiary of or body associated with the building society.

(2) The powers conferred by subsection (1) above may be exercised either—

(*a*) on the application of the requisite number of members of the society, or

(*b*) where no such application is made but the Commission is of opinion that an investigation should be held into the affairs of the society, or that the affairs of the society call for consideration by a meeting of its members.

(3) The powers conferred by subsection (1) above may be exercised in relation also to a subsidiary of or body associated with a building society either—

(*a*) where the application referred to in subsection (2)(*a*) above so requests, or

(*b*) where the application contains no such request but the Commission is of the opinion that it is necessary for the purposes of the investigation into or consideration of the affairs of the building society that the affairs of the subsidiary or associated body should also be investigated or considered.

(4) Where the inspectors are of the opinion mentioned in subsection (3)(*b*) above in relation to a subsidiary of or body associated with a building society they may, with the consent of the Commission, extend their investigation to the affairs of the subsidiary or associated body and make their report accordingly.

(5) For the purposes of subsections (1) to (3) above the requisite number of members—

(*a*) in the case of a building society having more than 1,000 members, is 100, and

(*b*) in the case of any other building society, is one-tenth of the whole number of members of the society.

(6) The following provisions shall have effect where an application is made as mentioned in subsection (2)(*a*) above, that is to say—

(*a*) the application shall be supported by such evidence as the Commission may require for the purpose of showing that the applicants have good reason for requiring an investigation by inspectors or consideration by a special meeting, as the case may be, and that the applicants are not actuated by malicious, frivolous, vexatious or scandalous motives in their application;

(*b*) such notice of the application shall be given to the building society and, in a case where the investigation is to extend to its affairs also, to the society's subsidiary or associated body, as the Commission may direct;

(*c*) the Commission shall require the applicants to give security for payment of the costs of the investigation or meeting before the inspector is appointed or the meeting is called subject, in the case of the costs of an investigation, to an amount not exceeding the corresponding Companies Act limit; and

(*d*) as regards the expenses of or incidental to the investigation or meeting—

(i) in the case of an investigation (in whichever way instituted), the expenses shall be defrayed in the first instance by the Commission but without prejudice to its rights to contribution under section 57(10);

(ii) in the case of a meeting, the expenses shall be defrayed by the applicants, or out of the funds of the society, or by the members or officers or former members or officers of the society, in such proportions as the Commission may direct.

(7) Before exercising its powers under subsection (1) above in a case falling within subsection (2)(*b*) above, the Commission shall inform the building society of the action which it proposes to take and the grounds for that action, and the society shall, within 14 days of receiving the information, be entitled to give the Commission an explanatory statement in writing by way of a reply.

(8) Where the Commission proposes to exercise its powers under subsection (1) above in a case falling within subsection (3)(*b*) above, subsection (7) above shall apply in relation to the subsidiary or associated body as it applies in relation to the society

(9) Inspectors appointed under this section shall, in addition to having the powers which are necessary for or incidental to the discharge of their functions under this section, have the powers specified in section 57.

(10) Where a special meeting is called under this section—

(*a*) the Commission may direct at what time and place the meeting is to be held, and what matters are to be discussed and determined at the meeting, and may give such other directions as it thinks fit with respect to the calling, holding and conduct of the meeting;

(*b*) the Commission may appoint a person to be chairman at the meeting or, in default of such an appointment, the meeting may appoint its own chairman;

(*c*) the meeting shall have all the powers of a meeting called according to the rules of the building society;

and the provisions of this subsection and any direction given under it shall have effect notwithstanding anything in thc rules of the building society.

(11) In this section "the corresponding Companies Act limit", in relation to security for the payment of the costs of an investigation, is £5,000 or such other sum as is specified for the time being in an order under section 431(4) of the Companies Act 1985 for the purposes of that section.

DEFINITIONS

"associated body": ss.18(17) and 119(1).
"Commission": ss.1 and 119(1).
"corresponding Companies Act limit": subs. (11).
"member": s.119(1).
"officer": s.119(1).
"subsidiary": s.119(1); Companies Act 1985, s.736.

GENERAL NOTE

This section enables the Commission either (i) to appoint one or more inspectors to investigate and report on the affairs of a society or (ii) to call a special meeting of the society to consider its affairs or (iii) to do both (either on the same or different occasions): subs. (1). The power under (i) above should be compared with that given by s.55; see the notes to that section. This section as a whole should also be compared with the similar provisions of ss.431 and 433 of the Companies Act 1985, which do not, however, extend to the calling of a special meeting.

Subs. (2)

Under this subsection, the powers mentioned above become exercisable by the Commission either on the application of the "requisite number" of members or when the Commission itself is of the opinion that there should be an investigation or meeting. The "requisite member" is 100 if the society's membership exceeds 1,000, or one-tenth of the membership if it does not: subs. (5).

Subss. (3) and (4)

Under subs. (3), the powers mentioned above may also be exercised in relation to a subsidiary of or other body associated with the society if the members asking the Commission to exercise its powers so request or if the Commission thinks it necessary. Subs. (4) permits any inspectors appointed under subs. (1) to extend their investigation to the affairs of a subsidiary of a body associated with the society, if they think it necessary and the Commission consents.

Subs. (6)

The purpose of this subsection is to protect societies from the risk of having to undergo an investigation, or to hold a special meeting, as a result of an unjustifiable application by members. Accordingly, where an application is made by members:

(*a*) it must be supported by such evidence as the Commission may require to show that it is made for good reason and that the applicants are not actuated by "malicious, frivolous, vexatious or scandalous" motives;

(*b*) notice of the application must be given to the society, and, where appropriate, its subsidiary or associated body, in accordance with the Commission's directions;

(*c*) the applicants must give security for the costs involved, subject, in the case of an application for an investigation, to a limit on the amount of the security corresponding to the limit imposed by s.431 of the Companies Act 1985 (currently £5,000, but subject to variation): see subs. (11);

(*d*) the expenses of or incidental to an investigation will be met in the first instance by the Commission, but without prejudice to its right to a contribution under s.57(10); the expenses of or incidental to a meeting will be met by the applicants or out of the funds of the society or by members or officers or former members or officers, as the Commission may direct.

Frivolous, vexatious or scandalous. These terms are used in the Rules of the Supreme Court, Order 18, rule 19, in connection with the power to strike out pleadings. See the commentary to that rule in the *Supreme Court Practice*, vol. 1, for a discussion of how the words are interpreted by the courts.

Costs. Expenses. It is not clear how these terms are to be distinguished.

Subss. (7) and (8)

Subs. (7) requires that before the Commission exercises its powers under this section, it must give the society notice of its proposed course of action and the grounds for it. The society has a right to provide an explanatory statement within 14 days thereafter. Subs. (8) applies subs. (7) to a subsidiary or associated body.

Subs. (9)

This subsection provides that inspectors appointed under this section have, in addition to their necessary incidental powers, the powers specified in s.57.

Subs. (10)

This subsection enables the Commission to give directions about a meeting held under this section and provides that such a meeting shall have all the powers of a meeting called in accordance with the rules.

Inspections: supplementary provisions

57.—(1) In this section—
"the body under investigation" means the building society whose affairs or, as the case may be, the building society whose affairs, and each subsidiary of or body associated with the building society whose affairs, are the subject of the investigation;
"the inspectors" means the persons appointed by the Commission under section 56 to conduct the investigation;
"the investigation" means the investigation under section 56 which the inspectors have been appointed to hold;
and references to officers or to agents include past, as well as present, officers or agents (as the case may be) and "agents", in relation to a building society or any subsidiary of or body associated with a building society, includes its bankers, its accountants and solicitors and auditors.

(2) When the inspectors have been appointed it is the duty of all officers and agents of the body under investigation—

(*a*) to produce to the inspectors all documents and material of or relating to the body under investigation which are in their custody or power;

(*b*) to attend before the inspectors when required to do so, and

(*c*) otherwise to give the inspectors all assistance in connection with the investigation which they are reasonably able to give.

(3) If the inspectors consider that a person other than an officer or agent of the body under investigation is or may be in possession of information concerning its affairs, they may require that person to produce to them any documents or material in his custody or power relating to the body under investigation, to attend before them and otherwise to give them all assistance in connection with the investigation which he is reasonably able to give; and it is that person's duty to comply with the requirement.

(4) The inspectors may examine on oath the officers and agents of the body under investigation, and any such person as is mentioned in subsection (3) above, in relation to the affairs of the body under investigation, and may administer an oath accordingly.

(5) An answer given by a person to a question put to him under the foregoing provisions of this section may be used in evidence against him.

(6) If an officer or agent of the body under investigation or any such person as is mentioned in subsection (3) above—

(*a*) refuses to produce any document or material which it is his duty under this section to produce, or

(*b*) refuses to attend before the inspectors when required to do so, or

(*c*) refuses to answer any question put to him by the inspectors with respect to the affairs of the body under investigation,

the inspectors may certify the refusal in writing to the High Court; and the court may thereupon inquire into the case and, after hearing any witnesses who may be produced against or on behalf of the alleged offender and after hearing any statement which may be offered in defence, may punish the offender in like manner as if he had been guilty of contempt of the court.

(7) The inspectors may, and if so directed by the Commission shall, make interim reports to the Commission, but they may at any time in the course of the investigation, without making an interim report, inform the Commission of matters coming to their knowledge as a result of the investigation tending to show that an offence has been committed.

(8) The Commission may, if it thinks fit—

(*a*) send a copy of any report made by the inspectors to the body whose affairs are or were the subject of the investigation;

(*b*) furnish a copy of any such report on request and on payment of the prescribed fee to—

(i) any member of the body whose affairs are or were the subject of the investigation;

(ii) the auditors of that body;

(iii) any person whose conduct is referred to in the report;

(iv) any other person whose financial interests appear to the Commission to be affected by matters dealt with in the report, whether as creditor or otherwise; and

(*c*) cause the report to be printed and published.

(9) A copy of a report of inspectors appointed under section 56 to hold an investigation under that section, certified by the Commission to be a true copy, is admissible in any legal proceedings as evidence of the opinion of the inspectors in relation to any matter contained in the report; and a document purporting to be such a certificate shall be received in evidence and be deemed to be such a certificate, unless the contrary is proved.

(10) The Commission shall be entitled to be repaid the expenses of the investigation defrayed by it under section 56(6)(*d*) as provided in the following paragraphs, that is to say—

  (*a*) by the applicants for the investigation, to such extent (if any) as the Commission may direct;
  (*b*) by any body whose affairs were the subject of the investigation, to such extent (if any) as the Commission may direct;
  (*c*) by any person convicted of an offence in proceedings instituted as a result of the investigation, to such extent (if any) as the court by or before which he was convicted may order;

and a person liable under any one of paragraphs (*a*) to (*c*) above is entitled to contribution from any other person liable under the same paragraph, according to the amount of their respective liabilities under it.

(11) In the application of this section to a building society whose principal office is in Scotland, any reference to the High Court shall be read as a reference to the Court of Session.

DEFINITIONS
  "agent": subs. (1).
  "associated body": ss.18(17) and 119(1).
  "body under investigation": subs. (1).
  "inspectors": subs. (1).
  "investigation": subs. (1).
  "member": s.119(1).
  "officer": s.119(1).
  "prescribed": s.119(1).
  "subsidiary": s.119(1); Companies Act 1985, s.736.

GENERAL NOTE
This section contains supplementary provisions in respect of investigations under s.56. It may be compared with the similar provisions in ss.434, 436, 437 and 439 of the Companies Act 1985.

Subs. (1)
Note that in this section, "officers and agents" includes past officers and agents.

Subss. (2) and (3)
Subs. (2) imposes a duty on every officer or agent of the society or other body under investigation to give to the inspectors all the assistance he reasonably can (including in particular assistance by the production of documents and material and by attendance before the investigators). *Cf.* s.55(3). Subs. (3) imposes a similar obligation on any other person whom the inspectors consider to be (or possibly to be) in possession of information concerning the affairs of the body under investigation. For sanctions for breach of those obligations, see subs. (6).

Subss. (4) and (5)
Subs. (4) empowers the inspectors to examine persons on oath and subs. (5) makes the answer of a person so examined admissible in evidence against him.

Subs. (6)
This subsection imposes sanctions for breach of the obligations imposed by subss. (2) and (3). The inspectors may certify in writing to the High Court the refusal to co-operate. The court may therefore inquire into the case and after hearing any evidence which may be tendered on either side may punish an offender as if he had been guilty of contempt of court (*i.e.* by a fine or by imprisonment: see the Rules of the Supreme Court, Order 52, in *Supreme Court Practice,* vol.1).

Subs. (7)
This subsection empowers the inspectors to make interim reports and obliges them to do so if so directed by the Commission. It also enables them to inform the Commission of matters coming to their knowledge tending to show that an offence has been committed, without a formal report.

Subs. (9)

Note that a copy of a report by inspectors, certified by the Commission to be a true copy, is admissible as evidence *of the opinion of the inspectors* in relation to any matter contained in the report. Presumably this means that the report can be treated as a form of expert evidence.

Subs. (10)

Under this subsection, the Commission is entitled to recover the expenses of an investigation from the applicants or the body the subject of the investigation (in either case to such extent as the Commission may direct) or from any person convicted of an offence in proceedings instigated as a result of the investigation (to such extent as the court by or before which he was convicted may direct). See the notes to s.56(6).

Part VII

Management of Building Societies

Directors and other officers

Directors: number

58.—(1) Every building society shall have at least two directors.

(2) One of the directors shall be appointed to be chairman of the board of directors.

General Note

Although there can have been few, if any, building societies in recent years without at least two directors, this section had no equivalent in the 1962 Act. It is, however, required by the EEC First Council Directive of December 12, 1977 that credit institutions should have at least two directors; accordingly, any society applying for authorisation after December 1, 1981, when the Building Societies (Authorisation) Regulations 1981 (S.I. 1981 No. 1488) came into operation, had to satisfy the Chief Registrar that the business of the society was effectively directed by at least two individuals (reg. 7). Under s.282 of the Companies Act 1985 a company other than a private company must also have at least two directors unless it was registered before November 1, 1929.

The Act provides no express sanction for the breach of s.58 as such but note that (i) the reduction of the number of directors below two is a ground on which a society may be wound up by the court (s.89(1)(c)), (ii) the criteria for prudent management, listed in s.45, include direction and management by a sufficient number of persons. Failure to observe those criteria may lead, ultimately, to the imposition of conditions on a society's authorisation to raise funds and borrow money or even to revocation of that authorisation: see ss.42 and 43.

Chief executive and secretary

59.—(1) Every building society shall have a chief executive, that is to say, a person who is employed by the society and who either alone or jointly with one or more other persons, is or will be responsible under the immediate authority of the directors for the conduct of the business of the society.

(2) Every building society shall have a secretary.

(3) The offices of chief executive and secretary of a building society may be held by the same person.

(4) The chief executive and the secretary of a building society shall be appointed by the directors of the society.

(5) The directors of a building society shall, as regards the appointment of the secretary or the chief executive of the society, take all reasonable steps to secure that the person appointed is a person who has the requisite knowledge and experience to discharge the functions of his office.

(6) Where a person becomes or ceases to be the chief executive of a building society, the society shall within one month give notice of that fact to the central office, stating the person's full name and address and

the date on which he became, or ceased to be, chief executive; and the central office shall record the person's name and the date on which he began to hold, or, as the case may be, ceased to hold office, in the public file of the society.

(7) Anything required or authorised to be done by or to the secretary or chief executive of a building society may, if the office is vacant or there is for any other reason no secretary or chief executive capable of acting, be done by or to any assistant or deputy secretary or assistant or deputy chief executive, as the case may be, or, if there is no assistant or deputy capable of acting, by or to any officer of the society authorised generally or specially for that purpose by the directors.

DEFINITIONS
"central office": s.119(1).
"officer": s.119(1).
"public file": s.119(1).

GENERAL NOTE
The primary purpose of this section is to promote the efficient management of societies by ensuring that every society has not only a secretary (a requirement carried over from the 1962 Act), but also a new officer, the chief executive, who has the immediate responsibility for the conduct of the society's business (subs. (1)) and whose identity will be readily discoverable from the public file (subs. (6)). Further, the directors must take all reasonable steps to ensure that the secretary and chief executive are capable of doing their respective jobs properly (subs. (5)). The Act provides no express sanction for the breach of s.59 but note that the criteria for prudent management, listed in s.45, include direction and management by a sufficient number of persons who are fit and proper to be officers. Failure to observe those criteria may lead, ultimately, to the imposition of conditions on a society's authorisation to raise funds and borrow money or to revocation of that authorisation: see ss.42 and 43.

Subs. (1)
"*Under the immediate authority of the directors.*" This does not mean that the chief executive himself may not be a director: see the definition of "executive" in s.119(1).

Subs. (5)
There is a parallel here with company law, in that s.286 of the Companies Act 1985 also requires steps to be taken to ensure that the secretary has the requisite knowledge and experience to discharge the functions of his office. The office of chief executive is not, as such, known to company law.

Subs. (7)
Cf. Companies Act 1985, s.283(4).

Directors: elections and retirements

60.—(1) Except in so far as they may be co-opted by virtue of subsection (13) below, the directors of a building society must be elected to office, either—
  (*a*) at the annual general meeting of the society, or
  (*b*) by postal ballot of the members conducted during that part of the financial year of the society which precedes the date on which the annual general meeting is held,
as the rules provide.

(2) The persons entitled to vote in an election of directors of a building society are those members of the society who, on the voting date, are entitled to vote on an ordinary resolution of the society.

(3) A person entitled to vote in an election of directors of a building society shall have one vote for every vacancy which is to be filled by the election but cannot be required to cast all or any of his votes.

(4) Subject to subsections (6), (7) and (9) below and to paragraph 5(3) of Schedule 2 to this Act, any person is eligible to be elected a director of a building society.

(5) The rules of a building society may require its directors to retire at a prescribed age without eligibility for re-election or reappointment; and, if the age so prescribed is no greater than the age which is the normal retirement age for the purposes of this section, subsection (7) below shall have no application to the directors of the society.

(6) If the rules of a building society make the provision authorised by subsection (5) above, a person who has attained the age so prescribed shall not be eligible to be elected as a director of the society.

(7) Except in a case where the operation of this subsection is excluded by subsection (5) above, if a person has attained the normal retirement age for directors, he shall not be eligible to be elected a director of a building society unless—

  (a) he has been approved as eligible for election by resolution of the board of directors, and

  (b) his age and the reasons for the board's approval of his eligibility have been notified to every person entitled to vote at the election.

(8) In this section "the normal retirement age", in relation to the directors of a building society, means 70 years or such lesser age as the rules of the society prescribe as the normal retirement age for its directors; and "the compulsory retirement age", for a society whose rules make the provision authorised by subsection (5) above, means the age so prescribed in its rules.

(9) The rules of a building society may impose, as a condition of a person's eligibility to be or to remain a director of the society, a requirement that he shall hold beneficially shares in the society not less in value than the amount prescribed by the rules, but the minimum holding to be required shall not exceed £1,000 or such other amount as may be subsituted for it by order of the Commission under this subsection.

(10) The rules of a building society may impose, as conditions of the validity of a person's nomination for election as a director, requirements as to—

  (a) the minimum number of members who must join in nominating him,

  (b) their qualifications as respects length of membership of and the value of shares held in the society, and

  (c) the depositing of money with the society in connection with his candidature,

but no other requirements; and rules made by virtue of this subsection must comply with section 61.

(11) A director of a building society shall retire from office—

  (a) in any case not provided for by paragraph (b) below, subsection (12) below or rules under section 61(10), at the third annual general meeting of the society following the date of his election, and

  (b) in a case where he had attained the normal retirement age at his election, at the next annual general meeting following that date;

subject (in either case) to any provision for his earlier retirement on the grounds of ceasing to hold the requisite shares in the society contained in the rules of the society.

(12) A director of a building society attaining the normal retirement age or, as the case may be, the compulsory retirement age shall, subject to any provision of the rules for earlier retirement, retire from office at the next annual general meeting of the society.

(13) If the rules of a building society so provide, the directors for the time being may appoint as additional directors or to fill any vacancy on the board of directors any person who—

(*a*) has not attained—
　　　(i) the normal retirement age, or
　　　(ii) the compulsory retirement age (where that age is less than the normal retirement age), and
(*b*) appears to them to be fit and proper to be a director,
not being a person who, having been nominated for election as a director at any election held within the preceding twelve months, was not elected as a director.

(14) A person who is co-opted under subsection (13) above shall cease to hold office at the end of the permitted period unless he is elected as a director of the society in accordance with this section within that period.

(15) A person who holds office as, or is to his knowledge nominated for election or proposed for appointment under subsection (13) above as, a director of a building society shall, not later than 28 days before he attains the normal retirement age or, as the case may be, the compulsory retirement age for directors of the society, give the society notice of the date on which he will attain that age; and if he fails to do so he shall be liable on summary conviction—
(*a*) to a fine not exceeding level 3 on the standard scale; and
(*b*) in the case of a continuing offence, to an additional fine not exceeding £40 for every week during which the offence continues.

(16) The power of the Commission to make an order under subsection (9) above—
(*a*) includes power to make such transitional provision as it considers necessary or expedient, and
(*b*) shall be exercisable by statutory instrument which shall be subject to annulment in pursuance of a resolution of either House of Parliament.

(17) In this section—
　　"ordinary resolution", means a resolution which will be effective without being passed as a special resolution or borrowing members' resolution;
　　"permitted period", in relation to a co-opted director, has the meaning given by section 61(12); and
　　"the voting date" means—
　　　(*a*) in the case of an election at a meeting, the date of the meeting, except where paragraph (*c*) below applies;
　　　(*b*) in the case of an election conducted by postal ballot, the date which the society specifies as the final date for the receipt of completed ballot papers;
　　　(*c*) in a case where a member appoints a proxy to vote at the meeting for him, the date which the society specifies as the final date for receipt of instruments appointing proxies to vote at the election;
and, for the purposes of this Act, the date of a person's election to office as a director of a building society, in a case where the rules provide for election by postal ballot, is the date of the meeting at which the declaration of the result of the ballot is made.

DEFINITIONS
　"borrowing members' resolution": s.119(1) and Sched. 2, para. 27.
　"Commission ": ss.1 and 119(1).
　"compulsory retirement age": subs. (8).
　"financial year": ss.117 and 119(1).
　"member": s.119(1).
　"normal retirement age": subs. (8).
　"ordinary resolution": subs. (17).
　"permitted period": subs. (17) and s.61(12).
　"special resolution": s.119(1) and Sched. 2, para. 27.

"the standard scale": Criminal Justice Act 1982, s.37.
"voting date": subs. (17).

GENERAL NOTE

Under Sched. 2, para. 3(4), the rules of a society must specify the manner in which directors are to be elected.

"*as the rules provide*". The section does not prohibit provisions in the rules of a society to the effect that, if the number of candidates nominated for election does not exceed the number of vacancies to be filled, those candidates shall be declared elected without a vote or ballot.

Subs. (2)

The voting rights of members must be covered by a society's rules: Sched. 2, para. 3(4).

Subs. (3)

Cannot be required to cast all or any of his votes. It has hitherto been the practice of some societies to include in their rules provisions requiring a particular number of votes to be cast in a particular election: *e.g.* as many votes as there are vacancies. Such provisions are intended to prevent "plumping"; that is, voting for one particular candidate only although there are several vacancies to be filled. The rationale for rules of this kind is that a voter having a number of votes who casts only one of them increases the chance of his favoured candidate's election, with the result that not all votes have equal weight; the rationale for preventing such rules is that a voter should not be obliged to vote for persons of whom he may have no knowledge. (See the debate in *Official Report*, Standing Committee A, February 11, 1986, cols. 335 to 342). The effect of this subsection is that anti-plumping provisions are no longer permitted.

Subs. (4)

This subsection has the effect that only excessive or insufficient age or, where a society's rules require its directors to hold a qualifying shareholding, failure to acquire such a shareholding makes a person ineligible for election as a director of a building society. (Note that the holding of a qualifying shareholding cannot be made a condition of valid nomination: see subs. (10).) The curious result is that a person may be elected although under the rules of the relevant society he must instantly vacate office by reason of his bankruptcy or mental incapacity or on some other similar ground.

Subss. (5) to (8)

These subsections, taken together, provide that, subject to any more stringent provisions in the rules, every society will have a normal retirement age of 70 for its directors. A society's rules could impose more stringent retirement conditions as follows: (i) a lower normal retirement age; (ii) a lower compulsory retirement age; (iii) a compulsory retirement age of 70; (iv) a normal retirement age (not exceeding 70) *and* a (higher) compulsory retirement age. In the absence of any provisions in the rules, the statutory normal retirement age of 70 will apply.

Subs. (9)

If a society wishes to impose a share qualification requirement on its directors, that requirement must appear in the rules: see Sched. 2, para. 3(4).

Subs. (11)

This subsection ensures that every director of a building society, including those holding executive positions, will stand for election at least once in every three years. Previously, the retirement of directors was a matter left entirely to each society's rules.

Subs. (13)

Under Sched. 2, para. 3(4), the rules of a society must specify whether or not directors may be co-opted. It may be noted that the power of co-option may not be exercised in favour of a candidate who was unsuccessful at an election of directors held within the previous twelve months or who, having been nominated at such an election, withdrew; a potential abuse is thus eliminated.

Subs. (14)

The effect of this subsection, when read with the definition of "permitted period", is to require a co-opted director to stand for re-election in the next round of elections (disregarding, for this purpose, any elections in respect of which the closing date for nominations has passed at the date of co-option).

Subs. (15)

Level 3: currently £400.

Directors: supplementary provisions as to elections, etc.

61.—(1) Rules made under section 60(10)(*a*), in order to comply with this section, must not require—

(*a*) in the case of a society with a qualifying asset holding, more than fifty members, and

(*b*) in the case of any other society, more than ten members, to join in nominating a person for election as a director.

(2) Rules under section 60(10)(*b*), in order to comply with this section, must not require a nominating member to have been a member for more than two years before the date of the nomination or to hold, or have at any time during that period held, shares in the society to a value greater than £100.

(3) Rules made under section 60(10)(*c*), in order to comply with this section—

(*a*) must not require more than £250 to be deposited with the society;

(*b*) must not require the money to be deposited before the date which, under the rules, is the closing date for the nomination of candidates for the election; and

(*c*) must provide for the return of the deposit to the candidate in the event of his securing—

(i) not less than 5 per cent. of the total number of votes cast for all the candidates in the election; or

(ii) not less than 20 per cent. of the number of votes cast for the candidate who is elected with the smallest number of votes.

(4) The Commission may, by order, amend subsection (1), (2) or (3)(*a*) or (*c*) above so as to substitute for the number, the maximum value of shares, the maximum amount of the deposit or the percentage of votes required to be secured respectively such other number, value, amount or percentage as it thinks appropriate.

(5) The power to make orders under subsection (4) above—

(*a*) includes power to make such transitional provision as the Commission considers necessary or expedient, and

(*b*) is exercisable by statutory instrument which shall be subject to annulment in pursuance of a resolution of either House of Parliament.

(6) If a building society, in a case where the board of directors has approved as eligible for election a person who has attained the normal retirement age, fails to notify every person entitled to vote at the election as required by section 60(7), the society shall be liable on summary conviction to a fine not exceeding level 4 on the standard scale and so shall any officer who is also guilty of the offence; but no such failure shall invalidate the election.

(7) If a duly nominated candidate for election as a director of a building society furnishes the society with an election address of not more than 200 words before the closing date for nominations, then, subject to subsection (8) below—

(*a*) it shall be the duty of the society to send a copy of the address to each member of the society who is entitled to vote in the election;

(*b*) each member's copy shall be sent in the same manner and, so far as practicable, at the same time as the notice of the meeting at which the election is to be conducted or the ballot papers are sent out, as the case may be, or as soon as is practicable thereafter; and

(c) if the building society fails to comply with the requirements of this subsection the society shall be liable on summary conviction to a fine not exceeding level 4 on the standard scale and so shall any officer who is also liable for the offence;

but no such failure shall invalidate the election.

(8) Subsection (7) above does not require a building society to send copies of an address to members of the society in any case where—

(a) publicity for the address would be likely to diminish substantially the confidence in the society of investing members of the public, or

(b) the rights conferred by that subsection are being abused to seek needless publicity for defamatory matter or for frivolous or vexatious purposes;

and that subsection shall not be taken to confer any rights on members, or to impose any duties on a building society, in respect of an address which does not relate directly to the affairs of the society.

(9) The Commission shall hear and determine any dispute arising under subsection (8)(a) above, whether on the application of the society or of any other person who claims to be aggrieved.

(10) The rules of a building society, if they provide for the retirement by rotation of its directors, may provide that a person elected to fill a vacant seat on the board must retire at the annual general meeting at which, in accordance with the rules for retirement by rotation, the seat is to fall vacant.

(11) Subsection (10) above applies to any vacancy arising when an elected director ceases to hold office for any reason before the annual general meeting at which (disregarding his age) the seat is due to fall vacant under section 60(11)(a).

(12) For the purposes of section 60(17) "the permitted period", with reference to the tenure of office of co-opted directors, is the period beginning with the date of the co-opted director's appointment and ending with whichever of the following first occurs, that is to say—

(i) in the case of a building society which elects its directors at its annual general meeting, the conclusion of the next such meeting following his appointment;

(ii) in the case of a building society which elects its directors by postal ballot, the declaration at its annual general meeting of the result of the next such ballot conducted after his appointment;

(iii) the expiration of the period of sixteen months beginning with the date of his appointment;

but a general meeting or postal ballot shall be disregarded for the purposes of this paragraph if the closing date for the nomination of candidates falls before the date of the co-opted director's appointment.

(13) Where a person becomes or ceases to be a director of a building society, the society shall within one month give notice of that fact to the central office, stating the person's full name and address and the date on which he became, or ceased to be, a director; and the central office shall record the person's name and the date on which he began to hold, or, as the case may be, ceased to hold office, in the public file of the society.

(14) If a building society fails to comply with subsection (13) above the society shall be liable on summary conviction to a fine not exceeding level 4 on the standard scale and so shall any officer who is also guilty of the offence.

"central office": s.119(1).
"Commission": ss.1 and 119(1).
"member": s.119(1).
"normal retirement age": s.60(8).
"officer": s.119(1).
"public file": ss.106 and 119(1).
"qualifying asset holding": ss.118 and 119(1).
"the standard scale": Criminal Justice Act 1982, s.37.

GENERAL NOTE
This section supplements s.60. The policy to be discerned from the detail of the provisions is that of encouraging democratic participation by building society members in their respective societies while protecting societies and their assets from the fringe activities of their most eccentric members or would-be directors.

Subs. (1)
The result of this subsection is that, where a society has commercial assets around the £100 million mark, then subject to the society's rules, a member's rights with regard to the nomination of a candidate for election as a director will be liable to fluctuate from year to year in a rather arbitrary fashion. Members of such a society who wish to nominate a candidate may well need to consider not only the provisions of the rules, but also the amount of the society's assets. Fortunately, they will be able readily to discover whether or not their society has a qualifying asset holding at any time by inspecting the previous year's annual accounts: see s.118(2).

Subss. (6), (7) and (14)
Level 4: currently £1,000.

Subss. (7), (8) and (9)
The right to have an election address circulated is new. It is intended to assist in ensuring that candidates do not attain office only if they have contacts with the existing Board. The right is not available, however, in the circumstances mentioned in subs. (8): *i.e.* (i) where publicity for the address would be likely substantially to diminish the confidence in the society of investing members of the public, or (ii) where the right is being abused to seek needless publicity for defamatory matter or for frivolous or vexatious purposes. It is for the Commission to decide whether (i) applies and for the High Court to decide whether (ii) applies (subject to any provision in the society's rules for arbitration on the question of frivolous or vexatious purposes: see Sched. 14, para. 4). Compare the very similar provisions relating to the right of members proposing a resolution to have a statement circulated: Sched. 2, para. 31. Compare also s.377 of the Companies Act 1985, relating to the similar rights of members of a company.
It shall be the duty of the society. The view expressed on behalf of the Government during the Committee stage of the Bill's passage through the House of Commons was that the duty to send involved the duty to pay for sending: see *Official Report*, Standing Committee A, February 11, 1986, at col. 349. *Sed quaere.*
Likely to diminish substantially the confidence in the society. The task of determining this issue is presumably given to the Commission because its members are thought to have the expertise to assess the effect of the intended address on the investing public. The would-be director may have a difficult path to tread; he may well wish to explain to his electorate how much better he could do the job than the present directors, but the more trenchant his criticisms, the greater the risk that they will diminish confidence in the society.
Defamatory or frivolous or vexatious purposes. The courts are, of course, well accustomed to considering questions of defamation. The expression "frivolous or vexatious" is to be found in the Rules of the Supreme Court, Order 18, rule 19, which includes provisions for striking out pleadings that are frivolous or vexatious. The commentary to the rule contained in the *Supreme Court Practice*, Vol. 1, indicates how the courts are likely to approach this issue.

Dealings with directors
Prohibition of tax-free payments to directors
62.—(1) A building society shall not pay a director remuneration (whether as director or otherwise) free of income tax, or otherwise

calculated by reference to or varying with the amount of his income tax, or to or with any rate of income tax.

(2) Any rule of a building society and any provision of any contract, or in any resolution of a building society, for payment to a director of remuneration falling within subsection (1) above has effect as if it provided for payment, as a gross sum subject to income tax, of the net sum for which the rule, contract or resolution actually provides.

GENERAL NOTE

A similar provision applies in respect of company directors under s.311 of the Companies Act 1985. The apparent purpose of the prohibition is to prevent directors from shifting the burden of meeting their personal tax bills. The society, of course, will have no knowledge of its directors' tax position and therefore may be unable to assess the effect of any agreement to pay remuneration net of tax. Note that directors' remuneration is a matter which must be covered by the rules of a society: Sched. 2, para. 3(4).

Directors to disclose interests in contracts and other transactions

63.—(1) It is the duty of a director of a building society who is in any way, whether directly or indirectly, interested in a contract or proposed contract with the society to declare the nature of his interest to the board of directors of the society in accordance with this section.

(2) In the case of a proposed contract, the declaration shall be made—

(*a*) at the meeting of the directors at which the question of entering into the contract is first taken into consideration; or

(*b*) if the director was not at the date of that meeting interested in the proposed contract, at the next meeting of the directors held after he became so interested.

(3) Where the director becomes interested in a contract after it is made, the declaration shall be made at the first meeting of the directors held after he becomes interested in the contract.

(4) For the purposes of this section, a general notice given to the directors of a building society to the effect that—

(*a*) he is a member of a specified company or firm and is to be regarded as interested in any contract which may, after the date of the notice, be made with that company or firm, or

(*b*) he is to be regarded as interested in any contract which may, after the date of the notice, be made with a specified person who is connected with him,

is a sufficient declaration of interest in relation to any contract made after that date with that company, firm or person.

(5) A director need not make a declaration or give a notice under this section by attending in person at a meeting of the directors if he takes reasonable steps to secure that the declaration or notice is brought up and read at the meeting.

(6) The foregoing provisions of this section apply in relation to any transaction or arrangement as they apply in relation to a contract and, for the purposes of this section, a transaction or arrangement of a kind described in section 65 made by a society for a director of the society or a person connected with a director of the society is to be treated (if it would not otherwise be so treated, and whether or not it is prohibited by that section) as a transaction or arrangement in which that director is interested.

(7) A director who fails to comply with this section shall be guilty of an offence and liable—

(*a*) on conviction on indictment, to a fine; or

(*b*) on summary conviction, to a fine not exceeding the statutory maximum.

DEFINITIONS
    "connected with": s.70(2) to (4).
    "statutory maximum": Criminal Justice Act 1982, s.74; Magistrates' Courts Act 1980, s.32.

GENERAL NOTE
    This section imposes on directors a duty to disclose their interest in contracts with their society and should be compared both with s.73 of the 1962 Act, which it substantially re-enacts, and with s.317 of the Companies Act 1985. The following differences from s.73 should be noted: (i) s.73(4) contained no provision for a general notice as respects a specified person connected with the director: *c.f.* the present subs. (4); (ii) subs. (6) is new; (iii) there is no equivalent in this section of s.73(7), which contained a saving for any rule of law restricting directors of building societies from having any interest in contracts with their respective societies. Curiously, s.317(9) of the Companies Act does contain such a saving. In other respects, s.317 is very similar to this section, although there are certain minor differences.
    The crucial word "interest" is not defined, but it is thought to mean "financial interest". Any wider construction would render the section unworkable in practice.
    The omission of any provision equivalent to the old s.73(7) naturally raises the question whether this section is intended to affect the general law. Under the general law, prior to this Act, a building society director, like a company director, might not make a profit at the expense of the society or through the use of the society's property and might not purchase the society's property: see Wurtzburg and Mills, *Building Society Law* (14th Ed.), p. 275. It was, however, open to the society to relax the restrictions of the general law by its rules, so that there could be a valid contract in which a director was interested. S.73 itself contained (and this section contains) no provision validating such contracts; there is simply a requirement that the director's interest be disclosed to the board. It appears, therefore, that s.73(7) was purely a declaratory provision and it seems to follow that this section will have the same effect as s.73 notwithstanding that there is no express saving for the general law. In other words, disclosure alone will not save a contract in which a director is interested if the society's rules do not permit such contracts to be made.
    The section makes no express provision for the effect of non-disclosure on the validity of a contract (contrast s.64(6) and (7)). In *Hely-Hutchinson* v. *Brayhead Limited* [1968] 1 Q.B. 549, non-disclosure was held to make the contract voidable, as would be the case if the general law applied. That decision, however, was based not only on s.199 of the Companies Act 1948 (which was in terms similar to those of the present section) but also on art. 99 of the particular company's articles, which permitted a director to be interested in a contract with the company provided that disclosure was made. No doubt the same result would be reached on a rule in similar terms to art. 99, but if a building society rule permitted a director to be interested in a contract with the society without requiring disclosure, it is not clear what the effect would be on the validity of the contract. The criminal sanction, of course, would be unaffected and it seems probable that as a matter of policy the section would be held to have the effect of making the contract voidable. The short and practical answer may be that no such rule would be permitted by the central office: see Sched. 2, paras. 3(3) and 4(4), requiring, in effect, that the rules should be consistent with the Act.
    Note that disclosure is to the board; directors are not obliged to make disclosure to the members generally. Under ss.73(8) and 74(4), however, the Commission, with the consent of the Treasury, may make regulations which would require, *inter alia*, that the annual accounts and the annual business statement would give particulars of directors' financial interests.

Subs. (4)
    This subsection seems necessarily to imply that a general notice cannot be given except as provided for in paras. (*a*) and (*b*). The result may sometimes appear anomalous: for example, a director may give a general notice under paragraph (*b*) in respect of a step-child (who is a "connected person") but not in respect of a brother or sister (who are not "connected persons") although the family relationship may well be closer. See the definition of persons "connected with" a director in s.70(2) to (4).

Subs. (6)
    Under this subsection, the disclosure requirements are applied to every "transaction or arrangement". Those words are not defined, but are clearly capable of a very wide meaning. Note that a transaction or arrangement of a kind described in s.65 and made for a director

or a person with whom he is connected must be disclosed whether or not the director is in fact interested.

Subs. (7)
　The statutory maximum. Currently £2,000.

Substantial property transactions involving directors and connected persons

64.—(1) A building society shall not enter into an arrangement—
  (*a*) whereby a director of the society, or a person connected with a director of the society, acquires or is to acquire one or more non-cash assets of the requisite value from the society; or
  (*b*) whereby the society acquires or is to acquire one or more non-cash assets of the requisite value from a director of the society or a person connected with a director of the society,
unless the arrangement is first approved by a resolution of the society passed at a general meeting.

(2) For this purpose a non-cash asset is of the requisite value if at the time the arrangement in question is entered into its value is—
  (*a*) except in a case falling within paragraph (*b*) below, not less than £50,000; and
  (*b*) where the last balance sheet of the society showed reserves amounting to less that £500,000, not less than the higher of £1,000 or the amount which represents 10 per cent. of the reserves so shown.

(3) The Commission may, by order made with the consent of the Treasury, amend subsection (2) above so as to substitute for any of the amounts for the time being specified in paragraphs (*a*) and (*b*) of that subsection such other amount as it thinks appropriate.

(4) The power to make an order under subsection (3) above is exercisable by statutory instrument which shall be subject to annulment in pursuance of a resolution of either House of Parliament.

(5) In this section "non-cash asset" means any property or interest in property other than cash and a reference to the acquisition of a non-cash asset includes the creation or extinction of an estate or interest in, or a right over, any property and also the discharge of any person's liability, other than a liability for a liquidated sum.

(6) An arrangement entered into by a building society in contravention of this section, and any transaction entered into in pursuance of the arrangement (whether by the society or any other person) is voidable at the instance of the society unless—
  (*a*) restitution of any money or other asset which is the subject matter of the arrangement or transaction is no longer possible or the society has been indemnified in pursuance of subsection (7)(*b*) below for the loss or damage suffered by it, or
  (*b*) any rights acquired in good faith, for value and without actual notice of the contravention by any person who is not a party to the arrangement or transaction would be affected by its avoidance, or
  (*c*) the arrangement is affirmed by the society at a general meeting held not later than the next annual general meeting after the entry into the arrangement.

(7) Where an arrangement or transaction is entered into with a building society by a director of the society or a person connected with him in contravention of this section then, without prejudice to any other liability but subject to subsections (8) and (9) below, that director and the person so connected, and any other director of the society who authorised the arrangement or any transaction entered into in pursuance of such an arrangement, is liable—
  (*a*) to account to the society for any gain which he has made directly or indirectly by the arrangement or transaction, and

(*b*) (jointly and severally with any other person liable under this subsection) to indemnify the society for any loss or damage resulting from the arrangement or transaction.

(8) Where an arrangement or transaction is entered into by a building society and a person connected with a director of the society in contravention of this section, that director is not liable under subsection (7) above if he shows that he took all reasonable steps to secure the society's compliance with this section.

(9) In any case, a person so connected and any such other director as is mentioned in subsection (7) above is not so liable if he shows that, at the time the arrangement was entered into, he did not know the circumstances constituting the contravention.

DEFINITIONS
    "Commission": ss.1 and 119(1).
    "connected with": s.70(2) to (4).
    "non-cash asset": subs. (5).
    "requisite value": subs. (2).

GENERAL NOTE
    This section broadly introduces into building society law the provisions relating to substantial property transactions involving directors and connected persons which are to be found in ss.320, 322 and 739 of the Companies Act 1985. The differences between the two sets of provisions are differences of drafting rather than of substance. The effect of the provisions may be summarised as follows: a transaction involving assets (other than cash) of the requisite value between a society and a director or a person connected with the director is voidable by the society unless—
    (1) the arrangement has the prior approval of the society in general meeting;
    (2) the arrangement is subsequently ratified by the society at a general meeting held not later than the next annual general meeting;
    (3) restitution is no longer possible;
    (4) the society has already been indemnified for the loss or damage suffered;
    (5) any rights acquired in good faith, for value and without actual notice of the contravention by a person who was not a party to the transaction would be affected by its avoidance.
    Note that only in case (1) above is there no contravention of this section. In the other cases, the section is still contravened (see subs. (6)), although the right to avoid the transaction is lost. It follows that in each of those cases the society will be entitled, in accordance with subs. (7), to an account and (except in case (4)) an indemnity—even in case (2), when the transaction has been ratified. Of course, it may be that ratification is the best way for the society to deal with the situation which arises following a contravention of this section, but that loss is still suffered.

Subs. (2)
    The effect of this subsection is that (i) any transaction involving assets worth £50,000 or more will always be subject to this section, (ii) no transaction involving assets worth less than £1,000 will be subject to the section, (iii) a transaction involving assets worth between £1,000 and £50,000 will be subject to the section if their value equals 10 per cent. or more of the reserves shown in the last balance sheet of the society. These amounts may be revised: subs. (3).

Subs. (5)
    The definitions of "non-cash asset" and "acquisition of a non-cash asset" are very wide. Note that an asset can be acquired not only by the creation of an estate or interest in or right over property, but also by the extinction of such an estate, interest or right. Presumably this would include not only such matters as the surrender of a lease or the release of a restrictive covenant but also, for example, the failure to exercise an option within the due time.

Subs. (7)
    The remedies provided by this subsection are standard equitable remedies in the case of a breach of fiduciary duty. The persons liable (subject to subss. (8) and (9)) are, it appears, the following:

(1) a director who enters into a transaction in contravention of the section;
(2) a person connected with a director who enters into such a transaction;
(3) the director to whom a person entering into such a transaction is connected;
(4) any other director who authorised the transaction.

A director in category (1) does not fall within subss. (8) or (9) and accordingly has no escape route. A person in category (2) or a director in category (4) will avoid liability if he can show that at the time of the transaction he did not know the circumstances constituting the contravention. A director in category (3), however, can only avoid liability, by virtue of subs. (8), if he can show that he took all reasonable steps to secure the society's compliance with this section. It seems to follow that such a director may be liable to the society although he was completely unaware that the transaction was even in contemplation. To take an extreme example, a society agrees to purchase, for office use, commercial premises with an open market value of £60,000. The society, being anxious to acquire the premises, agrees to pay £62,000. The vendors are the trustees of a trust one of the beneficiaries of which is a step-child of one of the directors. The director has no real relationship with his step-child and he is a non-executive director who has no concern with standard acquisitions and disposals by the society's premises department. Nevertheless, having regard to the provisions of this section and the definition of connected persons, it seems arguable that he could be sued for £2,000.

Restriction on loans, etc. to directors and persons connected with them

65.—(1) Subject to the following provisions of this section, a building society shall not—

(a) make an advance or other loan to a director or a person connected with a director of the society; or
(b) dispose of property by way of lease or hire to a director or a person connected with a director of the society; or
(c) make a payment on behalf of a director or a person connected with a director of the society in connection with the provision of any services for the time being specified in Part I of Schedule 8 to this Act; or
(d) enter into a guarantee or provide any security which is incidental to or connected with any such loan, disposal of property or payment; or
(e) take part in any arrangement whereby—
    (i) another person enters into a transaction which if it had been entered into by the society, would have contravened any of paragraphs (a) to (d) above; and
    (ii) that other person, in pursuance of the arrangement, has obtained or is to obtain any benefit from the society or a subsidiary of the society.

(2) Subsection (1)(a) above does not apply to—
(a) any loan of an amount which, when aggregated with any other relevant loans, does not exceed £2,500;
(b) any loan made in the ordinary course of the society's business and of an amount not greater and made on other terms not more favourable than it is reasonable to expect the society to have offered to a person of the same financial standing but unconnected with the society; or
(c) any loan, the amount of which, when aggregated with any other relevant loans, does not exceed £50,000, made for or towards the purchase or improvement of a dwelling-house used or to be used as the director's only or main residence if he is an executive director and loans of that description and on similar terms are ordinarily made by the society to its employees.

(3) Subsection (1)(b) above does not apply to—
(a) any lease or hiring of property the value of which, when aggregated with the value of any other relevant leases or hirings, does not exceed £5,000; or

(*b*) any lease or hiring made in the ordinary course of the society's business and on terms not more favourable than it is reasonable to expect the society to have offered to a person unconnected with the society.

(4) Subsection (1)(*c*) above does not apply to—

(*a*) any payment amounting, when aggregated with any other relevant payment, to no more than £1,000 in respect of which the person on whose behalf it is made is under an obligation to reimburse the society within a period not exceeding two months beginning with the date of the payment; or

(*b*) any payment of an amount not greater and on other terms not more favourable than it is reasonable to expect the society to have offered to a person of the same financial standing but unconnected with the society.

(5) Subject to compliance with the requirements of subsection (6) below, subsection (1) above does not preclude a building society from doing anything to provide a director with funds to meet expenditure incurred or to be incurred by him for the purposes of the society or for the purpose of enabling him properly to perform his duties as a director of the society nor does it preclude the society from doing anything to enable a director to avoid incurring such expenditure.

(6) The following are the requirements referred to in subsection (5) above—

(*a*) the things must either be done with the prior approval of the society given at a general meeting at which the requisite matters are disclosed or be done on condition that, if the approval of the society is not so given at the next annual general meeting, the loan is to be repaid, or any other liability arising under the transaction is to be discharged, within six months from the conclusion of that meeting; and

(*b*) the amount provided, when aggregated with any other relevant provision of funds, does not exceed £10,000.

(7) The following are the requisite matters which must be disclosed for the purposes of subsection (6) above—

(*a*) the purpose of the expenditure incurred or to be incurred, or which would otherwise be incurred, by the director;

(*b*) the amount of the funds to be provided by the society; and

(*c*) the extent of the society's liability under any transaction which is or is connected with the thing in question.

(8) The Commission may by order in a statutory instrument made with the consent of the Treasury substitute for any sum specified in this section a larger sum specified in the order.

(9) An order under subsection (8) above shall be subject to annulment in pursuance of a resolution of either House of Parliament.

(10) In this section—

"authorising provision" and "authorised", in relation to a transaction of a description falling within paragraph (*a*), (*b*) or (*c*) of subsection (1) above, mean respectively any provision of subsection (2), (3) or (4) or constituted by subsection (5) above and any transaction or thing done to which that paragraph does not apply or which is not precluded from being done by virtue of that provision;

"outstanding", in relation to loans, means outstanding in respect of principal and interest and, in relation to the provision of funds subject to a condition for repayment or discharge of any other liability, means unpaid or undischarged to any extent;

"provision of funds" includes anything else which, by virtue of subsection (5) above, a society is not precluded from doing by subsection (1) above; and

"relevant", in relation to a transaction of a description falling within paragraph (*a*), (*b*) or (*c*) of subsection (1) above, means an outstanding or, in the case of a lease or hiring, current transaction of that description (whether entered into by, or by arrangement with, the society) not being one authorised by any other authorising provision.

(11) Section 70 has effect for the interpretation, in the subsequent provisions of this Part, of references to transactions or arrangements contravening this section and to such transactions or arrangements being made "for" a person.

DEFINITIONS

"authorised", "authorising provision": subs. (10).
"Commission": ss.1 and 119(1).
"connected with": s.70(2) to (4).
"dispose of": s.119(1).
"executive": s.119(1).
"provision of funds": subs. (10).
"relevant": subs. (10).
"requisite matter": see subs. (7).

GENERAL NOTE

This section should be compared with ss.330 to 339 of the Companies Act 1985. Underlying both sets of provisions is a fairly straightforward object: to ensure that directors and persons connected with them do not make arrangements, directly or indirectly, with their society or company, on terms more favourable than the terms available to persons generally, or from which a substantial financial advantage is gained. In other words, directors must not abuse their position. The actual provisions by which this object is to be achieved are necessarily fairly detailed and there are differences between the two sets, arising, in large measure, from the fact that a company may carry on whatever kind of legal business its objects permit, whereas a building society may only carry on certain activities permitted by statute: see the notes to s.5 above. In the circumstances, these notes deal only with the provisions of s.65 itself and reference should be made to works on company law for the detail of ss.330 to 339. It is not thought, however, that the differences are intended to reflect any difference in policy; during the Bill's passage through the Commons, s.65 was said to be modelled on the Companies Act (*Official Report*, Standing Committee A, February 13, 1986, col. 357).

The structure of the section is as follows. Subs. (1) contains a basic prohibition on the following activities by a society:

(*a*) making a loan to a director or connected person;
(*b*) leasing or hiring property to a director or connected person;
(*c*) making a payment on behalf of a director or connected person for the provision of services specified in Sched. 8;
(*d*) guaranteeing or otherwise securing any such loan, lease, hiring or payment;
(*e*) taking part in any arrangement whereby another person does any thing which the society could not do under (1) to (4) above in return for a benefit from the society or a subsidiary.

The basic prohibition is thus very wide, but it is then substantially qualified. Subss. (2) to (4) qualify (*a*) to (*c*) above respectively. Subss. (5) to (7) contain a further qualification relating to the expenses of a director in acting as such. Subss. (8) and (9) provide for the increase of financial limits previously specified and subss. (10) and (11) contain definitions.

Note that in keeping with the fundamental object mentioned above, each of subss. (2) to (4) contains an exclusion for a transaction on terms no more favourable than those the society might reasonably have offered to a person of the same financial standing as the particular director but with no connection with the society.

The sanctions for breach of this section are set out in s.66. There should also be borne in mind the provisions of s.68, requiring each society to keep a register of transactions lawfully made under the permissive provisions of this section and to prepare an annual statement giving particulars of such transactions entered into during the financial year, and s.78(9) and (10), requiring the auditors to examine and report on the statement prepared under s.68.

Subs. (1)

Para. (*e*) of this subsection is designed to prevent evasion of the prohibitions in paras. (*a*) to (*d*) by the device of the society's procuring another person to enter into the transaction with the director or connected person. An example of such a device would be a "back-to-back" arrangement whereby one society offered loans on advantageous terms to the directors of another society in return for the second society's offering a similar facility to the directors of the first society.

Subs. (2)

Other relevant loans. By virtue of subs. (10), other relevant loans are loans (i) in respect of which money remains outstanding and (ii) which are not permitted under any paragraph of subs. (2) other than the one being considered. It follows that for example, a director who has received a loan of £2,500 under para. (*a*) may still receive an advance of £50,000 towards the purchase of a house under para. (*c*), provided that the other requirements of that paragraph are satisfied.

Subs. (3)

Other relevant leases or hirings. Again, by virtue of subs. (10), other relevant leases or hirings are leases or hirings (i) which are still current and (ii) which are not permitted under the paragraph of this subsection other than the one being considered.

Subs. (4)

Other relevant payment. The application of subs. (10) to this subsection is not quite as clear as its application to the preceding subsections, but it seems that other relevant payments are payments (i) in respect of which reimbursement by the person on whose behalf the payment was made has not been completed and (ii) which are not permitted under para. (*b*) of this subsection.

Subss. (5) to (7)

The effect of these subsections may be summarised as follows. A society may provide a director with funds to meet expenditure incurred or to be incurred for the purposes of the society or for the purposes of enabling him to perform his duties properly even if such provision of funds would otherwise be caught by subs. (1) if:

(1) the amount provided, together with any other relevant provision of funds (as to which see below), does not exceed £10,000; and

(2) either (*a*) the society gives its prior approval at a general meeting when the matters specified in subs. (7) are disclosed or (*b*) the provision is made on condition that if the society's approval is not given at the next annual general meeting, any liability is to be discharged within six months from the conclusion of that meeting.

Subs. (5) also permits a society to do "anything to enable a director to avoid incurring such expenditure" if the above conditions are satisfied.

Note that these provisions are not intended to cover the usual payment of out-of-pocket expenses or the usual direct discharge of a director's expenses because such payment or discharge would not usually involve a transaction within subs. (1). There are no very obvious examples of the sort of expenses that are to be covered.

Other relevant provision of funds. It seems that by virtue of subs. (10) this phrase means any other activity which is permitted by reason of subs. (5) and in respect of which a condition for repayment or discharge of any other liability has not been fully satisfied.

Sanctions for breach of s.65

66.—(1) If a building society enters into a transaction or arrangement contravening section 65, the transaction or arrangement is voidable at the instance of the society unless—

(*a*) restitution of any money or any other assets which is the subject matter of the arrangement or transaction is no longer possible, or the society has been indemnified in pursuance of subsection (2)(*b*) below for the loss or damage suffered by it, or

(*b*) any rights acquired in good faith, for value and without actual notice of the contravention by a person other than the person for whom the transaction or arrangement was made would be affected by its avoidance.

(2) Where a transaction or arrangement contravening section 65 is made by a building society for a director of the society or a person connected with a director of the society then, without prejudice to any other liability but subject to subsections (3) and (4) below, that director and the person so connected and any other director of the society who authorised the transaction or arrangement (whether or not it has been avoided in pursuance of subsection (1) above) is liable—

(a) to account to the society for any gain which he has made directly or indirectly by the transaction or arrangement; and

(b) (jointly and severally with any other person liable under this subsection) to indemnify the society for any loss or damage resulting from the transaction or arrangement.

(3) Where a transaction or arrangement contravening section 65 is entered into by a building society and a person connected with a director of the society, that director is not liable under subsection (2) above if he shows that he took all reasonable steps to secure the society's compliance with that section.

(4) In any case, a person so connected and any such other director as is mentioned in subsection (2) above is not liable if he shows that, at the time the transaction or arrangement was entered into, he did not know the circumstances constituting the contravention.

(5) A director of a building society who authorises or permits the society to enter into a transaction or arrangement knowing or having reasonable cause to believe that the society was thereby contravening section 65 is guilty of an offence.

(6) A building society which enters into a transaction or arrangement contravening section 65 for one of its directors is guilty of an offence unless it shows that, at the time the transaction or arrangement was entered into, it did not know the circumstances constituting the contravention.

(7) A person who procures a building society to enter into a transaction or arrangement knowing or having reasonable cause to believe that the society was thereby contravening section 65 is guilty of an offence.

(8) A person other than a building society who commits an offence under this section shall be liable—

(a) on conviction on indictment, to imprisonment for a term not exceeding two years or to a fine or both; or

(b) on summary conviction, to imprisonment for a term not exceeding six months or to a fine not exceeding the statutory maximum or both.

(9) A building society which commits an offence under this section shall be liable on conviction on indictment or on summary conviction to a fine which, on summary conviction, shall not exceed the statutory maximum.

DEFINITIONS
"the statutory maximum": Criminal Justice Act 1982, s.74; Magistrates' Courts Act 1980, s.32.
"transaction or arrangement contravening s.65": s.70(5).
"transaction or arrangement made for": s.70(5).

GENERAL NOTE
This section readily divides itself into two parts. Subss. (1) to (4) deal with civil liability for the contravention of s.65 and subss. (5) to (9) create criminal offences and impose criminal sanctions for such contravention. The corresponding provisions of the Companies Act 1985 are ss.341 and 342.

Subss. (1) to (4)
These subsections contain provisions very similar to those of subss. (6) to (9) of s.64 (substantial property transactions with directors) and reference may be made to the notes to

that section. In particular, it should be observed that subs. (2) appears to have the effect, commented on in relation to s.64(7), that liability may fall on a director who is connected with a person with whom a society enters into a transaction contravening s.65 but who has no knowledge at all of the transaction: morally speaking, an innocent party.

Subss. (5) to (7)
  Note that each of the offences created by these subsections either requires knowledge or reasonable cause to believe on the part of the alleged offender or makes it a defence to prove lack of knowledge. Compare the position in civil law, mentioned above.

Subss. (8) and (9)
  The statutory maximum. Currently £2,000.

Directors, etc, not to accept commissions in connection with loans

67.—(1) This section applies to any person who holds office in or is employed by a building society as director, secretary, chief executive, manager, solicitor, surveyor or valuer or in connection with the assessment of the adequacy of securities for advances secured on land.

(2) No person to whom this section applies shall (in addition to the remuneration prescribed or authorised by the rules or any resolution of the society) accept from any other person any commission for or in connection with any loan made by the society.

(3) If a person to whom this section applies accepts a commission in contravention of subsection (2) above—

  (*a*) both he and, subject to subsection (4) below, the person who paid it shall be liable on summary conviction to a fine not exceeding level 4 on the standard scale; and

  (*b*) if, having been convicted of an offence under paragraph (*a*) above, the person accepting the commission fails to pay over to the society the amount or value of the commission, as and when directed to do so by the court which convicted him, he shall be guilty of an offence under this paragraph and liable on summary conviction to imprisonment for a term not exceeding six months.

(4) No offence under paragraph (*a*) of subsection (3) above is committed by the person who paid the commission unless he did so knowing the circumstances that constituted the offence under that paragraph on the part of the person who accepted it from him.

(5) Where—

  (*a*) a charge upon a policy of life assurance is given as additional security for an advance made by a building society, or

  (*b*) a building society makes an additional advance to enable payment to be made of a premium on a policy of insurance, or

  (*c*) any policy of insurance is taken out so as to comply with the terms on which an advance is made by a building society, whether by way of insuring the property given as security for the advance or otherwise,

and the policy is effected through the building society, or the society nominates or selects a person by whom the policy is to be issued, it shall be unlawful for any person to whom this section applies, in connection with the effecting of the policy, to receive any commission from a person by or through whom the policy is issued.

(6) A person who pays, and a person who accepts, any commission which subsection (5) above makes it unlawful to receive shall be liable on summary conviction to a fine not exceeding level 4 on the standard scale.

(7) In this section—

  "charge upon a policy of life assurance", in relation to an advance secured on land in Scotland, means an assignation in security in respect of such a policy;

"commission" includes any gift, bonus or benefit;
"solicitor", in relation to England and Wales, includes licensed
conveyancer.

DEFINITIONS
"advance secured on land": ss.10(1) and 119(1).
"commission": subs. (7).
"manager": s.119(1).
"solicitor": subs. (7).
"the standard scale": Criminal Justice Act, 1982, s.37

GENERAL NOTE
The purpose of this section is to prohibit officers from accepting a commission in
connection with a loan or insurance policy. It is very largely a re-enactment of s.74 of the
1962 Act. It is of some interest to note that the provisions of that section relating to loans
were derived from the Building Societies Act 1894, s.23: the potential abuse has long been
recognised.

Subs. (1)
The list of persons subject to this section differs slightly from that contained in the 1962
Act. New to the section are the chief executive, the manager and the valuer. S.74(1) added
as a general term "or other officer", whereas the general description in this subsection is
"any person who holds office in or is employed by a building society . . . in connection with
the assessment of the adequacy of securities for advances secured on land". In practice, the
effect of the variations is likely to be small, but the new definition of persons to whom the
section applies is designed to link the prohibition on accepting a commission to those people
who are concerned with the assessment of the adequacy of the society's securities under s.13
and whose judgment might otherwise be influenced by the possibility of receiving a
commission.

Subss. (3) and (4)
The reference in subs. (3) to subs. (4), and subs. (4) itself, are both new. Presumably the
new Act provided a convenient opportunity of amending the section to ensure that the
person paying a commission is not guilty of an offence unless he is aware of the facts which
constitute a contravention of the section. Note, however, that subss. (5) and (6) contain no
equivalent provision. Unless it is thought that no payment under subs. (5) could be made in
ignorance of the contravention, the reason for this distinction is not clear.
Level 4. Currently £1,000.

Subs. (6)
Level 4. Currently £1,000.

Subs. (7)
The predecessor of this subsection, s.74(5), contained only the definition of commission.
Licensed conveyancer. See the Administration of Justice Act 1985, Part II.

Records of loans, etc. for directors falling within s.65

68.—(1) A building society shall maintain a register containing a copy
of every subsisting transaction or arrangement (other than an excepted
transaction or arrangement) falling within section 65(1) made for a
director or a person connected with a director of the society during the
current financial year or any of the preceding ten financial years.

(2) In the case of a transaction or arrangement which is not in writing,
there shall be kept in the register a written memorandum setting out its
terms.

(3) A building society shall make available for inspection by
members—

    (*a*) at its principal office during the period of 15 days expiring with the
date of its annual general meeting, and

    (*b*) at the annual general meeting,

a statement containing the requisite particulars of the transactions and arrangements falling within section 65(1) which were included in the register under subsection (1) above at any time during the last complete financial year preceding the meeting.

(4) The requisite particulars are those specified in Schedule 9 to this Act.

(5) Two copies of the statement required to be so made available to members shall be sent by the society to the Commission on the date on which the statement is required to be first made available to members and the central office shall keep one of them in the public file of the society.

(6) A copy of the statement required to be so made available shall also be sent, on demand and on payment of the prescribed fee, to any member of the society.

(7) There are excepted from the obligations imposed by this section on a building society with respect to a financial year all transactions or arrangements made or subsisting during that year for a person who was at any time during that year a director of the society or was connected with a director of the society if the aggregate of the values of each transaction or arrangement made for that person, less the amount (if any) by which the value of those transactions or arrangements has been reduced, did not exceed £1,000 at any time during that year.

(8) There are also excepted from the obligations imposed by this section on a building society with respect to a financial year all transactions or arrangements falling within paragraphs (*b*), (*d*) or (*e*) of section 65(1) made during that year for a person who was at any time during that year a director of the society or was connected with a director of the society if the aggregate of the values of each such transaction or arrangement so made for that director or any person connected with him, less the amount (if any) by which the value of those transactions or arrangements has been reduced, did not exceed £5,000 at any time during that year.

(9) The Commission may, by order made with the consent of the Treasury, amend subsection (7) or (8) above so as to substitute for the amount for the time being specified in that subsection such other amount as it thinks appropriate.

(10) The power to make an order under subsection (9) above is exercisable by statutory instrument which shall be subject to annulment in pursuance of a resolution of either House of Parliament.

(11) If a building society fails to comply with any provision of this section (or Schedule 9) the society shall be liable on conviction on indictment or on summary conviction to a fine not exceeding, on summary conviction, the statutory maximum, and so shall any officer who is also guilty of the offence.

DEFINITIONS
   "central office": s.119(1).
   "Commission": ss.1 and 119(1).
   "connected with": s.70(2) to (4).
   "excepted transaction or arrangement": subss. (7) and (8).
   "financial year": ss.117 and 119(1).
   "member": s.119(1).
   "prescribed fee": s.119(1).
   "public file": ss.106 and 119(1).
   "requisite particulars": see Sched. 9.
   "the statutory maximum": Criminal Justice Act 1982, s.74; Magistrates' Courts Act 1980, s.32.
   "transaction or arrangement made for": s.70(5).

GENERAL NOTE
   The purpose of this section is to ensure that a society maintains a proper record, available to its members, of the extent to which advantage is being taken of the permissive provisions

of subss. (2) to (5) of s.65 (restrictions on loans, etc., to directors and persons connected with them). That is obviously a matter in which some members, at least, will feel a keen interest and, indeed, the existence of the obligation to maintain such a record will provide an incentive to the society to give careful thought, not only to the legality but also to the desirability of a particular transaction; the possibility that justification may be called for will turn the society's mind to the question whether justification is possible.

Note that under s.78(9) and (10) the society's auditors are bound, in each financial year, to consider the statement of transactions to be prepared under subs. (3) and whether it includes the "requisite particulars". This, of course, is a further safeguard against abuse.

Similar provisions are to be found in the Companies Act 1985, ss.343 and 344 in relation to recognised banks. S.89 of the 1962 Act imposed a much more limited obligation on the society to make disclosure of certain advances in the annual return.

Subs. (1)
Every subsisting transaction. Presumably this phrase means that the transactions to be included in the register are ones in respect of which money is still payable by the director or the connected person to the society or the society's guarantee or other security is still in force.

Subs. (3)
Reference should be made to Sched. 9 and the notes thereto for the detail of the particulars to be included in a statement made under this subsection.

Subs. (6)
It is not clear by whom the statement is to be supplied to the member. One would normally expect it to be supplied by the society and that construction of the subsection is supported by the use of the word "also" in the second line. But there is apparently no provision either prescribing or permitting the society to prescribe a fee for supplying the statement. Contrast Sched. 2, para. 12, relating to the society's duty to supply a copy of the rules. The definition of "prescribed" in s.119(1) (prescribed by the Treasury or the Chief Registrar, depending upon whether the functions are those of the Commission or the central office) seems to suggest that one or other of those bodies may be obliged to supply the statement. The central office seems the more likely body: *c.f.* the provisions of s.106, under which any member of the public is entitled to be furnished with a copy of documents in the public file on payment of the prescribed fee. It is thought, on balance, that the duty is imposed on the society.

Subss. (7) and (8)
These two subsections specify the "excepted transactions and arrangements". Clearly, the intention is to exclude transactions or arrangements involving little financial value.

Subs. (11)
Note that the offence created by this subsection includes failure to comply with any provision of Sched. 9.
The statutory maximum. Currently £2,000.

Disclosure and record of related businesses

Disclosure and record of income of related businesses

69.—(1) Where, at any time during a financial year of a building society, a person both is a director or other officer of a building society and is, or is a director of or partner in, a business associate of the society, this section shall apply, as respects that year, to that person in relation to the business of the business associate.

(2) A person is a "business associate" of a building society in any financial year of the society if that person—

    (*a*) carries on a business which consists of or includes the provision of relevant services,

    (*b*) provides relevant services during that year to, or to other persons in connection with advances secured on land made by, the society, and

(c) is neither a subsidiary of nor a body associated with the society (within the meaning of section 18);
and "associated" has a corresponding meaning.

(3) The following are relevant services—

(a) conveyancing services provided by a solicitor;

(b) surveying and valuing land or other property;

(c) accountancy services;

(d) arranging for the provision of insurance against loss of or damage to property or on human life:

(e) any other services designated as relevant services.

(4) Where a business associate of a building society provides the society with services which are relevant services by virtue of subsection (3) above, any administrative services provided to the society by the business associate are also relevant services.

(5) The Commission may by order in a statutory instrument—

(a) designate as relevant services services of any description specified in the order which are normally provided to building societies; and

(b) make such incidental, supplementary or transitional provision as it considers necessary or expedient;
and in subsection (3)(e) above "designated" means designated by an order under this subsection.

(6) Where this section applies, as respects a financial year of a building society, to a person as a director or other officer of the society in relation to the business of a business associate, that person shall furnish the society with the requisite particulars of that business.

(7) The requisite particulars of the business of a business associate of a building society are—

(a) except where an election under paragraph (b) below is in force, those specified in Part I of Schedule 10 to this Act;

(b) if a building society elects to adopt Part II of that Schedule for its directors as respects a financial year, those specified in Part II of that Schedule; and

(c) as regards relevant services designated by an order under subsection (5) above, such particulars as are specified in the order;
and Part III of the Schedule has effect to supplement Parts I and II and includes a definition of "the volume of the business" for the purposes of this section.

(8) An election by a building society to adopt Part II of Schedule 10 as regards the requisite particulars to be furnished by its directors must be made in writing to the Commission before the beginning of the financial year as respects which it is made and the requisite particulars must be furnished in writing within the period of six weeks beginning with the end of the financial year for which they are required.

(9) For the purpose of enabling him to furnish the requisite particulars of the business of a business associate of a building society the person who is under the obligation to furnish them to the society may require any person who is a member of or partner in, or holds any office or employment with, the business associate to furnish him with such information relating to its business as he may reasonably require for that purpose.

(10) Any person who, without reasonable excuse—

(a) fails to furnish the particulars required by subsection (6) above or furnishes particulars which are false or misleading in a material particular or, in the case of particulars under Part II to Schedule 10, are not a justified estimate, or

(b) fails to furnish any information lawfully required of him under subsection (9) above or furnishes information which is false or misleading in a material particular, shall be liable on conviction on indictment or on summary conviction to a fine not exceeding, on summary conviction, the statutory maximum.

(11) Subject to subsection (12) below, a building society shall maintain at its principal office a register containing the particulars furnished to it under subsection (6) above as respects the last financial year and each of the ten financial years preceding that year.

(12) No particulars of the business of a business associate of a building society need be kept in the register provided for by subsection (11) above as respects any financial year of the society in which the volume of the business of which the requisite particulars are required did not exceed £5,000 or such other sum as may be substituted for it by order of the Commission in a statutory instrument under this subsection.

(13) A building society shall make available for inspection by members—

> (*a*) at its principal office during the period of 15 days expiring with the date of its annual general meeting, and
>
> (*b*) at the annual general meeting,

a statement containing the particulars required to be kept in the register under subsection (11) above as respects the last financial year.

(14) Two copies of the statement required to be so made available to members shall be sent by the society to the Commission on the date on which the statement is required to be first made available to members and the central office shall keep one of them in the public file of the society.

(15) A copy of the statement required to be so made available shall also be sent, on demand and on payment of the prescribed fee, to any member of the society.

(16) The power to make an order under subsection (5) or (12) above shall not be exercised except with the consent of the Treasury and any statutory instrument containing such an order shall be subject to annulment in pursuance of a resolution of either House of Parliament.

(17) In this section—

> "administrative services" means services necessary or incidental to the conduct of the society's business;
>
> "conveyancing services" in relation to—
>
>> (*a*) land in England and Wales or Northern Ireland, has the same meaning as it has in paragraph 1(3) of Schedule 21 to this Act with the modification, in relation to land in Northern Ireland, that "disposition" does not include any disposition in the case of such a lease as is excepted, by section 4 of the Landlord and Tenant Law Amendment Act (Ireland) 1860, from the requirements of that section, and
>>
>> (*b*) heritable property in Scotland, includes drafting all writs relating to such property and negotiating and concluding missives for its purchase, sale, transfer, lease and sublease; and
>
> "solicitor", in relation to England and Wales, includes licensed conveyancer, that is to say, a person who holds a licence under Part II of the Administration of Justice Act 1985.

DEFINITIONS

"administrative services": subs. (17).
"advances secured on land"; ss.10(1) and 119(1).
"business associate": subs. (2).
"central office": s.119(1).
"Commission": ss.1 and 119(1).
"conveyancing services": subs. (17).
"designated": subs. (5).
"financial year": ss.117 and 119(1).
"member" (in subs. (15)): s.119(1).
"officers": s.119(1).

"prescribed": s.119(1).
"public file": ss.106 and 119(1).
"relevant services": see subs. (3).
"requisite particulars": subs. (7).
"solicitor": subs. (17).
"the statutory maximum": Criminal Justice Act 1982, s.74; Magistrates' Court Act 1980, s.32.
"subsidiary": s.119(1); Companies Act 1985, s.736.
"volume of business": Sched. 10, para 10.

GENERAL NOTE
This section is designed to ensure that where a person is an officer in a building society and is also a business associate, or a director or partner in a business associate, of the society, a proper record is kept of the amount and value of the business done by the associate for the society. Underlying the section is a concern that in some cases there has been a marked channelling of business by the society in a particular direction which perhaps has not always been in the best interests of the society. The section does not attempt to prohibit such channelling (and clearly there would be considerable practical difficulties with any general prohibition); instead, it make sure that members and, indeed, anybody else who is interested, will be able to see what volume of business is going to associates.

The structure of the section is as follows. Subss. (1) to (5) set out the conditions for the application of the section. Subss. (6) to (10) make provision for the officer who also is, or is a director or partner in, a business associate to give certain particulars of the associate's business to the society. Subss. (11) to (15) make provision for the society to keep a register of the particulars with which it has been provided. Subs. (16) governs the Commission's power to alter certain financial limits in the section and subs. (17) is an interpretation provision.

Subss. (1) to (5)
By virtue of these provisions, a director or other officer of a society will owe a duty to give particulars to the society if in any financial year:

(1) he is or is a director or partner in a "person" which carries on a business which consists of or includes the provision of relevant services; and
(2) that person provides relevant services during that year to the society or to other persons in connection with advances secured on land made by the society.

A subsidiary or associated body within the meaning of s.18 is expressly excluded from being a business associate for the purposes of this section; information as to their business is otherwise available.

Note that (i) a person's status as a business associate may come and go from year to year, depending upon whether he provides any relevant services in the course of the year, (ii) it seems that "person" must include a partnership, although in English law a partnership has no legal personality of its own, (iii) it is not clear whether the words "in connection with advances secured on land made by the society" in subs. (2) extend to prospective advances which are not in fact completed. As a matter of policy, there seems no reason why such prospective advances should not be included, since the actual channelling of business occurs whether or not the advance is completed, but as a matter of language the position is doubtful.

The services expressly mentioned as relevant services are those where it is likely that there has been channelling of business in the past or which are so closely related to such services that there is likely to be channelling now that societies have acquired the additional powers given by this Act. The Commission, however, has power to designate further services and no doubt that power will be exercised if it appears that there are further areas in which there is a considerable channelling of business.

Subs. (7)
Reference should be made to Sched. 10 for the precise matters covered by "the requisite particulars". Parts I and II of that Schedule relate to the same matters, but Part I requires accurate figures to be given whereas Part II permits an estimate of the relevant band of figures to be given. It may be assumed that directors will be anxious to see their societies electing to adopt Part II.

For its directors. The right to elect on behalf of other officers is not expressly given. When subs. 7(*b*) is compared with subss. (1) and (6), an inference arises that the right cannot extend to other officers; this seems curious, to say the least.

Subs. (9)

This is clearly a sensible provision for the assistance of any director or officer trying to produce the required particulars. Note that it is backed by a criminal sanction: see subs. (10).

Subs. (10)

The statutory maximum. Currently £2,000.

Subss. (11) to (15)

These provisions are very similar to the provisions of s.68 and reference should be made to the notes to that section. See in particular the notes to s.68(6), discussing by whom a copy of the statement must be supplied. Note, however, that this section creates no offence of, and imposes no sanction for, breach of these subsections and there is no express obligation on the auditors to consider the statement prepared under subs. (13).

Interpretation

Interpretation of this Part

70.—(1) The following provisions apply for the interpretation of this Part.

(2) A person is "connected with" a director of a building society if, but only if, he (not being himself a director of it) is—

(*a*) that director's spouse, child or step-child; or

(*b*) a body corporate with which the director is associated; or

(*c*) a person acting in his capacity as trustee of any trust the beneficiaries of which include—

(i) the director, his spouse or any children or step-children of his, or

(ii) a body corporate with which he is associated, or of a trust whose terms confer a power on the trustees that may be exercised for the benefit of the director, his spouse, or any children or step-children of his or any such body corporate; or

(*d*) a person acting in his capacity as partner of that director or of any person who, by virtue of paragraph (*a*), (*b*) or (*c*) of this subsection, is connected with that director;

(*e*) a Scottish firm in which—

(i) that director is a partner,

(ii) a partner is a person who, by virtue of paragraph (*a*), (*b*) or (*c*) above, is connected with that director, or

(iii) a partner is a Scottish firm in which that director is a partner or in which there is a partner who, by virtue of paragraph (*a*), (*b*) or (*c*) above, is connected with that director.

(3) In subsection (2)—

(*a*) a reference to a child or step-child of any person includes an illegitimate child of his, and

(*b*) paragraph (*c*) does not apply to a person acting in his capacity as trustee under an employees' share scheme or a pension scheme.

(4) A director is "associated" with a body corporate if he, his spouse, his child or step-child or a person acting in his capacity as trustee of any trust the beneficiaries of which include the director, his spouse, child or step-child between them, either—

(*a*) own at lease one-fifth of that body's equity share capital (within the meaning of the Companies Act 1985), or

(*b*) are entitled to exercise or control the exercise of more than one-fifth of the voting power of that body at any general meeting.

(5) As regards transactions or arrangements falling within section 65, a "transaction contravening section 65" means a transaction to which subsection (1)(*a*), (*b*), (*c*) or (*d*) of that section applies and an "arrangement contravening section 65" means an arrangement to which subsection

(1)(*e*) of that section applies and such a transaction or arrangement is made "for" a person if—

(*a*) in the case of a loan, disposal or payment within paragraph (*a*), (*b*) or (*c*), it is made, in the case of paragraph (*a*) or (*b*), to him or, in the case of paragraph (*c*) on his behalf;

(*b*) in the case of a guarantee or security within paragraph (*d*), it is made as an incident of or in connection with a loan or disposal to him or a payment on his behalf; and

(*c*) in the case of an arrangement within paragraph (*e*), the transaction to which the arrangement relates was made for him.

DEFINITION

"equity share capital": Companies Act 1985, s.744.

GENERAL NOTE

This section provides for the interpretation of ss.58 to 70 of the Act. Subss. (2) to (4) are very closely based on s.346(2) to (4) of the Companies Act 1985, reflecting the introduction into this Part of this Act of several provisions derived from the 1985 Act. Such derivations are indicated in the notes to individual sections. Subs. (5) arises from specific provisions of this Act.

Subss. (2) to (4)

These subsections contain the definition of a person who is "connected with" a director. They cover a wide variety of relationships and are in general extremely broad. The only personal relationships included, however, are those of spouse, child and step-child. A curious point emerges in subs. (3)(*a*); the child or step-child here may be of any age, whereas under s.346(3)(*a*) of the 1985 Act, the connection ceases when the child or step-child attains 18.

PART VIII

ACCOUNTS AND AUDIT

Accounting records and systems of business control, etc.

Accounting records and systems of business control, etc.

71.—(1) Every building society shall—

(*a*) cause accounting records to be kept, and

(*b*) establish and maintain systems of control of its business and records and of inspection and report,

in accordance with this section.

(2) The accounting records of a society must be such as to—

(*a*) explain its transactions;

(*b*) disclose, with reasonable accuracy and promptness, the state of the business of the society at any time;

(*c*) enable the directors properly to discharge the duties imposed on them by or under this Act and their functions of direction of the affairs of the society; and

(*d*) enable the society properly to discharge the duties imposed on it by or under this Act;

and must be kept in an orderly manner.

(3) The accounting records shall in particular contain—

(*a*) entries from day to day of all sums received and paid by the society and the matters in respect of which they are received or paid;

(*b*) entries from day to day of every transaction entered into by the society which will or there is reasonable ground for expecting may give rise to liabilities or assets of the society other than insignificant assets or liabilities in respect of the management of the society; and

(c) a record of the assets and liabilities of the society and in particular of assets and liabilities of any class specifically regulated by or under any provision of Part II or Part III.

(4) The system of control which is to be established and maintained by a society is a system for the control of the conduct of its business in accordance with this Act and the decisions of the board of directors and for the control of the accounting and other records of its business.

(5) The system of inspection and report which is to be established and maintained by a society is a system of inspection on behalf of and report to the board of directors on the operation of the system of control of the society's business and records required by subsection (1)(b) above.

(6) The system of control and of inspection and report must be such as to—

(a) enable the directors properly to discharge the duties imposed on them by or under this Act and their functions of direction of the affairs of the society; and

(b) enable the society properly to discharge the duties imposed on it by or under this Act;

and no such system of control shall be treated as established or maintained unless there is kept available to the board a detailed statement in writing of the system as in operation for the time being.

(7) Without prejudice to the generality of subsection (6) above the systems of control and of inspection and report must be such as to secure that the society's business is so conducted and its records so kept that—

(a) the information necessary to enable the directors and the society to discharge their duties and functions is sufficiently accurate, and is available with sufficient regularity or at need and with sufficient promptness, for those purposes; and

(b) the information regularly obtained by or furnished to the Commission under or for the purposes of this Act is sufficiently accurate for the purpose for which it is obtained or furnished and is regularly furnished;

and in this subsection, in its application in relation to the Commission, "regularly" includes that regularity requested by or agreed with the Commission.

(8) The accounting records shall be kept at the society's principal office or at such other place or places as the directors think fit, and shall at all times be open to inspection by the directors.

(9) Accounting records shall be preserved for six years from the date on which they were made.

(10) Where a building society has subsidiaries or other associated bodies linked by resolution, the society shall also secure that such accounting records are kept and such systems of control and of inspection and report are established and maintained by the society and the subsidiaries or other associated bodies as will enable the society to comply with the requirements of this section in relation to the business of the society and those subsidiaries and other associated bodies.

(11) The directors and chief executive of every building society shall, within the period of three months beginning with the end of each financial year, make and send to the Commission a statement of their opinion whether the requirements of this section have been complied with in respect of that year; and the statement shall be signed by the chairman on behalf of the board of directors and by the chief executive.

DEFINITIONS
  "associated body": ss.18(17) and 119(1).
  "Commission": ss.1 and 119(1).
  "financial year": ss.117 and 119(1).
  "linked by resolution": ss.18(9) and 119(1).
  "subsidiary": s.119(1); Companies Act 1985, s.736.

GENERAL NOTE
  This section contains the basic provisions for a society's accounting records and systems of control of its business and records and of inspection and report. It goes very much further than its predecessor in the 1962 Act, s.76. The comparable provisions in the Companies Act 1985 are ss.221 and 222, but this section was drafted specifically to meet the accounting and control requirements of building societies and it is by no means identical to the company law provisions.
  Note that under s.79(1) the auditors, in preparing their report to the members, must consider whether this section has been complied with and further that under s.82 they must make an annual report to the Commission on the society's compliance.
  Maintenance of the requisite accounting records and systems of control and inspection and report is one of the criteria of prudent management listed in s.45. Failure to observe those criteria may lead, ultimately, to the imposition of conditions on a society's authorisation to raise funds and borrow money or even to revocation of that authorisation: see ss.42 and 43.

Subss. (2) and (3)
  These subsections contain the requirements with respect to accounting records. The form in which records may be kept is dealt with in s.114; records need not be kept, but must be capable of being reproduced, in legible form. Computerised records and microfilm are therefore permissible.
  Disclose . . . the state of the business. This replaces the previous formula "give a true and fair view". It is thought that accounting records themselves cannot give a true and fair view, although they provide the raw material from which accounts giving a true and fair view may be prepared. The Companies Act uses the more limited phrase "disclose . . . the financial position of the company".
  Entries from day to day. The object of these words is to ensure that transactions occurring on one day are shown to have occurred on that day and are distinguished from transactions occurring on another day. It is not always necessary for each transaction to be recorded in all the records on the day on which it occurred.

Subs. (5)
  Note that the system of inspection and report is a system of inspection of and report on the operation of the system of control. The system of control itself must be stated in writing and be available to the board: subs. (6).

Subs. (10)
  Under this subsection, subsidiaries and associated bodies are not obliged individually to comply with the requirements of the section, but the society must ensure that the records and system of control and of inspection and report are such that, when they are combined with the records and systems of the society, the requirements of the section are satisfied in relation to the business of the society, its subsidiaries and the other associated bodies to which the society is linked by resolution. Associated bodies to which the society is not so linked, and which are not subsidiaries, are not within the scope of this section.

Accounts

Duty of directors to prepare annual accounts

72.—(1) Subject to subsection (4) below, the directors of every building society shall prepare with respect to each financial year of the society—
  (*a*) an income and expenditure account showing the income and expenditure for that year,
  (*b*) a balance sheet showing the state of its affairs as at the end of that year, and
  (*c*) a statement of the source and application of the funds during that year.

(2) Except as provided in subsection (5) below, if, at the end of its financial year, a building society has subsidiaries, the directors shall also prepare, with respect to that year, group accounts dealing respectively with the income and expenditure, the state of the affairs and the source and application of the funds, of the society and the subsidiaries.

(3) The directors of a building society which has subsidiaries shall secure that, except where in their opinion there are good reasons against it, the financial year of each of its subsidiaries coincides with the society's own financial year.

(4) Where the directors prepare a statement of the source and application of the funds of the society and its subsidiaries under subsection (2) above they need not also prepare such a statement as to the society's funds under subsection (1) above.

(5) Subject to subsection (6) below, group accounts need not deal with a subsidiary if the society's directors are of the opinion that—

(a) it is impracticable, or would be of no real value to the society's members, in view of the insignificant amounts involved,

(b) it would involve expense or delay out of proportion to the value to members, or

(c) the result would be misleading or harmful to the business of the society or any of its subsidiaries;

and if the directors are of that opinion about each of the society's subsidiaries group accounts are not required.

(6) Except to the extent that regulations under section 73 otherwise allow, group accounts or group accounts dealing with a particular subsidiary shall not be dispensed with under subsection (5)(c) above without prior approval of the Commission.

(7) The Commission may by regulations made with the consent of the Treasury—

(a) add to the classes of documents to be comprised in a society's accounts to be prepared for each financial year under subsection (1) or (2) above;

(b) make provision as to the matters to be included in any document so added;

(c) modify the requirements of this Part as to the matters to be stated in any document comprised in the society's accounts; and

(d) reduce the classes of documents to be comprised in a society's accounts.

(8) Regulations under subsection (7) above may make different provision for different descriptions of society, and may include incidental and supplementary provisions.

(9) The power to make regulations under subsection (7) above is exercisable by statutory instrument which shall be subject to annulment in pursuance of a resolution of either House of Parliament.

(10) The accounts prepared with respect to a society's financial year under this section (whether as individual accounts or group accounts), with the notes to them, are referred to in this Part as "the annual accounts".

DEFINITIONS
"Commission": ss.1 and 119(1).
"financial year": ss.117 and 119(1).
"subsidiary": s.119(1); Companies Act 1985, s.736.

GENERAL NOTE
This section imposes on the directors an obligation to prepare the society's annual accounts; the form and contents of the accounts are dealt with in s.73. The section's predecessor in the 1962 Act was s.77, but that section contained none of the provisions for group accounts and for regulation by statutory instrument which are to be found here.

Corresponding company law provisions are to be found in ss.227 and 229 of the Companies Act 1985.

Subs. (3)

Good reasons against it. An example of a good reason why a subsidiary's financial year might not coincide with the society's financial year was offered to Standing Committee A during the Bill's passage through the House of Commons, *viz.*, that it is the practice for housing associations to end their year on March 31, because financial allocations are made for the year April 1 to March 31. December 31, however, is the prescribed year end for every society established after August 25, 1894. In such circumstances, clearly the financial years are unlikely to coincide and there is good reason why they should not be made to do so. (See *Official Report*, Standing Committee A, February 19, 1986, col. 429.)

Subs. (5)

This subsection contains certain exceptions to the requirement for group accounts imposed by subs. (2). Note that it does not follow that, because a subsidiary is not dealt with in group accounts, it will not feature in the society's accounts at all. The Commission in the exercise of its rule-making powers under s.73 may require the accounts to contain information about such a subsidiary (and also about other associated bodies, as defined in s.18(17)). Note also the possible impact of aggregation rules: see ss.7(10), 8(3) and 20(9).

Subs. (6)

The Commission's approval is required before a subsidiary can be omitted from group accounts on the ground that its inclusion would be misleading or harmful to the business of the society or any of its subsidiaries. The provision matches s.229(4) of the Companies Act 1985, which requires the approval of the Secretary of State for Trade and Industry in similar circumstances; it also reflects the view that the Commission will have considerable financial expertise. (*Cf.* s.61(9) and the notes thereto.)

Subs. (10)

It should be observed that the notes to the accounts form part of "the annual accounts".

Contents and form of annual accounts

73.—(1) The annual accounts of a building society shall conform to the requirements of this section and regulations made under it.

(2) Every income and expenditure account shall give a true and fair view of the income and expenditure of the society for the financial year.

(3) Every balance sheet shall give a true and fair view of the state of the affairs of the society as at the end of the financial year.

(4) Every statement of the source and application of funds shall give a true and fair view of the manner in which the business of the society has been financed and in which its financial resources have been used during the financial year.

(5) Subsections (2), (3) and (4) above, in their application to the group accounts of a society, are to be read as referring to the society and (so far as it concerns the members of the society) the subsidiaries dealt with in the group accounts.

(6) The annual accounts shall also contain, whether in the form of notes or otherwise, such supplementary information as is prescribed.

(7) The Commission shall, by regulations made with the consent of the Treasury, make provision with respect to the contents and the form of the annual accounts.

(8) Without prejudice to the generality of subsections (6) and (7) above, the regulations may—

(*a*) prescribe accounting principles and rules;

(*b*) require corresponding information for a preceding financial year;

(*c*) require the accounts of societies to deal also with bodies associated with them;

(*d*) make different provision for different descriptions of society;

(*e*) require the accounts to give particulars of the emoluments, pensions, compensation for loss of office and financial interests of directors, other officers and employees of prescribed descriptions of the society;

and may permit group accounts to be prepared in other than consolidated form.

(9) Where compliance with regulations under this section would not secure compliance with the requirements of subsection (2), (3) or (4) above the directors shall take such steps with regard to the contents or form of the accounts, in addition to or, if additions do not suffice, in derogation of the provisions of the regulations, as they think necessary to secure compliance with those subsections and record, in the notes to the accounts, what they have done, the reasons for it and its effects.

(10) The power to make regulations under this section is exercisable by statutory instrument which shall be subject to annulment in pursuance of a resolution of either House of Parliament.

(11) It is the duty of every director, other officer and employee of a building society as respects whom prescribed particulars are by virtue of subsection (8)(*e*) above required to be given in the accounts to give notice of such matters as may be necessary to enable the society to give those particulars in the accounts.

(12) In this section "prescribed" means prescribed in regulations under it.

DEFINITIONS

"the annual accounts": ss.72(10) and 119(1).
"associated": ss.18(17) and 119(1).
"Commission": ss.1 and 119(1).
"financial year": ss.117 and 119(1).
"officer": s.119(1).
"prescribed": subs. (12).
"subsidiary": s.119(1); Companies Act 1985, s.736.

GENERAL NOTE

This section makes provision for the contents and form of the annual accounts. In fact, most of the detailed provisions will be found in regulations to be made by the Commission under subs. (7). When the Bill was passing through the House of Commons, questions were raised as to the likely content of the regulations and it was said by Sir George Young on behalf of the Government that the regulations were expected to be very similar to the requirements for company accounts (see Sched. 5 to the Companies Act 1985). This should ensure compliance with an impending E.C. Directive on credit institution accounts. (See *Official Report*, Standing Committee A, February 18, 1986, col. 431).

The section's ancestry is s.78 of the 1962 Act and ss.228, 230 and 231 of the Companies Act 1985. The section elaborates and extends s.78 and, inevitably, is only broadly based on the company law provisions.

Subs. (7)

It was expressly stated by Sir George Young in Standing Committee A that among the matters which regulations under this section would require to be covered in the annual accounts was any change in the relationship between a building society and others in its group: see *loc.cit.*, col. 430.

Subs. (8)

Note that the remuneration of and award of pensions to directors must be covered by the rules: Sched. 2, para. 3(4).

Subs. (9)

This subsection empowers directors to add further matter to that prescribed or, where additions will not suffice, to depart from the requirements of the regulations if such addition or departure is necessary to ensure that subs. (2) to (4) are satisfied. Departure is made the last resort to achieve consistency with the Fourth Directive on company accounts (78/660/EEC), which requires that derogation from the provision of the regulations should be a power of last resort. That Directive does not apply to building societies, but it is believed that the relevant provisions of that Directive will be included in a proposed Directive to which societies will be subject.

Subs. (11)
C.f. s.74(8) and (9). It is curious that no sanction is prescribed for breach of this subsection.

Duty of directors to prepare annual business statement

74.—(1) The directors of every building society shall, by reference to the annual accounts and other records and information at their disposal, prepare with respect to each financial year of the society a statement (referred to in this Act as "the annual business statement") relating to prescribed aspects of the business of the society during the year.

(2) Where the society has subsidiaries or associated bodies the annual business statement shall deal also with prescribed aspects of the business of the subsidiaries or associated bodies during the year to which it relates.

(3) The annual business statement shall contain such information relating to such aspects of the business of the society and shall be in such form as the Commission prescribes by regulations made with the consent of the Treasury; and in this section "prescribed" means prescribed by regulations under this subsection.

(4) Without prejudice to the generality of subsections (1) to (3) above the regulations may require the annual business statements of building societies to include prescribed information about directors and past directors and persons connected with them and other officers and past officers and persons connected with them and their financial interests.

(5) The information comprising the annual business statement shall give a true representation of the matters in respect of which it is given.

(6) To such extent as may be prescribed matters contained in the society's annual business statement shall not be the subject of report by the auditors under section 78.

(7) The power to make regulations under subsection (3) above is exercisable by statutory instrument which shall be subject to annulment in pursuance of a resolution of either House of Parliament.

(8) It is the duty of every director or other officer of a building society to give notice to the society of such matters relating to himself or his financial interests as may be necessary for the purposes of compliance with the preceding provisions of this section.

(9) Any person who fails to comply with subsection (8) above shall be liable on summary conviction to a fine not exceeding level 5 on the standard scale.

(10) Any director who fails to comply with subsection (1) above shall be liable on conviction on indictment or on summary conviction to a fine not exceeding, on summary conviction, the statutory maximum.

DEFINITIONS
"the annual accounts": ss.72(10) and 119(1).
"associated": ss.18(17) and 119(1).
"financial year": ss.117 and 119(1).
"officer": s.119(1).
"prescribed": subs. (3).
"the standard scale": Criminal Justice Act 1982, s.37.
"the statutory maximum": Criminal Justice Act 1982, s.74; Magistrates' Courts Act 1980, s.32.
"subsidiary": s.119(1); Companies Act 1985, s.736.

GENERAL NOTE
This section establishes a new statutory document, the annual business statement, which will be annexed to the balance sheet: see s.80(2). Its form and contents are to be prescribed

by regulations to be made by the Commission under subs. (3) and the Act gives very little indication of what is likely to be prescribed. It was said, however, during the Bill's Committee stage in the House of Commons that the annual business statement would largely consist of statistical tables like the annual return made under s.88 of the 1962 Act. It is not intended to be a "free-ranging review of the business as a whole"; that is what the directors' report (provided for in s.75) should be. (See *Official Report*, Standing Committee A, February 18, 1986, cols. 431–2.)

Subject to subs. (6), the auditors have a duty to report on the annual business statement: see s.78(3).

Subs. (4)

Persons connected with. No definition of this phrase is contained in this Part of the Act or in the general interpretation section, s.119. It may be possible to apply the definition in s.70(2) to (4), although that definition is in terms limited by s.70(1) to Part VII of the Act.

Subs. (6)

This subsection provides for the exclusion of prescribed parts of the annual business statement from the general duty of the auditors under s.78(3) to report on the statement.

Subs. (9)

Level 5. Currently £2,000.

Subs. (10)

The statutory maximum. Currently £2,000.

Directors' report

75.—(1) The directors of a building society shall prepare for submission to the annual general meeting a report on the business of the society containing—

(*a*) a fair review of the development of its business during the financial year and of its position at the end of it, and

(*b*) such information relating to such aspects of the business of the society or of the society and any subsidiaries or other bodies associated with it as may be prescribed by regulations made by the Commission with the consent of the Treasury, and

(*c*) a statement whether any and, if so, what activities carried on during the year are believed to have been carried on outside the powers of the society.

(2) Where the society has subsidiaries or other associated bodies the report shall, in addition to containing the information prescribed in relation to them under subsection (1)(*b*) above, review the development of the business of the society and its subsidiaries and associated bodies during the year and their position at the end of it.

(3) The power to make regulations under subsection (1) above is exercisable by statutory instrument which shall be subject to annulment in pursuance of a resolution of either House of Parliament.

(4) If a directors' report does not contain the prescribed information or the information in the report is not given in accordance with the regulations, each director shall be liable on conviction on indictment or on summary conviction to a fine not exceeding, on summary conviction, the statutory maximum.

DEFINITIONS

"associated": ss.18(17) and 119(1).

"Commission": ss.1 and 119(1).

"financial year": ss.117 and 119(1).

"the statutory maximum": Criminal Justice Act 1982, s.74; Magistrates' Courts Act 1980, s.32.

This section requires the directors to prepare a report on the affairs of the society for submission to the members. The report will be attached to the balance sheet (s.80(4)) and will be considered at the annual general meeting. S.82 of the 1962 Act imposed a similar obligation on directors, but that section itself also prescribed matters to be included in the report. In this section, the contents of the report are in large part left to be prescribed by regulations to be made by the Commission; the only express requirements are that the report should contain a fair review of the development of the society's business during the financial year and its position at the end of it and that it should contain a statement whether any, and if so, what activities carried on during the year are believed to have been carried on outside the powers of the society. The section may be compared with s.235 of the Companies Act 1985.

Note that the auditors have a duty to report on the directors' report: s.78(3).

Subs. (1)

This subsection includes, in para. (*c*), the requirement of the statement as to activities carried on outside the power of the society. On its face, the requirement seems both new and rather curious. It should be noted, however, that (i) the particulars required under s.82(2) of the 1962 Act might reveal a breach of certain lending restrictions, (ii) the object of the requirement is not simply to extract a confession, but to provide an additional incentive for the directors of a society to ensure that no activities are carried on outside the society's powers by ensuring, indirectly, that the directors will apply their minds to the question whether a particular activity is lawful or not.

Subs. (4)

The statutory maximum. Currently £2,000.

Summary financial statement for members and depositors

76.—(1) The directors of a building society shall, with respect to each financial year, prepare for members and depositors a summary financial statement for that year, that is to say, a statement derived from the annual accounts, annual business statement and directors' report, giving a summary account of the society's financial development during and financial position at the end of the year.

(2) Where the society has subsidiaries or other associated bodies the statement shall (so far as they are dealt with in the group accounts) give an account of the financial development and position of the society and its subsidiaries and other associated bodies.

(3) The Commission may, by regulations made with the consent of the Treasury, make provision with respect to—

(*a*) the form of the summary financial statement, and

(*b*) the information which must be included in it.

(4) Every summary financial statement shall also include in the prescribed form statements to the effect that—

(*a*) it is only a summary of information in the accounts, business statement and directors' report;

(*b*) in so far as it summarises the information in the accounts, those accounts have been audited;

(*c*) the accounts, business statement and directors' report will be available to members and depositors free of charge on demand at every office of the society after a specified date.

(5) Every summary financial statement shall include a statement of the auditors' opinion as to its consistency with the accounts, business statement and directors' report and its conformity with the requirements of this section and regulations made under it.

(6) The power to make regulations under subsection (3) above is exercisable by statutory instrument which shall be subject to annulment in pursuance of a resolution of either House of Parliament.

(7) The summary financial statement shall be signed by two directors on behalf of the board of directors and by the chief executive of the society.

(8) A copy of the summary financial statement and, where this subsection extends under section 78(6) to the auditors' report also, of the auditors' report shall be sent by the society, not later than 21 days before the date of the annual general meeting at which the accounts and reports are to be considered, to—

(*a*) every member of the society who is entitled to receive notice of the meeting,

(*b*) the Commission, and

(*c*) the central office.

(9) A copy of the summary financial statement and, where this subsection extends under section 78(6) to the auditors' report also, of the auditors' report shall be given or sent by the society free of charge, at any time during the period ending with the publication of the next summary financial statement, to—

(*a*) any individual who for the first time subscribes for shares in, or deposits money with, the society, on his first subscribing for the shares or making the deposit, and

(*b*) any member of the society who was not sent a copy under subsection (8)(*a*) above, within seven days of his making a demand for a copy.

(10) If default is made by a building society in complying with subsection (8) above, the society shall be liable on summary conviction—

(*a*) to a fine not exceeding level 5 on the standard scale; and

(*b*) in the case of a continuing offence, to an additional fine not exceeding £200 for every day during which the offence continues,

and so shall any officer who is also guilty of the offence.

(11) If default is made by a building society in complying with subsection (9) above, the society shall be liable on summary conviction—

(*a*) to a fine not exceeding level 3 on the standard scale; and

(*b*) in the case of a continuing offence, to an additional fine not exceeding £40 for every day during which the offence continues,

and so shall any officer who is also guilty of the offence.

(12) The central office shall keep the copy of the summary financial statement received by it under subsection (8) above in the public file of the society.

DEFINITIONS
"the annual accounts": ss.72(10) and 119(1).
"the annual business statement": ss.74(1) and 119(1).
"associated": ss.18(17) and 119(1).
"auditors' report": see s.78(1).
"central office": s.119(1).
"Commission": ss.1 and 119(1).
"depositors": see s.119(1).
"directors' report": see s.75(1).
"financial year": ss.117 and 119(1).
"member": s.119(1).
"officer": s.119(1).
"public file": ss.106 and 119(1).
"the standard scale": Criminal Justice Act 1982, s.37.
"subsidiary": s.117(1); Companies Act 1985, s.736.
"summary financial statement": subs. (1).

GENERAL NOTE
This section introduces a new statutory document, the summary financial statement. Its purpose is to summarise the information contained in the annual accounts, annual business statement and directors' report and to present the summary in a way that will be relatively

comprehensible to the average investor. The detail of the form and contents is to be prescribed by regulations to be made by the Commission (subs. (3)).

The summary financial statement, rather than any of the other documents mentioned above, is likely to be, in future, the primary source of financial information for the average member. Members will receive copies of the statement, and not the other documents, before the annual general meeting (subs. (8)), although the other documents will be available on request (subs. (4) and s.81(3)). Members are safeguarded by the fact that the statement must include an auditors' statement as to its consistency with the other documents (subs. (5)). Moreover, if the auditors' report on the accounts is qualified, that report must accompany the summary financial statement (subs. (8) and s.78(6)). New investors will also receive the summary financial statement rather than the other documents (subs. (9)). Subss.(8) and (9) should be compared with s.83 of the 1962 Act and s.240 of the Companies Act 1985, under both of which the accounts and the directors' report are the primary source of financial information.

Note that the statement must carry a warning that it is a summary only: see subs. (4)(*a*). It must also indicate the availability of the summarised documents: subs. (4)(*c*).

Subs. (10)
Level 5. Currently £2,000.

Subs. (11)
Level 3. Currently £400.

Auditors and audit of accounts

Auditors: appointment, tenure, qualifications, etc.

77.—(1) Every building society shall at each annual general meeting appoint an auditor or auditors to hold office from the conclusion of that meeting until the conclusion of the next annual general meeting.

(2) Schedule 11 to this Act has effect as regards—

(*a*) the appointment of auditors;

(*b*) their qualifications and grounds of disqualification, and

(*c*) the resignation and removal of auditors.

GENERAL NOTE

Subs. (1) of this section, requiring the appointment of auditors at each annual general meeting, re-enacts s.84(1) of the 1962 Act. It may also be compared with s.384(1) of the Companies Act 1985 which is similar. Subs. (2) introduces Sched. 11, which, broadly, deals with the matters covered by the rest of s.84 and succeeding provisions of the 1962 Act, and the rest of s.384 and succeeding provisions of the Companies Act. The remuneration of the auditors is required to be covered by the rules: Sched. 2, para. 3(4).

Subs. (1)
To hold office. Note that the definition of "officer" in s.119(1) does not include the auditors of; *cf.* s.84(5) of the 1962 Act, which provided that a person holding the office of auditor was an officer of the society unless the rules otherwise provided.

Auditors' report

78.—(1) The auditors of a building society shall make a report to the members on the annual accounts which are to be laid before the society at the annual general meeting during their tenure of office.

(2) The auditors' report shall be read before the building society at the annual general meeting and shall be open to inspection by any member.

(3) The auditors shall, in their report under subsection (1) above, also make a report to the members on—

(*a*) the annual business statement, and

(*b*) the directors' report,

in so far as subsection (7) below requires them to do so.

(4) The auditors' report shall state whether the annual accounts have been prepared so as to conform to the requirements of this Part and the

regulations made under it and whether, in the opinion of the auditors, they give a true and fair view—

(a) in the case of the income and expenditure account, of the income and expenditure of the society for the financial year,

(b) in the case of the balance sheet, of the state of the affairs of the society as at the end of the financial year, and

(c) in the case of the statement of the source and application of funds, of the manner in which the business of the society has been financed and in which its financial resources have been used during the year.

(5) Subsection (4) above, in its application to the group accounts of a society, is to be read as referring to the society and (so far as it concerns the members of the society) the subsidiaries dealt with in the group accounts.

(6) If the auditors' report includes a qualification of their opinion that the annual accounts give a true and fair view of the matters specified in subsection (4) above, subsections (8) and (9) of section 76 extend also to the auditors' report.

(7) The auditors' report, in so far as it deals with the documents specified in subsection (3) above, shall state whether they have been prepared so as to conform to the requirements of sections 74 and 75 respectively and the regulations thereunder and whether, in the opinion of the auditors—

(a) the information given in the annual business statement gives a true representation of the matters in respect of which it is given, and

(b) the information given in the directors' report is consistent with the accounting records and the annual accounts for the year.

(8) The auditors' report on the annual business statement shall not deal with any matters which, by virtue of section 74(6), are not to be the subject of report under this section.

(9) The auditors of a building society shall, as regards the statement of particulars of transactions falling within section 65 which the society is to make available for inspection by members under section 68(3), examine the statement before it is made available to members and make a report to the members on it; and the report shall be annexed to the statement before it is so made available.

(10) The auditors' report under subsection (9) above shall state whether in their opinion the statement contains the particulars required by section 68; and where their opinion is that it does not, they shall include in their report, so far as they are reasonably able to do so, a statement giving the requisite particulars.

DEFINITIONS

"annual accounts": ss.72(10) and 119(1).

"annual business statement": ss.74(1) and 119(1).

"directors' report": see s.75(1).

"member": s.119(1).

"subsidiary": s.119(1); Companies Act 1985, s.736.

GENERAL NOTE

The object of this section, in summary, is to require auditors to check whether the directors have properly performed their duties under s.68 and ss.72 to 75 of the Act. It imposes on the auditors an obligation to prepare reports to members as follows:

(1) the main auditors' report must consider the annual accounts, the annual business statement (subject to the provisions of any regulations made under s.74(6)) and the directors' report: see subss.(1), (3) and (8);

(2) the auditors must further consider and report on the statement of particulars of transactions made under s.65 which is required to be prepared by s.68: see subs. (9).

The contents of the main report are prescribed by subss.(4), (5) and (7). That report is to be attached to the balance sheet (s.80(2)). The contents of the second report are prescribed by subs. (10). That report is to be annexed to the statement of particulars: subs. (9).

The basis of these provisions is to be found in s.89(1) to (3) of the 1962 Act and s.236 of the Companies Act 1985. The section is, however, cast in terms which reflect both the considerable changes from the previous law introduced by this Act and the special requirements of building societies.

Auditors' duties and powers

79.—(1) It is the duty of the auditors of a building society in preparing their report to the members under section 78, to carry out such investigations as will enable them to form an opinion as to the following matters—

(a) whether proper accounting records have been kept under section 71,

(b) whether the society has maintained satisfactory systems of control of its business and records and of inspection and report under that section, and

(c) whether the annual accounts are in agreement with the accounting records.

(2) If the auditors are of the opinion that the annual accounts are not in agreement with the accounting records they shall state that fact in their report.

(3) Every auditor of a building society has—

(a) a right of access at all times to the accounting and other records of the society and all other documents relating to its business, and

(b) a right to require from the officers of the society such information and explanations as he thinks necessary for the performance of the duties of the auditors.

(4) Where a building society has a subsidiary, then—

(a) if the subsidiary is a body corporate incorporated in any part of the United Kingdom, it is the duty of the subsidiary and its auditors to give to the society's auditors such information and explanation, and such access to documents, as those auditors may reasonably require for the purposes of their duties as auditors of the society;

(b) in any other case, it is the duty of the society, if required by its auditors to do so, to take all such steps as are reasonably open to it to obtain from the subsidiary such information and explanation and such access as are mentioned above.

(5) Subsection (4) above applies as regards any body associated with the society which is not a subsidiary as it applies as regards a subsidiary of the society.

(6) If the auditors fail to obtain all the information and explanations and the access to documents which, to the best of their knowledge and belief, are necessary for the purposes of their audit, they shall state that fact in their report.

(7) The auditors of a building society have the right—

(a) to attend any general meeting of the society, and to receive all notices of and other communications relating to any general meeting which any member of the society is entitled to receive, and

(b) to be heard at any meeting which they attend on any part of the business of the meeting which concerns them as auditors.

(8) If a building society or other body corporate fails to comply with subsection (4) above, the society or other body shall be liable on summary conviction to a fine not exceeding level 3 on the standard scale and so shall any officer of the society or, as the case may be, of the other body

who is also guilty of the offence; and if an auditor fails without reasonable excuse to comply with paragraph (*a*) of that subsection he shall be liable, on summary conviction, to such a fine.

(9) If a person who is an officer of a building society or of a body which is a subsidiary of or is associated with the society knowingly or recklessly makes to the auditors of that or another society or body a statement which—

(*a*) conveys or purports to convey any information or explanation which the auditors require, or are entitled to require, as auditors of the society or other body, as the case may be, and

(*b*) is false or misleading in a material particular,

that person shall be liable—

(i) on conviction on indictment, to imprisonment for a term not exceeding two years or to a fine, or both; and

(ii) on summary conviction, to imprisonment for a term not exceeding six months or to a fine not exceeding the statutory maximum, or both.

DEFINITIONS
"annual accounts": ss.72(10) and 119(1).
"associated": ss.18(17) and 119(1).
"member": s.119(1).
"officer": s.119(1).
"the standard scale": Criminal Justice Act 1982, s.37.
"the statutory maximum": Criminal Justice Act 1982, s.74; Magistrates' Courts Act 1980, s.32.
"subsidiary": s.119(1); Companies Act 1985, s.736.

GENERAL NOTE
This section contains further provisions as to the duties and rights of auditors and provides certain sanctions. Subss. (1) to (3), (6) and (7) are substantially derived from s.87(4) to (7) of the 1962 Act. (Similar provisions are also to be found in ss.237(1) to (4) and 387(1) of the Companies Act 1985.) Subss. (4) and (5) reflect the fact that other bodies (including subsidiaries) may now be associated with a building society. These subsections are therefore new. So are the penal provisions of subss. (8) and (9).

Subs. (6)
This is not a new provision, but clearly it may more frequently be invoked now that auditors may be dealing with overseas subsidiaries or other associated bodies which will not be subject to the same pressures to co-operate with the society's auditors as are U.K.-based subsidiaries or associated bodies. Note in particular the legal obligation imposed by subs. (4)(*a*).

Subs. (8)
Note that this subsection seems to assume that an auditor will not be an officer of a subsidiary or associated body; otherwise the express mention of an auditor would not be necessary. Curiously, there is no express reference to auditors in subs. (9) below.
Level 3. Currently £400.

Subs. (9)
See the note to subs. (8) above.
The statutory maximum. Currently £2,000.

Procedure on completion of accounts

Signing of balance sheet: documents to be annexed

80.—(1) Every balance sheet of a building society shall be signed by two directors on behalf of the board of directors and by the chief executive of the society.

(2) The income and expenditure account, the statement of the source and application of the funds and the annual business statement shall be

annexed to the balance sheet, and so shall any group accounts; and the auditor's report shall be attached to it.

(3) The income and expenditure account, the statement of the source and application of the funds and the annual business statement shall be approved by the board of directors before the balance sheet is signed on their behalf, and so shall any group accounts; and the date of their approval of those documents shall be endorsed on the balance sheet.

(4) The directors' report shall be attached to the balance sheet.

(5) If a balance sheet has not been signed as required by subsection (1) above, and a copy of it is issued, circulated or published, the building society shall be liable on summary conviction to a fine not exceeding level 3 on the standard scale and so shall any officer who is also guilty of the offence.

(6) If any copy of a balance sheet is issued, circulated or published—

(*a*) without having annexed to it a copy of the income and expenditure account, or

(*b*) without having annexed to it a copy of the source and application of funds statement, or

(*c*) without having annexed to it a copy of the annual business statement, or

(*d*) without having attached to it a copy of the auditors' report, or

(*e*) without having attached to it a copy of the directors' report,

the building society shall be liable on summary conviction to a fine not exceeding level 3 on the standard scale and so shall any officer who is also guilty of the offence.

DEFINITIONS
"annual business statement": ss.74(1) and 119(1).
"auditors' report": see s.78(1).
"directors' report": see s.75(1).
"officer": s.119(1).
"the standard scale": Criminal Justice Act 1982, s.37.

GENERAL NOTE
The purpose of this section is to ensure that unapproved, unsigned and incomplete copies of a society's accounts do not get into circulation. It establishes what is a complete and proper set of accounts. The ancestors of the section are ss.80 and 81 of the 1962 Act and s.238 of the Companies Act 1985.

Subss. (2) and (3)
The effect of the provisions for approval and annexure contained in these subsections is that only one set of signatures is required for the various documents comprising the annual accounts (see s.72(10)) and for the annual business statement.

Subs. (5)
Level 3. Currently £400.

Subs. (6)
The difference between annexure and attachment seems to be that the annexed documents are covered by signatures on the documents to which they are annexed. Attached documents require separate authentication.
Level 3. Currently £400.

Laying and furnishing accounts, etc., to members, Commission and central office

81.—(1) The directors of every building society shall lay before the society at the annual general meeting the annual accounts for the last financial year.

(2) The directors of every building society shall send a copy of the annual accounts for the last financial year to the Commission and to the

central office not later than 14 days before the annual general meeting at which the accounts are to be considered.

(3) Every building society shall, as from the date by which at the latest its directors are required to send them to the Commission, make copies of the annual accounts available free of charge to members of and depositors with the society at every office of the society and, free of charge, shall send copies of those documents to any member or depositor who demands it.

(4) If default is made in complying with subsection (1) or (2) above, every person who was a director at any time during the relevant period shall be liable on summary conviction—

(*a*) to a fine not exceeding level 5 on the standard scale; and

(*b*) in the case of a continuing offence, to an additional fine not exceeding £200 for every day during which the offence continues.

(5) If, on demand made of it under subsection (3) above, a building society fails, in accordance with that subsection, to make available or, as the case may be, within seven days of the demand, to send, to a person a copy of the annual accounts the society shall be liable on summary conviction—

(*a*) to a fine not exceeding level 3 on the standard scale; and

(*b*) in the case of a continuing offence, to an additional fine not exceeding £40 for every day during which the offence continues,

and so shall any officer who is also guilty of the offence.

(6) In subsection (4) above "the relevant period" means the period beginning at the end of the last financial year and ending with the date which falls 14 days before the annual general meeting following the end of that year.

(7) The central office shall keep the copy of the annual accounts of a building society received by it under subsection (2) above in the public file of the society.

(8) In this section any reference to the annual accounts includes a reference to the documents annexed or attached to them under section 80.

Definitions

"annual accounts": ss.72(10) and 119(1); see also subs. (8).
"central office": s.119(1).
"Commission": ss.1 and 119(1).
"depositor": see s.119(1).
"financial year": ss.117 and 119(1).
"member": s.119(1).
"officer": s.119(1).
"public file": ss.106 and 119(1).
"the relevant period": subs. (6).
"the standard scale": Criminal Justice Act 1982, s.37.

General Note

This section makes provision for the laying of the annual accounts, and documents annexed and attached thereto, before the annual general meeting and for their supply to the Commission, the central office and members. Compare ss.77, 83 and 88 of the 1962 Act (dealing respectively with: the laying of accounts before the annual general meeting; the duty to send copies of the accounts, the auditors' report and the directors' report to the Chief Registrar of Friendly Societies and to members; and the duty to make an annual return to the Chief Registrar). See also ss.241 and 242 of the Companies Act 1985.

Subs. (2)

Under this subsection, the relevant documents must be delivered to the Commission and the central office not later than 14 days before the annual general meeting, which must itself be held in the first four months of the new financial year: Sched. 2, para. 20. The effect is to impose a significantly stricter time limit on building societies than that applying to companies under s.242 of the 1985 Act (*viz.*, 10 months from the end of the financial year for a private company and seven months for a public company).

Subs. (3)
Note that copies of the annual accounts are no longer sent to members automatically; instead, they receive the summary financial statement prepared pursuant to s.76. See the notes to that section.

Subs. (4)
Level 5. Currently £2,000.

Subs. (5)
Level 3. Currently £400.

Auditors' duties to Commission and related rights

82.—(1) The auditors of a building society shall, with respect to each financial year of the society, make to the Commission in accordance with subsection (5) below a report on the conduct of the business of the society during that year in the respects specified in subsection (2) below.

(2) The auditor's report shall deal with—

(*a*) the accounting records kept by the society under section 71,

(*b*) the systems of control of its business and records of inspection and report maintained under that section, and

(*c*) the system of safe custody of documents maintained under section 12(12).

(3) The report shall state the auditors' opinion as respects the matters specified in subsection (2) above as follows, that is to say—

(*a*) as regards the accounting records of the society, whether or not they comply with the requirements of section 71 and, if not, specifying each requirement not complied with and the respects in which it was not complied with;

(*b*) as regards the system of control of its business and records, whether or not the system complies with the requirements of section 71 and, if not, specifying each requirement not complied with and the respects in which it was not complied with;

(*c*) as regards the system of inspection and report, whether or not the system complies with the requirements of section 71 and, if not, specifying each requirement not complied with and the respects in which it was not complied with;

(*d*) as regards the system of safe custody of documents, whether or not the system complies with the requirement of section 12(12) and, if not, specifying the respects in which it was not complied with.

(4) Where the society had, at any time during the year to which the report relates, subsidiaries or other associated bodies linked by resolution, the auditors' report shall deal also with and contain corresponding statements of their opinion as to compliance with the requirements of section 71 in its application to building societies having subsidiaries or other associated bodies linked by resolution.

(5) The auditors of a building society shall send their report under this section to the society and, subject to subsection (6) below, shall do so within the period of 72 days beginning with the end of the financial year to which it relates, and the society shall, within the period of 90 days so beginning, send the report to the Commission together with such comments as the board of directors think fit to make.

(6) A building society may allow its auditors a longer period in which to send their report than that specified in subsection (5) above, but not so as to prevent the society from complying with the duty imposed on it by that subsection as regards the Commission.

(7) If the board of directors of a building society make any comments to the Commission under subsection (5) above they shall cause a copy of the comments to be sent to the auditors before they send them to the Commission with the report under that subsection.

(8) The auditors of a building society, if they are satisfied that it is expedient to do so in order to protect the investments of shareholders or depositors or if they are requested to do so by the Commission on its being so satisfied, shall be entitled, notwithstanding any obligation of confidence incumbent on them and whether or not to do so would be contrary to the interests of the society, to furnish information to the Commission relating to the conduct of the society's business or the business of any of its subsidiaries or other associated bodies.

(9) The Treasury may by order impose on the auditors of building societies an obligation to furnish to the Commission, in such circumstances as may be prescribed in the order, relevant information available to them of such descriptions as may be prescribed in the order; and it shall be the duty of any auditor to furnish information to which the obligation extends notwithstanding any obligation of confidence incumbent on him.

(10) The power to make an order under subsection (9) above is exercisable by statutory instrument but no such instrument shall be made unless a draft of it has been laid before and approved by a resolution of each House of Parliament.

(11) In subsection (9) above "relevant information" means information relating to the conduct of the business of building societies or their subsidiaries or associated bodies.

DEFINITIONS
"associated": ss.18(17) and 119(1).
"Commission": ss.1 and 119(1).
"depositor": s.119(1).
"financial year": ss.117 and 119(1).
"linked by resolution": ss.18(9) and 119(1).
"relevant information": subs. (11).
"shareholder": s.119(1).
"subsidiary": s.119(1); Companies Act 1985, s.736.

GENERAL NOTE
This section is new. It contains three distinct elements, as follows.
(i) Subss. (1) to (7) oblige the auditors of a building society to report to the Commission annually on the society's accounting records, its system of control of its business and records, its system of inspection and report (for all of which see s.71) and its system of safe custody of documents (see s.12(12)). With respect to each of those subjects, the auditors must state whether, in their opinion, the statutory requirements are complied with and, if not, each requirement not complied with and the respects in which it was not complied with. Where the society has subsidiaries or associated bodies linked by resolution, the report must contain corresponding statements of the auditors' opinion as to compliance with s.71 as it applies to societies with subsidiaries or associated bodies linked by resolution. Subss. (5) and (6) provide for the report to come to the Commission via the society itself and for the directors to forward any comments to the Commission at the same time as they forward the report. They must supply a copy of such comments to the auditors before sending them to the Commission: see subs. (7).
(ii) Subs. (8) enables the auditors to give information to the Commission, notwithstanding that to do so involves a breach of confidence and may be contrary to the interests of the society, if the auditors are satisfied that it is expedient to do so to protect the investments of shareholders and depositors, or if they are requested to do so by the Commission on its being so satisfied.
(iii) Subss. (9) to (11) enable the Treasury to make regulations imposing on the auditors a duty to give available information of a prescribed nature to the Commission in prescribed circumstances.
Each of these three elements has considerable importance to the accountancy profession and represents something of a change in practice. The third element in particular, which was

only introduced by amendment at the Committee stage of the Bill's passage through the House of Lords, attracted much attention and was strongly opposed because it may lead to auditors being under a duty to break confidence with their clients. (Contrast subs. (8), which is enabling rather than imperative.)

Note that although provisions such as these are new to the Statute Book, it is intended that provisions covering (ii) and (iii) above at least should appear in the Financial Services Bill, which is expected to complete its Parliamentary progress shortly, and in the banking legislation proposed for 1986–7. No doubt there will be provisions similar to (i) above also, but their detailed terms must depend on the precise nature of the supervisory body and the activities supervised. It is believed that the accountancy profession will be issuing guidance as to proper professional practice in respect of these new provisions.

Subs. (5)

This subsection represents a compromise between requiring the auditors to report direct to the Commission, with the consequence that the directors would not know what was being said in the report, and requiring the report to be prepared in consultation with the directors, which might give the board an opportunity to influence the contents of the report.

Subs. (8)

During the Bill's progress through the House of Commons, concern was expressed in Committee that an auditor communicating with the Commission under this subsection might find himself open to an action for damages if, for example, closure or a change of management of the society followed. It was stated by Sir George Young, speaking for the Government, that he was advised that qualified privilege would attach because of the common and reciprocal interests of the Commission and the auditors in protecting share-holders and depositors. (See *Official Report*, Standing Committee A, February 18, 1986, cols. 452 to 453.)

Whether or not to do so would be contrary to the interests of the society. This phrase was introduced into the Bill at the Committee stage in the House of Lords. It is not clear what interests of the society (as opposed to interests of fraudulent or incompetent officers of the society) would be adversely affected if information were communicated to protect the investments of shareholders and depositors.

Subss. (9) and (10)

When these subsections were first introduced into the Bill, regulations made thereunder were to be subject to negative, rather than affirmative, resolution procedure; that is, they would have taken effect unless a resolution was passed for their annulment. It is very rare for regulations subject to the negative resolution procedure to receive careful scrutiny and debate. The chances of such scrutiny and debate are substantially increased if the affirmative resolution procedure is adopted. The latter procedure was adopted in this case at the Report stage in the House of Lords in order to allay some of the misgivings expressed at the prospect of compulsory disclosure of information by auditors.

In introducing these subsections, Lord Brabazon of Tara, speaking for the Government, made it clear that the power to make regulations was not to be exercised immediately. It was hoped that the professional accountancy bodies would produce appropriate guidance which would ensure that necessary information was communicated voluntarily. Particularly in the present climate of rapid change in financial markets, however, it was felt appropriate that this power should be included as a "reserve power." See *Official Report*, House of Lords, July 10, 1986, cols. 501 to 503. It is now necessary to wait to see what emerges from the accountancy profession.

PART IX

COMPLAINTS AND DISPUTES

Schemes for investigation of complaints

83.—(1) An individual shall, by virtue of and in accordance with schemes under this section, have the right, as against a building society, to have any complaint of his about action taken by the society in relation to a prescribed matter of complaint which affects him in prescribed respects investigated under the scheme.

(2) An individual shall also, by virtue of and in accordance with schemes under this section, have the right, as against any body which is associated with a building society, to have any complaint of his about action taken by that body in relation to a prescribed matter of complaint which affects him in prescribed respects investigated under the scheme.

(3) Every authorised building society shall be a member (and it may be the sole member) of one or more recognised schemes which or which between them confer the rights required to be conferred by subsection (1) above in relation to every matter (within its powers) which is for the time being a prescribed matter of complaint.

(4) The obligation imposed by subsection (3) above, in so far as it relates to a prescribed matter of complaint arising out of the exercise of adoptable powers, is to be construed as requiring a society to be a member of a recognised scheme conferring rights in relation to that matter not later than the date at which the alteration of the society's powers takes effect.

(5) Every authorised building society shall secure that each of the bodies associated with it is a member of one or more recognised schemes which or which between them confer the rights required to be conferred by subsection (2) above in relation to every matter (within the powers of that body) which is for the time being a prescribed matter of complaint.

(6) Schedule 12 to this Act has effect for the purposes of this section and, in that Schedule—

(a) Part I prescribes the matters for which provision must be made by a scheme if it is to be a scheme which qualifies for recognition for the purposes of this section;

(b) Part II prescribes the matters action in relation to any of which must be subject to investigation under a scheme if it is to qualify for recognition for the purpose of investigations in relation to that matter; and

(c) Part III contains other requirements to which a scheme must conform if it is to be so recognised.

(7) The Commission, with the consent of the Treasury, may by order vary Part II or Part III of Schedule 12 by adding to or deleting from it any provision or by varying any provision for the time being contained in it; and an order under this subsection may make such transitional provision as appears to the Commission to be necessary or expedient.

(8) The Commission shall have the function, in accordance with Schedule 13, of granting recognition of schemes and of withdrawing any recognition it has granted; but recognition does not extend to, and is not required for, provisions in a scheme which are not required to be made in pursuance of Schedule 12 to this Act.

(9) The Commission shall have power to do anything which is calculated to facilitate the discharge of its functions under subsection (8) above, or is incidental or conducive to their discharge, but this does not extend to expenditure for the purpose of operating a scheme.

(10) For the purpose of complying with the duty imposed on it by subsection (3) above, a building society may—

(a) make, or join with other building societies or other bodies in making, a scheme or schemes to be submitted to the Commission for approval by it as a recognised scheme; or

(b) accede as a member to any scheme, whether a scheme it has made or joined in making or a scheme made by other building societies or other bodies, which is for the time being a recognised scheme.

(11) A building society may also make or join in making, or accede to, schemes which are not required for the purposes of this section.

(12) The central office shall have the function, in accordance with Schedule 13, of recording accessions to schemes and of confirming any withdrawal from a scheme.

(13) A building society may withdraw from membership of a scheme but, if the scheme is a recognised scheme, its withdrawal is not effective except in accordance with the applicable provisions of Schedule 13.

(14) The power to make an order under subsection (7) above is exercisable by statutory instrument which shall be subject to annulment in pursuance of a resolution of either House of Parliament.

(15) In this section, section 84, Schedule 12 and Schedule 13—

"accede", in relation to a scheme, means assume the obligations and rights of membership and "accession" has a corresponding meaning;

"action" includes any failure to act, and so as regards "exercise" in relation to any power; and "action", in relation to a society, includes action on its behalf by any body associated with it;

"prescribed", in relation to matters of complaint, means prescribed for the time being in Part II of Schedule 12 and, in relation to the respects in which a complainant is affected by any action, means prescribed for the time being in Part III of that Schedule as grounds for making action subject to investigation under the scheme; and

"recognition" means recognition of a scheme by the Commission for the purposes of this section.

DEFINITIONS
"accede": subs. (15).
"action": subs. (15).
"adoptable powers": s.119(1) and Sched. 2, para. 1(4).
"associated": ss.18(17) and 119(1).
"authorised": s.119(1).
"central office": s.119(1).
"Commission": ss.1 and 119(1).
"exercise": subs. 15.
"prescribed": subs. (15).
"recognition": subs. (15).

GENERAL NOTE
This section, together with s.84 and Scheds. 12 and 13, introduces "ombudsman" provisions into building societies legislation. The effect of this section itself is broadly that:
  (a) an individual has a right, in prescribed circumstances, to have a complaint against a society or a body associated with a society investigated under an ombudsman scheme;
  (b) every authorised building society must be, and must secure that each body associated with it is, a member of one or more schemes conferring the right mentioned in (a) above;
  (c) Sched. 12 sets out the prescribed circumstances and the requirements to which a scheme must conform if it is to be recognised;
  (d) the Commission may recognise, or withdraw recognition from, a scheme in accordance with Sched. 13.
The section also contains further supplementary provisions.

Subss. (1) and (2)
These subsections confer the rights mentioned in (a) above. Note that (i) the rights are given to individuals only and not to corporate bodies (ii) the rights arise by virtue of and in accordance with the particular scheme. It seems to follow that although the rights must in each case cover "a prescribed matter of complaint" which affects the individual "in a prescribed respect" (or the scheme will not be recognised), there is no reason why a particular scheme should not confer additional rights if the participating societies so agree. See also subs. (8) (recognition would not extend to and is not required for such provisions) and the express provisions of subs. (11).

Subss. (1) and (2) refer to "a building society," but the obligation under subss. (3) and (5) to be a member, or to secure a body's membership, of a scheme extends only to "every *authorised* building society" and its associated bodies. Presumably an individual may enjoy the right against a building society which is not authorised if the society is a member of a scheme which so provides, whereas he will necessarily enjoy the right as against an authorised building society (unless it is in breach of its statutory duty). In practice, the point is likely to be unimportant.

The individual does *not*, of course, have to be a member of the society.

Subss. (3) to (5)

These subsections impose the obligations on authorised building societies mentioned above. Sanctions for breach of the obligations are contained in s.84. Subs. (4) qualifies the basic obligation under subs. (3) by providing that a society need not be a member of a scheme providing for investigation of matters arising out of the exercise of adoptable powers until the date on which an alteration of the society's rules to enable it to exercise those powers takes effect. The section as a whole proceeds on the footing that it is not necessary for every scheme to cover every prescribed matter of investigation; the essential point is that each society should be a member of sufficient schemes to cover every prescribed matter. If different schemes are set up, the exclusion of matters concerning adoptable powers will offer one obvious means of differentiation.

Subss. (6) and (7)

Note that subs. (7) provides flexibility. This is something of an experimental area and flexibility may be important if the "ombudsman" provisions are to be made to operate successfully.

Subs. (10)

This subsection and subs. (3) make it clear that a society may have its own scheme or schemes. No doubt some societies may wish to devise schemes of their own incorporating provisions in addition to those required by statute, and the existence of such a scheme may become an advertising point in the competition for business.

Subs. (13)

It follows from this subsection that a society which operates its own scheme additionally to the statutory scheme, or which together with others is a member of such a scheme, can cease to operate or can withdraw from that scheme at any time, because such schemes cannot be recognised schemes: see subs. (8).

Subs. (15)

It is worth noting that "action" includes any failure to act and "exercise" includes any failure to exercise.

Investigation of complaints: supplementary provisions

84.—(1) A building society, as a member of a recognised scheme, shall discharge any obligations and is entitled to enforce any rights imposed or conferred by the scheme or any determination of the adjudicator under the scheme, but nothing in section 83, this section or a scheme requires or authorises a building society to do anything which is outside its powers or otherwise contrary to any provision of this Act or any instrument under it.

(2) Determinations of complaints under recognised schemes shall be made by reference to what is, in the adjudicator's opinion, fair in all the circumstances of the case and any direction given to a building society or associated body by an adjudicator may (if the complainant accepts the determination) require it or the complainant not to exercise or require the performance of any of the contractual or other obligations or rights subsisting between them.

(3) Subject to subsections (4) and (5) below, a determination of the adjudicator under a recognised scheme, which is, by virtue of the complainant's acceptance of it, binding on the building society or associated body shall be final and conclusive and shall not be questioned in any court of law.

(4) Subsection (3) above does not apply where a society or associated body is authorised by the scheme to relieve itself of its obligation to take

the steps it is directed to take or pay the compensation awarded by the society's undertaking an obligation to give the requisite publicity for the reasons for not doing so and the society undertakes that obligation.

(5) Where a determination of the adjudicator under a recognised scheme is binding on the building society or associated body, the adjudicator shall, at the request of the society or associated body, state a case for the opinion of the High Court on any question of law and the High Court may direct the adjudicator to reconsider the complaint.

(6) A decision of the High Court under subsection (5) above shall be treated as a judgment of the High Court within the meaning of section 16 of the Supreme Court Act 1981 or section 39 of the Judicature (Northern Ireland) Act 1978 (which relate to the jurisdiction of the Court of Appeal to hear and determine appeals from any judgment of the High Court) but no appeal shall lie from the decision of the High Court on any case under subsection (5) above without the leave of the High Court or of the Court of Appeal.

(7) In the application of this section to Scotland—
  (a) for the references in subsection (5) to the High Court there shall be substituted references to the Court of Session; and
  (b) subsection (6) shall be omitted.

(8) If a building society fails to comply with section 83(3) the society shall be liable on summary conviction—
  (a) to a fine not exceeding level 4 on the standard scale; and
  (b) in the case of a continuing offence, to an additional fine not exceeding £100 for every day during which the offence continues;
and so shall any director of the society who is also guilty of the offence.

(9) If a building society fails, without reasonable excuse, to comply with section 83(5) the society shall be liable on summary conviction—
  (a) to a fine not exceeding level 4 on the standard scale; and
  (b) in the case of a continuing offence, to an additional fine not exceeding £100 for every day during which the offence continues;
and so shall any director of the society who is also guilty of the offence.

(10) If a building society fails to comply with section 83(3) or (5) the Commission may make an application to the High Court for an order directing the society to comply within a specified period with that subsection and the High Court may, if it thinks fit, make an order accordingly.

(11) In subsection (4) above the reference to an obligation to give the requisite publicity for a building society's or associated body's reasons is a reference to such an obligation undertaken in pursuance of a provision of the scheme authorised by paragraph 6(2) or (3) of Part III of Schedule 12.

DEFINITIONS
  "adjudicator": see Sched. 12.
  "associated": ss.18(17) and 119(1).
  "Commission": ss.1 and 119(1).
  "obligation to give the requisite publicity": subs. (11).
  "recognised scheme": see s.83(15).
  "the standard scale": Criminal Justice Act 1982, s.37.

GENERAL NOTE
  This section contains supplementary provisions relating to schemes for the investigation of complaints and should be read in conjunction with s.83 and Scheds. 12 and 13, which establish the framework for the operation of such schemes.

Subs. (1)
  The effect of this subsection is that a building society will be bound by, and will be able to enforce its rights under, a recognised scheme of which it is a member, provided always that it is neither compelled nor permitted to do anything which is outside its powers or otherwise contrary to any provision of the Act or any instrument under the Act.

Subs. (2)
This subsection has two parts. First, it provides the guideline by which the adjudicator is to approach the determination of complaints: namely what is fair in all the circumstances of the case. Second, it expressly permits the adjudicator to direct that a society, an associated body or a complainant shall not "exercise or require the performance of any of the contractual or other obligations or rights subsisting between them". Compare the notes to Sched. 12, Part III, para. 4.

Subs. (3)
Note that the determination is only binding on a society or an associated body if it has been accepted by the complainant. See Sched. 12, Part III, para. 6.

Subs. (4)
Note that the relieving provisions of para. 6 will be operable by a society or an associated body only if the scheme so provides.

Subs. (5)
Under this subsection, the adjudicator is obliged to state a case if requested to do so by the society or associated body. Note that the obligation arises only after the determination has become binding on the society or associated body by virtue of the complainant's acceptance of it (see subs. (3) and Sched. 12, para. 6). There can be no question of the application for the case having to be made before the determination is made, as was the position under s.98 of the 1962 Act (see Wurtzburg and Mills, *Building Society Law* (14th Ed.), p. 255). Note that the Act does not appear to provide any time limit within which an application for a case must be made. Presumably an adjudicator might refuse to state a case, and might have his refusal upheld by the court, if the society or body delayed excessively before making the application.

Subss. (8) and (9)
Level 4. Currently £1,000.

Settlement of disputes

85.—(1) Schedule 14 to this Act shall have effect for the settlement of certain disputes between a building society and a member, or a representative of a member, of the society or, as provided by Part II of the Schedule, between a building society and a depositor with the society.

(2) Nothing in that Schedule affects the jurisdiction of any court to hear and determine disputes arising out of any mortgage or any contract other than the rules of a society.

DEFINITIONS
"depositor": see s.119(1).
"member": s.119(1).
"mortgage": s.119(1).

GENERAL NOTE
This section introduces Sched. 14. Together with ss.83 and 84 and Scheds. 12 and 13, Sched. 14 establishes a new code for the settlement of disputes between a society and a member in his capacity as a member, or between the society and the representative of a member in that capacity, or, in Part II only, between the society and a depositor. The new code replaces ss.93 to 98 of the 1962 Act.

Note that s.85 refers only to a building society and not to bodies associated with a building society. Contrast the "ombudsman" provisions (*i.e.* ss.83 and 84 and Scheds. 12 and 13).

PART X

DISSOLUTION, WINDING UP, MERGERS AND TRANSFER OF BUSINESS

Dissolution and winding up

Modes of dissolution and winding up

86.—(1) A building society—
(*a*) may be dissolved by consent of the members, or

(*b*) may be wound up voluntarily or by the court,
in accordance with this Part; and a building society may not, except where
it is dissolved by virtue of section 93(5), 94(10) or 97(9), be dissolved or
wound up in any other manner.

(2) A building society which is in the course of dissolution by consent,
or is being wound up voluntarily, may be wound up by the court.

DEFINITION
"court": s.119(1).

GENERAL NOTE
The effect of this section is that a building society may now be dissolved or wound up in
any one of six ways. Those ways are:
(*a*) dissolution by consent of the members (see s.87);
(*b*) voluntary winding up (see s.88);
(*c*) winding up by the court (see s.89);
(*d*) dissolution consequent upon an amalgamation (see s.93);
(*e*) dissolution consequent upon a transfer of engagements (see s.94);
(*f*) dissolution consequent upon a transfer of business to a commercial company (see
    s.97).
Each method of dissolution or winding up is considered in detail in the notes to the relevant
section. As will appear from those notes, there has been a substantial overhaul of the
methods of dissolution or winding up which were permitted under the 1962 Act and the
regime now applicable to building societies is based very largely on the regime applicable to
companies.

Subs. (2)
Compare s.116 of the Insolvency Act 1986, which similarly permits a creditor or
contributory to seek a winding up by the court while a voluntary winding up is in progress.

Dissolution by consent

87.—(1) A building society may be dissolved by an instrument of
dissolution, with the consent (testified by their signature of that instrument) of three-quarters of the members of the society, holding not less
than two-thirds of the number of shares in the society.

(2) An instrument of dissolution under this section shall set out—
(*a*) the liabilities and assets of the society in detail;
(*b*) the number of members, and the amount standing to their credit
    in the accounting records of the society;
(*c*) the claims of depositors and other creditors, and the provision to
    be made for their payment;
(*d*) the intended appropriation or division of the funds and property of
    the society;
(*e*) the names of one or more persons to be appointed as trustees for
    the purposes of the dissolution, and their remuneration.

(3) An instrument of dissolution made with consent given and testified
as mentioned in subsection (1) above may be altered with the like consent,
testified in the like manner.

(4) The provisions of this Act shall continue to apply in relation to a
building society as if the trustees appointed under the instrument of
dissolution were the board of directors of the society.

(5) The trustees, within 15 days of the necessary consent being given
and testified (in accordance with subsection (1) above) to—
(*a*) an instrument of dissolution, or
(*b*) any alteration to such an instrument,
shall give notice to the central office of the fact and, except in the case of
an alteration to an instrument, of the date of commencement of the
dissolution, enclosing a copy of the instrument or altered instrument, as
the case may be; and if the trustees fail to comply with this subsection

they shall each be liable on summary conviction to a fine not exceeding level 3 on the standard scale.

(6) An instrument of dissolution under this section, or an alteration to such an instrument, shall be binding on all members of the society as from the date on which the copy of the instrument or altered instrument, as the case may be, is placed in the public file of the society under subsection (10) below.

(7) The trustees shall, within 28 days from the termination of the dissolution, give notice to the central office of the fact and the date of the termination, enclosing an account and balance sheet signed and certified by them as correct, and showing the assets and liabilities of the society at the commencement of the dissolution, and the way in which those assets and liabilities have been applied and discharged; and, if they fail to do so they shall each be liable on summary conviction—

(a) to a fine not exceeding level 2 on the standard scale, and

(b) in the case of a continuing offence, to an additional fine not exceeding £10 for every day during which the offence continues.

(8) Except with the consent of the Commission, no instrument of dissolution, or alteration of such an instrument, shall be of any effect if the purpose of the proposed dissolution or alteration is to effect or facilitate the transfer of the society's engagements to any other society or to a company.

(9) Any provision in a resolution or document that members of a building society proposed to be dissolved shall accept investments in a company or another society (whether in shares, deposits or any other form) in or towards satisfaction of their rights in the dissolution shall be conclusive evidence of such a purpose as is mentioned in subsection (8) above.

(10) The central office shall keep in the public file of the society any notice or other document received by it under subsection (5) or (7) above and shall record in that file the date on which the notice or document is placed in it.

DEFINITIONS
"central office": s.119(1).
"Commission": ss.1 and 119(1).
"depositors": see s.119(1).
"members": s.119(1).
"notice": s.119(1).
"public file": ss.106 and 119(1).
"the standard scale": Criminal Justice Act 1982, s.37.

GENERAL NOTE
This section enables the members of a society to dissolve their society by consent if the necessary agreement to an instrument of dissolution can be obtained. The provisions of the section are very closely modelled on ss.100 and 102 of the 1962 Act.

Note that by virtue of s.116 of the Insolvency Act 1986 as applied to this Act by Sched. 15, para. 14, a creditor or contributory can seek a winding up by the court notwithstanding that a dissolution by consent is in progress; but a contributory seeking such a winding up must satisfy the court that the rights of contributories will be prejudiced by the dissolution. See also s.86(2) and see Sched. 15, para. 9 for the meaning of "contributory".

Subs. (1)
This subsection lays down the conditions that have to be satisfied before an instrument of dissolution can take effect. First, the agreement of three-quarters of the members holding not less than two-thirds of the shares in the society must be obtained. Second, that agreement must be testified by the members having signed the instrument; it is not sufficient, in other words, for the members to pass a special resolution. It is not clear whether the signature must be that of the member himself or whether the signature of an agent is sufficient: see Wurtzburg and Mills, *Building Society Law*, (14th Ed.), pp. 305–6, suggesting that Scottish

law may require the member's own signature, whereas English law permits signature by an agent.

Subs. (2)

This subsection prescribes the contents of an instrument of dissolution. The effect is that the instrument will show in detail what the society's assets are at the date of the instrument, how they are to be dealt with and who is going to administer the dissolution. Note that the entitlement of members to participate in the distribution of any surplus assets is a matter required to be covered by the rules: Sched. 2, para. 3(4).

Subs. (5)

This subsection is somewhat stricter than its predecessors, ss.100(4) and 105 of the 1962 Act, in that it imposes a fairly short time limit for notification and attaches a criminal penalty to failure to notify. S.100(4) contains no penalty and neither provision specifies a time limit.

Level 3. Currently £400.

Subs. (7)

The account and balance sheet to be enclosed with notice of termination of the dissolution under this subsection should of course show that the assets have been applied in accordance with the instrument of dissolution, or the instrument as altered under subs. (3).

Level 2. Currently £100.

Subss. (8) and (9)

The purpose of these subsections is to ensure that a transfer of engagements to another society or to a company cannot be dressed up as a dissolution with the result that the restrictions and safeguards applying to transfers under ss.93 to 102 and Scheds. 2, 16 and 17 are avoided. An example of the sort of abuse against which these provisions are directed is as follows. An instrument of dissolution in respect of Society A is agreed under which all the officers are to receive substantial compensation for loss of office in priority to any distribution to members, who are to take their share of the surplus assets in the form of shares in Society B. The dissolution goes through and the officers of Society A are promptly re-employed by Society B, having first received a substantial nest egg at the expense of Society A's members.

Voluntary winding up

88.—(1) A building society may be wound up voluntarily under the applicable winding up legislation if it resolves by special resolution that it be wound up voluntarily.

(2) A copy of any special resolution passed for the voluntary winding up of a building society shall be sent by the society to the central office within 15 days after it is passed; and the central office shall keep the copy in the public file of the society.

(3) A copy of any such resolution shall be annexed to every copy of the memorandum or of the rules issued after the passing of the resolution.

(4) If a building society fails to comply with subsection (2) or (3) above the society shall be liable on summary conviction to a fine not exceeding level 3 on the standard scale and so shall any officer who is also guilty of the offence.

(5) For the purposes of this section, a liquidator of the society shall be treated as an officer of it.

DEFINITIONS

"applicable winding up legislation": s.90(3).
"central office": s.119(1).
"memorandum": s.119(1) and Sched. 2, para. 1.
"public file": ss.106 and 119(1).
"special resolution": s.119(1) and Sched. 2, para. 27.

GENERAL NOTE

This section provides for the voluntary winding up of a society under the "applicable winding up legislation". All that is required to set the procedure in motion is a special resolution of the society.

The applicable winding up legislation, in English law and for the purposes of this section, consists of those provisions of Parts IV, VI, VII and XII and ss.430 and 432 of, and Sched.

10 to, the Insolvency Act 1986 which relate to voluntary winding up, as modified by Sched. 15 to this Act. It would be inappropriate to attempt any detailed consideration of those provisions here; reference should be made to works on company law and insolvency. The following very brief indication of the matters covered by those provisions may, however, be of assistance.

Part IV. Ss.73 to 83 contain preliminary provisions applicable to winding up generally. Ss.84 to 90 contain general provisions as to voluntary winding up. S.90 provides that where the directors have made a declaration (under s.89) that they believe the society to be solvent, the winding up is a "members' voluntary winding up"; where no such declaration has been made, it is a "creditors' voluntary winding up". Ss.91 to 96 then deal with a members' voluntary winding up and (in ss.95 and 96) its conversion into a creditors' voluntary winding up where the liquidator forms the opinion that in fact the society is insolvent. Ss.97 to 106 deal with a creditors' voluntary winding up. Ss.107 to 116 contain further provisions applying to both kinds of voluntary winding up.

Ss.163 to 174 concern liquidators, their powers and duties, their removal and their release. Ss.175 to 200 contain further matters of general application in winding up, including preferential debts, power to appoint a special manager, power to disclaim and execution and attachment. Ss.201 to 205 make provision for dissolution after winding up. Ss.206 to 219 concern offences, penalisation of directors and officers and investigation and prosecution of malpractice.

Part VI. This Part consists of ss.230 to 246 and contains provisions relating to office holders, management and the adjustment of prior transactions.

Part VII. This Part contains interpretation provisions applicable to Parts I to VII of the Act.

Part XII. The only sections in this Part are ss.386 and 387, concerning preferential debts. Ss.430 and 432 and Sched. 10. These provisions relate to offences and penalties.

It is important to recall that in all cases provisions of the Insolvency Act must be read in conjunction with Sched. 15.

The 1962 Act made no express provision for a purely voluntary winding up, although such a winding up was possible if the rules so provided; s.99 of that Act permitted a society to be dissolved in any manner permitted by the rules. A society could, however, be wound up under the supervision of the court (as opposed to being wound up compulsorily): see s.32 of the Building Societies Act 1874 and s.103 of the 1962 Act.

Subs. (4)
Level 3. Currently £400.

Subs. (5)
It is thought that this subsection has the effect that a liquidator is to be treated as an officer of the society for all the purposes of the applicable winding up legislation, notwithstanding the words "for the purposes of this section".

Winding up by court: grounds and petitioners

89.—(1) A building society may be wound up under the applicable winding up legislation by the court on any of the following grounds in addition to the grounds referred to or specified in section 37(1), that is to say, if—

(*a*) the society has by special resolution resolved that it be wound up by the court;
(*b*) the number of members is reduced below ten;
(*c*) the number of directors is reduced below two;
(*d*) being a society registered as a building society under this Act or the repealed enactments, the society has not been granted authorisation under section 9 or been authorised under any corresponding enactment and more than three years has expired since it was so registered;
(*e*) the society has had its authorisation revoked under section 43 and has not been reauthorised thereafter;
(*f*) the society exists for an illegal purpose;
(*g*) the society is unable to pay its debts; or
(*h*) the court is of the opinion that it is just and equitable that the society should be wound up.

(2) Except as provided by subsection (3) below, section 37 or the applicable winding up legislation, a petition for the winding up of a building society may be presented by—

(*a*) the Commission,

(*b*) the building society or its directors,

(*c*) any creditor or creditors (including any contingent or any prospective creditor), or

(*d*) any contributory or contributories,

or by all or any of those parties, together or separately.

(3) A contributory may not present a petition unless either—

(*a*) the number of members is reduced below ten, or

(*b*) the share in respect of which he is a contributory has been held by him, or has devolved to him on the death of a former holder and between them been held, for at least six months before the commencement of the winding up.

(4) For the purposes of this section, in relation to a building society—

(*a*) the reference to authorisation under an enactment corresponding to section 9 is a reference to authorisation granted or deemed to have been granted under—

(i) in Great Britain, regulation 5 of the Building Societies (Authorisation) Regulations 1981, and

(ii) in Northern Ireland, regulation 5 of the Building Societies (Authorisation) Regulations (Northern Ireland) 1982, and

(*b*) the reference to its existing for an illegal purpose includes a reference to its existing after its purpose or principal purpose has ceased to be that required by section 5(1) for the establishment of a building society under this Act.

(5) In this section, "contributory" has the same meaning as in paragraph 9(2) or, as the case may be, paragraph 37(2) of Schedule 15 to this Act.

DEFINITIONS

"applicable winding up legislation": s.90(3).
"authorisation": s.119(1).
"Commission": ss.1 and 119(1).
"contributory": subs. (5) and Sched. 15, paras. 9 and 37.
"corresponding enactment": see subs. (4).
"court": s.119(1).
"repealed enactments": s.119(1).

GENERAL NOTE

This section provides for the winding up of a society by the court under the applicable winding up legislation. That legislation, in English law and for the purposes of this section, consists of those provisions of Parts IV, VI, VII and XII and ss.430 and 432 of, and Sched. 10 to, the Insolvency Act 1986 which relate to winding up by the court. As stated in the notes to s.88, no attempt is made to embark on a detailed discussion of those provisions in these notes. The very brief indication there given of the matters covered applies equally for the purposes of this section, save that mention should be made of ss.117 to 162, applying to winding up by the court, instead of ss.84 to 116, applying to voluntary winding up.

Prior to this Act, winding up by the court was an option open to a society under s.32 of the Building Societies Act 1874 and s.103 of the 1962 Act. Further, the Chief Registrar had power to present a petition for the winding up of a society in certain cases of default: see ss.22, 50 and 55 and Sched. 1, para. 5. A society could also be wound up as an unregistered company under the combined provisions of s.221 of the Insolvency Act 1986 and s.8 of the Building Societies Act 1894.

Subs. (1)

This subsection sets out the circumstances in which a society may be wound up by the court in addition to the circumstances set out in s.37. Compare Sched. 2, para. 1, as to the number of members a society must have before it can be registered and incorporated and s.58 as to the number of directors a society must have. Grounds (*a*), (*g*) and (*h*) are the same as grounds (*a*), (*f*) and (*g*) in s.122 of the Insolvency Act 1986, which sets out the

53–183

grounds on which a company may be wound up. By virtue of Sched. 15, para. 16, s.122 does not form part of the applicable winding up legislation.

Subs. (2)
This subsection makes provision for the persons who may present a winding up petition. The corresponding provision in the Insolvency Act 1986 is s.124 which again, by virtue of Sched. 15, para. 17, does not form part of the applicable winding up legislation.

Subs. (3)
This subsection is designed to prevent someone from becoming a contributory with a view to presenting a winding up petition forthwith. It is similar in intention to s.124(2) of the Insolvency Act. See the notes to Sched. 15, para. 9, for the meaning of "contributory".

Subs. (4)
The explanation offered in para. (*b*) of the reference to a society's existing for an illegal purpose seems to assume that the purpose is to be discovered not by reference to the society's memorandum but by reference to the purpose or principal purpose revealed by the society's activities. See also s.37(1)(*b*) and the notes thereto. Of course, a society could never obtain registration with a memorandum specifying an illegal purpose, or alter its memorandum to specify such a purpose: Sched. 2, paras. 1 and 4; Sched. 20, paras. 2 and 3.

Application of winding up legislation to building societies

90.—(1) In this section "the companies winding up legislation" means the enactments applicable in relation to England and Wales, Scotland or Northern Ireland which are specified in paragraph 1 of Schedule 15 to this Act (including any enactment which creates an offence by any person arising out of acts or omissions occurring before the commencement of the winding up).

(2) In its application to the winding up of a building society, by virtue of section 88(1) or 89(1), the companies winding up legislation shall have effect with the modifications effected by Parts I to III of Schedule 15 to this Act; and the supplementary provisions of Part IV of that Schedule shall also have effect in relation to such a winding up.

(3) In sections 37, 88, 89 and 103, "the applicable winding up legislation" means the companies winding up legislation as so modified.

DEFINITION
"the companies winding up legislation": subs. (1).

GENERAL NOTE
This section defines "the companies winding up legislation" and introduces Sched. 15. It further defines "the applicable winding up legislation" as being the companies winding up legislation as modified by Sched. 15.

Power of court to declare dissolution of building society void

91.—(1) Where a building society has been dissolved under section 87 or following a winding up, the High Court or, in relation to a society whose principal office was in Scotland, the Court of Session, may, at any time within 12 years after the date on which the society was dissolved, make an order under this section declaring the dissolution to have been void.

(2) An order under this section may be made, on such terms as the court thinks fit, on an application by the trustees under section 87 or the liquidator, as the case may be, or by any other person appearing to the Court to be interested.

(3) When an order under this section is made, such proceedings may be taken as might have been taken if the society had not been dissolved.

(4) The person on whose application the order is made shall, within seven days of its being so made, or such further time as the Court may allow, furnish the central office with a copy of the order; and the central office shall keep the copy in the public file of the society.

(5) If a person fails to comply with subsection (4) above, he shall be liable on summary conviction—

(*a*) to a fine not exceeding level 3 on the standard scale, and

(*b*) in the case of a continuing offence, to an additional fine not exceeding £40 for every day during which the offence continues.

DEFINITIONS
"central office": s.119(1).
"public file": ss.106 and 119(1).
"the standard scale": Criminal Justice Act 1982, s.37.

GENERAL NOTE
This section enables the court, on an application made by a person mentioned in subs. (2), to declare a dissolution void at any time within twelve years of the date of the dissolution. Subs. (1) seems to imply that the order of the court must be made within twelve years, but it is thought that it is sufficient if the application is made within twelve years: see the decision to similar effect in respect of s.294 of the Companies Act 1929 in *Re Scad Limited* [1941] Ch. 386. (The current equivalent of s.294 is s.651 of the Companies Act 1985, enabling the court to declare the dissolution of a company void within two years of the date of dissolution. It is not clear why the period allowed in respect of building societies is so much more generous.)

The object of the section is to allow a society to be restored to life for the purpose of recovering assets. Accordingly, the power exists only in the case of a dissolution under s.87 or following a winding up under s.88 or s.89, in all of which cases the society has no successor. The power is not required in the case of an amalgamation (s.93), a transfer of engagements (s.94), or a transfer of business to a commercial company (s.97).

The power is new.

Subs. (2)
The trustees under section 87. That is, the trustees appointed by the instrument of dissolution.

Subs. (3)
The effect of this subsection is not to restore the society to its pre-dissolution state, but simply to enable it to "take proceedings". In particular, there is no question of a society which was authorised to raise money and accept deposits before its dissolution having its authorisation automatically revived after its restoration to life.

Subs. (5)
Level 3. Currently £400.

Supplementary

92. Where a building society is being wound up or dissolved by consent, a member to whom an advance has been made under a mortgage or other security, or under the rules of the society, shall not be liable to pay any amount except at the time or times and subject to the conditions set out in the mortgage or other security, or in the rules, as the case may be.

DEFINITIONS
"member": s.119(1).
"mortgage": s.119(1).

GENERAL NOTE
This section is virtually identical to s.104 of the 1962 Act. Its purpose is to protect a borrowing member from having suddenly to repay the advance in full.
Being wound up. I.e., under s.88 or s.89.
Dissolved by consent. I.e., under s.87.

Mergers

Amalgamations

93.—(1) Any two or more building societies desiring to amalgamate may do so by establishing a building society as their successor in accordance with this section and Schedule 16 to this Act.

(2) In order to establish a building society as their successor the societies desiring to amalgamate must—

(*a*) agree upon the purpose or principal purpose of their successor and upon the extent of its powers in a memorandum which complies with the requirements of Schedule 2 to this Act;

(*b*) agree upon the rules for the regulation of their successor which comply with the requirements of that Schedule;

(*c*) each approve the terms of the amalgamation by two resolutions, of which—

(i) one is passed as a special resolution which also approves the memorandum and the rules of their successor, and

(ii) the other is passed as a borrowing members' resolution, in accordance with the applicable provisions of that Schedule;

(*d*) make a joint application to the Commission for confirmation of the amalgamation and send to the central office four copies of the rules and of the memorandum, each copy signed by the secretary of each of the societies.

(3) If the Commission confirms the amalgamation under section 95, the central office, if it is satisfied, as regards the proposed successor, of the matters relating to its rules, its purpose and powers and its name as to which it must, under paragraph 1 of Schedule 2 to this Act, be satisfied before it registers a society, shall—

(*a*) register the successor society,

(*b*) issue to it a certificate of incorporation, specifying a date ("the specified date") as from which the incorporation takes effect,

(*c*) retain and register one copy of the memorandum and of the rules,

(*d*) return another copy to the secretary of the successor, together with a certificate of registration, and

(*e*) keep another copy, together with a copy of the certificate of incorporation and of the certificate of registration of the memorandum and the rules, in the public file of the successor society.

(4) On the specified date all the property, rights and liabilities of each of the societies whose amalgamation was confirmed by the Commission (whether or not capable of being transferred or assigned) shall by virtue of this subsection be transferred to and vested in the society so incorporated as their successor.

(5) On the specified date, each of the societies to which the successor succeeds shall be dissolved by virtue of this subsection; but the transfer effected by subsection (4) above shall be deemed to have been effected immediately before the dissolution.

(6) If, on the specified date, the societies whose amalgamation was confirmed by the Commission are all authorised, their successor shall be treated as authorised for the purposes of this Act, whether or not the requirements of section 9(4) would be fulfilled in its case, as from that date.

(7) The central office shall record in the public file of the successor the fact that, by virtue of subsection (6) above, the society is to be treated as authorised for the purposes of this Act.

DEFINITIONS
"authorised": s.119(1).
"borrowing members' resolution": s.119(1) and Sched. 2, para. 29.

"central office": s.119(1).
"Commission": ss.1 and 119(1).
"memorandum": s.119(1) and Sched. 2, para. 1.
"public file": ss.106 and 119(1).
"special resolution": s.119(1) and Sched. 2, para. 27.
"the specified date": subs. (3).

GENERAL NOTE

This section provides for the creation of a new building society formed by the amalgamation of two or more existing societies. It replaces s.18 of the 1962 Act, providing for the "union" of two or more societies. It is, however, considerably more elaborate than s.18 and the opportunity has been taken to clarify the juridicial nature of the process. (See Wurtzburg and Mills, *Building Society Law* (14th Ed.), pp. 293–4, for a discussion of the obscurities under the 1962 Act.)

The section should be read in conjunction with s.95 and Sched. 16, which contain supplementary provisions.

Subs. (2)

This subsection lays down the procedure to be followed by societies desiring to amalgamate. The effect is that the societies must take virtually the same steps as are required under Sched. 2, para. 1 when persons establishing a new society desire to have that society registered and incorporated, but in addition the terms of the amalgamation must be approved by the members of the existing societies in accordance with subpara. (*c*) and the societies must apply to the Commission for confirmation of the amalgamation. Note the provisions of Sched. 16, Part II, as to the statements to be sent to members concerning proposals for amalgamation.

The applicable provisions of that Schedule. Paras. 27 and 29 of Sched. 2, dealing with special resolutions and borrowing members' resolutions respectively.

Subs. (3)

This subsection imposes on the central office duties very similar to those imposed under Sched. 2, para. 1 in connection with the registration and incorporation of a new society under that Schedule. The duties of the central office under this subsection, however, are conditional upon confirmation of the amalgamation by the Commission.

Subs. (4)

This subsection provides for the transfer of all the property, rights and liabilities of the amalgamating societies to the new society on the date on which the incorporation of the new society takes effect.

Subs. (5)

Under this subsection, the amalgamating societies are automatically dissolved on the date on which the incorporation of the new society takes effect, but the transfer effected under subs. (4) is deemed to have been made immediately prior to the dissolution.

Subs. (6)

This subsection has the effect that the new society need not seek authorisation to raise money and accept deposits under s.9 if on the date on which the incorporation of the new society takes effect, the amalgamating societies all have authority to do so.

Transfer of engagements

94.—(1) A building society may, in accordance with this section and Schedule 16 to this Act, transfer its engagements to any extent to another building society which, in accordance with this section and that Schedule, undertakes to fulfil the engagements.

(2) A building society, in order to transfer its engagements, must resolve to do so by two resolutions, of which one is passed as a special resolution and the other as a borrowing members' resolution in accordance with the applicable provisions of Schedule 2.

(3) A building society, in order to transfer some but not all of its engagements to its members in respect of shares held by them (with or without other engagements) must, in addition to resolving to transfer the

engagements by the two resolutions required by subsection (2) above, resolve to do so by an affected shareholders' resolution.

(4) For the purposes of this section in its application to a transfer by a society of engagements in respect of some shares in the society, an "affected shareholders' resolution" is a resolution passed by a majority of the holders of those shares who, under the rules of the society, would be entitled to vote on a special resolution, disregarding for this purpose any shares of theirs in respect of which the society's engagements are not to be transferred.

(5) A building society, in order to undertake to fulfil the engagements of another society, must resolve to do so—

(a) by two resolutions, of which one is passed as a special resolution and the other as a borrowing members' resolution in accordance with the applicable provisions of Schedule 2; or

(b) by a resolution of the board of directors, if the Commission consents to that mode of proceeding.

(6) The extent of the transfer, as so resolved by the society making and the society taking the transfer, shall be recorded in an instrument of transfer of engagements.

(7) A transfer of engagements between building societies shall be of no effect unless—

(a) the transfer is confirmed by the Commission under section 95; and

(b) a registration certificate is issued in respect of the transfer under subsection (8) below.

(8) Where the Commission confirms a transfer of engagements between building societies, the central office shall—

(a) register a copy of the instrument of transfer of engagements; and

(b) issue a registration certificate to the building society taking the transfer;

and, on such date as is specified in the certificate, the property, rights and liabilities of the society transferring its engagements (whether or not capable of being transferred or assigned) shall, by virtue of this subsection, be transferred to and vested in the society taking the transfer to the extent provided in the instrument of transfer of engagements.

(9) The central office shall keep a copy of the instrument and of the registration certificate issued under subsection (8) above in the public file of the building society taking the transfer.

(10) Where all its engagements have been transferred, the society shall, by virtue of this subsection, be dissolved on the date specified in the registration certificate; but the transfer effected by subsection (8) above shall be deemed to have been effected immediately before the dissolution.

DEFINITIONS
"affected shareholders' resolution": subs. (4).
"borrowing members' resolution": s.119(1) and Sched. 2, para. 29.
"central office": s.119(1).
"Commission": ss.1 and 119(1).
"registration certificate": see subs. (8).
"share": s.119(1).
"special resolution": s.119(1) and Sched. 2, para. 27.

GENERAL NOTE
This section provides for the transfer by one society to another of all or any of its engagements. It should be read in conjunction with s.95 and Sched. 16, which contain supplementary provisions. It replaces, and elaborates upon, s.19 of the 1962 Act, and in one respect it departs significantly from that section; it is clear from the words "to any extent" in subs. (1) and from subss. (3) and (5) that a partial transfer of engagements is permitted by this section. It is at best doubtful whether that was so under s.19. The instrument of transfer has to record the extent of the transfer (subs. (6)).

The phrase "transfer its engagements" is hallowed by long usage, but has never been the subject of statutory or judicial definition. It is understood, however, to mean a transfer of "power, rights and responsibilities"; "a transfer of membership as well as of property": Wurtzburg and Mills, *Building Society Law* (14th ed.), p. 295.

Subs. (2)
   The *applicable provisions of Schedule 2.* Paras. 27 and 29, dealing with special resolutions and borrowing members' resolutions respectively. Note that, under para. 29, in the case of a partial transfer only those borrowers whose mortgages are to be transferred are entitled to vote on a resolution for a transfer of engagements put to the transferor society's borrowing members.

Subs. (5)
   Under this section the transferee society may undertake to fulfil the engagements of the transferor society either by passing a special resolution and a borrowing members' resolution or, if the Commission consents, by a resolution of the board of directors. The latter course has very obvious economic advantages, particularly if the transferee society is very large. S.19(1) of the 1962 Act similarly required a special resolution in the absence of the consent of the central office to an ordinary resolution or a board resolution. In practice, the consent of the central office to a board resolution was frequently given. It seems probable that the Commission will adopt a similar approach.

Subs. (8)
   This subsection provides for the property, rights and liabilities of the transferor society, to the extent provided in the instrument of transfer, to be transferred to the transferee society on the date specified in the registration certificate.

Subs. (10)
   Under this subsection, if all its engagements are transferred, the transferor society is automatically dissolved on the date specified in the registration certificate, but the transfer effected under subs. (8) is deemed to have been made immediately prior to the dissolution.

Mergers: provisions supplementing ss.93 and 94

95.—(1) Part I of Schedule 16 to this Act shall have effect for imposing on building societies proposing to amalgamate or to transfer or undertake engagements requirements to issue statements to their members relating to the proposed amalgamation or transfer.

(2) Part II of Schedule 16 to this Act shall have effect for imposing requirements for notification by a building society, to its members and to the central office, of the receipt by the society of proposals for a transfer of engagements or an amalgamation.

(3) Where application is made to the Commission for confirmation of an amalgamation or transfer of engagements it shall, except as provided in subsections (4) to (9) below, confirm the amalgamation or transfer; and Part III of Schedule 16 to this Act shall have effect with respect to the procedure on an application for such confirmation.

(4) Subject to subsection (5) below, the Commission shall not confirm an amalgamation or transfer of engagements if it considers that—

  (*a*) some information material to the members' decision about the amalgamation or transfer was not made available to all the members eligible to vote; or

  (*b*) the vote on any resolution approving the amalgamation or transfer does not represent the views of the members eligible to vote; or

  (*c*) some relevant requirement of this Act or the rules of any of the societies participating in the amalgamation or transfer was not fulfilled or not fulfilled as regards that society.

(5) The Commission shall not be precluded from confirming an amalgamation or transfer of engagements by virtue only of the non-fulfilment of some relevant requirement of this Act or the rules of a society if it appears to the Commission that it could not have been material to the

members' decision about the amalgamation or transfer and the Commission gives a direction that the failure is to be disregarded for the purposes of this section.

(6) Where the Commission would be precluded from confirming an amalgamation or transfer of engagements by reason of any of the defects specified in paragraphs (*a*), (*b*), and (*c*) of subsection (4) above, it may direct any building society concerned—

(*a*) to take such steps to remedy the defect or defects, including the calling of a further meeting, as it specifies in the direction; and

(*b*) to furnish the Commission with evidence satisfying it that it has done so;

and, if the Commission is satisfied that the steps have been taken and the defect or defects has or have been substantially remedied, the Commission shall confirm the amalgamation or transfer; but, if it is not so satisfied, it shall refuse its confirmation.

(7) The Commission shall not confirm an amalgamation of or transfer of engagements between any two building societies one of which does not have a qualifying asset holding and is, for the purposes of this subsection, of disproportionate size in relation to the other unless the Commission is satisfied that, as regards the smaller society, the amalgamation or transfer—

(*a*) has the requisite support of its members, or

(*b*) is desirable in order to protect the investments of shareholders and depositors.

(8) For the purposes of subsection (7) above—

(*a*) one society is of "disproportionate size" in relation to another if its total assets amount to less than one-eighth of the total assets of the other;

(*b*) "the requisite support", in relation to the members of a society, is constituted by the votes of not less than 20 per cent. of the members qualified to vote on a special resolution of the society cast in favour of the special resolution approving the terms of the amalgamation or transfer of engagements; and

(*c*) "total assets", in relation to a building society, means its total assets as shown in the latest balance sheet.

(9) Where more than two building societies propose an amalgamation or transfer of engagements and, by virtue of subsection (7)(*a*) above the Commission refuses to confirm the amalgamation or transfer because of the failure of the smaller of any two of the societies that are of disproportionate size to secure the requisite support, the Commission shall refuse to confirm the amalgamation or transfer in relation to the other societies participating in the amalgamation or transfer.

(10) A failure to comply with a relevant requirement of this Act or any rules of a society shall not invalidate an amalgamation or transfer of engagements; but, if a society fails without reasonable excuse to comply with such a requirement the society shall be liable on summary conviction to a fine not exceeding level 4 on the standard scale and so shall any officer who is also guilty of the offence.

(11) In this section "relevant requirement", with reference to this Act or the rules of a society, means a requirement of section 93 or 94 or this section or of Schedule 16 to this Act or of any rules prescribing the procedure to be followed by the society in approving or effecting an amalgamation or transfer of engagements.

DEFINITIONS
"central office": s.119(1).
"Commission": ss.1 and 119(1).
"disproportionate size": subs. (8).

"member": s.119(1).
"officer": s.119(1).
"qualifying asset holding": ss.118 and 119(1).
"relevant requirement": subs. (11).
"requisite support": subs. (8).
"shareholder and depositor": s.119(1).
"special resolution": s.119(1) and Sched. 2, para. 27.
"the standard scale": Criminal Justice Act 1982, s.37.
"total assets": subs. (8).

GENERAL NOTE
  This section gives effect to Sched. 16 and contains supplementary provisions with respect to amalgamations (see s.93) and transfers of engagements (see s.94). It should be read in conjunction with that Schedule and those provisions.

Subs. (4)
  This subsection prevents the Commission from confirming an amalgamation or transfer if it considers that:
  (*a*) some material information was not made available to all members eligible to vote;
  (*b*) the vote on a resolution approving an amalgamation or transfer does not represent the views of the members eligible to vote;
  (*c*) any relevant requirement was not fulfilled.
The subsection is designed to ensure that the Commission will consider whether the resolutions approving the amalgamation or transfer represent the informed views of the members generally, reached by proper procedure. If it seems to the Commission that that is not the case, it cannot confirm the amalgamation or transfer. Note that under subs. (5) the Commission has power to direct that a failure to observe a relevant requirement be disregarded if it appears to the Commission that the failure could not have been material to the members' decision (but see subs. (10) for a criminal penalty). Presumably, a failure to fulfil a relevant requirement of the Act or the rules which renders invalid some step in the procedure, such as non-accidental failure to give notice of the resolution to members entitled to such notice, cannot be disregarded, as the conditions would not have been satisfied in which the Commission could even consider whether to give its confirmation.

Subs. (6)
  Under this subsection, when the Commission cannot, in consequence of a defect specified in subs. (4), confirm an amalgamation or transfer, it may direct any society concerned to take such steps as the Commission specifies to remedy the relevant defect or defects and to furnish the Commission with evidence satisfying it that the society has done so. If the Commission is satisfied that the defects have been substantially remedied, it may then confirm the amalgamation or transfer.

Subss. (7) and (8)
  These subsections are intended to offer a relatively small society some protection against the unwanted advances of a larger society. They should be considered together with Part II of Sched. 16, which obliges a society to give notice to its members of merger proposals (*i.e.* proposals for amalgamation or transfer) which have been received. By these two sets of provisions, the Act seeks to balance two possibly conflicting policies:
  (*a*) the policy of ensuring that the board of a society does not reject merger proposals out of hand, without notice to the members and contrary to their interests, for reasons such as personality differences between two boards or the fear of losing office;
  (*b*) the policy of ensuring that the energies of small societies are not continually diverted to the task of considering, advising members about and fighting off unwanted and unnecessary merger proposals.
Part II of Sched. 16 results from the first policy, which is discussed in more detail in the notes to that Schedule. These subsections result from the second policy. The aim is to make small local societies a less attractive target to large societies looking for a few extra branch offices or some additional resources, by imposing additional requirements which must be satisfied before a merger can be confirmed in cases in which one society is of "disproportionate size" in relation to the other within the meaning of subs. (8)(*a*).
  Those requirements are:
  (*a*) that the merger receives votes in favour from not less than 20 per cent. of the members qualified to vote on a special resolution; or

(b) that the Commission is satisfied that the merger is desirable in order to protect the interests of shareholders and depositors.

As to (a), such levels of support from the members of the smaller society are unlikely to be forthcoming unless the large society is making a genuinely advantageous offer. It will presumably be significantly harder to obtain such support if the board of the smaller society opposes the merger. Large societies will thus be discouraged from proceeding where the proposals are not agreed by the board of the smaller society. As to (b), it seems unlikely that this requirement would be satisfied if the sole concern of the large society was to obtain extra branches or additional reserves.

It seems to be implicit in subs. (7) that the large society will have a qualifying asset holding within the meaning of s.118 (currently total commercial assets of £100 million or more).

Subs. (9)

This subsection provides that where more than two societies propose an amalgamation or transfer but one of them is of disproportionate size (as defined in subs. (8)(a)) in relation to another and the requisite support cannot be obtained, the Commission shall refuse to confirm the whole proposed merger. This seems sensible, because clearly any merger excluding the small society would not be that in respect of which members voted.

Subs. (10)
Level 4. Currently £1,000.

Mergers: compensation for loss of office and bonuses to members

96.—(1) The terms of an amalgamation of or transfer of engagements between building societies may include provision for compensation to be paid by a society to or in respect of any director or other officer of that or any other society for loss of office or diminution of emoluments attributable to the amalgamation or transfer, but the provision must be authorised as follows, that is to say—

(a) except in so far as paragraph (b) below applies, the provision for such compensation to be paid by a society must be approved by the society by a resolution passed as a special resolution, not being the resolution required by section 93(2)(c) or 94(2) for the approval of the other terms of the amalgamation or transfer;

(b) if regulations are made under subsection (2) below authorising payments of such compensation within prescribed limits and the provision for such compensation includes only payments of amounts not exceeding the prescribed limits, the passing of the special resolution approving the terms of the amalgamation or transfer is sufficient authority for their payment.

(2) The Commission, with the consent of the Treasury, may by regulations authorise payments by building societies of compensation to directors or other officers for loss of office or diminution of emoluments attributable to amalgamations of, or transfers of engagements between, societies subject to limits specified in or determinable under the regulations and the regulations may make different provision for different classes of person.

(3) Nothing in subsection (1) or (2) above prevents a director or other officer from receiving payments from societies which, in the aggregate, exceed any limit applicable to him under subsection (2) above if the excess payment is included in provision approved as required by subsection (1)(a) above; but if any payment is received which has not been authorised under paragraph (a) or (b) of that subsection it shall be repaid.

(4) The terms of an amalgamation of, or transfer of engagements between, building societies may include provision for part of the funds of one or more of the participating societies to be distributed in consideration of the amalgamation or transfer among any of the members of the

participating societies, but the provision must be authorised as follows, that is to say—

    (a) subject to paragraph (b) below, the provision for such a distribution by a society shall not exceed the limits prescribed by regulations under subsection (5) below and the distribution must be approved by the special resolution giving the approval of the society to the terms of the amalgamation or transfer;

    (b) if the provision for such a distribution by a society exceeds the prescribed limits, it must be approved by the special resolution of that society and each of the other societies participating in the amalgamation or transfer by which each approved the terms of the amalgamation or transfer.

(5) The Commission, with the consent of the Treasury, shall by regulations authorise distributions of funds to members by building societies participating in amalgamations or transfers of engagements subject to limits specified in or determinable under the regulations and the regulations may make different provision for different circumstances.

(6) Where the terms of a transfer of engagements include provision for a distribution of the funds of the society transferring or the society undertaking the engagements and the society undertaking the engagements applies to the Commission for its consent to the society's approving the transfer by a resolution of the board of directors instead of a special resolution of the society, the Commission shall not give its consent unless it is satisfied that the distribution proposed to be made by each society will not exceed the prescribed limits.

(7) The power to make regulations under subsection (2) or (5) above is exercisable by statutory instrument which shall be subject to annulment in pursuance of a resolution of either House of Parliament.

(8) In this section—

    "compensation" includes the provision of benefits in kind;

    "distribution of funds" with reference to bonuses paid to members, includes distribution by means of a special rate of interest available to members for a limited period;

    "loss of office" includes, in relation to a director or other officer of a building society holding office in a subsidiary of that society or in an associated body by virtue of his position in that society, the loss of that office;

    "prescribed" with reference to limits on compensation or on distributions of assets, means prescribed by regulations under subsection (2) or (5) above, as the case may be.

DEFINITIONS
"associated body": ss.18(17) and 119(1).
"Commission": ss.1 and 119(1).
"compensation": subs. (8).
"distribution of funds": subs. (8).
"loss of office": subs. (8).
"member": s.119(1).
"officer": s.119(1).
"prescribed": subs. (8).
"special resolution": s.119(1) and Sched. 2, para. 27.
"subsidiary": s.119(1); Companies Act 1985, s.736.

GENERAL NOTE
Broadly speaking, the purpose of this section is to ensure that an amalgamation (see s.93) or transfer of engagements (see s.94) is not used as an occasion for the payment of substantial sums to the officers or members of a participating society without the proposals for that payment having received careful scrutiny.

Payment to any director or officer of a society of compensation for loss of office or diminution of emoluments is tackled in subss. (1) to (3). Under subs. (1), the terms of an amalgamation or transfer may permit such compensation to be paid by a society to any director or officer of that or any other society, provided that the relevant term is duly authorised.

In the absence of any regulations prescribing compensation limits, or if the sum payable exceeds any limits there may be, the authority required is a special resolution approving the payment in addition to the requisite transfer resolutions (subs. (1)(*a*)). If the Commission exercises its power under subs. (2) to make regulations for compensation with certain limits, and the proposed compensation is within those limits, the requisite transfer resolutions are sufficient authority themselves (subs. (1)(*b*)).

Subs. (3) covers the case where a director or officer is to receive compensation from more than one society. There is no difficulty if no regulations have been made; an additional special resolution will be required from each paying society under subs. (1). Similarly, there is no difficulty if regulations have been made and the total compensation does not exceed the prescribed limit; no additional resolution is required under subs. (1). The problem arises if the total exceeds the prescribed limit. Under subs. (3), the excess over the prescribed limit must be authorised by an additional special resolution and if not so authorised must be repaid. Presumably it will be necessary during the negotiations for the amalgamation or transfer to decide which society or societies is or are to be treated as paying the excess.

Note that, under subs. (8), "compensation" includes benefits in kind and "loss of office" includes loss of office in a subsidiary or other associated body.

Subss. (4) to (6) tackle the matter of distribution of funds to members. Again, different requirements are imposed for the authorisation of a distribution, depending upon whether or not prescribed limits will be exceeded. Subs. (5), however, unlike subs. (2), which is permissive only, provides that the Commission *shall* make regulations. Where the distribution does not exceed the prescribed limits, it must be approved by the society making the distribution by the special resolution approving the terms of the amalgamation or transfer: subs. (4) (*a*). Where the distribution exceeds the prescribed limits, it must be approved by each participating society by the special resolution approving the terms of the amalgamation or transfer: subs. (4)(*b*). Note, however, that under subs. (6), where on a transfer of engagements the transferee society applies to proceed by resolution of the board of directors and not by special resolution, the Commission may not give its consent unless it is satisfied that the distribution proposed to be made by each society will not exceed the prescribed limits.

Note that, under subs. (8), "distribution of funds" includes a distribution by means of a special interest rate available to members for a limited period.

Transfer of business to commercial company

Transfer of business to commercial company

97.—(1) A building society may, in accordance with this section and the other applicable provisions of this Act, transfer the whole of its business to a company (its "successor").

(2) The applicable provisions of this Act other than this section are section 98, section 99, section 100, section 101, section 102, paragraph 30 of Schedule 2 and Schedule 17.

(3) The successor may be a company formed by the society wholly or partly for the purpose of assuming and conducting the society's business in its place or an existing company which is to assume and conduct the society's business in its place; and for the purposes of the transfer the society may, notwithstanding anything in section 18, form, or acquire and hold shares in, a company whose objects extend to the carrying on of activities which the building society has no power to carry on.

(4) In order to transfer its business to its successor a building society must—

(*a*) in the case of a specially formed company, secure that it is formed having articles of association with the requisite protective provisions;

(*b*) agree conditionally with its successor in a transfer agreement on the terms of the transfer which, in so far as they are regulated terms, comply with section 99, section 100 and transfer regulations;

(*c*) approve the transfer and the terms of the transfer by the requisite transfer resolutions, that is to say, resolutions passed by the members of the society in accordance with paragraph 30 of Schedule 2 to this Act; and

(*d*) obtain the confirmation of the Commission of the transfer and its terms.

(5) In so far as the transfer agreement made between the society and its successor provides for rights to be conferred on members or officers of the society, whether or not in pursuance of regulated terms, the members or officers shall, in relation to those provisions, be treated as if they had been parties to the agreement and the rights shall be enforceable accordingly.

(6) If the Commission confirms the transfer under section 98 then, on the vesting date, all the property, rights and liabilities of the society making the transfer (whether or not capable of being transferred or assigned), except any shares in its successor, shall by virtue of this subsection and in accordance with transfer regulations be transferred to and vested in the successor.

(7) Where a building society continues to hold shares in its successor after the vesting date, the consideration (if any) for the disposal of the shares together with any other property, rights or liabilities of the society acquired or incurred after that date shall, by virtue of this subsection, be transferred to and vested in its successor on the date specified for its dissolution under subsection (10) below.

(8) A building society which has obtained confirmation of the transfer of its business shall send to the central office notice of the date which is to be the vesting date and shall do so not later than seven days before that date; and the central office shall record the date and, if a later date is notified under subsection (10) below, that date, in the public file of the society.

(9) Except where notice is given under subsection (10) below, a building society which, under this section, transfers its business to its successor shall, by virtue of this subsection, be dissolved on the vesting date; but the transfer effected by subsection (6) above shall be deemed to have been effected immediately before the dissolution.

(10) A building society may, for the purpose of facilitating the disposal of shares in its successor, include in the notice of the vesting date under subsection (8) above notice of a later date for the dissolution of the society; and if it does so, the society shall by virtue of this subsection be dissolved on that date instead of the vesting date, but the transfer effected by subsection (7) above shall be deemed to have been effected immediately before the dissolution.

(11) As from the vesting date, a society which has given notice under subsection (10 above shall cease to transact any business expect such as is necessary for the purpose of securing the disposal of the society's holding of shares in its successor.

(12) In this section, and the other applicable provisions of this Act—

"company" means a company within the meaning of the Companies Act 1985 or the Companies (Northern Ireland) Order 1986 which is a public company limited by shares; and a company is a "specially formed" company if it is formed by a building society (and by no others than its nominees) for the purpose of assuming and conducting its business in its place and is an "existing" company if it is a company carrying on business as a going concern on the date of the transfer agreement;

"confirmation", in relation to a transfer, means the confirmation of the Commission required by subsection (4)(*d*) above;

"regulated terms" means any terms of a transfer agreement which are regulated terms under section 99, section 100 or section 102;

"the requisite protective provisions" means the provisions required to be made by section 101(2);

"the requisite transfer resolutions" has the meaning given by subsection (4)(c) above;

"successor", in relation to a building society, has the meaning given by subsection (1) above;

"transfer agreement" means the agreement required by subsection (4)(b) above and, in relation to it, "conditionally" means conditional on the approval of the transfer by the requisite transfer resolutions and on confirmation of the transfer;

"transfer of business" means the transfer of the business of a building society to its successor under this section and "transfer" has a corresponding meaning;

"transfer regulations" means regulations under section 102; and

"the vesting date" means the date specified in or determined under the transfer agreement as the vesting date for the purposes of subsection (6) above.

DEFINITIONS
"central office": s.119(1).
"Commission": ss.1 and 119(1).
"company": subs. (12).
"confirmation": subs. (12).
"existing company": subs. (12).
"member": s.119(1).
"officer": s.119(1).
"regulated terms": subs. (12).
"requisite protective provisions": subs. (12).
"requisite transfer resolutions": subs. (12).
"specially formed company": subs. (12).
"successor": subss. (1) and (12)
"transfer agreement": subss. (4) and (12).
"transfer of business": subs. (12).
"transfer regulations": subs. (12).
"vesting date": subs. (12).

GENERAL NOTE
This section is one of the most controversial sections in the Act. It empowers a building society, on satisfying the various requirements imposed by ss.97 to 102, Scheds. 2 and 17 and transfer regulations, to transfer its business to a commercial company: either an existing company or one specially formed for the purpose (subs. (3)). The question of principle whether or not such a transfer should be permitted was debated at length at all stages of the Bill's progress through Parliament. The Government view, now embodied in the Act, was that, as a building society is a mutual institution, it should have power to transfer its business to a commercial company if the members so wished, but in order to effect such a transfer, which would involve radical changes for members, the society should be able to demonstrate a high level of support from members. The attraction of such a transfer is, of course, that a company is not confined by the "statutory straitjacket" worn by a society (see notes to s.5); it can pursue any lawful activity permitted by its objects.
"Company" means a public company limited by shares: subs. (12).

Subs. (4)
This subsection lays down the basic requirements for a transfer. They are:
(a) where the company is a specially formed company, the society must secure that it is formed having articles of association with the protective provisions required by s.101 (restricting outside investment in the new company for five years);
(b) the society must make a transfer agreement with its successor which (i) complies with ss.99 and 100 and transfer regulations made under s.102 and (ii) is conditional upon the approval of the transfer by the necessary resolutions and on confirmation;

(c) the society must approve the transfer and its terms by resolutions in accordance with Sched. 2, para. 30; and

(d) the society must obtain the confirmation of the Commission (as to which see s.98 and Sched. 17, Part II).

Note that the resolutions required under Sched. 2, para. 30, differ according to whether the successor is a specially formed, or an existing, company. In both cases there must be two resolutions approving the transfer, one a borrowing members' resolution within Sched. 2, para. 29, and the other a shareholders' resolution. In the case of a specially formed successor, the shareholders' resolution must be a special resolution passed on a poll on which not less than 20 per cent. of those qualified to vote did in fact vote. In the case of an existing successor, the shareholders' resolution must be a special resolution and must be passed either by not less than 50 per cent. of those qualified to vote or by the holders of shares representing not less than 90 per cent. of the total value of the shares of those entitled to vote. Experience suggests that it will be very difficult to get even 20 per cent. of the members to vote; the prospects of a transfer to an existing company must be remote indeed.

Subs. (5)

This subsection enables members and officers of the society to enforce rights conferred on them by the transfer agreement as if they were parties.

Subss. (6) to (10)

These subsections govern the transfer of property, rights and liabilities to the company and dissolution of the society. The basic principle is that all property, rights and liabilities of the society should be transferred to its successor on the vesting date specified in or determined under the transfer agreement (subs. (6)). That principle does not apply, however, to the society's shares (if any) in its successor (subs. (6)) which must nevertheless be disposed of before the society is dissolved (*c.f.* s.100(11)). It would have been possible to provide that the society's shares must be disposed of before the vesting date, so that that date could always be the date of dissolution; but such a provision might have had an adverse effect on the consideration realisable on a disposal. The section therefore empowers a society, when giving notice to the central office of the vesting date in accordance with subs. (8), to include a notice for the purpose of facilitating the disposal of shares that the dissolution date will be later (subs. (10)). If such a notice is given the society may hold those shares after the vesting date and will be dissolved on the dissolution date so specified (subs. (10)). If no such notice is given, the society is dissolved on the vesting date (subs. (9)). Where the society is still holding shares in its successor at the vesting date, the subsequent dissolution date specified in accordance with subs. (10) serves also as a supplementary vesting date on which the consideration (if any) for the shares and any other property, rights or liabilities incurred since the vesting date is transferred to the successor (subs. (7)).

As mentioned above, the successor will be a public limited company and shares in it may be disposed of accordingly, subject, as regards a specially formed company, to the provisions of s.101.

S.100 makes provision for regulating the terms in the transfer agreement governing what happens to shares in the society.

Transfers of business: supplementary provisions

98.—(1) Part I of Schedule 17 to this Act shall have effect for imposing on a building society proposing to transfer its business to a company an obligation to issue statements to its members relating to the proposed transfer.

(2) Where application is made to the Commission for confirmation of a transfer of business to a company it shall, except as provided in subsections (3) to (5) below, confirm the transfer; and Part II of that Schedule shall have effect with respect to the procedure on an application for such confirmation.

(3) Subject to subsection (4) below, the Commission shall not confirm a transfer of business if it considers that—

(a) some information material to the members' decision about the transfer was not made available to all the members eligible to vote; or (*b*) the vote on any resolution approving the transfer does not represent the views of the members eligible to vote; or

(*c*) there is a substantial risk that the successor will not become or, as the case may be, remain a recognised bank or licensed institution for the purposes of the Banking Act 1979: or

(*d*) some relevant requirement of this Act or the rules of the society was not fulfilled.

(4) The Commission shall not be precluded from confirming a transfer of business by virtue only of the non-fulfilment of some relevant requirement of this Act or the rules of the society if it appears to the Commission that it could not have been material to the members' decision about the transfer and the Commission gives a direction that the failure is to be disregarded for the purposes of this section.

(5) Where the Commission would be precluded from confirming a transfer of business by reason of any of the defects specified in paragraphs (*a*), (*b*), (*c*) and (*d*) of subsection (3) above, it may direct the society making the transfer—

(*a*) to take such steps to remedy the defect or defects as it specifies in the direction; and

(*b*) to furnish the Commission with evidence satisfying it that it has done so;

and, if the Commission is satisfied that the steps have been taken and the defect or defects has or have been substantially remedied, the Commission shall confirm the transfer; but, if it is not so satisfied, it shall refuse its confirmation.

(6) The steps that a society may be required under subsection (5)(*a*) above to take include the calling of a further meeting, securing the variation of the transfer agreement or securing the alteration of the approved protective provisions of the articles of association of its successor.

(7) A failure to comply with a relevant requirement of this Act or the rules of a building society shall not invalidate a transfer of the business of the society; but, if a society fails without reasonable excuse to comply with such a requirement, the society shall be liable on summary conviction to a fine not exceeding level 4 on the standard scale and so shall any officer who is also guilty of the offence.

(8) In this section "relevant requirement", with reference to this Act or the rules of a society, means a requirement of the applicable provisions of this Act or of any rules prescribing the procedure to be followed by the society in approving the transfer and its terms.

DEFINITIONS
"Commission": ss.1 and 119(1).
"company": s.97(12).
"licensed institution": Banking Act 1979, s.50(1).
"member": s.119(1).
"officer": s.119(1).
"protective provisions": see s.101.
"recognised bank": Banking Act 1979, s.50(1).
"relevant requirement": subs. (8).
"the standard scale": Criminal Justice Act 1982, s.37.
"transfer agreement": s.97(12).

GENERAL NOTE
This section gives effect to Sched. 17 and contains supplementary provisions with respect to a transfer of business to a commercial company under s.97. Subss. (3) to (6) and (7) to (8) are very similar in terms to s.95(4) to (6) and (10) and (11) respectively and reference should be made to the notes to that section, as indicated below.

Subs. (3)

This subsection specifies the grounds preventing the Commission from confirming a transfer of business. The grounds are the same as those specified in s.95(4), save that here there is an additional ground: that there is a substantial risk that the successor will not become or remain a recognised bank or licensed institution. Of course, if that risk materialised, the company could not carry on the transferred business consistently with banking legislation. The purpose of the subsection, like the purpose of s.95(4), is to ensure that the Commission will consider whether the resolutions approving the transfer expressed the informed views of the members generally, reached by proper procedure and (under this subsection) whether the company is likely to be able to carry on the business.

Subs. (4)

This subsection gives the Commission a dispensing power in respect of failure to observe a relevant requirement: *cf.* s.95(5) and the notes thereto.

Subss. (5) and (6)

These subsections enable the Commission to give directions to the society with a view to remedying any defects preventing the Commission from confirming the transfer: *cf.* s.95(6) and the notes thereto.

Subs. (7)

Level 4. Currently £1,000.

Regulated terms: compensation for loss of office, etc.

99.—(1) Subject to subsections (2) and (3) below, the terms of a transfer of business by a building society to the company which is to be its successor may include provision for compensation to be paid by the society or the company to or in respect of any director or other officer of the society for loss of office or diminution of emoluments attributable to the transfer.

(2) Any such provision must be authorised so far as the society is concerned as follows, that is to say—

   (a) except in so far as paragraph (*b*) below applies, the provision must be approved by a resolution passed as a special resolution, not being one of the requisite transfer resolutions;

   (b) if regulations are made under subsection (3) below authorising payments of such compensation within prescribed limits and the provision for such compensation includes only payments of amounts not exceeding the prescribed limits, the passing of the requisite transfer resolutions is sufficient authority for their payment.

(3) The Commission, with the consent of the Treasury, may by regulations authorise payments of compensation to directors or other officers attributable to transfers of business under section 97 subject to limits specified in or determinable under the regulations and the regulations may make different provision for different classes of persons.

(4) Nothing in subsection (2) or (3) above prevents a director or other officer from receiving payments which, in the aggregate, exceed any limit applicable to him under either of those subsections if the excess payment is included in provision approved as required by subsection (2)(*a*) above; but if any payment is received which has not been authorised under paragraph (*a*) or (*b*) of that subsection it shall be repaid.

(5) The power to make regulations under subsection (3) above is exercisable by statutory instrument which shall be subject to annulment in pursuance of a resolution of either House of Parliament.

(6) In this section—

   "compensation" includes the provision of benefits in kind;

   "loss of office" includes, in relation to a director or other officer of a building society holding office in a subsidiary of that society or in an associated body by virtue of his position in that society, the loss of that office; and

"prescribed", with reference to limits on compensation, means prescribed by regulations under subsection (3) above;

and any terms of a transfer of business to which subsection (2) or regulations under subsection (3) above apply are regulated terms for the purposes of section 97.

DEFINITIONS
"associated body": ss.18(17) and 119(1).
"Commission": ss.1 and 119(1).
"compensation": subs. (6).
"loss of office": subs. (6).
"officer": s.119(1).
"prescribed": subs. (6).
"requisite transfer resolutions": s.97(4) and (12).
"special resolution": s.119(1) and Sched. 2, para. 27.
"subsidiary": s.119(1); Companies Act 1985, s.736.
"successor": s.97(1).

GENERAL NOTE
The purpose of this section is to ensure that a transfer of business to a commercial company is not used as an occasion for the payment of substantial sums to the officers of a society without the proposals for that payment having received careful scrutiny. It is therefore very similar in object to s.96 and accordingly is similar in terms also.

Under subs. (1), compensation for loss of office or diminution of emoluments may be paid by the society or the company to directors or other officers of the society, but if compensation is to be made by the society, it must be duly authorised. In the absence of any regulations prescribing compensation limits, or if the sum payable exceeds any limits there may be, the authority required is a special resolution approving the payment in addition to the requisite transfer resolutions (subs. (2)). If the Commission exercises its power under subs. (3) to make regulations for compensation with certain limits, and the proposed compensation is within those limits, the requisite transfer resolutions are sufficient authority themselves (subs. (2)).

Subs. (4) is not easy to follow. It is thought, however, that it deals with the case where an officer is to receive compensation both from the company and from the society and the total compensation may exceed the prescribed limit or such higher limit as has been authorised by an additional special resolution. It might be argued that the excess is part of the company's contribution, but in view of this subsection, it seems that the safest course would be for the society to pass a resolution setting out the total sums to be paid and by whom they are to be paid, in any case in which the total compensation exceeds any prescribed limit there may be.

Note that under subs. (6), "compensation" includes benefits in kind and "loss of office" includes loss of office in a subsidiary or other associated body. Note also that compensation provisions are "regulated terms" for the purposes of s.97.

Regulated terms etc: distributions and share rights

100.—(1) Subject to subsections (2) to (10) below, the terms of a transfer of business by a building society to the company which is to be its successor may include provision for part of the funds of the society or its successor to be distributed among, or other rights in relation to shares in the successor conferred on, members of the society, in consideration of the transfer.

(2) The terms of a transfer of a society's business must—

(a) require its successor to assume as from the vesting date a liability to every qualifying member of the society as in respect of a deposit made with the successor corresponding in amount to the value of the qualifying shares held by him in the society; and

(b) confer a right, subject to subsection (7) below, to a distribution of funds, whether of the society or its successor, by way of bonus on every qualifying member of the society equal to the relevant proportion of the value of the qualifying shares held by him in the society; and

(c) in a case where the successor is a specially formed company, confer a right on every qualifying member of the society to a priority liquidation distribution by its successor calculated in the prescribed manner so as to represent the extent of his deposit under paragraph (a) above and secured on the property or undertaking of the successor.

(3) For the purposes of the liabilities assumed under subsection (2)(a) above by the society's successor, a member is a qualifying member if he held shares in the society on the day immediately preceding the vesting date and his qualifying shares are those held by him on that day.

(4) For the purposes of the rights conferred under subsection (2)(b) above on members of the society, a member is a qualifying member if he held shares in the society on the qualifying day and was not eligible to vote on the requisite transfer resolution, his qualifying shares are those held by him on that day and the relevant proportion is the proportion which (as shown in the latest balance sheet of the society) the society's reserves bear to its total liability to its members in respect of shares.

(5) For the purposes of the rights conferred under subsection (2)(c) above on former members of the society, a member is a qualifying member if he held shares in the society on the qualifying day, was eligible to vote on the requisite resolution and is a depositor with its successor.

(6) For the purposes of subsection (2)(c) above,—

(a) a right to a liquidation distribution by a society's successor is a right to a distribution of its assets in the event of its being wound up;

(b) the right shall confer priority in the distribution of the assets over all other creditors and members of the company other than those creditors the debts to whom are preferential debts for the purposes of the Insolvency Act 1986 or Article 570 of the Companies (Northern Ireland) Order 1986; and

(c) "prescribed" means prescribed by transfer regulations.

(7) The Commission may, where it confirms a transfer of a society's business to an existing company, as it thinks fit having regard to what is equitable between the members of the society, direct that no bonus distribution of funds in pursuance of subsection (2)(b) above shall be made or that the amount distributed shall be such lesser amount as it provides for in the direction; and where the Commission gives a direction under this subsection no liability to make such a distribution shall arise or, as the case may be, that liability shall be discharged by payment of the lesser amount.

(8) Where, in connection with any transfer, rights are to be conferred on members of the society to acquire shares in priority to other subscribers, the right shall be restricted to those of its members who held shares in the society throughout the period of two years which expired with the qualifying day; and it is unlawful for any right in relation to shares to be conferred in contravention of this subsection.

(9) Where the successor is an existing company, any distribution of funds to members of the society, except for the distribution required by subsection (2)(b) above, shall only be made to those members who held shares in the society throughout the period of two years which expired with the qualifying day; and it is unlawful for any distribution to be made in contravention of the provisions of this subsection.

(10) The following restrictions apply to any distribution of funds, or any conferring of rights in relation to shares, in connection with the transfer of its business from the society to its successor where the successor is a company specially formed by the society, that is to say—

(a) no distribution shall be made except that required by subsection (2)(b) above; and

(b) where negotiable instruments acknowledging rights to shares are issued by the successor within the period of two years beginning with the vesting date, no such instruments shall be issued to former members of the society unless they are also issued, and on the same terms, to all other members of the company;

and it is unlawful for any distribution of funds to be made in contravention of the provisions of this subsection.

(11) Where the successor is a specially formed company, the terms of the transfer must include provision to secure that the society ceases to hold any shares in the successor by the date on which the society is to dissolve.

(12) Any terms of a transfer of business to which subsection (2), (8), (9), (10) or (11) above apply are regulated terms for the purposes of section 97.

(13) In subsections (4), (5), (8) and (9) above, "qualifying day" means the day specified in the transfer agreement as the qualifying day for the purposes of this subsection.

DEFINITIONS
"Commission": ss.1 and 119(1).
"deposit": s.119(1).
"existing company": s.97(12).
"member": s.119(1).
"prescribed": subs. (6).
"priority liquidation distribution": see subs. (6).
"qualifying day": subs. (13).
"relevant proportion": subs. (4).
"requisite transfer resolutions": s.97(4) and (12).
"share": s.119(1).
"specially formed company": s.97(12).
"successor": s.97(1).
"vesting date": s.97(12).

GENERAL NOTE
This section contains detailed provisions governing the terms of a transfer of business to a commercial company in respect of the distribution of funds or rights in relation to shares in the successor company.

The first problem to be tackled is the question how the rights of shareholders in a building society are to be translated into rights in respect of a public company. The first part of the answer is to be found in subs. (2)(a) and subs. (3). The effect of those provisions, taken together, is to require the transfer agreement to include a term that every member of the society who held shares in the society on the day preceding the vesting date (which will be specified in the transfer agreement: see s.97(12)) will be treated as if he had a deposit with the successor of an amount equal to the value of his shareholding.

Thereafter the rights of members diverge according to whether they were or were not eligible to vote on the transfer resolutions and whether the successor is a specially formed or existing company. Subs. (2)(b), taken together with subs. (4), has the effect that a transfer agreement must further contain a term entitling every member who held shares on the "qualifying day" but who was not eligible to vote, to a distribution of funds by way of a bonus equal to the "relevant proportion" of the value of his shares on the qualifying day. "Qualifying day" means the day so specified in the transfer agreement and "relevant proportion" means the proportion, as shown in the latest balance sheet, borne by the society's reserves to its total liability to members in respect of shares. These provisions accordingly give an immediate benefit to members who were not eligible to vote (generally speaking, recent members or members with small shareholdings: see Sched. 2, para. 23). Note, however, that where the successor is an existing company, the Commission may, if it thinks fit having regard to what is equitable between members, direct that no such bonus distribution shall be made or that the distribution shall be of a lesser amount: subs. (7). It is not clear at this stage when and how that power is likely to be exercised. Note also that (i) where the successor is an existing company, no distribution of funds other than that under subs. (2)(*b*) shall be made except to members who held shares throughout the period of two years expiring on the qualifying day: subs. (9); (ii) where the successor is a specially formed company, no distribution of funds other than that under subs. (2)(*b*) shall be made: subs. (10).

Finally, under subs. (2)(*c*), taken together with subss. (5) and (6), a transfer agreement must contain a term, where the successor is a specially formed company, entitling every member who held shares on the qualifying day and who was eligible to vote on the transfer resolutions to priority in respect of that shareholding on the winding up of the successor company. The right is, of course, only available if the former member remains a depositor up to the time of the liquidation. The right gives priority over all other creditors and company members except creditors who are owed preferential debts within the meaning of s.386 of the Insolvency Act 1986 (in English law) *i.e.* fiscal liabilities, social security and pension scheme contributions and employees' remuneration. The amount in respect of which the right is granted will be calculated in accordance with regulations to be made by the Commission under s.102 so as to represent the extent of the deposit which the member is treated as having made under subs. (2)(*a*) and (3) of this section and will be secured on the property or undertaking of the successor.

The foregoing rights are the basic rights which must be given to members in a transfer agreement. Once those points have been covered, such further rights to a distribution of funds or in respect of shares in the successor as the society and the company may agree can be included, subject to the following:

(*a*) the restrictions on a distribution of funds contained in subss. (9) and (10) and noted above;

(*b*) the restriction that where rights are to be conferred on members to acquire shares in priority to other subscribers, the right shall be restricted to members who held shares throughout the period of two years ending on the qualifying day: subs. (8). The purpose of these restrictions (*i.e.* those in (*a*) and this restriction) is to minimise the risk of a sudden flow of investment into a particular society (and out of others) because of a rumour that that society is about to transfer its business to a company and there may be substantial bonuses for members. Under these provisions, only a limited class of members will receive such bonuses. The restriction should also help to allay fears that the directors of a society may in effect bribe members to vote for a transfer by the promise of substantial bonuses.

(*c*) the restriction, where the company is specially formed, that where negotiable instruments acknowledging rights to shares are issued by the successor within the period of two years beginning on the vesting date, no such instruments shall be issued to former members of the society unless they are also issued, on the same terms, to all other members of the company: subs. (10);

(*d*) the requirement that where the company is specially formed, the transfer must include provisions to secure that the society ceases to hold any shares in the successor by the date on which the society is to dissolve: subs. (11). *Cf.* the notes to s.97.

It is unlawful for any rights to be conferred or any distribution to be made in contravention of the prohibitions in subss. (8) to (10). Presumably, therefore, a member could not enforce the terms of an agreement which made such provision, notwithstanding the general right of enforcement given to members by s.97(5). In practice, the Commission would no doubt refuse to confirm a transfer if the agreement included such terms.

Note that terms to which subss. (2), (8), (9), (10) or (11) apply are regulated terms for the purposes of s.97: subs. (12).

Protective provisions for specially formed successors

101.—(1) No company specially formed by a building society to be its successor shall, at any time during the protective period—

(*a*) offer to the public, or allot or agree to allot with a view to their being offered for sale to the public, any shares in or debentures of the company, or

(*b*) allot or agree to allot any share in or debenture of the company, or

(*c*) register a transfer of shares in or debentures of the company,

if the effect of the offer, the allotment or the registration of the transfer would be that more shares or debentures than the permitted proportion would be held by, or by nominees for, any one person (other than the society).

(2) The articles of association of the company shall include provision such as will secure that the company does not offer the public, allot or register transfers of, shares or debentures in contravention of subsection (1) above and no alteration in those provisions may be made by the company during the protective period.

(3) Any provision (including any altered provision) of the company's articles of association which is to any extent inconsistent with subsection (1) above shall, to that extent, be void; and any allotment or registration of a transfer of shares or debentures in contravention of that subsection shall be void.

(4) The Bank of England, if it considers it desirable in the interests of the depositors and potential depositors of a successor to do so, may direct by notice to the successor that this section shall cease to apply to the successor.

(5) In subsections (1) to (3) above—

"the permitted proportion", in relation to shares in or debentures of the company, is 15 per cent. of, in the case of shares, the company's issued share capital and, in the case of debentures, the total indebtedness of the company on its debentures, as the case may be;

"the protective period" is the period beginning with the date of the company's incorporation and ending five years after the vesting date; and

"transfer", in relation to shares or debentures, does not include a transfer to a person to whom the right to any shares or debentures has been transmitted by operation of law;

and any expression used in those subsections and in the Companies Act 1985 or, as regards Northern Ireland, the Companies (Northern Ireland) Order 1986 has the same meaning in those subsections as in that Act or that Order.

DEFINITIONS

"permitted proportion": subs. (5).
"protective period": subs. (5).
"specially formed": s.97(12).
"successor": s.97(1).
"transfer": subs. (5).
"vesting date": s.97(12).

GENERAL NOTE

The purpose of this section, put broadly, is to give a specially formed company which has taken over a society's business five years of assured independent life in which to establish itself before any single person can acquire a substantial interest, whether with or without a view to a take-over. That purpose is carried into effect as follows:

(a) by subs. (1), the company may not make an offer or allotment or register a transfer if the effect would be that more than 15 per cent. of the issued share capital, or total indebtedness on debentures, would be concentrated in the hands of, or in the hands of nominees for, a single shareholder or debenture holder;

(b) by subs. (2), the company's articles must include provisions to ensure that the company does not make an offer or allotment or register a transfer in contravention of subs. (1) and no alteration in those articles may be made during the protective period (*i.e.,* from the date of incorporation to the expiration of five years from the vesting date specified in the transfer agreement);

(c) by subs. (3), any provision of the articles which is inconsistent with subs. (1) shall, to that extent, be void and any allotment or registration of a transfer in contravention of that section shall also be void.

The Bank of England has a discretion under subs. (4) to direct that this section shall cease to apply to the successor if it considers it desirable in the interests of depositors and potential depositors to do so.

Transfer regulations

102.—(1) The Commission, with the consent of the Treasury, may, by transfer regulations under this section, make provision regulating transfers of business under section 97.

(2) Transfer regulations may, in particular—

(*a*) make provision for and in connection with the transition from regulation by and under this Act to regulation by and under the Companies Act 1985 or, as regards Northern Ireland, the Companies (Northern Ireland) Order 1986 and the Banking Act 1979;

(*b*) make provision for the treatment, in the hands of companies taking such transfers, of the property, rights and liabilities transferred and for the modification of any enactment in its application to property, rights and liabilities so transferred;

(*c*) make provision for the purposes of and incidental to section 100 and section 101.

The power to make transfer regulations is exercisable by statutory instrument which shall be subject to annulment in pursuance of a resolution of either House of Parliament.

(4) Any terms of a transfer of business to which transfer regulations apply are regulated terms for the purposes of section 97.

DEFINITION
  "Commission": ss.1 and 119(1).

GENERAL NOTE
  This section empowers the Commission to make transfer regulations. From the list of matters specified in subs.(2) as matters which may in particular be covered, it seems that the regulations are envisaged as providing the detailed machinery for the transition from the building society regime to the company regime. Note that any terms of a transfer agreement to which transfer regulations apply are regulated terms for the purposes of s.97.

Cancellation of registration

Cancellation of registration

103.—(1) Where the central office is satisfied, with respect to a building society—

(*a*) that the society has been dissolved by virtue of section 93(5), 94(10), 97(9) or 97(10), or

(*b*) that the society has been wound up under the applicable winding up legislation and dissolved,

the central office shall cancel the registration of the society.

(2) Where the central office is satisfied, with respect to a building society—

(*a*) that a certificate of incorporation has been obtained for the society by fraud or mistake and that the society is not an authorised society, or

(*b*) that the society has ceased to exist,

the central office may cancel the registration of the society.

(3) Without prejudice to subsection (2) above, the central office may, if it thinks fit, cancel the registration of a building society at the request of the society, evidenced in such manner as the central office may direct.

(4) Before cancelling the registration of a building society under subsection (2) above, the central office shall give to the society not less than two months' previous notice, specifying briefly the grounds of the proposed cancellation.

(5) Where the registration of a building society is cancelled under subsection (2) above, the society may appeal to—

(*a*) the High Court, where the principal office of the society is situated in England and Wales or in Northern Ireland, or

(*b*) the Court of Session, where that office is situated in Scotland,

and on any such appeal the High Court or the Court of Session, as the case may be, if it thinks it just to do so, may set aside the cancellation.

(6) Where the registration of a building society is cancelled under subsection (2) or (3) above, then, subject to the right of appeal conferred by subsection (5) above, the society, so far as it continues to exist, shall cease to be a society incorporated under this Act (and accordingly shall cease to be a building society within the meaning of this Act).

(7) Subsection (6) above shall have effect in relation to a building society without prejudice to any liability actually incurred by the society; and any such liability may be enforced against the society as if the cancellation had not taken place.

(8) Any cancellation of the registration of a building society under this section shall be effected in writing signed by the central office.

(9) As soon as practicable after the cancellation of the registration of a society under this section the central office shall cause notice thereof to be published in the London Gazette, the Edinburgh Gazette or the Belfast Gazette according to the situation of the society's principal office, and if it thinks fit, in one or more newspapers.

DEFINITIONS

"applicable winding up legislation": s.90(3).
"central office": s.119(1).
"notice": s.119(1).

GENERAL NOTE

This section sets out the circumstances in which a society's registration must, or may, be cancelled by the central office and the effects of cancellation. It is derived largely from ss.113 to 115 of the 1962 Act. Those sections, however, included a power to suspend registration which is not included here. It is thought that that difference arises from the fact that s.113 of the 1962 Act included additional grounds for cancellation or suspension which, under the present Act, would bring into play the Commission's powers of control in Part VI. Suspension of registration is accordingly no longer a necessary sanction; nor is it now appropriate, having regard to the circumstances leading to cancellation which are now specified.

They are:

(*a*) that the society has been dissolved, either following an amalgamation (s.93(5)) or a transfer of engagements (s.94(10)) or a transfer of business (s.97(9) or (10)) or a winding up under the winding up legislation (see that legislation as amended by Sched.15). In any such case, cancellation is mandatory. See subs.(1);

(*b*) that a certificate of incorporation has been obtained by fraud or mistake and the society is not an authorised society, or that the society has ceased to exist. In any such case, cancellation is discretionary. See subs.(2);

(*c*) that the society has requested cancellation. Again, cancellation is discretionary. See subs.(3).

Where the central office is contemplating cancellation under subs.(2), it must give the society at least two months' previous notice, specifying briefly the proposed grounds for cancellation: subs.(4). If the cancellation is thereafter effected, subs.(5) gives a right of appeal to the High Court.

Once a registration is cancelled, then, subject to the right of appeal, the society ceases to be an incorporated society or a society within the meaning of this Act: subs.(6). Any liability it may have actually incurred, however, is not discharged, but may be enforced against the society as if cancellation had not taken place: subs.(7).

PART XI

MISCELLANEOUS AND SUPPLEMENTARY
AND CONVEYANCING SERVICES

Miscellaneous and supplementary

Power to amend, etc. to assimilate to company law

104.—(1) If, on any modification of the statutory provisions in force in Great Britain or Northern Ireland relating to companies, it appears to the Treasury to be expedient to modify the relevant provisions of this Act for the purpose of assimilating the law relating to companies and the law relating to building societies, the Treasury may, by order, make such modifications of the relevant provisions of this Act as they think appropriate for that purpose.

(2) The "relevant provisions of this Act" are the following provisions as for the time being in force, that is to say—

(*a*) so much of Part VI as relates to investigations or inspections;

(*b*) the provisions of Part VII (management);

(*c*) the provisions of Part VIII (accounts and audit); and

(*d*) so much of Part X as relates to winding up.

(3) The power conferred by subsection (1) above includes power to modify the relevant provisions of this Act so as to—

(*a*) confer power to make orders, regulations, rules or other subordinate legislation;

(*b*) create criminal offences; or

(*c*) provide for the charging of fees but not any charge in the nature of taxation.

(4) An order under this section may—

(*a*) make consequential amendments of or repeals in other provisions of this Act; or

(*b*) make such transitional or saving provisions as appear to the Treasury to be necessary or expedient.

(5) The power to make an order under this section is exercisable by statutory instrument but no such order shall be made unless a draft of it has been laid before and approved by a resolution of each House of Parliament.

(6) In this section—

"modification" includes any additions and, as regards modifications of the statutory provisions relating to companies, any modification whether effected by any future Act or by an instrument made after the passing of this Act under an Act whenever passed; and

"statutory provisions" includes the provisions of any instrument made under an Act.

DEFINITIONS
"modification": subs. (6).
"relevant provisions of this Act": subs. (2).
"statutory provisions": subs. (6).

GENERAL NOTE
This section gives the Treasury a useful power to modify the "relevant provisions" of this Act in order to assimilate company law and building society law following any future modifications to company law. The relevant provisions are set out in subs. (2) and are: provisions relating to investigations or inspections; management; accounts and audit; and winding up. The word "modifications" must imply a change which is fairly restricted in scope and certainly not one which involves a significant change in policy.
Note the following limits on the power:

(*a*) any order is subject to affirmative resolution procedure in Parliament (see subs. (5)) and is therefore much more likely to receive real consideration than if it were subject to negative resolution procedure;

(*b*) no order may provide for a charge in the nature of taxation: see subs. (3)(*c*).

Limited power to anticipate future statutory instrument powers

105.—(1) This section has effect as regards any power conferred under any provision of this Act on building societies or building societies of any description by—

(*a*) an instrument a draft of which has to be approved by a resolution of each House of Parliament before it can be made, or

(*b*) an instrument which is subject to annulment in pursuance of a resolution of either House of Parliament and which defers its operation until a future date;

and in this section "the anticipation date" is, in the case of an instrument falling within paragraph (*a*), the date on which either House approves the draft and, in the case of an instrument falling within paragraph (*b*), the date on which it was laid before Parliament.

(2) Every building society or, as the case may be, every building society of the description to which the instrument applies, has, as from the anticipation date, power, for the purposes of the power conferred by the instrument, to do such things, subject to subsection (3) below, as are reasonably necessary to enable it—

(*a*) to decide whether or not, and to what extent, to exercise (and in the case of an adoptable power to adopt) the power, and

(*b*) if it decides to exercise the power, to exercise it as from the date when it becomes exercisable by the society.

(3) Subsection (2)(*b*) above does not authorise a society—

(*a*) to make contracts, other than conditional contracts, for the acquisition of land, the acquisition of a business or the acquisition of shares in any company if that company offers the public any service or facility within the power,

(*b*) to issue invitations to members of the society or the public to apply for any power to be exercised for their benefit, or

(*c*) to retain shares in a company which offers the public any service or facility within the power;

and, in this subsection, "conditional", in relation to contracts with respect to the exercise of a power, means conditional on the power's becoming exercisable by the society.

(4) The power conferred by this paragraph, and activities carried on under it, for the purposes of an adoptable power are not to be treated as included in, or in activities comprised in, that adoptable power for the purposes of paragraph 16 of Schedule 2 to this Act.

DEFINITIONS

"adoptable power": s.119(1) and Sched. 2, para. 1.
"anticipation date": subs.(1).
"conditional": subs. (3).

GENERAL NOTE

This section gives societies a limited power to anticipate powers to be granted by a future statutory instrument. The limitation is both as to the time at which anticipation may begin and as to the acts which may be done.

Anticipation is permitted from the "anticipation date": that is, (i) where a proposed statutory instrument is subject to affirmative resolution procedure (subs. (1)(*a*)), the date on which either House of Parliament approves the draft, or (ii) where the proposed instrument is subject to negative resolution procedure (subs. (1)(*b*)), the date on which it was laid before Parliament.

The extent to which anticipation is permitted is the extent of doing such things as are reasonably necessary to enable the society (i) to decide whether or not and to what extent to exercise (and in the case of an adoptable power, to adopt) the power and (ii) (if it decides to exercise the power) to exercise it from the date on which it becomes exercisable: subs. (2). That subsection, however, is subject to the further restraints in subs. (3) that:

   (a) contracts connected with the new power must be conditional on the power's becoming exercisable by the society;

   (b) no invitation must be issued to members or to the public to apply for the power to be exercised for their benefit;

   (c) the society must not retain shares, in reliance on this section, in a company which offers the public any service or facility within the power.

The power of anticipation is, of course, available only to those societies which will be able to exercise the power which is being anticipated.

Subs.(4) ensures that a society exercising the power given by this section will not fall foul of the provisions in Sched. 2, Part II concerning unlawful anticipation of powers.

A similar power is conferred by Sched.20, para.7 for the purpose of allowing existing societies to consider and prepare for the exercise of the powers conferred under the new Act as it stands.

Public file of the society

106.—(1) The central office shall prepare and maintain a file relating to each building society (to be known as the public file) and the file shall—

   (a) contain the documents or, as the case may be, the copies of the documents and the records of the matters directed by or under any provision of this Act to be kept in the public file of the society; and

   (b) be available for inspection on reasonable notice by members of the public on payment of the prescribed fee.

(2) Any member of the public shall be entitled, on payment of the prescribed fee, to be furnished with a copy of all or any of the documents or records kept in the public file of a building society.

DEFINITIONS
   "central office": s.119(1).
   "prescribed": s.119(1).

GENERAL NOTE
This section imposes on the central office a duty to maintain a public file relating to each society. The file will contain the various documents directed by the Act to be kept in it and members of the public will be able to inspect the file and to obtain copies of its contents upon payment of fees prescribed by the Treasury.

It seems that members of the public should be able to ascertain from the public file what powers a society has, what its financial position was at the end of the latest year for which accounts are available and who are the directors and principal officers. Documents dealing with many other matters will also be found in the file (including documents resulting from certain defaults by the society in complying with the provisions of the Act: see, e.g. ss.37(4), 40(9), 41(8) and 43(9)).

Restriction of use of certain names and descriptions

107. (1) Subject to subsections (2) to (9) below, no person carrying on in the United Kingdom a business of any description shall, unless that person is a building society, use any name or in any other way so describe himself or hold himself out so as to indicate, or reasonably be understood to indicate—

   (a) that he is a building society,

   (b) that he, or his business, is connected with one or more building societies, or

   (c) that he, or his business, is connected with building societies generally.

(2) Subsection (1) does not prohibit the use by an institution carrying on the business of taking deposits and making loans secured on land which

has its principal place of business in a country or territory outside the United Kingdom, of the name under which the institution carries on business in that country or territory if—

    (*a*) the name is used in immediate conjunction with a description distinguishing the institution from a building society, being a description which has been approved for the purposes of this subsection by the Commission and the approval has not been revoked under subsection (7) below, and

    (*b*) where the name appears in writing, that description is sufficiently prominent to secure that a person who reads the name will also read the description.

(3) For a description to distinguish an institution from a building society for the purposes of subsection (2) above it must distinguish it by reference to all or any of the following matters,—

    (*a*) the situation of its principal place of business,

    (*b*) its legal status or constitution, and

    (*c*) the law (if any) which authorises it to take deposits in the United Kingdom,

as the Commission determines in its case, but need not indicate any other distinction.

(4) Subsection (1) above does not prohibit a person from carrying on a business under a name which indicates a connection between—

    (*a*) that person, or his business, and one or more building societies, or

    (*b*) that person, or his business, and building societies generally,

if the name has been approved for the purposes of this subsection by the Commission and the approval has not been revoked under subsection (7) below.

(5) No name shall be approved for the purposes of subsection (4) above unless the Commission, having regard to—

    (*a*) the true connection (if any) in fact existing between the person using, or proposing to use, the name and the particular society or societies in question or with building societies generally, as the case may be, and

    (*b*) in the cases referred to in subsection (4)(*a*) above, the respective natures of the business of that person and the society or societies in question,

is satisfied that the connection indicated by the name is not misleading; and, in so far as the name indicates investment or other financial support on the part of a building society the Commission shall not approve the use of the name unless it is satisfied that the name indicates no more investment or support than is the case and than is, in the opinion of the Commission, within the financial capacity of the building society to provide.

(6) An application for approval under subsection (2) or (4) above shall be made to the Commission in such form as it directs and accompanied by such information or evidence as it requires generally or in the particular case.

(7) The Commission may revoke any approval under subsection (2) or (4) above of a distinguishing description or a name, as the case may be, if it is of the opinion—

    (*a*) in the case of a distinguishing description, that, by reason of any change in the matters by reference to which the distinction is made, the description does not or does not any longer distinguish the institution as required by subsection (2) above, or

    (*b*) in the case of a name,

        (i) that the name has proved to be misleading to the public,

        (ii) that the approval has been obtained by fraud or mistake, or

(iii) that there has been a change in the facts to which the Commission had regard in giving its approval,
but it shall not do so without first giving the person to whom the approval was given an opportunity of making representations with respect to the proposed revocation of that approval.

(8) Subsection (1) above does not prohibit a person from using a description (other than his name) which, or from holding himself out in a way that, indicates a connection between himself or his business and one or more building societies if and to the extent he has been authorised to do so in writing by the society or societies in question.

(9) Subsection (1) above does not prohibit a person from using a description (other than his name) which, or from holding himself out in a way that, indicates a connection between himself or his business and building societies generally where the connection indicated is not misleading.

(10) Where on an application for—
(*a*) the first registration of a company, or the registration of a company by a new name, by the registrar under the Companies Act 1985 or the Companies (Northern Ireland) Order 1986, or
(*b*) approval by the Secretary of State of words or expressions for inclusion in a business name under section 2 of the Business Names Act 1985, or
(*c*) approval by the Department of Economic Development of words or descriptions for inclusion in a business name under Article 4 of the Business Names (Northern Ireland) Order 1986,
it appears to the registrar, the Secretary of State or the Department, as the case may be, that the use of the name or the words or description by the person seeking to register with it would contravene subsection (1) above, the registration shall not be made or the approval given.

(11) A person who contravenes subsection (1) above shall be liable on summary conviction to a fine not exceeding level 5 on the standard scale; and where the contravention involves a public display or exhibition of the offending name, description or other matter, there shall be a fresh contravention of the subsection on each day during which that person causes or permits the display or exhibition to continue for which that person shall be liable on summary conviction to a fine not exceeding £200.

(12) In this section—
"deposit" means a deposit within the meaning of the Banking Act 1979; and
"institution" has the same meaning as in that Act.

DEFINITIONS
"Commission": ss.1 and 119(1).
"deposit": subs.(12); Banking Act 1979, ss.1 and 50.
"institution": subs.(12); Banking Act 1979, s.50.
"the standard scale": Criminal Justice Act 1982, s.37.

GENERAL NOTE
The object of this section is to prevent any person from using a name or describing himself or holding himself out in such a way as to indicate that he is or is connected with a building society where such a description or holding out would be misleading. The section should be compared with s.51, dealing with the reverse case where a society may lead persons to believe that it is associated with, and has assumed an obligation to discharge the liabilities of, another body. See also s.108, covering the situation where the society's own name is misleading; and see Sched. 20, para. 14, for transitional provisions.

Subs. (1)
This subsection establishes the basic prohibition and is subject to the qualifications contained in subss.(2) to (9).

Subss. (2) and (3)

These subsections provide an exemption for an institution carrying on business of a nature akin to that of a building society which has its principal place of business in a country or territory outside the United Kingdom. The institution may use the name under which it carries on business in that country or territory, provided that the name is used in immediate conjunction with a description, approved by the Commission, distinguishing the institution from a building society as required by subs. (2). The distinction must be by reference to all or any of the following, as the Commission determines: (i) the situation of its principal place of business; (ii) its legal status or constitution; (iii) the law (if any) which authorises it to take deposits in the United Kingdom: subs. (3).

Subss. (4) and (5)

These subsections permit the use of a name indicating a connection with a building society if the name has been approved by the Commission. Before approval can be given, the Commission must be satisfied that the connection indicated by the name is not misleading. Further, if the name indicates investment or financial support by a society, the Commission must be satisfied that it indicates no more investment or support than is the case and than is, in the Commission's opinion, within the financial capacity of the society to provide.

Subs. (6)

Under this subsection, the Commission may direct in what form and accompanied by what information or evidence an application for approval must be made.

Subs. (7)

This subsection provides for the Commission to revoke its approval. Where the approval is of a distinguishing description under subs.(2), approval may be revoked on the ground of a change in the matters by reference to which the distinction is made. Where the approval is of a name under subs.(4), approval may be revoked on the grounds (i) that the name has proved misleading; (ii) that the approval was obtained by fraud or mistake; (iii) that there has been a change in the facts to which the Commission had regard when giving approval.

The Commission cannot revoke its approval without first giving the person to whom the approval was given an opportunity to make representations.

Subss. (8) and (9)

These subsections permit the use of a description or a holding out, but not the use of a name, indicating a connection with one or more societies if the society or societies in question have given written authorisation to do so, or indicating a connection with building societies generally where the connection indicated is not misleading. The subsections were inserted at the Report stage in the House of Commons after representations from the Building Societies Association that the section as originally drafted could cause difficulty for duly appointed agents of a society. (See *Official Report*, Standing Committee A, February 18, 1986, cols. 412–13.)

Subs. (10)

This subsection provides for the non-registration of any name of a company or any words for inclusion in a business name if the use of the name or words would contravene subs. (1).

Subs. (11)

Level 5. Currently £2,000.

Power to require building society to change misleading name

108.—(1) If, in the Commission's opinion, the name by which a building society is registered is misleading to the public as regards—

    (*a*) the scope of the society's activities,

    (*b*) the geographical area of its activities, or

    (*c*) the description of persons who are or may become members of it,

the Commission may, by notice served on the society, direct it to change its name.

(2) A direction must, if not duly made the subject of an application to the court under subsection (3) below, be complied with within a period of

six weeks from the date of the direction or such longer period as the Commission may think fit to allow.

(3) The building society may, within three weeks from the date of the direction, apply to the court to set it aside; and the court may set the direction aside or confirm it and, if it confirms the direction, shall specify a period within which it must be complied with.

(4) If a building society fails to comply with a direction under this section, it shall be liable on summary conviction—

(*a*) to a fine not exceeding level 3 on the standard scale; and

(*b*) in the case of a continuing offence, to an additional fine not exceeding £40 for every day during which the offence continues;

and so shall any officer who is also guilty of the offence.

(5) Where the Commission directs a building society under this section to change its name the society may change its name either by resolution of the board of directors or by a special resolution and paragraph 9 of Schedule 2 to this Act shall apply as if the change had been effected under that paragraph (but with the appropriate modifications).

DEFINITIONS
"Commission": ss.1 and 119(1).
"court": s.119(1).
"member": s.119(1).
"notice": s.119(1).
"officer": s.119(1).
"special resolution": s.119(1) and Sched. 2, para. 27.
"the standard scale": Criminal Justice Act 1982, s.37.

GENERAL NOTE
Under this section, the Commission is empowered to require a society to change its name if the Commission is of the opinion that the existing name is misleading to the public as regards (i) the scope of the society's activities or (ii) the geographical area of its activities or (iii) the description of persons who are or may become members: subs. (1). In the absence of an application to the court to set aside the Commission's direction, the society must comply with the direction within six weeks from its date or within such longer period as the Commission may allow: subs. (2). An application to the court must be made within three weeks of the date of the direction: subs. (3). Compare the similar provisions of s.32 of the Companies Act 1985.

It is not clear whether, on an application to the court, the court's role is simply to review the Commission's decision or whether it can make an independent determination of the question whether the name is misleading.

Note that where a society is required to change its name under this section, it may do so either by special resolution or by resolution of the board of directors. The latter course will no doubt be the speedier and certainly the cheaper. In the usual case, a change of name must be by special resolution: Sched. 2, para. 9.

Subs. (4)
Level 3. Currently £400.

Exemption from stamp duty

109. The following instruments shall be exempted from all such stamp duties (if any) as apart from this section would be chargeable on them, that is to say—

(*a*) any copy of the rules of a building society;

(*b*) any transfer of a share in a building society;

(*c*) any bond or other security to be given to, or on account of, a building society or by an officer of a building society;

(*d*) any instrument appointing an agent of a building society or revoking such an appointment; and

(*e*) any other instrument whatsoever which is required or authorised to be given, issued, signed, made or produced in pursuance of this Act or of the rules of a building society.

DEFINITIONS
  "officer": s.119(1).
  "share": s.119(1).

GENERAL NOTE
  This section is derived from s.117 of the 1962 Act. The list of exemptions is shorter, however, because, since 1962, certain of the instruments listed in s.117 have ceased to be liable to stamp duty.

Officers and auditors not to be exempted from liability

110.—(1) Subject to subsection (3) below, any provision to which this section applies, whether contained in the rules of a building society or in any contract with a building society or otherwise, shall be void.

(2) This section applies to any provision for—

(*a*) exempting any director, other officer or person employed as auditor of a building society from any liability which, by virtue of any rule of law, would otherwise attach to him in respect of the negligence, default, breach of duty or breach of trust of which he may be guilty in relation to the society, or

(*b*) indemnifying any such person against any such liability.

(3) Subsection (1) above shall not prevent a building society from indemnifying a person against any liability incurred by him in defending any proceedings (whether criminal or civil) in which judgment is given in his favour or in which he is acquitted.

(4) Section 727 of the Companies Act 1985 or, as the case may be, Article 675 of the Companies (Northern Ireland) Order 1986 (which empower the court to grant relief in certain cases of negligence, default, breach of duty or breach of trust) shall apply in relation to officers and auditors of a building society as it applies in relation to officers and auditors of a company.

DEFINITION
  "officer": s.119(1).

GENERAL NOTE
  The broad effect of this section is to make void any general provision in the rules of a society or in a contract with a society exempting any officer or auditor of a society from liability for negligence, default, breach of duty or breach of trust: see subss. (1) and (2). An officer or auditor may, however, be indemnified against any liability incurred by him in defending proceedings (whether civil or criminal) in which judgment is given in his favour or he is acquitted: subs. (3).
  Note that the liability against which he may not be indemnified is not in terms limited to liability to the society; it appears to include liability to third parties arising from any act which amounts to negligence, default, breach of duty or breach of trust to the society. The restrictive provisions of the section, and its uncertain ambit, provide a reason for not making more people than is necessary officers of the society.
  Subs. (4) applies to officers and auditors of a building society the provisions of s.727 of the Companies Act 1985. Under that section, broadly speaking, a person may be relieved from liability if he has acted "honestly and reasonably, and . . . having regard to all the circumstances of the case . . . ought fairly to be excused". It has been held that a director has acted "reasonably" if he has acted "in the way in which a man of affairs dealing with his own affairs with reasonable care and circumspection could reasonably be expected to act in such a case" (*per* Buckley J. in *Re Duomatic Limited* [1969] 2 Ch. 365, 377).
  The section is almost identical to s.92 of the 1962 Act and is similar to s.310 of the Companies Act 1985.

Time limit for commencing proceedings

111.—(1) Notwithstanding any limitation on the time for the taking of proceedings contained in any Act, summary proceedings for any offence under this Act may, subject to subsection (2) below, be commenced by the Commission at any time within the period of one year beginning with the date on which evidence sufficient in the opinion of the Commission to justify a prosecution for the offence, comes to its knowledge.

(2) Nothing in subsection (1) above shall authorise the commencement of proceedings for any offence at a time more than three years after the date on which the offence was committed.

(3) For the purposes of subsection (1) of this section a certificate, purporting to be signed by or on behalf of the Commission, as to the date on which such evidence as is mentioned in that subsection came to its knowledge, shall be conclusive evidence of that date.

(4) In the application of this section to Scotland, in subsection (1) the words "by the Commission" shall be omitted and in this section references to the Commission shall be read as references to the Lord Advocate.

(5) In the application of this section to Scotland, section 331(3) of the Criminal Procedure (Scotland) Act 1975 shall apply for the purposes of this section as it applies for the purposes of that section.

DEFINITION
"Commission": ss.1 and 119(1).

GENERAL NOTE
This section in effect re-enacts s.120 of the 1962 Act. It specifies a time limit for the commencement of summary proceedings, based on the date on which evidence sufficient, in the opinion of the Commission, to justify prosecution comes to its knowledge (subs. (1)) but with a final limit of three years from the date of the offence (subs. (2)). The Commission's certificate as to the date on which such evidence came to its knowledge is conclusive evidence of that date (subs. (3)).
S.731 of the Companies Act 1985 is to much the same effect.

Offences: liability of officers and defence of due diligence

112.—(1) Where an offence under any provision of this Act committed by a building society is proved to have been committed with the consent or connivance of, or to be attributable to any neglect on the part of, any officer of the society he, as well as the society, shall be guilty of that offence and liable to be proceeded against and punished in accordance with that provision.

(2) Where an offence under any of the following provisions of this Act, that is to say, section 9(11), section 48(5), section 52(11) or paragraph 3 of Schedule 3 is committed by a building society every director and the chief executive of the society shall also be guilty of that offence and liable to be proceeded against and punished accordingly.

(3) Where an offence under any provision of this Act committed by a body corporate other than a building society is proved to have been committed with the consent or connivance, or to be attributable to any neglect on the part of, any officer of the body corporate he, as well as the body corporate, shall be guilty of that offence and liable to be proceeded against and punished accordingly.

(4) In any proceedings for an offence under this Act, it shall be a defence for a person charged to prove that he took all reasonable precautions and exercised all due diligence to avoid the commission of such an offence by himself or any person under his control.

DEFINITIONS
"chief executive": see s.59.
"officer": s.119(1).

GENERAL NOTE

The purpose of this section is to ensure that when an offence is committed under this Act by any body corporate (whether or not a building society), the persons responsible for the commission of the offence are similarly liable to conviction and punishment. S.733 of the Companies Act 1985 makes similar provision with regard to officers of companies.

Subs. (1)

This subsection imposes liability on any officer of a society with whose consent and connivance the society committed an offence under the Act or to whose neglect the commission of the offence was attributable. Theoretically, an officer charged under this section could rely on the defence given by subs. (4), that he took all reasonable precautions and exercised all due diligence to avoid the commission of the offence. In practice, however, it is hard to see how such a defence could succeed if the elements of liability under subs. (1) (*i.e.* consent and connivance or neglect) are established.

Subs. (2)

This subsection imposes liability on every director and the chief executive of a society which raises money or accepts deposits without authorisation (s.9(11)), or intentionally alters, suppresses, conceals, destroys or refuses to produce a document which it has duly been required to produce (s.48(5)), or furnishes any information, provides any explanation or makes any statement which is false or misleading in a material particular (s.52(11) and Sched. 3, para. 3). The defence under subs. (4) mentioned above may be relied on.

Subs. (3)

This subsection is the same as subs. (1), save that references to building society have been replaced by references to any other body corporate. See the notes to that subsection.

Evidence

113.—(1) Any document purporting to have been signed by a registrar on behalf of the central office and to be a certificate of incorporation or registration or other document relating to a building society shall be received in evidence and shall, in the absence of any evidence to the contrary, be deemed to have been signed by a registrar on behalf of the central office.

(2) Any printed document purporting to be a copy of the rules or memorandum of a building society, and certified by the secretary or other officer of the society to be a true copy of its rules or memorandum as registered, shall be received in evidence and shall, in the absence of any evidence to the contrary, be deemed to be a true copy of its rules or memorandum.

DEFINITIONS

"central office": s.119(1).
"officer": s.119(1).
"memorandum": s.119(1) and Sched. 2, para. 1.

GENERAL NOTE

This section in effect re-enacts s.121 of the 1962 Act. It provides a convenient means of proving the documents to which it relates.

Records

114.—(1) Subject to any other provision of this Act or regulations under it, any record to be kept by a building society may be kept in any manner.

(2) Where any such record is not kept by making entries in a bound book, but by some other means, adequate precautions shall be taken for guarding against falsification and facilitating its discovery.

(3) The power in subsection (1) above includes power to keep the record by recording matters otherwise than in legible form so long as the recording is capable of being reproduced in a legible form; and any duty

imposed by or under this Act to allow inspection of, or to furnish a copy of, the record or any part of it is to be treated as a duty to allow inspection of, or to furnish, a reproduction of the recording or of the relevant part of it in a legible form.

(4) The Commission may, by regulations made with the consent of the Treasury, make such provision in addition to subsection (3) above as it considers appropriate in connection with such records as are kept otherwise than in legible form; and the regulations may make modifications of this Act so far as it relates to the records of building societies.

(5) If default is made in complying with this section the building society shall be liable on summary conviction—

(*a*) to a fine not exceeding level 4 on the standard scale, and

(*b*) in the case of a continuing offence, to an additional fine not exceeding £100 for every day during which the offence continues,

and so shall any officer who is also guilty of the offence.

DEFINITIONS
"Commission": ss.1 and 119(1).
"officer": s.119(1).
"the standard scale": Criminal Justice Act 1982, s.37.

GENERAL NOTE
This section:
(*a*) empowers a society to keep its records in any form which is capable of being reproduced in legible form (subject to any express provision of the Act or regulations);
(*b*) provides that any duty to allow inspection of, or to provide a copy of, a record, means inspection or a copy of the record in legible form;
(*c*) obliges the society, where the records are not kept by entry in a bound book, to take adequate precautions to guard against falsification and to facilitate its discovery.
The section is based on s.122 of the 1962 Act and ss.722 and 723 of the Companies Act 1985.

Note that the Commission has power to make regulations in connection with records kept otherwise than in legible form.

Subs. (5)
Level 4. Currently £1,000.

Service of notices

115.—(1) This section has effect in relation to any notice, directions or other document required or authorised by or under any provision of this Act or by the rules of a building society to be served on any person other than the Commission and the central office but subject, in the case of notices or other documents to be given or sent to members of a building society, to any provision of its rules.

(2) Any such document may be served on the person in question—

(*a*) by delivering it to him;

(*b*) by leaving it at his proper address; or

(*c*) by sending it by post to him at that address.

(3) Any such document may—

(*a*) in the case of a building society, be served on the secretary of the society;

(*b*) in the case of a body corporate (other than a building society), be served on the secretary or clerk of that body;

(*c*) in the case of a partnership, be served on any partner;

(*d*) in the case of an unincorporated association other than a partnership, be served on any member of its governing body.

(4) For the purposes of this section and section 7 of the Interpretation Act 1978 (service of documents) in its application to this section, the proper address of any person is—

(*a*) in the case of a building society or its secretary, the address of its principal office;

(*b*) in the case of a member of a building society, his registered address;

(*c*) in the case of a director or the chief executive of a building society, his officially notified address;

(*d*) in the case of a body corporate (other than a building society) its secretary or clerk, the address of its registered or principal office in the United Kingdom;

(*e*) in the case of an unincorporated association (other than a partnership) or a member of its governing body, its principal office in the United Kingdom;

and, in any other case, his last-known address (whether of his residence or of a place where he carries on business or is employed).

DEFINITIONS
    "central office": s.119(1).
    "chief executive": see s.59.
    "Commission": ss.1 and 119(1).
    "member": s.119(1).
    "notice": s.119(1).
    "officially notified address": s.119(1).
    "proper address": see subs. (4).
    "registered address": s.119(1) and Sched. 2, para. 13.

GENERAL NOTE
    This section makes provision for the service of notices. Note that, as regards notices and other documents to be given or sent to members of a society, an express provision in the rules will override the section: subs. (1).

Form of documents and power to prescribe fees

116.—(1) The Chief Registrar may, by directions under this subsection, make provision with respect to the form of, and the particulars to be included in, any document to be issued or sent by, or to be sent to, the central office under this Act.

(2) The Treasury may, by regulations under this subsection, make provision for the fees to be paid to the Chief Registrar for the inspection, or the furnishing of copies, of any documents in the custody of the central office, or in respect of the exercise by the central office of any of its functions, under this Act.

(3) The power to make regulations under this section is exercisable by statutory instrument which shall be subject to annulment in pursuance of a resolution of either House of Parliament.

(4) Any amounts received by the Chief Registrar under subsection (2) above shall be applied as an appropriation in aid of money provided by Parliament for the expenses of the Chief Registrar under this Act, and in so far as not so applied, shall be paid by the Chief Registrar into the Consolidated Fund.

DEFINITIONS
    "central office": s.119(1).
    "Chief Registrar": s.119(1).

GENERAL NOTE
    Under this section:
    (*a*) the Chief Registrar may make directions concerning the form of and the particulars to be included in any document to be issued or sent by, or to be sent to, the central office under this Act. *Cf.* the similar power conferred by s.123(1)(*a*) of the 1962 Act;
    (*b*) the Treasury may prescribe fees to be paid in respect of the exercise by the central office of any of its functions under the Act. *Cf.* s.123(1)(*b*) of the 1962 Act.

Subs. (4)
See the similar provision in respect of fees payable to the Commission in s.2(6).

Financial year of building societies

117.—(1) Subject to the provisions of this section and Schedule 20, the financial year of building societies shall be the period of twelve months ending with 31st December.

(2) The initial financial year of a building society shall be such period as expires with the end of the calendar year in which it is established and the final financial year of a building society shall be such shorter period than twelve months as expires with the date as at which the society makes up its final accounts.

(3) A building society whose financial year does not, by virtue of the saving provisions of Schedule 20, end with 31st December may alter its financial year by making up its accounts for one period of more than 6 months, and not more than 18 months, ending with 31st December; and in relation to a building society exercising the power conferred by this subsection, references in this Act to a financial year of the society include references to that period.

GENERAL NOTE
This section and Sched. 20, para. 16, substantially re-enact s.128 and Sched. 9, para. 11 of the 1962 Act. These notes deal both with this section and with Sched. 20, para. 16.
The effect of these provisions is that:
(a) any building society established after August 25, 1894, has a financial year ending on December 31 (see s.21 of the Building Societies Act 1894 and s.117(1) of this Act);
(b) any building society established before August 25, 1894 which has altered its financial year in exercise of the power conferred by s.70(2) of the Building Societies Act 1960 or s.128(2) of the 1962 Act has a financial year ending on December 31 (see Sched. 20, para.16);
(c) any other building society has a financial year ending on the date to which its accounts were annually made up at the commencement date of s.117 (see Sched. 20, para. 16). It is thought that this date will be January 1, 1987: see notes to s.126.
A society falling within (c) above is empowered by subs. (3) of this section to change its year end to December 31 by making up its accounts as indicated in that subsection.

Qualifying asset holding for certain powers

118.—(1) This section has effect for determining for the purposes of this Act whether, in any financial year, a building society has a "qualifying asset holding".

(2) A building society has a qualifying asset holding in any financial year, if, and only if, the aggregate value of its total commercial assets, as shown in its annual accounts for the previous year, is not less than £100 million or such other amount as may be substituted for it under subsection (3) below.

(3) The Commission, with the consent of the Treasury, may by order made by statutory instrument substitute for the amount for the time being specified in subsection (2) above such other amount as the Commission considers appropriate.

(4) An order under subsection (3) above may contain such transitional provisions as the Commission considers necessary or expedient.

(5) An instrument containing an order under subsection (3) above shall be subject to annulment in pursuance of a resolution of either House of Parliament.

DEFINITIONS
"annual accounts": ss.72(10) and 119(1).
"total commercial assets": s.119(1).

GENERAL NOTE
This section defines the "qualifying asset holding" which a society must have if it is to exercise certain of the powers conferred by or under this Act. Where such a holding is required, the fact is noted in respect of the particular power.

The test for whether or not a society has a qualifying asset holding is straightforward; it has such a holding if, and only if, its total commercial assets as shown in its annual accounts for the previous year amounted to at least £100 million. Clearly, there may be some societies which will fluctuate between having and not having a qualifying asset holding. Such societies will have to be particularly careful if they adopt powers which are only exercisable by societies with a qualifying asset holding.

Note that the Commission has power to alter the amount of £100 million.

Interpretation

119.—(1) In this Act, except where the context otherwise requires—

"adopt" and "adopted", in relation to powers, and "adoptable powers" have the meaning given by paragraph 1 of Schedule 2 of this Act;

"advance secured on land" and "advance fully secured on land" have the meanings given by section 10(1) and (11) and references to class 1 or class 2 advances are to be construed in accordance with sections 11 and 12;

"the annual accounts" has the meaning given by section 72(10);

"the annual business statement" has the meaning given by section 74(1);

"the applicable winding up legislation" and "the companies winding up legislation" have the meanings given by section 90;

"associated body" and, in that context, "associated" and "linked by resolution", in relation to a building society, have the meanings given by section 18(9) and (17) respectively;

"authorisation" means authorisation under section 9 or, on renewal, under section 41 or reauthorisation under section 44 or authorisation by virtue of section 93(6) or paragraph 6(1) of Schedule 20 to this Act and "authorised" in relation to any time, means having an authorisation current at that time;

"borrowing members' resolution" and "borrowing member" have the meanings given by paragraph 29 of Schedule 2 to this Act;

"building society" means a building society incorporated (or deemed to be incorporated) under this Act;

"the central office" means the central office of the registry of friendly societies except in relation to Scotland in relation to which it means the assistant registrar of friendly societies for Scotland;

"the Chief Registrar" means the Chief Registrar of Friendly Societies;

"the Commission" means the Building Societies Commission established by section 1;

"the court", in relation to a building society, except in relation to the winding up of the society, means—

(*a*) in the case of a society whose principal office is situated in England and Wales, the county court for the district in which the office is situated;

(*b*) in the case of a society whose principal office is situated in Scotland, the sheriff in whose jurisdiction the office is situated;

(*c*) in the case of a society whose principal office is situated in Northern Ireland, the county court for the division in which the office is situated;

and, in relation to the winding up of a building society, means the court which has jurisdiction under the applicable winding up legislation to wind up the society;

"the criteria of prudent management" means the criteria set out in section 45(3);

"deferred shares" means shares of a class defined by order of the Commission, with the consent of the Treasury, in a statutory instrument subject to annulment in pursuance of a resolution of either House of Parliament;

"deposit" includes loan, and cognate expressions shall be construed accordingly;

"dispose", in relation to any property, includes the granting of any interest in or right over it;

"executive", in relation to a director, means a person who holds office as a director and also as chief executive, secretary or manager;

"financial year" is to be construed in accordance with section 117;

"heritable security" means a security capable of being constituted over any land by disposition or assignation of that interest in security of any debt and of being recorded in the Register of Sasines or, as the case may be, in the Land Register of Scotland and includes a security constituted by a standard security and any other charge enforceable in the same manner as a standard security;

"Investor Protection Board" means the Board established by section 24;

"manager", in relation to a building society, means a person (other than the chief executive) employed by the society who, under the immediate authority of a director or the chief executive of the society exercises managerial functions or is responsible for maintaining accounts or other records of the society;

"member", in relation to a building society, includes any person who for the time being holds a share (whether advanced or not) in the society;

"memorandum" has the meaning given by paragraph 1 of Schedule 2 to the Act;

"mobile home loan" means a loan under section 15;

"mortgage" includes charge;

"mortgage debt", in relation to an advance secured on land, has the meaning given by section 11(14) and, in relation to a loan so secured, has a corresponding meaning;

"notice" means written notice and "notice to" a person means notice given to that person, and "notify" shall be construed accordingly;

"officer", in relation to a building society, means any director, chief executive, secretary or manager of the society; and, in relation to any offence, "officer" also includes any person who purports to act as an officer of the society; and in relation to any other body corporate means the corresponding officers of that body;

"officially notified", in relation to the appointment or address of a director or the chief executive of a building society, means respectively notified to, and the last address notified to, the central office under section 61(13) or 59(6), as the case may be;

"prescribed", in relation to fees, means prescribed under section 2 or 116 according as the fees are payable to the Commission or, in the case of functions of the central office, to the Chief Registrar;

"the public file", in relation to a building society, means the file relating to the society which the central office is required to maintain under section 106;

"qualifying asset holding", in relation to a building society, shall be construed in accordance with section 118;

"registered address", in relation to a member of a building society, has the meaning given by paragraph 13 of Schedule 2 to this Act;

"the repealed enactments" means the Building Societies Act 1962 or the Building Societies Act 1874, or, in relation to Northern Ireland, the Building Societies Act (Northern Ireland) 1967;

"share" includes stock;

"shareholder and depositor" includes a potential shareholder or depositor;

"special resolution" has the meaning given by paragraph 27 of Schedule 2 to this Act;

"subsidiary" has the same meaning as it has for the purposes of the Companies Act 1985;

"summary financial statement" has the meaning given by section 76(1);

"total commercial assets", in relation to a building society, means the aggregate of its class 1 assets, its class 2 assets and its class 3 assets.

(2) In relation to advances secured on land in Scotland, "mortgage" means a heritable security, "mortgagor" and "mortgagee" mean respectively the debtor and creditor in a heritable security and connected expressions shall be construed accordingly.

(3) For the purposes of any provision of this Act referring to the value of a person's shareholding in a building society—

(*a*) the value of a person's shares shall be taken as the amount standing to his credit in respect of payments made by him on the shares and interest credited to him by way of capitalisation; and

(*b*) shares held by a person to whom, as the holder of the share, the society has made an advance, shall be disregarded.

(4) The value in sterling of any transaction effected by or with a building society in another currency shall be determined for any purpose of this Act in accordance with directions given by the Commission under this subsection.

(5) The foregoing provisions of this Act shall be construed and have effect as if section 124 and Schedule 21 were contained in another Act and references in those provisions to this Act shall be construed accordingly.

GENERAL NOTE

This section is the principal interpretation section of the Act. Note subs. (3), making provision for the assessment of the value of a person's shareholding. *Cf.* s.129(4) of the 1962 Act, which contained no reference to interest.

Amendments, repeals, revocations and transitional and saving provisions

120.—(1) The enactments specified in Schedule 18 to this Act shall have effect with the amendments made by that Schedule.

(2) Subject to the saving provisions of Schedule 20, and of any order under section 121, the enactments specified in Schedule 19 to this Act are hereby repealed or revoked to the extent specified in the third column of that Schedule.

(3) Where any enactment amended or repealed or revoked by subsection (1) or (2) above extends to any part of the United Kingdom, the amendment or repeal or revocation extends to that part.

(4) The transitional and saving provisions of Schedule 20 to this Act shall have effect.

This section gives effect to Scheds. 18, 19 and 20, which contain, respectively, amendments to existing legislation, repeals and revocations and transitional and saving provisions.

Power to make transitional and saving provisions

121.—(1) The Treasury may, by order made by statutory instrument, make such provision as appears to them to be necessary or expedient for the purposes of the transition to the provisions of this Act from the existing enactments applicable in England and Wales, Scotland or Northern Ireland to building societies.

(2) An order under this section may—

(*a*) modify any of the existing enactments or provisions of this Act, in particular in their application to proceedings pending before the Chief Registrar or the Commission;

(*b*) create criminal offences or otherwise provide for the enforcement of obligations imposed by or under the order;

(*c*) provide for the charging of fees but not of any charge in the nature of taxation.

(3) An order under this section which contains any provision authorised by subsection (2)(*b*) or (*c*) above shall be subject to annulment in pursuance of a resolution of either House of Parliament.

(4) In this section "the existing enactments" means the enactments in force at the passing of this Act, including any enactment amended by Schedule 18 to this Act.

Definitions
"Chief Registrar": s.119(1).
"Commission": ss.1 and 119(1).
"existing enactments": subs. (4).

General Note
This section gives the Treasury a wide power to make such regulations as it thinks necessary or expedient for the purposes of the transition from the old regime to the new regime established by this Act.

Northern Ireland

122.—(1) With the exception of section 15, section 124 and Schedule 21 and subject to section 120(3), this Act extends to Northern Ireland.

(2) Subject to any Order made by virtue of subsection (1)(*a*) of section 3 of the Northern Ireland Constitution Act 1973 building societies shall not be a transferred matter for the purposes of that Act but shall for the purposes of subsection (2) of that section be treated as specified in Schedule 3 to that Act.

General Note
This section makes provision for the application of the Act to Northern Ireland.

Expenses

123. There shall be paid out of money provided by Parliament—

(*a*) any expenses incurred by the Commission which are attributable to the provisions of this Act, and

(*b*) any expenses incurred by the Chief Registrar which are attributable to any functions of his or of the central office under this Act.

Definitions
"central office": s.119(1).
"Chief Registrar": s.119(1).
"Commission": ss.1 and 119(1).

GENERAL NOTE
This section gives the necessary authority for payment of expenses by Parliament. See also ss.2(6) and 116(4), providing for fees paid to the Commission and to the Chief Registrar to be applied as an appropriation in aid of money provided under this section.

Provision of conveyancing services by recognised institutions and practitioners

Recognition of building societies, other institutions and individuals as suitable to provide conveyancing services

124. Schedule 21 to this Act shall have effect with respect to the provision by building societies, other institutions and individuals in England, Wales or Scotland, where they are for the time being recognised by the Lord Chancellor under that Schedule, of conveyancing services within the meaning of that Schedule; but nothing in that Schedule applies to the provision of such services in relation to land situated outside England and Wales.

DEFINITION
"conveyancing services": Sched. 21, para.1(3).

GENERAL NOTE
This brief section and Sched. 21 are the product of a considerable Parliamentary battle. Some building societies have for a long time been anxious to provide conveyancing services and have naturally regarded potential borrowers as likely customers for those services. They have been supported in that desire by those who think that if building societies could provide such services, the impact of the competition would reduce still further conveyancing costs (which have already fallen significantly over recent years) and that the would-be borrower would have the convenience of a "one stop" house-buying service: *i.e.* he could obtain conveyancing and lending services from the same source. The legal profession has tended to take the opposite point of view, perhaps largely because of fear of the effects of such competition on the solicitors' profession, but also because of concern as to the possible conflict of interest between borrower and building society and the borrower's need for independent advice.

The position in Parliament was additionally complicated by the fact that by letter dated January 12, 1984, an undertaking was given by the Solicitor-General on behalf of the Government to Mr. Austin Mitchell M.P. to introduce legislation which would permit a substantially wider range of persons and institutions to offer conveyancing services than was the case. Much of the debate on this section and Sched. 21 concerned the question whether that undertaking was being fulfilled. The provisions now included in the Act are in part derived from ss.32 to 35 of the Administration of Justice Act 1985 (introducing licensed conveyancers), but there are substantial differences.

There may be mentioned at this stage two matters which the Government envisages will be provided for in the regulations to be made under Sched. 21. First, institutions such as building societies will not be permitted to offer conveyancing services to potential borrowers, at least until the Lord Chancellor is satisfied, by the adoption of a code of practice or otherwise, that there will be adequate protection against conflicts of interest. (See *Official Report*, House of Commons, Standing Committee A, February 20, 1986, cols. 475–477 and 480). Second, the individuals within the institutions who will provide the services will be solicitors or licensed conveyancers. (See *Hansard,* H.L., vol. 478, col. 1106.)

The final result is rather curious. Tacked on to the end of an Act otherwise dealing exclusively with building societies, there is a provision to give effect to a Schedule whereby the Lord Chancellor is empowered to make rules for the recognition of building societies, other institutions and individuals as suitable to provide conveyancing services. The impact of the regulations is likely to be felt much further afield than in the offices of building societies. The degree of competition to be unleashed, however, will depend very much on the precise form of the regulations made under Sched. 21. For further comment, see the notes to that Schedule.

General

Short title

125. This Act may be cited as the Building Societies Act 1986.

Commencement

126.—(1) This Act shall come into operation as follows.

(2) Part I (and Schedule 1) shall come into operation at the end of the period of two months beginning with the day on which this Act is passed.

(3) The remaining provisions of this Act, except sections 121, 124, 125, this section, in Schedule 20, paragraph 7 (and section 120(4) so far as it relates to that paragraph) and Schedule 21, shall come into operation on such day as the Treasury may appoint by order made by statutory instrument and different days may be appointed for different provisions or different purposes.

(4) Section 124 and Schedule 21 shall come into operation on such day as the Lord Chancellor may appoint by order made by statutory instrument.

(5) Any reference to the commencement of or the commencement date for a provision of this Act is a reference to the date appointed under this section for that provision to come into operation.

GENERAL NOTE

This section provides for the coming into effect of the Act. By virtue of subs. (2), Part I (ss.1 to 4) and Sched. 1 came into effect on September 25, 1986, two months after the Act received the Royal Assent. Those are the provisions relating to the Commission. Clearly, the Commission will need a little time to get its tackle in order before it undertakes its full duties under the Act. Further, there remains a great deal of subordinate legislation to be made. Accordingly, it was announced by Mr Ian Stewart, the Economic Secretary to the Treasury, on July 25, 1986, that the main provisions would take effect on January 1, 1987, pursuant to orders made under subs. (3). Certain provisions will still not have effect on that date. At present it is envisaged that:

(1) s.14 will be given effect on January 1, 1987, but no regulations under that section will have been made in time for adoption of powers before that date. Regulations to permit direct lending in the Isle of Man, the Channel Islands and Gibraltar should be made soon and it is envisaged that they will provide that the power to lend in those territories does not have to be adopted;

(2) the power to establish subsidiaries or other associated bodies to operate in other E.C. Member States will be exercisable from January 1, 1988;

(3) the requirement under s.83 for the society to belong to a recognised scheme will come into effect on July 1, 1987, although powers to promote and join schemes will be available from January 1, 1987.

Note that ss.121, 124, 125 and 126 and Scheds. 20, para.7, and 21 (together with s.120(4) so far as it applies to Sched. 20, para. 7) are excepted from subs. (3). Subs. (4) provides for s.124 and Sched. 21 to take effect on an appointed date, but ss.121, 125 and 126 and Sched. 20, para. 7 (and s.120(4) to the extent indicated) are not subject to any provision preventing their taking immediate effect. Accordingly, those provisions came into force on July 25, 1986. That is particularly important as regards Sched. 20, para.7, which confers on existing societies a power, retrospective to December 19, 1985 (the date of the Bill's Second Reading in the House of Commons), to make the preparations there specified for the coming into force of the Act.

A final note: it should not be assumed that the whole of the 1962 Act will necessarily be repealed on January 1, 1987, when the main provisions of this Act are expected to come into force. In particular, it is thought that ss.28 to 31 of the 1962 Act (which are designed to guard against misunderstanding by potential borrowers about the implications of an offer of advance upon security) will not be repealed until the Building Societies Association has introduced a code of practice intended to achieve the same object. The new Act itself contains no equivalent of ss.28 to 31.

SCHEDULES

Section 1   SCHEDULE 1

THE BUILDING SOCIETIES COMMISSION

Status

1. The Commission shall be a body corporate.

The First Commissioner, etc

2. The person who holds office as Chief Registrar may also hold the office of chairman of the Commission and any person who holds office as an assistant registrar may also hold office as a member of the Commission.

Tenure of office of member

3.—(1) Subject to the provisions of this paragraph, a person shall hold and vacate office as a member or the chairman or deputy chairman of the Commission in accordance with the terms of the instrument appointing him to that office.

(2) A person may at any time resign office as a member or the chairman or deputy chairman of the Commission by giving the Treasury a signed notice stating that he resigns that office.

(3) When a member becomes or ceases to be the chairman or deputy chairman, the Treasury may vary the terms of his appointment so as to alter the date on which he is to vacate office as a member.

(4) If the chairman or deputy chairman ceases to be a member, he shall cease to be the chairman or deputy chairman, as the case may be.

(5) If the Treasury are satisfied that a member—
    (a) has been absent from meetings of the Commission for a period longer than three consecutive months without the permission of the Commission, or
    (b) has become bankrupt or made an arrangement with his creditors, or
    (c) is incapacitated by physical or mental illness, or
    (d) is otherwise unable or unfit to discharge the functions of his office,
the Treasury may declare his office as a member vacant, and shall notify the declaration in such manner as they think fit; and thereupon the office shall become vacant.

4. No person who has attained the age of 70 years is eligible to be or to remain a part-time member of the Commission.

Remuneration and pensions, etc. for part-time members

5. The Commission shall pay to its part-time members such fees for services and such allowances in respect of expenses as may be determined by the Treasury.

6.—(1) If the Treasury so determines in the case of any person who is or has been a part-time member of the Commission, the Commission shall pay or make arrangements for the payment of such pensions to or in respect of that person as the Treasury may determine.

(2) Where a person who is a part-time member of the Commission ceases to be a member otherwise than on the expiry of his term of office and it appears to the Treasury that there are special circumstances which make it right for that person to receive compensation, the Treasury may direct the Commission to make to that person a payment of such amount as the Treasury may determine.

Parliamentary disqualification

7.—(1) In Part II of Schedule 1 to the House of Commons Disqualification Act 1975 (bodies of which all members are disqualified under that Act) there shall be inserted at the appropriate place the entry: "The Building Societies Commission".

(2) A corresponding amendment shall be made in Part II of Schedule 1 to the Northern Ireland Assembly Disqualification Act 1975.

Staff

8. The Commission may appoint such staff as the chairman of the Commission thinks fit, subject to the approval of the Treasury as to numbers and as to terms and conditions of service.

Proceedings

9. The quorum of the Commission and arrangements relating to its meeting shall be such as the Commission may determine.

10. The validity of any proceedings of the Commission shall not be affected by any vacancy among the members or by any defect in the appointment of a member.

Performance of functions

11.—(1) With the exception specified in sub-paragraph (2) below, the Commission may authorise any member or members of the Commission to perform on behalf of the Commission such of the Commission's functions (including the power conferred by this paragraph) as are specified in the authorisation.

(2) The Commission shall not delegate any power it has under this Act to make orders, rules or regulations by statutory instrument.

12. The Statutory Instruments Act 1946 shall apply to all powers of the Commission of making statutory instruments under this Act as if the Commission were a Minister of the Crown.

13. In Schedule 2 to the Parliamentary Commissioner Act 1967 (which lists the authorities subject to investigation under that Act) there shall be inserted in the appropriate place in alphabetical order the words "Building Societies Commission".

Instruments

14. The fixing of the common seal of the Commission shall be authenticated by the signature of the chairman or deputy chairman or by some other person authorised by the Commission to act for that purpose.

15.—(1) A document purporting to be duly executed under the seal of the Commission shall be received in evidence and shall, unless the contrary is proved, be deemed to be so executed.

(2) A document purporting to be signed on behalf of the Commission shall be received in evidence and shall, unless the contrary is proved, be deemed to be so signed.

DEFINITIONS
"Chief Registrar": s.119(1)
"Commission": ss.1 and 119(1).

GENERAL NOTE
This Schedule makes provision for the constitution of the Commission and sets out the terms on which its members will hold office.
Para. 4. The retirement age of 70 applies only to part-time members of the Commission. However, full-time members will be subject to Civil Service retirement rules and will thus be obliged to retire at 60.
Para. 11. This provision enables the Commission to delegate the performance of any of its functions (other than the power to make orders, rules or regulations by statutory instrument) to any one or more of its members. The words in parenthesis in subpara. (1) make it clear that any member or members to whom a particular function is delegated may (if permitted under the terms of the original authorisation) sub-delegate the performance of that function to another member or members.
Para. 13. The effect of this paragraph is to empower the Parliamentary Commissioner for Administration to investigate complaints of maladministration made against the Commission in accordance with the provisions of the Parliamentary Commissioner Act 1967.

Sections 5, 93, 94 and 97   SCHEDULE 2

ESTABLISHMENT, INCORPORATION AND CONSTITUTION OF BUILDING SOCIETIES

PART I

GENERAL

Requirements for establishment

1.—(1) Any ten or more persons may establish a society under this Act by taking the following steps—
(a) agreeing upon the purpose or principal purpose of the society and upon the extent of its powers in a memorandum the provisions of which comply with the requirements of this Part of this Schedule;
(b) agreeing upon rules for the regulation of the society which comply with the require-ments of this Part of this Schedule;
(c) sending to the central office four copies of the memorandum and the rules, each copy

signed by at least ten of those persons (or, if there are only ten, by all of them) and by the intended secretary.

(2) Where copies of the memorandum and rules are sent to the central office in accordance with sub-paragraph (1)(*c*) above, the central office, if satisfied that—

(*a*) the provisions of the memorandum are in conformity with this Act and any instruments under it,

(*b*) the rules are in conformity with this Act,

(*c*) the intended name of the society is not, in its opinion, undesirable,

shall register the society and issue it with a certificate of incorporation.

(3) On registering a building society under sub-paragraph (2) above, the central office shall—

(*a*) retain and register one copy of the memorandum and of the rules,

(*b*) return another copy to the secretary of the society, together with a certificate of registration, and

(*c*) keep another copy, together with a copy of the certificate of incorporation, and of the certificate of registration of the memorandum and the rules, in the public file of the society.

(4) Subject to Schedule 20 in this Act, in relation to a building society—

"adoptable powers" means powers which, by any provision of this Act, must, in order to be exercisable, be adopted by the society;

"adopt" or "adopted" means adopt or adopted by agreement upon the establishment of the society or subsequently under paragraph 4 below; and

"assume" or "assumed" means assume or assumed by agreement upon the establishment of the society or subsequently under paragraph 4 below;

"memorandum" means the memorandum of the purpose and the extent of the powers of the society including the record of any alteration under paragraph 4 below.

The memorandum

2.—(1) The memorandum of a building society shall specify—

(*a*) the name of the society and the address of its principal office;

(*b*) the purpose or principal purpose of the society;

(*c*) the adoptable powers (if any) which the society has adopted, including the restrictions (if any) on their extent which it has assumed; and

(*d*) the restrictions (if any) which it has assumed on the extent of any of its other powers under this Act.

(2) Subject to sub-paragraph (3) below, in order to comply with sub-paragraph (1)(*c*) and (*d*) above the terms of each adoptable power and of each restriction on the extent of any power must be set out in the memorandum.

(3) For compliance with sub-paragraph (1)(*c*) above as respects the powers conferred by section 18 or under section 23, it shall be sufficient—

(*a*) in the case of section 18, to specify (as the case may be) the fact that the power of investment or support or both the powers of investment and support has or have been adopted in the case of companies, industrial and provident societies, corresponding European bodies and bodies included in designation orders under that section respectively, specifying, in the case of designated bodies, or descriptions of designated bodies, the body or description of body in relation to which the power or powers is or are exercisable;

(*b*) in the case of section 23, to specify the power in terms of subsection (1) of that section.

(4) The provisions of the memorandum of a building society, as read with the provisions of this Act as in force for the time being, are binding upon—

(*a*) each of the members and officers of the society; and

(*b*) all persons claiming on account of a member or under the rules;

and all such members, officers and persons so claiming and all persons dealing with the society shall be taken to have notice of those provisions.

(5) Where any adoptable power conferred by virtue of an instrument under a provision of this Act ceases, by reason of the amendment or revocation of the instrument, to be available to building societies or building societies of any description, every society affected by the amendment or revocation shall annex to its memorandum a note of the fact that, as from the operative date of the instrument, it no longer has that power and shall send a copy of the note to the central office which shall keep the copy in the public file of the society.

The rules

3.—(1) The rules of a building society shall provide for the matters specified in the Table in sub-paragraph (4) below.

(2) The rules of a building society are binding upon each of the members and officers of the society and on all persons claiming on account of a member or under the rules; and all such members, officers and persons (but no others) shall be taken to have notice of the rules.

(3) Nothing in this paragraph shall be taken to authorise any provision to be made which is inconsistent with this Act or an instrument made under it by the Commission or the Treasury or to affect the operation of any provision of this Act making rules void to any specified extent.

(4) The Table referred to in sub-paragraph (1) above is as follows:—

TABLE OF MATTERS TO BE COVERED BY THE RULES

1. The name of the society and the address of its principal office.

2. The manner in which the stock or funds of the society is or are to be raised.

3. The manner in which the terms are to be determined on which shares are to be issued and the manner in which shareholders are to be informed of changes in the terms on which their shares are held.

4. Whether any preferential or deferred shares are to be issued and, if so, within what limits.

5. The manner in which advances are to be made and repaid, and the conditions on which a borrower may redeem the amount due from him before the end of the period for which the advance was made.

6. The manner in which losses are to be ascertained and provided for.

7. The manner in which membership is to cease.

8. The manner of remunerating the auditors.

9. As respects directors—

(a) the manner of electing them and whether they may be co-opted;

(b) any conditions which must be satisfied with respect to the holding of shares in the society if a person is to become, or is to remain, a director;

(c) the manner of remunerating and, where it is not to be fixed by resolution at the annual general meeting, the maximum amount of the remuneration to be paid to, directors; and

(d) the circumstance in which pensions may be awarded to persons by virtue of their office as director and the method of determining the terms of such pensions.

10. The powers and duties of the board of directors.

11. The custody of the mortgage deeds and other securities belonging to the society.

12. The form, custody and use of the society's common seal.

13. The calling and holding of meetings and, in particular—

(a) the right of members to requisition meetings;

(b) the right of members to move resolutions at meetings;

(c) the manner in which notice of any resolutions to be moved at meetings is to be given to members;

(d) the procedure to be observed at meetings;

(e) the form of notice for the convening of a meeting and the manner of its service;

(f) the voting rights of members, the right to demand a poll and the manner in which a poll is to be taken.

14. The entitlement of members to participate in the distribution of any surplus assets after payments to creditors, on the winding up, or dissolution by consent, of the society.

Requirements for alteration of purpose, powers and rules

4.—(1) A building society may by special resolution—

(a) alter its purpose or principal purpose;

(b) alter its powers by the adoption or the rescission of the adoption of any adoptable power or by the assumption, rescission of the assumption or variation of a restriction on a power (whether an adoptable or other power); or

(c) alter its rules by the addition, rescission or variation of any rule.

(2) Where a building society alters its purpose or powers or its rules under this paragraph, it shall send to the central office—

(*a*) three copies of a record of the alteration signed by the secretary; and

(*b*) a statutory declaration by the secretary that the alteration was effected by a resolution passed as a special resolution and that the record is a true record of the resolution.

(3) On altering its purpose or powers or its rules under this paragraph the building society shall determine the date on which it intends the alteration to take effect; and the record of the alteration shall specify that date (in this paragraph referred to as "the specified date").

(4) Where copies of a record of an alteration of a building society's purpose, powers or rules are sent to the central office under sub-paragraph (2) above and the central office is satisfied that the alteration is in conformity with this Act and (where applicable) any instruments under it, the central office shall, subject to paragraph 19 below—

(*a*) retain and register one of the copies,

(*b*) return another to the secretary of the society together with a certificate of registration of the alteration, and

(*c*) keep another copy, together with a copy of the certificate of registration of the alteration, in the public file of the society.

(5) An alteration of the purpose or powers or of the rules of a building society under this paragraph shall take effect on the specified date or, if registration of the alteration is not effected under sub-paragraph (4) above until a later date, that later date.

(6) Any provision in the rules of a building society that the memorandum or rules may be altered without passing a special resolution shall be void.

(7) If a building society arranges for the publication in consolidated form of its rules or memorandum as altered for the time being, it shall send a copy to the central office and the central office—

(*a*) shall keep the copy in the public file of the society, but

(*b*) shall not register the copy.

(8) If a building society fails to comply with sub-paragraph (2) above, the society shall be liable on summary conviction to a fine not exceeding level 4 on the standard scale and so shall any officer who is also guilty of the offence.

Membership

5.—(1) The rules of a building society may allow a person to become a member without holding a share in the society.

(2) Such of the rules as concern the making of advances to members need not be expressed in terms which treat a member to whom an advance is made as being, by reason of the making of the advance, the holder of a share in the society.

(3) A person who is a minor—

(*a*) may, if the rules do not otherwise provide, be admitted as a member of a building society and give all necessary receipts; but

(*b*) may not vote or hold any office in the society; and

(*c*) may not nominate, or join in nominating, a person for election as a director of the society.

Liability of members

6.—(1) The liability of a member of a building society in respect of a share on which no advance has been made shall be limited to the amount actually paid, or in arrear, on the share.

(2) The liability of a member of a building society in respect of a share on which an advance has been made shall be limited to the amount payable on the share under any mortgage or other security or under the rules of the society.

(3) The liability of a member of a building society to whom an advance is made under rules made in pursuance of paragraph 5(1) or (2) above shall be no greater than it would be if the rules treated him as being, by reason of the making of the advance, the holder of a share in the society.

Joint shareholders

7.—(1) Two or more persons may jointly hold shares in a building society and the following provisions of this paragraph shall apply to any shares so held.

(2) In this paragraph, in relation to any shares jointly held, "representative joint holder" means that one of the joint holders who is named first in the records of the society.

(3) Except where the rules of the society otherwise provide, any notice or other document may be given or sent by the society to the joint holders by being given or sent to the

representative joint holder; but this sub-paragraph shall not prevent any of the joint holders from exercising the rights under this Act of a member of a building society to obtain from the society on demand a copy of the summary financial statement, the annual accounts and the annual business statement.

(4) For the purpose of determining—

(*a*) who is entitled to vote in an election of directors of the society;

(*b*) who is qualified to vote on a resolution of the society, and

(*c*) where it is relevant, the number of votes a person may then give,

the shares shall be treated as held by the representative joint holder alone; and accordingly a person who is a member of the society by reason only of being a joint holder of those shares (other than the representative joint holder) shall not be entitled to vote in any such election or qualified to vote on any such resolution.

(5) For the purposes of sections 87 and 93 to 102 the shares shall be treated as held by the representative joint holder alone; and accordingly a person who is a member of the society by reason only of being a joint holder of those shares (other than the representative joint holder) shall not be regarded as a member of the society for the purposes of those sections.

(6) The representative joint holder (but none of the other joint holders) shall have the right to join in making an application under section 56 and any reference in that section to the total membership of a building society shall be construed accordingly.

(7) In the register to be maintained under paragraph 13 below the entry of that one of the joint holders who is the representative joint holder shall indicate that fact.

(8) The joint holders shall be entitled to choose the order in which they are named in the records of the society.

Joint borrowers

8.—(1) Where an advance secured on land is made by a building society to two or more persons jointly the following provisions of this paragraph shall apply to their rights as borrowing members of the society.

(2) In this paragraph, in relation to any rights of theirs as borrowing members, "representative joint borrower" means that one of the joint borrowers who is named first in the record of the society.

(3) Except where the rules of the society otherwise provide, any notice or other document may be given or sent by the society to the joint borrowers by being given or sent to the representative joint borrower; but this sub-paragraph shall not prevent any of the joint borrowers from exercising the rights under this Act of a borrowing member of a building society to obtain from the society on demand a copy of the summary financial statement, the annual accounts and the annual business statement.

(4) For the purpose of determining—

(*a*) who is entitled to vote in any election of directors of the society, and

(*b*) who is qualified to vote on a resolution of the society,

the rights of the joint borrowers as borrowing members of the society shall be treated as the rights of the representative joint borrower alone; and accordingly a person who is a member of the society by reason only of being a joint borrower (other than the representative joint borrower) shall not be entitled to vote in any such election or qualified to vote on any such resolution.

(5) For the purposes of sections 87 and 93 to 102 the rights of the joint borrowers as borrowing members of the society shall be treated as the rights of the representative joint borrower alone; and accordingly a person who is a member of the society by reason only of being a joint borrower (other than the representative joint borrower) shall not be regarded as a borrowing member of the society for the purposes of those sections.

(6) The representative joint borrower (but none of the other joint borrowers) shall have the right to join in making an application under section 56 and any reference in that section to the total membership of a building society shall be construed accordingly.

(7) In the register to be maintained under paragraph 13 below the entry of that one of the joint borrowers who is the representative joint borrower shall indicate that fact.

(8) The joint borrowers shall be entitled to choose the order in which they are named in the records of the society.

Use and change of name

9.—(1) The common seal of a building society shall bear the registered name of the society.

(2) A building society shall not use any name or title other than its registered name.

(3) A building society may change its name by special resolution.

(4) Where a society changes its name in accordance with this paragraph notice of the change of name shall be sent to the central office and, unless the central office is of the opinion that the changed name is undesirable, the central office shall register the notice of the change of name and give the society a certificate of registration.

(5) A change of name shall take effect on the date on which the certificate of registration under sub-paragraph (4) above is issued or on such later date as may be specified in the certificate.

(6) The central office shall keep a copy of the certificate of registration issued under sub-paragraph (4) above in the public file of the society.

(7) A change of name shall not affect the rights and obligations of the society or of any of its members or of any other person concerned.

Offences relating to society's name

10.—(1) If a building society contravenes paragraph 9(2) above, the society shall be liable on summary conviction—

(a) to a fine not exceeding level 4 on the standard scale; and

(b) in the case of a continuing offence, to an additional fine not exceeding £100 for every week during which the offence continues;

and so shall any officer who is also guilty of the offence.

(2) If a building society fails to send to the central office a notice which it is required to send to it under paragraph 9(4) above, the society shall be liable on summary conviction to a fine not exceeding level 4 on the standard scale and so shall any officer who is also guilty of the offence.

Change of principal office

11.—(1) A building society may change its principal office—

(a) in such manner as its rules direct, or

(b) if there is no such direction in the rules, then at a general meeting specially called for the purpose in accordance with its rules.

(2) Notice of any such change and of the date of it shall, within seven days after the change, be sent to the central office and the central office shall keep the notice in the public file of the society.

(3) It is not necessary to alter the memorandum or rules of a building society by reason only that its principal office is changed.

(4) If a building society fails to send to the central office a notice which it is required to send to it under sub-paragraph (2) above, the society shall be liable on summary conviction to a fine not exceeding level 4 on the standard scale and so shall any officer who is also guilty of the offence.

Societies to supply copies of rules etc.

12.—(1) A building society shall, on demand, give a copy of its statutory documents—

(a) free of charge, to any member of the society to whom a copy of those documents has not previously been given, and

(b) to any other person, upon payment of such fee as the society may require, not exceeding the prescribed amount.

(2) The reference in sub-paragraph (1) above to a copy of a building society's statutory documents is a reference to—

(a) a printed copy of the society's rules for the time being, with a copy of the certificate of incorporation of the society annexed to it, and

(b) a printed copy of the memorandum of the society for the time being.

(3) If a building society fails to comply with the requirements of sub-paragraph (1) above, the society shall be liable on summary conviction to a fine not exceeding level 4 on the standard scale and so shall any officer who is also guilty of the offence.

(4) In sub-paragraph (1) above the "prescribed amount" means £1 or such other amount as the Commission prescribes by order made by statutory instrument.

Register of members

13.—(1) Every building society shall maintain a register of the names and addresses of the members of the society.

(2) The register shall be kept at the principal office or at such other place or places as the directors think fit.

(3) If a building society contravenes sub-paragraph (1) above, the society shall be liable on summary conviction to a fine not exceeding level 4 on the standard scale and so shall any officer who is also guilty of the offence.

(4) For the purposes of this Act "registered address" in relation to a member of a building society, means—

(a) the address shown in the register maintained under this paragraph, except in a case where paragraph (b) below applies;

(b) where the member has requested that communications from the society be sent to some other address, that other address.

Exception to duties to send documents

14.—(1) A building society is not obliged by any provision of this Act or its rules to send a notice or other document to a member in whose case the society has reason to believe that communications sent to him at his registered address are unlikely to be received by him.

(2) Where the requirement relates to notice of a meeting or postal ballot of the society, the society must, instead, comply with the advertising requirements of paragraph 35 below.

Right of members to obtain particulars from the register

15.—(1) At any time when a building society has had its authorisation revoked under section 43 and the society has not been re-authorised under section 44, a member of the society shall have the right to obtain, from the register kept under paragraph 13 above, the names and addresses of members of the society, for the purpose of communicating with them on a subject relating to the affairs of the society.

(2) If, at any time not falling within sub-paragraph (1) above, a member of a building society makes a written application to the Commission for the right to obtain names and addresses from the register, the Commission, if satisfied that the applicant requires that right for the purpose of communicating with members of the society on a subject relating to its affairs, and having regard to the interests of the members as a whole and to all the other circumstances, may direct that the applicant shall have the right to obtain from the register the names and addresses of the members for the purpose of communicating with them on such a subject.

(3) Any direction under sub-paragraph (2) above may be given subject to such limitations or conditions as the Commission may think fit.

(4) Before giving a direction under sub-paragraph (2) above, the Commission shall give particulars of the application to the building society and shall afford the society an opportunity of making representations with respect to the application; and the Commission shall, if the applicant or the society so requests, afford to the applicant and to the society an opportunity of being heard by it.

(5) A member entitled under this paragraph to obtain the names of members of a building society may apply in writing to the society, describing in the application the subject on which he proposes to communicate with other members of the society; and the society shall give him all necessary information as to the place or places where the register, or part of it, is kept, and reasonable facilities for inspecting the register and taking a copy of any names and addresses in the register.

(6) A building society shall not be obliged to disclose to a member making an application under this paragraph any particulars contained in the register other than the names of the members and their addresses, and may construct the register in such a way that it is possible to disclose the names and addresses to inspection without disclosing any such other particulars.

PART II

UNLAWFUL ANTICIPATION OF POWERS

Undertaking against and declaration of non-anticipation of powers

16.—(1) Where a building society adopts any adoptable power under paragraph 4 above then—

(a) it shall, by virtue of this paragraph, assume an obligation, enforceable as provided in paragraph 17 below, not to exercise that power until the date on which the alteration of its powers takes effect, and

(b) it shall send to the central office, with the documents required by paragraph 4(2) above, a declaration as respects that power made on behalf of the society which satisfies the requirements of this paragraph.

(2) The obligation assumed by virtue of this paragraph on the adoption of a power does not extend to the exercise of any power included in the adoptable power which the society has under the law in force at any time before the registration takes effect.

(3) A declaration, to satisfy the requirements of this paragraph, must be made by the chairman of the board of directors of the society, by one other director and by the chief executive of the society and it must either—

(a) state that, to the best of the knowledge and belief of the declarants, after due enquiry, the society has not, or has not with the permitted qualification, carried on any activity comprised in the power during the period which began one year before the specified date and expired with the date of the meeting at which the power was adopted, or

(b) state that, to the best of the knowledge and belief of the declarants, after due enquiry, the society, with specified exceptions, has not, or has not with the permitted qualification, carried on any activity comprised in the power during the period which began one year before the specified date and expired with the date of the meeting at which the power was adopted.

(4) The qualification of the statement so required which is permitted is that in so far as the society has, at any time during the said period, carried on any activity comprised in the power to which the statement relates, the society had the power to carry on that activity at that time under the law in force at that time.

(5) The exceptions to the statement so required must not include activities of the society which constitute significant excesses of its powers during the said period; and a declaration specifying activities as exceptions to the statement so required must also state the opinions of the declarants that the activities are believed not to constitute significant excesses of the society's powers during the period to which the declaration relates.

Penalty for breach of undertaking

17. If, in breach of the obligation assumed by virtue of paragraph 16 above, a building society exercises any power to which the obligation extends, then—

(a) the society shall be liable on conviction on indictment or on summary conviction to a fine not exceeding, on summary conviction, the statutory maximum, and

(b) any officer of the society who is also guilty of the offence shall be liable on summary conviction to a fine not exceeding the statutory maximum.

Penalty for false declaration

18. If the statement in a declaration made for the purposes of paragraph 16 above is false, then, any person who made the statement knowing it to be false or reckless as to whether it was true or false shall be liable—

(a) on conviction on indictment, to imprisonment for a term not exceeding two years or to a fine, or both, and

(b) on summary conviction to imprisonment for a term not exceeding six months or to a fine not exceeding the statutory maximum, or both.

Powers of central office

19.—(1) The central office, on receiving from a building society the declaration required by and the other documents referred to in paragraph 16 above, shall refer to the Commission for its determination the question whether or not the alteration of the society's powers is to be registered.

(2) On a reference to the Commission of the question whether or not the alteration of a society's powers is to be registered—

(a) if the declaration contains the statement specified in paragraph 16(3)(a) above and the Commission has no reasonable cause to believe that the society in question has carried on any activity comprised in the power to which the obligation imposed by paragraph 16 above extends at any time during the period which began one year before the specified date and expired on the date on which it considers the reference, the Commission shall direct the central office to register the alteration, and (*b*) in any other case, the Commission may, as it thinks fit, direct the central office to register, or not to register, the alteration.

(3) The Commission, in deciding, in a case falling within sub-paragraph (2)(*b*) above, whether or not to direct the registration of the alteration of a society's powers may have regard to all the circumstances of the case.

(4) No registration of an alteration shall be effected by the central office under paragraph 4(4) above before the expiry of the period of 21 days beginning with the date on which it receives the declaration required by and the other documents referred to in paragraph 16 above.

(5) If the central office, in pursuance of a direction of the Commission under sub-paragraph (2) above, refuses registration of the alteration of a society's powers under sub-paragraph (1) above it shall serve on the society a notice—

(*a*) recording its refusal,

(*b*) specifying the activity which is believed to constitute a breach of the society's obligation, and

(*c*) directing the society to make an application to the Commission under section 38 for a determination under that section whether the activity was or was not within the powers of the society at the time specified under sub-paragraph (*b*) above,

and shall send a copy of the notice to the Commission.

(6) The central office shall comply with any direction as regards the registration of the alteration of the society's powers given to it by the Commission consequent on the Commission's determination of the society's powers under section 38.

(7) In this paragraph "the specified date" has the same meaning as in paragraph 4 above.

PART III

MEETINGS, RESOLUTIONS AND POSTAL BALLOTS

Annual general meeting

20.—(1) Subject to sub-paragraph (2) below, every building society shall hold a meeting in the first four months of each financial year as its annual general meeting (in addition to any other meetings in that year) and shall specify the meeting as such in the notices calling it.

(2) Sub-paragraph (1) above does not require a building society to hold an annual general meeting in the calendar year in which it is incorporated.

(3) If default is made in holding a meeting in accordance with sub-paragraph (1) above, the Commission may—

(*a*) call, or direct the calling of, an annual general meeting in that financial year, and

(*b*) give such ancillary or consequential directions at it thinks expedient, including directions modifying or supplementing the operation of the rules of the society in relation to the calling, holding and conducting of the meeting.

(4) Notwithstanding anything in the rules of a building society, the business which may be dealt with at the annual general meeting shall include any resolution whether special or not.

(5) In any case where default is made—

(*a*) in holding an annual general meeting in accordance with sub-paragraph (1) above, or

(*b*) in complying with any directions of the Commission given under sub-paragraph (3) above,

the building society shall be liable on summary conviction to a fine not exceeding level 4 on the standard scale and so shall any officer who is also guilty of the offence.

Length of notice for calling meetings

21.—(1) Any provision contained in the rules of a building society shall be void to the extent that it provides for the calling of a meeting of the society (other than an adjourned meeting) by less than 21 days' notice expiring with the date of the meeting or, if earlier, the date specified by the society, under its rules, as the final date for the receipt of instruments appointing proxies to vote at the meeting.

(2) A meeting of a building society may be called by 21 days' notice, unless the rules provide for longer notice of the meeting to be given.

(3) Where notice of a meeting is given in accordance with sub-paragraph (2) above, the notice shall be taken for the purposes of this Act or any other enactment to have been duly given according to the rules of the building society.

Persons entitled to notice of meetings

22.—(1) Subject to the provisions of this Part of this Schedule, notice of a meeting of a building society shall be given to every member of the society who would be eligible to vote at the meeting if the meeting were held on the date of the notice.

(2) If the notice of the meeting includes notice of the intention to move a resolution as a borrowing members' resolution, notice of the meeting shall, subject to those provisions, be given also to every person who becomes a borrowing member of the society before the date which the society specifies as the final date for the receipt of instruments appointing proxies to vote on that resolution.

(3) Accidental omission to give notice of a meeting to, or non-receipt of notice of a meeting by, any person entitled to receive notice of the meeting does not invalidate the proceedings at that meeting.

Members' entitlement to vote on resolutions

23.—(1) A member of a building society is entitled to vote—
   (a) on a resolution, other than a borrowing members' resolution, if he was also a member at the end of the last financial year before the voting date; and
   (b) on a borrowing members' resolution if he was, at the end of that year, and is, on the voting date, a borrowing member of the society,
but subject, in either case, to paragraphs 5(3), 7(4) and 8(4) above and, in the case of paragraph (a), to sub-paragraph (3) below.

(2) Subject to the following provisions of this paragraph, any provision in the rules of a building society is void to the extent that it would have the effect of restricting the rights conferred on members by sub-paragraph (1) above.

(3) If the rules of the society so provide, a member is not entitled to vote on a resolution (other than a borrowing members' resolution) if—
   (a) he did not have a qualifying shareholding at the qualifying shareholding date; or
   (b) he does not have any shares on the voting date; or
   (c) although he was a member at the qualifying shareholding date and is a member on the voting date, he ceased to be a member at some time during the intervening period.

(4) Where a building society's rules provide that a member is not entitled to vote on a resolution (other than a borrowing members' resolution) unless he has a qualifying shareholding on the qualifying shareholding date, he shall be taken to satisfy that requirement if he had such a holding—
   (a) at the end of the last financial year before the voting date, except where paragraph (b) below applies; or
   (b) in a case where the voting date falls during that part of a financial year which follows the conclusion of the annual general meeting commenced in that year, at the beginning of the period of 56 days immediately preceding the voting date for members voting in person at a meeting or, as the case may be, on a postal ballot.

(5) For the purposes of this paragraph a member of a building society has a "qualifying shareholding" at any time if at that time he holds shares in the society to a value not less than the prescribed amount or such lesser amount as may be specified in the rules.

(6) In this paragraph "voting date", with reference to any resolution, means—
   (a) the date of the meeting at which the resolution is intended to be moved, except where paragraph (b) or (c) below applies;
   (b) where voting on the resolution is to be conducted by postal ballot, the date which the society specifies as the final date for the receipt of completed ballot papers;
   (c) in the case of a member appointing a proxy to vote instead of him at a meeting, the date which the society specifies as the final date for the receipt of instruments appointing proxies to vote on that resolution.

Proxies

24.—(1) A member of a building society who is entitled to attend and vote at a meeting of the society—
   (a) may appoint another person (whether a member of the society or not) as his proxy, to attend and, subject to sub-paragraph (3) below, to vote at the meeting instead of him, and
   (b) may direct the proxy how to vote at the meeting.

(2) Where the society, under its rules, specifies a final date for the receipt of instruments appointing proxies to vote at a meeting, a person appointed a proxy by a member who at that date is entitled to attend and vote at the meeting may act as his proxy at the meeting whether or not the member ceases to be so entitled after that date.

(3) A proxy is entitled to vote on a poll but, subject to any provision in the rules of the building society, not otherwise.

(4) In every notice calling a meeting of a building society there shall appear with reasonable prominence a statement—

(*a*) that a member entitled to attend and vote may appoint a proxy (or, where it is allowed, one or more proxies) to attend and vote at the meeting instead of him;

(*b*) that the proxy need not be a member of the society; and

(*c*) that the member may direct the proxy how to vote at the meeting.

(5) If default is made in complying with sub-paragraph (4) above in respect of a meeting of a building society, the society shall be liable on summary conviction to a fine not exceeding level 4 on the standard scale, and so shall any officer who is also guilty of the offence.

(6) Any provision contained in the rules of a building society shall be void in so far as it would have the effect of requiring the instrument appointing a proxy, or any other document necessary to show the validity of, or otherwise relating to the appointment of a proxy, to be received by the society or any other person more than seven days before a meeting or adjourned meeting in order that the appointment may be effective at the meeting or adjourned meeting.

Right to demand a poll

25.—(1) Any provision contained in the rules of a building society shall be void in so far as it would have the effect either—

(*a*) of excluding the right to demand a poll at a meeting of the society on any question other than the election of a chairman of the meeting or the adjournment of the meeting, or

(*b*) of making ineffective a demand for a poll on any such question which is made by not less than ten members having the right to vote at the meeting.

(2) The instrument appointing a proxy to vote at a meeting of a building society shall be taken also to confer authority to demand or join in demanding a poll; and for the purposes of sub-paragraph (1) above a demand by a person as proxy of a member shall be the same as a demand by the member.

Special resolutions

26. No resolution of a building society shall be passed as a special resolution unless it is required to be so passed by or under any provision of this Act or by the rules of the society.

27.—(1) A resolution of a building society shall be a special resolution when it has been passed by not less than three-quarters of the number of the members of the society qualified to vote on a special resolution and voting either—

(*a*) in person or by proxy on a poll on the resolution at a meeting of the society of which notice specifying the intention to move the resolution as a special resolution has been duly given; or

(*b*) in a postal ballot on the resolution of which notice specifying that the resolution will not be effective unless it is passed as a special resolution has been duly given.

(2) In any rules made by a building society on or after 1st October 1960, whether before or after the commencement of this Act, "special resolution", unless the context otherwise requires, means a special resolution as defined in this paragraph.

Borrowing members' resolutions

28. No resolution of a building society shall be passed as a borrowing members' resolution unless it is required to be so passed by or under any provision of this Act or by the rules of the society.

29.—(1) A resolution of a building society shall be a borrowing members' resolution when it has been passed by a majority of the borrowing members of the society voting either—

(*a*) in person or by proxy on a poll on the resolution at a meeting of the society of which notice specifying the intention to move the resolution as a borrowing members' resolution has been duly given; or

(*b*) in a postal ballot on the resolution of which notice specifying that the resolution will not be effective unless it is passed as a borrowing members' resolution has been duly given.

(2) For the purposes of this Part of this Schedule a person is a borrowing member of a building society at any time if at that time his indebtedness to the society is in respect of an advance fully secured on land and the amount of his mortgage debt is not less than the prescribed amount.

(3) Where a borrowing member's resolution approving a transfer of engagements by a building society is moved, only those borrowing members whose mortgages are to be transferred shall be entitled to vote on the resolution.

(4) In any rules made by a building society after the commencement of this paragraph, "borrowing members' resolution", unless the context otherwise requires, means a borrowing members' resolution as defined in this paragraph.

Transfer resolutions

30.—(1) The transfer resolutions required for the purposes of section 97 for the approval by members of a building society of a transfer of its business are two resolutions, of which—

(*a*) one is passed as a borrowing members' resolution, and
(*b*) the other ("the requisite shareholders' resolution") is passed in accordance with sub-paragraphs (2) to (5) below.

(2) In a case where the successor is to be a specially formed company, the requisite shareholders' resolution—

(*a*) must be passed as a special resolution, and
(*b*) must be passed on a poll on which not less than 20 per cent. of the members of the society qualified to vote on a special resolution voted;

and the notice of the resolution required by sub-paragraph (*a*) or sub-paragraph (*b*) of paragraph 27(1) above, as the case may be, must specify that the resolution will not be effective unless both of the requirements specified in this sub-paragraph are fulfilled.

(3) Subject to any direction under sub-paragraph (5) below, in a case where the successor is to be an existing company, the requisite shareholders' resolution must be passed as a special resolution and either—

(*a*) must be passed by not less than 50 per cent. of the members qualified to vote on a special resolution, or
(*b*) must be passed by the holders, being members qualified to vote on a special resolution, of shares in the society to a value, on the voting date, representing not less than 90 per cent. of the total value of the shares held on that date by the members so qualified to vote;

and, in either case, the resolution must be a resolution in relation to which the notice required by paragraph 27 above includes a statement specifying that the resolution will not be effective unless either of the above requirements is fulfilled has been duly given.

(4) If the Commission considers it expedient, in relation to a transfer of the business of a building society to an existing company, to do so for the purpose of protecting the investments of the shareholders of or depositors with the society, the Commission may give a direction under sub-paragraph (5) below.

(5) A direction under this sub-paragraph is a direction that, for the purposes of the transfer of business specified in the direction, the requisite shareholders' resolution is to be effective if it is passed as a special resolution.

(6) The Treasury, after consultation with the Commission, may by order amend sub-paragraph (2)(*b*), (3)(*a*) or (3)(*b*) above so as to substitute for the percentage for the time being specified in the sub-paragraph such other percentage as it thinks appropriate.

(7) The power to make orders under sub-paragraph (6) above is exercisable by statutory instrument which shall be subject to annulment in pursuance of a resolution of either House of Parliament.

(8) In this paragraph "voting date", with reference to a requisite shareholders' resolution, has the same meaning as in paragraph 23(6) above.

Members' right to propose and circulate resolutions

31.—(1) If at least the requisite number of qualified members of a building society give notice to the society of their intention to have moved on their behalf a resolution, other than a borrowing members' resolution, specified in the notice at an annual general meeting of the society, it shall be the duty of the society, subject to sub-paragraphs (4), (5) and (6) below—

(*a*) to include in the notice of the annual general meeting a notice specifying the intention to have the resolution moved on their behalf at the meeting and, where applicable, the intention to move it as a special resolution;

(*b*) at the request of the members intending to have the resolution moved on their behalf, to send to each member entitled to receive notice of the meeting a copy of any statement of not more than 100 words with respect to the matter referred to in the resolution.

(2) For the purposes of sub-paragraph (1) above—

(*a*) "the requisite number"—

    (i) in the case of a society with a qualifying asset holding, is fifty or such lesser number as is specified for the purpose in the rules of the society, and

    (ii) in the case of any other society is ten or such lesser number as is specified for the purpose in the rules of the society;

(*b*) every member of a building society is a "qualified member" unless the rules make other provision for the purpose which is not rendered void under sub-paragraph (3) below.

(3) Any provision contained in the rules of a building society shall be void to the extent that it would have the effect of requiring a qualified member, for the purposes of sub-paragraph (1) above,—

(*a*) to hold or have at any time held shares in the society to a value greater than the prescribed amount in force on the qualifying date, or

(*b*) to have held shares in the society at any time before the commencement of the period of two years ending with the qualifying date;

and for the purposes of this sub-paragraph the qualifying date is the date on which the notice is given to the society under sub-paragraph (1) above.

(4) Sub-paragraph (1) above does not require a building society to send notices of a resolution or copies of a statement to members of the society in any case where—

(*a*) publicity for the resolution or, as the case may be, the statement would be likely to diminish substantially the confidence in the society of investing members of the public; or

(*b*) the rights conferred by sub-paragraph (1) are being abused to seek needless publicity for defamatory matter or for frivolous or vexatious purposes;

and that sub-paragraph shall not be taken to confer any rights on members, or to impose any duties on a building society, in respect of a resolution or statement which does not relate directly to the affairs of the society.

(5) If the rules of a building society so provide, sub-paragraph (1) above does not require notice of a resolution to be given to members of the society if the resolution is in substantially the same terms as any resolution which has been defeated at a meeting or on a postal ballot during the period beginning with the third annual general meeting before the date on which notice of the resolution is given to the society.

(6) No copies of a statement with respect to a resolution shall be sent to members of a building society if, on any of the grounds in sub-paragraph (4) or (5) above, the society does not give the notice of the resolution to them required by sub-paragraph (1)(*a*) above.

(7) The Commission shall hear and determine any dispute arising under sub-paragraph (4)(*a*) above, whether on the application of the building society or of any other person who claims to be aggrieved.

(8) If a building society fails to comply with the requirements of sub-paragraph (1) above where notice is duly given under that sub-paragraph, the society shall be liable on summary conviction to a fine not exceeding level 4 on the standard scale and so shall any officer who is also guilty of the offence.

Members' resolutions: supplementary provisions

32.—(1) Notice of a resolution given under paragraph 31(1) above must be given to the building society not later than the last day of the financial year preceding the financial year in which is held the annual general meeting at which it is intended to move the resolution; and any statement to be sent to members under paragraph 31(1)(*b*) above must also be notified to the society not later than that day.

(2) The notice of a resolution and the copies of a statement required to be sent to members by paragraph 31(1)(*a*) or (*b*) above shall be sent to them in the same manner and (so far as practicable) at the same time as the notice of the annual general meeting at which the resolution is intended to be moved; and, where it is not practicable for them to be sent at the same time as the notice, they shall be sent as soon as practicable thereafter.

(3) Where notices of a resolution, or copies of a statement in respect of a resolution, intended to be moved at a meeting of a building society are required to be sent to any persons, the proceedings at the meeting are not invalidated by—

(a) the accidental omission to send a notice or copy to a person entitled to receive one, or

(b) the non-receipt of a notice or copy by such a person.

(4) The Commission may by order vary—

(a) the definition of "requisite number" or "qualified member" in sub-paragraph (2) of paragraph 31 above, or

(b) the descriptions of provisions which are rendered void by sub-paragraph (3) of that paragraph,

whether by the addition of any description or other provision or by the substitution or deletion of any definition, description or other provision for the time being specified or contained in that paragraph.

(5) An order under sub-paragraph (4) above shall be made by statutory instrument subject to annulment in pursuance of a resolution of either House of Parliament.

(6) An order under sub-paragraph (4) above may contain transitional, consequential or supplementary provision.

Postal ballots

33.—(1) The rules of a building society may provide for the voting in an election of directors or on any resolution of the society to be conducted in all, or in any particular, circumstances by postal ballot; and in this Act "ballot" or "postal ballot", in relation to an election or a resolution of the society, means the postal ballot, if any, taking place by virtue of those rules in the case of the election or the resolution in question.

(2) Where, under the rules of a society, a postal ballot is to take place, the following provisions of this paragraph have effect.

(3) Notice of a postal ballot shall be given not less than 21 nor more than 56 days before the date which the society specifies as the final date for the receipt of completed ballot papers (referred to in this paragraph as "the voting day").

(4) Subject to the provisions of this Part of this Schedule, notice of a postal ballot shall be given to every member of the society who would be entitled to vote in the election or on the resolution if the voting date for the election or the resolution fell on the date of the notice.

(5) If voting on the postal ballot is to be in respect of a resolution of which notice has been given of the intention to move it as a borrowing members' resolution, notice of the postal ballot shall, subject to those provisions, be given also to every person who becomes a borrowing member of the society before the voting day.

(6) Notice of a postal ballot—

(a) shall contain such other notices relating to the election or resolution, and

(b) shall be accompanied by such other documents,

as would be required to be given or sent to a member in connection with notice of a meeting, had it been intended to hold the election or vote on the resolution at a meeting instead of by postal ballot with the exception, however, of any notice relating to voting by proxy at a meeting.

(7) Accidental omission—

(a) to give notice of a postal ballot, or

(b) to send any document required by sub-paragraph (6) above to accompany such a notice,

to any person entitled to receive it, or non-receipt of such a notice or document by such a person, does not invalidate the postal ballot.

Declarations to be made in proxy and ballot forms

34.—(1) If a member of a building society who purports to exercise his rights—

(a) to appoint a proxy to vote instead of him at a meeting of the society, or

(b) to vote in a postal ballot, or

(c) to vote on a poll at a meeting of the society,

fails to make a declaration in accordance with sub-paragraph (2) below in the instrument of appointment or, as the case may be, on the voting paper, the appointment made or, as the case may be, the vote cast by him is invalid.

(2) The declaration to be made by a person in pursuance of sub-paragraph (1) above is as follows—

(*a*) that he has attained the age of 18 years or will have attained that age on or before the voting date or, where he is voting by proxy, on or before the date of the meeting;

(*b*) where the vote is to be cast otherwise than on a borrowing members' resolution, that on the voting date he is or, so far as he can reasonably foresee, will be a shareholder of the society;

(*c*) where the vote is to be cast on a borrowing members' resolution, that on the voting date he is or, so far as he can reasonably foresee, will be a borrowing member of the society; and

(*d*) where the member is not entitled to vote unless he had a qualifying shareholding at the qualifying shareholding date, that he had or, so far as he can reasonably foresee, will have such a shareholding on that date.

(3) A building society shall secure that every document issued by it for use as a voting paper or as an instrument for the appointment of a proxy incorporates a form of declaration under this paragraph for completion by the member using it.

(4) If a building society fails to comply with the requirements of sub-paragraph (3) above, the society shall be liable on summary conviction to a fine not exceeding level 4 on the standard scale and so shall any officer who is also guilty of the offence.

(5) In this paragraph—

"qualifying shareholding" shall be construed in accordance with paragraph 23(5) above;

"qualifying shareholding date" has the same meaning as it has for the purposes of paragraph 23 above; and

"voting date" has the meaning given by paragraph 23(6) above.

Advertising requirements in lieu of notice of meetings, etc.

35.—(1) The advertising requirements referred to in paragraph 14 above, in relation to notices of meetings or postal ballots of building societies, are as follows.

(2) Notice of the holding of the meeting or of the postal ballot must be given either—

(*a*) by displaying a notice in a prominent position in every branch office, or

(*b*) by advertisement in one or more newspapers circulating in the areas in which the members of the society reside,

according as the rules of the society provide.

(3) The notice must be so given not later than 21 days before the date of the proposed meeting or, as the case may be, the final date for the receipt of completed ballot papers.

(4) The notice shall state where members may obtain copies of the resolutions and any statements with respect to the matter referred to in a resolution, forms relating to voting by proxy and, in the case of a postal ballot, the ballot papers.

The prescribed amount

36.—(1) For the purposes of this Part of this Schedule, the "prescribed amount" is £100 or such other amount as the Commission, with the consent of the Treasury, by order specifies for the time being.

(2) The power to make an order under sub-paragraph (1) above shall be exercisable by statutory instrument subject to annulment in pursuance of a resolution of either House of Parliament.

(3) An order under sub-paragraph (1) above may contain transitional, consequential or supplementary provision.

DEFINITIONS

"adopt", "adopted", "adoptable powers": s.119(1) and para. 1(4).

"advance fully secured on land": ss.10(11) and 119(1).

"the annual business statement": ss.74(1) and 119(1).

"the annual accounts": ss.71 and 119(1).

"assume", "assumed": para. 1(4).

"authorisation", "authorised": s.119(1).

"borrowing members' resolution", "borrowing member": s.119(1) and para. 29.

"central office": s.119(1).

"Commission": ss.1 and 119(1).

"deferred shares": s.119(1).

"financial year": ss.117 and 119(1).

"member": s.119(1).

"memorandum": s.119(1) and para. 1(4).

"minor": Family Law Reform Act 1969, s.1.
"mortgage": s.119(1).
"mortgage debt": ss.11(14) and 119(1).
"notice", "notice to", "notify": s.119(1).
"officer": s.119(1).
"prescribed amount": para. 36(1).
"public file": ss.106 and 119(1).
"qualifying asset holding": ss.118 and 119(1).
"qualified member": para. 31(2).
"qualifying shareholding", "qualifying shareholding date": para. 23(4) and (5).
"registered address": s.119(1) and para. 13(4).
"requisite number": para. 31(2).
"requisite shareholders' resolution": para. 30(1).
"share": s.119(1).
"special resolution": s.119(1) and para. 27.
"the specified date": para. 3(4).
"the standard scale": Criminal Justice Act 1982, s.37.
"the statutory maximum": Criminal Justice Act 1982, s.74; Magistrates' Courts Act 1980, s.32.
"summary financial statement": ss.76 and 119(1).
"voting date": para. 23(6).
"voting day": para. 33(1).

GENERAL NOTE
This Schedule is divided into three parts as follows:
> *Part I*—General. This Part deals with the establishment of a building society; the contents of its memorandum and rules; requirements for the alteration of its purpose, powers and rules; membership; its name; and other related matters of an administrative nature.
> *Part II*—Unlawful anticipation of powers. This Part is concerned with ensuring that societies proposing to adopt additional powers under the relevant provisions of the Act (ss.15(10), 16(13), 17(11), 18(11), 19(4), 23(5) and 34(5)) do not exercise those powers before the date on which the alteration of powers takes effect.
> *Part III*—Meetings, resolutions and postal ballots. The various provisions in this Part concern members' rights in respect of their society.
It will be obvious that the Schedule contains many very detailed provisions. Two broad general threads may, however, be discerned. First, owing to the greatly increased range of activities which societies can now undertake, it is necessary for persons dealing with a society to have some means of ascertaining what powers that society has at any time. This leads to the requirements relating to the memorandum and the prohibition on the anticipation of powers. Second, the Schedule promotes the participation of shareholders in the affairs of their society while at the same time incorporating safeguards designed to protect societies against the lunatic fringe (*e.g.* para. 31(4)) and to avoid excessive administrative costs (*e.g.* paras. 14 and 35).
Many provisions of the Schedule are the same, or virtually the same, as provisions in the 1962 Act.

PART I

Para. 1
This paragraph deals with the three stages of establishment, registration and incorporation.*Cf.* s.5 of this Act and see ss.1 to 3 of the 1962 Act. Note that the minimum number of persons who may establish a society is ten. If the membership of a society which has already been incorporated falls below ten, the society may be wound up: see s.89(1)(*b*).
The intended name . . . is not undesirable. Cf. s.108, giving the Commission power to require a society to change a misleading name.

Para. 2
It will be observed that the memorandum of a building society will be broadly similar to the memorandum of association of a company: see the Companies Act 1985, s.2. The listing of powers will take the place of the listing of objects. On the other hand, "all persons dealing with the society" are taken to have knowledge of the provisions of the memorandum (subpara. (4)) and they have no general protection from the consequences of dealing with

a society which has no power to enter into the particular transaction. Contrast the position of persons dealing with a company: see s.35 of the 1985 Act.

It is clear from subparas. (2) and (3) that, except as mentioned in subpara. (3), it will not be sufficient, in a case where powers are to be created by an order made under a section, to include in the memorandum a formula such as "the society adopts every power which may hereafter be conferred on societies by order made under" the relevant section. It will be necessary to wait for orders under a particular section and then to set out the terms of every power thereby conferred which is adopted.

Specifying . . . the body or description of body. These words have the effect that the name of the particular body, or the actual description of the class of body, must be specified. A formula such as "any body or description of body for the time being designated" will not suffice.

Para. 3

S.4 of the 1962 Act required every society to provide for certain specified matters in its rules, so the existence of a table of this kind is nothing new. The contents of the new table, however, have been slightly revised, for example by the deletion of mention of fines and forfeiture and the inclusion of the provision relating to surplus assets (No. 14).

Para: 4

Much of this paragraph is based on s.17 of the 1962 Act. It should be noted that although a society must determine the date on which any alteration to its purpose, powers or rules is to take effect ("the specified date"), the date on which the alteration actually takes effect will be the later of the specified date and the date of registration. Note also that any alteration must be effected by a special resolution; it is not open to a society to provide otherwise (subpara. (6), re-enacting s.17(4) of the 1962 Act).

Level 4. Currently £1,000.

Para. 5

This paragraph repeats ss.8 and 9 of the 1962 Act with the addition in subpara. (3) of the prohibition on the nomination by minors of a candidate for election as a director. Subpara. (1) is intended primarily to ensure that borrowers can be admitted to membership of a society without being issued with borrowing or advanced shares. Presumably, however, it is also wide enough to permit a depositor to be a member of the society if the rules permit and by the terms of his deposit he undertakes to accept membership: see the discussion in Wurtzburg and Mills, *Building Society Law* (14th Ed.), p. 65.

Para. 6

This is a re-enactment of s.11 of the 1962 Act.

Para. 7

This paragraph in substance repeats the provisions of s.116 of the 1962 Act, with a few minor amendments. The change in terminology from "senior joint holder" to "representative joint holder" is intended to eliminate the suggestion of superiority contained in the word "senior".

Para. 8

This is a new paragraph putting joint borrowers on an equal footing with joint shareholders. Note, however, that in practical terms subpara. (4)(*a*) may frequently be otiose; borrowers can only vote on an election of directors if they are qualified to vote on an ordinary resolution: see s.60(2). It may be expected that societies will exercise their powers under para. 23 to restrict voting rights on an ordinary resolution to shareholders. Subpara. (4)(*b*) no doubt refers primarily to the new borrowing members' resolutions, defined in para. 29, which the Act requires on a merger or transfer (see ss.93, 94 and 97).

Para. 9

See ss.3(2), 15(1) and 16(1) to (3) of the 1962 Act. Note that under subpara. (5) the effective date for a change of name may be postponed beyond the date of registration. There was no similar provision in the 1962 Act. Subpara. (6) is also new. The name of the society and the form of the common seal must be covered by the rules: para. 3(4).

Para. 10
See ss.15(2) and 16(4) of the 1962 Act.
Level 4. Currently £1,000.

Para. 11
Save for the reference to the public file and the memorandum, this paragraph re-enacts s.108 of the 1962 Act. It is apparently for the society to decide on the date of the change. The address of the principal office must be covered by the rules: para. 3(4).
Level 4. Currently £1,000.

Para. 12
This paragraph is based on s.107 of the 1962 Act but has been somewhat altered.
Level 4. Currently £1,000

Para. 13
This paragraph is based on s.62 of the 1962 Act, but note that (i) it is left entirely to the directors to decide where the register should be kept; (ii) the definition of "registered address" is new and conveniently covers the case where a member has expressly asked that communications be sent to him at an address other than that appearing on the register.
Level 4. Currently £1,000.

Para. 14
This paragraph is new. It provides a convenient and inexpensive method of dealing with the member who has "gone away".

Para. 15
This paragraph is very largely derived from s.63 of the 1962 Act, although owing to the different powers of the Commission, subpara. (1) and s.63(1) are not in identical terms. It should be noted also that the Commission now exercises the functions formerly exercised by the Chief Registrar under s.63(2). *Cf.* the notes to s.1 above.

PART II

The provisions of this Part are necessarily new, since adoptable powers are a creation of this Act.

Para. 16
Under this paragraph, where a society adopts an adoptable power under para. 4, it assumes an obligation not to exercise that power until the alteration in its powers takes effect and it must send to the central office, with the documents required under para. 4(2), a declaration as to the power which satisfies the requirements of the paragraph (subpara. (1)). The obligation does not, however, prevent the society from exercising any power included in the adoptable power which the society has under the law at any time before the registration (sc. of the alteration) takes effect (subpara. (2)).

The declaration must be signed by the chairman of the board of directors, another director and the chief executive. There are two possible forms of declaration. The first states that, to the best of the knowledge and belief of the declarants, after due enquiry, the society has not, or has not "with the permitted qualification" carried on any activity comprised in the power during the period which began one year before the specified date (see para. 4(3)) and expired with the date of the meeting at which the power was adopted. The second form is the same, save that the words "with specified exceptions" appear after the words "after due enquiry, the society". The specified exceptions must not include activities which constitute "significant excesses" of its powers and a declaration specifying any exceptions must also state the opinion of the declarants that the activities are believed not to constitute significant excesses (subpara. (5)). It may well be that opinions will differ as to what constitutes a significant excess. A society would be unwise to rely on satisfying the Commission that any excesses were not significant; if the society is in doubt, it can always seek the Commission's guidance. *Cf.* s.38(13) and the notes thereto.

Paras. 17 and 18
The statutory maximum. Currently £2,000.

Para. 19
On receiving a declaration under para. 16 and the other documents required by para. 4(2), the central office must seek the Commission's determination of the question whether or not the alteration to the society's powers is to be registered (subpara. (1)). If the declaration is in the first form mentioned in the notes to para. 16 and the Commission has no reasonable cause to believe that the society was in breach of its obligation under para. 16 during the period which began a year before the specified date and expired on the date the Commission considers the question, the Commission must direct registration (subpara. (2)(*a*)). In any other case it has a discretion whether to do so or not (subpara. (2)(*b*)). If the Commission decides not to direct registration, the central office will notify the society that it refuses to register the alteration, will specify the activity which is believed to constitute a breach of the society's obligation and will direct the society to apply to the Commission under s.38 for a determination whether the suspect activity was or was not within the powers of the society (subpara. (5)).

If the Commission determines that an activity was outside the society's powers, the directors will be personally liable, jointly and severally, for any consequent loss or expense to the society: s.39(6). Further, the society will not be able to adopt the power in question, and so widen the scope of its business, until a period of twelve months has gone by during which the society has not anticipated its powers in the relevant respect.

See the very similar provisions in Sched. 20, paras. 8 to 11; but note the limited anticipating power in Sched. 20, para. 7.

PART III

Para. 20
Subparas. (1) to (3) replace s.64(1) to (4) of the 1962 Act and subpara. (5) replaces s.64(5). Subpara. (4) covers all resolutions but is limited to the annual general meeting and should be contrasted with s.69(4) of the 1962 Act which covered all meetings but was limited to special resolutions. The holding of meetings must be dealt with by the rules: para. 3(4).

Level 4. Currently £1,000.

Para. 21
This paragraph is based on s.65 of the 1962 Act, but omits the requirement that notice should not be sent more than 56 days before the meeting. The provisions of subpara. (1) relating to instruments appointing proxies are new. Note that, if the last date for the receipt of proxies is seven days before the meeting (*cf.* para. 24(6)), notice must be given 28 days before the meeting.

Para. 22
This paragraph replaces s.66 of the 1962 Act, but with substantial alterations to reflect the fact that there will now be no difference in the qualification provisions for those entitled to vote on a special and on an ordinary resolution and that borrowing members may, in certain circumstances, vote. Subpara. (2) has the curious effect that it will be necessary to give notice of a meeting at which a borrowing members resolution is to be moved to persons becoming borrowing members after the end of the previous financial year, although under para. 23(1)(*b*) they will have no right to vote on the resolution. Subpara.(3) is an important safeguard carried over from the 1962 Act.

Para. 23
This paragraph grants the same voting rights to members whether the resolution to be voted on is a special or an ordinary resolution. Under the 1962 Act, any member holding shares to the value of £1 or more at the end of the previous financial year was entitled to vote on a special resolution (s.69(2)). There was no obligatory rule for voting rights on an ordinary resolution; it was customary to restrict voting rights to those holding shares to the value of £25 or more, to whom alone notice of a meeting at which no special resolution was to be proposed had to be given (s.66(2)).

Under the new regime, the rules of a society may (but need not) restrict the right to vote on any resolution other than a borrowing members' resolution to members who:
(*a*) held a qualifying shareholding on the qualifying shareholding date; *and*
(*b*) held at least one share on the voting date; *and*
(*c*) remained a member (although not necessarily a shareholding member) throughout the intervening period. (Subpara. (3)).
A "qualifying shareholding" is a holding of shares to the value of the prescribed amount (currently £100, but variable: see para. 36) or such lesser amount as the rules of the society

may specify (subpara. (5)). The "qualifying shareholding date" is the end of the last financial year before the voting date (as to which see below) unless the voting date is later in the financial year than the conclusion of the annual general meeting, in which case it is the beginning of the period of 56 days immediately preceding the voting date for members voting in person at a meeting or, as the case may be, on a postal ballot (subpara. (4)). The "voting date" is the date of the meeting at which the resolution is intended to be moved or, in the case of a postal ballot, the final date specified for the return of completed ballot papers; however, in any case where a member appoints a proxy, it is the final date specified for the receipt of instruments appointing proxies.

The voting rights of members must be covered by the rules: para. 3(4).

Note that under para. 29, a borrowing member *must* owe a mortgage debt of at least the "prescribed amount" (currently £100: see above) to be entitled to vote on a borrowing members' resolution.

Para. 24

This paragraph is broadly similar to s.67 of the 1962 Act. It may be observed, however, that the paragraph expressly states that a proxy may be directed how to vote and that a society may now require proxy forms to be delivered up to seven days, rather than 48 hours, before the meeting. Subpara. (2) has the convenient, but perhaps curious, effect that a proxy may be able to vote although his principal could not. Note, however, the declarations as to entitlement to vote required in proxy forms by para. 34.

Level 4. Currently £1,000.

Para. 25

This is a re-enactment of s.68 of the 1962 Act. The right to demand a poll must be covered by the rules: para. 3(4).

Para. 26

This paragraph repeats a provision very commonly found in the rules of societies. Under the old law special resolutions differed from ordinary resolutions in that (i) the rules would almost certainly provide for a more limited franchise on an ordinary resolution than on a special resolution (*cf.* the notes to para. 23), (ii) any member had a right to give notice of intention to move a special resolution and the society then came under a duty to include in the notice of the meeting notice of that intention (s.70 of the 1962 Act), (iii) special resolutions required a three-quarters majority (s.69 of the 1962 Act). It is therefore understandable that societies were anxious to ensure that the special resolution procedure should not be used for a matter which could have been dealt with by ordinary resolution. Now that the differences numbered (i) and (ii) above no longer exist (see notes to paras. 23 and 31), it is not entirely clear what purpose this paragraph serves. Possibly it is intended to prevent attempts to defeat a resolution by making the majority required unnecessarily high, but if so, the word "passed" seems inappropriate.

Para. 27

This paragraph re-enacts s.69(1) and (5) of the 1962 Act, save that subpara. (1)(*b*) is new. The addition reflects the fact that postal ballots are now permissible in respect of all resolutions: see para. 33. Without that addition, a resolution could only be a special resolution if it was passed *at a meeting* of the society, as was the case under the old s.69(1).

Para. 28

This paragraph, of course, is new. Given the difference in franchise between borrowing members' resolutions and other resolutions, it is, perhaps, less obscure than para. 26. See the notes to that paragraph. Note that a borrowing members' resolution may be required under a society's rules in circumstances additional to those in which such a resolution is required under the Act (as to which see para. 29).

Para. 29

Again, this paragraph is new. It may be useful to mention that a borrowing members' resolution is required (i) on an amalgamation under s.93; (ii) on a transfer of engagements under s.94; (iii) on a transfer of business to a commercial company under s.97. There are no other occasions on which a borrowing members' resolution is required under the Act.

The prescribed amount. This has the same meaning as under para. 23 in respect of voting rights.

Para. 30

This paragraph should be read with s.97 which for the first time enables a building society to transfer its business to a commercial company. The policy considerations are mentioned in the notes to that section. Here it is relevant to observe, first, that the requirements for transfer to an existing company are very much more stringent than the requirements for transfer to a specially formed company and, second, that even the latter requirements are thought to constitute a very formidable obstacle for a society to surmount.

Para. 31

This paragraph replaces the much more limited right given to members in respect of special resolutions under s.70 of the 1962 Act. The following elements should be noted:
  (1) the "requisite number" of members have a right to give notice of intention to have moved on their behalf either an ordinary or a special resolution and, subject to certain qualifications, to have the notice circulated;
  (2) the requisite number of members also have a right, subject to certain qualifications, to have a statement in support of their resolution circulated;
  (3) in the absence of any other provision in the rules, the requisite number is fifty if the society has commercial assets of £100 million or more and ten if it has not. The society may specify a lower number and may require (broadly speaking) that each member giving notice has held shares of a value of up to £100 for a period up to two years.

Compare the provisions of s.61(1) and (2) relating to the right to join in nominating a candidate for election as a director.

The broad aim of the paragraph is to ensure that where a resolution has a certain level of support, the members wishing to have it moved have a reasonable opportunity to bring it to the attention of the general body of members, together with their arguments in its favour. The qualifications applicable to the right to have notice of a resolution and a statement circulated are the same, *mutatis mutandis*, as the provisions in respect of election addresses contained in s.61(8) and reference should be made to the notes to that subsection. See also s.61(9) concerning the functions of the Commission and the court (subpara. (7)). Subpara. (5) will be useful to prevent abuse of the above rights by members seeking to reintroduce a resolution that was recently defeated. Note that the right to move a resolution must be covered by the rules: para. 3(4).

Level 4. Currently £1,000.

Para. 32

This paragraph, as it states, supplements the preceding paragraph. Subpara. (3) is again a useful safeguard.

Para. 33

This is a new general provision covering postal ballots. Again, it contains a safeguard against accidental omissions or non-receipt of documents. Subpara. (5) creates an anomaly similar to that noted in relation to para. 22(2): notice must be given to persons who have only become borrowers since the end of the previous financial year and who are therefore not entitled to vote.

Para. 34

This paragraph is new. Presumably it is designed to ensure that there are brought to the member's attention the requirements which he must satisfy before he can vote. Curiously enough, the only sanction (other than invalidity) imposed by the paragraph is imposed not on persons falsely completing the declaration but on building societies which fail to incorporate the declaration in the relevant documents.

Level 4. Currently £1,000.

Para. 35

This paragraph should be read with paragraph 14. It is a very useful new provision designed to combat the problem of members who have "gone away". Similar methods of advertisement have long been used by many societies for matters such as changes in interest rates.

SCHEDULE 3

AUTHORISATION: SUPPLEMENTARY PROVISIONS

PART I

PRELIMINARY

1. In this Schedule—
   "authorisation" means authorisation under section 9 or on renewal under section 41
      or reauthorisation under section 44;
   "conditions" means conditions to be complied with by a building society and imposed
      on the grant of authorisation under section 9, on the renewal of authorisation
      under section 41, on reauthorisation under section 44 or under section 42;
   "revocation", with reference to authorisation, means revocation under section 43.

PART II

AUTHORISATION

Procedure for authorisation

2.—(1) An application for authorisation—
   (*a*) shall be made in such manner as the Commission may specify, either generally or in
          any particular case; and
   (*b*) shall be accompanied by such information as the Commission may reasonably require,
          either generally or in any particular case, in order to decide whether or not to grant
          authorisation and whether with or without conditions.
   (2) If required to do so by notice from the Commission given at any time after an
application for authorisation has been made and before a decision has been reached on the
application, the applicant shall furnish to the Commission such additional information as it
may reasonably require in order to reach a decision on the application.
   (3) If on an application for authorisation the Commission proposes to impose conditions
the provisions of Part III of this Schedule shall apply.
   (4) If the Commission proposes to refuse to grant authorisation it shall serve a notice on
the applicant stating—
   (*a*) that it proposes to grant authorisation;
   (*b*) the grounds for the proposed refusal; and
   (*c*) that the applicant may make representations with respect to the proposed refusal
          within such period of not less than 28 days as may be specified in the notice and that,
          if the applicant so requests, the Commission will afford to it an opportunity of being
          heard by the Commission within that period.
   (5) If the grounds for the proposed refusal include the ground that any officer of the
society is not a fit and proper person to hold office in the society the Commission shall also
serve the notice specified in sub-paragraph (4) above on the officer concerned giving him the
like right to make representations and to be heard with respect to his fitness and propriety
for office.
   (6) The Commission shall, before reaching a decision on the application, consider any
representations made to it in accordance with sub-paragraph (4) or (5) above.
   (7) If, on an application for authorisation, the Commission refuses to grant authorisation
it shall serve on the society and, subject to paragraph 10 below, on every director of and the
chief executive of the society, and every other person on whom a notice was served under
sub-paragraph (5) above, a notice stating the Commission's decision and the grounds for it
and, subject to sub-paragraph (8) below, shall do so before the expiry of the period of 6
months beginning with the date on which the application was received.
   (8) In any case where, under sub-paragraph (2) above, the Commission requires additional
information with respect to an application, the latest time for the giving of a notice under
sub-paragraph (7) above with respect to the application shall be the expiry of whichever of
the following periods first expires, namely—
   (*a*) the period of 6 months beginning with the date on which the additional information
          is furnished to the Commission; and
   (*b*) the period of 12 months beginning with the date on which the application was received
          by the Commission.

(9) In the application of this paragraph to an application for the renewal of authorisation under section 41—
  (a) sub-paragraph (7) shall have effect with the substitution of 3 for 6 months; and
  (b) sub-paragraph (8) shall have effect with the substitution of 3 for 6 months and of 6 for 12 months respectively.

Offences in connection with application

3.—(1) Any building society which furnishes any information or makes any statement which is false or misleading in a material particular in connection with an application for authorisation shall be liable, on conviction on indictment or on summary conviction, to a fine which, on summary conviction, shall not exceed the statutory maximum.

(2) Any person who knowingly or recklessly furnishes any information or makes any statement which is false or misleading in a material particular in connection with an application for authorisation shall be liable—
  (a) on conviction on indictment, to imprisonment for a term not exceeding two years or to a fine or both; or
  (b) on summary conviction, to a fine not exceeding the statutory maximum.

PART III

IMPOSITION OF CONDITIONS

4.—(1) If the Commission proposes to impose conditions it shall serve on the society and, subject to paragraph 10 below, on every director of the society and its chief executive a notice stating—
  (a) that the Commission proposes to impose conditions;
  (b) what the conditions will be;
  (c) the grounds for their imposition; and
  (d) that the society may make representations with respect to the proposed imposition of the conditions within such period of not less than 14 days as may be specified in the notice and that, if the society so requests, the Commission will afford to it an opportunity of being heard by the Commission within that period.

(2) If any condition proposed to be imposed on the society includes a requirement for the removal from office of any officer of the society the Commission shall also serve the notice specified in sub-paragraph (1) above on the officer whose removal is proposed giving him the like right to make representations and to be heard with respect to his proposed removal from office.

(3) The Commission shall, before reaching a decision on whether to impose conditions and, if so, what conditions, consider any representations made in accordance with sub-paragraph (1) or (2) above and, except where paragraph 5 below applies, the Commission shall serve on the society and, subject to paragraph 10 below, on every director of and the chief executive of the society and every other person on whom a notice was served under sub-paragraph (2) above, a notice stating its decision.

(4) If the Commission decides to impose conditions the notice under sub-paragraph (3) above shall—
  (a) specify the conditions, and
  (b) state the grounds for its decision to impose them.

(5) The Commission may not impose conditions on grounds other than those stated, or grounds included in those stated, in the notice served by it under sub-paragraph (1) above.

5.—(1) This paragraph applies where the Commission has decided to impose conditions but proposes to impose conditions different from and more onerous than those stated in the notice served by the Commission under paragraph 4(1) above.

(2) The Commission shall serve on the society and, subject to paragraph 10 below, on every director of the society and its chief executive, a notice stating—
  (a) what conditions the Commission proposes to impose;
  (b) the grounds for the imposition of those conditions instead of the conditions stated in the notice under paragraph 4(1) above; and
  (c) that the society may make representations with respect to the conditions the Commission proposes to impose within such period of not less than seven days as may be specified in the notice and that, if the society so requests, the Commission will afford to it an opportunity of being heard by the Commission within that period.

(3) If any condition proposed to be imposed on the society includes a requirement for the removal from office of any officer of the society the Commission shall also serve the notice

specified in sub-paragraph (2) above on the officer whose removal is proposed giving him the like right to make representations and to be heard with respect to his proposed removal from office.

(4) The Commission shall, before reaching a decision on whether to impose conditions different from those stated in the notice served under paragraph 4(1) above, and, if so, what conditions, consider any representations made in accordance with sub-paragraph (2) or (3) above and shall serve on the society and subject to paragraph 10 below, on every director of and the chief executive of the society and every other person on whom a notice was served under sub-paragraph (3) above, a notice stating its decision.

(5) If the Commission decides to impose conditions the notice under sub-paragraph (4) above shall—

(a) specify the conditions, and

(b) state the grounds for their imposition.

(6) The Commission may not impose conditions on grounds other than those stated, or grounds included in those stated, in the notice served by it under sub-paragraph (2) above.

PART IV

REVOCATION OF AUTHORISATION

Procedure for revocation

6.—(1) If the Commission proposes to revoke a society's authorisation it shall serve on the society and, subject to paragraph 10 below, on every director and its chief executive a notice stating—

(a) that the Commission proposes to revoke the authorisation,

(b) the grounds for the proposed revocation; and

(c) that the society may make representations with respect to the proposed revocation within such period of not less than 14 days as may be specified in the notice and that, if the society so requests, it will be afforded an opportunity of being heard by the Commission within that period.

(2) If the grounds for the proposed revocation include the ground that any officer of the society is not a fit and proper person to hold office in the society the Commission shall also serve the notice specified in sub-paragraph (1) above on the officer concerned giving him the like right to make representations and to be heard with respect to his fitness and propriety for office.

(3) The Commission shall, before reaching a decision on whether to revoke the authorisation, consider any representations made to it in accordance with sub-paragraph (1) or (2) above and, except where paragraph 7 below applies, the Commission shall serve on the society and, subject to paragraph 10 below, on every director of and the chief executive of the society and every other person on whom a notice was served under sub-paragraph (2) above, a notice stating its decision.

(4) If the Commission decides to revoke a society's authorisation, the notice under sub-paragraph (3) above shall state the grounds for the decision.

(5) The Commission may not revoke a society's authorisation on grounds other than those stated, or grounds included in those stated, in the notice served under sub-paragraph (1) above.

7.—(1) This paragraph applies where the Commission proposes, instead of revoking a society's authorisation, to impose conditions.

(2) The Commission shall serve on the society and, subject to paragraph 10 below, on every director of the society and its chief executive a notice stating—

(a) that it proposes to impose conditions instead of revoking the society's authorisation;

(b) what conditions it proposes to impose;

(c) the grounds for the imposition of conditions instead of revoking the society's authorisation; and

(d) that the society may make representations with respect to the conditions the Commission proposes to impose within such period of not less than seven days as may be specified in the notice and that, if the society so requests, it will be afforded an opportunity of being heard by the Commission within that period.

(3) If any condition proposed to be imposed on the society includes a requirement for the removal from office of any officer of the society, the Commission shall also serve the notice specified in sub-paragraph (2) above on the officer whose removal is proposed giving him a like right to make representations and to be heard with respect to his proposed removal from office.

(4) The Commission shall, before reaching a decision on whether to impose conditions and, if so, what conditions, consider any representations made in accordance with sub-paragraph (2) or (3) above and, except where paragraph 8 below applies, the Commission shall serve on the society and, subject to paragraph 10 below, on every director of and the chief executive of the society and every other person on whom a notice was served under sub-paragraph (3) above, a notice stating its decision.

(5) If the Commission decides to impose conditions the notice under sub-paragraph (4) above shall—

(*a*) specify the conditions, and

(*b*) state the grounds for their imposition.

(6) The Commission may not impose conditions on grounds other than those stated, or grounds included in those stated, in the notice served by the Commission under sub-paragraph (2) above.

8.—(1) This paragraph applies where the Commission has decided, instead of revoking a society's authorisation, to impose conditions but proposes to impose conditions different from and more onerous than those stated in the notice served by the Commission under paragraph 7(2) above.

(2) The Commission shall serve on the society and, subject to paragraph 10 below, on every director of the society and its chief executive, a notice stating—

(*a*) what conditions it proposes to impose;

(*b*) the grounds for the imposition of those conditions instead of the conditions stated in the notice under paragraph 7(2) above; and

(*c*) that the society may make representations with respect to the conditions the Commission proposes to impose within such period of not less than seven days as may be specified in the notice and that, if the society so requests, the Commission will afford to it an opportunity of being heard by the Commission within that period.

(3) If any condition proposed to be imposed on the society includes a requirement for the removal from office of any officer of the society the Commission shall also serve the notice specified in sub-paragraph (2) above on the officer whose removal is proposed giving him the like right to make representations and to be heard with respect to his proposed removal from office.

(4) The Commission shall, before reaching a decision on whether to impose conditions different from those stated in the notice served under paragraph 7(2) above and, if so, what conditions, consider any representations made in accordance with sub-paragraph (2) or (3) above and shall serve on the society and, subject to paragraph 10 below, on every director of and the chief executive of the society and every other person on whom a notice was served under sub-paragraph (3) above, a notice stating its decision.

(5) If the Commission decides to impose conditions the notice under sub-paragraph (4) above shall—

(*a*) specify the conditions, and

(*b*) state the grounds for their imposition.

(6) The Commission may not impose conditions on grounds other than those stated, or grounds included in those stated, in the notice served by it under sub-paragraph (2) above.

PART V

SUPPLEMENTARY

Imposition of conditions on appeal

9.—(1) The modifications of the provisions of Part III of this Schedule in their application to the imposition of conditions by the Commission in pursuance of a direction of an appeal tribunal under section 47(6) or (7) are as follows.

(2) The notice under paragraph 4(1) shall be served on the society and the other persons there specified within the period of 14 days beginning with the date on which the Commission received notice of the tribunal's decision under subsection (10) of that section; and a copy shall also be sent within that period to the tribunal.

(3) The notice under paragraph 4(1) may specify, as the period within which representations may be made, a period of not less than 7 days.

(4) If the Commission serves a notice under paragraph 5(2) on the society and the other persons there specified it shall send a copy of the notice to the tribunal.

Notice to directors and chief executives

10. Where any provision of this Schedule requires notice of any matter to be served on every director of a building society that requirement is satisfied by serving notice on each director whose appointment has been officially notified and the non-receipt of a notice of a matter by a director or the chief executive does not affect the validity of any action on the part of the Commission.

DEFINITIONS
"authorisation": para. 1 and ss.9, 41 and 44.
"chief executive": s.59(1).
"the Commission": ss.1 and 119(1).
"conditions": para.1 and ss.9, 41, 42 and 44.
"notice": s.119(1).
"officer": s.119(1).
"revocation": para.1 and s.43.
"statutory maximum": Criminal Justice Act 1982, s.74; Magistrates' Courts Act 1980, s.32.

GENERAL NOTE
Part II of this Schedule sets out the procedure to be followed:
(i) where a society applies for initial authorisation under s.9;
(ii) where a society applies for a renewal of its current authorisation pursuant to a direction given to it by the Commission under s.41; and
(iii) where a society whose authorisation has expired under s.41(7), or been revoked under s.43(1) or (3)(c), applies for reauthorisation under s.44.
Part III of the Schedule sets out the procedure to be followed where the Commission proposes to impose conditions:
(i) on an authorisation granted pursuant to an application made in any of the cases described above; and
(ii) in exercise of the power conferred by s.42 to impose conditions on a society's current authorisation.
Part IV of the Schedule sets out the procedure to be followed where the Commission proposes to revoke a society's authorisation under s.43(1), or where it proposes to impose conditions on a society's authorisation as an alternative to revoking it.
Part V of the Schedule modifies the provisions of Part III to enable the Commission to give effect to a direction of an appeal tribunal under s.47(6) or (7):
(i) that authorisation be granted conditionally instead of being refused (this will apply where the society has appealed from a refusal by the Commission to grant authorisation on an application brought under ss.9, 41 or 44);
(ii) that authorisation be continued subject to conditions instead of being revoked (this will apply where the society has appealed from a decision of the Commission to revoke its authorisation under s.43); or
(iii) that authorisation be granted or continued subject to conditions different from those imposed by the Commission (this will apply where the society has appealed from a decision of the Commission to impose conditions under ss.9, 41, 42 or 44; but note that there seems to be no right of appeal against conditions imposed by the Commission in lieu of revocation under Part IV of this Schedule: see ss.46 and 47 and the notes thereto).
The detailed provisions of the Schedule are largely self-explanatory and do not call for comment. It may be noted, however, that a society must be given the opportunity to make representations (including oral representations) if it so wishes before the Commission can reject an application for authorisation, or revoke an existing authorisation, or impose conditions on a new or continuing authorisation (see Part II, para. 2(4), Part III, paras. 4(1) and 5(2) and Part IV paras. 6(1), 7(2) and 8(2)). It may also be noted that, if the Commission proposes to refuse an application for authorisation, or to revoke an existing authorisation, on the ground that any officer of the society is not a fit and proper person to hold office, the officer concerned must be given an opportunity to make representations (or to be heard) as well as the society (see Part II, para. 2(5) and Part IV, para. 6(2)). A similar opportunity must also be given to any officer whose removal from office will be required by any condition proposed to be imposed by the Commission (see Part III, paras. 4(2) and 4(3) and Part IV, paras. 7(3) and 8(3)).
The provisions of this Schedule are based to some extent on regs. 6, 9 and 13 of the Building Societies (Authorisation) Regulations 1981; but the present provisions are considerably more detailed than their predecessors.

SCHEDULE 4

ADVANCES: SUPPLEMENTARY PROVISIONS

Provisions as to sale of mortgaged property

1.—(1) Where any land has been mortgaged to a building society as security for an advance and a person sells the land in the exercise of a power (whether statutory or express) exercisable by virtue of the mortgage, it shall be his duty—
  (*a*) in exercising that power, to take reasonable care to ensure that the price at which the land is sold is the best price that can reasonably be obtained, and
  (*b*) within 28 days from the completion of the sale, to send to the mortgagor at his last-known address by the recorded delivery service a notice containing the prescribed particulars of the sale.

(2) In so far as any agreement relieves, or may have the effect of relieving, a building society or any other person from the obligation imposed by sub-paragraph (1)(*a*) above, the agreement shall be void.

(3) Breach by a building society or any other person of the duty imposed by sub-paragraph (1)(*b*) above, if without reasonable excuse, shall be an offence.

(4) Any person guilty of an offence under sub-paragraph (3) above shall be liable on summary conviction—
  (*a*) to a fine not exceeding level 2 on the standard scale, and
  (*b*) to an additional fine for each week during which the offence continues not exceeding £10,
and, in relation to such an offence on the part of a building society, so shall any officer who is also guilty of the offence.

(5) Nothing in this section shall affect the operation of any rule of law relating to the duty of a mortgagee to account to his mortgagor.

(6) In sub-paragraph (1) above "mortgagor", in relation to a mortgage in favour of a building society, includes any person to whom, to the knowledge of the person selling the land, any of the rights or liabilities of the mortgagor under the mortgage have passed, whether by operation of law or otherwise.

Discharge of mortgages

2.—(1) When all money intended to be secured by a mortgage given to a building society has been fully paid or discharged, the society may endorse on or annex to the mortgage one or other of the following—
  (*a*) a receipt in the prescribed form under the society's seal, countersigned by any person acting under the authority of the board of directors;
  (*b*) a reconveyance of the mortgaged property to the mortgagor;
  (*c*) a reconveyance of the mortgaged property to such person of full age, and on such trusts (if any), as the mortgagor may direct.

(2) Where in pursuance of sub-paragraph (1) above a receipt is endorsed on or annexed to a mortgage, not being a charge or incumbrance registered under the Land Registration Act 1925, the receipt shall operate in accordance with section 115(1), (3), (6) and (8) of the Law of Property Act 1925 (discharge of mortgages by receipt) in the like manner as a receipt which fulfils all the requirements of subsection (1) of that section.

(3) Section 115(9) of the Law of Property Act 1925 shall not apply to a receipt in the prescribed form endorsed or annexed by a building society in pursuance of sub-paragraph (1) above; and in the application of that subsection to a receipt so endorsed or annexed which is not in that form, the receipt shall be taken to be executed in the manner required by the statute relating to the society if it is under the society's seal and countersigned as mentioned in sub-paragraph (1)(*a*) above.

(4) The foregoing sub-paragraphs shall, in the case of a mortgage of registered land, have effect without prejudice to the operation of the Land Registration Act 1925 or any rules in force under it.

(5) In this paragraph—
    "mortgage" includes a further charge;
    "the mortgagor", in relation to a mortgage, means the person for the time being
        entitled to the equity of redemption; and
    "registered land" has the same meaning as in the Land Registration Act 1925.

(6) This paragraph does not apply to Scotland.

(7) In the application of this paragraph to Northern Ireland—

(*a*) in sub-paragraph (1) for the words "on such trusts" there shall be substituted the words "on such uses";

(*b*) in sub-paragraph (2)—

(i) for the words from "charge" to "Property Act 1925" there shall be substituted the words "on registered land, the receipt to operate in accordance with Article 3(1), (7) and (9) of the Property (Discharge of Mortgage by Receipt) (Northern Ireland) Order 1983"; and

(ii) for the words "subsection (1) of that section" there shall be substituted the words "paragraph (1) of that Article";

(*c*) for sub-paragraphs (3) and (4) there shall be substituted—

"(3) If the mortgage is registered in accordance with the Registration of Deeds Act (Northern Ireland) 1970, the registrar under that Act shall—

(*a*) on production of the receipt mentioned in sub-paragraph (1) above make a note in the Abstract Book against the entry relating to the mortgage that the mortgage is satisfied; and

(*b*) grant a certificate, either on the mortgage or separately, that the mortgage is satisfied.

(4) The certificate granted under sub-paragraph (3)(*b*) above shall—

(*a*) be received in all courts and proceedings without further proof; and

(*b*) have the effect of clearing the register of the mortgage.";

(*d*) in sub-paragraph (5) for the definition of "registered land" there shall be substituted the following definition—

"registered land" means land the title to which is registered under Part III of the Land Registration Act (Northern Ireland) 1970;".

Power to prescribe form of documents

3.—(1) The Chief Registrar may make rules for prescribing anything authorised or required by any provision of this Schedule to be prescribed; and in this Schedule "prescribed" means prescribed by rules made under this paragraph.

(2) The power to make rules under this paragraph shall be exercisable by statutory instrument.

DEFINITIONS

"Chief Registrar": s.119(1).

"mortgage": s.119(1) and (in para. 2) para. 2(5).

"mortgagor" (in para. 1(1)): para. 1(6).

"mortgagor" (in para. 2): para. 2(5).

"officer": s.119(1).

"prescribed": para. 3(2).

"registered land": para. 2(5) and Land Registration Act 1925, s.3(xxiv).

"the standard scale": Criminal Justice Act 1982, s.37.

GENERAL NOTE

Para. 1

This paragraph substantially re-enacts s.36 of the 1962 Act; the only significant departures from the old section are to be found in sub-paras. (3) and (4), which modify and rationalise the provisions imposing the criminal sanctions for breach of the duty to send notice to the mortgagor containing the prescribed particulars of the sale. The duty imposed by what is now subpara. (1)(*a*) has been held to put the society exercising a power of sale over mortgaged property in the position of a fiduciary vendor: see *Reliance Permanent Building Society* v. *Harwood-Stamper* [1944] Ch. 362, discussed in Wurtzburg and Mills, *Building Society Law* (14th Ed.), pp. 209–211.

The prescribed particulars: the particulars to be contained in a notice sent under subpara. (1)(*b*) will be prescribed by rules to be made by the Chief Registrar of Friendly Societies (not, be it noted, by the Commission) under para. 3.

Level 2. Currently £100.

Para. 2

Sub-paras. (1)–(6) re-enact with minor variations the provisions of s.37 of the 1962 Act, and subpara. (7) makes provision for Northern Ireland. It appears that a receipt given in ignorance of the fact that moneys still remain due under the mortgage will discharge the mortgagor's personal liability under the mortgage covenants as well as the society's security over the mortgaged property: see *Harvey* v. *Municipal Permanent Investment Building Society* (1884) 26 Ch.D. 273 and *Erewash Borough Council* v. *Taylor* [1979] C.L.Y.B., para. 1831. *Sed quaere*.

In the prescribed form: the form will be prescribed by rules made by the Chief Registrar under para. 3. Presumably it remains the law that a society may, as an alternative, use the form of receipt provided for in s.115 of the Law of Property Act 1925 (see subs. (5) of that section and the Third Schedule to the Act): Wurtzburg and Mills, *Building Society Law* (14th Ed.), p. 202 but note pp. 204–5, explaining why the latter form is normally to be avoided.

Subpara. (4): as to the position regarding registered land, see Land Registration Act 1925, s.35 and rules 151 and 152 of the Land Registration Rules 1925 (which make provision for an instrument of discharge in Form 53).

Section 24   SCHEDULE 5

THE BUILDING SOCIETIES INVESTOR PROTECTION BOARD

Constitution

1.—(1) The Board shall consist of seven members as follows, namely—
   (*a*) the First Commissioner for the time being, who shall be the chairman of the Board,
   (*b*) two members appointed by the First Commissioner from among the other members of the Commission, and
   (*c*) four other members appointed under sub-paragraph (2) below;
and the First Commissioner shall appoint one of his two appointees to be deputy chairman of the Board.

(2) The four members to be appointed under this sub-paragraph shall be appointed by the Treasury, after consultation with the First Commissioner, and of those four, three shall be persons who are or have been directors, chief executives or managers of building societies.

(3) Each appointed member of the Board may, with the approval of the First Commissioner and subject to sub-paragraph (4) below appoint an alternate member to perform his duties as a member in his absence.

(4) In the case of a person appointed a member of the Board as a present or former director, chief executive or manager of a building society any alternate shall himself be or have been such a director, chief executive or manager.

Appointment and tenure of office

2.—(1) Subject to the following provisions of this paragraph a person shall hold and vacate office as a member or as deputy chairman of the Board in accordance with the terms of the instrument appointing him.

(2) A person appointed by the First Commissioner under paragraph 1(1)(*b*) above shall vacate his office as a member of the Board if he ceases to be a member of the Commission and the person appointed by the First Commissioner to be deputy chairman of the Board shall vacate his office as such in the same event.

(3) A person appointed under paragraph 1(2) above shall be appointed for a term not exceeding two years but he may be reappointed on his ceasing to hold office or at any time thereafter.

(4) A person appointed under paragraph 1(2) above may at any time resign his office as a member by giving to the Treasury a signed notice stating that he resigns from that office.

Allowances

3. The Board shall pay to each member such allowances in respect of expenses as the Board may, with the consent of the Treasury, determine.

Proceedings

4.—(1) The Board shall determine its own procedure, including the quorum necessary for its meetings.

(2) The validity of any proceedings of the Board shall not be affected by any vacancy among the members or by any defect in the appointment of any member.

5.—(1) The fixing of the common seal of the Board shall be authenticated by the signature of the chairman of the Board or some other person authorised by the Board to act for that purpose.

(2) A document purporting to be duly executed under the seal of the Board shall be received in evidence and deemed to be so executed, unless the contrary is proved.

Accounts, audit and annual report

6.—(1) The Board may determine its own financial year.

(2) It shall be the duty of the Board—

(*a*) to keep proper accounts and proper records in relation to the accounts; and

(*b*) to prepare in respect of any period (referred to in this paragraph as "the initial period") beginning with the commencement date for section 24 and ending with the beginning of the Board's first financial year and in respect of each of its financial years a statement of accounts showing the state of affairs and income and expenditure of the Board.

(3) A statement of accounts prepared in accordance with sub-paragraph (2)(*b*) above shall be audited by auditors appointed by the Board and the auditors shall report to the Board stating whether in their opinion the provisions of sub-paragraph (2) above have been complied with.

(4) A person shall not be qualified to be appointed as auditor by the Board under sub-paragraph (3) above unless—

(*a*) he is a member of, or a Scottish firm in which all the partners are members of, one or more bodies of accountants established in the United Kingdom and for the time being recognised for the purposes of section 389(1)(*a*) of the Companies Act 1985 by the Secretary of State; or

(*b*) he is for the time being authorised to be appointed as auditor of a company under section 389(1)(*b*) of that Act as having similar qualifications obtained outside the United Kingdom.

(5) It shall be the duty of the Board, as soon as possible after the end of the initial period and of each of its financial years, to prepare a report on the discharge of its functions during that period or, as the case may be, during that financial year.

(6) It shall be the duty of the Board to publish, in such manner as it thinks appropriate, every statement of account prepared in accordance with sub-paragraph (2)(*b*) above and every report prepared in accordance with sub-paragraph (5) above.

DEFINITIONS

"the Board": s.24(1).

"chief executive": s.59(1).

"the Commission": ss.1 and 119(1).

"the First Commissioner": s.1(2).

"initial period": para. 6(2)(*b*).

"manager": s.119(1).

GENERAL NOTE

Para.1 makes provision for the constitution of the Building Societies Investor Protection Board, which is to administer the Fund established under the protective scheme provisions contained in ss.25–29. The following paragraphs of the Schedule provide for the terms on which the members of the Board will hold office, the proceedings of the Board, and its accounts and annual report. Since contributions to the Fund will be called up from the contributory societies only in the event of a building society becoming insolvent, the requirement that the Board should make and publish an annual report on the discharge of its functions (see para. 6(5) and (6)) seems a little surprising. It is to be expected (and indeed hoped) that the annual reports for most years will make dull reading.

Section 27(12)   SCHEDULE 6

INSOLVENCY PAYMENTS: TRUSTS AND JOINT OR CLIENT ACCOUNT HOLDINGS

1.—(1) The following provisions of this Schedule have effect for the purposes of section 27.

(2) In this Schedule "investment", in relation to a building society, means the rights of a person arising from a deposit made by him, or a predecessor in title of his, with the society

or the interest of a person constituted by a share of his in the society; and that person is referred to as holding, or as the holder of, the investment.

2.—(1) Where any persons hold an investment in a building society as trustees then, unless the investment is held on trust for a person absolutely entitled to it as against the trustees, the trustees shall be treated as a single and continuing body of persons, distinct from the persons who may from time to time be the trustees and if the same persons hold different investments as trustees under different trusts, they shall be treated as a separate and distinct body with respect to each of those trusts.

(2) For the purpose of this Schedule an investment is held on trust for a person absolutely entitled to it as against the trustees where that person has the exclusive right, subject only to satisfying any outstanding charge, lien or other right of the trustees to resort to the investment for payment of duty, taxes costs or other outgoings, to direct how the investment shall be dealt with.

(3) Any reference in sub-paragraph (1) or (2) above to a person absolutely entitled to an investment as against the trustees includes a reference to two or more persons who are so entitled jointly; and in the application of sub-paragraph (2) to Scotland the words from "subject" to "outgoings" are omitted.

3. Where an investment is held on trust for any person absolutely entitled to it, or as the case may be, for two or more persons so entitled jointly, that person or, as the case may be, those persons jointly shall be treated as entitled to the investment without the intervention of any trust.

4.—(1) Except in the case of a partnership, where two or more persons are jointly entitled to an investment and paragraph 2(1) above does not apply, each of them shall be treated as having a separate investment of an amount produced by dividing the amount of the investment to which they are jointly entitled by the number of persons who are so entitled.

(2) Where two or more persons hold, or are absolutely entitled to, an investment as partners, the partnership shall be treated as holding, or as being absolutely entitled to, the investment as a single person distinct from the persons of whom the partnership is composed.

5. Where an investment is made by a person whose business is the provision of professional services or the carrying on of investment business (within the meaning of the Financial Services Act 1986) with money held to the account of clients of his, each of them shall be treated as having a separate investment of an amount equal to so much of the amount of the investment as represents money held to his account as a client.

6. The Board may decline to make any payment under section 27 in respect of an investment until the person claiming to be entitled to it informs the Board of the capacity in which he is entitled to the investment; and if it appears to the Board—

(*a*) that the persons entitled to an investment are so entitled as trustees, or

(*b*) that paragraph 3 above applies to an investment, or

(*c*) that two or more persons are jointly entitled to an investment other than as trustees, or

(*d*) that paragraph 5 above applies to an investment,

the Board may decline to make any payment in respect of the investment until sufficient information has been disclosed to it to enable it to determine what payment (if any) should be made under that section and to whom.

7. In this Schedule "jointly entitled" means—

(*a*) in England and Wales and Northern Ireland, beneficially entitled as joint tenants, tenants in common or as coparceners, and

(*b*) in Scotland, beneficially entitled as joint owners or owners in common.

DEFINITIONS
  "the Board": s.24(1).
  "deposit": s.119(1).
  "investment": para. 1(2).
  "jointly entitled": para. 7.
  "share": s.119(1).

GENERAL NOTE

Paras. 2 and 3
  The concept underlying these provisions is that, where a beneficiary under a trust has become entitled to call upon the trustees to transfer the trust property to him absolutely, then the beneficiary should be treated as the owner of the property (which in substance he is, subject only to satisfying any right of the trustees to be indemnified out of the trust property in respect of costs, taxes and so forth). Para. 2 is modelled on the Capital Gains

Tax Act 1979, ss.46(2) and 52(1), and reference should be made to works on revenue law for a full discussion of the concept of absolute entitlement as against trustees (see too *Stephenson* v. *Barclays Bank* [1975] 1 All E.R. 625, where the matter was considered in detail by Walton J.). In the present context, the effect of a beneficiary becoming absolutely entitled as against the trustees to shares in, or a deposit with, a building society is that the beneficiary rather than the trustees will be entitled to receive any payment out of the Fund in respect of the investment in the event of the society becoming insolvent: see para. 3 and s.27(1). Similar principles apply where two or more beneficiaries are jointly absolutely entitled to the investment: see *ibid.* In the case of joint entitlement, somewhat arbitrary results may arise from the combined operation of paras. 3 and 4(1). Suppose, for example, that trustees hold £20,000 in building society shares upon trust for two children contingently upon their attaining the age of 18. If the society becomes insolvent when the children are still under 18 (*i.e.* before they have become absolutely entitled to the shares) then the trustees will be entitled to any payment made in respect of the investment under s.27. The trustees will be treated as holding the investment as a single and continuing body of persons (see para. 2(1)), so that, in their hands, the shares will constitute a protected investment only to the extent of £10,000. Hence the maximum payment which the trustees can receive from the Fund under s.27 is £9,000 (see s.27(1), (2) and (5)). If, however, the society had become insolvent after the children had attained the age of 18, each child would have been treated as having a separate, and fully protected, investment of £10,000 (see paras. 3(2) and 4(1)), with the consequence that each child would have been entitled to receive a separate payment from the Fund of up to £9,000.

Para. 5

Or the carrying on of investment business (within the meaning of the Financial Services Act 1986.) These words were added to the Bill at the Report stage in the House of Lords. Their significance was explained by Lord Brabazon (speaking on behalf of the Government) as follows: "Under rules to be made under the financial services legislation, investment businesses will have to hold client money in separate accounts, which could be with both building societies and banks. However remote the contingency, the proper protection should be available to such accounts, so that the minimum [sic] protection of 90 per cent. up to £10,000 should be available to each client separately, as well as to the account as a whole" (see *Hansard*, H.L., Vol. 478, col. 1131).

Subs. 7(a)

The reference to coparceny is puzzling. There are some (highly exceptional) circumstances in which persons can still hold real property as coparceners, notwithstanding the changes to the old law of succession made by the 1925 property legislation. It seems highly doubtful, however, whether a building society investment (a form of personalty) could be held by persons as coparceners.

Section 32   SCHEDULE 7

INVESTORS: SPECIAL PROVISIONS

Members or depositors dying

1.—(1) The provisions of this paragraph have effect where a member of, or depositor with, a building society dies, testate or intestate, domiciled in any part of the United Kingdom leaving a sum of money in the funds of the society not exceeding £5000.

(2) If a person claiming to be beneficially entitled to the sum of money under the will or the applicable law of intestacy furnishes to the society—

(*a*) satisfactory evidence of the death, and

(*b*) a statutory declaration that the member or depositor has died and that the person claiming the amount is beneficially entitled under the will or the applicable law of intestacy to receive it,

the society may, without probate of the will or the grant of letters of administration or confirmation, as the case may be, pay the sum of money to that person.

(3) Where a building society has paid a sum of money to any person in reliance on evidence of death and a statutory declaration furnished as mentioned in sub-paragraph (2) above, the payment shall be valid and effectual with respect to any demand against the funds of the society from any other person claiming to be entitled to it but without prejudice to that person's pursuing his remedy for the amount against the person who received it.

(4) The Treasury may from time to time by order direct that this paragraph shall have effect as if for the reference in sub-paragraph (1) above to £5,000 there were substituted a reference to such higher amount as may be specified in the order.

(5) An order under sub-paragraph (4) above shall apply in relation to deaths occurring after the expiration of a period of one month beginning with the date on which the order comes into force.

(6) The power to make an order under sub-paragraph (4) above is exercisable by statutory instrument but no such order shall be made unless a draft of it has been laid before and approved by a resolution of each House of Parliament.

Receipts by depositors under age

2. Any receipt or acknowledgement given to a building society by a person who is a minor in respect of the payment to him of any sum due in respect of a deposit made by him with the society, shall not be invalid on the ground of his minority.

DEFINITIONS
   "deposit" and "depositor": s.119(1).
   "member": s.119(1)

GENERAL NOTE

Para. 1
   This paragraph substantially re-enacts s.46 of the 1962 Act (as amended by the Administration of Estates (Small Payments) Act 1965). However, the limit on the investments to which the provision applies has now been raised to £5,000 (from £1,500: see S.I. 1984 No. 539), and a measure of flexibility has been built in by reserving power to make subsequent increases in the limit by statutory instrument: see paras. (4) and (6). Note that sub-para. (2) requires satisfactory evidence of the death in addition to a statutory declaration stating (*inter alia*) that the investor had died.

Para. 2
   This paragraph substantially re-enacts s.47 of the 1962 Act. It will be noted that it applies only in cases where a minor has a deposit with the society, *cf.* Sched.2, para. 5(3)(*a*).
   Despite the protection afforded by the present provision, a society should still exercise care where a minor seeks to withdraw money deposited with the society. The minor's receipt will be effective if the fact of his minority is the *only* reason why, apart from this paragraph, the receipt would be invalid; but the paragraph will not validate a receipt which is open to challenge on other grounds (*e.g.* that the depositor had insufficient understanding to know what he was doing): *cf.* Wurtzburg and Mills, *Building Society Law* (14th Ed.) p. 66.

Section 34   SCHEDULE 8

POWERS TO PROVIDE SERVICES

PART I

THE SERVICES

1. Money transmission services.
2. Foreign exchange services.
3. Making or receiving of payments, as agents.
4. Management, as agents, or mortgage investments.
5. Management, as agents, of land.
6. Arranging for the provision of services relating to the acquisition or disposal of investments, whether on behalf of the investor or the person providing the service.
7. Establishment and management of personal equity plans.
8. Arranging for the provision of credit, whether on behalf of the borrower or the person providing credit, and providing services in connection with current loan agreements to the party providing credit.
9. Establishment and management of unit trust schemes for the provision of pensions.
10. Establishment and, as regards the contributions and benefits, administration, of pension schemes.

11. Arranging for the provision of insurance of any description, whether on behalf of the person effecting or the person providing the insurance.

12. Giving advice as to insurance of any description.

13. Estate agency services.

14. Surveys and valuations of land.

15. Conveyancing services.

Part II

General Restriction on Services Abroad

(1) Subject to sub-paragraph (2) below, no power to provide a service of a description specified in Part I of this Schedule includes power to maintain a place of business in a country or territory outside the United Kingdom for that purpose unless the society also conducts the principal business of a building society in that country or territory.

(2) This paragraph does not apply to the power to provide estate agency services.

Part III

Restrictions in Relation to Certain Services

Money transmission

1. No guarantee arising out of the operation of an account by means of which money transmission services are provided shall exceed, for any single operation, the prescribed limit.

Foreign exchange

2. The provision of foreign exchange services is restricted to their provision to individuals.

Estate management

3. Management of land is restricted to management of land which is or is to be used primarily for residential purposes or for purposes incidental to the use of adjoining land managed by the society which is or is to be used primarily for residential purposes.

4. The power to manage land is not available to a building society which does not for the time being have a qualifying asset holding.

Arranging for investment services

5. Arranging for the provision of investment services is restricted to their provision to individuals.

Personal equity plan management

6.—(1) The power to establish and manage personal equity plans is available only to a subsidiary of the society.

(2) The power to establish and manage personal equity plans is available only while the society has a qualifying asset holding.

Arranging for provision of credit

7. Arranging for the provision of credit and connected services is restricted to their provision by recognised banks or licensed institutions or other bodies for the time being approved for the purposes of this Schedule by the Commission, whether in relation to all building societies or specified classes of building society.

8. Arranging for the provision of credit is restricted to its provision to individuals except where the loan to the borrower is to be secured by—

(*a*) a mortgage of a legal estate in land in England and Wales or Northern Ireland, or

(*b*) a heritable security over land in Scotland,

being a mortgage or heritable security to which no other, or no more than one other, mortgage or heritable security, as the case may be, will have priority.

Pensions management etc.

9. The power to establish and manage unit trust schemes is available only to a subsidiary of the society.

Arranging for insurance

10. Arranging for the provision of insurance is restricted to its provision primarily to individuals; but this restriction does not apply to, nor in determining whether over any period insurance is being provided primarily to individuals is any account to be taken of income derived from, insurance relating to land which is to secure advances by the society.

Estate agency

11. The power to provide estate agency services is available only to a subsidiary of the society.

12. For the power to provide estate agency services to be available to the subsidiary of a building society, the following conditions must be fulfilled as regards the subsidiary and its business, that is to say—

(*a*) the subsidiary must have been formed in one of the following countries or territories, that is to say, the United Kingdom, a relevant British overseas territory or another member State and the principal business of the society must, at the time the society forms or acquires the subsidiary, be conducted in that country or territory;

(*b*) 40 per cent. or more of its total income in any financial year (wherever arising) must be derived from estate agency work done in countries or territories in which the society, at any time in that year, carried on the business of making advances secured on land; and

(*c*) its business must not include the lending of money, secured or unsecured, on its own account or the provision of any service which is a financial service for the purposes of this Schedule other than one which is for the time being specified in Part I of this Schedule.

13. No employee of a building society a subsidiary of which provides estate agency services shall act as agent for the subsidiary.

PART IV

SUPPLEMENTARY

Guarantees

1.—(1) The Commission, with the consent of the Treasury, may by order prescribe a limit of such amount as it considers appropriate for the purposes of paragraph 1 of Part III of this Schedule and in that paragraph "the prescribed limit" means the limit for the time being in force under this paragraph.

(2) The power to make an order under this paragraph shall be exercisable by statutory instrument and any instrument so made shall be subject to annulment in pursuance of a resolution of either House of Parliament.

2.—(1) Without prejudice to any other implied incidental power, the power conferred in Part I of this Schedule to provide money transmission services implies (subject to any specified restriction) power, as regards members as well as others, to give guarantees in relation to, or to permit occasional overdrawing on, accounts with the society.

(2) It shall be the duty of a building society which has become obliged by virtue of the provision of money transmission services under this Schedule to fulfill a guarantee on a person's account or has permitted an account to become overdrawn to recover as soon as practicable from the person the amount paid by it under the guarantee or, as the case may be, the amount due to it on the overdrawn account and any instrument embodying the guarantee.

Status as bankers

3.—(1) So far as regards the provision by it of a service which is a qualifying banking service for the purposes of this paragraph a building society shall be treated for all purposes as a bank and a banker and as carrying on the business of banking or a banking undertaking whether or not it would be so treated apart from this paragraph.

(2) A building society provides a qualifying banking service for the purposes of this paragraph if, with or without any restriction, it provides either or both of the services falling within paragraph 1 or 3 of Part I.

(3) This paragraph does not affect the determination of any question as to the status of a building society as a bank or banker for other purposes.

Foreign exchange services to individuals

4.—(1) For the purpose of determining whether a transaction consists in the provision of foreign exchange services to an individual it shall be presumed that a transaction does so consist if the value of the transaction is less than the standard amount.

(2) The standard amount is, subject to sub-paragraph (3) below, £5,000.

(3) The Commission, with the consent of the Treasury, may by order amend sub-paragraph (2) above so as to substitute for the amount for the time being specified in that sub-paragraph such other amount as it considers appropriate for the purposes of this paragraph.

(4) For the purposes of sub-paragraph (1) above the value of a transaction consisting in the provision of foreign exchange services is, where the society is selling the foreign currency, the sum paid to it and, where the society is purchasing the foreign currency, the sum paid by it.

Sanctions for breach of restrictions

5. If a person acts as agent in contravention of paragraph 13 of Part III of this Schedule he shall be liable on summary conviction to a fine not exceeding level 4 on the standard scale.

Interpretation

6. This Schedule is to be construed as relating only to the capacity of building societies to provide the services for the time being specified in it and not as making lawful any activity, whether of a building society or a subsidiary or other associated body of a building society, which would not be lawful apart from this Schedule.

7. In this Schedule—
    "conveyancing services" has the same meaning as in Schedule 21 to this Act;
    "estate agency work" has the same meaning as in the Estate Agents Act 1979;
    "investment services" means services falling within paragraph 6 of Part I;
    "mortgage investments" means investments consisting of rights arising out of advances secured on land;
    "pension scheme" means a personal pension scheme (within the meaning of the Social Security Act 1986) or an occupational pension scheme (as defined in section 66(1) of the Social Security Pensions Act 1975 or in relation to Northern Ireland, Article 2(2) of the Social Security Pensions (Northern Ireland) Order 1975) and the "provision of pensions" means the provision of benefits which are "money purchase benefits" within the meaning of that Act of 1986;
    "personal equity plan" means a personal equity plan for the purposes of Schedule 8 to the Finance Act 1986;
    "the principal business of a building society" means the business of raising funds (whether by the issue of shares or receiving deposits) for the purposes of the society or of making advances secured on land;
    "the prescribed limit", in relation to guarantees, has the meaning given by paragraph 1 of this Part;
    "recognised bank" and "licensed institution" have the same meaning as in the Banking Act 1979;
    "relevant British overseas territory" means any of the Channel Islands, the Isle of Man and Gibraltar; and
    "unit trust scheme" has the same meaning as in the Financial Services Act 1986.

DEFINITIONS

"advances secured on land": ss.5(10), 10(1) and 119(1).
"the Commission": ss.1 and 119(1).
"conveyancing services": Pt. IV, para. 7; and Sched. 21.
"estate agency work": Pt. IV, para. 7; Estate Agents Act 1979, s.1(1).
"financial services": s.34(11).
"financial year": ss.117 and 119(1).
"heritable security": s.119(1).
"investment services": Pt. IV, para. 7.
"licensed institution": Pt. IV, para. 7; Banking Act 1979, s.50(1).
"member State": European Communities Act 1972, s.1 and Sched. 1.
"pension scheme": see Pt. IV, para. 7 and the enactments there referred to.
"personal equity plan": Pt. IV, para. 7; Finance Act 1986, Sched. 8.
"the principal business of a building society": Pt. IV, para. 7.
"prescribed limit": Pt. IV, paras. 1 and 7.
"qualifying asset holding": ss.118 and 119(1).
"qualifying banking service": Pt. IV, para. 7; Banking Act 1979, s.50(1).
"relevant British overseas territory": Pt. IV, para. 7.
"standard amount": Pt. IV, para. 4(2).
"standard scale": Criminal Justice Act 1982, s.37.
"subsidiary": s.119(1); Companies Act 1985, s.736(1).
"unit trust scheme": Pt. IV, para. 7; Financial Services Act 1986.

GENERAL NOTE

A number of general points concerning the services specified in this Schedule were made in the notes to s.34. Those general points are not repeated here. The purpose of the present note is to add some further comments on the individual services specified in the Schedule.

1. *Money transmission services*

Hitherto, building societies have been inhibited in providing personal banking and money transmission services to their customers by the lack of any power to engage in unsecured lending. The lack of such power has prevented building societies from issuing cheque guarantee cards (since such cards require the issuer to meet payments to third parties whether or not sufficient funds are available in the customer's account) and has caused problems for societies wishing to make use of certain types of automatic teller machine networks. It was pointed out in the Green Paper that societies qualified to make use of the new power to make unsecured loans (now embodied in s.16) would be able to use it to overcome the problem of underwriting payments to third parties; but the Green Paper also proposed an additional power for all societies (*i.e.*, including those without a qualifying asset holding) to guarantee certain categories of payment, and to require customers to make good any debt arising from a call on that guarantee. It was further stated that the power would need to cover guarantees of up to £1,500 (30 times the present limit on current account cheque guarantee cards), thereby enabling building societies to issue cheque books, containing the customary 30 cheques, comparable to those of banks. (See the Green Paper, para.4.03.)

Those proposals are implemented by Part I, para. 1, Part III, para. 1 and Part IV, paras. 1 and 2 of the present Schedule. It will be seen that Part III, para. 1 provides that no guarantee arising out of the operation of an account by means of which money transmission services are provided is to exceed, for any single operation, the "prescribed limit"—that is, the limit to be prescribed by order made under Part IV, para. 1. Presumably, the limit will not be less than the figure of £50 per cheque contemplated in the Green Paper.

Part IV, para. 2(1) states that the power to provide money transmission services includes not only the power to give guarantees, but also the power to permit "occasional overdrawing" on the customer's account. It would appear that occasional overdrawings covered by this paragraph will not be treated as class 3 commercial assets of the society (since there is nothing in the Act to classify them as such); note, however, that where a society, pursuant to s.16(4), allows its members or depositors to borrow money on overdraft on a "non-occasional" basis, the amount lent by the society will be categorised as a class 3 commercial asset, and will accordingly count towards the limits imposed on such assets by s.20.

It is thought that the provisions of Part IV, para. 3 are intended to ensure that, when a society provides money transmission services, or makes or receives payments as agent (as to which, see Part I, para. 3), it can claim the protection given to bankers by the Bills of Exchange Act 1882 and the Cheques Act 1957.

2. *Foreign exchange services*

In view of the risks involved in large-scale dealings on the foreign exchange markets, this service has been limited to customers who are individuals (as opposed to corporate bodies). See Part III, para. 2 and *c.f. Official Report*, Standing Committee A, House of Commons, February 6, 1986, col. 244. Part IV, para. 4 (which was added to the Bill at the Report stage in the House of Commons) embodies a rather curious provision whereby it is to be "presumed" that a transaction consists in the provision of foreign exchange services to an individual if the value of the transaction (that is, the sum paid to the society where it is selling foreign currency, or the sum paid by the society where it is buying foreign currency) does not exceed "the standard amount"—initially £5,000, but capable of variation by order. The thinking behind this provision appears to be that, since the society may well be dealing with an off-the-street customer when it provides this service, some rule of thumb needs to be laid down to identify, on the one hand, cases in which it is safe for the society to assume that it is dealing with an individual acting on his own behalf and, on the other hand, cases where the society must take positive steps to satisfy itself that the individual is not in fact acting as agent for a corporate body. It is thought that, notwithstanding the statutory presumption, a society would not be entitled to enter into a foreign exchange transaction of a value less than the standard amount if it *knows* that it is dealing with a body corporate (or with an individual acting as agent for such body).

3. *Making or receiving of payments, as agents*

This will enable building societies to make fuller use of their branch networks by acting as paying and collecting agencies for other organisations *e.g.* by collecting local authority rent and rates, and bills for public utilities (see the Green Paper, para. 4.12). Note that in providing this service, the society will be treated as if it were a bank: see Part. IV, para. 3 and compare the last paragraph of the note on transmission services above.

4. *Management, as agents, of mortgage investments*

It was suggested in the Green Paper (para. 4.13) that this service might usefully be provided to local authorities wishing to sub-contract the management of their mortgage business.

5. *Management, as agents, of land*

Note the limitations on this power embodied in Part III, paras. 3 and 4. Para. 3 requires that the land, broadly speaking, must be used primarily for residential purposes, or for purposes incidental to the use of adjoining residential land managed by the society. Para. 4 restricts the availability of the power to societies with a qualifying asset holding within the meaning of s.118. These restrictions recall the comparable ones imposed by s.17 on the power of building societies to hold and develop land as a commercial asset. It may well be, therefore, that the present power will find its greatest use in cases where a building society, having previously acquired or developed residential land, wishes to dispose of the land while retaining the management of it in its own hands.

In para. 3, the expression "land . . . used . . . for purposes incidental to the use of adjoining land" no doubt covers land used for such things as estate roads and other communal areas. Compare the discussion of the similar expression in s.17(2)(*b*) in the notes to that section.

6. *Arranging for investment services*

Part III, para. 5 requires these services to be provided only to individuals (as opposed to corporate bodies). It should be noted that the power is a power to *arrange* for the provision of investment services, not a power to provide those services directly. It is not intended, therefore, that building societies should start giving investment advice to their customers. The point was explained by Sir George Young (speaking on behalf of the Government during the House of Commons Committee Stage) in the following terms: "We envisage [building societies] acting as intermediaries providing members of the public with easier access to the Stock Exchange and such like. They are, therefore, well placed to make investment opportunities more accessible, though they are arranging investment services rather than providing them directly." (See *Official Report*, House of Commons, Standing Committee A, February 6, 1986, col. 246.)

7. *Establishment and management of personal equity plans*

The power to provide this service is not available to societies themselves but only to their subsidiaries; further, the service may be provided only by subsidiaries of the larger societies (*i.e.* societies having a qualifying asset holding within the meaning of s.118). These limitations are no doubt intended, firstly, to ensure that the establishment and management of personal equity plans is not simply "tacked on" to a society's existing operations, but is entrusted to a separate subsidiary body in which the necessary specialist skills can be developed; and secondly, to ensure that each subsidiary providing this service has the backing of a substantial building society behind it (*c.f.* s.22). (Note, however, that while it is not open to a society without a qualifying asset holding to set up a subsidiary to establish and manage personal equity plans, there would be no objection to such a society *arranging* for its customers to invest in such plans under Part I, para. 6: see the preceding note.) The personal equity plan scheme is a creation of the Finance Act 1986. The broad outlines of the scheme may be discerned in Sched. 8 to that Act, but reference should be made to the regulations made by the Treasury under para. 1 thereof for the detailed provisions governing personal equity plans.

8. *Arranging for the provision of credit*

Again, this is a power to arrange for the provision of services, not a power to provide those services direct (*cf.* Part I, para. 6 and the notes thereto). The power is likely to be useful to societies without a qualifying asset holding (who lack the power to make unsecured loans under s.16) to arrange for the provision of credit to their customers. The power will be useful also to the larger societies by enabling them to arrange credit for their customers in excess of the limit on unsecured lending for the time being in force under s.16 (currently £5,000).

The power is restricted in two respects by Part III, paras. 7 and 8. The effect of para. 7 is that the lender providing the credit must be a recognised bank or a licensed institution within the meaning of the Banking Act 1979, or else a body approved for the purposes of this Schedule by the Commission. Para. 8 limits the power to arrange credit for corporate bodies (as opposed to individuals) to cases where the loan is to be secured by a first or second mortgage of land in the United Kingdom.

9. *Establishment and management of unit trust schemes for the provision of pensions*

The power to set up unit trust pension schemes is available only to subsidiaries of a building society (see Part III, para. 9). That, presumably, reflects the fact that the present power (in contrast to the following one) includes full power to manage the scheme following its establishment: the day-to-day management of a pension scheme is a task requiring specialist skills which can better be developed by a separate subsidiary body than by a building society as an offshoot of its existing operations (*cf.* the similar restriction imposed on the power to establish and manage personal equity plans: note, however, that the present power, somewhat surprisingly perhaps, does not embody the requirement that the parent society should have a qualifying asset holding).

10. *Establishment and administration of other pension schemes*

The present power, in contrast to the preceding one, is not limited in its availability to the subsidiaries of a building society. The reason for that, no doubt, is that this power (again unlike the preceding one) does not include power to undertake the management of pension schemes established under it, but merely to administer the collection of contributions and the payment of benefits.

11. *Arranging for the provision of insurance*

Like the powers to provide the services specified in Part I, paras. 6 and 8, the present power is a power to arrange for the provision of services, rather than a power to provide the service direct. By Part III, para. 10, the power is restricted to the provision of insurance "primarily" to individuals. It was indicated by Sir George Young (speaking for the Government) during the Report stage in the House of Commons that the word "primarily" in para. 10 was intended, for example, to enable a society to acquire an insurance broking business "which has some small business customers on its books", or, in a particular case, to arrange for the insurance of a customer's business at the same time as arranging for the insurance of his own house (see *Official Report*, House of Commons, June 4, 1986, col. 1008). It will be noted that the restriction imposed by para. 10 is wholly inapplicable in any case where the society is arranging for the insurance of property which is to secure an advance by the society (*e.g.* land which is to secure a class 2 advance to a corporate borrower).

12. *Giving advice as to insurance of any description*

This is self-explanatory. It has been separated from the preceding power to achieve consistency with the Financial Services Act 1986, Sched.1, which deals separately with the function of advising on investment business and arranging for its provision (see *ibid.*).

13. *Estate agency services*

This power is available only to subsidiaries of a building society: see Part III, para. 11. In the present context, the restriction is evidently intended primarily to avoid undesirable conflicts of interest arising. The nature of the possible conflict was explained in the Green Paper (para. 4.09) as follows: "Building societies would almost certainly wish to run estate agencies from their branch offices, rather than through separately housed subsidiaries. Branch managers could then be responsible both for arranging sales on behalf of the vendors and for financing the purchasers. As agents for the vendor, their duty would be to get as good a price as possible. Indeed the society would have a direct financial interest in achieving a high selling price. But its duty to a purchaser to whom it was also making a loan, and its duty to value its security adequately, would point in precisely the opposite direction." The requirement that estate agency services be provided exclusively through subsidiaries ought to avoid such conflicts of interest arising, at least in such an acute form. A further safeguard is provided by Part III, para. 13, which prohibits any employee of the parent society from acting as agent of the subsidiary: breach of this prohibition constitutes a criminal offence under Part IV, para. 5.

As to the circumstances in which an estate agency subsidiary may be established overseas, see Part III, para. 12(*a*) and (*b*), and *c.f.* the notes to s.34. It will be noted that the requirements in para. 12(*b*) and (*c*) must be satisfied whether the subsidiary is formed in the United Kingdom or overseas.

Estate agency services are not defined by the Act. Their scope must be wider than "estate agency work" (which is so defined by reference to the Estate Agents Act 1979: see Part IV, para. 7) and would probably include some things that estate agents normally do which would not otherwise be within the powers of a society, *e.g.* conducting auctions.

14. *Surveys and valuations of land*

This is a relatively modest development of existing practice under which societies (or some of them) have given mortgage applicants the opportunity, on payment of an appropriate fee, to have a report on the structure and condition of the property prepared for their use by the society's valuer at the same time as he makes a mortgage valuation of the property for the use of the society. There is not the same risk of a conflict of interest arising here as there is with the provision of estate agency and conveyancing services: both the society and the mortgage applicant have a common interest in ensuring that the property is sound and not over-valued (see the Green Paper, para. 4.07).

15. *Conveyancing services*

Reference should be made to s.124, Sched. 21 and the notes thereto.

Section 68(4)   SCHEDULE 9

DIRECTORS: REQUISITE PARTICULARS OF RESTRICTED TRANSACTIONS

Preliminary

1. In this Schedule—
    "the financial year" means the financial year to which the statement under section 68(3) relates;
    "restricted transaction or arrangement" means any transaction or arrangement falling within section 65(1) particulars of which are required to be included in that statement;
and other expressions have the same meaning as in those sections.

The requisite particulars

2.—(1) The particulars of a restricted transaction or arrangement required by section 68(3) are particulars of the principal terms of the transaction or arrangement.

(2) Without prejudice to the generality of sub-paragraph (1) above, the following particulars of a restricted transaction or arrangement are required—
    (*a*) a statement of the fact either that the transaction or arrangement was made or that is subsisted during the financial year;
    (*b*) the name of the person for whom it was made and, where that person is or was connected with a director of the building society, the name of that director;
    (*c*) in the case of an advance or other loan or any related guarantee—
        (i) the amount of the mortgage debt or corresponding liability both at the beginning and at the end of the financial year;
        (ii) the maximum amount of that debt or liability during that year;
        (iii) the amount of any interest which, having fallen due, has not been paid; and
        (iv) the amount of any provision made in the accounts in respect of any failure or anticipated failure by the borrower to repay the whole or part of the loan or to pay the whole or part of any interest on it;
    (*d*) in the case of a disposal of property by way of lease or hire—
        (i) the value of the property;
        (ii) the amount of any rental which, having fallen due, has not been paid; and
        (iii) the amount of any provision made in the accounts in respect of any failure or anticipated failure by the lessee or hirer to pay the whole or part of the rent;

(*e*) in the case of any payment made on behalf of the director or person connected with him, the amount of the payment; and

(*f*) in the case of a guarantee or security—

    (i) the amount for which the building society was liable under the guarantee or security both at the beginning and at the end of the financial year;

    (ii) the maximum amount for which the society may become liable; and

    (iii) any amount paid and any liability incurred by the society for the purpose of fulfilling the guarantee or security (including any loss incurred by reason of its enforcement).

DEFINITIONS

"connected with": s.70(2) to (4).
"financial year": para. 1.
"mortgage debt": s.119(1).
"person for whom": s.70(5).
"restricted transaction or arrangement": para. 1.

GENERAL NOTE

This Schedule sets out the particulars of transactions made under s.65(2) to (5) which are required by s.68(3) to be set out in the statement to be prepared under that subsection. The Schedule should be read in conjunction with ss.65 and 68.

Note that under para. 2(2)(*c*) and (*d*), the particulars must include not only a statement of what is outstanding but also a statement of any provision made in the accounts to cover any anticipated loss. That information may obviously prove useful in assessing the manner in which the society is using the provisions of s.65(2) to (5).

Broadly similar provisions appear in the Companies Act 1985, Sched. 6, para. 9.

Section 69(7)   SCHEDULE 10

REQUISITE PARTICULARS OF INCOME OF RELATED BUSINESSES

PART I

REQUISITE PARTICULARS WHERE NO ADOPTION OF PART II

Conveyancers

1. Where the business associate of the building society provides conveyancing services the requisite particulars of its business in any financial year are the following—

(*a*) the number of cases in which it has provided conveyancing services in respect of an advance secured on land and the purchase of the land both to the society and to the borrower;

(*b*) the number of cases in which it has provided the society (but not the borrower) with conveyancing services in respect of an advance secured on land;

(*c*) the aggregate amount of the fees paid to it by the society or by or on behalf of the borrower for the provision of conveyancing services falling within sub-paragraphs (*a*) and (*b*) above;

(*d*) the aggregate of the amounts paid to it by the society by way of commission for its having introduced investment business to the society;

(*e*) the aggregate amount of any fees paid to it by the society in consideration of the provision of conveyancing services in respect of any land held by the society under section 6, 10, 17 or 19;

(*f*) the aggregate amount of any fees paid to it by the society in consideration of the provision of management services to the society.

Valuers and surveyors

2. Where the business associate of the building society provides the services of surveying and valuing property the requisite particulars of its business in any financial year are the following—

(*a*) the number of cases in which it has, in respect of any land which is to secure an advance, surveyed the land or provided a valuation of it on behalf of the society or the borrower or both;

(*b*) the number of cases in which it has, on behalf of the society (but not the borrower), surveyed any land which is to secure an advance or provided the society with a valuation of it;

(c) the aggregate amount of the fees paid to it by the society or by or on behalf of the borrower for the provision of the services falling within sub-paragraphs (a) and (b) above;

(d) the aggregate of the amounts paid to it by the society by way of commission for its having introduced investment business to the society;

(e) the aggregate amount of any fees paid to it by the society in consideration of the provision of surveying or valuing services in respect of any property held by the society under section 6, 10, 17 or 19;

(f) the aggregate amount of any fees paid to it by the society in consideration of the provision of management services to the society.

Accountants

3. Where the business associate of the building society provides accountancy services the requisite particulars of its business in any financial year are the following—

(a) the aggregate amount of the fees paid to it by the society for the provision of accountancy services; and

(b) the aggregate amount of any fees paid to it by the society in consideration of the provision of management services to the society.

Insurance agents, etc.

4. Where the business associate of the building society arranges for the provision of relevant insurance the requisite particulars of its business in any financial year are the following—

(a) the aggregate of the amounts paid to it by the society or by way of commission by insurers in respect of relevant insurance effected by the society or by borrowers in compliance with the terms on which advances secured on land are made by the society; and

(b) the aggregate amount of any fees paid to it by the society in consideration of the provision of management services to the society.

PART II

REQUISITE PARTICULARS ON ADOPTION OF THIS PART

Conveyancers

5. Where the business associate of the building society provides conveyancing services the requisite particulars of its business in any financial year are the following—

(a) the prescribed band within which falls the estimated number of cases in which it has provided conveyancing services in respect of an advance secured on land and the purchase of the land both to the society and to the borrower;

(b) the prescribed band within which falls the estimated number of cases in which it has provided the society (but not the borrower) with conveyancing services in respect of an advance secured on land;

(c) the prescribed band within which falls the estimated aggregate amount of the fees paid to it by the society or by or on behalf of the borrower for the provision of conveyancing services falling within sub-paragraphs (a) and (b) above;

(d) the prescribed band within which falls the estimated aggregate of the amounts paid to it by the society by way of commission for its having introduced investment business to the society;

(e) the prescribed band within which falls the estimated aggregate amount of any fees paid to it by the society in consideration of the provision of conveyancing services in respect of any land held by the society under section 6, 10, 17 or 19;

(f) the prescribed band within which falls the estimated aggregate of any fees paid to it by the society in consideration of the provision of management services to the society.

Valuers and surveyors

6. Where the business associate of the building society provides the services of surveying and valuing property the requisite particulars of its business in any financial year are the following—

(*a*) the prescribed band within which falls the estimated number of cases in which it has, in respect of any land which is to secure an advance, surveyed the land or provided a valuation of it on behalf of the society or the borrower or both;

(*b*) the prescribed band within which falls the estimated number of cases in which it has, on behalf of the society (but not the borrower), surveyed any land which is to secure an advance or provided the society with a valuation of it;

(*c*) the prescribed band within which falls the estimated aggregate amount of the fees paid to it by the society or by or on behalf of the borrower for the provision of the services falling within sub-paragraphs (*a*) and (*b*) above;

(*d*) the prescribed band within which falls the estimated aggregate of the amounts paid to it by the society by way of commission for its having introduced investment business to the society;

(*e*) the prescribed band within which falls the estimated aggregate of any fees paid to it by the society in consideration of the provision of surveying or valuing services in respect of any property held by the society under section 6, 10, 17 or 19;

(*f*) the prescribed band within which falls the estimated aggregate amounts of any fees paid to it by the society in consideration of the provision of management services to the society.

Accountants

7. Where the business associate of the building society provides accountancy services the requisite particulars of its business in any financial year are the following—

(*a*) the prescribed band within which falls the estimated aggregate amount of the fees paid to it by the society for the provision of accountancy services; and

(*b*) the prescribed band within which falls the estimated aggregate amount of any fees paid to it by the society in consideration of the provision of management services to the society.

Insurance agents, etc.

8. Where the business associate of the building society arranges for the provision of relevant insurance the requisite particulars of its business in any financial year are the following—

(*a*) the prescribed band within which falls the estimated aggregate of the amounts paid to it by the society or by way of commission by insurers in respect of relevant insurance effected by the society or by borrowers in compliance with the terms on which advances secured on land are made by the society; and

(*b*) the prescribed band within which falls the estimated aggregate amount of any fees paid to it by the society in consideration of the provision of management services to the society.

Part III

Supplementary

Power to prescribe bands for Part II particulars

9.—(1) The Commission, with the consent of the Treasury, may by order prescribe, for the purposes of the provisions of Part II of this Schedule,—

(*a*) series of numbers by reference to limits specified in the order, or

(*b*) series of monetary amounts by reference to limits so specified;

and, in any provision of Part II, "prescribed band" means, in relation to cases, any series of numbers so prescribed for the purposes of that provision and, in relation to monetary amounts, any series of monetary amounts so prescribed for the purposes of that provision.

(2) The power conferred by this paragraph includes power to prescribe different series of numbers or of monetary amounts for the purposes of different provisions.

(3) The power to make an order under this paragraph is exercisable by statutory instrument which shall be subject to annulment in pursuance of a resolution of either House of Parliament.

Interpretation

10.—(1) In this Schedule—
"administrative services" means services falling within section 69(4);
"business associate" and "associated", in relation to a building society, have the same meaning as in section 69;
"financial year" means a financial year of the society with which the business associate is associated;
"prescribed band" has the meaning given by paragraph 9(1) above; and
"relevant insurance" means insurance falling within section 69(3)(*d*).

(2) In section 69, "the volume of the business", in relation to any business constituted by the provision of any services referred to in any provision of Part I or Part II of this Schedule means—

(*a*) in the case of a paragraph of Part I, the aggregate of all the fees and commissions which are the subject of the requisite particulars under that paragraph; and

(*b*) in the case of a paragraph of Part II, the aggregate of the amounts which are specified in orders under paragraph 9 above as the upper limits of the prescribed bands within which fall the estimated aggregates of the fees or commissions or other amounts received which are the subject of the requisite particulars under the provisions of that paragraph.

DEFINITIONS
"business associate": s.69 and para. 10(1).
"conveyancing services": s.69(17).
"financial year": para. 10(1).
"prescribed band": paras. 9(1) and 10(1).
"relevant insurance": s.69(3)(*d*) and para. 10(1).'

GENERAL NOTE
This Schedule specifies the particulars required under s.69(6) and should be read in conjunction with that section and the notes thereto. Part I of the Schedule requires particulars of exact numbers of transactions and exact amounts to be stated. When the Bill was originally published, there was no equivalent of Part II, which, if adopted, eases the requirements of Part I by permitting the particulars to specify within which of certain prescribed bands it is estimated that the numbers and amounts fall. Part II was introduced at the Report stage in the House of Commons (see *Hansard*, H.C., Vol. 98 col. 1039), following representations as to the administrative burden that compliance with Part I would require. The reduction in detail to be supplied should also reduce the risk that compliance would have the consequence of disclosing "sensitive commercial information" (see *Official Report*, House of Commons, Standing Committee A, February 13, 1986, col. 363). Part III, of course, supplements Part II.
Management services. This phrase is to be found throughout the Schedule except in the definition provision, para. 10. There, one finds a definition of "administrative services", which are mentioned in s.69, but not in the Schedule. It seems that there may have been a drafting oversight and that management and administrative services are to be treated as one and the same.

Section 77　　　　　　　　　　SCHEDULE 11

AUDITORS: APPOINTMENT, TENURE, QUALIFICATIONS

Appointment

1.—(1) The first auditors of a building society may be appointed by the directors at any time before the first general meeting of the building society following the end of the society's first financial year and auditors so appointed shall hold office until the conclusion of that meeting.

(2) If the directors fail to exercise their powers under sub-paragraph (1) above those powers may be exercised by the building society in general meeting.

2. The directors, or the building society in general meeting, may fill any casual vacancy in the office of auditor; but while any such vacancy continues, the surviving or continuing auditor or auditors (if any) may act.

3.—(1) If at any annual general meeting of a building society no auditors are appointed or re-appointed, the Commission may appoint a person to fill the vacancy; and the society shall, within one week of the power of the Commission becoming exercisable, give it notice of that fact.

(2) If a building society fails to give the notice required by sub-paragraph (1) above the society shall be liable on summary conviction—

(*a*) to a fine not exceeding level 3 on the standard scale, and

(*b*) in the case of a continuing offence, to an additional fine not exceeding £40 for every day during which the offence continues;

and so shall any officer who is also guilty of the offence.

4.—(1) A resolution at a general meeting of a building society—

(*a*) appointing as auditor a person other than a retiring auditor; or

(*b*) filling a casual vacancy in the office of auditor; or

(*c*) reappointing as auditor a retiring auditor who was appointed by the directors to fill a casual vacancy; or

(*d*) removing an auditor before the expiration of his term of office,

shall not be effective unless notice of the intention to move it has been given to the society not less than twenty-eight days before the meeting at which it is moved.

(2) A building society shall give to its members notice of any such resolution at the same time and in the same manner as it gives notice of the meeting, or, if that is not practicable, shall give them notice of the resolution, not less than twenty-one days before the meeting, either by advertisement in a newspaper having an appropriate circulation or in any other way allowed by the rules of the society.

(3) On receipt of notice of such an intended resolution as is mentioned above the society shall forthwith send a copy of it—

(*a*) to the person proposed to be appointed or removed, as the case may be;

(*b*) in a case within sub-paragraph (1)(*a*), to the retiring auditor; and

(*c*) where, in a case within sub-paragraph (1)(*b*) or (*c*), the casual vacancy was caused by the resignation of an auditor, to the auditor who resigned.

(4) Where notice is given of such a resolution as is mentioned in sub-paragraphs (1)(*a*) or (*d*) and the retiring auditor, or (as the case may be) the auditor proposed to be removed, makes with respect to the intended resolution representations in writing to the society (not exceeding a reasonable length) and requests their notification to the members, the society shall (unless the representations are received by it too late to do so)—

(*a*) in any notice of the resolution given to members, state the fact of the representations having been made, and

(*b*) send a copy of the representations to every member to whom notice of the meeting is or has been sent.

(5) If a copy of such representations is not sent out as required by sub-paragraph (4) above because it was received too late or because of the society's default, the auditor may (without prejudice to his right to be heard orally) require that the representations shall be read out at the meeting.

(6) The building society or any person claiming to be aggrieved may, within fourteen days of the receipt by the society of any representations made to it under sub-paragraph (4) above, apply in accordance with sub-paragraph (7) or (8) below to—

(*a*) the High Court, or

(*b*) the Commission,

for an order that copies of the representations need not or, as the case may be, shall not be sent out nor the representations read out at the meeting.

(7) An application under this sub-paragraph is an application to the High Court on the ground that the auditor is abusing the rights conferred by sub-paragraph (4) above to secure needless publicity for defamatory matter, and if the court is satisfied that the auditor is so abusing those rights it may by order direct that copies of the representations need not be sent out nor the representations read out at the meeting; and the court may further order the society's costs on the application to be paid in whole or in part by the auditor notwithstanding that he is not a party to the application.

(8) An application under this sub-paragraph is an application to the Commission on the ground that the sending out of copies of or the reading out at the meeting of the representations would be likely to diminish substantially the confidence in the society of investing members of the public and if the Commission is satisfied that the sending out of copies of the representations or the reading of them would have that effect it shall by order direct that copies of the representations shall not be sent out nor the representations read at the meeting.

(9) The building society shall—

(*a*) if the High Court makes an order under sub-paragraph (7) above or the Commission makes an order under sub-paragraph (8) above, send within fourteen days of the decision a statement setting out the effect of the order to the persons mentioned in sub-paragraph (4)(*b*) above; and

(*b*) if not, either send a copy of the written representations made under sub-paragraph (4) above to those persons or cause the representations to be read out the meeting.

(10) If default is made in complying with sub-paragraph (4) or (9) above the building society shall be liable—

(*a*) on conviction on indictment to a fine; or

(*b*) on summary conviction to a fine not exceeding the statutory maximum and, in the case of a continuing offence, to a fine not exceeding one tenth of the statutory maximum for every day during which the offence continues;

and so shall any officer who is also guilty of the offence.

Qualification and disqualification of auditors

5.—(1) A person is not qualified for appointment as auditor of a building society unless he is a member of one or more of the following bodies—

(*a*) the Institute of Chartered Accountants in England and Wales;

(*b*) the Institute of Chartered Accountants of Scotland;

(*c*) the Chartered Association of Certified Accountants;

(*d*) the Institute of Chartered Accountants in Ireland;

(*e*) any other body of accountants established in the United Kingdom and for the time being recognised by the Secretary of State for the purposes of section 389(1) of the Companies Act 1985; and

(*f*) any other body of accountants established in the United Kingdom or any other member State, being a body for the time being designated by order by the Commission with the consent of the Treasury.

(2) None of the following persons is qualified for appointment as an auditor of a building society—

(*a*) a director or employee of the society;

(*b*) a person who is a partner of, or in the employment of, or who employs, a director or employee of the society;

(*c*) a person who is disqualified from acting as auditor of any subsidiary of the society under section 389(6) of the Companies Act 1985;

(*d*) a body corporate.

(3) Nothing in this paragraph shall prevent the appointment as auditor of a Scottish firm if none of the partners of the firm is by virtue of this paragraph disqualified for appointment as auditor of the society.

(4) The power to make an order under sub-paragraph (1)(*f*) above is exercisable by statutory instrument subject to annulment by a resolution of either House of Parliament.

(5) No person shall act as auditor of a building society at a time when he knows that he is disqualified from appointment to that office; and if an auditor of a building society to his knowledge becomes so disqualified during his term of office he shall thereupon vacate his office and give notice to the society that he has vacated it by reason of that disqualification.

(6) A person who acts as auditor in contravention of sub-paragraph (5), or fails without reasonable excuse to give notice of vacating his office as required by that sub-paragraph, shall be liable—

(*a*) on conviction on indictment to a fine; or

(*b*) on summary conviction to a fine not exceeding the statutory maximum and, in the case of a continuing offence, to an additional fine not exceeding one-tenth of the statutory maximum for every day during which the offence continues.

Removal of auditors

6.—(1) A building society may by resolution in general meeting remove an auditor before the expiration of his term of office, notwithstanding anything in any agreement between it and him.

(2) Where a resolution removing an auditor is passed at a general meeting of a building society, the society shall within 14 days give notice of that fact to the central office.

(3) If a building society fails to give the notice required by sub-paragraph (2) above the society shall be liable on summary conviction to a fine not exceeding level 3 on the standard scale and, in the case of a continuing offence, to an additional fine not exceeding £40 for every day during which the offence continues and so shall every officer who is also guilty of the offence.

(4) Nothing in this paragraph is to be taken as depriving a person removed under it of compensation or damages that may be payable to him in respect of the termination of his appointment as auditor.

Resignation of auditors

7.—(1) An auditor of a building society may resign his office by depositing a notice to that effect at the principal office of the society; and any such notice operates to bring his term of office to an end on the date on which the notice is deposited, or on such later date as may be specified in it.

(2) An auditor's notice of resignation shall not be effective unless it contains either—

(*a*) a statement to the effect that there are no circumstances connected with his resignation which he considers should be brought to the notice of the members of, or depositors with, the society, or

(*b*) a statement of any such circumstances as are mentioned above.

(3) Where a notice under this paragraph is deposited at the principal office of a building society it shall within fourteen days send a copy of that notice—

(*a*) to the central office, and

(*b*) if the notice contains a statement under sub-paragraph (2)(*b*) above, to every person who under section 76(8) is entitled to receive a copy of the summary financial statement.

(4) The building society or any person claiming to be aggrieved may, within fourteen days of the receipt by the society of a notice containing a statement under sub-paragraph (2)(*b*), apply in accordance with sub-paragraph (5) or (6) below to—

(*a*) the High Court; or

(*b*) the Commission,

for an order that copies of the notice need not or, as the case may be, shall not be sent out.

(5) An application under this sub-paragraph is an application to the High Court on the ground that the auditor is using the notice to secure needless publicity for defamatory matter, and if the court is satisfied that the auditor is using the notice for that purpose it may by order direct that copies of it need not be sent out; and the court may further order the society's costs on the application to be paid in whole or in part by the auditor, notwithstanding that he is not a party to the application.

(6) An application under this sub-paragraph is an application to the Commission on the ground that the sending out of the notice would be likely to diminish substantially the confidence in the society of investment members of the public; and if the Commission is satisfied that the sending out of the notice would be likely to have that effect it shall by order direct that copies of it shall not be sent out.

(7) The building society shall, within fourteen days of the decision of the High Court or of the Commission, send to the persons mentioned in sub-paragraph (3)—

(*a*) if the court makes an order under sub-paragraph (5) above or the Commission makes an order under sub-paragraph (6), a statement setting out the effect of the order; and

(*b*) if not, a copy of the notice containing the statement under sub-paragraph (2)(*b*).

(8) If default is made in complying with sub-paragraph (3) or sub-paragraph (7) the building society shall be liable—

(*a*) on conviction on indictment to a fine; or

(*b*) on summary conviction to a fine not exceeding the statutory maximum and, in the case of a continuing offence, to a fine not exceeding one tenth of the statutory maximum for every day during which the offence continues;

and so shall any officer who is also guilty of the offence.

8.—(1) Where an auditor's notice of resignation contains a statement under paragraph 7(2)(*b*) above he may also deposit at the principal office of the society a requisition signed by him calling on the directors of the society forthwith duly to convene a special general meeting of the society for the purpose of receiving and considering such explanation of the circumstances connected with his resignation as he may wish to place before the meeting.

(2) Where an auditor's notice of resignation contains such a statement the auditor may request the society to sent to its members—

(*a*) before the general meeting at which his term of office would otherwise expire or expires, as the case may be; or

(*b*) before any general meeting at which it is proposed to fill the vacancy caused by his resignation,

a statement in writing (not exceeding a reasonable length) of the circumstances connected with his resignation.

(3) The society shall in that case (unless the statement is received by it too late for it to comply)—

(a) in any notice of the meeting given to members state the fact of the statement having been made, and

(b) send a copy of the statement to every member to whom notice of the meeting is or has been sent.

(4) If the directors of the society do not within 21 days from the date of the deposit of a requisition under this paragraph proceed duly to convene a meeting for a day not more than 28 days after the date on which the notice convening the meeting is given, every director who failed to take all reasonable steps to secure that a meeting was so convened shall be liable—

(a) on conviction on indictment to a fine; or

(b) on summary conviction to a fine not exceeding the statutory maximum.

(5) If a copy of the statement mentioned in sub-paragraph (2) is not sent out as required by sub-paragraph (3) because it was received too late or because of the society's default, the auditor may (without prejudice to his right to be heard orally) require that the statement be read out at the meeting.

(6) Copies of a statement need not be sent out and the statement need not be read out at the meeting if—

(a) on an application made to the High Court by the Society or a person aggrieved, the court is satisfied that the rights conferred by this paragraph are being abused to secure needless publicity for defamatory matter; or

(b) on an application to the Commission by the society or a person aggrieved, the Commission is satisfied that the circulating or reading out of the statement would be likely to diminish substantially the confidence in the society of investing members of the public.

(7) If the High Court makes an order under sub-paragraph (6)(a) above it may also order the society's costs of the application to be paid by the auditor notwithstanding that he is not a party to the application.

(8) Any auditor who has resigned his office is entitled to attend any such meeting as is mentioned in sub-paragraph (2)(a) or (b) and to receive all notices of, and other communications relating to, any such meeting which any member of the society is entitled to receive, and to be heard at any such meeting which he attends on any part of the business of the meeting which concerns him as former auditor of the society.

9. In the application of this Schedule to Scotland, references to the High Court shall be read as references to the Court of Session.

DEFINITIONS
"central office": s.119(1).
"Commission": ss.1 and 119(1).
"depositor": see s.119(1).
"financial year": ss.117 and 119(1).
"member": s.119(1).
"member State": European Communities Act 1972, s.1 and Sched. 1.
"notice": s.119(1).
"officer": s.119(1).
"standard scale": Criminal Justice Act 1982, s.37.
"statutory maximum": Criminal Justice Act 1982, s.74; Magistrates' Courts Act 1980, s.32.
"summary financial statement": ss.76(1) and 119(1).
"subsidiary": s.119(1); Companies Act 1985, s.736.

GENERAL NOTE
This Schedule contains provisions relating to the appointment, qualification, removal and resignation of auditors. It is closely based on the Companies Act 1985 and it also reflects some provisions of the 1962 Act, as indicated below. Its terms may be summarised broadly as follows.

Paras. 1 to 3 are designed to ensure that each society has an auditor. Para. 4 covers cases in which it is proposed to appoint an auditor who is not a retiring auditor appointed at an annual general meeting and cases in which an auditor is proposed to be removed before the expiration of his term of office. It contains detailed provisions enabling a retiring auditor or an auditor who is proposed to be removed to make representations to the society's members.

Para. 5 deals with qualification and disqualification of auditors and para. 6 with removal.

Paras. 7 and 8 are concerned with the resignation of auditors. An auditor cannot effectively resign unless his notice of resignation either (i) states that there are no circumstances connected with his resignation which he considers should be brought to the attention of members or depositors, or (ii) states such circumstances. Further provisions for giving publicity to the notice follow. The auditor also has a right to requisition a special meeting of the society to explain the circumstances of his resignation. These provisions are designed to ensure that if an auditor feels obliged to resign because in some way he becomes aware of irregularities within the society with which he cannot deal as auditor, he has an opportunity to make clear to the membership at large what the problem is. Note that no similar provisions apply to an auditor's decision not to seek re-election. Perhaps it is felt that in the circumstances postulated above, an auditor conforming to proper professional standards would take the positive step of resigning.

The following notes deal in detail with the derivation of the paragraphs of the Schedule and supplement the broad outline given above.

Para. 1

Broadly similar provisions are to be found in s.84(3) of the 1962 Act. S.384(1) and (2) of the Companies Act 1985 is in virtually identical terms.

Para. 2

This paragraph is identical to s.84(4) of the 1962 Act and s.384(4) of the Companies Act, save that the 1962 Act did not contain the words "or the building society in general meeting".

Para. 3

This paragraph corresponds with s.384(5) of the Companies Act.

Level 3. Currently £400.

Para. 4

Subparas. (1) and (3) to (5) follow almost exactly s.388(1) to (4) of the Companies Act 1985. They are similar to, but not identical with, s.85(1) to (4) of the 1962 Act. Subpara. (2) reflects s.85(2). Subpara. (7) is very similar to s.388(5) and s.85(5) respectively of the 1962 and 1985 Acts, but subpara. (8) (and therefore subpara. (6) also) is new.

Subparas. (7) and (8) should be compared with s.61(8) and (9) of the present Act and with Sched. 2, para. 31(4) and (7), which provisions also deal with the circulation of documents to members. The division of authority between court and Commission is the same in those cases also. Note, however, that those provisions offer an additional ground for non-circulation: that the right is being abused for "frivolous or vexatious purposes". Presumably it is assumed that, while the auditor's representations may be defamatory or damaging, they will be made for the purpose of securing his continuance in office and thus not for a frivolous or vexatious purpose.

The statutory maximum. Currently £2,000.

Para. 5

Subparas. (1) to (3) are broadly based on s.389(3) to (8) of the Companies Act 1985. S.86 of the 1962 Act contained similar provisions, but there has been some updating to take account of the United Kingdom's membership of the E.E.C. and the possibility that building societies will have subsidiaries. Subparas. (5) and (6) correspond with s.389(9) and (10).

The statutory maximum. Currently £2,000.

Para. 6

This paragraph is in terms very similar to those of s.386 of the Companies Act 1985. Note that although an auditor may be removed in breach of contract, a resolution for the removal of an auditor before the expiration of his term of office attracts the provisions of para. 4. The auditor will therefore at least have the opportunity to put his case before he is removed.

Para. 7

This paragraph follows closely s.390 of the Companies Act 1985. As to subparas. (4) to (6), see the notes to paras. 4(7) and (8) above.

The statutory maximum. Currently £2,000.

Para. 8

This paragraph follows closely s.391 of the Companies Act 1985. As to subpara. (6), see the notes to para. 4(7) and (8) above.

The statutory maximum. Currently £2,000.

Section 83
SCHEDULE 12

SCHEMES FOR INVESTIGATIONS OF COMPLAINTS

PART I

MATTERS TO BE PROVIDED FOR IN SCHEMES

The matters for which provision is, subject to Parts II and III of this Schedule, to be made are the following:

Administration

1. The establishment and functioning of an independent body (whether corporate or unincorporate) which is to administer the scheme.
2. The identity of the members.
3. The manner in which the expenses of the scheme are to be met by the members.

The adjudicator

4. The appointment of an independent adjudicator to conduct investigations under the scheme and his tenure of office and remuneration.

Scope of scheme

5. The matters action in relation to which is to be subject to investigation under the scheme and the grounds for making it subject to investigation.

Functions of adjudicator

6. The duty of the adjudicator to investigate, and make determinations on, actions duly referred for investigation.
7. The powers of, and procedure to be followed in the conduct of investigations by, the adjudicator.
8. The powers of the adjudicator on making of determinations.

Determinations and their effects

9. The extent to which determinations are binding.
10. The manner in which determinations are to be communicated and published.

Reports by investigators to administering body

11. The making to the body administering the scheme of regular reports by the adjudicator as to the discharge of his functions, and their publication.

Amendment or revocation of scheme

12. The manner of amending or revoking the scheme.

Accession to membership

13. Accession to membership of other societies.

Withdrawal from membership

14. Withdrawal from membership.

PART II

REQUIREMENTS FOR RECOGNISED SCHEMES: MATTERS OF COMPLAINT

Share accounts

1. The operation or termination of a share account and the grant or refusal to grant a shareholder other facilities normally available to shareholders of his description.

 Note: The operation or termination of a share account includes any aspect of the relationship or termination of the relationship between the society and a shareholder as such and in particular the operation or termination of any services incidental to such accounts.

 Note: The grant of facilities includes the terms on which they are granted.

Deposit accounts

2. The operation or termination of a deposit account and the grant or refusal to grant a depositor other facilities normally available to depositors of his description.

 Note: The operation or termination of a deposit account includes any aspect of the relationship or the termination of the relationship between the society and a depositor as such, including in particular the operation or termination of any services incidental to such accounts.

 Note: The grant of facilities includes the terms on which they are granted

Borrowing members: class 1 or class 2 advances

3. The operation or termination of the account of a member borrowing on a class 1 or class 2 advance and the grant or refusal to grant a borrowing member of that description other or further class 1, or as the case may be, class 2 advances secured on the same or different land or other facilities normally available to borrowing members of his description.

 Note: The operation or termination of the account of a borrowing member includes any aspect of the relationship or the termination of the relationship between the society and a borrowing member as such, including in particular the exercise of the right of foreclosure or any other power over the land by virtue of the mortgage.

 Note: The grant of advances includes the terms on which they are granted.

Borrowers: mobile home loans

4. The operation or termination of the account of a borrower under section 15 and the grant or refusal to grant a borrower under that section other facilities normally available to borrowers of his description.

 Note: The operation or termination of the account of a borrower under section 15 includes any aspect of the relationship or the termination of the relationship between the lender and such a borrower, including in particular the exercise of any power over the security.

 Note: The grant of facilities includes the terms on which they are granted.

Borrowers: other loans

5. The operation or termination of the account of a borrower under section 16 and the grant or refusal to grant a borrower under that section other facilities normally available to borrowers of his description.

 Note: The operation or termination of the account of a borrower under section 16 includes any aspect of the relationship or the termination of the relationship between the lender and such a borrower including in particular, in the case of a secured loan, the exercise of any power over the security.

 Note: The grant of facilities includes the terms on which they are granted.

Money transmission services

6. The terms on which are provided, the operation of, or the withdrawal of money transmission services.

Note: "Money transmission services" means the services of that description provided in accordance with Schedule 8 to this Act.

Foreign exchange facilities

7. The terms on which are provided, the operation of, or the withdrawal of foreign exchange services.
Note: "Foreign exchange services" means services of that description provided in accordance with Schedule 8 to this Act.

Agency payments and receipts

8. The terms on which payments are made or received as agents or the operation or withdrawal of the service.
Note: The payments made or received as agents are those made or received in accordance with Schedule 8 to this Act.

Provision of credit

9. The operation or termination of the account of a borrower with the person providing the credit.
Note: The credit provided is credit provided under arrangements for the provision of credit in accordance with Schedule 8 to this Act.

Part III

Minimum Requirements for Recognised Schemes: Other Provisions

Grounds of complaint

1. The grounds for making action by a building society or associated body subject to investigation under the scheme must be that the action constitutes—
   (*a*) in the case of a building society, a breach of the society's obligations under this Act, the rules or any other contract, or
   (*b*) in the case of an associated body, a breach of the associated body's obligations under its rules (if any) or any contract, or
   (*c*) unfair treatment, or
   (*d*) maladministration,
in relation to the complainant and has caused him pecuniary loss or expense or inconvenience.

Permissible exclusions from investigation

2. A scheme must not exclude action from investigation on any other than the following grounds, that is to say—
   (*a*) that the complaint is frivolous or vexatious;
   (*b*) that the action is the subject of proceedings in a court of law or was the subject of such proceedings in which a judgment on the merits was given;
   (*c*) that, where the society or associated body has a procedure for the resolution of complaints by it (an "internal procedure"), the procedure has not been invoked or has not been exhausted;
   (*d*) that there has been undue delay in having the matter investigated under the scheme; or
   (*e*) that the action in question occurred outside the United Kingdom.
   Note: An internal procedure for resolution of complaints is not to be treated as having been invoked unless the complainant has made his complaint to the principal office of the society or, as the case may be, the registered office of the associated body and is not to be treated as having been exhausted unless more than three months has elapsed since the complainant invoked it without any decision on his complaint having been communicated to him.
   Note: Delay in having a matter investigated under the scheme is not "undue delay" unless at least six months (disregarding the period for exhausting the society's or associated body's internal procedure) has expired since the matter came to the knowledge of the complainant; and a person is not, for this purpose, to be

presumed to have knowledge of the contents of a document which contains or relates to the terms or proposed terms of any transaction between him and the society.

Functions of adjudicator

3. A scheme must, as regards the duties and powers attached to the investigation of complaints under the scheme—

(*a*) impose on the adjudicator a duty, subject to the provision made in pursuance of sub-paragraph (*c*) below, to investigate and determine any complaint duly made;

(*b*) impose on the adjudicator a duty to afford the complainant and the society or associated body an opportunity to make representations (whether orally or in writing) in relation to the action complained of;

(*c*) confer power on the adjudicator to advise, mediate or act as conciliator before proceeding further with an investigation;

(*d*) confer power on the adjudicator to extend the scope of his investigation to other matters related to the action complained of; and

(*e*) confer on an adjudicator such powers to require information and documents relevant to the matter to be furnished to him as are necessary for the purposes of the investigation.

4.—(1) Subject to any provision made in pursuance of sub-paragraph (3) below, a scheme must authorise the adjudicator, in reaching his decision, to have regard to, but not to be bound by, any matter (whether or not of obligation) relevant to the action complained of and to question any decision.

(2) A scheme must impose on the adjudicator a duty, in reaching his decision, to have regard to—

(*a*) the rules (if any) of the society or associated body;

(*b*) the provisions of any deed or contract binding the society and the complainant or, as the case may be, the associated body and the complainant;

(*c*) the provisions of any code of conduct applicable to the conduct by the society or associated body of its affairs or business;

(*d*) any advertisement issued by the society or associated body in connection with any aspect of its activities and any communication with the complainant.

(3) Subject to sub-paragraph (4) below, a scheme may preclude the adjudicator, in his determination, from questioning the merits of any decision taken by the society or associated body with reference to—

(*a*) the taking or conduct of legal proceedings to enforce any right of the society or associated body; or

(*b*) the creditworthiness, for the purposes of any advance or other service or facility, of the complainant;

but not otherwise.

(4) Where investigation of a complaint on the ground of maladministration involves consideration by the adjudicator of any decision taken with reference to the creditworthiness of the complainant the scheme must confer power on the adjudicator to direct the society or associated body to take its decision again and reach it by proper procedures.

5.—(1) Subject to sub-paragraph (2) below, a scheme must confer power on the adjudicator, by his determination, to do either or both of the following, that is to say—

(*a*) direct the society or associated body whose action is complained of to take or desist from taking such steps as are specified in the determination;

(*b*) order the society or associated body whose action is complained of to pay the complainant a sum by way of compensation for the loss, expense or inconvenience caused by the action.

(2) A scheme may impose a limit on the amount of compensation that a society or associated body may be ordered to pay a complainant, but the limit must not be less than £100,000.

Effect of determinations and their communication

6.—(1) Subject to any provision made in pursuance of sub-paragraph (2) or (3) below, a scheme must provide that, if the complainant, by notice to the adjudicator within the period specified in the scheme, accepts his determination the society or associated body is under an obligation to take the steps it is directed to take or pay the compensation awarded or both.

(2) A scheme may relieve a society of the obligation imposed by a determination if, but only if, the society undertakes an obligation to give notice to its members of the reasons for

its non-fulfilment of the obligations imposed by the determination in the next directors' report under section 75 and to give notice of those reasons to the public in such manner as the adjudicator requires.

(3) A scheme may relieve an associated body of the obligations imposed by a determination if, but only if, each of the building societies with which it is associated undertakes an obligation to give notice to its members of the reasons for the non-fulfilment of the obligations imposed by the determination in the next directors' report under section 75 and to give notice of those reasons to the public in such manner as the adjudicator requires.

7. A scheme must impose on the adjudicator an obligation not to disclose, whether in his determination or otherwise, any information or opinion furnished in confidence to the society or, as the case may be, to the associated body for the purpose of any action on its part.

Reports by adjudicator to administering body

8. A scheme must require reports by the adjudicator as to the discharge of his functions to be made to the body administering the scheme not less frequently than once in every year.

Publication

9.—(1) A scheme must permit the body administering the scheme to publish the whole or any parts of the reports made to them by the adjudicator.

(2) A scheme, if it makes the provision authorised by paragraph 6(2) or (3) above, must require the body administering the scheme to send to the Commission, not less frequently than once in every year, particulars of the cases in which building societies have undertaken the alternative obligation authorised by either or both of those sub-paragraphs.

DEFINITIONS
"associated": ss.18(17) and 119(1).
"class 1 advance": ss.11(2) and 119(1).
"class 2 advance": ss.11(4) and 119(1).
"Commission": ss.1 and 119(1).
"deposit": s.119(1).
"internal procedure": Part III, para.2.
"notice": s.119(1).

GENERAL NOTE
This Schedule contains the basic provisions with which a scheme for the investigation of complaints by an individual against a society or an associated body must comply if it is to obtain recognition. It should be read with s.83, obliging societies and their associated bodies to be members of at least one such scheme, with s.84, containing supplementary provisions, and with Sched. 13, providing for recognition of, accession to and withdrawal from such schemes.

The Schedule contains three parts. Part I establishes the basic structure of schemes of this nature by laying down certain matters which must be provided for. Part II specifies the matters of complaint which are to be covered under recognised schemes. Broadly speaking, they are: matters relating to share or deposit accounts; borrowing of any kind from the society; and services which involve the handling of money. Part III contains further provisions as to what must and what must not, be included in any scheme if it is to obtain recognition.

PART I

Note the following points concerning the basic structure of a scheme:
(1) it is to be administered by an independent body (either corporate or unincorporate (para.1));
(2) the expenses are to be borne by the members (para. 3). *C.f.* s.83(9), expressly providing that the Commission has no power to incur expense for the purpose of operating a scheme;
(3) each scheme will have an "adjudicator" to conduct investigations, whose tenure of office and remuneration must be provided for (para. 4);
(4) the matters which may be investigated under the particular scheme must be specified (para. 5). A scheme will not necessarily cover all the matters listed in Part II;

(5) the scheme must set out the powers of the adjudicator and the procedure to be followed on an investigation (paras. 7 and 8). Note the further provisions of Part III, especially paras. 3 to 5;

(6) the scheme must cover withdrawal from membership. See, however, the restrictions imposed on withdrawal by s.83(13) and Sched. 13, para. 10.

PART II

Note that in relation to complaints as to the operation of share or deposit accounts or in connection with borrowing from the society (paras. 1 to 5) a relevant matter is whether or not the complainant has been treated differently from individuals of a similar description. He may have formed an expectation, quite reasonably, that he will be treated in a certain manner because other people are so treated. His failure to receive the same treatment is obviously likely to cause considerable dissatisfaction. See Part III, para. 1, under which "unfair treatment" is one of the grounds on which a matter may be subject to investigation.

PART III

Para. 1

This paragraph specifies the grounds which must be included as grounds for investigation under the scheme. Note that the complainant must allege "pecuniary loss or expense or inconvenience" in addition to the other matters set out. This may prove a very small restriction, however, if "inconvenience" is given the wide construction which it is obviously capable of bearing.

Para. 2

This paragraph sets out the only grounds on which a matter may be excluded from investigation.

Frivolous or vexatious. This expression is to be found in the Rules of the Supreme Court, Order 18, rule 19, which includes provisions for striking out pleadings that are frivolous or vexatious. The commentary to that rule in the *Supreme Court Practice*, vol.1, indicates how the courts have approached the question what is frivolous or vexatious.

Judgment on the merits. It follows from the use of this phrase that, for example, if the complainant brought legal proceedings which were struck out for any reason, or, indeed, if the society did not defend the proceedings and judgment in default was obtained, a complaint under the scheme would not be barred under para. 2(*b*). In practice, it might well be excluded under one of the other heads.

Undue delay. See the explanatory provisions in the note to this paragraph. It seems fairly clear that the complainant can require a matter to be investigated even after six months if there were good reasons for the delay. Para. 2(*d*) could simply have imposed a six month time limit if that was what was intended.

Para. 3

Presumably if the adjudicator is obstructed in the exercise of his powers under subparas. (*c*), (*d*) and (*e*), he may record the fact in his report to the body administering the scheme under para. 8. Thereafter it will be for that body to decide what action to take. For example, the adjudicator's report could be published: see para. 9.

Para. 4

This paragraph requires the adjudicator to have regard to a wide variety of matters in reaching his decision. Note in particular the obligation to have regard to codes of conduct and advertisements. It is not intended, however, that the adjudicator should have power to review the merits of a decision as to creditworthiness; he can only review the procedure by which the decision was reached and require a fresh decision to be made by proper procedures where that course is appropriate: see subparas. (3) and (4).

To have regard to, but not to be bound by. This phrase indicates that although the adjudicator must have regard to the provisions of any relevant contract, he need not be bound by those provisions. This point caused considerable concern both in the House of Commons and the House of Lords: see *Hansard*, H.C. vol. 98, cols. 929 to 932 and H.L. vol. 478, cols. 504 to 507. At the end of the day, it appears that the adjudicator is indeed not limited by contractual provisions in reaching his decision. It is not intended, however, that he should ride rough-shod over contractual relationships; the circumstances in which it is envisaged that he might depart from the contract are cases where it would be unfair to rely on the particular provision: for example, if the complainant had been led reasonably to believe that there would be no such reliance. Much will obviously depend on how adjudicators exercise their discretion in all the circumstances: note that the guiding principle is "what is fair in all the circumstances of the case": s.84(1). See also the provision of para.

6, providing that in certain circumstances a society or associated body will not be obliged to abide by the adjudicator's determination.

Para. 6

Note that the obligation on a society or associated body to comply with the adjudicator's determination arises only if the complainant gives notice (*i.e.* notice in writing: see s.119(1)) to the adjudicator accepting his determination within the period specified in the scheme.

Note also that a scheme need not include provisions under which a society or associated body is not obliged to abide by the adjudicator's determination.

Section 83   SCHEDULE 13

SCHEMES FOR INVESTIGATION OF COMPLAINTS: RECOGNITION, ACCESSION, ETC.

Preliminary

1. For the purposes of this Schedule, a scheme—

"qualifies for recognition" if it makes provision for the matters specified in Part I of Schedule 12 and the matters action in relation to which is subject to investigation under the scheme consist of or include one or more of the prescribed matters of complaint; and

"conforms to the relevant requirements" if, in relation to a prescribed matter of complaint, it makes action in relation to that matter subject to investigation in accordance with Part III of that Schedule;

and any reference to a scheme qualifying for recognition, or being recognised, to any "extent" indicates recognition of it for the purpose of investigations of action in relation to one or more prescribed matters of complaint.

2.—(1) The function of the Commission of granting recognition of schemes is exercisable, in accordance with paragraph 4 or 5 below, on the Commission's own motion or on a submission for its approval made by or on behalf of any building societies.

(2) In this Schedule, in relation to a scheme recognised by the Commission to any extent, a "direction for its recognition" means a direction that the scheme is, to the extent specified in the direction, a scheme recognised by the Commission.

The register of recognised schemes

3.—(1) The central office shall maintain a register of recognised schemes for the investigation of complaints ("the register"), and the register shall—

(a) contain a copy of every scheme and the direction for its recognition a copy of which is directed to be kept in it by any provision of this Part of this Schedule; and

(b) be available for inspection on reasonable notice by members of the public on payment of the prescribed fee.

(2) Any member of the public shall be entitled, on payment of the prescribed fee, to be furnished with a copy of any scheme and the direction for its recognition kept in the register.

Procedure for recognition: Commission's initiative

4.—(1) If it appears to the Commission, from its own enquiries or from information made available to it, that a scheme has been made or is in operation which qualifies for recognition the Commission shall consider the scheme and the extent to which it qualifies for recognition.

(2) If, on consideration of a scheme, the Commission is satisfied that the scheme qualifies for recognition and conforms to the relevant requirements in relation to one or more prescribed matters of complaint, the Commission shall approve the scheme as a recognised scheme to such extent as it considers appropriate.

(3) The Commission shall, on approving a scheme under this paragraph, give a direction for its recognition.

(4) On giving a direction for the recognition of a scheme, the Commission shall send a copy of the scheme and of the direction to the central office; and the central office shall keep the copy of the scheme and of the direction in the register.

Procedure for recognition: submission by societies

5.—(1) Submission by or on behalf of building societies of a scheme for approval by the Commission as a recognised scheme shall be made by an application for recognition which shall be—

(*a*) made in such manner as the Commission specifies, either generally or in any particular case; and

(*b*) accompanied by such information as the Commission may reasonably require, either generally or in any particular case, in order to make its decision on the application;

and in this paragraph "the applicants" means those societies or the person acting on their behalf for the purposes of the application.

(2) Where an application is made to the Commission for recognition of a scheme then—

(*a*) if it appears to the Commission that the scheme qualifies for recognition and conforms to the relevant requirements in respect of one or more of the prescribed matters of complaint, the Commission shall approve the scheme as a recognised scheme to such extent as it considers appropriate;

(*b*) if it appears to the Commission that the scheme, with modifications, will, in addition to qualifying for recognition, conform to the relevant requirements in respect of one or more of the prescribed matters of complaint, and the applicants agree on appropriate modifications within the period of 21 days from the date on which the Commission notifies the applicants of the modifications it proposes for their agreement, the Commission shall approve the scheme as modified as a recognised scheme to such extent as it considers appropriate;

but otherwise it shall withhold its approval.

(3) The Commission shall, on approving a scheme, give a direction for its recognition and send copies of the direction to the applicants.

(4) On giving a direction for the recognition of a scheme, the Commission shall also send a copy of the scheme and of the direction to the central office; and the central office shall keep the copy of the scheme and of the direction in the register.

Procedure on accession to schemes

6.—(1) A building society which accedes to a recognised scheme or has acceded to a scheme which becomes a recognised scheme shall, within the period of 21 days beginning with the date of its accession or on which it receives a copy of the direction for its recognition, as the case may be, send a notice of that fact to the central office and to the Commission.

(2) A notice by a society under sub-paragraph (1) above shall specify the prescribed matters of complaint action in relation to which by the society is subject to investigation under the scheme.

(3) The central office, on receiving such a notice from a society, shall, if satisfied that the scheme is a recognised scheme to the extent required to enable the society to comply with its duty under section 83(3) in relation to the prescribed matters of complaint specified in the notice record the accession of the society to the scheme in the public file of the society.

(4) If a building society fails to comply with sub-paragraph (1) above, the society shall be liable on summary conviction—

(*a*) to a fine not exceeding level 4 on the standard scale, and

(*b*) in the case of a continuing offence, to an additional fine not exceeding £100 for every day during which the offence continues;

and so shall any director of the society who is also guilty of the offence.

Withdrawal of recognition

7.—(1) The Commission may withdraw its recognition of a scheme if it appears to the Commission that—

(*a*) the scheme does not conform to the relevant requirements; or

(*b*) the scheme is so operated as not to conform to those requirements.

(2) Withdrawal of recognition of a scheme under this paragraph may operate in relation to the scheme as a whole or to the extent to which the scheme makes one or more prescribed matters of complaint subject to investigation under it.

8.—(1) If the Commission proposes at any time to withdraw recognition of a scheme to any extent, it shall serve on each member, on the body administering the scheme and on the adjudicator under the scheme, a notice stating—

(*a*) that the Commission proposes to withdraw recognition and to what extent;

(*b*) the grounds for the proposed withdrawal of recognition; and

(*c*) that the person receiving the notice may make representations with respect to the proposed withdrawal within such period of not less than 14 days as may be specified in the notice.

(2) The Commission shall, before reaching a decision on whether to withdraw recognition, consider any representations made to it in accordance with sub-paragraph (1) above and shall serve on every person on whom it served a notice under that sub-paragraph a notice stating its decision and the grounds for it.

9. Withdrawal of recognition by the Commission shall take effect as from such date as is specified in the notice of its decision, being a date not less than one year nor more than two years after the date of the notice.

Withdrawal from membership

10.—(1) A building society wishing to withdraw from membership of a recognised scheme shall send notice of its proposed withdrawal to the central office and to the Commission.

(2) A notice by a society under sub-paragraph (1) above shall specify the prescribed matters of complaint action in relation to which by the society is subject to investigation under the scheme and the recognised scheme or recognised schemes of which it is or, on its withdrawal, will become a member under which, as regards each of the prescribed matters of complaint specified in the notice, action by the society is or will be subject to investigation.

(3) The central office, on receiving such a notice from a society, if satisfied that its withdrawal from the scheme will not result in a failure by it to comply with the duty imposed on it by section 83(3), shall confirm the withdrawal of the society from the scheme; but, if the central office is not so satisfied, the central office shall withhold its confirmation

(4) If the central office withholds its confirmation of a society's withdrawal from a scheme, the society shall continue to be a member of the scheme and bound and entitled under the scheme accordingly.

(5) On confirming the withdrawal of a society from a scheme the central office shall send to the society and to the Commission notice of its decision and the central office shall record the decision in the public file of the society.

DEFINITIONS

"accede": s.83(15).
"adjudicator": see Sched. 12.
"applicants": para. 5.
"central office": s.119(1).
"Commission": ss.1 and 119(1).
"conforms to the relevant requirements": para. 1.
"direction for its recognition": para. 2.
"extent": para. 1.
"notice": s.119(1).
"prescribed fee": s.119(1).
"prescribed matter of complaint": s.83(15).
"public file": ss.106 and 119(1).
"qualifies for recognition": para. 1.
"register": para. 3.
"the standard scale": Criminal Justice Act 1982, s.37.

GENERAL NOTE

This Schedule makes provision for: the maintenance of a register of recognised schemes for dealing with complaints by an individual against a society or an associated body (as defined in s.18(17)); the recognition of such schemes; accession to such schemes; withdrawal of recognition from such schemes; and withdrawal from membership of such schemes. It should be read in conjunction with ss.83 and 84 and Sched. 12.

Para. 1

This paragraph may be paraphrased as follows:

(*a*) a scheme "qualifies for recognition" if it covers the matters mentioned in Part I of Sched.12 and permits investigation of one or more of the matters specified in Part II of that Schedule;

(*b*) a scheme "conforms to the relevant requirements" if any investigation is to be made in accordance with Part III of that Schedule;

(*c*) the "extent" of a scheme's recognition means the number of Part II matters which it is recognised as covering. That extent will be specified in the direction for the scheme's recognition (para. 2).

Paras. 4 and 5

As is expressly stated in para. 2, the Commission may consider whether to grant recognition either on its own motion (covered by para. 4) or on a submission for approval made by or on behalf of any building societies (covered by para. 5). Rather curiously, para. 4 obliges the Commission to consider any scheme which qualifies for recognition of which it becomes aware, regardless, apparently, of whether the participating bodies wish the scheme to be recognised. There is no provision in this paragraph enabling the Commission to suggest modifications to such a scheme so that recognition can be granted. Para. 5 does contain such a provision.

An application under para. 5 is to be made in such a manner as the Commission specifies and is to be accompanied by such information as the Commission may reasonably require in order to make its decision.

Para. 6

This paragraph lays down the procedure to be followed when a society joins a recognised scheme or when a scheme to which a society already belongs becomes recognised. The procedure is designed to ensure that members of the public can find out which scheme or schemes a society belongs to and which matters are covered under each such scheme. Note that there are no similar provisions in respect of associated bodies.

Level 4. Currently £1,000.

Paras. 7–9

Para. 7(2) has the effect that recognition can be withdrawn from the scheme as a whole or the number of Part II matters in respect of which it is recognised can be reduced.

Notice must be given of any proposal to withdraw recognition to the members of the scheme, the body administering it and the adjudicator, so that representations may be made and considered before recognition is withdrawn (para. 8). Withdrawal of recognition is not effective at once, but only from a specified date between one and two years from the notice of withdrawal (para. 9); no doubt the delay is to allow suitable alternative arrangements to be made.

Para. 10

Under this paragraph, before a society can withdraw from membership of a scheme, the withdrawal must be confirmed by the central office. Such confirmation can only be given if the central office is satisfied that even after the withdrawal, the society will still be a member of one or more schemes covering each of the Part II matters. There are no similar provisions in respect of associated bodies.

Section 85   SCHEDULE 14

SETTLEMENT OF DISPUTES

PART I

PROCEEDINGS IN COURT

Jurisdiction of the court

1.—(1) No court other than the High Court or, in the case of a building society whose principal office is in Scotland the Court of Session, shall have jurisdiction to hear and determine disputes to which this paragraph applies; and, in this Part of this Schedule, "the court" means the High Court or, as the case may be, the Court of Session.

(2) This paragraph applies to any dispute—

(*a*) between a building society and a member of the society in his capacity as a member, or

(*b*) between a building society and a representative of such a member in that capacity, in respect of any rights or obligations arising from the rules of the society or any provision of this Act or any statutory instrument under it.

(3) Except in the cases referred to in sub-paragraph (5) below, no disputes to which this paragraph applies may be referred to arbitration.

(4) The court shall not hear and determine any dispute arising out of section 61(8)(*a*) or paragraph 31(4)(*a*) of Schedule 2 to this Act.

(5) The court shall not hear and determine any dispute which is required to be referred to arbitration under paragraph 4 below or which is referred to the Commission under paragraph 6 or to an adjudicator under paragraph 7 below except as provided in paragraph 2 below.

2. The court may hear and determine a dispute falling within paragraph 1(5) above in any case where, on the application of any person concerned, it appears to the court—

(*a*) that application has been made by either party to the dispute to the other party for the purpose of having the dispute settled by arbitration, and (*b*) that either arbitrators have been appointed within 40 days of that application or the arbitrators have refused, or have neglected for a period of 21 days, to proceed with the reference or make an award.

Right of central office to be heard

3.—(1) Any person who institutes proceedings in the court in relation to a dispute to which paragraph 1 above applies shall give notice of the fact and of the matter in dispute to the central office.

(2) The court shall not proceed to hear a dispute to which paragraph 1 applies until the court is satisfied that the notice required by sub-paragraph (1) above has been given.

(3) The central office shall be entitled, with the leave of the court, to attend and to be heard at any hearing of a dispute to which paragraph 1 applies.

PART II

ARBITRATION

Circulation of election addresses, resolutions and statements

4.—(1) If the rules of the society so provide, any dispute in respect of a refusal by a building society to send to its members—

(*a*) copies of an election address, in accordance with section 61(7), or

(*b*) any document required to be sent under paragraph 31(1) of Schedule 2 to this Act,

shall, unless the refusal is on one of the grounds specified in sub-paragraph (2) below, be referred to arbitration.

(2) Those grounds are—

(*a*) that publicity for the document in question would be likely to diminish substantially the confidence in the society of investing members of the public, or

(*b*) that the rights conferred by section 61(7) or paragraph 31(1) are being abused to seek needless publicity for defamatory matter.

Procedure on a reference to arbitration

5.—(1) This paragraph has effect in relation to an arbitration under paragraph 4(1) above.

(2) One or more arbitrators shall be appointed in the manner provided for by the rules of the building society; and so shall another arbitrator if an appointed arbitrator dies or refuses to act.

(3) No arbitrator acting on a reference shall be beneficially interested (whether directly or indirectly) in the funds of the society.

(4) The rules of the society may provide for the procedure to be followed on a reference to arbitration.

(5) An award made by arbitrators, or the majority of them, shall be final and binding.

(6) For the purposes of the Arbitration Act 1950 and the Arbitration Act 1979 or, in Northern Ireland, the Arbitration Act (Northern Ireland) 1937 the rules of the society shall be treated as an arbitration agreement.

(7) In relation to Scotland, sub-paragraph (6) above shall be omitted.

Access to register of members

6.—(1) Any dispute as to the rights of a member of a building society under paragraph 15 of Schedule 2 to this Act shall be referred to the Commission.

(2) The reference of a dispute to the Commission under this paragraph shall be treated as a reference to arbitration; and its award shall have the same effect as that of an arbitrator acting in a reference under paragraph 4(1) above.

Disputes cognizable under a scheme

7.—(1) Any dispute relating to a prescribed matter of complaint action in relation to which is subject to investigation under a scheme under section 83 may, if the complainant and the society or, as the case may be, the complainant and the associated body agree, instead of being determined by the adjudicator under the scheme, be referred to him as arbitrator.

(2) The reference of a dispute to an adjudicator under sub-paragraph (1) above shall be treated as a reference to arbitration, and his award shall have the same effect as that of an arbitrator acting in a reference under paragraph 4(1) above.

(3) Any expression used in this paragraph and section 83 has the same meaning in this paragraph as in that section.

General

8. In this Part of this Schedule, in relation to an arbitration in Scotland, references to an arbitrator shall be read as references to an arbiter.

DEFINITIONS
"adjudicator": see Sched. 12.
"associated": ss.18(17) and 119(1).
"central office": s.119(1).
"Commission": ss.1 and 119(1).
"complainant": see Sched. 12.
"court": para. 1.
"member": s.119(1).
"prescribed matter of complaint": s.83(15).

GENERAL NOTE
This Schedule provides for the mode in which disputes between a society and a member in his capacity as a member, or between the society and a representative of a member in that capacity, or, in Part II only and as hereinafter mentioned, between the society and a depositor, are to be settled. The Schedule applies in all cases except where the matter is to be investigated pursuant to a scheme under ss.83 and 84 and Scheds. 12 and 13. Those provisions, together with s.85 and this Schedule, replace ss.93 to 98 of the 1962 Act with a new code for the settlement of disputes such as are mentioned above. In these notes "dispute" means a dispute of that kind.

Para. 1
The effect of this paragraph is that the court hears every dispute unless:
(*a*) it is a dispute expressly referred to the Commission under s.61(8)(*a*) or para. 31(4) of Sched. 2. (See the notes to those provisions and para. 1(4) of this Schedule);
(*b*) it is a dispute under s.61(8)(*b*) or para. 31(4)(*b*) of Sched. 2 which, in accordance with para. 4, is required by the rules of the society to be referred to arbitration. (See the notes to those provisions and see para. 1(5));
(*c*) it is a dispute as to the right of a member to have access to the register of members under para. 15(2) of Sched. 2: see para. 1(5) and para. 6, providing for determination of such disputes by the Commission;
(*d*) it is a dispute relating to a "prescribed matter of complaint" which may be investigated under a scheme under s.83 and Sched. 12 and which the complainant and the society have agreed to refer to the adjudicator as arbitrator: see para. 1(5) and para. 7.
(*e*) it is a dispute relating to a prescribed matter of complaint for the purposes of a scheme under s.83 and Sched. 12 and is being or will be dealt with as such (as opposed to being dealt with by arbitration as in (*d*) above).

Para. 2
This paragraph qualifies (*b*) under the notes to para. 1 above by providing for the court to hear a dispute where one party has applied to the other for arbitration but the arbitrators have not been appointed within 40 days of the application or have refused, or neglected for 21 days to proceed with the reference or make an award. (*C.f.* s.96(2) of the 1962 Act.) In theory, this paragraph will also qualify (*d*) above, if the steps leading to an agreement for arbitration under para. 7 amount to an application within para. 2(*a*).

Para. 3
This paragraph ensures that the central office will have an opportunity to be heard in any proceedings in court if it wishes to be heard.

Para. 4
As indicated in (*b*) under the notes to para. 1 above, the court's jurisdiction is excluded if a society provides in its rules for the reference to arbitration of disputes arising out of a refusal to send to its members (i) an election address, (ii) a resolution or (iii) a statement supporting a resolution to members. In fact, however, the right under this paragraph to provide for arbitration is a limited right only. Under s.61(8) and Sched. 2, para. 31, the society may refuse to send an address, resolution or statement on the grounds that:

(1) publicity for the address, the resolution or the statement (as the case may be) would be likely to diminish substantially the confidence in the society of investing members of the public; or

(2) the right to have the address, the resolution or the statement (as the case may be) circulated is being abused:

(*a*) to seek needless publicity for defamatory matter; or

(*b*) for frivolous or vexatious purposes.

Both (1) and (2)(*a*) above are excluded from the operation of the paragraph by subpara. (2). It follows that the scope for arbitration is not large. (Note that in addition to disputes on the issue of "frivolous or vexatious purposes", there might be disputes as to, *e.g.*, the date when a document reached the society or whether a document relates directly to the affairs of the society.)

Para. 5

Note that under this paragraph the rules of a society which permits arbitration *must* provide for the appointment of one or more arbitrators (subpara. (2)) and *may* provide for the procedure to be followed (subpara. (4)). As to the paragraph generally, compare s.94 of the 1962 Act. Presumably rules permitting arbitration will not be approved by the central office under Sched. 2, para. 1 or 4 or Sched. 20, para. 3 if they contain no provision for the appointment of arbitrators. In the absence of provisions except as to appointment, presumably the Arbitration Acts 1950 and 1979 will apply.

Para. 6

See the notes to Sched. 2, para. 15.

Para. 7

The previous paragraphs of this Schedule have been concerned solely with disputes between members, or their representatives, and a society. The effect of this paragraph is to permit an investigation under a scheme under s.83 to proceed, by agreement, as a reference to the adjudicator as arbitrator. The field of possible parties is therefore widened. S.85(1) seems to contemplate that a depositor might be a party to the dispute and para. 7 itself expressly refers to associated bodies. It is not clear how the inclusion of associated bodies is to be reconciled with s.85 which specifies the disputes for settling which Sched. 14 has effect and which mentions only members, depositors and societies as potential parties to the dispute. Moreover, by using the word "complainant", which is introduced by Sched. 12, where it plainly includes a person who is neither a member nor a depositor (*e.g.* a borrower who was granted a loan under s.16 and is not a member), para. 7 seems to contemplate a further extension of potential parties; but again there is the difficulty of reconciliation with s.85.

Section 90   SCHEDULE 15

APPLICATION OF COMPANIES WINDING UP LEGISLATION TO BUILDING SOCIETIES

PART I

GENERAL MODE OF APPLICATION

1. The enactments which comprise the companies winding up legislation (referred to in this Schedule as "the enactments") are the provisions of—

(*a*) Parts IV, VI, VII and XII of the Insolvency Act 1986, or

(*b*) Part XX of the Companies (Northern Ireland) Order 1986,

and, in so far as they relate to offences under any such enactment, sections 430 and 432 of, and Schedule 10 to, the Insolvency Act 1986 or Article 678 of, and Schedule 23 to, the Companies (Northern Ireland) Order 1986.

2. Subject to the following provisions of this Schedule, the enactments apply to the winding up of building societies as they apply to the winding up of companies limited by shares and registered under the Companies Act 1985 or (as the case may be) the Companies (Northern Ireland) Order 1986.

3.—(1) The enactments shall, in their application to building societies, have effect with the substitution—

(*a*) for "company" of "building society";

(*b*) for "the registrar of companies" or "the registrar" of "the central office";

(*c*) for "the articles" of "the rules"; and

(*d*) for "registered office" of "principal office".

(2) In the application of the enactments to building societies—

(*a*) every reference to the officers, or to a particular officer, of a company shall have effect as a reference to the officers, or to the corresponding officer, of the building society and as including a person holding himself out as such an officer; and

(*b*) every reference to an administrator, an administration order, an administrative receiver, a shadow director or a voluntary arrangement shall be omitted.

4.—(1) Where any of the enactments as applied to building societies requires a notice or other document to be sent to the central office, it shall have effect as if it required the central office to keep the notice or document in the public file of the society concerned and to record in that file the date on which the notice or document is placed in it.

(2) Where any of the enactments, as so applied, refers to the registration, or to the date of registration, of such a notice or document, that enactment shall have effect as if it referred to the placing of the notice or document in the public file or (as the case may be) to the date on which it was placed there.

5. Any enactment which specifies a money sum altered by order under section 416 of the Insolvency Act 1986, or, as the case may be, Article 614 of the Companies (Northern Ireland) Order 1986, (powers to alter monetary limits) applies with the effect of the alteration.

Part II

Modified Application of Insolvency Act 1986

Parts IV and XII

Preliminary

6. In this Part of this Schedule, Part IV of the Insolvency Act 1986 is referred to as "Part IV"; and that Act is referred to as "the Act".

Members of a building society as contributories in winding up

7.—(1) Section 74 (liability of members) of the Act is modified as follows.

(2) In subsection (1), the reference to any past member shall be omitted.

(3) Paragraphs (*a*) to (*d*) of subsection (2) shall be omitted; and so shall subsection (3).

(4) The extent of the liability of a member of a building society in a winding up shall not exceed the extent of his liability under paragraph 6 of Schedule 2 to this Act.

8. Sections 75 to 78 and 83 in Chapter I of Part IV (miscellaneous provisions not relevant to building societies) do not apply.

9.—(1) Section 79 (meaning of "contributory") of the Act does not apply.

(2) In the enactments as applied to a building society, "contributory"—

(*a*) means every person liable to contribute to the assets of the society in the event of its being wound up, and

(*b*) for the purposes of all proceedings for determining, and all proceedings prior to the determination of, the persons who are to be deemed contributories, includes any person alleged to be a contributory, and

(*c*) includes persons who are liable to pay or contribute to the payment of—

    (i) any debt or liability of the building society being wound up, or

    (ii) any sum for the adjustment of rights of members among themselves, or

    (iii) the expenses of the winding up;

but does not include persons liable to contribute by virtue of a declaration by the court under section 213 (imputed responsibility for fraudulent trading) or section 214 (wrongful trading) of the Act.

Voluntary winding up

10.—(1) Section 84 of the Act does not apply.

(2) In the enactments as applied to a building society, the expression "resolution for voluntary winding up" means a resolution passed under section 88(1) of this Act.

11. In subsection (1) of section 101 (appointment of liquidation committee) of the Act, the reference to functions conferred on a liquidation committee by or under that Act shall have effect as a reference to its functions by or under that Act as applied to building societies.

12.—(1) Section 107 (distribution of property) of the Act does not apply; and the following applies in its place.

(2) Subject to the provisions of Part IV relating to preferential payments, a building society's property in a voluntary winding up shall be applied in satisfaction of the society's liabilities to creditors (including any liability resulting from the variation to the liquidator's duty effected by section 28 or 31 of this Act) pari passu and, subject to that application, in accordance with the rules of the society.

13. Sections 110 and 111 (liquidator accepting shares, etc. as consideration for sale of company property) of the Act do not apply.

14. Section 116 (saving for certain rights) of the Act shall also apply in relation to the dissolution by consent of a building society as it applies in relation to its voluntary winding up.

Winding up by the court

15. In sections 117 (High Court and county court jurisdiction) and 120 (Court of Session and sheriff court jurisdiction) of the Act, each reference to a company's share capital paid up or credited as paid up shall have effect as a reference to the amount standing to the credit of shares in a building society as shown by the latest balance sheet.

16. Section 122 (circumstances in which company may be wound up by the court) of the Act does not apply.

17. Section 124 (application for winding up) of the Act does not apply.

18.—(1) In section 125 (powers of court on hearing of petition) of the Act, subsection (1) applies with the omission of the words from "but the court" to the end of the subsection.

(2) The conditions which the court may impose under section 125 of the Act include conditions for securing—

(a) that the building society be dissolved by consent of its members under section 87, or

(b) that the society amalgamates with, or transfers its engagements to, another building society under section 93 or 94, or

(c) that the society transfers its business to a company under section 97,

and may also include conditions for securing that any default which occasioned the petition be made good and that the costs, or in Scotland the expenses, of the proceedings on that petition be defrayed by the person or persons responsible for the default.

19. Section 126 (power of court, between petition and winding-up order, to stay or restrain proceedings against company) of the Act has effect with the omission of subsection (2).

20. If, before the presentation of a petition for the winding up by the court of a building society, an instrument of dissolution under section 87 is placed in the society's public file, section 129(1) (commencement of winding up by the court) of the Act shall also apply in relation to the date on which the instrument is so placed and to any proceedings in the course of the dissolution as it applies to the commencement date for, and proceedings in, a voluntary winding up.

21.—(1) Section 130 of the Act (consequences of winding-up order) shall have effect with the following modifications.

(2) Subsections (1) and (3) shall be omitted.

(3) A building society shall, within 15 days of a winding-up order being made in respect of it, give notice of the order to the central office; and the central office shall keep the notice in the public file of the society.

(4) If a building society fails to comply with sub-paragraph (3) above, it shall be liable on summary conviction to a fine not exceeding level 3 on the standard scale; and so shall any officer who is also guilty of the offence.

22. Section 140 (appointment of liquidator by court in certain circumstances) of the Act does not apply.

23. In the application of sections 141(1) and 142(1) (liquidation committees), of the Act to building societies, the references to functions conferred on a liquidation committee by or under that Act shall have effect as references to its functions by or under that Act as so applied.

24. The conditions which the court may impose under section 147 (power to stay or sist winding up) of the Act shall include those specified in paragraph 18(2) above.

25. Section 154 (adjustment of rights of contributories) of the Act shall have effect with the modification that any surplus is to be distributed in accordance with the rules of the society.

26. In section 165(2) (liquidator's powers) of the Act, the reference to an extraordinary resolution shall have effect as a reference to a special resolution.

Winding up: general

27. Section 187 (power to make over assets to employees) of the Act does not apply.

28.—(1) In section 201 (dissolution: voluntary winding up) of the Act, subsection (2) applies without the words from "and on the expiration" to the end of the subsection and, in subsection (3), the word "However" shall be omitted.

(2) Sections 202 to 204 (early dissolution) of the Act do not apply.

29. In section 205 (dissolution: winding up by the court) of the Act, subsection (2) applies with the omission of the words from "and, subject" to the end of the subsection; and in subsections (3) and (4) references to the Secretary of State shall have effect as references to the Commission.

Penal provisions

30. Sections 216 and 217 of the Act (restriction on re-use of name) do not apply.

31.—(1) Sections 218 and 219 (prosecution of delinquent officers) of the Act do not apply in relation to offences committed by members of a building society acting in that capacity.

(2) Sections 218(5) of the Act and subsections (1) and (2) of section 219 of the Act do not apply.

(3) The references in subsections (3) and (4) of section 219 of the Act to the Secretary of State shall have effect as references to the Commission; and the reference in subsection (3) to section 218 of the Act shall have effect as a reference to that section as supplemented by paragraph 32 below.

32.—(1) Where a report is made to the prosecuting authority (within the meaning of section 218) under section 218(4) of the Act, in relation to an officer of a building society, he may, if he thinks fit, refer the matter to the Commission for further enquiry.

(2) On such a reference to it the Commission shall exercise its power under section 55(1) of this Act to appoint one or more investigators to investigate and report on the matter.

(3) An answer given by a person to a question put to him in exercise of the powers conferred by section 55 on a person so appointed may be used in evidence against the person giving it.

Preferential debts

33. Section 387 (meaning in Schedule 6 of "the relevant date") of the Act applies with the omission of subsections (2) and (4) to (6).

PART III

MODIFIED APPLICATION OF THE COMPANIES

(NORTHERN IRELAND) ORDER 1986, PART XX

Preliminary

34. In this Part of this Schedule, Part XX of the Companies (Northern Ireland) Order 1986 is referred to as "Part XX", that Order is referred to as "the Order" and references to "Articles" are references to Articles of that Order.

Members of building society as contributories in winding up

35.—(1) Article 468 (liability of members) is modified as follows.

(2) In paragraph (1), the reference to any past member shall be omitted.

(3) Sub-paragraphs (*a*) to (*d*) of paragraph (2) shall be omitted; and so shall paragraph (3).

(4) The extent of the liability of a member of a building society in a winding up shall not exceed the extent of his liability under paragraph 6 of Schedule 2 to this Act.

36. Articles 469 to 472 and 477 in Chapter I of Part XX (miscellaneous provisions not relevant to building societies) do not apply.

37.—(1) Article 473 (meaning of "contributory") does not apply.

(2) In the enactments as applied to a building society, "contributory"—

(*a*) means every person liable to contribute to the assets of the society in the event of its being wound up, and (*b*) for the purposes of all proceedings for determining, and all proceedings prior to the determination of, the persons who are to be deemed contributories, includes any person alleged to be a contributory, and

(*c*) includes persons who are liable to pay or contribute to the payment of—
    (i) any debt or liability of the building society being wound up, or
    (ii) any sum for the adjustment of rights of members among themselves, or
    (iii) the expenses of the winding up;

but does not include persons liable to contribute by virtue of a declaration by the court under Article 583 (imputed responsibility for fraudulent trading).

Voluntary winding up

38.—(1) Article 529 does not apply.

(2) In the enactments as applied to a building society, the expression "resolution for voluntary winding up" means a resolution passed under section 88(1) of this Act.

39. Articles 539, 540 and 551 (liquidator accepting shares, etc. as consideration for sale for company property) do not apply.

40. In the application of Article 548 (committees of inspection) to building societies, a committee of inspection shall exercise only those functions conferred by or under the Order as so applied.

41.—(1) Article 555 (distribution of property) does not apply; and the following applies in its place.

(2) Subject to the provisions of Part XX relating to preferential payments, a building society's property in a voluntary winding up shall be applied in satisfaction of the society's liabilities to creditors (including any liability resulting from the variation to the liquidator's duty effected by section 28 or 31 of this Act) pari passu and subject to that application, in accordance with the rules of the society.

42. Article 562 (saving for certain rights) shall also apply in relation to the dissolution by consent of a building society as it applies in relation to its voluntary winding up.

Winding up by the court

43. Article 479 (circumstances in which company may be wound up by the court) does not apply.

44. Article 481 (application for winding up) does not apply.

45.—(1) Article 482 (powers of court on hearing of petition) applies with the omission of the words from "but the court" to the end of the Article.

(2) The conditions which the court may impose under Article 482 include conditions for securing—

(*a*) that the building society be dissolved by consent of its members under section 87, or

(*b*) that the society amalgamates with, or transfers its engagements to, another building society under section 93 or 94, or

(*c*) that the society transfers its business to a company under section 97,

and may also include conditions for securing that any default which occasioned the petition be made good and that the costs of the proceedings on that petition be defrayed by the person or persons responsible for the default.

46. Article 483 (power of court, between petition and winding-up order, to stay or restrain proceedings against company) has effect with the omission of paragraph (2).

47. If, before the presentation of a petition for the winding up by the court of a building society, an instrument of dissolution under section 87 is placed in the society's public file, Article 486(1) (commencement of winding up by the court) shall also apply in relation to the date on which the instrument is so placed and to any proceedings in the course of the dissolution as it applies to the commencement date for, and proceedings in, a voluntary winding up.

48.—(1) Article 487 (consequences of winding-up order) shall have effect with the following modifications.

(2) Paragraphs (1) and (3) shall be omitted.

(3) A building society shall within 15 days of a winding-up order being made in respect of it, give notice of the order to the central office, and the central office shall keep the notice in the public file of the society.

(4) If a building society fails to comply with subparagraph (3) above, it shall be liable on summary conviction to a fine not exceeding level 3 on the standard scale; and so shall any officer who is also guilty of the offence.

49. In the application of Article 507 (committees of inspection) to building societies, a committee of inspection shall exercise only those functions conferred by or under the Order as so applied.

50. The conditions which the court may impose under Article 510 (power to stay winding up) shall include those specified in paragraph 45(2) above.

51. Article 519 (adjustment of rights of contributories) shall have effect with the modification that any surplus is to be distributed in accordance with the rules of the society.

52. In Article 556(1) (liquidator's powers), the reference to an extraordinary resolution shall have effect as a reference to a special resolution.

Winding up: general

53.—(1) Article 610 (power to make over assets to employees) does not apply.

(2) Article 543(5) and Article 553(6) (final meeting and dissolution: voluntary winding up) shall apply without the words from "and on the expiration" to "dissolved; but".

Penal provisions

54.—(1) Articles 585 and 586 (prosecution of delinquent officers) do not apply in relation to offences committed by members of a building society acting in that capacity.

(2) Article 585(3) and paragraphs (1) and (2) of Article 586 do not apply.

(3) The references in paragraphs (3) and (4) of Article 586 to the Department of Economic Development shall have effect as references to the Commission; and the reference in paragraph (3) to Article 585 shall have effect as a reference to that Article as supplemented by paragraph 55 below.

55.—(1) Where a report is made to the prosecuting authority (within the meaning of Article 585) under Article 585(2) in relation to an officer of a building society, he may, if he thinks fit, refer the matter to the Commission for further enquiry.

(2) On such reference to it the Commission shall exercise its power under section 55(1) of this Act to appoint one or more investigators to investigate and report on the matter.

(3) An answer given by a person to a question put to him in exercise of the powers conferred by section 55 on a person so appointed may be used in evidence against the person giving it.

Part IV

Dissolution of Building Society wound up

(England and Wales, Scotland and Northern Ireland)

56.—(1) Where a building society has been wound up voluntarily, it is dissolved as from 3 months from the date of the placing in the public file of the society of the return of the final meetings of the society and its creditors made by the liquidator under—

(a) section 94 or (as the case may be) 106 of the Insolvency Act 1986 (as applied to building societies), or on such other date as is determined in accordance with section 201 of that Act, or

(b) Article 543 or (as the case may be) 553 of the Companies (Northern Ireland) Order 1986 (as so applied), or on such other date as is determined in accordance with that Article,

as the case may be.

(2) Where a building society has been wound up by the court, it is dissolved as from 3 months from the date of the placing in the public file of the society of—

(a) the liquidator's notice under section 172(8) of the Insolvency Act 1986 (as applied to building societies), or

(b) the notice of the completion of the winding up from the official receiver or the Official Assignee for company liquidations,

or on such other date as is determined in accordance with section 205 of that Act, as the case may be.

57.—(1) Sections 654 to 658 of the Companies Act 1985 or Articles 605 to 609 of the Companies (Northern Ireland) Order 1986 (provisions as to corporate property as bona vacantia) shall have the same effect in relation to the property of a dissolved building society (whether dissolved under section 87 or following its winding up) as they have in relation to the property of a dissolved company, but with the following modifications.

(2) Paragraph 3(1) above shall apply to those sections for the purpose of their application to building societies.

(3) Subsection (2) of section 654 and subsections (1) and (3) of section 655 apply without the words "or 653"; and the references in those subsections to section 651 shall have effect as references to section 91 of this Act.

(4) Paragraph (2) of Article 605 and paragraph (1) of Article 606 apply without the words " or 604"; and references in those paragraphs to Article 602 shall have effect as references to section 91 of this Act.

Insolvency rules and fees: England and Wales and Scotland

58.—(1) Rules may be made under section 411 of the Insolvency Act for the purpose of giving effect, in relation to building societies, to the provisions of the applicable winding up legislation.

(2) An order made by the competent authority under section 414 of the Insolvency Act 1986 may make provision for fees to be payable under that section in respect of proceedings under the applicable winding up legislation and the performance by the official receiver or the Secretary of State of functions under it.

Insolvency rules and fees: Northern Ireland

59.—(1) Rules may be made under Article 615 of the Companies (Northern Ireland) Order 1986 for the purpose of giving effect in relation to building societies, to the provisions of the applicable winding up legislation.

(2) Rules made by the Department of Economic Development under paragraph (6) of Article 613 may make provision for fees to be payable under that paragraph in respect of proceedings under the applicable winding up legislation and the performance by the Official Assignee for company liquidations or that Department of functions under it.

DEFINITIONS
"central office": s.119(1).
"Commission": ss.1 and 119(1).
"contributory": paras. 9 and 37.
"the enactments": para. 1.
"member": s.119(1).
"officer": s.119(1).
"public file": ss.106 and 119(1).

GENERAL NOTE
This Schedule contains the necessary provisions for adapting the relevant sections of the Insolvency Act 1986 to the winding up of building societies, whether voluntarily or by the court. It has four parts. Part I contains general provisions; Part II makes the necessary detailed modifications to the Insolvency Act, which applies to England and Wales, and Scotland; Part III makes similar modifications to the Companies (Northern Ireland) Order 1986; and Part IV makes provision for the dissolution of building societies which have been wound up.

It follows from the nature and purpose of the Schedule that much of its substance is concerned with detailed modification which does not call for annotation and accordingly many paragraphs receive no express mention in the following notes. Notes on paragraphs in Part II (paras. 6 to 33) apply generally to the corresponding paragraphs in Part III (paras. 34 to 55).

Para. 1
This paragraph specifies the enactments covered by the term "companies winding up legislation" in s.90 (in the Schedule called "the enactments").

Para. 3
This paragraph contains general substitutionary provisions for application throughout the enactments.

Para. 4
Under this paragraph, documents which in company law are to be registered are to be placed in the public file of a building society.

Paras. 7 and 9
Taken together, these paragraphs have the important effect of establishing who is a contributory and who can therefore present a petition for winding up in that capacity. By s.74 of the Insolvency Act as modified:

(*a*) every member is liable to contribute to the assets of the society to any amount sufficient for payment of its debts and liabilities, the expenses of winding up and the adjustment of the rights of the contributories; but

(*b*) the extent of liability shall not exceed the extent of liability under Sched. 2, para. 6: *i.e.* in the case of a holder of shares on which no advance has been made, the amount actually paid or in arrears on the share, and in the case of an advanced member, the amount payable under the terms of the advance.

By s.79 of the Insolvency Act as modified, "contributory" means every person liable to contribute to the assets of the society in the event of its being wound up.

It follows that both shareholders and advanced members are contributories, the shareholder being liable to contribute the amount of his share (by reason of the fact that he will get none of his money back until the creditors have been paid) and the advanced member being liable to contribute the sums payable under the advance.

Para. 12

This paragraph makes provision for the distribution of property on a voluntary winding up. After payment of creditors, it is to be applied in accordance with the rules of the society. Note that the distribution of surplus assets is a matter which must be covered by the rules: Sched. 2, para. 3(4).

Para. 14

See the notes to s.87.

Paras. 16 and 17

See the notes to s.89.

Para. 18

This paragraph enables the court, under s.125 of the Insolvency Act, to adjourn a petition for a winding up on conditions designed to ensure that the society is dissolved in one of the other ways provided for in ss.87, 93, 94 and 97 of this Act.

Para. 24

This paragraph enables the court, under s.147 of the Insolvency Act, to stay a winding up after a winding up order has been made on conditions such as are mentioned in para. 18.

Para. 25

Under this paragraph, any surplus arising on a winding up by the court is to be applied in accordance with the society's rules. See the note to para. 12 above.

Para. 56

The broad effect of this paragraph is that as a general rule a society which has been wound up will be dissolved three months after the date on which notice of the completion of the winding up is placed in its public file.

Para. 57

By virtue of this paragraph, any property of a dissolved society is deemed to be *bona vacantia*, subject to the further provisions of ss.654 to 658 of the Companies Act 1985 as modified.

Sections 93, 94 and 95   SCHEDULE 16

MERGERS: SUPPLEMENTARY PROVISIONS

PART I

ISSUE OF STATEMENTS TO MEMBERS

1.—(1) A building society which desires—

(*a*) to amalgamate with one or more other building societies, or

(*b*) to transfer its engagements to another building society, or

(*c*) to undertake to fulfil the engagements of another building society,

shall, unless the Commission, in the case of a society desirous of undertaking to fulfil another's engagements, has consented under section 94(5) to its proceeding by resolution of the board of directors, send to every member entitled to notice of a meeting of the society a statement concerning the matters specified in sub-paragraph (4) below.

(2) A building society shall include the statement referred to in sub-paragraph (1) above in or with the notice to be sent to its members of the meeting of the society at which the resolutions required for the approval of the amalgamation or, as the case may be, the transfer are to be moved.

(3) No statement shall be sent unless its contents, so far as they concern the matters specified in sub-paragraph (4) below, have been approved by the Commission.

(4) Those matters are the following, namely—

(a) the financial position of the building society and that of the other building society or societies participating in the amalgamation or transfer:

(b) the interest of the directors of the building society in the amalgamation or transfer of engagements;

(c) the compensation or other consideration (if any) proposed to be paid to or in respect of the directors or other officers of the building society and of the other building society or societies participating in the amalgamation or transfer;

(d) the payments (if any) are to be made to members of the building society and of the other building society or societies participating in the amalgamation or transfer by way of a distribution of funds in consideration of the amalgamation or transfer;

(e) the changes (if any) to be made, in connection with the amalgamation or transfer of engagements, in the terms governing outstanding class 1 or class 2 advances made by the building society;

(f) any other matter which the Commission requires in the case of the particular amalgamation or transfer of engagements.

(5) The statement shall be sent so that any member to whom the building society sends notice of the meeting at which the resolutions to approve the amalgamation or transfer are to be considered will receive the statement not later than he receives the notice.

(6) Any expression used in this paragraph and in section 96 has the same meaning in this paragraph as in that section.

PART II

NOTIFICATION OF PROPOSALS FOR MERGER

Preliminary

2. In this Part of this Schedule—

"merger" means an amalgamation of building societies under section 93 or a transfer of all the engagements of one building society to another under section 94; and "merge" has a corresponding meaning;

"merger proposal", in relation to a building society, means a proposal in writing, by another building society desiring to merge with it, for the societies to merge, with or without terms for the merger; and "prosper" has a corresponding meaning;

"merger resolutions", in relation to a building society, means the resolutions required for the approval of a merger of the society with another building society under section 93(2) or 94(2);

"merger statement" means a statement containing the requisite particulars of a merger proposal; and

"requisite particulars", in relation to a merger proposal, means the particulars required by paragraph 3(2) below to be given in a merger statement.

Duty to notify members

3.—(1) Subject to sub-paragraph (3) below, it shall be the duty of a building society receiving a merger proposal to send, in accordance with this Part of this Schedule, a merger statement in respect of the proposal to every member entitled to notice of a meeting of the society.

(2) A merger statement must contain the following particulars—

(a) the fact that a merger proposal has been made, and

(b) the identity of the proposer;

with or without other particulars regarding the proposal.

(3) Sub-paragraph (1) above does not require a merger statement to be sent to members if the proposer has requested in writing that the requisite particulars are to be treated as confidential; and, where such a request is made and is at a later date withdrawn in writing, the society receiving the proposal shall, for the purposes of this Part of this Schedule, treat the proposal as having been received on that date instead of any earlier date.

4.—(1) A building society shall include in or with every notice of its annual general meeting a merger statement with respect to any merger proposal, other than a proposal of which notice has already been given under this paragraph,—

(a) received by it during the period of 12 months ending with the ninth month of the last financial year of the society before that meeting; or (*b*) treated by paragraph 3(3) above as having been received by it during the last three months of that financial year;

and the society may also include, under this sub-paragraph, a merger statement with respect to any proposal received, or treated as received, by it after the end of either period.

(2) In any case where merger resolutions are to be moved at any meeting of a building society, every notice of the meeting shall have included in or with it a merger statement with respect to any merger proposal, other than a proposal of which notice has already been given under this paragraph, received by it more than 42 days before the date of the meeting.

Duty to notify central office

5.—(1) Where a building society sends a merger statement to its members under paragraph 4 above in connection with a meeting of the society, it shall send a copy of the statement to the central office at least 14 days before the date of the meeting.

(2) The central office shall keep the copy of a merger statement received by it from a building society in the public file of that society.

Penalty

6. If default is made by a building society in complying with paragraph 4(1), 4(2) or 5 above, the society shall be liable on summary conviction to a fine not exceeding level 4 on the standard scale; and so shall any officer who is also guilty of the offence.

PART III

CONFIRMATION BY COMMISSION: PROCEDURE

7. An application for confirmation by the Commission of an amalgamation or transfer of engagements shall be made in such manner as the Commission may prescribe.

8.—(1) Where a building society applies to the Commission for confirmation of an amalgamation or transfer of engagements, the society shall publish notice of the application in any one or more of the London Gazette, the Edinburgh Gazette or the Belfast Gazette, as the Commission directs and, if it so directs, in one or more newspapers.

(2) A notice published in pursuance of sub-paragraph (1) above shall—

(*a*) state that any interested party has the right to make representations to the Commission with respect to the application; and

(*b*) specify a date determined by the Commission before which any written representations or notice of a person's intention to make oral representations must be received by the Commission; and

(*c*) specify a date determined by the Commission as the day on which it intends to hear any oral representations.

9.—(1) After the date specified in pursuance of paragraph 8(2)(*b*) above, the Commission shall—

(*a*) determine the time and place at which oral representations may be made;

(*b*) give notice of that determination to the building societies participating in the amalgamation or transfer and any persons who have given notice of their intention to make oral representations; and

(*c*) send copies of the written representations received by the Commission to the building societies participating in the amalgamation or transfer.

(2) The Commission shall allow any building society participating in the amalgamation or transfer an opportunity to comment on the written representations, whether at a hearing or in writing before the expiration of such period as the Commission specifies in a notice to the society.

DEFINITIONS

"central office": s.119(1).
"class 1 advance": ss.11(2) and 119(1).
"class 2 advance": ss.11(4) and 119(1).
"Commission": ss.1 and 119(1).
"financial year": ss.117 and 119(1).
"member": s.119(1).
"merger", "merger proposal", "merger resolutions" and "merger statement": para. 2.
"notice": s.119(1).
"officer": s.119(1).

"proposer": para. 2.
"public file": ss.106 and 119(1).
"requisite particulars": para. 2.
"the standard scale": Criminal Justice Act 1983, s.37.

GENERAL NOTE

This Schedule contains supplementary provisions relating to amalgamations (see s.93) and transfers of engagement (see s.94). It should be read in conjunction with those sections, and with s.96 (compensation for loss of office and bonuses to members).

PART I

Para. 1

This paragraph obliges a society which desires to amalgamate, or to transfer its engagements, or to undertake the engagements of another society (subject, in the last case, to the exception mentioned below), to send to every member entitled to notice of a meeting a statement concerning the matters specified in para. 1(4). The statement is to be sent with the notice of the meeting at which the necessary resolutions for the amalgamation or transfer are to be moved.

The purpose of requiring the statement to be sent is, of course, to ensure that the specified information is available to members in deciding which way to vote. The matters to be covered are: the financial position of the societies concerned; the interest of the directors of the member's society in the proposed amalgamation or transfer; the compensation or other consideration to be paid to the directors or other officers of the societies concerned; the changes to be made to the terms governing outstanding class 1 and class 2 advances; any other matter required to be covered by the Commission. On receiving the statement the member should be in a position to judge how all interested parties will be affected.

The exception referred to above applies when the Commission has consented, under s.94(5), to a society proceeding by resolution of the board of directors instead of by a special resolution and a borrowing members' resolution. Plainly the statement is not required in such a case.

Note that the Commission must approve the statement as far as concerns the specified matters (subpara. (3)).

It is not clear what effect subpara. (5) is intended to have, when it is read together with subpara. (2).

The paragraph is largely derived from s.20 of the 1962 Act.

PART II

This Part of the Schedule is intended to give effect to the first policy mentioned in the notes to s.95(7) and (8): that is, the policy of ensuring that the board does not for personal or other improper reasons, reject merger proposals (*i.e.* proposals for amalgamation or transfer), without notice to the members and contrary to their interests. That object is to be achieved by obliging the society to give notice to its members of the fact that a proposal has been made and the identity of the proposer (para. 3). Further particulars can be given if the board so wishes. Note that the proposer may request that the "requisite particulars" (see para. 3(2)) may be treated as confidential and if such a request is made, the society is not obliged to send a statement until after the request has been withdrawn in writing.

When the Bill was first introduced, it contained further provisions under which a society wishing to take over another society might, in certain specified circumstances, approach the members of the other society directly if the directors of the other society were unwilling to put merger proposals before the members. Those provisions were felt likely to place an undue burden on smaller societies and were removed at the Report stage in the House of Commons: see *Hansard*, H.C. Vol. 98, col. 1020. Under the present provisions members will learn that a proposal has been made and it is then for them to decide what, if anything, to do about it.

Para. 4

The purpose of this paragraph is to ensure that members are in a position to consider merger proposals at the annual general meeting if they so desire.

Para. 5

Note that not only must the central office be kept informed of merger proposals, but the merger statement will be kept on the public file.

Para. 6

Level 4: Currently £1,000.

PART III

This Part lays down the procedure to be followed on an application to the Commission for confirmation of an amalgamation or transfer. Note that any "interested party" has the right to make representations and such representations may be written or oral (para. 8). The societies concerned must be given an opportunity of commenting on any written representation.

Presumably it is hoped that this procedure will bring to light any failure to give information, disagreement on the part of members, or non-compliance with a relevant requirement which might prevent the Commission from confirming the amalgamation or transfer. See the provisions of s.95 and the notes thereto.

Sections 97 and 98   SCHEDULE 17

TRANSFERS OF BUSINESS: SUPPLEMENTARY PROVISIONS

PART I

ISSUE OF STATEMENT TO MEMBERS

Preliminary

1. In this Part of this Schedule—
  "prescribed matters" in relation to any transfer of the business of a building society to its successor, means the matters relating to the transfer, the society, its officers, members or depositors, or the successor, which are prescribed in regulations made under paragraph 5 below; and
  "transfer statement", in relation to a transfer of business by a building society, means the statement with respect to the transfer to be sent to members of the society under paragraph 2 below.

Duty to send transfer statements to members

2. A building society which desires to transfer its business shall, in accordance with this Part of this Schedule, send a transfer statement to every member entitled to notice of a meeting of the society.

3. A transfer statement, in relation to a transfer of business by a building society, shall contain—
  (*a*) the particulars required, in relation to the prescribed matters, by the regulations made under paragraph 5 below, and
  (*b*) particulars of any other matters required by the Commission in the case of the particular transfer,
with or without other particulars regarding the transfer.

4.—(1) Subject to sub-paragraph (2) below, a building society shall, in relation to a transfer of business, include a transfer statement in or with the notice to be sent to its members of the meeting of the society at which the requisite transfer resolutions are to be moved.

(2) No transfer statement shall be sent unless its contents, so far as they concern the prescribed matters or any matter of which particulars are required to be given under paragraph 3(*b*) above, have been approved by the Commission.

5.—(1) The Commission, with the consent of the Treasury, may make regulations for the purpose of specifying, as prescribed matters, the matters of which transfer statements are to give particulars; and the regulations may also require particulars to be given of any alternatives to the particular transfer which were available to the society making the transfer.

(2) The power to make regulations under this paragraph is exercisable by statutory instrument which shall be subject to annulment in pursuance of a resolution of either House of Parliament.

PART II

CONFIRMATION BY COMMISSION: PROCEDURE

6. An application by a building society for confirmation by the Commission of a transfer of its business to a company shall be made in such manner as the Commission may prescribe.

7.—(1) Where a building society applies for confirmation of a transfer of its business, the society shall publish a notice of the application in any one or more of the London Gazette, the Edinburgh Gazette or the Belfast Gazette, as the Commission directs and, if it so directs, in one or more newspapers.

(2) A notice published in pursuance of sub-paragraph (1) above shall—

(*a*) state that any interested party has the right to make representations to the Commission with respect to the application;

(*b*) specify a date determined by the Commission before which any written representations or notice of a person's intention to make oral representations must be received by the Commission; and

(*c*) specify a date determined by the Commission as the day on which it intends to hear any oral representations.

8.—(1) After the date specified in the notice in pursuance of paragraph 7(2)(*b*) above, the Commission shall—

(*a*) determine the time and place at which oral representations may be made;

(*b*) give notice of that determination to the building society making the transfer and any persons who have given notice of their intention to make oral representations; and

(*c*) send copies of the written representations received by the Commission to the building society making the transfer.

(2) The Commission shall allow the building society making the transfer an opportunity to comment on the written representations, whether at a hearing or in writing, before the expiration of such period as the Commission specifies in a notice to the society.

DEFINITIONS

"Commission": ss.1 and 119(1).
"depositor": see s.119 (1).
"member": s.119(1).
"notice": s.119(1).
"officer": s.119(1).
"prescribed matters": para. 1.
"requisite transfer resolutions": s.97(4) and (12).
"successor": s.97(1).
"transfer statement": para. 1.

GENERAL NOTE

This Schedule contains two parts. Part I concerns the issue of a statement to members in respect of the proposed transfer of a society's business to a commercial company and Part II provides for the procedure on an application for the confirmation of such a transfer by the Commission. The Schedule should be read in conjunction with ss.97 and 98, to which it is supplementary.

PART I

Para. 2 obliges a society wishing to transfer its business to send a transfer statement to every member entitled to notice of a meeting. The statement must contain the particulars required by regulations in respect of the "prescribed matters" and any other particulars the Commission may require in the particular case and may contain other particulars: para. 3. Para. 5. empowers the Commission to make regulations as to the particulars to be included in respect of the prescribed matters, which are defined in para. 1 as matters relating to the transfer, the society, its officers, members or depositors, or the successor. The statement is to be sent together with the notice of the meeting at which the requisite transfer resolutions are to be moved: para. 4. Note that the contents of the statement, so far as they concern the prescribed matters or any other matter required by the Commission to be included, must be approved by the Commission: para. 4.

This Part is very similar to Part I of Sched. 16, which provides for the sending of statements to members in respect of a proposed amalgamation or transfer of engagements. It has the same purpose of ensuring that members have certain information available in deciding which way to vote.

Para. 5

Any alternatives to the particular transfer. The precise scope of this phrase is not clear. The broad purpose is presumably to give the Commission power to make regulations to ensure that members are not led to believe that the proposal before them represents the only possibility for the future and this would tend to suggest a fairly broad construction. It is thought, however, that the phrase would not cover alternative terms of the particular transfer.

PART II

This Part lays down the procedure to be followed on an application for confirmation of a transfer to a commercial company and is virtually identical to Part II of Sched. 16, dealing with confirmation of an amalgamation or transfer of engagements. As under that Part, any "interested party" has the right to make representations and such representations may be written or oral: para. 7. The society must be given an opportunity of commenting on any written representation.

Presumably it is hoped that this procedure will bring to light any failure to give information, disagreement among members, doubt as to the successor's future status or non-compliance with a relevant requirement which might prevent the Commission from confirming the transfer. See s.98 and the notes thereto.

Section 120   SCHEDULE 18

AMENDMENTS OF ENACTMENTS

PART I

UNITED KINGDOM

Bankers' Books Evidence Act 1879 (c.11)

1. In section 9(1) of the Bankers' Books Evidence Act 1879 (meaning of "bank" and "banker" for purposes of that Act), after paragraph (*a*) there shall be inserted the following—

"(*aa*) a building society (within the meaning of the Building Societies Act 1986);".

Land Registration Act 1925 (c.21)

2. In section 25(1) (proprietor's power to create charges) of the Land Registration Act 1925, in paragraph (*b*), for the words from "under" to "with" there shall be substituted "(within the meaning of the Building Societies Act 1986), in accordance with."

Payment of Wages Act 1960 (c.37)

3.—(1) This paragraph amends the Payment of Wages Act 1960 as follows.

(2) In section 1(3) (authorised means of payment of wages), after paragraph (*a*) there shall be inserted—

"(*aa*) payment into an account at a building society, being an account standing in the name of the person to whom the payment is due, or an account standing in the name of that person jointly with one or more other persons,".

(3) In section 2(1) (requirements applicable to authorised payments) after "bank" there shall be inserted "or building society".

(4) In section 7(1) (interpretation)—

(*a*) after "way)" in the definition of "account", there shall be inserted "and, in relation to a building society, includes a share account and a deposit account (however described)",

(*b*) after the definition of "bank", there shall be inserted—

"building society" means a building society within the meaning of the Building Societies Act 1986;" and

(*c*) in the definition of "branch", after "head office of the bank" there shall be inserted, "and, in relation to a building society, includes the principal office of the society;".

Trustee Investments Act 1961 (c.62)

4.—(1) This paragraph amends the Trustee Investments Act 1961 as follows.

(2) In Part II of Schedule 1 (narrower range investments requiring advice), for paragraph 12 there shall be substituted—

"12. In deposits with a building society within the meaning of the Building Societies Act 1986.".

(3) In Part III of Schedule 1 (wider range investments), for paragraph 2 there shall be substituted—

"2. In shares in a building society within the meaning of the Building Societies Act 1986.".

Stock Transfer Act 1963 (c.18)

5. In section 1(4) of the Stock Transfer Act 1963 (simplified transfer of certain securities, not to apply to building society securities), for "1962" there shall be substituted "1986".

Industrial and Provident Societies Act 1965 (c.12)

6. In section 31(*b*) of the Industrial and Provident Societies Act 1965 (authorised investments), for "society registered under the Building Societies Acts" there shall be substituted "building society within the meaning of the Building Societies Act 1986".

Income and Corporation Taxes Act 1970 (c.10)

7.—(1) This paragraph amends the Income and Corporation Taxes Act 1970 as follows.

(2) In section 343(8) (arrangements for payment of tax by building societies) for "Building Societies Act 1962 or the Building Societies Act (Northern Ireland) 1967" there shall be substituted "Building Societies Act 1986".

(3) In section 415(5) (contractual savings schemes) for "Building Societies Act 1962 or the Building Societies Act (Northern Ireland) 1967" there shall be substituted "Building Societies Act 1986".

Banking and Financial Dealings Act 1971 (c.80).

8.—(1) This paragraph amends the Banking and Financial Dealings Act 1971 as follows.

(2) In section 2(1) (power to suspend financial dealings on bank holidays) after paragraph (*g*) there shall be inserted—

"; and

(*h*) a direction that, subject as aforesaid, no building society shall, on that day, except with permission so granted, effect in the course of its business any transaction or, according as may be specified in the order, a transaction of such kind as may be so specified."

(3) In section 2(6) after the definition of "authorised dealer in gold" there shall be inserted—

"building society" means a building society within the meaning of the Building Societies Act 1986.".

Local Government Act 1972 (c.70)

9. In Schedule 12A (access to information: exempt information) to the Local Government Act 1972—

(*a*) in Part II, in paragraph 2(*d*) for "1962" there shall be substituted "1986"; and

(*b*) in Part III, in paragraph 1(1), after the definition of 'protected informant' there shall be inserted the following definition—

"'registered', in relation to information required to be registered under the Building Societies Act 1986, means recorded in the public file of any building society (within the meaning of that Act);".

Consumer Credit Act 1974 (c.39)

10.—(1) This paragraph amends the Consumer Credit Act 1974 as follows.

(2) In section 16(1) (consumer credit agreement with certain bodies exempt from regulation) the words "or building society" shall be omitted and, after paragraph (*f*), there shall be inserted the words ", or

(*g*) a building society.".

(3) In section 16(3) (Secretary of State's duty to consult before making orders), after paragraph (*d*) there shall be inserted the words "or

(*e*) under subsection (1)(*g*) without consulting the Building Societies Commission and the Treasury.".

(4) In section 189(1) (definitions), for the definition of "building society" there shall be substituted the following definition—

"building society" means a building society within the meaning of the Building Societies Act 1986;".

Solicitors Act 1974 (c.47)

11.—(1) This paragraph amends the Solicitors Act 1974 as follows.

(2) In section 32 (accounts rules and trust accounts rules), in subsections (1) and (2), in paragraph (*a*), after "banks", there shall be inserted "or with building societies" and, in the words following paragraph (*c*), the word "banks'" shall be omitted.

(3) In section 33 (interest on clients' money) in subsections (1) and (3), after "bank", there shall be inserted "or with a building society."

(4) In section 85 (bank accounts)—

(*a*) after "account with a bank" there shall be inserted "or a building society," and

(*b*) in paragraphs (*a*) and (*b*) after "bank" there shall be inserted "or society".

(5) In section 87(1) (interpretation), after the definition of "bank" there shall be inserted—

"building society" means a building society within the meaning of the Building Societies Act 1986; and a reference to an account with a building society is a reference to a deposit account."

Home Purchase Assistance and Housing Corporation Guarantee Act 1978 (c.27)

12. In section 3(1) (building society law) of the Home Purchase Assistance and Housing Corporation Guarantee Act 1978, after "determining" there shall be added the word "(a)" and at the end of that subsection there shall be added the words—

"(*b*) the classification of the advance, or any such further advance, for the purposes of Part III of the Building Societies Act 1986.".

Banking Act 1979 (c.37)

13.—(1) This paragraph amends the Banking Act 1979 as follows.

(2) In section 34(1) (Treasury regulations controlling advertisements for deposits), after the word "Bank" there shall be inserted the words "and, in so far as they relate to building societies, the Building Societies Commission".

(3) In section 36(4) (exemption from restriction on use of description "banking services") there shall be inserted—

(*a*) after the word "Act", the words "or an authorised building society,", and

(*b*) after the words "the institution", the words "or society, as the case may be".

(4) In section 41(5) (consents for prosecutions), in paragraph (*a*) after the words "Public Prosecutions or" and in paragraph (*b*) after the words "Ireland or", there shall be inserted the words ", in the case of proceedings against a building society, the Building Societies Commission or, in any other case".

(5) In section 50(1) (definitions), after the definition of "the Bank" there shall be inserted the following definition—

"building society" means a building society within the meaning of the Building Societies Act 1986 and, in that context, "authorised" has the meaning given by section 119(1) of that Act;".

Charging Orders Act 1979 (c.53)

14. In section 6(1) (interpretation) of the Charging Orders Act 1979, in the definition of "building society", for "1962" there shall be substituted "1986".

Finance Act 1982 (c.39)

15.—(1) This paragraph amends the Finance Act 1982 as follows.

(2) In section 28(5) (variation of terms of repayment of certain loans) for "Building Societies Act 1962 or the Building Societies Act (Northern Ireland) 1967" there shall be substituted "Building Societies Act 1986".

(3) In paragraphs 2(4), 4(1) and 14(1) of Schedule 7 (deduction of tax from certain loan interest), for "Building Societies Act 1962 or the Building Societies Act (Northern Ireland) 1967" there shall be substituted "Building Societies Act 1986".

Companies Act 1985 (c.6)

16.—(1) This paragraph amends the Companies Act 1985 as follows.

(2) In section 295(3) (disqualification orders against directors of companies; meaning of "company"), after "Part XXI" there shall be inserted "and a building society (within the meaning of the Building Societies Act 1986).".

(3) In section 302(4) (provision against undischarged bankrupt acting as director, etc.; meaning of "company"), after "unregistered company" there shall be inserted ", a building society (within the meaning of the Building Societies Act 1986)".

Insolvency Act 1985 (c.65)

17.—(1) This paragraph amends the Insolvency Act 1985 as follows.

(2) In section 1 (prohibition of unqualified persons acting as insolvency practitioners) for the definition of "company" in subsection (5) there shall be substituted—
> "company" means a company within the meaning given by section 735(1) of the 1985 Act, a company which may be wound up under Part XXI of that Act or a building society within the meaning of the Building Societies Act 1986.".

(3) In section 12 (duty of court to disqualify unfit directors of insolvent companies) after subsection (9) there shall be inserted—
> "(10) In this section and in sections 14 to 19, a reference to a company or to a director (but not a shadow director) of a company includes a reference to a building society within the meaning of the Building Societies Act 1986 or to a director of a building society.".

(4) In Schedule 2 (matters for determining unfitness of directors) there shall be inserted the following paragraph—
> "5A. In the application of this Schedule to the directors of a building society, references to sections of this Act or of the 1985 Act other than sections which apply to building societies or their directors in any event, whether by virtue of this Act or of the Building Societies Act 1986, shall be construed as references to the corresponding provisions (if any) of the Building Societies Act 1986.".

Housing Act 1985 (c.68)

18.—(1) This paragraph amends the Housing Act 1985 as follows.

(2) In section 442(5) (consultations by Secretary of State regarding forms of local authority indemnity agreement) for "Chief Registrar of Friendly Societies" in paragraph (*a*), there shall be substituted "Building Societies Commission".

(3) In section 447 (recognised lending institutions) and in section 448 (recognised savings institutions) for "designated building societies" there shall be substituted "building societies".

(4) For section 450 (modifications of building society law) there shall be substituted the following section—

> "Modifications of building society law.
> 450. So much of an advance by building society which is partly financed under section 445 (assistance for first-time buyers) or the corresponding Scottish or Northern Ireland provisions as is so financed shall be treated as not forming part of the advance for the purpose of determining—
> (*a*) whether the advance, or any further advance made within two years of the date of purchase, is beyond the powers of the society, and
> (*b*) The classification of the advance, or any such further advance, for the purposes of Part III of the Building Societies Act 1986.".

(5) In section 622 (minor definitions) for the definition of "building society" there shall be substituted—
> "building society" means a building society within the meaning of the Building Societies Act 1986".

Housing Associations Act 1985 (c.69)

19.—(1) This paragraph amends the Housing Associations Act 1985 as follows.

(2) Sections 63 to 66 (building society advances) and in section 72 (minor definitions) the definitions of, and in section 73 (index of definitions) the entries relating to, "building society", "Chief Registrar" and "officer" shall be ommitted.

(3) In sections 84(5) and 86(4) (consultation by Secretary of State regarding building society indemnities) for "Chief Registrar of Friendly Societies" there shall be substituted "Building Societies Commission".

(4) In section 101 (minor definitions), for the definition of "building society" there shall be substituted—

> "building society" means a building society within the meaning of the Building Societies Act 1986;".

Part II

Northern Ireland

Industrial and Provident Societies Act (Northern Ireland) 1969 (c.24 N.I.)

20. In section 31(*b*) of the Industrial and Provident Societies Act (Northern Ireland) 1969 (authorised investments) for "society registered under the Building Societies Act" there shall be sustituted "building society within the meaning of the Building Societies Act 1986.".

Payment of Wages Act (Northern Ireland) 1970

21.—(1) This paragraph amends the Payment of Wages Act (Northern Ireland) 1970 as follows.

(2) In section 1(3) (authorised means of payment of wages), after paragraph (*a*) there shall be inserted—

> "(*aa*) payment into an account at a building society, being an account standing in the name of the person to whom the payment is due, or an account standing in the name of that person jointly with one or more persons,".

(3) In section 2(1) (requirements applicable to authorised payments), after "bank" there shall be inserted "or building society".

(4) In section 7(1) (interpretation)—

(*a*) in the definition of "account", after "way)" there shall be inserted "and, in relation to a building society, includes a share account and a deposit account (however described)".

(*b*) after the definition of "bank" there shall be inserted—

> "building society" means a building society within the meaning of the Building Societies Act 1986;", and

(*c*) in the definition of "branch", after "head office of the bank" there shall be inserted "and, in relation to a building society, includes the principal office of the society;".

Private Streets (Northern Ireland) Order 1980 (S.I. 1980/1086 (N.I.12))

22. In Article 33 (security not to be deemed prior mortgage under Building Societies Acts) of the Private Street (Northern Ireland) Order 1980 for the words from "section 32" where they first occur onwards there shall be substituted "section 11(2)(*d*) or (4)(*d*) of the Building Societies Act 1986".

Housing (Northern Ireland) Order 1981 (S.I. 1981/156 (N.I.3))

23.—(1) This paragraph amends the Housing (Northern Ireland) Order 1981 as follows.

(2) In Article 2(2) (interpretation) after the definition of "building regulations" there shall be inserted—

> "building society" means a building society within the meaning of the Building Societies Act 1986".

(3) For Article 155 (building society law) there shall be substituted the following section—

"Modifications of building society law.

155. So much of an advance by a building society which is partly financed under this Part or sections 445 to 449 of the Housing Act 1985 or the Home Purchase Assistance and Housing Corporation Guarantee Act 1978 as is so financed shall be treated as not forming part of the advance for the purpose of determining—

(a) whether the advance, or any further advance made within two years of the date of purchase, is beyond the powers of the society, and

(b) the classification of the advance, or any such further advance, for the purposes of Part III of the Building Societies Act 1986.".

(4) In Article 155A (exclusion of Restrictive Trade Practices Act 1976), after "Scottish Provisions" there shall be inserted "(namely, sections 445 to 447 of the Housing Act 1985 or the Home Purchase Assistance and Housing Corporation Guarantee Act 1978)".

(5) In Article 156(5)(b) (consultations by the Department regarding forms of indemnity agreements) for "Registrar of Friendly Societies for Northern Ireland" there shall be substituted "Building Societies Commission".

(6) For paragraph 1 of Schedule 10 there shall be substituted—

"1. Building Societies.".

Property (Discharge of Mortgage by Receipt) (Northern Ireland) Order 1983 (S.I. 1983/766 (N.I.9))

24. In Article 3(10) of the Property (Discharge of Mortgage by Receipt) (Northern Ireland) Order 1983, after "applies" in the definition of "mortgage" there shall be inserted "and, subject to paragraph 2(7) of Schedule 4 to the Building Societies Act 1986, does not include a mortgage to which that paragraph 2 applies.".

Housing (Northern Ireland) Order 1983 (S.I. 1983/1118 (N.I. 15))

25. In Article 3(4) of the Housing (Northern Ireland) Order 1983, in the definition of "building society" for the words from "1962" onwards there shall be substituted "1986".

Companies (Northern Ireland) Order 1986

26.—(1) This paragraph amends the Companies (Northern Ireland) Order 1986 as follows.

(2) In Article 303(3) (disqualification orders against directors of companies; meaning of "company"), after "Part XXI" there shall be inserted "and a building society (within the meaning of the Building Societies Act 1986).".

(3) In Article 310(3) (provision against undischarged bankrupt acting as director, etc.; meaning of "company"), after "unregistered company" there shall be inserted ", a building society (within the meaning of the Building Societies Act 1986)".

GENERAL NOTE

This Schedule makes detailed amendments as set out therein where required in view of the extended powers of building societies (and in particular their powers to offer banking services) or for the purpose of updating statutory references.

Section 120   SCHEDULE 19

REPEALS AND REVOCATIONS

PART I

REPEALS: GENERAL

Chapter	Short title	Extent of repeal
37 & 38 Vict. c.42.	The Building Societies Act 1874.	Section 1. Section 4. Section 32.
57 & 58 Vict. c.47.	The Building Societies Act 1894.	Section 8(1). Section 29.

Chapter	Short title	Extent of repeal
8 & 9 Eliz. 2 c.64.	The Building Societies Act 1960.	Section 72. Section 73(1). Section 77. In Schedule 5, the entry relating to paragraph 4 of section 32 of the Building Societies Act 1874.
9 & 10 Eliz. 2 c.62.	The Trustee Investments Act 1961.	In Part IV of Schedule 1, paragraphs 3A and 7.
10 & 11 Eliz. 2 c.37.	The Building Societies Act 1962.	The whole Act.
1965 c.32.	The Administration of Estates (Small Payments) Act 1965.	In Schedules 1 and 3, the entries relating to the Building Societies Act 1962.
1969 c.46.	The Family Law Reform Act 1969.	In Schedule 1, the entry relating to the Building Societies Act 1962.
1970 c.10.	The Income and Corporation Taxes Act 1970.	In section 343(5), the words "union or".
1974 c.39.	The Consumer Credit Act 1974.	In section 16, in subsection (1) the words "or building society," and, in subsections (1)(*e*) and (3)(*c*), the word "or".
1974 c.46.	The Friendly Societies Act 1974.	In Schedule 10, paragraph 9.
1974 c.47.	The Solicitors Act 1974.	In section 32, in subsections (1) and (2), the word "banks'".
1974 c.49.	The Insurance Companies Act 1974.	In Schedule 1, the entries relating to the Building Societies Act 1962.
1978 c.27.	The Home Purchase Assistance and Housing Corporation Guarantee Act 1978.	In section 3, subsections (2) to (4).
1979 c.37.	The Banking Act 1979.	In paragraph 6 of Schedule 1, the words from "within" to the end. In Schedule 6, paragraphs 6, 7, 16, and 17.
1982 c.50.	The Insurance Companies Act 1982.	In Schedule 5, paragraphs 3 and 5.
1984 c.28.	The County Courts Act 1984.	In Schedule 2, paragraph 26.
1985 c.9.	The Companies Consolidation (Consequential Provisions) Act 1985.	In Schedule 2, the entries relating to the Building Societies Act 1962.
1985 c.58.	The Trustee Savings Banks Act 1985.	In Schedule 1, paragraph 11(2)(*a*) and so much of that sub-paragraph as relates to the section 59 specified therein.
1985 c.61.	The Administration of Justice Act 1985.	Section 66.
1985 c.68.	The Housing Act 1985.	In section 458, the definition of "designated building society". In section 459, the entry relating to "designated building society".
1985 c.69.	The Housing Associations Act 1985.	Sections 63 to 66. In section 72, the definitions of "building society", "Chief Registrar" and "officer". In section 73, the entries relating to "building society", "Chief Registrar" and "officer".
1985 c.71.	The Housing (Consequential Provisions) Act 1985.	In Schedule 2, paragraphs 5 and 6.

PART II

REVOCATION EXTENDING TO GREAT BRITAIN

Number	Title	Extent of revocation
S.I. 1981/1488.	The Building Societies (Authorisation) Regulations 1981.	The whole Regulations.

PART III

REPEALS AND REVOCATIONS EXTENDING ONLY TO NORTHERN IRELAND

Chapter or number	Short title	Extent of repeal or revocation
1967 c.5 (N.I.).	The Administration of Estates (Small Payments) Act (Northern Ireland) 1967.	In Schedule 1, the entry relating to the Building Societies Act 1874.
1967 c.31 (N.I.).	The Building Societies Act (Northern Ireland) 1967.	The whole Act.
1969 c.24 (N.I.).	The Industrial and Provident Societies Act (Northern Ireland) 1969.	In section 101(1), the definition of "Building Societies Acts".
1969 c.28 (N.I.).	The Age of Majority Act (Northern Ireland) 1969.	In Schedule 1, the entry relating to the Building Societies Act (Northern Ireland) 1967.
1969 c.31 (N.I.).	The Age of Majority Act (Northern Ireland) 1969.	In Part I of Schedule 1, the entry relating to the Building Societies Act (Northern Ireland) 1967.
1970 c.18 (N.I.).	The Land Registration Act (Northern Ireland) 1970.	In Schedule 12 the entry relating to the Building Societies Act (Northern Ireland) 1967.
1978 c.23.	The Judicature (Northern Ireland) Act 1978.	In Schedule 5, in Part II the entry relating to the Building Societies Act (Northern Ireland) 1967.
S.I. 1979/1573 (N.I. 12).	The Statutory Rules (Northern Ireland) Order 1979.	In Schedule 4 the entry relating to the Building Societies Act (Northern Ireland) 1967.
1980 c.25.	The Insurance Companies Act 1980.	In Schedule 3, paragraph 3.
S.I. 1981/156 (N.I. 3).	The Housing (Northern Ireland) Order 1981.	Article 156(6). In Part II of Schedule 2, the entry relating to the Building Societies Act (Northern Ireland) 1967.
S.R. 1982/155 (N.I.).	The Building Societies (Authorisation) Regulations (Northern Ireland) 1982.	The whole Regulations.
S.I. 1983/776 (N.I. 9).	The Property (Discharge of Mortgage by Receipt) (Northern Ireland) Order 1983.	In Article 3(10), in the definition of "mortgage" the words "section 37 of the Building Societies Act (Northern Ireland) 1967".
S.I. 1983/1118 (N.I. 15).	The Housing (Northern Ireland) Order 1983.	In Schedule 10, the entry relating to the Building Societies Act (Northern Ireland) 1967.
1985 c.71.	The Housing (Consequential Provisions) Act 1985.	In Schedule 2, paragraphs 13, 51(2) and 51(5)(*a*).
S.I. 1986/1035 (N.I. 9).	The Companies Consolidation (Consequential Provisions) (Northern Ireland) Order 1986.	In Part I of Schedule 1, the entry relating to the Building Societies Act (Northern Ireland) 1967.

Section 120   SCHEDULE 20

TRANSITIONAL AND SAVING PROVISIONS

Preliminary

1. In this Schedule—
    "the commencement date for" any provision of this Act means the date on which that provision comes into operation;
    "existing society" means a building society registered at the passing of this Act under the repealed enactments; and
    "existing rules" means the rules of a society in force immediately before the commencement date for section 5.

Adoption of powers and alteration of rules

2.—(1) At any time during the period beginning two months after the passing of this Act and ending with the relevant commencement date, a building society may, for the purposes of the transition to this Act,—
    (*a*) by special resolution, agree in a memorandum upon—
        (i) the purpose or principal purpose of the society,
        (ii) whether to adopt any and, if so, what adoptable powers (with or without restrictions),
        (iii) whether to assume any and, if so, what restrictions on the extent of its other powers under this Act, and
        (iv) any alterations to its rules required for conformity with any provision made in pursuance of (ii) or (iii) above; and
    (*b*) send to the central office four copies of the memorandum and of any altered rules accompanied by a statutory declaration by the secretary that the agreement was effected by a resolution passed as a special resolution.

(2) The commencement date relevant to the matters specified in sub-paragraph (1) above is—
    (*a*) in the case of the society's purpose, the commencement date for section 5,
    (*b*) in the case of an adoptable power, the commencement date for the provision of this Act which confers the power,
    (*c*) in the case of a restriction on the extent of any other power, the commencement date for section 5, and
    (*d*) in the case of a rule altered for conformity, the commencement date applicable to the provision of the memorandum which requires the alteration.

(3) On agreeing upon its purpose, on the adoption of, or the assumption of a restriction on the extent of, a power or on any alteration of any of its rules for conformity, under this paragraph, the building society shall determine the date on which the society intends it to take effect and the memorandum and altered rules (if any) sent to the central office shall be accompanied by a record specifying that date (in this paragraph referred to as "the specified date").

(4) Subject to paragraph 11 below, the central office, if satisfied that the provisions of the memorandum and any altered rules are in conformity with this Act and any instruments under it, shall—
    (*a*) retain and register one copy of the memorandum and of the altered rules,
    (*b*) return another copy to the secretary of the society, together with a certificate of registration, and
    (*c*) keep another copy, together with the record of the specified date sent to it under sub-paragraph (3) above and a copy of that registration certificate, in the public file of the society.

(5) The provisions of a memorandum registered under this paragraph shall take effect on the specified date for that provision or, if registration of the memorandum is not effected until a later date, that later date, and so with the rules altered for conformity with a provision of the memorandum.

3.—(1) Before the end of the transitional period each existing building society shall—
    (*a*) by special resolution agree in a memorandum upon—
        (i) the purpose or principal purpose of the society,
        (ii) whether to adopt any and, if so, what adoptable powers (with or without restrictions), and

      (iii) whether to assume any and, if so, what restrictions on the extent of its other powers under this Act;

  (*b*) by special resolution agree upon the alterations to be made to its rules so that they conform to this Act; and

  (*c*) send to the central office four copies of the memorandum and of the rules as altered each signed by the secretary and accompanied by a statutory declaration by the secretary that the agreement was effected by a resolution passed as a special resolution.

(2) On agreeing upon its purpose, on the adoption of, or the assumption of a restriction on the extent of, a power, or on any alteration to its rules, under this paragraph, the building society shall, subject to sub-paragraph (3) below, determine the date on which the society intends it to take effect and the memorandum and rules sent to the central office shall be accompanied by a record specifying that date (in this paragraph referred to as "the specified date").

(3) No date shall be specified under sub-paragraph (2) above in relation to a society's purpose or its rules which falls more than six months after the date of the meeting at which the society agreed upon the memorandum or the rules, as the case may be.

(4) Subject to paragraph 11 below, the central office, if satisfied that—

  (*a*) the provisions of the memorandum are in conformity with this Act and any instruments under it, and

  (*b*) the rules, as altered, are in conformity with this Act,

shall retain and register a copy of the memorandum and of the altered rules.

(5) On registering a copy of the memorandum and of the altered rules under sub-paragraph (4) above, the central office shall—

  (*a*) return another copy to the secretary of the society, together with a certificate of registration, and

  (*b*) keep another copy, together with the record of the specified date sent to it under sub-paragraph (2) above and a copy of that certificate, in the public file of the society.

(6) The provisions of a memorandum registered under this paragraph shall take effect on the specified date for that provision or, if registration of the memorandum is not effected until a later date, that later date.

(7) The rules registered under this paragraph shall take effect on the specified date for the rule or, if registration of the rules is not effected until a later date, that later date.

(8) In this paragraph "the transitional period" means the period beginning with the commencement date for section 5 and expiring with such day as the Commission, with the consent of the Treasury, prescribes by order in a statutory instrument.

Default powers

4.—(1) If the central office has not, before the end of the transitional period, received from an existing building society copies of the memorandum in accordance with paragraph 2 or 3 above, the society shall be treated as having agreed upon the purpose specified as its purpose in its existing rules or on such purpose conforming to section 1(1) of the Building Societies Act 1962 as the central office directs as its apparent purpose.

(2) If the central office has not, before the end of the transitional period, received from an existing building society copies of its rules as altered in accordance with paragraph 3 above, the society shall be treated as having agreed upon such alteration of its rules as, in conformity with model rules made under this paragraph, the central office directs.

(3) The Commission may, by order in a statutory instrument made with the consent of the Treasury, prescribe model rules for building societies for the purposes of this paragraph.

(4) Where, under this paragraph, a society is treated as having agreed upon a purpose or as having agreed upon altered rules then the central office shall prepare three copies of a memorandum and of rules for the society and shall—

  (*a*) retain and register one copy,

  (*b*) return another to the secretary of the society, together with a certificate of registration, and

  (*c*) keep another copy, together with a copy of that certificate, in the public file of the society.

(5) The memorandum and rules so registered shall be for all purposes the memorandum and rules of the society until altered under paragraph 4 of Schedule 2 to this Act.

(6) Such fee as is prescribed shall be due from the society to the Chief Registrar for the registration of a memorandum and rules under this paragraph.

(7) In this paragraph "the transitional period" means the period beginning with the commencement date for section 5 and expiring with such day as the Commission, with the consent of the Treasury, prescribes by order in a statutory instrument.

Registration with existing authorities

5. A building society which, at the commencement date for section 5, was registered under the Building Societies Act (Northern Ireland) 1967 or registered or deemed to be registered in Northern Ireland under the enactments repealed by that Act shall be treated, for the purposes of this Act, as registered with the central office immediately before the commencement of that section.

Authorisation under existing enactments

6.—(1) A building society which, at the commencement date for section 9 is authorised to raise money and accept deposits under—
(*a*) the Building Societies (Authorisation) Regulations 1981, or
(*b*) the Building Societies (Authorisation) Regulations (Northern Ireland) 1982,
shall be treated, whether or not the requirements of subsection (4) of section 9 would be fulfilled in its case, at the commencement of that section as authorised for the purposes of this Act (in particular Part VI).
(2) The central office shall record in the public file of each building society to which sub-paragraph (1) above applies the fact that, by virtue of that sub-paragraph, the society is to be treated as authorised for the purposes of this Act.

Anticipation of powers: declaratory provision

7.—(1) It is hereby declared that every building society has had, as from 19th December 1985, power, for the purposes of any power conferred by this Act on building societies or building societies of its description, to do such things, subject to sub-paragraph (2) below, as are reasonably necessary to enable it—
(*a*) to decide whether or not, and to what extent, to exercise (and in the case of an adoptable power to adopt) the power, and
(*b*) if it decides to exercise the power, to exercise it as from the date when it becomes exercisable by the society.
(2) Sub-paragraph (1)(*b*) above does not authorise a society—
(*a*) to make contracts, other than conditional contracts, for the acquisition of land, the acquisition of a business or the acquisition of shares in any company if that company offers the public any service or facility within the power,
(*b*) to issue invitations to members of the society or the public to apply for any power to be exercised for their benefit, or
(*c*) to retain shares in a company which offers the public any service or facility within the power;
and, in this sub-paragraph, "conditional", in relation to contracts with respect to the exercise of a power, means conditional on the power's becoming exercisable by the society.
(3) The power conferred by this paragraph, and activities carried on under it, for the purposes of an adoptable power are not to be treated as included in, or in activities comprised in, that adoptable power for the purposes of paragraph 8 of this Schedule.

Unlawful anticipation of powers

8.—(1) Where a building society adopts any adoptable power under paragraph 2 or 3 above—
(*a*) it shall, by virtue of this paragraph, assume an obligation, enforceable as provided in paragraph 9 below, not to exercise that power until the date on which the memorandum of its powers takes effect as respects that power, and
(*b*) it shall send to the central office, with the documents required by paragraph 2(1) or 3(1) above a declaration as respects that power made on behalf of the society which satisfies the requirements of this paragraph.
(2) The obligation assumed by virtue of this paragraph on the adoption of a power does not extend to the exercise of any power included in the adoptable power which the society has under the law in force at any time before the registration takes effect.

(3) A declaration, to satisfy the requirements of this paragraph, must be made by the chairman of the board of directors of the society, by one other director and by the chief executive of the society and it must either—

(*a*) state that, to the best of the knowledge and belief of the declarants, after due enquiry, the society has not, or has not with the permitted qualification, carried on any activity comprised in the power during the period which began one year before the specified date (or with 1 April 1986, if later) and expired with the date of the meeting at which the power was adopted, or

(*b*) state that, to the best of the knowledge and belief of the declarants, after due enquiry, the society, with specified exceptions, has not, or has not with the permitted qualification, carried on any activity comprised in the power during the period which began one year before the specified date (or with 1 April 1986, if later) and expired with the date of the meeting at which the power was adopted.

(4) The qualification of the statement so required which is permitted is that in so far as the society has, at any time during the said period, carried on any activity comprised in the power to which the statement relates, the society had the power to carry on that activity at that time under the law in force at that time.

(5) The exceptions to the statement so required must not include activities of the society which constitute significant excesses of its powers during the said period; and a declaration specifying activities as exceptions to the statement so required must also state the opinion of the declarants that the activities are believed not to constitute significant excesses of the society's powers during the period to which the declaration relates.

Penalty for breach of undertaking

9. If, in breach of the obligation assumed by virtue of paragraph 8 above, a building society exercises any power to which the obligation extends, then—

(*a*) the society shall be liable on conviction on indictment or on summary conviction to a fine not exceeding, on summary conviction, the statutory maximum, and

(*b*) every officer of the society who is also guilty of the offence shall be liable, on summary conviction to a fine not exceeding the statutory maximum.

Penalty for false declaration

10. If the statement in a declaration made for the purposes of paragraph 8 above is false, then, any person who made the statement knowing it to be false or reckless as to whether it was true or false shall be liable—

(*a*) on conviction on indictment, to imprisonment for a term not exceeding two years or to a fine or both, and

(*b*) on summary conviction to imprisonment for a term not exceeding six months or to a fine not exceeding the statutory maximum or both.

Powers of central office

11.—(1) The central office, on receiving from a building society the declaration required by and the other documents referred to in paragraph 8 above, shall refer to the Commission for its determination the question whether or not the memorandum of the society's powers is to be registered.

(2) On a reference to the Commission of the question whether or not the memorandum of a society's power is to be registered—

(*a*) if the declaration contains the statement specified in paragraph 8(3)(*a*) above and the Commission has no reasonable cause to believe that the society in question has carried on any activity comprised in the power to which the obligation imposed by paragraph 8 above extends at any time during the period which began one year before the specified date (or with 1st April 1986, if later) and expired on the date on which it considers the reference, the Commission shall direct the central office to register the memorandum, and

(*b*) in any other case, the Commission may, as it thinks fit, direct the central office to register, or not to register, the memorandum.

(3) The Commission, in deciding, in a case falling within sub-paragraph (2)(*b*) above, whether or not to direct the registration of the memorandum of a society's powers may have regard to all the circumstances of the case.

(4) No registration of a memorandum shall be effected by the central office under paragraph 2(2) or 3(2) above before the expiry of the period of 21 days beginning with the

date on which it receives the declaration required by and the other documents referred to in paragraph 8 above.

(5) If the central office, in pursuance of a direction of the Commission under subparagraph (2) above, refuses registration of the memorandum of a society's powers under sub-paragraph (1) above it shall serve on the society a notice—

(*a*) recording its refusal,

(*b*) specifying the activity which is believed to constitute a breach of the society's obligation, and

(*c*) directing the society to make an application to the Commission under section 38 for a determination under that section whether the activity was or was not within the powers of the society at the time specified under sub-paragraph (*b*) above,

and shall send a copy of the notice to the Commission.

(6) The central office shall comply with any direction as regards the registration of the memorandum of the society's powers given to it by the Commission consequent on the Commission's determination of the society's powers under section 38.

(7) Nothing in the foregoing provisions of this Schedule implies that it is improper for any of the following, that is to say—

(*a*) the Chief Registrar or any assistant registrar of the central office,

(*b*) the assistant registrar of friendly societies for Scotland,

(*c*) the registrar of building societies for Northern Ireland, or

(*d*) the Commission,

to give a building society or building societies generally an indication of the action the Commission might or might not take in exercising its functions under this paragraph; and no decision of the Commission under this paragraph shall be liable to be set aside by reason of the indication having been given.

(8) In this paragraph "the specified date" has the same meaning as in paragraph 2 or, as the case may be, 3 above.

Permissible securities for advances

12.—(1) Until provision is made by an order under section 10(6) prescribing the descriptions of equitable interests in land which may be taken as security for advances secured on land, building societies may advance money on the security of an equitable interest in land in England and Wales or Northern Ireland in addition to a mortgage of the freehold or leasehold estate where the lease or a related instrument includes provision entitling the leaseholder to acquire a beneficial interest of any extent in the freehold or a greater leasehold interest and the right to acquire that interest is assigned as additional security.

(2) Until such provision is made, section 17(10) shall have effect with the substitution of a reference to an equitable interest of the description specified in sub-paragraph (1) above for the reference to an equitable interest specified in an order under section 10(6).

(3) On the making of the first order under section 10(6) this paragraph shall cease to have effect.

13. Until provision is made by an order under section 12(3) prescribing indemnities given by a local authority as a description of additional security for the purposes of section 11(4)(*c*), an indemnity given under section 442 of the Housing Act 1985, under section 31 of the Tenants' Rights, Etc. (Scotland) Act 1980 or under Article 156 of the Housing (Northern Ireland) Order 1981 shall be such a security; and on the making of the first order under section 12(3) this paragraph shall cease to have effect.

Existing business names

14. Any person who, at the commencement date for section 107, uses a name for business purposes which indicates a connection between—

(*a*) that person, or his business, and a building society, or

(*b*) that person, or his business, and building societies generally,

shall be deemed for the purposes of section 107 to have been given approval, under subsection (4) of that section, by the Commission for the continued use of that name.

Directors in office

15.—(1) Except as provided in this paragraph, an existing director shall be treated for the purposes of sections 60 and 61 as having been duly elected a director on the date of his appointment as a director or, as the case may be, of his most recent re-appointment to that office before the commencement date.

(2) An existing director who holds office as director by virtue of holding some other position in the society shall, except in a case within sub-paragraph (4) below, be treated for the purposes of sections 60 and 61 as having been duly elected a director at the commencement date.

(3) If the term of office of an existing director would, in accordance with the terms on which he holds office, expire on an earlier date than is provided for by sub-paragraph (1) above, he shall vacate office on that earlier date.

(4) An existing director who has attained the normal retirement age, or the compulsory retirement age (if any), as the case may be, before the commencement date shall retire from office at the first annual general meeting of the society after the commencement date.

(5) If, at the commencement date, an existing director, other than a director falling within sub-paragraph (2) above, has held office since the date of his appointment or most recent re-appointment for a period longer than is provided for in section 60(11)(*a*), he shall retire from office at the first annual general meeting of the society after the commencement date.

(6) In this paragraph—

    "the commencement date" means the commencement date for sections 60 and 61;

    "existing director" means any director of a building society in office immediately before the commencement date; and

    "the compulsory retirement age" and "the normal retirement age" have the meanings given in section 60(8).

Existing financial years

16. In the case of a building society established before 25th August 1894—

(*a*) if—

    (i) before 1st October 1962 the society had altered its financial year in exercise of the power conferred by section 70(2) of the Building Societies Act 1960, or

    (ii) after that date and before the commencement date for section 117, the society has exercised the corresponding power conferred by section 128(2) of the Building Societies Act 1962,

    "financial year" shall, after the date on which the society exercised the power, have the meaning given in section 117 and shall (so far as may be relevant for the purposes of this Act) include the period for which the society made up its accounts in the exercise of the power, and

(*b*) subject to the preceding provisions of this paragraph, "financial year" means a period of 12 months ending with the time up to which, at the commencement date for section 117, the accounts of the society were annually made up.

Qualifying assets

17. For the purposes of the application of section 118 by reference to the annual accounts of a building society prepared before the first financial year for which accounts under Part VIII of this Act are prepared, the reference to the total commercial assets of a society shall have effect as a reference to the amount in the last balance sheet prepared under the Building Societies Act 1962 which represents the total assets constituted by mortgage debts outstanding to the society.

Provision of conveyancing services for building societies

18.—(1) A building society may, at any time during the period of three years beginning with the day on which section 66 of the Administration of Justice Act 1985 ("section 66") comes or came into force or for such shorter period as is prescribed by the Commission by order in a statutory instrument, alter the rules of the society by resolution of the board of directors so as to provide for conveyancing services to be carried out on the society's behalf, in relation to estates or interests in land in England and Wales, by all or any of the following, namely—

(*a*) a recognised body within the meaning of section 9 of that Act;

(*b*) a licensed conveyancer within the meaning of section 11(2) of that Act; and

(*c*) a recognised body within the meaning of Part II of that Act.

(2) If, on the day on which this paragraph comes into operation, no day has been appointed for the commencement of section 66, the rules of a building society may be so

altered within the period of three years from the commencement of this paragraph or such shorter period as is prescribed by the Commission by order in a statutory instrument.

(3) Where any alteration of the rules of a society is effected under sub-paragraph (1) above, the society shall send to the central office three copies of the alteration signed by the secretary and a statutory declaration by an officer of the society that the alteration was effected by resolution of the board of directors.

(4) Where copies are sent to the central office in accordance with sub-paragraph (3) above, and the central office is satisfied that the alteration is in conformity with this Act and (where applicable) any instrument under it, it shall—

(*a*) retain and register one of the copies,

(*b*) return another to the secretary of the society together with a certificate of registration of the alteration, and

(*c*) keep another copy, together with a copy of that certificate, in the public file of the society.

(5) If a building society fails to comply with sub-paragraph (3) above, the society shall be liable on summary conviction to a fine not exceeding level 4 on the standard scale, and so shall any officer who is also guilty of the offence.

(6) The power to alter the rules under sub-paragraph (1) above shall cease to be exercisable by a building society if, during the period of three years mentioned in that sub-paragraph or sub-paragraph (2) or within such lesser period as is prescribed under those sub-paragraphs, as the case may be, a special resolution is passed altering (in any respect) the rules of the society in pursuance of paragraph 4 of Schedule 2 to this Act.

(7) In this paragraph, "conveyancing services" has the same meaning as in paragraph 1(3) of Schedule 21 to this Act.

Definitions

"adoptable powers": s.119(1) and Sched. 2, para. 1.
"assume": see Sched. 2, para. 1.
"central office": s.119(1).
"Chief Registrar": s.119(1).
"commencement date for": para. 1.
"Commission": ss.1 and 119(1).
"compulsory retirement date": s.60(8) and para. 15.
"conditional": para. 7.
"conveyancing services": para. 18 and Sched. 21, para. 1.
"existing director": para. 15.
"existing rules": para. 1.
"existing society": para. 1.
"memorandum": s.119(1) and Sched. 2, para. 1.
"mortgage debt": s.119(1).
"normal retirement age": s.60(8) and para. 15.
"officer": s.119(1).
"prescribed": s.119(1).
"public file": ss.106 and 119(1).
"repealed enactments": s.119(1).
"section 66": para. 18.
"special resolution": s.119(1) and Sched. 2, para. 27.
"the standard scale": Criminal Justice Act 1982, s.37.
"the statutory maximum": Criminal Justice Act 1982, s.84; Magistrates' Courts Act 1980, s.32.
"transitional period": paras. 3 and 4.

General Note

This Schedule contains transitional and saving provisions to ease the change from the old regime to the new.

Para. 2

This paragraph enables a society to agree upon a memorandum during the period starting two months after the passing of this Act (*i.e.* September 25, 1986) and ending with "the relevant commencement date" (subpara. (1)). The phrase "the relevant commencement date" is explained in subpara. (2), which clearly envisages a number of possible dates. It seems, therefore, to follow that there may be different periods under subpara. (1) during which different parts of the memorandum can be agreed upon: *sed quaere.* It is thought that, in practice, the only relevant commencement date will be the commencement date for s.5 (*i.e.* January 1, 1987: see the notes to s.126); the transitional period under para. 3 begins on that date (see para. 3(8)) and it seems that any agreement upon a memorandum once that transitional period has begun will be governed by para. 3.

The memorandum must specify: the purpose or principal purpose of the society; which (if any) adoptable powers are adopted and with what restrictions (if any); whether any restrictions are assumed on the society's other powers under the Act; and any alterations to its rules required for conformity with provisions as to the adoption of powers or assumption of restrictions: subpara. (1)(*a*). Four copies of the agreed memorandum and any altered rules must be sent to the central office: subpara. (1)(*b*). The society must also determine the date on which its purpose, its adoption of a power, its assumption of a restriction on a power, or any alteration of rules for conformity is to take effect and the memorandum and rules sent to the central office must be accompanied by a record specifying that date: subpara. (3). (Note that subpara. (5), referring to "the specified date for that provision", envisages that there may be different dates specified for different purposes.)

Thereafter, the procedure is similar to that under Sched. 2, para. 1 in respect of a new society, but an existing society will receive a certificate of registration and not a certificate of incorporation.

Presumably the provisions of Sched. 2, paras. (2) and (3) as to the terms of specification in a memorandum of adoptable powers will apply equally here.

Para. 3

This paragraph in effect imposes two requirements. First, a society which has not exercised the power given by para. 2 must adopt a memorandum during the transitional period starting with the date on which s.5 comes into force (*i.e.* January 1, 1987: see the notes to s.126) and ending on a date to be specified (but intended to be September 1, 1988). Second, it obliges every society, during the same transitional period, to agree upon the alterations to be made to its rules so that they comply with the Act. (In theory, alterations will not necessarily be required, but it is thought very unlikely that any society's rules will in fact comply with the Act in all respects.) The remaining provisions of the paragraph are very similar to those of para. 2, but note:

(*a*) the words "the alterations to be made to [the] rules so that they conform to this Act" (subpara. (1)) cover a much wider field than the power given by para. 2(1)(*a*)(iv) to make alterations required for conformity with the adoption of powers or the assumption of restrictions under para. 2(1)(*a*)(ii) or (iii). It follows that a society which has exercised its power under para. 2 will almost certainly need to make further rule changes to comply with this paragraph;

(*b*) the society is prohibited from specifying a date in relation to its purpose or altered rules which falls more than six months after the date of the meeting at which the society agreed on the memorandum or rules, as the case may be;

(*c*) alterations made to the rules under this paragraph will not be contained in the memorandum itself, unlike alterations made under para. 2.

See para. 4 for the default powers exercisable if a society fails to comply with its obligations under this paragraph.

Para. 4

This paragraph in effect enables the central office to impose a memorandum and altered rules on a society which has not complied with para. 3. The purpose in the memorandum will be the purpose specified in the existing rules or such purpose conforming to s.1(1) of the 1962 Act as the central office directs as the society's apparent purpose (subpara. (1)). The rules will be altered to conform with model rules as the central office may direct (subpara. (2)). The Commission has power under subpara. (3) to prescribe model rules.

Para. 5

This paragraph preserves the registration of societies registered in Northern Ireland with existing bodies. S.5(4) has the same effect for societies registered elsewhere in the United Kingdom.

Para. 6

This paragraph provides that a society which at the commencement date for s.9 (intended to be January 1, 1987: see the notes to s.126) is authorised to raise money and accept deposits is to be treated as authorised for the purposes of this Act.

Para. 7

This paragraph took effect immediately upon the passing of the Act (see the notes to s.126) and is retrospective to December 19, 1985, the date of the Bill's Second Reading in the House of Commons. The terms of the paragraph are very similar to those of s.105, permitting a limited anticipation of powers to be conferred under a statutory instrument, and reference should be made to the notes to that section. The purpose of the paragraph is to protect societies which have spent money on preliminary research and other preparatory work in anticipation of the new powers. Although the paragraph is expressed to be declaratory, it is not very obvious that the 1962 Act did indeed empower societies to carry out such work.

Paras. 8 to 11

These paragraphs are very similar to paras. 16 to 19 of Sched. 2 and reference should be made to the notes to those provisions for a detailed discussion of their effect. The following differences from paras. 16 to 19 should be observed:

(1) April 1, 1986 is not a relevant date for the purposes of those paragraphs. References to April 1, 1986 are included here because it was thought that after publication of the Bill, societies should have the period up to April 1, 1986 to make quite sure that their business was being conducted strictly within the bounds of the old legislation (with the possible exception of work permitted under para. 7 above) and that no declaration of non-anticipation should be demanded in respect of the period prior to April 1, 1986. In effect, societies had a period of grace to set their affairs in order. A society which has failed to take advantage of that period is likely to be viewed unfavourably by the Commission when it considers whether or not to direct registration under para. 11;

(2) para. 19 of Sched. 2 contains no provision equivalent to para. 11(7). The purpose of para. 11(7) is to ensure that societies have material on which to make a reasonable assessment of the prospect of getting a memorandum approved, notwithstanding that there has been an anticipation of powers. Compare the somewhat similar provisions of s.38(13).

The statutory maximum: Currently £2,000.

Para. 12

This paragraph is considered in the notes to s.10(6).

Para. 13

This paragraph makes transitional provisions pending the making of an order under s.12(3).

Para. 14

This paragraph protects persons who at the commencement date of s.107 (intended to be January 1, 1987: see the notes to s.126) have an existing business name. Such names are deemed to have been approved by the Commission for the purposes of that section.

Para. 15

This paragraph governs the application of ss.60 and 61 to existing directors. The commencement date of those provisions is intended to be January 1, 1987: see the notes to s.126. The sections will apply as follows:

(1) generally a director is treated as duly elected on the date of his appointment, or most recent appointment, to office;

(2) a director who holds office as director by virtue of holding another office in the society is treated as duly elected on the commencement date, unless he falls within (4) below;

(3) if a director's term of office would otherwise expire earlier than if (1) above applied, the director shall vacate office on that earlier date;

(4) a director who has attained the normal retirement age, or the compulsory retirement age (if any), at the commencement date shall vacate office at the next annual general meeting;

(5) a director who, at the commencement date, has held office for a longer period since his appointment, or most recent appointment, than is permitted by s.60(11)(*a*) shall vacate office at the next annual general meeting.

Para. 16

This paragraph is discussed in the notes to s.117.

Para. 17

This paragraph provides for the application of s.118 during the period before the first annual accounts under Part VIII of this Act have been prepared.

Para. 18

This paragraph enables a society to amend its rules, within the specified time limits, so as to provide for conveyancing services to be carried out *on its behalf* by recognised bodies or licensed conveyancers under the Administration of Justice Act. The paragraph very largely repeats s.66 of that Act, which will be repealed when Sched. 19 comes into effect (intended to be January 1, 1987: see the notes to s.126).

Note that (i) under subpara. (1), the alteration may be made by resolution of the board of directors, (ii) the alteration may no longer be so made after other rules of the society have been altered under Sched. 2, para. 4 (not under paras. 2 or 3 or this Schedule) by special resolution.

Level 4. Currently £1,000.

Section 124   SCHEDULE 21

PROVISION OF CONVEYANCING SERVICES BY RECOGNISED INSTITUTIONS AND PRACTITIONERS

Power of Lord Chancellor to make recognition rules

1.—(1) The Lord Chancellor may, in accordance with the provisions of this Schedule, make rules with respect to the recognition by him of institutions as being suitable to undertake the provision of conveyancing services.

(2) In this Schedule—

"institution" means any building society or other body corporate or any unincorporated association;

"officer", in relation to a recognised institution which is a body corporate, includes a director, manager or secretary;

"recognised institution" means an institution for the time being recognised under this Schedule;

"recognised practitioner" means a sole practitioner for the time being recognised under this Schedule;

"recognition rules" means rules made by the Lord Chancellor under this Schedule;

"sole practitioner" means an individual carrying on a business or profession otherwise than as a member of an unincorporated association;

"unicorporated association" means a partnership or any other association of two or more persons which is not a body corporate.

(3) References in this Schedule to conveyancing services are references to the preparation of transfers, conveyances, contracts and other documents in connection with, and other services ancillary to, the disposition or acquisition of estates or interests in land; and for the purposes of this sub-paragraph—

(*a*) "disposition"—

(i) does not include a testamentary disposition or any disposition in the case of such a lease as is referred to in section 54(2) of the Law of Property Act 1925 (short leases); but

(ii) subject to that, includes in the case of leases both their grant and their assignment; and

(*b*) "acquisition" has a corresponding meaning.

Recognition of institutions

2.—(1) Recognition rules may prescribe—

(*a*) the circumstances in which institutions, or institutions of any specified description, may be recognised by the Lord Chancellor under this Schedule as being suitable to undertake the provision of conveyancing services; and

(*b*) the conditions which (subject to any exceptions provided by the rules) must at all times be complied with by institutions so recognised if they are to remain so recognised.

(2) Without prejudice to the generality of sub-paragraph (1)(*b*) above, rules made by virtue of that provision may prescribe such conditions as appear to the Lord Chancellor to be appropriate for the purpose of—

(*a*) protecting persons for whom conveyancing services are provided by recognised institutions from conflicts of interest that might otherwise arise in connection with the provision of such services; and

(*b*) securing that compensation is available to such persons in respect of negligence, fraud or other dishonesty on the part of officers or employees of recognised institutions or (in the case of recognised institutions which are unincorporated associations) on the part of members of such institutions.

(3) Recognition rules may make provision for enabling the Lord Chancellor to require a recognised institution to furnish him with such information or documents as he considers necessary or expedient for the purpose of ascertaining whether or not the institution is complying with any conditions prescribed in pursuance of sub-paragraph (1)(*b*) above.

Grant and revocation of recognition

3.—(1) Recognition rules may make provision—
(*a*) for the manner and form in which applications for recognition under this Schedule are to be made, and for the payment of fees in connection with such applications;
(*b*) as to the period (whether determinate or otherwise) for which any recognition granted under this Schedule shall (subject to the provisions of any recognition rules) remain in force; and
(*c*) for the revocation by the Lord Chancellor of any such recognition on any of the grounds referred to in sub-paragraph (2) below.
(2) Those grounds are—
(*a*) that an institution's recognition was granted as a result of any error or fraud;
(*b*) that while an institution was a recognised institution—
    (i) the institution, or
    (ii) where it is a body corporate, any director, manager, secretary or other similar officer of the institution, or
    (iii) where it is an unincorporated association, any member of the institution, has been convicted by any court in the United Kingdom of a criminal offence which, in the opinion of the Lord Chancellor, renders the institution unsuitable to be recognised under this Schedule; or
(*c*) the institution has, while a recognised institution, failed to comply with any conditions prescribed in pursuance of paragraph 2(1)(*b*) above or with any requirement imposed in pursuance of paragraph 2(3) above.
(3) Recognition rules may—
(*a*) prescribe the manner and form in which any revocation of an institution's recognition under this Schedule is to be notified to the institution; and
(*b*) provide for any such revocation to be effective as from the time when the institution is notified of it in accordance with the rules.

Recording of recognised status

4.—(1) Recognition rules may make provision—
(*a*) for the keeping by the Lord Chancellor of a list containing the names and principal places of business of all institutions which are for the time being recognised under this Schedule;
(*b*) for requiring such institutions to notify the Lord Chancellor of changes in their principal places of business; and
(*c*) for the information contained in any list kept in pursuance of paragraph (*a*) above to be available for inspection.
(2) Recognition rules may make provision with respect to the giving of evidence of an institution's status as a recognised institution (or lack of such status) at any particular time by means of a certificate of a description specified in the rules.

Delegation of functions

5.—(1) Recognition rules may make provision—
(*a*) for enabling the Lord Chancellor to delegate the exercise of any functions exercisable by him by virtue of any of the other paragraphs of this Schedule (apart from the power to make recognition rules) to any officer or officers of his nominated in accordance with the rules: and
(*b*) for a decision made by any such officer in pursuance of paragraph (*a*) above to be treated, for the purposes of any provision of recognition rules or this Schedule, as a decision of the Lord Chancellor.
(2) Any such rules may provide for a person who is aggrieved by any such decision to be entitled, in such cases as may be prescribed by the rules, to have the matter in question determined by the Lord Chancellor.

Supplementary provisions as to recognition rules

6.—(1) Recognition rules shall be made by statutory instrument subject to annulment in pursuance of a resolution of either House of Parliament.
(2) Any such rules may make different provision for different circumstances.
(3) Without prejudice to the generality of sub-paragraph (2) above—

(*a*) recognition rules may provide for the Lord Chancellor to refuse an application by an institution for recognition under this Schedule where it appears to him that it would be more appropriate for the institution to apply for recognition under section 32 of the Administration of Justice Act 1985 (recognition of bodies managed and controlled by licensed conveyancers); and

(*b*) any rules prescribing a fee may provide for that fee to be reduced, or not to be payable, in such circumstances as may be specified in the rules.

Restrictions on conveyancing by unqualified persons not to apply in case of recognised institutions

7.—(1) Section 22(1) of the Solicitors Act 1974 (restriction on person preparing certain instruments when not qualified to act as a solicitor)—

(*a*) shall, notwithstanding section 24(2) of that Act (application of penal provisions to bodies corporate), not apply to a body corporate by reason of any act done by an officer or employee of the body if, at the time it was done, the body was a recognised institution; and

(*b*) shall not apply to a member of an unincorporated association by reason of any act done by an officer or employee, or by another member, of the association if, at the time it was done, the association was a recognised institution.

(2) Section 22(1) of that Act shall also not apply to any officer or employee of an institution by reason of any act done by him if—

(*a*) at the time it was done the institution was a recognised institution; and

(*b*) it was done by him at the direction and under the supervision of another person who was at the time an officer or employee of the institution or (in the case of an unincorporated association) a member of the institution; and

(*c*) it could have been done by that other person for or in expectation of any fee, gain or reward without committing an offence under section 22 of that Act.

Legal professional privilege

8. Any communication made to or by a recognised institution in the course of its acting as such for a client in connection with providing conveyancing services for him shall in any legal proceedings be privileged from disclosure in like manner as if the institution had at all material times been acting as the client's solicitor.

Modification of enactments relating to conveyancing

9. In the following provisions, namely—

(*a*) sections 10(2), 48 and 182 of the Law of Property Act 1925;

(*b*) sections 113 and 144(1)(xxiv) of the Land Registration Act 1925;

(*c*) section 12 of the Land Charges Act 1972;

(*d*) section 13 of the Local Land Charges Act 1975;

(*e*) section 11(8) of the Estate Agents Act 1979; and

(*f*) sections 4(3) and 6(2) of the Matrimonial Homes Act 1983,

any reference to a solicitor shall be construed as including a reference to a recognised institution, and any reference to a person's solicitor shall be construed as including a reference to a recognised institution acting for that person in connection with providing conveyancing services for him.

Penalty for pretending to be a recognised institution

10.—(1) An institution shall not describe itself or hold itself out as an institution for the time being recognised under this Schedule unless it is so recognised.

(2) Any institution which contravenes sub-paragraph (1) above shall be guilty of an offence and liable on summary conviction to a fine not exceeding level 4 on the standard scale.

Offences committed by bodies corporate and unincorporated associations

11.—(1) Where an offence under paragraph 10 above which has been committed by a body corporate is proved to have been committed with the consent or connivance of, or to be attributable to any neglect on the part of, any director, manager, secretary or other similar officer of the body corporate, or any person purporting to act in any such capacity, he as well as the body corporate shall be guilty of the offence and shall be liable to be proceeded against and punished accordingly.

(2) Proceedings for an offence alleged to have been committed under paragraph 10 by an unincorporated association shall be brought in the name of that association (and not in that

of any of its members) and, for the purposes of any such proceedings, any rules of court relating to service of documents shall have effect as if the association were a corporation.

(3) A fine imposed on an unincorporated association on its conviction of an offence under paragraph 10 shall be paid out of the funds of the association.

(4) Schedule 3 to the Magistrates' Courts Act 1980 (procedure on charge of offence against a corporation) shall have effect in a case in which an unincorporated association is charged in England or Wales with an offence under paragraph 10 in like manner as it has effect in the case of a corporation so charged.

(5) Where any unincorporated association is guilty of an offence under paragraph 10, then—

(*a*) in the case of a partnership, every partner, or

(*b*) in the case of any other unincorporated association, every member of the committee or other similar governing body,

other than a partner or member who is proved to have been ignorant of or to have attempted to prevent the commission of the offence, shall be guilty of that offence and be liable to be proceeded against and punished accordingly.

Power of Lord Chancellor to make recognition rules in the case of sole practitioners

12.—(1) The Lord Chancellor may, in accordance with the provisions of this paragraph, make rules with respect to the recognition by him of sole practitioners as being suitable to undertake the provision of conveyancing services.

(2) Subject to sub-paragraph (3) below, paragraphs 2 to 6 and 8 and 9 above shall apply in relation to the recognition of sole practitioners as they apply in relation to the recognition of institutions, and accordingly, in the application of those paragraphs in accordance with this sub-paragraph, any reference to an institution shall have effect as if it were a reference to a sole practitioner and any reference to a recognised institution shall have effect as if it were a reference to a recognised practitioner.

(3) In the application of those paragraphs in accordance with sub-paragraph (2) above—

(*a*) the reference in paragraph 2(2)(*b*) to negligence, fraud or other dishonesty on the part of officers or employees of recognised institutions shall have effect as if it were a reference to negligence, fraud or other dishonesty on the part of recognised practitioners or their employees; and

(*b*) paragraph 6(3)(*a*) shall be omitted.

Restrictions on conveyancing by unqualified persons not to apply to recognised practitioners in relation to acts done by their employees

13. Section 22(1) of the Solicitors Act 1974 shall not apply to an individual by reason of any act done by any employee of his, if at the time it was done, the individual was a recognised practitioner.

Penalty for pretending to be a recognised practitioner

14.—(1) A person shall not describe himself or hold himself out as a sole practitioner for the time being recognised under this Schedule unless he is so recognised.

(2) Any person who contravenes sub-paragraph (1) above shall be guilty of an offence and liable on summary conviction to a fine not exceeding level 4 on the standard scale.

DEFINITIONS
The Schedule has its own interpretation provisions in para.1.
"the standard scale": Criminal Justice Act 1982, s.37.

GENERAL NOTE
This Schedule should be read in conjunction with s.124 and the notes thereto. It confers on the Lord Chancellor the power to make rules for the recognition of certain institutions and practitioners as being suitable to provide conveyancing services (defined in para.1(3)). As such, it is a part of the policy, to which the Government is now committed, of increasing competition in the conveyancing field.

It will be observed that the Schedule contains no provisions of a disciplinary nature as to the manner in which individual employees of an institution perform conveyancing services. That is because such employees will be solicitors or licensed conveyancers and will be amenable to the disciplinary codes of their respective professions: see the notes to s.124.

Para. 2

This paragraph contains the fundamental power to prescribe the circumstances in which institutions may be recognised and the conditions with which they must comply if they are to remain so recognised. It appears that the conditions will include the employment of solicitors or licensed conveyancers only to provide conveyancing services, and compliance with any restrictions on persons to whom services may be provided or with any code of conduct: see the notes to s.124. Note the specific power in subpara. (2)(*b*) to make provision for securing that compensation is available in cases of negligence, fraud or other dishonesty.

Para. 3

This paragraph contains provisions for the grant and revocation of recognition. There is no express right for institutions to make representations against revocation of recognition; possibly such a right may be included in the rules to be made under subpara. (1).

Para. 4

This paragraph enables recognition rules to provide for the maintenance of an up-to-date list of recognised institutions, for inspection of the list and for certificates giving evidence of an institution's status as recognised.

Para. 5

Under this paragraph, the rules may enable the Lord Chancellor to delegate all his functions under this Schedule except his rule-making power. Subpara. (2) envisages a limited power for a person aggrieved by the decision of an officer to whom a function has been delegated to take the matter to the Lord Chancellor himself.

Para. 6

Note that this paragraph envisages that the rules may provide for recognition to be refused on the ground that it would be more appropriate for the institution to apply for recognition under s.32 of the Administration of Justice Act 1985 (*i.e.* as being a body managed and controlled by licensed conveyancers). It is not yet apparent why such a body might prefer to apply in accordance with rules made under this Schedule.

Para. 7

This paragraph contains consequential provisions as to the application of s.22 of the Solicitors Act 1974, which imposes restrictions on the preparation of certain instruments by unqualified persons.

Para. 8

This paragraph contains a consequential extension of legal professional privilege.

Para. 9

This paragraph makes consequential amendments to existing legislation.

Paras. 10 and 11

Under para. 10, it is an offence for an institution to describe itself or hold itself out as a recognised institution unless it is so recognised. Para. 11 contains supplementary provisions as to the commission of offences and how proceedings are to be brought.

Level 4: Currently £1,000.

Para. 12

Broadly speaking, this paragraph applies the provisions of paras. 2 to 6, 8 and 9 to the recognition of sole practitioners. It is not clear who these sole practitioners will be if they are not solicitors or licensed conveyancers (who do not need to be included in these provisions).

Paras. 13 and 14

These paragraphs have functions similar to those of paras. 7 and 10.

Level 4: Currently £1,000.

RATE SUPPORT GRANTS ACT 1986*

(1986 c. 54)

An Act to validate certain block grant determinations already approved by the House of Commons; and to clarify and amend the law relating to rate support grants. [21st October 1986]

INTRODUCTION AND GENERAL NOTE

The need for this Act arose as a result of a successful application by Birmingham City Council for judicial review of the determination by the Secretary of State for the Environment of their multiplier in the Rate Support Grant Report for 1986–87.

S.59(1) of the Local Government, Planning and Land Act 1980 allows the Secretary of State to determine a multiplier to adjust the amount of block grant payable to a local authority. This power may only be exercised for any purpose specified in s.59(6). S.59(6)(*a*) specifies the purpose of limiting changes in the amount of block grant payable to an authority for a year compared to the amount payable in a previous year.

This power had been used, in each year since 1981, to limit some factors affecting grant entitlements but not others. In 1986–87 it was used to set "caps" to limit the grant gains that some authorities made as a result of the abandonment of expenditure targets and penalties under s.59(6)(*cc*) of the 1980 Act. Caps were also applied to eliminate the effects of grant changes as a result of abolition of the Greater London Council and the metropolitan county councils.

The Birmingham Council sought judicial review on the grounds that s.59(6)(*a*) enabled the Secretary of State to limit only the *overall* change in a local authority's grant entitlement from one year to the next, and the power had been wrongly used to limit grant changes due to individual factors. When the case came to court it was accepted on behalf of the Secretary of State that he had no power to act as he did and that accordingly the determination of Birmingham's multiplier for 1986–87 was *ultra vires* and invalid. The court was satisfied that the concession was a proper one and a declaration was made accordingly: *R.* v. *Secretary of State for the Environment, ex p. City of Birmingham District Council*, April 15, 1986, unreported.

Following this judgment the Government concluded that legislation was necessary to preserve the position as they had believed it to be before the Birmingham challenge, since it would otherwise have been necessary to recalculate all rate support grant entitlements from 1981 onwards leading to possibly unmanageable grant losses for many authorities. The Act preserves the previously believed position in three ways. S.1 validates all past determinations of multipliers up to and including those for 1986–87. S.2 provides clear powers to enable the Secretary of State in future to limit the effects from year to year of particular factors on grant entitlements. Thirdly, Sched. 1 clarifies and amends other minor aspects of the legislation where current practice might be open to challenge on technical grounds.

PARLIAMENTARY DEBATES

Hansard: H.C. Vol. 99, col. 519; Vol. 100, col. 77; Vol. 102, col. 108; H.L. Vol. 479, cols. 275, 992.

The Bill was considered in Committee by the House of Commons in Standing Committee G between July 1–15, 1986.

Validation of approved block grant determinations

1. The enactments relating to determinations under section 59 of the Local Government, Planning and Land Act 1980 (adjustment of block grant by use of multipliers) shall be deemed to have been complied with in the case of all determinations made or purporting to be made under that section and specified in Rate Support Grant Reports or supplementary reports approved by the House of Commons on or before 21st January 1986.

---

* Annotations by Reginald Jones, Barrister, former Inspector of Audit, District Audit Service.

GENERAL NOTE

This section validates the determination of multipliers under earlier Rate Support Grant Reports in so far as they were invalid for the reasons indicated in the General Note to the Act, above, or otherwise. The date of January 21, 1986, in the section is the date on which the latest Rate Support Grant Report was approved.

Adjustment of block grant to limit effects of changes

2.—(1) As respects determinations made under section 59 of the said Act of 1980 after the passing of this Act the following provisions shall have effect instead of subsection (6)(*a*) of that section and section 8(3)(*a*) of the Local Government Finance Act 1982.

(2) The power conferred by section 59(1) may be exercised for the purpose of limiting or avoiding the effect on—

(*a*) the amount of block grant payable to a local authority for any year; or

(*b*) the contribution made or to be made by ratepayers in any year to the expenditure of the local authorities exercising fu. ctions in their area,

of any difference or differences between that year and the previous year in any of the matters relevant to the calculation of block grant.

(3) The power may be exercised for the purpose mentioned in subsection (2) above in respect of such difference or differences and, in the case of a limitation, to such extent as the Secretary of State thinks desirable; but he shall not exercise the power for that purpose so as to decrease the amount of block grant payable to a local authority for any year unless he is satisfied that it is necessary to do so in order to prevent the difference in question having an unreasonable effect on the way in which block grant for that year is distributed or on the contribution made or to be made by ratepayers in that year to the expenditure of local authorities.

(4) Where the Secretary of State decides to exercise the power for the purpose mentioned in subsection (2) above in respect of any difference, the effect that the difference would have had shall be calculated, and any limit imposed by him shall be determined, in such manner as he thinks appropriate.

DEFINITIONS

"local authority": s.4(2); Local Government, Planning and Land Act 1980, s.53(5).

"year": s.4(2); Local Government, Planning and Land Act 1980, s.68(1).

GENERAL NOTE

This section, in providing for purposes for which multipliers may be determined to adjust block grant payable to a local authority, replaces s.59(6)(*a*) of the Local Government, Planning and Land Act 1980 and s.8(3)(*a*) of the Local Government Finance Act 1982, which are repealed: subs. (1).

Subs. (2) provides that the power to determine multipliers conferred by s.59(1) of the 1980 Act may be exercised for the purpose of limiting or avoiding the effect on the amount of block grant payable to a local authority, or on the contributions of ratepayers to the expenditure of local authorities in their area, of any differences between that year and the previous year in any of the matters relevant to the calculation of block grant. This means it can be exercised in relation to individual constituent factors and not merely, as declared in the *Birmingham* case, above, in relation to the overall change in an authority's entitlement from one year to the next.

The provision that the power may be used to limit the effect of changes in grant-related matters on ratepayers' contributions to all the authorities in their area is also new (subs. (2)(*b*)). This would apply, for example, to the effects of the changes in the structure of local government in London and the metropolitan counties under the London Government Act 1985.

Subs. (3) allows the power to be exercised for the purpose in s.2(2) in respect of such differences and to such extent as the Secretary of State thinks desirable. It also provides that he shall not exercise the power for that purpose so as to decrease an authority's grant unless he is satisfied that it is necessary to do so in order to avoid an unreasonable effect on the way in which grant is distributed or on the contribution to be made by ratepayers to local authorities' expenditure. This replaces the narrower provision of s.8(3)(*a*) of the Local Government Finance Act 1982, under which an authority's grant could not be reduced unless the Secretary of State was satisfied that otherwise there would be an unreasonable increase in the amount of block grant payable to that authority. This did not allow for the justification for limiting grant increases on the ground that other authorities might be adversely affected if caps were not applied to gainers (since the total block grant available to all authorities is limited).

Subs. (4) empowers the Secretary of State to calculate the effects of any year-to-year differences in grant-related matters, and to determine any limits imposed in respect thereof, in such manner as he thinks appropriate. This enables him, for example, to specify notional reference points or "base positions" from which the effect can be calculated of each of the changes whose effect on grant is to be limited. It also allows him to determine the limit in appropriate terms, *i.e.* as a rate poundage figure. (For example, in 1986–87, the first base position was an estimate of the grant authorities would have received if no changes had been made from 1985–86 in matters affecting grant. Subsequent base positions incorporated successively the effect of the abolition of targets and penalties, the abolition of the G.L.C. and metropolitan counties, and changes in methods of calculating grant-related expenditure. Limits on the effect of each change in rate poundage terms were set separately before moving on to the next base position).

Other rate support grant amendments

3.—(1) Part VI of the Local Government, Planning and Land Act 1980 and Part II of and Schedule 2 to the Local Government Finance Act 1982 shall have effect with the amendments specified in Schedule 1 to this Act, being amendments for clarifying and amending the provisions relating to rate support grants and amendments consequential on section 2 above.

(2) Those amendments shall have effect in relation to any exercise after the passing of this Act of the powers conferred by those provisions in relation to any year beginning on or after 1st April 1982 except that the amendments in paragraphs 1, 2, 3, 8, 9, 11 and 12 shall be deemed always to have had effect.

GENERAL NOTE
This section gives effect to the various amendments to the Local Government, Planning and Land Act 1980 and the Local Government Finance Act 1982, which are contained in Sched. 1.

These are mainly consequential or clarificatory amendments. Some are given retrospective effect by subs. (2) in order to remove doubts about the exercise of the relevant powers in previous years.

Short title, interpretation, repeals, and extent

4.—(1) This Act may be cited as the Rate Support Grants Act 1986.

(2) In sections 1 and 2 above references to section 59 of the said Act of 1980 include references to paragraph 5(1) of Schedule 2 to the Local Government Finance Act 1982 (which makes corresponding provision for the Receiver for the Metropolitan Police District) and in section 2 above "local authority" means any body (including the Receiver) which is a local authority for the purposes of Part VI of the said Act of 1980 and "year" has the same meaning as in that Part.

(3) The enactments mentioned in Schedule 2 to this Act are hereby repealed to the extent specified in the third column of that Schedule.

(4) This Act extends to England and Wales only.

SCHEDULES

Section 3   SCHEDULE 1

AMENDMENTS

Determination of grant-related poundages

1.—(1) Section 57 of the Local Government, Planning and Land Act 1980 shall be amended as follows.

(2) For subsection (1) there shall be substituted—

"(1) A local authority's grant-related poundage shall be calculated and their grant-related expenditure shall be determined by the Secretary of State in accordance with principles to be applied to all local authorities or to all local authorities belonging to the appropriate class".

(3) In subsection (2) for the words "the principles on which the grant-related poundage and the grant-related expenditure are determined" there shall be substituted the words "the principles on which the grant-related poundage is calculated and the grant-related expenditure is determined".

2. After section 61(6) of the said Act of 1980 there shall be inserted—

"(6A) A supplementary report may specify fresh principles for the calculation of a grant-related poundage in place of those specified in the Rate Support Grant Report and in that event that poundage shall be re-calculated on the fresh principles."

3.—(1) In paragraph 1(1) of Schedule 2 to the Local Government Finance Act 1982, in the definition of "Receiver's grant-related poundage" for the word "determined" there shall be substituted the word "calculated".

(2) In paragraph 5(2)(*b*) of that Schedule for the words "any fresh determination of his grant-related poundage" there shall be substituted the words "any re-calculation of his grant-related poundage on fresh principles specified".

———————

GENERAL NOTE

S.57(1) of the Local Government, Planning and Land Act 1980 required grant-related poundages to be "determined". By s.60(6)(*a*) "determinations" must be specified in a Rate Support Grant Report. In practice, the principles on which the determinations have been based were specified in the Reports, but not the determinations for each authority. Paragraphs 1 to 3 make amendments so that grant-related poundages are required to be "calculated" on principles to be applied to all local authorities. The principles must still be specified in the Rate Support Grant Reports, as required by s.57(2) of the 1980 Act. These amendments are retrospective: s.3(2).

———————

Multipliers

4.—(1) Section 59 of the said Act of 1980 shall be amended as follows.

(2) In subsection (5)(*b*) for the words "in paragraphs (*a*) to (*d*) of subsection (6) below" there shall be substituted the words "in paragraphs (*b*) to (*d*) of subsection (6) below or in section 2(2) of the Rate Support Grants Act 1986".

(3) Subsection (6)(*a*) shall be omitted.

(4) After subsection (6) there shall be inserted—

"(6A) A multiplier may be subject to a maximum determined by the Secretary of State."

(5) In subsection (11) for paragraph (*c*) there shall be substituted—

"(*c*) as if paragraph (*e*) referred to two classes, namely—

(i) councils of inner London boroughs; and

(ii) councils of outer London boroughs;".

5. In section 8(3) of the said Act of 1982 paragraph (*a*) shall be omitted and in paragraph (*b*) for the words "that subsection" there shall be substituted the words "subsection (6) of that section".

6. In paragraph 5(2) of Schedule 2 to the said Act of 1982 for the words from the beginning to "paragraph (*c*) or (*d*) of that subsection" there shall be substituted the words "In paragraph (*b*) of subsection (6) of section 59 of the principal Act references to a local authority shall include references to the Receiver and the power conferred by this paragraph may only be exercised—

(*a*) for the purposes specified in paragraph (*b*), (*c*) or (*d*) of that subsection or in section 2(2) of the Rate Support Grants Act 1986;".

7. After paragraph 5(2) of Schedule 2 to the said Act of 1982 there shall be inserted—

"(2A) A multiplier determined under this paragraph may be subject to a maximum determined by the Secretary of State."

GENERAL NOTE

Paras. 4 to 7 make amendments to the law on multipliers, mainly consequential on s.2. Sub-para. (4) is a new provision enabling the Secretary of State to specify an upper limit for multipliers.

Explanation of determinations in rate support grant reports

8.—(1) In section 60(6)(*b*) of the said Act of 1980 for the words "the considerations leading the Secretary of State to make any such determination" there shall be substituted the words "such explanation as the Secretary of State thinks desirable of the main features of any such determination".

(2) In section 61(6) of that Act for the words "the considerations leading to them" there shall be substituted the words "such explanation as the Secretary of State thinks desirable of their main features".

9. In section 8(9)(*b*) of the said Act of 1982 for the words "the considerations leading the Secretary of State to make the determination" there shall be substituted the words "such explanation as the Secretary of State thinks desirable of the main features of the determination."

GENERAL NOTE

Paras. 8 and 9 relax the requirements that the Secretary of State should specify the considerations leading him to make any of the determinations in a Rate Support Grant Report. To avoid the possibility of legal challenge on the ground that some minor consideration has not been specified, these paragraphs change the requirement so that he must give such explanation as he thinks desirable of the main features of determinations. These paragraphs are retrospective: s.3(2).

Supplementary reports

10. After section 61(4) of the said Act of 1980 there shall be inserted—

"(4A) The Secretary of State shall not in a supplementary report vary a multiplier so far as previously determined for the purpose specified in section 2(2) of the Rate Support Grants Act 1986 (or previously determined or purported to be determined for the purpose specified in section 59(6)(*a*) above) unless he is satisfied that the variation is required in consequence of the principles specified by him in relation to the original determination not having been correctly applied to it on the basis of the information available to him when it was made."

GENERAL NOTE

Para. 10 precludes the Secretary of State from varying a multiplier previously determined unless there was an error in applying the principles specified by him for the original determination on the basis of information available to him at the time. The intention is to rule out the possibility of varying multipliers in the light of subsequent information about expenditure, since this would result in unacceptable uncertainty in grant entitlements.

Adjustments for matching amount available for block grant

11. For section 62 of the said Act of 1980 there shall be substituted—
   "Adjustments for matching amount available for block grant
   62.—(1) Where at any time after a Rate Support Grant Report or supplementary report for any year has been approved by the House of Commons it appears to the Secretary of State from information as to the expenditure incurred or to be incurred by local authorities during that year that the aggregate amount of block grant to which local authorities would be entitled in accordance with the report, or any previous adjustment under this section, differs from the aggregate amount available for that grant in that year he may adjust the amount payable to each authority (whether by increasing or reducing it) so as to reconcile those aggregate amounts.
      (2) An adjustment under this section may be made either—
   (a) so that the amount payable to an authority is adjusted in the same ratio as the aggregate amounts mentioned in subsection (1) above bear to one another; or
   (b) in accordance with principles applicable to all local authorities or to all local authorities belonging to the appropriate class and specified in the report mentioned in that subsection."
12. Paragraph 8(2) of Schedule 2 to the said Act of 1982 shall be omitted.

GENERAL NOTE
   Para. 11 substitutes a new section for s.62 of the Local Government, Planning and Land Act 1980, dealing with adjustments for matching the aggregate amount of local authorities' block grant settlements with the total amount made available by Parliament, a process known as "close-ending". The new section enables the adjustment to be made either by a common percentage, as under the original s.62, or otherwise in accordance with principles applicable to all local authorities, or all authorities belonging to a class specified in the relevant report. Para. 12 makes a consequential amendment. These amendments are retrospective: s.3(2).

Submission of information

13.—(1) Section 65 of the said Act of 1980 shall be amended as follows.
   (2) In subsection (1) before the words "by such date as he may specify" there shall be inserted the words "in such form and" and after the words "sections 53 to 63 above" there shall be inserted the words "and section 2 of the Rate Support Grants Act 1986".
   (3) After subsection (2) there shall be inserted—
      "(3) Where no or no sufficient information as to the expenditure incurred or to be incurred by a local authority during any year has been submitted to the Secretary of State, whether under subsection (1) above or otherwise, he may for the purpose of making a supplementary report, an adjustment under section 62 above or an estimate under section 66(1) below make such assumptions as to that expenditure as he thinks appropriate; and where any information as to that expenditure is submitted to him under subsection (1) above after the date specified by him, or otherwise than under that subsection, he may for any of those purposes disregard it if he considers that it is not reasonably practicable to take it into account for that purpose."

GENERAL NOTE
   Para. 13 amends s.65 of the Local Government, Planning and Land Act 1980, which empowers the Secretary of State to require local authorities to submit returns of expenditure for the purpose of calculating block grant. Para. 13(2) allows the Secretary of State to specify the form in which the information is to be supplied. Para. 13(3) gives him the power to make assumptions as to expenditure in the absence of information and to disregard late information if he thinks it impracticable to take account of it. This provision modifies the effect of s.66 of the 1980 Act which requires him to use the best information available to him for the purpose of block grant calculations.

Section 4(3)   SCHEDULE 2

REPEALS

Chapter	Short title	Extent of repeal
1980 c.65	The Local Government, Planning and Land Act 1980.	Section 59(6)(*a*)
1982 c.32.	The Local Government Finance Act 1982.	Section 8(3)(*a*). In Schedule 2, paragraph 8(2).
1985 c.51.	The Local Government Act 1985.	Section 69(5)(*a*). Section 80(1).

FAMILY LAW ACT 1986*

(1986 c.55)

ARRANGEMENT OF SECTIONS

PART I

CHILD CUSTODY

CHAPTER I

PRELIMINARY

---

* Annotations by M. D. A. Freeman, Professor of English Law, University College London, Barrister, and K. McK. Norrie, Lecturer in Law, University of Aberdeen.

CHAPTER VI

MISCELLANEOUS AND SUPPLEMENTAL

PART II

RECOGNITION OF DIVORCES, ANNULMENTS AND LEGAL SEPARATIONS

Divorces, annulments and judicial separations granted in the British Islands

Overseas divorces, annulments and legal separations

Supplemental

PART III

DECLARATIONS OF STATUS

PART IV

MISCELLANEOUS AND GENERAL

An Act to amend the law relating to the jurisdiction of courts in the United Kingdom to make orders with regard to the custody of children; to make provision as to the recognition and enforcement of such orders throughout the United Kingdom; to make further provision as to the imposition, effect and enforcement of restrictions on the removal of children from the United Kingdom or from any part of the United Kingdom; to amend the law relating to the jurisdiction of courts in Scotland as to tutory and curatory; to amend the law relating to the recognition of divorces, annulments and legal separations; to make further provision with respect to the effect of divorces and annulments on wills; to amend the law relating to the powers of courts to make declarations relating to the status of a person; to abolish the right to petition for jactitation of marriage; to repeal the Greek Marriages Act 1884; to make further provision with respect to family proceedings rules; to amend the Child Abduction Act 1984, the Child Abduction (Northern Ireland) Order 1985 and the Child Abduction and Custody Act 1985; and for connected purposes.   [7th November 1986]

PARLIAMENTARY DEBATES

Hansard: H.L. Vol. 472, col. 1398; Vol. 473, col. 1078; Vol. 476, col. 9; Vol. 477, cols. 418, 1036; H.C. Vol. 102, col. 1439.

INTRODUCTION AND GENERAL NOTE

Despite its title this Act is not a Family Law Act in the conventional sense. It makes few alterations to substantive family law. It in no way facilitates the construction of a Family Court or a framework for conciliation. The Act is, in the main, a private international law measure. It gives effect to the recommendations of two Law Commission reports and, subject to modifications, to a third report.

Part I of the Act gives effect to the recommendations of the Law Commission and the Scottish Law Commission, contained in their joint report "Custody of Children—Jurisdiction and Enforcement within this United Kingdom" (Law Com. No. 138, Scot. Law Com. No. 91, Cmnd. 9419). A new statutory code laying down the jurisdictional bases for the granting of custody orders in England and Wales, Scotland and Northern Ireland is set out. Such orders will be recognised in each of the other parts of the U.K. A procedure for recognition and enforcement in each part of the U.K. of custody orders made in another part is set out in Chapter V. The key to recognition and enforcement lies in registration (see s.27). The powers of the courts, when making or enforcing custody orders, is also widened. There are powers, wider than in existing law, to order disclosure of a child's whereabouts (s.33), to order the recovery of a child (s.34), to restrict the removal of a child from the jurisdiction (s.35), etc.

Part II of the Act in substance gives effect in the recommendations of the Law Commission and the Scottish Law Commission, contained in their report "Recognition of Foreign Nullity Decrees and Related Matters" (Law Com. No. 137, Scot. Law Com. No. 88, Cmnd. 9341). The Law Commissions proposed that the recognition of foreign nullity decrees should be assimilated to the grounds of recognition of divorces and legal separations, then contained in the Recognition of Divorces and Legal Separations Act 1971. Part II of the Act does this. The 1971 Act is thus re-enacted with a number of modifications. There is to be automatic recognition in the U.K. of divorces, annulments and judicial separations granted by courts of civil jurisdiction anywhere in the British Islands (s.44). In dealing with the recognition of *overseas* divorces, annulments and legal separations, a more restricted approach is adopted than that recommended by the Law Commissions. A distinction is drawn (s.46) between overseas divorces, etc., obtained *by means of proceedings* and overseas divorces, etc. obtained *otherwise* than by means of proceedings. The latter will be recognised only if granted and effective in the countries where the parties to the marriage were domiciled, and only where this is officially certified. Moreover, they will not be recognised if one (or other) of the parties was habitually resident in the U.K. for at least one year before the divorce, etc., was obtained. As far as foreign divorces, etc., obtained by proceedings are concerned, the Act enacts the Law Commission's proposals. They are to be recognised if they are effective under the law of the country in which they were obtained, provided that *either* party was, at the date of the commencement of the proceedings, habitually resident in, or domiciled in, or a national of that country.

Part III of the Act, which extends only to England and Wales, gives effect to the recommendations of the Law Commission in its report "Declarations In Family Matters" (Law Com. No. 132). The Law Commission recommended that "a new legislative code, based on consistent principles, should replace the existing hotchpotch of statutory and discretionary relief". This the Act seeks to do. It sets out a legislative framework to determine declaratory relief in matters of marital status, legitimacy and legitimation and adoptions effected overseas. There are procedural safeguards (see in particular s.59).

This part of the Act also abolishes the right to petition for jactitation of marriage (s.61) and repeals the Greek Marriages Act 1884, which was designed to validate 36 marriages celebrated in England between 1836 and 1837 between members of the Greek Orthodox Church.

S.64, the most controversial provision in the Act ("a black mark upon what is otherwise an admirable piece of law reform" *per* Lord Elwyn-Jones at H.C. Vol. 437, col. 1087), enlarges the rule-making powers of the Matrimonial Causes Rules Committee. This is to enable a "greater degree of flexibility, in particular the ability to distinguish different cases and different circumstances" (*per* Lord Chancellor at H.C. Vol. 473, col. 1084).

EXTENT

The whole Act applies to the whole of the U.K. with the following *exceptions*.

The following provisions extend to *England and Wales only*:

Ss.2–7
S.53
Ss.55–63
Ss.64, 65
S.68(3) and
paras. 9–17, 19, 23–27 of Sched. 1 (and s.68(1), so far as relating to those paragraphs) (see s.69(5)).

The following provisions extend to *Scotland only*:

Ss.8–18
S.26
Paras. 1, 3–8, 18, 21, 22 of Sched. 1 (and s.68(1), so far as relating to those paragraphs) (see s.69(6)).

The following provisions extend to *Northern Ireland only*:

Ss.19–24
S.66
S.68(4)
Paras. 2, 32–34 of Sched. 1 (and s.68(1), so far as relating to those paragraphs) (see s.69(7)).

COMMENCEMENT

Ss.64–67 came into operation on January 7, 1987 (see s.69(2)). The rest of the Act is to come into force on such day or days as the relevant Minister (as to which see s.69(4)) may by order made by statutory instrument appoint (s.69(3)). No dates have as yet been appointed.

PART I

CHILD CUSTODY

CHAPTER I

PRELIMINARY

Orders to which Part I applies

1.—(1) Subject to the following provisions of this section, in this Part "custody order" means—

(*a*) an order made by a court in England and Wales under any of the following enactments—
  (i) section 9(1), 10(1)(*a*), 11(*a*) or 14A(2) of the Guardianship of Minors Act 1971 or section 2(4)(*b*) or 2(5) of the Guardianship Act 1973;
  (ii) section 42(1) of the Matrimonial Causes Act 1973;
  (iii) section 42(2) of the Matrimonial Causes Act 1973;
  (iv) section 33(1) of the Children Act 1975 or section 2(4)(*b*) of the Guardianship Act 1973 as applied by section 34(5) of the Children Act 1975;
  (v) section 8(2) or 19(1)(ii) of the Domestic Proceedings and Magistrates' Courts Act 1978;
(*b*) an order made by a court of civil jurisdiction in Scotland under any enactment or rule of law with respect to the custody, care or control of a child, access to a child or the education or upbringing of a child, excluding—
  (i) an order committing the care of a child to a local authority or placing a child under the supervision of a local authority;
  (ii) an adoption order as defined in section 12(1) of the Adoption (Scotland) Act 1978;
  (iii) an order freeing a child for adoption made under section 18 of the said Act of 1978;
  (iv) an order for the custody of a child made in the course of proceedings for the adoption of the child (other than an order made following the making of a direction under section 53(1) of the Children Act 1975);
  (v) an order made under the Education (Scotland) Act 1980;
  (vi) an order made under Part II or III of the Social Work (Scotland) Act 1968;
  (vii) an order made under the Child Abduction and Custody Act 1985;
  (viii) an order for the delivery of a child or other order for the enforcement of a custody order;
  (ix) an order relating to the tutory or curatory of a child;
(*c*) an order made by a court in Northern Ireland under any of the following enactments—
  (i) section 5 of the Guardianship of Infants Act 1886 (except so far as it relates to costs);
  (ii) Article 45(1) of the Matrimonial Causes (Northern Ireland) Order 1978;
  (iii) Article 45(2) of the Matrimonial Causes (Northern Ireland) Order 1978;
  (iv) Article 10(2) or 20(1)(ii) of the Domestic Proceedings (Northern Ireland) Order 1980;
(*d*) an order made by the High Court in the exercise of its jurisdiction relating to wardship so far as it gives the care and control of a child to any person or provides for the education of, or for access to, a child, excluding an order relating to a child of whom care or care and control is (immediately after the making of the order) vested in a local authority or in the Northern Ireland Department of Health and Social Services.
(2) In this Part "custody order" does not include—
  (*a*) an order within subsection (1)(*a*) or (*c*) above which varies or revokes a previous order made under the same enactment;
  (*b*) an order under section 14A(2) of the Guardianship of Minors Act 1971 which varies a previous custody order; or
  (*c*) an order within paragraph (*d*) of subsection (1) above which varies or revokes a previous order within that paragraph.

(3) Subject to sections 32 and 40 of this Act, in this Part "custody order" does not include any order which—

(a) was made before the date of the commencement of this Part;

(b) in the case of an order within subsection (1)(b) or (d) above or an order under any of the enactments mentioned in subsection (4) below, is made on or after that date on an application made before that date; or

(c) in any other case, is made on or after that date in proceedings commenced before that date.

(4) The said enactments are—

(a) sections 9(1) and 14A(2) of the Guardianship of Minors Act 1971 and section 33(1) of the Children Act 1975; and

(b) section 5 of the Guardianship of Infants Act 1886.

(5) For the purposes of subsection (3) above an order made on two or more applications which are determined together shall be regarded as made on the first of those applications.

(6) Provision may be made by act of sederunt prescribing, in relation to orders within subsection (1)(b) above, what constitutes an application for the purposes of this Part.

GENERAL NOTE

This part of the Act gives effect to the recommendations of the Law Commission and the Scottish Law Commission contained in their Joint Report (Law Com. No. 138; Scot. Law Com. No. 91). Chapters II, III and IV lay down for England and Wales, Scotland and Northern Ireland respectively, the jurisdictional bases for the granting of custody orders which will be recognised in each of the other parts of the U.K. Chapter V provides the procedure for the recognition and enforcement in each part of the U.K. of custody orders made in another part. Chapter VI widens the powers of the courts when making or enforcing custody orders, giving powers, *inter alia*, to order the disclosure of a child's whereabouts, power to order the recovery of a child and powers to restrict the removal of a child from the jurisdiction.

Chapter I is in one section. This defines "custody order" for the purposes of Part I of the Act. "Custody order" is defined differently for the three parts of the U.K. This is necessary both because each of the three parts of the U.K. has its own statutory provisions, and because the term "custody" is used in different senses in different contexts.

The English orders, affected by the Act, are listed in s.1(1)(a) and (d). The Northern Irish orders, so affected, are listed in s.1(1)(c) and (d). It follows that English and Northern Irish orders not so listed are not "custody" orders within the meaning of the term as used in the Act, however they are described in the legislation under which they are made. Custody law in Scotland is partly statutory and partly common law. This necessitates a different approach to drafting as far as Scotland is concerned (see s.1(1)(b) with its reference to "any enactment or rule of law").

Subs. (1)

Means: custody orders not listed are not "custody orders" within the meaning of the term as used in the Act. Excluded are care orders, place and safety orders and supervision orders, as well as orders made as a step in adoption proceedings (see ss.19 and 25 of Children Act 1975).

Section 9(1): this enables the court, on application of the mother or father, including the father of an illegitimate child (see s.14) to make such order relating to the child's legal custody or the right of access to him as the court thinks fit, having regard to the child's welfare and to the conduct and wishes of the mother and father.

Section 10(1)(a): this empowers the court to make a custody order or order as to access where it has ordered (under s.4(4)) that a person shall be sole guardian to the exclusion of a parent.

Section 11(1): this empowers the court to make a custody order or an order as to access where joint guardians disagree.

Section 14A: this relates to access to minors by grandparents.

Section 2(4)(a) *and* (5): this enables the court to make interim orders pending a final decision.

Section 42(1) *and* (2): this refers to custody orders made under the Matrimonial Causes Act 1973 in proceedings for divorce, nullity or judicial separation and to orders made as ancillary to financial orders made in consequence of the failure by one spouse to maintain the other spouse and/or the children of the marriage. It is necessary to distinguish these two types of order because they are treated differently in the Act for jurisdictional purposes (see ss.2(1) and 4(1)).

Section 33(1): this refers to custodianship orders made under Children Act 1975 (operative from December 1, 1985) and includes orders as to access and interim orders. See, further, M. D. A. Freeman, *The Law and Practice of Custodianship* (1986).

Section 8(2) *or* 19(1)(ii): this refers to custody orders made under Part I of the 1978 Act, enabling a magistrates' court to make orders for financial provision for parties to a marriage or children of a family, and also, where such financial provision has been applied for, to make orders relating to the legal custody of and access to such children of the family. The main power is to be found in s.8 of the 1978 Act. S.19 gives the court power to make interim orders, including interim custody orders. See, further, M. D. A. Freeman and C. M. Lyon, *The Matrimonial Jurisdiction of Magistrates' Courts* (1980).

Civil jurisdiction: thus excluding all orders made by criminal courts.

Any enactment or rule of law: in Scotland custody orders are to a large extent governed by the common law.

Excluding . . . : note all orders *except* those listed in (i) to (ix) are "custody orders".

Northern Ireland: the technique applied here parallels that in relation to England and Wales. Subs. (1)(*c*)(i) to (iv) corresponds to subs. (1)(*a*)(i), (ii), (iii) and (v).

The High Court: in England and Wales or Northern Ireland (as appropriate; see Interpretation Act 1978, Sched. 1).

Wardship: the wardship order itself is not a "custody order". A child becomes a ward of court by virtue of the making of the application but this fact will not of itself enable the main provisions of the Act to be invoked (see however s.38). If, on the other hand, the High Court in the exercise of its wardship jurisdiction makes an order giving care and control of the child to any person, or an order relating to access to the child or his education, that will be a "custody order" governed by the Act.

Care and control . . . to a person: i.e. a named individual. Cases where the court, when exercising wardship jurisdiction, commits the ward to a local authority, or orders that the ward be under the supervision of a welfare officer or of a local authority (whether under the Family Law Reform Act 1969, s.7(2) or under its inherent powers) are specifically excluded.

Subs. (2)

This subsection provides that certain orders made in England and Wales and in Northern Ireland are not custody orders for the purposes of the Act. It excludes variation and revocation orders from the definition of "custody order" and means that the jurisdictional rules in Parts II and IV relating to the making of custody orders in England and Wales and Northern Ireland will not apply to variations and revocations, except where they are specifically mentioned (and see s.6(3)). Subject to these exceptions and to cases where the Act specifically restricts the jurisdiction to vary, a court in England and Wales or in Northern Ireland will retain any jurisdiction it had to revoke or vary a custody order made by it, even though it would no longer have jurisdiction under the Act to make the order which is varied or revoked (see further Law Com. No. 138, para. 4.30).

Subs. (3)

Before: and see s.1(5).

Any of the enactments: see s.1(4).

CHAPTER II

JURISDICTION OF COURTS IN ENGLAND AND WALES

Jurisdiction in cases other than divorce, etc.

2.—(1) A court in England and Wales shall not have jurisdiction to make a custody order within section 1(1)(*a*) of this Act, other than one under section 42(1) of the Matrimonial Causes Act 1973, unless the condition in section 3 of this Act is satisfied.

(2) The High Court in England and Wales shall have jurisdiction to make a custody order within section 1(1)(*d*) of this Act if, and only if,—

   (*a*) the condition in section 3 of this Act is satisfied, or (*b*) the ward is present in England and Wales on the relevant date (within the meaning of section 3(6) of this Act) and the court considers that the immediate exercise of its powers is necessary for his protection.

GENERAL NOTE
This part of the Act prescribes the jurisdiction of courts in England and Wales to make custody orders. Ss.2 and 3 provide that in proceedings, other than divorce proceedings, habitual residence is to be the main basis of jurisdiction for the making of custody orders. The alternative basis for jurisdiction is "presence". S.4 makes some amendments to s.42 of the Matrimonial Causes Act 1973 (dealing with jurisdiction to make custody orders in divorce proceedings). S.5 enables a court which has jurisdiction to make a custody order to exercise a discretion to refuse or to stay an application for the custody of a child, pending the outcome of proceedings elsewhere. S.6 provides for the duration and variation of an English custody order, when a court in either Scotland or Northern Ireland subsequently obtains jurisdiction to make a custody order in respect of the same child.

Subs. (1)
Section 42(1): a custody order on divorce, nullity or judicial separation.
The condition: *i.e.* the child is habitually resident in England and Wales on the relevant date or is present there and not habitually resident in any part of the U.K.

Subs. (2)
Within section 1(1)(*d*): *i.e.* in wardship.
The ward is present: this preserves the special emergency jurisdiction of the High Court in wardship. It enables the court to deal with any ward who is present in England and Wales, where the court considers the immediate exercise of its powers is necessary for his protection.
Relevant date: as to which see s.3(6).
Immediate exercise: "Where a child is in immediate danger, his protection must take precedence over procedural considerations" *per* Law Com. para. 4.19.

Habitual residence or presence of child

3.—(1) The condition referred to in section 2 of this Act is that on the relevant date the child concerned—
(*a*) is habitually resident in England and Wales, or
(*b*) is present in England and Wales and is not habitually resident in any part of the United Kingdom,
and, in either case, the jurisdiction of the court is not excluded by subsection (2) below.
(2) For the purposes of subsection (1) above, the jurisdiction of the court is excluded if, on the relevant date, proceedings for divorce, nullity or judicial separation are continuing in a court in Scotland or Northern Ireland in respect of the marriage of the parents of the child concerned.
(3) Subsection (2) above shall not apply if the court in which the other proceedings there referred to are continuing has made—
(*a*) an order under section 13(6) or 21(5) of this Act (not being an order made by virtue of section 13(6)(*a*)(i)), or
(*b*) an order under section 14(2) or 22(2) of this Act which is recorded as made for the purpose of enabling proceedings with respect to the custody of the child concerned to be taken in England and Wales,
and that order is in force.
(4) Subject to subsections (5) and (6) below, in this section "the relevant date" means the date of the commencement of the proceedings in which the custody order falls to be made.
(5) In a case where an application is made for a custody order under section 9(1) or 14A(2) of the Guardianship of Minors Act 1971 or section 33(1) of the Children Act 1975, "the relevant date" means the date of the application (or first application, if two or more are determined together).

(6) In the case of a custody order within section 1(1)(*d*) of this Act "the relevant date" means—

(*a*) where an application is made for an order, the date of the application (or first application, if two or more are determined together), and

(*b*) where no such application is made, the date of the order.

GENERAL NOTE

This section lays down *habitual residence* as the new basis of jurisdiction in proceedings other than proceedings for divorce, nullity or judicial separation. It is also provided that physical presence of the child is a ground for the exercise of jurisdiction where the child is not habitually resident in any part of the U.K. In the absence of such a provision, the applicant might have been left without any remedy in any part of the U.K.

Subs. (1)

Relevant date: see s.3(4).

The child: *i.e.* a person who has not attained the age of eighteen (see s.7).

Habitually resident: this is not defined in the Act or in any other previous Act in which the concept has been used (but see s.41—provisions as to habitual residence after removal without consent of all the persons having the right to determine where the child is to reside or in contravention of a court order). According to the Law Commission, "habitual residence points better than the tests of nationality and domicile to the forum with which the child and, in the majority of cases, the other persons concerned have the closest long-term connections" (para. 4.15). In *Cruse* v. *Chittum* [1974] 2 All E.R. 940 habitual residence was defined as regular physical presence, enduring for some time. In more recent cases (*R.* v. *Barnet London Borough Council, ex p. Shah* [1983] 2 A.C. 309, 340, 342 and *Kapur* v. *Kapur* [1984] F.L.R. 920) it has been suggested that there is no substantial difference between ordinary residence and habitual residence. But it has been said that one can be ordinarily resident in more than one country at the same time (see *I.R.C.* v. *Lysaght* [1928] A.C. 234). It surely cannot be right that one can be habitually resident in more than one country at the same time. See, for agreement, J. Blom [1973] 22 J.C.L.Q. 109, 136; L. De Winter (1969) 128 Recueil Des Cours 357.

It has been held that a child of tender years is ordinarily resident in his parents' matrimonial home, and that this ordinary residence cannot be changed by one parent without the consent of the other (see *P. (G. E.), Re* [1965] Ch. 568, 585–86). If habitual residence is to be equated with ordinary residence, as recent cases suggest, the court would have the jurisdiction to make a custody order when the child was out of the jurisdiction and had been so for a considerable time.

Present: *i.e.* physically present. The Law Commission envisaged three examples where this jurisdiction might be valuable:

(*a*) the child is taken from the parent entitled to custody in a foreign country and brought to the U.K. The child is not habitually resident anywhere in the U.K.;

(*b*) the child, though present in the U.K., is habitually resident in a country which does not accept habitual residence as a ground for jurisdiction, and is not prepared to assume jurisdiction on any other ground;

(*c*) the child, though present in the U.K., is habitually resident in a country which applies criteria for the determination of custody issues which are contrary to U.K. public policy (*e.g.* the father always gets custody). The U.K. court might refuse to enforce the foreign order, but it should be possible for the U.K. court to make a custody order on the basis of the child's physical presence (see para. 4.25).

Part of the United Kingdom: *i.e.* in Scotland or Northern Ireland (see s.42(1)).

Excluded: see s.3(3): There is no jurisdiction if proceedings for divorce, nullity or judicial separation are continuing in a court in Scotland or Northern Ireland in respect of the marriage of the parents of the child concerned.

Subs. (2)

Relevant date: see s.3(4).

Proceedings . . . continuing: see s.42(2) and (3).

Marriage of the parents of the child: in relation to a child, who is not a child of both parties to the marriage, but is a child of the family (*i.e.* a child who has been "treated" by both parties as a child of their family), the reference to "marriage . . . ." is to be construed as a reference to proceedings in respect of that marriage (see s.42(4)).

Subs. (3)

This subsection restores the jurisdiction taken away by s.3(2) in cases where the divorce, etc., in Scotland or Northern Ireland decides to waive its custody jurisdiction or to sist or stay custody proceedings before it, in favour of an English court.

Subs. (4)

This subsection defines the term "relevant date" for the purpose of the preceding subsections.

Relevant date: important because this is the point of time with reference to which jurisdiction is determined. Where the court makes an order of its own motion in other proceedings, the "relevant date" is the date of commencement of those proceedings. For example, if a magistrates' court is asked under Part I of the Domestic Proceedings and Magistrates' Courts Act 1978 to make provision for the maintenance of a child, and subsequently decides to make a custody order, the "relevant date" is the date of the application for an order under Part I of the Act.

Subs. (5)

Section 9(1): applications for custody under s.9(1) may be made after or in the course of proceedings for the appointment of a guardian to deal with the child's property. In this case the "relevant date" is the date of the application for custody.

Section 14A(2): applications may be made by grandparents for access, where one or both of the child's parents has died. The "relevant date" is the date of the application by the grandparent.

Section 33: this refers to applications for custodianship. An application may be deemed to be made, if the court so directs, in the course of adoption proceedings, under powers given to it by s.37 of the Children Act 1975 (see, for an example, *Re, M, The Times*, October 13, 1986). In this case, the "relevant date" is the date on which the application is made, or treated as made, under s.33.

Two or more: where there are cross-applications, the "relevant date" is the date of the *first* application.

Subs. (6)

This subsection refers to custody orders made in wardship proceedings, *i.e.* orders relating to the care and control or education of or access to a child who is a ward of court. Such orders may be applied for. They may also be made by the court of its own motion.

The date of the application: the question whether a custody order should be made may arise some time after the child has become a ward of court.

Jurisdiction in divorce proceedings, etc.

4.—(1) The enactments relating to the jurisdiction of courts in England and Wales to make orders under section 42(1) of the Matrimonial Causes Act 1973 shall have effect subject to the modifications provided for by this section.

(2) In section 42(1)(*b*) of that Act (which enables orders as to custody and education to be made immediately, or within a reasonable period, after the dismissal of proceedings for divorce, etc.) for the words "within a reasonable period" there shall be substituted the words "(if an application for the order is made on or before the dismissal)".

(3) A court shall not have jurisdiction to make a custody order under section 42(1)(*a*) of that Act after the grant of a decree of judicial separation if, on the relevant date, proceedings for divorce or nullity in respect of the marriage concerned are continuing in Scotland or Northern Ireland.

(4) Subsection (3) above shall not apply if the court in which the other proceedings there referred to are continuing has made—

    (*a*) an order under section 13(6) or 21(5) of this Act (not being an order made by virtue of section 13(6)(*a*)(i)), or

    (*b*) an order under section 14(2) or 22(2) of this Act which is recorded as made for the purpose of enabling proceedings with respect to the custody of the child concerned to be taken in England and Wales,

and that order is in force.
 (5) Where a court—
   (*a*) has jurisdiction to make a custody order under section 42(1) of
        the Matrimonial Causes Act 1973 in or in connection with
        proceedings for divorce, nullity of marriage or judicial separ-
        ation, but
   (*b*) considers that it would be more appropriate for matters relating
        to the custody of the child to be determined outside England
        and Wales,
the court may by order direct that, while the order under this subsection
is in force, no custody order under section 42(1) with respect to the child
shall be made by any court in or in connection with those proceedings.
 (6) In this section "the relevant date" means—
   (*a*) where an application is made for a custody order under section
        42(1)(*a*), the date of the application (or first application, if two
        or more are determined together), and
   (*b*) where no such application is made, the date of the order.

GENERAL NOTE
 It follows from s.3(2) that the court in which proceedings for divorce, nullity or judicial
separation of the parents are continuing has exclusive jurisdiction in relation to the custody
of a child of the family, even though the child in question is habitually resident in another
part of the U.K. To enable this principle to be carried through, specific provision is made
in s.4 for the following possibilities: (a) the application for divorce, nullity, judicial separation
may be dismissed; (b) a decree of judicial separation may be followed by proceedings for
divorce or nullity; (c) the court dealing with divorce, nullity or judicial separation may itself
wish to waive its jurisdiction in favour of another court.

Subs. (2)
 This subsection limits jurisdiction to make a custody order after the dismissal of
proceedings for divorce, nullity and judicial separation to the case where the application for
the order was made on or before the dismissal of the main proceedings. Under the existing
law an application could be made "within a reasonable period after the dismissal". The Law
Commission thought this "imprecise" (para. 4.98). Since under s.3(2) jurisdiction to make
custody orders on the basis of the child's habitual residence or presence in England and
Wales is excluded by divorce, etc., proceedings elsewhere in the U.K. *only* when those
proceedings are "continuing", it is clearly desirable that the jurisdiction to make a custody
order after dismissal of divorce, etc., proceedings is limited. This is what this subsection
does.

Subs. (3)
 There is no jurisdiction to make a custody order after the grant of a decree of judicial
separation if proceedings for divorce or nullity are continuing in Scotland and Northern
Ireland.
 Relevant date: see s.4(6).

Subs. (4)
 This subsection restores the jurisdiction taken away by s.4(3) in cases where the divorce,
etc., court in Scotland or Northern Ireland decides to waive its custody jurisdiction or to sist
or stay custody proceedings before it, in favour of an English court.

Subs. (5)
 This subsection gives the English court the power to waive its custody jurisdiction in
favour of a court outside England and Wales.
 The court may . . . direct: note the court is not obliged to do so. It has a power, not a
duty.
 No custody order: where the court waives its custody jurisdiction, a court in Scotland or
Northern Ireland is enabled by s.13(5) (Scotland) and s.20(3) (Northern Ireland) to exercise
the jurisdiction it could have exercised under the Act but for the English divorce, judicial
separation or nullity proceedings.

Subs. (6)

This subsection defines "relevant date" for the purpose of this section.

No such application: *i.e.* where the court makes a custody order of its own motion. The "relevant date" to determine whether it has jurisdiction to do so is the date on which it makes the order.

Power of court to refuse application or stay proceedings

5.—(1) A court in England and Wales which has jurisdiction to make a custody order may refuse an application for the order in any case where the matter in question has already been determined in proceedings outside England and Wales.

(2) Where, at any stage of the proceedings on an application made to a court in England and Wales for a custody order, or for the variation of a custody order, it appears to the court—

(a) that proceedings with respect to the matters to which the application relates are continuing outside England and Wales, or

(b) that it would be more appropriate for those matters to be determined in proceedings to be taken outside England and Wales,

the court may stay the proceedings on the application.

(3) The court may remove a stay granted in accordance with subsection (2) above if it appears to the court that there has been unreasonable delay in the taking or prosecution of the other proceedings referred to in that subsection, or that those proceedings are stayed, sisted or concluded.

(4) Nothing in this section shall affect any power exercisable apart from this section to refuse an application or to grant or remove a stay.

GENERAL NOTE

This section gives the courts a *discretion* either to refuse an application relating to the custody or a child or to stay custody proceedings before them pending the outcome of other proceedings elsewhere.

Subs. (1)

Which has jurisdiction: see ss.2 and 3.

May refuse: the court has a discretion. There have been doubts expressed in the past about the freedom of the courts to disclaim jurisdiction in custody cases (see *Re X's Settlement* [1945] Ch. 44, 47; *Babington* v. *Babington*, 1955 S.C. 115, 121). The matter is now placed beyond doubt.

Has already been determined: the case cannot be re-opened, even where circumstances have changed since the order.

Outside England and Wales: the exercise of the discretion is not limited to cases where the other proceedings are or were in the U.K. It may also be exercised in favour of proceedings in foreign countries. Such proceedings include proceedings before a tribunal or other authority having power under the law having effect there to determine questions relating to the custody of children (s.42(7)).

Subs. (1)

This subsection deals with two further situations:

(i) proceedings relating to custody are continuing outside England and Wales;

(ii) although no such proceedings have been commenced, the English court considers it would be more appropriate for the custody matters to be determined in proceedings outside England and Wales.

In either circumstance, the court is given a discretion to stay the proceedings before it. The discretion is designed, *inter alia*, to enable courts to dispose of applications which are made as a delaying tactic or to resolve cases in which more than one court has jurisdiction.

At any stage: the discretion covers every stage of the proceedings.

Outside England and Wales: including foreign countries.

More appropriate: there are many circumstances in which it might be more appropriate, most obviously where the child is habitually resident outside England and Wales.

May stay: the court has a discretion.

This subsection enables a court which has granted a stay under the previous subsection to revoke that stay and resume hearing the proceedings if, in the event, the other proceedings originally expected to continue or to be begun in another country are unreasonably delayed or are themselves stayed, sisted or concluded.

This subsection preserves any other existing powers to refuse an application or to grant or remove a stay.

Duration and variation of custody orders

6.—(1) If a custody order made by a court in Scotland or Northern Ireland (or a variation of such an order) comes into force with respect to a child at a time when a custody order made by a court in England and Wales has effect with respect to him, the latter order shall cease to have effect so far as it makes provision for any matter for which the same or different provision is made by (or by the variation of) the order made by the court in Scotland or Northern Ireland.

(2) Where by virtue of subsection (1) above a custody order has ceased to have effect so far as it makes provision for any matter, a court in England or Wales shall not have jurisdiction to vary that order so as to make provision for that matter.

(3) A court in England and Wales shall not have jurisdiction—

    (*a*) to vary a custody order, other than one made under section 42(1)(*a*) of the Matrimonial Causes Act 1973, or

    (*b*) after the grant of a decree of judicial separation, to vary a custody order made under section 42(1)(*a*) of that Act,

if, on the relevant date, proceedings for divorce, nullity or judicial separation are continuing in Scotland or Northern Ireland in respect of the marriage of the parents of the child concerned.

(4) Subsection (3) above shall not apply if the court in which the proceedings there referred to are continuing has made—

    (*a*) an order under section 13(6) or 21(5) of this Act (not being an order made by virtue of section 13(6)(*a*)(i)), or

    (*b*) an order under section 14(2) or 22(2) of this Act which is recorded as made for the purpose of enabling proceedings with respect to the custody of the child concerned to be taken in England and Wales,

and that order is in force.

(5) Subsection (3) above shall not apply in the case of a variation of a custody order within section 1(1)(*d*) of this Act if the ward is present in England and Wales on the relevant date and the court considers that the immediate exercise of its powers is necessary for his protection.

(6) Where any person who is entitled to the actual possession of a child under a custody order made by a court in England and Wales ceases to be so entitled by virtue of subsection (1) above, then, if there is in force an order for the supervision of that child made under—

    (*a*) section 7(4) of the Family Law Reform Act 1969,

    (*b*) section 44 of the Matrimonial Causes Act 1973,

    (*c*) section 2(2)(*a*) of the Guardianship Act 1973

    (*d*) section 34(5) or 36(3)(*b*) of the Children Act 1975, or

    (*e*) section 9 of the Domestic Proceedings and Magistrates' Courts Act 1978.

that order shall cease to have effect.

(7) In this section "the relevant date" means—

    (*a*) where an application is made for a variation, the date of the application (or first application, if two or more are determined together), and

    (*b*) where no such application is made, the date of the variation.

GENERAL NOTE

This section provides for the duration and variation of an English custody order when a court in either Scotland or Northern Ireland subsequently obtains jurisdiction to make a custody order in respect of the same child.

Subs. (1)

This subsection provides that if a custody order (or a variation of one) made in another part of the U.K. by a court with jurisdiction under this Act comes into force at a time when an order made in England and Wales has effect, the *later* order will prevail over the English order to the extent that it overlaps. This would happen where a child's habitual residence has changed.

Subs. (2)

Where an English order has ceased to have effect in whole or in part by reason of a later order (in Scotland or Northern Ireland), the English court does not have power to vary its own order, so as to make provision for the matters covered by that later order.

Subs. (3)

This provides that if, on the relevant date, proceedings in respect of the marriage of the child's parents are continuing in Scotland or Northern Ireland, the English court is not to have jurisdiction to vary its own custody order, unless the English order itself was made (a) in divorce or nullity proceedings or (b) in judicial proceedings and the variation is made before the decree.

Relevant date: see s.6(7).

Continuing: see s.42(2) and (3).

Marriage of the parents: for the case where a child is a "child of the family" and not of the marriage, see s.42(4).

Subs. (4)

This subsection provides for the possibility that the court in Scotland or Northern Ireland in which the divorce, etc., proceedings are continuing decides to waive its jurisdiction to make a custody order or to sist or stay custody proceedings before it, in favour of the English court. If it does this, the power to vary an English order revives.

Subs. (5)

This subsection preserves the overriding right of the High Court in wardship to vary its own order in respect of a ward who is present in England on the relevant date, if the court considers that the immediate exercise of its powers is necessary for the child's protection.

Present: presence is sufficient to ground jurisdiction.

Immediate exercise: thus indicating that such powers are only exercised in cases of emergency.

Subs. (6)

This subsection provides for the cessation of supervision orders attached to custody orders which themselves have ceased to have effect. The only supervision orders affected are those listed: supervision orders made in criminal proceedings or in care or adoption proceedings are not affected (they are outside the scope of the Act).

Actual possession: *i.e.* has "actual custody" (see s.87(1) of the Children Act 1975).

Subs. (7)

This subsection defines "relevant date" as the date of the application for the variation, or of the first application for variation where two or more are determined together, or, where no application is made, the date on which the variation falls to be made.

No such application: *i.e.* where the court is considering making a variation of a custody order of its own motion or in the course of proceedings for some other purpose, *e.g.* an application for variation of an order for periodical payments for the child's maintenance under Part I of the Domestic Proceedings and Magistrates' Courts Act 1978.

Interpretation of Chapter II

7. In this Chapter "child" means a person who has not attained the age of eighteen.

GENERAL NOTE

Has not attained: age is attained at the commencement of the anniversary of birth (see Family Law Reform Act 1969, s.9(1)).

Eighteen: it should be noted that an order made in England and Wales relating to a child of 16 or over will not be recognised or enforced in Scotland (see s.25(1)) or Northern Ireland (see s.27(5)). See, further, para. 1.22 of the Law Commission report. In practice, custody orders are not likely to be made in respect of children of 16 or over. See *Hewer* v. *Bryant* [1970] 1 Q.B. 357, 369 ("Custody is a dwindling right which the courts will hesitate to enforce against the wishes of the child, and the more so the older he is. It starts with a right of control and ends with little more than advice" *per* Lord Denning M.R.). See also *Gillick* v. *West Norfolk and Wisbech Area Health Authority* [1985] 3 All E.R. 402 and [1986] A.C. 112.

CHAPTER III

JURISDICTION OF COURTS IN SCOTLAND

GENERAL NOTE TO CHAPTER III
The purpose of this chapter is to lay down for the Scottish courts a scheme for jurisdiction to grant custody orders which is uniform with the scheme laid down in Chapter II for England and Wales and in Chapter IV for Northern Ireland. The present chapter also allocates jurisdiction between courts in Scotland.
Following the uniform scheme, the primary basis for jurisdiction of a Scottish court to grant custody orders is the existence of matrimonial proceedings, for it is felt that whenever a court is dealing with matrimonial proceedings, its ability to deal with the family as a whole should supersede the right of any other court. The Scottish court in which such proceedings are taking place will therefore always have jurisdiction during the matrimonial proceedings, and afterwards until the child reaches the age of 16, or until the proceedings are dismissed or decree of absolvitor granted.
If matrimonial proceedings are not taking place anywhere in the U.K., then jurisdiction to make custody orders is granted to the Court of Session on the basis of the child's habitual residence within Scotland; and to the sheriff if the child is habitually resident in the sheriffdom. S.16 provides the same grounds for jurisdiction for orders relating to tutory and curatory. If the child is not habitually resident in any part of the U.K., then the Court of Session will have jurisdiction to make a custody order on the basis of the child's presence, and the sheriff will have jurisdiction on the same basis if the further condition is satisfied that either the pursuer or the defender in the application is habitually resident in the sheriffdom. Provision is also made (s.12) for the Court of Session or the sheriff to exercise jurisdiction on an emergency basis if such is necessary for the protection of the child.
If the court has jurisdiction to make a custody order, then it shall also have the power to make orders for the delivery of the child from one parent to the other. Various consequential powers are also laid down.

Jurisdiction in independent proceedings

8. A court in Scotland may entertain an application for a custody order otherwise than in matrimonial proceedings only if it has jurisdiction under section 9, 10, 12 or 15(2) of this Act.

DEFINITIONS
"custody order": see s.1.
"matrimonial proceedings": see s.18(1).

GENERAL NOTE
This section makes it clear that the only grounds of jurisdiction of the Scottish court in independent custody proceedings are those laid down in ss.9, 10, 12 and 15(2).

Habitual residence

9. Subject to section 11 of this Act, an application for a custody order otherwise than in matrimonial proceedings may be entertained by—
   (*a*) the Court of Session if, on the date of the application, the child concerned is habitually resident in Scotland;
   (*b*) the sheriff if, on the date of the application, the child concerned is habitually resident in the sheriffdom.

"child": see s.18(1).
"custody order": see s.1.
"date of the application": see s.18(2).
"matrimonial proceedings": see s.18(1).

GENERAL NOTE
The primary basis for jurisdiction of the Scottish court to make a custody order in independent proceedings (*i.e.* those not connected with matrimonial proceedings) is that of habitual residence of the child, such residence being determined at the date of the application. The Court of Session will have jurisdiction if the child is habitually resident in Scotland, and the sheriff will have jurisdiction if the child was habitually resident in the sheriffdom. This ground of jurisdiction is subject to s.11 which allows the court seized in matrimonial proceedings in relation to the parents of the child to supersede the jurisdiction granted in this section.

"Habitual residence". This term is not defined in the Act, but it is one commonly used as a connecting factor in family law matters (see *e.g.* the Recognition of Divorces and Legal Separations Act 1971 (repealed in Part II of the present Act) and the Domicile and Matrimonial Proceedings Act 1973). For a judicial discussion of the term, see *Cruse* v. *Chittum* [1974] 2 All E.R. 940. See also note to s.3(1) above. Provision is made in s.41 for the situation in which a child's habitual residence is changed due to its wrongful removal from the jurisdiction. In such a case, the child's original habitual residence is deemed to continue for one year after such removal.

Presence of child

10. Subject to section 11 of this Act, an application for a custody order otherwise than in matrimonial proceedings may be entertained by—
(*a*) the Court of Session if, on the date of the application, the child concerned—
  (i) is present in Scotland; and
  (ii) is not habitually resident in any part of the United Kingdom;
(*b*) the sheriff if, on the date of the application,—
  (i) the child is present in Scotland;
  (ii) the child is not habitually resident in any part of the United Kingdom; and
  (iii) either the pursuer or the defender in the application is habitually resident in the sheriffdom.

"child": see s.18(1).
"custody order": see s.1.
"date of the application": see s.18(2).
"matrimonial proceedings": see s.18(1).

GENERAL NOTE
This section is intended as a safety net to ensure jurisdiction to make custody orders over children not habitually resident in the U.K. and for whom the emergency jurisdiction (s.12 below) would not be appropriate, but over whom it is felt that nevertheless there ought to be jurisdiction. It would cover, for example, the situation of a child abducted abroad (*i.e.* outwith the U.K.) from a parent entitled to custody and then brought to Scotland. There may be no emergency threatening the child, but unless the Scottish court has jurisdiction to hear an application from the person entitled to custody, that person would be denied an effective remedy (unless there was a foreign decree awarding custody to such a person and that decree was entitled to recognition and enforcement in Scotland under s.26: see below).

If the child is not habitually resident in any part of the U.K. then (a) the Court of Session has jurisdiction to make a custody order if the child concerned is present in Scotland, and (b) the sheriff has jurisdiction to make a custody order if the child concerned is present in Scotland and either the pursuer or the defender is habitually resident in the sheriffdom. This is a new jurisdiction conferred upon the sheriff, and the extra element of habitual residence of one of the parties to the application ought to obviate conflicts of jurisdiction between different sheriff courts.

"Either the pursuer or the defender": *i.e.* normally but not necessarily the parents of the child.

"May": the discretion lies with the court.

Provisions supplementary to sections 9 and 10

11.—(1) Subject to subsection (2) below, the jurisdiction of the court to entertain an application for a custody order with respect to a child by virtue of section 9, 10 or 15(2) of this Act is excluded if, on the date of the application, matrimonial proceedings are continuing in a court in any part of the United Kingdom in respect of the marriage of the parents of the child.

(2) Subsection (1) above shall not apply in relation to an application for a custody order if the court in which the matrimonial proceedings are continuing has made one of the following orders, that is to say—

(*a*) an order under section 4(5), 13(6) or 21(5) of this Act (not being an order made by virtue of section 13(6)(*a*)(ii)); or

(*b*) an order under section 5(2), 14(2) or 22(2) of this Act which is recorded as made for the purpose of enabling proceedings with respect to the custody of the child concerned to be taken in Scotland or, as the case may be, in another court in Scotland,

and that order is in force.

DEFINITIONS

"child": see s.18(1).

"continuing": see s.42(2) and (3).

"custody order": see s.1.

"date of the application": see s.18(2).

"matrimonial proceedings": see s.18(1).

"proceedings . . . in respect of the marriage of the parents of the child": see s.42(4).

GENERAL NOTE

The Law Commissions (Law Com. No. 138, Scot. Law Com. No. 91 (1985)) consider that "It is in the interest of the child's welfare and generally to the advantage of all concerned that a court which is dissolving or annulling a marriage or effecting a judicial separation should be able to deal with the affairs of the family as a whole" (at para. 4:7). Primarily for this reason, but also because of the extra expense and inconvenience it would cause if the divorce court were not also the custody awarding court, the design of the Act is to ensure that the court dealing with the matrimonial affairs of the family is primarily the court which will have jurisdiction over the granting of a custody order. This section gives effect to this principle.

Subs. (1)

This excludes, subject to subs. 2 below, jurisdiction based on ss.9, 10, and 15(2) if there are matrimonial proceedings continuing in any court in any part of the U.K. in respect of the marriage of the parents of the child concerned.

"A court in any part of the United Kingdom": this includes both other courts within Scotland, and courts outwith Scotland.

"The marriage of the parents of the child": s.42(4) defines this phrase to include a marriage between one of the parents of the child and another person who accepts the child as one of the family.

"Continuing": matrimonial proceedings are deemed by s.42(2) to be "continuing" in a court in England and Wales or in Northern Ireland until the child reaches the age of 18; and by s.42(3) to be "continuing" in a court in Scotland until the child reaches the age of 16, unless the proceedings have been dismissed, or decree of absolvitor granted before then.

Subs. (2)

See note under s.13(6).

Emergency jurisdiction

12. Notwithstanding that any other court, whether within or outside Scotland, has jurisdiction to entertain an application for a custody order,

the Court of Session or the sheriff shall have jurisdiction to entertain such an application if—
(a) the child concerned is present in Scotland or, as the case may be, in the sheriffdom on the date of the application; and
(b) the Court of Session or sheriff considers that, for the protection of the child, it is necessary to make such an order immediately.

DEFINITIONS
"child": see s.18(1).
"custody order": see s.1.
"date of the application": see s.18(2).

GENERAL NOTE
This section grants a residual jurisdiction to both the Court of Session and the sheriff court based on presence of the child if there exists such emergency as renders it necessary for the protection of the child to make a custody order. This jurisdiction exists whether or not any other court in Scotland or outwith Scotland has jurisdiction and irrespective of the basis of that jurisdiction. This fulfils the Law Commissions' recommendations (at para. 4:99) that, "the ability to invoke the jurisdiction of the court on this basis should [never] be excluded by reason of the fact that some other basis of jurisdiction may be available". So, for example, even although matrimonial proceedings are taking place in England, the Scottish court may still exercise this essentially protective jurisdiction.
"Shall have jurisdiction": though jurisdiction is recognised it is within the discretion of the court as to whether or not to exercise that jurisdiction.
"Necessary": the nature of the emergency which must exist before this section is operable is nowhere defined, and is therefore a matter within the discretion of the court asked to exercise the jurisdiction under this section. It is to be imagined that the necessity must be in some sense immediate. At common law, the Court of Session and (probably) the sheriff had the power to exercise jurisdiction in cases of emergency, and the sort of situations in which that power was exercisable included threats of the child being abducted from its parents (*Murray* v. *Forsyth* 1917 S.C. 721) and threats of "injury, physical or moral, to the child" (*Westergaard* v. *Westergaard* 1914 S.C. 977, *per* Lord Justice-Clerk Macdonald at p.981).

Jurisdiction ancillary to matrimonial proceedings

13.—(1) The jurisdiction of a court in Scotland to entertain an application for a custody order in matrimonial proceedings shall be modified by the following provisions of this section.

(2) A court in Scotland shall not have jurisdiction, after the dismissal of matrimonial proceedings or after decree of absolvitor is granted therein, to entertain an application for a custody order under section 9(1) of the Matrimonial Proceedings (Children) Act 1958 unless the application therefor was made on or before such dismissal or the granting of the decree of absolvitor.

(3) Where, after a decree of separation has been granted, an application is made in the separation process for a custody order, a court in Scotland shall not have jurisdiction to entertain that application if, on the date of the application, proceedings for divorce or nullity of marriage in respect of the marriage concerned are continuing in another court in the United Kingdom.

(4) A court in Scotland shall not have jurisdiction to entertain an application for the variation of a custody order made under section 9(1) of the Matrimonial Proceedings (Children) Act 1958 if, on the date of the application, matrimonial proceedings in respect of the marriage concerned are continuing in another court in the United Kingdom.

(5) Subsections (3) and (4) above shall not apply if the court in which the other proceedings there referred to are continuing has made—
(a) an order under section 4(5) or 21(5) of this Act or under subsection (6) below (not being an order made by virtue of paragraph (a)(ii) of that subsection), or

(*b*) an order under section 5(2), 14(2) or 22(2) of this Act which is recorded as made for the purpose of enabling proceedings with respect to the custody of the child concerned to be taken in Scotland or, as the case may be, in another court in Scotland,
and that order is in force.

(6) A court in Scotland which has jurisdiction in matrimonial proceedings to entertain an application for a custody order with respect to a child may make an order declining such jurisdiction if—

    (*a*) it appears to the court with respect to that child that—

        (i) but for section 11(1) of this Act, another court in Scotland would have jurisdiction to entertain an application for a custody order, or

        (ii) but for section 3(2), 6(3), 20(2) or 23(3) of this Act, a court in another part of the United Kingdom would have jurisdiction to make a custody order or an order varying a custody order; and

    (*b*) the court considers that it would be more appropriate for matters relating to the custody of that child to be determined in that other court or part.

(7) The court may recall an order made under subsection (6) above.

DEFINITIONS
    "child": see s.18(1).
    "custody order": see s.1.
    "date of the application": see s.18(2).
    "matrimonial proceedings": s.18(1).

GENERAL NOTE
    S.11 above enacted that the pre-eminent ground of jurisdiction to make a custody order was the continuance in the court of matrimonial proceedings. By s.42(2) these would continue in a court in Scotland until the child reaches the age of 16, or until the proceedings are dismissed or decree of absolvitor granted. Consequently, this jurisdiction shall exist to the exclusion of any court which might otherwise have jurisdiction to entertain an independent action for custody even after the matrimonial decree has been granted. S.13 modifies these rules in certain circumstances.

Subs. (2)
    Under s.9(1) of the Matrimonial Proceedings (Children) Act 1958 the court could entertain an application to make a custody order notwithstanding the fact that the matrimonial proceedings themselves are dismissed or decree of absolvitor granted so long as the application is made "on or within a reasonable period" after the dismissal of the proceedings. This was felt to be unsatisfactory in respect of the imprecision of the phrase "reasonable period". It would also be inconsistent with the scheme of the present Act which grants jurisdiction to the matrimonial court only until the proceedings are dismissed. Consequently, this subsection restricts the court's power to make a custody order when the matrimonial proceedings are dismissed, or decree of absolvitor granted, to the case where the application has been made on or before the said dismissal or decree.

Subs. (3)
    If after a decree of separation has been granted, an application is then made for a custody order, the court will generally have jurisdiction to entertain it, since (s.42(2) and (3)) the proceedings will still be continuing. This subsection deals with the situation of a separation decree having been granted in one court and divorce or nullity proceedings being raised in another court in the U.K.: the subsection deprives the former court of its jurisdiction over the custody application, and vests that jurisdiction in the court in which the divorce or nullity proceedings are continuing.
    "Another court in the United Kingdom": the other court could either be in Scotland or in any other part of the U.K.

Subs. (4)
    If matrimonial proceedings have been dismissed or decree of absolvitor granted but an application for a custody order has been made on or before such dismissal or absolvitor then the general rule is that the original court may still make the custody order (s.9(1) of the

Matrimonial Proceedings (Children) Act 1958 and s.13(2) of the present Act), and will also have jurisdiction to vary such orders. This subsection modifies this by denying the original court jurisdiction to vary the order if on the date of the application matrimonial proceedings are continuing in respect of the marriage in another court in the United Kingdom. Jurisdiction over custody passes to the court in which the matrimonial proceedings are continuing.

"Another court in the United Kingdom": the other court could either be in Scotland or in any other part of the U.K.

Subs. (5)

The above two subsections will not apply (*i.e.* (a) the court which granted a decree of separation will have jurisdiction to make a custody order notwithstanding that divorce or nullity proceedings are continuing in another court in the U.K.; and (b) the court which dismissed matrimonial proceedings but made a custody order will have power to vary such order notwithstanding that matrimonial proceedings are continuing in another court in the U.K.) if the second court (*i.e.* the one which would otherwise be given jurisdiction under subss. 3 or 4) has waived its jurisdiction in favour of the original court (as it may do under s.4(5) or 21(5) or has sisted or stayed its proceedings in order to allow custody to be determined by the original court (as it may do under ss.5(2), 14(2) or 22(2)). In the latter case it must be recorded that the staying or sisting order has been made specifically to allow the original court to determine the issue of custody.

Subs. (6)

Sometimes the court in which matrimonial proceedings are continuing may consider that the court which would have jurisdiction over custody had that issue arisen independently is the more appropriate one to determine custody. This subsection therefore allows the court with primary jurisdiction to decline that jurisdiction. The other court which would have jurisdiction had the issue of custody arisen on its own would then be empowered to decide the issue of custody by virtue of s.11(2).

This covers the situation in which the matrimonial court has not made a custody order during the matrimonial proceedings, but is asked for such later. Matrimonial proceedings may still be "continuing" (s.42(3)), but it might no longer be appropriate for that court to determine custody, for example because all the parties have moved to another part of the U.K. The matrimonial court may then make an order declining jurisdiction, and jurisdiction would become exercisable on the basis available had the issue of custody arisen independently, *i.e.* habitual residence or presence.

Subs. (7)

This allows the court to recall the declinature order made under subsection (6), and so re-acquire jurisdiction.

Power of court to refuse application or sist proceedings

14.—(1) A court in Scotland which has jurisdiction to entertain an application for a custody order may refuse the application in any case where the matter in question has already been determined in other proceedings.

(2) Where, at any stage of the proceedings on an application made to a court in Scotland for a custody order, it appears to the court—

(*a*) that proceedings with respect to the matters to which the application relates are continuing outside Scotland or in another court in Scotland; or

(*b*) that it would be more appropriate for those matters to be determined in proceedings outside Scotland or in another court in Scotland and that such proceedings are likely to be taken there,

the court may sist the proceedings on that application.

DEFINITION

"custody order": see s.1.

GENERAL NOTE

This section allows the court with jurisdiction to refuse the application if the matter has already been decided in another court, or to sist the proceedings on the application if the proceedings are continuing in another court or proceedings are likely to be taken in a more appropriate court. This provision clears up any doubt there may be that the court can decline its essentially protective jurisdiction in custody cases.

Subs. (1)

"May": the court has the discretion as to whether or not to refuse the application on the ground that the question has already been determined.

"Other proceedings": the court can, if it wishes, refuse the application under this section when there have been other proceedings in Scotland, elsewhere in the U.K., or in any foreign country: there is no territorial limit placed on the "other proceedings".

Subs. (2)

"It appears to the court": it is for the Scottish court seized to determine whether the other court is a more appropriate one to determine the issue of custody.

"Outside Scotland or in another court in Scotland": the proceedings can be taking place or likely to take place in any other court with jurisdiction in Scotland, elsewhere in the U.K., or in any foreign country.

"Likely": this is not a condition existing in the analogous English provision (s.5(2) above). Presumably the court will require some evidence of intention to take proceedings elsewhere. But it is submitted that this need not be construed too onerously, since the court may recall the sist if in fact proceedings are not taken or if there is undue delay in taking such proceedings elsewhere.

Duration, variation and recall of orders

15.—(1) Where, after the making by a court in Scotland of a custody order ("the existing order") with respect to a child,—

(a) a custody order, or an order varying a custody order, competently made by another court in any part of the United Kingdom with respect to that child; or

(b) an order for the custody of that child which is made outside the United Kingdom and recognised in Scotland by virtue of section 26 of this Act,

comes into force, the existing order shall cease to have effect so far as it makes provision for any matter for which the same or different provision is made by the order of the other court in the United Kingdom or, as the case may be, the order so recognised.

(2) Subject to sections 11(1) and 13(3) and (4) of this Act, a court in Scotland which has made a custody order ("the original order") may, notwithstanding that it would no longer have jurisdiction to make the original order, make an order varying or recalling the original order; but if the original order has by virtue of subsection (1) above ceased to have effect so far as it makes provision for any matter, the court shall not have power to vary that order under this subsection so as to make provision for that matter.

(3) In subsection (2) above, an order varying an original order means any custody order made with respect to the same child as the original order was made.

(4) Where any person who is entitled to the custody of a child under a custody order made by a court in Scotland ceases to be so entitled by virtue of subsection (1) above, then, if there is in force an order made by a court in Scotland under section 12(1) of the Matrimonial Proceedings (Children) Act 1958 or section 11(1)(b) of the Guardianship Act 1973 providing for the supervision of that child by a local authority, that order shall cease to have effect.

DEFINITIONS

"child": see s.18(1).

"custody order": see s.1.

GENERAL NOTE

Subs. (1)

This subsection deals with the situation in which a custody order has been made by a court in Scotland and then either another order is competently made by a court in the U.K.

or a foreign order is recognised in Scotland under the terms of s.26: in both cases the later order is given precedence and will thus supersede the earlier order insofar as it is inconsistent therewith.

"After . . . comes into force": the later custody order, or the recognised foreign custody order, will take precedence if it comes into force (rather than having been made) after the making of the original order.

Subs. (2)

A court which had jurisdiction to make a custody order and which did so will retain the power to vary or recall that order even although it no longer has jurisdiction to make the original order. This is subject to certain exceptions:

(1) where the original order has been superseded in terms of subs. (1) above;
(2) where the original court no longer has jurisdiction because matrimonial proceedings are continuing in another court in the U.K. (ss.11(1) and 13(4)); and
(3) where there are divorce or nullity proceedings continuing in a court in the U.K. which superseded (by s.13(3)) the jurisdiction of the court making a custody order during a separation process.

Subs. (3)

"Custody order": as defined in s.1(1)(*b*).

Subs. (4)

Where a custody order is superseded by a later order in terms of subs. (1) above then any supervision order which has been made with the custody order in terms of s.12(1) of the Matrimonial Proceedings (Children) Act 1958, or s.11(1)(*b*) of the Guardianship Act 1973 shall also cease to have effect.

Tutory and curatory

16.—(1) Subject to subsections (2) and (3) below, an application made after the commencement of this Part for an order relating to the tutory or curatory of a pupil or minor may be entertained by—

(*a*) the Court of Session if, on the date of the application, the pupil or minor is habitually resident in Scotland,

(*b*) the sheriff if, on the date of the application, the pupil or minor is habitually resident in the sheriffdom.

(2) Subsection (1) above shall not apply to an application for the appointment or removal of a factor loco tutoris or of a curator bonis or any application made by such factor or curator.

(3) Subsection (1) above is without prejudice to any other ground of jurisdiction on which the Court of Session or the sheriff may entertain an application mentioned therein.

(4) Provision may be made by act of sederunt prescribing, in relation to orders relating to the tutory or curatory of a pupil or minor, what constitutes an application for the purposes of this Chapter.

DEFINITION

"date of the application": see s.18(2).

GENERAL NOTE

The Scottish Law Commission felt that it would be undesirable that different forms of order relating to parental rights should be subject to very different rules for jurisdiction. It has already recommended, in its Report on *Illegitimacy* (Scot. Law Com. (No. 82) 1984) that the court should have jurisdiction to make orders relating to tutory and curatory in matrimonial proceedings. Consequently, jurisdiction based on habitual residence is provided as an additional ground of jurisdiction by this section.

Subs. (1)

"Date of the application": as in s.9 (which provides habitual residence as a ground for jurisdiction in relation to custody orders) the date at which habitual residence is to be determined is the date on which the application is made.

Subs. (2)

The above subsection will not apply to applications relating to the administration of the property of the pupil or minor.

Subs. (3)

"Any other ground": according to Anton (*Private International Law*, at p.381) "It may be said that the domicile of the incapax is the primary ground of jurisdiction". There is however very little clear authority for this (see Anton at pp.380–381).

Orders for delivery of child

17.—(1) Subject to subsection (2) below, an application by one parent of a child for an order for the delivery of the child from the other parent, where the order is not sought to implement a custody order, may be entertained by the Court of Session or a sheriff if, but only if, the Court of Session or, as the case may be, the sheriff would have jurisdiction under this Chapter to make a custody order with respect to the child concerned.

(2) Subsection (1) above is without prejudice to the grounds of jurisdiction on which the Court of Session or a sheriff may entertain an application by a parent who is entitled to the custody of a child for an order for the delivery of the child from a parent who is not so entitled.

(3) Subsection (1) above shall apply to an application by one party to a marriage for an order for the delivery of the child concerned from the other party where the child is the child of one of the parties and has been accepted as one of the family by the other party as it applies to an application by one parent of a child for an order for the delivery of the child from the other parent.

DEFINITIONS
   "child": see s.18(1).
   "custody order": see s.1.

GENERAL NOTE
   In a dispute between parents it was at one time common for one parent, instead of applying for a custody order, to apply for a delivery order against the other parent. In order to ensure that this tactic does not detract from the jurisdictional scheme laid down by the Act, this section provides that the jurisdictional rules in relation to the making of a delivery order are to be identical to the jurisdictional rules in relation to the making of a custody order.

Subs. (1)

"If, but only if": only when there is jurisdiction to make a custody order will a Scottish court have jurisdiction to make a delivery order. If there is no jurisdiction to make one, there shall be no jurisdiction to make the other.

"As the case may be": each court is to be looked at individually, and the very court asked to make a delivery order must be the one with jurisdiction to make the custody order (*i.e.* it is not a sufficient ground of jurisdiction for the sheriff to make a delivery order that the Court of Session has jurisdiction to make a custody order).

Subs. (2)

"Entitled": this subsection deals with the case of one parent having a positive right of custody against the other parent (*e.g.* when a custody order has already been made in that parent's favour).

Subs. (3)

"Accepted as one of the family": this reflects the definition of "child of the family" given in s.42(4).

Interpretation of Chapter III

18.—(1) In this Chapter—
   "child" means a person who has not attained the age of sixteen;
   "matrimonial proceedings" means proceedings for divorce, nullity of marriage or judicial separation.

(2) In this Chapter, "the date of the application" means, where two or more applications are pending, the date of the first of those applications;

and, for the purposes of this subsection, an application is pending until a custody order or, in the case of an application mentioned in section 16(1) of this Act, an order relating to the tutory or curatory of a pupil or minor, has been granted in pursuance of the application or the court has refused to grant such an order.

GENERAL NOTE

Subs. (1)
"Child" is defined as a person who has not attained the age of 16. This reflects the rule of Scots law that a custody order may be made over a child only until it reaches that age. In the rest of the U.K., "child" is defined as a person who has not attained the age of 18. This allows the English and Northern Irish courts to continue to make custody orders over children until the age of 18. However, with recognition and enforcement of such orders (see Chapter V below) the scheme laid down by the Act applies only for children below the age of 16. This is to prevent the Scottish courts having to deal with any custody issue for a child over the age that Scots law itself recognises.

CHAPTER IV

JURISDICTION OF COURTS IN NORTHERN IRELAND

Jurisdiction in cases other than divorce, etc.

19.—(1) A court in Northern Ireland shall not have jurisdiction to make a custody order within section 1(1)(*c*) of this Act, other than one under Article 45(1) of the Matrimonial Causes (Northern Ireland) Order 1978, unless the condition in section 20 of this Act is satisfied.

(2) The High Court in Northern Ireland shall have jurisdiction to make a custody order within section 1(1)(*d*) of this Act if, and only if,—

(*a*) the condition in section 20 of this Act is satisfied, or

(*b*) the ward is present in Northern Ireland on the relevant date (within the meaning of section 20(6) of this Act) and the court considers that the immediate exercise of its powers is necessary for his protection.

GENERAL NOTE
This section sets out the jurisdiction of courts in Northern Ireland to make custody orders in cases other than divorce, nullity or judicial separation.

Subs. (1)
This subsection sets the scene for s.20 by providing that the court in Northern Ireland shall not have jurisdiction to make a custody order within the meaning of s.1(1)(*c*) of the Act other than an order under Art. 45(1) of the Matrimonial Causes (Northern Ireland) Order 1978, unless the condition set out in s.20 is satisfied. The proceedings referred to are proceedings for a custody order under the Guardianship of Infants Act 1886, under Art. 45(2) of the 1978 Order (*i.e.* ancillary to an application for financial relief under Art. 29 of that Order) or under Art. 10(2) or 20(1)(ii) of the Domestic Proceedings (Northern Ireland) Order 1980 (*i.e.* ancillary to proceedings for financial provision in magistrates' courts under Part I of that Order).

Subs. (2)
This subsection relates to the jurisdiction of the High Court in wardship. It preserves the special emergency jurisdiction to deal with any ward who is present in Northern Ireland, where the court considers that the immediate exercise of its powers is necessary for his protection. Otherwise, the provisions of s.20 apply.

Habitual residence or presence of child

20.—(1) The condition referred to in section 19 of this Act is that on the relevant date the child concerned—

(*a*) is habitually resident in Northern Ireland, or

(*b*) is present in Northern Ireland and is not habitually resident in any part of the United Kingdom,

and, in either case, the jurisdiction of the court is not excluded by subsection (2) below.

(2) For the purposes of subsection (1) above, the jurisdiction of the court is excluded if, on the relevant date, proceedings for divorce, nullity or judicial separation are continuing in a court in England and Wales or Scotland in respect of the marriage of the parents of the child concerned.

(3) Subsection (2) above shall not apply if the court in which the other proceedings there referred to are continuing has made—

(*a*) an order under section 4(5) or 13(6) of this Act (not being an order made by virtue of section 13(6)(*a*)(i)), or

(*b*) an order under section 5(2) or 14(2) of this Act which is recorded as made for the purpose of enabling proceedings with respect to the custody of the child concerned to be taken in Northern Ireland,

and that order is in force.

(4) Subject to subsection (5) and (6) below, in this section "the relevant date" means the date of the commencement of the proceedings in which the custody order falls to be made.

(5) In the case of a custody order under section 5 of the Guardianship of Infants Act 1886 "the relevant date" means the date of the application for the order (or first application, if two or more are determined together).

(6) In the case of a custody order within section 1(1)(*d*) of this Act "the relevant date" means—

(*a*) where an application is made for an order, the date of the application (or first application, if two or more are determined together), and

(*b*) where no such application is made, the date of the order.

GENERAL NOTE

Subs. (1)

This subsection establishes the habitual residence of the child as a new basis of jurisdiction in proceedings other than proceedings for divorce, nullity or judicial separation.

Habitually resident: not defined in the Act (though see s.41). See commentary on s.3.

Part of the United Kingdom: see s.42(1).

Present: otherwise the applicant might be left without a remedy in any part of the U.K.

Subs. (2)

This subsection gives priority over custody proceedings in Northern Ireland based on the habitual residence of the child to proceedings in England and Wales or Scotland for divorce, nullity or judicial separation in respect of the marriage of the parents. It follows that if, on the "relevant date" proceedings are "continuing" in England and Wales or Scotland, the Northern Ireland court, except the High Court in an emergency (see s.19(2)(*b*)), will have no jurisdiction to make a custody order.

Relevant date: see s.20(4).

Marriage of the parents: see s.42(4)(*c*).

Subs. (3)

This subsection restores the jurisdiction taken away by s.20(2) in cases where the divorce etc. court in England and Wales or Scotland decides to waive its custody jurisdiction or to sist or stay custody proceedings before it, in favour of the Northern Ireland court.

Subs. (4)

This subsection defines the term "relevant date" for the purpose of the preceding subsections.

Subs. (5)

Applications for custody order s.5 of the Guardianship of Infants Act 1886 may be made after or in the course of proceedings for the appointment of a guardian to deal with the child's property.

The *"relevant date"*: *i.e.* the date of the application for custody. This wording is used to cover the possibility of cross-applications.

Subs. (6)

This subsection refers to custody orders made in wardship proceedings, *i.e.* orders relating to the care and control or education of or access to a child who is a ward of court. Such orders may be applied for or be made by the court of its own motion.

Relevant date: this takes account of the possibility that the question whether a custody order should be made may arise some considerable time after the child has become a ward of court, and that, when the question does arise, jurisdiction in custody now rests, under the scheme embodied in the Act, with a court elsewhere.

Jurisdiction in divorce proceedings, etc.

21.—(1) The enactments relating to the jurisdiction of courts in Northern Ireland to make orders under Article 45(1) of the Matrimonial Causes (Northern Ireland) Order 1978 shall have effect subject to the modifications provided for by this section.

(2) In Article 45(1)(*b*) of that Order (which enables orders as to custody and education to be made immediately, or within a reasonable period, after the dismissal of proceedings for divorce, etc.), for the words "within a reasonable period" there shall be substituted the words "(if an application for the order is made on or before the dismissal)".

(3) A court shall not have jurisdiction to make a custody order under Article 45(1)(*a*) of that Order after the grant of a decree of judicial separation if, on the relevant date, proceedings for divorce or nullity in respect of the marriage concerned are continuing in England and Wales or Scotland.

(4) Subsection (3) above shall not apply if the court in which the other proceedings there referred to are continuing has made—

(*a*) an order under section 4(5) or 13(6) of this Act (not being an order made by virtue of section 13(6)(*a*)(i)), or

(*b*) an order under section 5(2) or 14(2) of this Act which is recorded as made for the purpose of enabling proceedings with respect to the custody of the child concerned to be taken in Northern Ireland,

and that order is in force.

(5) Where a court—

(*a*) has jurisdiction to make a custody order under Article 45(1) of the Matrimonial Causes (Northern Ireland) Order 1978 in or in connection with proceedings for divorce, nullity of marriage or judicial separation, but

(*b*) considers that it would be more appropriate for matters relating to the custody of the child to be determined outside Northern Ireland,

the court may by order direct that, while the order under this subsection is in force, no custody order under Article 45(1) with respect to the child shall be made by any court in or in connection with those proceedings.

(6) In this section "the relevant date" means—

(*a*) where an application is made for a custody order under Article 45(1)(*a*), the date of the application (or first application, if two or more are determined together), and

(*b*) where no such application is made, the date of the order.

GENERAL NOTE

The general effect of this Act is that a court in which proceedings for divorce, nullity or judicial separation of the parents are continuing has exclusive jurisdiction in relation to the custody of a child of the family, even though the child in question is habitually resident in another part of the U.K.

To enable this principle to be applied, specific provision has to be made for the following possibilities;

(i) the application for divorce, etc., may be dismissed;

(ii) a decree of judicial separation may be followed by proceedings for divorce or nullity;

(iii) the court dealing with the divorce, etc., may itself wish to waive its jurisdiction in favour of another court.

S.21 makes specific provision for these matters.

Subs. (1)

This subsection specifies the jurisdiction affected.

Subs. (2)

This subsection limits jurisdiction to make a custody order after the dismissal of proceedings for divorce, nullity or judicial separation to the case where the application for the order was made on or before the dismissal of the main proceedings. This narrows the existing Order, which allowed such an application to be entertained if made "within a reasonable period after the dismissal".

Subs. (3)

This subsection provides for the possibility that proceedings for divorce or nullity are begun in one part of the U.K. after the grant of a decree of judicial separation in another part. In that event, the jurisdiction to make a custody order passes to the divorce etc. court.

The effect of the subsection is to prevent a further order relating to custody being made in the court by which the judicial separation was granted, even though the proceedings for judicial separation might still be regarded as "continuing" within the meaning of the term as defined in s.42(2) of the Act.

Continuing: see s.42(2).

Subs. (4)

This subsection restores the jurisdiction taken away by s.21(3) in cases where the divorce, etc., court in England and Wales or Scotland decides to waive its custody jurisdiction or stay or sist proceedings before it, in favour of the Northern Ireland court.

Subs. (5)

This subsection gives power to a Northern Ireland court before which proceedings for divorce, nullity or judicial separation are "continuing" to waive its jurisdiction in favour of a court outside Northern Ireland. The power of a Northern Ireland court to waive custody jurisdiction is *not* limited to the case where the court thinks it would be more appropriate for the custody issue to be determined in England and Wales or Scotland. It extends also to cases where it thinks it more appropriate that the issue be determined in *another* country.

Subs. (6)

This subsection defines "relevant date" for the purpose of limiting jurisdiction in judicial separation proceedings under s.21(3).

The "relevant date" will normally be the date of the application for a custody order under Art 45(1)(*a*) of the Matrimonial Causes (Northern Ireland) Order 1978, or the date of the first application where two or more are determined together (see para. (a)). But where there is no application, and the court concludes on the facts that it should make a custody order of its own motion, the "relevant date" is the date on which it makes the order.

Power of court to refuse application or stay proceedings

22.—(1) A court in Northern Ireland which has jurisdiction to make a custody order may refuse an application for the order in any case where the matter in question has already been determined in proceedings outside Northern Ireland.

(2) Where, at any stage of the proceedings on an application made to a court in Northern Ireland for a custody order, or for the variation of a custody order, it appears to the court—

(*a*) that proceedings with respect to the matters to which the application relates are continuing outside Northern Ireland, or

(*b*) that it would be more appropriate for those matters to be determined in proceedings to be taken outside Northern Ireland,

the court may stay the proceedings on the application.

(3) The court may remove a stay granted in accordance with subsection (2) above if it appears to the court that there has been unreasonable delay in the taking or prosecution of the other proceedings referred to in that subsection, or that those proceedings are stayed, sisted or concluded.

(4) Nothing in this section shall affect any power exercisable apart from this section to refuse an application or to grant or remove a stay.

GENERAL NOTE

This section gives courts a discretion either to refuse an application relating to the custody of a child or to stay custody proceedings before them pending the outcome of other proceedings elsewhere. The exercise of this discretion is not limited to the case where the other proceedings are or were in the U.K. It may also be exercised in favour of proceedings in foreign countries.

Subs. (1)

This covers the case where the matter in question has already been determined in proceedings outside Northern Ireland. The court is allowed to say that the custody issue will not be reopened, even though the court has jurisdiction, where it is considered that the issue has already been fully explored and there has been no change of circumstances.

Jurisdiction: see ss.19, 20, 21.

May refuse: the court has complete discretion.

Outside Northern Ireland: including outside the U.K.

Subs. (2)

This subsection deals with two further possibilites:

(i) proceedings relating to custody are continuing outside Northern Ireland;

(ii) although no such proceedings have been commenced, the Northern Ireland court considers it would be more appropriate for the custody matters to be determined in proceedings outside Northern Ireland.

In either circumstance, the court is given a *discretion*, if it thinks fit, to stay the proceedings before it.

Subs. (3)

This enables a court which has granted a stay under s.22(2) to revoke that stay and resume hearing the proceedings if, in the event, the other proceedings originally expected to continue or to be begun in another country are unreasonably delayed or are themselves stayed, sisted or concluded. This could occur where, for example, the court in the other country has not dealt with the custody issues, or where one of the parties has said he intends to raise the issue of custody but has failed to do so.

Subs. (4)

This subsection preserves any other existing powers to refuse an application or to grant or remove a stay.

Duration and variation of custody orders

23.—(1) If a custody order made by a court in England and Wales or Scotland (or a variation of such an order) comes into force with respect to a child at a time when a custody order made by a court in Northern Ireland has effect with respect to him, the latter order shall cease to have effect so far as it makes provision for any matter for which the same or different provision is made by (or by the variation of) the order made by the court in England and Wales or Scotland.

(2) Where by virtue of subsection (1) above a custody order has ceased to have effect so far as it makes provision for any matter, a court in Northern Ireland shall not have jurisdiction to vary that order so as to make provision for that matter.

(3) A court in Northern Ireland shall not have jurisdiction—

(a) to vary a custody order, other than one made under Article 45(1)(a) of the Matrimonial Causes (Northern Ireland) Order 1978, or

(b) after the grant of a decree of judicial separation, to vary a custody order made under Article 45(1)(a) of that Order,

if, on the relevant date, proceedings for divorce, nullity or judicial separation are continuing in England and Wales or Scotland in respect of the marriage of the parents of the child concerned.

(4) Subsection (3) above shall not apply if the court in which the proceedings there referred to are continuing has made—

(a) an order under section 4(5) or 13(6) of this Act (not being an order made by virtue of section 13(6)(a)(i)), or

(b) an order under section 5(2) or 14(2) of this Act which is recorded as made for the purpose of enabling proceedings with respect to the custody of the child concerned to be taken in Northern Ireland, and that order is in force.

(5) Subsection (3) above shall not apply in the case of a variation of a custody order within section 1(1)(d) of this Act if the ward is present in Northern Ireland on the relevant date and the court considers that the immediate exercise of its powers is necessary for his protection.

(6) Where any person who is entitled to the actual possession of a child under a custody order made by a court in Northern Ireland ceases to be so entitled by virtue of subsection (1) above, then, if there is in force an order for the supervision of that child made under—

(a) Article 47 of the Matrimonial Causes (Northern Ireland) Order 1978, or

(b) Article 11 of the Domestic Proceedings (Northern Ireland) Order 1980,

that order shall also cease to have effect.

(7) In this section "the relevant date" means—

(a) where an application is made for a variation, the date of the application (or first application, if two or more are determined together), and

(b) where no such application is made, the date of the variation.

GENERAL NOTE
This section deals with the duration of, and powers to revoke, a custody order.

Subs. (1)
This provides that if a custody order (or a variation of one) made in England and Wales or Scotland by a court with jurisdiction under this Act comes into force when an order made in Northern Ireland is in effect, then the *later* order will prevail over the Northern Ireland order to the extent to which it overlaps.

Subs. (2)
Where a Northern Ireland order has ceased to have effect in whole or in part by reason of a later order having been made in England and Wales or Scotland, the Northern Ireland court is not to have power to vary its own order.

Subs. (3)
If, on the relevant date, proceedings in respect of the marriage of the child's parents are "continuing", the Northern Ireland court is not to have jurisdiction to vary its own custody order, unless the Northern Ireland order was made in divorce or nullity proceedings or in judicial separation proceedings and the variation is made before the decree.
Relevant date: see s.23(7).
Continuing: see s.42(2) and (3).
Marriage of the parents . . . . : see s.42(4)(c).

Subs. (4)
This provides for the possibility that the court in England and Wales or Scotland in which the divorce, etc., proceedings are continuing decides to waive its jurisdiction to make a custody order or to stay or sist custody proceedings before it, in favour of the Northern Ireland court. If that happens, the power to vary an earlier Northern Ireland order revives.

Subs. (5)
This preserves the overriding right of the High Court in wardship to vary its own order in respect of a ward who is present in Northern Ireland on the relevant date, if the court considers that the immediate exercise of this power is necessary for the child's protection.

Subs. (6)
This provides for the cessation of supervision orders which were made in conjunction with custody orders which have ceased to have effect.

Subs. (7)

This section defines "relevant date". Paragraph (*b*) covers the situation where the court makes a custody order of its own motion in the course of proceedings for some other purpose (*e.g.* an application for variation of an order for periodical payments for the child's maintenance under Part I of the Domestic Proceedings (Northern Ireland) Order 1980).

Interpretation of Chapter IV

24. In this Chapter "child" means a person who has not attained the age of eighteen.

GENERAL NOTE

This defines "child" as a person who has not attained the age of 18. Note an order made in Northern Ireland relating to a child of 16 or more, though valid in Northern Ireland by reason of the definition of this section, will not be recognised or enforced in England and Wales or Scotland, by reason of s.25(1) and s.27(5) (and see Law Com., para. 1.22).

CHAPTER V

RECOGNITION AND ENFORCEMENT

Recognition of custody orders: general

25.—(1) Where a custody order made by a court in any part of the United Kingdom is in force with respect to a child who has not attained the age of sixteen, then, subject to subsection (2) below, the order shall be recognised in any other part of the United Kingdom as having the same effect in that other part as if it had been made by the appropriate court in that other part and as if that court had had jurisdiction to make it.

(2) Where a custody order includes provision as to the means by which rights conferred by the order are to be enforced, subsection (1) above shall not apply to that provision.

(3) A court in a part of the United Kingdom in which a custody order is recognised in accordance with subsection (1) above shall not enforce the order unless it has been registered in that part of the United Kingdom under section 27 of this Act and proceedings for enforcement are taken in accordance with section 29 of this Act.

GENERAL NOTE

This section provides that a custody order relating to a child under 16 made by a U.K. court is to be recognised in other parts of the U.K. as having the same effect as if it had been made in that part, and as if that court had had jurisdiction to make it. But where enforcement of such an order is required, the order must first be registered (see s.27), and proceedings for enforcement must be taken in accordance with s.29.

Subs. (1)

Custody order: see s.32(1).

Part of the United Kingdom: see s.42(1).

Attained the age of sixteen: attained at the commencement of the sixteenth anniversary of the child's birth.

Appropriate court: see s.32(1).

Subs. (2)

The Law Commission did not consider that "recognition should extend to those parts of custody orders, or to subsequent ancillary orders, which form part of the enforcement process, such as orders to hand over a child at a particular time and place, or authorising the use of force to seize a child" (para. 5.10). This subsection implements this limitation.

Subs. (3)

Unless it has been registered: the importance of registering a custody order in other parts of the U.K., where relevant, is thus stressed.

Recognition: special Scottish rule

26. Any rule of law whereby an order for the custody of a child made outside the United Kingdom is recognised in Scotland shall continue to have effect, except that, after the commencement of this Part, the ground for such recognition shall be that the order was made in the country where the child was habitually resident and not where he was domiciled.

GENERAL NOTE

Under Scots Law custody orders made by a court outside Scotland are recognised if pronounced by the court of the domicile (see *Westergaard* v. *Westergaard*, 1914 S.C. 977 and Anton, *Private International Law*, pp. 378–79). But, where the question of enforcement arises in Scotland, the court treats the child's welfare as the first and paramount consideration: a custody order made by a court of competent jurisdiction outside Scotland is given "the fullest respect and consideration" and is not "blindly enforced" (see *Campins* v. *Campins*, 1979 S.L.T.(Notes) 41, 42 *per* Lord Cameron). This rule is superseded by s.25(1) as regards orders made in England and Wales and Northern Ireland. This section *amends* Scots Law by substituting the child's habitual residence for the child's domicile as the jurisdictional criterion for recognition of orders made outside the U.K.

Any rule of law: *i.e.* the common law rule that Scottish courts will recognise a custody order made by the court of the domicile of the child.

Outside the United Kingdom: this section applies only to foreign custody orders. Custody orders made in another part of the U.K. are to be recognised and enforced in accordance with the new rules laid down by this Chapter.

Habitually resident: this is not defined in the Act. But see commentary on s.3.

Registration

27.—(1) Any person on whom any rights are conferred by a custody order may apply to the court which made it for the order to be registered in another part of the United Kingdom under this section.

(2) An application under this section shall be made in the prescribed manner and shall contain the prescribed information and be accompanied by such documents as may be prescribed.

(3) On receiving an application under this section the court which made the custody order shall, unless it appears to the court that the order is no longer in force, cause the following documents to be sent to the appropriate court in the part of the United Kingdom specified in the application, namely—

(*a*) a certified copy of the order, and

(*b*) where the order has been varied, prescribed particulars of any variation which is in force, and

(*c*) a copy of the application and of any accompanying documents.

(4) Where the prescribed officer of the appropriate court receives a certified copy of a custody order under subsection (3) above, he shall forthwith cause the order, together with particulars of any variation, to be registered in that court in the prescribed manner.

(5) An order shall not be registered under this section in respect of a child who has attained the age of sixteen, and the registration of an order in respect of a child who has not attained the age of sixteen shall cease to have effect on the attainment by the child of that age.

GENERAL NOTE

This section specifies a procedure, similar to that in the Maintenance Orders Act 1950, for the registration of a custody order made in one part of the U.K. in the "appropriate court" in another part of the U.K. Such registration is a necessary pre-condition to enforcement of the order in that part.

Subs. (1)

This subsection provides that any person on whom any rights are conferred by a custody order may apply for registration, and that the application should be made to the court which made the order.

Part of the United Kingdom: see s.42(1).

Subs. (2)

This subsection provides that the manner of application and the information to be supplied are to be prescribed by rules of court (not as yet made).

Subs. (3)

This subsection provides that the court which made the order is to forward the application, together with a certified copy of the order, to the appropriate court in the part of the U.K. specified in the application, unless it appears to the court that the order is no longer in force.

Appropriate court: see s.32(1).

Part of the United Kingdom: see s.42(1).

Subs. (4)

This subsection provides that the prescribed officer in the court to which the application is transmitted is to cause the order to be registered forthwith. He has no discretion as to registration. Any person who wishes to challenge the order or its enforcement should use the procedures set out in ss.30 and 31.

Appropriate court: see s.32(1).

Certified copy: see s.42(1).

Custody order: see s.32(1).

Forthwith: it is submitted this means "immediately." Although time-honoured, the expression is unfortunate because it does not specify a time limit.

Prescribed manner: prescribed by rules of court or Acts of Sederunt (see s.42(2)).

Subs. (5)

This subsection restricts the orders which may be registered to those relating to a child under 16. It further provides that a previously registered order is to cease to have effect when the child in question reaches the age of 16. This limitation rejects the Scots law on custody. An order made in England and Wales or Northern Ireland will continue in force in the part of the U.K. in which it was made until the child reaches the age of 18, but will be outside the scheme for recognition and enforcement in other parts of the U.K. after the child attains the age of 16.

Attained the age of sixteen: "attained" at the commencement of the sixteenth anniversary of the child's birth (Family Law Reform Act 1969, s.9(1)).

Cancellation and variation of registration

28.—(1) A court which revokes, recalls or varies an order registered under section 27 of this Act shall cause notice of the revocation, recall or variation to be given in the prescribed manner to the prescribed officer of the court in which it is registered and, on receiving the notice, the prescribed officer—

    (*a*) in the case of the revocation or recall of the order, shall cancel the registration, and

    (*b*) in the case of the variation of the order, shall cause particulars of the variation to be registered in the prescribed manner.

  (2) Where—

    (*a*) an order registered under section 27 of this Act ceases (in whole or in part) to have effect in the part of the United Kingdom in which it was made, otherwise than because of its revocation, recall or variation, or

    (*b*) an order registered under section 27 of this Act in Scotland ceases (in whole or in part) to have effect there as a result of the making of an order in proceedings outside the United Kingdom, the court in which the order is registered may, of its own motion or on the application of any person who appears to the court to have an interest in the matter, cancel the registration (or, if the order has ceased to have effect in part, cancel the registration so far as it relates to the provisions which have ceased to have effect).

GENERAL NOTE
This section provides for the possibility that a registration may need to be cancelled, or a registered order varied, because of subsequent events.

Subs. (1)
The order may be revoked, recalled or varied in the country in which it was originally made, *e.g.* by the court which made it (or by another court in the same country). This subsection provides that the court which revokes, recalls or varies the order is to notify the registering court, and the prescribed officer is then to cancel the registration, or, as the case may be, to cause the particulars of the registration to be registered.
Prescribed: see s.42(1).

Subs. (2)
The registered order may cease to have effect in the country in which it was made because it has been superseded by a later order made by a U.K. court with jurisdiction (see ss.6(1), 15(1), 23(1)). This subsection provides for this by allowing the court in which the order is registered to cancel the registration, of its own motion or on the application of any person who appears to the court to have an interest in the matter.
Part of the United Kingdom: see s.42(1).
Revocation . . . : as to which see s.28(1).

Enforcement

29.—(1) Where a custody order has been registered under section 27 of this Act, the court in which it is registered shall have the same powers for the purpose of enforcing the order as it would have if it had itself made the order and had jurisdiction to make it; and proceedings for or with respect to enforcement may be taken accordingly.

(2) Where an application has been made to any court for the enforcement of an order registered in that court under section 27 of this Act, the court may, at any time before the application is determined, give such interim directions as it thinks fit for the purpose of securing the welfare of the child concerned or of preventing changes in the circumstances relevant to the determination of the application.

(3) The references in subsection (1) above to a custody order do not include references to any provision of the order as to the means by which rights conferred by the order are to be enforced.

GENERAL NOTE
This section provides that the registering court is to have the same powers of enforcement as it would have in respect of its own orders. The registering court is given power to give interim directions to secure the welfare of the child concerned or to prevent circumstances being changed (*e.g.* the child being removed from the U.K.).

Subs. (1)
Custody order: not including provisions as to the means by which rights conferred by the order are to be enforced (see s.29(3)).
The court: *i.e.* the High Court in England and Wales or Northern Ireland, the Court of Session in Scotland. This is regardless of the level of the court which made the registered order.
Proceedings . . . enforcement: the procedures and safeguards of the registering court are to be complied with.

Subs. (2)
Preventing changes: *e.g.* the court might direct that the child is not to be removed from the U.K.

Subs. (3)

This subsection provides that any provision of the registered order as to the means by which rights conferred by the order are to be enforced is not to be treated as having been made by the registering court.

Means by which rights . . . enforced: e.g. contempt proceedings.

Staying or sisting of enforcement proceedings

30.—(1) Where in accordance with section 29 of this Act proceedings are taken in any court for the enforcement of an order registered in that court, any person who appears to the court to have an interest in the matter may apply for the proceedings to be stayed or sisted on the ground that he has taken or intends to take other proceedings (in the United Kingdom or elsewhere) as a result of which the order may cease to have effect, or may have a different effect, in the part of the United Kingdom in which it is registered.

(2) If after considering an application under subsection (1) above the court considers that the proceedings for enforcement should be stayed or sisted in order that other proceedings may be taken or concluded, it shall stay or sist the proceedings for enforcement accordingly.

(3) The court may remove a stay or recall a sist granted in accordance with subsection (2) above if it appears to the court—

(*a*) that there has been unreasonable delay in the taking or prosecution of the other proceedings referred to in that subsection, or

(*b*) that those other proceedings are concluded and that the registered order, or a relevant part of it, is still in force.

(4) Nothing in this section shall affect any power exercisable apart from this section to grant, remove or recall a stay or sist.

GENERAL NOTE

The purpose of this section is to indicate the grounds on which a person with an interest may ask the court in which a custody order made in another U.K. country has been registered to suspend enforcement of the order, and the action the court may take if such an application is made.

Subs. (1)

This subsection specifies the grounds on which application may be made for enforcement to be suspended: *viz.* that the applicant has taken or intends to take other proceedings which might result in the registered order being superseded or changed.

Registered: if registered in Scotland, see also ss.26 and 28(2)(*b*).

Other proceedings: it may be that the original order was made without jurisdiction.

Subs. (2)

The court considers . . . : it thus has discretion. A stay (or sist) may be refused if the court considers that the objector has made out a prima facie case.

Subs. (3)

The registering court is given discretion to remove a stay or recall a sist where there has been unreasonable delay in the taking or prosecution of the other proceedings or where the other proceedings are concluded and the registered order is still in force. The registering court is thus enabled to retain some control over objections, thereby being able to prevent the exploitation of the provisions of the section to delay enforcement indefinitely.

Subs. (4)

This subsection preserves the registering court's residual power to grant a stay or sist on grounds not covered by s.30(1). The Law Commission does not anticipate this subsection being invoked frequently. It draws attention, however, to possibilities which cannot be defined in advance, such as that the child is undergoing medical treatment which it would be inadvisable to interrupt at the time enforcement is sought.

Dismissal of enforcement proceedings

31.—(1) Where in accordance with section 29 of this Act proceedings are taken in any court for the enforcement of an order registered in that court, any person who appears to the court to have an interest in the matter may apply for those proceedings to be dismissed on the ground that the order has (in whole or in part) ceased to have effect in the part of the United Kingdom in which it was made.

(2) Where in accordance with section 29 of this Act proceedings are taken in the Court of Session for the enforcement of an order registered in that court, any person who appears to the court to have an interest in the matter may apply for those proceedings to be dismissed on the ground that the order has (in whole or in part) ceased to have effect in Scotland as a result of the making of an order in proceedings outside the United Kingdom.

(3) If, after considering an application under subsection (1) or (2) above, the court is satisfied that the registered order has ceased to have effect, it shall dismiss the proceedings for enforcement (or, if it is satisfied that the order has ceased to have effect in part, it shall dismiss the proceedings so far as they relate to the enforcement of provisions which have ceased to have effect).

GENERAL NOTE

This section provides for the possibility that the registered order, for which enforcement is sought, has since ceased to have effect in the U.K. In general this will occur where a later order has been made.

Subs. (1)

Ceased to have effect: because it has been superseded by a later order. The decision whether the original order has ceased to have effect in such circumstances is to be taken by the court of registration.

Subs. (2)

This subsection, which relates only to Scotland, provides for the possibility that an order registered in Scotland (but made in England and Wales or in Northern Ireland) is superseded in Scots law by a later order made in the country of the child's habitual residence, though it remains valid in that part of the U.K. in which it was made. That country will be outside the U.K.

Subs. (3)

In part: the powers in this subsection extend to orders which have partially ceased to have effect, and then apply to that part only.

It shall dismiss: if the registering court is satisfied that the registered order has ceased to have effect, it must dismiss the proceedings.

Interpretation of Chapter V

32.—(1) In this Chapter—
"the appropriate court", in relation to England and Wales or Northern Ireland, means the High Court and, in relation to Scotland, means the Court of Session;
"custody order" includes (except where the context otherwise requires) any order within section 1(3) of this Act which, on the assumptions mentioned in subsection (3) below—
   (a) could have been made notwithstanding the provisions of this Part;
   (b) would have been a custody order for the purposes of this Part; and
   (c) would not have ceased to have effect by virtue of section 6, 15 or 23 of this Act.

(2) In the application of this Chapter to Scotland, "custody order" also includes (except where the context otherwise requires) any order within section 1(3) of this Act which, on the assumptions mentioned in subsection (3) below—

(*a*) would have been a custody order for the purposes of this Part; and

(*b*) would not have ceased to have effect by virtue of section 6 or 23 of this Act,

and which, but for the provisions of this Part, would be recognised in Scotland under any rule of law.

(3) The said assumptions are—

(*a*) that this Part had been in force at all material times; and

(*b*) that any reference in section 1 of this Act to any enactment included a reference to any corresponding enactment previously in force.

GENERAL NOTE

This is the definition section of Chapter V of Part I of this Act. It defines "appropriate court" as the High Court in England and Wales and Northern Ireland, and the Court of Session in Scotland. The concept of "custody order" is further explained.

CHAPTER VI

MISCELLANEOUS AND SUPPLEMENTAL

Power to order disclosure of child's whereabouts

33.—(1) Where in proceedings for or relating to a custody order in respect of a child there is not available to the court adequate information as to where the child is, the court may order any person who it has reason to believe may have relevant information to disclose it to the court.

(2) A person shall not be excused from complying with an order under subsection (1) above by reason that to do so may incriminate him or his spouse of an offence; but a statement or admission made in compliance with such an order shall not be admissible in evidence against either of them in proceedings for any offence other than perjury.

(3) A court in Scotland before which proceedings are pending for the enforcement of an order for the custody of a child made outside the United Kingdom which is recognised in Scotland shall have the same powers as it would have under subsection (1) above if the order were its own.

GENERAL NOTE

This section confers on *all* courts powers in proceedings for or relating to a custody order, including enforcement of a registered order, to require any person who it has reason to believe may have information relevant to where the child is to disclose that information to the court. The High Court in England and Wales already has power to make a summary order to this effect in wardship proceedings (see *Ramsbotham* v. *Senior* (1869) L.R. 8 Eq. 575). The Court of Session in Scotland has power to compel a person who is a party to proceedings and who knows the child's whereabouts to disclose to the court what he knows. It also has power (see *Abusaif* v. *Abusaif*, 1984 S.L.T. 90, 91) to order the hearing of evidence from anyone, even if not a party to the proceedings, who, it has reasonable grounds to believe, may have information which would assist the discovery of the child. It is, however, uncertain what powers are exercisable in custody proceedings by other courts, or what the extent of the High Court's powers may be where the child in question is not a ward of court. This section covers *all* courts in *all* parts of the U.K.

Subs. (1)

Order: the subsection does not indicate what measures may be taken in the event of non-compliance. The Law Commission envisages that failure to comply would be punishable as a contempt or, in the case of a magistrates' court in England and Wales, under s.63 of the Magistrates' Courts Act 1980.

Subs. (2)

This subsection relates to protection against self-incrimination. It provides that a person shall not be excused from supplying information relevant to a child's whereabouts by reason that to do so might incriminate him or his spouse of an offence, but that any statement or admission made in complying with an order for disclosure is not admissible in evidence against either of them in proceedings for an offence other than perjury.

Any offence: *e.g.* a person who has unlawfully removed or detained a child contrary to s.2 of the Child Abduction Act 1984 cannot refuse to say where the child is on the grounds that his answer might incriminate him of an offence under the 1984 Act, but anything he says cannot be used in evidence against him in criminal proceedings for that offence, though it could be used in a prosecution brought for perjury.

Subs. (3)

This subsection makes it clear that in Scotland the power to require disclosure of a child's whereabouts is to apply where the proceedings are for the enforcement of a custody order made outside the U.K.

There is no corresponding provision in relation to courts in England and Wales or Northern Ireland, because the courts in those countries have no power to enforce an order made outside the U.K., and this Act confers no such power on them.

Power to order recovery of child

34.—(1) Where—

(*a*) a person is required by a custody order, or an order for the enforcement of a custody order, to give up a child to another person ("the person concerned"), and

(*b*) the court which made the order imposing the requirement is satisfied that the child has not been given up in accordance with the order,

the court may make an order authorising an officer of the court or a constable to take charge of the child and deliver him to the person concerned.

(2) The authority conferred by subsection (1) above includes authority—

(*a*) to enter and search any premises where the person acting in pursuance of the order has reason to believe the child may be found, and

(*b*) to use such force as may be necessary to give effect to the purpose of the order.

(3) Where by virtue of—

(*a*) section 13(1) of the Guardianship of Minors Act 1971, section 43(1) of the Children Act 1975 or section 33 of the Domestic Proceedings and Magistrates' Courts Act 1978, or

(*b*) Article 37 of the Domestic Proceedings (Northern Ireland) Order 1980,

a custody order (or a provision of a custody order) may be enforced as if it were an order requiring a person to give up a child to another person, subsection (1) above shall apply as if the custody order had included such a requirement.

(4) This section is without prejudice to any power conferred on a court by or under any other enactment or rule of law.

GENERAL NOTE

This section gives the courts in England and Wales or Northern Ireland power to enforce delivery orders. The section does not extend to Scotland (see s.69(6)).

Subs. (1)

This subsection is designed to give to courts in England and Wales or Northern Ireland, when seeking to enforce the delivery of a child to another person in accordance with a custody order, a power to authorise an officer of the court or a constable to take charge of the child and deliver him to the person concerned.

Authorising: for what the authority includes see s.34(2).

Constable: magistrates' courts in England and Wales do not have officers of court to whom an authorisation could appropriately be issued. Hence, the addition of "constable" in this subsection.

Subs. (2)

This subsection gives authority to a person authorised under subsection (1) to enter and search premises and to use such force as may be necessary to give effect to the purpose of the order. The powers thereby extended to constables and to court officers of all courts are analogous to those already possessed by the staff in relation to a ward of court in England and Wales. The Law Commission hopes that "the existence of the powers [in this subsection] will save time and money by reducing the need to resort to wardship proceedings for the purpose of recovering a child" (Law Com., para. 6.37).

Such force as may be necessary: note the subsection does not say "reasonable" force (*cf.* Police and Criminal Evidence Act 1984, s.117).

Subs. (3)

This subsection provides an *additional* method of enforcement of custody orders made by magistrates' courts in England and Wales or Northern Ireland. The statutory provisions cited in the subsection provide that once a copy of a custody order has been served on a person who has the child, the custody order may be enforced as if it were an order of a magistrates' court requiring that person to give up the child to the person entitled to actual custody. The powers specified in s.34(1) and (2) can now be used in support of the listed provisions.

Subs. (4)

This makes it clear that the powers conferred by this section are in *addition* to and not in substitution for any existing powers a court may possess (*e.g.* Magistrates' Courts Act 1980, s.63(3) in relation to s.34(3)).

Powers to restrict removal of child from jurisdiction

35.—(1) In each of the following enactments (which enable courts to restrict the removal of a child from England and Wales)—

(*a*) section 13A(1) of the Guardianship of Minors Act 1971,

(*b*) section 43A(1) of the Children Act 1975, and

(*c*) section 34(1) of the Domestic Proceedings and Magistrates' Courts Act 1978,

for the words "England and Wales" there shall be substituted the words "the United Kingdom, or out of any part of the United Kingdom specified in the order,".

(2) In Article 38(1) of the Domestic Proceedings (Northern Ireland) Order 1980 (which enables courts to restrict the removal of a child from Northern Ireland) for the words "Northern Ireland" there shall be substituted the words "the United Kingdom, or out of any part of the United Kingdom specified in the order,".

(3) A court in Scotland—

(*a*) at any time after the commencement of proceedings in connection with which the court would have jurisdiction to make a custody order, or

(*b*) in any proceedings in which it would be competent for the court to grant an interdict prohibiting the removal of a child from its jurisdiction,

may, on an application by any of the persons mentioned in subsection (4) below, grant interdict or interim interdict prohibiting the removal of the child from the United Kingdom or any part of the United Kingdom, or out of the control of the person in whose custody the child is.

(4) The said persons are—

(*a*) any party to the proceedings,

(*b*) the tutor or curator of the child concerned, and

(*c*) any other person who has or wishes to obtain the custody or care of the child.

(5) In subsection (3) above "the court" means the Court of Session or the sheriff; and for the purposes of subsection (3)(*a*) above, proceedings shall be held to commence—

(*a*) in the Court of Session, when a summons is signeted or a petition is presented;

(*b*) in the sheriff court, when the warrant of citation is signed.

GENERAL NOTE

This section (and the next one) remove the existing anomaly whereby a restriction imposed by a court in one part of the U.K. on taking a child abroad is of no effect in the two other parts.

This section clears the ground for s.36 by modifying the existing powers of certain courts to make orders restricting a child's removal, in particular, by enabling courts to make orders prohibiting a child's removal from the U.K.

Subs. (1)

This subsection amends certain statutory provisions enabling courts to prohibit the removal of a child from England and Wales so as to allow for orders prohibiting or restricting the removal of a child either from the U.K. as a whole or from any part of the U.K. specified in the order.

Subs. (2)

This subsection amends a Northern Ireland provision in a similar way to that in s.35(1).

Subs. (3)

This subsection (and the next) clarify and extend existing Scots law as to the granting of interdict and interim interdict prohibiting the removal of a child from the U.K. or any part of it or out of the control of the person in whose custody the child is. The Court of Session's powers are already extensive, but there was doubt as to how far the powers of the sheriff court extended.

These subsections replace s.13 of the Matrimonial Proceedings (Children) Act 1958, which is repealed (see Sched. 2).

A court in Scotland: *i.e.* the Court of Session or a sheriff court. See further s.35(5).

Subs. (4)

The said persons: the list is *exclusive*.

Any other person: the application will probably have to be made in the course of proceedings in which the person was seeking custody or care of the child.

Effect of orders restricting removal

36.—(1) This section applies to any order made by a court in the United Kingdom prohibiting the removal of a child from the United Kingdom or from any specified part of it.

(2) An order to which this section applies shall have effect in each part of the United Kingdom other than the part in which it was made—

(*a*) as if it had been made by the appropriate court in that other part, and

(*b*) in the case of an order which has the effect of prohibiting the child's removal to that other part, as if it had included a prohibition on his further removal to any place except one to which he could be removed consistently with the order.

(3) The references in subsections (1) and (2) above to prohibitions on a child's removal include references to prohibitions subject to exceptions; and in a case where removal is prohibited except with the consent of the court, nothing in subsection (2) above shall be construed as affecting the identity of the court whose consent is required.

(4) In this section "child" means a person who has not attained the age of sixteen; and this section shall cease to apply to an order relating to a child when he attains the age of sixteen.

GENERAL NOTE

This section is designed to ensure (so far as practicable) that an order made in one part of the U.K. prohibiting the removal of a child from the U.K. or any part of it shall *automatically* have effect in other parts of the U.K.

The provision is necessary to enable *civil* remedies to be invoked.

It is complementary to the Child Abduction Act 1984, under which the unlawful removal of a child may be a criminal offence.

Subs. (1)

Prohibiting the removal: including "prohibitions subject to exceptions" (see s.36(3)).

Child: *i.e.* a person who has not attained the age of sixteen (s.36(4)).

Subs. (2)

Appropriate court: see s.40(1) and s.32(1).

Subs. (3)

Subject to exceptions: *e.g.* allowing a short visit to a parent in another part of the U.K.

Subs. (4)

Attains the age of sixteen: *i.e.* on the sixteenth anniversary of his birth (Family Law Reform Act 1969, s.9(1)). If an English court prohibits the removal of a child until he reaches 18, the child, if 16, could be removed from Scotland without any breach of Scots law, although the removal would still constitute a contempt of the English court.

Surrender of passports

37.—(1) Where there is in force an order prohibiting or otherwise restricting the removal of a child from the United Kingdom or from any specified part of it, the court by which the order was in fact made, or by which it is treated under section 36 of this Act as having been made, may require any person to surrender any United Kingdom passport which has been issued to, or contains particulars of, the child.

(2) In this section "United Kingdom passport" means a current passport issued by the Government of the United Kingdom.

GENERAL NOTE

The purpose of this section is to extend to all U.K. courts with jurisdiction to forbid the removal of a child from the U.K. or any part of it the power already possessed by the High Court in England and Wales (see *Practice Direction (Minor: Passport)* [1981] 1 W.L.R. 558) to order the surrender of any U.K. passport issued to or containing particulars of that child. Obviously, the provision only applies to U.K. passports.

Subs. (1)

Treated under section 36: the power to require surrender of a passport is exercisable by the courts of a part of the U.K. other than the part in which the prohibition or restriction on removal had been imposed.

Contains particulars: this does not necessarily mean that an adult with a child on his or her passport will be deprived of his or her ability to travel overseas. The reference to the child may easily be deleted on the authority of the passport office.

Automatic restriction on removal of wards of court

38.—(1) The rule of law which (without any order of the court) restricts the removal of a ward of court from the jurisdiction of the court shall, in a case to which this section applies, have effect subject to the modifications in subsection (3) below.

(2) This section applies in relation to a ward of court if—

(*a*) proceedings for divorce, nullity or judicial separation in respect of the marriage of his parents are continuing in a court in another part of the United Kingdom (that is to say, in a part of the United Kingdom outside the jurisdiction of the court of which he is a ward), or

(*b*) he is habitually resident in another part of the United Kingdom, except where that other part is Scotland and he has attained the age of sixteen.

(3) Where this section applies, the rule referred to in subsection (1) above shall not prevent—

(*a*) the removal of the ward of court, without the consent of any court, to the other part of the United Kingdom mentioned in subsection (2) above, or

(*b*) his removal to any other place with the consent of either the appropriate court in that other part of the United Kingdom or the court mentioned in subsection (2)(*a*) above.

GENERAL NOTE

The purpose of this section is to limit the effect of the rule of law applying in England and Wales and in Northern Ireland which, without any order of the court, restricts the removal of a ward of court from the court's jurisdiction. The rule, emphasised in *Practice Direction* [1977] 1 W.L.R. 1067, is that it is a criminal contempt to take a ward out of England and Wales (or Northern Ireland, as the case may be) without the prior leave of the court. This rule takes effect immediately on the making of the application to make the child a ward, and operates for 21 days or, if an application for an appointment for a hearing is made within that period, until the determination of the application (see Supreme Court Act 1981, s.41, and R.S.C., Ord. 90, r.4(1)).

The limitation in this section is designed to enable the child to be removed to another part of the U.K., if he is habitually resident there or if proceedings for divorce, nullity or judicial separation are continuing there in respect of the marriage of his parents.

Subs. (1)

This subsection specifies the scope of the section.

Rule of law: see General Note to this section. Note the section *only* applies to *wardship*.

Subs. (2)

Marriage of his parents: and see s.42(4).

Part of the United Kingdom: see s.42(1).

Habitually resident: not defined in the Act. See note on s.3.

Other part is Scotland: the provision does not apply where the other part of the U.K. is Scotland and the child is 16 or more.

Subs. (3)

This limits the general provision in s.38(1). Removal of the ward to another part of the U.K. is thus permitted (see para. (*a*)) as is removal to anywhere else with the consent of either the appropriate court or the court where proceedings for divorce, nullity or judicial separation in respect of the marriage of the ward's parents are pending (see para. (*b*)).

Part of the United Kingdom: see s.42(1).

Appropriate court: see s.40(1).

Duty to furnish particulars of other proceedings

39. Parties to proceedings for or relating to a custody order shall, to such extent and in such manner as may be prescribed, give particulars of other proceedings known to them which relate to the child concerned (including proceedings instituted abroad and proceedings which are no longer continuing).

GENERAL NOTE

This section requires parties to proceedings for or relating to a custody order, including proceedings for the enforcement of a custody order, to give particulars of any other proceedings known to them which relate to the child concerned, wherever they took place, and whether or not they are continuing. The provision is *not* limited to proceedings in the U.K.

Custody order: see s.40(1).

Prescribed: means prescribed by rules of court or act of sederunt (see s.42(1)).

Interpretation of Chapter VI

40.—(1) In this Chapter—
"the appropriate court" has the same meaning as in Chapter V;
"custody order" includes (except where the context otherwise requires) any such order as is mentioned in section 32(1) of this Act.

(2) In the application of this Chapter to Scotland, "custody order" also includes (except where the context otherwise requires) any such order as is mentioned in section 32(2) of this Act.

Habitual residence after removal without consent, etc.

41.—(1) Where a child who—
  (*a*) has not attained the age of sixteen, and
  (*b*) is habitually resident in a part of the United Kingdom,
becomes habitually resident outside that part of the United Kingdom in consequence of circumstances of the kind specified in subsection (2) below, he shall be treated for the purposes of this Part as continuing to be habitually resident in that part of the United Kingdom for the period of one year beginning with the date on which those circumstances arise.

(2) The circumstances referred to in subsection (1) above exist where the child is removed from or retained outside, or himself leaves or remains outside, the part of the United Kingdom in which he was habitually resident before his change of residence—
  (*a*) without the agreement of the person or all the persons having, under the law of that part of the United Kingdom, the right to determine where he is to reside, or
  (*b*) in contravention of an order made by a court in any part of the United Kingdom.

(3) A child shall cease to be treated by virtue of subsection (1) above as habitually resident in a part of the United Kingdom if, during the period there mentioned—
  (*a*) he attains the age of sixteen, or
  (*b*) he becomes habitually resident outside that part of the United Kingdom with the agreement of the person or persons mentioned in subsection (2)(*a*) above and not in contravention of an order made by a court in any part of the United Kingdom.

GENERAL NOTE

This section is designed to deter the unauthorised removal of a child from one jurisdiction to another for the purpose of delaying enforcement of a custody order, or of initiating or reopening custody proceedings in a forum which the person removing the child thinks may be more favourable to him. The section also provides for the possibility of a child not being returned at the end of a period of staying access. The aim of the provision is that, despite a wrongful removal or retention, the courts of the part of the U.K. in which the child was *habitually resident* immediately before the removal or retention will retain jurisdiction for *one year*.

Subs. (1)

Not attained the age of sixteen: attained on the sixteenth anniversary of birth (see Family Law Reform Act 1969, s.9(1)).

Habitually resident: see note on s.3.

Part of the United Kingdom: see s.42(1).

Subs. (2)

Retained outside: after leaving with "authority", *e.g.* not returning from a holiday abroad or a period of staying access.

The right to determine where he is to reside: where there is no court order parents have equal rights to determine where a child shall reside (see Guardianship Act 1973, s.1). If one takes the child out of the part of the U.K. where the child habitually resides, or keeps him outside that part, without the consent of the court, s.41 will apply.

Subs. (3)

This subsection covers two circumstances in which subs. (1) should become inapplicable within the one-year period. In para. (1), the child reaches the age of 16 during the course of the year. In para. (*b*), the lack of authority for the removal or retention is remedied by the agreement (of all the persons entitled to determine where he is to reside) to his acquiring a new habitual residence. An example would be the removal by one parent of a child from England to Scotland without the other parent's consent, where the other parent subsequently agrees to the child's remaining in Scotland. Case (b) *only* applies where the removal, or retention, is not in contravention of a court order.

General interpretation of Part I

42.—(1) In this Part—

"certified copy", in relation to an order of any court, means a copy certified by the prescribed officer of the court to be a true copy of the order or of the official record of the order;

"part of the United Kingdom" means England and Wales, Scotland or Northern Ireland;

"prescribed" means prescribed by rules of court or act of sederunt.

(2) For the purposes of this Part proceedings in England and Wales or in Northern Ireland for divorce, nullity or judicial separation in respect of the marriage of the parents of a child shall, unless thay have been dismissed, be treated as continuing until the child concerned attains the age of eighteen (whether or not a decree has been granted and whether or not, in the case of a decree of divorce or nullity of marriage, that decree has been made absolute).

(3) For the purposes of this Part, matrimonial proceedings in a court in Scotland which has jurisdiction in those proceedings to make a custody order with respect to a child shall, unless they have been dismissed or decree of absolvitor has been granted therein, be treated as continuing until the child concerned attains the age of sixteen.

(4) Any reference in this Part to proceedings in respect of the marriage of the parents of a child shall, in relation to a child who, although not a child of both parties to the marriage, is a child of the family of those parties, be construed as a reference to proceedings in respect of that marriage; and for this purpose "child of the family"—

(*a*) if the proceedings are in England and Wales, means any child who has been treated by both parties as a child of their family, except a child who has been boarded out with those parties by a local authority or a voluntary organisation;

(*b*) if the proceedings are in Scotland, means any child of one of the parties who has been accepted as one of the family by the other party;

(*c*) if the proceedings are in Northern Ireland, means any child who has been treated by both parties as a child of their family, except a child who has been boarded out with those parties by or on behalf of the Department of Health and Social Services or a voluntary organisation.

(5) References in this Part to custody orders include (except where the context otherwise requires) references to custody orders as varied.

(6) For the purposes of this Part each of the following orders shall be treated as varying the custody order to which it relates—

(a) an order which provides for a person to be given access to a child who is the subject of a custody order, or which makes provision for the education of such a child,

(b) an order under section 42(6) of the Matrimonial Causes Act 1973 or Article 45(6) of the Matrimonial Causes (Northern Ireland) Order 1978,

(c) an order under section 42(7) of that Act or Article 45(7) of that Order, and

(d) an order under section 19(6) of the Domestic Proceedings and Magistrates' Courts Act 1978 or Article 20(6) of the Domestic Proceedings (Northern Ireland) Order 1980;

and for the purposes of Chapter V of this Part and this Chapter, this subsection shall have effect as if any reference to any enactment included a reference to any corresponding enactment previously in force.

(7) References in this Part to proceedings in respect of the custody of a child include, in relation to proceedings outside the United Kingdom, references to proceedings before a tribunal or other authority having power under the law having effect there to determine questions relating to the custody of children.

GENERAL NOTE

This section is the interpretation section of Part I of the Act.

Subs. (2)

This subsection is ancillary to the operation of sections in the Act which refer to "continuing" proceedings for divorce, nullity or judicial separation. Those sections provide in effect the jurisdiction of a court to make an order relating to the custody of a child is excluded if on the relevant date proceedings for divorce, etc., in respect of the marriage of the parents of the child concerned are continuing in a court in another part of the U.K. The effect of this subsection is that, once proceedings for divorce, etc., have begun in England and Wales or in Northern Ireland, they are to be treated as continuing until the child in question reaches the age of 18, or until the proceedings are dismissed.

Subs. (3)

This subsection makes provisions for Scotland similar to those made in s.42(2) for England and Wales and Northern Ireland.

Scottish proceedings, however, are only treated as continuing until the child in question reaches the age of 16.

Subs. (4)

This subsection defines "proceedings in respect of the marriage of the parents of a child" and "child of the family" in accordance with definitions found in s.52(1) of the Matrimonial Causes Act 1973 and s.88(1) of the Domestic Proceedings and Magistrates' Courts Act 1978.

It is required to assist in the interpretation of ss.3(2), 6(3), 20(2), 23(3) and 38.

The definition, so far as Northern Ireland is concerned, is taken from Article 2(2) of the Matrimonial Causes (Northern Ireland) Order 1978.

The definition, so far as Scotland is concerned, follows that in Matrimonial Proceedings (Children) Act 1958, s.7(1).

Subs. (5)

This subsection provides that references to custody orders include references to custody orders as varied (except where the context otherwise requires).

Subs. (6)

This subsection provides that certain orders are to be treated for the purposes of the Act as variations of the custody orders to which they relate.

Subs. (7)

This subsection defines the meaning of "proceedings in a country outside the United Kingdom" as including proceedings before a tribunal or other authority having power under the law having effect in that country to determine questions relating to children. In some countries (Switzerland, Denmark, Norway) decisions on custody are taken by administrative authorities.

Application of Part I to dependent territories

43.—(1) Her Majesty may by Order in Council make provision corresponding to or applying any of the foregoing provisions of this Part, with such modifications as appear to Her Majesty to be appropriate, for the purpose of regulating—

(*a*) in any dependent territory;

(*b*) as between any dependent territory and any part of the United Kingdom; or

(*c*) as between any dependent territory and any other such territory,

the jurisdiction of courts to make custody orders, or orders corresponding to custody orders, and the recognition and enforcement of such orders.

(2) In subsection (1) above "dependent territory" means any of the following territories—

(*a*) the Isle of Man,

(*b*) any of the Channel Islands, and

(*c*) any colony.

(3) An Order in Council under subsection (1) above may contain such consequential, incidental and supplementary provisions as appear to Her Majesty to be necessary or expedient.

(4) An Order in Council under subsection (1)(*b*) above which makes provision affecting the law of any part of the United Kingdom shall be subject to annulment in pursuance of a resolution of either House of Parliament.

GENERAL NOTE

This section gives Her Majesty by Order in Council the power to make provision corresponding to, or applying, any of the foregoing provisions of the Act to dependent territories.

PART II

RECOGNITION OF DIVORCES, ANNULMENTS AND LEGAL SEPARATIONS

Divorces, annulments and judicial separations granted in the British Islands

Recognition in United Kingdom of divorces, annulments and judicial separations granted in the British Islands

44.—(1) Subject to section 52(4) and (5)(*a*) of this Act, no divorce or annulment obtained in any part of the British Islands shall be regarded as effective in any part of the United Kingdom unless granted by a court of civil jurisdiction.

(2) Subject to section 51 of this Act, the validity of any divorce, annulment or judicial separation granted by a court of civil jurisdiction in any part of the British Islands shall be recognised throughout the United Kingdom.

GENERAL NOTE

This part of the Act deals with the recognition of divorces, annulments and judicial and legal separations. The same *grounds* are to apply for the recognition of a decree of divorce, nullity or legal separation. It draws a distinction between those granted *in the British Islands* and *overseas* divorces, annulments and legal separations, though the grounds for recognition are the same for both British Islands and overseas decrees.

S.44 deals with the recognition in the U.K. of divorces, annulments and judicial separations granted in the British Islands. It provides that (i) the validity of a divorce, annulment or judicial separation granted by a court of civil jurisdiction in any part of the British Islands is to be recognised throughout the U.K.

There are two *exceptions* to this: (a) recognition may be refused if the divorce, etc., was granted or obtained at a time "when it was irreconcilable with a decision determining the question of the subsistence or validity of the marriage of the parties previously given . . . by a court of civil jurisdiction in that part of the U.K. or by a court elsewhere and recognised or entitled to be recognised in that part of the U.K." (s.51(1)); and (b) recognition may be refused if the divorce or separation was granted or obtained at a time when, according to the law of that part of the U.K. (including its rules of private international law and the provisions of this Part (of the Act)), "there was no subsisting marriage between the parties" (s.51(2)).

Only divorces and annulments obtained in a court of civil jurisdiction are to be recognised (s.44(12)), though divorces obtained before January 1, 1974 and recognised as valid under rules of law applicable before that date are saved from this provision (see s.52(5)(*a*)).

The law contained in this part of the Act applies to divorces etc. obtained before the commencement of the Act (see s.52(1)).

Subs. (1)

Subject to section 52(4) and (5)(a): which saves divorces obtained before January 1, 1974, which were not granted by a court of civil jurisdiction and were recognised as valid under rules of law applicable before that date. A unilateral, non-judicial divorce will thus merit recognition if it was granted (i) before January 1, 1974; (ii) by a person whose personal law allowed him so to divorce his wife. See *Qureshi* v. *Qureshi* [1972] Fam. 173.

Annulment: includes any decree or declarator of nullity of marriage, however expressed (see s.54(1)).

Part of the United Kingdom: see s.54(1).

Subs. (2)

This subsection preserves the existing law as found in the 1971 Act, though it clarifies matters left in doubt by that Act. The 1971 Act in s.1 talked of recognition of divorce decrees "granted under the law of any part of the British Isles". Taken literally this would have required recognition under s.1 of any decree of a foreign court which purported to apply the law of some part of the British Isles. That cannot have been Parliament's intention, but the matter remained in doubt. The new provision refers instead to the validity of any divorce, annulment or judicial separation "granted by a court of civil jurisdiction in any part of the British Islands".

Subject to section 51: there are two exceptions to the general rule. They are (i) the divorce, etc., was irreconcilable with a decision determining the question of the subsistence or validity of the marriage of the parties previously given by a court of civil jurisdiction in that part of the U.K. or by a court elsewhere, and recognised or entitled to be recognised in that part of the U.K. (s.51(1)), and (ii) the divorce or separation was granted or obtained at a time when, according to the law of that part of the U.K., including its rules of private international law, there was no subsisting marriage between the parties (s.51(2)). The second qualification is broadly similar to that in s.8(1) of the 1971 Act, as amended by s.15(2) of the 1973 Act. It means that recognition can be refused if there was no valid marriage between the parties according to English law, including its conflicts rules. So, for example, an English court will remain able to refuse recognition to a Scots divorce because the marriage had already been dissolved either in England or in some other jurisdiction whose divorce is recognised under the 1971 Act or this Act. It would also be able to refuse recognition if it considered that the marriage had already been annulled or had never been validly created.

These are the *only* exceptions. So want of jurisdiction or the fact that the divorce is contrary to public policy are *not* grounds for non-recognition. Clearly, a person who wishes to challenge the validity of the divorce etc. should do so in the jurisdiction in which it was granted, and not in that where recognition is sought. But note s.51(5) which states that "nothing in this part shall be construed as requiring the recognition of any finding of fault made in any proceedings for divorce, annulment or separation or of any maintenance, custody or other ancillary order made in any such proceedings". This provision is broadly similar to s.8(3) of the 1971 Act.

Part of the British Islands: so Channel Island divorces etc. are to be recognised in England and Wales, Scotland and Northern Ireland.

Overseas divorces, annulments and legal separations

Recognition in the United Kingdom of overseas divorces, annulments and legal separations

45. Subject to sections 51 and 52 of this Act, the validity of a divorce, annulment or legal separation obtained in a country outside the British

Islands (in this Part referred to as an overseas divorce, annulment or legal separation) shall be recognised in the United Kingdom if, and only if, it is entitled to recognition—

(a) by virtue of sections 46 to 49 of this Act, or

(b) by virtue of any enactment other than this Part.

GENERAL NOTE

This section provides that a divorce, annulment or legal separation obtained outside the British Islands will only be recognised if it is entitled to recognition under ss.46–49 or by virtue of any other enactment. Such divorces, etc., are classed as "overseas divorces, etc.". This section makes it clear that overseas divorces, legal separations and annulments are not entitled to recognition otherwise than under legislation, that is they are not entitled to recognition under the old common law rules. The common law rules for recognition of annulments and those common law rules for recognition of divorce which survived the 1971 Act are thus effectively swept away.

A divorce, etc., obtained in a country outside the British Isles, but in which proceedings were commenced in a different country from that in which it was obtained (a "transnational divorce") is governed by this Act. It would be an "overseas divorce, annulment or legal separation". The House of Lords held in *Fatima's* case ([1986] 2 All E.R. 32) that a transnational divorce could not be an "overseas" divorce within the 1971 Act. This is overturned by the wording of s.45.

Subject to sections 51 and 52: an overseas divorce, etc., may be refused recognition if (i) it was granted or obtained at a time when it was irreconcilable with a decision determining the question of the subsistence or validity of the marriage of the parties previously given by a court of civil jurisdiction in that part of the U.K. or by a court elsewhere and recognised or entitled to be recognised in that part of the U.K. (s.52(1)); (ii) it was granted or obtained at a time when, according to the law of that part of the U.K. (including its conflicts rules) there was no subsisting marriage between the parties (s.52(2)); (ii) it was obtained without such steps having been taken for giving notice of the proceedings to a party to the marriage as, having regard to the nature of the proceedings, and all the circumstances, should reasonably have been taken (s.52(3)(a)(i)) (this only applies where the divorce, etc., was obtained by means of "proceedings"); (iv) without a party to the marriage having been given, for any reason other than lack of notice, such opportunity to take part in the proceedings as, having regard to those matters, he should reasonably have been given (s.52(3)(a)(ii)) (again, only where there have been proceedings); (v) where there is no official document certifying that the divorce, etc., is effective under the law of the country in which it was obtained or where either party to the marriage was domiciled in another country at the relevant date, there is no official document certifying that the divorce etc., is recognised as valid under the law of that other country (s.52(3)(b)); (vi) the divorce etc., is manifestly contrary to public policy.

Divorce, annulment or legal separation: the same grounds of recognition apply to all three.

Obtained in a country: a divorce obtained in a country outside the British Isles in which the proceedings were commenced in a different country from that in which it was obtained (a "transnational" divorce) is governed by the legislation. Presumably this applies even if those proceedings were commenced in the British Isles. A *talaq* registered in Pakistan having been pronounced in the U.K. is "obtained" in Pakistan (*per* Lord Ackner in *Fatima*. Further, there is no reason why "obtained in a country" should be limited to "obtained in a single country in which all the relevant proceedings took place". A divorce instituted in India (*e.g.* by pronouncement of the words of *talaq* and "obtained" in Pakistan (by completion of that country's administrative requirements) will be a divorce "obtained in a country outside the British Islands".

Outside the British Islands: foreign diplomatic premises in the U.K. are part of the U.K. (*Radwan* v. *Radwan* [1973] Fam. 24).

Any enactment other than this Part: this preserves in relation to the present law as to recognition of overseas divorces and legal separations, and extends to overseas annulments, their recognition under any enactment. But most other enactments (*e.g.* Colonial and Other Territories (Divorce Jurisdiction) Acts 1926 to 1950 and the Matrimonial Causes (War Marriages) Act 1944) are repealed by this Act (see s.68(2) and Sch. 2).

Grounds for recognition

46.—(1) The validity of an overseas divorce, annulment or legal separation obtained by means of proceedings shall be recognised if—

(*a*) the divorce, annulment or legal separation is effective under the
law of the country in which it was obtained; and
(*b*) at the relevant date either party to the marriage—
   (i) was habitually resident in the country in which the divorce,
   annulment or legal separation was obtained; or
   (ii) was domiciled in that country; or
   (iii) was a national of that country.
(2) The validity of an overseas divorce, annulment or legal separation
obtained otherwise than by means of proceedings shall be recognised
if—
(*a*) the divorce, annulment or legal separation is effective under the
law of the country in which it was obtained;
(*b*) at the relevant date—
   (i) each party to the marriage was domiciled in that country; or
   (ii) either party to the marriage was domiciled in that country and
   the other party was domiciled in a country under whose law
   the divorce, annulment or legal separation is recognised as
   valid; and
(*c*) neither party to the marriage was habitually resident in the United
Kingdom throughout the period of one year immediately preceding
that date.
(3) In this section "the relevant date" means—
(*a*) in the case of an overseas divorce, annulment or legal separation obtained by means of proceedings, the date of the
commencement of the proceedings;
(*b*) in the case of an overseas divorce, annulment or legal separation obtained otherwise than by means of proceedings, the
date on which it was obtained.
(4) Where in the case of an overseas annulment, the relevant date fell
after the death of either party to the marriage, any reference in subsection
(1) or (2) above to that date shall be construed in relation to that party as
a reference to the date of death.
(5) For the purpose of this section, a party to a marriage shall be
treated as domiciled in a country if he was domiciled in that country either
according to the law of that country in family matters or according to the
law of the part of the United Kingdom in which the question of recognition
arises.

GENERAL NOTE
This section sets out the grounds for recognition of overseas divorces, annulments and
legal separations.
A distinction is drawn beween divorces, etc., obtained by means of *proceedings* and one
obtained *otherwise than by means of proceedings*.
In the 1971 Act, also reflected in the 1973 Act, the basic dichotomy was between judicial
divorces and non-judicial divorces. The Law Commission in their draft Bill effectively
recommended the scrapping of that distinction by giving a very wide definition to the phrase
"judicial or other proceedings" and applying the same rules to all (Law Com. No. 137, para.
6.11). The Act ignores this recommendation and creates a dichotomy instead between
divorces, etc., obtained by means of proceedings and those obtained otherwise than by
means of proceedings. Ostensibly to give greater protection to women (see *per* Lord
Hailsham, H.L. Vol. 473, col. 1082), the thrust of s.46 is to make it more difficult to satisfy
the requirements for recognition of "non-proceedings divorces" than for "proceedings
divorces". Indeed, to make it more difficult to satisfy the necessary requirements for non-
proceedings divorces than it was before the passing of the Act.
A preliminary question must thus be answered whenever the recognition of an overseas
divorce, etc., is in question: has it been obtained by means of proceedings, or otherwise
than by means of proceedings? This is *not* the same question as whether the divorce, etc.,
has been obtained judicially or non-judicially. Certain non-judicial divorces are obtained by
means of proceedings (*e.g.* the *talaq* in *Quazi* v. *Quazi* [1980] A.C. 744 and the Iranian
administrative divorce in *Makouipour* v. *Makouipour,* 1967 S.C. 116).

Subs. (1)

Proceedings: this is defined in (s.54(1)) as "judicial or other proceedings". Accordingly, judicial discussion of that phrase since 1971 remains of great relevance. Unfortunately, the courts did not interpret the phrase with any real consistency. In *Quazi* v. *Quazi* [1980] A.C. 744, a Pakistani national resident in England had gone back to Pakistan and there pronounced a *talaq* in accordance with the procedures laid down by the Pakistan Muslim Family Laws Ordinance of 1961. Wood J. recognised the *talaq* on the ground that the husband was a national of the country in which the divorce was obtained (and therefore fulfilled the condition in s.3(1)(*b*) of the 1971 Act). The Court of Appeal overruled this on the ground that a *talaq* of this nature was not an "overseas divorce" within the meaning of s.2 because it had not been obtained by "means of judicial or other proceedings" and was not, therefore, entitled to recognition under s.3. The court held that the word "other" ought to read *ejusdem generis* with the word "judicial", so that "proceedings" would mean "quasi-judicial proceedings". The House of Lords overruled the Court of Appeal and held that a "full" *talaq* in this sense was entitled to recognition under the 1971 Act. They held the *ejusdem generis* rule to be inapplicable. They further held that a *talaq* such as the one in *Quazi*, which required various administrative procedures to be followed before it became effective, though not of a judicial character, fell within the description of other proceedings in s.2(*a*), for it constituted an act officially recognised by the law of Pakistan as leading to an effective divorce. Lord Scarman said: "I construe s.2 as applying to any divorce which has been obtained by means of any proceeding, *i.e.* any act or acts, officially recognised as leading to divorce in the country where the divorce was obtained, and which itself is recognised by the law of the country as an effective divorce" (p.824). It is worth comparing this with the test subsequently adopted by the Court of Appeal in *Chaudhary* v. *Chaudhary* [1984] 3 All E.R. 1017. The parties were Pakistani nationals from Azad Kashmir, where the pronouncement of words of *talaq* is sufficient to constitute a divorce. The husband purported to divorce the wife in Kashmir by pronouncing a *talaq* before two witnesses. The husband responded to the wife's divorce petition in England by arguing that the marriage no longer existed, since it had been dissolved by the 'bare' *talaq* he had pronounced in Kashmir. The Court of Appeal held that the divorce was not an "overseas divorce" because it had not been obtained by "other proceedings". The Court of Appeal was unanimous in holding that the mere pronouncement of the words, though possibly a "procedure" was not a proceeding. " 'Proceedings' must at least bear in the statute a meaning which the word would have in normal speech where . . . no one would ordinarily refer to a private act conducted by parties *inter se* or by one party alone, as a proceeding. . . . The word must import a degree of formality and at least the involvement of some agency . . . of or recognised by the state having a function that is more than simply probative" *per* Oliver L.J. (pp.1030–1031).

The Act reflects the policy of *Chaudhary* rather than that of *Quazi*. This may be seen as an invitation to courts to follow the *Chaudhary* line. It is, at the very least, implicit disapproval of the House of Lords in *Quazi*.

Effective: this may be in issue in the case of extra-judicial divorces. But see also a situation like that in *Torok* v. *Torok* [1973] 1 W.L.R. 1066 (Hungarian "partial" decree of divorce not yet "effective", so that marriage not dissolved and petition could be brought in England). Also it might be argued that foreign forum could permit an attack on the validity of its own divorce because procedural requirements (falling short of s.51) are not complied with (*cf. Pemberton* v. *Hughes* [1899] 1 Ch. 781). Another situation in which a divorce, etc., might be ineffective is where the jurisdictional requirements of the foreign forum were not met: if the circumstances are such that the foreign court would itself rescind the decree, it would be "ineffective" and of no effect in England (Scotland or Northern Ireland) (*cf. Papadopoulos* v. *Papadopoulos* [1930] P.55).

Law of the country: what is a country? Are the U.S.A. and Canada countries? Or should one look for connections with New York and Ontario? S.49(2) states that each territory should be regarded as a separate country. Accordingly, at least where the test is domicile or habitual residence, country means New York, not U.S.A., Ontario, not Canada.

Relevant date: see s.46(3)(*a*).

Either party: either petitioner or respondent, husband or wife.

Annulment; see s.54(1).

Habitually resident: see note on s.3.

Domiciled: either according to the law of that country in family matters *or* according to the law of the part of the United Kingdom in which the question of recognition arose (s.46(5)). *Cf.* 1971 Act. s.3(2).

National: according to the law of that country (see for example *Torok* v. *Torok*). "National" is not defined in the Act.

Subs. (2)

A divorce, etc., which has not been obtained by means of proceedings (and so would not have been recognised under s.3 of the 1971 Act, but would have been open to recognition under s.6 of that Act), can be recognised if it fulfils the stated requirements. These requirements are not only stricter than those laid down in s.46(1), but are also stricter than those required before the passing of the Act. (i) Under s.46(2) a divorce, etc., may be recognised if obtained in the country in which both parties were domiciled, or in a country in which one party is domiciled if the other party is domiciled in a country which would recognise the divorce, etc., as valid. But under s.6 of the 1971 Act there was no requirement that either party be domiciled in the country in which the divorce, etc., was obtained, and it was sufficient that both be domiciled in a country (or two countries) in which the divorce, etc., would be recognised (and see *per* Lord Meston, H.L. Vol. 473, col. 1093–1094); (ii) Under s.16(2) of the 1973 Act a non-judicial divorce obtained abroad would not be recognised if *both* parties had been habitually resident in the U.K. for a period of one year immediately preceding the institution of the proceedings (*i.e.* the proceedings leading to the divorce). S.46(2)(c) of this Act precludes recognition of the divorce if either party has been habitually resident in the U.K. for a period of one year immediately preceding the date on which the divorce was obtained. In both the above situations, divorces which might have been entitled to recognition under s.6 of the 1971 Act will not now be so entitled (but see Lord Hailsham, H.L. Vol. 473, col. 1082: "it would be wrong not to continue to afford recognition on a similar basis" to that laid down in s.6).

Otherwise than by means of proceedings: see note on s.46(1), above.

Effective: see note on s.46(1), above.

Law of the country: see note on s.46(1), above.

Relevant date: see note on s.46(3)(b).

Each party . . . domiciled: cf. s.46(1)(b)(ii). On domicile, see s.46(5) and note on s.46(1), above.

Neither habitually resident: the condition in (i) is *in addition* to either (a) or (b). This restriction only applies to divorces, etc., obtained otherwise than by means of proceedings. The previous law applied this restriction to all non-judicial divorces. A "full *talaq*" is not obtained in a court of law and was, therefore, subject to s.16(2) of the 1973 Act. But, since a full *talaq* is one obtained by means of proceedings (*Quazi*), such a divorce will come within the terms of s.46(1) (and this contains no restriction like that in s.16(2) of the 1973 Act). The restriction is, however, *retained for non-proceedings* divorces in s.46(2). Under s.16(2), if both parties were habitually resident in the U.K., they had to be divorced judicially. Under the 1986 Act, if *either* party is habitually resident in the U.K. he will have to obtain a divorce by means of proceedings (including, for these purposes, non-judicial proceedings such as a "full *talaq*").

Subs. (3)

This sorts out the definitional problems of the 1971 Act which identified the "relevant date" as "the date of the institution of the proceedings in the country in which [the divorce] was obtained". As was pointed out in *Fatima*, this pre-supposes that the proceedings were instituted in the same country as that in which the divorce was eventually obtained. In *Fatima*, it was held that the use of these words imparted a condition that, to be recognised under s.3 of the 1971 Act, all proceedings had to take place in one country, so that a "transnational" divorce could not be recognised. Now there is only *one* date to be looked at; that is the date on which the connecting factor is determined, *i.e.* the date of the *institution* of the proceedings in relation to divorces, etc., *obtained* by means of proceedings, and the date the divorce, etc., is *obtained* in relation to divorces, etc., *not* obtained by means of proceeding.

Subs. (4)

This applies only to the recognition of overseas annulments. It adopts the date on which the jurisdictional requirement has to be satisfied in the case of an annulment obtained after the death of one or both spouses as the date of the death of the spouse with whom the jurisdictional link is to be established.

Subs. (5)

This makes it clear that reference to the domicile basis of jurisdiction is reference to *two alternative* concepts of domicile. First, an overseas divorce, etc., will be recognised if it was obtained in the country of either party's domicile in the sense in which that term is used in the foreign country in matters of family law. Secondly, domicile as that concept is understood in the part of the U.K. in which the question of recognition arises.

Cross-proceedings and divorces following legal separations

47.—(1) Where there have been cross-proceedings, the validity of an overseas divorce, annulment or legal separation obtained either in the original proceedings or in the cross-proceedings shall be recognised if—

 (a) the requirements of section 46(1)(b)(i), (ii) or (iii) of this Act are satisfied in relation to the date of the commencement either of the original proceedings or of the cross-proceedings, and

 (b) the validity of the divorce, annulment or legal separation is otherwise entitled to recognition by virtue of the provisions of this Part.

(2) Where a legal separation, the validity of which is entitled to recognition by virtue of the provisions of section 46 of this Act or of subsection (1) above is converted, in the country in which it was obtained, into a divorce which is effective under the law of that country, the validity of the divorce shall be recognised whether or not it would itself be entitled to recognition by virtue of those provisions.

GENERAL NOTE

This embodies the substance of a provision in s.4(1) of the 1971 Act. It has been extended to recognition of overseas annulments and to the recognition of overseas divorces and legal separations on the jurisdictional basis of domicile as that term is used in the U.K. Subs. (2) has similar effect to s.4(2) of the 1971 Act. It applies merely to the conversion of legal separations into divorce but is slightly wider than its counterpart in the 1971 Act (it applies to recognition on the basis of domicile as that term is used in the U.K., as well as to other jurisdictional bases listed in s.46). It also makes it clear that the conversion must be effective in the country in which the legal separation was obtained.

Proof of facts relevant to recognition

48.—(1) For the purpose of deciding whether an overseas divorce, annulment or legal separation obtained by means of proceedings is entitled to recognition by virtue of section 46 and 47 of this Act, any finding of fact made (whether expressly or by implication) in the proceedings and on the basis of which jurisdiction was assumed in the proceedings shall—

 (a) if both parties to the marriage took part in the proceedings, be conclusive evidence of the fact found; and

 (b) in any other case, be sufficient proof of that fact unless the contrary is shown.

(2) In this section "finding of fact" includes a finding that either party to the marriage—

 (a) was habitually resident in the country in which the divorce, annulment or legal separation was obtained; or

 (b) was under the law of that country domiciled there; or

 (c) was a national of that country.

(3) For the purposes of subsection (1)(a) above, a party to the marriage who has appeared in judicial proceedings shall be treated as having taken part in them.

GENERAL NOTE

This section is similar to s.5 of the 1971 Act. The main differences are (i) the section extends to overseas annulments and also to recognition on the basis of domicile as used in the U.K.; (ii) this extension to the English concept of domicile has required subsection (2) not to include within the term "finding of fact" a finding by the foreign court as to domicile in the sense in which the term is used in the U.K.

If the foreign court makes a finding of fact, expressly or by implication, on the basis of which jurisdiction is assumed, that finding is conclusive evidence of that fact if *both* parties to the marriage took part in the proceedings, and in any other case is sufficient proof of that fact unless the contrary is shown. If the proceedings are "judicial" in character, entering an appearance is treated as taking part (s.48(3)). For example, see *Torok* v. *Torok* [1973] 1

W.L.R. 1066 and *Cruse* v. *Chittum* [1974] 2 All E.R. 940 (Mississippi Court finding of fact as to either habitual residence or domicile).

Supplemental

Modifications of Part II in relation to countries comprising territories having different systems of law

49.—(1) In relation to a country comprising territories in which different systems of law are in force in matters of divorce, annulment or legal separation, the provisions of this Part mentioned in subsections (2) to (5) below shall have effect subject to the modifications there specified.

(2) In the case of a divorce, annulment or legal separation the recognition of the validity of which depends on whether the requirements of subsection (1)(*b*)(i) or (ii) of section 46 of this Act are satisfied, that section and, in the case of a legal separation, section 47(2) of this Act shall have effect as if each territory were a separate country.

(3) In the case of a divorce, annulment or legal separation the recognition of the validity of which depends on whether the requirements of subsection (1)(*b*)(iii) of section 46 of this Act are satisfied—

    (*a*) that section shall have effect as if for paragraph (*a*) of subsection (1) there were substituted the following paragraph—

        "(*a*) the divorce, annulment or legal separation is effective throughout the country in which it was obtained;"; and

    (*b*) in the case of a legal separation, section 47(2) of this Act shall have effect as if for the words "is effective under the law of that country" there were substituted the words "is effective throughout that country".

(4) In the case of a divorce, annulment or legal separation the recognition of the validity of which depends on whether the requirements of subsection (2)(*b*) of section 46 of this Act are satisfied, that section and section 52(3) and (4) of this Act and, in the case of a legal separation, section 47(2) of this Act shall have effect as if each territory were a separate country.

(5) Paragraphs (*a*) and (*b*) of section 48(2) of this Act shall each have effect as if each territory were a separate country.

GENERAL NOTE

This section modifies the general provisions in sections 46–48 to provide for the case where the country in which the jurisdictional connection is established is one which comprises several territories which have different systems of law.

Non-recognition of divorce or annulment in another jurisdiction no bar to re-marriage

50. Where, in any part of the United Kingdom—

    (*a*) a divorce or annulment has been granted by a court of civil jurisdiction, or

    (*b*) the validity of a divorce or annulment is recognised by virtue of this Part,

the fact that the divorce or annulment would not be recognised elsewhere shall not preclude either party to the marriage from re-marrying in that part of the United Kingdom or cause the re-marriage of either party (wherever the re-marriage takes place) to be treated as invalid in that part.

GENERAL NOTE

This section deals with the effect of the recognition of a divorce or annulment on the capacity of either party to remarry. It goes further than s.7 of the 1971 Act (which only applies to marriages in the U.K.) in that it applies not only to the recognition of annulments, but in that it extends to capacity to remarry whether in the U.K. or elsewhere, following a divorce or annulment. The section applies both to U.K. and to overseas divorces and annulments recognised in any part of the U.K. This means, therefore, that if for example a French divorce or Northern Irish divorce (or annulment) is recognised in England under s.44 or 45, the fact that it is not recognised in the Republic of Ireland, where the parties are domiciled, will not affect the validity in England of any re-marriage by one of the parties, whether the re-marriage takes place in England, elsewhere in the U.K. or overseas.

Wherever the marriage takes place: this fills the gap in s.7 of the 1971 Act, identified by the Court of Appeal in *Lawrence* v. *Lawrence* [1985] 2 All E.R. 733 (only Purchas L.J. accepted it was a gap).

Refusal of recognition

51.—(1) Subject to section 52 of this Act, recognition of the validity of—

    (*a*) a divorce, annulment or judicial separation granted by a court of civil jurisdiction in any part of the British Islands, or

    (*b*) an overseas divorce, annulment or legal separation,

may be refused in any part of the United Kingdom if the divorce, annulment or separation was granted or obtained at a time when it was irreconcilable with a decision determining the question of the subsistence or validity of the marriage of the parties previously given (whether before or after the commencement of this Part) by a court of civil jurisdiction in that part of the United Kingdom or by a court elsewhere and recognised or entitled to be recognised in that part of the United Kingdom.

(2) Subject to section 52 of this Act, recognition of the validity of—

    (*a*) a divorce or judicial separation granted by a court of civil jurisdiction in any part of the British Islands, or

    (*b*) an overseas divorce or legal separation,

may be refused in any part of the United Kingdom if the divorce or separation was granted or obtained at a time when, according to the law of that part of the United Kingdom (including its rules of private international law and the provisions of this Part), there was no subsisting marriage between the parties.

(3) Subject to section 52 of this Act, recognition by virtue of section 45 of this Act of the validity of an overseas divorce, annulment or legal separation may be refused if—

    (*a*) in the case of a divorce, annulment or legal separation obtained by means of proceedings, it was obtained—

        (i) without such steps having been taken for giving notice of the proceedings to a party to the marriage as, having regard to the nature of the proceedings and all the circumstances, should reasonably have been taken; or

        (ii) without a party to the marriage having been given (for any reason other than lack of notice) such opportunity to take part in the proceedings as, having regard to those matters, he should reasonably have been given; or

    (*b*) in the case of a divorce, annulment or legal separation obtained otherwise than by means of proceedings—

        (i) there is no official document certifying that the divorce, annulment or legal separation is effective under the law of the country in which it was obtained; or

        (ii) where either party to the marriage was domiciled in another country at the relevant date, there is no official document certifying that the divorce, annulment or legal separation is recognised as valid under the law of that other country; or

    (*c*) in either case, recognition of the divorce, annulment or legal separation would be manifestly contrary to public policy.

(4) In this section—

"official", in relation to a document certifying that a divorce, annulment or legal separation is effective, or is recognised as valid, under the law of any country, means issued by a person or body appointed or recognised for the purpose under that law;

"the relevant date" has the same meaning as in section 46 of this Act;

and subsection (5) of that section shall apply for the purposes of this section as it applies for the purposes of that section.

(5) Nothing in this Part shall be construed as requiring the recognition of any finding of fault made in any proceedings for divorce, annulment or separation or of any maintenance, custody or other ancillary order made in any such proceedings.

GENERAL NOTE

This section lays down the only grounds on which a divorce, annulment or separation, which satisfies the other provisions of the Act, may be denied recognition in the part of the U.K. in which the recognition issue is raised. It is based on s.8 of the 1971 Act. It extends to annulments and this extension has meant that specific provision has had to be made for the doctrine of *res judicata*.

Subs. (1)

Irreconcilable with a decision: a *discretion* is conferred on a court in any part of the U.K. to deny recognition to a divorce, annulment or separation on the basis of *res judicata*. And see *Vervaeke* v. *Smith* [1983] 1 A.C. 145.

Subs. (2)

This re-enacts the substance of s.8(1) of the 1971 Act. It applies to the recognition of divorces and separations, not annulments. It applies whether the decree has been granted elsewhere in the British Islands or overseas.

There is an overlap between s.51(1) and (2). If a marriage has already been dissolved or annulled (in the U.K. or elsewhere), before the divorce was obtained whose recognition is in issue in that part, the effect of the earlier decision on the recognition of the later divorce will fall within both s.51(1) and (2). S.51(2) is inappropriate in the case of recognition of *annulments*. Its retention is necessary in the case of recognition of divorces and separations in certain cases where there is no subsisting marriage between the parties at the time of the divorce, etc., according to the law of that part of the U.K. where recognition is sought, as, for example, where the marriage is regarded as void *ab initio*, but no nullity decree has ever been granted.

May: s.51(2) confers a *discretion* to deny recognition. *Cf.* s.8(1) of the 1971 Act which was a mandatory provision.

Subs. (3)

This provides three further discretionary grounds for denying recognition to an overseas divorce, annulment or legal separation. It does *not* apply to the recognition of other *British* divorces, etc. It is similar to s.8(2) of the 1971 Act. It extends also to annulments. Paragraph (*b*) is a new departure, not recommended by the Law Commissions and added by the Government. It is a ground for refusing the recognition of a divorce, etc., obtained otherwise than by means of proceedings. Such a divorce, etc., *may* be refused recognition if there is no official document certifying that the divorce, etc., is effective where it is obtained, or certifying that it is recognised as valid where it is obtained. This official document is not one which certifies the divorce, etc., itself, for if such were necessary for the constitution of the divorce, etc., then, we must assume, the divorce would be obtained by means of proceedings. Rather the document is one of proof which must be granted officially. "Official" is defined (s.51(4)) as meaning "issued by a person or body appointed or recognised for the purpose under that law".

May be refused: the court has a discretion. It may "refuse recognition in the absence of official certification". However, since there is increasing reluctance on the part of English courts to grant recognition to start with (see *Chaudhary, Fatima,* above), it is to be supposed that discretion will normally be exercised in favour of withholding recognition. We would suggest that if a foreign legal system has no official procedure for the granting of certification, an English, etc., court ought to be very slow to refuse recognition on the ground of absence of such a document. But, recognition is normally in the hands initially of administrators (marriage registrars, tax inspectors, immigration officials, etc.) and they are likely to place higher regard on the existence or absence of documentary proof.

Obtained by means of proceedings: see s.46(1).

Steps . . . notice: see *Hack* v. *Hack* (1976) 6 Fam. Law 177; *Newmarch* v. *Newmarch* [1978] Fam. 79; *cf. Joyce* v. *Joyce* [1979] 2 W.L.R. 770.

Obtained otherwise than by means of proceedings: see s.46(2).

Manifestly contrary to public policy: this suggests that discretion should be exercised sparingly (and see *Newmarch* v. *Newmarch* at p.95). An example of a divorce refused recognition on this ground is the case of *Kendall* v. *Kendall* [1977] Fam. 208.

Provisions as to divorces, annulments etc. obtained before commencement of Part II

52.—(1) The provisions of this Part shall apply—

    (*a*) to a divorce, annulment or judicial separation granted by a court of civil jurisdiction in the British Islands before the date of the commencement of this Part, and

    (*b*) to an overseas divorce, annulment or legal separation obtained before that date,

as well as to one granted or obtained on or after that date.

(2) In the case of such a divorce, annulment or separation as is mentioned in subsection (1)(*a*) or (*b*) above, the provisions of this Part shall require or, as the case may be, preclude the recognition of its validity in relation to any time before that date as well as in relation to any subsequent time, but those provisions shall not—

    (*a*) affect any property to which any person became entitled before that date, or

    (*b*) affect the recognition of the validity of the divorce, annulment or separation if that matter has been decided by any competent court in the British Islands before that date.

(3) Subsections (1) and (2) above shall apply in relation to any divorce or judicial separation granted by a court of civil jurisdiction in the British Islands before the date of the commencement of this Part whether granted before or after the commencement of section 1 of the Recognition of Divorces and Legal Separations Act 1971.

(4) The validity of any divorce, annulment or legal separation mentioned in subsection (5) below shall be recognised in the United Kingdom whether or not it is entitled to recognition by virtue of any of the foregoing provisions of this Part.

(5) The divorces, annulments and legal separations referred to in subsection (4) above are—

    (*a*) a divorce which was obtained in the British Islands before 1st January 1974 and was recognised as valid under rules of law applicable before that date;

    (*b*) an overseas divorce which was recognised as valid under the Recognition of Divorces and Legal Separations Act 1971 and was not affected by section 16(2) of the Domicile and Matrimonial Proceedings Act 1973 (proceedings otherwise than in a court of law where both parties resident in United Kingdom);

    (*c*) a divorce of which the decree was registered under section 1 of the Indian and Colonial Divorce Jurisdiction Act 1926;

    (*d*) a divorce or annulment which was recognised as valid under section 4 of the Matrimonial Causes (War Marriages) Act 1944; and

    (*e*) an overseas legal separation which was recognised as valid under the Recognition of Divorces and Legal Separations Act 1971.

GENERAL NOTE

This section deals with the recognition of divorces, annulments and legal separations granted or obtained before the Act comes into force.

It is modelled on s.10(4) of the 1971 Act. It applies to the recognition of annulments, as well as of divorces and legal separations.

Subs. (1)

This preserves the retrospective effect of the 1971 Act in relation to the recognition of overseas divorces and legal separations, *i.e.* applying to those obtained both before and after the 1971 Act came into force.

Subs. (2)

This makes the recognition (or denial of recognition) of both British and overseas divorces, etc., granted or obtained before the Act comes into force, subject to the two provisions in paras. (a) and (b) (as in s.10(4)(*b*) of the 1971 Act.)

Subs. (3)

This makes clear the implementation of the policy (see Law Com. No. 137, para. 4.13) that not only should the Act apply to the recognition of British nullity decrees granted before the Act comes into force, but the law should be changed in relation to the recognition of British decrees of divorce and judicial separation.

Subs. (4)

This preserves the recognition of the validity of certain divorces, annulments and legal separations obtained before the Act comes into force. They are listed in subs. (5), and constitute exceptions to the retrospective and preclusive effect of s.51(1) and (2).

Subs. (5)

This lists five categories of divorce, etc., obtained before the Act comes into force, the recognition of the validity of which is preserved by s.52(4).

Effect of divorces and annulments on wills

53. In subsection (1) of section 18A of the Wills Act 1837 (effect of a decree of divorce or nullity of marriage on wills)—

   (*a*) after the word "court" there shall be inserted the words "of civil jurisdiction in England and Wales"; and

   (*b*) for the words "or declares it void" there shall be substituted the words "or his marriage is dissolved or annulled and the divorce or annulment is entitled to recognition in England and Wales by virtue of Part II of the Family Law Act 1986".

GENERAL NOTE

This section (which *only* applies to England and Wales) amends s.18A of the Wills Act 1837 (which was introduced by the Administration of Justice Act 1982). It is intended to make clear that the effects on a will or bequest of the dissolution or annulment of the testator's marriage shall apply whether the divorce or annulment was *granted* in England and Wales *or* was *recognised* in England and Wales by virtue of this Act.

Interpretation of Part II

54.—(1) In this Part—

   "annulment" includes any decree or declarator of nullity of marriage, however expressed;

   "part of the United Kingdom" means England and Wales, Scotland or Northern Ireland;

   "proceedings" means judicial or other proceedings.

(2) In this Part "country" includes a colony or other dependent territory of the United Kingdom but for the purposes of this Part a person shall be treated as a national of such a territory only if it has a law of citizenship or nationality separate from that of the United Kingdom and he is a citizen or national of that territory under that law.

GENERAL NOTE

This section provides definitions of "annulment", "part of the United Kingdom" and "proceedings". Subs. (2) is in the same terms as s.10(3) of the 1971 Act. It makes it clear that references to "country" include a colony or other dependent territory and that references to nationality only apply, in the case of a dependent territory, if it has a law of citizenship or nationality independent of that of the U.K.

PART III

DECLARATIONS OF STATUS

Declarations as to marital status

55.—(1) Subject to the following provisions of this section, any person may apply to the court for one or more of the following declarations in relation to a marriage specified in the application, that is to say—

(a) a declaration that the marriage was at its inception a valid marriage;

(b) a declaration that the marriage subsisted on a date specified in the application;

(c) a declaration that the marriage did not subsist on a date so specified;

(d) a declaration that the validity of a divorce, annulment or legal separation obtained in any country outside England and Wales in respect of the marriage is entitled to recognition in England and Wales;

(e) a declaration that the validity of a divorce, annulment or legal separation so obtained in respect of the marriage is not entitled to recognition in England and Wales.

(2) A court shall have jurisdiction to entertain an application under subsection (1) above if, and only if, either of the parties to the marriage to which the application relates—

(a) is domiciled in England and Wales on the date of the application, or

(b) has been habitually resident in England and Wales throughout the period of one year ending with that date, or

(c) died before that date and either—

(i) was at death domiciled in England and Wales, or

(ii) had been habitually resident in England and Wales throughout the period of one year ending with the date of death.

(3) Where an application under subsection (1) above is made by any person other than a party to the marriage to which the application relates, the court shall refuse to hear the application if it considers that the applicant does not have a sufficient interest in the determination of that application.

GENERAL NOTE

This part of the Act implements the proposals of the Law Commission's paper *Declarations In Family Matters* (Law Com. No. 132, February 1984). The Law Commission recommended "a new legislative code, based on consistent principles, should replace the existing hotchpotch of statutory and discretionary relief available in matters of matrimonial status, legitimacy, legitimation and adoption" (para. 2.13). There were, as the Law Commission recognised (see the summary in para. 2.12) a number of unsatisfactory features in the former law, contained in s.45 of the Matrimonial Causes Act 1973 and in the court's inherent jurisdiction (R.S.C., Ord. 15, r.16).

Subs. (1)

This subsection sets out the declarations as to marital status which the court may make. The applicant will be able to apply for more than one declaration, *e.g.* he may ask for a declaration that the marriage was initially valid and, in addition, that it subsisted on certain dates and, in the alternative (in case he fails) that it did not subsist on those dates.

Any person: not just the parties to a marriage. Any one with a sufficient interest in obtaining a declaration as to marital status may apply (see s.55(3)). The applicant must satisfy the jurisdictional tests in s.55(2).

The court: *i.e.* the High Court or a county court (s.63).

One or more: the applicant may apply for more than one declaration.

A marriage: as in the previous law (see M.C.A. 1973 s.45(1)), "marriage" is not limited to a monogamous marriage or one now monogamous even if polygamous at its inception (*cf. Ali* v. *Ali* [1968] P. 564: *Cheni* v. *Cheni* [1965] P. 85). An application may be made in respect of a polygamous marriage.

Inception: if any doubt should arise as to what constitutes the "inception" of a marriage (*e.g.* a proxy marriage: *Apt* v. *Apt* [1948] P. 83; *Ponticelli* v. *Ponticelli* [1958] P. 204; *Birang* v. *Birang* (1977) Fam.Law 172 or a marriage invalid at its inception but retrospectively validated: *Starkowski* v. *Att.-Gen.* [1954] A.C. 155), the question should be referred to the *lex loci celebrationis* on the principle *locus regit actum*. But it is difficult to see how on the facts of *Starkowski* it would be possible to hold that the marriage was valid at its inception (it only became valid after registration some years after the ceremony). Presumably, though, an English court would have jurisdiction to make a declaration where a marriage was valid at its inception but subsequently retrospectively invalidated by the *lex loci celebrationis*. Whether it would recognise the invalidation is another question (French courts in the aftermath of the Spanish civil war recognised such legislation where French nationals' marriages were not affected).

Valid marriage: There is no power to make a declaration that a marriage was initially invalid (see s.58(5)(*a*)). An applicant who wishes to have it declared that his marriage was initially invalid will have to apply for a decree of nullity. Under the previous law it was held (see *Kassim* v. *Kassim* [1962] P. 224) that the court had the power to make such a declaration but where it found the marriage to be void it should grant a decree of nullity. But in *Kunstler* v. *Kunstler* [1969] 1 W.L.R. 1506 such an application under R.S.C., Ord. 15, r.16 was entertained. See also *Woyno* v. *Woyno* [1960] 1 W.L.R. 986; *Gray* v. *Formosa* [1963] P. 259; *Merker* v. *Merker* [1963] P. 283. The matter is now put beyond doubt by this statutory provision.

Subsisted: declarations under R.S.C., Ord.15, r.16 have been made to this effect in the past. See *Garthwaite* v. *Garthwaite* [1964] P. 356 ("the marriage remains a valid and subsisting marriage"); *Qureshi* v. *Qureshi* [1972] Fam. 173 ("her marriage to the respondent subsisted and that her status was that of a married woman") and *Re Meyer* [1971] P. 298 ("the marriage subsisted on" a specified date).

The value of such a declaration is evident from the facts of a case such as *Re Meyer*. In *Re Meyer*, the wife divorced her husband in Nazi Germany in 1939 under duress. Both parties lived together in England for some years and, on the husband's death, his widow became entitled in Germany to a pension from a Compensation Fund for the benefit of victims of the Nazi regime. The German court ordered the wife to prove by production of a suitable English document that she was validly married according to English law on certain specified dates. The wife successfully sought from the English court a declaration that the 1939 German decree was invalid and that she was lawfully married to the husband on the relevant dates. A declaration might also be useful if an applicant were seeking to establish succession rights in a foreign country (see Law Com., para. 3.8).

Did not subsist: see note on "subsisted".

Validity of divorce . . . .: such declarations were made under the previous law. See *Har-Shefi* v. *Har-Shefi* [1953] P. 161; *Lee* v. *Lau* [1967] P. 14; *Cruse* v. *Chittum* [1974] 2 All E.R. 940; *Quazi* v. *Quazi* [1980] A.C. 744 (all on divorce); and *Abate* v. *Abate* [1961] P. 29; *Merker* v. *Merker* [1963] P. 283; *Law* v. *Gustin* [1976] Fam. 155; *Perrini* v. *Perrini* [1979] Fam. 84 (all on annulment). Note the term "decree of divorce" is not used. It is thus possible for a declaration to be sought as to the validity of an extra-judicial divorce obtained before s.16(1) of the Domicile and Matrimonial Proceedings Act 1973 came into force. This section is not retrospective and does not affect the validity of an extra-judicial divorce obtained before 1974 which would be recognised as valid by the old recognition rules (the common law: see *Qureshi* v. *Qureshi* [1972] Fam. 173).

Outside England and Wales: *i.e.* in the British Islands or overseas.

Entitled to recognition: see Part II of this Act.

So obtained: *i.e.* in the British Islands (outside England and Wales) or overseas.

Not entitled to recognition: see Part II of this Act.

Subs. (2)

A court: *i.e.* the High Court or a county court (see s.63).

Either of the parties: the jurisdictional test need only be satisfied by *one* of the parties to the marriage.

Domiciled: domiciled according to English law (see *Re, Martin* [1900] P. 211). For the meaning of "domicile", Dicey and Morris, *Conflict of Laws* (10th ed., 1980), ch. 7 should be consulted.

Habitually resident: there is no authoritative definition of this. The word "habitual" indicates a quality of residence rather than a period of residence (*Cruse* v. *Chittum* [1974] 2 All E.R. 940, 942–43). In an earlier Law Commission report (Law Com. No. 48), it was said that the residence must be more than transient or casual; once established, however, it is not necessarily broken by a temporary absence" (para. 42).

Throughout the period: this does not mean that one of the parties must have lived in England and Wales throughout the whole of the one year period preceding the application. An applicant could be "habitually resident" in England and Wales for the preceding year without living in England and Wales for any of that period. What is in question are "durable ties" (Law Com. No. 48, *loc. cit.*) and not actual residence.

Died: there is no jurisdiction if the applicant is neither domiciled nor habitually resident in England and Wales, if the other party to the marriage satisfied either of these jurisdictional requirements at his (or her) death. The applicant need not be a party to the marriage (see s.55(3)). An application may be brought after the death of one party or of both parties to the marriage, provided *one* of the parties to the marriage satisfied one of the jurisdictional requirements.

Subs. (3)

Any person (not just a party to the marriage) may apply for a declaration as to the marital status. This subsection accordingly limits applications to those with a "sufficient interest" in the determination of the application.

Sufficient interest: this is not defined. It will be for the court to decide, in the light of all the circumstances of the case, whether the applicant has a sufficient interest. The Law Commission does not think the courts will have any difficulty in determining whether the test has been satisfied (para. 3.33). Examples where applications may be made are to test the validity of a parent's marriage where there is a property or succession claim.

Declarations as to legitimacy or legitimation

56.—(1) Any person may apply to the court for a declaration that he is the legitimate child of his parents.

(2) Any person may apply to the court for one (or for one or, in the alternative, the other) of the following declarations, that is to say—

(*a*) a declaration that he has become a legitimated person;

(*b*) a declaration that he has not become a legitimated person.

(3) A court shall have jurisdiction to entertain an application under subsection (1) or (2) above if, and only if, the applicant—

(*a*) is domiciled in England and Wales on the date of the application, or

(*b*) has been habitually resident in England and Wales throughout the period of one year ending with that date.

(4) In this section "legitimated person" means a person legitimated or recognised as legitimated—

(*a*) under section 2 or 3 of the Legitimacy Act 1976; or

(*b*) under section 1 or 8 of the Legitimacy Act 1926; or

(*c*) by a legitimation (whether or not by virtue of the subsequent marriage of his parents) recognised by the law of England and Wales and effected under the law of any other country.

GENERAL NOTE

This section allows for declarations as to legitimacy and legitimation. The existing law Matrimonial Causes Act 1973, s.45(1) and (2) is extended to cover legitimations recognised at common law.

Subs. (1)

This subsection gives the court power to grant a declaration that the applicant is legitimate. For jurisdiction, see s.56(3).

The court: *i.e.* the High Court or a county court (s.63).

He is: the court does not have the power to make a declaration as to the legitimacy of any person other than the applicant.

Legitimate child: but not to make a declaration that the applicant is or was illegitimate (s.58(5)(*b*)). Included in "legitimacy" is the putative marriage concept. A declaration may thus be applied for by a child of a putative marriage rendered legitimate by s.1 of the Legitimacy Act 1976 (see *F and F* v. *Att.-Gen.* [1980] 10 Fam. Law 60).

Subs. (2)

This subsection gives the court power to grant a declaration that the applicant has, or has not, become a legitimated person, as the case may be. For jurisdiction, see s.56(3).

The court: *i.e.* the High Court or a county court (s.63).

He has: only the person whose legitimation is in issue may apply.

Legitimated person: as to which see s.56(4).

Not become a legitimated person: the Law Commission believes "there may well be cases in which such a declaration could serve a useful purpose, particularly where the alleged legitimation has occurred as a result of formal acknowledgement, or governmental act, in a foreign country" (p.18, n.124).

Subs. (3)

Domiciled: the domicile of origin of a legitimate child is that of his father. Until the child attains the age of 16 (or marries under that age), his domicile will follow that of his father. If the father dies it will thereafter usually follow that of his mother, as it will where the parents are separated and the child has his home with his mother and has no home with his father (Domicile and Matrimonial Proceedings Act 1973, s.4). A circular argument will, accordingly, develop when considering whether the court has jurisdiction where the applicant for a declaration of legitimacy is an unmarried child under 16. His domicile depends on whether he is legitimate. Jurisdiction to entertain the application depends on his domicile. The Law Commission envisages that courts will resolve this problem by not declining jurisdiction until it has been ascertained whether or not the alleged fact upon which its jurisdiction is found is true. As the Law Commission notes (p.33, n.224): "in practice this will mean that jurisdiction will depend on the domicile of the child's mother or father, as the case may be". See also for an analogy *Garthwaite* v. *Garthwaite* [1964] P. 356.

Habitually resident: see note in s.55(2), above.

Subs. (4)

This subsection defines "legitimated person" for the purposes of this section. The definition corresponds to that in s.10(1) of the Legitimacy Act 1976. The effect of paragraphs (a) and (b) is that a declaration of legitimation may be granted in respect of legitimation by virtue of the Legitimacy Act 1976, or recognised under either of those Acts; and paragraph (c) makes it clear that a declaration may also be granted that the applicant is recognised as legitimated at common law.

Not by virtue of subsequent marriage: for example, by recognition: see *Luck's Settlement Trusts, Re* [1940] Ch. 864.

Recognised by the law of England . . . effected under the law of any other country: note where the legitimation is by an act other than marriage, the Legitimacy Act has no application. It will be recognised only if the common law rules are satisfied: *i.e.* the father must be domiciled in a country, the law of which accepts the validity of the legitimation, both at the time of the child's birth and at the time of the act effecting the legitimation (see *Luck's Settlement Trusts, Re* [1940] Ch. 864).

Declarations as to adoptions effected overseas

57.—(1) Any person whose status as an adopted child of any person depends on whether he has been adopted by that person by either—

    (*a*) an overseas adoption as defined by section 72(2) of the Adoption Act 1976, or

    (*b*) an adoption recognised by the law of England and Wales and effected under the law of any country outside the British Islands,

may apply to the court for one (or for one or, in the alternative, the other) of the declarations mentioned in subsection (2) below.

(2) The said declarations are—

    (*a*) a declaration that the applicant is for the purposes of section 39 of the Adoption Act 1976 the adopted child of that person;

    (*b*) a declaration that the applicant is not for the purposes of that section the adopted child of that person.

(3) A court shall have jurisdiction to entertain an application under subsection (1) above if, and only if, the applicant—

    (*a*) is domiciled in England and Wales on the date of the application, or

    (*b*) has been habitually resident in England and Wales throughout the period of one year ending with that date.

(4) Until the Adoption Act 1976 comes into force—

    (*a*) subsection (1) above shall have effect as if for the reference to

section 72(2) of that Act there were substituted a reference to
section 4(3) of the Adoption Act 1968; and
(*b*) subsection (2) above shall have effect as if for the reference to
section 39 of that Act there were substituted a reference to
Part II of Schedule 1 to the Children Act 1975.

GENERAL NOTE
This section empowers the court to grant a declaration that English law recognises, or
does not recognise, that the applicant has been validly adopted abroad. There is no reported
case in which a court has had to consider an application for a declaration as to the validity
of a foreign adoption. Nor is there any reason to suppose that the courts did not have
inherent power under R.S.C.; Ord. 15, r.16. But, as the Law Commission expressed it
(para. 3.16), "declarations as to foreign adoptions . . . determine a person's status." They,
accordingly, thought it "desirable, in the interests of certainty and convenience, that
legislation . . . should deal comprehensively with declarations as to family status, and at the
same time provide clear and satisfactory jurisdictional rules for declarations as to the validity
of foreign adoptions" (*idem*).
The Adoption Act 1976 is not yet in force: hence the need to provide a transitional
provision in subs. (4).

Subs. (1)
Any person whose status . . .: only the child himself may apply for a declaration.
Overseas adoption: *i.e.* defined as "an adoption of such a description as the Secretary of
State may by order specify, being a description of adoptions of children appearing to him to
be effected under the law of any country outside Great Britain" (see s.72(2) of the Adoption
Act 1976).
An adoption recognised . . .: An adoption may fall to be recognised either under the
Adoption Act 1968 (or Adoption Act 1976 when it is brought into operation), or under the
common law. The Secretary of State may specify any adoption effected under the law of any
country outside Great Britain as an "overseas adoption" (see above). The intention is to
recognise not only Convention adoptions made in countries which are parties to the Hague
Convention of 1965, but also adoptions made in countries whose adoption law is broadly
similar to that in England. S.I. 1973 No. 19 specifies a large number of countries as within
the category of "overseas adoptions". These include the whole Commonwealth, except India
and Bangladesh, all Western European countries, the U.S.A., South Africa, Israel, Turkey,
Greece, Yugoslavia. Under this Order, there need be no juristic link of any kind between
the adopters and the country where the adoption was made. Recognition is automatic,
subject to two qualifications: (i) recognition must not be contrary to public policy; (ii) the
adoption must have been effected under statutory, not common or customary law. *Other*
adoptions still depend on the common law. On this see *Re Valentine's Settlement* [1965] Ch.
226, where the C.A. refused to recognise an adoption granted in a country where the
adopters were not domiciled. There were differing opinions expressed as to whether in
addition it was necessary for the children to be ordinarily resident in the country where the
adoption took place. It is possible that the rule in *Armitage* v. *Att.-Gen.* [1906] P. 135 may
apply by analogy to adoption. (See, further, Dicey and Morris, *Conflict of Laws,* 10th ed.
1980) rule 69.

Subs. (2)
For the purposes of section 39 . . . which deals with the status conferred by adoption.

Subs. (3)
Domiciled: according to English law.
Habitually resident: see note on s.3.
Until the Adoption Act 1976 . . .: there are no plans to bring this into force in the
immediate future. It is unlikely to come into force until all of its provisions are operative.

General provisions as to the making and effect of declarations

58.—(1) Where on an application for a declaration under this Part the
truth of the proposition to be declared is proved to the satisfaction of the
court, the court shall make that declaration unless to do so would
manifestly be contrary to public policy.
(2) Any declaration made under this Part shall be binding on Her
Majesty and all other persons.

(3) The court, on the dismissal of an application for a declaration under this Part, shall not have power to make any declaration for which an application has not been made.

(4) No declaration which may be applied for under this Part may be made otherwise than under this Part by any court.

(5) No declaration may be made by any court, whether under this Part or otherwise—

(a) that a marriage was at its inception void;

(b) that any person is or was illegitimate.

(6) Nothing in this section shall effect the powers of any court to grant a decree of nullity of marriage.

GENERAL NOTE

This section provides that the matter in question in respect of which a declaration is sought must be proved to the satisfaction of the court. It further provides that declarations should be available as of right, subject to the power of the court to withhold relief as a matter of public policy. The section stresses that a declaration under the Act operates *in rem* and lays down that the court, in dismissing an application for a declaration, shall not be able to make another declaration for which an application has not been made. The declarations provided for in this Act are only available under this Act, so that they are not available under R.S.C., Ord. 15, r.16. Lastly, this section lays down that the court is not able to grant a declaration that a marriage was initially invalid, or one that a person is or was illegitimate.

Subs. (1)

Satisfaction of the court: "this formulation is intended to make it clear that the standard of proof is high and that the court should only grant a declaration when the evidence in support of it is clear and convincing. As in other civil proceedings, the burden of proof will be on the applicant" *per* Law Commission, p.37, n. 265. A declaration ought not to be granted if the evidence in support of it cannot be properly investigated and verified (*Aldrich* v. *Att.-Gen* [1968] P. 281, 291).

Manifestly be contrary to public policy: public policy should only be invoked in exceptional circumstances.

Subs. (2)

Shall be binding: that is to say, it is binding *in rem*. "If the judgment is as to the status of a person, it is called a judgment *in rem* and everyone must accept it" *per* Lord Simon of Glaisdale in *The Ampthill Peerage* [1977] A.C. 547, 576. Lord Wilberforce, *ibid.*, p.568, stressed the importance of finality in litigation as to a person's status: "It is vitally necessary that the law should provide a means for any doubts which may be raised to be resolved once and for all and that they should not be capable of being reopened whenever, allegedly, some new material is brought to light which might have been borne upon the question. How otherwise could a man's life be planned?" A declaration can, of course, be rescinded if obtained by fraud (in this context "fraud" means "dishonesty": "there must be conscious and deliberate dishonesty and the declaration must be obtained by it" *per* Lord Wilberforce in *The Ampthill Peerage* [1977] A.C. 547, 571).

Subs. (3)

Any declaration: but the court will be able to make a declaration applied for by the *respondent* in answer to the petition: *e.g.* the respondent may cross-pray for a declaration that a foreign divorce is invalid in answer to an application for a declaration that the divorce is valid if he has a sufficient interest in obtaining the declaration, and in those circumstances the court may grant this declaration.

Subs. (4)

No declaration . . . may be made otherwise: so declarations which may be applied for in this Part of this Act may not now be applied for under R.S.C., Ord. 15, r.16. But declarations which may not be applied for may presumably still be sought under the inherent jurisdiction of the court. However, the two most obvious exclusions from declarations under this Part of the Act (that a marriage was at its inception void; that any person is or was illegitimate) cannot be sought under R.S.C. Ord., 15, r.16 (see s.58(5)).

Subs. (5)
Or otherwise: *i.e.* under the inherent jurisdiction of the court.
Void: a nullity decree should be sought. See also s.58(6) making it clear that the court retains powers to grant a decree of nullity of marriage. Forcing parties to resort to nullity (*e.g.* where the parties to a marriage are of the same sex, as in *Corbett* v. *Corbett* [1971] P. 83) prevents the circumvention of ancillary proceedings by an application for a declaration.
Illegitimate: this exclusion is confined to declarations *in rem*. "It would not prevent a finding that a person is illegitimate where such a finding is necessary in the course of litigation, for instance in a succession case" *per* Law Commission, para. 3.22.

Subs. (6)
Decree of nullity: which, in relation to marriages void *ab initio*, declares that there never was a marriage. This subsection is thus a saving provision and makes it clear that subs. (5) does not prevent the court from making a decree of nullity in respect of a void marriage.

Provisions relating to the Attorney-General

59.—(1) On an application for a declaration under this Part the court may at any stage of the proceedings, of its own motion or on the application of any party to the proceedings, direct that all necessary papers in the matter be sent to the Attorney-General.
(2) The Attorney-General, whether or not he is sent papers in relation to an application for a declaration under this Part, may—
    (*a*) intervene in the proceedings on that application in such manner as he thinks necessary or expedient, and
    (*b*) argue before the court any question in relation to the application which the court considers it necessary to have fully argued.
(3) Where any costs are incurred by the Attorney-General in connection with any application for a declaration under this Part, the court may make such order as it considers just as to the payment of those costs by parties to the proceedings.

GENERAL NOTE
This section, which sets out the Attorney-General's role in relation to declarations, is intended to provide innocent parties with some protection against the force of *in rem* declarations.

Subs. (1)
The court may: the Attorney-General under the previous law (M.C.A. 1973, s.45(6)) had to be brought in in all cases. There is now a discretion on the court.

Subs. (2)
Sent papers: see s.59(1).

Subs. (3)
Costs: there is a similar provision in divorce and nullity proceedings in relation to costs incurred by the Queen's Proctor (see M.C.A. 1973, ss.8(2) and (5)).

Supplementary provisions as to declarations

60.—(1) Any declaration made under this Part, and any application for such a declaration, shall be in the form prescribed by rules of court.
(2) Rules of court may make provision—
    (*a*) as to the information required to be given by any applicant for a declaration under this Part;
    (*b*) as to the persons who are to be parties to proceedings on an application under this Part;
    (*c*) requiring notice of an application under this Part to be served on the Attorney-General.

(3) No proceedings under this Part shall affect any final judgment or decree already pronounced or made by any court of competent jurisdiction.

(4) The court hearing an application under this Part may direct that the whole or any part of the proceedings shall be heard in camera, and an application for a direction under this subsection shall be heard in camera unless the court otherwise directs.

GENERAL NOTE

This section, *inter alia*, makes provision for hearings *in camera*.

Subs. (1)

Rules of court: the Law Commission envisages that the procedure for the declarations would be "substantially similar" to that applicable in cases under s.45 of the M.C.A. 1973 (para.3.62).

Subs. (2)

This reproduces the existing s.45(8) of the M.C.A. 1973.

Subs. (4)

This corresponds to s.49(9) of the M.C.A. 1973.

Abolition of right to petition for jactitation of marriage

61. No person shall after the commencement of this Part be entitled to petition the High Court or a county court for jactitation of marriage.

GENERAL NOTE

This section abolishes the right to petition for jactitation of marriage. A previous attempt to abolish it failed in 1857. Since it was "not now very familiar to this court" in 1820 (*Hawke* v. *Corri* (1820) 2 Hag.Con. 280, 281, 284), "had fallen into disuse" in 1900 (*Cowley* v. *Cowley* [1900] P. 305, 313), it is surprising that it has survived till now. There are about six reported cases this century.

False claims about the existence of a marriage may, of course, be defamatory, in which case an action in defamation may lie. If they are merely embarrassing to the aggrieved party, there will be henceforth no remedy.

After the commencement of this Part: any proceedings for jactitation of marriage begun before the commencement are not affected by this section (see s.68(3)(*b*)).

Repeal of Greek Marriages Act 1884

62.—(1) The Greek Marriages Act 1884 shall cease to have effect.

(2) Any marriage in respect of which a declaration that it was a valid marriage could before the commencement of this Part have been made under the Greek Marriages Act 1884 is hereby declared to have been a valid marriage; but nothing in this subsection shall affect any status or right which would not have been affected by a declaration under that Act.

GENERAL NOTE

Between 1836 and 1837 marriages between members of the Greek Orthodox Church were celebrated in England in the belief (which was probably wrong) that they were valid in English law. The Greek Marriages Act 1884 was passed to remove doubts as to the validity of these marriages (some 36 marriages were in question). The Act left these marriages invalid unless an interested party applied for a declaration of validity with regard to any particular marriage. Two applications are reported, but it is not known whether any other applications have been made. Applications could still have been made since the 1884 Act can be invoked by "any persons interested in the validity of any such marriage." This section finally puts the matter to rest by declaring the marriages in 1836 and 1837 to have been valid. This enables the 1884 Act to be repealed and its procedure to be abolished.

Subs. (1)

Shall cease to have effect: the Act is repealed (see Sched. 2).

Subs. (2)
   Any marriage: as noted above there were only 36 marriages in question.
   Hereby declared: *i.e.* the marriage was valid when celebrated.
   Status or right: see Greek Marriages Act 1884, s.2.

Interpretation of Part III

63. In this Part "the court" means the High Court or a county court.

GENERAL NOTE
   This section gives jurisdiction over declarations in this part of the Act to the High Court and to county courts. All county courts, not just divorce county courts, are given jurisdiction. Applications to the High Court should be made to the Family Division of the High Court (see Sched. 1, para. 26).

PART IV

MISCELLANEOUS AND GENERAL

Family proceedings rules

64.—(1) Rules of court made by the rule-making authority constituted by section 40 of the Matrimonial and Family Proceedings Act 1984 (family proceedings rules) which relate to the costs of proceedings—

   (*a*) may amend or repeal any statutory provision relating to the practice and procedure of the Supreme Court or county courts so far as may be necessary in consequence of provision made by the rules; and

   (*b*) may make different provision for different cases or descriptions of cases, for different circumstances or for different areas.

   (2) Notwithstanding anything in the Legal Aid Act 1974, the power conferred by subsection (1)(*b*) above includes power to make different provision according to whether each or any of the parties is entitled to legal aid in connection with the proceedings.

   (3) In this section—

   "legal aid" means legal aid under Part I of the Legal Aid Act 1974;
   "statutory provision" means any enactment, whenever passed, or any provision contained in subordinate legislation (as defined in section 21(1) of the Interpretation Act 1978), whenever made.

   (4) In relation to any time before the coming into force of section 40 of the Matrimonial and Family Proceedings Act 1984, this section shall have effect as if the reference in subsection (1) above to that section were a reference to section 50 of the Matrimonial Causes Act 1973 (matrimonial causes rules).

GENERAL NOTE
   This section, far and away the most controversial provision in the Act (see, *e.g.* the debate at the Committee Stage of the House of Lords at Vol. 476, cols. 9–23) gives additional powers to the Matrimonial Causes Rules Committee and the rule-making authority constituted by s.40 of the Matrimonial and Family Proceedings Act 1984. The section is "badly needed" in order that matrimonial work, "from having the status of a poor relation, a second-class citizen, can be brought into line with the rest of the Supreme Court" *per* Lord Chancellor, Vol. 476, col. 17. The intention is that "any future rules will allow unassisted litigants to have their costs taxed by the taxing master, because there will be no prescribed scales for them at all" *per* Lord Chancellor at col. 21.

Amendments of Child Abduction Act 1984

65. In section 1(2)(*b*), 3(*a*) and (5) of the Child Abduction Act 1984 (offence of abduction of child by parent etc.), for the words "a court in

England and Wales" there shall be substituted the words "a court in the United Kingdom".

GENERAL NOTE
This section makes an amendment to several provisions in the Child Abduction Act 1984 to take account of changes in the law on custody effected by this Act.

Amendments of Child Abduction (Northern Ireland) Order 1985

66. In Article 3(2)(*b*), (3) and (5)(*a*) of the Child Abduction (Northern Ireland) Order 1985 (offence of abduction of child by parents etc.), for the words "a court in Northern Ireland" there shall be substituted the words "a court in the United Kingdom".

GENERAL NOTE
This section makes an amendment to several provisions in the Child Abduction (Northern Ireland) Order 1985 to take account of changes effected in the law on custody effected by this Act.

Amendments of Child Abduction and Custody Act 1985

67.—(1) The Child Abduction and Custody Act 1985 shall be amended as follows.

(2) In section 20 (suspension of court's powers), after subsection (2) there shall be inserted the following subsection—

"(2A) Where it appears to the Secretary of State—

(*a*) that an application has been made for the registration of a decision in respect of a child under section 16 above (other than a decision mentioned in subsection (3) below); or

(*b*) that such a decision is registered,

the Secretary of State shall not make, vary or revoke any custody order in respect of the child unless, in the case of an application for registration, the application is refused."

(3) In subsection (3) of that section, after the words "subsection (1)" there shall be inserted the words "or (2A)".

(4) Immediately before section 25 there shall be inserted the following section—

"**Power to order disclosure of child's whereabouts**

24A.—(1) Where—

(*a*) in proceedings for the return of a child under Part I of this Act; or

(*b*) on an application for the recognition, registration or enforcement of a decision in respect of a child under Part II of this Act,

there is not available to the court adequate information as to where the child is, the court may order any person who it has reason to believe may have relevant information to disclose it to the court.

(2) A person shall not be excused from complying with an order under subsection (1) above by reason that to do so may incriminate him or his spouse of an offence; but a statement or admission made in compliance with such an order shall not be admissible in evidence against either of them in proceedings for any offence other than perjury."

(5) In section 27(1) (interpretation), in the definition of "custody proceedings" for the words from "made" onwards there shall be substituted the words "made, varied or revoked".

GENERAL NOTE

This section amends the Child Abduction and Custody Act 1985 to bring the provision in that Act into line with this Act. In particular there is inserted into the 1985 Act a new power (modelled on s.33 of this Act) to order disclosure of a child's whereabouts.

Subs. (2)

Custody order: as defined in s.27(1) of the 1985 Act as amended by s.67(5) of this Act. An order placing a child in the care of a local authority is a custody order for the purposes of the 1985 Act.

Minor and consequential amendments, repeals and savings

68.—(1) The enactments and orders mentioned in Schedule 1 to this Act shall have effect subject to the amendments specified in that Schedule, being minor amendments and amendments consequential on the provisions of this Act.

(2) The enactments mentioned in Schedule 2 to this Act (which include some that are spent or no longer of practical utility) are hereby repealed to the extent specified in the third column of that Schedule.

(3) Nothing in this Act shall affect—

(*a*) any proceedings under section 45 of the Matrimonial Causes Act 1973 begun before the date of the commencement of Part III of this Act;

(*b*) any proceedings for jactitation of marriage begun before that date; or

(*c*) any proceedings for a declaration begun in the High Court before that date by virtue of rules of court relating to declaratory judgments.

(4) The repeal of section 2 of the Legitimacy Declaration Act (Ireland) 1868 shall not affect any proceedings under that section begun before the commencement of that repeal.

GENERAL NOTE

This section provides for the minor and consequential amendments set out in Sched. 1, and for the repeals set out in Sched. 2, to have effect. Repealed are enactments some of which "are no longer of practical utility". An example is the Greek Marriages Act of 1884 (and see also s.62(1)). S.68(3) contains transitional provisions.

Subs. (3)

Section 45: which is repealed by this Act (see Sched. 2) and replaced by provisions in Part III of the Act (see in particular ss.55.56).

Before the date of the commencement of Part III: (see s.69(3)) as date has yet to be appointed.

Jactitation of marriage: (see s.61) Since there have been so few such petitions, it seems extremely unlikely that one has been commenced.

That date: *i.e.* the date appointed for Part III to come into force.

Rules of Court: *i.e.* R.S.C., Ord. 15, r.16.

Short title, commencement and extent

69.—(1) This Act may be cited as the Family Law Act 1986.

(2) Sections 64 to 67 of this Act shall come into force at the end of the period of two months beginning with the day on which this Act is passed.

(3) Subject to subsection (2) above, this Act shall come into force on such day as the relevant Minister or Ministers may by order made by statutory instrument appoint; and different days may be so appointed for different provisions or for different purposes.

(4) In subsection (3) above "the relevant Minister or Ministers" means—

(*a*) in the case of an order which appoints a day only for Part III of this Act and its associated amendments and repeals, the Lord Chancellor;

(b) in any other case, the Lord Chancellor and the Lord Advocate.

(5) The following provisions of this Act, namely—

Chapter II of Part I;

section 53;

Part III;

sections 64 and 65;

section 68(3); and

paragraphs 9 to 17, 19 and 23 to 27 of Schedule 1 and section 68(1) so far as relating to those paragraphs,

extend to England and Wales only.

(6) The following provisions of this Act, namely—

Chapter III of Part I;

section 26; and

paragraphs 1, 3 to 8, 18, 21 and 22 of Schedule 1 and section 68(1) so far as relating to those paragraphs,

extend to Scotland only; and sections 34 and 38 of this Act do not extend to Scotland.

(7) The following provisions of this Act, namely—

Chapter IV of Part I;

section 66;

section 68(4); and

paragraphs 2 and 32 to 34 of Schedule 1 and section 68(1) so far as relating to those paragraphs,

extend to Northern Ireland only; and paragraph 20 of Schedule 1 to this Act and section 68(1) of this Act so far as relating to that paragraph do not extend to Northern Ireland.

GENERAL NOTE

This section deals with citation, commencement and extent of the Act.

SCHEDULES

Section 68(1)   SCHEDULE 1

MINOR AND CONSEQUENTIAL AMENDMENTS ACTS

The Conjugal Rights (Scotland) Amendment Act 1861 (c.86)

1. In section 9 of the Conjugal Rights (Scotland) Amendment Act 1861—
   (a) after the words "decree make" there shall be inserted the words "an order making";
   (b) at the end there shall be added the following subsection—
       "(2) An order made by a court under subsection (1) above may, on the application of any person concerned, be varied, recalled or set aside by a subsequent order by that court made at any time before the child concerned attains the age of sixteen."

The Guardianship of Infants Act 1886 (c.27)

2. In section 9 of the Guardianship of Infants Act 1886, in the paragraph beginning "In Ireland" for the words from "the county court" to the end there shall be substituted the words "any county court, except that provision may be made by county court rules that in the case of such applications to county courts as are prescribed by county court rules only such county courts as are so prescribed shall be authorised to hear those applications".

The Sheriff Courts (Scotland) Act 1907 (c.51)

3. In section 6 of the Sheriff Courts (Scotland) Act 1907, after the words "Act 1973" there shall be inserted the words "and Chapter III of Part I of the Family Law Act 1986".

The Matrimonial Proceedings (Children) Act 1958 (c.40)

4. In section 8(1) of the Matrimonial Proceedings (Children) Act 1958—
  (*a*) for the words from "custody" to "jurisdiction" there shall be substituted the words "custody the court has power";
  (*b*) at the end there shall be added the words "In this subsection "child" does not include a child with respect to whom the court has made an order under section 13(6) or 14(2) of the Family Law Act 1986".

5. In section 9(1) of the said Act of 1958, for the words from "either forthwith" to "granted therein" there shall be substituted the words ", subject to section 13(2) of the Family Law Act 1986."

6. In section 10(1) of the said Act of 1958, for the words from "custody" to "jurisdiction" there shall be substituted the words "custody the court has power".

7. In section 11(1) of that Act, for the words from "custody" to "jurisdiction" there shall be substituted the words "custody the court has power".

The Law Reform (Miscellaneous Provisions) (Scotland) Act 1966 (c.19)

8. In section 8(6) of the Law Reform (Miscellaneous Provisions) (Scotland) Act 1966, in the definition of "sheriff"—
  (*a*) after the word "means" there shall be inserted the words—
    "(*a*) in relation to an order under subsection (1)(*a*), (*b*) or (*c*) above or an order varying any such order";
  (*b*) at the end there shall be added the words—
    "(*b*) in relation to an order mentioned in subsection (1)(*d*) above or an order varying any such order, the sheriff having jurisdiction under section 9, 10 or 12 of the Family Law Act 1986."

The Domestic and Appellate Proceedings (Restriction of Publicity) Act 1968 (c.63)

9. In section 2 of the Domestic and Appellate Proceedings (Restriction of Publicity) Act 1968 (restriction of publicity for certain proceedings)—
  (*a*) in subsection (1) paragraph (*a*) shall cease to have effect and there shall be inserted at the end the following paragraph—
    "(*d*) proceedings under Part III of the Family Law Act 1986";
  (*b*) in subsection (3) for the words "subsection (1)(*a*)" there shall be substituted the words "subsection (1)(*d*)".

The Guardianship of Minors Act 1971 (c.3)

10.—(1) Section 15 of the Guardianship of Minors Act 1971 shall be amended as follows.
(2) For subsection (1) there shall be substituted the following subsection—
  "(1) Subject to the provisions of this section "the court" for the purposes of this Act means the High Court, any county court or any magistrates' court, except that provision may be made by rules of court that in the case of such applications to a county court, or such applications to a magistrates' court, as are prescribed, only such county courts, or as the case may be such magistrates' courts, as are prescribed shall be authorised to hear those applications."
(3) After subsection (2) there shall be inserted the following subsections—
  "(2A) It is hereby declared that any power conferred on a magistrates' court under this Act is exercisable notwithstanding that any party to the proceedings is residing outside England and Wales.
  (2B) Where any party to the proceedings on an application to a magistrates' court under this Act resides outside the United Kingdom and does not appear at the time and place appointed for the hearing of the application, the court shall not hear the application unless it is proved to the satisfaction of the court, in such manner as is prescribed, that such steps as are prescribed have been taken to give to that party notice of the application and of the time and place appointed for the hearing of it.
  (2C) In this section "prescribed" means prescribed by rules of court."
(4) Subsections (3) to (6) shall cease to have effect.
11. After section 15 of that Act there shall be inserted the following section—

"Financial provision for minor resident in country outside England and Wales
  15A.—(1) Where one parent of a minor resides in England and Wales and the other parent and the minor reside outside England and Wales, the court shall have power, on an application made by that other parent, to make one or both or the orders

mentioned in section 9(2)(*a*) and (*b*) of this Act against the parent resident in England and Wales, notwithstanding that no order has been made under section 9(1) of this Act regarding the custody of the child; and in relation to such an application section 9(2)(*a*) and (*b*) shall have effect as if for any reference to the parent excluded from actual custody there were substituted a reference to the parent resident in England and Wales.

(2) Any reference in this Act to the powers of the court under section 9(2) of this Act or to an order made under the said section 9(2) shall include a reference to the powers which the court has by virtue of subsection (1) above or, as the case may be, to an order made by virtue of subsection (1) above."

12. In section 17 of that Act subsection (2) shall cease to have effect.

The Matrimonial Causes Act 1973 (c.18)

13. In section 41(1) of the Matrimonial Causes Act 1973, at the end of paragraph (*b*) there shall be inserted the following sub-paragraph—

"(iii) such arrangements have been made in respect of every child named in the order except any child with respect to whom the court has made an order under section 4(5) or 5(2) of the Family Law Act 1986 (orders precluding or staying proceedings for a custody order), or".

14. In section 47 of that Act (declarations in respect of polygamous marriages), for subsection (3) there shall be substituted the following subsection—

"(3) In this section 'a declaration concerning the validity of a marriage' means any declaration under Part III of the Family Law Act 1986 involving a determination as to the validity of a marriage".

15. In section 50 of that Act (matrimonial causes rules)—
  (*a*) in subsection (1) at the end of paragraph (*a*) there shall be inserted the words "and Part III of the Family Law Act 1986";
  (*b*) in subsection (2) in paragraph (*a*) for the words "38 or 45 above" there shall be substituted the words "or 38", in paragraph (*b*) the words "proceedings in a county court under section 45 above or to" shall cease to have effect and in paragraph (*c*) the words "or to any aspect of section 47 above which is excepted by paragraph (*b*) above" shall cease to have effect.

The Guardianship Act 1973 (c.29)

16. The following provisions of the Guardianship Act 1973 shall cease to have effect—
  (*a*) in section 1(6), the words from "except that" to the end of the subsection;
  (*b*) in section 2(1), the words "15", "and section 15(3) to (6)" and "they are";
  (*c*) section 5(3);
  (*d*) in Part I of Schedule 2, paragraph 3;
  (*e*) in Part II of Schedule 2, the text of section 15(3) to (6) of the Guardianship of Minors Act 1971.

17. In section 1(6) of the said Act of 1973 for the words "15(1) to (3)" there shall be substituted the words "15(1) to (2A), section 15(2C)".

18. In section 10(3) of that Act, for the words from "any sheriff" to "1886" there shall be substituted the words "the sheriff court".

The Children Act 1975 (c.72)

19. In section 33(1) of the Children Act 1975 the words "if the child is in England or Wales at the time the application is made" shall cease to have effect.

20.—(1) Section 100 of that Act shall be amended as follows.

(2) In subsection (2) after the word "If" there shall be inserted the words "in the case of an application for any order other than an order under Part II of this Act".

(3) For subsection (7) there shall be substituted the following subsection—

"(7) In the case of an application for an order under Part II of this Act, the following are authorised courts—
  (*a*) the High Court,
  (*b*) for the purposes of such applications under the said Part II as are prescribed by rules made under section 75 of the County Courts Act 1984, any county courts so prescribed in relation to those applications;
  (*c*) for the purposes of such applications under the said Part II as are prescribed by rules made under section 144 of the Magistrates' Courts Act 1980, any magistrates' court so prescribed in relation to those applications.".

(4) In subsection (8) the words "or 42" shall cease to have effect.

The Marriage (Scotland) Act 1977 (c.15)

21. In proviso (ii) to section 3(5) of the Marriage (Scotland) Act 1977 (certificate as to capacity to marry)—

(*a*) after the word "above" there shall be inserted the word "(*a*)"; and

(*b*) at the end there shall be added the words "or (*b*) if no such certificate has been issued only by reason of the fact that the validity of a divorce or annulment granted by a court of civil jurisdiction in Scotland or entitled to recognition in Scotland under section 44 or 45 of the Family Law Act 1986 is not recognised in the state in which the certificate would otherwise have been issued."

22. In section 26(2) of the said Act of 1977 there shall be inserted in the appropriate alphabetical position the following definition—

'"annulment" includes any decree of declarator of nullity of marriage, however expressed.'

The Domestic Proceedings and Magistrates' Courts Act 1978 (c.22)

23. In section 8(2) of the Domestic Proceedings and Magistrates' Courts Act 1978, after the words "the said section 2, 6 or 7" there shall be inserted the words "(but subject to section 2 of the Family Law Act 1986)".

24. In section 30(1) of the said Act of 1978, after the words "subject to" there shall be inserted the words "section 2 of the Family Law Act 1986 and".

The Supreme Court Act 1981 (c.54)

25. In section 26(*b*) of the Supreme Court Act 1981 the words "or jactitation of marriage" shall cease to have effect.

26. In paragraph 3 of Schedule 1 to that Act (business assigned to Family Division of the High Court) there shall be added at the end the following sub-paragraph—

"(*e*) applications under Part III of the Family Law Act 1986."

The Matrimonial and Family Proceedings Act 1984 (c.42)

27. In section 32 of the Matrimonial and Family Proceedings Act 1984 (what is family business), in the definition of "matrimonial cause" for the words "judicial separation or jactitation of marriage" there shall be substituted the words "or judicial separation".

The Child Abduction and Custody Act 1985 (c.60)

28. In section 9 of the Child Abduction and Custody Act 1985 (suspension of court's powers in cases of wrongful removal), after paragraph (*a*) there shall be inserted the following paragraph—

"(*aa*) enforcing under section 29 of the Family Law Act 1986 a custody order within the meaning of Chapter V of Part I of that Act;".

29. In section 20(2) of the said Act of 1985 (suspension of court's powers), after paragraph (*a*) there shall be inserted the following paragraph—

"(*aa*) in the case of proceedings under section 29 of the Family Law Act 1986 for the enforcement of a custody order within the meaning of Chapter V of Part I of that Act, enforce that order;".

30. In section 27(1) of the said Act of 1985 (interpretation), in the definition of "custody order" after the word "means" there shall be inserted the words "(unless the contrary intention appears)".

31. In paragraph 5 of Schedule 3 of the said Act of 1985 (custody orders in Scotland), after sub-paragraph (ii) there shall be inserted the following sub-paragraph—

"(ii*a*) an order freeing a child for adoption made under section 18 of the Adoption (Scotland) Act 1978".

ORDERS

The Matrimonial Causes (Northern Ireland) Order 1978 S.I. 1978/1045 (N.I. 15)

32. In Article 44(1) of the Matrimonial Causes (Northern Ireland) Order 1978, at the end of sub-paragraph (*b*) there shall be inserted the following head—

"(iii) such arrangements have been made in respect of every child named in the order except any child with respect to whom the court has made an order under section

21(5) or 22(2) of the Family Law Act 1986 (orders precluding or staying proceedings for a custody order); or".

The Domestic Proceedings (Northern Ireland) Order 1980 S.I. 1980/563 (N.I. 5)

33. In Article 10(2) of the Domestic Proceedings (Northern Ireland) Order 1980, after the words "that Article" there shall be inserted the words "(but subject to section 19 of the Family Law Act 1986)".

34. In Article 32(1) of that Order, for the words "Without prejudice" there shall be substituted the words "Subject to section 19 of the Family Law Act 1986 and without prejudice".

Section 68(2)   SCHEDULE 2

REPEALS

Chapter	Short title	Extent of repeal
31 & 32 Vict. c.20.	The Legitimacy Declaration Act (Ireland) 1868.	Section 2.
47 & 48 Vict. c.20.	The Greek Marriages Act 1884.	The whole Act.
49 & 50 Vict. c.27.	The Guardianship of Infants Act 1886.	In section 9, the words from "court within" to "reside".
16 & 17 Geo. 5. c.40.	Indian and Colonial Divorce Jurisdiction Act 1926.	The whole Act.
3 & 4 Geo. 6. c.35.	Indian and Colonial Divorce Jurisdiction Act 1940.	The whole Act.
7 & 8 Geo. 6. c.43.	Matrimonial Causes (War Marriages) Act 1944.	The whole Act.
10 & 11 Geo. 6. c.30.	Indian Independence Act 1947.	Section 17.
11 & 12 Geo. 6. c.3.	Burma Independence Act 1947.	Section 4(3).
11 & 12 Geo. 6. c.7.	Ceylon Independence Act 1947.	Section 3. In Schedule 2, paragraph 9.
14 Geo. 6. c.20.	Colonial and Other Territories (Divorce Jurisdiction) Act 1950.	The whole Act.
14 Geo. 6. c.37.	The Maintenance Orders Act 1950.	Section 7.
6 & 7 Eliz. 2. c.40.	The Matrimonial Proceedings (Children) Act 1958.	Section 13.
8 & 9 Eliz. 2. c.52.	Cyprus Act 1960.	In the Schedule, paragraph 14.
8 & 9 Eliz. 2. c.55.	Nigeria Independence Act 1960.	In Schedule 2, paragraph 14.
9 & 10 Eliz. 2. c.16.	Sierra Leone Independence Act 1961.	In Schedule 3, paragraph 15.
10 & 11 Eliz. 2. c.1.	Tanganyika Independence Act 1961.	In Schedule 2, paragraph 15.
10 & 11 Eliz. 2. c.23.	South Africa Act 1962.	In Schedule 3, paragraph 9.
10 & 11 Eliz. 2. c.40.	Jamaica Independence Act 1962.	In Schedule 2, paragraph 14.
10 & 11 Eliz. 2. c.54.	Trinidad and Tobago Independence Act 1962.	In Schedule 2, paragraph 14.
10 & 11 Eliz. 2. c.57.	Uganda Independence Act 1962.	In Schedule 3, paragraph 13.
1963 c.54.	Kenya Independence Act 1963.	Section 7.

Chapter	Short title	Extent of repeal
1964 c.46.	Malawi Independence Act 1964.	Section 6.
1964 c.65.	Zambia Independence Act 1964.	Section 7.
1966 c.19.	The Law Reform (Miscellaneous Provisions) (Scotland) Act 1966.	In section 8(2), the words "made in a consistorial action".
1966 c.29.	Singapore Act 1966.	Section 2.
1968 c.63.	The Domestic and Appellate Proceedings (Restriction of Publicity) Act 1968.	Section 2(1)(*a*).
1969 c.29.	Tanzania Act 1969.	Section 2. In section 4(3), the words "or the Divorce Jurisdiction Acts". Section 7(1).
1971 c.3.	The Guardianship of Minors Act 1971.	Section 15(3) to (6). Section 17(2).
1971 c.53.	Recognition of Divorces and Legal Separations Act 1971.	The whole Act.
1973 c.18.	The Matrimonial Causes Act 1973.	Section 45. In section 50(2), in paragraph (*b*), the words "proceedings in a county court under section 45 above or to" and, in paragraph (*c*), the words "or to any aspect of section 47 above which is excepted by paragraph (*b*) above".
1973 c.29.	The Guardianship Act 1973.	In section 1(6), the words from "except that" to the end. In section 2(1), the words "15", "and section 15(3) to (6)" and "they are". Section 5(3). In Schedule 2, in Part I, paragraph 3, and in Part II, the text of section 15(3) to (6) of the Guardianship of Minors Act 1971.
1973 c.45.	Domicile and Matrimonial Proceedings Act 1973.	Section 2. Sections 15 and 16.
1973 c.48.	The Pakistan Act 1973.	In section 4(5), the words from the beginning to "1940, and".
1975 c.72.	The Children Act 1975.	In section 33(1), the words from "if" to the end. In section 53(1), the words from "but where" to the end. Section 54. In section 100(8), the words "or 42".
1981 c.54.	The Supreme Court Act 1981.	In section 26(*b*), the words "or jactitation of marriage".
1984 c.42.	The Matrimonial and Family Proceedings Act 1984.	In Schedule 1, paragraph 14.
1985 c.73.	The Law Reform (Miscellaneous Provisions) (Scotland) Act 1985.	Section 16.

PARLIAMENTARY CONSTITUENCIES ACT 1986

(1986 c. 56)

A Table showing the derivation of the provisions of this consolidation Act will be found at the end of the Act. The Table has no official status.

ARRANGEMENT OF SECTIONS

An Act to consolidate the House of Commons (Redistribution of Seats) Acts 1949 to 1979 and certain related enactments.

[7th November 1986]

PARLIAMENTARY DEBATES

Hansard: H.L. Vol. 475, col. 546; Vol. 476, col. 592; Vol. 477, cols. 758, 1036, H.C. Vol. 102, col. 1439.

Parliamentary constituencies

1.—(1) There shall for the purpose of parliamentary elections be the county and borough constituencies (or in Scotland the county and burgh constituencies), each returning a single member, which are described in Orders in Council made under this Act.

(2) In this Act and, except where the context otherwise requires, in any Act passed after the Representation of the People Act 1948, "constituency" means an area having separate representation in the House of Commons.

The Boundary Commissions

2.—(1) For the purpose of the continuous review of the distribution of seats at parliamentary elections, there shall continue to be four permanent Boundary Commissions, namely a Boundary Commission for England, a Boundary Commission for Scotland, a Boundary Commission for Wales and a Boundary Commission for Northern Ireland.

(2) Schedule 1 to this Act shall have effect with respect to the constitution of, and other matters relating to, the Boundary Commissions.

Reports of the Commissions

3.—(1) Each Boundary Commission shall keep under review the representation in the House of Commons of the part of the United Kingdom with which they are concerned and shall, in accordance with subsection (2) below, submit to the Secretary of State reports with respect to the whole of that part of the United Kingdom, either—

(*a*) showing the constituencies into which they recommend that it should be divided in order to give effect to the rules set out in paragraphs 1 to 6 of Schedule 2 to this Act (read with paragraph 7 of that Schedule), or

(*b*) stating that, in the opinion of the Commission, no alteration is required to be made in respect of that part of the United Kingdom in order to give effect to the said rules (read with paragraph 7).

(2) Reports under subsection (1) above shall be submitted by a Boundary Commission not less than ten or more than fifteen years from the date of the submission of their last report under that subsection.

(3) Any Boundary Commission may also from time to time submit to the Secretary of State reports with respect to the area comprised in any particular constituency or constituencies in the part of the United Kingdom with which they are concerned, showing the constituencies into which they recommend that that area should be divided in order to give effect to the rules set out in paragraphs 1 to 6 of Schedule 2 to this Act (read with paragraph 7 of that Schedule).

(4) A report of a Boundary Commission under this Act showing the constituencies into which they recommend that any area should be divided shall state, as respects each constituency, the name by which they recommend that it should be known, and whether they recommend that it should be a county constituency or a borough constituency (or in Scotland a county constituency or a burgh constituency).

(5) As soon as may be after a Boundary Commission have submitted a report to the Secretary of State under this Act, he shall lay the report before Parliament together, except in a case where the report states that no alteration is required to be made in respect of the part of the United Kingdom with which the Commission are concerned, with the draft of an Order in Council for giving effect, whether with or without modifications, to the recommendations contained in the report.

(6) Schedule 2 to this Act which contains the rules referred to above and related provisions shall have effect.

Orders in Council

4.—(1) The draft of any Order in Council laid before Parliament by the Secretary of State under this Act for giving effect, whether with or without modifications, to the recommendations contained in the report of a Boundary Commission may make provision for any matters which appear to him to be incidental to, or consequential on, the recommendations.

(2) Where any such draft gives effect to any such recommendations with modifications, the Secretary of State shall lay before Parliament together with the draft a statement of the reasons for the modifications.

(3) If any such draft is approved by resolution of each House of Parliament, the Secretary of State shall submit it to Her Majesty in Council.

(4) If a motion for the approval of any such draft is rejected by either House of Parliament or withdrawn by leave of the House, the Secretary of State may amend the draft and lay the amended draft before Parliament, and if the draft as so amended is approved by resolution of each House of Parliament, the Secretary of State shall submit it to Her Majesty in Council.

(5) Where the draft of an Order in Council is submitted to Her Majesty in Council under this Act, Her Majesty in Council may make an Order in

terms of the draft which (subject to subsection (6) below) shall come into force on such date as may be specified in the Order and shall have effect notwithstanding anything in any enactment.

(6) The coming into force of any such Order shall not affect any parliamentary election until a proclamation is issued by Her Majesty summoning a new Parliament, or affect the constitution of the House of Commons until the dissolution of the Parliament then in being.

(7) The validity of any Order in Council purporting to be made under this Act and reciting that a draft of the Order has been approved by resolution of each House of Parliament shall not be called in question in any legal proceedings whatsoever.

Notices

5.—(1) Where a Boundary Commission intend to consider making a report under this Act they shall, by notice in writing, inform the Secretary of State accordingly, and a copy of the notice shall be published—

   (*a*) in a case where it was given by the Boundary Commission for England or the Boundary Commission for Wales, in the London Gazette,

   (*b*) in a case where it was given by the Boundary Commission for Scotland, in the Edinburgh Gazette, and

   (*c*) in a case where it was given by the Boundary Commission for Northern Ireland, in the Belfast Gazette.

(2) Where a Boundary Commission have provisionally determined to make recommendations affecting any constituency, they shall publish in at least one newspaper circulating in the constituency a notice stating—

   (*a*) the effect of the proposed recommendations and (except in a case where they propose to recommend that no alteration be made in respect of the constituency) that a copy of the recommendations is open to inspection at a specified place within the constituency, and

   (*b*) that representations with respect to the proposed recommendations may be made to the Commission within one month after the publication of the notice;

and the Commission shall take into consideration any representations duly made in accordance with any such notice.

(3) Where a Boundary Commission revise any proposed recommendations after publishing a notice of them under subsection (2) above, the Commission shall comply again with that subsection in relation to the revised recommendations, as if no earlier notice had been published.

Local inquiries

6.—(1) A Boundary Commission may, if they think fit, cause a local inquiry to be held in respect of any constituency or constituencies.

(2) Where, on the publication of the notice under section 5(2) above of a recommendation of a Boundary Commission for the alteration of any constituencies, the Commission receive any representation objecting to the proposed recommendation from an interested authority or from a body of electors numbering one hundred or more, the Commission shall not make the recommendation unless, since the publication of the notice, a local inquiry has been held in respect of the constituencies.

(3) Where a local inquiry was held in respect of the constituencies before the publication of the notice mentioned in subsection (2) above, that subsection shall not apply if the Commission, after considering the matters discussed at the local inquiry, the nature of the representations received on the publication of the notice and any other relevant circumstances, are of opinion that a further local inquiry would not be justified.

(4) In subsection (2) above, "interested authority" and "elector" respectively mean, in relation to any recommendation, a local authority whose area is wholly or partly comprised in the constituencies affected by the recommendation, and a parliamentary elector for any of those constituencies; and for this purpose "local authority" means—

(*a*) in England and Wales, the council of a county, London borough or district,

(*b*) in Scotland, the council of a region, islands area or district, and

(*c*) in Northern Ireland, the council of a district.

(5) Subsections (2) and (3) of section 250 of the Local Government Act 1972 (which relate to the attendance of witnesses at inquiries) shall apply in relation to any local inquiry which the Boundary Commission for England or the Boundary Commission for Wales may cause to be held in pursuance of this Act.

(6) In relation to any local inquiry which the Boundary Commission for Scotland may cause to be held in pursuance of this Act, the said subsections (2) and (3) shall apply as if that Act applied to Scotland but with the substitution of references to an order for references to a summons.

(7) In relation to any local inquiry which the Boundary Commission for Northern Ireland may cause to be held in pursuance of this Act, sections 19 and 20 of the Poor Relief (Ireland) (No. 2) Act 1847 shall apply.

Consequential amendments

7. Schedule 3 to this Act shall have effect.

Repeals and revocation

8.—(1) The enactments specified in Schedule 4 to this Act are hereby repealed to the extent specified in the third column of that Schedule.

(2) Article 2(7) of the Local Government Reorganisation (Consequential Provisions) (Northern Ireland) Order 1973 is hereby revoked.

(3) Where a period of time specified in any enactment repealed by this Act is current at the commencement of this Act, this Act shall have effect as if the corresponding provision of this Act had been in force when the period began to run.

Citation, commencement and extent

9.—(1) This Act may be cited as the Parliamentary Constituencies Act 1986, and shall be included among the Acts which may be cited as the Representation of the People Acts.

(2) This Act shall come into force at the end of the period of three months beginning with the day on which it is passed.

(3) This Act extends to Northern Ireland.

SCHEDULES

Section 2   SCHEDULE 1

THE BOUNDARY COMMISSIONS

Constitution

1. The Speaker of the House of Commons shall be the chairman of each of the four Commissions.

2. Each of the four Commissions shall consist of the chairman, a deputy chairman and two other members appointed by the Secretary of State.

3. The deputy chairman—
   - (*a*) in the case of the Commission for England shall be a judge of the High Court appointed by the Lord Chancellor,
   - (*b*) in the case of the Commission for Scotland shall be a judge of the Court of Session appointed by the Lord President of the Court of Session,
   - (*c*) in the case of the Commission for Wales shall be a judge of the High Court appointed by the Lord Chancellor,
   - (*d*) in the case of the Commission for Northern Ireland shall be a judge of the High Court in Northern Ireland appointed by the Lord Chief Justice of Northern Ireland.

4. A member of any Commission (other than the chairman) shall hold his appointment for such term and on such conditions as may be determined before his appointment by the person appointing him.

Officers

5. The officers of each Commission shall include, as assessors, the following persons—
   - (*a*) in the case of the Commission for England, the Registrar General for England and Wales and the Director General of Ordnance Survey,
   - (*b*) in the case of the Commission for Scotland, the Registrar General of Births, Deaths and Marriages for Scotland and the Director General of Ordnance Survey,
   - (*c*) in the case of the Commission for Wales, the Registrar General for England and Wales and the Director General of Ordnance Survey,
   - (*d*) in the case of the Commission for Northern Ireland, the Registrar General of Births and Deaths in Northern Ireland, the Commissioner of Valuation for Northern Ireland and the Chief Electoral Officer for Northern Ireland.

6.—(1) The Secretary of State may, at the request of any Commission, appoint one or more assistant Commissioners to inquire into, and report to the Commission upon, such matters as the Commission think fit.

(2) Any such assistant Commissioner shall be appointed either for a certain term or for the purposes of a particular inquiry, and on such conditions as to remuneration and otherwise as may be determined before his appointment by the Secretary of State with the approval of the Treasury.

7. The Secretary of State shall appoint a secretary to each of the Commissions, and may appoint such other officers of any Commission as he may determine with the approval of the Treasury, and the term and conditions of any such appointment shall be such as may be so determined.

Expenses

8. The expenses of each Commission, including the travelling and other expenses of the members and the remuneration and expenses of the assistant Commissioners, secretary and other officers, shall be paid out of money provided by Parliament.

Proceedings and instruments

9. A Commission shall have power to act notwithstanding a vacancy among their members, and at any meeting of a Commission two, or such greater number as the Commission may determine, shall be the quorum.

10. For the purpose of considering any matter of common concern, the Commissions, or any two or three of them, may hold joint meetings.

11. Subject to the provisions of this Act, each of the Commissions shall have power to regulate their own procedure.

12. Every document purporting to be an instrument made or issued by a Commission and to be signed by the secretary or any person authorised to act in that behalf, shall be received in evidence and shall, until the contrary is proved, be deemed to be an instrument made or issued by the Commission.

Section 3   SCHEDULE 2

RULES FOR REDISTRIBUTION OF SEATS

The rules

1.—(1) The number of constituencies in Great Britain shall not be substantially greater or less than 613.

(2) The number of constituencies in Scotland shall not be less than 71.

(3) The number of constituencies in Wales shall not be less than 35.

(4) The number of constituencies in Northern Ireland shall not be greater than 18 or less than 16, and shall be 17 unless it appears to the Boundary Commission for Northern Ireland that Northern Ireland should for the time being be divided into 16 or (as the case may be) into 18 constituencies.

2. Every constituency shall return a single member.

3. There shall continue to be a constituency which shall include the whole of the City of London and the name of which shall refer to the City of London.

4.—(1) So far as is practicable having regard to rules 1 to 3—

    (*a*) in England and Wales,—

        (i) no county or part of a county shall be included in a constituency which includes the whole or part of any other county or the whole or part of a London borough,

        (ii) no London borough or any part of a London borough shall be included in a constituency which includes the whole or part of any other London borough,

    (*b*) in Scotland, regard shall be had to the boundaries of local authority areas,

    (*c*) in Northern Ireland, no ward shall be included partly in one constituency and partly in another.

(2) In sub-paragraph (1)(*b*) above "area" and "local authority" have the same meanings as in the Local Government (Scotland) Act 1973.

5. The electorate of any constituency shall be as near the electoral quota as is practicable having regard to rules 1 to 4; and a Boundary Commission may depart from the strict application of rule 4 if it appears to them that a departure is desirable to avoid an excessive disparity between the electorate of any constituency and the electoral quota, or between the electorate of any constituency and that of neighbouring constituencies in the part of the United Kingdom with which they are concerned.

6. A Boundary Commission may depart from the strict application of rules 4 and 5 if special geographical considerations, including in particular the size, shape and accessibility of a constituency, appear to them to render a departure desirable.

General and supplementary

7. It shall not be the duty of a Boundary Commission to aim at giving full effect in all circumstances to the above rules, but they shall take account, so far as they reasonably can—

    (*a*) of the inconveniences attendant on alterations of constituencies other than alterations made for the purposes of rule 4, and

    (*b*) of any local ties which would be broken by such alterations.

8. In the application of rule 5 to each part of the United Kingdom for which there is a Boundary Commission—

(a) the expression "electoral quota" means a number obtained by dividing the electorate for that part of the United Kingdom by the number of constituencies in it existing on the enumeration date,

(b) the expression "electorate" means—

    (i) in relation to a constituency, the number of persons whose names appear on the register of parliamentary electors in force on the enumeration date under the Representation of the People Acts for the constituency,

    (ii) in relation to the part of the United Kingdom, the aggregate electorate as defined in sub-paragraph (i) above of all the constituencies in that part,

(c) the expression "enumeration date" means, in relation to any report of a Boundary Commission under this Act, the date on which the notice with respect to that report is published in accordance with section 5(1) of this Act.

9. In this Schedule, a reference to a rule followed by a number is a reference to the rule set out in the correspondingly numbered paragraph of this Schedule.

Section 7   SCHEDULE 3

CONSEQUENTIAL AMENDMENTS

The Northern Ireland Constitution Act 1973

1.—(1) Section 28 of the Northern Ireland Constitution Act 1973 shall be amended as follows.

(2) In subsection (2) for the words "section 2(1) or (3) of the House of Commons (Redistribution of Seats) Act 1949" there shall be substituted the words "section 3(1) or (3) of the Parliamentary Constituencies Act 1986".

(3) In subsection (3) for the words "Act of 1949" there shall be substituted the words "Act of 1986".

(4) In subsection (4) for the words from the beginning to "in report)" there shall be substituted the words "Sections 3(4) and (5), 4 and 5(1) (implementation of recommendations in report of Boundary Commission and publication of notice of proposed report)".

(5) For subsection (5) there shall be substituted—

"(5) An Order in Council under the said Act of 1986 for giving effect, with or without modifications, to the recommendations contained in a report or supplementary report of the Boundary Commission for Northern Ireland may make amendments consequential on giving effect to those recommendations in section 1(1) of and in the Schedule to the said Act of 1973".

2. The said section 28 shall (notwithstanding the repeal by this Act of the House of Commons (Redistribution of Seats) Act 1979) continue to have effect with the substitution for subsection (6) of—

"(6) The coming into force of any such Order in Council shall not affect any election to the Assembly before the next general election to the Assembly or affect the constitution of the Assembly then in being."

The House of Commons Disqualification Act 1975

3. In Part III of Schedule 1 to the House of Commons Disqualification Act 1975 for the words "Part I or Part II of Schedule 1 to the House of Commons (Redistribution of Seats) Act 1949" there shall be substituted the words "Schedule 1 to the Parliamentary Constituencies Act 1986.

The Northern Ireland Assembly Disqualification Act 1975

4. In Part III of Schedule 1 to the Northern Ireland Assembly Disqualification Act 1975 for the words "Part I or Part II of Schedule 1 to the House of Commons (Redistribution of Seats) Act 1949" there shall be substituted the words "Schedule 1 to the Parliamentary Constituencies Act 1986".

The European Assembly Elections Act 1978

5.—(1) Schedule 2 to the European Assembly Elections Act 1978 shall be amended as follows.

(2) In paragraph 1—

    (*a*) for the words "section 3 of the 1949 Act" there shall be substituted the words "the 1986 Act", and

    (*b*) for the words "section 2(1)", in both places where they occur, there shall be substituted the words "section 3(1)".

(3) In paragraph 3—

    (*a*) for the words "section 3 of the 1949 Act" there shall be substituted the words "the 1986 Act", and

    (*b*) for the words "section 2(3)" there shall be substituted the words "section 3(3)".

(4) For paragraph 4 there shall be substituted—

"4. A supplementary report of a Boundary Commission under this Schedule showing the Assembly constituencies into which they recommend that any area should be divided shall state, as respects each Assembly constituency, the name by which they recommend that it should be known.

4A—(1) Where the Boundary Commission for any part of Great Britain intend to consider making a supplementary report under this Schedule, they shall, by notice in writing, inform the Secretary of State accordingly, and a copy of the notice shall be published—

    (*a*) in a case where it was given by the Boundary Commission for England or the Boundary Commission for Wales, in the London Gazette, and

    (*b*) in a case where it was given by the Boundary Commission for Scotland, in the Edinburgh Gazette.

(2) As soon as may be after a Boundary Commission have submitted a supplementary report to the Secretary of State under this Schedule, he shall lay the report before Parliament together, except in a case where the report states that no alteration is required to be made in respect of the part of Great Britain with which the Commission are concerned, with the draft of an Order in Council for giving effect, whether with or without modifications, to the recommendations contained in the report.

4B—(1) The draft of any Order in Council laid before Parliament by the Secretary of State under this Schedule for giving effect, whether with or without modifications, to the recommendations contained in a supplementary report of a Boundary Commission may make provision for any matters which appear to him to be incidental to, or consequential on, the recommendations.

(2) Where any such draft gives effect to any such recommendations with modifications, the Secretary of State shall lay before Parliament together with the draft a statement of the reasons for the modifications.

(3) If any such draft is approved by resolution of each House of Parliament, the Secretary of State shall submit it to Her Majesty in Council.

(4) If a motion for the approval of any such draft is rejected by either House of Parliament or withdrawn by leave of the House, the Secretary of State may amend the draft and lay the amended draft before Parliament, and if the draft as so amended is approved by resolution of each House of Parliament, the Secretary of State shall submit it to Her Majesty in Council.

(5) Where the draft of an Order in Council is submitted to Her Majesty in Council under this Schedule, Her Majesty in Council may make an Order in terms of the draft which (subject to paragraph 8 below) shall come into force on such date as may be specified in the Order and shall have effect notwithstanding anything in any enactment.

(6) The validity of any Order in Council purporting to be made under this Schedule and reciting that a draft of the Order has been approved by resolution of each House of Parliament shall not be called in question in any legal proceedings whatsoever."

(5) After sub-paragraph (2) of paragraph 5 there shall be inserted—

"(3) Where a Boundary Commission revise any proposed recommendations after publishing a notice of them under this paragraph the commission shall publish a further notice under this paragraph in relation to the revised recommendations, as if no earlier notice had been published."

(6) After paragraph 5 there shall be inserted—

"5A—(1) A Boundary Commission may, if they think fit cause a local inquiry to be held in respect of any Assembly constituency or constituencies.

(2) Where, on the publication of the notice under paragraph 5 above of a recommendation of a Boundary Commission for the alteration of any Assembly constituencies, the Commission receive any representation objecting to the proposed recommendation from an interested authority or from a body of electors numbering five hundred or more, the Commission shall not make the recommendation unless, since the publication of the notice, a local inquiry has been held in respect of the Assembly constituencies.

(3) Where a local inquiry was held in respect of the Assembly constituencies before the publication of the notice mentioned in sub-paragraph (2) above, that sub-paragraph shall not apply if the Commission, after considering the matters discussed at the local inquiry, the nature of the representations received on the publication of the notice and any other relevant circumstances, are of opinion that a further local inquiry would not be justified.

(4) In sub-paragraph (2) above, "interested authority" and "elector" respectively means, in relation to any recommendation, a local authority whose area is wholly or partly comprised in the Assembly constituencies affected by the recommendation and an elector for any of those Assembly constituencies; and for this purpose "local authority" means—

(*a*) in England and Wales, the council of a county, London borough or district, and

(*b*) in Scotland, the council of a region, islands area or district."

(7) In paragraph 6 for the words "paragraph 4" there shall be substituted the words "paragraph 5A".

(8) In paragraph 7 for the words "paragraph 4" there shall be substituted the words "paragraphs 4A and 4B".

(9) In paragraph 8 for the words "the provisions applied by paragraph 4 above", in both places where they occur, there shall be substituted the words "this Schedule".

(10) In paragraph 11—

(*a*) for the words from "the 1949 Act", in the first place where they occur, to "Act 1958" there shall be substituted the words—

" 'the 1986 Act' means the Parliamentary Constituencies Act 1986", and

(*b*) for the words "established by the 1949 Act" there shall be substituted the words "provided for by the 1986 Act".

(11) In paragraph 12 for the words "section 2(4) of the 1949 Act" there shall be substituted the words "paragraph 4A above".

The Finance (No. 2) Act 1983

6. In section 7(1) of the Finance (No. 2) Act 1983 for the words "section 3 of the House of Commons (Redistribution of Seats) Act 1949" there shall be substituted the words "the Parliamentary Constituencies Act 1986".

SCHEDULE 4

                               REPEALS

Chapter	Short title	Extent of Repeal
11 & 12 Geo. 6 c.65.	The Representation of the People Act 1948.	Section 1(1). Section 81.
12, 13 & 14 Geo. 6. c.66	The House of Commons (Redistribution of Seats) Act 1949.	The whole Act.
6 & 7 Eliz. 2. c.26.	The House of Commons (Redistribution of Seats) Act 1958.	The whole Act.
1963 c.33.	The London Government Act 1963.	Section 4(7)(*c*). Section 8(1). In Schedule 3, in Part II, paragraph 21.
1973 c.36.	The Northern Ireland Constitution Act 1973.	Section 28(7).
1973 c.65.	The Local Government (Scotland) Act 1973.	In Schedule 3, paragraphs 1 and 19.
1979 c.15.	The House of Commons (Redistribution of Seats) Act 1979.	The whole Act.
1986 c.12.	The Statute Law (Repeals) Act 1986.	In Schedule 2, paragraph 4(1).

TABLE OF DERIVATIONS

Note: The following abbreviations are used in this Table:—

1949	=	The House of Commons (Redistribution of Seats) Act 1949 (12, 13 & 14 Geo. 6. c.66)
1958	=	The House of Commons (Redistribution of Seats) Act 1958 (6 & 7 Eliz. 2. c.26)
1963	=	The London Government Act 1963 (c.33)
1972	=	The Local Government Act 1972 (c.70)
1973	=	The Local Government (Scotland) Act 1973 (c.65)
1979	=	The House of Commons (Redistribution of Seats) Act 1979 (c.15)
SL(R) 1986	=	The Statute Law Repeals Act 1986 (c.12)
S.I. 1951/753	=	The Transfer of Functions (Minister of Health and Minister of Local Government and Planning) (No. 2) Order 1951 (S.I. 1951/753)
S.I. 1968/1656	=	The Minister for the Civil Service Order 1968 (S.I. 1968/1656)
S.I. 1970/1681	=	The Secretary of State for the Environment Order 1970 (S.I. 1970/1681)
S.I. 1973/2095	=	The Local Government Reorganisation (Consequential Provisions) (Northern Ireland) Order 1973 (S.I. 1973/2095)
S.I. 1981/1670	=	The Transfer of Functions (Minister for the Civil Service and Treasury) Order 1981 (S.I. 1981/1670)

Provision	Derivation
1(1)	Representation of the People Act 1948 (c.65) s.1(1); SL(R) 1986 Sch. 2, para. 4(1).
(2)	1949 s.4.
2(1)	1949 s.1(1).
(2)	Introduces Schedule 1.
3(1)	1949 s.2(1); 1958 s.2(2).
(2)	1958 s.2(1).
(3)	1949 s.2(3); 1958 s.2(2).
(4)	1949 ss.3(1), 6.
(5)	1949 s.2(5).
(6)	Introduces Schedule 2.
4(1)–(4)	1949 s.3(2)–(5).
(5), (6)	1949 s.3(6).
(7)	1949 s.3(7).
5(1)	1949 s.2(4).
(2)	1949 Sch. 1 Pt. III, para. 3.
(3)	1958 s.4(1).
6(1)	1949 Sch. 1 Pt. III, para. 4.
(2), (3)	1958 s.4(2).
(4)	1958 s.4(3), (4); 1972 s.179(3); 1973 Sch. 3, para. 19; S.I. 1973/2095 Art. 2(7).
(5), (6)	1949 Sch. 1 Pt. III, para. 5(1)(2); 1972 s.272(2).
(7)	1949 Sch. 1 Pt. III, para. 5(3).
7–9	—
Sch. 1	
para. 1	1949 Sch. 1 Pt. I, para. 1.
2	1949 Sch. 1 Pt. I, paras. 2–5; 1958 Sch., para. 1; S.I. 1951/753 Art. 8(1); S.I. 1970/1681 Art. 6(3).
3	1958 s.1(1), Sch. para. 1.
4	1949 Sch. 1 Pt. I, para. 8; 1958 s.1(1).
5	1958 s.1(2); Northern Ireland Constitution Act 1973 (c.36) s.28(7).
6, 7	1949 Sch. 1 Pt. II, paras. 1, 2; S.I. 1968/1656 Art. 3(2); S.I. 1981/1670 Art. 3(5).
8	1949 Sch. 1 Pt. II, para. 3.
9, 10	1949 Sch. 1 Pt. III, paras. 1, 2.
11, 12	1949 Sch. 1 Pt. III, paras. 6, 7.

Provision	Derivation
Sch. 2	
para. 1(1)–(3)	1949 Sch. 2, para. 1.
(4)	1949 Sch. 2, para. 1; 1979 s.1(1), (2).
2, 3	1949 Sch. 2, paras. 2, 3.
4	1949 Sch. 2, para. 4; 1963 Sch. 3 Pt. II, para. 21; 1973 Sch. 3, para. 1; S.I. 1973/2095 Art. 2(7).
5, 6	1949 Sch. 2, paras. 5, 6.
7	1958 s.2(2).
8	1949 Sch. 2, para. 7; 1958 s.3, Sch., para. 2.
9	Interpretation.
Sch. 3	—
Sch. 4	—

PUBLIC TRUSTEE AND ADMINISTRATION OF FUNDS ACT 1986

(1986 c. 57)

ARRANGEMENT OF SECTIONS

Public Trustee and Funds Administration

An Act to make provision with respect to certain functions of the Public Trustee, the Accountant General of the Supreme Court and the Court of Protection as respects the management, protection or administration of the funds and other property and, if under disability, the affairs of private persons; and with respect to the investment expenses of the National Debt Commissioners.   [7th November 1986]

PARLIAMENTARY DEBATES
Hansard: H.L. Vol. 472, col. 1399; Vol. 474, col. 830; Vol. 475, col. 407; Vol. 476, col. 9; H.C. Vol. 102, col. 1438.

Public Trustee and Funds Administration

Public Trustee and Accountant General: appointment, tenure of office etc.

1.—(1) The office of Public Trustee and the office of Accountant General of the Supreme Court may be held by one person.

(2) The office of Accountant General of the Supreme Court may, but need not, be held by the Permanent Secretary to the Lord Chancellor.

(3) The enactments specified in the Schedule to this Act shall have effect with the amendments specified in that Schedule.

Exercise by Public Trustee of functions of Court of Protection

2.—(1) Part VII of the Mental Health Act 1983 (which provides for the protection and management of the property and affairs of mental patients) shall have effect with the following amendments.

(2) In section 94 (exercise of judge's functions)—

  (*a*) in subsection (1), at the beginning there shall be inserted the words "Subject to subsection (1A) below" and after the words "Master of the Court of Protection" there shall be inserted the words ", by the Public Trustee";

  (*b*) in subsection (1), there shall be inserted, in paragraph (*a*), after the word "Master" the words ", the Public Trustee" and, after that paragraph, the following paragraph—

    "(*aa*) in the case of the Public Trustee, subject to any directions of the Master and so far only as may be provided

by any rules made under this Part of this Act or (subject to
any such rules) by directions of the Master,"; and

(c) after subsection (1) there shall be inserted the following
subsection—

"(1A) In such cases or circumstances as may be prescribed
by any rules under this Part of this Act or (subject to any
such rules) by directions of the Master, the functions of the
judge under this Part of this Act shall be exercised by the
Public Trustee (but subject to any directions of the Master
as to their exercise)".

(3) In section 111 (exercisability of functions conferred by other
Acts)—

(a) in subsection (2), after the words "subsection (3)" there shall
be inserted the words "and (3A)" and after the words "Master
of the Court of Protection" there shall be inserted the words
", by the Public Trustee";

(b) after subsection (2) there shall be inserted the following
subsection—

"(2A) The exercise of the functions referred to in subsection (2) above by the Public Trustee shall be subject to any
directions of the Master and they shall be exercisable so far
only as may be provided by any rules made under this Part
of this Act or (subject to any such rules) by directions of the
Master."; and

(c) after subsection (3) there shall be inserted the following
subsection—

"(3A) In such cases or circumstances as may be prescribed
by any rules under this Part of this Act or (subject to any
such rules) by directions of the Master, the functions referred
to in subsection (2) above shall be exercised by the Public
Trustee (but subject to any directions of the Master as to
their exercise)."

Functions of the Public Trustee

3.—(1) The Public Trustee shall have, in addition to his powers and
duties under the Public Trustee Act 1906 ("the 1906 Act"), the following
functions.

(2) Subject to subsections (4), (5) and (6) below, the Public Trustee
shall have all the functions expressed to be conferred by Part VII of the
Mental Health Act 1983 ("the 1983 Act") on the judge with respect to the
property and affairs of a patient and, notwithstanding anything in the 1906
Act, if authorised, appointed or directed (as the case may be) to do so,
he may—

(a) act as, as well as appoint a person to act as, a receiver for a patient,
or

(b) carry on, as well as authorise or direct a suitable person to carry
on, a patient's profession, trade or business.

(3) Subject to subsections (4), (5) and (6) below, the Public Trustee
shall have all the functions expressed to be conferred by any enactment
not contained in Part VII of the 1983 Act on the authority having
jurisdiction under that Part of that Act.

(4) The Public Trustee shall not exercise the functions conferred on
him by subsection (2) or (3) above except where those functions are made
exercisable or are to be exercised by him by virtue of rules made or
directions given to him under Part VII of the 1983 Act.

(5) Where, under any such rules or directions, functions become
exercisable or are to be exercised by the Public Trustee he shall discharge

the duties and may exercise the powers so imposed or conferred on him (and, where directions are given by the Master, in accordance with the directions) whether or not, under any provision of the 1906 Act, he would be obliged or empowered to decline to accept any trust or other duty.

(6) The discharge by the Public Trustee of any functions under this section shall not be treated as the discharge of the duties of his office for the purposes of the following provisions of the 1906 Act, that is to say—

(*a*) section 7 (liability of Consolidated Fund);

(*b*) section 9 (fees); and

(*c*) section 10 (appeal to court);

but persons may be appointed as his officers and expenses paid under section 8 and rules may be made under section 14 of that Act for the purposes of this section as for the purposes of that Act.

(7) In this section "the judge" and "patient" have the same meaning as in Part VII of the 1983 Act and "the Master" means the Master of the Court of Protection.

Accountant General's powers of investment

4. In section 38 of the Administration of Justice Act 1982 (management and investment of funds in court), subsection (5) (power of court to specify manner of investment by Accountant General) and, in subsection (4), the words "subject to subsection (5) below" shall be omitted.

Investment expenses of National Debt Commissioners

Deduction by National Debt Commissioners of investment expenses of money in court

5.—(1) In section 39 of the Administration of Justice Act 1982 (investment of money in court transferred to National Debt Commissioners) in subsection (2) (payment of excess into Consolidated Fund) after paragraph (*b*) there shall be inserted the words—

"and

(*c*) an amount equal to the expenses incurred by the Commissioners in that year in making investments under subsection (1) above and disposing of investments so made".

(2) In subsection (3) of that section (deficiencies to be made good out of the Consolidated Fund) for the words "paragraphs (*a*) and (*b*)" there shall be substituted the words "paragraphs (*a*) to (*c*)".

(3) After subsection (4) of that section there shall be inserted the following subsection—

"(4A) Any sum deducted by the Commissioners under subsection (2)(*c*) above shall be applied as an appropriation in aid of moneys provided by Parliament for the expenses of the National Debt Commissioners; and, so far as not so applied, shall be paid into the Consolidated Fund."

General

Short title, commencement and extent

6.—(1) This Act may be cited as the Public Trustee and Administration of Funds Act 1986.

(2) This Act shall come into force on such day as the Lord Chancellor appoints by order made by statutory instrument.

(3) With the exception of the amendments in the Administration of Justice Act 1982, this Act extends to England and Wales only.

Section 1

SCHEDULE

OFFICES OF PUBLIC TRUSTEE AND ACCOUNTANT GENERAL

Public Trustee

1. For subsection (1) of section 8 of the Public Trustee Act 1906 (appointment and tenure of office of public trustee) there shall be substituted the following—

"(1) The Lord Chancellor shall appoint such person as he thinks fit to the office of Public Trustee and the person so appointed shall hold and vacate office in accordance with the terms of his appointment.

(1A) The Public Trustee shall be paid such salary or fees as the Lord Chancellor determines with the consent of the Treasury.

(1B) If one person holds office both as the Public Trustee and as the Accountant General of the Supreme Court then, if he ceases to be the Accountant General, he shall also cease to be the Public Trustee unless the Lord Chancellor otherwise directs.

(1C) If a vacancy occurs in the office of Public Trustee or the person appointed to hold office is for any reason unable to act for any period such person as the Lord Chancellor appoints as deputy in that office shall, during the vacancy or that period, perform the functions of that office (and any property vested in the Public Trustee may accordingly be dealt with by the deputy in all respects as if it were vested in him instead)."

Accountant General of the Supreme Court

2. In section 93(1) of the Supreme Court Act 1981 (status of officers for purposes of salary and pension), after the words "Schedule 2" there shall be inserted the words "or the office of Accountant General of the Supreme Court".

3. For subsections (2) and (3) of section 97 of the Supreme Court Act 1981 (office of Accountant General) there shall be substituted the following—

"(2) The Lord Chancellor shall appoint such person as he thinks fit to the office in the Supreme Court of Accountant General of the Supreme Court and the person so appointed shall hold and vacate office in accordance with the terms of his appointment.

(3) The Accountant General shall be paid such salary or fees as the Lord Chancellor determines with the consent of the Treasury.

(4) If one person holds office both as the Accountant General and as the Public Trustee then, if he ceases to be the Public Trustee, he shall also cease to be the Accountant General unless the Lord Chancellor otherwise directs.

(5) If a vacancy occurs in the office of Accountant General or the person appointed to hold the office is for any reason unable to act for any period such person as the Lord Chancellor appoints as deputy in that office shall, during the vacancy or that period, perform the functions of that office (and any property vested in the Accountant General may accordingly be dealt with by the deputy in all respects as if it were vested in him instead)."

4. In Schedule 2 to the Parliamentary Commissioner Act 1967 (which lists the authorities subject to investigation under that Act), after note 1, there shall be inserted the following note—

"1A. The reference to the Lord Chancellor's Department includes the department of the Accountant General of the Supreme Court (whether or not that office is held by the Permanent Secretary to the Lord Chancellor).".

EUROPEAN COMMUNITIES (AMENDMENT) ACT 1986*

(1986 c.58)

An Act to amend the European Communities Act 1972 so as to include in the definition of "the Treaties" and "the Community Treaties" certain provisions of the Single European Act signed at Luxembourg and The Hague on 17th and 28th February 1986 and extend certain provisions relating to the European Court to any court attached thereto; and to amend references to the Assembly of the European Communities and approve the Single European Act. [7th November 1986]

INTRODUCTION AND GENERAL NOTE

This Act makes legislative changes which are necessary in order to enable the United Kingdom to comply with the obligations entailed by the Single European Act. The Single European Act was approved by the European Council in December 1985 and signed at Luxembourg and The Hague on February 17 and February 28, 1986. The Single European Act has to be ratified by all national Parliaments of the Member States of the European Communities before entering into force. It was intended that all necessary ratifications should occur by the end of December 1986, so that the Single European Act could come into force by January 1, 1987.

The Single European Act is divided into four Titles:

Title I contains certain common provisions. By Art. 1 the European Council, *i.e.* the meeting of the Heads of State of the Member States and the Commission's President, is formally recognised as part of the European Communities' institutional framework. By Art. 2 the European Council must meet, at least twice a year.

Title II contains provisions amending the Treaties establishing the European Communities, namely the Treaty establishing the European Coal and Steel Community, the Treaty establishing the European Economic Community and the Treaty establishing the European Atomic Energy Community.

The most important changes are as follows:

(a) A new decision-making procedure is established (the "co-operation procedure") involving the Council, the European Parliament and the Commission of the European Communities. It strengthens the role of the European Parliament in the legislative process of the European Economic Community (Arts. 6 and 7).

(b) The Council is given the power to create a Court of First Instance, attached to the European Court of Justice (Arts. 4, 5, 11, 12, 26 and 27).

(c) The Internal Market is to be completed by December 31, 1992 (Arts. 13, 14 and 15).

(d) Qualified majority voting by the Council is to apply in an increased number of areas concerning the Internal Market (Arts. 16, 18 and 19).

(e) The European Economic Community's competence is extended to cover co-operation in economic and monetary policy (Art. 20), social policy (Arts. 21 and 22), economic and social cohesion (Art. 23), research and technological development (Art. 24) and the environment (Art. 25).

Title III contains provisions on European Co-operation by Member States of the European Communities in the sphere of foreign policy.

Title IV contains general and final conditions. Art. 33 provides for ratification by Member States of the European Communities. Art. 34 provides that the Single European Act shall be drawn up in a single original in the Danish, Dutch, English, French, German, Greek, Irish, Italian, Portuguese and Spanish languages, the text in each of these languages being equally authentic.

The European Communities (Amendment) Act 1986 contains certain amendments to the European Communities Act 1972, namely:

S.1 of the Act provides that the definition of "the Treaties" and "the Common Treaties" in s.1(2) of the European Communities Act 1972, shall be extended to include Title II and, so far as they relate to any of the Communities or any Community institution, the preamble and Titles I and IV of the Single European Act.

S.2(a) of the Act provides that references in s.3(1) of the European Communities Act

---

* Annotations by Alison A. Green, LL.M., Barrister.

1972, to the "decision of the European Court and any court attached thereto" should be substituted for the words "decision of the European Court."

S.2(b) of the Act provides that in ss.3(2) and (3) and 11(1) of the European Communities Act 1972 the following should be added after "the European Court," namely the words "or any court attached thereto."

The European Communities (Amendment) Act 1986 provides in s.3 for the substitution of the words "European Parliament" for "Assembly of the European Communities" and for the substitution of the words "European Parliamentary" for the words "Assembly" and "European Assembly" in certain enactments and instruments.

S.4(1) of this Act provides for it to be cited as the European Communities (Amendment) Act 1986.

S.4(3) provides that enactments and instruments set out in the Schedule to this Act are to be repealed or revoked to the extent specified in the third column of the Schedule.

COMMENCEMENT

Royal Assent was received on November 7, 1986. The Act should come into force on January 1, 1987.

PARLIAMENTARY DEBATES

Hansard: H.C. Vol. 94, col. 1083; Vol. 96, col. 316; Vol. 99, col. 800; Vol. 100, cols. 483, 597, 927; Vol. 101, col. 504. H.L. Vol. 478, col. 656; Vol. 479, col. 1004; Vol. 480, cols. 246, 1035; Vol. 481, cols. 509, 913.

The Bill was considered in Committee by the House of Commons, June 16, 26 and 27, 1986.

Extended meaning of "the Treaties" and "the Community Treaties"

1. In section 1(2) of the European Communities Act 1972, in the definition of "the Treaties" and "the Community Treaties", after paragraph (*h*) (inserted by the European Communities (Spanish and Portuguese Accession) Act 1985) there shall be inserted the words "and

　　(*j*) the following provisions of the Single European Act signed at Luxembourg and The Hague on 17th and 28th February 1986, namely Title II (amendment of the treaties establishing the Communities) and, so far as they relate to any of the Communities or any Community institution, the preamble and Titles I (common provisions) and IV (general and final provisions);".

DEFINITIONS

S.1(2) and Schedule 1 to the European Communities Act 1972 set out the definition of "the Treaties" and of "the Community Treaties." The "Treaties," as defined in s.1(2) of that Act, include:
　(i) the Treaty concerning the accession of the United Kingdom to the European Economic Community and the European Atomic Energy Community,
　(ii) the six principal pre-accession Treaties which are listed in Part I of Schedule 1 to the Act,
　(iii) Treaties entered into by any of the Communities, and
　(iv) ancillary Treaties to which the United Kingdom becomes a party,
　(v) the Treaties relating to the accession of Denmark, Ireland, the Hellenic Republic, Spain and Portugal to the European Economic Community and the European Atomic Energy Community,
　(vi) decisions by the United Kingdom, Denmark, Ireland, the Hellenic Republic, Spain and Portugal, relating to their accession to the European Coal and Steel Community.

S.1 adds certain provisions of the Single European Act to the definition of "the Treaties and the Community Treaties" in s.1(2) of the European Community Act 1972, namely Title II, and, so far as they relate to any of the Communities or any Community institution, the preamble and Titles I and IV.

GENERAL NOTE

The effect of this amendment is that references in the European Communities Act 1972 to "the Treaties" or "the Community Treaties" are intended to cover Title II of the Single

European Act, which contains amendments to Treaties establishing the European Coal and Steel Community, the European Economic Community and the European Atomic Energy Community and, so far as they relate to any of the Communities or any Community institution, the preamble and Title I (common provisions) and Title IV (general and final provisions) of the Single European Act. The two most important consequences of this is that first, s.2(1) of the European Communities Act 1972 gives the force of law in the United Kingdom to those provisions of the Treaties which are directly applicable in Member States of the European Communities, without further implementing legislation, and, secondly, s.3(1) of the European Communities Act 1972 provides that any questions as to the meaning or effect of any of the Treaties shall be treated as a question of law and, if not referred to the European Court, has to be determined in accordance with principles laid down by the European Court.

Extension of provisions to courts attached to European Court

2. In the European Communities Act 1972—
   (*a*) in section 3(1) (which requires certain questions, if not referred to the European Court, to be determined in accordance with the principles laid down by and any relevant decision of the European Court), for "decision of the European Court)" there shall be substituted "decision of the European Court or any court attached thereto)"; and
   (*b*) in sections 3(2) and (3) and 11(1) (which, as regards the European Court, provide for judicial notice to be taken of its pronouncements, for proof of its judgments and orders, and for the trial and punishment of persons who in sworn evidence before it make statements which they know to be false or do not believe to be true), after "the European Court", wherever occurring, there shall be inserted "or any court attached thereto".

DEFINITIONS
   The words "any court attached thereto" refers to a court of first instance which the Council has power to attach to the European Court of Justice at Luxembourg. Such a court is to have jurisdiction to hear and determine at first instance, subject to a right of appeal to the Court of Justice on points of law, certain classes of actions or proceedings brought by natural or legal persons. Such a court is not to have competence to hear and determine actions brought by Member States or by Community institutions or questions referred for a preliminary ruling by the courts of Member States (see Arts. 4, 5, 11, 12, 26 and 27 of the Single European Act). Such a court has not yet been created.

GENERAL NOTE
   Para. (a) of this section extends s.3(1) of the European Communities Act 1972 so that in legal proceedings within the United Kingdom, all questions of law concerning the Treaties or Community instruments, if not referred to the European Court, are to be determined in accordance with principles laid down by the European Court or any court attached thereto.
   Para. (b) of this section extends to s.3(2) of the European Communities Act 1972 so that judicial notice may be taken of any decisions of or expressions of opinion on questions of law, as described above, by a court attached to the European Court. S.2(*b*) also extends s.3(3) to enable proof of judgments and orders of courts attached to the European Court to be given in legal proceedings within the United Kingdom by production of certified copies of such judgments and orders. Further, s.2(*b*) extends s.11(1) of the European Communities Act 1972 so that people, who in sworn evidence before a court attached to the European Court make statements which they know to be false or do not believe to be true, may be prosecuted and punished in the United Kingdom for making such statements.

Provisions relating to European Assembly

3.—(1) Subject to subsection (2) below and to the repeals and revocations made by section 4(3) below, any enactment or instrument passed or made before the day on which the Single European Act enters into force shall have effect on and after that day with the substitution—

(*a*) of a reference to the (or, as the case may be, a) European Parliament for any reference (however worded) to the (or an) Assembly of the European Communities; and

(*b*) of the words "European Parliamentary" for the word "Assembly" and for the words "European Assembly" wherever that word or those words are used adjectivally with reference to the European Assembly (together with, where necessary, the consequential substitution of "a" for "an").

(2) The provisions on which subsection (1) above operates do not include that subsection itself or subsection (3) below or the long title of this Act but, subject to those exceptions, include—

(*a*) the long titles of Acts passed before the day mentioned in subsection (1) above;

(*b*) any provision of an Act or instrument passed or made before that day specifying how that Act or instrument may be cited; and

(*c*) so much of any Act or instrument so passed or made as uses a mode of citation authorised by another such Act or instrument to refer to that other Act or instrument.

(3) On and after the day mentioned in subsection (1) above the enactments and instruments amended by this section shall have effect as if the Assembly of the European Communities had always been named the European Parliament.

(4) For the purpose of section 6 of the European Assembly Elections Act 1978 the Single European Act is hereby approved.

DEFINITIONS

The Assembly of the European Communities was the previous title of the European Parliament. References to the "Assembly of the European Communities" are to be replaced by the "European Parliament". Where the words "Assembly" or "European Assembly" are used adjectivally they are to be replaced by the words "European Parliamentary".

GENERAL NOTE

S.3 of this Act is intended to substitute references to the "European Parliament" for the words "Assembly of the European Communities" and to substitute references to "European Parliamentary" where the words "Assembly" or "European Assembly" are used adjectively.

Subs. (1)

Subject to subs. (2) and to the repeals and revocations made by s.4(3), references to "European Parliament" and "European Parliamentary" are to be substituted as described in the General Note, in enactments or instruments passed or made in the United Kingdom before the day on which the Single European Act enters into force. Such substitution shall take effect on and after the day on which the Single European Act enters into force.

Subs. (2)

This subsection includes provisions where the substitution of wording, as referred to in subs. (1), is to occur.

Subs. (4)

S.6 of the European Assembly Elections Act 1978 requires Parliamentary approval by way of an Act of Parliament for treaties increasing the powers of the Assembly. Subs. (4) gives such approval in relation to the Single European Act.

Short title, interpretation and repeals

4.—(1) This Act may be cited as the European Communities (Amendment) Act 1986.

(2) In this Act "the Single European Act" means the Single European Act signed at Luxembourg and The Hague on 17th and 28th February 1986.

(3) The enactments and instruments mentioned in the Schedule to this

Act are hereby repealed or revoked to the extent specified in the third column of that Schedule as from the day mentioned in section 3(1) above.

GENERAL NOTE

Subs. (3)

This subsection effects certain repeals and revocations as listed in the Schedule to this Act. The repeals and revocations abolish the definition of "Assembly," as set out in various enactments and instruments.

Section 4(3)   SCHEDULE

REPEALS

Acts

Chapter	Short title	Extent of repeal
1978 c.10.	European Assembly Elections Act 1978.	In section 1, the words "(in this Act referred to as the Assembly)".
1979 c.50.	European Assembly (Pay and Pensions) Act 1979.	In section 8(1), the definition of "the Assembly".
1985 c.50.	Representation of the People Act 1985.	In section 27(1), the definition of "the Assembly".

Instruments

Reference	Title	Extent of revocation
S.I. 1979 No. 521.	European Assembly Election Petition Rules 1979.	In Rule 2(1), the definition of "Assembly".
S.R. (N.I.) 1979 No. 179.	European Assembly Election Petition Rules (Northern Ireland) 1979.	In Rule 2(1), the definition of "Assembly".
S.I. 1984 No. 137.	European Assembly Elections Regulations 1984.	In Regulation 2(1), the definition of "Assembly".
S.I.1984 No. 198.	European Assembly Elections (Northern Ireland) Regulations 1984.	In Regulation 2(1), the definition of "Assembly".

SEX DISCRIMINATION ACT 1986*

(1986 c. 59)

An Act to amend the Sex Discrimination Act 1975 and sections 64 and 73 of the Employment Protection (Consolidation) Act 1978; to make provision with respect to requirements to discriminate in relation to employment which are contained in public entertainment licences; to provide for the removal of certain restrictions applying to the working hours and other working conditions of women; and to repeal the Baking Industry (Hours of Work) Act 1954.   [7th November 1986]

INTRODUCTION AND GENERAL NOTE

The first six sections of this Act amend the SDA 1975 and the EqPA 1970 to bring them into line with European Community law. The amendments were prompted by two major cases in which the European Court of Justice found that the U.K.'s sex discrimination legislation failed to comply with the Equal Treatment Directive (76/207/EEC). In the remainder of the Act, protective legislation applying to one sex only is repealed.

Ss.1 and 6 were introduced to comply with the European Court's findings in *E.C. Commission* v. *U.K.* (Case 165/82 [1984] I.C.R. 192). S.1 extends the protection of SDA 1975 to undertakings with five employees, or less, and partnerships of five partners, or less, with an exception to maintain privacy. S.6 provides for the avoidance of discriminatory terms in collective agreements, internal rules of undertakings, and rules governing the independent occupations and professions. No new remedial measures are, however, established (see General Note to s.6).

Ss.2 and 3 were introduced as a result of the case of *Marshall* v. *Southampton and South West Hampshire Area Health Authority (Teaching)* [1986] I.R.L.R. 140, in which the European Court held that the Equal Treatment Directive is contravened if men and women are required to retire at different ages. The case held that the Directive was directly applicable to State employees, but legislation was needed to provide a remedy for private sector employees. The present Act amends both the SDA 1975 and the EqPA 1970 to comply with the ruling, and applies to partnerships as well as employees. S.2 makes it unlawful to discriminate against a woman solely on the grounds of her age, for example by dismissing or demoting her or by refusing her promotion or training because she is nearing 60. By s.3, the upper age limit for unfair dismissal cases is equalised. This section only comes into effect on November 7, 1987, to give employers 12 months to adjust to the new requirements. The case did not require amendment of the State pension age, which therefore remains at 65 for men and 60 for women. The upper age limit for redundancy compensation remains likewise unchanged, at 65 for men and 60 for women. (s.82(1) EPCA 1978).

S.4 amends the provisions whereby training may be offered to women only or men only where members of that sex are under-represented in an area of work, or are in special need of training because they have been out of the labour market discharging domestic or family responsibilities. Under the 1975 Act, such training could only be offered by a body designated for that purpose by the Secretary of State. S.4 removes the requirement for designation, allowing anyone to provide such training. S.5 closes a loophole in the SDA

---

* Annotations by Sandra Fredman, B.A.(Rand), M.A., B.C.L.(Oxon), Lecturer in Law, King's College, University of London.

1975 by preventing local authorities from using public licensing powers in a discriminatory fashion.

Ss. 7 and 8 provide for the repeal of protective legislation restricting the hours of work for women, and in the case of the baking industry, of men. Hours of work of young people are unaffected. It is arguable that these repeals infringe the U.K.'s obligations under the European Social Charter (see note to Section 7 below).

PARLIAMENTARY DEBATES
Hansard: H.L. Vol. 470, col. 1286; Vol. 471, col. 1176; Vol. 472, col. 510; Vol. 473, col. 418; Vol. 474, col. 198. H.C. Vol. 98, col. 569; Vol. 102, cols. 1195, 1326.

The Bill was considered in Committee by the House of Commons in Standing Committee A, June 12 to July 1, 1986.

ABBREVIATIONS
EOC: Equal Opportunities Commission
EqPA 1970: Equal Pay Act 1970
RRA 1976: Race Relations Act 1976
SDA 1975: Sex Discrimination Act 1975
SC: Standing Committee
TULRA: Trade Union and Labour Relations Act 1974

Private households and small undertakings and partnerships

1.—(1) In section 6 of the Sex Discrimination Act 1975 (in this Act referred to as "the 1975 Act"), subsection (3) (which excludes private households and undertakings of five employees or less from the operation of the provisions of subsections (1) and (2) of that section) shall cease to have effect.

(2) After paragraph (*b*) of subsection (2) of section 7 of the 1975 Act (cases where being a man is a genuine occupational qualification) there shall be inserted the following paragraph—

"(*ba*) the job is likely to involve the holder of the job doing his work, or living, in a private home and needs to be held by a man because objection might reasonably be taken to allowing to a woman—

(i) the degree of physical or social contact with a person living in the home, or

(ii) the knowledge of intimate details of such a person's life,

which is likely, because of the nature or circumstances of the job or of the home, to be allowed to, or available to, the holder of the job; or".

(3) In section 11 of the 1975 Act, in subsection (1) (which deals with discrimination against a woman in relation to a position as partner in a firm consisting of six or more partners), the words "consisting of six or more partners" shall cease to have effect.

COMMENCEMENT: s.10(2) (February 7, 1987).

GENERAL NOTE
In *E.C. Commission* v. *U.K.* [1984] I.C.R. 192, the European Court held that there was no justification for excluding small undertakings or private households from the protection of the SDA. However, it did acknowledge the importance of respect for privacy. This section therefore aims to protect all workers from discrimination, while maintaining a narrower exception in situations in which privacy is genuinely at stake. Thus s.1(1) repeals the exception in s.6(3) of the 1975 Act, which excluded private households and undertakings of five employees or less from the operation of the employment provisions of the Act, while s.1(2) creates a new exception for employment in a private home involving physical or social contact with a person living there or knowledge of intimate details of the person's life. Although not explicitly required by the European Court decision, the section also repeals the exemption for firms of fewer than six partners previously contained in s.11(1) of the

1975 Act. (It is noteworthy that similar exemptions contained in the RRA 1976 are not repealed).

Subs. (1)

Notwithstanding this amendment, the Government has proposed that Community law be amended to allow member states to exempt very small enterprises from national provisions implementing the Equal Treatment Directive. (*Hansard*, H.L. Vol. 571, No. 52, cols. 1177, 1178).

Subs. (2)

The European Court held that the exception for all private households was broader than necessary to protect legitimate interests in privacy. This section indroduces a more limited exception to protect privacy, by adding a new subsection to s.7 of the 1975 Act, which lists employments where being a man is a "genuine occupational qualification." While employees having relatively little social or physical contact with the householder (such as a gardener or cook in a large household) will be protected against discrimination, the amendment permits an employer to discriminate in relation to jobs which involve working or living in a private home and which entail physical or social contact with a member of a household or knowledge of intimate details of such a person's life, such that there could be reasonable objection to the job being held by a person of a particular sex. It should be noted that s.7 only permits discrimination in respect of the arrangements made for the purposes of determining who should be offered employment (s.6(1)(a)), or a refusal or deliberate omission to offer employment (s.6(1)(c)) or in the access given to opportunities for promotion and other benefits (s.6(2)(a)). It does not permit discrimination in the terms on which employment is offered (s.6(1)(b)), nor is an employer allowed to discriminate against an employee by dismissing or subjecting him or her to any other detriment (s.6(2)(b)). Nor does the exception apply to discrimination by way of victimisation (s.4). "Private home" is not defined.

"objection might reasonably be taken": Mere subjective preference will not be sufficient.

"knowledge of intimate details": This section is intended to deal with situations in which, even if there is little physical or social contact with a person living in the home, the job involves knowledge of intimate details of that person's life. "The intention is to protect, for example, a woman who would suffer embarrassment and indignity to think of a man washing and ironing her underclothes or performing other very personal services even if she were out of the house at the time or bedridden upstairs so that there was no physical or social contact." (*Hansard,* H.L., Vol. 474, No. 83, col. 199).

Discrimination as to retirement etc.

2.—(1) In subsection (4) of section 6 of the 1975 Act (exclusion of provisions discriminating against employees etc. in relation to death or retirement), at the end there shall be inserted the words "except in so far as, in their application to provision in relation to retirement, they render it unlawful for a person to discriminate against a woman—

> (*a*) in such of the terms on which he offers her employment as make provision in relation to the way in which he will afford her access to opportunities for promotion, transfer or training or as provide for her dismissal or demotion, or
>
> (*b*) in the way he affords her access to opportunities for promotion, transfer or training or by refusing or deliberately omitting to afford her access to any such opportunities; or
>
> (*c*) by dismissing her or subjecting her to any detriment which results in her dismissal or consists in or involves her demotion."

(2) In subsection (4) of section 11 of the 1975 Act (exclusion of provisions discriminating against partners etc. in relation to death or retirement), at the end there shall be inserted the words "except in so far as, in their application to provision made in relation to retirement, they render it unlawful for a firm to discriminate against a woman—

> (*a*) in such of the terms on which they offer her a position as partner as provide for her expulsion from that position; or
>
> (*b*) by expelling her from a position as partner or subjecting her to any detriment which results in her expulsion from such a position."

(3) In section 82 of the 1975 Act (interpretation), after subsection (1) there shall be inserted the following subsection—

"(1A) References in this Act to the dismissal of a person from employment or to the expulsion of a person from a position as partner include references—

(a) to the termination of that person's employment or partnership by the expiration of any period (including a period expiring by reference to an event or circumstance), not being a termination immediately after which the employment or partnership is renewed on the same terms; and

(b) to the termination of that person's employment or partnership by any act of his (including the giving of notice) in circumstances such that he is entitled to terminate it without notice by reason of the conduct of the employer or, as the case may be, the conduct of the other partners."

(4) In section 6 of the Equal Pay Act 1970 (exclusions of sections 1 to 5)—

(a) in subsection (1A)(b) (terms related to, or provision in connection with, death or retirement), at the end there shall be inserted the words "other than a term or provision which, in relation to retirement, affords access to opportunities for promotion, transfer or training or provides for a woman's dismissal or demotion"; and

(b) in subsection (2) (meaning of retirement), at the end there shall be inserted the words "and the reference in subsection (1A) above to a woman's dismissal shall be construed in accordance with section 82(1A) of the Sex Discrimination Act 1975 as a reference to her dismissal from employment."

COMMENCEMENT: s.10(3) & (4).

GENERAL NOTE

This section was introduced as a result of the European Court ruling that dismissal of a woman solely because she has attained the qualifying age for a State pension, which age is different for men and women under national legislation, constitutes discrimination on the grounds of sex, contrary to Article 5(1) of the Equal Treatment Directive No. 76/207 (*Marshall* v. *Southampton and South West Hampshire Area Health Authority (Teaching)* [1986] I.R.L.R. 140). According to this case, the Equal Treatment Directive was directly applicable to State employees, but not private employees. This amendment applies the decision to all employees.

The State pension age itself is unaffected by this Act. By virtue of Article 7 of EEC Directive 79/7 on Social Security, Member States are free to decide for themselves at what age State pensions are payable. Retirement age and the age at which State pensions are payable may therefore differ. This disjuncture has some problematic implications. A woman over the age of 60 has the option of retiring, in which case she receives a State pension, or of continuing at work, in which case she can defer her pension until she retires, and receive an enhanced pension on retirement (or, if she earns below a given limit, she can receive her State pension while working). Since many women may have interrupted working lives and therefore inadequate pensions, they may opt to continue working to improve their pensions. They are not required to pay national insurance contributions during the years worked over the age of 60. Men, on the other hand receive no State pension if they retire before 65, and continue to pay national insurance contributions during the years worked up to 65. The Government has argued that it would be too expensive to equalise pensionable age.

What effect does the amendment have on occupational pension schemes and other benefits linked to retirement? The intention behind the wording of the amendment was to preserve the present position in this respect. Prior to the amendment, it was permissible to offer different benefits under occupational pension schemes, although employers have since 1978 been required to provide equal access to membership of such schemes (ss.53–56 Social Security Pensions Act 1975). The unamended s.6(4) of the SDA 1975 accordingly provided that s.6(1)(b) and (2) did not apply to provision in relation to death or retirement. The amendment does not repeal s.6(4), but creates an exception to the exception, deliberately leaving elements in the realms of legitimate discrimination. Thus, the amendment deliberately omits the words "or to any other benefits, facilities or services, or by omitting to afford her access to them" in s.6(2)(*a*). It also omits the words "any other detriment", referring instead to a detriment which results in her dismissal or consists in or involves her demotion. The result is that occupational pensions, provision in relation to death and redundancy payment schemes, are kept out of the purview of the Act.

The extent to which this complies with European law is questionable. It is submitted that s.6(4) as amended, complies with European law in so far as it permits the age at which an occupational pension is payable to be linked to the State pensionable age; but not in so far as it purports to permit discrimination in the quantum of benefits themselves. Differential ages are permitted because Directive 79/7 allows Member States to exclude from its scope the determination of pensionable ages, and possible consequences for other benefits. In *Burton* v. *British Railways Board* [1982] I.R.L.R. 116, the European Court held that since States may determine their own pensionable ages, any benefits tied to the pensionable age may lie outside Directive 79/7 (reiterated in *Marshall* v. *Southampton and South West Hampshire Area Health Authority (Teaching)* [1986] I.R.L.R. 140, para. 35). The *Marshall* case itself specifically excluded the question of access to statutory or occupational retirement schemes from consideration. (para. 31). However, *Burton* was limited to the age at which benefits are payable. To the extent that s.6(4) permits discrimination in the quantum of benefits as against the age at which benefits are payable, it is submitted that it may continue to be contrary to European law. In *Marshall*, it was stated that Article 1(2) of the Equal Treatment Directive (allowing the progressive implementation in respect of social security matters), must be construed strictly. Moreover, in *Bilka-Kaufhaus Gmbh* v. *Weber von Hartz* [1986] I.R.L.R. 317, the European Court of Justice held that an occupational pension scheme was not a social security scheme if it was based on agreement between the employer and employees, even if this was adopted in accordance with statutory obligations. Only if there is no element of agreement, and the scheme is compulsory for general categories of workers, is it a social security scheme. In other cases, an occupational pension scheme could count as "pay" for the purposes of Article 119, being consideration which the worker received indirectly in respect of his or her employment from the employer. (See also *Worringham and Humphreys* v. *Lloyds Bank,* Case 69/80 [1981] I.C.R. 558 (E.C.J.)). Article 119 is directly applicable, allowing a worker to sue directly, without the need for enabling legislation. Thus where s.6(4) fails to provide a remedy, an employee can base a claim on Article 119 itself.

A similar argument applies to access to redundancy payments. It remains lawful to link access to redundancy payments to State pension age under *Burton* above. With respect to quantum, it is submitted that where severance pay is the subject of agreement either with the individual worker or the worker's trade union, it counts as pay for Article 119 under the *Bilka-Kaufhaus* decision, and discrimination is outlawed.

Again, discrimination in access to other facilities remains lawful. However, this exception should have limited impact. First, the facilities must relate to retirement. Secondly, if the treatment is a fundamental breach of contract, then the person is entitled to resign and claim to have been unfairly dismissed (subs. (3) below). Thirdly, if the facilities amount to consideration in respect of employment (for example, discount cash facilities), they may be "pay" for the purposes of Article 119 on the argument above.

Further legislation eliminating discrimination in occupational pension schemes is to be expected following the adoption on July 24, 1986 of a new Directive on equal treatment in occupational and social security schemes (86/378 EEC, (1986) 10 *Equal Opportunities Review*). This provides for elimination of discrimination in schemes designed to supplement State pensions. However, it is limited in several important ways. In particular, it permits equalisation of access to be deferred until State pension ages are equalised; it allows discrimination in respect of survivors' pensions; and it does not outlaw differentiation based on actuarial calculations (Article 9). Implementing legislation is required by January 1, 1993.

Note that commencement is delayed for 12 months following Royal Assent, in order to give employers time to make new arrangements, unless the Secretary of State decides to bring them into force earlier (s.10). This means that this section will probably come into force on November 7, 1987. In the meantime, the *Marshall* case continues to apply to State employees. (The definition of "State employees" for these purposes is for the national courts to determine). Moreover, according to the E.A.T. in *Parsons* v. *East Surrey Health Authority* ((1986) 10 *Equal Opportunities Review* 35), State employees dismissed before the *Marshall* case may rely on *Marshall*, the latter decision being declaratory of the existing law. In addition, the continuing lawfulness of different retirement ages in the light of *Marshall* is being questioned in the Appeal Court case of *Duke* v. *Reliance Systems*. (See generally (1986) 10 *Equal Opportunities Review* 11).

Subs. (1)

"except in so far as in their application to provision in relation to retirement": The exception in s.6(4) in respect of provision in relation to death is untouched by this amendment; it remains lawful to discriminate in this respect (*e.g.* a pension may be payable to the dependent spouse of a deceased male employee, but not of a deceased female employee. But see now Social Security Act 1986.)

"provision in relation to death or retirement": The unamended s.6(4) has been broadly construed to mean everything which is "part and parcel of the employers' system for catering for retirement." (*Barber* v. *Guardian Royal Exchange Assurance Group*; *Roberts* v. *Tate & Lyle Food and Distribution* [1983] I.R.L.R. 240). It is submitted that, although these words have the opposite effect in the amendment, they should be construed with similar breadth.

"access to promotion, transfer or training": The amendment deliberately omits the words "or to any other benefits, facilities or services, or by omitting to afford her access to them" in s.6(2)(*a*). It also omits the words "any other detriment", referring only to a detriment which results in her dismissal or consists in or involves her demotion. This was intended to permit discrimination in respect of access to occupational pensions and voluntary redundancy schemes.

For the relationship between this and European law, see General Note to section 2 above.

"demotion": The statute goes beyond the strict requirements of the *Marshall* case in including demotion. Thus, an employer cannot remove major responsibilities from women or reduce their status unless the same is done for men of the same age. (*Hansard*, H.L. Vol. 481, No. 161, col. 955).

"subject her to any detriment which results in her dismissal": "Dismissal" is defined in subs. (3) to include constructive dismissal. S.6(2)(*a*) uses the words "any other detriment". These words were deliberately omitted, again to allow discrimination in respect of occupational pensions (SC 1990). (See General Note above).

"Discriminate": Indirect discrimination is included. Thus a rule that full-time employees must retire at 65 and part-timers at 60 may be unlawful indirect discrimination if disproportionate numbers of women work part-time.

Subs. (2)

This subsection limits the exclusion in relation to death and retirement in respect of partnerships. As in subs. (1) above, the exclusion remains in effect in so far as it affects provision relating to death. In addition, it remains lawful to discriminate against a woman in respect of provision in relation to retirement which may concern access to benefits facilities or services, or which subject her to any detriment not leading to her expulsion. This allows discrimination in pensionable age and the age at which voluntary redundancy payments are made if linked to State pensionable age. As to whether it is lawful to discriminate in respect of the nature of the benefits themselves, see note to subs. (1) above.

"Expulsion": Defined in subs. (3) below.

Subs. (3)

"expiration of any period, (including a period expiring by reference to an event or circumstance)": As in the cases of unfair dismissal and redundancy compensation, the concept of "dismissal" includes the expiry without renewal of a fixed term contract (s.55(2)(*b*) EPCA 1978). This section, in addition, goes beyond s.55 EPCA in including periods which expire by reference to an event or circumstance. "Purpose" contracts, or contracts which expire by reference to an uncertain future event, have been held to be excluded from s.55 EPCA (*Wiltshire County Council* v. *NAFTHE* [1980] I.C.R. 455, *Brown* v. *Knowsley Borough Council* [1986] I.R.L.R. 102). The present definition would include such contracts, and *a fortiori*, contracts which specify that they will expire at a given age.

"Termination in circumstances such that he is entitled to terminate it without notice by reason of the conduct of the employer": This is identical to the concept of "constructive dismissal" in s.55(2)(*c*) EPCA (unfair dismissal) and s.83(2) EPCA (redundancy). The test is whether the employer has fundamentally breached the contract of employment, rather than whether the employer has behaved unreasonably (*Western Excavating* v. *Sharp* [1978] I.C.R. 221). However, there is an implied term of mutual trust and cooperation. Breach of this term by the employer may entitle an employee to resign and claim to have been constructively dismissed (*Post Office* v. *Roberts* [1980] I.R.L.R. 347).

Subs. (4)

The EqPA 1970 is concerned with contractual issues, whereas the SDA 1975 deals with non-contractual issues. The effect of this section is to narrow the exclusion in relation to death or retirement so that the EqPA applies to contractual terms concerning retirement related elements such as dismissal, demotion, and access to opportunities for promotion, transfer or training. One result is that an employee can complain to an industrial tribunal about the contractual terms before being retired. As in subsections (1) and (2) above, provision in relation to death is unaffected, and reference to access to benefits, facilities or services is deliberately omitted. However, any benefits which amount to "pay" for the purposes of Article 119 (consideration directly or indirectly in respect of employment) remain discriminatory under that Article, which is directly applicable. (See *Worringham* v. *Lloyds Bank* [1981] I.C.R. 558 (E.C.J.) and *Garland* v. *British Railway Engineering* [1982] I.R.L.R. 257). (See General Note above).

As in subss. (1) and (2), retirement includes the expiry without renewal of a term, and constructive dismissal (subs. (3)). With respect to the latter, however, where a term is included in the contract, it is difficult to see how application of the term can be construed as a fundamental breach, as required by the definition of "constructive dismissal" in *Western Excavating* v. *Sharp* ([1978] I.C.R. 221).

Note that under the Social Security Pensions Act 1975 (ss.53–56), equal access to occupational pension schemes must be afforded to men and women, and by s.6(1A)(*a*) EqPA 1970, an equality clause operates in relation to membership of such a scheme. However, that Act does not prevent discrimination in the nature of the benefits provided.

Age of retirement etc.: unfair dismissal

3.—(1) For paragraph (*b*) of subsection (1) of section 64 of the Employment Protection (Consolidation) Act 1978 (upper age limit for unfair dismissal cases) there shall be substituted the following paragraph—

"(*b*) attained the following age on or before the effective date of termination, that is to say—

(i) if in the undertaking in which he was employed there was a normal retiring age for an employee holding the position which he has held and the age was the same whether the employee holding that position was a man or a woman, that normal retiring age; and

(ii) in any other case, the age of sixty-five."

(2) In subsection (6) of section 73 of the said Act of 1978 (definitions for the purpose of the provision for reducing a basic award for unfair dismissal), for the words from " 'the specified anniversary' " to "her birth" there shall be substituted the words " 'the specified anniversary' in relation to an employee means the sixty-fourth anniversary of the day of his birth".

(3) Subsection (2) above shall not affect any award for the unfair dismissal of an employee in relation to whom the effective date of termination (within the meaning of Part V of the said Act of 1978) was before the coming into force of that subsection.

COMMENCEMENT: s.10(2), (3).

GENERAL NOTE

This section amends s.64 EPCA 1978 to equalise the age at which men and women cease to be eligible to claim unfair dismissal. The section deliberately omits to amend s.82(1) EPCA 1978, which provides that male employees cease to be entitled to statutory redundancy payments on reaching the age of 65 while female employees cease to be eligible at 60. The differential age entitlement for redundancy payments thus remains on the statute book. One result is that a woman over 60, who is unfairly selected for redundancy, may be eligible to claim that she has been unfairly dismissed (unless the normal retirement age for both men and women is 60), whereas she is not eligible for statutory redundancy pay. (*Hansard*, H.L. Vol. 481, No. 161, col. 971.)

The justification given in Parliament for retaining the differential age requirement was that redundancy payments, like pensions, were covered by the Social Security Directive

(79/7), which allows Member States to determine their own pensionable ages. As in s.2 above, it remains lawful under *Burton* v. *British Railways Board* [1982] I.R.L.R. 116 (E.C.J.), to link benefits to the State pension age.

Subs. (1)
"*normal retirement age*": Normal retirement age is not necessarily the age specified in the contract. There is a strong presumption that the contractual age is the normal retirement age, but this can be rebutted if in practice there is some other age at which employees are regularly retired. The question is: What would be the reasonable expectation of an employee at the relevant time? (*Waite* v. *GCHQ* [1983] I.C.R. 653 (H.L.)). Note that the normal retirement age applies unless there is no such age (*e.g.* employees generally retire at different ages), or there is a different normal retirement age for men and women. Only then does the age of 65 apply.

Subs. (2)
S.73(5) and (6) provide for the tapering of the basic award payable to an employee who has been unfairly dismissed in the last year before retirement age, previously 59 for women and 64 for men. This age is now 64 for both men and women.

Discrimination in relation to training

4.—(1) Section 47 of the 1975 Act (discrimination in relation to training by a training body) shall be amended as follows.
(2) In subsections (1) and (3)—
    (*a*) for the words "a training body" there shall be substituted the words "any person"; and
    (*b*) for the words "it appears to the training body" there shall be substituted the words "it reasonably appears to that person".
(3) In subsection (2)—
    (*a*) for the words "it appears to a training body" there shall be substituted the words "it reasonably appears to any person"; and
    (*b*) for the words "the training body" there shall be substituted the words "that person".
(4) For subsection (4) (definition of, and power to designate, training body) there shall be substituted the following subsection—
    "(4) the preceding provisions of this section shall not apply in relation to any discrimination which is rendered unlawful by section 6."

COMMENCEMENT: November 7, 1986 (Royal Assent).

GENERAL NOTE
S.47 SDA 1975 permits single sex training facilities to be established where persons of that sex are under-represented in an area of work or have left the labour market for domestic or family reasons. Prior to the amendment, such facilities could only be set up by the Manpower Services Commission, industrial training boards, (s.14(2)(*a*) and (*b*) SDA 1975), or persons designated for these purposes by the Secretary of State. By October 1986, over 170 training bodies had been designated. (*Hansard*, H.L. Vol. 481, No. 161, col. 973). The amendment removes the need for administrative sanction. Instead, it permits anyone to set up such a training course, provided it "reasonably appears" to that person that the criteria in s.47(1), (2) and (3) have been satisfied. Policing is to be done by individuals: an individual who is refused access to training facilities because they are limited to one sex, may complain of unlawful discrimination on the basis that s.47 has not been complied with. Complaints of actions unlawful by virtue of Part II SDA 1975 (*e.g.* s.14 SDA 1975) lie to an industrial tribunal (s.63 SDA 1975); complaints under Part III lie to the county court (s.66 SDA 1975). Note that training projects may be eligible for assistance from the European Social Fund. (SC 207).

Subss. (2) and (3)
"*reasonably appears*": The test is objective.

Subs. (4)

S.47 does not permit employers to discriminate positively in offering employment or in any of the other employment related factors mentioned in s.6 SDA 1975. However, by s.48, employers may offer single sex training to existing employees if the criteria in that section (substantially the same as those in s.47), are satisfied.

Discrimination required by public entertainment licences

5.—(1) Nothing in—
  (*a*) any licence granted (whether before or after the coming into force of this section) under Schedule 1 to the Local Government (Miscellaneous Provisions) Act 1982 or Schedule 12 to the London Government Act 1963 (public entertainment licences); or
  (*b*) any regulations made for the purpose of prescribing the terms, conditions or restrictions on or subject to which any such licence is deemed to be granted,

shall have effect, at any time after the coming into force of this section, so as to require any person to do any act which, apart from section 51 of the 1975 Act (acts done under statutory authority), is rendered unlawful by Part II of the 1975 Act (discrimination in relation to employment) or by so much of Part IV of the 1975 Act as relates to acts rendered unlawful by the said Part II.

(2) In this section "act" has the same meaning as in the 1975 Act.

COMMENCEMENT: November 7, 1986.

GENERAL NOTE

As a result of this amendment, a public entertainments licence, or regulation under which such a licence is granted, is unlawful if it requires discrimination which would be unlawful under Part II SDA 1975 (discrimination in relation to employment). The section reverses the effects of *Greater London Council* v. *Farrar* [1980] I.C.R. 226, in which it was held that, by virtue of s.51 SDA 1975 (acts done under statutory authority), it was lawful for the Greater London Council (using its powers under Sched. 12 to the London Government Act 1963) to issue a licence to an entertainer subject to the provision that no women wrestlers were permitted. The present section was prompted by the European Commission, which advised that the result of the *Farrar* case was in breach of the Equal Treatment Directive (76/207 EEC). The amendment does not, however, change the position with respect to college statutes, such as those under the Universities of Oxford and Cambridge Act 1923, which may lawfully exclude women from membership of the college (*Hugh-Jones* v. *St. Johns College, Cambridge* [1979] I.C.R. 848 (E.A.T.)). At present, the majority of colleges in Oxford and Cambridge allow fellows of both sexes, with the exception of some women's colleges, on the basis that it is important to retain greater access for women. Their position is under discussion (SC 217).

"whether before or after": Unlike s.51 of the 1975 Act (acts done under statutory authority), this section is retrospective.

Collective agreements and rules of undertakings

6.—(1) Without prejudice to the generality of section 77 of the 1975 Act (which makes provision with respect to the validity and revision of contracts), that section shall apply, as it applies in relation to the term of a contract, to the following, namely—
  (*a*) any term of a collective agreement, including an agreement which was not intended, or is presumed not to have been intended, to be a legally enforceable contract;
  (*b*) any rule made by an employer for application to all or any of the persons who are employed by him or who apply to be, or are, considered by him for employment;

(*c*) any rule made by an organisation, authority or body to which subsection (2) below applies for application to all or any of its members or prospective members or to all or any of the persons on whom it has conferred authorisations or qualifications or who are seeking the authorisations or qualifications which it has power to confer;

and that section shall so apply whether the agreement was entered into, or the rule made, before or after the coming into force of this section.

(2) This subsection applies to—

    (*a*) any organisation of workers;

    (*b*) any organisation of employers;

    (*c*) any organisation whose members carry on a particular profession or trade for the purposes of which the organisation exists;

    (*d*) any authority or body which can confer an authorisation or qualification which is needed for, or facilitates, engagement in a particular profession or trade.

(3) For the purposes of the said section 77 a term or rule shall be deemed to provide for the doing of an act which would be rendered unlawful by the 1975 Act if—

    (*a*) it provides for the inclusion in any contract of employment of any term which by virtue of an equality clause would fall either to be modified or to be supplemented by an additional term; and

    (*b*) that clause would not be prevented from operating in relation to that contract by section 1(3) of the Equal Pay Act 1970 (material factors justifying discrimination).

(4) Nothing in the said section 77 shall affect the operation of any term or rule in so far as it provides for the doing of a particular act in circumstances where the doing of that act would not be, or be deemed by virtue of subsection (3) above to be, rendered unlawful by the 1975 Act.

(5) The avoidance by virtue of the said section 77 of any term or rule which provides for any person to be discriminated against shall be without prejudice to the following rights except in so far as they enable any person to require another person to be treated less favourably than himself, namely—

    (*a*) such of the rights of the person to be discriminated against; and

    (*b*) such of the rights of any person who will be treated more favourably in direct or indirect consequence of the discrimination,

as are conferred by or in respect of a contract made or modified wholly or partly in pursuance of, or by reference to, that term or rule.

(6) In this section "collective agreement" means any agreement relating to one or more of the matters mentioned in section 29(1) of the Trade Union and Labour Relations Act 1974 (meaning of trade dispute), being an agreement made by or on behalf of one or more employers or one or more organisations of employers or associations of such organisations with one or more organisations of workers or associations of such organisations.

(7) Any expression used in this section and in the 1975 Act has the same meaning in this section as in that Act, and this section shall have effect as if the terms of any service to which Parts II and IV of that Act apply by virtue of subsection (2) of section 85 of that Act (Crown application) were terms of a contract of employment and, in relation to the terms of any such service, as if service for the purposes of any person mentioned in that subsection were employment by that person.

DEFINITIONS
  "collective agreement": s.2(6).
  "employment": s.2(7) (s.82(1) SDA 1975).
  "profession": s.2(7) (s.82(1) SDA 1975).

COMMENCEMENT: s.10(2) (February 7, 1987).

GENERAL NOTE

This section was introduced to comply with the ruling of the European Court in *E.C. Commission* v. *U.K.* ([1984] I.C.R. 192) in which it was held that British law violated Article 3 of Directive 76/207/EEC which states: "Any provisions contrary to the principle of equal treatment which are included in collective agreements, individual contracts of employment, internal rules of undertakings and rules governing independent occupations and professions shall be, or may be declared, null and void or may be amended".

The section provides that s.77 SDA 1975 should apply to collective agreements, employers' rules and rules of professional bodies in the same way as it applies to contractual terms. (subss. (1) and (2)). Thus, a term of a collective agreement or of a relevant rule is void where its inclusion renders the making of the collective agreement or rule unlawful by virtue of the SDA 1975; or it is included in furtherance of an act rendered unlawful by virtue of that Act or it provides for the doing of an act which would be rendered unlawful by that Act (s.77(1) SDA 1975). S.77(2) SDA 1975 provides that where the victim of the discrimination is a party to the contract, the term will not be void but unenforceable against that party, and s.77(5) provides for a county court, on application by any person "interested in a contract to which subs. (2) applies", to make an order removing or modifying any term made unenforceable by that subsection. These two subsections of s.77 are unlikely to apply in the case of collective agreements since the parties to collective agreements, the employer and the trade union, are not the victims of discrimination; but it may apply to members of organisations specified in subs. (2) below. S.6 of the current Act also extends s.77 SDA 1975 to terms which contravene the EqPA (s.6(3)).

The avoidance of a term in a collective agreement or rule is without prejudice to the rights of the victim of discrimination or anyone treated more favourably as a result of discrimination (subs. (5)). Thus, if a collective agreement is incorporated into an individual contract, the term remains part of the contract until a new agreement has been negotiated. Otherwise, the Government argued, the avoidance of a term relating, for example, to holiday pay would leave individuals without any holiday entitlement pending the negotiation of new agreements.

The Government chose to implement the Directive by declaring discriminatory terms void, rather than amending them. No new remedies are established. The impact is therefore minimal. By s.18 TULRA, collective agreements are presumed not to be intended to be legally binding unless the parties state otherwise in writing, and in practice, the vast majority of collective agreements are not legally binding. Merely to declare discriminatory terms in such agreements void therefore adds nothing to the present legal framework. The only remedies are at individual level, (as was already the case prior to the present Act), in the form of an application to an industrial tribunal under the EqPA 1970 or SDA 1975, or to a county court under s.77 SDA 1975.

With respect to employer's rules (subs. (1)(*b*)), the impact is similarly minimal, since no additional remedies have been provided. The 1975 Act in any case provides that if the employer's rules are discriminatory in the arrangements made for determining who should be offered employment or in the terms on which employment is offered, or in access to promotion, etc., or any of the other areas covered by s.6 SDA 1975, the employee has recourse to an industrial tribunal. Where the rule is incorporated into an individual contract, the employee's remedy again lies to an industrial tribunal, usually under the EqPA 1970. Although the present section declares a discriminatory rule void *per se*, the term incorporated into the individual contract will in most circumstances remain in force (subs. (5)) until a tribunal has decided otherwise, or the rule has been changed by the employer.

Similarly, little has changed with respect to the rules of an organisation to which subs. (2) applies (subs. (1)(*c*)). Such rules are usually construed as a contract between the members and any discriminatory terms would have been void under s.77 before the 1986 Act. This section therefore merely reiterates the point.

The decision to rely on individual remedies does not, however, take into account the severe limitations to which individuals are subject. As the European Court recognised in the non-compliance case (*E.C. Commission* v. *U.K.*, above), the main function of a collective agreement is to lay down a code of terms and conditions for a whole sector or area of employment. A discriminatory collective agreement could therefore give rise to thousands of individual claims, an expensive and slow process, potentially leading to different conclusions by different tribunals. A more effective amendment would be to create a mechanism for remedying the collective agreement itself; for example, by extending the limited jurisdiction of the Central Arbitration Committee (CAC) under s.3 EqPA, as suggested by the Advocate General in the European Court and strenuously urged by the

Opposition in Parliament. However, the Government regarded the European Court judgment as requiring changes which were "merely presentational," arguing that individual remedies were adequate and that the main effect of the section was to act as an incentive to unions and employers to renegotiate agreements. Indeed, it used the occasion of the Act to repeal s.3 EqPA rather than extending it (see Schedule). Voluntary references to the CAC do remain possible, and the EOC has the power to undertake a formal investigation in the case of a discriminatory collective agreement.

Subs. (1)
  "*collective agreement*": defined in subs. (6).

"*including an agreement which was not intended, or is presumed not to have been intended, to be a legally enforceable contract*": By s.18 TULRA, collective agreements are presumed not to be intended to be legally binding unless the parties state otherwise and the vast majority of collective agreements are, in practice, not legally binding. For the effect of this section, see General Note (above).

"*employer's rules*": See General Note above.

"*employed by him*": By subs. (7), all expressions have the same meaning as in the 1975 Act. Thus, "employed" includes all those who work under a contract of service or apprenticeship, or a contract personally to execute any work or labour (s.32(1) SDA 1975).

"*who apply to or are considered by him for employment*": Thus, arrangements for recruiting employees are covered.

"*prospective members*": This synchronises with applicants in subs. (*b*) above.

Subs. (2)
  This sets out the relevant organisations to whose rules s.77 now applies by virtue of subs. 1(*c*) above. These are identical to those mentioned in ss. 12 and 13 of the 1975 Act, which already gave individual remedies for victims of discrimination by these organisations or authorities.

Subs. (3)
  Although the European Court judgment only concerned the Equal Treatment Directive, the Equal Pay Directive (75/117) contains a similar requirement that provisions in collective agreements be declared null and void or amended (Art. 4). This section therefore extends s.77 SDA 1975 to any term in a collective agreement or rule specified in subs. (1)(*b*) or (*c*) which provides for the inclusion in a contract of employment of a term which would contravene the EqPA 1970. The defence contained in s.1(3) EqPA 1970 (material factors justifying discrimination) is applicable here.

Subs. (4)
  The exceptions in the SDA 1975 and EqPA 1970 apply here.

Subs. (5)
  The effect of subs. (5)(*a*) is that where a relevant term or rule has been incorporated into the individual contract of employment of a victim of the discrimination, the rights of the victim under the contract are unaffected by the avoidance of the term or rule. For example, if a term in a collective agreement provides for discriminatory holiday entitlement, the term remains until a new collective agreement is renegotiated. If this were not the case, and the avoidance of the term at collective level also meant its avoidance at individual level, the employee would be entitled to no holiday leave at all. (If the EqPA 1970 applies, an equality clause will, however, be implied).

"*discriminated*": defined in SDA 1975, s.1. (see subs. (7) below). Thus, both direct and indirect discrimination are covered.

"*except in so far as they enable any person to require another person to be treated less favourably than himself*": Although the rights of a person to be treated more favourably in direct or indirect consequence of the discrimination are preserved by subs. (5)(*b*), this does not extend to a term requiring another person to be treated less favourably. Thus, if rules of an association provide that no women shall be senior members of the association, then the contracts of membership of existing members, made in pursuance of those rules, remain in force, but a member could not sue the association for breach of contract if a woman were made a senior member since that term would be void.

"such of the rights of the person to be discriminated against": For example, holiday entitlement incorporated into a woman's contract of employment is not avoided under this section even if it is less than the holiday entitlement of comparable men. The victim may however complain to an industrial tribunal, and, where EqPA 1970 applies, an equality clause may be implied.

"such of the rights of any person who will be treated more favourably": Holiday entitlement of male employees, for example, will not be avoided even though it is more than that afforded to women, subject to the exception above, namely that the term does not enable that person to treat another person less favourably.

"made or modified wholly or partly in pursuance of, or by reference to that term or rule": This would cover terms incorporated from a collective agreement, or contracts, such as contracts of membership or employment, made in pursuance of a discriminatory rule, as well as any modifications due to changes in rules or collective agreements.

Subs. (6)

The definition of "collective agreement" is almost identical to that in s.30(1) TULRA 1974 except that the latter refers to an agreement "or arrangement."

Subs. (7)

Thus, "discrimination" includes direct and indirect discrimination, and the definition of "employment" includes all those who work under a contract of service or apprenticeship, or a contract personally to execute any work or labour (s.82(1) SDA 1975). As in the SDA 1975, this section applies to Crown employees despite the fact that they are not employed under contracts of employment.

Removal of restrictions on working hours and conditions of women

7.—(1) Section 1 of and Part I of Schedule 1 to the Hours of Employment (Conventions) Act 1936 (which impose restrictions on the employment of women by night in industrial undertakings) shall cease to have effect.

(2) The following provisions of the Mines and Quarries Act 1954 (which contain provisions with respect to women and young persons employed at a mine or quarry) shall cease to have effect with respect to women employed at a mine or quarry, that is to say—

(*a*) section 125 (provisions as to hours worked);

(*b*) section 126 (periods of employment);

(*c*) section 128 (notice fixing periods of employment); and

(*d*) section 131 (register of women and young persons employed).

(3) The following provisions of the Factories Act 1961 (which contain provisions with respect to women and young persons employed in factories) shall cease to have effect with respect to women employed in factories, that is to say—

(*a*) section 86 (general conditions as to hours of employment);

(*b*) section 88 (notice fixing hours of employment);

(*c*) section 91) restriction of employment inside and outside factory on the same day);

(*d*) section 92 (restriction of use during intervals of rooms where a process is being carried out);

(*e*) section 93 (prohibition of Sunday employment); and

(*f*) section 94 (annual holidays);

and accordingly, in section 89(9)(*a*) of that Act (which relates to overtime working), for the words from "no woman" to "young person" there shall be substituted the words "no young person shall be employed".

(4) The Secretary of State may by order made by statutory instrument make such provision amending or revoking any subordinate legislation (within the meaning of the Interpretation Act 1978) as he considers appropriate—

(*a*) in consequence of the preceding provisions of this section; or (*b*) for removing any restriction which is contained in that subordinate legislation and appears to him to be equivalent to a restriction removed by this section;

and an order under this section may contain such consequential and transitional provision as appears to the Secretary of State to be expedient.

(5) A statutory instrument containing an order under subsection (4) above shall be subject to annulment in pursuance of a resolution of either House of Parliament.

COMMENCEMENT: s.10(3).

GENERAL NOTE

This section repeals most of the existing statutory provisions restricting the hours of work and other terms and conditions of women. Unlike some other European countries, there is no comprehensive statutory regulation of hours and holidays for all employees. The statutory regulation which does exist applies in a piecemeal and disjointed fashion to women and young persons, largely because the unions and reform groups in the nineteenth century were unable to achieve comprehensive protection for all workers. For the rest, limits on hours of work have generally been achieved by collective bargaining. (See *Hepple and Fredman Labour Law and Industrial Relations in Great Britain* (Kluwer 1986) paras. 55 and 56).

The present Act repeals the bulk of the protective legislation, rather than extending some protections to men. By contrast, the Equal Opportunities Commission, in a report in 1979, had suggested that where health, safety and welfare demanded, legislation protecting the hours of work of women should be replaced so that it applied equally to men and women ("Health and Safety Legislation: Should we distinguish between men and women?"). Many European countries, including Scandinavia, Belgium and Finland restrict night work for both sexes, and several studies, including a large study of French industrial workers, have illustrated the difficulties many people face in adapting themselves to nightwork. The Health and Safety at Work, etc. Act 1974 may be available to protect some workers in this regard.

Some protective legislation is being retained, such as protection of pregnant and nursing women, restrictions on women employed on cleaning moving parts in factories (s.60 Factories Act 1961) and restrictions on women working underground in mines (s.124 Mines and Quarries Act 1954). The repeals do not apply to young persons.

In repealing this protective legislation, the U.K. is violating its commitment under Article 8(4) of the European Social Charter, which requires contracting parties: "(*a*) to regulate the employment of women workers on night work in industrial employment; and (*b*) to prohibit the employment of women workers in underground mining and, as appropriate, all other work which is unsuitable by reason of its dangerous, unhealthy and arduous nature." (Article 8(4)). The Government has announced its intention to denounce Article 8(4)(*a*) with effect from February 26, 1988, with notice required by August 26, 1987. Until then, the requirements of the Charter will be complied with. Thus, the Hours of Employment (Conventions) Act 1936, which restricts night work for women, remains in force until at least February 1988. The other legislation, however, is to be repealed by statutory instrument, sooner than that. (*Hansard*, H.L. Vol. 481, No. 162, cols. 1004–1005). Article 8(4)(*b*) is not to be denounced, on the basis that the obligation is complied with by virtue of the general duty under the Health and Safety at Work, etc. Act 1974 and other special protections for women which remain on the statute book, such as the prohibition on women working underground in the Mines and Quarries Act 1954. Nevertheless, it is arguable that repeal of some of the protections such as the provisions against night work and other arduous work in the Factories Act, contravenes the obligation in Article 8. (*Hansard*, H.L. Vol. 481, No. 162, col. 1006).

It should be noted that where an employer wishes to change the contractual hours of work as a result of these repeals, the consent of the employee is required. If the employee is dismissed for refusing to agree to such a variation, she may be able to claim to have been unfairly dismissed (s.54 EPCA 1978), provided she fulfils the eligibility criteria (*eg.* employment under a contract of service for at least two years). However, such a dismissal is not automatically unfair; an amendment which would have had that effect was rejected by the House of Commons after being inserted by the House of Lords.

The Department of Employment is to issue leaflets to employers outlining the changes and giving guidance to employers on their implementation. In particular, employers will be encouraged to give full consideration to employee consultation and the availability of transport. (*Hansard* H.L. Vol. 481, No. 161, col.994). A House of Lords amendment requiring a Code of Conduct was rejected by the House of Commons.

Subs. (1)

S.1 of the Hours of Employment (Conventions) Act 1936, implementing ILO Convention No. 4 of 1919 (as revised by Conventions 41 of 1934 and 89 of 1948), prevents the employment of women by night in any industrial undertaking, which includes mines, quarries, manufacture, construction, maintenance, etc. The section is subject to several exceptions, *eg.* for family members and women in managerial positions; and the Secretary of State has the power to exempt undertakings for women over 16. Once s.1 and its associated sections are repealed, only s.3 of this Act will remain in force, anomalously restricting the hours of work of sheet glass workers.

The repeal of the Hours of Employment (Conventions) Act 1936, violates the UK's commitments under Article 8 of the European Social Charter. (See introductory General Note). Thus its commencement is to be delayed until at least February 1988, when the denunciation by the UK of that Article will take effect. (*Hansard*, H.L. Vol. 481, No. 162, col. 1994).

Subs. (2)

This subsection withdraws the protections in the Mines and Quarries Act 1954 for women employed at a mine or quarry, while preserving them for young persons. The protections withdrawn include those restricting the number of hours worked (s.125), and preventing night work and Sunday working (s.126).

Certain restrictions remain. For example, s.124, which prevents the employment of women for a significant amount of time underground, is not repealed; nor is s.93, which provides that women shall not be employed to lift, carry or move a load so heavy as to be likely to cause injury. This complies with the UK's obligations under Article 8(4)(*b*) of the Social Charter which requires contracting parties to prohibit the employment of women workers in underground mining and other work which is unsuitable by reason of its dangerous, unhealthy or arduous nature. The Government does not intend to withdraw from Article 8(4)(*b*) (*Hansard*, H.L. Vol. 481, No. 162, col. 1005), although it is arguable that the repeal of the other sections of the Mines and Quarries Act violates this article (*Hansard*, H.L. Vol. 481, No. 162, col. 1002).

Subs. (3)

The Factories Act 1961 is the major consolidating measure concerning restrictions on hours worked by women and young persons in factories. Subs. (3) repeals these insofar as they relate to women. The provisions are similar to those in the Mines and Quarries Act 1954, repealed in subs. (2) above, including restrictions on the number of hours worked in factories, the prohibition of nightwork, obligations for rest periods (ss.86, 94) and holidays (s.94), and prohibitions on Sunday working (s.93).

These sections were in any case subject to numerous exceptions, and both the Health and Safety Executive and the Secretary of State have the power to grant exemptions. In 1984–1985, more than 4,000 special exemption orders had been granted covering about 200,000 of the 1·5m women in manufacturing industry. (*Hansard*, H.L. Vol. 471, No. 52, col. 1181).

It is arguable that the provisions here repealed are subject to Article 8(4)(*b*) of the European Social Charter, as concerning work which is dangerous, unhealthy or arduous. However, the Government takes the opposite view and does not intend to repeal that part of the Charter. Hence the repeals in this subsection are not to be delayed. (Compare subs. (1) above).

Repeal of Baking Industry (Hours of Work) Act 1954

8. The Baking Industry (Hours of Work Act 1954 (which imposes restrictions on the hours for which a bakery worker may do work in relation to which restrictions on the working hours of women are removed by virtue of section 7 above) shall cease to have effect.

COMMENCEMENT: s.10(3).

GENERAL NOTE

The repeal of the Baking Industry (Hours of Work) Act 1964, which subjected night work in bakeries to strict limits, brings to an end one of the few statutes which restrict the hours of work of male employees. (Their female counterparts are covered by the Factories Act 1961, to be repealed by s.4 above.) The aim of the statute was to deal with the problem of regulating nightwork in the baking industry, after persistent failure to achieve this end by collective bargaining. S.9 gave the Minister the power to make exceptions if there was an appropriate collective agreement: about two-thirds of employees in the industry are accordingly exempt (*Hansard*, H.L. Vol. 471, No. 52, col. 1182). The EOC had recommended that the Act be retained and extended to women (with the anomalies removed) on the basis that permanent nightwork and exceptionally long hours (averaging 49·9 hours a week) continue to be problematic in the baking industry (*Hansard*, H.L. Vol. 472, No. 58, cols. 597, 599). The Government defended its repeal on the basis that it was no longer justified (*Hansard*, H.L. Vol. 471, No. 52, col. 1182).

With the repeal of this Act, relatively few statutory limits on the hours of work of adult men remain. These include limits on the hours spent underground by miners, (Mines and Quarries Act 1954) as well as on the hours of work of sheet glass workers (Hours of Employment (Conventions) Act 1936), shop assistants, (Shop (Early Closing Days) Act 1965) and vehicle drivers (Transport Act 1968).

Consequential amendment, repeals and saving

9.—(1) In section 6(1) of the Equal Pay Act 1970 (exclusion of operation of equality clause and section 3(4) in relation to certain matters), for the words from the beginning to "shall" there shall be substituted the words "An equality clause shall not".

(2) The enactments mentioned in the Schedule to this Act (which include enactments that are no longer of practical effect) are hereby repealed to the extent specified in the third column of that Schedule.

(3) Neither the repeal by this Act of section 3 of the Equal Pay Act 1970 (collective agreements and pay structures) nor the amendment made by subsection (1) above shall affect—

(*a*) the continuing effect, after the coming into force of that repeal, of any declaration made under that section before the coming into force of that repeal; or

(*b*) the operation, at any time after the coming into force of that repeal, of section 5(1) of that Act in so far as it refers to the rules which apply under subsection (4) of the said section 3.

COMMENCEMENT: s.10(2) and (3).

GENERAL NOTE

Subs. (1)

This amendment is consequential on the repeal of s.3 EqPA 1970 (see note to subs. (2) below).

Subs. (2)

The most significant repeal mentioned in the Schedule is that of s.3 EqPA 1970, which enabled either party to a collective agreement, or the Secretary of State, to refer a collective agreement to the Central Arbitration Committee (CAC) if the agreement contained any provision applying specifically to men only or to women only. The CAC was given limited powers to amend such agreements. The number of references to the CAC in recent years has dwindled to almost nothing, partly as a result of the restrictive interpretation of its powers given by the Divisional Court in *R*. v. *CAC, ex p. Hymac* ([1979] I.R.L.R. 461), and this was the reason given for its repeal. Both the European Commission in *E.C. Commission Communities* v. *U.K.* ([1984] I.C.R. 192) and the Opposition had argued that instead of repealing s.3, the powers of the CAC should be extended to enable it to amend collective agreements with terms declared void by s.6 above. (See General Note to s.6).

The repeals mentioned in Part II of the Schedule, including s.3 of EqPA, come into force three months after the passing of this Act. (s.10(2)). Those in Part III, come into force on a day appointed by the Secretary of State (s.10(3)).

Subs. (3)

Subs. (3)(*a*) preserves the operation of any declaration amending a collective agreement made by the (CAC) under s.3 EqPA prior to the coming into force of the Act. Subs. (3)(*b*) preserves the operation of ss.4(1) and 5(1) EqPA 1970, which give the CAC the power to amend orders made by Wages Councils or agricultural wages orders containing provisions applying to men only or to women only. The way in which such orders are to be amended is laid down in s.3(4) EqPA 1970. However, s.4 EqPA 1970 is repealed by the Wages Act 1986 (Sched. 5, Part II).

Short title, commencement and extent

10—(1) This Act may be cited as the Sex Discrimination Act 1986.

(2) Sections 1, 6 and 9(1) and (3) above and Part II of the Schedule to this Act shall come into force at the end of the period of three months beginning with the day on which this Act is passed.

(3) Subject to subsection (4) below, sections 2, 3, 7 and 8 above and Part III of the Schedule to this Act shall come into force on such day as the Secretary of State may by order made by statutory instrument appoint, and different days may be so appointed for different provisions or for different purposes.

(4) Except in so far as they come into force at an earlier time under subsection (3) above, sections 2 and 3 above shall come into force at the end of the period of twelve months beginning with the day on which this Act is passed.

(5) This Act does not extend to Northern Ireland except for the purpose of repealing, in their application to Northern Ireland, sections 1 and 4(1) of and Part I of Schedule 1 to the Hours of Employment (Conventions) Act 1936.

GENERAL NOTE

Subs. (4)

Employers are given 12 months from Royal Assent to change their practices to accord with the new legislation (*Hansard*, H.L. Vol. 481, No. 161, col. 998).

Section 9   SCHEDULE

REPEALS

PART I

REPEAL COMING INTO FORCE AT ROYAL ASSENT

Chapter	Short title	Extent of repeal
1975 c.65	The Sex Discrimination Act 1975.	In section 81, in subsections (1) and (2), "47(4)(*b*)".

PART II

REPEALS COMING INTO FORCE AFTER THREE MONTHS

Chapter	Short title	Extent of repeal
1970 c.41.	The Equal Pay Act 1970.	Section 3. In section 6(1A), the words "and those provisions". Section 10.
1975 c.65.	The Sex Discrimination Act 1975.	In section 6— subsection (3); and in subsection (5), the words "or by reference to a collective agreement". In section 11(1), the words "consisting of six or more partners". In section 80(1), paragraph (*d*). In Part I of Schedule 1, in paragraph 6(2), the words "and 10".

Chapter	Short title	Extent of repeal
1975 c.71.	The Employment Protection Act 1975.	In Schedule 16, in paragraph 13 of Part IV— in sub-paragraph (2), the words "3" and "and 10"; in sub-paragraph (3), the words "and 10"; and sub-paragraphs (4) and (5).

PART III

REPEALS COMING INTO FORCE ON APPOINTED DAY

Chapter	Short title	Extent of repeal
26 Geo. 5 and 1 Edw. 8. c.22.	The Hours of Employment (Conventions) Act 1936.	Section 1. Section 4(1). In Schedule 1, Part I.
2 & 3 Eliz. 2. c.57.	The Baking Industry (Hours of Work) Act 1954.	The whole Act.
2 & 3 Eliz. 2. c.70.	The Mines and Quarries Act 1954.	In section 125(1), the words "woman or", wherever occurring. In section 126— subsection (1); in subsection (4), the words from the beginning to "quarry and"; and in subsection (5), the words "No woman and". In section 128— in subsection (1), the words "women and", wherever occurring, and the words "woman or"; in subsection (2), the words "women and"; and in subsection (3), the words "women or". In section 131(1), the words "women and". In Schedule 4, the entry relating to the Hours of Employment (Conventions) Act 1936.
9 & 10 Eliz. 2. c.34.	The Factories Act 1961.	In section 86, the words "woman or", wherever occurring, and the words "women and". In section 88(1), the words "women and", wherever occurring, and the words "woman or". In section 89— in subsection (1), the words "women and"; in subsection (2), the words "woman or", wherever occurring, and the words from "except" onwards; in subsection (3), the words "women or", wherever occurring; subsection (6);

Chapter	Short title	Extent of repeal
9 & 10 Eliz. 2. c.34—*cont.*	The Factories Act 1961—*cont.*	*in subsection (9)(b)*, the words "woman or"; and in subsection (10), the words "woman or", wherever occurring. In section 90— in subsection (1), the words "woman or"; and in subsection (2), the words "women or". In section 91— in subsection (1), the words "woman or", wherever occurring; in subsection (2), the words "woman or a"; and in subsection (3), the words "woman or and the words "her or". In section 92, the words "woman or", wherever occurring. In section 93, the words "woman or", wherever occurring. In section 94— in subsection (1), the words "woman and"; and in subsection (6), the words "woman or", wherever occurring. Section 95. In section 96, the words "women or". In section 97— in subsections (1) and (5), the words "of women and", wherever occurring; and in subsection (6), the words "women and". In section 98, the words "women and", wherever occurring. In section 99(7), the words "women and". In section 100— in subsection (1), the words "women and", in the first place where they occur, and the words "of women and"; and in subsection (2), the words "women and" and the words "woman or". In section 101, the words "women and". In section 102(1), the words "women and". In section 106(1), the words "women and", wherever occurring. In section 107(2), the words "women and". In section 108, the words "women and", wherever occurring. In section 109— in subsection (1), the words "woman or"; and in subsection (2), the words "women and". Sections 110 and 111. In section 112(1), the words "women and", in the first two places where they occur, and the words "women and of".

Chapter	Short title	Extent of repeal
9 & 10 Eliz. 2. c.34—*cont.*	The Factories Act 1961—*cont.*	In section 113— in subsection (1), the words "women and", in the first two places where they occur, and the words "women and to"; and in subsection (2), the words "woman or". In section 114, the words "women or". In section 115(5), the words "women and".
1968 c.64.	The Civil Evidence Act 1968.	In the Schedule, the entry relating to the Baking Industry (Hours of Work) Act 1954.
1974 c.37.	The Health and Safety at Work etc. Act 1974.	In Schedule 1, the entry relating to the Baking Industry (Hours of Work) Act 1954.
1975 c.65.	The Sex Discrimination Act 1975.	In Schedule 5, paragraph 3.
1985 c.9.	The Companies Consolidation (Consequential Provisions) Act 1985.	In Schedule 2, the entry relating to the Baking Industry (Hours of Work) Act 1954.